THE OXFORD HANDBOOK

INTERNATIONAL

# BUSINESS

# THE OXFORD HANDBOOK OF

# INTERNATIONAL BUSINESS

*Edited by*

## ALAN M. RUGMAN

AND

## THOMAS L. BREWER

OXFORD

UNIVERSITY PRESS

# OXFORD
## UNIVERSITY PRESS

Great Clarendon Street, Oxford OX2 6DP

Oxford University Press is a department of the University of Oxford.
It furthers the University's objective of excellence in research, scholarship,
and education by publishing worldwide in

Oxford New York

Auckland Bangkok Buenos Aires Cape Town Chennai
Dar es Salaam Delhi Hong Kong Istanbul Karachi Kolkata
Kuala Lumpur Madrid Melbourne Mexico City Mumbai Nairobi
São Paulo Shanghai Taipei Tokyo Toronto

Oxford is a registered trade mark of Oxford University Press
in the UK and in certain other countries

Published in the United States
by Oxford University Press Inc., New York

British Library Cataloguing in Publication Data
Data available

Library of Congress Cataloging in Publication Data
Oxford handbook of international business/
edited by Alan M. Rugman and Thomas L. Brewer.
p. cm.
Includes bibliographical references and index.
1. International trade. I. Rugman, Alan M. II. Brewer, Thomas L., 1941–
HF1379 .O996 2001    658.8 48—dc21    2001016400

ISBN 0–19–924182–1
ISBN 0–19–925841–4 (Pbk.)

3 5 7 9 10 8 6 4 2

Typeset by Kolam Information Services Pvt. Ltd. Pondicherry, India
Printed in Great Britain
on acid-free paper by
Biddles Ltd, King's Lynn, Norfolk

# PREFACE

In response to the new initiative of OUP to launch the Oxford Handbook series we invited leading scholars in the field of international business to write original state of the art literature reviews for this book. These chapters are designed to survey and synthesize the relevant literature. Each author has been encouraged to bring analytical insight and critical thinking to this task.

Each of the potential authors identified is an authority on the topic, as recognized by an extensive set of publications in leading refereed journals and by citations to this body of work. All have been active as leaders in the Academy of International Business, the professional body for scholars in the field of international business with a worldwide membership of approximately 3,000 academics. All have attended the annual conferences of the AIB or published in the *Journal of International Business Studies*. One of the two editors of this book is Professor Thomas Brewer, the current editor of *JIBS* and thereby positioned at the centre of the most extensive network of authors and referees in the area of international business. The second editor, Professor Alan Rugman, has been identified as one of the five most influential scholars in the field of international business, based on citation counts. He is the author or editor of thirty books in the field.

In order to determine appropriate contributors to the *Oxford Handbook of International Business*, and therein its content, the editors have consulted two 'domain' statements. First is that of the Academy of International Business, as reflected in the statement of the editorial board of *JIBS*.

*The Journal of International Business Studies (JIBS)* welcomes manuscripts on multinational and other firms' business activities, strategies and managerial processes that cross national boundaries. The journal also welcomes manuscripts on the interactions of such firms with their economic, political and cultural environments. We are interested in papers that are exceptional in terms of theory, evidence, or methodology and that significantly advance social scientific research on international business. As a methodologically pluralistic journal, *JIBS* welcomes conceptual and theory-development papers, empirical hypothesis-testing papers, mathematical modelling papers, case studies, and review articles. The journal has a special interest in research on important issues that transcend the boundaries of single academic disciplines and managerial functions. We therefore welcome inter-disciplinary scholarship and commentaries that challenge the paradigms and assumptions of individual disciplines or functions; such papers, however, should be grounded in conceptual and/or empirical literature. The journal does not accept manuscripts about teaching materials or methods.

The second statement is that of the International Management Division of the Academy of Management.

*International Management.* Specific domain: content pertaining to theory, research and practice with an international or cross-cultural dimension. Major topics include investigations of the adjustments organizations make in order to succeed in various countries; investigations of the cross-border management of operations, including multi-country, multi-unit strategy formulations and implementations; investigations of evolving organizational forms and management practices that are the consequence of the interaction of two or more socially-embedded, multi-level, evolving business processes (from individual to supranational) and their outputs; investigations of the cross-border differential impact of cultural, social, economic, technological, and political forces on organizational forms and management practices; comparative management studies; and other research with an international dimension.

Based on these two domain statements, Professors Brewer and Rugman met and interacted on numerous occasions to develop and refine the list of twenty-eight chapters. These chapters cover all of the major themes identified in these domain statements. The book is arranged in six parts dealing in turn with:

   I.  History and Theory of the Multinational Enterprise: six chapters;
   II. The Political and Policy Environment: five chapters;
   III. Strategy for MNEs: four chapters;
   IV. Managing the MNE: six chapters;
   V.  Regional Studies: five chapters;
   VI. Conclusions: two interdisciplinary and thematic chapters.

This structure, and the potential contributions, have been discussed with several other senior scholars in the field of international business. The design of the book reflects the current content of the field and also covers the major intellectual issues of current and likely future interest. For example, a key long-term intellectual debate stems from the contrasting disciplinary perspectives of economics and political science as they analyze the role of multinational enterprises and public policy. In Part II our chapters are linked to address this core issue; and authors in Parts I, III, IV, and V were requested to consider this issue in their particular chapters. Another debate relates to the influence of culture on firm strategy and structure. Besides Chapters 18 and 22 which specifically address the issue, this was also considered by the authors of Chapters 13–15 and 24–8.

A.R. *and* T.B.

# ACKNOWLEDGEMENTS

Without the support of Templeton College, University of Oxford, this book would not have been possible. Dean Rory Knight in particular helped to facilitate an authors' conference at the College in April 2000. This was partly funded by a gift from The Friends of Templeton, Chair Mr John Morrell.

Invaluable secretarial assistance with the book, conference, and ongoing support for Professor Rugman was provided by Mrs Denise Edwards: other support was provided by Corinne Wride and Anne Greening.

The editors are pleased to acknowledge the insight and editorial support of David Musson and Sarah Dobson of Oxford University Press.

We are also extremely grateful to all the contributors for their professional attention to detail, delivery of abstracts, drafts, and revised chapters in a prompt manner, and their good humour and tolerance throughout this long process.

*Alan M. Rugman, Oxford University*
*Thomas Brewer, Georgetown University*

# CONTENTS

# PART II THE POLITICAL AND POLICY ENVIRONMENT

# PART III STRATEGY FOR MNEs

# PART IV MANAGING THE MNE

# PART V REGIONAL STUDIES

# PART VI CONCLUSIONS

# Figures

# TABLES

....................................

# LIST OF CONTRIBUTORS

**David M. Berg**, Assistant Professor, School of Management, University of Texas at Dallas.

**Julian Birkinshaw**, Associate Professor, London Business School.

**Michael Bowe**, Senior Lecturer in Economics and International Finance, Manchester School of Management, UMIST.

**Thomas L. Brewer**, Editor of *Journal of International Business Studies*, and Associate Professor, Georgetown University.

**Peter Buckley**, Professor and Director, Centre for International Business, University of Leeds.

**John Cantwell**, Professor of Economics, University of Reading.

**Mark Casson**, Professor of Economics, University of Reading.

**John Child**, Chair of Commerce, University of Birmingham, and Visiting Professor of Management, University of Hong Kong.

**James W. Dean**, Professor of Economics, Simon Fraser University and Kaiser Professor of International Business, Western Washington University.

**John H. Dunning**, Emeritus Professor of International Business, University of Reading and Emeritus State of New Jersey Professor of International Business, Rutgers University.

**Lorraine Eden**, Associate Professor, Department of Management, Texas A&M University.

**John L. Graham**, Professor, Graduate School of Management, University of California, Irvine.

**Robert Grosse**, Professor of World Business and Director of Research, Thunderbird, The American Graduate School of International Management.

**Stephen E. Guisinger**, Professor of International Management, University of Texas at Dallas.

**Jean-François Hennart**, Professor of International Management, Tilburg University, the Netherlands.

**Andrew C. Inkpen**, Associate Professor, Thunderbird, American Graduate School of International Management.

**Stephen J. Kobrin**, William Wurster Professor of Multinational Management, The Wharton School, University of Pennsylvania.

**Bruce Kogut**, The Dr Felix Zandman Professor of International Management, The Wharton School, University of Pennsylvania.

**Masaaki (Mike) Kotabe**, The Washburn Chair of International Business and Marketing, Temple University.

**James R. Markusen**, Professor of Economics, University of Colorado, Boulder, NBER and CEPR.

**Klaus E. Meyer**, Associate Professor, Center for East European Studies, Copenhagen Business School.

**Sylvia Ostry**, Distinguished Research Fellow, Munk Centre for International Studies, University of Toronto.

**Gordon Redding**, Affiliate Professor of Asian Business, INSEAD.

**Alan M. Rugman**, L. Leslie Waters Chair of International Business, Indiana University, and Fellow, Templeton College, University of Oxford.

**Debora L. Spar**, Professor, Harvard Business School.

**Stephen B. Tallman**, Professor of Management, David Eccles School of Business, University of Utah.

**Alain Verbeke**, Professor of International Business, University of Brussels and Associate Fellow, Templeton College, University of Oxford.

**D. Eleanor Westney**, Sloan Fellows Professor, Sloan School of Management, Massachusetts Institute of Technology.

**Mira Wilkins**, Professor of Economics, Florida International University.

**George S. Yip**, Professor of Strategic and International Management, London Business School.

**Stephen Young**, Professor and Co-Director, Strathclyde International Business Unit, University of Strathclyde.

**Srilata Zaheer**, Professor, Carlson School of Management, University of Minnesota.

# PART I

## HISTORY AND THEORY OF THE MULTINATIONAL ENTERPRISE

# CHAPTER 1

# THE HISTORY OF MULTINATIONAL ENTERPRISE

## MIRA WILKINS

## 1.1 PREFACE

OVER the last four decades, using the evolving theories of multinational enterprise as a measure and means of asking questions and, at the same time, developing their own theoretical perspective, economic and business historians have been engaged in writing works on the history of multinational enterprise. The method of the historian is first and foremost to look at what happened; business historians have gone into archives to study the growth of individual firms; but as they penetrate archives, they have had to ask what is important and make selections. They ask questions of their data. Single firms are but trees in a forest. Some business historians have gone much farther—and asked is there a pattern? What does the forest look like? The most valuable contribution of business historians to the field of multinational enterprise is to provide a sense of process, change, accumulated experience, paths taken and not taken, the limits of choice, and the basis for the development of the tissue of multinational enterprise behavior. Students of multinational enterprise have recognized the need for 'longitudinal' (or 'sequential') data, which is, of course, the forte of the business historian.

A second contribution of economic and business historians is to instill a recognition of complexity, of the multi-faceted aspects of business enterprises as they emerge and mature, as managers and managerial directions change, and as the environment in which managers operate takes on different characteristics. The boundaries of the firm are often porous and alter through time. The historian faces questions of defining the firm and the recognition that extension of management matters in that definition. Business historians are not only interested in entries and start-ups. They are concerned with the entire firm as it evolves and changes through time. They monitor retreats as well as growth. They recognize that the individual firm often engages in both horizontal and vertical integration, as well as related and unrelated diversification over borders.

A third major benefit of the research of economic and business historians is the reminder on context. When four decades ago, students of the history of multinational enterprise began to do intensive research specifically on the history of international businesses, there was a belief afloat that foreign direct investments began in the post-World War II era. The long history of American multinational enterprise was then chronicled—and the misconception well documented. There still remains—in otherwise thoughtful works—the erroneous view that the international spread of foreign direct investment from home countries other than the United States was a post-World War II phenomenon. Research by economic and business historians has shown that to be patently false. The evolution of the *modern* multinational enterprise dates back roughly to the last half, or better still the last third, of the nineteenth century. Yet, there were also earlier multinational enterprises that shared certain features with the modern multinational enterprise.

The fourth key contribution of this literature is the strong warning against linearity. The stories told by the economic and business historians are never linear. They demonstrate continuities, but also major discontinuities—both in the specific story of individual firms and in the general one of group behavior. Historians seek to interpret change and delve into the nature of the firm. They teach that *ex ante* there have always been surprises. These can, to be sure, be explained—but only *ex poste*. There are patterns, which alter through time. The literature of economic and business history shows the dynamic, evolving nature of the firm as it experiences internal problem-solving and as it responds to new configurations within the world economy. Both continuities and discontinuities require study.

A fifth contribution by business and economic historians has been their search for an understanding of the varying linkages over time between individual firms and the 'outside' world. How and to what extent do intra-firm and also inter-firm relationships provide efficiencies in the allocation of resources over borders and add to overall economic growth? Sometimes multinational enterprises (individually or in network associations) have not only responded to conditions within the world economy, but have had profound impact on the course of those circumstances. Firms react to public policies, and also at times take part in the shaping of these policies. The interaction between what is endogenous and what is exogenous is never stable. Moreover, the extent to which multinational enterprises penetrate in a 'shallow' or 'deep' manner within a particular host economy alters over time; impacts must be seen as multi-dimensional.

# 1.2 GENERAL WORKS ON THE HISTORY OF MULTINATIONAL ENTERPRISE

The definition of a multinational enterprise becomes important in a discussion of the literature on the history of multinational enterprise. This has been a source of confusion. In the phrase 'international business', the term business can be defined as a firm or as an activity.[1] If the former, it is synonymous with multinational enterprise; if the latter it is not. Most (not all) students of the history of international business have used the terms international, multinational, transnational, global, as an adjective; and business, company, corporation, enterprise, firm, as the noun that it modifies. Except where otherwise noted, this is the way I will use the words in the present essay, the adjective connoting business over borders and the noun defining the producer of goods and services.

Another confusion in definition has been associated with the phrases 'multinational enterprise', and 'foreign direct investments'. Often writers have used the terms interchangeably.[2] Historians have long recognized that

---

[1]  See the approaches in Toyne and Nigh (1997). Toyne and Nigh hosted a conference in South Carolina in 1992 on international business. As a business historian, I defined business as a firm (Toyne and Nigh 1997, 31–50), but soon recognized that this was not to be taken for granted and that others wanted to define it as an activity.

[2]  Particularly in the theoretical literature on multinational enterprise the phrases 'theory of foreign direct investment' and 'theory of multinational enterprise' were (and are) frequently used interchangeably.

they are not the same. The appropriate formulation is that the multinational enterprise in extending itself over borders makes foreign direct investments (no matter how small).[3] Foreign direct investment is one of a multinational enterprise's many activities, albeit an essential one for without the investment (however small) there is no extension of the firm and no internalization that is fundamental to an analysis of the international business. A multinational enterprise provides intra-firm connections, a tissue that unifies on a regular basis; it is not merely a channel for one-time transactions but a basis for different sorts of internal and external organizational relationships. The study of the history of multinational enterprise (with the firm as the unit for analysis) is, moreover, distinct from the rich and extensive literature on the history of the world economy.[4]

A number of general works on the history of multinational enterprise exist. In 1970 and 1974, Mira Wilkins published her *The Emergence of Multinational Enterprise: American Business Abroad from the Colonial Era to 1914* and *The Maturing of Multinational Enterprise: American Business Abroad from 1914 to 1970* (Wilkins 1970, 1974a). These studies were prepared during the 1960s at the time when US-headquartered multinational corporations were expanding globally and capturing headlines. The books—based on archival research—demonstrated that the international expansion of US business was not a post-World War II phenomenon, but rather had a long history, that the modern multinational enterprise was associated with the general growth pattern of US business, and that in the late nineteenth century, leading US industrial enterprises as they became national, had become international businesses. Wilkins in the Epilogue to *The Maturing of Multinational Enterprise* developed a model on the evolution of multinational enterprise (Wilkins 1974a, 414–39, 565–6). Wilkins's work was influenced by the business

[3] As historians describe experiences of multinational enterprises over time, they have always included more than foreign direct investment, but they, like others in the international business field, have often erred in using the terms as though they were interchangeable. I like to define a multinational enterprise (MNE) as a firm that is headquartered in one country and extends itself over borders—as a firm. In some (exceptional) cases there may be more than one headquarters (as with Unilever, or Royal Dutch Shell). The phrase 'no matter how small' is necessary, for an historian recognizes that a firm has to start the process and so will begin with a single investment abroad in a host country; typically, however, MNEs move into more than one host country—sometimes immediately, sometimes very rapidly, sometimes very slowly. Indeed, today a single MNE may operate in more than 100 different host countries. What seems important in discussing MNE is that it has a presence abroad, no matter how small; it does not merely export to other unaffiliated firms or consumers. It is internalizing its operations over borders.

[4] Some scholars unfamiliar with the extensive literature on the history of multinational enterprise have erroneously equated the scholarship on the history of the multinational enterprise with that on the history of the world economy. Some histories of the world economy do cover multinational enterprise; most do not do so effectively; they do provide fine background for the stories of evolving firms.

historian, Alfred D. Chandler, who in his *Strategy and Structure* had chronicled the rise of American multi-functional, multi-regional, multi-divisional, corporations (Chandler 1962). Chandler stressed that as a firm grew in size and altered its strategies, efficiency only came about with appropriate changes in managerial structures. Wilkins and Chandler were interested in the business firm and how it emerged and matured through time. Raymond Vernon also in the 1960s developed a data-set on large American (and then subsequently non-US headquartered) multinational enterprises and, in the course of doing so, assembled a formidable amount of information on the historical background of the corporations that he studied.[5]

In the early 1970s, there came to be extensive research on the history of European multinational enterprises. The entire issue of the Autumn, 1974, *Business History Review* (the journal of US business historians, published at Harvard Business School) was on the history of multinational enterprise; it contained essays by two of Vernon's students, John Stopford on the history of British manufacturing multinational enterprises and Lawrence Franko on European manufacturing multinationals (Stopford 1974; Franko 1974).[6] Franko later followed up on this article with a 1976 book on European multinationals that contained a sizable historical segment (Franko 1976). Meanwhile, in 1972, at a conference on the evolution of international management structures, and in 1974 at the first of the Fuji Business History conferences in Japan, the prominent historian of modern Europe, Charles Wilson, presented papers on 'Multinationals, Management, and World Markets: A Historical View', and 'The Multinational in Historical Perspective' (Wilson 1975, 1976?).

It became very apparent that the history of European (including British) multinationals needed additional exploration. In 1977, Mira Wilkins published an essay in *The Journal of European Economic History*, urging trained historians to pay more heed to the development of European multinationals, suggesting that the history of the expansion of enterprise across borders was an important subject (Wilkins 1977). What followed in the 1980s and early 1990s was an explosion of inquiries into the history of multinational enterprise. Alice Teichova, Maurice Lévy-Leboyer, and Helga Nussbaum edited a volume entitled *Multinational Enterprise in Historical Perspective* (Teichova, Lévy-Leboyer, and Nussbaum 1986).[7] Geoffrey Jones (joined in one instance with Peter Hertner and in another with Harm Schröter) edited and contributed to a group of books that added substantially to our knowledge of the

---

[5] This was in connection with a huge project on multinational enterprise at Harvard Business School.

[6] This same issue also contained other articles on American business abroad, including Kindleberger (1974).

[7] Three years later the same group of editors published a sequel (Teichova, Lévy-Leboyer, and Nussbaum 1989).

history of multinational enterprise: Peter Hertner and Geoffrey Jones (eds.), *Multinationals: Theory and History*; Geoffrey Jones (ed.), *British Multinationals: Origins, Management and Performance*; and Geoffrey Jones and Harm G. Schröter (eds.), *The Rise of Multinationals in Continental Europe* (Hertner and Jones 1986; Jones 1986*b*; Jones and Schröter 1993).[8] Meanwhile, Stephen Nicholas, in an innovative essay in the *Journal of Economic History*, discussed 'Agency Contracts, Institutional Modes, and the Transition to Foreign Direct Investment by British Manufacturing Multinationals before 1939' (Nicholas 1983). Wilkins added to the general discussion with her 'European and North American Multinationals, 1870–1914: Comparisons and Contrasts', published in *Business History* (Wilkins 1988*a*). All of these works were influenced by Alfred Chandler's *Visible Hand*, and then a new set would be nourished in the 1990s by his *Scale and Scope* (Chandler 1977, 1990).[9] Chandler dealt with the growth of the large modern industrial corporation and, thus, with the history of US, British, and German multinational enterprise. With the coming of age of Japanese multinationals, business historians also examined their backgrounds. In one of what would eventually be three articles on the history of Japanese multinationals, all published in *Business History Review*, in 1986 Wilkins wrote on 'Japanese Multinational Enterprise before 1914' (Wilkins 1986*c*, 1982, 1990).

These (and numerous other) studies had their vantage point from the home, the headquarters country, perceiving the firm as it stretched outwards over borders. At the same time, this literature was supplemented by an expanding number of contributions on the history of multinational enterprises that observed them from the perspective of host countries or regions. As early as 1958, John Dunning's study (recently updated and republished), *American Investment in British Manufacturing Industry*, had an introductory chapter on the growth of US companies' direct investments in British manufacturing (Dunning 1958). Subsequently, Geoffrey Jones prepared an extensive data base on multinational enterprise activity in Britain, including far more than US investments.[10] Antje Hagen published in German a detailed study of

---

[8] Smith (1998) and Kogut (1998) dealt with French multinationals (and foreign firms in France), which had been short-changed in the initial research on multinationals from continental European countries.

[9] In addition, Chandler wrote several articles specifically on the history of multinational enterprise, including Chandler (1980); Chandler, Amatori, and Hikino (1997) edited a volume on the history of big business that contained substantial data on the history of multinational enterprise. Meanwhile, Christopher J. Schmitz (1993) had done a short study of the growth of big business in the United States and western Europe, 1850–1939, that contained materials on the history of multinational enterprise.

[10] He used this data collection in Jones (1988); Bostock and Jones (1994); and Jones and Bostock (1996). For other studies of the history of foreign multinational enterprise in Britain, see Godley (1999). Scott Fletcher and Andrew Godley have done extensive work on foreign investment in British retailing (Fletcher and Godley 2000)

German direct investments in Great Britain, 1871–1918, which she supplemented with articles on the same subject in *Business History* and *Business History Review* (Hagen 1997*a*, 1997*b*, 1999). Mira Wilkins's history of foreign investment in the United States (which covers both direct and portfolio investments) has a large segment on the history of non-US multinationals in that country. The first volume of her history was published in 1989; sequels are forthcoming (Wilkins 1989, in process); a very useful article on foreign multinationals in the United States in the post-World War II years has been done by Robert Lipsey (1993).[11] The activities of certain multinationals in central Europe, 1918–39, are documented in Alice Teichova and P. L. Cottrell (eds.), *International Business and Central Europe, 1918–1939* (Teichova and Cottrell 1983).

Indeed, the historical literature on multinationals in host countries is vast and covers less developed as well as developed countries—and countries on all continents. It includes, for example, Mira Wilkins, 'The Impact of American Multinational Enterprise on American–Chinese Economic Relations, 1786–1949'; Takeshi Yuzawa and Masaru Udagawa (eds.), *Foreign Business in Japan before World War II*; and Mark Mason, *American Multinationals and Japan: The Political Economy of Japanese Capital Controls, 1899–1980* (Wilkins 1986*b*; Yuzawa and Udagawa 1989; Mason 1992). R. P. T. Davenport-Hines and Geoffrey Jones (eds.), *British Business in Asia since 1860* has chapters on the history of British business in Iran, India, Thailand, Malaysia and Singapore, China, and Japan (Davenport-Hines and Jones 1989). Thomas O'Brien, *The Century of US Capitalism in Latin America* provides a brief overview of American business in Latin America, while Carlos Marichal (ed.), *Foreign Investment in Latin America: Impact on Economic Development, 1850–1930* contains articles on such diverse topics as the origins of British multinationals in Latin America (Charles Jones), French enterprise and Latin America (Frédéric Mauro), German banks and German direct investment in Latin America (George F. W. Young), Canadian firms in public sector activities in Mexico and Brazil (H. V. Nelles and C. Armstrong), and foreign banks in the early industrialization of Sao Paulo (Tamás Szmrecsányi and Flavio A. M. de Saes) (O'Brien 1999; Marichal 1994). Rory Miller has done and is doing important work on British multinationals in Latin America (Miller 1993, 1995, 1999). So, too, D. C. M. Platt's edited volume, *Business Imperialism 1840–1930: An Inquiry based on British Experience in Latin America* (Platt 1977) includes valuable contributions on British multinational commercial

---

[11] A few years after John Dunning published his work on American investment in British manufacturing industry, he collected a wonderful body of historical data on the direct investments of British companies in the United States, which material Wilkins found invaluable. Wilkins has published articles on the history of Japanese direct investment in the United States (Wilkins 1982, 1990, 1994*b*), French direct investment in the United States (Wilkins 1993), and Swiss direct and portfolio investments in the United States (Wilkins 1999*a*).

banks, mortgage, and insurance companies (Charles Jones), public utilities (Charles and Linda Jones and Robert Greenhill), and those British firms operating in Peru (Rory Miller).

These studies (and there are hundreds of others) supplemented a broad range of many much earlier ones, for example, Frank A. Southard, *American Industry in Europe*, C. F. Remer, *Foreign Investment in China*, Herbert Marshall, Frank A. Southard, and Kenneth W. Taylor, *Canadian–American Industry*, and Dudley Maynard Phelps, *Migration of Industry to South America* (Southard 1931; Remer 1933; Marshall, Southard, and Taylor 1936; Phelps 1936).[12] None of these volumes published during the 1930s had used the phrase 'multinational enterprise' (Platt's contributors in the mid-1970s were also not yet using the term), but each—and a large number of added ones—dealt with business over borders through a lens of a particular recipient country or region. While some of the many such books and articles were simply descriptive of the enterprises in the foreign country, others dealt with the firms' impact on development (all gave background and history).

Part of the difficulties of host country or regional views of the multinational enterprise is that by definition such an approach 'truncates' the firm, dividing its host country impact from the overall context of its activity as a multinational enterprise. This became evident in an attempt that Mira Wilkins made to compare hosts to multinationals: see her 'Comparative Hosts' (Wilkins 1994a).

As foreign direct investment rose in the post-World War II period and as scholars began to try to measure that path, business historians joined others in the collection of statistics. Business historians have, however, had trouble in presenting statistical series on the extent of multinational enterprise involvements over long periods of time. The US Department of Commerce has since the 1920s collected direct investment statistics on US business abroad and on foreign business in the United States. Cleona Lewis in her seminal *America's Stake in International Investments* (Lewis 1938) supplemented the US Department of Commerce studies and added more historical data. There are approximations (albeit not necessarily consistent information) on US outward and inward direct investments that go back to 1914. As for figures on direct investments that do not involve the United States, John Dunning and T. A. B. Corley have made valiant efforts to try to reconstruct such historical statistics. John Dunning has long been interested in the history of international production—and has added to the literature on the history of international business in important manners—see, for example, his 'Changes

---

[12] Marshall, Southard, Taylor (1936) dealt with US business in Canada *and* Canadian business in the United States.

in the Level and Structure of International Production: the Last One Hundred Years' (Dunning 1983; Corley 1989, 1994*a*, 1998).[13] Other attempts to assemble historical data on direct investments include P. Svedberg, 'The Portfolio-Direct Composition of Private Foreign Investment in 1914 Revisited', and more recently Michael J. Twomey, in 'Patterns of Foreign Investment in Latin America in the Twentieth Century' (Svedberg 1978; Twomey 1998).

Significant findings have surfaced from the numerous historical studies as well as from the attempts to construct statistical series to document them. (1) Clearly, the modern multinational enterprise is not a post-World War II phenomenon. (2) There were substantial differences from one home (head-quarters) country to the next in the patterns of the evolution of multinational enterprise. (3) As was perhaps more obvious (since there were many more of them), host countries differed in the composition of and the digestion of multinational enterprises's contributions. (4) While changing political borders and the end to Empires (in the aftermath of World War I, in the interwar years, as well as in the post-World War II years) were part of the narrative of historians who attempt to understand the nature of multinational enterprise, they posed formidable problems of consistency in *measuring* foreign direct investments through time. (5) The early research had placed too much emphasis on the history of manufacturing multinationals; there was an important history of service-sector multinationals that needed to be explored (and was often inadequately reflected in the statistical data on foreign direct investments). In addition, there had not been adequate discussion of multi-national enterprises with direct investments in primary-sector activities. (6) Historians grappled with a range of problems associated with the definition of multinational enterprise; changing definitions of the multinational enterprise (as well as changing geographical boundaries) frustrated efforts to obtain consistent time series data over long periods. (7) As it became ever more evident that foreign direct investment and multinational enterprise were not the same, once again the statistical data on foreign direct investment would often fail to capture the fundamentals of the story of multinational enterprise. (8) Although much of the contemporary theoretical discussions of multi-nationals cast light on the history of multinationals, certain historical experi-ences defied conventional (or contemporary) patterns. A 'Whig' approach to history (that is, looking back from the present rather than beginning with the historical circumstances themselves) sometimes had introduced blinders that obscured important past occurrences. Indeed, it was some of the dis-tinctive features of times past that posed major problems in defining

[13] Lewis (1945) made a pioneer attempt to assemble worldwide foreign direct investment figures for 1938.

multinational enterprises (and raised fundamental questions as to whether it was even possible to establish satisfactory statistical time series on direct investment and worse still on the course of multinational enterprise); yet, reservations notwithstanding, all those writing on multinational enterprise have welcomed and applauded the efforts to try to provide appropriate, meaningful longitudinal statistical information. As the present essay progresses, I will indicate how these eight findings together have served to enlarge the scope of research and will discuss some of the newly emerging theoretical constructs.

But first, more on the most recent work. On the general history, Geoffrey Jones, *The Evolution of International Business* (Jones 1996), has incorporated the latest insights into the first overall history of multinational enterprise. Mira Wilkins, in an ambitious 1997 A. C. Davidson Lecture in Canberra, Australia, attempted to cover 'Multinational Enterprises and Economic Change', from the late nineteenth century to the late 1990s (Wilkins 1998a). There now exist—accompanied by editors' introductions—two anthologies on the history of multinationals: Mira Wilkins (ed.), *The Growth of Multinationals* and Geoffrey Jones (ed.), *Transnational Corporations: A Historical Perspective* (Wilkins 1991; Jones 1993b). Mark Casson, adding his own interpretative introductions, has, in addition, assembled three book reprint series (Casson 1999, 2000, forthcoming).[14] For a brief state-of-the-art survey on the history of multinationals, written at the dawn of the 21st century, see Mira Wilkins, 'The Historical Development of Multinational Enterprise to 1930: Discontinuities and Continuities', and Geoffrey Jones, 'The Historical Development of Multinationals from the 1930s to the 1980s' (Wilkins forthcoming 2001?; Jones forthcoming 2001?). In this summary of the literature, I have not traced the actual historical evolution of the multinational enterprise, for to do so would not only mean doubling the length of this article but would involve repeating what is in the materials provided above. I refer my reader to the above publications.

---

[14] Casson's reprint series have original introductions. Lacking such original introductions, there were other book reprint series covering volumes relevant to the history of multinational enterprise by Arno Press: notably, ones on American Business Abroad (50 books, 1976), with an editorial board of Stuart Bruchey, Eleanor Bruchey, Raymond Vernon, and Mira Wilkins, and on European Business: Four Centuries of Foreign Expansion (59 books, 1977) with an editorial board of Mira Wilkins, Rondo Cameron, and Charles Wilson. So, too, Arno Press's International Finance Series (53 books, 1978), with an editorial board of Mira Wilkins, Peter B. Kenen, and Charles Kindleberger, had some selections on banks as multinationals. A Garland Press reprint series (44 books, 1983) on The World Economy (editorial board: Mira Wilkins, Charles P. Kindleberger, and Raymond Vernon) also contained a number of reprinted books that dealt with the history of multinational enterprise.

## 1.3 CASE STUDIES

To understand the history of multinational enterprise, it is vital to know the experiences of individual firms through time. General histories of multinational enterprise are only valid if they can capture the story-lines of evolving specific businesses. Some business historians have wrangled over how many case studies constitute an appropriate 'sample'. Others have been impatient with such questions. They want to read as many company histories as possible—and then ask, when is it legitimate to generalize and when is it illegitimate. The best case studies involve an author's spending years in a firm's archives—considering the strategies of top management and separating the important from the insignificant. Such case studies take time. The modern multinational enterprise is huge; decision making is complex; managements change over the decades, as does the world in which the firm operates. Business histories of individual enterprises are grist to the mill of the general historian of multinational enterprise. He or she should be reading literally hundreds of such histories, if he or she is going to generalize effectively. At the same time, the general historian needs to do original research on at least some companies.

There are a formidable number of business histories, which vary in quality and substance—from excellent archive-based studies to capsule historical sketches. All can be useful, some far more than others. The first business history specifically dedicated to international business history was Mira Wilkins and Frank Ernest Hill, *American Business Abroad: Ford on Six Continents* (Wilkins and Hill 1964). It told of the growth of a major multinational enterprise and was written based on data from Ford Motor Company's archives in the United States and outside that country. It was an extraordinary story: Ford exported its sixth car and had a foreign direct investment in a factory in Canada in its second year of existence. While Wilkins and Hill (1964) was the first history designed to focus exclusively on the evolution of a global business, it was far from alone in covering the history of major multinational enterprises. There were, for example, excellent archive-based histories of Standard Oil of New Jersey (the predecessor of EXXON), Unilever, and in 1970 and 1975 a splendid two-volume history of Imperial Chemical Industries would appear (Hidy and Hidy 1954; Gibb and Knowlton 1955; Wilson 1968; Reader 1970, 1975).[15] In addition to these, D. C. Coleman's fine

---

[15] The third volume of the Standard Oil of New Jersey/Exxon history was not published until 1971 (Larson, Knowlton, and Popple 1971); the fourth came out in 1988 (Wall 1988). The first two volumes of Charles Wilson's history of Unilever were published in 1954 and then republished in a series, when in 1968, the third volume was completed (Wilson 1968). David Fieldhouse would subsequently contribute two important additions to the history of Unilever (Fieldhouse 1978,

history of Courtaulds covered that company's important international business in the rayon industry (Coleman 1969). There are first-class business histories on Royal Dutch Shell (the early years only), British Petroleum, Burmah Oil, Rio Tinto, Swedish Match, British American Tobacco, Hoffmann-La Roche, the Hongkong and Shanghai Bank, the British Bank of the Middle East, and the Deutsche Bank. And this is but a tiny sample of the many books on the history of individual international businesses. At present, major histories of Merck and Burroughs Wellcome are in process (Gerretson 1953–7; Ferrier 1982; Bamberg 1994, 2000; Corley 1983; Harvey 1981; Lindgren 1979; Hassbring 1979; Wikander 1979; Modig 1985; Cox 2000; Peyer 1996; King 1987–91; Jones 1986a, 1987; Gall et al. 1995; Galambos in process; Church in process).

Articles also abound on particular businesses abroad. Thus, Dong-Woon Kim has done a series of essays on J. & P. Coats, the giant Scottish multinational enterprise in the thread industry, with global manufacturing operations before World War I (Kim 1995, 1997, 1998). Geoffrey Jones wrote papers on the history of key British manufacturing multinationals, including Dunlop Tire Company (Jones 1984).[16] Tetsuo Abo's essay, 'ITT's International Business Activities, 1920–1940'—on International Telephone and Telegraph—was one of the first on the history of worldwide telecommunication companies (Abo 1982–3). Jeff Merron, 'Putting Foreign Consumers on the Map: J. Walter Thompson's Struggle with General Motors' International Advertising Account in the 1920s' offers a recent examination of the international business of a leading advertising agency (Merron 1999).

Especially noteworthy volumes that considered individual multinational enterprises in particular countries (as distinct from general histories) include Fred V. Carstensen's *American Enterprise in Foreign Markets: Studies of Singer and International Harvester in Imperial Russia* and Sherman Cochran, *Big Business in China: Sino-Foreign Rivalry in the Cigarette Industry, 1890–1930* (Carstensen 1984; Cochran 1980). These titles constitute a small selection from the panoply of books and articles (and pamphlets and short blurbs) on the history of individual companies, but the sample should portray the richness and variety of historical materials.

---

1994). Fieldhouse's history of United Africa Company, a subsidiary of Unilever, gives a better appraisal of the history of foreign business in Africa than any other study that I have read (Fieldhouse 1994). Geoffrey Jones is in the process of carrying Charles Wilson's history of Unilever up to more recent years. Reader (1970, 1975) covers the forerunners of Imperial Chemical Industries, 1870–1926 in the first volume, while Imperial Chemical Industries' history, 1926–1952 is covered in the second volume.

[16] Other articles were included in Jones (1986b).

# 1.4 INDUSTRY STUDIES

Business historians supplement individual company histories with studies on industrial sectors; these often include within them histories of companies in the industry and those firms' relationships with one another within an industry. Here again a short essay allows the inclusion of barely a limited, albeit hopefully a somewhat representative group of publications, from the existing vast array. Many industry histories on international oil, for example, prove invaluable historical information; Daniel Yergin's *The Prize* is outstanding and has a long and full bibliography (Yergin 1991). For background on the modern copper industry, Thomas R. Navin, *Copper Mining and Management* has not been surpassed, although one would like to have something comparable that is more up-to-date, covering the last quarter of the century (Navin 1978).[17] There are excellent histories of the chemical industry, from the work of Williams Haynes to that of L. F. Haber to the more recent historical scholarship of Fred Aftalion (Haynes 1945–54; Haber 1971; Aftalion 1991).[18] For the history of the international construction industry, Marc Linder, *Projecting Capitalism: A History of the Internationalization of the Construction Industry*, stands alone (Linder 1994). In banking, Geoffrey Jones, *British Multinational Banking 1830–1990* and Rondo Cameron and V. I. Bovykin (eds.), *International Banking 1870–1914* are wonderfully helpful works by historians that incorporate current thinking on multinational enterprises (Jones 1993*a*; Cameron and Bovykin 1991).[19] A group of studies on trading companies has contributed immensely to our comprehension of modern mercantile enterprise, where the trade is internalized within the firm. On this subject, particularly valuable are Geoffrey Jones, *Merchants to Multinationals*, and his edited collection, *The Multinational Traders* (Jones 2000, 1998).[20] There are studies of the international history of advertising (e.g. West 1988). Numerous other industries, in primary sectors, secondary sectors, and a wide range of services have had their historians. Mark Casson and

[17] Part 3 of Navin (1978) contains brief company histories of the major US and foreign copper companies in existence in the mid-1970s. More narrow, but also extremely useful is Moran (1974).

[18] Vol. 6 of Haynes (1945–1954) contains brief histories of American chemical companies, including their international business. While there are excellent histories of the global chemical industry, the sometimes associated and sometimes separate global pharmaceutical industry has been the subject of a number of studies but none is comprehensive. For a fine short summary of recent history (1970 to the present), see Galambos and Sturchio (1998). These all are general; some studies get very specific, for example, Wilkins (2000) on the history of German chemical companies in the United States.

[19] See also Jones (1990), a set of original articles, and Jones (1992), an anthology of previously published articles many of which are on the history of banks as multinationals.

[20] See also Yonekawa and Yoshihara (1987), Chalmin (1985), and Chapman (1992).

associates, in *Multinationals and World Trade: Vertical Integration and the Division of Labour in World Industries* (1986), provided a set of industry studies, which had substantial historical content (Casson *et al.* 1986).[21] Historical studies of industries offer insights on the formidable differences that relate to the industry (or industries) in which an individual multinational enterprise participates. Research on industries has also led to discourses on the history of cartels, and their relationships with alliances and networks.[22]

# 1.5 DIPLOMATIC HISTORY AND THE HISTORY OF PUBLIC POLICY

In many ways diplomatic and business historians should be companions in their pursuit of international business history. The published volumes *Foreign Relations of the United States*, US State Department archival records, as well as the diplomatic records of other nations offer rich materials for the historian of international business.[23] There have, in particular, been a number of historical monographs on oil and diplomacy—for example those by Stephen Randall, Irvine H. Anderson, Michael B. Stoff, Marian Kent, and Gregory P. Nowell (Randall 1985; Anderson 1975, 1981; Stoff 1980; Kent 1976; Nowell 1994). Each of these offers important data on business–government relationships in an international context. Nowell's *Mercantile States and the World Oil Cartel 1900–1939* provides an especially provocative approach to what he calls 'transnational structuring' (Nowell 1994).

Other works in diplomatic history open up hidden stories. Thus, diplomatic historian Noel H. Pugach found in US government archives wonderful material on the history of the Chinese American Bank of Commerce, 1919–37 (Pugach 1997). Many of the contributors to Sébastian Guex's edited volume, *Switzerland and the Great Powers 1914–1945: Economic Relations with the United States, Great Britain, Germany and France*, effectively combined

---

[21] The essays in Casson, *et al.* (1986) covered the motor (James Foreman-Peck), bearings (Bernard Wolf), synthetic fiber, copper, and bananas (Robert A. Read), tin (Jean-François Hennart), and shipping (Mark Casson) industries.

[22] See, for example, Schröter (1996).

[23] In the 1970s, Mira Wilkins looked at US government records with an eye to understanding diplomatic involvements in the oil industry in certain South American countries in the 1920s. She looked at the differences in perspectives of the US State and Commerce departments. See Wilkins (1974*b*).

diplomatic with business history, furnishing new insights on multinational enterprise (Guex 1999). These examples seem idiosyncratic, but should reveal some of the manners in which diplomatic and business history are synergetic.

The history of public policies toward multinational enterprise, of business–government relationships, has emerged in connection with works on diplomatic history, but also in many other contexts. Thus, legal historians have written on the history of international telecommunications policies, including a great deal on the regulation of multinationals (see, for example, Sidak 1997). Business historians have used the literature on anti-trust policies in their studies of multinational enterprise (for instance, Wilkins 1974a). To my knowledge, there has been no good history on the global taxation of multinationals. Much of the large existing business-and-government literature contains historical data that are relevant to the study of multinational enterprise. Thus, Stephen Kobrin's careful work on mass-expropriating political regimes and expropriation acts is immensely helpful in understanding a crucial time in the history of multinationals (Kobrin 1980, 1984).[24] Accordingly, while no general history of public policies toward multinational enterprise exists, the topic is addressed in many specialized studies as well as in most of the more general histories of particular firms and industries.

# 1.6 EARLY HISTORY

A broad consensus prevails among most students of the history of multinational enterprise that the modern multinational dates from the mid- or late nineteenth century—that it is in fact a post-industrial revolution phenomenon. Only with steamships, railroads, and cables was it possible for managers to exercise control over business operations across borders in a meaningful manner. Transportation and communication revolutions were prerequisites for the existence of effective coordination within an individual firm.

Over the years, however, this consensus has been challenged. Indeed, for decades it has been recognized that certain aspects of the modern multinational enterprise have had a long history. Wilkins's 1970 history of American business abroad began with the sentence: 'From the period of the earliest

[24] See also summary, reclassification, and update of this information in Kennedy (1992).

known civilization in 2500 BC, Sumerian merchants found in their foreign commerce that they needed men stationed abroad to receive, to store, and to sell their goods' (Wilkins 1970, 3). Yet, little attention was paid to this suggestion and the proposition was put forth (by Charles Wilson, Rondo Cameron, and others) that the first multinationals were thirteenth-century Italian bankers (Wilson 1976?, 265–6; Cameron and Bovykin 1991, 3; see also Kindleberger 1984). At a conference in the early 1970s, a heated dispute arose over whether the East India Company (England) and the Dutch East India Company would qualify as multinational enterprises. These were large corporations that spread over borders and developed a sizable international business.

Past debates have now been replaced by new elements. First, there has been the publication of Karl Moore and David Lewis, *Birth of the Multinational: 2000 Years of Ancient Business History: From Ashur to Augustus*, which documents early far-reaching trade routes and argues that the trader in the ancient world extended the firm (Moore and Lewis 1999). This is a fascinating study that shows the importance of looking at the nature of mercantile activities over borders before the current era. The book has been criticized, as using the words multinational or international, before there were nation-states.[25] That aside, if one defines a multinational enterprise as a firm that moves over political borders (however loosely defined), there would seem to be a legitimacy in their argument.

As historians and the discipline itself have become less Euro-centric, the 'jump' from Greece and Rome to the Middle Ages has been challenged; studies will be forthcoming on the international business forms that emerged in the interim years.[26] The points made by Charles Wilson and Rondo Cameron on the bankers' direct investments (extensions of the firm) over borders seem valid; they now need to be placed in a broader historical context (see also Teichova, Kurgan-van Hentenrik, and Ziegler 1997). Ann Carlos and Stephen Nicholas, in a group of articles, have argued that it is appropriate to include as multinational enterprises not only the East India companies, but

[25] Comments by historian Herman Van der Wee, at Conference on Mapping the Multinationals, 30 Sept.–3 Oct. 1999. For a provocative essay on the more general questions of how one defines political borders and sovereignty, see Kobrin (1998).

[26] In the first draft of Wilkins (forthcoming 2001?), she used the phrase 'to jump' and was appropriately chastised by Gunder Frank (E-mail: Gunder Frank to Mira Wilkins, 28 Jan. 2000). There is a growing literature on non-European activities in the period before 'the West Became Rich'. As historians continue to broaden their perspectives, there are studies in process of the multinational enterprise that will fill the temporal space between the birth of Christ (or the fall of Rome) and the 13th-century Italian bankers (Karl Moore tells me that he and David Lewis are preparing such a work). These will include businesses outside of Europe, and certainly cover the organization of Arabian trade, about which we at present know very little, although we do know that the trade itself appears to have been far flung and probably was accompanied by some sorts of foreign direct investments (in foreign outposts).

also other chartered companies including the Hudson Bay Company that lasted for centuries (see in particular, Carlos and Nicholas 1988; and also Chaudhury and Morineau 1999). All these studies (and the newer research agendas) take the view that in the centuries before fast transportation and communication, mechanisms emerged to provide for effective internalization within the firm. Carlos and Nicholas (1988) have documented sizable intra-firm transactions and coordination and control.[27] Coordination and control often came from cultural conditioning, from trust, from shared assumptions on the 'way things were done'.

As the gap in research between the work of Moore and Lewis on the ancient world and that on the thirteenth-century multinationals based in Europe is filled, it is already clear that the businesses examined will be traders (and shippers) and perhaps merchant bankers. What seems apparent is that all the parent enterprises of the pre-nineteenth-century multinationals appear to be traders (and shippers) or bankers or individual investors, including entrepreneurial partnerships and family groups. There were direct investments abroad by these 'parent' enterprises in manufacturing, mining, and plantations. However, until the nineteenth-century (with the development of the modern multinational enterprise), Mira Wilkins has recently noted that try as hard as she could, and after consultation with many other scholars, she was unable to identify a single manufacturing company that extended as a firm over borders to sell and/or manufacture its products abroad. Likewise, the parents of mining companies abroad were not existing mining enterprises. This kind of internalization is associated with the modern multinational enterprise (Wilkins forthcoming 2001?).

Some historians have argued that there was no industrial revolution, that there was incremental industrial progress over the many centuries.[28] This is a minority viewpoint and most (not all) students of the history of multinational enterprises would, I believe, now accept the proposition that there is a basis for (a legitimacy to) the separation of the multinationals of earlier epochs from those of post-industrial revolution enterprises that have occupied (and continue to occupy) the main attention of historians of multinational enterprise. At the same time, most historians would also agree that it is imperative to study and to understand the coordination of business activities over borders as it existed in its various pre-industrial forms.

In sum, the research on pre-industrial age multinational enterprise is very exciting. It broadens our vision on what is significant and helps in

---

[27] Where there were corporate structures, as in the case of the East India companies, for example, the corporation was set up to trade and its managerial structure coordinated and controlled the activities within the firm.

[28] Rondo Cameron has been the leading advocate of this point of view.

clarifying what distinguishes contemporary multinational enterprises. It adds new insights into the nature and history of this most important institution. Yet, it does not effectively challenge the notion that the modern multinational enterprise dates from the late nineteenth and early twentieth centuries.

## 1.7 EMERGING IDEAS

What are the other new frontiers in research on the history of multinational enterprises? One set of issues deals with 'conduits and structures'. As the multinational enterprise evolves, it is obvious that the chain of strategies adopted by managers is highly complex. In 1998, Mira Wilkins and Harm Schröter published *The Free-Standing Company in the World Economy, 1830–1996* (Wilkins and Schröter 1998). This collection of essays, by authors who presently live in eight different countries, tapped sources in ten different languages and dealt with a particular type of multinational enterprise (a managed business over borders) that was very prevalent in the fifty years before 1914; the form continued to be used after 1914, but in relative terms it was never as important as in the pre-1914 period. The free-standing company made foreign direct investments, but these did not involve the growth of a firm from activities and competencies developed within the headquarters-firm in the home environment. The form was a way of mating capital riches with opportunities abroad, while reducing uncertainties. Its origins and early years of existence required clusters of separate companies acting in tandem. Discussions of free-standing companies have stimulated a considerable rash of research on the history of multinational enterprise.[29]

The conduits/structures approach deals with different kinds of and forms of cross-border transactions within the context of the history of the multinational enterprise. In this spirit, Mark Casson has emphasized the importance of information flows within the multinational enterprise, considering this intermediation role over time (Casson 2000 for the latest rendition).

---

[29] The first full article on (and the 'introduction' of the concept of) the free-standing company came in Wilkins 1988. *Business History,* the journal of British business historians, in particular, has published a large number of essays on free-standing companies; see, e.g. Casson 1994; Corley 1994*b*; Hennart 1994; Greenhill 1995; Charles Jones 1997. The German historian Thomas Fischer has looked at gold and silver mining in Colombia, using a framework on free-standing companies (Fischer 1995). In considering French business abroad, Smith (1998, 54–5) and Kogut (1998, 22–3) have found the concept useful. There were numerous other articles.

Others have thought about the significance of information asymmetry (moral hazard and adverse selection) and how it contributes to the understanding of the history of multinational enterprise. There has been much research on technology flows. In the course of this, business historians have provided crucial material on the utilization and diffusion of technology (and specifically of patent use); John Cantwell has contributed new insights on this subject (Cantwell 1999*a*, 1999*b*).[30] Historians have also paid attention to the history of other intangible assets, for example, brand names and trade marks (Wilkins 1992; Jones and Morgan 1994).

As business historians have enlarged their research horizons to more often include service sector as well as industrial multinationals, the nature of and varieties of conduits and structures grow in importance. There are discussions of networks and alliances, far beyond the cartel structures and the clusters associated with free-standing companies. Gordon Boyce's *Information, Mediation, and Institutional Development: The Rise of Large-Scale Enterprise in British Shipping, 1870–1914* explores how private information flows shape institutional development (Boyce 1995).

With the 1990s and early twenty-first century privatizations and the multinational enterprise extension into public utilities (both in telecommunications and power and light), business historians are pointing to a prior age of such multinational enterprise direct investments in cables, telephones, as well as electric light and power facilities. At the Buenos Aires International Economic History meetings in 2002 there will be a session on the history of and role of multinational enterprise in the global spread of electrification. It will trace the complex process of internationalization, sometimes with managerial direction, engineering talent, and finance coming from different nations to be mobilized and to converge in assisting host country projects. It will also show how the 'domestication' of these once international activities occurred.[31] Studies of business history offer data on the kinds of alliances that companies

---

[30] One of the early contributions on firms as conduits for technological transfer and diffusion was Wilkins (1974*c*). For historical information on technology transfer and multinational enterprise, see also the articles collected in Jeremy (1994*b*). A particularly stimulating set of essays, combining business history insights with those on the diffusion of technology, is in Chandler, Hagström, and Sölvell (1998).

[31] William Hausman, Peter Hertner, and Mira Wilkins have had approved a session on global electrification at the International Economic History Congress in 2002 in Buenos Aires; they are organizing a pre-session at Wittenberg, Germany, for 2001 (Hausman, Hertner, and Wilkins 2002). A vast historical literature exists that is binational or biregional that covers multinational enterprise and the spread of electric public utilities. But the pattern does not fit comfortably with conventional models of multinational enterprise, nor with the free-standing company model. Using insights from both and tracing the managerial and financial patterns, the conveners of these sessions hope to study the differing forms that multinational enterprise can take as business firms contributed to global electrification. Historian Kenneth Lipartito has on his future agenda assembling a group of scholars to provide comparable research on the history of telecommunications.

undertake through time, how these vary, and how they are associated with 'conduits' and what is internalized within the firm. The networks, alliances, clusters, porous boundaries of firms, and differences over time that emerge from this research are of fundamental concern to the business historian. What is becoming increasingly evident is that mapping the multinational enterprise in terms of legal, administrative (who reports to whom), and operational structures (general information, technology on products and processes, financial, personnel, and trade flows) result in different configurations not only over the decades but also in any one single period. Notions of control, 'centralization', and 'decentralization', and the meanings of headquarters and sub-headquarters are fraught with nuances and the business historian has available a broad collection of insights to cast on these matters.[32] The concepts of business as an actor and defining differing conduits for investments have illuminated the relationships between foreign portfolio and direct investments over time (Dunning and Dilyard 1999; Wilkins 1999*b*).[33]

In the context of an absence of neat hierarchial relationships, there has been research on the role of 'trust' and 'family' in supplying the cement for enterprise and as identified with enterprise culture. I mentioned this in the context of pre-industrial revolution investments, but the subject spans the years. Mark Casson has been particularly interested in the associations between information costs and 'trust' (Casson 1995).[34] There have been deliberations on size and the limits of size.[35] The business historian

---

[32]   Some of these complexities were hinted at in Wilkins (1986*a*). Jean-François Hennart, in his numerous articles that apply transaction cost theory to the history of multinational enterprise, has grappled with some of these problems. The complications become more formidable as the scale and scope of the modern multinational enterprise increases and as cross border mergers multiply.

[33]   The group (Hausman, Hertner, and Wilkins 2002) studying global electrification has been grappling with how to handle the admixture of international investment that combines foreign portfolio and foreign direct investments. One of the problems with developing statistical series on foreign direct investment is that over time foreign portfolio investments may be transformed into foreign direct investments (and vice versa).

[34]   Geoffrey Jones has pointed out that in the development of multinational banking a culture emerged within the British banks based on trust (Jones 1993*a*). As noted the research on trust helps explain some of the pre-industrial multinational enterprises, where communication was slow, but well-established norms signaled appropriate behavior (strategies and tactics).

[35]   The work of Alfred Chandler, with his emphasis on large-scale enterprise and economies of scale and scope, has dominated the business history field; however, in the last decade, a number of scholars have been concerned that in considering US business history in particular, Chandler did not pay adequate attention to the importance of 'specialty production'. See Scranton (1998). Was Chandler remiss in omitting smaller businesses from his narrative? The emphasis by some business historians 'on the small' has had little impact on the study of the history of multinational enterprise, albeit scholars have pointed out that certain small innovative firms became multinational (a firm did not need to be large to start the process of becoming multinational) but then by definition the firm becomes multi-unit and usually 'large'. Wilkins's 'Thinking Big,

is interested in what constitutes 'advantage' over time in the spread of international business: Is, as some (in particular, Jean-François Hennart) have claimed, internalization itself enough, or does there need to be some kind of intangible asset in process or product, in technology or trade-marked good? How is advantage renewed through time? Is the 'culture' of a particular business part of the 'advantage'? For backward integration of the manufacturing firm, can advantage be defined in terms of information on markets for the raw material? Hennart 1998 has much to say on what constitutes advantage.

This brings business historians to the question of performance, and how it is measured. How do business historians evaluate the 'success' of firms over time? Is it appropriate only to describe firm behavior, or should there be evaluations on efficiency and equity matters involving the firm? What criteria (profitability, market penetration, shareholder value, introduction of new technologies, size of assets, size of employment, size of sales, longevity, economic impact and linkages, for example) should be used to analyze 'performance'? Given that each of these criterion brings forth different conclusions, the shaping of the questions to be answered becomes ever more important. Business historians have tended to avoid normative judgements on particular firms. Social activists have often, as a consequence, seen their work as an 'apologetic' for the giant business enterprise.

While business historians have focused on an 'internalist analysis of corporate dynamics', some find themselves dissatisfied with that approach, believing that it neglects so much beyond the individual firm. Business historian Richard John, for example, sees future business historians devoting more attention to 'the wider political, cultural, and social context in which American [and presumably other nations'] business evolved' (John 1997). He believes there is a dichotomy between the attention to the changing firm and the broad context. Other business historians perceive no such separation and accept that managers of multinational enterprise do not formulate strategies in a vacuum (either internal to the firm or external). Indeed, taking up the gauntlet put down by John and combining it with the existing literature on multinationals as conduits not merely of direct investment but of the entire package of a managed enterprise, it is worth reevaluating, for example, the direct investments in third world countries in the late nineteenth and early twentieth century and asking more precisely exactly where multinationals fit

Thinking Small, but Thinking Internationally' (Wilkins 1996) served as the focal point for discussion at a plenary session at the Business History Conference in the Spring of 1996. The notion of size and multinational enterprise activities becomes very apparent in the history of post-World War II US business (Whitman 1999). But, the scaling back, 'down-sizing', has reflected the 'limits of size'. For a brilliant discussion on this (as germane today as when it was written), see Arrow (1974).

(Wilkins 1998*b*).[36] With some exceptions, business historians have often left to sociologists and political scientists, a number of different topics that should in effect be within their sphere of interest. Thus, while the literature on 'staples theory' is extensive (staples theory deals with the impact of raw material exports on the economy of the primary product producer), business historians have not systematically considered the implications (political scientists and sociologists have: see Topik and Wells 1998, which is very useful on this topic, as is Laxer 1989). Critiques from the standpoint of power relationships are once again more in the sphere of sociologists and political scientists than business historians.

In the business history literature of today, a number of additional insights contribute importantly to studies of the history of multinational enterprise. These include applications from economics on path dependency and the general thinking about accumulated learning and learning curves. Economic and business historians who do not write about the history of multinational enterprise stimulate those who do. Thus, the work of Paul David and Brian Arthur dealing with path dependency has energized the thinking of many students of the history of international business (David 1985; Arthur 1989); the influential book by Richard R. Nelson and Sidney G. Winter, *An Evolutionary Theory of Economic Change* should also be mentioned, not for path dependency but for its overall impact (Nelson and Winter 1982). Its impact is probably comparable to that of Edith Penrose on an earlier generation (Penrose 1959). Naomi R. Lamoreaux, Daniel M. G. Raff, and Peter Temin's edited volume, *Learning by Doing in Markets, Firms, and Countries* (Lamoreaux, Raff, and Temin 1999) is full of ideas applicable to the history of international business, from the presentation on the effects of learning on the evolution of markets, licensing, and sale *of patents* (Lamoreaux and Kenneth Sokoloff), to the role of different types of organizational forms in pricing decisions (David Genesove and Wallace Mullins), to the nature of the learning curve versus economies of scale and scope in business development (Kazuhiro Mishina), to organizational responses through time to existing plant configurations (David A. Hounshell). In a similar vein, a volume edited by Ross Thomson, *Learning and Technological Change* (Thomson 1993), provides a variety of approaches that are congenial with and enlarge the range for studies on the history of multinational enterprise (see also Lamoreaux and Raff 1995).

---

[36] Wilkins (1998*b*) tried to apply insights from international business history to the understanding of three important exports from Latin America. The new research on trading companies was particularly useful in this analysis.

# 1.8 BUSINESS HISTORY JOURNALS

Business historians have a number of journals, including *Business History Review* (published at Harvard Business School), *Business History* (the British journal), *Entreprises et Histoire* (published in Paris), and *Itinerario* (published at the University of Leiden). These have regularly included valuable materials on the history of multinational enterprise. The first issue of *Enterprise and Society* (the journal of the Business History Conference) appeared in March 2000; it, like its predecessor, *Business and Economic History*, will provide a forum for new work on the history of multinational enterprise (whereas *Business and Economic History* covered the proceedings of the Business History Conference, *Enterprise and Society* is a refereed journal).

# 1.9 CONCLUSIONS

The literature on the history of multinational enterprise is large and growing—and there is substantial interest in the field. The journals in business history are publishing on the history of multinational enterprise. New ideas proliferate that keep up with the changes in the world of international business and seek out historical precedents and explanations. Yet, the business historian cannot, as noted, use exclusively the lens of the present. To do so will distort the past. The past must be captured from behind and the vast variety and discontinuities cannot be (and should not be) neglected.

Many scholars in international business have recognized the importance of historical data. This article has noted the contributions of Dunning, Vernon, Casson, Kindleberger, Hennart, Kogut, and Kobrin to this literature.[37] Richard Caves in the *Journal of International Business Studies* has called for more 'longitudinal data' and more 'longitudinal profiles' (Caves 1998). Alan Rugman and other leaders in international business studies have seen the firm as a dynamic unit, changing through time (Rugman 1996a, 1996b). There is no absence of appreciation in the field of international business of the historical dimension.

---

[37] None of these individuals was a member of the Business History Conference (the professional society of business historians), albeit all have participated in enriching the literature. Only Mark Casson is listed in a recent directory of business historians (Jeremy 1994a).

## REFERENCES

ABO, TETSUO (1982–3). 'ITT's International Business Activities, 1920–1940', *Annals of the Institute of Social Science*, 24: 104–28.

AFTALION, FRED (1991). *A History of the International Chemical Industry*. Philadelphia: University of Pennsylvania Press.

ANDERSON, IRVINE H. (1975). *Standard-Vacuum Oil Company and United States East Asian Policy 1933–1941*. Princeton: Princeton University Press.

—— (1981). *ARAMCO, the United States, and Saudi Arabia: A Study of the Dynamics of Foreign Oil Policy, 1933–1950*. Princeton: Princeton University Press.

ARNO PRESS SERIES (1976). American Business Abroad (50 books). Editorial board: Stuart Bruchey, Eleanor Bruchey, Raymond Vernon, and Mira Wilkins.

—— (1977). European Business: Four Centuries of Foreign Expansion (59 books). Editorial board: Mira Wilkins, Rondo Cameron, and Charles Wilson.

—— (1978). International Finance (53 books). Editorial board: Mira Wilkins, Peter B. Kenen, and Charles Kindleberger.

ARROW, KENNETH J. (1974). *The Limits of Organization*. New York: W. W. Norton.

ARTHUR, W. BRIAN (1989). 'Competing Technologies, Increasing Returns, and Lock-In by Historical Events', *Economic Journal*, 99/Mar.: 116–31.

BAMBERG, J. H. (1994). *The History of the British Petroleum Company, Vol. 2: The Anglo-Iranian Years, 1928–1954*. Cambridge: Cambridge University Press.

—— (2000). *The History of the British Petroleum Company, Vol. 3*. Cambridge: Cambridge University Press.

BOSTOCK, FRANCES, and JONES, GEOFFREY (1994). 'Foreign Multinationals in British Manufacturing 1850–1962', *Business History*, 36/Jan.: 89–126.

BOYCE, GORDON (1995). *Information, Mediation, and Institutional Development: The Rise of Large-Scale Enterprise in British Shipping, 1870–1914*. Manchester: Manchester University Press.

CAMERON, RONDO, and BOVYKIN, V. I. (eds.) (1991). *International Banking 1870–1914*. New York: Oxford University Press.

CANTWELL, JOHN (1999a). 'Firms as the Source of Innovation and Growth: The Evolution of Technological Competence', *Journal of Evolutionary Economics*, 9: 331–66.

—— (ed.) (1999b), *Foreign Direct Investment and Technological Change*. 2 vols. Cheltenham: Edward Elgar.

CARLOS, ANN M., and NICHOLAS, STEPHEN (1988). 'Giants of an Earlier Capitalism: The Chartered Trading Companies as Modern Multinationals', *Business History Review*, 62/Autumn: 398–419.

CARSTENSEN, FRED V. (1984). *American Enterprise in Foreign Markets: Studies of Singer and International Harvester in Imperial Russia*. Chapel Hill: University of North Carolina Press.

CASSON, MARK (1994). 'Institutional Diversity in Overseas Enterprise: Explaining the Free-Standing Company', *Business History*, 36/Oct.: 95–108.

—— (1995). *Organization of International Business: Studies in the Economics of Trust, Vol. 2*. Aldershot: Edward Elgar.

——(1999). 'Introduction to The Emergence of International Business 1200–1800 Series', in Phillipe Dollinger, *The German Hansa*. Reprint London: Routledge: vii–xxiii.

——(2000). 'Introduction to The Evolution of International Business 1800–1945 Series', in J. F. Rippy, *British Investments in Latin America 1822–1949*. Reprint London: Routledge: 1–28.

——(forthcoming). 'Introduction to The Hegemony of International Business 1945–1970 Series'.

——and associates (1986). *Multinationals and World Trade: Vertical Integration and the Division of Labour in World Industries*. London: Allen & Unwin.

CAVES, RICHARD E. (1998). 'Research on International Business: Problems and Prospects', *Journal of International Business Studies*, 29/First Quarter: 9.

CHALMIN, PHILIPPE (1985). *Negociants et Chargeurs*. Paris: Economica.

CHANDLER, ALFRED D. (1962). *Strategy and Structure*. Cambridge, Mass: MIT Press.

——(1977). *Visible Hand*. Cambridge, Mass.: Harvard University Press.

——(1980). 'The Growth of the Transnational Industrial Firm in the United States and the United Kingdom: A Comparative Analysis', *Economic History Review*, 2nd ser., 33/Aug.: 396–410.

——(1990). *Scale and Scope*. Cambridge, Mass.: Harvard University Press.

——AMATORI, FRANCO, and HIKINO, TAKASHI (eds.) (1997). *Big Business and the Wealth of Nations*. Cambridge: Cambridge University Press.

——HAGSTRÖM, PETER, and SÖLVELL, ÖRJAN (eds.) (1998). *The Dynamic Firm: The Role of Technology, Strategy, Organization, and Regions*. Oxford: Oxford University Press.

CHAPMAN, STANLEY (1992). *Merchant Enterprise in Britain*. Cambridge: Cambridge University Press.

CHAUDHURY, SUSHIL, and MORINEAU, MICHEL (1999). *Merchants, Companies, and Trade*. Cambridge: Cambridge University Press.

CHURCH, ROY (in process). 'History of Burroughs Wellcome'.

COCHRAN, SHERMAN (1980). *Big Business in China: Sino-Foreign Rivalry in the Cigarette Industry, 1890–1930*. Cambridge, Mass: Harvard University Press.

COLEMAN, D. C. (1969). *Courtaulds*. Vol. 2. Oxford: Oxford University Press.

CORLEY, T. A. B. (1983). *A History of the Burmah Oil Company 1886–1924*. London: Heinemann.

——(1989). 'The Nature of Multinationals, 1870–1939', in Alice Teichova, Maurice Lévy Leboyer, and Helga Nussbaum (eds.), *Historical Studies in International Corporate Business*. Cambridge: Cambridge University Press, 45.

——(1994*a*). 'Britain's Overseas Investments in 1914 Revisited', *Business History*, 36/Jan.: 71–88.

——(1994*b*). 'Free-Standing Companies, their Financing, and Internalisation Theory', *Business History*, 36/Oct.: 109–17.

——(1998). 'The Free-Standing Company, in Theory and Practice', in Mira Wilkins and Harm Schröter (eds.), *The Free-Standing Company in the World Economy, 1830–1996*. Oxford: Oxford University Press, 136.

COX, HOWARD (2000). *The Global Cigarette: Origins and Evolution of British American Tobacco, 1880–1945*. Oxford: Oxford University Press.

DAVENPORT-HINES, R. P. T., and JONES, GEOFFREY (eds.) (1989). *British Business in Asia since 1860*. Cambridge: Cambridge University Press.

DAVID, PAUL A. (1985). 'Clio and the Economics of QWERTY', *American Economic Review*, 75/May: 332–7.

DUNNING, JOHN H. (1958). *American Investment in British Manufacturing Industry*. London: George Allen & Unwin (rev. and updated edn., London: Routledge, 1998).

—— (1983). 'Changes in the Level and Structure of International Production: The Last One Hundred Years', in Mark Casson (ed.), *The Growth of International Business*. London: Allen & Unwin, 84–139.

—— and DILYARD, JOHN R. (1999). 'Toward a General Paradigm of Foreign Direct and Foreign Portfolio Investment', *Transnational Corporations*, 8/Apr.: 1–52

FERRIER, R. W. (1982). *The History of the British Petroleum Company, Vol. 1: The Developing Years, 1901–1932*. Cambridge: Cambridge University Press.

FIELDHOUSE, D. K. (1978). *Unilever Overseas: The Anatomy of a Multinational 1895–1965*. London: Croom Helm.

—— (1994). *Merchant Capital and Economic Decolonization: The United Africa Company 1929–1989*. Oxford: Oxford University Press.

FISCHER, THOMAS (1995). 'Empresas extranjeras en el sector del oro y la plata en Colombia, 1870–1914: la free-standing company como modelo aplicado por inversionistas extranjeros', *Boletin Cultural y Bibliografico*, 39: 60–84.

FLETCHER, SCOTT R., and GODLEY, ANDREW (2000). 'Foreign Direct Investment in British Retailing, 1850–1962', *Business History*, 42/Apr.: 43–62.

FRANKO, LAWRENCE (1974). 'The Origins of Multinational Manufacturing by Continental European Firms', *Business History Review*, 48/Autumn: 277–302.

—— (1976). *The European Multinationals*. Stamford, Conn.: Greylock Publishers.

GALL, LOTHAR, and associates (1995). *The Deutsche Bank, 1870–1995*. London: Weidenfeld & Nicolson.

GALAMBOS, LOUIS (in process). 'History of Merck'.

—— and STURCHIO, JEFFREY L. (1998). 'Pharmaceutical Firms and the Transition to Biotechnology: A Study in Strategic Innovation', *Business History Review*, 72/Summer: 250–78.

GARLAND PRESS SERIES (1983). World Economy (44 books). Editorial board: Mira Wilkins, Charles Kindleberger, and Raymond Vernon.

GERRETSON, F. C. (1953–1957). *History of Royal Dutch*, 4 vols. Leiden: E. J. Brill.

GIBB, GEORGE SWEET, and KNOWLTON, EVELYN H. (1956). *The Resurgent Years 1911–1927*. New York: Harper & Brothers.

GODLEY, ANDREW C. (1999). 'Pioneering Foreign Direct Investment in British Manufacturing', *Business History Review*, 73/Autumn: 394–429.

GREENHILL, ROBERT (1995). 'Investment Group, Free-Standing Company or Multinational? Brazilian Warrant, 1909–52', *Business History*, 37/Jan.: 86–111.

GUEX, SÉBASTIAN (ed.) (1999). *La Suisse et les Grandes Puissances 1914–1945: Relations économiques avec les Etats-Unis, la Grande-Bretagne, l'Allemagne et la France/Switzerland and the Great Powers 1914–1945: Economic Relations with the United States, Great Britain, Germany and France*. Geneva: Droz.

HABER, L. F. (1971). *The Chemical Industry 1900–1930: International Growth and Technological Change*. Oxford: Clarendon Press.

HAGEN, ANTJE (1997a). *Deutsche Direktinvestitionen in Grossbritannien, 1871–1918.* Stuttgart: Franz Steiner Verlag.

—— (1997b). 'Patent Legislation and German FDI in the British Chemical Industry before 1914', *Business History Review,* 71/Autumn: 351–80.

—— (1999). 'German Direct Investment in the United Kingdom, 1871–1918', *Business History,* 41/Apr: 37–68.

HARVEY, CHARLES E. (1981). *The Rio Tinto Company: An Economic History of a Leading International Mining Concern, 1873–1954.* Penzance: Alison Hodge.

HASSBRING, LARS (1979). *The International Development of the Swedish Match Company, 1917–1924.* Stockholm: LiberFörlag.

HAUSMAN, WILLIAM, HERTNER, PETER, and WILKINS, MIRA (2002). Projected session at International Economic History Congress, Buenos Aires.

HAYNES, WILLIAMS (1945–54). *American Chemical Industry.* 6 vols. New York: Van Nostrand.

HENNART, JEAN-FRANÇOIS (1994). 'Free-Standing Firms and the Internalisation of Markets for Financial Capital: A Response to Casson', *Business History,* 36/Oct.: 118–32.

—— (1998). 'Transaction Cost Theory and the Free-Standing Firm', in Mira Wilkins and Harm Schröter (eds.), *The Free-Standing Company in the World Economy.* Oxford: Oxford University Press, 65–93.

HERTNER, PETER, and JONES, GEOFFREY (eds.) (1986). *Multinationals: Theory and History.* Aldershot: Gower Publishing Co.

HIDY, RALPH W., and HIDY, MURIEL E. (1955). *Pioneering in Big Business, 1882–1911.* New York: Harper & Brothers.

JEREMY, DAVID J. (ed.) (1994a). *An International Directory of Business Historians.* Aldershot: Edward Elgar.

—— (ed.) (1994b). *Technology Transfer and Business Enterprise.* Cheltenham: Edward Elgar.

JOHN, RICHARD R. (1997). 'Elaborations, Revisions, Dissents: Alfred D. Chandler, Jr.'s *Visible Hand* after Twenty Years', *Business History Review,* 71/Summer: 151–200.

JONES, CHARLES (1997). 'Institutional Forms of British Direct Investment in South America', *Business History,* 39/Apr.: 21–41.

JONES, GEOFFREY (1984). 'The Growth and Performance of British Multinational Firms before 1939: The Case of Dunlop', *Economic History Review,* 2nd ser. 36/Feb.: 35–53.

—— (1986a). *Banking and Empire in Iran. The History of the British Bank of the Middle East, Vol. 1.* Cambridge: Cambridge University Press.

—— (ed.). (1986b). *British Multinationals: Origins, Management and Performance.* Aldershot: Gower Publishing Co.

—— (1987). *Banking and Oil. The History of the British Bank of the Middle East, Vol. 2.* Cambridge: Cambridge University Press.

—— (1988). 'Foreign Multinationals and British Industry before 1945', *Economic History Review,* 2nd ser. 41/Aug.: 429–53.

—— (ed.) (1990). *Banks as Multinationals.* London: Routledge.

—— (ed.) (1992). *Multinational and International Banking.* Aldershot: Edward Elgar.

JONES, GEOFFREY (cont.) (1993a). *British Multinational Banking: 1830–1990*. Oxford: Clarendon Press.

—— (ed.) (1993b). *Transnational Corporations: A Historical Perspective*. London: Routledge.

—— (1996). *The Evolution of International Business: An Introduction*. London: Routledge.

—— (ed.) (1998). *The Multinational Traders*. London: Routledge.

—— (2000). *Merchants to Multinationals*. Oxford: Oxford University Press.

—— (forthcoming 2001?). 'The Historical Development of Multinationals from the 1930s to the 1980s', in Alfred D. Chandler, Bruce Mazlish, and Paul de Sa (eds.), *Mapping the Multinationals*. New York: Westview/Harper Collins, Global History Series.

—— and BOSTOCK, FRANCES (1986). 'Multinationals in British Manufacturing before 1962', *Business History Review*, 70/Summer: 207–56.

—— and MORGAN, NICHOLAS (eds.) (1994). *Adding Value: Brands and Marketing in Food and Drink*. London: Routledge.

—— and SCHRÖTER, HARM G. (eds.) (1993). *The Rise of Multinationals in Continental Europe*. Aldershot: Edward Elgar.

KENNEDY, CHARLES R. (1992). 'Relations between Transnational Corporations and Governments of Host Countries', *Transnational Corporations*, 1/Feb.: 73.

KENT, MARIAN (1976). *Oil and Empire: British Policy and Mesopotamian Oil 1900–1920*. London: Macmillan.

KIM, DONG-WOON (1995). 'J. & P. Coats in Tsarist Russia, 1889–1917', *Business History Review*, 69/Winter: 465–93.

—— (1997). 'J. & P. Coats as a Multinational before 1914', *Business and Economic History*, 26/2: 525–39.

—— (1998). 'The British Multinational Enterprise in the United States before 1914: The Case of J. & P. Coats', *Business History Review*, 72/Winter: 523–51.

KINDLEBERGER, CHARLES (1974). 'The Origins of US Direct Investment in France', *Business History Review*, 48/Autumn: 382–413.

—— (1984). 'International Banks and International Business in Historical Perspective' (1983), repr. in Charles Kindleberger, *Multinational Excursions*. Cambridge, Mass.: MIT Press, 155–70.

KING, FRANK H. H. (1987–91). *The Hongkong Bank*. 4 vols. Cambridge: Cambridge University Press.

KOBRIN, STEPHEN J. (1980). 'Foreign Enterprise and Forced Divestment in the LDCs', *International Organization*, 34/1 Winter: 65–88.

—— (1984). 'Expropriation as an Attempt to Control Foreign Firms in LDCs: Trends from 1969 to 1979', *International Studies Quarterly*, 18: 329–48.

—— (1998). 'Back to the Future: Neomedievalism and the Postmodern Digital World Economy', *Journal of International Affairs*, 51/2 Spring: 361–86.

KOGUT, BRUCE (1998). 'The Evolution of the Large Firm in France in Comparative Perspective', *Entreprises et Histoire*, 19: 1–41.

LAMOREAUX, NAOMI R., and RAFF, DANIEL M. G. (eds.) (1995). *Coordination and Information: Historical Perspectives on the Organization of Enterprise*. Chicago: University of Chicago Press.

———— and TEMIN, PETER (eds.) (1999). *Learning by Doing in Markets, Firms, and Countries.* Chicago: University of Chicago Press.

LARSON, HENRIETTA M., KNOWLTON, EVELYN H., and POPPLE, CHARLES S. (1971). *New Horizons 1927–1950.* New York: Harper & Row.

LAXER, GORDON (1989). *Open for Business: The Roots of Foreign Ownership in Canada.* Toronto: Oxford University Press.

LEWIS, CLEONA (1938). *America's Stake in International Investments.* Washington, DC: Brookings Institution.

—— (1945). *Debtor and Creditor Countries: 1938, 1944.* Washington, DC: Brookings Institution.

LINDER, MARC (1994). *Projecting Capitalism: A History of the Internationalization of the Construction Industry.* Westport, Conn.: Greenwood Press.

LINDGREN, HAKAN (1979). *Corporate Growth: The Swedish Match Industry in its Global Setting.* Stockholm: LiberFörlag.

LIPSEY, ROBERT (1993). 'Foreign Direct Investment in the United States: Changes over Three Decades', in Kenneth A. Froot (ed.), *Foreign Direct Investment.* Chicago: University of Chicago Press.

MARICHAL, CARLOS (ed.) (1994). *Foreign Investment in Latin America: Impact on Economic Development, 1850–1930.* Milan: Universita Bocconi.

MARSHALL, HERBERT, SOUTHARD, FRANK A., and TAYLOR, KENNETH W. (1936). *Canadian-American Industry.* New Haven: Yale University Press.

MASON, MARK (1992). *American Multinationals and Japan: The Political Economy of Japanese Capital Controls, 1899–1980.* Cambridge, Mass.: Harvard University Press.

MERRON, JEFF (1999). 'Putting Foreign Consumers on the Map: J. Walter Thompson's Struggle with General Motors' International Advertising Account in the 1920s', *Business History Review,* 73/Autumn: 465–503.

MILLER, RORY (1993). *Britain and Latin America in the Nineteenth and Twentieth Centuries.* London: Longman.

—— (1995). 'British Investment in Latin America, 1850–1950: A Reappraisal', *Itinerario* 19/3: 21–52.

—— (1999). 'Business History in Latin America: An Introduction', in Carlos Dávila and Rory Miller (eds.), *Business History in Latin America: The Experience of Seven Countries.* Liverpool: Liverpool University Press.

MODIG, HANS (1985). *Swedish Match Interests in British Industry during the Interwar Years.* Stockholm: LiberFörlag.

MOORE, KARL, and LEWIS, DAVID (1999). *Birth of the Multinational: 2000 Years of Ancient Business History—From Ashur to Augustus.* Copenhagen: Copenhagen Business School Press.

MORAN, THEODORE (1974). *Multinational Corporations and the Politics of Dependence: Copper in Chile.* Princeton: Princeton University Press.

NAVIN, THOMAS R. (1978). *Copper Mining and Management.* Tucson: University of Arizona Press.

NELSON, RICHARD R., and WINTER, SIDNEY G. (1982). *An Evolutionary Theory of Economic Change.* Cambridge, Mass.: Harvard University Press.

NICHOLAS, STEPHEN (1983). 'Agency Contracts, Institutional Modes, and the Transition to Foreign Direct Investment by British Manufacturing Multinationals before 1939', *Journal of Economic History*, 43/Sept.: 675–86.

NOWELL, GREGORY P. (1994). *Mercantile States and the World Oil Cartel 1900–1939*. Ithaca: Cornell University Press.

O'BRIEN, THOMAS (1999). *The Century of US Capitalism in Latin America*. Albuquerque: University of New Mexico Press.

PENROSE, EDITH (1959). *The Theory of the Growth of the Firm*. New York: Wiley.

PEYER, HANS CONRAD (1996). *Roche: A Company History 1896–1996*. Basel, Switzerland: Editiones Roche.

PHELPS, DUDLEY MAYNARD (1936). *Migration of Industry to South America*. New York: McGraw Hill.

PLATT, D. C. M. (ed.) (1977). *Business Imperialism 1840–1930: An Inquiry based on British Experience in Latin America*. Oxford: Oxford University Press.

PUGACH, NOEL H. (1997). *Same Bed, Different Dreams: A History of the Chinese American Bank of Commerce, 1919–1937*. Hong Kong: University of Hong Kong.

RANDALL, STEPHEN J. (1985). *United States Foreign Oil Policy, 1919–1948*. Kingston: McGill-Queen's University Press.

READER, W. J. (1970, 1975). *Imperial Chemical Industries*. 2 vols. London: Oxford University Press.

REMER, C. F. (1933). *Foreign Investment in China*. New York: Macmillan.

RUGMAN, ALAN M. (1996a). *The Theory of Multinational Enterprises: The Selected Scientific Papers of Alan M. Rugman, Vol. 1*. Cheltenham: Edward Elgar.

—— (1996b). *Multinational Enterprises and Trade Policy: The Selected Scientific Papers of Alan M. Rugman, Vol. 2*. Cheltenham: Edward Elgar.

SCHMITZ, CHRISTOPHER (1993). *The Growth of Big Business in the United States and Western Europe, 1850–1939*. Houndmills: Macmillan Press.

SCHRÖTER, HARM G. (1996). 'Cartelization and Decartelization in Europe, 1870–1995: Rise and Decline of an Economic Institution', *The Journal of European Economic History*, 25/Spring: 129–53.

SCRANTON, PHILIP (1998). *Endless Novelty. Specialty Production and American Industrialization, 1865–1925*. Princeton: Princeton University Press.

SIDAK, J. GREGORY (1997). *Foreign Investment in American Telecommunications*. Chicago: University of Chicago Press.

SMITH, MICHAEL S. (1998). 'Putting France in a Chandlerian Framework', *Business History Review*, 72/Spring: 46–85.

SOUTHARD, FRANK A. (1931). *American Industry in Europe*. Boston: Houghton-Mifflin.

STOFF, MICHAEL B. (1980). *Oil, War, and American Security: The Search for a National Policy on Foreign Oil, 1941–1947*. New Haven: Yale University Press.

STOPFORD, JOHN M. (1974). 'The Origins of British-Based Multinational Manufacturing Enterprises', *Business History Review*, 48/Autumn: 303–35.

SVEDBERG, P. (1978). 'The Portfolio-Direct Composition of Private Foreign Investment in 1914 Revisited', *Economic Journal*, 80: 763–77.

TEICHOVA, ALICE, and COTTRELL, P. L. (eds.) (1983). *International Business and Central Europe, 1918–1939*. Leicester: Leicester University Press.

—— KURGAN-VAN HENTENRIK, GINETTE, and ZIEGLER, DIETER (eds.) (1997). *Banking, Trade and Industry: Europe, America and Asia from the Thirteenth to the Twentieth Century.* Cambridge: Cambridge University Press.

—— LÉVY-LEBOYER, MAURICE, and NUSSBAUM, HELGA (eds.) (1986). *Multinational Enterprise in Historical Perspective.* Cambridge: Cambridge University Press.

—— —— —— (eds.) (1989). *Historical Studies in International Corporate Business.* Cambridge: Cambridge University Press.

THOMSON, ROSS (ed.) (1993). *Learning and Technological Change.* New York: St. Martin's Press.

TOPIK, STEVEN C., and WELLS, ALLEN (eds.) (1998). *The Second Conquest of Latin America: Coffee, Henequen, and Oil during the Export Boom, 1850–1930.* Austin: University of Texas Press.

TOYNE, BRIAN, and NIGH, DOUGLAS (eds.) (1997). *International Business: An Emerging Vision.* Columbia: University of South Carolina Press.

TWOMEY, MICHAEL J. (1998). 'Patterns of Foreign Investment in Latin America in the Twentieth Century', in John H. Coatsworth and Alan M. Taylor (eds.), *Latin America and the World Economy Since 1800.* Cambridge, Mass.: Harvard University Press, 171–201.

WALL, BENNETT H. (1988). *Growth in a Changing Environment: A History of Standard Oil Company (New Jersey), 1950–1972 and Exxon Corporation 1972–1975.* New York: McGraw-Hill.

WEST, DOUGLAS. (1988). 'Multinational Competition in the British Advertising Agency Business, 1936–1987', *Business History Review,* 62/Autumn: 467–501.

WHITMAN, MARINA V. N. (1999). *New World, New Rules: The Changing Role of the American Corporation.* Boston, Mass.: Harvard Business School Press.

WIKANDER, ULGA (1979). *Kreuger's Match Monopolies, 1925–1930. Case Studies Market Control through Public Monopolies.* Stockholm: LiberFörlag.

WILKINS, MIRA (1970). *The Emergence of Multinational Enterprise: American Business Abroad from the Colonial Era to 1914.* Cambridge, Mass: Harvard University Press.

—— (1974a). *The Maturing of Multinational Enterprise: American Business Abroad from 1914 to 1970.* Cambridge, Mass: Harvard University Press.

—— (1974b). 'Multinational Oil Companies in South America in the 1920s: Argentina, Bolivia, Brazil, Chile, Colombia, Ecuador, and Peru', *Business History Review,* 48/Autumn: 414–46.

—— (1974c). 'The Role of Private Business in the International Diffusion of Technology', *Journal of Economic History,* 34/March: 166–88.

—— (1977). 'Modern European Economic History and the Multinationals', *Journal of European Economic History,* 6/Winter: 575–95.

—— (1982). 'American–Japanese Direct Foreign Investment Relationships, 1930–1952', *Business History Review,* 56/Winter: 497–518.

—— (1986a). 'Defining a Firm: History and Theory', in Peter Hertner and Geoffrey Jones (eds.), *Multinationals: Theory and History.* Aldershot: Gower Publishing Co., 80–95.

—— (1986b). 'The Impacts of American Multinational Enterprise on American–Chinese Economic Relations, 1786–1949', in Ernest R. May and John K. Fairbank (eds.), *America's China Trade in Historical Perspective*. Cambridge, Mass: Harvard University Press, 259–92, 337–42.

—— (1986c). 'Japanese Multinational Enterprise before 1914', *Business History Review*, 60/Summer: 199–231.

—— (1988a). 'European and North American Multinationals, 1870–1914: Comparisons and Contrasts', *Business History*, 30/Jan.: 8–45.

—— (1988b). 'The Free-Standing Company, 1870–1914: An Important Type of British Foreign Direct Investment', *Economic History Review*, 2nd ser., 41/May: 259–82.

—— (1989). *The History of Foreign Investment in the United States to 1914*. Cambridge, Mass: Harvard University Press.

—— (1990). 'Japanese Multinationals in the United States: Continuity and Change, 1879–1990', *Business History Review*, 64/Winter: 585–629.

—— (ed.) (1991), *The Growth of Multinationals*. London: Edward Elgar.

—— (1992). 'The Neglected Intangible Asset: The Influence of the Trade Mark on the Rise of the Modern Corporation', *Business History*, 34/Jan.: 66–95.

—— (1993). 'The History of French Multinationals in the United States', *Entreprises et Histoire*, 3/May: 14–29.

—— (1994a). 'Comparative Hosts', *Business History*, 36/Jan.: 18–50.

—— (1994b). 'Epilogue: More than One Hundred Years: A Historical Overview of Japanese Direct Investments in the United States', in Tetsuo Abo (ed.), *Hybrid Factory*. New York: Oxford University Press, 257–83, 290–6.

—— (1996). 'Thinking Big, Thinking Small, but Thinking Internationally', *Business and Economic History*, 25:2/Winter: 119–30.

—— (1998a). 'Multinational Enterprises and Economic Change', *Australian Economic History Review*, 38/2 July: 103–34.

—— (1998b). 'An Alternative Approach', in Steven C. Topik and Allen Wells (eds.), *The Second Conquest of Latin America: Coffee, Henequen, and Oil during the Export Boom, 1850–1930*. Austin: University of Texas Press, 188–214.

—— (1999a). 'Swiss Investments in the United States, 1914–1945', in Sébastian Guex (ed.), *La Suisse et les Grandes Puissances 1914–1945 (Switzerland and the Great Powers 1914–1945)*. Geneva: Droz, 91–139.

—— (1999b). 'Two Literatures, Two Story-lines: Is a General Paradigm of Foreign Portfolio and Foreign Direct Investment Feasible?', *Transnational Corporations*, 8/Apr.: 53–116.

—— (2000). 'German Chemical Firms in the United States from the Late 19th Century to the Post-World War II Period', in John Lesch (ed.), *The German Chemical Industry in the Twentieth Century*. Dordrecht, Netherlands: Kluwer, 285–321.

—— (forthcoming 2001?). 'The Historical Development of Multinational Enterprise to 1930: Discontinuities and Continuities', in Alfred D. Chandler, Bruce Mazlish, and Paul de Sa (eds.), *Mapping the Multinationals*. New York: Westview/Harper Collins, Global History Series.

—— (in process). 'The History of Foreign Investment in the United States after 1914'.

—— and HILL, FRANK ERNEST (1964). *American Business Abroad: Ford on Six Continents*. Detroit: Wayne State University Press.

—— and SCHRÖTER, HARM (eds.) (1998). *The Free-Standing Company in the World Economy, 1830–1996*. Oxford: Oxford University Press.

WILSON, CHARLES (1968). *The History of Unilever*. 3 vols. London: Praeger.

—— (1975). 'Multinationals, Management, and World Markets: A Historical View', in Harold F. Williamson (ed.), *Evolution of International Management Structures*. Newark, Del.: University of Delaware Press, 193–216.

—— (1976?). 'The Multinational in Historical Perspective', and 'Remarks', in Keiichiro Nakagawa (ed.), *Strategy and Structure of Big Business*. Tokyo: University of Tokyo Press, 265–303.

YERGIN, DANIEL (1991). *The Prize*. New York: Simon & Schuster.

YONEKAWA, SHIN'ICHI, and YOSHIHARA, HIDEKI (eds.) (1987). *Business History of General Trading Companies*. Tokyo: University of Tokyo Press.

YUZAWA, TAKESHI, and UDAGAWA, MASARU (eds.) (1989). *Foreign Business in Japan before World War II*. Tokyo: University of Tokyo Press.

# CHAPTER 2

# THE KEY LITERATURE ON IB ACTIVITIES: 1960–2000

## JOHN H. DUNNING

## 2.1 INTRODUCTION

IN considering the origin, form, and global spread of the value-added activities of multinational enterprises (MNEs) over the past four decades, this chapter traces the main thrust and content of two influential strands of literature.

The two strands are closely inter-related. The first examines the development of scholarly thought on the determinants of the ownership, sectoral pattern, and geographical scope of MNE activity; and the second, the main changes in the external technological, economic, and political environment that, in part at least, have helped fashion these explanations. In identifying and reviewing both literatures, and the interface between them, we shall consider three main time periods, viz. the 1960s to the mid 1970s, the mid 1970s to the late 1980s, and the late 1980s to the turn of the century.

We shall present only the broad statistical trends of MNE activity in the text of this chapter, but for a comprehensive data review of the changing profile of international business (IB) activity over the past forty years, the reader is invited to consult the annual *World Investment Reports* of UNCTAD[1] between 1991 and 2000; *The World Investment Directory Reports* (five volumes, issued between 1992 and 1997), also prepared by UNCTAD; and, prior to these publications, a series of quinquennial surveys by the UNCTC[2] in 1973, 1978, 1983, and 1988.

# 2.2 THE MAIN INTELLECTUAL STRANDS

## 2.2.1 The 1960s–mid 1970s

Most scholars trace the first attempt to systematically explain the activities of firms outside their national boundaries to Stephen Hymer, a Ph.D. student who, under the supervision of Charles Kindleberger, completed his Ph.D. thesis at M.I.T., in 1960.[3] Hymer observed, as had others before him, that, in the 1950s, there was a substantial growth in the foreign value-adding activities of US firms, especially in Canada and Western Europe; and that these activities tended to be concentrated in particular industrial sectors. Why was this?

In turning to the traditional explanation of international capital flows, viz. differences in interest rates between countries, Hymer found this of little use in explaining the territorial expansion of firms. Indeed, he quickly made it clear that he was not so much interested in explaining foreign direct investment (fdi) *per se*, but rather the foreign value-adding activities of firms, irrespective of how these were financed. Hymer's orientation of interest was strongly influenced by the work of a leading industrial economist, Joe Bain, of the University of California at Berkeley, who, four years earlier, had sought to explain the ownership and competitive structure of different US industrial sectors according to whether firms found it easy or difficult to enter or exit these sectors (Bain 1956). In particular, he developed a typology of entry barriers which gave firms in industries protected by these barriers competitive advantages over those which were not. Such advantages included the

[1] United Nations Conference on Trade and Development.
[2] United Nations Centre on Transnational Corporations.
[3] See particularly Hymer (1960, 1976, and 1968).

ownership of proprietary rights, absolute cost and scale economies, and the privileged access to product or factor markets.

Hymer sought to use this approach to explain the industrial composition of fdi. He was also interested in examining why firms should wish to *own* or *control* their foreign activities; but it was not until several years later (Hymer 1968), that he explicitly used Coasian analysis to explain the rationale behind the cross-border vertical and horizontal integration of firms.[4] Moreover, apart from his emphasis on the desire of firms to appropriate the maximum economic rent of their assets to strengthen their market positions, Hymer paid little or no attention to strategic or managerial related issues.[5]

In contrast to that of Hymer, Raymond Vernon's approach, when he penned his classic article in 1966 on the product cycle and international investment, was more macro and trade oriented; although, like Hymer, he was mainly concerned with explaining the foreign activities of *US* firms. In his work, Vernon laid more emphasis on country specific factors influencing both the *origin* of the competitive advantages of firms, and the location of the value-added activities arising from them. Vernon argued that these kind of advantages, which enabled US firms to penetrate the markets of their foreign rivals (and, at the same time, create barriers to potential competitors), were essentially those which US factor endowments, patterns of demand, and market structures were best suited to produce. Vernon suggested that, initially at least, these advantages were best exploited, i.e. have value added to them, in their country of origin, but subsequently, as the products arising from them became standardized and/or reached some degree of maturity, and as the threat of competition from foreign firms became more pronounced, production might be shifted abroad.

Vernon's analytical framework paid only scant attention to the organizational structure of firms. He did not concern himself with why the firms should choose to engage in fdi rather than license the right of use of their proprietary assets to foreign firms, nor, indeed, with the gains which might arise from the act of multinationality *per se*. However, in a later contribution, Vernon (1983) did pay more attention to the organization of institutional risk as a factor influencing the outward fdi of firms.

For the decade or so following Hymer and Vernon's pioneering work, research on the theory of international production followed four main paths. The first was the formalization and testing of Hymer-type hypotheses.

---

[4] In his Ph.D. thesis, Hymer, like Edith Penrose in her earlier writings (see e.g. Penrose 1958), used the word 'integration', to describe the internalization of intermediate product markets as the main vehicle for the growth of firms.

[5] For a comprehensive assessment of Hymer's contribution to the theory of the multinational firm, see Horaguchi and Toyne (1990).

This empirical work drew, almost exclusively, on data on the activity of US affiliates in a number of developed host countries.[6] Some of this research, especially that of Caves (1971, 1974a,b) touched upon the systemic advantages of firms which uniquely arose from the common governance of trans-border activities. However, for the most part, attention was focused on those advantages which enabled the firms to penetrate foreign markets in the first place. The second was an extension of Vernon's analysis of US MNEs to embrace those of UK, Continental European, and Japanese origin.[7] Each of these studies confirmed the importance of the location-bound characteristics of home countries in influencing both the sectoral distribution of outward fdi, and its geographical profile. Each, too, hinted at the possibility, later more rigorously researched by other scholars, (eg. Pavitt 1987; Cantwell 1989; and Cantwell and Hodson 1990), that there was a link between the innovatory capabilities of countries in particular sectors, and the propensity of their firms to engage in fdi.

Third, in the early 1970s, scholars—and particularly those of a business school tradition—started to pay more attention to the strategic behavior of firms. Knickerbocker (1973), for example, discovered that there was tendency for US oligopolists to bunch the timing of their fdi in particular sectors and countries, while Flowers (1976) and Graham (1978) found that similar behavioral patterns could be observed in the activities of the foreign competitors of US multinationals, including the penetration by the former of the US itself.

A fourth, and related, line of theoretical advance stemmed from the interests of international finance scholars.[8] They reasoned that fdi was essentially a means by which firms could spread exchange rate and other risks, and internalize imperfect foreign exchange and capital markets. While some of these scholars (notably Aliber 1971) acknowledged the competitiveness of source and recipient countries as a factor influencing the competence of firms to engage in fdi, the risk diversification hypothesis, articulated especially by Rugman (1975, 1979) was principally predicated on the response of firms to market failure, and, in particular, their desire to lessen, or insure against, trans-border costs of environmental uncertainty and volatility.

---

[6] Reviews of this work are contained in Dunning (1993) and Caves (1996).

[7] See e.g. the writings of Stopford (UK 1974, 1976), Franko (Continental Europe, 1976), and Yoshino (Japan, 1976).

[8] Notably Agmon and Lessard (1977), Grubel (1968) and Rugman (1975, 1979) and Lessard (1992).

## 2.2.2 The 1970s to the late 1980s

In the following decade, the major intellectual thrust of IB scholars shifted away from the act of foreign direct investment as such to the institution making this investment, and, in particular, why it should want to extend its value added activities outside its home country.[9] In part, this was a reflection of changes in the world economic and political environment (to which we shall return later) and, in part, to the somewhat different intellectual background and interests of a new generation of IB scholars.

Two main streams of literature emerged during these years. The first was that identified with a group of the Scandinavian researchers[10] who were primarily concerned with explaining the *process* by which firms internationalized their activities. They put forward a sequential or incremental approach to understanding a deepening of the foreign commitments of firms as they learned more about the particular market and supply conditions of foreign countries. Their model also postulated that firms would first enter the foreign markets about which they were most familiar and then, capitalizing on the knowledge acquired from exporting to, or investing in, those markets, move on to less familiar territories. Though the interests of this group of scholars was largely confined to the market seeking activities of firms, theirs was one of the first dynamic models of the mode of entry into foreign markets.

The second stream of literature adopted a different approach to explaining the existence and growth of IB activity; and essentially addressed the questions 'What is distinctive about MNEs?' and 'Why, in fact, do firms headquartered in one country prefer to own value-adding activities in another country, rather than engage in arm's length or contractual transactions with foreign firms?' Quite independently, four groups of economists, respectively from Canada, the US, Sweden, and the UK became interested in explaining the foreign production of firms as a market replacing activity. Each essentially argued that this would occur whenever and wherever firms perceived that the net benefits of using cross-border markets to organize the transactions of intermediate goods and services were perceived to be lower than those of hierarchical control (i.e. their own internal administrative mechanisms).

---

[9] This is not to say that there no advances in our understanding of the determinants of fdi, and how these varied between countries, industries, and firms. The investment development path (IDP) for example, sought to relate the propensity of countries to engage in outbound fdi or receive inbound fdi, to their stage of development and other variables such as their industrial structure, size and propensity to engage in international transactions (Dunning 1981). In the last two decades, the ideas behind the IDP have helped explain the changing international investment position of several countries (Dunning and Narula 1996).

[10] Notably those of Uppsala University, Sweden e.g. Johanson and Vahlne (1977), and of the Helsinki School of Economics, e.g. Luostarinen (1979).

This idea, had, in fact, been earlier explored (but not developed) by the French economist Maurice Bye (1958) and later (as we have seen) by Hymer in a paper which was only translated in 1990 into English.[11] It was also implicit in Edith Penrose's study of the growth of firms (Penrose 1958). However, unlike Hymer, the internalization economists presupposed not only that the kind of firm specific advantages he (and others) identified were exogenously determined; but also that such advantages were not a necessary prerequisite for fdi. For—so the argument went—it was quite possible that the act of fdi itself, which involved internalizing the cross-border markets for the technology, management skills, and other intermediate products exported by the parent company to its foreign affiliates, conferred certain unique benefits. These benefits all stemmed from the endemic failure of arm's length transactions to either provide such benefits, or not provide them as efficiently as the firm could itself.

The economists recognized there was nothing new in the concept of market failure; the idea had been worked over nearly forty years earlier in a classic article by Ronald Coase (Coase 1937). And it was presently being reinterpreted in a behavioral context by Oliver Williamson (1975), and other organizational scholars. Indeed, this was a decade in which the study of organizations made some of its most exciting advances. The very *raison d'être* for the firm itself was being questioned; and many of the issues raised were debated in the context of the MNE. 'Why do firms, rather than markets, internalize cross-border transactions?' became *the* question of the day. Market failure—as identified, for example, in the costs of opportunism, bounded rationality, information asymmetry, moral hazard, adverse selection, reputation protection, agency misrepresentation, and uncertainty; or in the inability of the market for any good, asset or service, to capture economies external to the transaction involved; or its failure to permit firms to engage in price discrimination—became *the* leading explanation of the existence and growth of the MNE qua MNE.

In the late 1970s and early 1980s, then, the MNE became increasingly to be perceived as an institution which coordinates the use of intermediate assets generated in one country, with value-added activities arising from these assets in another country, (or countries), rather than as a firm which owns or controls production facilities in two or more countries. As it happens, both perceptions are correct, but while the latter focuses on the role of enterprises as *producers*, the former focuses on their role as *transactors*. Similarly, whereas earlier scholars were interested in why firms, which became MNEs, had advantages over their uninational or indigenous competitors in the countries in which they operated, the internalization economists, of which J. C. McManus,—the first to publish on this subject in 1972—Peter Buckley and Mark

---

[11] See Hymer (1968) in Casson (1990).

Casson (1976), Jean-François Hennart (1977, 1982), Nils Lundgren (1977), and Birgitta Swedenborg (1979), were the leading exponents, were concerned with the reasons why which cross-border transactions in intermediate products are coordinated *within* MNE hierarchies, rather than through external markets.

While the internalization economists acknowledged that country specific factors might influence the form and extent of market failure,—e.g. the market for pharmaceutical patents between the US and the UK was likely to be different from that of between the US and Pakistan,—and accepted that location specific variables would largely determine *where* the value added activities of MNEs would take place, the main focus of their attention was directed to identifying and evaluating the kinds of market failure promoting fdi; and, particularly, to the extent to which the internalization of cross-border markets might itself influence these advantages.

For much of the last two decades, as Jean-François Hennart enlarges upon in Chapter 5, the theory of internalization (or, we believe, paradigm is a more appropriate word) has been the dominant explanation for the existence and growth of the MNE. It has natural appeal to micro-economists, business historians, and organizational theorists. But it has not been without its critics, and, since the early 1980s, these have become more vocal. We will identify just four of these.[12] First there are the Marxist or neo-Marxist scholars who do not accept the neoclassical approach to resource allocation and organization on which internalization theory is predicated.[13] Second, there are the neo-classical trade economists, notably Kiyoshi Kojima, (1973, 1978) who prefer to explain fdi by use of traditional macro-models of trade in which the unit of analysis is the *country* rather than the business *enterprise*. At the same time, other trade economists—notably Hirsch (1976), Elhanen Helpman (1985), James Markusen (1995), and Peter Gray (1982, 1996, 1999)—by acknowledging that, in our contemporary global economy, firm- as well as country-specific assets influence the comparative advantages of countries, have come closer to reconciling the analytical approaches towards determining trade and foreign production.

Third, there are those who seek to explain the growth of MNEs in terms of their ability to create and sustain income generating advantages, *vis à vis* those of their competitors. Taking a Schumpeterian rather than a Walrasian approach to economic activity, they assert that, many of the unique assets of firms should be treated as endogenous rather than exogenous variables. Here the resource based theory of the firm, whose heritage can be traced back to the writings of Edith Penrose in the 1950s, took root, particularly among business scholars (Wernerfelt 1984, Barney 1991, Conner 1991). However, although the theory provided useful insights into the origin and sustainability

---

[12] These are explored in more detail in Dunning (2000)
[13] See e.g. the writings of Radice (1975), Cowling and Sudgen (1987), and Jenkins (1987).

of the competitive advantages of firms[14]—be they MNEs or not—it shed little light on the geographical sourcing or exploitation of these advantages; nor, indeed, of the modality by which these tasks were achieved.

Fourth, the early 1980s, saw the emergence of the evolutionary theory of the firm (Nelson and Winter 1982) which was later used to explain the pattern and trajectory of growth of some kind of MNEs—both at home and overseas (Cantwell 1989). Though related to the resource based and internalization theories of the firm, the evolutionary approach tends to take a more dynamic and path-dependency perspective; and in so doing, stresses such endogenous competitive advantages as the content and path of firm specific asset accumulation, learning capabilities and the innovation of new routines. However, IB theory, until very recently, like the resource based theory, largely neglected the locational dimension of MNE activity. This is now being given increasing attention by some of its leading proponents.[15]

The second phase of scholarly research on IB activities, also saw an attempt to offer a more integrated approach on the 'why', 'where', and 'how' of such activities. In 1976, at a Nobel Symposium in Stockholm, the present author put forward the eclectic theory (later to be renamed paradigm) of MNE activity (NB not of the MNE qua MNE), (Dunning 1977). The paradigm—also known as the OLI paradigm—asserted, and continues to assert, that the determinants of MNE activity, rested (rests) on the juxtaposition of three inter-related factors.

(1) The competitive (or O specific) advantages of existing or potential MNEs (*inter alia* as identified by the resource based, evolutionary, and organizational theories of the firm).

(2) The locational (or L specific) advantages of particular countries in offering complementary assets, for these advantages to the exploited or augmented, and

(3) The propensity of the firms possessing the O specific advantages to combine these with those of foreign based assets, by fdi, rather than by (or in addition to) the market mechanism, or some kind of non-equity cooperative venture.

We chose to call the paradigm 'eclectic' as we believed, and still believe, that a full explanation of MNE activity needed to draw upon and integrate a *variety of contextually related* theories; and most noticeably, those which took

---

[14] The authors referred to those competitive advantages arising from a bundle of scarce, unique, non-imitatible, and sustainable resources and capabilities. These advantages were presumed to stem from, or create, some kind of barrier to entry to factor, or *intermediate*, product markets by firms not possessing them. Compare this approach to industrial organizational models which seek to identify firm specific advantages based on obstacles to entry in *final* product markets.

[15] See particularly some of the recent writings of John Cantwell and his associates on technology enhancing fdi (e.g. Cantwell and Piscitello 1999), and also Chapter 14 of this volume.

account of the different types of MNE activity. Later described as *market seeking, resource seeking, efficiency seeking*, and *strategic asset seeking*, the first three types were initially identified by Jack Behrman in 1974.

Although the paradigm purports to offer a framework for examining all forms and modalities of MNE activity,—or indeed of foreign direct divestment—(Boddewyn 1979, 1983) it is important to note that it can also be translated into a number of testable theories by contextualizing the OLI configuration of variables. Thus the configuration likely to explain the extent and geographical scope of IB activity of the US telecommunications industry in Brazil is likely to be different, or differently valued, than that required to explain the fdi by Japanese banks in France or Korean fdi in consumer electronics sector in Hungary, or Chinese fdi in mineral exploration in Australia.

Over the past twenty-five years, the eclectic paradigm has been frequently modified and fine-tuned in the light of scholarly debate and the changing world economic scenaria.[16] Several tests of the significance of particular OLI variables were made, both by the author of this chapter, and by other researchers, in the late 1970s and 1980s. A selection of these are summarized in Dunning (1981, 1988, 1993, 1995, and 2000) and in Caves (1982 and 1996).

## 2.2.3 The late 1980s to 2000

Over the last two decades, in addition to the modification and refinement of the extant theories of IB activity, several new and for the most part complementary explanations have emerged and taken root. We use the word complementary deliberately, as it is clear—at least to the author of this chapter— that many of the insights about the determinants of fdi and the foreign activities of MNEs are either *country* (or region), *industry* or *firm* specific, or are seeking to explain different facets of these activities. At the same time, the contributions to our theorizing about IB activities have become increasingly multidisciplinary. Until the early 1980s, for example, most of the theories and paradigms were put forward by economists. More recently—as a comprehensive volume by Toyne and Nigh (1997) has shown—business strategists, organizational theorists, business history scholars, political scien-

---

[16] Some of these of the 1990s are described in later sections of this Chapter, but the first major reassessment of the paradigm was made in 1988 when a distinction was made between the competitive or ownership advantages of firms, viz. Oa derived from the possession of particular assets, advantages, and those which arose from the coordination and integration of related value added activities viz. Ot advantages.

tists, and economic geographers have all helped enhance our understanding of the 'why', 'where', and 'how' of IB activity.

Some of these approaches are described in more detail elsewhere in this volume. In this chapter, we shall limit our attention to identifying three major contemporary intellectual thrusts. Again, as in the previous two decades, the content and trajectory of IB research has sometimes been pro-active, and sometimes reactive, to the kind of events identified in the following section.

The three strands of scholarly thinking are closely interconnected. We shall deal briefly with each in turn.

(1) First, there has been a growing awareness among scholars that firms go abroad, or increase their multinationality, in order to *augment* their competitive advantages and/or to create new advantages, as well as to *exploit* these advantages. Such asset seeking and learning related fdi has been acknowledged as a *raison d'etre* for MNE activity by several groups of researchers, and a growing literature is emerging on the rationale and determinants of such investment; and particularly of how firms organize the spatially dispersed assets under their ownership and control. In a recent paper, Doz, Asakawa, Santos, and Williamson (1997) have coined the term 'metanational' corporation to refer to the type of MNE which harnesses resources and intellectual capabilities from throughout the world, and integrates these in a way which best advances its long term strategic objectives. Tom Wesson (Wesson 1993, 1997) and Shige Makino (1998) have both argued that extant explanations of MNE activity cannot easily accommodate asset seeking fdi. This view is also shared by economists seeking to explain Third World fdi in advanced industrial economies (e.g. Moon 1999). The logistics and strategic implications of the spatial dimensions of asset augmenting and learning related IB activity have been actively explored by Malmberg, Sölvell, and Zander (1996) and Sölvell and Birkinshaw (2000); while business scholars and economic geographers have pinpointed the advantages of intranational spatial clustering and network linkages in the accessing and accumulation of knowledge and social capital (Florida 1995, Enright 1998, 2000). At a micro level, researchers such as Kogut and Zander (1994), Dunning (1996), Kuemmerle (1999), Chen and Chen (1998), and Dunning and Lundan (1998) have assembled a powerful body of evidence of both why firms should seek to protect or advance their global competitive advantages by fdi, and also of the kind of foreign based resources and capabilities they are likely to target. Most recently of all, there has been a renewal of interest by economists and business strategists in the role of the foreign subsidiaries of MNEs in the dynamics of knowledge accumulation and organizational efficiency—an issue first addressed in several of the fdi-impact studies of the 1950s and 60s.[17]

---

[17] For further details, see Chapter 14 by Julian Birkinshaw in this volume.

(2) Second, IB scholars, again from various disciplinary persuasions, have observed, and attempted to explain, the increasing *diversity* of forms of foreign involvement. In particular, the growth of foreign portfolio investment, mergers and acquisitions, strategic alliances and a host of network relationships has been particularly spectacular over the last two decades (UNCTAD 1999, 2000). Not only have academic researchers sought to incorporate these new (or revived) modes into the received theories of fdi; (Dunning and Dilyard 1999) but—and this reflects their distinctive characteristics and the age in which we live—to pay more attention to the determinants and implications of their volatility. In turn, this is also causing scholars to revisit some of the traditional models of risk, uncertainty, and strategic interaction and to explore new analytical techniques such as signaling and real option theory (Kogut and Kulatilaha 1994; Lin 1998; Casson 2000, and Chapter 4 of this volume).

(3) Third, we see increasing attention being given to embracing the growing variety of cross-border non-equity cooperative associations within a general theory of international economic involvement. Some of the implications of the growth of such alliances on the OLI configuration facing MNEs, or potential MNEs, were first set out by the present author (Dunning 1995). At the same time, over the last decade or so, several monographs and papers have explored the increasing propensity of firms to form cross-border alliances to:

(1) help them upgrade their research and development capabilities, and/or speed up the process of innovation;
(2) to identify, and utilize externally owned resources and capabilities from throughout the world; and to coordinate these with those internally owned and controlled (Doz, Asakawa, Santos, and Williamson 1997); and
(3) to take advantage of being part of spatial clusters of economic activity, thereby benefiting from lower spatial transaction costs and enhanced learning opportunities (Storper and Scott 1995, Florida 1995).

At the same time, more attention is also being paid to the determinants of acquisitions and mergers (A&M) as a form of IB activity.[18] We shall give more attention to these issues in the next section of the chapter.

In each of these three areas, received paradigms and theories of the MNE and of IB activity are being critically scrutinized, and new paradigms and theories are being suggested. At the same time, there continues to be a robust testing of a variety of context-specific hypotheses. This has been facilitated by an improvement in the statistical data, and an increasing number of IB researchers—including several from developing and ex-communist countries. *Inter alia* this has resulted in several new and unfamiliar country-related studies (eg inbound fdi in East European Countries, China and the Mekong

---

[18] Most recently UNCTAD's *World Investment Report,* 2000 has addressed this issue.

Delta, and outbound fdi by developing Asian countries); a widening of sectoral case studies, including previously under-studied sectors, e.g. regulated industries and services; and an increasing number of business histories of individual MNEs. Also worthy of note is the increasing attention being paid to some of the environmental, social, political, and cultural implications of IB activity—particularly within the context of globalization.[19]

As a summary to this section of the chapter, we reproduce a table (Table 2.1), which was first published in a chapter written for a volume edited by Neil Hood and Stephen Young in 1999. It identifies some of the main changes both in the chapter of MNE activity, and its determinants which have occurred over the past two to three decades. We present this table without commenting further on it.

## 2.3 THE EXTERNAL CONDITIONS INFLUENCING MNE ACTIVITY

### 2.3.1 The 1960s to the mid 1970s

For most of these years, the US was at the peak of its economic and technological hegemony. Europe and Japan were still recovering from World War II. Many developing nations were struggling to find their way in their first flush of political independence, and were attractive to foreign investors only as natural resource providers. Most national governments operated some form of exchange control. The international capital market was largely dormant. By contemporary standards, cross-border information and telecommunications technologies were at an extremely rudimentary stage.

In such a scenario, the world was made up of a number of self-contained and fragmented markets. Even so, trade followed the dictates of comparative advantage. International direct investment flows were dominated by the US. As Table 2.2 shows, in the mid 1960s, the US was still accounting for over one-half of the world's stock of fdi. MNE activity at this time was predominantly

---

[19] The reader is referred to OECD (1999) on environmental issues, Donaldson (1996), Donaldson and Dufee (1998), and Santoro (2000), on ethical issues, Kogut and Singh (1988), Casson (1997), and Dunning and Bansal (1997) on cultural issues, and Kobrin (1997) on the sovereignty of nation-states.

## Table 2.1 The changing characteristics of paradigms and theories: some stylized facts

| 1970s–1980s | 1990s |
| --- | --- |
| Fdi mainly undertaken to exploit O specific advantages of investing firms; one way flow of resources and capabilities. | Multiple motives for fdi; more global sourcing of assets. |
| Largely greenfield fdi and sequential fdi financed by reinvested profits. | Fdi (particularly in Triad) largely in form of A & Ms and reinvested profits. |
| O advantages largely based on privileged possession of (home) country-specific assets (Oa). | O advantages more firm specific and related to degree of multinationality, and ability to harness and utilize created assets throughout the world. |
| Clear cut choice between alternative modalities of exploiting O advantages (licensing compared to fdi, etc.). | Systemic approach to organization of MNE activities. Alternative modalities often complementary to each other. More institutional pluralism. |
| Comparatively little foreign-based innovatory activity; foreign affiliates less embedded in the host countries. | Considerable foreign based innovatory activity (carried out mainly in advanced industrial countries) and/or via strategic alliances with foreign firms. |
| Significant inter-country barriers to both trade and fdi. | Reduced barriers to trade and fdi. |
| Clear cut international division of labor based on H-O type distribution of factor endowments. | International specialization of MNEs based more on Schumpeterian type trade and fdi. |
| Locational choices made mainly in respect to asset usage. | Locational choices also made with respect to asset augmentation. |
| Relatively little attention paid to 'spatial' market failure and location specific external economies. | More attention paid to gains arising from being part of a complex, or cluster, of firms, and from spatially linked learning economies. |
| Static nature of major paradigms. | Better appreciation of need to consider dynamic aspects of IB activity. |
| Role of MNE affiliates mainly to carry out delegated value added activities by parent company. | Affiliates now regarded as integral part of asset augmenting activities of MNEs of which they are part nature of OLI variables; and to extend the theory to embrace path dependent asset creation and learning capabilities. |

**Table** 2.1 *continued*

| 1970s–1980s | 1990s |
| --- | --- |
| Hierarchical organizational structure of MNEs. | Flattened pyramids; more heterarchical structures; more delegation of responsibilities to line managers. |
| Most strategies towards market failure 'exit' rather than 'voice' strategies. | More voice strategies towards market failure; and particularly towards capturing dynamic externalities of common governance. |
| Cautious attitudes by many governments to fdi. | Welcoming attitude to fdi by most governments. |
| Few attempts to integrate inter-disciplinary approaches to understand MNE activity. | Recognition of need to draw upon inter-disciplinary theories to construct a meaningful and robust systemic paradigm of MNE activity. |

*Source* Adapted from Table 2.1 in Dunning (1999)

of two kinds. The first was that in manufacturing and related service industries. This was primarily designed to produce products for host country markets, and was largely determined by the production and spatially related cost advantages[20] of supplying these markets from a local production facility. Such activity was mainly directed to other developed and a handful of the more advanced developing countries. The second was natural resource based activity, the purpose of which was to supply agricultural products and minerals for the home markets of the investing companies and/or that of other industrialized countries. Such fdi was mainly attracted to locations which had a competitive advantage in producing these goods, and in transporting them to foreign consumers.

In these years, researchers were mainly interested in answering three main questions. The first was 'Under what conditions will fdi replace trade?' The second was 'What determines the sectoral composition of such investment?' The third was 'In what countries is such investment likely to take place?' The main subject to be explained was the foreign value-adding activities of US owned firms; although some analysts seemed all too ready to assume that the behavior of US MNEs could be generalized to explain that of other foreign

[20] e.g. transport costs and government imposed barriers to trade.

Table 2.2 Stock of outward foreign direct investment by major home countries and regions (billions of US dollars) 1967–98

| Countries/Regions | 1967 | | | 1973 | | | 1980 | | | 1990 | | | 1998 | | |
|---|---|---|---|---|---|---|---|---|---|---|---|---|---|---|---|
| | Value | % of total | % of GDP | Value | % of total | % of GDP | Value | % of total | % of GDP | Value | % of total | % of GDP | Value | % of total | % of GDP |
| Developed market economies | 109.3 | 97.3 | 4.8 | 205.0 | 97.1 | 5.1 | 499.7 | 97.4 | 6.43 | 1640.7 | 95.7 | 9.4 | 3714.9 | 90.2 | 13.9 |
| United States | 56.6 | 50.4 | 7.1 | 101.3 | 48.0 | 7.7 | 220.2 | 42.9 | 8.1 | 435.2 | 25.4 | 7.9 | 993.6 | 24.1 | 10.6 |
| United Kingdom | 15.8 | 14.1 | 14.5 | 15.8 | 7.5 | 9.1 | 80.4 | 15.7 | 15.0 | 232.6 | 13.6 | 23.8 | 498.6 | 12.1 | 29.1 |
| Japan | 1.5 | 1.3 | 0.9 | 10.3 | 4.9 | 2.5 | 19.6 | 3.8 | 1.9 | 201.4 | 11.8 | 6.9 | 296.1 | 7.2 | 6.5 |
| Germany(FDR) | 3.0 | 2.7 | 1.6 | 11.9 | 5.6 | 3.4 | 43.1 | 8.4 | 5.3 | 151.6 | 8.4 | 9.2 | 390.1 | 9.5 | 14.4 |
| Switzerland | 2.5 | 2.2 | 10.0 | 7.1 | 3.4 | 16.2 | 21.5 | 4.2 | 21.1 | 65.7 | 3.8 | 29.1 | 176.7 | 4.3 | 62.4 |
| Netherlands | 11.0 | 9.8 | 33.1 | 15.8 | 7.5 | 25.8 | 42.1 | 8.2 | 24.4 | 109.1 | 6.4 | 38.5 | 263.0 | 6.4 | 58.1 |
| Canada | 3.7 | 3.3 | 5.3 | 7.8 | 3.7 | 6.1 | 23.8 | 4.6 | 9.0 | 84.8 | 4.9 | 14.9 | 156.6 | 3.8 | 23.3 |

| | | | | | | | | | | | | | | | |
|---|---|---|---|---|---|---|---|---|---|---|---|---|---|---|---|
| France | 6.0 | 5.3 | 7.0 | 8.8 | 4.2 | 3.8 | 18.0 | 3.5 | 2.7 | 110.1 | 6.4 | 9.2 | 242.3 | 5.9 | 13.6 |
| Italy | 2.1 | 1.9 | 2.8 | 3.2 | 1.5 | 2.4 | 7.3 | 1.4 | 1.6 | 56.1 | 3.3 | 5.1 | 170.7 | 4.1 | 10.9 |
| Sweden | 1.7 | 1.5 | 5.7 | 3.0 | 1.4 | 6.1 | 3.7 | 0.7 | 3.0 | 46.5 | 2.7 | 21.5 | 93.5 | 2.3 | 34.7 |
| Other[a] | 5.4 | 4.8 | 0.8 | 20.0 | 9.5 | 1.7 | 20.0 | 3.9 | – | 147.6 | 8.6 | 4.7 | 434.1 | 10.6 | 20.8 |
| Developing countries | 3.0 | 2.7 | 0.6 | 6.1 | 2.9 | 0.6 | 13.4 | 2.6 | 0.8 | 73.1 | 4.3 | 2.3 | 390.9 | 9.5 | 5.8 |
| Central & East Europe | nsa | nsa | nsa | nsa | nsa | nsa | nsa | nsa | nsa | neg | 0.0 | nsa | 11.3 | 0.3 | 1.2 |
| World | 112.3 | 100.0 | 4.0 | 211.1 | 100.0 | 4.2 | 513.1 | 100.0 | 5.3 | 1714.1 | 100.0 | 8.4 | 4117.1 | 100.0 | 11.9 |

For 1997

[a] Australia, Austria, Belgium, Denmark, Finland, Greece, Ireland, New Zealand, Norway, Portugal, South Africa, and Spain.

nsa (not separately available)

*Source* UN *World Investment Report* (various editions), Dunning J.H. and Cantwell J. *The IRM Directory of Statistics of International Investment and Production* (New York: Macmillan 1987)

investors. Moreover, as we have already pointed out, the attention was focused on the act of fdi *per se* rather than on the institution making the investment.

One exception to this approach was the work of Stephen Hymer. Indeed his thesis was entitled 'The International Operation of National Firms'. However, even he could not quite make up his mind which he was interested in: explaining the activities of firms *in toto*, or the growth of the firm *per se*. In any case, until the 1970s, his approach was much less influential than that of Ray Vernon, who, as we have already seen, largely ignored the organizational attributes of firms in his seminal 1996 article.

Another feature of the early studies on IB activity was that they were heavily oriented towards trade type explanations, although later the focus shifted to industrial organization models. For example, the unique O advantages of US firms were hypothesized to reflect the factor endowments, demand conditions, and the market structure of their country of origin. During these years, little if any weight was given to the role of home governments in influencing the ability or motivation of their domestic enterprises to engage in fdi; although, most surely, one factor which tempted American companies to extend their territorial horizons in the 1950s and 1960s, was US antitrust policy, which limited the opportunities for domestic growth via acquisition and mergers (Bergsten, Horst, and Moran 1978).

The interplay between the strategies of MNEs and the competitiveness of their home countries was not generally high on the agenda of policy makers. This was partly because the foreign activities of firms were not generally regarded as substitutes for their home based activities; but mainly because, as far as the leading overseas investor (namely the US) was concerned, the great majority of firms were not, at that time, involved in foreign production; and those that were (apart from a few resource based MNEs) tended to treat their foreign operations quite separately from their domestic counterparts.[21]

Yet the situation was changing fast. In 1957, the foreign assets of the 500 largest US industrial corporations were only 5 per cent of their domestic assets. By 1996, this proportion had increased to 7.6 per cent and by 1977 to 16.9 per cent (UNCTC 1988). Over the same period, the proportion of the global sales and employment of US firms accounted for by their foreign affiliates more than doubled.

However, in the 1960s, there was one policy issue of some importance to the two leading international investing countries; that was the likely impact of outward fdi on their balance of payments. In both the US and UK, studies were commissioned on this subject (Hufbauer and Adler 1968), (Reddaway, Potter, and Taylor 1968); and some not very successful attempts were made by

---

[21] For an early analysis of the strategy of US firms towards their foreign operations see Kolde (1968), Farmer and Richman (1966), Robinson (1967), Fayerweather (1969). A classic text on the strategy of UK MNEs published at this time was that of Brooke and Remmers (1970).

both governments to discourage capital outflows to help reduce balance of payments deficits.

By contrast, much more attention was directed to evaluating the impact of US multinational activity on the economies of host countries. Indeed, this was the main topic of research by economists throughout much of the 1960s. For the most part, these studies were apolitical and were conducted by scholars from developed countries. Most showed that inbound fdi generally benefited the recipient economies, especially by transferring new technologies, management and marketing skills, organizational competences, and new forms of entrepreneurship. They also demonstrated that the presence of foreign affiliates provided an important impetus to indigenous competitors to upgrade their own resources and capabilities, and raise their productivities.[22]

## 2.3.2  The 1970s to the late 1980s

As we have seen, by the mid 1970s there was a redirection in the interests and perspectives of IB scholars. Increasingly, the center of attention turned away from fdi as a modality for resource transference to the international firm (now renamed the multinational enterprise) as the owner of these resources, and the controller of the way in which they were deployed. A number of exogenous events combined to prompt this shift of interest. The first was in 1968, when Jacques Servan Schreiber published his book *The American Challenge*. This treatise warned of the increasing domination by US firms in high technology industries in Western Europe. The concern lay less with the growing proportion of European production accounted for by US affiliates, and more with the implications of this phenomena for the long-term competitiveness of the host economies. The basic assertion of Servan Schreiber was that, by drawing upon the technological, entrepreneurial, and managerial assets of their parent companies, at a zero or below market price, US affiliates could not only out-compete European firms in a wide variety of markets, but, because the former undertook most of their higher value activities in their home countries, they would weaken the latter's innovatory capacity, and thus endanger their future economic viability.

The second event was the setting up, in 1972, of a Group of Eminent Persons, by the Economic and Social Council (ECOSOC) of the United Nations, to examine the impact of MNEs on economic development.[23] The

---

[22]  See fn. 20.

[23]  Earlier work by various UN agencies on the role of fdi in economic development is described in Dell (1990). In retrospect, the title of his book was significant, as all the previous work of the ECOSOC in this area had been on evaluating the consequences of fdi qua fdi.

investigation was prompted by one of the most publicized events in the history of international business—viz. the unacceptable involvement of the ITT Company in the political affairs of Chile (Dell 1990). The group, like Servan Schreiber, explored issues related to the behavior of firms pursuing integrated strategies towards their global activities; and sought to identify the economic and social impact of these strategies for the institutions and people of the countries which were host to their affiliates.

The group pinpointed several reasons for the emergence of the global (as distinct from the multi-domestic) enterprise.[24] The first was the increase in the *degree* of multinationalization by the leading foreign investors. The foreign production component of the world production of the largest 800 or so industrial firms rose from 15 per cent in 1962 to 26 per cent in 1972; and with it the number of foreign subsidiaries owned or controlled by them (Dunning and Pearce 1985). The second was the growth of non-US multinational firms, first those from Europe and then those from Japan (Cantwell and Randaccio 1990; Franko 1989). This was accompanied by a decline in US economic hegemony, and a gradual convergence of the resources, capabilities and industrial structures of the major industrialized countries.

The third reason was the slowing down of the rate of technological innovation throughout the world in the 1970s, and an increase in the size and product diversification of the leading MNEs. The fourth was the increasing interdependence among the market economies of the world. The most forceful expression of such interdependence was the formation of a number of regional customs unions and free trade areas, e.g. the European Economic Community (EEC) and the Latin American Free Trade Area (LAFTA). However, also significant was the rapid growth of intra-firm trade and intra-trade fdi, which, itself, was symptomatic of the convergence of cross-border demand patterns and innovatory capabilities, and of the internationalization of oligopolistic market structures—at least within the industrially developed nations. Increasingly too, at a macro level, at least in these same countries, national governments were beginning to accept the need for some harmonization of their monetary and exchange rate policies.

These factors all combined to help to switch the attention of IB researchers away from trade related variables to the characteristics of firms and markets. Two main schools of thought emerged at this time. One was in direct descent of Hymer. It saw the international firm as an exploiter and creator of monopolistic advantages, which used its foreign value-added activities to reduce rather than promote competition. Most noticeably this was the perception of the 'dependencia' school (e.g. Dos Santos 1970; Sunkel 1972, 1973; Weisskopf

---

[24] The findings of the Group were set out in full in UNCTC (1974); and summarized in Dell (1990). For an analysis of the differences in the organizations and strategies of the global of multi-domestic enterprises, see Porter (1986).

1972), and of neo-Marxist scholars (e.g. Baran 1957, Radice 1975). The other view articulated by mainstream neo-classical economists (e.g. Caves 1971, 1982) was that, in most cases, the MNE was more appropriately viewed as a compensating instrument for intrinsic cross-border market failures, and a more efficient allocator of scarce resources and capabilities than would otherwise have occurred. This was also the position taken by the national governments of most industrialized economies, and of the more prosperous Asian developing countries.

There were two main exceptions to this shift of emphasis. One was the burgeoning research on Third World MNEs, which was prompted by the emergence of Brazil, Korea, Taiwan, Hong Kong, Singapore, and India as exporters of capital. Here, the particular question of interest was whether there were any differences in the determinants and structure of the foreign activities of this group of international actors compared with that of their first world counterparts. The answer by scholars such as Louis Wells (1983) and Sanjaya Lall (1983) was that there were, but these were no less important than the differences which existed *among* developing countries in their propensity to invest overseas; and those which might be expected to reflect variations in the age, experience, kind of products supplied, and extent of overseas commitment of the investing firms.

The second and, perhaps, more influential exception to the shift towards more firm specific explanations of IB activity was that of the Japanese scholar Kiyoshi Kojima. Since the mid 1970s, Kojima has consistently argued that country-specific differences between Japan and the US explain most of the differences in the level and structure of their foreign investments (see, for example Kojima 1973, 1978, and 1982). In particular, he focuses on, first, the differences in the home institutional and social structure in which firms operate, and second on the strategic goals and industrial policies of the home governments.

While Kojima's macro-economic approach to explaining fdi has been strongly criticized by internalization scholars (see especially Buckley 1986), there is little doubt that, by emphasizing the role of the home government in shaping domestic factor endowments and demand conditions, trade patterns, innovation systems, market structures, and fdi policies, he identified a lacuna in the thinking of scholars about the determinants of MNE activity. At the same time, Kojima failed to properly appreciate, first the growing significance of firm specific advantages of Japanese firms, and, second, that at least some of the country-specific advances reflected the advice or assistance given by the Japanese government to their own hierarchies, to better cope with the demands of structural change and that of the cross-border failure in intermediate product markets. Rather paradoxically, it was left to Western trade economists, noticeably Gray (1982, 1996), Helpman (1985), Hirsch (1976), Horstman and Markusen (1986), Markusen (1995), and Markusen and

Venables (1998) to later offer an integrated model of trade and fdi.[25] Some key relationships between contemporary trade and fdi models are set out in UN (1996), Dunning (1997), and Gray (1999).

## 2.3.3 The late 1980s to 2000

Kojima was not alone in feeling uncomfortable that the IB literature in the 1980s was so much dominated by micro or business oriented approaches. Other economists, not to mention political scientists and industrial geographers, were beginning to give more attention to the role of factors exogenous to firms, in affecting the extent, pattern and modes of MNE activity; and, indeed, it is perfectly clear that the political, technological and economic events of the last two decades have resulted in a very different international economic scenario than that which existed in the mid 1980s.

Most noticeably, as the data in Tables 2.2, 2.3, and 2.4 show, not only have the foreign based activities of MNEs become the main modality for serving foreign markets but there has been a considerable reconfiguration in the importance of the leading outward and inward foreign direct investors. On the other hand, notwithstanding the emergence of China as the second largest recipient of new fdi flows (UN 1999), in 1998, nearly 70 per cent of the inward stock of fdi continued to be located in three great trading blocs—North America, Western Europe, and Japan; and in that same year more than four-fifths of the innovatory activities of MNEs was also undertaken within the Triad countries. The rapid growth of all kinds of fdi in Europe, including intra-EU investment, and new opportunities for more fdi in the US—and more recently in Japan—suggests that intra-industry foreign owned production and other forms of cross-border activity, e.g. non-equity alliances within the Triad, may well rise further in the future.

At the same time, the renaissance of the market economy, new technological advances, the globalization—or, as Rugman (2000) would have it, the regionalization—of production have brought about widespread consequences for the locational attractiveness of all countries, which in turn, have affected the propensity of MNEs to invest in and out of these countries. Over the last few years, all the signs are that these are becoming increasingly important. Let us explain what we mean. One of the most significant characteristics about MNE activity is the extent to which it aids the cross-border movement and/or geographical dispersion of assets, notably money capital and innovatory capacity, and of intermediate products, technology, and

[25] See also James Markusen's contribution to this volume (Chapter 3)

management skills. *Inter alia*, this mobility—which is currently being dramatically enhanced by the advent of electronic commerce and money (Cohen 2000)—is offering MNEs wider locational options in respect of both the creation and use of these assets and products. At the same time, the imperatives of new technologies and global competitive pressures are leading to an explosion of cross-border acquisitions and mergers (A&Ms) and strategic alliances. According to the UN (1999) the volume of the former has risen eight times over the past decade, and, as Table 2.4 shows is growing at twice the rate of fdi flows.

In almost all the major economies in the world, the role of domestic and/or foreign based MNEs is increasing. Referring again to Tables 2.2 and 2.3, it can be seen that the ratio of stock of inward and outward direct investment to gross national product more than doubled between 1980 and 1998. Erstwhile Communist countries, notably those in Central and Eastern Europe, China, and in the Mekong Delta, whose borders were effectively closed to MNE activity until only fifteen years ago, accounted for 11.1 per cent of all new fdi inflows in 1998. Widespread privatization and the deregulation of many service sectors have opened up huge new opportunities for fdi in the utility, telecommunications and banking and finance sectors, while the demands of the knowledge-based economy are resulting in a no less impressive internationalization of all kinds of professional and business services.[26] Regional economic integration, especially in Europe, by making possible more Smithian division of labor, has also increased the propensity of MNEs to internalize trade flows. Direct investment earnings and payments for cross-border technology and management services are currently one of the fastest growing components of world invisible trade.

Each and all of these events has helped fashion (and is likely to continue to fashion) the orientation of IB literature. Globalization, and the critical importance of upgrading intellectual capital as a wealth-enhancing process, is demanding that scholars should give more attention to the harnessing, creation, and organization of a range of knowledge-related assets from different locations as a competitive advantage in its own right. The variables affecting the 'where' of MNE activity, as firms seek to reconcile the mobility of many of their intangible assets with the need to deploy these with other assets which are not only location bound, but concentrated in a limited spatial area, is also under scrutiny. So, indeed are the appropriate policies for national and regional governments to pursue, if their own economic and social investments are to be protected and advanced by such activities.

---

[26] As, for example, is shown in the data on the activities of US MNEs annually published by the US Department of Commerce; and in the five years benchmark surveys on *US Direct Investment Abroad* (e.g. US Department of Commerce 1998).

Table 2.3 Stock of inbound foreign direct investment by major host countries and regions (billions of US dollars) 1967–98

| Countries/Regions | 1967 | | | 1973 | | | 1980 | | | 1990 | | | 1998 | | |
|---|---|---|---|---|---|---|---|---|---|---|---|---|---|---|---|
| | Value | % of total | % of GDP | Value | % of total | % of GDP | Value | % of total | % of GDP | Value | % of total | % of GDP | Value | % of total | % of GDP |
| Developed market economies | 73.2 | 69.4 | 3.2 | 153.7 | 73.9 | 3.8 | 373.6 | 73.7 | 4.8 | 1394.9 | 78.9 | 8.4 | 2785.4 | 68.3 | 10.5 |
| Western Europe | 31.4 | 29.8 | 4.2 | 73.8 | 35.5 | 5.6 | 200.4 | 39.6 | 5.7 | 784.4 | 44.4 | 11.1 | 1571.4 | 38.4 | 8.6 |
| UK | 7.9 | 7.5 | 7.2 | 24.1 | 11.6 | 13.9 | 63.0 | 12.4 | 11.7 | 218.7 | 12.4 | 22.4 | 326.8 | 8.0 | 18.6 |
| Germany | 3.6 | 3.4 | 1.9 | 13.1 | 6.3 | 3.8 | 36.6 | 7.2 | 4.5 | 86.5 | 4.9 | 6.8 | 228.8 | 5.6 | 2.3 |
| Switzerland | 2.1 | 2.0 | 8.4 | 4.3 | 2.1 | 9.8 | 8.5 | 1.7 | 8.4 | 33.7 | 1.9 | 14.9 | 60.1 | 1.5 | 9.9 |
| United States | 9.9 | 9.4 | 1.2 | 20.6 | 9.9 | 1.6 | 83.0 | 16.4 | 3.1 | 394.9 | 22.3 | 7.2 | 875.0 | 21.4 | 9.3 |
| Other[a] | 31.9 | 30.2 | 4.2 | 59.3 | 28.5 | 4.2 | 90.2 | 17.8 | – | 215.6 | 12.2 | – | 339.0 | 8.3 | – |
| Japan | 0.6 | 0.6 | 0.3 | 1.6 | 0.8 | 0.4 | 3.3 | 0.7 | 0.3 | 9.9 | 0.6 | 0.3 | 30.3 | 0.7 | 0.3 |
| Developing countries | 32.3 | 30.6 | 6.4 | 54.7 | 26.3 | 5.4 | 132.9 | 26.2 | 5.9 | 370.6 | 21.0 | 10.5 | 129.3 | 29.8 | 10.3 |

| Africa | 5.6 | 5.3 | 9.0 | 10.2 | 4.9 | 8.7 | 13.8 | 2.7 | 4.8 | 37.6 | 2.1 | 12.1 | 75.3 | 1.8 | 8.3 |
|---|---|---|---|---|---|---|---|---|---|---|---|---|---|---|---|
| Asia | 8.3 | 7.9 | 3.9 | 15.3 | 7.4 | 3.6 | 70.0 | 13.8 | 6.0 | 214.0 | 12.1 | 10.3 | 716.6 | 17.5 | 8.4 |
| Latin America and the Caribbean | 18.5 | 17.5 | 15.8 | 28.9 | 13.9 | 12.3 | 47.7 | 9.4 | 6.4 | 114.1 | 6.5 | 10.1 | 415.6 | 10.2 | 16.1 |
| Other[b] | na | na | na | 0.3 | 0.1 | 0.1 | neg | neg | nsa | nsa | nsa | nsa | 11.8 | 0.3 | nsa |
| Central & Eastern Europe | nsa | nsa | nsa | nsa | nsa | nsa | nsa | nsa | nsa | 3.0 | 0.2 | 1.5 | 83.3 | 2.0 | 10.5 |
| World | 105.5 | 100.0 | 3.8 | 208.1 | 100.0 | 4.1 | 506.6 | 100.0 | 5.0 | 1768.0 | 100.0 | 8.7 | 4088.1 | 100.0 | 11.7 |

[a]Other developed economies include Australia, Canada, Japan, New Zealand, South Africa, Africa Sub-Saharan.

[b]Africa, Algeria, Egypt, Tunisia, and Morocco.

Other developing countries and Central & Eastern Europe (up until 1988).

nsa (not separately available)

na (not available)

*Source* As for Table 2.2

Table 2.4 Selected indicators of FDI and international production, 1986–98

| ITEM | Value at current prices (billion dollars) | | | Annual growth rate (per cent) | | | | | |
|---|---|---|---|---|---|---|---|---|---|
| | 1996 | 1997 | 1998 | 1989–90 | 1991–95 | 1996 | 1997 | 1998 |
| FDI inflows | 359 | 464 | 644 | 24.3 | 19.6 | 9.1 | 29.4 | 38.7 |
| FDI outflows | 380 | 475 | 649 | 27.3 | 15.9 | 5.9 | 25.1 | 36.6 |
| FDI inward stock | 3,086 | 3,437 | 4,088 | 17.9 | 9.6 | 10.6 | 11.4 | 18.9 |
| FDI outward stock | 3,145 | 3,423 | 4,117 | 21.3 | 10.5 | 10.7 | 8.9 | 20.3 |
| Cross-border M&As | 163 | 236 | 411 | 21.0 | 30.2 | 15.5 | 45.2 | 73.9 |
| Sales of foreign affiliates | 9,372 | 9,728 | 11,427 | 16.6 | 10.7 | 11.7 | 3.8 | 17.5 |
| Gross product of foreign affiliates | 2,026 | 2,286 | 2,677 | 16.8 | 7.3 | 6.7 | 12.8 | 17.1 |
| Total assets of foreign affiliates | 11,246 | 12,211 | 14,620 | 18.5 | 13.8 | 8.8 | 8.6 | 19.7 |
| Exports of foreign affiliates | 1,841 | 2,035 | 2,338 | 13.5 | 13.1 | −5.8 | 10.5 | 14.9 |
| Employment of foreign affiliates (thousand) | 30,941 | 31,630 | 35,074 | 5.9 | 5.6 | 4.9 | 2.2 | 10.9 |
| Memorandum: | | | | | | | | |
| GDP at factor cost | 29,024 | 29,360 | – | 12.0 | 6.4 | 2.5 | 1.2 | – |
| Gross fixed capital formation | 6,072 | 5,917 | – | 12.1 | 6.5 | 2.5 | −2.5 | – |
| Royalties and fees receipts | 57 | 60 | – | 22.4 | 14.0 | 8.6 | 3.8 | – |
| Exports of goods and non-factor services | 6,523 | 6,710 | 6,576 | 15.0 | 9.3 | 5.7 | 2.9 | −2.0 |

Source UNCTAD, based on FDI/TNC database and UNCTAD estimates

The challenges of an innovation-driven economy and the emergence of new forms of IB activities, together with the increasing volatility of many cross-border transactions, are also presenting major challenges to scholars whose main task is to study alternative ways in which MNEs organize their varied cross-border value-adding activities. It is also necessitating a reappraisal of the roles played, and the relationships between, the myriad of decision-taking entities comprising these enterprises. How can one accommodate the increasing significance of A&Ms, and the constant reconfiguration of assets and capabilities owned or controlled by MNEs into the established theories of the MNE, and of MNE activity? How does the emergence of a new set of interdependent technologies, of electronic commerce and the internet, affect the ownership and control of their cross-border activities, and their relationships with other institutions? How does the increasing instability of financial and exchange markets, and the changing architecture of supranational institutions such as the WTO, World Bank, and IMF, affect their ability to organize and shift inputs and outputs across the globe, and to price these appropriately? And how, indeed, can such tasks be accomplished in a way which balances the advantages of flexibility and organizational cohesion with a coordinated yet specialized trajectory of asset enhancement (Buckley and Casson 1998; Rangan 1998)?

These are just a few of the ways in which the intellectual interests of IB scholars and the events in the global economy—which is the stage on which these interests are played out—are currently relating to each other.

## 2.3 A CONCLUDING REMARK

One of the main conclusions of this chapter is that, over the past four decades, not only has the literature on IB activity grown at an exponential rate[27] but that the scholarly contributors to our understanding of the subject have become much more multi-disciplinary and geographically diffuse.

---

[27] In 1960, there was no specialized journal dealing with IB issues, and according to an early survey conducted by Sanjaya Lall (1975) only 40 or so research monographs on the subject had been published. At the time of Lall's survey (1973) some of the most prolific contemporary writers on IB issues, including all of the authors of the chapters in this volume, apart from Mira Wilkins and myself, had not begun publishing. Forty years on there are at least eight journals and the number of books and papers published *each* year run into hundreds if not thousands!

The issues addressed have also widened out a great deal. While business historians, organizational, management, and marketing scholars still continue to focus on the behavioral strategy of individual corporations; increasingly the interaction between IB entities and the global environment in which they operate has come to take a major place in the literature. Here international political economists, political scientists, economic geographers, sociologists, and environmentalists have all made, and are continuing to make, a major contribution to our thinking.[28] IB, after all, comprises an eclectic (*sic*) set of related disciplines, and this is one of its main strengths. Perhaps, in the next half-century, its scholarly reach will embrace even more disciplines. Indeed, this is to be applauded whenever and wherever this adds to our knowledge about the phenomena of the global economy and the role of MNE-related activity in promoting economic and social welfare.

## REFERENCES

AGMON, T., and LESSARD D. R. (1977). 'Investor Recognition of Corporate International Diversification', *Journal of Finance*, 32: 1049–55.

ALIBER, R. Z. (1971). 'The Multinational Enterprise in a Multiple Currency World', in J. H. Dunning (ed.), *The Multinational Enterprise*. London: Allen & Unwin.

BARAN, P. A. (1973). *The Political Economy of Growth*. New York: Monthly Review Press.

BARNEY, J. B. (1991). 'Firm Resources and Sustained Competitive Advantage', *Journal of Management*, 17: 99–120.

BEHRMAN, J. (1974). *Decision Criteria for Foreign Direct Investment in Latin America*. New York: Council of the Americas.

BERGSTEN, C. F., HORST, T., and MORAN, T. H. (1978). *American Multinational and American Interests*. Washington, DC: The Brookings Institution.

BODDEWYN, J. (1979). 'Foreign Investment: Magnitude and Factors', *Journal of International Business*, 10, Spring/Summer: 21–7.

—— (1983). 'Foreign Divestment Theory: Is it the Reverse of Fdi Theory?', Weltwirtschaftliches Archiv *119*, 345–55.

---

[28] Most certainly the best sources for tracing these developments over the past three decades have been the various reports of the United Nations Center on Transnational Corporations (now the Transnationals and Investment Division of UNCTAD). In particular, their annual publication, *The World Investment Report* (WIR) contains a wealth of factual data, as well as exploring, each year, a particular aspect of the role of TNCs (e.g. with respect to technology, transfer, human resource development, international trade, market structure, and competition, the challenge of development and so on). Moreover, each of the WIRs contains an extensive bibliography. Of the other international agencies, the OECD provides useful statistical data on fdi, and occasional reports on the role of fdi in member countries and on various aspects of MNE activity; while the World Bank and International Finance Corporation frequently publish surveys on the interface between fdi and economic and social development.

BRASH, D. (1966). *American Investment in Australian Industry*. Canberra: Australian University Press.

BROOKE, M. Z., and REMMERS, H. L. (1970). *The Strategy of Multinational Enterprise*. London: Longmans.

BUCKLEY, P. J. (1983). 'Macroeconomic Versus International Business Approach to Direct Foreign Investment: A Comment on Professor Kojima's Interpretation', *Hitosubashi Journal of Economics*, 24/1: 95–100.

—— and CASSON, M. C. (1976). *The Future of the Multinational Enterprise*. London: Macmillan.

——1985). *The Economic Theory of the Multinational Enterprise*. London: Macmillan.

——— —— (1998). 'Models of the Multinational Enterprise', *Journal of International Business Studies*, 29/1: 25–44.

BYE, M. (1958). 'Self Financed Multi-Territorial Units and Their Time Horizon', *International Economic Papers*, 8: 147–78.

CANTWELL, J. A. (1989). *Technological Innovation and Multinational Corporations*. Oxford: Basil Blackwell.

—— and HODSON, C. (1991). 'Global R&D and UK Competitiveness', in Casson, M. C. (ed.), *Global Research Strategy and International Competitiveness*. Oxford: Basil Blackwell, 133–82.

—— and PISCITELLO, L. (1999). 'The Emergence of Corporate International Networks for the Accumulation of Dispersed Technological Competencies', *Management International Review*, 39 (Special Issue 1): 123–47.

—— and RANDACCIO, F. S. (1990). 'Catching Up amongst the World's Largest Multinationals', *Economic Notes*, 19: 1–23.

CASSON, M. C. (ed.) (1990). *The Multinational Enterprise*. London: Edward Elgar.

—— (1991). *Economics of Business Culture. Game Theory, Transactional Costs and Economic Performance*. Oxford: Clarendon Press.

—— (2000). *Economics of International Business: A New Research Agenda*. Cheltenham: Edward Elgar.

CAVES, R. E. (1971). 'Industrial Corporations: The Industrial Economics of Foreign Investment', *Economica*, 38: 1–17.

—— (1974a). 'Causes of Direct Investment: Foreign Firms' Shares in Canadian and United Kingdom Manufacturing Industries', *Review of Economics and Statistics*, 56: 272–93.

—— (1974b). 'Multinational Firms, Competition and Productivity in Host Country Markets', *Economica*, 41: 176–93.

—— (1982 and 1996). *Multinational Firms and Economic Analysis*. Cambridge: Cambridge University Press, 1st and 2nd edns.

CHEN, H., and CHEN, T-J. (1998). 'Network Linkages and Location Choice in Foreign Direct Investment', *Journal of International Business Studies*, 29/3: 445–68.

COASE, R. H. (1937). 'The Nature of the Firm', *Economica* (New Series), 4: 386–405.

COHEN, B. J. (2000). 'Marketing Money: Currency Policy in a Globalized World', in Prakash, A., and Hart, J. A. (eds.), *Coping with Globalization*. London: Routledge, 173–97.

CONNER, K. (1991). 'A Historical Comparison of Resource Based Theory and Five Schools of Thought Within Industrial Organization Economics. Do we Have a New Theory of the Firm?', *Journal of Management*, 17: 121–54.

COWLING, K., and SUGDEN R. (1987). *Transactional Monopoly Capitalism*. Brighton: Wheatsheaf.

DEANE, R. S. (1970). *Foreign Investment in New Zealand*. Wellington: Sweet and Maxwell.

DELL, S. (1990). *The United Nations and International Business*. Durham and Landan: Duke University Press.

DONALDSON, T. (1996). 'Values in Tension: Ethics Away from Home', *Harvard Business Review*, Sept./Oct.: 48–62.

——and DUFEE, T. (1998). *Ties That Bind: A Social Contracts Approach to Business Ethics*. Cambridge, Mass.: Harvard Business School Press.

DOS SANTOS, J. (1970). 'The Structure of Dependence', *American Economic Review*, Papers and Proceedings: 231–36.

DOZ, Y. L., ASA KAWA, K., SANTOS, J. F. P., and WILLIAMSON, P. J. (1997). *The Metanational Corporation*. Fontainebleau, France: INSEAD working paper, 97/60/SM.

DUNNING, J. H. (1958). *American Investment in British Manufacturing Industry*. London: Allen & Unwin, (repr. New York: Arno Press, 1976).

——(1977). 'Trade, Location of Economic Activity and the MNE: A Search for an Eclectic Approach', in Ohlin, B., Hesselborn, P. O., and Wijkman, P. M. (eds.), *The International Allocation of Economic Activity*. London: Macmillan, 395–418.

——(1981). *International Production and the Multinational Enterprise*. London: Allen & Unwin.

——(1988). *Explaining International Production*. London: Unwin Hyman.

——(1993). *Multinational Enterprises and the Global Economy*. Wokingham, Berkshire: Addison Wesley.

——(1995). 'Reappraising the Eclectic Paradigm in the Age of Alliance Capitalism', *Journal of International Business Studies*, 26: 461–91.

——(1996). 'The Geographical Sources of Competitiveness of Firms: The Results of a New Survey', *Transnational Corporations*, 5/3: 1–30.

——(1997). *Alliance Capitalism and Global Business*. London: Routledge.

——(1999). 'Globalization and the Theory of MNE Activity', in Hood, N., and Young, S. (eds.), *The Globalization of Multinational Enterprises Activity*. Basingstoke: Macmillan, 21–54.

——(2000). 'The Eclectic Paradigm as an Envelope for Economic and Business Theories of MNE Activity', *International Business Review*, 9: 163–90.

——and BANSAL, S. (1997). 'The Cultural Sensitivity of the Eclectic Paradigm', *Multinational Business Review*, Winter, 1–16.

——and LUNDAN, S. (1998). 'The Geographical Sources of Competitiveness', *International Business Review*, 7/2: 115–33.

——and NARULA, R. (eds.) (1997). *Foreign Direct Investment and Governments*. London: Routledge.

ENRIGHT, M. J. (1998). 'Regional Clusters and Firm Strategy', in Chandler, A. D., Jr., Hagstrom, P., and Solvell, O. (eds.), *The Dynamic Firm*. Oxford: Oxford University Press, 315–42.

—— (2000). 'The Globalization of Competition and the Localization of Competitive Advantage: Policies towards Regional Clustering', in Hood, N., and Young, S. (eds), *The Globalization of Multinational Enterprise Activity*. Basingstoke: Macmillan, 303–31.

FARMER, R. N., and RICHMAN, B. M. (1966). 'International Business, An Operational Theory', *Comparative Management and Economic Progress*. Homewood, Ill.: Irwin.

FAYERWEATHER, J. (1969). *International Business Management: A Conceptual Framework*. New York: McGraw Hill.

FLORIDA, R. (1995). 'Towards the Learning Region', *Futures*, 27 (b): 527–36.

GRAHAM, E. M. (1978). 'Transatlantic Investment by Multinational Firms: A Rivalistic Phenomenon', *Journal of Post Keynesian Economics*, 1: 82–99.

GRAY, H. P. (1982). 'Towards a Unified Theory of International Trade, International Production and Direct Foreign Investment', in Black, J., and Dunning, J. H. (eds.), *International Capital Movements*. London: Macmillan, 58–83.

—— (1996). *Incorporating Firm Specific Variables into Trade Theory*. Newark Rutgers University, mimeo.

—— (1999). *Global Economic Involvement: A Synthesis of Modern International Economics*. Copenhagen: Copenhagen Business Press.

GRUBEL, H. G. (1968). 'Internationally Diversified Portfolio, Welfare Gains and Capital Flows', *American Economic Review*, 58: 299–314.

HELPMAN, E. (1985). 'The Multinational Firm and the Structure of Trade', *Review of Economic Studies*, 52: 443–57.

HENNART, J.-F. (1977). *A Theory of Foreign Direct Investment*. University of Maryland Ph.D. dissertation.

—— (1982). *A Theory of Multinational Enterprise*. Ann Arbor: University of Michigan Press.

—— (2000). 'The Transaction Cost Theory of the Multinational Enterprise', in Pitelis, C. N., and Sugden, R. (eds.), *The Nature of the Transactional Firm*. (2nd edn.). London: Routledge, 72–118.

HIRSCH, S. (1976). 'An International Trade and Investment Theory of the Firm'. *Oxford Economic Papers*, 28: 258–70.

HOFSTEDE, G. (1991). *Cultures and Organization*. London: McGraw-Hill.

HOOD, N., and YOUNG, S. (eds.) (1999). *The Globalization of Multinational Enterprise Activity*. Basingstoke: Macmillan.

HORAGUCHI, H., and TOYNE, B. (1990). 'Setting the Record Straight, Hymer, Internalization Theory and Transaction Cost Economics: A Note', *Journal of International Business Studies*, 21(3): 487–94.

HORSTMAN, I., and MARKUSEN, J. R. (1987). 'Strategic Investments and the Development of Multinationals', *International Economic Review*, 28: 109–21.

HUFBAUER, G. C., and ADLER, M. (1968). *US Manufacturing Investment and The Balance of Payments*. Washington US Treasury Department, Tax Policy Research Study No. 1.

HYMER, S. (1960). *The International Operations of National Firms: A Study of Direct Investment*. Ph.D. thesis, MIT, published by MIT Press under same title in 1976.

—— (1968). 'La Grande Firme Multinationale', *Revue Economique*, 14(b): 949–73.

JENKINS, R. (1987). *Transactional Corporations and Uneven Development: The Internationalization of Capital and the Third World*. London: Methuen.

JOHANSON J., and VAHLNE, J. E. (1977). 'The Internationalization Process of the Firm: A Model of Knowledge Development and Increasing Market Commitments', *Journal of International Business Studies*, 8: 23–32.

KNICKERBOCKER, F. T. (1973). *Oligopolistic Reaction and the Multinational Enterprise*. Cambridge, Mass.: Harvard University Press.

KOBRIN, S. (1997). 'The Architecture of Globalization: State Sovereignty in a Networked Global Economy', in Dunning, J. H. (ed.), *Governments. Globalization and International Business*. Oxford: Oxford University Press, 146–72.

KOGUT, B., and KULATILAKA, N. (1994). 'Operational Flexibility, Global Manufacturing and the Option Value of a Multinational Network', *Management Science*, 40/1: 123–39.

——— and SINGH, A. (1988). 'The Effect of National Culture in the Choice of Entry Mode', *Journal of International Business Studies*, 19: 411–32.

——— and ZANDER, U. (1994). 'Knowledge of the Firm and the Evolutionary Theory of the Multinational Corporation', *Journal of International Business Studies*: 24/4: 625–46.

KOJIMA, K. (1973). 'A Macroeconomic Approach to Foreign Direct Investment', *Hitosubashi Journal of Economics*, 14: 1–21.

——— (1978). *Direct Foreign Investment: A Japanese Model of Multinational Business Operations*. London: Croom Helm.

——— (1982). 'Macroeconomic Versus International Business Approaches to Foreign Direct Investment', *Hitosubashi Journal of Economics*, 25: 1–19.

KOLDE, E. (1968). *International Business Enterprises*. London: Prentice Hall.

KUEMMERLE, W. (1999). 'The Drivers of Foreign Direct Investment into Research and Development: An Empirical Investment', *Journal of Investment Business Studies*, 30/1: 1–24.

LALL, S. (1975). *Foreign Private Manufacturing Investment and Multinational Corporations: An Annotated Bibliography*. New York: Praeger.

——— (1983). *The New Multinationals. The Spread of Third World Enterprises*. Chichester: Wiley.

LESSARD, D. R. (1982). 'Multinational Diversification and Direct Foreign Investment', in Eiteman, D. K., and Stonehill A. (eds.), *Multinational Business Finance*. Reading, Mass.: AddisonWesley.

LUI, Sx (1998). *Foreign Direct Investment and The Multinational Enterprise. A Reexamination using Signalling Theory*. Westport, Conn: Greenwood Publishing.

LUNDGREN, N. (1977). Comment (on a chapter by J. H. Dunning), in Ohlin, B., Hesselborn, P. O., and Wijkman, P. M. (eds.), *The International Allocation of Economic Activity*. London: Macmillan, 419–25.

LUOSTARINEN, R. (1979). *Internationalization of the Firm*. Helsinki: Academie Oeconomicae, Helsinki School of Economics.

MALMBERG, A., SÖLVELL, Ö., and ZANDER, I. (1996). 'Spatial Clustering, Local Accumulation of Knowledge and Firm Competitiveness', *Geographical Annals* 78(B)/2: 85–97.

MARKUSEN, J. R. (1995). 'The Boundaries of Multinational Enterprise and the Theory of International Trade', *Journal of Economic Perspectives*, 9/2: 169–89.

MARKUSEN, J., and VENABLES, A. (1998). 'Multinational Enterprises and the New Trade Theory', *Journal of International Economics*, 46: 183–203.

McMANUS, J. C. (1972). 'The Theory of the Multinational Firm', in Paquet, G. (ed.), *The Multinational Firm and the Nation State.* Toronto: Collier-MacMillan.

MOON, H.-C. (1999). *An Unconventional Theory of Foreign Direct Investment.* Seoul: Seoul National University (mimeo).

NARULA, R. (1996). *Multinational Enterprises and Economic Structure.* London: Routledge.

PAVITT, K. (1987). 'International Patterns of Technological Accumulation', in Hood, N., and Vahlne, J. E. (eds.), *Strategies in Global Competition.* New York: Wiley, 126–57.

PENROSE, E. (1958). *The Theory of the Growth of the Firm.* Oxford: Basil Blackwell.

PORTER, M. E. (ed.) (1986). *Competition in Global Industries.* Boston: Harvard University Press.

—— (1990). *The Competitive Advantage of Nations.* New York: The Free Press.

—— (1998). 'Location, Clusters and the New Microeconomics of Competition', *Journal of Business Economics*, 33, Jan., 7–13.

RADICE, H. (ed.) (1985). *International Firms and Modern Imperialism.* Harmondsworth: Penguin.

RANGAN, S. (1998). 'Do Multinationals Operate Flexibly? Theory and Evidence', *Journal of International Business Studies*, 29/2: 17–37.

REDDAWAY, W. B., POTTER, S., and TAYLOR, C. (1968). *The Effects of UK Direct Investment Overseas.* Cambridge: Cambridge University Press.

ROBINSON, R. D. (1967). *International Management.* New York: Holt, Rinehart & Winston.

RUGMAN, A. M. (1975) 'Motives for Foreign Investment: The Market Imperfections and Risk Diversification Hypotheses', *Journal of World Trade Law*, 9: 567–73.

—— (1979). *International Diversification and the Multinational Enterprise.* Lexington, Mass.: Lexington Books.

—— (2000). *The End of Globalisation.* London: Random House Business Books.

SAFARIAN, A. E. (1966). *Foreign Ownership of Canadian Industry.* Toronto: McGraw Hill.

SANTORO, M. (2000). *Global Capitalism and Human Rights in China.* New York: Cornell University Press.

SERVAN SCHREIBER, J. (1968). *The American Challenge.* London: Hamish Hamilton.

SÖLVELL, Ö., and BIRKINSHAW, J. (2000). 'Multinational Enterprises and the Knowledge Economy: Leveraging Global Practices', in Dunning, J. H. (ed.), *Regions. Globalization and the Knowledge Based Economy.* Oxford: OUP, 82–106.

STONEHILL, A. (1965). *Foreign Ownership in Norwegian Enterprises.* Oslo: Central Bureau of Statistics.

STOPFORD, J. M. (1974). 'The Origins of British-based Multinational Enterprises', *Business History Review*, 48: 303–35.

—— (1976). 'Changing Perspective of Investment by British Manufacturing Multinationals', *Journal of International Business Studies*, 7: 15–28.

STORPER, M., and SCOTT, H. J. (1995). 'The Wealth of Regions', *Futures*, 27/5: 505–26.

STUBENITSKY, F. (1970). *American Direct Investment in the Netherlands.* Rotterdam: Rotterdam University Press.

SUNKEL, O. (1972). 'Big Business and Dependencia: A Latin-American View', *Foreign Affairs*, 50: 517–31.

SUNKEL, O. (*cont.*)(1973). 'The Pattern of Latin-American Dependence', in Urquidi, V. L., and Thorp, R. (eds), *Latin America in the International Economy.* London: Macmillan, 3–25, 26–34.

SWEDENBORG, B. (1979). *The Multinational Operation of Swedish Firms: An Analysis of Determinants and Effects.* Stockholm: Industriens Utredmrngsinstut.

TOYNE, B., and NIGH, D. (eds.) (1997). *International Business: An Emerging Vision.* Columbia, SC: University of South Carolina Press.

UN (1973). *Multinational Enterprises and Economic Development.* New York: UN.

—— (1996). *World Investment Report 1996. Investment. Trade and International Policy Arguments.* New York: UN.

—— (various dates, 1991–2000). *World Investment Report.* New York: UN, (annual publication).

—— (1999). *World Investment Report: Foreign Investment and the Challenge of Development.* New York: UN.

—— (2000). *World Investment Report: Cross Border Mergers and Acquisitions.* New York: UN.

UNCTC (1982). *Transnational Corporations and World Development.* New York: United Nations Center on Transnational Corporations.

US DEPARTMENT of COMMERCE (1998). *US Direct Investment Abroad: Benchmark Survey for 1994.* Washington Department of Commerce.

VERNON, R. (1966). 'International Investment and International Trade in the Product Cycle', *Quarterly Journal of Economics,* 80: 90–207.

—— (1974). 'The Location of Economic Activity', in Dunning, J. H. (ed.), *Economic Analysis and the Multinational Enterprise.* London: Allen & Unwin, 89–114.

—— (1983). 'Organizational and Institutional Responses to International Risk', in Herring, R. J. (ed.), *Managing International Risk.* Cambridge: Cambridge University Press, 191–216.

WEISSKOPF, T. E. (1972). 'Capitalism Underdevelopment and the Future of the Poor Countries', in Bhagwati, J. (ed.), *Economics and the World Order.* London: Macmillan, 43–77.

WELLS, L. T., JR. (1983). *Third World Multinationals.* Cambridge, Mass.: MIT Press.

WERNERFELT, B. (1984). 'A Resource-based View of the Firm', *Strategic Management Journal,* 5/2: 171–80.

WESSON, T. J. (1993). *An Alternative Motivation for Foreign Direct Investment.* (Ph.D. dissertation), Cambridge, Mass.: Harvard University Press.

—— (1997). 'A Model of Asset-Seeking Foreign Direct Investment', *Proceedings of International Business Division,* The Administration Science Association of Canada, 18/8: 110–20.

WILLIAMSON, O. E. (1975). *Markets and Hierarchies: Analysis and Antitrust Implications.* New York: Free Press.

YOSHINO, M. Y. (1976). *Japan's Multinational Enterprises.* Honolulu: Hawaii University Press.

ZEILE, W. J. (1997). 'US Intra-firm Trade in Goods', *Survey of Current Business,* February: 23–8.

CHAPTER 3

..................................................................................................

# INTERNATIONAL TRADE THEORY AND INTERNATIONAL BUSINESS

..................................................................................................

## JAMES R. MARKUSEN

## 3.1 INTRODUCTION

..................................................................................................

INTERNATIONAL trade theory and the study of international business have never had much to say to each other. It doesn't help that practitioners of these two disciplines generally reside in economics departments and business schools respectively. But that aside, there are fundamental differences in the types of questions, objectives, and tools of analysis in the two fields. The tradition of trade theory is primarily one of general-equilibrium analysis, and by its very nature this requires researchers to adopt very simple models of firms. Indeed, in competitive models with constant returns to scale, the firm has no real meaning and researchers speak of 'industries', not firms. This focus is consistent with the objectives of trade theory, which are to explain the overall pattern of production, consumption, and trade in the world economy.

General-equilibrium analysis brings a great strength and discipline to this endeavor. But this strength leaves it ill equipped to deal with individual firms and the important role that the latter play in the real economy.

International business studies provide rich detail on the strategies, decisions, and organization of individual firms, but leave it unclear how these individual decisions aggregate up to explain the pattern of overall international economic activity. Since I am an international trade economist, I am likely ignorant of much that has been learned in international business. But from the little I know, I do not see how international business studies allow me to explain certain stylized facts of aggregate activity, such as why so much direct investment is concentrated among the high-income countries, or why direct investment has grown much faster than trade for two decades.

The purpose of this chapter is to acquaint researchers in the field of international business with recent research in the field of international trade, which is moving toward incorporating aspects of international business and multinational firms into our general-equilibrium trade models. Conversely, I and other international trade economists look forward to learning more about developments in international business from this volume.

The paper begins with a discussion of the interests of trade economists in explaining the 'big picture'; that is, explaining the pattern of ownership, production, and trade in the world economy. I will discuss what I consider to be the strengths and weaknesses of current trade theory *vis-à-vis* international business studies as just noted.

I then move to a discussion of how trade theory attempts to link up different economic variables, particularly technology characteristics, country characteristics, and the costs of doing business abroad. I then turn to the formulation of a simple model with endogenous location decisions by multinational firms. This model of the firm is absurdly simple from the point of view of international business economists, but it has the advantage of allowing the individual firm to be linked with country characteristics and costs of business. I term this the 'knowledge-capital model' of the multinational enterprise, and it can be embedded in a simple two-country general-equilibrium model. It permits either strictly national firms, horizontal multinationals, and/or vertical multinationals to arise in equilibrium as a function of country characteristics and international business costs.

The following section of the paper will then show how the conceptual model leads to testable empirical predictions about how multinational activity should relate to characteristics of parent and host countries. Multinational activity is measured by the production and sales of affiliates of country i firms in country j. Country characteristics include total market size, size differences between the countries, the skilled-labor endowments of the countries, interactions between size differences and endowment differences, investment costs, and trade costs.

I will then turn to empirical studies that 'test' and estimate the knowledge-capital model, using US data on bilateral affiliate activity with the US as parent or host. These tests have generally given good support to the theory, allowing the pattern of world affiliate activity to be explained by country characteristics and the costs of international business.

# 3.2 THE INDUSTRIAL-ORGANIZATION APPROACH TO TRADE THEORY

For many decades, international trade theory was dominated by the Arrow-Debreu general-equilibrium model, in which perfect competition and constant returns to scale are the principal assumptions. This is a very powerful tool, and allows trade economists great leverage in seeking to explain the pattern of ownership, production, and trade in the world economy. General-equilibrium analysis allows economists to explain indirect but important channels of influence, such as the effect of protection on the distribution of income via changing factor prices.

Beginning in about 1980, trade economists began to move away from the assumptions of perfect competition and constant returns, while maintaining a general-equilibrium structure. This was motivated in part by the observation of a very large volume of trade among the high-income developed countries, which did not seem to be well-explained by traditional models, such as the Heckscher-Ohlin model. The introduction of imperfect competition, increasing returns to scale, and product differentiation led to models that could predict large volumes of trade among similar countries. Nevertheless, firms were typically modeled as producing a single product in a single location, serving foreign markets by exports if at all.

Somewhat later, simple general-equilibrium models in which multi-nationals arise endogenously were constructed. The exogenous variables are such things as technology, market size, relative factor endowments, trade costs, and investment costs. Firms choose whether or not to serve foreign markets by exports or by branch plants, and/or whether or not to vertically fragment production according to factor intensities and international differences in factor prices. More specifically, the typical exogenous variables in these models can be divided into three sets.

*Technology characteristics*
(1) firm-level scale economies;

(2) plant-level scale economies;
(3) factor intensities of different stages of production;
(4) ease of geographically fragmenting stages of production.

*Country characteristics*
(1) total factor endowments;
(2) relative factor abundance (especially skilled labor);
(3) physical, institutional, and legal infrastructure.

*Cost of international business*
(1) costs of trading goods (tariffs, quotas, transport costs);
(2) costs of direct investment (restrictions on ownership, use of foreign personnel, capital controls, taxation, corruption, etc.);
(3) agency costs (moral hazard, asymmetric information, contract enforceability, credibility of commitments, etc.).

The question that trade economists are often interested in is how these variables combine to determine equilibrium market structure. By market structure, let me limit the discussion to a fairly basic taxonomy, which excludes things like joint ventures, subcontracting, and so forth. Assume that a firm may assume one of three organizational modes:

1. National firm—all stages of production and production units located in one country. These will be referred to as type-n firms.
2. Horizontal multinational—'headquarters' in one country, production facilities producing roughly the same goods and services in several countries. These will be referred to as type-h firms.
3. Vertical multinational—geographic fragmentation of production by stages (e.g. R&D, intermediates, final assembly). These will be referred to as type-v firms.

By market structure, we then mean: what types of firms (n, h, v) are active in equilibrium, and where are the firms headquartered? The types of firms active in equilibrium and the countries in which their headquarters are located will be referred to as the 'regime'. The principal focus of my research has then been to determine how the equilibrium regime depends on the three sets of variables noted above.

# 3.3 THE KNOWLEDGE-CAPITAL MODEL OF THE MNE

In several previous articles, I have reviewed a great deal of empirical evidence about multinational firms, and I don't have the enthusiasm for repeating that discussion here (Markusen 1995, 1998). One principal idea that emerges from the data is that multinational firms are intensive in the use of knowledge-based assets. From this result together with the many stylized facts behind it, I have advanced the concept of the 'knowledge-capital model' of the multinational enterprise. This theory is constructed around the idea that multinational firms are intensive in the use of knowledge-based assets, and that these assets have three important properties. These are as follows.

1. *Transportability or fragmentation*: knowledge-based assets can be supplied to geographically dispersed production facilities at low cost.
2. *Factor intensity*: knowledge-based assets are skilled-labor intensive relative to production.
3. *Jointness*: knowledge-based assets can be supplied to additional production facilities without reducing their value in existing facilities.

Properties 1 and 2 provide motives for the vertical fragmentation of production, locating activities where the factors they use intensively are cheap. Property 3 provides a motive for horizontal multinationals which replicate roughly the same activities in multiple locations. Jointness leads to firm-level scale economies that give multi-plant firms a cost advantage over single-plant firms. The idea is that knowledge is a joint input or 'public good' within the firm.

These properties suggest a simple technology for the firm, perhaps too simple for international business, yet tractable in a general-equilibrium model. Consider the following two-sector, two-country, two-factor general-equilibrium model.[1]

4. Two countries, i and j,
   Two goods, X and Y,
   Two factors, skilled (S) and unskilled (L) labor.
5. Good Y is produced with constant returns by a perfectly competitive industry, and is unskilled-labor intensive.
6. Good X is produced with increasing returns, by an imperfectly competitive industry and is skilled-labor intensive.
7. X-sector technology:
   F—firm-specific fixed costs (skilled-labor intensive),
   G—plant-specific fixed costs (less skilled-labor intensive than F),
   c—constant marginal cost (less skilled-labor intensive than F),
   t—transport cost between countries (unskilled-labor intensive).
8. X-sector firms may:
   choose a country for a 'headquarters' (location of F), and a single plant in either country,

[1] This model is drawn from Markusen and Venables (1998, 2000). See also Markusen (1984), Horstmann and Markusen (1987, 1992), and Helpman (1984, 1987).

choose a country for a 'headquarters' (location of F) and plants in both countries.

9. X-sector firm types:

n—national firms with one plant in the same country as its headquarters,

h—horizontal firms with plants in both countries,

v—vertical firms with one plant, headquarters and plant in different countries.

10. Other assumptions:

Cournot competition,

segmented markets,

free entry and exit.

11. Determined in equilibrium:

the number of each type of firm active in equilibrium,

the pattern of production, ownership and trade in goods and intangibles.

Before discussing the formal structure of this model, it might be useful to relate it to Dunning's (1977, 1981) 'eclectic paradigm'. As noted above, the firm-level fixed cost F creates multi-plant economies of scale, and we could think of the asset created by F (e.g. blueprints, formulae, procedures, patents) as Dunning's ownership advantage. Location advantages come in two forms, primarily related to whether or not the investment is horizontal or vertical as defined above. If it is horizontal, then the transport cost t creates a location advantage for producing in the foreign market rather than exporting to it. But the plant-level fixed cost G is a location disadvantage for having a second plant. There is thus a tension between G and t and, as we shall discuss shortly, one prediction is that investment will be more likely in large host-country markets.

For vertical investments in which the production process is fragmented into stages with different factor intensities, different factor prices between countries will create a location advantage. So, for example, a significant difference between skilled and unskilled labor prices between countries may mean that the headquarters are located in the skilled-labor-abundant country where F is cheap, and the plant is located in the unskilled-labor-abundant countries where c is cheap. Note that for vertical investments, the transport cost t will generally be a location disadvantage, since it raises the cost of shipping final output back to the home market.

It is beyond the scope of the paper to discuss internalization advantage. But let me mention that there are a number of trade papers that do deal with internalization, and it basically arises in these models from the same properties of knowledge-based assets that lead to multi-plant economies and firm-level scale economies. The same joint-input property of knowledge that makes it easily transported to foreign plants make that knowledge easily dissipated.

## Table 3.1  Notation

| | |
|---|---|
| $Y_i$ | Production of Y in country i |
| $W_i$ | Welfare of country i |
| $X_{ij}^k$ | Production of X by a firm type k, headquartered in i, selling in j |
| $N_i^k$ | Number of firms of type k headquartered in country i active in equilibrium |
| $P_y$ | Price of good Y |
| $mc_{yi}$ | Marginal cost of producing good Y in country i |
| $p_{ui}$ | Price of a unit of welfare (utility) in country i |
| $mc_{ui}$ | Marginal cost of producing a unit of welfare (utility) in country i |
| $P_{xi}$ | Price of good X in country i |
| $mc_{xij}^k$ | Marginal production (and shipping if relevant) cost of X for firm type k headquartered in country i and selling in country j |
| $P_{fci}^k$ | Price of fixed costs for firm type k, headquartered in i |
| $fc_i^k$ | Fixed costs for firm type k, headquartered in i |
| $w_i$ | Wage of unskilled labor in country i |
| $v_i$ | Wage of skilled labor in country i |
| $cons_i$ | The representative consumer in country i |
| $entre_i^k$ | The 'owner' of firm type k headquartered in country i |
| $mk_{ij}^k$ | Markup of firm type k headquartered in country i and selling in j |
| $mkrev_i^k$ | Markup revenue of firm type k headquartered in country i |

Now let me describe how the formal model is specified. Note that it is useful to think of welfare as being 'produced' (with inputs of commodities), and having a unit 'price' and 'cost' of production, which is in fact the unit expenditure function for the representative consumer. It is similarly useful to think of fixed costs as being produced, and the demand coming from entrepreneurs (firm owners) out of markup revenues. A list of notation is given in Table 3.1. Superscript 'k' denotes firm type, k = (n, h, v). Superscripts i and j refer to countries. When used in combination (ij) the first subscript refers to the country in which the firm is headquartered, and the second denotes the country in which the output is sold.

A large model of this type is formulated as a complementarity problem; that is, as a set of inequalities subject to non-negative values of

## Table 3.2 Inequalities and complementary variables

| Inequalities | Complementary variables number | |
|---|---|---|
| pricing inequalities | activity level | number |
| $p_y \leq mc_{yi}$ | $Y_i$ | 2 |
| $p_{ui} \leq mc_{ui}$ | $W_i$ | 2 |
| $p_{xj}(I - mk_{ij}^k) \leq mc_{xij}^k$ | $X_i^k$ | 12 |
| $p_{fci}^k \leq fc_i^k$ | $N^k$ | 6 |
| market clearing inequalities | price | number |
| $\sum_i$ demand $Y_i \leq \sum_i$ supply $Y_i$ | $p_y$ | 1 |
| demand $W_i \leq$ supply $W_i$ | $p_{ui}$ | 2 |
| demand $X_j \leq \sum_k \sum_i$ supply $X_{ij}^k$ | $p_{xj}$ | 2 |
| demand $N_i^k \leq$ supply $N_i^k$ | $p_{fci}^k$ | 6 |
| demand $L_i \leq$ supply $L_i$ | $w_i$ | 2 |
| demand $S_i \leq$ supply $S_i$ | $v_i$ | 2 |
| income balance | incomes | number |
| expenditure $cons_i \leq$ income $cons_i$ | income $cons_i$ | 2 |
| demand $N_i^k \leq mkrev_i^k$ | income $entre_i^k$ | 6 |
| auxiliary constraints | markups | number |
| $km_{ij}^k \leq$ (Cournot formula)$m_{ij}^k$ | $mk_{ij}^k$ | 12 |

complementary variables. Either an inequality holds as a strict equality and the complementary variable is positive, or it holds as a strict inequality and the associated variable is zero. As noted above, a useful trick is to view fixed costs as being produced and demand by entrepreneurs out of markup revenues. In equilibrium, fixed costs equal markup revenues, which is the free-entry condition of zero profits. The model is calibrated so that the activity level of fixed costs production in equilibrium corresponds to the number of firms active in equilibrium (N).

What follows are the inequalities and complementary variables of the model. Pricing inequalities (marginal revenue equal to marginal cost) have quantities ('activity levels') as complementary or 'dual' variables, and market clearing inequalities have prices as complementary or dual variables. Remaining inequalities are income balance inequalities for agents, including firm owners, and the equations giving the Cournot markup formulae.

## 3.4 TESTABLE HYPOTHESES

An attractive feature of the above model is that it offers testable hypotheses about the relationship between the pattern of multinational investment and country characteristics such as size, relative size, relative factor endowments, and trade costs. Figures 3.1 and 3.2 are taken from simulations of a model similar to that above found in Carr, Markusen, and Maskus (2001). These diagrams are Edgeworth boxes, in which the dimensions of the floor are the total two-country endowment of skilled and unskilled labor. The origin for country i is as shown, with the origin for country j at the opposite corner of the box. Different points in this box correspond to differences in country sizes and differences in relative endowments. Along the southwest-northeast (SW-NE) diagonal, the countries differ in size (except at the midpoint) but not in relative endowments. Movements away from this diagonal toward the northwest or southeast (NW-SE) corner allows the countries to differ in relative endowments, with country i skilled-labor abundant toward the NW corner.

The vertical axis of Figures 3.1 gives the volume of affiliate production in the world economy, measured as the production in country j of plants owned by country i firms (i.e., the firm's headquarters are in country i) and vice versa. Consider first the SW-NE diagonal where the countries differ in size but not in relative endowments. Affiliate production is an inverted U, reaching a maximum when the countries are identical. At this midpoint, the solution is symmetric and only horizontal multinationals exist. Each firm produces half its output in its home plant and half in its branch plant. Thus exactly half of all world production is affiliate production. As the countries become different in size, single-plant national firms enter in the large country, serving the smaller market by exports rather than through an expensive branch plant. This leads to two hypotheses. First, affiliate sales by country i firms in country j should be related to the sum of their GDPs, but decreasing in the difference in their GDPs, holding their sum constant.

Figure 3.1 shows that the highest levels of total affiliate activity occur when one country is small and skilled-labor abundant. Consider the region between

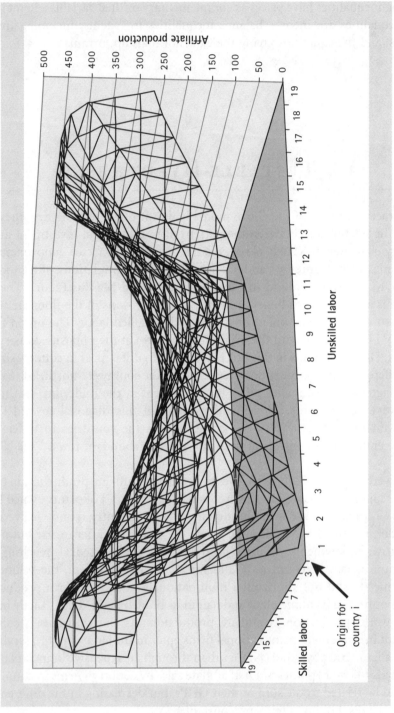

Fig. 3.1 Volume of affiliate production: 25% trade costs

the SW and NW corners of Figure 3.1 where country i is small and skilled-labor abundant. In this region, production of X in the world economy is dominated by vertical multinationals headquartered in country i. The headquarters of firms are concentrated in country i due to the general-equilibrium price of skilled labor. The plants are concentrated in country j for two reinforcing reasons. First, factor prices favor production in the skilled-labor-scarce country. Second, with transport costs, if a firm has only one plant then it will want to locate that plant in the large country, other things equal. Thus factor-price and country-size motives reinforce one another, and potentially all of world X production could be affiliate production. These results lead to two further hypotheses. First, production by affiliates of country i firms in country j is related to the relative skilled-labor abundance of country i. Second there is an interaction effect between skilled-labor abundance and country size, so that production by affiliates of country i firms in country j is particularly high when country i is both skilled-labor abundant and small (e.g. Sweden, Switzerland, the Netherlands).

Figure 3.2 has the same dimensions and definitions for the 'floor' as in Figure 3.1. The vertical axis is different, however. Figure 3.2 presents results for a comparative-statics exercise in which trade protection in both directions is raised from 5 per cent to 25 per cent. Second, Figure 3.2 presents affiliate production only in one direction, production by affiliates of country i firms in country j. Figure 3.2 shows that an increase in trade costs raise affiliate production in a central region of the Edgeworth box, and lower it when country i (the parent country) is skilled-labor abundant and somewhat small. These two regions correspond both to different firm types, and to different directions of trade costs. The central region, where trade costs increase affiliate production is due to national firms in country i switching to serving country j (the host country) by branch plant production rather than exports (i.e., the national firms in country i become type-h multinationals). The second point to note is that this change is due entirely to host-country (country j) protection alone. That is, the region of increased affiliate production in Figure 3.2 would look essentially the same if we had only increased host-country j's import tariff, for example. We thus have the hypothesis that host-country trade (import) costs increase affiliate production. We could add an interaction effect as well, noting that the effect of the host-country trade cost is highest when the countries are similar in relative endowments.

The region in which the increase in trade costs reduces affiliate production in Figure 3.2 is due to vertical (type-v) multinationals in country i switching to being type-n or even type-h firms. Affiliate production in country j that was for export back to country i ceases with the high trade cost (production in country i by a type-h firm headquartered in that country

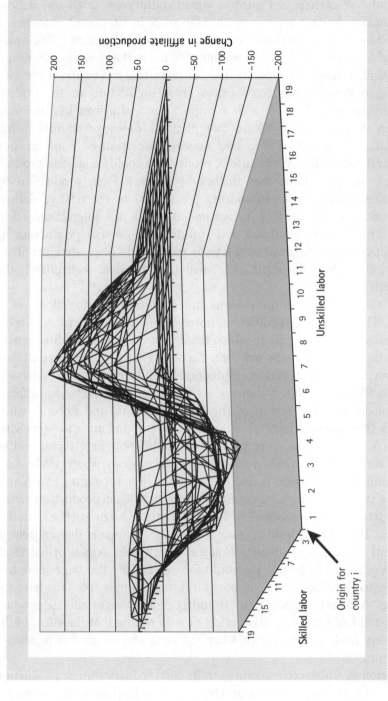

Fig. 3.2 Change in affiliate production, country i plants in country j: 25% trade costs minus 5% trade costs in both directions

does not count as affiliate production). Second, this region of decreasing affiliate activity in Figure 3.2 is due entirely to the home country (country i) trade cost, and this region would look essentially the same if we only considered an increase in country i's trade (import) cost. We thus have the hypothesis that the home-country trade (import) costs reduce affiliate production.

# 3.5 Empirical Results

Table 3.3 lists some recent empirical results from Carr, Markusen, and Maskus (2000), which employ the model outlined above and incorporate the hypotheses just discussed.[2] Country i is the home (parent) country and country j is the host country. The dependent variable is affiliate production by country i firms in country j. Definitions of the variables are as follows, where k = i,j.

$GDP_k$ – real gross national production of country k in \$US

$SK_k$ – the proportion of the labor force in country k that is skilled;

$INC_j$ – an index of the difficulty/cost of investing in the host country (from the World Economic Forum);

$TC_k$ – an index of the difficulty/cost of exporting to (importing into) country k (from the World Economic Forum);

DIST – a control variable, the distance between the capital cities of countries i and j.

The column of Table 3.3 labeled 'predicted sign' follows from the discussion of the previous section and Figures 3.1 and 3.2. The first two variables relate to horizontal investments in particular: affiliate production by country i firms in country j will be highest where total income is high and the countries are similar in size (hence a negative sign on the squared difference in size). The third and fourth variables relate especially to vertical investments: affiliate production by country i firms in country j will be high when country i is skilled-labor abundant relative to j, and when country i is skilled-labor abundant $(SK_i - SK_j > 0)$ and small $(GPD_i - GDP_j < 0)$. Host country investment costs $(INC_j)$ is expected to have a negative sign, while host-

---

[2] See also related and supporting evidence in Brainard (1993, 1997), Caves (1996), Eaton and Tamura (1994), Ekholm (1995, 1997, 1998a, b), Hummels and Stern (1994), and Lipsey (1993).

## Table 3.3 Empirical results

Dependent variable: affiliate sales by country i firms in country j

| Variable | Predicted sign | Sign as predicted? | Statistically significant? |
|---|---|---|---|
| $GDP_i + GPD_j$ | + | Yes | Yes |
| $(GDP_i - GPD_j)^2$ | – | Yes | Yes |
| $(SK_i - SK_j)$ | + | Yes | Yes |
| $(GDP_i - GPD_j)(SK_i - SK_j)$ | – | Yes | Yes |
| $INC_j$ | – | Yes | Yes/No* |
| $TC_j$ | + | Yes | Yes/No* |
| $TC_j(SK_i - SK_j)^2$ | – | Yes | No |
| $TC_i$ | – | Yes | Yes/No* |
| Dist | – | Yes | Yes |

*Yes/No indicates that the variable is significant in some regressions but not in others (e.g., a variable may be significant with country fixed effects, insignificant without or vice versa).

*Source* Carr, Markusen, and Maskus 2001

country trade costs ($TC_j$) are expected to have a positive sign. The interactive term between host-country trade costs and the squared difference in endowments should have a negative sign (the protective effect encouraging inward horizontal investment is strongest when the countries are similar). Home (parent) country trade costs ($TC_i$) should have a negative sign. Distance should discourage direct investment, but the case for this in theory is not overwhelming. It could lead to a substitution from serving a more distant market by exports to serving it with a branch plant.

Carr, Markusen, and Maskus (2001) report a number of regressions, such as with and without country fixed effects, weighted least squares using only observations with positive affiliate activity from i to j, and Tobit regressions which include zero observations on the dependent variable. The latter carry important information and not surprisingly, are typically found when the parent country i is a small, relatively skilled-labor-scarce country. The data is a panel of bilateral observations on thirty-four countries over an eight-year period, 1987–94. This is US Commerce Department data, so unfortunately all observations have the US as either country i or country j.

Table 3.3 gives results which, apart from the magnitudes and statistical significance of the coefficients, are broadly consistent across all specifications. The knowledge-capital model receives good support from the data. It is interesting that the GDP and SK variables always have the right sign and are strongly statistically significant. The trade and investment-cost variables basically always have the right signs, but sometimes they are statistically insignificant. One implication of these results is that we might have some confidence in using the knowledge-capital model for public policy discussions.

One limitation of the Carr, Markusen, and Maskus (2001) is that it does not give a good picture of horizontal versus vertical activity. The latter is notoriously difficult to do with existing data and of course, almost all firms do a combination of horizontal and vertical activities, with both intermediate and final goods traded between production units in different countries. One indirect way of getting at this problem which can be tackled with the data is to look at affiliate production for local sale, versus production that is exported back to the home country or to third countries. It seems reasonable to suppose that production for local sale is related to horizontal activity while production for export, particularly back to the home country, may be more closely related to vertical activity. If we accept this hypothesis, then production for local sale should be more closely related to market size than to factor endowment (and factor price) differences, while production for export should be the opposite.

The same US Commerce Department data just described does break down affiliate production into local sales and export sales. For US affiliates abroad, the latter is in fact broken down into exports back to the US and exports to third countries. Maskus and I used this data to produce the results shown in Table 3.4 (Markusen and Maskus, 2001). The first two rows of Table 3.4 have both inward and outward (US affiliates in country j, and country j affiliates in the US) observations as dependent variables. The inward observations (country j affiliates in the US) do not discriminate whether or not the exports are going back to the parent country or to some third country, so all export sales are lumped together. Results in these two rows are consistent with production for local sale being related to horizontal activity and 'market seeking' motives, while production for export appears more related to vertical and 'resource seeking' motives. The elasticity of production for local sales with respect to host-country GDP is considerably higher than the GDP elasticity for export sale. Elasticities of these two variables with respect to the skilled-labor proportion (running from 0 to 100) in host country j are negative. But the elasticity for production for local sale is essentially zero, while the elasticity for export sale is significantly negative: production for export sale seeks out unskilled-labor-abundant countries.

Table 3.4 Effects of host–country size and skilled–labor abundance on foreign affiliate production for local sale and export: derivatives evaluated at the mean of independent variables

| Effect on: | Elasticity wrt an increase in country j's GDP | Elasticity wrt a one point increase in SK$_j$ | One point increase in INVC$_j$ (millions) | One point increase in TC$_j$ (millions) |
|---|---|---|---|---|
| Local sales of country i affiliates in country j (inward and outward data) | $\varepsilon = 1.56^*$ | $\varepsilon = -0.02$ | $-\$633.4$ | $\$366.6$ |
| Export sales of country i affiliates in j to all countries (inward and outward data) | $\varepsilon = 1.12$ | $\varepsilon = -0.68$ | $-\$277.2$ | $\$52.1$ |
| Local sales of US affiliates in country j (US outward data only) | $\varepsilon = 1.04$ | $\varepsilon = 0.60$ | $-\$517.8$ | $\$314.8$ |
| Export sales of US affiliates in j to the US (US outward data only) | $\varepsilon = 0.21$ | $\varepsilon = 0.06$ | $-\$346.6$ | $\$207.6$ |

$^*\varepsilon$ denotes elasticity

Source Markusen and Maskus 2001

We do not report elasticities of sales with respect to INV$_j$ and TC$_j$, just levels, since these variables are qualitative indices, running from 0 to 100. Figures are in millions of US$. Both production for local sale and export sale respond negatively to INV$_j$ (the larger magnitude of the former does not mean more sensitivity since production for local sale is quantitatively much more important). Production for local sale is much more strongly encouraged by the host-country's trade cost as we would expect.

In the third and fourth rows of Table 3.4, we look at the US outward data only, so we can explicitly identify production for export back to the US. Results are quantitatively different, but qualitatively similar to those for the inward-outward sample. Production of US affiliates abroad for local sale is much more sensitive to local market size than is production for export back to the US as we would expect. In contrast to the inward-outward sample, US production abroad seeks out skilled labor, but production for local sale is much more skilled-labor seeking than production for export back to the US. The latter is insensitive to the labor-force composition in the host country. Thus in both samples, we could say that production for local sale responds more positively or less negatively to the skilled-labor abundance of the host country than production for export sale. The last two columns of rows three and four give results similar to the first two rows concerning the effects of $INV_j$ and $TC_j$. The large coefficient on $TC_j$ for export sales is somewhat puzzling however, since the theory predicts that exports sales should be relatively insensitive to host-country trade costs. Of course, one thing that the very simple model presented here does not consider is intermediate inputs imported by the affiliate, and host-country trade costs obviously raise the prices of these intermediates to the affiliate.

# 3.6 SUMMARY AND CONCLUSIONS

The purpose of this paper is to explain recent efforts by international trade economists to incorporate multinational firms endogenously into general equilibrium trade models, generate testable hypotheses, and then subject the models to estimation and testing. The models of the firms *per se* are extremely simple, with important details being sacrificed in order to provide general-equilibrium tractability. The model is however rich enough to provide motives for both horizontal and vertical expansion across international borders. The horizontal motive derives from the assumption of firm-level scale economies, while the vertical motive derives from differences in factor intensities among stages of production combined with differences in factor endowments across countries.

This model provides testable hypotheses as to how production of affiliates in country j of firms headquartered in country i should be related to characteristics of both countries, including absolute and relative country sizes, differences in skilled-labor abundance, host-country investment costs, and the trade costs of both parent and host country. Recent empirical tests give good support to the theory, indicating that it should be useful for policy analysis as well as for positive analysis.

## REFERENCES

BRAINARD, S. LAEL (1993). 'An Empirical Assessment of the Factor Proportions Explanation of Multinationals' Sales', NBER working paper No. 4580.

—— (1997). 'An Empirical Assessment of the Proximity-Concentration Tradeoff between Multinational Sales and Trade', *American Economic Review*, 87: 520–44.

CARR, DAVID, MARKUSEN, JAMES R., and MASKUS, KEITH E. (2001, forthcoming). 'Estimating the Knowledge-Capital Model of the Multinational Enterprise', *American Economic Review*.

CAVES, RICHARD E. (1996). *Multinational Enterprise and Economic Analysis* (2nd edn.). London: Cambridge University Press.

DUNNING, JOHN H. (1977). 'Trade, Location of Economic Activity and MNE: A Search for an Eclectic Approach', in B. Ohlin, P. O. Hesselborn, and P. M. Wijkman (eds.), *The International Allocation of Economic Activity*. London: Macmillan.

—— (1981). *International Production and the Multinational Enterprise*. London: George Allen & Unwin.

EATON, JONATHAN, and TAMURA, AKIKO (1994). 'Bilateralism and Regionalism in Japanese and US Trade and Foreign Direct Investment Relationships', *Journal of Japanese and International Economics*, 8: 478–510.

EKHOLM, KAROLINA (1995). *Multinational Production and Trade in Technological Knowledge*. Lund Economic Studies, no. 58. Lund: University of Lund.

—— (1997). 'Factor Endowments and the Pattern of Affiliate Production by Multinational Enterprises', CREDIT working paper no. 97/1997. Nottingham: University of Nottingham.

—— (1998a) 'Headquarter Services and Revealed Factor Abundance', *Review of International Economics*, 6: 545–53.

—— (1998b). 'Proximity Advantages, Scale Economies, and the Location of Production', in P. Braunerhjelm and K. Ekholm (eds.), *The Geography of Multinationals*. Dordrecht: Kluwer Academic Publishers, 59–76.

HELPMAN, ELHANAN (1984). 'A Simple Theory of Trade with Multinational Corporations', *Journal of Political Economy*, 92: 451–71.

—— (1985). 'Multinational Corporations and Trade Structure', *Review of Economic Studies*, 52: 443–58.

HORSTMANN, IGNATIUS J., and MARKUSEN, JAMES R. (1987). 'Strategic Investments and the Development of Multinationals,' *International Economic Review*, 28: 109–21.

—— (1992). 'Endogenous Market Structures in International Trade,' *Journal of International Economics*, 32: 109–29.

HUMMELS, DAVID L., and STERN, ROBERT M. (1994). 'Evolving Patterns of North-American Merchandise Trade and Foreign Direct Investment, 1960–1990', *The World Economy* 17: 5–29.

LIPSEY, ROBERT E. (1993). 'Foreign Direct Investment in the United States: Changes over Three Decades', in K. Froot (ed.), *Foreign Direct Investment*. Chicago: University of Chicago Press, 113–72.

MARKUSEN, JAMES R. (1984). 'Multinationals, Multi-Plant Economies, and the Gains from Trade', *Journal of International Economics*, 16: 205–26.

—— (1995). 'The Boundaries of Multinational Firms and the Theory of International Trade', *Journal of Economic Perspectives*, 9: 169–89.

—— (1998). 'Multinational Firms, Location and Trade', *The World Economy*, 21: 733–56.

—— and MASKUS, KEITH E. (2001). 'Multinational Firms: Reconciling Theory and Evidence', in M. Blomstrom and L. Goldberg (eds.), *Topics in Empirical International Economics: A Festschrift in Honor of Robert E. Lipsey*. Chicago: University of Chicago Press, (forthcoming).

—— and VENABLES, ANTHONY J. (1998). 'Multinational Firms and the New Trade Theory', *Journal of International Economics*, 46: 183–203.

—— (2000.) 'The Theory of Endowment, Intra-Industry and Multinational Trade', *Journal of International Economics*, 52/2: 209–34.

CHAPTER 4

........................................................................................

# STRATEGIC COMPLEXITY IN INTERNATIONAL BUSINESS

........................................................................................

PETER BUCKLEY

MARK CASSON

## 4.1 THE CURRENT CHALLENGES FACING INTERNATIONAL BUSINESS THEORY

........................................................................................

MOST contributions to a handbook are necessarily retrospective, but there is also scope for a prospective view of the kind offered in this chapter. In retrospect there have been significant theoretical achievements in international business (IB) over the past forty years, but the prospects are not so good.

(1) A comparison of the periods 1972–82 and 1990–2000 suggests a declining dynamic of theoretical innovation; developments in IB were once ahead of those in related areas, whereas now they seem to follow behind;

(2) Every answer raises new questions: but many of the new questions raised in the 1970s literature remain unresolved;

(3) The 'strategic alliances' literature exhibits the weaknesses as well as the strengths of a multi-disciplinary perspective; there are so many different propositions about different aspects of alliances, often based on different definitions, that it becomes unclear whether they are coherent or not;

(4) The debate between transaction costs and resource-based theories has become increasingly sterile; and

(5) Excessive dependence on case studies means that the 'strategic management' literature increasingly confuses consultancy with research, and equates the development of executive teaching materials with original contributions to knowledge.

If IB is to regain its influence within the social sciences as a whole, it is necessary to re-integrate it into mainstream intellectual debate. One way in which this can be done is to introduce more refined analytical techniques into IB theory. This chapter recommends that the rational action approach to modelling should be expanded in order to address a wider range of IB issues. It provides practical examples of how this can be done, based mainly on our own recent work.

The rational action approach has achieved its greatest successes in addressing economic issues, but it can also elucidate issues in strategic management and organizational behaviour. By working with formal models whose assumptions are explicit it is possible to eliminate ambiguity, and thereby foster informed criticism that serves to eliminate logical error (Elster 1986; Hargreaves-Heap 1989). Modern IB texts tend to present the subject as a multi-disciplinary field of research that addresses issues that are specific to international business operations. This was not the view of IB that prevailed at the time of its greatest intellectual vitality in the 1970s, however. Many scholars of that time perceived IB as a field of applied economics—a useful 'laboratory' in which to test general theories against newly gathered statistical evidence (Buckley and Casson 1976).

Since the 1970s the methods of economics have been extended to other fields of social science, such as politics, law, and sociology (Buckley and Casson 1993). This has been made possible by the increasing power of rational action modelling techniques. As a result, it is possible to update the 1970s view: IB is now best regarded as a field of applied social science, rather than just a field of applied economics, as before. But in this context social science must be understood, not a collection of different disciplines, each with its own tradition and methodology, but an integrated social science based upon the rational action approach.

This chapter does not present a forecast of how the subject will evolve, but simply makes a proposal, with which others may well disagree. It begins with a critique of recent calls for the use of 'softer' theories in IB. In particular, it considers whether the increasing complexity of the IB environment makes formal modelling impractical. It concludes that it does not. Much of what is called complexity, it suggests, is subjective, and merely reflects the confusion of scholars who rely on softer theories. Such confusions can be dispelled by invoking the intellectual rigour of the rational action approach.

Two main sources of complexity are identified. One is the uncertainty involved in long-term planning. It reflects the 'strategic' nature of certain decisions, such as those concerned with irreversible investments. There is a distinctive set of rational action modelling techniques that is available for analysing such decisions.

Another source of complexity is connected with networks. Networks in IB take both physical and social forms. A physical network comprises a set of production plants, distribution centres, and retail outlets. These various facilities are connected by transport infrastructure. Several facilities may be owned by the same firm, depending upon where the boundaries of the firm are drawn. Boundaries of firms that span international boundaries lead to multinational firms. Formal models of IB networks are now available which determine simultaneously where all the boundaries of the different firms within a system are drawn. These models can also incorporate flows of knowledge generated by R&D and marketing activities, as explained below.

Social networks are concerned with communications between decision-makers. Networks can be high-trust or low-trust, and either formal or informal. Communication through social networks allows different decision-makers to coordinate their decisions. Coordination within a firm involves internal networks, which often take a hierarchical form, whereas coordination between firms involves external networks which typically take a 'flatter' form. Formal analysis of communication costs makes it possible to analyse what kind of networks will emerge to coordinate different types of activity.

## 4.2 COMPLEXITY OR CONFUSION?

It is often asserted that the modern global environment is so complex that it is impossible to capture reality with the aid of any formal model. As a result, a good deal of effort has gone into developing heuristic approaches that use analogy and metaphor, rather than formal theory, to articulate key ideas (Parkhe 1993). For example, writers on joint ventures and strategic alliances have argued that as the boundaries of the firm become increasingly 'fuzzy', so theory must become 'fuzzy' too in order to handle the issue. Fuzzy theories are difficult to refute, however, because it is usually unclear what they mean, so that errors in these theories go undetected for a considerable time. Researchers who attempt to build on 'fuzzy' foundations can waste a good deal of time before the weaknesses of their foundations are properly exposed.

Another example of fuzzy thinking arises when people apply general systems theory to try to understand the complexity of the global economy. General systems theory talks a lot about 'complex systems', and so it seems intuitively reasonable that it should be invoked to explain the nature and causes of complex IB phenomena. The fact that the theory is opaque only adds to its credibility so far as the uninitiated are concerned.

But a lot of what is described as 'complexity' is often just confusion. When people do not understand something, they tend to assume that it must be 'complex', and so turn to 'complexity theory' for a solution. This theory introduces them to new jargon—such as 'chaos', 'catastrophe', 'emergent properties', and the like (Arthur 1988; Coriat and Dosi 1998). It is suggested that these concepts derive from advanced mathematics, or 'rocket science'. In fact, many of the terms are little more than labels applied to areas of ignorance. While it is true that the mathematical theory of non-linear systems can explain chaotic behaviour, for example, such behaviour has little or nothing to do with the kind of behaviour that is observed in the IB system. If there is some connection, then it has certainly not been spelled out rigorously so far.

Popular perceptions of complexity may also be a response to a quickening pace of change. The world economy of today appears to be radically different from what it was only fifty years ago. It can be argued that radical changes call for radically new theories to explain them. A new brand of IB theory must be developed to meet the intellectual challenges of the new millennium, it may be said. Complexity provides an impressive range of novel jargon for describing change in the international business system. 'The global economy is a dynamic self-organizing system based on co-evolving institutions' seems to be a profound statement, even though it says little more than that the global economy is undergoing change.

Radical changes in theory are very expensive, however, because a whole new set of concepts needs to be developed and disseminated. Investing in radically new theory is extremely wasteful if existing theory is perfectly adequate. This chapter argues that complexity can be addressed perfectly adequately using existing concepts derived from the rational action approach.

# 4.3 TWO CONCEPTS OF COMPLEXITY

Systems theorists distinguish between combinatorial complexity and what may be termed organic complexity. Combinatorial complexity is created when a large number of different cases have to be analysed before a decision can be made, and in each case a large number of different factors have to be taken into account. Organic complexity arises because of numerous inter-dependencies and feedback loops within a system. Everything depends upon everything else in such a way that cause and effect are difficult to disentangle. Organic complexity, it is suggested, cannot be addressed through rational analysis. In organically complex systems agents cannot understand the system of which they form a part. As a result, they have to commit themselves arbitrarily to certain rules, and the interactions between different agents playing according to different rules then generates the very kind of complexity in the system that defies analysis.

The techniques illustrated in this chapter approach complexity as a combinatorial problem. They address combinatorial complexity using a range of simplifying techniques. This reflects a methodological stance that complexity is best addressed by simplifying the representation of reality, rather than by making theory itself more complex. The problem of organic complexity is not ignored altogether, however. Organic complexity is handled by the traditional method of focusing on an equilibrium. For more than a century, economists have tackled system interdependencies by analysing the mathematical properties of equilibrium. Systems theorists often ridicule this approach. The fact remains, however, that the qualitative features of a system's dynamic behaviour are largely determined by its equilibrium properties. All stable systems have a propensity to converge to an equilibrium. Systems that exhibit localized instabilities usually do so because they have more than one equilibrium. The number of equilibria is therefore an important guide to the out-of-equilibrium behaviour of a complex system. Although an equilibrium model cannot track the out-of-equilibrium behaviour of a system over time, it can identify the equilibrium to which the system will tend to converge from any given initial condition. For many purposes, this is all that a satisfactory model is required to do.

Certain types of disequilibrium behaviour can also be modelled in mathematical terms. This is normally achieved by assuming that agents follow certain simple myopic rules: the agent makes little attempt to look far ahead (Nelson and Winter 1982). This contrasts sharply with the situation in rational action modelling, where agents are far sighted. Similarly, in simple disequilibrium models agents do not adapt their rules to the environment in which they operate, as a rational agent would do. These extreme assumptions are relevant in certain special cases: they are useful, for example, in explaining the sudden build up of traffic jams, the persistence of stock exchange 'bubbles', and the formation of crowds around sensational events. It is not at all clear that they are useful in explaining IB phenomena, however. A successful multinational enterprise is unlikely to be controlled by a myopic rule-driven manager who is unable to adapt his behaviour to the circumstances he is in. It is more likely to be managed by a successful entrepreneur who can take a long-term view of a situation, and can adapt his behaviour to different sets of conditions.

Nevertheless, it is often claimed that disequilibrium models with system effects can provide a more realistic account of the global economy than a rational action model can. One reason for this is that some disequilibrium models predict that almost anything can happen out of equilibrium. When behaviour is highly sensitive to certain parameter values, which are difficult to measure, then it can always be claimed that the model has explained reality because the parameters took on whatever values they needed to. This kind of explanation is vacuous, because as long as key parameter values cannot be independently measured the explanation is impossible to verify.

'Path-dependence' is a good example of this type of non-explanation. Almost any historical aspect of the IB system can be explained in path-dependent terms. Path dependent explanations usually begin with unspecified initial conditions which have been lost way back in the mists of time. 'Given the way things began, and all the things that have happened since, things are bound to be the way they are', goes this kind of explanation. The problem is that data on how things began, and on many of the things that happened since, are usually incomplete. In many applications of path dependence, even the pattern of causation linking one step to the next is unclear. Path dependence can be used to rationalize almost any sequence of events, and can give any simple narrative of events the appearance of a being a scientific test of systems theory.

This is not to deny that path-dependence occurs. Agents are 'locked in' by their actions whenever there are adjustment costs, because their actions cannot be costlessly reversed. But 'lock in' is only a serious problem under certain conditions, and rational action models explain what these conditions are. It is often suggested that 'lock in' is a direct consequence of myopic decision-making, but this is incorrect. Everyone is locked in by adjustment costs, whether they are rational or not. Rational agents may be locked in less than irrational ones, however, because when they realize that they still have much to learn about a situation they will choose a course of action which maximizes flexibility. To establish that agents are myopic it is necessary to show that they are worse off than a rational agent would have been, and not simply that they were locked in by a situation. Few systems theorists have addressed this crucial issue.

An important reason why 'lock in' is of limited importance in IB is that multinational firms have access to a wide range of factor and product markets. For example, a firm that has over-extended its capacity at an upstream stage of production can use external intermediate products to sell off surplus output to independent downstream firms. Alternatively, the firm could sell off surplus plant and equipment in markets for second-hand assets, or even divest the entire upstream operation as a going concern. All of these strategies incur adjustment costs, of course, but the costs are nowhere near as large as they would be in the absence of the market system. While it highly desirable for IB theory to take account of adjustment costs, therefore, it is unnecessary to suppose that adjustment costs are a major source of instability in the IB system.

# 4.4 RATIONAL ACTION AND INTERNATIONAL BUSINESS STRATEGY

During the 1980s and 1990s the concept of strategy came to occupy an important role in the IB literature, although the term was hardly used at all before then (Porter 1991). None of the key theoretical developments of the 1970s invoked the concept of strategy at all. It is interesting to note that very few of the writers who use the concept of strategy most regularly ever bother to define the term. Sometimes they employ it simply as a synonym for 'chosen course of action', while in other cases they use it to signal that some particular decision is of crucial importance.

The rational action approach clearly implies that some decisions are more important than others, and indicates why this is the case. A strategic decision may be defined, in rational action terms, as a decision with the following characteristics:

(1) long-term perspective creates a need for inter-temporal planning;
(2) uncertain environment;
(3) information needs to be collected in the most efficient and reliable manner;
(4) irreversible commitment of resources;

(5) determines the context in which future tactical (short-term) decisions are taken: the implications for tactical decisions need to be considered before strategic decisions are made;

(6) inter-actions with other strategists: either competition, co-operation, or both.

There is now a 'critical mass' of rational action technique that can be used to analyse strategic issues. These techniques address strategic complexity through clarification and simplification of the decision problem (see for example Kreps 1990). The repertoire includes the following:

*Information costs*
- decision theory: rational choice under uncertainty
- sequential analysis
- search theory.

*Dynamic optimization*
- optimal timing of investment
- irreversibility and switching costs.

*Real option theory*
- deferring decisions to avoid mistakes
- valuing flexibility.

*Game theory*
- Nash equilibria of a non-co-operative game
- sequential games
- repeated games.

There is insufficient space to review all of the relevant techniques at this stage. This chapter focuses on the first three sets of techniques, as these have achieved the widest acceptance in IB theory (see, for example, Allen and Pantzalis 1996; Buckley and Casson 1981; Casson 1995; DeMeza and van der Ploeg 1987). The final set of techniques—game theory—affords major opportunities for IB which have so far been exploited to only a limited extent (Graham 1990).

# 4.5 Example: Analysing Foreign Market Entry

The application of these new techniques is best illustrated by means of an example. One of the classic issues in IB is foreign market entry strategy

(Buckley and Casson 1981, 1998*a*). This is a decision by a firm in a home country (country 1) to supply the market in a foreign country (country 2). Foreign market entry involves uncertainty, relating to either demand side factors, such as the size of the foreign market, or supply side factors, such as foreign costs of production.

The simplest way of introducing uncertainty into the rational action approach is to assume that decision-makers partition the state of the environment into a number of different categories, or 'states of the world', and then assign a subjective probability to each. A sophisticated decision-maker may distinguish a large number of different states, whereas a naïve decision-maker may distinguish just a few. The simplest categorization of states is a binary one (Hirshleifer and Riley 1992).

For the sake of simplicity, it is assumed that uncertainty relates to the supply side only, and that the decision-maker distinguishes just two states of the world: state 1, in which foreign cost conditions are bad, and state 2, in which they are good. The key issue is whether the foreign market is served by domestic production or foreign production. Under domestic production the foreign market is supplied through exports (strategy 1) whilst under foreign production (strategy 2) the firm undertakes foreign direct investment (FDI).

Suppose that the firm is already committed to serving the market, and that market size is fixed, so that the revenue obtained is the same for either strategy. Thus only the costs of the two strategies are different. Production takes place under constant returns to scale, with a unit cost of production $c_0$ in country 1. Unit cost is $c_1$ in country 2 when conditions are bad, and $c_2$ when conditions are good, where $c_1 > c_0 > c_2$. It follows that the firm should export when foreign cost conditions are bad and invest abroad when they are good. The probability that conditions are good is $p$ $(0 \leq p \leq 1)$.

The firm's objective, it is assumed, is to maximize expected profit. This is a reasonable objective for a firm with a large number of shareholders who hold well-diversified portfolios. With given revenues, this translates into minimizing expected unit costs. The expected cost of foreign production is $E(c) = (1 - p) c_1 + pc_2$ while the unit cost of domestic production is already known to be $c_0$. Comparing the expected unit cost of foreign production with the cost of domestic production shows that the firm should produce abroad when $p > p^* = (c_1 - c_0)/(c_1 - c_2)$. In other words, the firm should produce abroad when the probability of good production conditions exceeds a critical level $p^*$.

A simple way of understanding this result is to recognize that there are two types of error that the firm can make. The first is to reject the export strategy when it is correct (a Type I error), and the second is to accept the export strategy when foreign production is appropriate instead (a Type II error). The nature of these errors, and the costs associated with them, are set out in Table 4.1. The cost of a Type I error is $c_1 - c_0$, and the cost of a Type II

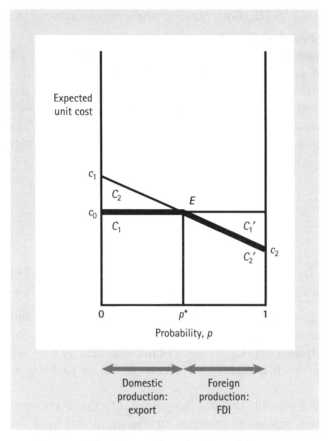

**Fig. 4.1 Diagrammatic solution of the entry
strategy under uncertainty**

error is $c_0 - c_2$. It follows that the critical probability value may be expressed as:

$p^* =$ Cost of Type I error/ Total cost of both errors.

The solution is illustrated in Figure 4.1. The horizontal axis measures the probability that foreign cost conditions are good and the vertical axis measures corresponding expected unit cost. The horizontal schedule $C_1 C_1'$ indicates that domestic costs are constant, independently of foreign costs, whilst the downward-sloping schedule $C_2 C_2'$ shows that expected foreign costs decrease as the probability of good conditions increases. The minimum attainable expected unit cost is indicated by the thick line $C_1 E C_2'$, which is the lower envelope of the two schedules, and has a kink at the switch-point $E$. The rational decision-maker minimizes expected costs by choosing to export for low probabilities, to the left of $E$, and to produce abroad for high probabilities, to the right of $E$.

The economic implications of the analysis may be summarized as follows:

(1) Optimists undertake FDI; pessimists export;
(2) The greater the cost of Type I error relative to the cost of a Type II error, the more optimistic an investor needs to be;
(3) The costs of a Type I error are greater, the higher the cost of foreign production under bad conditions relative to domestic costs; and
(4) The costs of a Type II error are greater, the lower the cost of foreign production under good conditions relative to domestic costs.

# 4.6 COLLECTING INFORMATION

It is often suggested that uncertainty is a basic 'fact of life', but this is not quite correct. Uncertainty can be dispelled by collecting information. Even if it cannot be dispelled entirely, its impact can be reduced by narrowing down the margin for error. It is therefore irrational to always passively accept uncertainty.

But how is it possible to know how much information is worth collecting? Rational action modelling provides an answer to this question. All that is required is that the decision-maker can estimate the cost of collecting relevant items of information, and attach subjective probabilities to what the results of investigation will turn out to be. This allows the decision-maker to estimate both the costs and the benefits of collecting information, and therefore to arrive at a rational information strategy (Casson 2000a, chs. 4, 7).

Decision-making becomes a two-stage procedure: in the first stage the decision-maker decides how much information to collect, and in the second stage he uses the information he has collected to take the decision. These two stages are interdependent, and the rational decision-maker arrives at his strategy by considering them in reverse order. He knows that it would be a waste of time collecting information that would not influence his decision. He therefore needs to determine in advance how he would use any item of information if he had it. If he would not use it whatever it turned out to be, then it is a waste of time collecting it. Only once he has decided how he would use it is he in a position to decide whether he wants to collect it or not.

Suppose, for example, that the decision-maker could research the costs of foreign production at a cost $q$. Once he has collected the cost information, he can avoid both the Type I and Type II errors shown in Table 4.1. If he discovers

Table 4.1  Two possible errors in strategic choice
under uncertainty

|  | State 1: Foreign cost conditions bad | State 2: Foreign cost conditions good |
| --- | --- | --- |
| Strategy 1 | 0 | *Type II error* |
| Produce at home: Exporting | | $c_0 - c_2$ |
| Strategy 2 | *Type I error* | 0 |
| Produce abroad: | $c_1 - c_0$ | |
| FDI | | |

that the conditions are good then he can commit to invest abroad, while if he discovers that conditions are bad then he can export instead. As a result, the expected cost of market entry is $(1 - p)c_0 + pc_2$, which is always lower than the expected cost of either the ordinary export strategy or the ordinary foreign investment strategy, except when the decision-maker is certain at the outset what the conditions will be $(p = 0,1)$.

The expected cost of market entry using information on foreign costs is illustrated by the line $C_1C_2'$ in Figure 4.2. This figure is similar to Figure 4.1, but with the addition of the research strategy. To evaluate the total cost of the research strategy, the cost $q$ must be added to the cost of market entry. Since this cost is independent of what the information runs out to be, its effect is simply to shift the schedule $C_1C_2'$ in parallel fashion up to $C_3C_3'$. If the cost of research is suitably low, this will determine two new critical values, $p_1^*$, $p_2^*$, at which the decision-maker switches into and out of the information-gathering strategy. These critical points are determined by constructing the lower envelope $C_1E_1E_2C_2'$ of the three schedules, and identifying the kinks $E_1$ and $E_2$.

The following results may be derived from the figure:

(1) research is most efficient when uncertainty is high—i.e. the probability $p$ is in the mid range
$$p_1^* < p < p_2^*;$$
(2) research is most valuable when the variability of foreign production costs, $c_1 - c_2$, is large; and

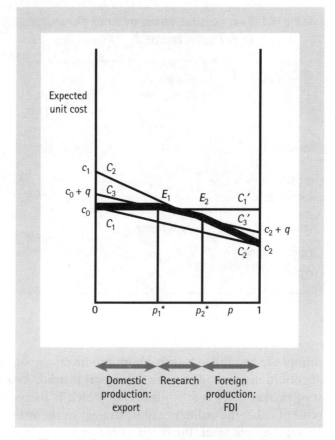

**Fig. 4.2 Strategy for information gathering**

(3) the range of probability values for which research is efficient is greater, the
   lower the research cost, $q$.

# 4.7 USING DECISION TREES

The fundamental point about research is that it alters the information set
available to the decision-maker at the time of the decision. The easiest way to
appreciate the significance of this is with the aid of a decision tree. Figure 4.3
uses a decision tree to compare decision-making with and without research.
Without research, the decision-maker acts first and the true situation reveals

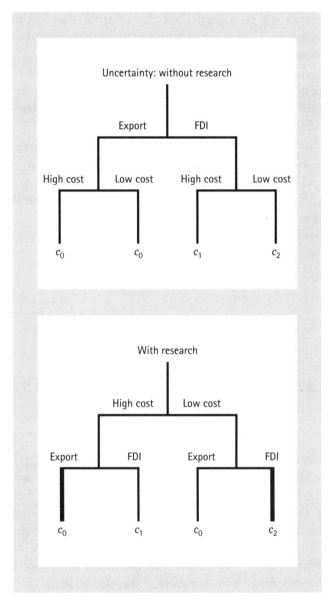

**Fig. 4.3  Comparison of decision trees with and without research**

itself later, whereas with research the situation is revealed before the decision-maker acts.

A complete description of a research strategy involves specifying not only what information will be collected but also what the decision-maker will do with the information once it has been collected. In the previous example there are only two ways in which it could be used. Once of these—to invest if foreign cost conditions are good, and otherwise to export—is obviously sensible, whilst the alternative—to invest only if foreign cost conditions are bad, is obviously absurd. The use of the information is indicated by the thick vertical lines in the bottom half of the figure.

The gist of this discussion so far may be summarized as follows:

(1) research strategies enlarge the information set available to the decision-maker and thereby reduce the risk of error;

(2) research strategies involve rules for using the information that has been collected in the course of the research; and

(3) as new strategies are introduced, new critical points are introduced at which switching between strategies occurs.

# 4.8 DEFERRING DECISIONS: REAL OPTIONS

Research is not the only way of augmenting the information set. If a decision-maker waits long enough, the information they require may reveal itself anyway. Deferring a decision may save the cost of collecting the information at the outset. The reason why firms do not delay decisions is because there is a cost involved. For example, if market entry will be profitable right away, profits will be lost if entry is deferred. Furthermore, there is a risk that another firm may enter the market and pre-empt the profit opportunity. Comparing deferment with research, therefore, there is a trade-off between saving information costs on the one hand, and losing revenue on the other.

If market entry decisions were fully reversible then there would be no need to defer a decision at all. A provisional decision would be made on the basis of the information that was freely available at the outset, and when additional information became available this decision would be changed as appropriate. The revenue stream would therefore commence immediately, and the cost of information would be avoided altogether. The only losses would relate to errors made at the outset, and corrected later.

In practice, of course, most decisions are not reversible. If the firm invests in a foreign production plant, for example, it will not be able to sell it off for as much as it cost to build. The 'illiquidity' of the plant means that the firm incurs a capital loss. Similarly, if the firm adapts the plant to some alternative use then adjustment costs will be incurred. Some investments are more readily reversed than others. Strategies that involve reversible investments afford more flexibility than those which do not. High levels of uncertainty favour the selection of flexible strategies, since mistakes are easier to put right (Buckley and Casson 1998b).

# 4.9 EXAMPLE: OPTIMIZING THE DYNAMICS OF FOREIGN MARKET ENTRY USING RESEARCH, DEFERMENT, AND SWITCHING STRATEGIES

The demand for flexibility can be analysed using real option theory (Dixit and Pindyck 1994; Kogut 1991; Kogut and Kulatilaka 1994; Rivoli and Salorio 1996). The specific approach followed here is based on Casson (2000a), chapter 7. Continuing with the previous example, suppose that there are now two periods, 1 and 2, and that the overall market entry strategy must be set at the beginning of period 1. The first period is short—of unit length, in fact— while the second period is of infinite length. The firm now maximizes expected net present value rather than expected profit; it discounts future costs and revenues at a fixed interest rate, $r$.

Entry into the foreign market is profitable right away, but information about the state of foreign cost conditions is not available until the end of period 1. Both exporting and foreign investment incur a fixed set-up cost, $f$, which is the same whether it is incurred in period 1 or period 2. An investment in foreign production is much more difficult to liquidate than an equivalent investment in export production: it can be sold off for only $h_2$ instead of $h_1$, where $h_2 < h_1 < f$.

At the beginning of period 1 the firm decides whether to carry out research to discover foreign production costs. It also decides whether to invest in foreign production right away, to commit itself to exporting right away, or to defer the decision on the method of market entry until period 2. If it carries out research then it will produce abroad only if it discovers that foreign costs are low; otherwise it will export instead. These commitments will be made right away since with the information at its disposal it has no reason to defer a decision.

In period 2 the firm can reverse any commitments it made in period 1 in the light of new information. Alternatively, if the firm deferred its decision, then it can decide its entry strategy unconstrained by the legacy of previous decisions.

The decision tree is shown in Figure 4.4. There are six dominant entry strategies, which are listed in Table 4.2. If the firm could costlessly obtain all the information it required at the outset then its profit would be

$$v = s(1+r)/r - f - pc_2 - (1-p)c_0$$

In practice none of the available strategies can achieve this level of profit, but they can be ranked by their shortfalls compared to this norm. The shortfalls are shown in the right-hand column of the table.

The number of strategies that need to be considered can be reduced using one or more of the following conditions:

1. If the firm exports initially then it will switch to foreign investment when cost conditions turn out to be good (i.e. strategy 5 is preferred to strategy 1) if and only if the sunk costs are lower than the capitalized savings on subsequent production costs:

$$f - h_1 < (c_0 - c_2)(1+r)/r.$$

2. If the firm invests abroad initially then it will switch to exporting when cost conditions turn out to be bad (i.e. strategy 6 is preferred to strategy 2) if and only if

$$f - h_2 < (c_1 - c_0)(1+r)/r.$$

3. Deferment is preferred to research (i.e. strategy 4 is preferred to strategy 3) if and only if the expected profit lost from the first period trading is less than the costs of research:

$$s < q + c_0 - p(c_0 - c_2) + (fr/(1+r)).$$

The overall solution can be determined using a four-way comparison: this involves the cheapest from each of the two pairs of strategies (1, 5), (2, 6), together with the research strategy (3) and the deferment strategy (4). The solution is illustrated graphically in Figure 4.5. In contrast to Figure 4.2, which plotted the absolute costs of each strategy, Figure 4.5 plots the costs of each strategy relative to the full-information norm as defined above. The schedule $C_1C_1'$ shows the costs associated with the cheapest of strategies 1 and 5; the

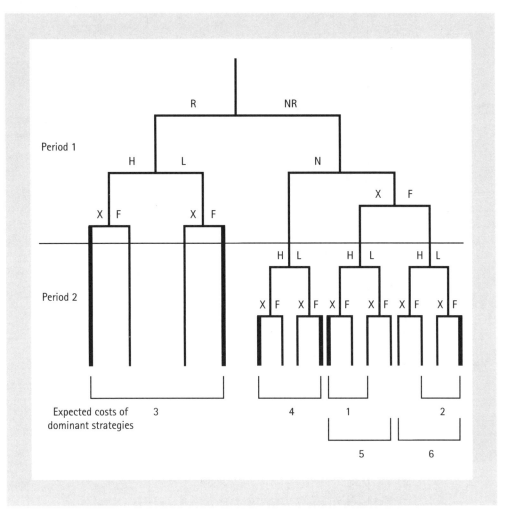

**Fig. 4.4 Decision tree for integrated research/waiting/switching problem**

Key  F  Foreign direct investment      NR  No research
     H  High foreign production costs  R   Research
     L  Low foreign production costs   X   Exporting
     N  Null strategy

schedule $C_2 C_2'$ shows the costs associated with the cheapest of the strategies 2 and 6, while $C_3 C_3'$ and $C_4 C_4'$ show respectively the costs associated with strategies 3 and 4.

Because of the way that costs are defined, the horizontal axis represents the base-line performance of the full-information strategy. The figure shows that none of the strategies attains base-line performance except at the two ends of the axis, where the decision-maker is subjectively certain about the level of foreign production costs ($p = 0,1$). The figure has been drawn to illustrate the

Table 4.2 Foreign entry strategy set encompassing research, deferment, and switching, assuming that it is always profitable to serve the market

| Strategies | Research? | Entry under uncertainty | If cost high | If cost low | Expected cost relative to norm |
|---|---|---|---|---|---|
| 1. Commit to X | NR | X | X | X | $p(c_0 - c_2)(1+r)/r$ |
| 2. Commit to F | NR | F | F | F | $(1-p)(c_1 - c_0)(1+r)/r$ |
| 3. Research | R | | X | F | $q$ |
| 4. Defer | NR | N | X | F | $s - c_0 + p(c_0 - c_2) - fr/(1+r)$ |
| 5. Conditional switch from X to F | NR | X | X | F | $p((c_0 - c_2) + (f - h_1)/(1+r))$ |
| 6. Conditional switch from F to X | NR | F | X | F | $(1-p)((c_1 - c_0) + (f - h_2)/(1+r))$ |

Key   F Foreign direct investment
      N Null strategy
      NR No research
      R Research
      X Exporting

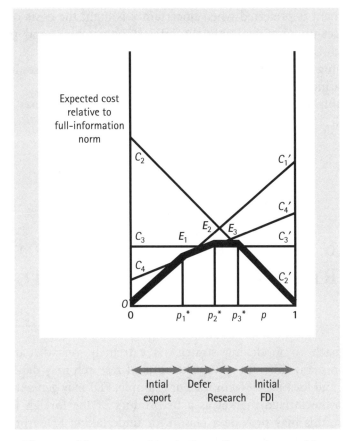

**Fig. 4.5 Diagrammatic solution of an entry problem encompassing research, deferment, and switching**

case where both research costs and the profits generated by foreign sales are relatively modest. This means that both research and deferment are optimal strategies for certain values of $p$. There are now three critical probability values at which the firm switches strategies: $p_1^*$, where the firm switches from initial exporting to deferment; $p_2^*$, where it switches from deferment to research; and $p_3^*$ where it switches from research to initial FDI.

A selection of the results that can be obtained (in addition to the previous results) is given below:

(1) As the decision-maker becomes more optimistic, the chosen strategy switches in turn from exporting to deferment to research to FDI; some of the steps may be omitted when one of the strategies is completely dominated by the others, but the basic sequence is never reversed;

(2) Deferment is preferred when uncertainty is high, the costs of error are high, set-up costs are high, the interest rate is high, and the cost of research is high;

(3) Switching is more likely to take place, the lower are the losses incurred by liquidating a fixed investment; and

(4) Switching is more likely to take place when foreign costs are highly variable.

# 4.10 FURTHER EXTENSIONS OF THE REAL OPTIONS APPROACH TO STRATEGY

This approach to modelling strategy is extremely versatile and can be extended in many different ways. The costs of research may depend on the ownership and location of facilities. For example, FDI may generate information about the foreign market as a by-product of the foreign location of production; this may provide a reason for undertaking FDI from the outset—but in a flexible form, so that it can be divested if the market turns out to be poor. Similarly a foreign-owned plant may be more useful in capturing information than a plant operated by a licensee, because ownership gives more effective access to information by-products. Hence not only does information-gathering affect ownership and location strategy, but ownership and location strategies affect information-gathering too. Ownership issues are considered in more detail below.

So long as there remains just a single source of uncertainty, most problems of this type can be solved using the graphical technique described above. The following properties of Figure 4.5 are common to all graphical solutions:

(1) The envelope of minimum expected cost, indicated by the thick line, is (weakly) convex;

(2) The convex envelope is constructed from a series of straight-line graphs representing the expected costs of the various dominant strategies;

(3) There are critical probabilities defining the switch-points between strategies;

(4) Changes in the parameters—such as costs, sales revenues, and interest rates—cause the straight-line graphs to shift and/or rotate, and thereby

lead to previously efficient strategies becoming inefficient, and vice versa. This generates a wide range of inter-related hypotheses about the effects of various parameters on the dynamics of foreign market entry under uncertainty.

Additional sources of uncertainty can also be introduced: for example, the reactions of established foreign firms in the foreign market, or the reactions of other potential foreign entrants into that market. In this context, it is important to distinguish two types of situation:

(1) The initial entrant wins customer loyalty, and subsequent entrants can only access the 'residual' market that was not captured by the initial entrant; and

(2) There is no customer loyalty, so an initial entrant must subsequently defend their market share through price warfare, or other competitive weapons. The initial entrant can deter followers by making an irreversible commitment to the foreign market, which means that it will always pay him to 'stay and fight' rather than 'quit the market'. The method of entry then becomes important in determining the strength of this threat.

These issues (especially the second) can be analysed using game-theoretic techniques.

# 4.11 The IB System as a Global Network

As noted earlier, the rational action approach emphasizes combinatorial complexity rather than analytical complexity. An important source of combinatorial complexity in the IB system lies in its network structure. This network structure was only implicit in the previous analysis, and it now needs to be made explicit.

A simple network structure is represented schematically in Figure 4.6, using a set of conventions established in earlier work (Casson 1995, 1997, 2000a,b). The figure illustrates a two-country world, comprising a home country (country 1) and a foreign country (country 2). It focuses on a single industry, assumed, for convenience, to be a manufacturing industry. Physical processes, such as production and distribution, are represented by square boxes. Each box indicates a facility, such as a factory or warehouse, at a specific location.

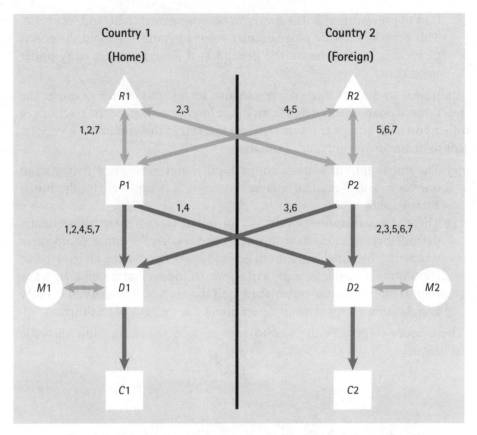

**Fig. 4.6 Schematic representation of a simple international business system**

*Note* The letter indentifying a facility denotes the type of the facility, as described in the text. The number indentifies the country in which the facility is located.

The numbers associated with the flows indentify the location strategies that involve these flows. The strategies concerned are described in Table 4.5.

Flows of tangible products are represented by black lines: thus factory output awaiting distribution flows from production, *P*, to distribution, *D*, and onwards from distribution to the final customer, *C*; the customer may be household consumers, the government, or firms in some other industry. The direction of flow is indicated by an arrow.

Intangible flows such as knowledge are represented by grey lines. Two types of knowledge are identified: technological know-how, produced by R&D, and local market knowledge, accumulated through experience in distribution of the product. Technological know-how is generated in scientific laboratories, *R*, indicated by a triangle, whilst marketing expertise is accumulated by a marketing department, *M*, indicated by a circle. Unlike product flows, which

Table 4.3 Tabular representation of flows illustrated in Figure 4.6

| From/to | R1 | R2 | M1 | M2 | P1 | P2 | D1 | D2 | C1 | C2 |
|---------|----|----|----|----|----|----|----|----|----|----|
| R1 | | | | | Know-how | Know-how | | | | |
| R2 | | | | | Know-how | Know-how | | | | |
| M1 | | | | | | | Experi-ence | | | |
| M2 | | | | | | | | Experi-ence | | |
| P1 | Feed-back | Feed-back | | | | | Wholesale product | Wholesale product | | |
| P2 | Feed-back | Feed-back | | | | | Wholesale product | Wholesale product | | |
| D1 | | | Feed-back | Feed-back | | | | | Retail product | |
| D2 | | | Feed-back | Feed-back | | | | | | Retail product |
| C1 | | | | | | | | | | |
| C2 | | | | | | | | | | |

are one-way, knowledge flows are two-way, as indicated by the two arrows on each grey line.

In principle any configuration of production plants, distribution facilities, research laboratories, and marketing offices located in any number of different countries can be represented in this way. Mapping out the entire IB system would, of course, prove extremely complex, and generate a very complicated diagram (Isard 1956). However, the network structure of the IB system can also be conveniently summarized in tabular form, as indicated in Table 4.3; this tabular form can be more readily expanded to accommodate additional detail as required.

## 4.12 LEVELS OF AGGREGATION

The IB system can be represented at different levels of aggregation. For example, when discussing international trade and investment flows at a macroeconomic level it may be sufficient to analyse the system in terms of a single representative plant in each country. In this case each of the boxes, triangles, or circles indicates a single representative facility of a given type. The number of facilities of that type in a given country may be indicated by placing a number adjacent to the corresponding box; thus a number 'three' placed adjacent to the box P2 would indicate that there are three production plants in country 2.

By contrast, a microeconomic view of a particular industry in a particular country might require different regional locations to be identified, and the transport infrastructure linking these locations to be mapped out, including ports, airports, railway junctions, and major road hubs. In general, the existence of specialized nodes where traffic is switched between linkages is fully apparent only with disaggregation.

The extreme of disaggregation occurs when individual workspaces are identified within each plant, and the roles of separate individuals are identified. This level of disaggregation is extremely useful for discussing the organizational structure of the firm, as explained below.

Each element identified at a high level of aggregation appears as a system in its own right when viewed at a lower level of aggregation. There is a hierarchy of sub-systems within the system as a whole. The representation of a system using a high level of aggregation is analogous to the 'desk top' on a computer screen, whilst a representation using a low level of aggregation opens up the 'windows' to reveal the contents of the drives or files.

Different variants of IB work with different levels of aggregation:

- the individual person
- the firm
- the industry
- the global economy
- the socio-political-ecological system.

Economic theories of IB—such as internalization theory, and theories of international business strategy—operate at the firm and industry level, and these are the levels on which this chapter focuses.

Scholars working at one level of aggregation often criticize others for making unwarranted assumptions. This sometimes leads to unnecessary controversy. Typically those who work at low levels of aggregation criticize those working at higher levels of aggregation for making sweeping assumptions, whilst those who work at high levels of aggregation tend to criticize those working at lower levels of aggregation for cluttering their analysis with irrelevant detail, and being 'unable to see the wood for the trees'. It is important for those working at one level of aggregation to bear in mind that other scholars work at other levels of aggregation and that considerable care is needed in reconciling work at adjacent levels of aggregation.

It is not only the level of aggregation that is important when describing a system. There is an important distinction between short run and long run analysis too. In the short run the IB system comprises a fixed number of facilities which have been inherited from the past. In the long run, by contrast, the number of facilities is variable because new facilities can be created and established facilities may be closed down. In a long run context it is therefore important to distinguish between actual and potential facilities.

# 4.13 IMPLEMENTING THE NETWORK RESEARCH AGENDA

The network view of the IB system is well suited to addressing two of the major issues in IB: the issue of where IB facilities will be *located* and the issue of who will *own* them. These questions can be considered separately or together. It is possible to analyse, for a given pattern of ownership, where facilities will be located. Similarly, for a given pattern of location, it is possible to analyse the structure of ownership. Finally, it is also possible to determine simultaneously what the patterns of location and ownership within the system will be.

Issues of location, considered in isolation from issues of ownership, are addressed by theories of geography and trade. Relevant theories include the the Ricardian theory of comparative advantage, the Heckscher-Ohlin-Stopler-Samuelson theory of factor intensities, and theories of transport costs and economies of scale (Krugman 1995).

IB theory has tended to concentrate on issues of ownership: in particular, internalization theory, as developed in the 1970s, focused on the question of why a firm that owned facilities in one country would wish to own facilities in another country, and how it could survive against international competition if it did so. The theory emphasized the gains from internalizing knowledge flow, and allowed for gains from internalizing intermediate flows of material product too—e.g. components and raw materials.

A major justification for distinguishing IB as a special field of study is that pattern of ownership used to coordinate international linkages in a network are different from those used to coordinate purely domestic ones. If there were no substantial difference then the international dimension would be of limited significance so far as the interaction of ownership and location are concerned. A key feature of an IB system is that the costs and benefits of internalization vary according to whether an international or domestic linkage is involved. This cost differential can impact on both ownership and location decisions. Thus a firm may license internationally a technology that it exploits internally in the domestic market; similarly, it may produce at home instead of abroad because it can only afford to produce abroad by licensing its technology and it is reluctant to do so because of the costs involved.

To illustrate this point, it is useful to consider the structure of costs within an IB network. Consider first location strategy. Suppose that in the previous example both the national markets have to be served, and that both are of fixed size. Market sizes are normalized to unity for simplicity. Since the markets cannot be served without distribution facilities, nor without market knowledge, the costs incurred by marketing and distribution activities are sunk costs, and so can be omitted from the analysis. This leaves just the costs that are shown in Table 4.4. The key elements in this table are the production costs in the two countries, $c_1$, $c_2$, R&D costs in the two countries, $a_1$, $a_2$, costs of transferring technology internationally, $m$, and the cost of transporting the product internationally, $z$. All of these costs are assumed to be known for

**Table 4.4 Structure of location costs for the flows illustrated in Figure 4.1 (excluding sunk costs of marketing and distribution)**

| From/to | R1 | R2 | P1 | P2 | D1 | D2 |
|---|---|---|---|---|---|---|
| R1 | Domestic R&D cost; fixed cost: $a_1$ | | Domestic transfer cost (zero) | International transfer cost; fixed cost: $m$ | | |
| R2 | | Foreign R&D cost; fixed cost: $a_2$ | International transfer cost; fixed cost: $m$ | Domestic transfer cost (zero) | | |
| P1 | | | Domestic production cost; unit cost: $c_1$ | | Domestic transport cost (zero) | International transport cost; unit cost: z |
| P2 | | | | Foreign production cost; unit cost: $c_2$ | International transport cost; unit cost: z | Domestic transport cost (zero) |

## Table 4.5 Dominant locational strategies

| Location strategy | Description | Active facilities | Cost |
|---|---|---|---|
| | *Research in country 1 only* | | |
| 1 | Export from country 1 | $R1, P1$ | $a_1 + 2c_1 + z$ |
| 2 | Produce in both countries | $R1, P1, P2$ | $a_1 + m + c_1 + c_2$ |
| 3 | Export from country 2 | $R1, P2$ | $a_1 + m + 2c_2 + z$ |
| | *Research in country 2 only* | | |
| 4 | Export from country 1 | $R2, P1$ | $a_2 + m + 2c_1 + z$ |
| 5 | Produce in both countries | $R2, P1, P2$ | $a_2 + m + c_1 + c_2$ |
| 6 | Export from country 2 | $R2, P2$ | $a_2 + 2c_2 + z$ |
| | *Research in both countries* | | |
| 7 | Produce in both countries | $R1, R2, P1, P2$ | $a_1 + a_2 + c_1 + c_2$ |

*Note* All the strategies utilize both distribution facilities $D1, D2$; these are omitted from the third column for reasons of simplicity.

certain; the analysis can be extended to allow for uncertainty by using the techniques described in the earlier part of this chapter.

It is easy to deduce that:

(1) it is never efficient to carry out research in both countries unless there is production in both countries;
(2) when there is research in both countries, it is never efficient to 'cross haul' research by linking R&D in country 1 to production in country 2, and vice versa; and;
(3) when there is production in both countries it is never efficient to 'cross-haul' the product by exporting from country 1 to country 2 at the same time as exporting from country 2 to country 1.

It follows that just seven location strategies need to be distinguished. These seven strategies dominate all other conceivable strategies, in the sense that one of these seven strategies will always afford the lowest overall system cost. The dominant strategies are listed in Table 4.5. Note that because of locational specialization, strategies 1–6 utilize only some, and not all, of the available facilities.

The optimal location strategy is derived by comparing the costs set out in the final column of the table and identifying the strategy associated with the lowest cost. The following principles characterize an efficient location strategy in general terms:

1. Produce in both countries if and only if international transport costs exceed the savings from concentrating all production in the lower cost country:

   $$z > max[c_1 c_2] - min[c_1, c_2].$$

2. Research in both countries if and only if producing in both countries, and if the cost of transferring technology exceeds the cost of researching in the higher-cost country:

   $$m > max[a_1 a_2].$$

3. Produce and research in different countries if and only if the cost of transferring technology is less than the smaller of the savings in research costs and production costs achieved by switching one of the locations:

   $$m < min[|a_2 - a_1|, |c_2 - c_1|].$$

4. If producing and researching in the same country, choose the country for which the sum of research and production costs is lowest:

   choose country 1 if $(a_2 - a_1) + (c_2 - c_1) > 0$, and otherwise choose country 2.

5. Similarly, if producing and researching in different countries, choose the combination for which the sum of research and production costs is lowest:

   choose to research in 1 and produce in 2 if $(a_2 - a_1) - (c_2 - c_1) > 0$, and otherwise choose the opposite combination.

# 4.14 TRANSACTION COSTS: OPTIMIZING OWNERSHIP PATTERNS

From a network perspective, ownership patterns are driven by the need to minimize the costs of coordinating the system. Each facility is allocated an owner. Since no two owners can own the same facility outright, the ownership strategies of different firms constrain each other: what is owned by one firm cannot be owned by other firms as well. Although ownership can be shared through joint ventures, the partners must still harmonize their strategies, so that their shares add to 100 per cent. The interdependence of ownership strategies is missing from conventional expositions of internalization theory, which focus on the strategies of a single firm. This weakness is often mitigated by assuming that the firm invests in new facilities, such as a greenfield production plant, but the problem remains when discussing take-overs, where several firms may be competing to acquire the same facility, and only one of them can succeed. In general, the internalization strategies of all firms in a system need to be analysed simultaneously, and this can only be done using a network approach.

The pattern of ownership that emerges in an IB system depends crucially on the structure of transactions costs (Coase 1937). For present purposes transaction costs may be equated with the costs of coordinating linkages, although a more refined analysis would distinguish different aspects of transaction costs (Casson 2000a, chs. 3, 5). The transaction costs associated with any given linkage in a network depend, in general, upon three main factors:

(1) the nature of the flow along the linkage and, in particular, whether the flow is an intangible flow of knowledge ($i = 1$) or a tangible flow of product ($i = 2$);
(2) whether the flow is internal to a firm ($j = 1$), or external, connecting two independent firms ($j = 2$); and
(3) whether the flow is domestic ($k = 1$) or international ($k = 2$).

The transactions cost incurred by the IB system is the sum of the transaction costs associated with the individual linkages utilized by the system. The linkages that are active at any one time depend on the location strategy that is being used. Thus different location strategies, when applied in conjunction with a given pattern of ownership, are liable to generate different transaction costs, as well as different location costs.

The total cost of the system is the sum of the transaction costs and the location costs. In general, there is a trade-off between location costs and transaction costs, because economizing on location costs through the international rationalization of research and production locations will tend to increase the number of international linkages, and international linkages typically incur higher transaction costs than purely domestic ones. In order to mitigate the increase in transaction cost patterns of ownership may change. In this way, changes in the system driven by location factors may induce a change in patterns of ownership; conversely, changes in ownership patterns may induce changes in location strategies, although in practice this effect appears to be less common.

When all the different location strategies are permuted with all the different ownership patterns, a very large number of possible system structures emerge.

All of these structures can, however, be ranked in terms of their overall system costs, and so in principle the least-cost configuration of the system can always be ascertained. Although it is complex, the problem remains finite.

The solution of this problem determines how many different firms will exist within the system, and where their individual boundaries will lie. Firms must be large enough to internalize all the linkages that benefit from internalization, but small enough to allow other linkages to be external instead. The importance of internalizing knowledge flows means that a higher proportion of knowledge flows will be internal to firms than will flows of ordinary products. It follows that the boundaries of firms will be determined mainly by the structure of knowledge flows, and only secondarily by the structure of product flows. This highlights a major difference between the IB literature and some of the other literature on transaction costs (e.g. Williamson 1985) where the emphasis of internalization is erroneously placed on ordinary product flows.

For many purposes, however, it is unnecessary to consider all of the permutations referred to above. IB scholars are typically interested in more specific issues which can be 'projected out' of the network model. For example, they are primarily concerned with the coordination of international linkages rather than domestic linkages. They also tend to be concerned with the choice between a subset of all the possible location strategies discussed above.

Consider, for example, the issue of foreign market entry strategy, as discussed in the first part of this chapter. Before internalization theory was developed it was normally assumed that FDI was the natural form of the local production strategy. Internalization theory pointed out that licensing was also an option. The network model presented above indicates that there are other options too. Foreign market servicing involves establishing a link between the R&D carried out in the home country (country 1) and the marketing and distribution of the product carried out in the foreign country (country 2). This involves two separate linkages: a flow of knowledge between R&D and production, and a flow of product between production and R&D. Either of these flows can be internal or external to the firm (see Table 4.6). Under the export strategy the flow of knowledge is domestic but the flow of product is international, whereas under local production the converse applies: the flow of knowledge is international and the flow of product is domestic. As a result, different location strategies generate different pattern of transactions costs, and the resulting differences in transactions costs can influence the choice of location strategy. They also determine the form of ownership structure used to implement the chosen location strategy.

Suppose, for example, that internalization of knowledge flow is always cheaper than external knowledge flow, but that the internalization of product flow is only cheaper where domestic rather than international linkages are

**Table 4.6** Alternative contractual arrangements for linking domestic R&D to foreign distribution

|  | Domestic production | Foreign production |
|---|---|---|
| *Internalize knowledge flow* | | |
| Internalize product flow | (1) | (2) |
|  | FDI in distribution | FDI in production & distribution |
|  | $t_{111} + t_{212}$ | $t_{112} + t_{211}$ |
| Externalize product flow | (3) | (4) |
|  | Export to independent foreign sales agent | FDI in production; sell through an independent foreign sales agent |
|  | $t_{111} + t_{222}$ | $t_{112} + t_{221}$ |
| *Externalize knowledge flow* | | |
| Internalize product flow | (5) | (6) |
|  | License a firm that undertakes FDI in distribution | License a foreign producer that integrates forward into distribution |
|  | $t_{121} + t_{212}$ | $t_{122} + t_{211}$ |
| Externalize product flow | (7) | (8) |
|  | License an exporter that sells through an independent foreign sales agent | License a foreign producer that sells through an independent local agent |
|  | $t_{121} + t_{222}$ | $t_{122} + t_{221}$ |

*Note* It is assumed that the domestic market is always supplied through domestic production. Domestic distribution is either integrated with domestic production, or undertaken by an independent agent, whichever affords the lower transaction costs. This decision can be made independently of all other decisions and, since it does not bear directly on IB strategy, is omitted from the analysis.

concerned. Under these conditions it always pays to internalize the linkage between production and R&D. The structure of transaction costs for knowledge flow implies that the cheapest foreign production strategy involves FDI rather than licensing. The structure of transaction costs for product flow implies that foreign production will be integrated with foreign distribution, so that FDI in production implies FDI in distribution too. It also implies, however, that exporting will be carried out at arm's length, so that domestic production will be sold to an independent distributor in the foreign market. So far as the domestic situation is concerned, domestic production will be integrated with domestic distribution, so that the firm will be vertically integrated in both countries.

The actual choice between exporting and FDI depends on the structure of both location costs and transaction costs. The costs of domestic R&D are common to both strategies. The exporting strategy derived above incurs transaction costs

$$t_1 = t_{111} + t_{222}$$

while the FDI strategy incurs transaction costs

$$t_2 = t_{112} + t_{211}$$

where $t_{ijk}$ is the transaction cost associated with a flow of type $i$ through a market of type $j$ along a linkage of geographical type $k$ (as defined above). Combining these expressions with the expressions for location costs in Table 4.5 shows that FDI is preferred to exporting when:

$$z + c_1 - c_2 > m + t_2 - t_1$$

This condition states that the savings in international transport costs *plus* any savings in production costs effected by FDI must exceed the costs of international technology transfer *plus* any additional transaction costs that stem from internationalizing internal technology transfer *less* any savings in distribution costs that arise from using an internal domestic market rather than an external international one. This result demonstrates how embedding an analysis of foreign market entry within a network view can enrich understanding of the issue.

# 4.15 The Distribution of Information Within a Global System

In the first part of this paper foreign market entry was discussed from the standpoint of an individual firm, whereas in the second part it has been discussed from the standpoint of the overall system. In the first part the existence of the firm was given, whereas in the second part the structure of the firm emerged from an analysis of internalization. The first part also assumed uncertainty, whereas the second did not. Intuitively, the system perspective is that of an all-knowing planner who controls the whole system, while the firm perspective is that of a decision-maker who only understands a part of the system—specifically, that part of the system to which their personal knowledge and experience relates. Another difference is that the planner begins from scratch, and moves directly to the optimal configuration, whereas the individual decision-maker is constrained by the legacy of their previous decisions.

The link between the system-wide view of the planner and the partial view of the individual firm is that in a private enterprise economy, where indvidual entrepreneurs compete to establish firms, competition between them will tend to drive the system towards the planner's system-wide optimum (Hayek 1937; Richardson 1960). Different entrepreneurs will select different locations for their facilities, and choose to operate with different boundaries for their firms. They will compete to own facilities in highly desirable locations. The entrepreneurs with the most efficient strategies will be able to outbid those with less efficient strategies, and so competition for the ownership and control of scarce resources will reward those entrepreneurs whose partial plans are most closely aligned with the system-wide optimum.

In practice, of course, there is no planner who possesses all the information of the kind required to fully optimize the system. Planning has encountered numerous problems at national level, and these would only be further compounded if planning were attempted at the global level. This does not mean that the network view is irrelevant, however, because for reasons already noted a well-functioning private enterprise economy will tend to converge on the optimum through incremental trial and error. Competition between individual entrepreneurs within the system leads to a pooling of local knowledge—the knowledge being encoded in the prices that the entrepreneurs quote when bidding for the use of facilities and when competing for customers. So long as the competitive system remains stable, therefore, the network approach will successfully identify the long-run tendencies in the system by identifying the equilibrium to which it is converging through localized iterations.

Because an individual entrepreneur perceives only a small part of the global system, he faces considerable uncertainty regarding the consequences of his decisions. He cannot track the full implications of any decision that he makes. Conversely, because decision-making has been decentralized to many different entrepreneurs like himself, he is continuously exposed to unexpected changes caused by decisions made by other people—notably his customers and his competitors. The efficiency with which the global system works will therefore depend on the skill of entrepreneurs in handling uncertainties of this kind.

# 4.16 SOCIAL NETWORKS AND ORGANIZATIONS

An important strategy for handling uncertainty is to construct a network of contacts that act as sources of information (Ebers 1997). An entrepreneur can develop two main types of network for this purpose. First, he can build a network involving other entrepreneurs, who own independent firms, and secondly he can turn his own firm into a networking organization. External networks may encompass not only other firms, but governments, banks, and opinion-leaders too. Internal networking may involve a hierarchical structure of reporting based on authority relations, or a flatter structure where people of similar status consult with each other.

There is insufficient space to describe in detail how social networks can be analysed using the rational action approach. It is sufficient to note that the rational action approach explains very simply why people are motivated to join social networks in order to gain access to information. Networks generate efficiency gains by exploiting the 'public good' property of knowledge and information. The rational action approach also explains how social and physical networks interact. Social networks are used to coordinate physical networks—for example, by planning the flow of product along the linkages between facilities. At the same time, social networks utilize physical networks as inputs—as, for example, when people travel to face-to-face meetings by road, rail, or air.

It is worth noting that the rational action approach to social networks has significant implications for the modelling of organizational behaviour within multinational firms (Egelhoff 1991). Where a large amount of information on the global environment needs to be routinely collected, a division of labour may be introduced that allows different members of an internal network to specialize in collecting different sorts of information. Where multiple sources of uncertainty are involved, multiple sources of information are normally required. The information obtained from these various sources needs to be synthesized for decision-making purposes. This requires communication between the specialists involved. Some of the communication may be 'intermediated' by other specialists, and these intermediators may sometimes take overall responsibility for the decisions. Thus the nature of the division of labour applied to information processing determines the organization of the multinational firm.

The efficiency of internal communication is a major factor in the overall cost of decision-making, and hence a major determinant of the performance of the firm. The 'entrepreneurial' qualities of the firm's key decision-makers govern its ability to synthesize information successfully. This in turn affects the overall quality of decisions (e.g. the frequency with which potential mistakes are avoided) and so determines overall performance.

The organization of decision-making can be introduced into the previous model of foreign market entry under uncertainty by formally splitting the final period into an infinite number of sub-periods, and allowing new information of a particular type to become available each period. Foreign costs of production fluctuate from one period to the next, and foreign output each period therefore needs to be adjusted in response. This encourages the firm to invest in information systems for predicting changes in cost. It also encourages the firm to invest in highly versatile capital equipment, thereby establishing a link between the structure of the organization and the type of physical capital that it employs (Capel 1992).

# 4.17 CONCLUSION

All of these research avenues need to be fully explored before any claim that the challenge of complexity warrants the introduction of more radical or unorthodox techniques into IB theory can be accepted. It is only sensible to follow the simplest and most straightforward path of theoretical development before investing too heavily in untried concepts and techniques. This chapter has suggested that the most productive theoretical developments in IB over the next ten years or so are likely to be those that build upon the rational action approach.

When the rational action approach is along the lines described above, many of the notions found in systems theory emerge in their proper light. Rule-driven behaviour, of the kind assumed in systems theory, is shown to be a rational response to information costs (Baumol and Quandt 1964). It is only rational in certain types of environment, however: in other environments, entrepreneurial improvization is shown to be the order of the day.

Economy of coordination calls for a division of labour in information processing, and this in turn calls for cooperative behaviour of a social nature. It is rational to adapt the rules governing social behaviour to the long-term features of the environment within which decisions have to be made. The environment differs between locations, and it is therefore to be expected that there will be differences between locations in the kinds of rules that are used. In other words, social interactions will follow different rules in different places.

It is not expected that everyone will agree with these recommendations. But the onus is on those who disagree to set out their own agenda with a similar degree of analytical rigour, and to demonstrate that their favoured approach can deliver practical results. Talking about 'strategy' or 'complexity' in non-specific ways may be adequate for consultancy assignments, or for teaching certain types of courses, but it is not an adequate response to the research challenges that currently face IB.

# REFERENCES

ALLEN, LINDA, and PANTZALIS, CHRISTOS (1996). 'Valuation of the Operating Flexibility of Multinational Corporations', *Journal of International Business Studies*, 27/4: 633–53.

ARTHUR, BRIAN W. (1988). 'Competing Technologies: An Overview', in Giovanni Dosi, C. Freeman, R. Nelson, G. Silverberg, and L. Soete (eds.), *Technical Change and Economic Theory*. London: Francis Pinter.

BAUMOL, WILLIAM J., and QUANDT, RICHARD E. (1964) 'Rules of Thumb and Optimally Imperfect Decisions', *American Economic Review*, 54/1: 23–46.

BUCKLEY, PETER J., and CASSON, MARK C. (1976). *The Future of the Multinational Enterprise*. London: Macmillan.

—— (1981). 'The Optimal Timing of a Foreign Direct Investment', *Economic Journal*, 91: 75–87.

—— (1993). 'Economics as an Imperialist Social Science', *Human Relations*, 46/9: 1035–52.

—— (1998a). 'Analysing Foreign Market Entry Strategies: Extending The Internalisation Approach', *Journal of International Business Studies*, 29/3: 539–61.

—— (1998b). 'Models of the Multinational Enterprise', *Journal of International Business Studies*, 29/1: 21–44.

CAPEL, JEANETTE (1992). 'How to Service a Foreign Market Under Uncertainty: A Real Option Approach', *European Journal of Political Economy*, 8: 455–75.

CASSON, MARK C. (1995). *Organization of International Business*. Aldershot: Edward Elgar.

—— (1997). *Information and Organisation: A New Perspective on the Theory of the Firm*. Oxford: Clarendon Press.

—— (2000a). *Economics of International Business: A New Research Agenda*. Cheltenham: Edward Elgar.

CASSON, MARK C. (*cont.*) (2000*b*). *Enterprise and Leadership: Studies on Firms, Networks and Institutions.* Cheltenham: Edward Elgar.

COASE, RONALD H. (1937). 'The Nature of the Firm', *Economica*, NS, 4: 386–405.

CORIAT, B., and DOSI, GIOVANNI (1998). 'The Institutional Embeddedness of Economic Change: An Appraisal of the 'Evolutionist' and 'Regulationist' Research Programmes', in K. Nielsen and E. J. Johnson (eds.), *Institutions and Economic Change.* Cheltenham: Edward Elgar.

DEMEZA, DAVID and VAN DER PLOEG, FREDERICK (1987). 'Production Flexibility as a Motive for Multinationality', *Journal of Industrial Economics*, 35/3: 343–51.

DIXIT, AVRINASH, and PINDYCK, ROBERT S. (1994). *Investments under Uncertainty.* Princeton, NJ: Princeton University Press.

EBERS, MARK (ed.) (1997). *The Formation of Inter-Organizational Networks.* Oxford: Clarendon Press

EGELHOFF, WILLIAM G. (1991). 'Information-processing theory and the Multinational Enterprise', *Journal of International Business Studies*, 22/3: 341–68.

ELSTER, JOHN (ed.) (1986). *Rational Choice.* Oxford: Blackwell.

GRAHAM, E. M. (1990). 'Exchange of Threat Between Multinational Firms as an Infinitely Repeated Game', *International Trade Journal*, 4: 259–77.

HARGREAVES-HEAP, SHAUN (1989). *Rationality in Economics.* Oxford: Blackwell.

HAYEK, FRIEDRICH VON A. (1937). 'Economics and Knowledge', *Economica*, NS, 4: 33–54.

HIRSHLEIFER, JACK, and RILEY, JOHN G. (1992). *The Analytics of Uncertainty and Information.* Cambridge: Cambridge University Press.

ISARD, WALTER (1956). *Location and Space Economy.* Cambridge, Mass.: MIT Press.

KOGUT, BRUCE (1991). 'Joint Ventures and the Option to Expand and Acquire', *Management Science*, 37/1: 19–33.

KOGUT, BRUCE, and KULATILAKA, NALIN (1994). 'Operating Flexibility, Global Manufacturing, and the Option Value of a Multinational Network', *Management Science*, 40/1: 123–39.

KREPS, DAVID M. (1990). *Game Theory and Economic Modelling.* Oxford: Oxford University Press.

KRUGMAN, PAUL (1995). *Development, Geography and Economic Theory.* Cambridge, Mass.: MIT Press.

NELSON, RICHARD, and WINTER, SIDNEY G. (1982) *An Evolutionary Theory of Economic Change.* Cambridge, Mass.: Harvard University Press.

PARKHE, AVIND (1993). 'Messy' Research, Methodological Predispositions, and Theory Development in International Joint Ventures', *Academy of Management Review*, 18: 227–68.

PORTER, MICHAEL E. (1991). 'Towards a Dynamic Theory of Strategy', *Strategic Management Journal*, 12 (Special Issue): 95–117.

RICHARDSON, GEORGE B. (1960). *Information and Investment.* Oxford: Oxford University Press.

RIVOLI, PIETRA, and SALORIO, EUGENE (1996). 'Foreign Direct Investment under Uncertainty', *Journal of International Business Studies*, 27/2: 335–54.

WILLIAMSON, OLIVER E. (1985). *The Economic Institutions of Capitalism.* New York: Free Press.

CHAPTER 5

..................................................................................................

# THEORIES OF THE MULTINATIONAL ENTERPRISE

..................................................................................................

## JEAN-FRANÇOIS HENNART

THIS chapter provides a critical survey of some of the theories that have sought to explain why multinational enterprises (MNEs) exist, with special emphasis on the transaction costs/internalization approach. While scholars have quibbled over the definition of a MNE (and whether it ought to manufacture in at least two countries to qualify for that title), I define it as a private institution devised to organize, through employment contracts, interdependencies between individuals located in more than one country.[1] Hence a domestic manufacturer who only uses local distributors abroad is not an MNE, but a domestic department store with its own overseas buying offices, but no foreign manufacturing, is. Due to stringent page limits, this is not a complete survey, both because it omits many important theories, and because it fails to acknowledge many authors who have contributed to the

I thank Alexander Eapen and participants in the author's conference at Templeton College, Oxford, April 2000, for their comments.
[1] Legally, are part of a firm whose agents who are linked to it through an employment contract. Hence subcontractors (long-term suppliers, franchisees, licensees) are not part of the firm which contracts with them.

transaction cost/internalization approach. For a more complete survey of the various theories, see Chapter 2 in this volume. Readers looking for a somewhat fuller survey of transaction costs/internalization theories are referred to Hennart (2000).

Progress in our understanding of why MNEs exist has been slow because answering the question requires an understanding of a firm as one of many alternative social institutions that endeavor to organize economic activities. Many economists are not interested in institutions. Many scholars interested in firms do not see them as alternatives to markets.[2] The result is that progress in our understanding of the MNE has been slow, with each discipline (economics, strategy, organization theory) pursuing its research in splendid isolation, and many theories surviving in spite of their inability to account for the existence and growth of MNEs.

The first section briefly discusses early capital flow and industrial organization theories before focusing on transaction costs/internalization theories, the now dominant theories of the MNE. I focus on my own brand of the theory, developing first the basic foundations, then applying them to the MNE. Because internalization theory (Buckley and Casson 1976; Rugman 1981) and the eclectic paradigm (Dunning 1977, 1981, 1993, 1997) share many features with transaction cost theory, I do not describe them separately, but rather indicate where they differ.

# 5.1 THE EVOLUTION OF THE THEORY OF THE MULTINATIONAL ENTERPRISE

## 5.1.1 Trade theories

An economics graduate student seeking in the 1960s to understand why multinational enterprises (MNEs) exist, and their impact on society, would have been directed to look in International Trade textbooks under 'Foreign Direct Investment'. Trade economists of the time (and still to a large extent today) saw the MNE as a component in the long-term capital section of the balance of payment. MNEs caused one type of capital exports, foreign direct

[2] They implicitly assume that firms are not constrained by their competition with other institutions, for example markets.

investment (FDI), with FDI occurring when investors had control of foreign assets, and portfolio investment when they did not (hence FDI was undertaken mostly by business firms, and portfolio investment mostly by individuals). What caused FDI? Like any type of factor movement, capital flowed from one country to another in response to differences in real interest rates.

This view has two main limitations. First, there is no exact match between FDI and the growth of MNEs. Second, differences in real interest rates provide neither a necessary nor a sufficient reason for the existence of MNEs.

FDI measures the export of capital from one country to the rest of the world. But this is an imperfect measure of the evolution of MNEs because a firm establishing a plant or an office in a foreign country can expand without capital export from the home country by borrowing locally and/or reinvesting its profits. For example, over the 1966–72 period only 13 per cent of the funds invested abroad by a sample of American MNEs came from US sources, the rest being borrowed locally (or from other foreign countries) or reinvested (Mantel 1975).

The view that the existence of MNEs could be explained by international differences in interest rates was generally accepted by economists until Steven Hymer attacked it in his Ph.D. thesis (1970).[3] Hymer asked why, if FDI was motivated by the search for higher returns, it was undertaken by firms, and sought control of foreign assets. After all, banks are better intermediators than firms, and taking a small stake gives the investor more liquidity. Hymer also noted the presence of simultaneous FDI crossflows, with the US both exporting and importing FDI from the same country.

FDI crossflows are, however, compatible with a portfolio view of capital flows in which investors invest in assets bearing low returns because including these assets in their portfolio cause a reduction in overall risk that more than compensates for lower returns (Markowitz 1959). Unfortunately, this improvement does not rescue the theory because there are still the questions of why those who undertake FDI are manufacturers, rather than financial intermediaries, and why they tend to take majority stakes in foreign firms. Only 18 per cent of the foreign affiliates in Vernon's sample of 391 US MNEs were minority owned by their parents (Vernon 1977, 34). This is strange, since the smaller the stake, the greater the diversification. An overwhelming proportion of foreign affiliates are also in the same narrow industry as their parents. For example, in a sample of Japanese firms investing in the US, 75 per cent manufactured in the US a product they also manufactured in Japan (Hennart and Reddy 1997). This is not the way to buy diversification. Lastly, one can build an optimally diversified portfolio for a given country by looking at both rates of return by country and the correlation of those returns between

---

[3] He was however unable to publish it in main economic journals because reviewers found it 'too obvious' (Kindleberger 1976).

pairs of countries. If FDI is explained by portfolio diversification, then the geographical pattern of FDI for a given country will closely match that of an optimally diversified portfolio. Levy and Sarnat (1970) built such an optimal portfolio for a US investor. The actual distribution of US investment bears, however, very little resemblance to this optimal portfolio (Hennart 1982). Hence neither interest rate theory nor its more sophisticated portfolio variant can explain the existence of MNEs.[4]

## 5.1.2 Industrial organization theories

Hymer's (1960) theory of the MNE brought the focus from the nation to the firm. Hymer considered what happened in a world of segmented national markets dominated by home-grown monopolists when lower transportation costs and trade barriers brought two such monopolists into contact. He argued that competition between these two firms would generate (pecuniary) externalities, which a merger of these two firms, or the acquisition of one by the other—i.e. the creation of a firm spanning the two countries, i.e. an MNE—would internalize. This could explain the creation of MNEs. The same logic could explain why a domestic monopolist would set up a green-field venture abroad to preempt the development of a local competitor, or would choose not to license to a local firm, but instead to expand abroad on its own. Hence the crux of Hymer's theory was that MNEs were instruments by which competitors reduced competition in industries where large barriers to entry had created and were sustaining local monopolies.[5]

Hymer's thesis was therefore that MNEs were internalizing externalities due to competition on markets for final products. In other words, as firms compete with one another, they lower the price they can charge consumers, and end up giving up their monopoly profits. These externalities are pecuniary externalities, insofar as their internalization is zero-sum: what the MNE loses, the consumer gains. While there is no doubt that in some cases an MNE (through mergers/acquisitions or preemptive greenfield investments) is set up to limit competition, the theory does not provide a set of necessary and

---

[4] In recent years, a new stream of literature has appeared that seeks to relate 'geographical diversification' and 'product diversification' to performance. Geographical diversification is often measured as a simple count of countries where the MNE is doing business (hence it is not diversification in a portfolio sense). This literature is developing in seeming ignorance of theories of the MNE. For a critique of this literature see Dess *et al.*, (1995).

[5] In his dissertation, Hymer hints at a transaction costs approach by arguing that horizontal investment can be caused by imperfections in markets for intangibles. This viewpoint is clearer in subsequent work published in French (Hymer 1968). Hymer did not, however, systematize the argument.

sufficient reasons for the emergence and development of MNEs. First, Hymer fails to explain the presence of MNEs in highly competitive industries, such as textiles, car rental, and fast food. Second, an MNE is only one way of internalizing pecuniary externalities. Others are cartels (Casson 1985) or tacit collusion, based for example on the division of geographical territories (possibly joined with cross-licensing), as was common in the interwar period (Hennart 1985).

Hymer's thesis triggered a stream of literature that looked at the foreign forays of MNEs as manifestations of oligopolistic reaction, focusing on 'follow the leader' and 'exchange of hostages' behavior. The early literature (Flowers 1976; Graham 1978) erroneously assumed that this was the only driver of a firm's foreign expansion. Later researchers have incorporated strategic interaction in transaction costs models, on the assumption that exchange of hostages and follow the leader increase the probability a follower will move abroad over that predicted by transaction costs variables. Results show that some of these strategic factors increase the probability a firm will venture abroad if it belongs to 'loose oligopolistic' industries (Yu and Ito, 1988; Hennart and Park 1994).

## 5.1.3  Transaction cost/internalization theories

Hymer saw MNEs as internalizers of pecuniary externalities due to structural market imperfections. But, as the traditional literature on externalities shows, markets are not perfectly efficient, and suffer from natural market imperfections as well (Dunning and Rugman 1985). These imperfections arise because agents are 'boundedly rational' and 'opportunistic'. Economic agents do not always know prices and are not always able to measure outputs. They cannot always trust others to be honest (Williamson 1975; 1985). When natural market imperfections are high, the expansion of firms across national boundaries may be a more efficient way to internalize these non-pecuniary externalities. In contrast to Hymer's pecuniary externalities, internalizing these non-pecuniary externalities is a positive sum game in which both producers and consumers gain. This is the argument of the transaction costs/internalization theory of the MNE (Buckley and Casson 1976; Hennart 1977, 1982; Rugman 1981). Transaction cost theories thus seek to explain why MNEs organize international interdependencies that could also be handled by markets. Since this is the dominant theory in international business (Caves 1998) the following sections will develop it in greater depth.

# 5.2 THE TRANSACTION COST THEORY OF THE MULTINATIONAL ENTERPRISE

Some authors mistakenly believe that the transaction cost/internalization theory of the MNE originated with Williamson (1975). In fact, it was independently developed by Buckley and Casson (1976) and Hennart (1977, 1982), himself inspired by McManus (1972). Because these authors developed their theories quite early, the application they make of transaction costs differs in significant ways from that of Williamson (1985). Specifically, the concept of asset specificity, which plays a large role in Williamson's theory, is less central to why MNEs expand abroad. As we will see below, many cases of foreign expansion can be explained by the high cost of using the market when property rights are imperfectly defined and enforced, and not by asset specificity, which is only a special case of narrow, and hence inefficient markets.

Another very common misconception is that transaction costs theory is coherent and monolithic. Transaction costs theory should be seen as an approach, a way of looking at the world. Its rather recent development means that researchers are likely to exhibit significant differences in the way they apply it. The following pages summarize the rather idiosyncratic approach I have been developing over the years (Hennart 1982, 1986, 1993a, 1993b).

## 5.2.1 Basic transaction costs theory

Transaction cost theory focuses on the problem of organizing interdependencies between individuals. These individuals can generate rents by pooling together different or similar capabilities. Transaction cost theory argues that firms arise when they are the most efficient institution to organize these interdependencies. Likewise, MNEs thrive when they are more efficient than markets and contracts in organizing interdependencies between agents located in different countries.[6] For example, firm A may have established a distribution system and a manufacturing capacity in its own country, but may be looking for foreign licenses to manufacture and distribute complementary products; while on the other hand a foreign manufacturer may have already developed such a product and can sell its technology to Firm A at very low

---

[6] Hence the transaction cost theory of the MNE is a general theory of economic institutions which is applicable to domestic institutions as well. The only difference is that MNEs face the additional difficulty of having to manage across political and cultural barriers.

marginal cost. However, such cooperation, which would be profitable to both parties, will not automatically take place. Both parties must be aware of the potential gains of cooperating, they must be able to agree on a price for the technology, and they must prevent protracted bargaining from eating all the potential gains from cooperation. Because economic agents suffer from cognitive limitations (they are boundedly rational) and because at least some of them are opportunistic, organizing this cooperation will incur positive information, enforcement, and bargaining costs. These are called transaction costs (Williamson 1975, 1985).

The basic argument of transaction cost theory is that the cost of organizing a given transaction varies with the method of organization chosen to organize it. This is because each of the two basic methods of organization, the price system and hierarchy, experiences different levels of costs for a given transaction. And they experience different costs because they use different methods.

The price system focuses on outputs. In a price system, prices for outputs convey to all agents the value of goods and services. Prices also reward agents in proportion to their measured output. And lastly, if there are enough buyers and sellers, prices are exogenous and thus eliminate opportunities for bargaining. In practice, bounded rationality and opportunism make markets less than perfectly efficient. Consequently, (1) agents will sometimes be unable to define and measure property rights and therefore prices will not convey an accurate estimate of the value of goods and services; (2) agents will find it sometimes difficult to measure output, so that money will have to be spent to enforce trades and/or there will be some residual amount of cheating; (3) agents will engage in bargaining when there is an insufficient number of buyers and sellers.

The price system is thus heavily dependent on the definition and measurement of outputs in all their dimensions. If some dimensions are not measured, then agents will be incited to maximize the measured dimensions at the expense of the non-measured (and hence non-rewarded) ones. I call 'cheating' the behavior of some market participants who take advantage of measurement difficulties to overprice and/or underperform.

When measurement and enforcement costs are high, and the small number of buyers and sellers renders prices endogenous, switching to hierarchy may be preferable. Hierarchy replaces the *output constraints* of markets by *behavior constraints* (Hennart 1982, 1986, 1993a).[7]

Behavior constraints can be external or internal: external behavior constraints are imposed on the individual from the outside, either through direct

---

[7] Note that we use the term 'hierarchy' to describe a method of control, not the managers who implement it in firms. As we will argue shortly, 'firm' and 'hierarchy' are not the same thing, and neither is 'market' equivalent to 'price'. Prices and hierarchy are methods of organization, while markets and firms are institutions. Both institutions make use of both methods simultaneously, but markets use predominantly prices, and firms hierarchy.

observation by a hierarchical superior, or through bureaucratic rules and procedures. Internal behavior constraints rely on interiorized rules so that employees behave as if they were being observed. This can be achieved by (1) selecting employees who have the same goals as management and/or (2) persuading employees through training and socialization that they have the same goals as their employer. Establishing both external and internal behavior constraints is costly. Given bounded rationality and opportunism, neither of these two methods will perfectly constrain behavior.

If output is hard to measure, then rewarding it will lead to biases, as agents will try to produce too much of the bads that are not being measured (and for which they are therefore not accountable), and too little of the goods. One way to alleviate this problem is to reduce the incentive to produce the bads (and to increase that of producing the goods) by severing the connection (established by market prices) between output and reward. Instead agents can be rewarded based on their behavior, i.e. for obeying the directives of a central party, the boss.

This relationship by which agents agree to do as told in exchange for a salary that is at least partly independent of market-measured output is called the employment contract, and the agent is called an employee. Through employment contracts the boss can then direct the behavior of the agent so as to produce less bads (or more goods).[8] Naturally the former transactors, now employees, will only let the boss direct their behavior if their reward becomes independent of the specific transaction. Employees are no longer motivated to cheat because their reward is now independent of their output measured at market prices, but this decoupling of output and reward has the unavoidable but unfortunate consequence of lowering their incentives to work, and of encouraging them to 'shirk'.[9] A self-employed individual who slacks pays the full cost of this behavior in terms of reduced income. An employee, who is rewarded for obeying managerial directives, may not, as long as his behavior is not perfectly observable. If work demands more effort than leisure, then, just like market transactors will take advantage of the high cost of measuring output to cheat, employees will take advantage of the high cost of monitoring behavior to shirk. The extent of shirking will depend on the cost of imposing internal or external behavior constraints. That cost is likely to vary across activities, across time periods, and across firms. Controlling shirking through observation or bureaucratic rules is easy when behavior

---

[8] Note that this explanation of why firms can be more efficient than markets differs from that of Buckley and Casson (1976) and Rugman (1981) who argue that firms set up more efficient 'internal markets'. For a criticism of this argument see Hennart (1986).

[9] A firm would like to enlist the energy and initiative of its employees, but the fact that employees are not rewarded in direct proportion of their output can lead them sometimes to live by the letter, but not by the spirit, of their employment contract. This is what is meant by shirking.

is a good guide to performance, for example in machine-paced processes, but not when employees are spread out over space or when tasks involve quick responses to unforeseen events. Then asking supervisors for directions, or applying standard operating procedures, will incur high costs. In such cases, internalized behavior control, such as a strong company culture, may make sense, but we would expect it to be very costly in firms with multicultural workforces, i.e. in MNEs.

The analysis up to now has focused on enforcement costs. Firms also differ from markets in the way they handle information. In firms agents rely on prices to know what to do. Prices give them much of the information they need to carry on their business. The system will break down if prices fail to provide accurate signals to coordinate the behavior of agents. It then pays for a central party, the boss, to replace the decentralized price system by a centralized system of managerial directives. Each agent will now collect a limited amount of information, transfer it to the boss, who will synthesize it and send back directives to agents for execution. Because prices can no longer be trusted, employees must be told what to do. But the reward of employees is independent of their market-measured output, so they will have less incentive than self-employed individuals to collect and pass on information necessary to carry out business. The ability of management to know what employees must do is a clear limit to the efficiency of hierarchy (Hennart 1993*b*).

The above contrast between prices and hierarchy has been seen by some (e.g. Perrow 1986) as overdrawn because most real-world institutions use simultaneously both methods of organization. The solution to this apparent problem lies in the distinction between methods of organization (prices and hierarchy) and institutions (markets and firms). Markets and firms make use of both methods of organization, but in various proportions, with firms relying mostly on hierarchy, and markets on prices (Hennart 1993*a*).

Why would institutions use simultaneously both methods of organization? Just like increased application of fertilizers leads to diminishing returns, increased investments in setting up ever more sophisticated behavior or output constraints will have the same consequences. At some point the imposition of additional behavior constraints (over-monitoring and micro-managing) will result in less and less shirking reduction, and may even at some point increase it, a point persuasively made by Ghoshal and Moran (1996) (even though they see it as a major criticism of transaction cost theory, which it is not). Hence whenever it is important to elicit initiative and effort from employees, the firm may selectively introduce output constraints, such as bonuses, piecework, or stock options. Inversely, diminishing returns to the measurement of outputs may lead market traders to seek to add behavior to the usual market output constraints. This results in what we call 'contracts'.

Contracts add a superstructure of behavior constraints on what are basically output constraints. Consider franchising. Franchisers get to keep the bulk of what they make (their main constraint is output-based), but the difficulty of pricing the impact of their behavior on the goodwill capital of the franchise chain has led franchisors to impose a set of behavioral constraints on them. For example, franchisees of Domino's Pizza are rated on their obedience to eighty-six rules—such as whether employees meet grooming standards—which are enforced by surprise visits (Dussauge 1998). Diminishing returns to the increased use of either method of organization means that in practice we will observe firms and markets using a mix of both output and behavior constraints. This simultaneous use of price and hierarchy fits comfortably within a transaction cost model, and does not call for a special theory of 'hybrids' or 'alliances' (Hennart 1993a).[10]

## 5.2.2 Application of transaction cost theory to the multinational firm

The preceding paragraphs have argued that MNEs arise to organize through employment contracts interdependencies between agents located in different countries. These interdependencies give rise to two types of externalities: competition in the market for final products generates pecuniary externalities which can potentially be internalized by mergers, cartels, or collusion. Natural market imperfections generate non-pecuniary externalities which can potentially be internalized by spot markets, contracts, or MNEs. It is on these non-pecuniary externalities that the rest of this section will focus.

An MNE will expand abroad (will organize interdependencies through hierarchy, i.e. through employment contracts) when it can organize interdependencies between agents located in different countries more efficiently than markets. This implies that three conditions must be met: (1) interdependent agents must be located in different countries (otherwise we would have a domestic firm), (2) the MNE must be the most efficient way to organize these interdependencies (otherwise we would have international markets transactions), and (3) given condition (2) the costs incurred by MNEs to organize these interdependencies are lower than the benefits of doing so.[11]

---

[10] Naturally, there is a limit to the use of behavior constraints in markets since the more numerous the constraints, the lower the incentives to exert effort. Likewise output constraints in firms re-introduce incentives to cheat (see Hennart 1993a).

[11] This is an important, but neglected, condition (Hennart 1982). At a given level of technology, some interdependencies are just too expensive to organize, whether by firms or by markets.

When are these conditions likely to be met? The transaction cost literature of the MNE has identified the characteristics of interdependencies that make their organization within markets more costly than within MNEs. Interdependencies involving some types of know-how, some types of raw materials and components, some types of marketing and distribution services, and in some cases, financial capital, fit this category. Let us review them in turn.

### 5.2.2.1 *Know-how*

Most applications of transaction cost/internalization theory to the MNE have focused on international interdependencies involving know-how (Buckley and Casson 1976; Magee 1977, Rugman 1981; Teece 1981, Cantwell 1989). Know-how developed in one country is often potentially useful in others, and can be transferred at low marginal cost. Markets for know-how suffer, however, from the fundamental problem of information asymmetry. For markets to function well, buyers and seller must have perfect knowledge of what is being sold. As Arrow (1962) first argued, the buyer of know-how does not generally know its exact characteristics, and the seller cannot provide the buyer with that information, since by doing this he would be transferring his know-how to the buyer free of charge. One way to go around this problem is to set up a patent system. By giving to the seller of know-how a monopoly in its use, and by providing mechanisms for enforcement, the patent system makes it possible for him to disclose his know-how to potential buyers without losing property rights to it. However, patent systems have clear limitations that are due to the difficulty of writing tacit knowledge into patents and to the imperfect enforcement of patent rights (Hennart 1982; Levin *et al.* 1987). There are considerable differences between products and between countries in the degree of protection patents provide. When patents are well protected, knowledge interdependencies will be organized by licensing contracts (Davies 1977; Caves, Crookell, and Killing 1983; Contractor 1984; Davidson and McFetridge 1985). In the opposite case, the lack of protection will incite firms not to disclose information about their know-how. This will cause potential buyers to underbid, and no knowledge transfer will take place—a dynamic similar to Ackerlof's (1970) market for lemons.

Transfer within a firm can then be more efficient, because both the sender and the receiver of the know-how are now rewarded for effective transfer, and not for cheating each other as in a market setting. Buyers and sellers of knowledge will therefore form an MNE and put their behavior under the control of a central party charged with maximizing their joint income (Hennart 1982).[12]

---

[12] This means that the way a firm is organized does affect its relative efficiency compared to the market. Putting the internal transferor and transferee of know-how into separate profit

Note that this analysis is not in terms of exploiting advantages. It is not know-how advantages that are being internalized by MNEs, but *markets for know-how*. The initiative to establish an MNE to organize know-how inter-dependencies may come from a firm seeking to acquire knowledge or from one seeking to exploit it. Thinking of the MNE as internalizing markets is therefore more general than thinking of it as internalizing advantages, since no separate theory of 'asset seeking FDI' is then necessary.[13]

### 5.2.2.2 *Reputation*

Just like knowledge, reputation developed in country A can sometimes be profitably exploited in country B. The simplest case is to cater to country A investors or tourists permanently or temporarily present in country B. Such sharing of reputation can be organized through franchising contracts or within an MNE. Franchising contracts typically stipulate that agents pay a royalty on sales for the use of the franchisor's trademark (and ancillary business know-how) and agree to subject themselves to the franchisor's behavior constraints.

Free-riding is the main problem with franchising. Franchisees can max-imize their income by reducing the quality of the goods they sell that bear the franchisor's trademark. As long as free-riding is costly to detect and to punish and most customers are non-repeat, only a small part of the damage thus inflicted on the goodwill capital of the franchise chain will be borne by the free-rider. If the quality of the franchisee's output can be easily described and enforced by contract, then franchising will be used. If it is difficult to con-tractually define quality, then a better way to curb free-riding is to transform the franchisee into an employee. Paid a fixed amount unrelated to sales, the erstwhile franchisee, now an employee, has no longer incentives to reduce quality. But because he is no longer rewarded for his output, he is also incited to shirk, and this will have to be controlled by behavior constraints.[14] Every-thing else constant, international goodwill interdependencies will be organ-ized through international franchising contracts if (1) it is relatively easy to write contracts which specify a certain level of quality and whose violation is

centers and granting bonuses to their bosses based on the unit's profits may recreate in firms a level of opportunism similar to that found in markets.

[13] This is in contrast to Dunning's OLI theory (Dunning 1977, 1981, 1993, 1997) that argues that a firm becomes an MNE if it has 'ownership advantages'. This makes it difficult to explain cases like Daewoo's acquisition of a British car design firm. Daewoo did not invest in the UK because it had advantages, but because it wanted to acquire 'advantages'.

[14] As evidence that franchised units are more efficiently run than company-owned ones, or, in other words, that shirking does take place in firms, consider the following: in February 1996 McDonald's reported that the ratio of cash flow to sales for its domestic units was 13.7 per cent for franchised units and 10.4 per cent for company-owned ones (Gibson 1996).

easy to detect and prove to third parties and (2) it would be relatively costly to control shirking by employees. When the reverse is the case, goodwill interdependencies will be organized within the MNE (through employee-staffed overseas units). Fast food, hotels, employment agencies, and car rentals belong to the first category, and banking, advertising, management consulting, and high level legal advice to the second (Hennart 1982).[15]

Note that international interdependencies in know-how and reputation go a long way to explain MNEs in services. No special theory of service MNEs is therefore necessary.

### 5.2.2.3 *Raw materials and components*

Interdependencies involving raw materials and components arise when different stages of the value chain are optimally handled by different agents located in different countries. This occurs when, for example, the optimal location of component manufacture differs from that of assembly; or when raw materials are located in a different country than processing plants. Many of the interdependencies involving raw materials and components are handled by international spot markets or by long term procurement contracts. In some cases, however, organization of these interdependencies within MNEs is more efficient.

Well functioning markets require a large number of buyers and sellers. Sometimes that number is limited and we have 'small numbers conditions'. Small number conditions result from economies of scale, high transportation costs, government barriers, and asset specificity. This later condition obtains when one of the parties to the transaction makes investment the value of which is conditional on the continuation of the relationship. Asset specificity makes spot trades risky, because the party making transaction-specific investments runs the risk of having the other party opportunistically renegotiating the terms of trade after he has made the investments—the so-called 'holdup problem' (Williamson 1985). One way for parties with transaction-specific investments to protect themselves is to write a long-term contract that specifies *ex ante* the terms and conditions of the exchange and the penalties to be paid in case of breach. But even long-term contracts do not protect the parties in conditions of high uncertainty, because specifying in advance all potential contingencies becomes then impossible.[16] When transaction-specific investments are large (and the useful life of the equipment is long),

---

[15] For some empirical evidence, see Caves and Murphy (1976) and Brickly and Dark (1987). Franchisors can also be expected to free-ride. They may collect money up-front by selling the right to franchise large territories, and then leave the business. To reassure franchisees that they will not act that way, most franchisors own some outlets.

[16] What matters here is 'non-indexable' uncertainty. The vagaries of the price of oil do not cause problems for contracts as long as oil is traded on commodity exchanges. On the other

contracts must have such duration that the risk of unforeseen events becomes very large. They then provide only limited protection (Stuckey 1983; Franz, Sternberg, and Strongman 1986).

Here as elsewhere, the alternative to contracts is to have buyers and sellers become employees of the same firm. Employees are now paid to facilitate transfers, and no longer benefit from holding up their partners.

The preceding considerations explain why we find MNEs internalizing trade in some raw materials and components. They explain, *inter alia*, why aluminum companies have vertically integrated into bauxite, but tin smelting firms have not integrated into alluvial tin mining (Hennart 1988) and why car assemblers own engine plants but subcontract many other car components. The case of raw materials and components show clearly the advantages of reasoning in terms of *internalization of markets* rather than *exploitation of advantages*, since the expansion of MNEs in this case proceeds generally in the absence of advantages. For example, US steel companies which have vertically integrated into iron ore mining use specialist companies to run their captive iron ore mining operations, because they do not have much experience (and hence probably zero advantages) in this business.

### 5.2.2.4 *Distribution and marketing*

Selling a product in a foreign market generally requires physical (warehouses, inventories, repair facilities, transportation equipment) as well as intellectual investments (salespeople must be trained to demonstrate and repair the product). These investments can be small and 'general purpose' or large and specific to a particular manufacturer. As in the case of raw materials and components, the market for distribution services will be inefficient (and will thus be internalized by firms) if it is narrow. This may be due to small number conditions *ex ante* or *ex post*. *Ex ante* small number conditions are due to the economies of scale that often characterize distribution. *Ex post* small number conditions arise because the effective sale of a particular product may require that the distributor make manufacturer-specific investments. *Ex ante* small number conditions encourage bargaining, which can be reduced by including both parties within a MNE. *Ex post* small number conditions expose the party who is making manufacturer-specific investments to holdup (Williamson 1985). As a result, distributors may be reluctant to make these investments, fearing that, once such investments are made, they could be held up by manufacturers. As in the case of raw materials, contracts (here distribution contracts) can protect distributors, but only when investments are relatively modest and the environment is predictable. When the physical or intellectual

hand, the end of the Bretton Woods system of fixed exchange rate parities created serious problems for the contracts between Japanese buyers and Australian sellers of bauxite.

investments necessary to effectively sell a product are large and manufacturer-specific, and the environment is hard to predict, the integration of manufacturing and distribution within an MNE will often be the best solution (Anderson and Coughlan 1987; Klein, Frazier, and Roth 1990).

The difficulty of separating the performance of manufacturers from that of distributors is another reason for integrating manufacturing and distribution within a firm. Most products are sold with accompanying services in a product-cum-service bundle—for example household appliances are installed and serviced by the retailers that sell them, while machine tool dealers provide operator training and service contracts. Consumers find it sometimes difficult to separate the respective contributions of manufacturers and retailers to that bundle. For example, it is often difficult for a car owner to know whether problems with her car are due to a defective product or inept servicing. This makes it possible for one party to free ride on the other(s), and hence difficult for manufacturer and distributor to jointly provide the optimal level of service (Chen and Hennart 1999). At low levels of interdependence, manufacturers will impose behavioral constraints on service providers (for example, they will demand that they follow training sessions) or retailers on manufacturers (they may ask them to follow particular manufacturing procedures and use approved raw materials). Imposing behavioral constraints through franchised distribution or contract manufacturing requires that quality standards be contractually defined and enforced. When this is not the case, manufacturers and distributors will find it efficient to be joined within a MNE (manufacturers will vertically integrate into foreign distribution or distributors will vertically integrate into foreign manufacturing). Business history provides considerable evidence of manufacturers integrating into foreign distribution for products the quality of which could be affected by improper handling and service (Wilkins 1970; Nicholas 1983). The case of Singer is well documented. That firm found it initially necessary to integrate vertically into domestic and foreign retailing because independent agents were unwilling to learn to demonstrate its sewing machines, and did not want to risk carrying stocks and financing the sale of what was then a new and costly product (Hennart 1982, 87).

Inversely, distributors have backward integrated into foreign production (rather than bought products at arm's length or through purchase contracts) when the quality of the products they were buying was difficult to assess *ex ante*. The most famous case is that of bananas. The quality of bananas is affected by rough handling at the cutting and shipping stages, but this only shows up when bananas reach the customer. Hence it is difficult to assure quality if grower, shipper, and distributor are separate concerns because it is difficult to ascertain who is to blame for poor quality. This explains why US banana distributors have integrated into banana plantations (Read 1986; Litvak and Maule 1977; Wilkins 1970).

### 5.2.2.5 *Financial capital*

Consistent with the view of trade theorists, financial capital that is raised in one country can often be profitably invested in another. But temporarily granting property rights to money (lending money) is fraught with special risks. Besides the problem of the two parts of the transaction not being simultaneous (money is lent today to be repaid in the future), there is that of fungibility. A person who rents an apartment gets the apartment back (more or less) at the expiration of the lease. Money lent to an entrepreneur may be spent in ways that leave zero collateral and therefore prevent the lender from getting back his principal. This can happen because the borrower is (in various proportions) unlucky, incompetent, or dishonest. As a protection, lenders typically impose behavior constraints on borrowers (i.e. money is generally lent by contracts that constrain the behavior of lenders—for example first mortgages only authorize disbursement to the house seller and require the borrower to post some collateral and to take insurance on the property, etc.). In spite of this, the transaction costs of lending are high.

Given bounded rationality and opportunism, lenders cannot easily distinguish lucky, smart, and honest borrowers from unlucky, stupid, and dishonest ones. They therefore use three second-best strategies: (1) they lend to borrowers and projects with which they are familiar, (2) they control how their funds are used, and/or (3) they ask for collateral. Those three strategies will tend to prevent many good projects from being funded, especially if borrowers and lenders reside in different countries and are thus not personally acquainted. Strategy 2 only works if the lender knows the borrower's business. Strategy 3 means that projects with poor collateral will not get funded.

One solution to the problems experienced by international markets for financial capital is to join lenders and borrowers within a firm.[17] This means that entrepreneurs with projects will use their own funds or find other individuals willing to become co-owners of the project (they will form 'syndicates' or float the company on stock exchanges). Inversely, potential lenders, uncomfortable about lending to unknown entrepreneurs or for unknown projects, will become owners or co-owners of the projects that use their money. Being equity owners has then three main advantages: (1) it provides them with more control than loan contracts, as they have much greater access to internal information and can affect decisions *ex ante* rather than *ex post*; (2) they now have greater flexibility than lenders when problems

---

[17]   Casson (1998) argues that capital markets cannot be internalized because capital is a factor of production, and 'according to internalization theory, it is intermediate product markets that are internalized, and not factor markets. Factor markets link households with firms, and cannot normally be internalized.' Technology, however, is also a factor of production, and the internalization of markets for technology is at the center of internalization theory. The only factor of production that normally cannot be internalized is labor, because it cannot be owned (although there are exceptions, as in slavery and in certain sport businesses).

occur (Williamson 1988); (3) lastly, the former borrower-entrepreneurs are now employees, and, since they are no longer exclusively rewarded by the profits they generate with the borrowed funds, they do not have the same incentives to take excessive risk (but this has also the unintended consequence of decreasing their incentives to exert effort) (Jensen and Meckling 1976).

In other words, when domestic and international markets for loanable funds are characterized by high transaction costs (because of information asymmetry between lenders and borrowers and the lack of collateral), the solution will be for lenders and borrowers to be joined within a firm, i.e. for lenders to become co-owners of the venture, or for borrowers to raise their own funds (Hennart 1994, 1998). Then MNEs, rather than bank loans or bonds, will be used to transfer financial capital across countries.

The preceding argument implies that long-term lending (through bank loans or corporate bonds) should play a more important role domestically than internationally and should be directed to firms with good collateral. Inversely, the financing of projects with poor collateral that rely on foreign sources of finance should be disproportionately undertaken by MNEs (or by their predecessor, the so-called 'Free Standing Firm').[18]

I believe that what we know of the mechanisms used for the international transfer of long-term financial capital is roughly consistent with this prediction. Historically, MNEs and free standing firms have played an important role in the international transfer of private flows of long-term financial capital to fund projects in sectors poorly understood by lenders and/or offering limited collateral, for example in mining and in research intensive activities (Mikesell and Whitney 1987; Hennart 1994, 1998). In contrast, banks have limited their international lending to short-term loans on receivables. In the nineteenth century, long-term international lending was through bonds issued by governments (which have taxing powers, and hence good collateral) or by firms with strong collateral assets (mortgage companies and railways, which owned land) (Wilkins 1989; Hennart 1994). When banks have deviated from this and lent long term to foreign firms with poor collateral, as they did in the 1960s and 70s, the results have been disastrous.

# 5.3 CONCLUSIONS

The transaction cost theory of the MNE argues that they arise to organize interdependencies between agents located in different countries. This will

---

[18] For more on Free Standing Firms see Wilkins and Schroeter (1998).

occur (1) when organizing these interdependencies within the firm is more efficient than organizing them through the market and (2) when the benefits of organizing interdependencies within the firm are higher than their costs.

The theory is therefore based on a comparison of the cost of organizing interdependencies in firms and in markets. Just looking at the costs of running markets is not enough. Market failure is not a sufficient reason why MNEs exist, since it is quite possible that the costs that both MNEs and markets experience in organizing an interdependency are higher than the gains. A theory of the MNE must also be a theory of why firms can be efficient. I have argued that the reason why firms can, in some cases, be more efficient than markets is that they replace output by behavior constraints. But we have seen that this reliance on behavior constraints leads also to biases, and these biases go a long way in explaining control processes in MNEs. For example, the difficulty of observing behavior across distance and of setting up rules specifying the behavior of foreign subsidiary managers (because headquarters has insufficient knowledge of foreign environments) means that the mix of constraints imposed on foreign subsidiaries is likely to have, *ceteris paribus*, more output and less behavior constraints than that imposed on managers of domestic affiliates. Hence the often noted phenomenon of 'quasi-independent' subsidiaries (Hennart 1993*b*).

Any factor that increases the efficiency of international markets, such as, *inter alia*, improvements in the definition and enforcement of property rights, should, *ceteris paribus*, increase the scope of international markets and decrease that of MNEs. Inversely, improvements in business technology that reduce the costs of running firms tend to increase the efficiency of MNEs, and the role they play in the international economy. Interdependencies that used to be managed by markets will now be managed by MNEs. It will now pay for firms to organize some interdependencies that were previously too costly to organize by either firms of markets. This may explain, for example, why American technological and managerial innovations led to the development of US-based MNEs in the 1960s, while British technological innovations in the first half of the nineteenth century did not lead to a similar expansion of UK-based MNEs (Hennart 1982). While such broad-based analysis may be over-ambitious, the same model can (and has been) applied in smaller settings, for example to changes through time in the extent of international vertical backward integration for a particular product.[19] But a lot remains to be done in this area.

The theory can also account for the simultaneous use of output and behavior constraints in firms and in markets. We can, for example, explain the benefits and the limits of using output constraints in firms. Inversely, we

---

[19] See for example Stuckey's (1983) study of changes in the extent of international vertical integration between alumina refining and aluminum smelting.

can account for the introduction of behavior constraints in transactions where output constraints predominate. The resulting institutions are contracts, and we can model their benefits and costs. The model is useful in explaining the strengths and limitations of alliances.

Lastly, the model has been described in terms of interdependencies. The reason is that some authors have erroneously thought that the use of the word 'transaction' by transaction cost theorists meant that the model was limited to the analysis of existing transactions, and could not handle the creation of new capabilities. This mistaken view may have arisen from an earlier emphasis on exploitation of advantages. Almost by definition, a firm can only exploit advantages it already owns.

In reality, the process by which MNEs get established is always one of merging complementary capabilities. A firm located in country X has some assets which have potential value in country Y if successfully combined with some country Y factors. These factors can be available on the market, or embedded in some local firm. This is what I mean by 'interdependencies'. Agents located in two different countries have the potential, if they combine their capabilities through international markets or within MNEs, of creating rents. MNEs arise when they offer the most efficient way to realize these potentialities, when they are the most efficient method of combining local and foreign assets. The process of establishing MNEs (i.e. market entry) can thus be seen as one of creating new combinations. Transaction costs theory tries to explain the institutional forms they will take.

Thinking in terms of 'interdependencies' also underlines that when the complementary assets are embedded in firms A and B located in two different countries, the concept of who takes the initiative to combine the assets is irrelevant to the major question of why MNEs exist. MNEs exist because the combination of the assets is more efficiently done within an MNE than through spot markets or contracts, but the initiative can come from either A or B. A firm with a mineral deposit in a given country but no mining expertise can set up a joint venture with a mining firm in another country which has the expertise it lacks, it can sell its deposit to that firm, or it can acquire the mining firm to obtain the expertise. In all three cases, an MNE will result. A theory of why MNEs exist should be able to handle all three cases with the same model, as we can if we think in terms of interdependencies.

# References

ACKERLOF, G. (1970). 'The Market for "Lemons": Qualitative Uncertainty and the Market Mechanism', *Quarterly Journal of Economics*, 74: 448–500.

ANDERSON, E., and COUGHLAN, A. (1987). 'International Market Entry through Expansion via Independent or Integrated Channels of Distribution', *Journal of Marketing*, 51: 71–82.

ARROW, K. (1962). 'Economic Welfare and the Allocation of Resources for Invention', in K. Arrow (ed.), *The Rate and Direction of Inventive Activity*. Princeton: Princeton University Press, 609–25.

BRICKLY, J., and DARK, F. (1987). 'The Choice of Organizational Form: the Case of Franchising', *Journal of Financial Economics*, 18: 401–20.

BUCKLEY, P. (1983). 'New Theories of International Business', in Mark Casson (ed.), *The Growth of International Business*. London: George Allen & Unwin.

—— and CASSON, M. (1976). *The Future of Multinational Enterprise*. London: Macmillan.

CANTWELL, J. (1989). *Technological Innovations and Multinational Corporations*. Oxford: Basil Blackwell.

CASSON, M. (1985). 'Multinational Monopolies and International Cartels', in Buckley, P. J., and Casson, M. C. (eds.), *The Economic Theory of the Multinational Enterprise: Selected Papers*. London: Macmillan, 60–97.

—— (1998). 'An Economic Theory of the Free Standing Company', in Wilkins, M., and Schroeter, H., *The Free Standing Company in the World Economy*. New York: Oxford University Press.

CAVES, R. (1998). 'Research in International Business: Problems and Prospects', *Journal of International Business Studies*, 29: 5–19.

—— and MURPHY, W. (1976). 'Franchising: Firms, Markets, and Intangible Assets', *Southern Economic Journal*, 42: 572–86.

—— CROOKELL, H., and KILLING, P. (1982). 'The Imperfect Market for Technology Licenses', *Oxford Bulletin of Economics and Statistics*, 45: 249–67.

CHEN, S., and HENNART, J.-F. (1999). 'A Property Rights Theory of Private Branding', working paper, Center for Economic Research, Tilburg University.

CONTRACTOR, F. (1984). 'Choosing between Foreign Direct Investment and Licensing: Theoretical Considerations and Empirical Tests', *Journal of International Business Studies*, 15: 167–88.

DAVIDSON, WILLIAM H., and McFETRIDGE, D. (1984). 'International Technology Transactions and the Theory of the Firm', *Journal of Industrial Economics*, 32: 253–64.

DAVIES, H. (1977). 'Technological Transfer through Commercial Transactions', *Journal of Industrial Economics*, 26: 161–75.

DESS, G., GUPTA, A., HENNART, J.-F., and HILL, C. (1995). 'Conducting and Integrating Strategy Research at the International, Corporate, and Business Levels: Issues and Directions', *Journal of Management*, 21: 357–93.

DUNNING, J. (1977). 'Trade, Location of Economic Activity, and the Multinational Enterprise: A Search for an Eclectic Approach', in *The International Allocation of Economic Activity*, ed. B. Ohlin, P. O. Hesselborn, and P. M. Wijkman. New York: Holmes and Meier.

—— (1981). *International Production and the Multinational Enterprise*. London: George Allen & Unwin.

—— (1993). *Multinational Enterprises and the Global Economy*. New York: Addison-Wesley.

—— (1997). *Alliance Capitalism and Global Business*. London: Routledge.

—— and RUGMAN, A. (1985). 'The Influence of Hymer's Dissertation on the Theory of Foreign Direct Investment', *American Economic Review*, May: 228–32.

DUSSAUGE, P. (1998). *Domino's Pizza International Inc*. Wharley End: European Case Clearing House.

FLOWERS, E. (1976). 'Oligopolistic Reaction in European and Canadian Direct Investment to the US', *Journal of International Business Studies*, 7: 43–55.

FRANZ, J., STERNBERG, B., and STRONGMAN, J. (1986). *Iron Ore: Global Prospects for the Industry*. Washington, DC: World Bank.

GHOSHAL, S., and MORAN P. (1996). 'Bad for Practice: A critique of Transaction Cost Theory', *Academy of Management Review*, 21: 13–47.

GIBSON R. (1996). 'McDonald's, US-Franchisee Ventures are on the Rise', *Wall Street Journal*, June 26.

GRAHAM, E. (1978). 'Transatlantic Investment by Multinational Firms: A Rivalistic Phenomenon', *Journal of Post-Keynesian Economics*, 1: 82–99.

HENNART, J.-F. (1977). *A Theory of Foreign Direct Investment*. Ph.D dissertation, University of Maryland.

—— (1982). *A Theory of Multinational Enterprise*. Ann Arbor: University of Michigan Press.

—— (1985). 'Comment on Intra-Industry Direct Foreign Investment, Market Structure, Firm Rivalry, and Technological Performance, by Edward M. Graham', in *Multinationals as Mutual Invaders: Intraindustry Foreign Direct Investment*, ed. Asim Erdilek. Beckenham, England: Croom Helm, 88–93.

—— (1986). 'What is Internalization?', *Weltwirtschaftliches Archiv*, Winter: 791–804.

—— (1988*a*.) 'Vertical Integration in the Aluminum and Tin Industries', *Journal of Economic Behavior and Organization*, 9/3: 281–300.

—— (1993*a*). 'Explaining the Swollen Middle: Why Most Transactions are a Mix of Market and Hierarchy', *Organization Science*, 4/4: 529–47.

—— (1993*b*). 'Control in Multinational Firms: The Role of Price and Hierarchy', in Sumantra Ghoshal and Eleanor Westney (eds.), *Organization Theory and the Multinational Corporation*. New York: St Martin's Press.

—— (1994). 'International Capital Transfers: A Transaction Cost Framework', *Business History*, 36: 51–70.

—— (1998). 'Transaction Cost Theory and the Free-Standing Firm', in M. Wilkins and H. Schroeter (eds.), *The Free Standing Company in the World Economy*. London: Oxford University Press.

—— (2000). 'Transaction Costs Theory and the Multinational Enterprise', in C. Pitelis and R. Sugden (eds.), *The Nature of the Transnational Firm, 2nd edn*. London: Routledge.

—— and PARK, Y. R. (1994). 'Location, Governance and Strategic Determinants of Japanese Manufacturing Investment in the United States', *Strategic Management Journal*, 15: 419–36.

HENNART, J.-F. (*cont.*), and REDDY, S. (1997). 'The Choice between Mergers/Acquisitions and Joint Ventures: the Case of Japanese Investors in the United States', *Strategic Management Journal*, 18/1: 1–12.

HYMER, S. (1960). *The International Operations of National Firms*. Ph.D. dissertation, Massachusetts Institute of Technology.

—— (1968). 'La Grande Firme Multinationale', *Revue Economique*, 14: 949–73.

—— (1976). *The International Operations of National Firms*. Boston: MIT Press.

JENSEN, M., and MECKLING, W. (1976). 'Theory of the Firm: Managerial Behavior, Agency Costs, and Capital Structure', *Journal of Financial Economics*, 3: 305–60.

JOHANSON, J., and VAHLNE, J. E. (1977). 'The Internalization Process of the Firm', *Journal of International Business Studies*, 8/Spring/Summer: 23–32.

KINDLEBERGER, C. P. (1976), Preface to Hymer, S. (1976). *The International Operations of National Firms*. Boston: MIT Press.

KLEIN, S., FRAZIER, G., and ROTH, V. (1990). 'A Transaction Cost Analysis Model of Channel Integration in International Markets', *Journal of Marketing Research*, 23: 196–208.

LEVIN, R., KLEVORICK, A., NELSON, R., and WINTER, S. (1987). 'Appropriating the Returns from Industrial Research and Development', *Brookings Papers on Economic Activity*, 3: 783–820.

LEVY, H., and SARNAT, M. (1970). 'International Diversification and Investment Portfolios', *American Economic Review*, 60: 668–75.

LITVAK, I., and MAULE, C. (1977). 'Transnational Corporations and Vertical Integration: The Banana Case', *Journal of World Trade Law*, 11/6: 537–49.

MAGEE, S. (1977). 'Information and the Multinational Corporation: An Appropriability Theory of Direct Foreign Investment', in J. N. Bhagwhati (ed.), *The New International Economic Order*. Cambridge, Mass.: MIT Press.

MANTEL, I. (1975). 'Sources and Uses of Funds for a Sample of Majority-Owned Foreign Affiliates of US Companies, 1966–72', *Survey of Current Business*, 55: 29–52.

MARKOWITZ, H. (1959). *Portfolio Selection*. New York: Wiley.

McMANUS, J. (1972). 'The Theory of the Multinational Firm', in Gilles Paquet (ed.), *The Multinational Firm and the Nation State*. Don Mills, Ont.: Macmillan.

MIKESELL, R., and WHITNEY, J. (1987). *The World Mining Industry*. Boston: Allen & Unwin.

NICHOLAS, S. J. (1983). 'Agency Contracts, Institutional Modes, and the Transition to Foreign Direct Investment by British Manufacturing Multinationals before 1935', *Journal of Economic History*, 48: 675–86.

PERROW, C. (1986). *Complex Organizations: A Critical Essay (3rd edn)*. New York: Random House.

READ, R. (1986). 'The Banana Industry: Oligopoly and Barriers to Entry', in Mark Casson and associates, *Multinationals and World Trade*. London: Allen & Unwin.

RUGMAN, A. (1981). *Inside the Multinationals*. New York: Columbia University Press.

STUCKEY, J. (1983). *Vertical Integration and Joint Ventures in the Aluminum Industry*. Cambridge, Mass.: Harvard University Press.

TEECE, D. (1981). 'The Multinational Enterprise: Market Failure and Market Power Considerations', *Sloan Management Review*, Spring/22 (3): 3–17.

VERNON, R. (1977). *Storm Over the Multinationals.* Cambridge, Mass.: Harvard University Press.

WILKINS, M. (1970). *The Emergence of Multinational Enterprise: American Business Abroad from the Colonial Era to 1914.* Cambridge, Mass.: Harvard University Press.

—— and SCHROETER, H. (1998). *The Free Standing Company in the World Economy.* New York: Oxford University Press.

WILLIAMSON, O. (1975). *Markets and Hierarchies: Analysis and Antitrust Implications.* New York: Free Press.

—— (1985). *The Economic Institutions of Capitalism.* New York: Free Press.

—— (1988). 'Corporate Finance and Corporate Governance', *Journal of Finance,* 63/3: 567–98.

YU, C-M., and ITO, K. (1988). 'Oligopolistic Reaction and Foreign Direct Investment: the Case of the US Tire and Textile Industries', *Journal of International Business Studies,* 49: 449–60.

CHAPTER 6

························································

# LOCATION, COMPETITIVENESS, AND THE MULTINATIONAL ENTERPRISE

························································

## ALAN M. RUGMAN
## ALAIN VERBEKE

## 6.0 Introduction

························································

THIS chapter provides an overview of the key insights resulting from recent
international business research on the interactions between location advantages and the competitiveness of multinational enterprises (MNEs). It consists of four main sections. First, the evolution of the location advantage
concept in the international economics literature is discussed. Here, it appears
that the international economics literature has substantially broadened its
analytical scope in the last few decades. However, the field of international

business research had gone even further in its analysis of the interactions between location and MNE competitiveness because of its in-depth focus on the actual behaviour of MNEs. The complex nature of location advantages for MNEs is discussed in more detail in the chapter's second section. The third section describes the intellectual foundations of a spatial analysis of MNE activities. Finally, the chapter's fourth section discusses the relative contribution of home country specific advantages (CSAs) and host CSAs to MNE competitiveness: it concludes that host CSAs may become increasingly important to achieve global competitiveness.

# 6.1 A CRITICAL ASSESSMENT OF THE ECONOMIC THEORY OF COMPARATIVE ADVANTAGE

## 6.1.1 Traditional international economics

An analysis of the academic literature on location advantages first requires a classification and positioning of the different conceptual perspectives on this issue. Figure 6.1 provides a simple framework which allows us to classify these different conceptual perspectives on the basis of two key parameters. The first parameter is related to the unit of analysis. Here, the focus can be on location advantages at the level of a country, a single industry, or an individual firm. The second parameter makes a distinction between trade and foreign direct investment (FDI) as the outcome of specific location advantages. This distinction is critical because the location advantages instrumental to exports or imports may be very different from the location advantages conducive to outward or inward FDI. Here, it should be emphasized that FDI may itself influence trade flows: it may through local production substitute for trade or even create new intermediate or final goods trade flows.

Conventional international trade theory which attempts to explain trade patterns can be largely positioned in cell 1 of Figure 6.1. The standard Ricardian model, valid in a 2 country–2 product situation, concludes that comparative rather than absolute advantage of nations leads to trade and gains from trade. Even if the first country possesses a superior technology that would make it the more efficient producer of any good, it will, subject to a

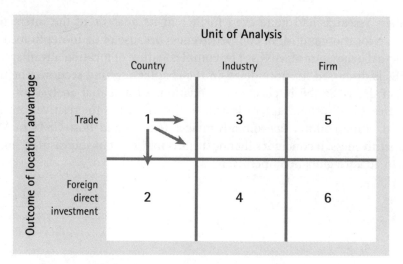

**Fig. 6.1 A classification of the international economics perspectives on location advantage**

number of conditions,[1] specialize in only that product for which it is comparatively most efficient in terms of labour productivity. This also implies that the second country, with an inferior technology, will still have an implicit location advantage in producing the second product.

The Heckscher-Ohlin model builds upon the availability of identical technologies in the two countries, but also the presence of two production factors (labour and capital) and concludes, again subject to several critical assumptions,[2] that each country will specialize in the product that, in relative terms, requires the most intensive use of its most abundant production factor. More specifically, the labour abundant and capital abundant country will export the labour intensive and capital intensive product respectively.

Follow-up work, building upon the Heckscher-Ohlin thinking has led to a relaxation of most assumptions of the original model, allowing analyses to be performed that recognize the presence of many goods and many production factors. The two key conclusions usually continue to hold, however; first, an abundance of a particular production factor in one country gives this country a location advantage for the manufacturing of products that make an intensive use of the abundant production factor. Second, an increase of a specific production factor will not lead to a homogeneous expansion of the country's

---

[1] These conditions include, *inter alia*, the presence of only two countries, two products, one scarce production factor (labour) but a different production technology (and therefore a different labour productivity) in each country, with constant returns to scale.

[2] These assumptions include, *inter alia*, identical production factor prices and identical homothetic tastes in the two countries.

output. It will shift production and trade toward products that make the most intensive use of the expanding factor, hence strengthening the country's apparent location advantage for that product.

The explanation of trade based upon the comparative, macro-level advantage of countries in terms of the availability of technology or production factor abundance has undoubtedly proven useful to explain trade patterns between countries at very different levels of economic development. Leamer and Levinsohn (1995) provide an overview of the empirical literature. However, it has also appeared less useful to explain trade patterns and therefore location advantages of countries with access to similar technologies and similar factor endowments.

## 6.1.2 New international economics

Most trade between developed countries is intra-industry trade (Grubel and Lloyd 1975), which means that at a high level of aggregation of products (e.g. electronics or automobiles), developed countries have similar macro-level location advantages. The key explanation of this phenomenon is product differentiation, combined with the presence of scale economies and therefore imperfect competition (Dixit and Stiglitz 1977; Greenaway and Milner 1986; Helpman and Krugman 1985; Krugman 1980).

The analysis of intra-industry trade has pushed international economics scholars to largely shift their focus from analysing the comparative advantage of nations merely at the macro-level toward the joint analysis of country level, industry level, and even firm level location advantages. The modern trade theory literature has thereby systematically shifted from merely covering cell 1 in Figure 6.1, to also including cells 3 and 5. One key study in this context is Cox and Harris' (1985) study on the likely impact of free trade between Canada and the United States. The study not only concludes that both countries may actually benefit from gains of trade at the macro-level but also that the higher potential to obtain scale economies and lower prices will lead to an exit of small, inefficient producers. Although freer trade with the United States will lead to a stronger location advantage for Canadian exporters at the macro and industry level, it simultaneously implies the elimination of the main location advantages, i.e. trade barrier protection, benefiting small, but previously economically viable firms. Similar conclusions arise from the Smith and Venables' (1988) study on the likely impact of a single EU market (the 'Europe 1992' programme) on trade patterns.

Modern international economics has also developed substreams of thinking that give the multinational firm (MNE) a critical place in the analysis

(Batra and Ramachandran 1980; Cantwell 1994; Ethier 1986; Helpman and Krugman 1985; and Markusen 1984). Here, the various activities performed by the MNE are spatially dispersed, with R&D and other upstream activities typically performed in home countries, depending upon these home countries' comparative advantages.

Some work has also investigated the dynamic effects of institutional changes such as trade liberalization on location advantages. *Ceteris paribus*, trade liberalization affects location in two ways. First, domestic firms with an interest in serving the more accessible foreign markets will be attracted by locations with a better 'exposure' to serving the foreign markets, e.g. through lower transport costs, better geographic proximity, the potential to capitalize on agglomeration economies, etc. Hanson (1998) studied the effects of North American economic integration on industry location and found a significant impact of transport costs and inter-industry agglomeration economies. Second, foreign firms may enter the market through FDI and contribute to industry specialization in the goods and services for which comparative advantages exist, to serve both the local and international markets.

Hence, increasingly the international economic analysis of location advantages has spread its area of inquiry to fill the six cells of Figure 6.1., as evidenced by the content of articles published in mainstream economics journals such as the *American Economic Review* and the *Journal of International Economics*. Caves (1996) provides a useful, albeit selective, overview of the recent international economics literature contributions to the linkages between location advantages and MNE behaviour.

An interesting feature of much recent research on location advantages in the international economics literature, is the increasing attention devoted to 'created' location advantages, such as R&D, as opposed to the conventional factor endowments location advantages such as labour pools or the availability of capital. For example, investments in R&D allow countries to specialize in high technology sectors and to have high growth rates (Grossman and Helpman 1991). These investments may constitute a major location advantage, depending upon international technology diffusion rates and the extent to which an advantage can be maintained over time.

The international economics literature on comparative advantage has thus evolved from a very narrow discipline largely positioned in cell 1, to a much broader research area that now spans the six cells of Figure 6.1 with perhaps cells four and six as the most promising ones for future research, given that R&D investments and the 'intentional' upgrading of location advantages largely occur at the industry or firm level (Rugman and Verbeke 1990).

## 6.1.3 The upgrading of location advantages

Dunning's (1977, 1988, 1992, 1999, 2000) eclectic paradigm as well as the modern internalization perspective on the functioning of MNEs (Rugman 1981, 1996; Rugman and Verbeke 1992, 1998) start from the premise that location advantages may be very different for each firm.

In this context, it is also important to emphasize that firm level knowledge creation appears very much embedded in localized innovation systems. As a result, much of the trade resulting from MNE activity is driven by differences in these innovation systems (Dosi, Pavitt, and Soete 1990). MNEs may also further strengthen the location advantages of the countries in which they operate through reciprocal spill-over effects with the local networks they associate themselves with, both through cooperation and competition (see Rugman and D'Cruz 2000; and Dunning 2000).

Thus, it is not clear whether either investment incentives favouring FDI or TRIMS (trade related investment measures) discriminating against foreign MNEs such as local content requirements, export performance requirements, and trade balancing measures can ultimately contribute much to long-run location advantages of a particular country. The assessment of costs and benefits of such measures appears in any case very difficult (Guisinger *et al.* 1985). TRIMS in particular do not appear very effective. When inhibited to achieve an 'organic symbiosis' with local innovation systems and to contribute as a 'workhorse' in such systems, MNEs are then forced to adopt a 'Trojan horse' policy. For example, local content conflicts in Europe have prompted Japanese motor vehicle companies to bring with them their Japanese component suppliers (Ozawa 1991; Saucier 1991).

Foreign MNEs can contribute to further develop and exploit the most promising knowledge bundles in a localized innovation system. The value added of a localized innovation system to the MNE is twofold. First, it allows the firm to tap into a complementary knowledge base that would otherwise remain out of reach. Second, it provides flexibility and options to the MNE, as it allows the firm to 'hedge its bets' in the innovation area.

Increasingly, however, and this precisely reflects the importance of localized knowledge creation, it also appears that even the six cells of Figure 6.1 do not allow us to adequately position all of the relevant recent international business literature on location advantages. As regards the horizontal axis of Figure 6.1, a substantial body of literature on location advantages and competitiveness now suggests the importance of additional units of analysis. The country level analysis can be extended to include on the one hand regional trade and investment blocks as in the Triad Power concept (Ohmae 1985; Rugman 2000) and on the other hand subnational, regional 'clusters' (Porter 1990, 1998). In the former case, the concept of region largely results from political decision making (albeit reflecting efforts to increase economic integration);

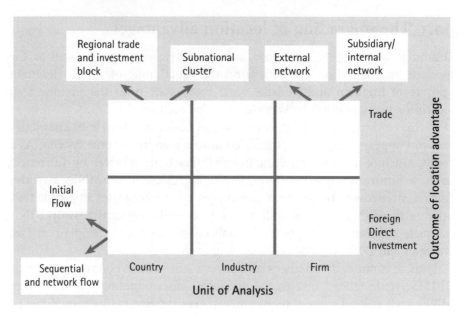

**Fig. 6.2 New perspectives on location advantages**

in the latter case, a variety of socio-economic, demographic, cultural, etc. characteristics of a geographically defined area determine the region's boundaries.

In addition, the firm-level analysis can be extended to include two points. First, is the study of location advantages of subsidiaries, whereby optimization needs to occur benefiting the MNE's entire internal network (Rugman and Verbeke 2001). Second, much recent work has been done on location advantages of firms within the context of their external networks (e.g. forward and backward linkages). In these cases, the distinction between the firm level and industry level analysis of location advantages has become increasingly blurred (Rugman and D'Cruz, 2000).

With respect to the vertical axis of Figure 6.1, the 'trade focus' on goods and services and the 'investment focus' on initial capital flows (although belatedly recognizing the importance of intangible know-how flows associated with the capital flows), have largely neglected the ongoing, sequential, and internal 'network' flows of know-how, whereby the direction and complexity of flows may substantially change over time (Birkinshaw 2000; Cantwell and Piscitello 1999). In other words the 'optimal location' for know-how development and the optimal diffusion patterns of this know-how may change over time, within the context of effectively functioning international business networks, irrespective of initial FDI flows (Rugman and Verbeke 2001). The above modifications to the analysis are represented in Figure 6.2.

# 6.2 THE ROLE OF LOCATION ADVANTAGES FOR MULTINATIONAL ENTERPRISES

## 6.2.1 Location advantages and international business theory

Hymer (1960, published 1976) was the first author to focus on foreign direct investment as a tool used by MNEs to transfer and exploit abroad proprietary resources. Interestingly, his view was that they would face location disadvantages *vis-à-vis* indigenous firms in host countries such as language and cultural barriers, lack of knowledge on the local socio-economic and business system, expropriation risks, etc. which have been synthesized under the heading of 'liability of foreignness'. This implies that MNEs producing in host countries would not benefit to the same extent as indigenous firms from either localized network spillover effects or synergies from the combination of firm level and host country location advantages.

Vernon's (1966) well known product cycle focused on the symbiosis between home country location advantages in technological innovation and the resulting proprietary assets at the MNE level. From a dynamic perspective, MNEs were then observed to be capable of linking their firm specific advantages (FSAs) with specific location advantages of host countries (in terms of demand patterns, supply capabilities, and labour costs) as the maturing or standardization of products occurred (Rugman 1999). This dynamic approach, aimed at explaining market seeking FDI, neglected two key aspects of the linkages between MNEs and location advantages. First, the fact that MNEs may use foreign markets to reduce risks, although this was taken into account in a later publication (Vernon 1983). Second, the contribution of host country location advantages to the MNE's rejuvenation or extension of its knowledge base. Yet, Vernon's dynamic approach went far beyond conventional models that attempted to explain FDI flows as an almost mechanistic reaction to exogenous macro-level location advantages such as favourable exchange rates or relative labour costs (Aliber 1970; Cushman 1985; Culem 1988).

At the beginning of the twenty-first century, Dunning's eclectic paradigm has become the leading conceptual framework for the analysis of international expansion patterns of business firms. This paradigm builds upon the interactions among ownership specific variables, internalization incentive advantages, and location-specific variables. A first important contribution of this framework within the context of this chapter is that the location-specific characteristics which contribute to competitive advantage are recognized to vary for different countries, sectors, and firms (Dunning 1992, Table 4.3, 84). The eclectic paradigm thereby allows us to span the three units of analysis of Figure 6.1. It is interesting to observe that, at the firm level, the location advantages appear to include several 'soft' elements such as the firm's experience with foreign involvement, psychic distance variables, attitudes to risk diversification, attitudes towards the centralization of functions such as R&D etc.

A second contribution is that it allows identification of the key location advantages of four different types of international production: natural resource seeking, market seeking, efficiency seeking, strategic asset seeking (Dunning 1998). One of the eclectic model's great strengths is that it highlights the complexity of determining the practical implications for managers and public policy makers of specific location advantages.

## 6.2.2 Four types of FDI

First, *natural resource seeking FDI* occurs when firms identify specific host country locations as an attractive source of natural resources at the lowest real cost. However, even in this case, additional location advantages such as good transport infrastructure, an effective institutional and legal framework, etc. have been identified as critical. In this case, FDI is usually associated with the exports of resource based products from the host country. However, this may in turn improve the location advantages of the home country both for the production and exports of goods which use the imported resources as a low cost or high quality input. As intra-firm trade replaces inter-firm trade, an unfavourable taxation regime in a specific country—whether the home or host nation—can even be overcome as a location disadvantage by shifting profit, but not the production itself from the nation with the unfavourable regime. FDI should therefore not be viewed solely as an outcome of existing location advantages but it may be instrumental to the creation of new location advantages.

Although the identification of location advantages clearly becomes much more complex when international production is involved, the predicted direction of the trade flows associated with natural, resource seeking FDI is largely consistent with conventional trade theory. The home country will export capital intensive products with a high knowledge content. The host country will primarily export resource based or labour intensive products with a low technology content.

Second, *market seeking FDI* is more difficult to reconcile with conventional trade theory because it usually has an immediate import substitution effect (except if trade barriers made imports impossible in the first place), but often also leads to trade creation (Lipsey and Weiss 1984; Rugman 1990). This occurs, for example, when the newly established subsidiary uses intermediate outputs from the home country in its own production process, when it becomes a leveraging platform for additional exports in other product areas for the home country and finally, when its production is not used only to serve a host country market but also third country markets.

Here, a first complexity is that location advantages of specific countries may shift over time as exemplified by the international product cycle (Vernon 1966). A net exporter of innovative products may switch to market seeking FDI and may later become a net importer of the same, but now standardized, product. A second complexity is that substantial intra-industry FDI can now be observed, reflecting the differential FSAs of rivals in an industry but also the similar location advantages of countries, as both the source nation and recipient of FDI. A third complexity is that, even within a single MNE, complex intra-firm flows of knowledge and goods can often be observed, reflecting sophisticated bundles of location advantages and firm specific advantages, and resulting in complex network linkages among the various affiliates (Rugman and Verbeke 2000).

Dunning (1973) in an early survey of the field studies on FDI, already identified thirty location advantages viewed as determinants of especially market seeking FDI including host country market characteristics, trade barriers, cost factors, investment climate components, etc. Here, an interesting observation was that many location advantages are actually industry specific (Dunning and Norman 1987).

The third type of FDI, *efficiency seeking FDI*, leads to even higher complexity as regards the location advantages of the countries involved. First, this type of FDI is usually trade creating at the firm level, because it reflects a rationalization of the MNE's operations and typically a specialization of the various affiliates in its internal network. This increases both intra-firm knowledge and goods flows, and the international exposure of the affiliates. An in-depth, fine grained analysis, of FSA and location advantage bundles at the affiliate level is then required to understand exactly how location matters to the firm. Here, it is important to understand the specific role given to or earned by affiliates in the company (Rugman 1990). They may act as 'globally rationalized' subsidiaries performing a particular set of activities in the vertical chain or have a regional or world product mandate. In the case of a vertically integrated chain consisting of several, globally rationalized businesses, intra-firm trade is likely to increase, building upon the location advantages benefiting each subsidiary, thereby leading to an increase of both intermediate goods trade and international production (Cantwell 1994).

An interesting observation regarding internationally integrated production is, however, that the key location advantages do not appear to be related to low wages. MNEs export primarily from high labour cost countries with large markets, implying to some extent the presence of local scale economies (Kravis and Lipsey 1982). Even more importantly MNEs seek location advantages complementary to their own firm specific advantages, typically in the form of an appropriate infrastructure, technology development, and supporting institutions (Cantwell 1995).

The fourth main type is *strategic asset seeking FDI* (Wesson 1993). Here, assets of foreign firms are secured by new plants and acquisitions or joint ventures, to create synergies with the existing pool of assets through common ownership, see e.g. Kogut and Chang (1991). Here, it is, e.g. the R&D performed in host countries rather than the home country which constitutes the key location advantage leading to FDI. To the extent that the acquired assets sourced from a host country are also linked to a localized innovation system, the MNE as a whole may get access to at least some spillovers from that innovation system. Conversely, the localized innovation system may benefit from being associated with the foreign MNE.

Dunning (2000) provides a brilliant synthesis of the key location advantages identified by ten schools of thought on location advantages as they apply to these four main types of FDI.[3]

In addition to the four main motives for FDI, additional motives appear equally related to location factors. First, escape investments, typically made to avoid home country restrictions (e.g. regulation of laboratory tests on animals, limitations on the range of services that can be provided in the financial services industry, etc.) obviously reflect the absence of government restrictions elsewhere.

Second, trade supporting investments (e.g. to aid in purchasing of inputs, logistics activities, after sales service, the liaison with host governments, etc.) precisely aim to facilitate home country imports or exports through building on host country location advantages.

## 6.2.3 Operationalization of CSA–FSA framework

Dunning's eclectic framework is clearly related to Rugman's (1996) and Rugman and Verbeke's (1992) extended internalization perspective. This perspec-

---

[3] These ten schools include (1) traditional location theories; (2) theories related to the process of internationalization; (3) agglomeration theories; (4) theories related to spatially specific transaction costs; (5) theories related to the presence of complementary assets; (6) theories related to government induced incentives; (7) theories related to oligopolistic behaviour and product cycles; (8) theories of risk diversification; (9) exchange rate theories; (10) knowledge enhancing (dynamic) theories of location.

tive suggests that it is precisely the nature of a company's FSAs and the type of country specific advantages (CSAs) it faces, that will determine whether a particular production activity will be located in a foreign country through FDI, i.e. whether internalization will occur.

An interesting feature of the FSA–CSA framework is that it can be operationalized at three levels. First, as a strategic management tool to guide top management decision making at the firm level. Here, it should be recognized that the CSA–FSA configuration may be different for every strategic business unit, subsidiary and even value added activity, within a single firm (Rugman, Verbeke, and Luxmore 1990; and Rugman and Verbeke 2001). Second, as a public policy tool, to describe at the national level and by industry both the revealed comparative advantages (RCA; use of Balassa index) and the revealed firm specific advantages of domestic companies, (RFSA; ratio of sales by domestic MNEs to sales by foreign based MNEs in an industry, relative to the total sales by domestic MNEs to total sales by foreign based MNEs) (Sleuwaegen and Veugelers 2001). Third, at the level of cross-country analyses, whereby a country's relative attractiveness *vis-a-vis* other countries can be described in terms of on the one hand general location parameters (in principle exogenous to companies, such as the quality of the educational system) and on the other hand characteristics of the 'average' firm. For example, the competitiveness rankings of countries established in the yearly World Competitiveness reports of the World Economic Forum can be decomposed in a 'CSA' and an 'FSA' part.

The normative implications of possessing weak or strong location advantages are, however, very different for firms, industries, and countries. At the firm level, location advantages contribute to the firm's performance (in terms of survival, profitability, and growth) *vis-à-vis* rival companies. Managerial decision making should therefore attempt to optimize this contribution. At the industry level, location advantages do not usually bear similar implications, for two reasons. First, an industry usually does not act to optimize its location advantages, although public agencies may select specific industries as beneficiaries of location enhancement measures. The much debated strategic trade policy case reflects such a normative policy position. Here, the aim is either to shift profits to domestic firms through helping them attain first-mover advantages and learning curve effects or to generate localized technological spill-over effects (Rugman and Verbeke 1991). Second, a 'bandwagon' effect has often been observed, whereby several firms in an industry attempt to penetrate foreign markets almost simultaneously. However, such collective moves do not aim to optimize an industry's location advantages but on the contrary to prevent rivals from gaining privileged access to benefits associated with specific locations.

At the country level, the intentional 'creation' of location advantages for either domestic firms or foreign firms (or both) has been the subject of an enormous literature recently synthesized by Rugman and Verbeke (1998). The conclusion of their study is threefold.

First, the creation of location advantages favouring either domestic firms or foreign MNEs through specific incentive programmes and regulatory policies by government has become very difficult as many countries have become both major source nations and recipients of FDI. Hence, national treatment of foreign firms is mostly the appropriate policy. Second, many MNEs have adopted strategies of national responsiveness which makes a natural symbiosis with indigenous clusters much easier than in the past. Third, given the first two comments, many governments and MNEs now share a preference for international trade and investment agreements, either at the level of a regional block (e.g. EU, NAFTA) or at the multilateral level. In such cases, the concept of location advantages takes the form of a public good shared by all firms and countries covered by the agreements (Rugman and Verbeke 1994). From a comparative institutional perspective, the question shifts from asking who enjoys the strongest, government-induced location advantages to assessing the overall benefits of the international regulatory system, *vis-à-vis* a system of anarchy in creating national and subnational location advantages.

International regulatory systems to constrain the creation of artificial location advantages obviously do not make national government policy in this area obsolete. Instead they suggest a redirection towards innovation and knowledge accumulation, in line with a country's technological trajectory and national innovation system characteristics.

An important question is whether the nature of CSAs has changed in the recent past. Dunning (1998) has argued that in the 1980s and 1990s three important changes have occurred. First, the emergence of knowledge as the 'key wealth creating asset'. As a result, and with the exception of some natural resource and cheap labour seeking FDI, MNEs now attach much more importance to locations with excellent infrastructure and institutional facilities, rather than conventional location advantages such as low labour costs or easy access to raw materials. Second, the rise of 'transactional benefits' of spatial proximity in the knowledge development process between the non-location bound FSAs of MNEs and the location bound, immobile clusters of complementary assets in host countries. These benefits of spatial proximity have led affiliates of MNEs to become increasingly embedded in host country innovation systems, as demonstrated by the growing geographic dispersion of R&D and the number of patents registered by MNEs outside their home country (Almeida 1996; Shan and Song 1997; Cantwell 1989; Kuemmerle 1999; Pearce 1990).

Third, the emergence of 'alliance capitalism', i.e. a collaborative, stakeholder approach guiding both intra-firm relationships and inter-firm cooperative agreements, especially in knowledge creation. In this context, it appears, for example, that localized networks of related and supporting activities act as an agglomerative magnet on FDI (Wheeler and Mody 1992; Audretsch and Feldman 1996). This does not imply, however, that within a single country, the location distribution of foreign owned and domestically owned production operations is necessarily the same. For example, Shaver (1998) found that foreign owned manufacturing operations in the United States were located comparatively more in coastal states where it is more cost effective to receive imports. In addition, they were also located more in non-union, low wage, right-to-work states, reflecting, *inter alia*, an attempt to reduce the liability of foreignness on the cost side *vis-à-vis* domestic rivals. Shaver (1998) also suggested that foreign firms might prefer low wage states because they perceive employee skills, to be 'upgraded' by the company, as largely uniform across the country. If this were correct, it would also imply that FDI location would not be determined as much as domestic investment by the potential to benefit from cluster spillover effects. This view, however, is in contrast with the more convincing empirical evidence of Chen and Chen (1998) that much recent FDI, especially by small companies, should be viewed as a linkage to a foreign network, i.e. as a tool to tap into resources such as 'market intelligence, technological know-how, management enterprise, or simply reputation for being established in a prestigious market'.

These three elements largely explain the growth of strategic asset seeking FDI and the paradox of observing 'sticky places within slippery space' (Markusen 1996).

# 6.3 SPATIAL ASPECTS OF FDI AND MNE ACTIVITY

One of the key observations in economic geography is that both internationally and within a single country, economic activities are characterized by a specific level of geographic dispersion/concentration (Amiti 1998). Building upon Krugman (1991a,b, 1998), three forces can be identified that foster concentration and three forces that stimulate dispersion. The former forces include (1) the presence of large markets that allow economies of scale in local production, a reduction in logistics costs, and agglomeration economies with related and supporting industries (backward and forward linkages), (2) abundant markets for specialized knowledge inputs (e.g. highly skilled labour), (3) knowledge spillovers that lead to geographically localized positive externalities. The latter forces consist of (1) dispersed, immobile production factors such as land, natural resources, and some types of labour, as well as immobile demand requiring localized service provision, (2) scarcity rents, when an initial concentration of economic activity pushes up prices of scarce production factors in a particular location, and (3) negative externalities such as congestion and technological 'lock-in'.

Apart from the above factors, a localized culture of interdependence and exchange and institutions such as universities, specialized services, and service organizations supporting this culture, may greatly aid superior innovative performance (Audretsch 1998; and Saxenian 1990).

Two types of knowledge spillovers exist (Audretsch 1998). The first type, reflects intra industry knowledge spillovers that benefit all firms located within a region, but limited to a single industry (Glaeser *et al.* 1992). The reason for this regional specialization of spillovers is that firms within a specific industry may be very similar in terms of the type of individuals they attract, the way these individuals develop, absorb, and communicate knowledge and the networking institutions they build, contribute to, and draw upon in the region. The second type, consisting of inter-industry spillovers in contrast, reflects the exchange of complementary knowledge among firms in different industries. Here, it is the diversity of geographically concentrated knowledge transfers that leads to new richness.

The main contribution of international business scholars has been to analyse geographical concentration/dispersion of FDI, not mainly as the result of exogenous forces but to a large extent as the outcome of MNE behaviour (Mucchielli 1998; Porter 1998*a*). For example, the existence of an economic centre, close to a large market, may attract foreign entry, which in turn makes this centre even more attractive to other firms. The presence of such path dependencies explains why the international expansion of MNEs is usually also restricted to a limited number of locations, because agglomeration economies and spillover effects only arise over time and are created through a process of cumulative causation. It is a self-reinforcing set of firm level actions that largely contributes to the spatial concentration of industries and the creation of specialized geographic areas.

Here too, the FSA/CSA framework can be used. More specifically, the creation of 'sticky places' fundamentally depends upon the synergies between strong mobile or non-location bound FSAs and immobile CSAs. Here, not all synergies are internalized by the firms involved. The spatial proximity between firms in a specific industry and, e.g. a pool of workers with specialized skills, the non-business infrastructure, etc. leads to technological and organizational spillover effects benefiting the entire, localized industrial district.

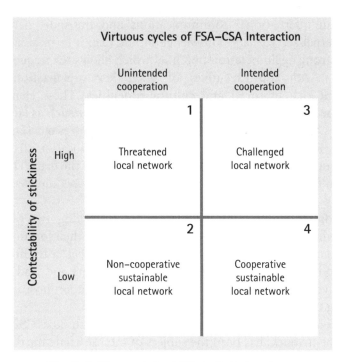

**Fig. 6.3 The sustainability of sticky places**

From a sustainability perspective, four types of 'sticky places' can be distinguished, as shown in Figure 6.3. The horizontal axis measures the degree of cooperation within the localized network among the various actors, i.e. the presence or absence of intended efforts to create virtuous cycles of FSA–CSA interaction. Here, the key issue is whether these actors aim to create local network externalities or whether these spillover effects just arise unintentionally. This distinction may be important within the context of the vertical axis, which represents the international contestability of the local network. If the contestability of stickiness is high, as a result of international competition, the defence mechanisms of the local network will be much weaker in quadrant 1 than quadrant 3, which explains the growing efforts of many local and regional governments to contribute to the creation and functioning of structured clustering mechanisms (Porter 1998*b*).

An important empirical question is obviously whether clustering benefits in the form of, e.g. agglomeration economies, access to 'thick' markets for knowledge inputs, and technological spillover effects are equally important for all MNE value added activities. Porter (1986) has argued that, within the firm, the determinants favouring a specific geographic configuration may be very different for each value chain activity. For example, corporate and regional MNE headquarters, typically require a 'strategic location', with easy access to an international communications and transport network, high quality external services and knowledge inputs (e.g. information processing workers), strong agglomeration potential which allows for frequent personal interactions with top executives of other key organizations, and an environment rich in social and cultural amenities. These elements must obviously be weighted against the cost of scarce inputs such as land, negative externalities associated with large, dense economic centres etc. (Dicken 1998). In contrast, R&D facilities may require very different location characteristics, depending upon the precise role of the R&D facility in the firm. This role may be either to exploit existing knowledge or to create new knowledge (Kuemmerle 1999).

As regards activities such as production and marketing, two MNEs facing broadly similar external 'location pulls' may still make their location decisions largely dependent on their administrative heritage (e.g. a tradition of centralized production building upon home nation CSAs and leading to scale economies versus decentralized operations, building upon host nation CSAs and leading to benefits of national responsiveness).

The issue of relative contribution of home CSAs versus host CSAs to overall MNE competitiveness has been the subject of intense academic debate in the recent past. This is discussed in the next section.

# 6.4 THE RELATIVE CONTRIBUTION OF HOME CSAS AND HOST CSAS TO MNE COMPETITIVENESS

The most influential work on the impact of location on international competitiveness in the 1990s has undoubtedly been Porter's study on the 'diamond' of competitive advantage (Porter 1990). Porter argues that four interrelated elements at the level of each industry within an individual nation determine international competitiveness. These determinants include factor conditions, demand conditions, related and supporting industries, and firm strategy, structure, and rivalry. Two other elements, namely government and chance are viewed by Porter as secondary determinants that may affect the strength of the primary elements.

Porter's (1990) approach undoubtedly constitutes an important advance on conventional economics thinking on the sources of competitiveness at the industry level. His comments on the importance of (1) created, advanced factor conditions as opposed to natural resource endowments; (2) sophisticated rather than large scale demand; (3) linkages with related and supporting firms; and (4) intense domestic competition, have undoubtedly been useful to both managers and public policy makers. However, from an international business perspective, Porter's (1990) framework is also associated with substantial weaknesses, especially when applying his perspective at the firm level. His framework assumes that for each business in a firm, a single home base exists which acts as the sole source of this firm's key location advantages. These CSAs can then be absorbed within the firm, i.e. contribute to the development and exploitation of its FSAs. Foreign nations' diamonds can only be tapped into selectively, because a firm aiming to draw upon a foreign diamond's strengths is viewed as always being at a disadvantage *vis-à-vis* firms 'inside' this foreign diamond system.

Porter's (1990) perspective has been rightfully criticized by several international business scholars. Dunning (1993) has argued: 'To suggest the competitive position of MNEs like IBM, Philips of Eindhoven, SKF, Nestle, BAT, rests only on their access to the diamond of competitive advantage of their home countries is ludicrous—however much their initial foray overseas may have been based on such advantages.' Porter did acknowledge the strategic option for firms to 'shift' the 'home base' for specific businesses from the home country to a host country, in function of their relative CSAs. However, firms and industries from small open economies largely rely on international linkages, especially through inward and outward FDI as sources of competitiveness. For example, in relatively small economic systems such as Belgium in the European Union (EU) context, or Canada in the context of the North American Free Trade Agreement (NAFTA), any analysis of the sources of domestic firms' international competitiveness needs to take into account the issue of access to foreign diamond components. Hence, a 'multiple diamond' approach is clearly required, as demonstrated by several conceptual and empirical studies (Moon, Rugman, and Verbeke 1995, 1998).

One of the key problems of Porter's (1990) framework is his concentration on non-location bound FSAs developed by companies in their home country prior to engaging in FDI. As a result, he largely neglects (a) the systemic advantages of MNEs resulting precisely from the common governance of internationally dispersed value added activities, each building upon an idiosyncratic bundle of CSAs, and (b) the benefits of strategic asset seeking FDI, accruing to the MNE, whereby these assets may largely have been created on the basis of host CSAs.

Dunning (1996) has empirically assessed the geographical sources of MNE competitiveness through a survey of 144 of the Fortune global 500 industrial firms. He found that the relative contribution of host nation CSAs to the MNE overall competitiveness is increasing. On average, between 40 and 50 per

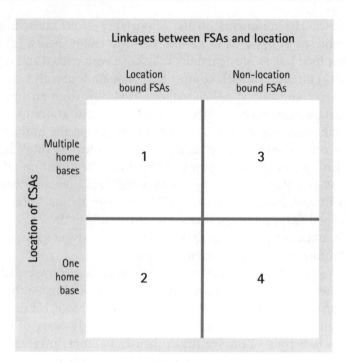

**Fig. 6.4 Firm (or business) level sources of
international competitive advantage**

cent of the location advantages' contribution to MNE competitiveness is
viewed as being derived from host countries, particularly in the areas of
natural resources, linkages with suppliers and rivals, and through foreign
market size. In contrast, technological capabilities and skilled labour capital
still appeared to be derived largely from the home country.

The relative importance of home versus host CSAs to the MNE's overall
competitiveness is thus clearly an empirical question. Rugman and Verbeke
(1995) have developed a conceptual framework that allows to position firms
(or businesses within the firm) according to their reliance on specific bundles
of CSAs as sources of international competitiveness. This is illustrated in
Figure 6.4. The vertical axis measures the number of locations relied upon by
the firm or each business within the firm as key sources of CSAs for any given
business. Here, it is critical to know whether the firm or business within the
firm builds primarily on one or several locations as a source of key CSAs,
i.e., whether it has one or several home bases. The horizontal axis investigates
whether the firm or business within the firm relies primarily on location
bound or non-location bound FSAs.

The former reflect strengths that provide a favourable competitive position
to a firm in a particular geographical area, such as a country or a limited set of
countries, but cannot easily be transferred abroad, whether as an intermediate

output (e.g. managerial skills, R&D knowledge) or embodied in a final product. In contrast, non-location bound FSAs represent company strengths that can easily be transferred across locations at low costs and with only limited adaptation; this transfer can again take place in the form of intermediate or final outputs. The significance of the distinction between location bound FSAs and non-location bound FSAs has been explained in Rugman and Verbeke (1991, 1992). In fact, this distinction reflects a resource based interpretation of the integration-national responsiveness framework as developed by Bartlett (1986).

Porter's single home base perspective is clearly located in quadrant 4 of Figure 6.4. For each business, the firm relies on CSAs of a single nation as the key source of competitiveness. The firm then creates non-location bound FSAs building upon the home base CSAs, leading to exports and outward FDI. This perspective is consistent with Vernon's (1966) product life cycle. Quadrant 1 describes the firms that consist of largely independent, country based business units. They derive their competitive advantages primarily from location-bound FSAs that allow them to be nationally responsive. Quadrant 2 reflects the case whereby the firm (or its businesses) again relies on a single home base, but here it does not lead to the firm becoming a successful exporter or outward investor. Instead, the only way to achieve survival, profitability and growth is to develop specific domestic niches.

Finally, Quadrant 3 represents firms or individual businesses within the firm which function primarily through international network linkages. These units operate in a more integrated fashion, within a structure that may take the form of a 'global web', Reich (1991). MNEs engaged in strategic asset seeking usually also operate in this quadrant. It is in this case that the management of both the intra-organizational and inter-organizational networks may become very complex (Campbell and Verbeke 2001; Rugman and Verbeke 2001).

The question arises where firms should be positioned that work with subsidiary world product mandates (WPMs) (Rugman and Bennett 1982). Here, it should be emphasized that if the 'businesses' within an MNE are defined sufficiently narrowly, it can usually be argued that individual 'business units' with WPMs indeed all function with a single home base, thus requiring their positioning in quadrant 4 rather than quadrant 3. However, the single home base concept then becomes largely tautological (see below).

It should be mentioned that Porter has refined his perspective on the importance of a single home base in more recent work (Porter 1998a), recognizing the importance of foreign locations to the overall competitiveness of MNEs. However, rather than acknowledging the existence in many cases of the importance of multiple home bases for MNEs, even for individual businesses, he has now chosen to define the concept of 'business' or 'product line' in such a narrow fashion that the prevalence of a single home base can indeed be defended in most cases of world product mandates.

For example, rather than recognizing that Honda now functions with at least two home bases in the automobile business, namely Japan and the United States, with the latter country being specialized in the design, development, and upgrading of station wagons, Porter (1998a, 335) argues that station wagons actually constitute a distinct business or product line, thus building upon a single home base, namely the United States. In addition, according to Porter (1998a, 335) even the development of the 'two door Civic Coupe' in the United States will be achieved using the United States as a 'single' home base! A home base is thus defined as the location in which the most important decisions can be taken, largely independently from other locations: here, the definition of a product line can be adapted and narrowed as much as necessary to conform to the requirement that strategic decision making be concentrated in one location.

However, it is rather difficult to believe that all strategic decision making regarding the two-door Honda Civic Coupe would be divorced throughout the value chain from decisions on other cars in the Civic line or even other Honda car models. Indeed, Prahalad and Hamel (1990) have precisely identified as one of Honda's core competencies, its ability to share knowledge on small engines across very broad businesses such as automobiles, motorcycles, and lawn mowers. In this context, it is interesting to observe, however, that when talking about Honda as a whole, Porter (1998a, 333–4) attempts to demonstrate, in contradiction with his own product line based analysis, the existence of a single home base for this firm in the automobile business using, *inter alia*, data of R&D geographic concentration.

The fallacy of the single home base argument becomes even clearer when Porter discusses the Hewlett Packard case (Porter 1998a, 339). He argues that 77 per cent of HP's physical space dedicated to manufacturing, R&D, and administration in fact is the United States, reflecting in his view, the existence of a single home base, especially since the 'specialized expertise' of 'worldwide experts' is also concentrated in that home base. This raises two interesting issues. First, the fact that 23 per cent of physical space dedicated to manufacturing, R&D, and administration is not located in the United States, obviously does not qualify for a multiple home base designation. In that case, what percentage would? Second, on what basis can a distinction be made between 'specialized expertise' of worldwide experts, which appears to qualify for 'home base' branding and for example 'process-oriented R&D, product localization and local marketing', Porter (1998a, 334), activities which do not appear to deserve a home base qualification.

In terms of description, the discussion on whether a firm or business unit functions with a single home base or multiple home bases appears to be a largely semantic issue. At the firm level, Porter's (1998a) analysis suggests that a high percentage of core assets, competencies, and strategic decision making power concentrated in one country would lead to the qualification of a firm as being a single home based company. In contrast, the authors of this chapter would argue that (1) there must be a 'threshold percentage' of core assets, competencies, and strategic decision making power concentration below which a firm would be viewed as functioning with several home bases, and (2) when one or various foreign units have built up a substantial critical mass of, e.g., R&D knowledge and are able to substantially augment this knowledge base through virtuous interactions with location advantages in host countries, the firm would again be viewed as functioning with several home bases.

At the business unit level, Porter's (1998a) perspective suggests that any business unit can be defined sufficiently narrowly (typically as a product line) so as to allow the identification of a single home base. In contrast, the authors of this chapter would argue that business units should be defined *ex ante*. A business unit with several product lines using different home bases would then reflect the presence of a multiple home base structure.

From a normative perspective, Porter's (1998a) view is more problematic as he suggests that it is impossible at the firm or business unit level to have more than one home base. His approach therefore is not testable. In contrast, the authors of this chapter view the presence of one or multiple home bases as an empirical question, whereby factual evidence suggests an increased use of multiple home bases.

# CONCLUSION

This chapter has suggested that the main challenge facing MNEs today in the location area is to combine effective access to—and participation in—foreign knowledge clusters, with efficient firm-level leveraging of the resulting knowledge base. To meet this challenge may be fraught with difficulties, for two reasons.

First, the benefits from setting up a subsidiary in a foreign, local cluster may not be easy to assess *ex ante*, as these benefits may largely depend on the actual absorption of cluster know-how. The absorption effectiveness may be very difficult to predict, given that a substantial portion of these benefits consists of cluster spill-over effects. Subjective perceptions may be critical here. This also implies that existing participants in a cluster, as well as local/regional public agencies responsible for the economic development of a cluster, may substantially affect the perceived cluster attractiveness through the external image they are able to create for it.

Second, the international leveraging of know-how derived from participation in a cluster may also be difficult, when various MNE operations build upon diverging, specialized technological capabilities and when knowledge transfer costs are high.

A complementary issue is related to the effect of MNEs on the local knowledge clusters themselves. Whether MNEs will consistently enhance the upgrading of local knowledge clusters, rather than eliminate domestic expertise and reduce long-run cluster stability in host countries is at present a much debated policy issue and an empirical question which requires substantial further research.

However, on the positive side, two categories of potential benefits to clusters from MNE activity have so far been largely ignored in the literature.

First, high profile MNEs may through their presence in a cluster provide legitimacy to this cluster and alter the cluster's attractiveness as perceived by other MNEs and domestic firms. In other words, a global signalling effect may arise, which may greatly contribute to the cluster's visibility, as well as its expansion and sustainability.

Second, MNEs may well act as intermediaries in the international cross-fertilization of localized knowledge clusters.

The mainstream international business literature has traditionally viewed the MNE as an efficiency driven, transaction cost reducing, and welfare enhancing institution, as exemplified in this book by J. Dunning (Chapter 2), and J.-F. Hennart (Chapter 5). In their work, the MNE is considered an appropriate vehicle for the transfer and exploitation of proprietary knowledge, as well as for knowledge development, and extension or acquisition across borders when alternative modes of operation are inefficient. As a result of FDI, the MNE benefits from foreign location advantages, whereas foreign locations may benefit from various beneficial MNE spill-over effects, such as the upgrading of the local supplier base, the productivity improvement of the local human resources pool, the increase in sophistication of local demand, and better customer service as an outcome of stronger competition. However, MNEs may also increasingly act as a link between sticky, localized innovation clusters. In such a case they are the unintended lubricant for international exchanges and spill-overs among these centres. MNEs could thus increase the foreign knowledge absorption capacity of localized innovation clusters and contribute to the global diffusion of knowledge. Such a diffusion process may be tempered by the MNEs' limited capabilities to absorb and transfer knowledge (i.e. create a 'bumblebee' effect) within their own internal network, especially when multiple home bases are used, with distinct approaches to knowledge development and transfer.

## REFERENCES

ALIBER, R. Z. (1970). 'A Theory of Foreign Direct Investment', in C. P. Kindleberger (ed.), *The International Corporation* Cambridge, Mass.: MIT Press.

ALMEIDA, P. (1996). 'Knowledge Sourcing by Foreign Multinationals: Patent Citation Analysis in the US Semi-conductor Industry', *Strategic Management Journal*, 17 (Winter): 155–65.

AMITI, M. (1998). 'New Trade Theories and Industrial Location in the EU: A Survey of Evidence', *Oxford Review of Economic Policy*, 14(2): Oxford: Oxford University Press.

AUDRETSCH, D. B. (1998). 'Agglomeration and the Location of Innovative Activity', *Oxford Review of Economic Policy*, 14(2): Oxford: Oxford University Press.

—— and FELDMAN, M. P. (1996). 'R&D Spillovers and the Geography of Innovation and Production', *American Economic Review*, 86(4): 253–73.

BARTLETT, C. (1986). 'Building and Managing the Transnational: The New Organizational Challenge', in M. E. Porter (ed.), *Competition in Global Industries*. Boston: Harvard Business School Press, 367–401.

BATRA, R. N., and RAMACHANDRAN, R. (1980). 'Multinational Firms and the Theory of International Trade and Investment', *American Economic Review*, 70: 278–90.

BIRKINSHAW, J. (2000). *Entrepreneurship in the Global Firm*. London: Sage.

CAMPBELL, A., and VERBEKE, A. (2001). 'The Multinational Management of Multiple External Networks', in D. Van Den Bulcke and A. Verbeke (eds.), *Globalization and the Small Open Economy*. Cheltenham: Elgar.

CANTWELL, J. (1989). *Technological Innovation and Multinational Corporations*. Oxford: Basil Blackwell.

—— (1994). 'The Relationship Between International Trade and International Production', in D. Greenaway and L. A. Winters (eds.), *Surveys in International Trade*. Oxford: Blackwell, 303–28.

—— (1995). 'The Globalization of Technology: What Remains of the Product Cycle?', *Cambridge Journal of Economics*, 19: 155–74.

—— and PISCITELLO (1999). 'The Emergence of Corporate International Networks for the Accumulation of Dispersed Technological Competence', *Management International Review*, 39(1): 123–47

CAVES, R. (1996). *Multinational Firms and Economic Analysis*. Cambridge: Cambridge University Press.

CHEN, H., and CHEN, T-J. (1998). 'Network Linkages and Location Choice in Foreign Direct Investment', *Journal of International Business Studies*, 29(3): 445–67.

COX, D., and HARRIS, R. (1985). 'Trade Liberalization and Industrial Organization', *Journal of Political Economy*, 93: 115–45.

CULEM, C. (1988). 'The Locational Determinants of Direct Investment Among Industrialized Countries', *European Economic Review*, 32: 885–904.

CUSHMAN, D. O. (1985). 'Real Exchange Rate Risk, Expectations and the Level of Direct Investment', *Review of Economics and Statistics*, May: 297–308.

DICKEN, P. (1998). *Global Shift: Transforming the World Economy*. London: Paul Chapman Publishing Ltd.

DIXIT, A. K., and STIGLITZ, J. E. (1977). 'Monopolistic Competition and Optimum Product Diversity', *American Economic Review*, 67: 297–308.

Dosi, G., Pavitt, K., and Soete, L. L. G. (1990). *The Economics of Technical Change and International Trade*. Hemel Hempstead: Harvester Wheatsheaf.

Dunning, J. H. (1973). 'The Determinants of International Production', *Oxford Economic Papers*, 25(3), Nov.: 289–336.

—— (1977). 'Trade, Location of Economic Activity and the MNE: A Search for an Eclectic Approach', in B. Ohlin, P. O. Hesselborn, and P. M. Wijkman (eds.), *The International Allocation of Economic Activity*. London: Macmillan, 395–418.

—— (1988). 'The Eclectic Paradigm of International Production: An Update and Some Possible Extensions', *Journal of International Business Studies*, 19: 1–31.

—— (1992). *Multinational Enterprises and the Global Economy*. Wokingham: Addison-Wesley.

—— (1993). *The Globalization of Business*. London: Routledge.

—— (1996). 'The Geographical Sources of Competitiveness of Firms: Some Results of a New Survey', *Transnational Corporations*, 5(3): 1–30.

—— (1998). 'Location and the Multinational Enterprise: A Neglected Factor?' *Journal of International Business Studies*, 29(1): 45–66.

—— (1999). 'Forty Years on: American Investment in British Manufacturing Industry Revisited', *Transnational Corporations*, 8(2): 1–34.

—— (2000). 'The Eclectic Paradigm as an Envelope for Economic and Business Theories of MNE Activity', *International Business Review*, 9: 163–90.

—— and Norman, G. (1987). 'The Location Choice of Offices of International Companies', *Environment and Planning*, A, 613–31.

Ethier, W. J. (1986). 'The Multinational Firm', *Quarterly Journal of Economics*, 80: 805–33.

Glaeser, E., Kallal, H., Scheinkman, J., and Shleifer, A. (1992). 'Growth of Cities', *Journal of Political Economy*, 100: 1126–52.

Greenaway, D., and Milner, C. (1986). *The Economics of Intra-Industry Trade*. Oxford: Basil Blackwell.

Grossman, G. M., and Helpman, E. (1991). *Innovation and Growth in the Global Economy*. Cambridge, Mass.: MIT Press.

Grubel, H. G., and Lloyd, P. (1975). *Intra-Industry Trade: The Theory and Measurement of International Trade in Differentiated Products*. London: Macmillan.

Guisinger, S. E., and associates (1985). *Investment Incentives and Performance Requirements*. New York: Praeger.

Hanson, G. H. (1998). 'North American Economic Integration and Industry Location', *Oxford Review of Economic Policy*, 14(2): Oxford: Oxford University Press.

Helpman, E., and Krugman, P. R. (1985). *Market Structure and Foreign Trade*. Cambridge, Mass.: MIT Press.

Hymer, S. H. (1960). *The International Operations of National Firms: A Study of Direct Investment*. Ph.D. thesis, MIT: published by MIT Press. (Also published under same title in 1976.)

Kogut, B. (1983). 'Foreign Direct Investment as a Sequential Process', in C. P. Kindleberger and D. B. Audretsch (eds.), *The Multinational Corporation in the 1980s*. Cambridge, Mass.: MIT Press, 38–56.

—— and Chang, S. J. (1991). 'Technological Capabilities and Japanese Direct Investment in the United States', *Review of Economics and Statistics*, LXXIII: 401–13.

KRAVIS, I. B., and LIPSEY, R. E. (1982). 'The Location of Overseas Production for Exports by US Multinational Firms', *Journal of International Economics*, 12: 201–23.

KRUGMAN, P. R. (1980). 'Scale Economies, Product Differentiation and the Pattern of Trade', *American Economic Review*, 70: 950–9.

—— (1991*a*). 'Increasing Returns and Economic Geography', *Journal of Political Economy*, 99: 483–99.

—— (1991*b*). *Geography and Trade*. Cambridge, Mass.: MIT Press.

—— (1998). 'What's New about the New Economic Geography?', *Oxford Review of Economic Policy*, 14(2): Oxford: Oxford University Press.

KUEMMERLE, W. (1999). 'The Drivers of Foreign Direct Investment into Research and Development: An Empirical Investigation', *Journal of International Business Studies*, 30(1): 1–24.

LEAMER, E. E., and LEVINSOHN, J. (1995). 'International Trade Theory: The Evidence', in G. M. Grossman and K. Rogoff (eds.), *Handbook of International Economics*, III. Amsterdam: Elsevier-North Holland.

LIPSEY, R. E., and WEISS, M. Y. (1984). 'Foreign Production and Exports of Individual Firms', *Review of Economics and Statistics*, 66: 304–8.

MARKUSEN, A. (1996). 'Sticky Places in Slippery Space: A Typology of Industrial Districts', *Economic Geography*, 72(3): 293–313.

MARKUSEN, J. R. (1984). 'Multinationals, Multi-plant Economies, and the Gains from Trade', *Journal of International Economics*, 16: 205–26.

MOON, H. C., RUGMAN, A. M., and VERBEKE, A. (1995). 'The Generalized Double Diamond Approach to International Competitiveness', in A. M. Rugman, J. Van den Broeck, and A. Verbeke (eds.), *Research in Global Strategic Management, Vol. 5: Beyond the Diamond*. Greenwich, Conn.: JAI Press, 97–114.

—— (1998). 'A Generalized Double Diamond Approach to the Global Competitiveness of Korea and Singapore', *International Business Review*, 7: 135–50.

MUCCHIELLI, J.-L. (1998). *Research in Global Strategic Management, Volume 6: Multinational Location Strategy*. London: JAI Press.

OHMAE, K. (1985). *Triad Power*. New York: Free Press.

OZAWA, T. (1991). 'Japanese Multinationals and 1992', in B. Burgenmeier and J.-L. Mucchielli (eds.), *Multinationals and Europe 1992*. London: Routledge, 135–54.

PEARCE, R. D. (1990). *The Internationalization of Research and Development*. London: Macmillan.

PORTER, M. E. (ed.) (1986). *Competition in Global Industries*. Boston: Harvard Business School Press.

—— (1990). *The Competitive Advantage of Nations*. New York: Free Press.

—— (1998). *On Competition*. Boston: Harvard Business School Press.

—— (1998*a*). 'Competing Across Locations', in Porter 1998, ibid., 309–48.

—— (1998*b*). 'Clusters and Competion', in Porter 1998, ibid., 197–287.

PRAHALAD, C. K., and HAMEL, G. (1990). 'The Core Competence of the Corporation', *Harvard Business Review*, 68(3): 79–81.

REICH, R. B. (1991). *The Work of Nations*. New York: Knopf.

RUGMAN, A. M. (1981). *Inside the Multinationals: The Economics of Internal Markets*. New York: Columbia University Press.

RUGMAN, A. M. (*cont.*) (1990). *Multinationals and Canada–United States Free Trade.* Columbia: University of South Carolina Press.

—— (1996). *The Theory of Multinational Enterprises.* Cheltenham: Elgar.

—— (1999). 'Forty Years of the Theory of the Transnational Corporation', *Transnational Corporations,* 8(12): 51–76.

—— (2000). *The End of Globalization.* London: Random House Business Books.

—— and BENNETT, J. (1982). 'Technology Transfer and World Product Mandating in Canada', *Columbia Journal of World Business,* 17(4): 58–62.

—— and D'CRUZ, J. (2000). *Multinationals as Flagship Firms: Regional Business Networks.* Oxford: Oxford University Press.

—— and VERBEKE, A. (1990). *Global Corporate Strategy and Trade Policy.* London: Routledge.

———— (1991). 'Strategic Trade Policy is not Good Strategy', *Hitotsubashi Journal of Commerce and Business,* 25(1): 75–97.

———— (1992). 'A Note on the Transnational Solution and the Transaction Cost Theory of Multinational Strategic Management', *Journal of International Business Studies,* 23(4): 761–71.

———— (1994). 'Foreign Direct Investment and NAFTA: A Conceptual Framework', in A. Rugman (ed.), *Foreign Investment in NAFTA.* Columbia: University of South Carolina Press, 80–104.

———— (1995). 'Transnational Networks and Global Competition: An Organizing Framework', in A. M. Rugman, J. Van den Broeck, and A. Verbeke (eds.), *Research in Global Strategic Management Vol. 5: Beyond the Diamond.* Greenwich, Conn.: JAI Press, 3–23.

———— (1998). 'Multinational Enterprises and Public Policy', *Journal of International Business Studies,* 29(1): 115–36.

———— (2001). 'Subsidiary Specific Advantages in Multinational Enterprises', *Strategic Management Journal,* 22(3): 237–50.

———— and LUXMORE, S. (1990). 'Corporate Strategy and the Free Trade Agreement: Adjustment by Canadian Multinational Enterprises', *Canadian Journal of Regional Science,* 13(2/3): 307–30.

SAUCIER, P. (1991). 'New Conditions for Competition Between Japanese and European Firms', in B. Burgenmeier and J.-L. Mucchielli (eds.), *Multinationals and Europe 1992: Strategies for the Future.* London: Routledge, 121–34.

SAXENIAN, A. (1990). 'Regional Networks and the Resurgence of Silicon Valley', *California Management Review,* 33: 89–111.

SHAN, W., and SONG, J. (1997). 'Foreign Direct Investment and the Sourcing of Technological Advantage: Evidence from the Biotechnology Industry', *Journal of International Business Studies,* 28(2): 267–84.

SHAVER, J. M. (1998). 'Do Foreign-owned and US-owned Establishments Exhibit the Same Location Pattern in US Manufacturing Industries?', *Journal of International Business Studies,* 29(3): 469–92.

SLEUWAEGEN, L., and VEUGELERS, R. (2001). 'Competitive and Comparative Advantage: The Performance of Belgium in a Global Context', in D. Van Den Bulcke and A. Verbeke (eds.), *Globalization and the Small Open Economy.* Cheltenham: Elgar.

SMITH, A., and VENABLES, A. J. (1988). 'Completing the Internal Market in the European Community: Some Industry Simulations', *European Economic Review*, 32: 1501–25.

VERNON, R. (1966). 'International Investment and International Trade in Produce Cycle', *Quarterly Journal of Economics*, 80: 190–207.

—— (1983). 'Organizational and Institutional Responses to International Risk', in R. J. Herring (ed.), *Managing International Risk*. Cambridge, Mass.: Cambridge University Press, 191–216.

WESSON, T. J. (1993). 'An Alternative Motivation for Foreign Direct Investment', Ph.D. dissertation, Harvard University.

WHEELER, K., and MODY, A. (1992). 'International Investment and Location Decisions: The Case of US Firms', *Journal of International Economics*, 33: 57–76.

# PART II

## THE POLITICAL AND POLICY ENVIRONMENT

# CHAPTER 7

# SOVEREIGNTY@BAY: GLOBALIZATION, MULTINATIONAL ENTERPRISE, AND THE INTERNATIONAL POLITICAL SYSTEM

STEPHEN J. KOBRIN

## 7.1 INTRODUCTION

ALTHOUGH modern multinational firms date from the late nineteenth century, the term 'multinational corporation' did not appear until 1960. At a conference at Carnegie Mellon University, David Lilienthal (1960) distinguished between portfolio and direct investment and then defined multi-national corporations as 'such corporations—which have their home in one country but which operate and live under the laws of other countries as well'.[1] It is of interest that from the start the multinational corporation was defined in terms of jurisdiction and potential jurisdictional conflict.

Given the considerable attention paid to foreign investment by economists since the late nineteenth century, one would have expected extensive discussion of the multinational corporation's 'special features' well before 1960 (Fieldhouse 1986). The literature, however, focused primarily on the macro-economic (and macropolitical) aspects of capital flows, often in capital exporting countries. There was little interest in the political impact of foreign direct investment (FDI) other than the somewhat abstract ideas of Marx and his followers about the internationalization of capital.[2] Lenin's one line definition may be the best known: 'If it were necessary to give the briefest possible definition of imperialism we should have to say that imperialism is the monopoly stage of capitalism' (Lenin 1970: 85).

That changed dramatically in the late 1950s and early 1960s. First, contributions by Edith Penrose, Stephen Hymer, and John Dunning revolutionized the study of FDI approaching it as a function of the growth of the firm rather than the export of capital (Dunning 1976; Hymer 1976; Penrose 1959). One result of the shift in emphasis from capital flows to firm and transaction based theories of FDI was to draw attention to the broader economic (and noneconomic) impact of MNCs on host and home countries.

The dramatic expansion of the multinational enterprise (MNE) after 1960 produced a 'first wave' of literature in the popular and academic press. The opening lines of Raymond Vernon's best-known book capture its tenor well: 'Suddenly, it seems, the sovereign states are feeling naked. Concepts such as sovereignty and national economic strength appear curiously drained of meaning' (Vernon 1971: 3).[3]

In a seminal series of lectures two years before the publication of *Sovereignty at Bay*, Charles Kindleberger (1969: 207) argued that the 'nation-state is just about through as an economic unit'. George Ball (1967) predicted increased conflict between the MNE, a 'modern concept evolved to meet

---

[1] D. K. Fieldhouse corroborates Lilienthal's first use of the term and provides an interesting intellectual history of the development and use of *multinational enterprise* (Fieldhouse 1986). Lilienthal defined direct investment in terms of 'industrial or commercial operations abroad which directly involve corporate managerial responsibility'.

[2] e.g. Marx and Engels's famous statement from the Communist Manifesto that 'Modern Industry has Established the World Market.'

[3] To be fair, Vernon certainly did not predict the end of the nation-state or the end of sovereignty. As he has pointed out, the book's subtitle, 'The Multinational Spread of US Enterprises', is a much more accurate descriptor of its contents. The title did, however, squarely raise the issue.

the requirements of the modern age' and the nation-state which is 'a very old-fashioned idea and badly adapted to serve the needs of our present complex world'. *Global Reach*, a widely read polemic, cited Dow Chemical's CEO's dream of establishing his headquarters on an neutral island 'beholden' to no nation and concluded that the managers of global corporations are demanding 'the right to transcend the nation-state, and in the process, to transform it' (Barnet and Muller 1974: 16).

In this chapter I am concerned with only one aspect of the vast literature on MNE–state relations: the impact of the MNE on sovereignty, autonomy, and control. I argue that the mainstream literature of the sovereignty at bay era (including Vernon's book) did not predict the end of the nation-state or conclude that sovereignty is critically compromised either in theory or practice. In fact, while the terms 'sovereignty', 'autonomy', and 'control' appear frequently in these discussions, they are rarely defined or even used precisely.

At the end of the day MNEs are international or cross-border entities which are *of* the existing interstate system firmly rooted in national territorial jurisdiction. The problems posed by the traditional MNE for both states and the interstate system tend to involve issues of jurisdictional asymmetry, jurisdictional overlap and control, rather than sovereignty in its formal sense. The hierarchical or *Fordist* structure of the traditional MNE reinforces the core values of the modern international political system: state sovereignty and mutually exclusive territoriality. To the extent that MNEs serve as a means for nation-states to exert, and even increase, national power they are sovereignty affirming rather than sovereignty violating (Bergsten, Horst, and Moran 1978).

As we enter the twenty-first century sovereignty has become much more problematic; it is reasonable to describe it as 'at bay' or perhaps '@bay.' Globalization has compromised territorial sovereignty, the basic idea that economic (and political) governance are based on geographic jurisdiction. MNEs play a central role in that process as a result of dramatic increases in the scale of technology, the rise of strategic alliances, the emergence of an electronically networked world economy, and the increased importance of transnational actors and international civil society.

I next turn to a brief review of the nature of the modern interstate system and the meaning of autonomy, control, and sovereignty. I will then discuss (rather than review) the 'sovereignty at bay' literature, arguing that the impacts of MNEs on states and the state system were limited and did not threaten territorial sovereignty directly. Last, I will examine the impact of globalization and the MNE on states and sovereignty.

# 7.2 THE POST-WESTPHALIAN SYSTEM

The Peace of Westphalia, which ended the Thirty Years War in 1648, is generally accepted as marking the end of medieval universalism and the origin of the modern state system (Krasner 1993).[4] The medieval to modern transition entailed the *territorialization* of politics, the replacement of overlapping and interlaced feudal hierarchies by geographically defined territorially sovereign states. It entailed the evolution of political geography from 'scattered islands of political power' to solid block of authority in which one ruler had final authority (Strayer 1970: 31).

The cardinal organizing principle of the modern international system is the division of the globe's surface into mutually exclusive geographically defined jurisdictions enclosed by discrete and meaningful borders (Ruggie 1993). Joseph Camilleri and Jim Falk (1992: 238) argue that *the* primary function of the state is the organization of space; that 'The spatial qualities of the state, understood as a geometric entity with precisely demarcated boundaries, is integral to the notion of sovereignty and international relations theory.' The modern state—and perhaps modernity itself—are inherently geographic constructs; political authority is based upon, and defined by, geographical parameters (Anderson 1986; Spruyt 1994).

Robert Keohane (1993) observes that sovereignty is typically discussed rather than defined. Formal sovereignty is a legal concept: within an exclusive territorial enclave demarcated by unambiguous borders each state is recognized as supreme and independent of outside authorities in the exercise of authority (Barkin and Cronin 1994; Jarvis and Paolini 1995). *Internal sovereignty* defines the legitimization of the state *vis-à-vis* competing domestic claimants. It assumes a monopoly of force within its territory, the 'undisputed right to determine the framework of rules, regulations and policies within a territory and to govern accordingly' (Held and McGrew 1993: 265).

*External sovereignty* is a more amorphous construct. It underlies or legitimates the modern interstate order by assuming both mutually exclusive territoriality as an organizing principle and mutual recognition by like (i.e. territorially defined) units that each state represents a specific society within an exclusive domain (Barkin and Cronin 1994; Ruggie 1983). External sovereignty defines relations among states in the international system, and indeed,

---

[4] Krasner argues that the conventional view is wrong and Westphalia did not represent a clean break with the past; that political organizations based on territoriality existed before 1648 and that universal institutions long outlasted it. Nonetheless, it is a convenient point of demarcation when thinking about the origin of the modern state system.

the system itself in terms of an absence of central authority (Hall 1999; Reinicke and Witte 1999).[5]

Autonomy is a political idea which implies that a state can make its own decisions about how it will deal with internal and external problems (Keohane 1993). Autonomy is related to control and policy effectiveness, the belief that territorial sovereignty translates into unambiguous control over economies and economic actors, for example, and that policy effectiveness is not constrained by outside forces. (It has also been described as operational sovereignty.) The line between autonomy and internal sovereignty is far from sharp; Kenneth Waltz (1969: 96), for example, defines sovereignty in terms of a state deciding 'for itself how it will cope with its internal and external problems'.

In his retrospective review of *Sovereignty at Bay* ten years after its publication, Vernon (1981: 517) expresses concern that readers remember the book's title rather than its message; that he is unfairly associated with the argument that the nation-state is 'done for, finished off by the multinational enterprise'. However, both the title and the opening lines of the book, which argue that concepts such as sovereignty seem 'curiously drained of meaning', appear unambiguous. The apparent contradiction is resolved when one pays closer attention to what Vernon actually means by 'sovereignty'. In *Sovereignty at Bay*, (and his other writing) he is concerned with autonomy and control, with the problems posed by overlapping and intertwining jurisdictions rather than formal or legal sovereignty.

I argue that despite the 'end of sovereignty' arguments which abounded during the reaction to the first wave of multinational expansion, the traditional MNE did not compromise sovereignty in any fundamental sense. It did constrain autonomy and control and thus may be said to have placed some limits on the *implementation* of internal sovereignty. However, the MNE reinforced the critical system defining construct of external sovereignty: mutually exclusive territoriality, borders, and geographically-based political and economic governance.

## 7.3 SOVEREIGNTY AT BAY?

Vernon justified the title *Sovereignty at Bay* in terms of three propositions, none of which dealt with sovereignty directly: (1) most governments will be

---

[5] One explanation suggested for the spread of sovereign territorial institutions, that is important for our purposes here, is that it allowed respective jurisdictions, and thus limits to authority, to be specified precisely through agreement on fixed borders (Spruyt 1994).

reluctant to give up the advantages of the MNE; (2) given the global interests of the MNE subsidiaries can never respond single mindedly to the interests of any single jurisdiction; and (3) the network of the MNE cannot escape serving as a 'conduit' through which states exert influence on other states (Vernon 1981). A broader review of the literature of the sovereignty at bay era reveals four major interrelated sets of problems that MNEs pose for states and the state system:

(1) the distribution of the costs and benefits associated with the MNE. This applies both within and across states;
(2) jurisdictional asymmetry between the state's control over geographic jurisdiction and the international network of the MNE and its affiliates;
(3) jurisdictional conflict and overlap and 'underlap', including the problem of extraterritoriality; and
(4) a weakening of national control over the economy and economic actors.

The issue of the distribution of costs and benefits arising from MNEs is certainly important, especially in the North–South context. However, most of the discussion of this issue revolves about transfers of resources, capabilities and/or power among states (or among groups within states) within the existing system. Furthermore, to the extent that the distribution of costs and benefits of multinational enterprise relates directly to my primary concern here, it is subsumed under the rubric of 'national control'. Thus, my discussion will thus focus on the last three issues.

## 7.3.1 Jurisdictional asymmetry

Over seventy years ago in an article about the League of Nations, *The Economist* (1930) argued that the 'supreme difficulty of our generation' results from economics and politics perpetually 'falling out of gear with one another'. While the world economy has been organized into a single 'all-embracing' unit, the international political system remains partitioned into sovereign national states. This asymmetry between economics and politics manifest when the centrally controlled, transnational, multinational enterprise confronts an international political order organized in terms of territorially sovereign states has given rise to what James Rosenau (1992) calls the problem of governance without government.

There is a lack of correspondence between the scope of the multinational enterprise and the jurisdictional reach of the nation-state either singularly or collectively. The MNE is not accountable to any authority which matches its ambit or which represents the aggregate interests of all of the countries in which it operates (Vernon 1971). The MNE's ability to operate as a worldwide system combined with the limited view and extent of authority of any national government creates asymmetries of both information and jurisdiction.

While MNEs are, in theory, responsive to all of the national jurisdictions in which they operate, in practice, none has complete control, either individually or collectively. No single territorial state has sufficient information to fully comprehend the operations of an MNE. Furthermore, authority cannot be summed across jurisdictions; each nation attempting to regulate the MNE through the portion 'residing' within its borders may not provide sufficient leverage over the firm as a whole to achieve its policy objectives.

Many of the authors writing in reaction to the first wave of MNE investment dealt with this topic directly. In a well-known article, Ball (1968: 164) argued that there is a 'lack of phasing between the development of our archaic political and modern business structures', that the political boundaries of nation-states are too constricted to allow the mobilization and deployment of the factors needed for production and consumption. He went on to note the problem of governance of the international firm, given the asymmetry between its scope and that of national authorities, and called for the evolution of some sort of supranational political structure. Recognizing that was not likely, he suggested 'denationalizing' MNEs as a second-best solution, governing world corporations through a treaty-based international companies law administered by an international institution.

## 7.3.2 Jurisdictional conflict and extraterritoriality

The subsidiary of an MNE is both a local corporation—typically incorporated under local law—subject to the same rights and responsibilities as any other national firm *and* a unit in a multinational network under the control of its headquarters. In Vernon's (1977: 193) words, 'each affiliate includes the elements of a double personality. It is an entity created under the laws of the country in which it operates, responsive to the sovereign that sanctions its existence. Yet at the same time, as a unit in a multinational network, each affiliate must be responsive to the needs and strategies of the network as a whole.'

This duality was at the root of much of the MNE–state conflict during the sovereignty at bay era. Citizens of one country 'resident' in another create situations of jurisdictional overlap or conflict: do the tax codes, regulations, or laws of the home or host country apply? Multinational networks also served as vehicles facilitating the extraterritorial reach of one state into the domain of another: conduits or transmission belts 'through which the power of one sovereign state is projected into the territory of another' (Vernon 1977: 177).

In an early proposal for a 'GATT' for multinational firms, Paul Goldberg and Charles Kindleberger (1970: 298) concluded that 'fortunately' the substantial and recurring problems posed by the international corporation were limited to taxation, antitrust policy, balance of payments, export controls, and securities regulation. They note that 'Each has a common denominator: the international corporation is either unregulated, having slipped between the cracks of national jurisdictions, or is cabined by the overlapping regulation of two countries having varying political or economic goals.'

As Bergsten, Horst, and Moran note, 'Perhaps the messiest issue confronting policy makers is allocating taxable income within the multinational enterprise.' To some extent, jurisdictional conflict is a zero-sum game, 'US tax gains must come from the multinationals or from foreign tax authorities' (1978: 211). Furthermore, the problem of 'underlap' is certainly significant; corporate tax revenues as a proportion of the total have fallen over the past decade, at least in part due to the difficulty of collecting taxes from MNEs.

Antitrust actions are also responsible for jurisdictional conflict. Differences between American and European law, for example, led to conflicts over actions of subsidiaries of US multinational firms. Perhaps more important, American courts have held that non-nationals can be held responsible for acts committed outside of US territory that restrict competition in the US market. This has led to situations—the ICI–Dupont case, for example—where American courts required action which the British courts then prohibited (Rubin 1971). (Anti-trust conflicts have abated over time as American and European competition policies have converged.)

Last, attempts to extend a country's jurisdictional reach extraterritorially through a multinational firm's networks were responsible for a great deal of the conflict 'caused' by multinational firms during the 1960s and 70s. Jack Berhman, for example, found that twelve of sixteen conflicts among Atlantic countries arising from the activities of MNEs involved American attempts to apply The Trading with the Enemy Act extraterritorially.[6] Similarly, David Leyton-Brown found that most of the sixty-one public conflicts he studied in Canada, Britain, and France involving multinationals involved extraterritoriality (both were cited in Nye Jr. 1974).

While the combination of internal sovereignty and mutually exclusive jurisdiction gives the state control over everything that transpires within its borders, or within its territory, international law extends that jurisdiction to the actions of nationals abroad (Rubin 1971: 11). Thus 'international law is

---

[6] For a review of American attempts to apply the Trading with the Enemy Act extraterritorially see Kobrin (1989).

considered to give a state jurisdiction over conduct within its own territorial borders, and over the actions of its own nationals anywhere'. That being said, territoriality is generally considered to prohibit *extraterritorial* acts, the prosecution of foreigners for acts committed outside of a state's territories (Craig 1970).

Although the US government accepts the principle of territoriality, it also argues that it has jurisdiction over its nationals anywhere, and that control—and ownership—determine nationality (Craig 1970). That ambiguity makes determining the 'nationality' of the subsidiary of a multinational firm problematic, and raises questions about whose law applies.

The case of Fruehauf in France is not atypical. In 1964 the Treasury Department learned that Fruehauf's French subsidiary had entered into a contract to supply trailers to a French truck manufacturer for assembly and eventual delivery to China. At that time US commercial relations with the PRC were prohibited by the Trading with the Enemy Act, but were both legal and encouraged in France. Treasury demanded that the American headquarters of Fruehauf force their subsidiary to withdraw from the contract, under penalty of the law.

Several points are of interest here. First, France considered the subsidiary a French firm subject to French law and policy while the American government clearly considered it subject to its law and policy. Second, the US Government did not go to the subsidiary directly, but exercised its control over the headquarters located within the borders of the US and thus exercised its will through the hierarchical structure of the MNE. While there is no question that Freuhauf's corporate headquarters is a US firm within US jurisdiction, from a French point of view, the US government implemented its law extraterritorially through the subsidiary of a multinational.

While the results of this particular case were mixed, the Trading with the Enemy Act was applied regularly from the 1950s to the 1970s and in most instances US multinationals prevented their subsidiaries from doing business with proscribed countries (Kobrin 1989; Rubin 1971).[7] Efforts to apply American law through the network of MNEs culminated in the early 1980s when the Reagan administration attempted to prevent construction of a Soviet natural gas pipeline into Western Europe through the extraterritorial enforcement of export controls, using both FDI and licenses as vehicles. While the episode caused serious problems for a number of firms, it ended in failure due to the united and vigorous opposition of most European countries (Kobrin 1989). (The Helms-Burton legislation which attempts to sanction Canadian and

[7] Using multinational networks to extend jurisdictional reach extraterritorially was not limited to the US, or even to headquarters countries. During the 1973 oil embargo, for example, Saudi Arabia and some of the other Arab states were able to use the networks of the oil multinationals to prevent virtually any Arab oil from being delivered to the boycotted countries (Nye Jr. 1974).

European firms doing business with Cuba certainly indicates that the US Government has not given up trying to extend its reach abroad.)

### 7.3.3 National control

The emergence of MNEs has diminished state control over both economies and economic actors. To some extent, the loss of national control over the domestic economy resulted from increasing interdependence; multinational enterprise can be seen as effect rather than cause in that regard, as a vehicle rather than prime mover. One can argue that it is developments in the technology of communications and transport as well as increases in the scale, pace, and complexity of product and process technology that account for both interdependence and the MNE. That it is really the former—including the emergence of a global financial system—that accounts for diminished national control over economic actors and economic policy. In Robert Gilpin's words 'national economies [are] enmeshed in a web of interdependence from which they cannot escape', (1975).

Be that as it may, the multinational enterprise is the primary agent of interdependence and its increasing importance does limit state control over the domestic economy. As I have argued elsewhere (Kobrin 1997), MNEs organize international economic transactions through internalization; MNEs are the vehicle through which production has become international and factors of production such as management, labor, and technology have become mobile across borders. That combined with the increasing linkages between trade and foreign direct investment diminishes the ability of national governments to control domestic economies and achieve economic policy objectives (Stopford and Strange 1991).

As Vernon observed, the twentieth century was one in which governments took on the task of promoting the welfare of their citizens. In modern societies, political leaders find themselves dependent on the private sector, on the nation's enterprises, to achieve this and other goals. As noted above, however, there is a marked asymmetry in scope of operations and objectives between the nation-state and the MNE, between the 'global strategies of MNEs designed to advance corporate profitability and growth, and the strategies of governments intended to promote the economic and social welfare of their citizens' (Dunning 1991). Put simply, the MNE is global and the nation-state local.

Thus, multinational enterprises are transnational organizations which have their own interests which may or may not be closely related to the interests of any or all of the nations in which they are resident (Huntington 1973). There may well be an inherent conflict between the state attempting to achieve its objectives through the operations of private sector firms and the broader objectives of the MNE. As Vernon (1977: 15) notes well, 'Whenever the loyalty and commitment of a substantial enterprise in the economy seems ambiguous, tension is unavoidable.'

While there is no reason to assume that the MNE and a state will have conflicting objectives, there is no reason to assume that they will be identical or even overlap substantially. They are very different entities. Given the increased reliance of governments on the private sector to accomplish economic objectives, the emergence of multinational enterprise has resulted in a higher probability of a divergence between state and firm objectives. Increased economic interdependence and the system optimizing nature of the MNE has reduced the degree of control that governments exert over their economies and economic actors.

## 7.3.4 The modern state system and the MNE

While internal sovereignty is absolute in theory, it is rarely absolute in practice. The 'exclusive right to determine the framework of rules, regulations and policies within a territory' is compromised every time a state enters into a bilateral treaty or agrees to conform to the rules of an international organization. While, again in theory, the absence of a central authority makes each state the final arbiter of whether or not it will abide by treaties and remain in an international organization, the interdependent world economy of the last half of the twentieth century imposed serious constraints on states' room for maneuver (Keohane and Nye 1977).

External sovereignty, on the other hand, is much closer to an absolute construct. In the modern interstate system, economic and political governance are a function of borders and geographic jurisdiction. The defining principles of the system are mutually exclusive territorial sovereignty and mutual recognition by like units. Compromising external sovereignty compromises the state and the system.

The question at hand is whether the rapid growth of multinational enterprise from the late 1950s through the early 1980s—what I have called the sovereignty at bay era—actually compromised formal sovereignty. There is certainly a point where degree becomes kind, where the erosion of autonomy and control over an economy and economic actors renders the presumptive right of states as the supreme authority within their borders relatively meaningless. While the line between autonomy and internal sovereignty is diffuse, I do not believe that it was crossed by the traditional MNE.

To the contrary, MNEs of the sovereignty at bay era actually reinforced the core values of the post-Westphalian state system. Legally, there is no such thing as a multinational corporation as incorporation is possible only under national law. The multinational enterprise 'must content itself with stringing together corporations created by the laws of different states' (Vagts 1970: 740). The MNE is an assemblage of national corporations and thus a creature of national jurisdiction, the corporation's very existence 'conditioned upon a grant from the state' (Berle and Means 1939).

The nationality and control of the vast majority of MNEs remained national rather than multinational (Hu 1992). During the era in question, transnational actors (i.e. a MNE) linked interest groups (i.e. national sub-sidiaries) across borders but were dependent on access to territory to do so. In that sense they are sovereignty affirming: 'The national governments who control access will thus be strengthened . . . the growth of transnational oper-ations does not challenge the nation-state but reinforces it' (Huntington 1973). Similarly, Krasner (1995) argues that transnational actors require the basic structure of the modern state system, multiple centers of authority, to exist.

In conclusion, the primary problems raised by the MNE during the sover-eignty at bay era were those of jurisdictional conflict (underlap and overlap) and extraterritoriality; they invloved conflict between territorially defined states. The question was whose jurisdiction, whose laws and regulation, applied? While that makes the principle of mutually exclusive territoriality more difficult to apply in practice, it certainly does not make it less valid. MNEs remained dependent on access to territory to function and on national jurisdiction for their legal identity.

The problem posed by the traditional MNE is one of national regulation of international phenomena and certainly is not new. The various attempts at governance of the MNE over the last three decades have involved interna-tional cooperation among sovereign states and international organizations that are comprised of sovereign states as members. These certainly include the various attempts at the United Nations and OECD to develop codes of conduct for MNEs and the ill-fated Multilateral Agreement on Investment (MAI) negotiated in the mid-1990s (see Brewer and Young 1998; Kobrin 1998). All of these efforts represent attempts to exert some degree of control over the MNE through international action. Again, the issue here is control and autonomy rather than sovereignty.

I now ask whether globalization has changed this conclusion. Whether 'the sovereignty of the nation state [has] remained intact while the autonomy of the state has altered, or has the modern state actually faced a diminution of sovereignty in the face of the globalization of politics?' (Held, McGrew, Goldbaltt, and Perraton 1999: 52).

# 7.4 GLOBALIZATION AND THE MNE

The world in which the traditional MNE found itself was international rather than global, a profoundly geographic world of territoriality and borders.[8] An international economy is unambiguously *modern*; it involves relations between sovereign units of the post-Westphalian state system and hierarchically structured, often vertically integrated, discrete economic actors.

International transactions are cross-border economic and political interactions which assume the existence of clearly defined, delineated, and separable national markets and nation-states (Kobrin 1998). The expansion of MNEs during the sovereignty at bay era was consistent with this framework: most MNEs are national firms with a clear center or home country which engage in international operations and require access to territory to function.[9]

Globalization is difficult to define precisely. As David Held *et al.* note, it is in danger of becoming the cliché of our times: a 'big idea which encompasses everything from global financial markets to the Internet but which delivers little substantive insight into the contemporary human condition' (1999: 1). It is important to note that globalization transcends economics, it includes social, cultural, and political processes which are enmeshed in a larger 'global' order; forms of social, political, and economic organization beyond the pale of the state (Albrow 1997).

Globalization implies both deep integration and interconnectedness; networks of relationships between a large number of heterogeneous social, cultural, political, and economic organizations. 'The spatial reach and density of global and transnational interconnectedness weave complex webs and networks of relations between communities, states, international institutions, non-governmental organizations, and multinational corporations which make up the global order' (Held *et al.* 1999: 27).

I have argued elsewhere that globalization represents a fundamental change in the mode of organization of the world economy (and world politics) that compromises territorial sovereignty, a systemic change comparable in scope to the emergence of the post-Westphalian state system in Europe in the seventeenth century (Kobrin 1997, 1998). The question here is whether the MNE—which is both a cause and effect of globalization—compromises territorial sovereignty to the point where the phrase 'sovereignty at bay' is

---

[8] The concept of international affairs is relatively recent, dating from the late 18th century; it was not relevant before the emergence of territorially defined nation-states. The *Oxford English Dictionary* attributes the first use of the term *international* to Bentham in 1780 in a discussion of international jurisprudence in which he explicitly states that the word is a new one.

[9] Some of the material in this section is drawn from Kobrin (1997).

meaningful literally. MNEs in a global world economy impact the modern interstate system and sovereignty in multiple ways, all interrelated:

(1) MNEs are agents of deep economic integration and the internationalization of production;
(2) a dramatic increase in the scale of technology in many strategic industries renders minimal effective market size larger than that of even the larger national markets;
(3) networks are replacing hierarchies and markets as modes of economic integration;
(4) non-territorial networks are developing into a transnational 'civil' society linking a variety of economic, social, and political actors electronically. MNEs represent nodes of private authority in the international system; and
(5) markets are migrating to cyberspace or some combination of physical and virtual space.

## 7.4.1 Deep integration

By the late 1990s, 60,000 Transnational Corporations with over 500,000 foreign affiliates accounted for about 25 per cent of global output. The United Nations Programme on Transnationals concluded that 'international production...is at the core of the process of globalization' (UNCTAD 1999: xvii, xix). Deep integration and mutual interdependence are a reality; the internationalization of production implies that MNEs coordinate international economic flows. It would be difficult, if not impossible, to disentangle the complex transnational production networks of the MNE in order to allow a state to exert a significant degree of control over the system.

With the internationalization of production, political-economic emphasis has shifted from trade to investment and thus, from border controls to the domestic regulatory framework at large, blurring the line between 'domestic' and 'international' to the point where the distinction may no longer be meaningful. Everything from environmental to health and safety regulations affect both international as well as domestic investment and can, and have, been taken as constraints on 'trade' or restrictions on international competitiveness.

In 1991 John Stopford and Susan Strange (1991: 1) argued that upheavals in the international political economy had resulted in a mutual interdependence which limits state's options; 'firms have become more involved with governments and governments have come to recognize their increased dependence on the scarce resources controlled by firms'. Again, the issue here is whether deep integration has reached the point where degree has become kind, where national autonomy and control have eroded to the extent that internal sovereignty has become problematic.

## 7.4.2  The scale of technology

In sectors such as semiconductors, aerospace, pharmaceuticals, biotechnology, or telecommunications, a competitive R&D budget cannot be sustained by sales in even the largest national market (Mytelka and Delapierre 1999). International expansion is a necessity if a firm is to fully amortize the enormous research and development expenses associated with rapidly evolving process and product technology. These dramatic increases in the cost, risk, and complexity of technology render national markets problematic both as the primary units of the state system and as vehicles for control over the economy and economic actors.

First, in these strategic sectors even the largest national markets are too small to be meaningful economic units; they are no longer the 'principal entities' of the world economy. National markets are *fused* transnationally rather than linked across borders. Put differently, in these industries the market, in the most fundamental sense, no longer coincides with the state.

Second, and as a result, states have become increasingly dependent on MNEs to maintain technological competitiveness. MNEs are required to integrate or fuse markets to achieve the scale necessary to support the development of technology. Attempts to exert control over MNEs may limit access to technology and negatively affect national competitiveness.

## 7.4.3  Networks and alliances

Increases in the scale of technology are one of the primary drivers of a significant change in the mode of organization of the world economy: the shift from hierarchical *Fordist*[10] multinational firms to networked alliances, many of which are not based on equity links. Increasingly, network metaphors are used to describe the emerging world economy: a transition from standardized mass production to flexible production, from vertically integrated, large scale organizations to disaggregation of the value chain and horizontally

---

[10]  See Harvey (1990) for a discussion of Fordism and post-modernity.

networked economic units (Michalet 1991; UNCTAD 1994). In Dunning's (1994) terms, hierarchical enterprises are being replaced by alliance capitalism.

A networked world economy entails a complex web of transactions rather than a series of dyadic or triadic cooperative arrangements between firms. A large multinational firm may well be involved in tens if not hundreds of alliances linking various parts of its organization with others. These webs of alliances are multilateral rather than bilateral and polygamous rather than monogamous (Dicken 1994).

Networks and alliances affect state control, autonomy, and sovereignty directly. As noted above, the vast majority of traditional, hierarchical MNEs are responsive to their headquarters government; even the most international have a clear center in terms of operations and management. That is not the case for alliances and emerging knowledge-based networks.

Networks are diffuse and relational rather than hierarchical. It is difficult, if not impossible, to locate the center and borders are diffuse and ambiguous. Many alliances are not equity based, but rather constellations of interacting companies or parts of companies—often on a project basis. It is far from clear which, if any, government represents the home country and whether any state can exert substantial regulatory control over these diffuse networks of firms. Alliances and other multinational networks may not be creatures of 'national jurisdiction'; incorporation under a national legal system and access to territory are much less critical than for MNEs during the sovereignty at bay era.

Firms (Nike is a classic example) may be disaggregated to the point where the firm approaches a name attached to a large number of subcontractors, a 'virtual' corporation (Cutler, Haufler, and Porter 1999). The degree of control or even knowledge of the firm's center, much less the home country government, over labor practices or environmental standards of subcontractors in other countries, for example, is questionable.

Mytelka and Delapierre (1999) argue that new, global, knowledge-based networked oligopolies are emerging in industries where technologies are characterized by very high costs and risks in research and development. Again, the impact of these new forms of organization is to disengage the market from the state (and from state control) and to increase dependence of the state on the MNE for technology and technological development.

## 7.4.4 MNEs, transnational actors, and global civil society

In their 1971 book Robert Keohane and Joseph Nye define transnational relations as 'contacts, coalitions, and interactions across state boundaries not controlled by the central foreign policy organs of governments' (Nye and Keohane 1971: xi). Transnational organizations are autonomous or quasi-autonomous actors in world politics; they command significant resources, extend their reach across national borders, and can influence world politics directly; that is, without the mediation of the state foreign policy apparatus. While there are a wide variety of transnational organizations, the prototype is certainly the multinational enterprise.

The increased salience of multinational enterprise (and other transnational actors) results in what James Rosenau has termed a dual system of sovereignty bound and sovereignty free actors coexisting together (Rosenau 1990). Significant transnational actors compromise the core principles of the modern interstate system: the supremacy of the state domestically and the idea of a system constructed in terms of, and limited to, mutual recognition by functionally equivalent units.

The importance of transnational actors, and global 'civil' society in general, has increased dramatically with the emergence of the Internet and the world wide web. Space and distance are no longer barriers to the linking of interest groups and advocacy organizations across borders: Greenpeace, Amnesty International, Neo-nazi hate groups, and terrorist organizations are all linked tightly via the Net. The successful opposition to the Multilateral Agreement on Investment (MAI) negotiated at OECD and much of the opposition to the World Trade Organization during the Seattle meeting in 1999 was organized electronically by very large numbers of geographically disparate groups over the Web (Kobrin 1998).

MNEs are only a part of this emerging world of relatively autonomous transnational actors. They are, however, an important part. Ronald Diebert (1997: ix) has characterized the post-modern world order as 'a place inhabited by de-territorialized communities, fragmented identities, transnational corporations, and cyber spatial flows of finance'; a world that is a pastiche of multiple and overlapping authorities (also see Kobrin 1998).

MNEs have emerged as a source of private authority in world politics. In many cases, the governance of international economic transactions falls under the provenance of the private sector, of MNEs, rather than sovereign states or international organizations; 'Private actors are increasingly engaged in authoritative decision-making that was previously the prerogative of sovereign states' (Cutler *et al.* 1999: 16).

There is no question that the emergence of significant transnational actors and a global 'civil' society have transformed the interstate system and directly affect the construct of sovereignty. They further blur the line between the domestic and the international, compromise the idea of states as the ultimate authority domestically, limit the importance of access to territory, and raise questions about the definition of significant actors in the international system.

## 7.4.5 MNEs and cyberspace

Markets, and MNEs, are migrating to cyberspace as electronic commerce grows rapidly in both the business to consumer and business to business spheres. We are entering an era when information in the form of an electronic book, a symphony, movie, software, or medical advice will be exchanged over the Internet for information in the form of electronic cash (Kobrin 1997).

Electronic supply networks are becoming common. General Motors, Ford, and DaimlerChrysler have announced plans for a multibillion dollar supply network (Covisent) that may grow to include both Renault and Nissan. Several large petroleum companies, including Shell, have also formed electronic supply networks.

While this is not the place for a complete exploration of the impact of the information revolution on states and the state system, it is clear that the movement of markets and MNEs to cyberspace will have serious implications for geographic jurisdiction and sovereign territoriality. If software, for example, is imported in the form of disks and manuals it is subject to border controls and tariffs. However, if it is transmitted digitally—downloaded from the Internet—control becomes problematic and autonomy is directly constrained.

The Indian software industry has evolved from sending Indian programmers abroad to work at a client's site (known as 'body-shopping') to satellite linkages through which programmers physically situated in India work directly on the client's host computer, wherever in the world it is located (Kobrin 2000). If an Indian programmer located in New Delhi edits a program on a computer in New York there is no question that economic value has been created. Did the transaction take place in India or the US? Which jurisdiction gets to tax it or control it? Does either government even know that this sort of transaction has taken place?

In a fundamental sense, cyberspace is inherently nongeographic, characterized by nonterritorial spaces that, to some extent, are subjective. Cyberspace destroys rather than weakens the significance of physical location (Post 1996: 159). It is difficult to map physical space onto cyberspace; Net addresses are relational organizational constructs and often do not reflect physical location. Servers routinely shift clients from 'location' to 'location' to balance loads; a buyer can log on to any server remotely. Following just three or four hypertext links removes any sense of physical location—one could be in Bangalore as well as Boston. The chief executive of Shell Services International discussing their Web-based electronic supply network was quoted as saying 'we don't actually know where we procure' (*Financial Times* 2000).

During the sovereignty at bay era the multinational enterprise was at the center of jurisdictional conflict. Most MNE–state conflict, however, involved questions of overlap and ambiguity; territorial jurisdiction, *per se*, was not at issue, rather the problem was sorting out when jurisdiction should be based on location or nationality. In the era of the Internet and electronic commerce the issue is not jurisdictional conflict, but whether the basic idea of territorial jurisdiction is still relevant.

# 7.5 SOVEREIGNTY@BAY

Strange (1996: 95) believes that 'the center of gravity in world politics has shifted ... from the public agencies of the state to private bodies of various kinds, and from states to markets and market operators'. She argues that the authority of the governments of all states has weakened as a result of technological and financial change and the integration of national economies into a single global economy.

The thesis of the first part of this paper is that while MNEs of the sovereignty at bay era may have compromised state autonomy and control, and while they may have facilitated jurisdictional conflict and extraterritorial reach, they did not compromise fundamentally formal sovereignty in either its internal or external sense. The question at hand is whether that conclusion still applies given the massive changes in the world economy subsumed under the rubric of globalization.

I believe that the answer is a qualified 'no'. I see no evidence that the nation-state will become obsolete, that other sources of allegiance and identity will replace it.[11] However, globalization is weakening territorial sovereignty to the point where economic and political governance based primarily on geographic jurisdiction may no longer be viable. The MNE is a primary actor in this process, it cannot be separated from globalization. It acts as both cause and effect, motivator and agent. Many of the changes wrought by economic globalization are made manifest through the strategy, structure, and operations of the MNE.

Degree has become kind; the attenuation of authority and control has compromised the idea of the state as the ultimate domestic authority. Strange (1996: 72) puts it well. She argues that the state as an institution is not disappearing, but rather the metamorphosis brought on by structural change in the world economy means that states are no longer entitled to make the exceptional claims they once did. 'It [the state] is becoming, once more as in

[11] See Appadurai (1996) for an argument that the state is becoming obsolete.

the past, just one source of authority among several, with limited powers and resources.'

The globalization of production has political as well as economic impacts: it transforms both the creation and distribution of wealth and 'the context in which, and the instruments through which, state power and authority are exercised' (Held *et al.* 1999: 281). The deepening of integration, fusion of markets, shift to networked organizations, and migration to cyberspace have dramatically changed the relationship between states and firms, lessen the importance of access to territory, and raise serious questions about the continued viability of economic governance exercised through territorially defined national markets.

Interdependence has deepened to the point where the costs of policy autonomy are prohibitive. More important, the networked and relational structure of MNEs and of the world economy makes it almost impossible for any state, or all states collectively, to disentangle the web. The sharp distinction between the domestic and international that was a fundamental characteristic of the modern political-economy has now blurred. In many instances, it is virtually impossible to distinguish between domestic and international production, actors, or policy. (Is where a product is made still a relevant question? Or the nationality of a networked strategic alliance?)

Furthermore, economic and political space no longer coincide. Markets are 'larger' than states and, more important, economies and economic actors (e.g. virtual firms) are increasingly nonterritorial. John Ruggie (1993: 172) puts it well, arguing that a nonterritorial 'region' has been created in the world economy, 'a decentered yet integrated space-of-flows, operating in real time' which exists alongside national economies. While these conventional 'space-of-places' (national economies) continue to engage in economic relations which are mediated by the state, 'in the non-territorial global economic region, however, the conventional distinctions between internal and external are once again problematic...'

The emergence of MNEs as transnational actors, and the rise of international civil society in general, challenges the idea that international politics is the sole province of sovereign states in the formal interstate system (Deibert 1997). MNEs are certainly not completely autonomous actors. However, they have enough autonomy to function as significant actors in the system. The idea of private political authority is no longer an oxymoron (Cutler *et al.* 1999).

Perhaps most important looking to the future is the emergence of the Internet and electronic commerce. One of the primary arguments for the continued viability of internal and external sovereignty was that MNEs (and other transnational actors) require access to territory to function. In that sense they were sovereignty affirming, reinforcing the core values of the post-Westphalian system.

The Net and electronic commerce render that argument problematic. Krasner, who has always argued for the dominance of states in the system, recognizes that technology has weakened the authority of states and the bargaining power that flows from the ultimate right to grant access to territory. In cases where technology facilitates 'disembodied transnational movements' state authority is weakened (Krasner 1995). (He does go on to argue that further erosion of state control is not evident.)

As noted above, geographic jurisdiction may not be meaningful in cyberspace. To the extent that markets migrate to cyberspace, and especially to the extent that digital transactions gain in importance, territorial sovereignty will not provide the basis for effective or efficient economic governance. That certainly raises questions about the viability of an interstate system constructed on the basis of mutually exclusive geography and the recognition of and by, and *only* of and by, like units.

The emerging world order is likely to involve a range of heterogeneous units in multiple, interwoven, and overlapping layers of governance. Effective economic (and political) governance may well involve governments, the private sector (MNEs), a broad range of civil society groups, and international organizations. The meaning of sovereignty may evolve to mean no more than a very prominent seat at the table in international negotiations. Furthermore, the line separating what is domestic and what is international is rapidly being erased in many issue areas.

States will not disappear and will certainly continue to play a major, if not the major role in the international order. That however, is not the same as saying that they will remain the supreme authority domestically or the only constituent units of the international system. This time around, sovereignty in terms of both domestic authority and mutually exclusive territoriality may really be 'at bay'.

## References

ALBROW, MARTIN (1997). *The Global Age*. Stanford: Stanford University Press.

ANDERSON, JAMES (1986). 'The Modernity of States', in Anderson, James (ed.), *The Rise of the Modern State*. Atlantic Highlands, NJ: Humanities Press International, Inc.

APPADURAI, ARJUN (1996). *Modernity at Large: Cultural Dimensions of Globalization*. Minneapolis: University of Minnesota Press.

BALL, GEORGE W. (1968). 'COSMOCORP: The Importance of Being Stateless', *The Atlantic Community Quarterly*, IV (Summer): 163–70.

—— (1967). 'The Promise of the Multinational Corporation', *Fortune*, 75 (June): 80.

BARKIN, J. S., and CRONIN, B. (1994). 'The State and Nation: Changing Norms and the Rules of Sovereignty in International Relations', *International Organization*, 48: 107–30.

BARNET, RICHARD J., and MULLER, RONALD E. (1974). *Global Reach: The Power of the Multinational Corporations*. New York: Simon & Schuster.

BERGSTEN, C., HORST, FRED THOMAS, and MORAN, THEODORE H. (1978). *American Multinationals and American Interests*. Washington, DC: The Brookings Institution.

BERLE, ADOLPH A., JR., and MEANS, GARDNER C. (1939). *The Modern Coporation and Private Property*. New York: The MacMillan Company.

BREWER, THOMAS L., and YOUNG, STEPHEN (1998). *The Multilateral Investment System and Multinational Enterprises*. Oxford: Oxford University Press.

CAMILLERI, JOSEPH, and FALK, JIM (1992). *The End of Sovereignty*. Cheltenham: Edward Elgar.

CRAIG, WILLIAM LAWRENCE (1970). 'Application of the Trading with the Enemy Act to Foreign Corporations Owned by Americans', *Harvard Law Review*, 85: 579–90.

CUTLER, A. CLAIRE, HAUFLER, VIRGINIA, and PORTER, TONY (1999). 'Private Authority and International Affairs', in Cutler, A. Claire, Haufler, Virginia, and Porter, Tony (eds.), *Private Authority and International Affairs*. Albany, NY: State University of New York Press.

DEIBERT, RONALD J. (1997). *Parchment, Printing, and Hypermedia: Communication in World Order Transformation*. New York: Columbia University Press.

DICKEN, PETER (1994). 'The Roepke Lecture in Economic Geography. Global Local Tensions: Firms and States in the Global Space-Economy', *Economic Geography*, 70: 101–20.

DUNNING, JOHN H. (1976). *American Investment in British Manufacturing Industry*. New York: Arno Press.

—— (1991). 'Governments and Multinational Enterprise: From Confrontation to Co-operation?', *Millennium*, 20: 225–44.

—— (1994). *Globalization, Economic Restructuring and Development*. Geneva: UNCTAD.

ECONOMIST, THE (1930). 'The Prospects of the League', (Oct. 11): 652.

FIELDHOUSE, D. K. (1986). 'The Multinational: A Critique of a Concept', in Alice Teichova, Maurice Levy-Leboyer, and Helga Nussbaum (eds.), *The Multinational Enterprise in Historical Perspective*. Cambridge: Cambridge University Press.

*Financial Times*, (2000). E-Procurement: A Network of Suppliers to be Woven on the Web, accessed electronically.

GILPIN, ROBERT (1975). *US Power and the Multinational Corporation*. New York: Basic Books.

GOLDBERG, PAUL M., and KINDLEBERGER, CHARLES P. (1970). 'Toward a GATT for Investment: A Proposal for Supervision of the International Corporation', *Law and Policy in International Business*, 2: 295–323.

HALL, RODNEY BRUCE (1999). *National Collective Identity: Social Constructs and International Systems*. New York: Columbia University Press.

HARVEY, DAVID (1990). *The Condition of Postmodernity*. Cambridge, Mass.: Blackwell Publishers.

HELD, D., and McGREW, A. (1993). 'Globalization and the Liberal Democratic State', *Government and Opposition*, 28: 265.

———— GOLDBALTT, DAVID, and PERRATON, JONATHAN (1999). *Global Transformations*. Stanford: Stanford University Press.

HU, YAO-SU (1992). 'Global or Stateless Corporations are National Firms with International Operations', *California Management Review*, Winter: 107–26.

HUNTINGTON, SAMUEL P. (1973). 'Transnational Organizations in World Politics', *World Politics*, 25 (April): 333–68.

HYMER, STEPHEN (1976). *The International Operations of Nation Firms: A Study of Direct Foreign Investment*. Cambridge, Mass.: MIT Press.

JARVIS, ANTHONY P., and PAOLINI, ALBERT J. (1995). 'Locating the State', in Camilleri, Joseph A., Jarvis, Anthony P., and Paolini, Albert J. (eds.), *The State in Transition: Reimagining Political Space*. Boulder, Colo.: Lynn Riener Publishers.

KEOHANE, ROBERT O. (1993). 'Sovereignty, Interdependence, and International Institutions', in Miller, Linda B., and Smith, Michael Joseph (eds.), *Ideas and Ideals: Essays in Honor of Stanley Hoffman*. Boulder, Colo.: Westview Press.

KEOHANE, ROBERT O., and NYE, JOSEPH S. (1977). *Power and Interdependence: World Politics in Transition*. Boston: Little, Brown & Co.

KINDLEBERGER, CHARLES P. (1969). *American Business Abroad: Six Lectures on Direct Investment*. New Haven: Yale University Press.

KOBRIN, STEPHEN J. (1997). 'The Architecture of Globalization: State Sovereignty in a Networked Global Economy', in Dunning, John H. (ed.), *Governments, Globalization and International Business*. Oxford: Oxford University Press.

—— (1998). 'Back to the Future: Neomedievalism and the Postmodern Digital World Economy', *Journal of International Affairs*, 51(2): 361–86.

—— (2000). 'Development After Industrialization: Poor Countries in an Electronically Integrated Global Economy', in Hood, Neil, and Young, Stephen (eds.), *The Globalization of Multinational Enterprise Activity and Economic Development*. New York: St Martin's Press, Inc.

—— (1997). 'Electronic Cash and the End of National Markets', *Foreign Policy*, (107 Summer): 65–77.

—— (1989). 'Enforcing Export Embargoes Through Multinational Corporations: Why it Doesn't Work Anymore', *Business in the Contemporary World*, 1 (2 Winter): 31–42.

—— (1998). 'The MAI and the Clash of Globalizations', *Foreign Policy*, (112): 97–109.

KRASNER, STEPHEN D. (1993). 'Westphalia and All That', in Goldstein, Judith, and Keohane, Robert O. (eds.), *Ideas and Foreign Policy*. Ithaca: Cornell University Press.

—— (1995). 'Power Politics, Institutions, and Transnational Relations', in Risse-Kappen, Thomas (ed.), *Bringing Transnational Relations Back In*. Cambridge: Cambridge University Press.

LENIN, V. I. (1970). *Imperialism, the Highest Stage of Capitalism*. Moscow: Progress Publishers.

LEVY-LEBOYER, MAURICE, and NUSSBAUM, HELGA (eds.), *Multinational Enterprise in Historical Perspective*. Cambridge: Cambridge University Press.

LILIENTHAL, DAVID (1960). 'The Multinational Corporation', in Melvin, Ashen, and Bach, G. L. (eds.), *Management and Corporations, 1985*. New York: McGraw-Hill.

MICHALET, CHARLES-ALBERT (1991). 'Strategic Partnerships and the Changing Internationalization Process', in Mytelka, Lynn K. (ed.), *Strategic Partnerships and the World Economy*. Rutherford, NJ: Fairleigh Dickenson Press.

MYTELKA, LYNN K., and DELAPIERRE, MICHEL (1999). 'Strategic Partnerships, Knowledge-Based Network Oligopolies, and the State', in Cutler, A. Claire, Haufler, Virginia, and Porter, Tony (eds.), *Private Authority and International Affairs*. Albany, NY: State University of New York Press.

NYE, JOSEPH S., JR. (1974). 'Multinational Corporations in World Politics', *Foreign Affairs*, 53(1, Oct.): 153–75.

—— and KEOHANE, ROBERT (1971). 'Transnational Relations and World Politics: An Introduction', in Keohane, Robert O., and Nye, Joseph S., JR. (eds.), *Transnational Relations and World Politics*. Cambridge, Mass.: Harvard University Press.

PENROSE, EDITH (1959). *The Theory of the Growth of the Firm*. Oxford: Oxford University Press.

POST, DAVID (1996). 'Governing Cyberspace', *The Wayne Law Review*, 43(1): 155–71.

REINICKE, WOLFGANG H., and WITTE, JAN MARTIN (1999). 'Globalization and Democratic Governance: Global Public Policy and Trisectoral Networks', in Lankowski, Carl (ed.), *Governing Beyond the Nation-State: Global Public Policy, Regionalism or Going Local*. Washington, DC: American Institute for Contemporary German Studies.

ROSENAU, JAMES (1990). *Turbulence in World Politics*. Princeton: Princeton University Press.

—— (1992). 'Governance, Order and Change in World Politics', in Rosenau, James N., and Czempiel, Ernst-Otto (eds.), *Governance without Government: Order and Change in World Politics*. Cambridge: Cambridge University Press.

RUBIN, SEYMOUR J. (1971). 'Multinational Enterprise and National Sovereignty: A Skeptic's Analysis', *Law and Policy in International Business*, 3: 1–41.

RUGGIE, JOHN GERARD (1983). 'Continuity and Transformation in World Politics: Toward a Neorealist Synthesis', *World Politics*, xxxv (2, Jan.): 261–85.

—— (1993). 'Territoriality and Beyond: Problematizing Modernity in International Relations', *International Organization*, 47 (1, Winter): 139–74.

SPRUYT, HENDRIK (1994). *The Sovereign State and its Competitors*. Princeton: Princeton University Press.

STOPFORD, JOHN, and STRANGE, SUSAN (1991). *Rival States, Rival Firms: Competition for World Market Shares*. Cambridge: Cambridge University Press.

STRANGE, SUSAN (1996). *The Retreat of the State: The Diffusion of Power in the World Economy*. Cambridge: Cambridge University Press.

STRAYER, JOSEPH R. (1970). *On The Medieval Origins of the Modern State*. Princeton: Princeton University Press.

UNCTAD (1994). *World Investment Report: 1993*. New York: United Nations.

—— (1999). *World Investment Report: 1999*. New York: United Nations.

VAGTS, DETLEV F. (1970). 'The Multinational Enterprise: A New Challenge for Transnational Law', *Harvard Law Review*, 83.

VERNON, RAYMOND (1971). *Sovereignty at Bay*. New York: Basic Books.

—— (1977). *Storm Over the Multinationals: The Real Issues.* Cambridge, Mass.: Harvard University Press.

—— (1981). 'Sovereignty at Bay: Ten Years After', *International Organization*, 35 (Summer): 517–29.

WALTZ, KENNETH (1969). *Theory of International Politics.* Reading, Mass.: Addison-Wesley.

# CHAPTER 8

## NATIONAL POLICIES AND DOMESTIC POLITICS

### DEBORA L. SPAR

IN 1945 Albert Hirschman published *National Power and the Structure of Foreign Trade*, a pathbreaking examination of the politics of trade. Set amidst the European intrigues of the 1930s, *National Power and the Structure of Foreign Trade* painstakingly demonstrated how countries could use trade to extract political and economic benefit from their trading partners. For Hirschman and the legion of scholars who followed in his footsteps trade was indeed economic statecraft, the continuation of politics by commercial means.[1] It was a way of advancing state interests and gaining allies; of using the flow of goods and services to create political dependency and enhance state power.

At the turn of the twenty-first century, such arguments seem outdated already, positively quaint in an era marked now by global capitalism and 'boundaryless' firms.[2] Yet despite the undeniable surge of international business, and despite a sweeping embrace of liberal economic policies, there is still more than a touch of relevance to Hirshman's argument and his work. Trade

---

[1] Other works in this vein include Hawtrey 1930; Fichte 1845–6; List 1991.
[2] See e.g. Ohmae 1990, 1995.

is still a political activity and the firms that conduct it are political actors. States still use trade to achieve noncommercial aims and firms can still get entangled in the pursuit of these goals.

Indeed trade, by its very nature, is a political event. Whenever firms move goods or services across international borders, they affect society on both sides of the transaction. They enhance industrial revenues, for example, or augment the comparative development of national economies or create dependencies—on resources, strategic inputs, or capital—that persist over time. Even though firms may have no explicit intentions along these lines, the impact is the same: by transferring resources and commercial activity across borders, firms also shift the distribution of rewards and power. And this, after all, is the very lifeblood of politics.

When international business takes the form of investment rather than trade, the effect is even more pronounced. For when firms from one country invest directly into the territory of another, they are physically transplanting the means of production from one place to another, taking with them the jobs, technology, taxes, and suppliers that their operation produces. The impact of this shift can be dramatic, so dramatic, indeed, that states frequently spend vast sums of money in an effort to woo multinational investors and make them stay.[3] This is a far cry from the situation that prevailed earlier in the twentieth century, when nations derided multinationals as invaders and often entangled them in years of negotiation and yards of red tape. Yet both reactions reveal how important foreign investment can be for a host country, and thus how closely these countries are bound to regulate, and monitor, and administer investment flows. In the abstract, of course, foreign direct investment looks rather bloodless. It is an aggregate flow of capital and technology across international borders, a simple transfer of resources from one location to another. Yet under the surface lurk the same issues that intrigued Hirschman, and the same political notes. Investment means a movement of wealth, a movement of people, a movement often of ideas or technology or culture. All of these movements have political ramifications and all, therefore, are potentially subject to the long arm of domestic policy.

Formally, the interaction between domestic policy and international business runs in two directions.[4] States erect policies that affect firms' ability to trade and invest across borders; and the actions of trading and investing firms affect the political climate of the states in which they do business. The relationship, of course, is interactive and changes over time: states influence firms, and firms influence states, and both operate simultaneously in a number of domestic and international arenas.[5] The present essay, though,

---

[3]  See e.g. Goodman, Spar, and Yoffie 1996; Spar 1998; Wells and Wint 1990.
[4]  See Milner and Yoffie 1989.
[5]  See Dixit and Pindyck 1994.

concentrates on just one piece of this complex arrangement. Arguing that international business is essentially, incontrovertibly political, it describes the range of state policies that can shape and constrain the behavior of firms. Specifically, it examines five different kinds of domestic policy: trade policy, foreign direct investment, capital controls, regulation, and competition policy. This list is by no means exhaustive. Indeed, there is a far wider set of policies that shape the environment in which firms trade and invest. Yet these are some of the most common policies to affect firms, and some of the most important. The first section of this essay thus describes how policies tend to emerge in each of these areas; what objectives they are often directed towards; and how they affect the course of international business. The second section then moves to the politics behind the policies—that is, to an examination of how the policies that affect international business are created and by whom. A concluding section examines the emerging role of transnational groups in shaping and defining a country's national policies.

# 8.1 Trade Policy

Of all the rules that impinge upon the conduct of international business, the rules of trade are perhaps the most obvious. Because trade so clearly crosses national borders and can affect a national economy so deeply, governments have nearly always tried to govern the trading economy and shape the performance of trading firms. While the recent advent of international institutions such as the GATT and WTO has blunted some of the sharper instruments of trade policy, governments nevertheless maintain a considerable arsenal of policy tools. They create rules that directly and indirectly affect the ability of firms to compete across borders.

At some level of abstraction, nearly any economic policy undertaken by the state can be seen as exerting an influence on trade. Any policy that affects relative costs, or demand, or labor markets can shift the international trading environment, favoring some firms at the expense of others. But below this broad macro level is a series of policies that target directly the conduct of trade. States use these policies for different ends, and with differing intensities. Sometimes their aim is explicitly to enhance the competitive performance of nationally based firms; sometimes, competitive advantage is wholly tangential to the state's policy aims. Whenever these policies are in force, however, firms contemplating either a trading relationship or a foreign investment need to investigate the commercial impact of these trading rules. Three kinds of rules demand particular attention: export controls, protectionism, and strategic trade policy.

# 8.2 EXPORT CONTROLS

Export controls rank among the oldest tools of trade policy. Ever since the early days of mercantilist trade, states have tried to limit, from time to time, the goods that producers can ship across their borders. Occasionally these controls serve an economic object, insulating the domestic economy from the inflationary impact of excess foreign demand. More often, however, controls serve a distinctly political purpose. They are designed to prevent a rival state from gaining access to key resources and technology, or to punish a state for some perceived wrongdoing. In both of these instances, export controls are employed as a 'force short of war', a way for the state to enhance its geopolitical aims without having to risk military confrontation.

Customarily, export controls fall into one of two related categories. Sometimes they are part of a standard policy of restriction: a government will compose a list of 'strategic' goods (computers or encryption codes or, in one case, buttons) and a matching list of countries to which the export of these goods is prohibited. Such was the structure of CoCom (the Coordinating Committee), an informal organization of the United States and its post-war allies that regulated the export of military technologies and strategic resources to the countries of the Soviet bloc.[6] In other instances, states impose specific sanctions or embargoes to protest the actions of a rival state. During the period of apartheid, for example, many countries prohibited their firms from exporting to South Africa. Politically motivated sanctions have also been applied to Chile (1970–3), El Salvador (1977–81), Iran (1979–81), and a host of other countries.[7]

Ideally, the aim of sanctions or export controls is to force the target country to change its behavior. In the process, however, these policies directly affect commercial conditions—in the target state, the sending state, and peripheral countries. For firms in the target, or recipient, state, the effects are obvious.

---

[6] For more on the history of export controls and CoCom, see Bergsten 1974; Mastanduno 1988 and 1992; and Bergenstein and Yoffie 1984.

[7] The most exhaustive study of sanctions and their efficacy is Hufbauer and Schott 1985.

Strategic imports are liable to disappear from the market, leaving importers and import-dependent firms at a loss, while massively increasing demand for locally available substitutes. Exporters from the sending states, meanwhile, will face an immediate decline in sales and the potential loss of long-term relationships. When the United States imposed sanctions against the Soviet Union in the early 1980s, for example, American farmers experienced a precipitous decline in grain exports and General Electric lost a $175 million contract to provide rotors to a planned Soviet gas pipeline. Such losses, though, can clearly be a boon for firms in peripheral states; when GE and other US firms were forced out of the pipeline deal, European competitors readily stepped in.[8]

Fortunately, sanctions are a relatively rare phenomenon. But for the firms affected, their impact can be dramatic. Firms need, therefore, to keep a careful watch on political events that could lead to sanctions or other export controls. If they deal in strategic goods, or sell to highly volatile states, they need to think carefully about how to hedge their operations and what to do in case sanctions are imposed. Otherwise, they are likely to get caught, as was Conoco in 1995, when President Clinton cited national security concerns to block a $1 billion deal to develop Iranian oil fields.[9] Firms also need to be aware of the political forces and particular rules that drive sanction policy; in the mid-1990s, a number of Canadian firms found themselves in violation of US law due to their trading activities with Cuba.[10] An absurd situation, perhaps, but also a highly uncomfortable one. Finally, if firms are caught by sanctions or seek to benefit from them, they need to gauge the probable longevity of the controls. A short 'signalling' episode deserves a very different response than does an extended period of commercial and political strain.[11]

# 8.3 PROTECTIONISM

Protectionist policies are a common feature of the international economy. All states employ protectionism in one guise or another; all firms have felt its

---

[8] The European firms were also torn, however, since the US government threatened to retaliate by denying exports to any firms that did not comply with the US-initiated sanctions. Eventually, the US government backed down. For a full story of this episode, see Jentleson 1986; and Crawford and Lenway 1985.

[9] Sanger 1995.

[10] See Farnsworth 1996.

[11] Numerous scholars have tried to understand when sanctions are most likely to succeed, and how long they are likely to endure. See e.g. Hufbauer and Schott 1985; and Martin 1992.

various effects. The challenge for managers is to understand as precisely as possible where protectionism lies, and how best to avoid or exploit its rules.

Sometimes protectionism is flagrant. In its oldest and most obvious form, protectionism is tariffs, quotas, and other mechanical barriers to trade. Because it wants to protect its domestic producers from the strains of international competition, or because it wants to nurture and support domestic production, the state imposes quantitative or price-based restrictions.[12] Foreign firms hoping to sell into the protected market either have to fit in under the requisite quota, or see the tariff included in the cost of their product. Both responses, presumably, damage the competitiveness of foreign firms relative to their domestically based competitors. A similar relationship holds for less direct forms of trade protection. Under international pressure to reduce tariffs and eliminate quotas, many states resort to more discreet means. They offer research funding or export credits to their own firms, or impose regulatory conditions that disadvantage foreign firms against their domestic rivals. Such 'nontariff barriers' are legion, and the subject of intense international acrimony. Germany's 'health code' for beer is said to bar foreign competitors, as is Italy's definition of precisely what constitutes pasta. Canada's regulation of cultural content limits penetration by US media firms, while Japan's impenetrable distribution system acts to impede the entry of foreign products and retail outlets.[13] Even rules that are entirely domestic in their intent can have subtle protectionist effects.

Yet protectionism, by itself, is not necessarily bad for firms. In fact, it often presents firms with distinct opportunities to mold and employ the rules to serve their own commercial interest. Consider the case of Lenzing AG, an Austrian rayon manufacturer that established an Indonesian joint venture in 1978. Like many developing countries at that time, Indonesia followed a strict policy of import substitution industrialization, levying high tariffs on all imported goods, and particularly on those essentials—such as clothing—that it hoped to develop internally. As the sole domestic producer of rayon, Lenzing was the happy beneficiary of Indonesia's protectionism. Between 1980 and 1994, revenues expanded by roughly 15 per cent each year. Similar examples abound. When Japan's automakers perceived an impending wave of protectionism in the United States, they invested aggressively and directly in the US market, pre-emptively leaping the tariff barriers and even increasing their total US market share. In related cases, the US imposition of quotas on Japanese television sets and steel proved a windfall for Korean manufacturers, who seized the market share left vacant by the restricted Japanese.[14]

[12] For a discussion of these various motives, see Chacholiades 1978; Goldstein 1988; and Yoffie 1983.
[13] For a particularly provocative argument of how the Japanese system discriminates against foreign firms, see Ballantine 1995.
[14] See Goodman, Spar, and Yoffie 1996.

# 8.4 STRATEGIC TRADE POLICY

Essentially, strategic trade policy is old-fashioned protectionism nudged to a higher theoretical and industrial level. It rests on a series of well-formulated propositions about the national advantages of protecting certain large and critical industries.[15] In these industries (such as semiconductors and aircraft) the presence of externalities and scale economies means that firms must be global to compete, and that only a handful of competitors will survive in the global marketplace. In these industries, therefore, trade approaches a zero-sum game. Either countries foster the growth of their own firms or they risk losing the industry entirely.

For firms in these industries, the politics of strategic trade policy are straightforward. If they want to compete, firms need to garner governmental support. In most cases, this support entails not only domestic assistance, but also a willingness to fight and negotiate at the international level. Thus the growth and globalization of the semiconductor industry saw the formation of a powerful and well-connected Semiconductor Industry Association in the United States, and the eventual negotiation of international agreements limiting Japanese sales of semiconductors in the US market.[16] Similarly, the growth and commercial success of Europe's Airbus Industrie has undeniably been facilitated by governmental credit, sales assistance, and ongoing negotiations at the international level. Note that in both of these cases, firms from related industries are also significantly affected: component suppliers and airlines feel the impact of aircraft policies; and computer manufacturers are influenced by restrictions on semiconductor sales. Just like firms in the 'strategic' sectors, therefore, they need to heed the politics of trade policy, gauging the rules that will emerge and responding strategically to them.

# 8.5 RULES OF FOREIGN DIRECT INVESTMENT

The second type of rules that affect the environment of international business are rules of foreign direct investment. These are rules that influence the

---

[15] For an excellent brief summary of the theoretical argument, see Krugman 1987 and 1990; and Tyson 1992.

[16] See Yoffie 1988.

conditions under which firms can invest directly in the territory of foreign states.[17]

Historically, the rules and context of foreign investment have been driven by conflict. Fearful of the economic and industrial power of foreign investors (and particularly of Western multinational corporations), many states in the nineteenth and early twentieth centuries kept exceedingly tight reins over the companies that invested in their territory. Investments were negotiated on a case-by-case basis and the state retained a unique ability to wrest further concessions from foreign investors once their capital had been sunk into the country and their technologies rendered obsolete by the passage of time.[18] States often also retained the right to expropriate or nationalize the property of foreign investors. Such occurrences were fairly common in the 1960s and 1970s.[19]

Recently, the use of such draconian measures has declined precipitously. Instead, hungry for the capital and technology of foreign firms, many states are anxiously competing to attract investors, offering them financial incentives and the promise of preferential treatment. This apparent about-face, however, does not mean that foreign investment has lost its political undercurrents, or that domestic rules no longer affect the environment for investing firms. Foreign investment remains inherently political, and rules can have a dramatic impact on the success of investing firms.[20]

Rules shape the investment climate in a number of ways. First, even as states increasingly welcome foreign investments, they still customarily restrict it. As of 1994, not a single country in the world permitted an unrestricted right of entry to all sectors and activities.[21] Many states maintain formal licensing procedures for foreign firms; most prohibit, or at least limit, investment in certain 'strategic' sectors. Japan, for example, limits foreign investment in the banking, insurance, radio, telecommunications, transport, fishing, and utilities sectors, and prohibits foreign firms from investing at all in its mining, oil, and gas sectors. The United Kingdom limits foreign participation in its radio, telecommunications, mining, fishing, and tourist sectors; it forbids foreign participation in its rail transport and public utility sectors.[22] Second, even

[17] The literature on foreign direct investment is vast. Some important recent works include Kuemmerle 1999; Gliberman and Shapiro 1999; Dunning 1998; Buckley and Casson 1998.

[18] This relationship between the state and the investor has been classified as the 'obsolescing bargain', and subjected to a tremendous amount of academic scrutiny and debate. See Vernon 1971; Wells 1982; Moran 1974; and Kobrin 1987.

[19] See Kobrin 1985.

[20] For an interesting and balanced appraisal of the politics behind foreign direct investment, see Graham and Krugman 1992; Vernon 1977; Moran 1974. For a more extreme view, see Barnet and Muller 1974; and Hymer 1976. A full compendium of materials is available in Gomes-Casseres and Yoffie 1993.

[21] United Nations 1994.

[22] From United Nations 1994.

where investment is permitted, it may nevertheless be conditional—on the participation of a local joint venture partner, the import of certain technologies, or a promise to manufacture for export. IBM's initial entry into Japan, for instance, was made contingent on its low-cost licensing of patents to Japanese firms.[23] More recently, in 1995, a dispute over technology transfer to China apparently cost Chrysler a potential $1 billion minivan deal.[24] In other cases, states can influence foreign investment through operational restrictions, such as limits on the employment of aliens and specific performance requirements.

On the other hand, states can also use the rules of foreign investment to attract and advantage particular firms. In general, most states now comply (at least in principle) with international guidelines on national treatment. That means that states promise not to discriminate against foreign, as compared with domestic, firms. Compliance with the international guidelines, however, does not prevent states from offering specific incentives to potential investors. And thus states regularly strike preferential deals. They can offer preferential treatment on taxes; improved access to infrastructural goods such as water, transportation links, and electricity; or assistance in securing an appropriate labor force. Sometimes this preferential treatment is bundled into special investment zones, such as Malaysia's 'multimedia supercorridor' or the export processing zones (EPZs) of the Philippines. Sometimes preferential treatment is offered on an *ad hoc*, negotiated basis. And often it is local officials, rather than the central government, who have the most to offer.

For firms contemplating a foreign investment, the restrictions and incentives on foreign investment operate similarly. They shift the playing field, favoring some deals and opportunities while disadvantaging others. They force the investing firms to think strategically about how to avoid the limits imposed by domestic law as well as how to reap the benefits that the law and particular circumstances are capable of providing. Consider the case of Gerber Products Company. In 1991, Gerber was contemplating the acquisition of Alima S. A., a Polish food processing facility. Having just recently broken from decades of communist doctrine and Soviet domination, Poland was eager for foreign investment and rapidly rewriting its rules of commerce. Gerber found itself in the midst of this political change. There was still a long and tedious process of investment review, an equally long list of officials who needed to approve various pieces of the deal, and general confusion about the tax incentives available to foreign investors. Yet rather than running from this chaos, Gerber's management used it to their advantage. They negotiated at various levels throughout the government, struck tough bargains, and won most of the rule-based concessions they desired. In the process, they realized

[23]  US Congress, Office of Technology Assessment 1993.
[24]  Wong 1996.

that their leverage lay in being first. Because Gerber was a high-visibility company with an apparent long-term interest in Poland, the Polish government was eager to package an attractive deal and structure its rules in a conciliatory fashion. Subsequent investors found the Polish government still responsive, but far less willing to negotiate the terms of their investment.[25]

In other cases, however, the politics of foreign investment can create a far more hostile environment and discouraging set of rules. Consider the United States in the late 1980s, when fear of Japan's growing economic prowess drove a heightened scrutiny of Japanese investment in the US market. In late 1986, Fujitsu fell victim to this scrutiny when it announced plans to acquire an 80 per cent interest in the Fairchild Semiconductor Corporation from its French parent, Schlumberger Ltd. The Committee on Foreign Investment in the United States (CFIUS), which investigated the matter, emphasized national security concerns, a rather dubious tack since the company was already under foreign ownership. Although CFIUS lacked the authority to block the sale, growing Defense Department involvement made all the parties increasingly uncomfortable. Under these circumstances, the investors' only options were either to leave the market or fight their battles directly with those who made the rules. And that is precisely what the Japanese firms did. Some, like Fujitsu, just left, while others marched in effect on Washington, launching a powerful, expensive, and ultimately successful lobbying campaign.

# 8.6 CAPITAL CONTROLS

At the end of World War II, nearly all countries imposed some level of control over the export of capital. Fearful of 'disequilibrating' swings in short term capital movements, they intermittently regulated how much capital investors could take abroad with them, and under what circumstances.[26]

In the 1990s, capital controls are far less common. Indeed, all developed countries allow free repatriation of capital invested abroad and, generally, the free transfer of profits and dividends from overseas subsidiaries.[27] In the

---

[25] For more on Gerber's investment in Poland, see Young and Spar 1993. For more on the general background of foreign investment in Poland, see Spar 1993.

[26] There is a voluminous literature on the progressive liberalization of capital controls among the developing countries, and the relationship between domestic policies and the increasingly global nature of capital markets. See e.g. Strange 1986; Kindleberger 1987; and Frieden 1991.

[27] United Nations 1994.

developing world, however, capital controls are more far prevalent. They constitute another area of rules that impinge upon the conduct of international trade and investment.

Essentially, countries use capital controls to buffer the domestic economy from the free-flowing forces of the international capital market. As this market grows in size and intensity, with over a trillion dollars streaming daily across national borders, developing countries occasionally find themselves caught between two opposing tensions. On the one hand, the globalization of capital flows reduces the efficacy of any unilateral rules on capital and risks isolating any country that attempts to stem or control the flow. On the other hand, though, the sheer force of the global market increases the financial vulnerability of a developing state.[28] After Mexico's peso collapse in 1995, repercussions swept across the developing countries, causing Morgan Stanley's emerging market index to fall 14.91 per cent in just two months.[29] The reverse situation is also possible. In 1996, Indonesia was overwhelmed by short-term capital flows and saw its money supply grow by a wholly unpredicted 30 per cent.[30] To blunt the impact of such external shocks, developing countries often maintain a series of controls on capital and foreign exchange flows. As of 1996, 92 of the 156 countries classified by the IMF as 'developing countries' restricted, to some degree, the use of foreign exchange for the purchase of goods and services. Of these countries, 130 maintained restrictions on capital account (i.e. financial) transactions.[31] While many of these controls are targeted most directly at short term, or portfolio, flows, they have a strong peripheral impact on flows associated with trade and foreign investment. They also tend to fall most heavily on foreign firms, since governments that grant licenses of foreign exchange typically distinguish between foreign and domestic applicants.

Where capital controls are in place, multinational firms need to include them as part of the strategic landscape, and respond to them accordingly. For countries that are economically volatile, firms also need to consider the possibility of dramatic policy shifts. Take the recent case of China. In the early 1990s, China strictly regulated the amount of hard currency that foreign investors were allowed to repatriate. While promising to liberalize these restrictions over time, the Chinese authorities never pronounced either their precise timetable for reform or their conception of full liberalization. Some firms, lured by China's burgeoning markets and promise of reform, assumed these controls would soon disappear, or at least that sufficient hard currencies could be procured from the country's handful of permitted 'swap markets'. Many of these companies soon found themselves at odds in China,

---

[28] For a further elaboration of this tension, see US Congress, Office of Technology Assessment (1993, 135–58).

[29] Flaherty 1995.          [30] Ali 1997.          [31] Vernon, Wells, and Rangan 1996.

scrambling not only to repatriate funds, but even to gather sufficient currency to purchase the imports needed for their production. Other firms understood the full complexity of China's currency system, as well as the political difficulties that were likely to squash any rapid attempts to dismantle it. Accordingly, once they decided to go to China they went explicitly for the long term. Rather than trying to maneuver around the currency controls, they made a strategic decision to reinvest all Chinese profits in China, building local supply networks and deferring repatriation until the business was fully self-sufficient and the currency controls lifted.

# 8.7 REGULATION

Unlike the rules of trade or foreign investment or capital controls, the rules of regulation do not adhere solely to transnational transactions. They are directed instead to the domestic economy, and to the mass of policy objectives that economic activity both facilitates and demands. Because these policies vary so widely across national borders, however, they are inherently important to the conduct of international business.

In theory, governments regulate in order to promote a public good or redress a public 'bad', known more formally as positive and negative externalities. They regulate to improve economic efficiency by correcting naturally existing market imperfections, or by controlling egregious excesses that the market has produced. They also regulate in order to guide market forces towards certain noneconomic, socially desirable ends: cleaner air, for example, or more effective medical treatments. To achieve these societal goals, regulators employ a multitude of policy tools: price caps; rate regulation; wage controls; health and safety standards; environmental reviews. In theory, again, regulators choose from among these options those policies that best advance their economic and social goals. In practice, regulatory policy is also often subject to the usual pulling and hauling of politics. Rather than running from regulators (as is often the impression), firms or other interested parties petition the state for regulations that advance their own position. This results in the well-documented practice of 'regulatory capture'.[32]

Whether driven by public goods or political maneuvers, however, the rules and politics of regulation affect foreign firms in a number of different ways.

---

[32] Analysts of this phenomenon include Stigler 1971; Posner 1974; Peltzman 1976; and Wilson 1974.

First, they establish which specific industries are subject to regulation, and thus which firms will need to participate in a direct and ongoing relationship with the state. In some industries (pharmaceuticals, food processing, health care services) regulation is nearly universal. In others (mining, entertainment, retailing, telecommunications), firms are heavily regulated in some countries and left to their own devices elsewhere. Thus, firms that are accustomed to working in a regulated environment in one country may find themselves in a wholly unregulated and competitive market in another country. And firms accustomed to the free market may find themselves in a heavily controlled environment once they cross national borders. In either case, foreign investment demands a considerable amount of commercial adaptation. Firms that thrive in an unregulated environment will have to learn to play by a different and more constraining set of rules, and to develop political ties with their new regulatory authorities. Firms that have grown up in a regulated market, by contrast, may suffer from the full force of competition and the absence of familiar regulators.

Second, even when firms move from one regulated market to another, the forms of regulation can still be radically different. Take the pharmaceutical industry. In the United States, it is regulated through a combination of patents, approval procedures, and strictly defined distribution. To sell prescription drugs, pharmaceutical firms must obtain the necessary patents, gain approval from the Food and Drug Administration, and then market their product to doctors, hospitals, and health maintenance organizations. When US pharmaceutical firms go to China, however, they encounter an entirely different regulatory structure. Patent laws are far less effective and 'theft' of prescription formulas quite common. Approvals come from two agencies, and the dispensing of drugs occurs not only through hospitals and doctors' offices, but also at a multitude of factory- and enterprise-run clinics. These differences in regulatory policy compel US pharmaceutical firms to adopt distinctly different commercial strategies in the Chinese market. They can still enter the market and do business there, but only if they reverse quite substantially their normal mode of operation.

# 8.8 ANTITRUST AND COMPETITION POLICY

A final set of rules that impinge upon firms' foreign activities are rules of competition and antitrust. These are rules that provide the basic guidelines for market activity, rules that are deeply embedded in the political culture of a country and thus tend to vary widely across national borders.

The foundation for antitrust and competition policy lies with the economics of industrial organization and the belief that market forces can occasionally produce anti-competitive outcomes.[33] Developed first in English common law and expanded during the heyday of the late nineteenth century American trusts, antitrust policy seeks to maintain the efficacies of competition by keeping capitalist firms from growing too large or working too closely with their would-be rivals. Essentially, antitrust policy is intended to prevent firms from exerting undue control over the markets in which they operate. It customarily targets several kinds of presumed anti-competitive behavior: predatory pricing; excessive market concentration; and collusion.[34]

Like regulation, antitrust is a form of state intervention directed almost entirely at the domestic market. States employ antitrust to gain what they believe to be a more efficient use of national resources, higher levels of domestic growth, greater stability in prices, output, or employment, or a more equitable distribution of incomes. Sometimes governments also just use antitrust as a means to limit the reach of firms they perceive as being too large or powerful.[35] None of these motives has any explicit implication for trading or investing firms. Insofar as antitrust affects the domestic environment of business, however, it peripherally affects any foreign firm operating within the domestic market. It forces foreign firms to play by particular and often unfamiliar rules of competition.

Arguably, the greatest impact is felt by foreign firms that move into the US market. Because US antitrust rules are amongst the most stringent in the world and because they are applied with varying levels of intensity by successive administrations, they are a constant source of frustration for foreign firms that operate in the US market. In 1994, for instance, the US Justice Department brought suit against Pilkington plc, a British glass making firm. The Justice Department accused the British firm of monopolizing a key technology through the use of restrictive licensing agreements. Even though these practices had little effect on the US market, the Justice Department claimed jurisdiction on account of Pilkington's 80 per cent ownership of Libby-Owens-Ford, a US-based firm.[36] In a more spectacular and protracted

[33] Antitrust policy is thus deeply rooted in both political and economic theory. For more on this point, see Baron 1993. For more on the economic theory itself, see Posner 1976.

[34] There is a voluminous literature on the origins, intent, and implementation of antitrust policy. For a standard legal account, see Areeda 1967; for a simpler overview, see Shenefield and Stelzer 1993. More controversial works include Bork 1978.

[35] This is especially prevalent in the United States, where the Justice Department has occasionally been accused of using size, in and of itself, as an indicator of anti-competitive behavior.

[36] See Bradsher 1994. For other attempts by the US government to extend the extraterritorial jurisdiction of its antitrust policies, see Vernon and Spar 1989.

case, the Justice Department has tried for decades to prosecute DeBeers, the South African diamond company that oversees the world's most successful cartel.[37] Well aware of the long arm of US law, however, DeBeers has become somewhat of an expert on US antitrust policy, and has carefully structured its entire organization to avoid any entanglement with the US rules. Although the United States is the world's largest market for the diamonds DeBeers produces, the company has no corporate presence on US soil.

While the American cases present perhaps the starkest examples, competition policies in other countries also affect the prospects of foreign firms. And once again, the prospects are not necessarily bleak. Sometimes, antitrust and competition policy can provide dramatic opportunity for competitive advantage. In the European Union, for example, tightly enforced competition policies in the telecommunications and banking sectors have provided a windfall for foreign firms. In India, competition policies enacted since the mid-1990s promise to break the stranglehold of large local enterprises and open the way for enterprising foreign entrants. In both of these cases, the lessons are clear: changes in the rules of competition can fundamentally alter the relative competitiveness of firms operating within a given market.

# 8.9 DOMESTIC POLITICS

When firms encounter protectionism, or capital controls, or environmental regulation, it can often seem as if these policies have just descended from the heavens. Either that, or policies appear as some impenetrable relic, the remnant of earlier objectives or long-forgotten whim. And sometimes they are. Yet generally, the policies that affect international business are generated through some kind of a rational process and by particular, often even predictable, sources. They are created, most importantly, by *politics*—by the struggle for power and interests that characterizes nearly all human societies. If firms want to understand the policies that are liable to affect their businesses, they need to consider as well the process by which these policies are established. They need, in other words, to understand the domestic politics of the countries in which they trade or invest.

So where do policies come from? And how are they created? It depends. In some countries, according to some scholars, rules emerge through a rational

---

[37] For more on DeBeers and the international diamond cartel see Spar 1994.

and predictable process of rent-seeking. Various interest groups express their preferences to a political system which arbitrates their interests and rewards those with the most votes, the greatest clout, or the staunchest coalition.[38] Though this view of the political process is stark and almost certainly over-simplified, it rings true in many cases, especially those concerning the forma-tion of trade policy in democratic states.[39] Recall the Cuban trade embargo described above. Why does the United States persist in sanctioning trade with Cuba? Largely because there is a powerful domestic lobby in favor of the sanctions, and a relatively uncommitted and uncoordinated group of oppon-ents. Precisely the reverse pattern characterizes US trade policy towards China. Here, the strongly held interests of large and diverse domestic firms consistently overwhelm the narrower interests of human rights and (occa-sionally) labor groups. To track the likely outcome of trade policy in either of these cases, one would need only to follow the interest group politics that surround them.

In other instances, rules spring much more directly from the will and power of the central leadership. For decades, policy in China was essentially the political desires of Chairman Mao; after his death, the mantle passed to Deng who, without Mao's monomaniacal fervor, nevertheless set the rules for China. Accordingly, analysts of China during this time focused almost ex-clusively on the leader's pronouncements and the personal cohort that sur-rounded him. For these, they knew, were the source of China's rules. A similar relationship holds whenever power concentrates in a single personality or faction: Stalin's Russia; Qaddafi's Libya; Hussein's Iraq; Suharto's Indonesia. If firms want to understand what drives the business environment in these countries, they need to understand the interests and desires of the leadership. If they want to modify the rules to suit their own interests, they need to go directly to the leader.

Such excessive concentrations of power, however, are increasingly rare. In most countries, power is split among various groups and agencies, and rules emerge from a continuous bargaining among them—from the 'pulling and hauling that is politics', to borrow Graham Allison's memorable phrase.[40] The outcomes of these struggles depend on the institutional structure of the various agencies and the relative weights of power distributed among them. In the United States, for instance, some rules are controlled almost entirely by particular agencies (the FCC for broadcast television; the Justice Department for antitrust) while others (particularly trade policy) are more susceptible to legislative and electoral politics. In Japan, by contrast, the lines of bureaucratic

[38] The outlines of so-called 'public choice theory' are laid out in Downs 1957; Buchanan and Tullock 1962; and Brown 1974.
[39] For more specific discussion of trade issues, see Baldwin 1986; Bauer, Pool, and Dexter 1972; Cline 1984; Destler, Odell, and Elliott 1987; Destler 1986; Lavergne 1983; Milner 1988.
[40] Allison 1999.

discretion are both broader and more clearly demarcated. Powerful agencies such as MITI and MOF have, for decades at least, been essentially removed from political vacillation and armed with rule-making and enforcement capabilities. For decades, therefore, firms that traded with or invested in Japan maintained the closest ties they could with these agencies, and watched carefully for any changes in their regulatory agenda.

A very different view of the rule-making process comes from left of the mainstream, from a band of scholars associated either with Marxism or with the expanding field of 'critical legal studies'.[41] Though they vary widely in the scope and focus of their inquiries, these scholars essentially argue that rules follow power and that power, more often than not, clusters around wealth. Rules, these scholars argue, do not emerge from a tussle among interest groups, or a personal agenda, or a bureaucratic process: they are simply set by those with an ability to control policy and a desire to maintain their own privileged position. It is easy to dismiss such claims as ideologically motivated, rather than empirically drawn. But in certain cases they ring true. Consider the United Fruit Company (UFC) and its successor, Chiquita Brands. For years, UFC was an indomitable force throughout the banana-producing world. It wrote the rules that met its needs and enforced them through local alliances and the strong arm of US diplomacy. So great was the company's power that it gave rise to the term 'banana republic'—an apt description for most of the region in which UFC held sway. Similar allegations have periodically been made against the US multinational oil majors, although the data here is more jumbled, and the rule-making story harder to substantiate. Nevertheless, it does seem clear that in some places and under some circumstances, clout can carry the rules. This possibility raises both obstacles and opportunities for foreign firms.

Another possibility that firms must consider is the paradoxical chance that rules simply won't matter, or even exist. Though such circumstances are rare, they do occur. Sometimes, countries or even industries stumble through stretches of anarchy, times when the rules that normally prevail are under attack, or in flux, or incapable of enforcement. In the aftermath of communism, for example, Russia underwent a massive legal and political transformation. The central institutions of the old regime—the overarching authoritarian party, the vast and centrally controlled bureaucracy, the network of state-run factories and collective farms—were dismantled as newly elected leaders strove to establish the basic institutions of democracy and market capitalism. Yet in Russia, the evolution of these institutions suffered sorely from social and political attack. The basic structure of the state remained ambiguous throughout the transition period and laws were widely and regularly disregarded. As a result, foreign firms hoping to do business in

[41] Seminal works in this field include Kairys 1982; Unger 1976; and Horwitz 1977.

Russia faced a rule-less environment—and, in many cases, a commercial nightmare.

The Russian case is admittedly extreme. But it also demonstrates the critical link between the norms that prevail in a given society and the rules that emerge from it. One of the few relationships that both political scientists and legal scholars agree upon is that rules derive, at some basic level, from the norms that already prevail within a given society.[42] If rules are imposed upon a wholly alien environment, enforcement will nearly always be hobbled by an inherently awkward fit. Thus the chaos of Russia is made comprehensible by a history of dictatorship and centralized planning. When Western-style laws descend, as they did, into such an inhospitable environment, they simply don't take hold. The same is true, on a smaller scale, in China, where certain kinds of rules (particularly those pertaining to intellectual property and legal due process) run contrary to the deeply embedded norms of society. Formally, China offers full protection to both intellectual and physical property. It has documented laws and legal procedures which claim to protect copyrights, trademarks, and patented technologies. Yet numerous Western companies have encountered basic difficulties in preserving the sanctity of their property. McDonald's, for example, was informed in November 1994 that its 20-year lease of a 700-seat restaurant in Beijing was to be revoked after only three years to make way for an apartment complex; no compensation was offered until the restaurant chain won a court battle two years later. For Disney, intellectual property was completely insecure, with counterfeit goods so widespread that the company found it necessary to cancel a television show rather than promote a tide of illegitimate merchandise. Microsoft, too, has found it difficult to profit in the Chinese market due to widespread piracy of its popular software. In each of these cases, the firm's problems lay not with the letter of the law but rather with a deep-seated disinterest in the law's enforcement. The laws of China protect property, but the accepted and customary norms of interaction do not yet agree.

This gap between *politics* and *policy* is subtle but important. All national policy, it seems safe to conclude, is the product of domestic politics, of the struggle for power and interest that defines a national system and creates its rules. Yet not all of a country's political forces are encapsulated in its formal policies. There remain pockets of norms and beliefs and standards, informal rules that shape the business environment without actually dictating its terms. These informal rules are more difficult to codify than are national policies; they are rarely written down and lack the legal presence of laws. Yet they can be equally important in shaping a nation's behavior and its attitude towards

---

[42] For more on the sometime contentious distinction between law and norms, see Austin 1954; Shklar 1986; Schauer 1991.

trade and investment. In trying to understand the policies of any given country, therefore, firms must consider the full range of political action that resides there: the political forces that give rise to actual policy, as well as the quieter, dimmer, but no less powerful forces that shape the unwritten rules of business.[43]

# 8.10 THE ROLE OF INTERNATIONAL FORCES

A final aspect of national policy comes from an unlikely source. It comes, indeed, from the international arena and from the growing array of external groups who claim some voice in a country's ostensibly internal affairs. Some of these voices, to be sure, have existed for centuries. States have always defined their rules of trade in relation to those of their neighbors; political alliances and enmities have long shaped the policy options available to any individual state.[44] None of this has changed. What has happened in recent years, however, is that new actors have appeared on the world stage, armed with a distinctly international agenda and explicitly determined to shape the ways in which national rules are created and enforced.

The first of these developments is the advent of international institutions such as GATT and the WTO.[45] Devoted to the expansion of global (or at least regional) trade, these institutions contain their own complex sets of rules and their own mechanisms for enforcement. As countries comply with internationally negotiated rules, they shift simultaneously their domestic environment for trade and investment. When, say, India conforms to GATT schedules for tariff and quota reduction, it opens its markets to an increased flow of foreign goods and removes the barriers that formerly relegated foreign trading firms to a distinctly uncompetitive position. Yet, India's acceptance of GATT rules also reduces the incentives of foreign firms to engage in tariff-jumping investment. A change in the rules of trade at the international level may thus necessitate a change in corporate strategy in a particular domestic

---

[43] For more on these informal rules, see Spar 1999.    [44] Waltz 1979.
[45] For more on the advent and implications of the WTO, see Nicolaidis 1998; Gopalan, Moss, and Wells 1996.

market. A similar dynamic holds at the regional level, where rules promulgated by institutions such as the European Union or NAFTA can dramatically rearrange the contours of competition. Under NAFTA, for example, local content rules that previously adhered to the individual states apply instead across the North American region. So Japanese firms whose Mexican investments made sense in a pre-NAFTA world subsequently have to expand local sourcing in order to gain free access to the US and Canadian markets. And Canadian firms, previously unable to sell freely into Mexico without a Mexican presence, no longer face any constraint.

The second development is less obvious but perhaps even more powerful and enduring. It is the dramatic growth of nongovernmental organizations, transnational groups that form around a particular shared interest: in human rights, for instance, or environmentalism. These groups have no official political standing. They are sponsored neither by the home states of their members nor by international institutions such as GATT. Yet they can exert significant pressure on both national policy and corporate decisions.[46] In a highly publicized 1995 incident, for example, Shell Oil decided to abandon a $16 million plan to dump a disused oil rig on the bottom of the Atlantic Ocean because Greenpeace had succeeded in inciting a massive consumer boycott against the company. In Indonesia, both the government and Freeport McMoran, the country's largest foreign investor, have scrambled to ward off environmental attacks on the vast Irian Jaya copper mine. China persistently revisits plans for its massive Three Gorges Dam at the behest of international pressure groups; so does India, with its own Sardar Sardovar Dam. Elsewhere, chemical companies have been besieged by allegations of laxer safety standards in their foreign facilities, and garment and footwear manufacturers have been accused of unfair and abusive labor practices in their Asian operations.[47] Note that none of these accusations allege illegal conduct on the part of the corporate participants. And all of them focus on rules that apply primarily at the domestic level. Yet transnational groups are able, increasingly, to exert pressure on how these rules are created and enforced. Through a variety of tactics, they compel governments to revisit their own policies and cede, perhaps, a portion of their own power.[48]

---

[46]  See e.g. Kapstein 1996; Collingsworth, Goold, and Harvey 1994; Leonard 1988. The ability of special interest groups to affect the foreign policy making process seems particularly marked in the United States, and particularly strong with regard to trade policy. See e.g. the comparative analyses in Katzenstein 1978; Ikenberry, Lake, and Mastanduno 1988; Risse-Kappen, Ropp, and Sikkink 1999.

[47]  See Burns and Spar 2000.

[48]  For more on this phenomenon, see Spar 1999.

# 8.11 Conclusions

At the turn of the twenty-first century, it is difficult to predict just how closely international forces will move towards the threshold of the state. Many suggest that the transformation is already upon us, with multinational corporations and international nongovernmental organizations moving to accept the power that was once bestowed only on states.[49] In this view, the age of sovereignty is already passed, replaced by some new, possibly medieval, system where nations are obsolete and domestic politics fades to background noise in a crowded global system. Perhaps. Yet despite the most convincing arguments of post-Westphalian prophets, despite the undeniable growth of international pressure groups and multinational firms, reports of the death of sovereignty seem somewhat premature—even in the area of trade and investment. With the possible exception of capital controls, most nations still employ most of the policies described above. They favor certain domestic industries for protection or growth; they restrict or encourage foreign investment in particular sectors; they regulate commerce along a multitude of dimensions; and they determine the composition of 'fair' competition. Some of these policies may be shrinking somewhat in scope, some may be simultaneously negotiated and applied at the national level. But nations remain largely able and fully willing to impose their own policies on the firms that operate across their territory.

To be sure, the days of Hirschman may have passed. Trade is only rarely a tool of economic statecraft today, and the proliferation of overseas locations has softened the national identity of many multinational firms.[50] Yet the underlying components of international business remain unchanged. Trading or investing still entails a shift of resources and economic potential across national borders; it still means that some groups will benefit at the perceived expense of others, or that some will receive favors or bear costs that are not distributed evenly. This is the most basic stuff of politics: the struggle over resources and power. So long as nation-states can intermediate in this struggle, they are likely to remain influential actors in the world of international business, shaping the rules that firms follow and the environment in which they compete.

[49] See e.g. Kobrin Ch. 7 in this volume, and elsewhere.
[50] See Ohmae 1990; for a contrasting view, see Pauly 1997.

# REFERENCES

ALI, MUKLIS (1996). 'Indonesia Warns of High Short-Term Capital Inflows', *Reuter Asia-Pacific Business Report*, (Aug. 8).

—— (1997). 'Indonesia to Maintain Prudent Fiscal Policy', *Reuter Asia-Pacific Business Report*, (Jan. 8).

ALLISON, GRAHAM (1999). *Essence of Decision: Explaining the Cuban Missile Crisis*. New York: Longman.

AREEDA, PHILLIP (1967). *Antitrust Analysis: Problems, Text, Cases*. Boston: Little, Brown & Co.

AUSTIN, JOHN (1954). *The Province of Jurisprudence Determined and The Uses of the Study of Jurisprudence*. New York: Noonday Press.

BALDWIN, ROBERT E. (1986). *The Political Economy of US Import Policy*. Cambridge, Mass.: MIT Press.

BALLANTINE, DEWEY (1995). 'Privatizing Protection: Japanese Market Barriers in Consumer Photographic Films and Consumer Photographic Paper', Eastman Kodak Company memorandum in support of a petition filed pursuant to section 301 of the Trade Act of 1974, as amended. Washington, DC: Dewey Ballantine (May).

BARNET, RICHARD J., and MULLER, RONALD E. (1974). *Global Reach: The Power of the Multinational Corporations*. New York: Simon & Schuster.

BARON, DAVID P. (1993). *Business and Its Environment*. Englewood Cliffs, NJ: Prentice Hall.

BAUER, RAYMOND A., DE SOLA POOL, RAYMOND, and DEXTER, LEWIS ANTHONY (1982). *American Business and Public Policy: The Politics of Foreign Trade*. Chicago: Aldine Atherton.

BERGENSTEIN, SIGRID, and YOFFIE, DAVID (1984). 'Export Controls', Harvard Business School Case 384-008, Boston: Harvard Business School Publishing.

BERGSTEN, C. FRED (1974). *Completing the GATT: Toward New International Rules to Govern Export Controls*. Washington, DC: The British–North American Committee, National Planning Association.

BORK, ROBERT H. (1978). *The Antitrust Paradox*. New York: Basic Books.

BRADSHER, KEITH (1994). 'US Sues British in Antitrust Case', *New York Times* (May 27): A1.

BROWN, ALBERT (1974). *The Economic Theory of Representative Government*. Chicago: Aldine.

BUCHANAN, JAMES M., and TULLOCK, GORDON (1962). *The Calculus of Consent*. Ann Arbor: University of Michigan Press.

BUCKLEY, PETER J., and CASSON, MARK C. (1998). 'Analyzing Foreign Market Entry Strategies: Extending the Internalization Approach', *Journal of International Business*, 29/3: 539.

BURNS, JENNIFER, and SPAR, DEBORA L. (2000). 'Hitting the Wall: Nike and International Labor Practices', Harvard Business School Case 700-047, Boston: Harvard Business School Publishing.

CHACHOLIADES, MILTIADES (1978). *International Trade Theory and Policy*. New York: McGraw Hill.

CLINE, WILLIAM R. (1984). *Exports of Manufactures from Developing Countries.* Washington, DC: Brookings Institution.

COLLINGSWORTH, TERRY J., GOOLD, WILLIAM, and HARVEY, PHARIS J. (1994). 'Labor and Free Trade', *Foreign Affairs*, 73(1): 8–13.

CRAWFORD, BEVERLY, and LENWAY, STEFANIE (1985). 'Decision Modes and International Regime Change: Western Collaboration on East–West Trade', *World Politics*, 37 (April): 385–407.

DESTLER, I. M. (1986). *American Trade Politics: System Under Stress.* Washington, DC: Institute for International Economics, New York: Twentieth Century Fund.

——ODELL, JOHN S., and ELLIOTT, KIMBERLY ANN (1987). *Antiprotection: Changing Forces in United States Trade Politics.* Washington, DC: Institute for International Economics.

DIXIT, AVINASH K., and PINDYCK, ROBERT S. (1994). *Investment Under Uncertainty.* Princeton: Princeton University Press.

DOWNS, ANTHONY (1957). *An Economic Theory of Democracy.* New York: Harper Row.

DUNNING, JOHN H. (1998). 'Location and the Multinational Enterprise: A Neglected Factor?', *Journal of International Business*, 29/1: 45.

ENCARNATION, DENNIS J. (1992). *Rivals Beyond Trade: America Versus Japan in Global Competition.* Ithaca: Cornell University Press.

FAGRE, N., and WELLS, LOUIS T. (1982). 'Bargaining Power of Multinationals and Host Governments', *Journal of International Business Studies*, 13 (Fall): 19–24.

FARNSWORTH, CLYDE H. (1996). 'Canada Warns US on Law Penalizing Cuba Commerce', *New York Times*, (June 18): D6

FICHTE, J. G. (1845–46). *Sammtliche Werke.* Berlin: Veit.

FLAHERTY, FRANCIS (1995). 'The Emerging Markets, Mexico is Everywhere', *The New York Times*, (Jan. 14): 37.

FRIEDEN, JEFFREY (1991). 'Invested Interest: The Politics of National Economic Policies in a World of Global Finance', *International Organization*, 45/4: 425–51.

GLIBERMAN, STEVE, and SHAPIRO, DANIEL M. (1999). 'The Impact of Government Policies on Foreign Direct Investment: The Canadian Experience', *Journal of International Business*, 30/3: 513.

GOLDSTEIN, JUDITH (1988). 'Ideas, Institutions, and American Trade Policy', in Ikenberry, G. John, Lake, David A., and Mastanduno, Michael (eds.), *The State and American Foreign Economic Policy.* Ithaca: Cornell University Press.

GOMES-CASSERES, BENJAMIN, and YOFFIE, DAVID B. (1993). *The International Political Economy of Direct Foreign Investment.* Cheltenham: Edward Elgar.

GOODMAN, JOHN B., SPAR, DEBORA L., and YOFFIE, DAVID B. (1996). 'Foreign Direct Investment and the Demand for Protection in the United States', *International Organization*, 50/4: 565–91.

GOPALAN, LAKSHMI, MOSS, DAVID, and WELLS, LOUIS T., JR. (1996). 'International Institutions', HBS Case 796116, Boston: HBS Publishing.

GRAHAM, EDWARD M., and KRUGMAN, PAUL R. (1991). *Foreign Direct Investment in the United States.* Washington, DC: Institute for International Economics.

HAWTREY, R. G. H. (1930). *The Economic Aspects of Sovereignty.* London: Longmans, Green & Co.

HORWITZ, MORTON J. (1977). *The Transformation of American Law, 1977–1860*. Cambridge, Mass.: Harvard University Press.

HUFBAUER, GARY CLAUDE, and SCHOTT, JEFFREY J. (1985). *Economic Sanctions Reconsidered: History and Current Policy*. Washington, DC: Institute for International Economics.

HYMER, STEPHEN (1976). *The International Operations of National Firms : A Study of Direct Foreign Investment*. Cambridge, Mass.: MIT Press.

IKENBERRY, JOHN G., LAKE, DAVID A., and MASTANDUNO, MICHAEL (eds.) (1988). *The State and American Foreign Economic Policy*. Ithaca: Cornell University Press.

JENTLESON, BRUCE W. (1986). *Pipeline Politics: The Complex Political Economy of East–West Energy Trade*. Ithaca: Cornell University Press.

KAIRYS, DAVID (ed.) (1982). *The Politics of Law: A Progressive Critique*. New York: Pantheon Books.

KAPSTEIN, ETHAN (1996). 'Workers and the World Economy', *Foreign Affairs*, 75(3): 16–37.

KAPSTEIN, PETER (ed.) (1978). *Between Power and Plenty: Foreign Economic Policies of Advanced Industrial States*. Madison: University of Wisconsin Press.

KINDLEBERGER, CHARLES (1987). *International Capital Movements*. Cambridge: Cambridge University Press.

KOBRIN, STEPHEN J. (1985). 'Expropriation as an Attempt to Control Foreign Firms in LDCs: Trends from 1960 to 1979', *International Studies Quarterly*, 29: 329–48.

—— (1987). 'Testing the Bargaining Hypothesis in the Manufacturing Sector in Developing Countries', *International Organization*, 41/4: 609–38.

KRUGMAN, PAUL R. (1987). 'Is Free Trade Passé?' *Economic Perspectives*, 1/2, 131–44.

—— (1990). *Rethinking International Trade*. Cambridge, Mass.: MIT Press.

KUEMMERLE, WALTER (1999). 'The Drivers of Direct Investment into Research and Development: An Empirical Investigation', *Journal of International Business*, 30/1: 1.

LAVERGNE, REAL P. (1983). *The Political Economy of US Tariffs*. New York: Academic Press.

LEONARD, J. (1988). *Pollution and the Struggle for World Product*. Cambridge: Cambridge University Press.

LIST, FREDRICH (1991). *The National System of Political Economy*. Trans. from the original German by Sampson S. Lloyd; with J. S. Nicholson's introductory essay to the 1904 edn. Fairfield, NJ: A. M. Kelley.

MARTIN, LISA (1992). *Coercive Cooperation : Explaining Multilateral Economic Sanctions*. Princeton, NJ: Princeton University Press.

MASTANDUNO, MICHAEL (1988). 'Trade as a Strategic Weapon: American and Alliance Export Control Policy in the Early Postwar Period', in Ikenberry, G. John, Lake, David A., and Mastanduno, Michael (eds.), *The State and American Foreign Economic Policy*. Ithaca: Cornell University Press.

—— (1992). *Economic Containment: CoCom and the Politics of East–West Trade*. Ithaca: Cornell University Press.

MILNER, HELEN (1988). *Resisting Protectionism: Global Industries and the Politics of International Trade*. Princeton: Princeton University Press.

MILNER, HELEN (*cont.*), and YOFFIE, DAVID B. (1989).'Between Free Trade and Protectionism: Strategic Trade Policy and a Theory of Corporate Trade Demands', *International Organization*, 43/1: 239–72.

MORAN, THEODORE H. (1974). *Multinational Corporations and the Politics of Dependence: Copper in Chile.* Princeton: Princeton University Press, 135–58.

NICOLAIDIS, KALYPSO (1998). *Mutual Recognition Regimes: Towards a Comparative Analysis.* Cambridge: Weatherhead Center for International Affairs.

OHMAE, KENICHI (1990). *The Borderless World: Power and Strategy in the Interlinked Economy.* New York: HarperBusiness.

—— (1995). *The End of the Nation State: the Rise of Regional Economies.* New York: Free Press.

PAULY, LOUIS W. (1997). *Who Elected the Bankers?: Surveillance and Control in the World Economy.* Ithaca: Cornell University Press.

PELTZMAN, SAM (1976). 'Toward a More General Theory of Regulation', *Journal of Law and Economics*, 19: 211–40.

POSNER, RICHARD A. (1974). 'Theories of Economic Regulation', *Bell Journal of Economics and Management Science*, 5 (Autumn): 335–58.

—— (1976). *Antitrust Law: An Economic Perspective.* Chicago: University of Chicago Press.

RISSE-KAPPEN, THOMAS, ROPP, STEVE C., and SIKKINK, KATHERINE (1999). *The Power of Human Rights: International Norms and Domestic Change.* New York: Cambridge University Press.

SANGER, DAVID E. (1995). 'Conoco Told US Years Ago of Oil Negotiations with Iran', *New York Times*, (March 17): A.1, col. 3.

SCHAUER, FREDERICK F. (1991). *Playing by the Rules: A Philosophical Examination of Rule-based Decision-making in Law and in Life*, Oxford: Clarendon Press.

SHENEFIELD, JOHN H., and STELZER, IRWIN M. (1993). *The Antitrust Laws: A Primer.* Washington, DC: American Enterprise Institute.

SHKLAR, JUDITH (1986). *Legalism: Law, Morals, and Political Trials.* Cambridge, Mass.: Harvard University Press.

SPAR, DEBORA (1993). 'Foreign Direct Investment in Eastern Europe', in Keohane, Robert O., Nye, Joseph S., and Hoffmann, Stanley (eds.), *After the Cold War: International Institutions and State Strategies in Europe, 1989–1991.* Cambridge, Mass.: Harvard University Press, 286–309.

—— (1994). *The Cooperative Edge: The Internal Politics of International Cartels.* Ithaca: Cornell University Press.

—— (1999). 'Note on Rules', Harvard Business School Case 799-013, Boston: Harvard Business School Publishing.

—— (1998). 'The Spotlight and the Bottom Line', *Foreign Affairs*, 77/2: 7–12.

—— (1998). 'Attracting High Technology Investment: Intel's Costa Rica Plant', *Foreign Investment Advisory Service*, Occ. Paper 11.

STIGLER, GEORGE J. (1971). 'The Theory of Economic Regulation', *Bell Journal of Economics*, 2: 3–21.

STRANGE, SUSAN (1986). *Casino Capitalism.* Oxford: Basil Blackwell.

TYSON, LAURA D'ANDREA (1992). 'Who's Bashing Whom?' Washington, DC: Institute for International Economics.

UNGER, ROBERTO MANGABEIRA (1976). *Law in Modern Society: Toward a Criticism of Social Theory.* New York: Free Press.

UNITED NATIONS (1994). World Investment Report: 294, 295, and 307.

US CONGRESS, Office of Technology Assessment (1993). *Multinationals, and the National Interest: Playing by Different Rules.* Washington, DC: US Government Printing Office, (Sept.): 72.

VERNON, RAYMOND (1971). *Sovereignty at Bay: The Multinational Spread of US Enterprise.* New York: Basic Books.

——(1977). *Storm Over the Multinationals.* Cambridge, Mass.: Harvard University Press.

——and SPAR, DEBORA L. (1989). *Beyond Globalism: Remaking American Foreign Economic Policy.* New York: Free Press, 113–17.

——WELLS, LOUIS T., JR., and RANGAN, SUBRAMANIAN (1996). *The Manager in the Global Economy.* Upper Saddle River, NJ: Princeton Hall (7th edn.), 141.

WALTZ, KENNETH N. (1979). *Theory of International Politics.* Reading, Mass.: Addison-Wesley.

WELLS, LOUIS T. (1982). 'Bargaining Power of Multinationals and Host Governments', *Journal of International Business Studies*, 13/Fall: 19–24.

——and WINT, A. (1990). 'Marketing a Country: Promotion as a Tool for Attracting Foreign Investment', *Foreign Investment Advisory Service*, Occ. Paper 1.

WILSON, JAMES Q. (1974). 'The Politics of Regulation', in McKie, James W. (ed.), *Social Responsibility and the Business Predicament.* Washington, DC: The Brookings Institute.

WONG, LANA (1996). 'Technology Seen as Price of Access', *South China Morning Post* (Feb. 8): 4.

YOFFIE, DAVID B. (1983). 'Note on Free Trade and Protectionism', Harvard Business School Case 383-174, Boston: Harvard Business School Publishing.

——(1988). 'How an Industry Builds Political Advantage', *Harvard Business Review*, repr. 88314.

YOUNG, ALLEGRA, and SPAR, DEBORA (1993). 'Gerber Products Company: Investing in the New Poland', Harvard Business School Case 793-069, Boston: Harvard Business School Publishing.

# CHAPTER 9

# THE MULTILATERAL TRADING SYSTEM

## SYLVIA OSTRY

## 9.1 INTRODUCTION

IN the ongoing discussion about the world trading system it's important to make a distinction between the possibility versus the probability of the failure to launch a new round as in Seattle in November 1999. The latter required a catalyst to trigger the outcome of failure. But the transformation of the trading system combined with the structural weakness of the WTO (World Trade Organization) would have ensured that even 'success' could not guarantee the future of a rules-based multilateral system in the absence of fundamental reform of the WTO.

The following discussion will first summarize the main transformative changes in the system which include the impact of the Uruguay Round as well as changes in the policy *ambience* and the policy *process*. I will then highlight the most urgent reforms needed to keep the system going and briefly note the longer-term changes required in the international governance architecture.

Without exaggeration, one could say that the ambience of trade policy-making has profoundly changed since the end of the Uruguay Round in 1994. This discussion will track the roots of this change to the transformation in the nature of the trading system initiated by the Uruguay Round. This transformation, however, is a necessary but not sufficient explanation of that event. Equally important is the impact of the spread of Internet use in the mid-1990s, a phenomenon which is transforming the *policy process*—as exemplified by the role of the NGOs in contesting the terms of the policy debate. In addition there are ongoing changes in the climate of ideas which raise questions about the neoclassical model at the core of economics and of trade policy. Finally, it will be argued that coping with these changes will require structural reform, not only of the WTO, but also the postwar international architecture if the multilateral rules-based system is to endure. So let's begin at the beginning of the story: the Uruguay Round.

## 9.2 THE TRADING SYSTEM IS NOT JUST ABOUT TRADE: THE URUGUAY ROUND

The inclusion of the so-called new issues (intellectual property and services) in the Uruguay Round was entirely an American initiative. A number of developing countries, led by India and Brazil, were bitterly opposed. But, as the government was aware, without a fundamental rebalancing of the GATT, it seems highly improbable that the American business community would have continued to support the multilateral system for much longer (Ostry 1990: 23). So the American multinational enterprises (MNEs) undertook a major role in shaping the negotiations. On the intellectual property issue the main impetus came from the pharmaceutical, software, and entertainment industries with the CEO of Pfizer playing a lead role as Chairman of the Intellectual Property Rights Committee (IPC). At the Punta del Este meeting in September 1986 many delegates were somewhat surprised to learn that the top priority of President Reagan for the Uruguay Round was to stop piracy since, unlike the services issue, the position of the US on intellectual property had only been formalized a few months earlier (Preeg 1995: 65). But by May 1988 the IPC, which had created an international business coalition including European and Japanese business organizations, presented a proposal which went well beyond eliminating piracy and included 'minimum standards, enforcement mechanisms, and dispute settlement' (Ostry 1990: 24). This became the official American position and was eventually supported by the EU and Japan, who had been lukewarm or even hostile to including IPRs in a 'trade' negotiation until prodded by their corporations. Moreover some academics had questioned the rationale for including intellectual property rights in the trading system especially since the effect of such rights on trade was ambiguous.

While TRIPS (Trade-related aspects of intellectual property rights) delivered the basic elements of the IPC agenda, because all complex negotiations involve trade-offs, some key issues were left unsettled. These must be reviewed as part of the so-called built-in agenda mandated by the Uruguay Round. Of all these issues by far the most contentious—explosive might be a better adjective—concerned Article 27.3(b) which allowed members to exclude from patentability certain plant and animal inventions. A hint of what was to come might have been observed in Geneva during the final stages of the negotiations when environmental NGOs covered Swiss highway bridges with graffiti admonishing 'GATT: no patents on life!' and draped the GATT headquarters building with a huge banner carrying the same message (Croome 1995: 255). But even those who took note of the message could hardly have predicted the attack on GMOs (genetically modified organisms) and the 'life science' industry which erupted by the end of the decade and has become a rallying point for a wide and diverse range of groups opposed to the WTO and to the role of corporations in shaping the system. Moreover, the profound differences between the attitudes of European and American consumers with respect to food made from genetically modified plants, and growing signs of a division between small farmers and large agribusiness corporations illustrate the complexity of this issue as compared with a 'distributional' issue such as agricultural subsidies. The GATT model of reciprocity was premised on the idea that protectionist lobbies could be offset by export interests. The debate was over the *division* of the pie. But although the debate over GMOs has important distributional implications (both within and among countries) the central concern involves the *recipe* for making the pie and for this concern the old GATT model of reciprocity is largely irrelevant.

Moreover, it's important to underline that, in the services negotiations, reciprocity was also largely irrelevant to securing the GATS (General Agreement on Trade in Services). By the end of the 1980s a major change in economic policy was underway. The revolution of what might be termed Ronald Thatcherism began in the OECD countries but was adopted by many developing countries, including countries in Latin America and in Central and Eastern Europe by the onset of the 1990s. Economic reform—deregulation, privatization, liberalization—were seen as essential elements for launching and sustaining higher growth. Even without the regulatory reform thrust from the Uruguay Round, the postwar economic regulatory state was no longer a dominant paradigm and reform of key service sectors such as telecommunications and finance were regarded as essential building blocks in the soft infrastructure underpinning growth.

With the inclusion of the 'new issues' of intellectual property and trade in services, the Uruguay Round marked a watershed in the evolution of the global trading system, ushering in the agenda of deeper integration. Thus, although the 'new issues' are not identical—obviously negotiations on tele-communications or financial services differ from intellectual property rights—they do have one common or generic characteristic. They deal with the *institutional infrastructure* of the economy. The barriers to access for service providers stem from laws, administrative actions, or regulations which impede cross-border trade and investment. Further, since these laws and administrative actions are for the most part invisible, a key element in any negotiation is transparency—i.e. the publication of all relevant laws, regula-tions, and administrative procedures. In the case of intellectual property the negotiations covered not only comprehensive standards for domestic laws but, perhaps more importantly, detailed provisions for enforcement proced-ures. It's important to underline that this deeper integration agenda not only involves an inherently intrusive focus on domestic policy but also greatly reinforces the legalization trend in the trading system as will be clear in the discussion of the WTO dispute settlement.

Given this radical transformation of the system and the arduous task of completing the Round, it certainly seemed that in January 1995, at the official birth of the WTO, as a result of a favorable confluence of different forces, support by member governments for domestic and international liberaliza-tion appeared to be near-universal.

But the law of unintended consequences was at work. Because of the focus of attention on *economic* regulation, the negotiations on *social* regulation concerning product standards, health and safety measures, and environment received little publicity and little attention from the senior policy ranks. In the OECD countries social regulation started in the late 1960s and has been accelerating since then. The OECD has called the phenomenon 'regulatory inflation'. One could—with a bit of a stretch perhaps—say that the postwar economic regulatory state of the advanced countries is withering away, while the social regulatory state is alive, well, and growing. Thus social regulation, covering the environment, labor, food safety, product labeling, etc., has grown by 300–400 per cent in the industrialized countries since 1970 (Organization for Economic Cooperation and Development (OECD) 1997: 191–248). (This is decidedly not the case in the developing countries, nor are they likely to embrace the social regulatory state unilaterally: *au contraire!*) While there are a number of reasons for this bout of regulatory inflation a major factor has been the increasing influence of nongovernmental organizations (NGOs) in the rich countries. For this and other reasons, it would be unwise to evaluate the implications of these new transnational actors simply on the basis of the street theatre in Seattle because they have and will continue to play an important role in the changing ambience of the policy process.

# 9.3 THE AMBIENCE OF TRADE POLICY

There was very little public interest in the Uruguay Round negotiations. As the new Director-General of the WTO, Mike Moore, has described it: 'The Uruguay Round was launched in the silence of public apathy,' (World Trade Organization (WTO) 1999a). The same could be said about the previous seven rounds since the creation of the GATT in 1948. The negotiations were handled by governments although, as noted earlier, the reciprocity model involved lobbying by so-called distributional coalitions, chiefly business and trade unions, as an important element in the process and outcome. In the Uruguay Round, the role of multinational corporations and farmers was unique because of the unique character of the new issues and the centrality of agriculture as a deal-maker or breaker in the ultimate settlement. While the US was the leader in launching and guiding all GATT negotiations, it's fair to argue that all the negotiations ultimately depended on cooperations between the two big players, the Americans and the European Community. It's true that in the Uruguay Round some developing countries were more prominent than in earlier negotiations in which they negotiated mainly to secure unreciprocated access to OECD markets. But in the end the big North–South trade-off (the new issues in exchange for agricultural reform and reduction of barriers in textiles and clothing) required a transatlantic accord.

Today there are many governments who sorely miss the 'silence of public apathy'. The publicity surrounding international institutions is not only due to the role of the NGOs, (of which more shortly). I would argue that the absence of apathy also reflects a broader and more pervasive secular change in the industrialized countries—an alienation from the elite. The American sociologist V. O. Key, Jr. (1963: 27–53), wrote about the 'permissive consensus' of the earlier postwar decades. While the broad public had little detailed knowledge of international policy, opinion polls demonstrated consistent support for the government's foreign policy which would, of course, include trade policy. As Key noted: 'when a permissive consensus exists, a government may be relatively free to work out a solution of the issue or it may be free to act or not to act,' (1963: 35). The deference to government, and more broadly to the establishment as it was then termed, underlay the permissive consensus and has dramatically declined since the 1960s in all OECD countries as many recent analyses of opinion polls have demonstrated (*The Economist* 1999: 49–50). Perhaps the Uruguay Round was the last gasp of the permissive consensus—and barely that.

Of course there are many reasons for the decline in deference to government and to the elites—a word of opprobrium in North America and even in Europe today. One major cause has been the much wider access to information and the role of the media. The latest stage in the information technology revolution—the accelerating use of the Internet since the mid-90s as exemplified by the role of the NGOs in Seattle—will be described shortly. But another development, more difficult to discern, is also at work—the ongoing change in the climate of ideas which is raising doubts about the received wisdom on trade and economic growth and will likely, over time, have an effect on policy. As Keynes famously observed:

The ideas of economists and political philosophers, both when they are right and when they are wrong, are more powerful than is commonly understood. Practical men, who believe themselves quite exempt from any intellectual influences, are usually the slaves of some defunct economist. Madmen in authority, who hear voices in the air, are distilling their frenzy from some academic scribbler from a few years back.

# 9.4 THE CLIMATE OF IDEAS

## 9.4.1 Academic scribblers

One of the most important academic scribblers of this century was Joseph Schumpeter whose work on the capitalist engine of innovation, or creative destruction as he termed it, is enjoying a major revival in the new growth theory. But when read today his views about the future of capitalism, as expressed in his 1942 book *Capitalism, Socialism and Democracy*, seem absurd. His lengthy and brilliantly argued answer to the question heading Part II—Can Capitalism Survive?—boils down to one word—'no'.

He argued that the fatal flaw at the heart of the capitalist system is that its fundamental ethos—rationality—cannot be defended against the attacks of its progeny, the intellectual. The intellectuals—defined as people 'who wield the power of the spoken and the written word' (Schumpeter 1942: 147), live on criticism and their 'whole position depends on criticism that stings', (Schumpeter 1942: 15). Capitalism is based on freedom so the intellectuals cannot be controlled. But the 'unheroic and rationalist' defense of the capitalist is no match for the criticism that 'nothing is sacrosanct' (Schumpeter 1942: 15) and renders indefensible the system's institutions.

So the weakness of the system which provides the target for the intellectuals (who, he notes, have many more outlets as books become cheaper, newspaper chains spread, and radios proliferate) is the absence of a heroic and binding ethos, or set of moral values. As he so trenchantly put it: 'The stock exchange is a poor substitute for the Holy Grail' (Schumpeter 1942: 137). But there it is—how wrong could he get? In the United States, at least, the Stock Exchange *is* the Holy Grail!

From the vantage point of the new millennium, when capitalism has been embraced by all but a few countries in the world, Schumpeter's dire prediction seems almost bizarre. Nor is it just capitalism that reigns supreme. It's core ethos—economics—can well boast of having invaded most of the other social sciences, a phenomenon (proudly) termed 'economic imperialism' (Lazear 1999). Even, *pace* Schumpeter, religion has not been safe from the discipline's imperial reach. For example, one can develop a really neat model of church attendance as investment under uncertainty—the uncertainty being whether or not you go to heaven (Lazear 1999: 20).

Yet despite his erroneous forecast, was Schumpeter all wrong? Perhaps it would be unwise to dismiss the penetrating insight of his core argument about moral values. Echoes of the diatribes of his 'intellectuals' can be heard daily—and certainly can be read hourly on the Internet.

Let's move forward thirty or so years to another scribbler, the American sociologist and philosopher Daniel Bell. In his 1976 book *The Cultural Contradictions of Capitalism* we can hear faint echoes of Schumpeter but with a very different twist. The intellectuals no longer exist. They have been replaced by a growing cadre in the knowledge and communications industry dedicated to the promotion of hedonism as the guiding principle for production and consumption. In the early days of American capitalism this unrestrained economic impulse was 'held in check by Puritan restraint and the Protestant ethic' (Bell 1976: 21). But the Protestant ethic was destroyed by the granting of credit: 'with credit cards one could indulge in instant gratification' in an unending cycle of creating new wants and new means of gratifying those wants (Bell 1976: 21). The result is that the capitalist system lacks a 'transcendental tie' or some set of 'ultimate meanings' to bind the society and defend the system. And that is Bell's cultural contradiction of capitalism.

His description of the consequences of this 'hollowing out' makes fascinating reading. Among them are environmental degradation; a rise of religious fundamentalism; a growing attack on the idea that economic growth can solve all problems; and a rise of anti-cognitive, anti-intellectual culture which yearns for a simpler, less technocratic society. He describes the sensibility of the 1960s, which spawned the new culture, as 'rebellious but not revolutionary' in the sense that the rebels had no clear idea of what they wanted as an alternative social model. But the rebellion did have the effect of undermining authority and, in its attack against the hated government and business 'technocrats', insistently raised the cry for 'participation'.

Bell describes at some length his proposals for coping with this 'crisis of belief'. He rejects the view that it is a crisis of capitalism with its implication that socialism is an alternative. He argues that since the consumerist, free-enterprise society no longer has moral standing with the citizenry a new public philosophy is required if liberal society is to survive. Central to his discussion of these philosophic rules is 'the balance between equity and efficiency in the competition between social claims and economic performance' (Bell 1976: 256). Indeed, he argues that the question of equality 'has become a central issue for the public household today' (Bell 1976: 262).

A good deal of what Bell wrote about the sixties generation and hedonistic society rings true today. There is little respect for authority and apparently no limit to the creation of consumption needs and wants. What is out of synch, however, is the view that equality would be the central issue in American domestic policy dialogue. In a recent analysis of American views about the role of government in reducing differences in income, in 1973 48 per cent agreed that it is the government's responsibility, in 1998 only 30 per cent held the same view (Blendon *et al.* 1999: 14–17). This apparent tolerance for inequality is unique to the United States. And this has international implications worth a brief digression (Kenen and Ostry 1999: 3–22).

In a period of ongoing and pervasive change in the external environment, institutions mediate the impact of that change and hence the pace and nature of adaptation. We live in such a period today; the change is called globalization; and the most flexible system, the American, comes out on top.

The contrast between the US, Europe, and Japan can be characterized as a contrast between Exit and Voice, a widely-used metaphor. An Exit paradigm is far more adaptable because change is governed by an anonymous mechanism that rewards the most efficient—winners prosper and losers appear to disappear. A Voice paradigm, by contrast, gives losers influence. Governments must then engage in a long and difficult process to renegotiate the social contract. 'Rigidities' designed to deliver stability and social cohesion under high growth and predictable incremental change become powerful impediments to adaptability at a time of pervasive and unrelenting transformation. In Europe the Voice is loud and explicit. In Japan it is quiet and discreet. But in both systems Exit is difficult to arrange.

To a considerable degree, the difficulty stems from the 'equality' issue. The new technologies driving globalization are high-skill biased so that widening income disparity, so evident in the US over the past two decades, is *endogenous* to the technology trajectory. Ongoing changes in technology and in the global economy ensure that the pressures for convergence to the American model will not soon abate. In Europe and Asia globalization has become a synonym for Americanization and 'globaphobia' is on the rise driven, in part, by rising inequality within and among countries.

So was Bell completely off the mark when he said that equality would be the central concern for reformulating the public philosophy of the United States? Perhaps the answer is yes and no. Yes, in terms of domestic policy where the superbly adaptable Exit model rules. No, if we listen to the voices of the AFL-CIO (American Federation of Labor and Congress of Industrial Organizations) and demanding the inclusion of labor standards in trade agreements. Is the Voice model being externalized? The implications of an external Voice compensating for domestic Exit are worrisome indeed. But more of that below. For now let's return to our academic scribblers.

In his contribution to the 1993 meeting of the British Association for the Advancement of Science, Samuel Brittan explains that he had suggested the theme *Market Capitalism and Moral Values* because 'the relationship between moral evaluation and economic analysis has come back into fashion. It went underground in the heyday of the belief in economics as a supposedly technical guide to action: but now it has resurfaced,' (Brittan and Hamlin (eds.) 1993: 1). Among the several reasons he suggests for this resurgence is a growing misunderstanding, especially in the media, of the positive role of markets; a misunderstanding based on a confusion between self-interest and materialism (Brittan and Hamlin (eds.) 1993: 6). What is of particular concern to him is the 'blank incomprehension' about 'the role of relative prices, including pay'—i.e. the role of inequality in the allocative mechanism (Brittan and Hamlin (eds.) 1993: 20). He is particularly scathing about the new wave of 'social responsibility' decrying the movement as 'the codes that kill jobs' (Brittan and Hamlin (eds.) 1993: 8).

Brittan was not alone in his concern about the 'blank incomprehension' and indeed, during the 1990s the issue of the trend to increasing inequality, especially but not only in the US, spawned a minor growth industry in the discipline. Was it due to trade or technology? Was it an economic 'good' essential to the effective functioning of the market economy (Welch 1999)? Was it an inevitable result of economic growth and therefore defensible in instrumental terms (Barro 1999)? Were those attacking a rising disparity due to the astonishing proliferation of millionaires in the US best described as 'spiteful egalitarians' (Feldstein 1998)?

Perhaps the single best indicator of the revival of the equality issue was the awarding of the Nobel Prize in Economics to Amartya Sen in 1998. Sen's work has proceeded on two fronts: development policy (where he has had a considerable influence on the World Bank) and welfare economics or policy analysis concerned with the 'social good'. In his 1999 book *Development as Freedom: Human Capability and Global Need*[1] he brings the two strands together and spells out his defense of the need to shift the focus of development from the single objective of economic growth, as measured by national income, to a quite different and far more complex concept he calls freedom. Rejecting the economist's metric of income as the sole measure of well-being means that the market is not the sole allocative mechanism, so he's *really* back to basics. The basics include defining and measuring the objectives governing individual behavior—what it is that individuals seek to maximize—and defining and measuring the 'social good'—the aggregate of individuals' well-being. And the distribution of income and property is central to his concept of the social good.

This is not the place to review the complex mathematical/philosophical reasoning about 'functionings' and 'capabilities'. Suffice it to say that in rejecting the metric of income and in the absence of a market, someone must make judgments about weighting and comparability, i.e. someone must define freedom and the good life in practical, concrete terms. Sen, of course, recognizes this but his answer is that although economists 'pine for some wonderful formula that would simply give us ready-made weights that are *just right*', no such formula exists and the alternative he comes up with is that of public discussion based on information about the different components of the quality of life. But this doesn't get over the basic hurdle of who's to define and judge. In the end these are issues of metaphysics or moral philosophy—but also of economics?

Needless to say, Sen's work has generated considerable debate and not only among development economists. In presenting his case for social justice, Sen rejects the libertarian concept of negative freedom and endorses positive freedom, including the rights to income, health, education, and so on. He also rejects the Rawlsian concept of procedural justice, i.e. a system of fair rule. He is indeed arguing that morals are an integral part of the discipline. In response, there has been a vigorous defense of negative liberty—the freedom to choose. The battle lines have been drawn and as the debate proceeds between the competing schools of scribblers it will be interesting to see which will most influence the 'practical men' in power.

---

[1] This is taken from Ostry 1999. See also Sugden, Robert (1993). 'Welfare, Resources, and Capabilities: A Review of Inequality Re-examined by Amartya Sen', *Journal of Economic Literature*, XXXI. 1947–1962.

In addition to the debate over morals and equality, another battle has emerged in the last few years about the benefits of free trade. In addition to the debate over the impact of trade—and, more broadly, globalization—on labor markets a number of economists are raising questions concerning the link between trade and growth.[2] The implications for policy are significant: if trade is not a major engine of growth then, *ceteris paribus*, the costs of protectionism have been overestimated and indeed, the causality may run in the opposite direction. Of course the issue is not put in such simplistic terms and the *ceteris paribus* is heavily loaded with other considerations. Nonetheless, by raising the question itself, these scribblers will likely have some influence on the trade policy dialogue, especially in non-OECD countries.

To summarize the discussion thus far I would argue that Schumpeter's assertion that the Achilles heel of the capitalist system was the absence of a binding set of moral values has now been revived, certainly in public discussion but also in the academy. Issues such as the link between growth and trade are part of the same climate of change. Maybe this is simply an example of the old aphorism that yesterday's heresy is today's dogma and the reaction to globalization is relatively minor. And are the demonstrations against international institutions just a replay of the 1960s rebels without a cause? My own view is that it was not, which brings me to my last lot of academic scribblers—the ecological economists.

## 9.4.2 Ecological economics

Environmental or ecological economics is also a product of the 1990s. The environmental movement is, of course, far older but the launch of an interdisciplinary journal that brought together biologists and economists took place in 1989. A constant theme in the writings has been that the laws of economics and ecology are not contradictory but incommensurable (Gowdy 1999: 321–498). Many reasons are given for this uncompromising view but the main argument rests on the concept of scale. In neoclassical theory economic production is a self-contained process: scarcity of inputs are overcome by substitution (or innovation) and externalities should be handled by internalization and relative prices. But the scale of the economy *vis-à-vis* the global environment is not part of the model. To

---

[2] For a full review of the recent literature see Rodriguez and Rodrik 1999; and also Harrison and Hanson 1999. For a recent survey of the debate see articles in *The Economic Journal*, Oxford, Sept. 1998.

counter this, the ecological economists have coined a saying—that the economy is a wholly-owned subsidiary of the environment—which has gained widespread usage.

The economists' response that technology and effective implementation of market mechanisms can overcome the basic problem of scale have, thus far, been firmly rejected. It is argued that there are no technological substitutes for climatic stability, or the ozone layer, or bio-diversity and that environmental degradation is irreversible. There are many other intractable issues such as appropriate discount rates or an agreed definition of sustainability, so we can be assured that the debate will be ongoing for some time. But meanwhile the new discipline has mounted a major attack on current economic policy—not least of all trade policy.

The most comprehensive and uncompromising critique of trade policy has been presented by Herman Daly, one of the founding fathers of the new discipline (Daly 1993: 121–32). He argues that in order for one country to internalize environmental externalities and not suffer a loss of competitiveness, tariff protection would be required. But even if this were agreed (which he thinks is unlikely) he is opposed to free trade and to capital mobility because globalization destroys local communities, and for ecological economists the preservation of community and the assurance of equity are values integral to 'sustainability'. But worst of all, free trade obscures the scale limits both local as well as global. He is thus opposed to the economists' proposals for tradable emissions and even to significant developing country imports of environmental technologies which would increase growth beyond local carrying capacity. There's much more to his exposition but what it boils down to is that since ecosystems can't grow, the subsystem (economy) must develop without growth and with very limited trade. If this seems utopian, it is. (But then, John Gray the eminent British political philosopher has attacked the global market as 'an experiment in utopian social engineering' (Gray 1999: 235).

Of course there are many environmentalists who do not subscribe to such extreme views. Indeed the ecological economics school is largely rejected by many of the mainstream academics and NGOs. But some version of a new ecological paradigm, when combined with the other changes in the climate of ideas, certainly provided powerful ammunition to the anti-globalization movement. An inchoate and informed new paradigm stressing equality, ecology, and community may perhaps be emerging. Maybe the rebels will find a cause.

# 9.5 DIFFERENT GAME: DIFFERENT PLAYERS

'You taught me language; and my profit on't is I know how
to curse.'

Shakespeare: *The Tempest*

While economists, business and trade officials ponder how E-commerce will
affect the global market, few seem to have given much thought as to how the
Internet has and will affect the market for policy ideas and therefore the
policy-making *process*.

A major impact of the Internet has and will be to make the market for ideas
contestable, a radical transformation which will affect the domestic and
international policy-making process. Inexpensive, borderless, real time
networking provides the NGOs with economics of scale and also of scope
by linking often widely disparate groups with one common theme.
Equally important, it offers the opportunity to disseminate strategic knowledge formerly concentrated in governments and business. To illustrate this
it's worth describing the first major policy impact of this technological
revolution, the demise of the OECD's multilateral agreement on investment
or MAI.

In October 1997, forty-seven NGOs from twenty-three countries and five
continents met in Paris at OECD headquarters. The consultation had been
arranged at the request of the World Wildlife Fund and some national
representatives who had been lobbied by domestic advocacy organizations.
The NGOs argued that the MAI would undermine sustainable development
and national sovereignty. The most powerful case for this argument concerned the MAI's investor protection mechanism. This replicated the investment provisions in NAFTA (North American Free Trade Association) which
included procedures for resolving disputes by which private parties as well as
governments could take action and adopted a very broad definition of
investment expropriation, so broad it could lead to investor claims against
government regulation in, say, environmental or health areas, which negatively affect the value of investment. In Canada, American corporations had
launched several cases against the government that aroused a storm of
opposition led by a coalition of NGOs. These same NGOs were among the
most prominent in Paris in October 1997. And these same NGOs had been
active in launching the anti-NAFTA debate by building coalitions in Canada,
the US, and Mexico.

After the consultation the groups at the meeting organized an anti-MAI
coalition and launched an international campaign to stop the negotiations.

A world wide MAI website list[3] displays fifty-five sites mainly from OECD countries and covering a wide range of interests. But environmental and legal groups together accounted for more than half the total. Groups in Canada and the United States provided a constant flow of information to coordinate the campaign. By October 1998 the negotiations had been suspended and in December, after the official withdrawal of the French government at the request of the red–green members of the coalition, they were officially terminated. (The action of the French government is not without significance. While North American greens have chosen an advocacy route to contest the market for policy ideas, the European environmentalists formed political parties and greens are now members of government coalitions in four EU countries: Germany, France, Italy, and Finland as well as increasingly prominent in the European parliament.)

Of course there were a number of reasons why the MAI failed but there seems little doubt that the NGOs played a key role (Smythe and Smith 1999). It's worth underlining the importance of the role of both environmentalists and lawyers in the networks. On the environmental front the MAI defeat echoed earlier events in Geneva. In 1991, after a panel ruling that the US violated its GATT obligations by banning Mexican tuna caught by a process which killed dolphins—the famous or infamous tuna–dolphin decision— American environmental groups mounted a major attack on GATT-zilla. The campaign in Washington raged against the cabal of faceless bureaucrats in Geneva who were undermining American sovereignty and subverting democracy. Although GATT survived and the Uruguay Round created the WTO, many of the themes, albeit for the most part in less colorful terms, are at the core of the continuing environmentalist critique of the WTO. The coalition between the greens and a wide range of other advocacy groups who, although for different reasons, see the WTO as an institution captured by and serving only corporate interests is of considerable significance. Despite a wide range of views about the 'evils' of globalization the green message seems to be very effective in coalescing dissent. Indeed global environmental coalitions were first launched in preparation for and during the Rio Summit in 1992, a watershed event in increasing the role of NGOs and the first global summit to take place in the age of the new information technology. And the networks created at Rio were also part of the anti-NAFTA coalitions (Preston 1994).

It's also worth underlining the role of lawyers in North American advocacy groups. This role is indeed virtually unique and neither European nor Asian NGOs share the 'legalistic' culture of the US and Canada. In a report on the MAI issued by European MP Catherine Lalumière she stresses the role played by the 'Anglo-Saxon' environmental NGOs but also emphasizes their 'deep capacity for legal analysis' and recommends that the French government

---

[3] See world wide MAI website lists, *jeaton@fox.nstn.ca*, 3 April 1998.

hire more lawyers and that French universities train more lawyers 'knowledgeable in international law which is still largely anglo-saxon', (Lalumière
1998). Keynes reportedly said during the negotiations over the International
Trade Organization in the early 1940s that he had always believed that the
Mayflower was peopled by lawyers but he had changed his mind and now
knew that only missionaries were on board. Maybe he was right both times!
But humor aside, the legalistic approach to advocacy has become an important (and divisive) issue in the WTO as we will discuss below.

The campaign against the MAI was made possible by the Internet as use
accelerated in the mid-1990s. But as pointed out above, the campaign in Paris
was based on learning acquired in earlier anti-globalization experiences
utilizing the new technology, albeit in a less sophisticated form. As is characteristic of any innovation, learning by doing is a key element. Thus, while
building on the experience of the anti-MAI campaign, which had built on
NAFTA from experience at Rio, the mobilization of dissent against the WTO
Seattle meeting was far broader and deeper, and illustrates the potential of the
Internet to make the market for ideas contestable, a radical transformation
which will affect the domestic and international policy-making process.
Inexpensive, borderless, real time networking provides the NGOs with economics of scale and also of scope by linking often widely disparate groups
with one common theme. Equally important, it offers the opportunity to
disseminate strategic knowledge formerly concentrated in governments and
business.

An analysis of a large number of websites concerning Seattle and post-
Seattle developments suggests that there are three broad functional categories
of NGO coalitions or networks: what might be termed 'mobilization networks' whose chief objective is to rally support for a specific set of activities:
'technical networks' designed to facilitate and provide specific information;
networks dedicated to servicing, developing, and providing specific information; and networks dedicated to servicing developing countries which I call a
'virtual secretariat'.

Two examples of mobilization networks preparing for Seattle were the
International Civil Society Opposing a Millennium Round (ICS) and People's
Global Action (PGA). The ICS claimed to represent more than 1,400 local,
regional, and international NGOs from over eighty-seven countries. The list is
attached to their statement and includes environmentalist, religious and
human rights organizations, labor coalitions, women's groups, student
groups, and small farmer groups who are opposed to the agribusiness oligopoly, from all OECD countries and a large number of developing countries.[4]
The PGA is also a very broad coalition which was dedicated to organizing a
conference in Seattle on 30 November, at the outset of the WTO meetings. On

---

[4] See *http://www.twnside.org.sg/souths/twn/title/wtomr-cx.htm*.

the Internet the conference was termed N30. The PGA describes itself as 'an instrument for coordination, not an organization' and was formed in Geneva in February 1998.[5] The PGA organized a 'carnival against capitalism' in the city of London on 18 June 1999. The J18 carnival, as reported in *The Daily Telegraph*, deteriorated into violence, resulting in more than six hours of rioting and vandalism in the financial district. (*The Daily Telegraph* 1999: 1, 4, 5).

The mobilization networks are coalitions of a widely diverse set of NGOs often with conflicting interests. They pride themselves on their pure form of 'participatory democracy' with no center and no hierarchy. However in Seattle (and Washington during the April 2000 International Monetary Fund and World Bank meetings) both the libretto of the carefully choreographed street operas and the sound bites on television carried a simple, common theme—anti-globalization or, rather, anti-corporate globalization and pro-democracy. The charge was that the WTO (or the International Monetary Fund or the World Bank) is dominated by the interests of transnational corporations; that rules and procedures are 'undemocratic'; that it is harming the environment; and increasing inequality both within and among countries. The sound bite versions were the slogans: 'fix it or nix it'; 'no new round but turnaround'; 'shrink it or sink it'.

So one must distinguish between the loose mobilization networks of diverse NGOs around the world and the 'headquarters executives' responsible for creating and marketing the message. These HQ organizations such as Ralph Nader's 'Public Citizen' and 'Global Trade Watch'; the US-based 'Preamble Centre'; 'Friends of the Earth' in the UK (which organized the ICS manifesto) were aided in logistics planning by a number of groups including the 'Direct Action Network' or DAN, and the 'Ruckus Society', and in press relations and media management by 'Turning Point', an NGO formed only in 1999 to produce a series of advertisements in the *New York Times* on the effects of globalization on the environment. Some analysts have argued that NGOs like these are part of a new industry—the protest business (Jordan and Maloney 1997).

The protest business could be a new market created by the Internet—after all, technological innovation can generate wholly new products and services. It's difficult at this point in time to predict the viability of the new business but it seems to have combined three key ingredients or what I've termed the three Ms; a saleable *message*; a skillful *media* strategy; and *money* (from mass-mailings and a number of philanthropic institutions, mainly American).[6] The

---

[5]  See *http://www.agp.otg/agp/en/PGAenfos/about.html*.

[6]  The Chronicle of Philanthropy (*acewald@mindspring.ca*) noted that after Seattle and Washington a conference of the National Network of Grantmakers drew some 350 participants to Boston to discuss why philanthropies should care about globalization and promote NGOs concerned with the issue.

objective is to influence the policy process through public opinion. It's very important to underline, as noted earlier, that these new actors do not resemble the distributional coalitions sparring over the division of the pie. Indeed in the traditional version of the political economy of trade, their support is quite irrational because of the free rider problem associated with collective action for public goods. This definition of rationality needs a re-examination.

Following from that, it's important to distinguish the very prominent role of a traditional distributional lobby, the American unions in Seattle (less so in Washington) from the mobilization networks. The so-called Turtle–Teamster alliance between the unions and the greens was probably a marriage of convenience to influence American trade policy but it seems unlikely that a lasting alliance could be forged given the profound divisions between these two groups. What was heard in the streets of Seattle was, as suggested, the Voice externalized but workers of the world are more likely to compete than unite.

In marked contrast to the mobilization networks are the technical networks such as, for example, the Centre for International Environmental Law in Geneva and Washington; the International Institute for Sustainable Development in Winnipeg; the Institute for Agriculture and Trade Policy in Minneapolis; the International Centre for Trade and Sustainable Development in Geneva; WEED (World Economy, Ecology and Development) in Bonn; and the Institute for Global Communications in Palo Alto, California, which directs and supports the Association for Progressive Communication (APC) linking 15,000 NGO computers in 95 countries. It was the APC that played a major role in providing communications services for NGOs at Rio. The primary purpose of these, and a number of similar networks, is to facilitate the greater participation of NGOs in the policy process by providing a flow of strategic and technical information, very heavily weighted to environmental and legal issues. Some were present in Seattle and Washington, etc., but probably not many on the streets.

These technical groups are interested in influencing policy mainly by operating through institutional channels both governmental and intergovernmental. Events like Seattle provide an opportunity to access national delegations and network with other NGOs. One example of their operational effectiveness has been the ongoing debate over GMOs (genetically modified organisms). The meeting in Montreal on the Cartagena Biosafety Protocol at the end of January 2000 was widely expected to be another Seattle but, in fact, ended in an agreement (albeit as a result of brilliantly ambiguous drafting!) (*Economist* 2000a, 2000b; World Trade Agenda 2000). The large number of NGOs engaged in the meeting proclaimed victory, especially in inserting the precautionary principle, a very contentious subject at the WTO. *En route* to the WTO there will be a number of other steps being carefully planned including meetings of the Codex Alimentarius, the institution that establishes international food standards recognized by the WTO.

Finally, a remarkable and recent development has been the proliferation of NGOs dedicated to providing information and undertaking advocacy on behalf of developing countries—a virtual secretariat. Examples are 'Third World Network' in Malaysia with offices in India, Uruguay, Ghana, London, and Geneva, and established links with other NGOs in both north and south and a wide range of publications; TWN collaborates with the 'South Centre' in Geneva which is funded by LDC members with the mission of networking with other institutions 'to promote South solidarity' on policy; SEATINI (Southern and East African Trade and Information and Negotiations Initiative) with several offices in African countries and funding from UNDP and UNCTAD and a mission to build the knowledge base and capabilities of African countries; 'Focus on the Global South' in Thailand with a mission to link grassroots NGOs working on development issues to broader policy concerns including WTO and APEC; and CUTS (Consumer Unity and Trust Society) in India with a research and advocacy mission in trade and sustainable development. In addition, there are also a number of northern NGOs with a focus on Southern issues in the WTO such as 'Rongead' (European NGO Network on Agriculture, Trade Environment and Development) based in France, and funded by the European Commission, the French government, and a private Foundation; 'Intrac' (International NGO Research Centre) based in Oxford to train NGOs in developing countries and act as a consultancy; as well as a number of traditional development NGOs (such as Oxfam, Christian Aid, and other religious organizations) which are now focusing on trade and environmental issues.

This South 'virtual secretariat' provided a continual flow of information on negotiations in Geneva; helped formulate policy positions on all major issues; and many of their leaders were present in Seattle and at the UNCTAD meeting in Bangkok in February 2000. Once again, they are not a homogenous group and may differ on specific subjects but, the strategic assets of information and political know-how can provide a base for a significant increase in bargaining power in the WTO.

The new prominence of the NGOs in trade policy-making should be evaluated in a broader context. Thus the American business community— in marked contrast to their activist transnational role in the Uruguay Round—has maintained a low profile with respect to WTO negotiations. Apart from the service industries, the business community in both Europe and the United States has demonstrated little in the way of what might be termed generic or systemic interest, and even in the case of services the interest is sector-specific rather than cross-cutting, although that may well change over time, and perhaps E-commerce will be the catalyst. However, the current lack of activism is remarkable and one can only speculate as to the reasons. Perhaps the Uruguay Round was truly a singular event because it involved a radical transformation of the GATT system and the stakes were very high. Moreover, the global span of many corporations today facilitates direct negotiation with host governments so, ask many of them, why bother with lengthy and tedious intergovernmental negotiations? Privatization of trade policy may be an attractive option. Another factor is the restructuring of American corporations over the past decade which has required a sharper focus on a limited number of specific governmental lobbying objectives with shorter-term impact on the bottom line. Thus Chinese accession to the WTO was a top priority. (That also seemed to be the case for the US government whose objectives for a new round were minimal and defensive, while the EU position was far more assertive, including new issues such as investment and competition policy.) In the absence of a multilateral option which would require a narrowing of the transatlantic divide not only over agriculture but also more fundamental issues (of which more below), as the 1980s so clearly demonstrated, a revival of unilateralism, bilateralism, and regionalism should not be ruled out.

To sum up, if one were asked to predict the future of the world trading system the best single word would be 'uncertain'. But maybe that's too terse a reply. A layman's definition of Heisenberg's uncertainty principle is: we can know where we are but not where we are going, or we can know where we're going but not where we are. So, how about Heisenberg squared as a more specific response? Yet that too is not adequate. Many lessons can be learned from the anti-globalization upsurge. But most important is the urgent need to reform the WTO, a necessary but not sufficient condition to ensure the survival of a global rules-based trading system. The postwar architecture for international cooperation also needs restructuring.

# 9.6 REFORM OF THE WTO PLUS

The political compact which created the postwar economic architecture, the Bretton Woods institutions and what was to have been the International Trade Organization or ITO, rested on an assurance that international rules would preserve space for domestic policy autonomy. The ITO never came into existence but one piece of it, the GATT, survived and indeed thrived. The objectives of the GATT were: liberalizing trade through successive multilateral negotiations aimed at reducing border barriers; and creating rules to govern and sustain the liberalizing momentum. The domestic policy space, defined in terms of economic regulation and the maintenance of full employment, was safeguarded by rules to permit temporary blockage of imports under clearly specified terms (dumping, subsidies, and safeguards against import surges) as well as the rarely used but very broad Article 23 concerning 'nullification and impairment'. These rules were intended to provide a buffer or interface between the international objective of sustained liberalization and the objectives of domestic policy, in other words *sovereignty*. But with the Uruguay Round, the central domain of trade policy became domestic regulation, and legal systems and the definition of domestic policy space today not only differs from that of the postwar period (with the decline in economic regulatory intervention) but also differs significantly among the members of the WTO, especially with respect to social policy. The protective buffers have become protectionist tools, and in any case are largely irrelevant as a means of safeguarding the diverse and changing concept of sovereignty among the 130-plus members of the WTO.

It is not simply the move inside the border which represents the radical break between the GATT and the WTO. Of equal significance, as mentioned earlier, is the greatly strengthened Dispute Settlement Mechanism. It's important to note once again that the business groups who lobbied so successfully to include intellectual property in the Uruguay Round did so because the UN agency, the World Intellectual Property Organization (WIPO) has no dispute mechanism to enforce these rights. And, of course, the same is true for labor rights in the ILO or environmental policy in UNEP, the United Nations Environment Program. That's why the WTO is not simply a *magnet for discontent* but also for *policy overload*.

Since the establishment of the WTO, the most high-profile and contentious disputes have concerned environmental or food safety issues (but this is likely to change as services negotiations extend agreements into the areas of education, health, and culture.) The WTO does not regulate environmental or social policy but its rules, negotiated in the original GATT consensus, seek to constrain the trade restrictive impact of domestic regulation in order to prevent such regulation being used as a disguised barrier to trade. In recent cases, dispute panels and especially the Appellate Body (AB) have been forced to interpret the WTO rules which govern domestic environmental or food safety policies. Thus as is the case with all courts and all legal rules in such complex areas, that interpretation has essentially involved these judges in an international institution making law that defines the boundary for domestic policy space. And, not surprisingly, this has spawned the criticism, especially by the North American NGOs, that the WTO suffers a 'democratic deficit'. Here is the echo of the 1960s cry for participatory democracy.

The NGO demand for democratization really comprises three requests: more transparency (publication of WTO documents, etc.) more access to

WTO activities such as meetings of committees (this usually stops short of a request to be included in negotiations); and, for the legal advocacy NGOs, the right to observer status and to present *amicus curiae* briefs in dispute settlement panels and the Appelate Body. Of these three the first—transparency—is generally agreed by most member countries, and indeed a great deal of WTO documentation is now available on its website. The second—the right to greater participation—is far more controversial and needs to be carefully considered (see below). And the third is opposed by many southern NGOs as well as a large number of governments. This is worth spelling out.

Whatever the merits of the case for participation as *amicus curiae* in dispute settlement procedures by NGOs, it is clear that if it were granted other non-governmental actors would, in the name of fairness, demand equal treatment: for example corporations, unions, and private legal firms. Further, since *amicus* briefs often carry little weight in judicial decisions, it seems likely that the next step would be a demand for the right to bring cases directly. The result would be to transform the mechanism into a purely litigious and adversarial process. It's difficult to comprehend how this would 'democratize' the WTO unless, of course, one subscribed to the view that in a 'true' democracy private litigation is preferable to government regulation. While some would argue that the United States is moving to a system where 'lawsuits make policy' this combination of *laissez-faire* and *laissez-litiger* is not a model appropriate to an international institution. Indeed, there are now a number of proposals for reform of the dispute settlement system to make it less litigious and to promote mediation and arbitration in contentious cases.[7]

However, the NGO demand for democracy in terms of participation is perhaps the most difficult and controversial. The WTO is an intergovernmental organization and most member governments want to keep it that way. They argue that NGOs should deal with their own governments if they wish to play a role in the policy process. The response of the NGO advocates of participation is that only they have a truly transnational vision which is lacking in national governments so that, for example, 'a citizen who cares very deeply about ending whaling ... will find his or her views better represented in international fora by the Worldwide Fund for Nature than by his or her own government, which has many goals it must simultaneously pursue' (Esty 1998: 133). But it's not clear what the word citizen means in this context. There are no 'world' citizens but only citizens of nation-states. Governments are accountable to their citizens, albeit some more so than others. How would we define accountability in the case of nongovernmental organizations? And what about transparency? Who and where are their members? What is their source of funding? Are they 'accountable' to their membership or to their

---

[7] See e.g. Barfield, Claude (1999). 'More Than You Can Chew?', *The New Dispute Settlement System in the World Trade Organization*, paper prepared for the International Institution Advisory Commission, draft 15. *http://www.aei.org/past-event/conf1209b.htm*.

funders? These are simply examples of some of the questions that would have to be settled before a meaningful proposal on 'participatory democracy' in the WTO could be debated. But any such proposal would be fiercely opposed by most developing countries in the WTO—especially after their experience in Seattle.

For these countries, especially the poorest, the democratic deficit of the WTO stems from its governance structure. They feel—and are—excluded from many of the decision-making fora. The WTO is a member-driven organization governed by a rule of consensus: there is no weighted voting as is the case in the Bretton Woods institutions. But, of course, an organization with over 130 members, often with widely different views on important issues, cannot function when key and contentious policy issues must be negotiated. So other decision-making processes must be and are established. And, not surprisingly, these are dominated by the so-called Quad (the US, EU, Japan, and Canada) and the larger and more influential developing countries. This process worked in the past but the issues today are far more divisive and likely to become even more so. Thus the most urgent requirement to enhance the flexibility, adaptability, and legitimacy of the WTO is to establish a smaller body or Executive Committee which would in effect be a policy forum without rule-making power.

The Executive Committee would be able to meet on a regular basis and, with the assistance of the director-general and the secretariat, review current and prospective policy issues in order to advise the biennial Ministerial Conference, which would retain full decision-making authority. With such a forum, at both a ministerial and senior official level, the norms and principles of policy and the fundamental issue of forging a new international contract could be discussed and debated. It is essential to underline that forging a consensus in a smaller group aided by expert policy-analytic information is facilitated by peer group pressure. The Executive Committee can then play a role, at both the official and ministerial level, in promoting the extension of that consensus to the entire membership.

In establishing such a committee, the most difficult problem, of course, is membership and the various formulae tried out in the Uruguay Round failed to secure agreement. But the establishment of the Trade Policy Review Mechanism (TPRM), created a precedent for a possible formula. Thus different countries were subject to different review schedules on the basis of the member's share of world trade. This same formula could be used for establishing a committee of reasonable size and rotating membership which would ensure that all countries and regions would be represented within a given time frame (Ostry 1998: 25).

Another function of the Executive Committee supported by a high quality (although not necessarily large) expert secretariat would be the diffusion of knowledge in national capitals, another essential ingredient of consensus-building. This, in turn, would facilitate a 'democratization' of the policy-making process in member countries by making the debate more transparent and more inclusive.

In order to keep up to date and reasonably small in size, the WTO could not possibly generate all its policy analysis in-house. Like most research bodies today, the WTO secretariat would have to establish a research network linked to other institutions such as the OECD, the Bretton Woods institutions, private think tanks, universities, and the like. Knowledge networks are key elements in promoting cooperation and coordination. This networking should also include NGOs; business groups (the International Chamber of Commerce, for example); international labor associations, and so on.

While establishing an Executive Committee and improving the WTO's analytic and networking capabilities would help entrench the legitimacy and credibility of the institution, these reforms alone wouldn't do much to prevent further marginalization of many developing countries, especially the least developed. Technical assistance and more effective coordination with other international institutions will be required.

The gap between rich and poor countries has been widening over the past three decades largely due to differences in trend rates of growth of per capita income. The knowledge gap is far greater than the income gap and in the absence of change in domestic policies, as well as development policies directed at upgrading the institutional infrastructure, is bound to widen. This growing marginalization has little to do with trade but that fact has not prevented the anti-globalization movement from blaming the WTO.

Clearly, the WTO, with very limited technical training resources (less than one per cent of its budget) cannot deal alone with the marginalization problem. That may have been acceptable when trade policy was only about trade. But the much more demanding WTO agenda and the litigious and evidentiary-intensive dispute process has placed a burden on many non-OECD countries. The richer countries have access to analytical expertise at the OECD, at their home base, and also have far larger Geneva missions. So an upgrading of WTO training resources is urgently required. And this would also facilitate more effective coordination with the World Bank's efforts to improve the governance and institutional infrastructure, including legal systems and regulatory policies.

Reform of the WTO governance structure and enhanced research and training resources would help tackle the 'democratic deficit' but the so-called 'trade and...' issues will require confronting the inadequacy of the postwar international architecture. In the absence of a stronger (ILO) International Labor Organization and a new environmental institution, the WTO will continue to be a magnet for policy overload.

If the objective of the American and other OECD unions is to improve working arrangements in developing countries, the mandate rests with the

ILO. (If it's not, then it's a matter for domestic policy designed to ameliorate the distributional consequences of adjustment to global forces.) But the ILO has no power of enforcement. Moreover, many of its developing country members have resisted repeated attempts to improve enforcement capacity—while at the same time opposing labor standards in the WTO. Indeed in 1997 when the Director-General of the ILO proposed that the ILO could act to oversee a multilateral system of voluntary social labeling the initiative was rejected by the Non-Aligned Movement (O'Brien *et al.* 2000: 104). This dilemma (or hypocrisy) must be resolved and the ILO monitoring and enforcement mechanisms strengthened. But development institutions will also have to play their role since labor standards are clearly linked to growth. What will be needed, in effect, is reform of the ILO and more effective coordination with the WTO, the World Bank and UNCTAD, i.e. improved coherence in international policy-making which was in fact one of the objectives of the Uruguay Round, although at the time of the launch coherence was conceived in terms of coordination only with the Bretton Woods institutions.

It's worth noting that while this 'macro' approach to labor standards would rest on government policy, an innovative 'micro' policy is now rapidly evolving independently of government and, indeed, generated by 'technical' NGOs. The Washington-based Council on Economic Priorities (CEP), is a consumer organization established in 1969. In 1998 SA8000 was launched—on the Fiftieth Anniversary of the Universal Declaration of Human Rights. CEP had established a separate accreditation agency (CEPAA) only the year before which developed a 'social accountability' code that includes the ILO basic labor rights plus rules on wages and hours. The codes are technically designed for auditors and their development involved large corporations, unions, and NGOs. They have been endorsed by international certification agencies. Monitoring of the developing country subsidiaries of the transnational corporations which have adopted SA8000 will be carried out by a network of NGOs linked to CEPAA. While the information is designed for a consumer audience, the next step will be to involve investors, beginning with large pension funds. The core strategy of this micro policy is market-like: consumer and investor pressure will force an increasing number of firms to join the SA8000 crowd with a little help from global whistleblowers and the media! This policy innovation is very new (and but one example of a burgeoning of 'soft law' projects) (Clapp 1998: 295–316; Diller 1999: 99–128), but certainly it is worthy of further research, especially as it is also a spin-off from the information technology revolution. As CEP has noted, 'With instantaneous media connection and the internet . . . today's remote factory scandal can become tomorrow's global headline.'[8]

---

[8] See SA8000 in References.

While labor standards have no place in the WTO, the same cannot be said of environmental issues. Trade and the environment are linked in both positive and negative ways as the recent report by the WTO has clearly demonstrated (World Trade Organization (WTO) 1999b). But using trade policy as an instrument of environmental policy is both ineffective in terms of achieving environmental objection and costly in terms of growth. However, in the absence of a strong environmental institution (which the United Nations Economic Program or UNEP is not) using the dispute settlement mechanism to define the boundary between domestic and international policies will not work and the WTO will continue to be under attack. Perhaps as a first step, housing all the multilateral environmental agreements in a reinforced UNEP could help the process but, in effect, only a new WEO (World Environmental Organization) with a clearly defined mission, political influence, and analytic and technical resources could effectively launch the policy dialogue on the relationship between ecology and economy, including, of course, the role of trade. This will not be easy because there really are significant differences between the two models—the economic and the ecological—even if we reject both utopian formulations. The economists' concepts of maximization and trade-offs; of equilibrium; and the primacy of efficiency, yield unambiguous policy statements. A defining characteristic of the ecological sciences is uncertainty, seen most vividly today in the rapid and unprecedented changes in biotechnology. If risk can't be accurately estimated then unambiguous assessments are precluded. Moreover, the ecological paradigm stresses the goals of equality, and community as well as efficiency, so the two paradigms, even in modified versions, will not be easy to reconcile. What the eventual outcome of the debate will be remains to be seen. But an optimist would opine that where there's a political will there's a policy way. The best hope is that, unlike the Asian financial crisis in 1997, which led to much talk about architecture but little action, the ongoing assault on the global trading system may prove to be the catalyst for a serious rethinking of global policy.

## REFERENCES

BARRO, ROBERT J. (1999). 'Inequality, Growth and Investment', *National Bureau of Economic Research Working Paper 7038.* Cambridge, Mass.: National Bureau of Economic Research.

BELL, DANIEL (1976). *The Cultural Contradictions of Capitalism.* New York: Basic Books.

BLENDON, ROBERT J., and associates (1999). 'The 60's and the 90's', *Brookings Review.* Washington, DC: Brookings Institution.

BRITTAN, SAMUEL, and HAMLIN, ALAN (eds.) (1993). 'Market Capitalism and Moral Values', *Proceedings of Section F (Economics) of the British Association for the Advancement of Science.*

*Chronicle of Philanthropy, The* (*acewald@mindspring.ca*).

CLAPP, JENNIFER (1998). 'The Privatization of Global Environmental Governance: ISO 14000 and the Developing World', *Global Governance,* 4.

CROOME, JOHN (1995). *Reshaping the World Trading System.* Geneva: World Trade Organization.

*Daily Telegraph, The* 'Mobs Put City Under Siege', (London, 19 June 1999).

DALY, HERMAN E. (1993). 'From Adjustment to Sustainable Development: The Obstacle of Free Trade', *The Case Against Free Trade.* San Francisco, Calif.: Earth Island Press.

DILLER, JANELLE (1999). 'A Social Conscience in the Global Market Place? Labour, Dimensions of Codes of Conduct, Social Labeling and Investor Initiatives,' *International Labour Review,* CXXXVIII/2: 99–128.

*Economist, The* (17 July 1999, 29 January 2000, and 5 February 2000).

ESTY, DANIEL C. (1998). 'Non-Governmental Organizations at the World Trade Organization: Cooperation, Competition or Exclusion', *Journal of International Economic Law,* 1/1: 133.

FELDSTEIN, MARTIN (1998). 'Income Inequality and Poverty', *National Bureau of Economic Research Working Paper 6770.* Cambridge, Mass.: National Bureau of Economic Research.

GOWDY, JOHN M., and FERRERI CARBONELL, ADA (1999). *Ecological Economics,* 29/3: 321–498.

GRAY, JOHN (1999). *False Dawn: The Delusions of Global Capitalism.* London: Granta Books.

HARRISON, ANN, and HANSON, GORDON (1999). 'Who Gains from Trade Reform: Some Remaining Puzzles', *Journal of Development Economics,* 59: 125–54.

*http://www.agp.org/agp/en/PGAenfos/about.html.*

*http://www.twnside.org.sg/souths/twn/title/wtomr-cx.html.*

JORDAN, GRANT, and MALONEY, WILLIAM A. (1997). *The Protest Business? Mobilizing Campaign Groups.* Manchester: Manchester University Press.

KENEN, PETER, and OSTRY, SYLVIA (1999). 'Overview: The Evolving Corporation', *The Evolving Corporation.* Washington, DC.: Group of Thirty Study Group Report.

KEY, JR., V. O. (1963). *Public Opinion and American Democracy.* New York: Alfred A. Knopf.

LALUMIÈRE, CATHERINE, European MP, and LANDAU, JEAN-PIERRE, Inspector General of Finance (Republic of France: Ministry of the Economy, 1998). Original available at *http://www.finances.gouv.fr/pole.*

LAZEAR, EDWARD P. (1999). 'Economic Imperialism', *National Bureau of Economic Research Working Paper 7300.* Cambridge, Mass.: National Bureau of Economic Research.

O'BRIEN, ROBERT, GOETZ, ANNE MARIE, SCHOLTE, JAN AART, and WILLIAMS, MARC (2000). *Contesting Global Governance: Multilateral Economic Institutions and Global Social Movements.* Cambridge: Cambridge University Press.

OECD (1997). *Report of Regulatory Reform,* ii: Thematic Studies/2: 191–248 (Paris).

OSTRY, SYLVIA (1990). *Governments and Corporations in a Shrinking World*. New York: Council on Foreign Relations.

—— (1998). *Reinforcing the WTO*. Washington, DC: Group of Thirty Study Group Report.

—— (1999). 'The Sen Commandments: A Review of Development as Freedom: Human Capability and Global Need', *National Post*, Toronto (Sept. 25).

PREEG, ERNEST H. (1995). *Traders in a Brave New World*. Chicago: University of Chicago Press.

PRESTON, SHELLEY (1994). 'Electronic Global Networking and the NGO Movement: The 1992 Rio Summit and Beyond', *Swords and Ploughshares: A Chronicle of International Affairs*, iii/2, Spring. Washington, DC: The Graduate Student Council of the School of International Service, The American University.

RODRIGUEZ, FRANCISCO, and RODRIK, DANI (1999). 'Trade Policy and Economic Growth: A Skeptic's Guide to the Cross-National Evidence', *National Bureau of Economic Research Working Paper 7081*. Cambridge, Mass.: National Bureau of Economic Research.

'SA8000: Setting the Standard for Corporate Social Accountability', *http://www. cepaa.org*.

SCHUMPETER, JOSEPH A. (1942). *Capitalism, Socialism and Democracy*, 3rd edn. New York: Harper and Bros.

SMYTHE, ELIZABETH, and SMITH, PETER J. (1999). 'Globalization, Citizenship and Technology: The MAI meets the Internet', paper presented at the annual meeting of the Canadian Political Science Association. Sherbrooke, Quebec (mimeo.).

WELCH, FINIS (1999). 'Richard T. Ely Lecture: In Defense of Inequality', *American Economic Review*, 89/2: 1–17.

*World Trade Agenda* (14 February 2000), Geneva.

*World Trade Organization*, Press Release (28 Sept. 1999), Geneva.

—— Special Studies 4, 'Trade and Environment', (1999), Geneva.

*World Wide MAI Website Lists, jeaton@fox.nstn.ca* (3 April 1998).

CHAPTER 10

..................................................

# CAPITAL FLOWS, CAPITAL CONTROLS, AND INTERNATIONAL BUSINESS RISK

..................................................

DAVID M. BERG

STEPHEN E. GUISINGER

AMONG the critical elements in the political and policy environment facing firms involved in international business are the flow, regulation, and risk surrounding international capital flows, for both direct and portfolio investment outside the firm's domestic environment. Much like trade flows, capital flows can be either stimulated or suppressed, can be regulated or allowed free movement, can contribute to the integration or isolation of national economies. In this chapter, we review the literature on capital flows in the world economy, along with those on the utilization of capital controls and the broader issues of international business risks associated with debt and equity capital flows for both firms and financial institutions active internationally. We then conclude with a brief discussion of some of the research topics facing the field of international business in these areas.

Table 10.1 Annual average growth rates GDP vs. FDI

|  | 1960–70 | 1970–80 | 1980–90 |
|---|---|---|---|
| World GDP growth | 5.3% | 3.6% | 2.8% |
| FDI growth (stock) | 8.1% | 13.7% | 12.3% |

# 10.1 CAPITAL FLOWS

Since 1960, growth rates for foreign direct investment (FDI) have been far higher than those of world GDP. Table 10.1 above, drawn from Thomas (1997), illustrates this growth phenomenon through 1990. International Monetary Fund (IMF) data for the period from 1991–97 continue this dramatic trend, depicting an increase in worldwide direct investment outflows from $193 billion in 1991 to nearly $419 billion in 1997—an increase of 117 per cent in six years (*Balance of Payments Statistics Yearbook* 1998).

This increasing level of cross-national investment reflects the growing importance of multinational firms in total world production. Thomas also notes that the stock of FDI emanating from the developed countries rose from $67 billion in 1960 to $1.87 trillion in 1992, and that foreign sales rose from 30 per cent of overall sales in 1971 to 40 per cent in 1980 (p. 70). Not only has the *potential* for capital mobility increased, due, in part, to factors like decreasing transportation and communication costs, but *actual* mobility has increased. In the remainder of his 1997 book, Thomas focuses on the increased inter-nationalization of the automobile industry, but such has been the experience of many other industries as well, during this period. In a survey of overall financial liberalization in thirty-four countries, Williamson and Mahar (1998) found that in 1973, only nine countries—the US, Canada, West Germany, Hong Kong, Indonesia, Malaysia, Singapore, Mexico, and South Africa—had 'liberalized' or 'largely liberalized' international capital flows, while by 1996, twenty-eight of the thirty-four fit into one of those two categories.

Why has such integration in capital flows occurred? Fischer and Reisen (1994) suggest three reasons: (1) controls have become less effective due to growing integration of trade and financial innovation, as well as capital flow relaxation by other countries, leading to a sort of *de facto* opening; (2)

bilateral trade talks have exerted pressure on some countries to open their financial systems and let currencies float; and (3) the OECD (Organization for Economic Cooperation and Development) Codes of Liberalization commit member countries (and thus, those pursuing membership) to 'eliminate any restrictions between member countries on current invisible operations and capital movements' (p. 1). Kindleberger (1987) also points to the advent of flexible exchange rates in 1973, innovations in communications and transportation bringing world markets closer, and new financial instruments. Drabek and Griffith-Jones (1999) echo the factors of increased overall liberalization and communications technologies, adding that of the growth of institutional investors who both can and will invest internationally. Finally, Popper points to the elimination of withholding taxes in countries such as the US, France, Germany, and the United Kingdom, as well as the way in which 'many Latin American countries liberalized their markets as part of broader stabilization packages' (1997: 5).

In his introduction to a volume of multi-industry, multi-national case studies in FDI and development, Chan (1995) points out that these investment flows have, until recently, remained largely concentrated in the developed countries, who received 83 per cent of global FDI in 1990, although Chan notes the increase of outward FDI from some newly industrializing countries like Taiwan, due, perhaps, to 'concerns of rising labor costs, wages, pollution costs and foreign protectionism' (p. 2). Chan goes on to note several trends with regard to capital and investment flows: first, that rising FDI, to some extent, has replaced arm's length trading relationships with more efficient intrafirm trade; second, that ongoing globalization and regionalization tend to increase FDI; third, that FDI has become more acceptable in some countries as official development aid has decreased; and fourth, that these developments have been perhaps most noticeable in the former socialist economies of Central and Eastern Europe.

Indeed, despite the large volume of capital flows among the developed countries, significant growth has occurred in the share and volume of worldwide FDI sent into developing countries, and much research attention in the 1990s has focused on issues of capital flows to and from the developing countries, perhaps since that phenomenon is not only newer, but also growing at a faster rate from a smaller base. Perhaps in confirmation of this, Kant (1996) notes that 'foreign direct investment (FDI) has been the largest single source of external finance for developing countries since 1993. In 1995, the share of developing countries in global FDI inflows reached an historic high of 38 per cent' (p. 1)—more than double the 17 per cent reported by Chan (1995) for 1990. Two years later, for 1997, the IMF figures set that percentage at nearly 44 per cent (*Balance of Payments Statistics Yearbook*, 1998). Park and Song (1996) report that the developing countries of Asia received a net inflow of $261 billion in foreign capital from 1990–4, more than double the amount received in the prior decade. They go on to study the experiences of Korea, Thailand, Malaysia, and Indonesia in managing those flows. Drabek and Griffith-Jones edited a 1999 volume on the management of such inflows in the emerging market economies of Europe, which also attracted high levels of foreign capital during the 1990s.

Increased financial integration on a global basis, facilitating capital inflows and outflows, is generally seen as a good thing for the world economy. Fischer and Reisen note among the benefits of such liberalization: 'Dismantling capital controls is generally presumed to generate economic benefits through cross-border portfolio diversification in both assets and liabilities and increased opportunities for intertemporal trade, by imposing macroeconomic discipline on national governments, and from the rising costs and ineffectiveness of controls as economic development proceeds' (1994: 3). Bayoumi (1997) suggests that integrated international capital markets connect potential lenders and borrowers, leading to higher savings and investment and increased efficiency in capital markets, resulting in higher consumer welfare.

However, in the introduction to his study of the Taiwanese case, Kuo (1991) points out that such liberalization is a relatively new phenomenon, even among the industrialized countries. He points out that the US used the Interest Equalization Tax and the Voluntary Foreign Credit Restraint Program in support of relatively segmented financial markets from 1963–74, and that Japan maintained significant barriers to capital movements in both directions as recently as 1979. While the industrialized countries are now generally liberal with regard to capital flows, the newly industrialized and lesser developed countries (NICs and LDCs) have traditionally been importers, rather than exporters, of capital, and therefore, more sensitive to the impact created by inflows of foreign capital. From a position of strict economic efficiency, Kuo concedes that open capital markets support the principle of comparative advantage, allowing capital to flow 'from where it is plentiful to where it is scarce, thereby maximizing national and world productivity' (Kuo 1991: 34), but notes that such overall gains, as is often the case, are not necessarily evenly distributed.

In fact, much attention has been focused on the potential risks of too much openness too soon when it comes to developing countries and capital flows. Fischer and Reisen note that: '(b)ased on some dismal liberalization experiences... most economists recommend a late opening of the capital account in the reform process' (1994: 3). Manzocchi titles a section of his 1999 book: 'Liberalisation and Instability: The Debate of the 1990s' (p. 21). Drabek and Griffith-Jones (1999) point out three main challenges for policymakers in Central and Eastern Europe: (1) attracting foreign capital, (2) managing surges of large capital inflows, and (3) managing volatility and decline in those flows. Williamson titles his chapter in the 1997 edited volume *Capital*

*Controls in Emerging Economies*, 'Orthodoxy is Right: Liberalize the Capital Account Last', and goes on to point out that too-soon-liberalized capital flows may lead to misdirected investment, too-easily-funded budget deficits, and an overvalued currency. Williamson and Mahar provide a report of the various effects of overall financial liberalization in thirty-four countries (including liberalizing international capital flows), including post-liberalization financial crises (1998). After the Latin American debt crises of the 1980s and the Asian financial crises of the late 1990s, Beddoes suggests: 'The recent spate of crises in emerging markets around the world has shattered the consensus over the benefits of unfettered capital flows' (1999: 16), but goes on to suggest that radical restructuring of the global financial system would be going too far. So what can countries do?

Some researchers have proposed tools. Williamson (1999) provides a list of twelve policy options a government faced with large capital inflows may use to manage those flows. Wihlborg and Dezseri (1997) compile a series of eight preconditions for capital account liberalization put forth in the literature, including fiscal discipline, stable domestic macroeconomic conditions, and the ability to limit tax base erosion. Thus, while international capital flows have significantly increased in the past decades, it is not clear that the era of capital controls, or the rational justification of them, is at an end.

Complicating the study of capital controls is the widespread use of tax incentives by host countries to divert capital inflows to priority sectors. It is not unusual to find host countries maintaining restrictions on capital inflows while simultaneously offering generous tax incentives for capital flowing to certain sectors of the economy. Developing countries, such as Indonesia, may screen foreign direct investment on a case-by-case basis, but then offer tax holidays to investors in a particular industrial sector or in a particular location within the host country. One study (Guisinger 1985) identified more than fifty different instruments, including capital controls, used by host governments to encourage or discourage investment to achieve various social objectives.

Some economists have questioned the effectiveness of tax incentives in altering the allocation of investment within a country or in raising the aggregate level of investment. They argue that investment decisions are made on the basis of commercial and long run economic factors and not tax policies that are subject to sudden revision. However, evidence compiled in a number of different settings suggests that, at the margin, tax policies affect investor behavior. Guisinger (1985) found that in seventy-four foreign direct investment projects studied, the absence of all incentives would have caused investors to locate new projects in other countries in almost two-thirds of the investments studied. Michael Boskin and William Gale (1987: 215) found that 'a tax policy [for the United States] which raises the after-tax rate of return enough to lead to a dollar of increased domestic investment in the US brings with it between 8 and 27 cents of FDI'.

In the next section, we detail further the rationale, impacts, and debate over capital controls in the international arena.

# 10.2 CAPITAL CONTROLS

## 10.2.1 Objectives/motivations

Governments impose controls on capital movements for a variety of reasons. Governments use capital controls to pursue short-term concerns– maintaining a desired value of the exchange rate, for example. They also use controls in an effort to achieve long-term objectives, such as building and maintaining the country's stock of capital. Sometimes, controls are applied narrowly to only certain sectors. At other times, controls are broad based, addressing macroeconomic concerns affecting all sectors. Governments may attempt to control both capital inflows and outflows. The complex scope of capital controls is apparent in Table 10.2, which provides a stylized account of focus, instruments, and motivation for capital controls. Motivations for capital controls (shown below in Table 10.2) can be grouped under three broad headings: macroeconomic management; development; and risk abatement.

### 10.2.1.1 *Macroeconomic management*

1. Maintaining pegged exchange rates: perhaps the most widely cited reason for capital controls is macroeconomic management, especially to avoid balance of payments disequilibrium. The Mundell-Fleming model rests on the assumption that government efforts to stabilize the economy are welfare-enhancing (Dooley 1995). When governments use fiscal policy to stabilize the domestic economy, the Mundell-Fleming framework suggests that capital controls may be necessary to achieve goals of internal and external balance. Some governments regard controls on short-term capital as their principal defense against speculators who seek to profit from changes in pegged exchange rates.

2. Capturing an inflation tax: another objective of a government's macroeconomic policy may be to finance government spending through the use of

## Table 10.2 Scope and rationale for capital controls

| Focus of control | Inflow instrument | Rationale | Outflow instrument | Rationale |
|---|---|---|---|---|
| Capital and money markets (shares; mutual funds; debt instruments; money market instruments; derivatives) | Limit purchases of financial instruments by non-residents; limit sale abroad by residents | Macroeconomic management | Limit sale of foreign financial instruments by non-residents; limit purchases abroad by residents | Macroeconomic management |
| Credit operations | Limit loans to residents by non-residents | Risk abatement; Development | Limit loans to non-residents by residents | Macroeconomic management |
| Direct investment | Tax and direct controls, including negative list of banned sectors | Development | Controls on liquidation of direct investments; taxes or direct controls on purchases of controlling interests abroad | Development |
| Real estate transactions | Limit purchases by non-residents | Development | Limit purchases by residents | Development |
| Commercial bank regulations | Limit non-resident deposits | Risk abatement | Regulate deposits overseas | Risk abatement |
| Personal portfolios | Limit transfers to residents from non-residents | Development; Risk abatement; Macroeconomic management | Limit transfers from residents to non-residents | Development; Risk abatement; Macroeconomic management |

inflationary finance. Governments can tax domestic savers indirectly by allowing inflation to reduce the real value of the money balances. Giovanni and de Melo (1993) showed that financial repression serves as an important source of government revenue for some countries. By closing off the opportunity for savers to move funds abroad, governments can maximize their returns from this tax.

### 10.2.1.2 *Development objectives*

1. Correct distortions: one of the most common reasons offered by governments for controls on the movement of capital is that they are necessary to offset distortions elsewhere in the economy. The economic theory of the second-best claims that governments can enhance national welfare by imposing new distortions in an economy riddled by pre-existing distortions that cannot be easily removed. These countervailing distortions in effect nullify the welfare-reducing properties of pre-existing distortions and partially restore welfare to the level achievable under distortion-free conditions.

Conditions in developing countries provide fertile ground for second-best theorizing. Razin and Sadka (1991) argue that governments face a structural problem in taxing resident's income from foreign capital compared to their ability to tax income from resident's holdings of domestic capital. In their model, capital outflow restrictions increase the feasible tax base. Harberger (1986) has argued that the cost of foreign borrowing is a function of country risk, which increases in proportion to the amount of resident's foreign borrowing. A resident's decision to borrow abroad may not take into account the increased cost to other resident borrowers—i.e. the private marginal cost to one borrower may be less than the increased social cost to the country. Under these conditions, a government restriction limiting foreign borrowing would be welfare maximizing.

In practice, governments have difficulty fine-tuning second-best policies. Second-best policies that overshoot or undershoot the optimal policy level could reduce welfare compared to a policy of non-intervention.

2. Infant industry protection: many governments view their financial institutions as underdeveloped in comparison with those in developed countries. At the core of many of the infant industry protection arguments for capital controls are the poorly defined property rights that exist in developing countries. As an example, Tornell and Velasco (1992) have developed a model in which resident investors prefer foreign to domestic investment when the social returns on domestic investments exceed private returns that are depressed because investors are concerned about preserving their property rights. This argument applies also to limitations on capital inflows. Reduced competition from foreign investors is one way of raising rates of return to domestic investors.

### 10.2.1.3 *Risk abatement*

Governments regulate domestic financial institutions to ensure sound institutions with prudent lending policies. This same motivation extends to international risk exposure. Governments may choose to limit their financial sector's international exposure out of a desire to limit systemic risk. Dornbusch (1986), for example, has argued that capital controls may slow down short-term capital movements but this can only be a transitory measure. Van Wijnbergen (1985) has noted that investors recognize the option value of waiting in the presence of uncertainty. Consequently, government efforts to reduce uncertainty can lower the option value of waiting and bring domestic investment closer to its optimal level.

1. Experience with capital control instruments: the arguments for capital controls lead logically to two related questions. First, what has been the pattern of capital controls that have been erected on the basis of these theoretical constructs? Second, have these controls been effective? Even where theoretically persuasive, capital controls must be evaluated in the light of practical experience. As noted in the case of second-best arguments, governments have difficulty in setting policies to optimal levels and in enforcing other regulations and laws that permit capital control policies to operate effectively.

On the first question, Johnston and Tamirisa (1998) develop a number of stylized facts about controls, using a sample of forty-five developing and transition countries.

1. Controls on outflows are more prevalent than controls on inflows, except for direct foreign investment and real estate purchases.
2. High correlations exist between controls on inflows and outflows, suggesting that they are imposed concurrently.
3. Lower correlation on direct investment controls with capital and money market controls, suggesting unique reasons for these controls.

2. Do capital controls achieve their objectives? Because of the complexity of capital control systems, this question defies straightforward answers. Countries differ greatly in their stage of development and degree of economic distress when capital controls are first applied. General conclusions drawn about capital controls may not apply to individual countries at different stages of development or in different phases of the business cycle. The measure of success is also open to question. Controls may affect a variety of economic variables but still fail to raise the welfare of a country by more than the cost of the control system.

Dooley (1995) has surveyed a number of studies that attempted to measure the effectiveness of control systems. His survey suggests the following:

1. Capital control systems can be effective for short periods of time in maintaining spreads between spot exchange rates in dual currency regimes.
2. Attempts to control capital outflows are doomed to failure unless all possible substitute avenues for capital export are also controlled.
3. Governments can defend their currencies against speculative attacks for short periods of time but they cannot end the threat of future speculative attacks.

4. Capital controls have not prevented changes in exchange rates when the balance of payments was in fundamental disequilibrium.
5. Developing countries markedly increase the breadth and restrictiveness of control systems in the year prior to devaluations in their currencies.
6. Developing countries are less adept at managing control systems.
7. Controls on capital inflows prevent risk diversification and discourage high-risk projects with potentially large social returns.

# 10.3 INTERNATIONAL BUSINESS RISK ENVIRONMENTS

The implications of capital controls for international businesses are just one aspect of the uncertainties or risks involved in doing business outside a firm's domestic market. Much has been written on the interface of multinational enterprises with their international business environments. Both academics and financial market practitioners have published 'how-to' manuals and rankings of countries based on their risk profiles. Some focus on the assessment of such risk (Rogers 1983, 1986, 1988, 1997; Jodice 1985), while others emphasize ways in which firms may manage such risk, or at least their approach to it (Kobrin 1982; Kennedy 1987). The labeling of this risk, however, has not always been consistent. Scholars have written of country risk as both the composite of generic risks inherent in a host country environment (Roberts 1988) and as 'the possibility that a sovereign state or sovereign borrowers of a particular country may be unable or unwilling...to fulfill their obligations towards a foreign lender and/or investor' (Krayenbuehl 1985: 3), while others have labeled this latter risk as sovereign risk (Heffernan 1986). Another term which has seen wide use is 'political risk', which is generally used to refer to 'potentially significant managerial contingencies generated by political events and processes' (Kobrin 1982: 29), but, as noted by Haendel, 'the implications of the term *political risk* vary with the interests and needs of the definer' (1979: 5). While it has been suggested that these three characterizations of risk may, in fact, be nested (Sovereign Risk nested within Political Risk nested within Country Risk), the inconsistent labeling of these risks makes this initially problematic. Thus, in exploring the literature on these types of risk, it seems appropriate to define and differentiate among the three types of risk to be discussed here: political risk, country risk, and sovereign risk. Following this discussion of the three types of risk, we will again address the relationships among these risk characterizations based on their common and distinctive aspects.

## 10.3.1 Political risk

The first, and perhaps most restrictive definition of risk we will address is that of *political risk*. Kobrin (1979) comprehensively reviews the literature on political risk, noting that, up to that point, most writing on political risk had focused on either host country interference in business operations, or events such as political acts or constraints imposed on the firm. He then goes on to suggest that firms develop means of assessing and responding to that risk; Kobrin, Basek, Blank, and La Palombara (1980), in surveying 455 firms, found such assessment to be an emerging function in large international firms, but still more reactive than active. Building on previous research, Kobrin (1982) defines political risk as politically generated circumstances which may have significant implications for management. He goes on to refine this definition by distinguishing between political processes and those resulting from normal supply- and demand-related economic forces (excluding those economically generated contingencies from his definition), by defining 'significant contingencies' in relation to 'their potential effect on the magnitude and distribution of cash flows' (p. 48)—thus introducing an element of uncertainty (an alternative definition of risk), and finally by specifying the nature of the relationship between the firm and the relevant political environment. In this final case, Kobrin suggests that the 'relationship between the political environment and the firm's operations may be direct or indirect and negative or positive. In most instances government policy provides the linkage between environment and impacts of the organization' (p. 49). Kobrin also notes that the contingencies mentioned in this definition are more likely defined as micro or firm/industry-specific, rather than macro or country-wide. Kennedy suggests: '(a) political risk event is one that threatens a firm with a financial, strategic, or personnel loss *due to non-market forces* [emphasis added] . . . definitions of political risk, therefore, that focus on environmental uncertainties or changes as such are misplaced' (1987: 5). In essence, this definition coincides with the major points of Kobrin's, emphasizing political rather than market forces, firm-specific threats, and allowing for the possibility that some changes may not be detrimental to the firm. Finally, in compiling an extensive bibliography of work on political risk assessment, Jodice (1985) defines political risk as 'Changes in the operating conditions of foreign enterprises that arise out of the political process . . . that affect ownership and behavior of the firm. Political risk can be conceptualized as events, or a series of events, in the national and international environments that can affect the physical assets, personnel, and operations of foreign firms' (p. 5).

Empirically, Brewer (1983) focuses on the relationship between political instability and policy instability, finding that the former is not necessarily strongly associated with the latter. He later further explores the role of government policies in increasing or decreasing market imperfections and FDI (1993), reporting on the effects of host country actions ranging from protectionist import policies to export subsidies, many of which fall under the political risk umbrella. Nigh (1985) also explores the relationship between political events and manufacturing foreign direct investment (MFDI) from the US, finding differences between developed and less developed countries. He finds that US MFDI in developed countries is only affected by conflict and cooperation between nations, while US MFDI in less developed countries is also affected by conflict and cooperation within the host country. Jain and Nigh (1989) also test the effects of conflict and cooperation on bank lending to foreign countries, finding that banks tend to focus on cooperative political events between home and host country in making their lending decisions.

Interest in researching the impact of host country political developments on a firm's activities is driven by what Jodice refers to as:

the increased perception (based on real experience) of greater risk in foreign operations derived directly from war, revolution, and civil violence or indirectly through government policy change (expropriation or nationalization of ownership; regulation of behavior; restrictions on sourcing or remission of earnings ... With the end of the major colonial empires in 1960, came a surge in national assertiveness toward the foreign investor. (1985: 4)

The rapid post-World War II internationalization of many firms coincided with this rise in national sentiments and growing interdependence in the world economy, adding what Kennedy (1987) refers to as 'more complexity and uncertainty to the corporate external environment' (p. 2). Firm assets and activities were increasingly impinged upon by host governments. The political risk environment of the 1960s and 1970s focused on this rise in national sentiment, and a growing literature on nationalization spoke of expropriation as a 'psychic commodity' (Jodice 1985: 10); and as early as 1953–4, Bronfenbrenner produced a list of eight risk-generating factors in the political environment of the twentieth century, including the awareness of income disparities, frustration at limited upward social mobility, and the favoring of domestic groups versus foreigners.

Minor (1994) reports on a number of studies done in the 1970s and 1980s to tally the expropriation ('forced divestment of equity ownership of a foreign direct investor', p.178) of foreign firms' operations in developing countries from 1960–79, most notably, Kobrin (1984), and then goes on to update that survey through 1994. He supports Kobrin's conclusion that 'expropriation has declined because developing countries have found other effective and efficient methods of dealing with multinational investors' (p. 178). The rate of expropriations was found to increase during the 1960s and sharply in the early 1970s, peaking in 1974–5, declining markedly through the late 1970s, and basically disappearing after 1986. The last expropriations noted by Minor were in Peru in the mid-1980s. This does not imply, however, that political risk for internationally active firms disappears at this time, since Minor also echoes Kobrin's suggestion that the relatively heavy-handed expropriation has been replaced by more regulatory controls and an increased confidence in the host country's bargaining power.

More recent work on political risk, therefore, focuses on the impact of this type of regulation and negotiation on foreign investments, as well as on the inherent risks of international political change or instability. Makhija (1993) speaks of the 'increasing government sophistication in regulating multinational firms' (p. 531), and creates a political risk model which focuses on government intervention, which she defines as: 'those acts stemming from the host government that are designed to precipitate change in the behavior of the multinational firms in a direction compatible with host government objectives . . . in the form of regulations and policies that are official in nature and require a certain level of compliance' (p. 533). She then tests her model on the Venezuelan petroleum industry from 1947–76, finding some support for her hypothesis: 'that government decision makers take into account certain types of industry-related information when making the decision to intervene in a particular manner' (p. 548). This fine-tuned approach, while still posing potential risks to the individual firm or industry, is far more sophisticated than simple expropriation, and provides the potential for ongoing mutual benefit.

From a portfolio diversification standpoint, Cosset and Suret (1995) find that diversifying investment among politically risky countries not only improves risk-return characteristics, but also reduces overall risk in an investment portfolio, demonstrating that, at least as far as portfolio investment goes, investment in countries seen as politically risky may not be detrimental. This reflects the more recent emphasis on firm level strategies as means of coping with or controlling both political and country-level risk at the same time the nation is furthering its own goals. For example, Lenway and Murtha title their 1994 article 'The State as Strategist in International Business Research', emphasizing the fact that both firms and nations have agendas and means of carrying them out. Therefore, since political risk, as defined here, is but one component of the international or country-level risk faced by a multinational firm in carrying out its aims, we now move on to our second, most inclusive, category of international business risk, country risk.

## 10.3.2 Country risk

While we have characterized political risk as being firm- or industry-specific, the term has also been used in a more generic sense, to represent not only firm-level but overall host country environmental risk. For our purposes, however, we will refer to such a country-level construct as *Country Risk*. Prior to introducing their country-level risk ratings and overall risk assessments for over seventy countries worldwide, Business International Corporation sets forth their definition:

country risk refers to exposure to either an outright loss or to an unanticipated lower earnings stream in cross-border business, caused by *economic, financial, or socio-political events or conditions* [emphasis added] in a particular country that are not under the control of a private enterprise or individual. This risk exposure can apply to direct foreign investment, import-export relationships, technology and know-how, licensing or lending. It refers to uncertainty about future conditions within a country or those current conditions that cause inherent instability in or uncertainty about the future. (1981: 2)

They then go on to elaborate on the components of country risk: (1) financial risk (currency uncertainties, financial policy uncertainties, and financial ramifications of economic performance; (2) economic risk (such as the size and growth of the economy, export composition, and external dependencies); and (3) operating environment factors (including legal structure, red tape, local labor unions, and the country's cultural basis), as well as a dozen examples of political risk, including radical change in government policy or composition, expropriation, and nationalization. For them, political risk is only one part of the country risk equation. This broader characterization of country risk is consistent with that used by Roberts (1988): 'a spectrum of risks arising from the economic, social, and political environments of a given country (including government policies framed in response to trends in these environments), having potential favorable or adverse consequences for foreigners' debt and/or equity investments in that country' (p. 2). Thus, country-risk factors go beyond the political actors and environment of the host country to encompass nonpolitical risks which can still impact significantly on the profitability and operations of MNCs in that country. Many of these risks are more generic, applying to a broader range of firms and industries, and not necessarily put in place by specific actors within the host country. Stapenhurst (1992) speaks of four components of 'country-specific risk': (1) domestic climate (including level of national violence, political turmoil, recurring governmental crisis), (2) economic climate (likelihood of government intervention in the economy, rate of inflation, persistent balance of payments deficits), (3) social conditions (animosities and skewed income distribution patterns, government social policy), and (4) foreign relations (defense budget, conflict with neighbors, trade permit requirements), bridging in some sense the gap between the specifics of political risk and the general environmental overview of country risk. He further clarifies: 'political risk assessment in international banks is often combined with economic risk assessment in a distinct corporate function: *country risk analysis*. Such analysis seeks to "marry" economic and political analysis' (p. 53).

Much recent scholarly work on country risk, in fact, has been directed towards characterizing it in the most exhaustive categorization possible, so that firms may identify and address it in a structured and meaningful way. Shan (1991) speaks of the country-level 'environmental risks peculiar to a traditional centrally planned economy' (p. 555) in examining joint ventures in China. His definition of risk refers to the magnitude of exposure the firm experiences, suggesting that risk varies with the dollar amount, temporal duration, scope, location, and timing of the investment, and that as perceived risk or uncertainty increases, the foreign firm's share in the Chinese joint venture is likely to decrease. Here, while the characterization of country risk is not particularly well-defined, the contribution is the recognition that the level of country risk experienced can be mitigated by sharing it with a local partner to a larger degree. Risk, in Shan's depiction is not just the uncertainty of the environment, but the degree to which the individual firm can be affected by that risk.

Perhaps the most significant recent contribution to the categorization and development of a meaningful and useable country risk framework for internationally active firms is that of Miller (1992, 1993), in his integrated risk management framework for international business. He points out that even defining the term 'risk' has proven problematic for the literature, and suggests that treating various components of risk and uncertainty in isolation from each other is a suboptimal strategy. Miller (1992) suggests that managers face uncertainties at three levels: the general environment, the industry, and the firm. In his empirical testing of this model, Miller (1993) finds that using a multidimensional approach to measuring uncertainty allowed for greater differentiation in risk assessment. He also concludes that '(t)ests for country effects on managers' uncertainty perceptions supported the relevance of country-level assessments of political, policy, and macroeconomic uncertainties' (p. 709)—the major components of what we have traditionally characterized as country risk. He also finds, however, that country-level analysis does not suffice in predicting uncertainties along the lines of competition, resource/service inputs, or market demand, which can be seen as more firm- or industry-specific, and require more detailed analysis than simply at the level of the country.

In addition to Miller's work, Brouthers (1995) also supports the notion of a more complete perception of international risk than that supplied by simple political or financial risk analysis. Brouthers speaks of 'Total Strategic

International Risk'—incorporating both control risk and market complexity risk, then uses that composite risk to predict entry mode, in some sense, combining the work of Miller and Shan to demonstrate that an increase in overall perceived risk (both firm control-related and market/country-related) will lead to lower equity entry modes. Brouthers, Brouthers, and Nakos (1998) also find, in their study of firms entering Central and Eastern European markets, that investment risk perceptions influence entry mode choices, and note that: 'Changes in the economic, social, or political system of a country can have an adverse impact on investments. This may occur because of nationalization of industries, restrictions imposed on the repatriation of profits, preferences being given to domestically owned firms, or high inflation which quickly decreases the value of invested funds' (p. 490)—again supporting the examination of a full slate of risk factors in a specific country before engaging in business there. Finally, Werner, Brouthers, and Brouthers (1996), again confirm the need for a more unified approach to international business risk, noting that: 'according to more recent research, given the large number of different types of international risks, actions taken to avoid one type of risk, such as exchange-rate risk, may actually increase exposure to another type of risk, such as political risk...it is important to incorporate a number of international risk variables into investigations of international risk.' (p. 572). In their 1996 article, Werner *et al.* assess, confirm, and refine slightly the dimensions of Miller's 1993 measures of Perceived Environmental Uncertainty (PEU). Of the three international business risk measures discussed here, country risk is clearly the broadest and forms, along with more firm/industry-specific measures, the basis for a multidimensional overall assessment of risk in a given country venture.

## 10.3.3  Sovereign risk

In the financial community, Sovereign Risk is distinguished from country risk as follows: 'sovereign risk refers to the possibility that the servicing of a long-term debt obligation owed by a government entity (or guaranteed by one) may be interrupted for some reason...country risk, on the other hand, is a broader, more generic term' (Nye 1988: 25). This assignment of sovereign risk to represent the financial risks directly associated with the host country government and its guarantees is echoed by Cantor and Packer (1997): 'Like other credit ratings, sovereign ratings are assessments of the relative likelihood that a borrower will default on its obligations' (p. 66)—thus the ratings serve as an external or third-party assessment of sovereign risk. Heffernan (1986) further clarifies:

academics (including this author) have tended to equate country risk with sovereign risk because this is the only aspect of country risk analysis to which truly measurable probabilities can be attached. On the other hand, practitioners in the field of finance who use the terms risk and uncertainty interchangeably would be critical of the narrow interpretation given to it by academics. There is nothing wrong with either approach, but a problem arises because two conventions are being used. (1986: xv)

In this chapter, we will follow the convention of differentiating between the two as noted above—sovereign risk applying directly to the government and its guarantees, country risk representing an overall assessment of the risk associated with doing business in a specific country.

While interest and research in political risk largely grew out of the nationalizations and expropriations experienced by MNCs in the 1960s and 1970s, interest and research in sovereign risk stems to a great extent from the experiences of banks with the debt crises of the 1970s and 1980s. While Krayenbuehl (1985) titles his book *Country Risk*, his table of contents makes it clear he is really addressing sovereign risk, as his chapter headings include: 'The political element: the will to honour obligations', 'The economic element: the capability to honour obligations and to incur foreign debt', and 'New lending to countries in difficult financial situations'. His preface begins: 'The international debt situation has, over the past few years, been one of the major items of discussion in the international financial community as well as in government circles... What more can be done in the future in order to avoid similar problems—that is, to find ways of managing the international debt situation with a minimum of crises?' (p. vii). The debt renegotiation, rescheduling, and moratoria of the post-oil-shock era led to greater interest in ascertaining and controlling for country-level risk on the part of financial institutions. Krayenbuehl's book was only one of a number which came out in the mid-1980s, including Heffernan (1986) and Calverly (1985), who notes that: '(t)he euphoria of the 1970s when many banks relied on international lending for much of their asset and earnings growth has been replaced by a new caution. Many banks have been reappraising their approaches to risk and are giving country risk factors a much more prominent, if not dominant, position among the various factors going into decision-making' (p. v). While recent pre-crisis lending to Asia may arguably have followed a similar pattern (Delhaise 1998), the tools for more systematic analysis of sovereign risk have been in place since the 1980s. Banks at various levels, from regional (Suzman and Srivastava 1986), to international (McCulloch 1986), developed more structured means of analyzing sovereign risk. Snider (1988) suggests that:

Lack of political 'will' of the debtor countries' governments is often cited as a catchall political explanation of these governments' suspension of interest payments on their external debt... No systematic attention has been paid to how the political strength of debtor governments affects a country's economic performance that in turn impacts on its ability to earn foreign exchange with which to service its external debt. (p. 117)

The 1980s seem to have been largely devoted to attempting to systematize the sovereign debt assessment process. In the 1990s, academic attention seems to have shifted to the effects, accuracy, and usefulness of such assessments. Tarzi (1997) provides an overview of methodologies used by banks to assess sovereign risk: Country Evaluation Reports (relatively unstructured), Qualitative Spreadsheets (more structured but limited), Checklist Systems and Questionnaires, and Quantitative Systems (statistical, more objective, but arbitrary). Tarzi proposes that such assessments cannot be made in an isolated sense, and should also be comparative and focus more on cause-effect relationships than on static measurements. Nye (1997) echoes, to some extent, Tarzi's concerns about subjectivity, noting that the ratings of firms like Moody's and Standard and Poor's, like any rating, have aspects of subjectivity in them. Cantor and Packer (1997), both economists with the Federal Reserve Bank of New York, explore not only the determinant, but also the impact of the sovereign assessments assigned by Moody's and S&P, finding that:

to a large extent, Moody's and Standard and Poor's rating assignments are based on a small number of well-defined criteria, which the two agencies appear to weight similarly. We also find that the market...broadly shares the relative rankings of sovereign credit risks made by the two rating agencies. In addition, credit ratings appear to influence yields independently. (p. 66)

They also found that the impact of the ratings appeared to be higher for lower-rated sovereign debt. Finally, Ramcharran (1999) analyzes the impact of sovereign risk on bank lending to developing countries during the early-to-mid 1990s, and finds that, of political risk, access to capital markets, and debt in default or management in the past three years, only political risk (characterized as 'the risk of nonpayment or non-servicing of payment for goods or services, loans, trade-related finance and dividends and the non-repatriation of capital' (p. 87) ), significantly affected bank lending to individual countries. Thus, the 1990s appeared to be a time in which the evaluation of assessment systems put in place in the wake of the 1980s debt crisis took center stage. The recent Asian financial crisis should provide additional data for such analyses and, perhaps, for further revision in the models of sovereign risk assessment.

Having now reviewed the literature on these three major types of international business risk, we can attempt a better differentiation among them. First, the standard interpretation of Political Risk seems to deal with two factors: a risk which arises either politically or from non-market forces, and which affects or has implications for the firm (Kennedy 1987; Kobrin 1982). Country Risk seems to incorporate these emphases, but also broadens the source of the risk to include more generic economic, financial, and other nonpolitical factors (Business International Corporation 1981). The focus remains, however, on the effects these risk factors may have on the firm's actions and results. Thus, it appears that Political Risk may be seen as a subset of Country Risk, reflecting one, but not all of the forces operating on the firm in a foreign environment. Sovereign Risk, however, has a different focus than the other two—that of the risks associated with accepting the obligations and/or guarantees of a specific national government—it is not the locus of operation which is important here, but rather the partner or guarantor (Nye 1988). As noted above, Heffernan (1986) highlights the difficulties of establishing a consistent labeling standard for these terms, but this may be one important distinction to make: that Political Risk and Country Risk are environmental risks, while Sovereign Risk is tied more to the government's role as a provider or guarantor of support.

# 10.4 CONCLUSION

The interface between the firm and its country environment(s) continues to be a complex and changing one. With the increase in capital flows over the past decades, capital controls have been eased in many cases, but not eliminated. Other international business risks remain, generated by economic and political forces outside the firm's control. Future research in this area may provide further insights into the nature of these interactions, as well as into how they may be effectively managed at the firm level.

## REFERENCES

*Balance of Payments Statistics Yearbook* (1998). Washington, DC: International Monetary Fund.

BAYOUMI, T. (1997). *Financial Integration and Real Activity.* Ann Arbor: University of Michigan Press.

BEDDOES, Z. M. (1999). 'The International Financial System: Think Again', *Foreign Policy*, Fall, 16–27.

BOSKIN, M. J., and GALE, W. G. (1987). 'New Results on the Effects of Tax Policy on the International Location of Investment', in Feldstein, Martin (ed.), *The Effects of Taxation on Capital Accumulation.* Chicago: University of Chicago Press.

BREWER, T. L. (1983). 'The Instability of Governments and the Instability of Controls on Funds Transfers by Multinational Enterprises: Implications for Political Risk Analysis', *Journal of International Business Studies*, 14/3: 147–57.

—— (1993). 'Government Policies, Market Imperfections, and Foreign Direct Investment', *Journal of International Business Studies*, 24/1: 101–20.

BRONFENBRENNER, M. (1955). 'The Appeal of Confiscation in Economic Development', *Economic Development and Cultural Change*, 3: 201–18.

BROUTHERS, K., BROUTHERS, L., and NAKOS, G. (1998). 'Entering Central and Eastern Europe: Risks and Cultural Barriers', *Thunderbird International Business Review*, 40/5: 485–504.

BROUTHERS, L. (1995). 'The Influence of International Risk on Entry Mode Strategy in the Computer Software Industry', *Management International Review*, 35/1: 7–28.

BUSINESS INTERNATIONAL CORPORATION (1981). *Managing and Evaluating Country Risk.* New York: Business International Corporation.

CALVERLY, J. (1985). *Country Risk Analysis.* London: Butterworth.

CANTOR, R., and PACKER, F. (1997). 'Determinants and Impact of Sovereign Credit Ratings', in Rogers, J. (ed.). *Global Risk Assessments: Issues, Concepts and Applications.* Riverside, Calif.: Global Risk Assessments Inc., 65–100.

CHAN, S. (1995). 'Introduction: Foreign Direct Investment in a Changing World', in Chan, S. (ed.), *Foreign Direct Investment in a Changing Global Political Economy.* New York: St Martin's Press.

COSSET, J., and SURET, J. (1995). 'Political Risk and the Benefits of International Portfolio Diversification', *Journal of International Business Studies*, 26/2: 301–18.

DELHAISE, P. (1998). *Asia in Crisis: The Implosion of the Banking and Finance Systems.* Singapore: John Wiley & Sons (Asia).

DOOLEY, M. (1995). 'A Survey of Academic Literature on Controls over International Capital Tranactions', *National Bureau of Economic Research*, No. 5352, 1–48.

DORNBUSCH, R. (1986). 'Special Exchange Rates for Capital Account Transactions', *World Bank Economic Review*, 1/1: 3–33.

DRABEK, Z., and GRIFFITH-JONES, S. (1999). 'Summary and Conclusions: Managing Capital Flows in Central and Eastern Europe', in Drabek, Z., and Griffith-Jones, S. (eds.), *Managing Capital Flows in Turbulent Times: The Experience of Europe's Emerging Market Economies in Global Perspective.* Armonk, NY: M. E. Sharpe, 213–46.

FISCHER, B., and REISEN., H. (1994). 'Financial Opening: Why, How, When', *International Center for Economic Growth, Occasional papers, Number 55.* San Francisco: ICS Press.

GIOVANNI, A., and DE MELO, M. (1993). 'Government Revenue from Financial Repression', *American Economic Review*, 83/4: 953–63

GUISINGER, S., and associates (1985). *Investment Incentives and Performance Requirements.* New York: Praeger.

HAENDEL, D. (1979). *Foreign Investments and the Management of Political Risk.* Boulder, Colo.: Westview Press.

HARBERGER, A. (1986). 'Welfare Consequences of Capital Inflows', in Choksi, A., and Papageorgiou, D. (eds.), *Economic Liberalization in Developing Countries.* Oxford: Basil Blackwell, 157–63.

HEFFERNAN, S. (1986). *Sovereign Risk Analysis.* London: Allen & Unwin.

JAIN, A. K., and NIGH, D. (1989). 'Politics and the International Lending Decisions of Banks', *Journal of International Business Studies*, 20: 349–59.

JODICE, D. (1985). *Political Risk Assessment: An Annotated Bibliography*. Westport, Conn.: Greenwood Press.

JOHNSTON, B., and TAMIRISA, N. (1998). 'Why do Countries use Capital Contols?', *International Monetary Fund*, Working Paper (98/181).

KANT, C. (1996). 'Foreign Direct Investment and Capital Flight', *Princeton Studies in International Finance (80)*, Princeton, NJ: Princeton University Department of Economics Finance Section.

KENNEDY, C. (1987). *Political Risk Management: International Lending and Investing Under Environmental Uncertainty*. New York: Quorum Books.

KINDLEBERGER, C. P. (1987). *International Capital Movements: Based on the Marshall Lectures given at the University of Cambridge 1985*. Cambridge: Cambridge University Press.

KOBRIN, S. J. (1979). 'Political Risk: A Review and Reconsideration', *Journal of International Business Studies*, 10/1: 67–80.

—— (1982). *Managing Political Risk Assessment: Strategic Responses to Environmental Change*. Berkeley: University of California Press.

—— (1984). 'Expropriation as an Attempt to Control Foreign Firms in LDCs: Trends from 1960–1979'. *International Studies Quarterly*, 3: 329–48.

—— BASEK, J., BLANK, S., and LA PALOMBARA, J. (1980). 'The Assessment and Evaluation of Non-economic Environments by American Firms: A Preliminary Report', *Journal of International Business Studies*, 11/1: 32–47.

KRAYENBUEHL, T. (1985). *Country Risk: Assessment and Monitoring*. Lexington, Mass.: Lexington Books.

KUO, C. (1991). *International Capital Movements and the Developing World*. New York: Praeger.

LENWAY, S., and MURTHA, T. (1994). 'The State as Strategist in International Business Research', *Journal of International Business Studies*, 25/3: 513–36.

MAKHIJA, M. (1993). 'Government Intervention in the Venezuelan Petroleum Industry: An Empirical Investigation of Political Risk', *Journal of International Business Studies*, 24/3: 531–55.

MANZOCCHI, S. (1999). *Foreign Capital in Developing Economies: Perspectives from the Theory of Economic Growth*. New York: St Martin's Press.

McCULLOCH, W. (1986). 'Country Risk Assessment by Banks', in Rogers, J. (ed.), *Global Risk Assessments: Issues, Concepts and Applications*. Riverside, Calif.: Global Risk Assessments Inc., 121–35.

MILLER, K. (1992). 'A Framework for Integrated Risk Management in International Business', *Journal of International Business Studies*, 23/2: 311–31.

—— (1993). 'Industry and Country Effects on Managers' Perceptions of Environmental Uncertainties', *Journal of International Business Studies*, 24/3: 693–714.

MINOR, M. (1994). 'The Demise of Expropriation as an Instrument of LDC Policy, 1980–1992', *Journal of International Business Studies*, 25/1: 177–88.

NIGH, D. (1985). 'The Effect of Political Events on United States Direct Foreign Investment: A Pooled Time-Series Cross-Sectional Analysis', *Journal of International Business Studies*, 16/1: 1–17.

NYE, R. (1988). 'Capital Markets and Country Risk: Sovereign Credit Assessment at Moody's', in Rogers, J. (ed.), *Global Risk Assessments: Issues, Concepts and Applications*. Riverside, Calif.: Global Risk Assessments Inc., 13–35.

—— (1997). 'Sovereign Credit Ratings: A Subjective Assessment', in Rogers, J. (ed.), *Global Risk Assessments: Issues, Concepts and Applications*. Riverside, Calif.: Global Risk Assessments Inc., 101–18.

PARK, Y. C., and SONG, C. (1996). 'Managing Foreign Capital Flows: The Experiences of Korea, Thailand, Malaysia and Indonesia', Jerome Levy Economics Institute Working Papers (163): Annandale-on-Hudson, NY: Bard College.

POPPER. H. A. (1997). *Issues in International Capital Mobility*. New York: Garland.

RAMCHARRAN, H. (1999). 'International Bank Lending to Developing Countries: An Empirical Analysis of the Impact of Country Risk', *Multinational Business Review*, Spring: 83–91.

RAZIN, A., and SADKA, E. (1991). 'Efficient Investment Incentives in the Presence of Capital Flight', *Journal of International Economics*, 31: 171–81.

ROBERTS, E. (1988). 'Country Risk Assessment: The Union Carbide Experience', in Rogers, J. (ed.), *Global Risk Assessments: Issues, Concepts and Applications*. Riverside, Calif.: Global Risk Assessments Inc., 1–12.

ROGERS, J. (ed.) (1983, 1986, 1988, 1997). *Global Risk Assessments: Issues, Concepts and Applications*. Riverside, Calif.: Global Risk Assessments Inc.

SHAN, W. (1991). 'Environmental Risks and Joint Venture Sharing Arrangements', *Journal of International Business Studies*, 22(4), 555–78.

SNIDER, L. (1988). 'Political Capacity and the Credit Worthiness of LDC Debtors: Combining Aggregate Data With Quantified Judgement', in Rogers, J. (ed.), *Global Risk Assessments: Issues, Concepts and Applications*. Riverside, Calif.: Global Risk Assessments Inc., 117–52.

STAPENHURST, F. (1992). *Political Risk Analysis around the North Atlantic*. New York: St Martin's Press.

SUZMAN, C., and SRIVASTAVA, M. (1986). 'Country Risk Assessment by Regional Banks', in Rogers, J. (ed.), *Global Risk Assessments: Issues, Concepts and Applications*. Riverside, Calif.: Global Risk Assessments Inc., 101–20.

TARZI, S. (1997). 'Country Risk Analysis, International Banking and the Developing Countries', *The Journal of Social, Political and Economic Studies*, 22/4: 481–95.

THOMAS, K. P. (1997). *Capital Beyond Borders: States and Firms in the Auto Industry, 1960–94*. New York: St Martin's Press.

TORNELL, A., and VELASCO, A. (1992). 'The Tragedy of the Commons and Economic Growth: Why Does Capital Flow from Poor to Rich Countries?', *Journal of Political Economy*, 100/6: 1208–31.

VAN WIJNBERGEN, S. (1985). 'Capital controls and the Real Exchange Rate', *Economica*, 57: 15–28.

WERNER, S., BROUTHERS, L., and BROUTHERS, K. (1996). 'International Risk and Perceived Environmental Uncertainty: The Dimensionality and Internal Consistency of Miller's Measure', *Journal of International Business Studies*, 27/3: 571–87.

WIHLBORG, C., and DEZSERI, K. (1997). 'Preconditions for Liberalization of Capital Flows: A Review and Interpretation', in Ries, C., and Sweeney, R. (eds.), *Capital Controls In Emerging Economies*. Boulder, Colo.: Westview Press.

Williamson, J. (1997). 'Orthodoxy is Right: Liberalize the Capital Account Last', in Ries, C., and Sweeney, R. (eds.), *Capital Controls in Emerging Economies*. Boulder, Colo.: Westview Press.

—— (1999). 'The Management of Capital Inflows' in Drabek, Z., and Griffith-Jones, S. (eds.), *Managing Capital Flows in Turbulent Times: The Experience of Europe's Emerging Market Economies in Global Perspective*. Armonk, NY: M.E. Sharpe, 10–27.

—— and Mahar, M. (1998). 'A Survey of Financial Liberalization', *Essays in International Finance (211)*. Princeton, NJ: Princeton University Department of Economics Finance Section.

# CHAPTER 11

# MULTILATERAL INSTITUTIONS AND POLICIES: THEIR IMPLICATIONS FOR MULTINATIONAL BUSINESS STRATEGY

## THOMAS L. BREWER
## STEPHEN YOUNG

## 11.1 INTRODUCTION

THE topic of this chapter—the multilateral regime for FDI—lies within the domain of international business studies that focus on multinational enterprises and their political environment. The topic is of central and increasing importance for MNEs' strategies and operations. It has also become more salient among scholars, business executives, and public sector officials, as a result of the suspension of negotiations in the OECD for a Multilateral Agreement on Investment (MAI) in 1998; and failure to gain agreement for the launch of a new 'millennium round' of negotiations at the 3rd World Trade Organization (WTO) Ministerial Conference in Seattle, USA in December 1999[1].

The relevance of the WTO to business strategy is evident in existing agreements, in negotiations to revise those agreements, in disputes, and in the expansion of its membership. In regard to the latter, for instance, a General Motors executive in China noted that Chinese membership in the WTO (under negotiation in 2001) would have major effects on one of its FDI projects in China—an auto assembly facility:

[ In the executive's] view, an international company's enthusiasm for China's entry could probably be measured in inverse proportion to the size of its investment in China.

The larger the investment, the more negative a foreign business [in China] is likely to feel about greater competition. General Motors has invested more than $2 billion in China, a large chunk of it in an auto-assembly plant in Shanghai that began making a new version of the Buick for the China market.

Since the autos sell for about $36,000, it will not be competitive once steep import duties are reduced. The new agreement [for China's membership in the WTO] calls for the reduction of auto import duties by 2006 to 25 per cent, from the current 80 per cent to 100 per cent (*International Herald Tribune* 2000).

Despite the importance of such WTO-related issues for business strategy, the implications for MNEs of the WTO system have not received much attention by scholars of international business. International strategy scholars, as a group, have a strong tradition of focusing on *national governments* in studies of international business–government relations. At the same time, economists, political scientists, and legal scholars have tended to focus on international regimes concerning international *trade* and/or *financial* capital flows, including portfolio flows, rather than foreign direct investment (see Chapters 9 and 10 in this volume by Ostry and Guisinger).

At least a minimal understanding of the institutional features of the multilateral regime is needed in order that the totality of the literature can be more conveniently and effectively evaluated. Section 2 of the chapter therefore describes the main elements of the system and illustrates the implications of the system for business strategy and operations; Section 3 summarizes and evaluates diverse bodies of literature—from business studies, as well as economics, political science, and law; and Section 4 proposes directions for future research.

---

[1] The event also attracted worldwide publicity because of the protests and associated violence and vandalism accompanying the talks. Extensive discussions of the negotiations preceding, during, and after the ministerial meeting are available in *Inside US Trade* (<http://insidetrade. com/secure/seattle_archive.asp>). See also Ch. 9 in this volume by Ostry.

## 11.1.1 The significance of the topic

As the literature review in Section 3 reveals, there are several different approaches to, and perspectives on, this subject. Graham (1996; see also Caves 1996; Brewer and Young 2000c) has presented the economic case for multilateral investment liberalization which parallels that for multilateral trade liberalization; basically the equivalent of the gains from trade argument. The application of unilateral policies to achieve this goal is not optimal, hence the requirement for multilateral cooperation and a multilateral investment regime. These arguments underly the core principles of multilateral investment agreements such as those contained in the draft MAI or the WTO (see Appendix 11.1 at the end of this chapter).

In keeping with the business strategy focus of this chapter, Table 11.1 lists the core principles and proposes some common MNE responses to them. Since the principles revolve around investment liberalization, there is considerable synergy with the requirements of multinationals. However, MNEs benefit from discrimination where it leads to incentive bidding among host countries to attract their inward investments (Brewer and Young 1997). In a similar manner, new investors tend to favor the banning of performance requirements (as is partially undertaken in the Trade Related Investment Measures (TRIMs) agreement in the WTO) which may require high cost local sourcing; whereas existing investors may oppose their removal, which could place them at a competitive disadvantage.

Modal neutrality is an important principle which leaves firms to decide the optimal method of market servicing. Thus, for example, investment decisions become more a function of efficiency considerations stemming from countries' comparative advantages, and less a function of market access considerations created by host countries' import substitution policies.

From a public policy standpoint, however, there are additional issues which are of major significance, where economic efficiency and equity conditions would necessitate regulation of multinationals, and which are high on the agenda. These include the potentially anti-competitive behavior of large MNEs operating in oligopolistic industries, which would require international competition policy; and issues pertaining to country economic development including environmental protection, and corporate social responsibility. The latter, in particular, have become a major focus for the activities (including direct action) of civil society groups which argue that MNEs have done little to live up to their obligations in a more liberal global economy (UNCTAD 1999d: ch. 12; Picciotto and Mayne 1999).

## Table 11.1 Core principles of multilateral agreements, and perspectives of MNEs

| | |
|---|---|
| Multilateral rules | Permit global strategies by reducing patchwork of overlapping and conflicting rules at different levels. However, multilateral rules reduce possibilities for playing off one jurisdiction against another. |
| National treatment | Non-discrimination against MNEs. Although a central principle, there are widespread country/sectoral exceptions in all agreements. Since equal treatment is not required, investment subsidies to MNEs are still possible and welcomed by firms. |
| Most favored nation treatment (MFN) | Prohibits discrimination against products or firms of one foreign country against those of another. |
| Transparency | Government policies should be stated clearly and implemented fairly. MNE preference for transparency; although some may benefit from ability to negotiate independently in opaque systems. |
| Modal neutrality | No discrimination in favor of one modality (e.g. trade, FDI, licensing) rather than another. Non-tariff barriers are still widespread and encourage FDI. Anti-dumping duties permitted under Uruguay Round rules and may lead to 'duty-jumping' FDI. Some performance requirements banned under Uruguay Round (TRIMs agreement): new investors favor abolition; but existing investors may prefer retention of TRIMs. |
| Investment protection / protection of intellectual property rights (IPR) | Important for security of investment, especially significant in developing countries. IPR protection important for prevention of counterfeiting: some progress in Uruguay Round TRIPs Agreement. |

*Source* Authors. See also UNCTAD 1996a: chs. v and vi and Brewer and Young 2000c: section 1.4

# 11.2 THE PUBLIC POLICY REGIME FOR FOREIGN DIRECT INVESTMENT

## 11.2.1 Levels of public policy

In operating internationally, the MNE faces a plethora of institutions and regulatory regimes, at multilateral, regional, bilateral, national, and sub-national levels. The emphasis in this chapter is upon the multilateral level, but it is important to recognize the partial patchwork of instruments and arrangements which characterize the investment policy scene, and which can create confusion and conflict.

Within the *bilateral* sphere, there is a vast network of more than 1,400 bilateral investment treaties (BITs). For a capital exporting country, the major objective is to obtain legal protection for FDI under international law; and for a capital importing country, BITs supplement host country laws in respect of protection standards and thus assist the attraction of investment. There are also many regional integration arrangements (RIAs) that complement and overlap with the WTO system; 109 of these were notified to the GATT over the period 1947 to 1994 (WTO 1995). A detailed analysis of BITs and RIAs is not within the scope of this chapter; some RIAs, however, are included within the regionally focused chapters in the book. For readers who are interested in these topics, the following are useful: On BITs, see Khalil (1992), Muchlinski (1995), Sornarajah (1994), UNCTAD (1996a). On RIAs, see Brewer and Young (1995) for the EU; see Eden (1996), Gestrin and Rugman (1996), and Rugman (1994, 2000) on NAFTA. See Kobrin (1995) on the issue of RIAs and their interactions with MNEs. Many regional and other international organizations have useful websites with detailed information about RIAs and their provisions concerning FDI. They include:

EU: *www.europa.eu.int*
NAFTA: *www.nafta-sec-alena.org*
OAS (NAFTA, FTAA, Mercosur): *www.oas.org*
OECD: *www.oecd.org*
USTR: *www.ustr.gov*
WTO: *www.wto.org*

## 11.2.2 Characteristics of multilateral rules

Regarding the multilateral regime *per se*, Brewer and Young (2000c: 35–7) have highlighted the diversity of rules in respect of:

1. The organizations involved, which include the WTO, OECD, United Nations (ILO and UNCTAD), the World Bank, International Monetary Fund (IMF), and others. While this chapter focuses upon the WTO, it is worth noting the calls for reform of the IMF and the World Bank in the wake of the Asian financial crisis; and for improved coordination between institutions so as to improve regulatory effectiveness, which would clearly involve the WTO (Picciotto 1999; Griffith-Jones 1999).

2. Issue coverage and interrelationships. The emphasis in this chapter is on areas such as the central rules of investment, settlement of disputes, employment, and labor relations, etc. However, trade and trade-related measures are also of major significance for the MNE. For other issues—taxation and finance, bribery and illicit payments, consumer protection, social policy and labor standards, environmental protection, and human rights—see Picciotto (1999: Table 1.1).

3. Binding or nonbinding agreements. As illustrations, the WTO rules are binding; whereas the OECD's Declaration on International Investment and Multinational Enterprises is nonbinding.

4. Year of establishment. UNCTAD (1996a: Table V.2) lists seventy-three regional or multilateral investment instruments covering the period 1948–96, of which forty-three are binding and sixty-three have been adopted. All these instruments are reproduced in UNCTAD-DTCI (1996b), *International Investment Instruments: A Compendium.*

5. Country coverage. As at March 2000, there were 135 members of the WTO, with a further thirty-five observer governments, making it effectively a global body. Indeed the vast majority of the latter had applied to join, including most notably the Russian Federation and China. The OECD membership is no longer limited to the traditional developed countries. Non-OECD governments were periodically briefed on the ill-fated MAI negotiations and were being encouraged to accede subsequent to completion of the negotiations—arrangements that were regarded as smacking of paternalism (Waelde 1999; Picciotto and Mayne 1999).

## 11.2.3 The evolution of the multilateral system

The current features of the system can be traced in part to the evolution of the proposal for an International Trade Organization (ITO) during the 1940s and the subsequent defeat of it by the US Congress (Brewer and Young 2000c). In the negotiations of the charter for an ITO, investment issues were among the most important and most controversial, and in the end they were a major factor in the rejection by the US of the Havana Charter that would have created it. As a result, investment issues were largely ignored in the GATT until the Uruguay Round negotiations (Christy 1991; GATT 1994*a*; Croom 1995).[2]

Table 11.2 summarizes the landmarks in the evolution of the multilateral investment regime; and Table 11.3 summarizes the essential characteristics of the major multilateral and regional investment agreements in effect in 2001. Interest has ebbed and flowed over a period of fifty years, involving a range of institutions, and a changing balance of interest between liberalization and regulation in rule-making. The suspension of the MAI negotiations (effectively termination) in 1998 may well have marked the end of the 'liberalization' phase, and Table 11.3 suggests a new phase of 'uncertainty' from the late 1990s.

The details of the MAI negotiations and related issues at the OECD are covered in Ley (1996), Smith (1996), and Witherell (1996). See Kobrin (1998) on the political context of the MAI negotiations, especially including the domestic politics in the US. However, there are several other OECD agreements that have been in effect for many years and that are still important elements of the international regime for FDI. These are the Code of Liberalization of Capital Movements, the Code of Liberalization of Current Invisible Operations, and the Declaration on International Investment and Multinational Enterprises (which includes Guidelines for Multinational Corporations and a National Treatment Instrument).

As noted, the period from the early 1980s to the mid 1990s was one of widespread liberalization of FDI-related policies at all levels from the multilateral to the national and sub-national. However, Mashayekhi and Gibbs (1999: 1) have observed that 'All multilateral negotiations on this subject since the Havana Charter have been marked by the reluctance to subject investment policies to international rules and disciplines'. At national and regional levels, too, there remain many barriers to FDI even among the US, the EU countries, and other members of the OECD. Such barriers are illustrated and documented, for instance, in the numerous exceptions to the 'National Treatment Instrument' of the OECD, which otherwise provides for nondiscrimination against foreign firms (OECD 1994). Further evidence is available in annual reports issued by the EU and by the US. Each year, the former's 'Report on United States Barriers to Trade and Investment' (e.g. EU 1999) and latter's section on Europe in its 'National Trade Estimate' (e.g. USTR 1999) is filled with observations about the other's barriers to FDI. (The latest annual versions are available on their respective websites at *www.europa.eu.int* and *www.ustr.gov.*)

---

[2] There were a few exceptions, though—for instance, in the context of a dispute concerning the domestic content requirements of Canada's Foreign Investment Review Agency (Brewer and Young 2000*c*: 121–2).

## Table 11.2 Landmarks in the evolution of the multilateral regime for FDI

| Period | Features of period | Landmark events |
|---|---|---|
| Mid 1940s–late 1960s | *Inauguration of institutional framework* Honeymoon period: little concern about regulating MNEs or about liberalizing government FDI policies. | Havana Charter for *International Trade Organization* published in 1948 but not ratified. Postwar international economic order constructed around establishment of the International Monetary Fund/World Bank and the General Agreement on Tariffs and Trade. |
| | | Binding OECD *Codes on Liberalization of Capital Movements* and *Current Invisible Operations* introduced in 1963. Former required liberalization of policies on inward and outward capital flows over long term. |
| Late 1960s–early 1980s | *Control of MNEs* Negative attitudes towards MNEs, especially in developing countries. | Discussions commenced on binding United Nations *Code of Conduct on Transnational Corporations* in mid-1970s with aim of controlling MNEs. Draft of voluntary code finally submitted in 1990, but not ratified. |
| | | Voluntary OECD *Guidelines for Multinational Enterprises* published in 1976: set standards on employment and industrial relations, information disclosure, financing, taxation etc. Little evidence of implementation by MNEs. |
| Early 1980s–mid 1990s | *Liberalization of Policies* Liberalization of government policies, including FDI policies, at national, bilateral, regional and multilateral levels. | Completion of GATT Uruguay Round negotiations, and establishment of the *World Trade Organization* in 1995. Mainly trade agreement but some investment powers in respect of services, local content rules, and intellectual property rights. |

**Table 11.2** *Continued*

| Period | Features of period | Landmark events |
|---|---|---|
| Late 1990s – | *Uncertainty*<br>Liberalization trend continued, but increasing concerns of developing countries and conflicts between developed nations. Other issues include multiplicity of agreements at different levels and overlapping relationships | Negotiations on OECD *Multilateral Agreement on Investment* suspended without agreement in 1998.<br><br>WTO's enhanced dispute settlement procedures began to be implemented, including some investment cases. Agreements reached in 1997 on liberalizing telecommunications, information technology, and financial services' industries worldwide. Membership of 135 countries in March 2000.<br><br>3rd WTO Ministerial Conference (Seattle, USA) failed to agree launch of new Trade Round. Reform of WTO, environmental issues, labor standards, and income inequality high on agenda. |

*Source* Updated from Young and Brewer 2000c, Table 2.1; see also original sources: US Department of State (1948); OECD (1976a, b); OECD (1993a, b); GATT (1994b)

There thus remain many government policies that prohibit or otherwise constrain the FDI-related strategic and operational decisions of firms; and other areas where policies are required in order to achieve a better balance between the rights and obligations of firms and the rights and obligations of countries.

At the same time, there has emerged in the form of the World Trade Organization a new, complex, and far-reaching multilateral regime affecting FDI. To be sure, in a narrow sense, many of the agreements and dispute cases are not part of an FDI regime because they do not explicitly include provisions concerning FDI; rather, they concern trade or intellectual property. However, rules concerning such matters are nevertheless directly relevant to firms' decisions concerning FDI and thus to the topic of this chapter. Furthermore, both the TRIMs agreement and the General Agreement on Trade in Services (GATS) do contain explicit provisions concerning FDI.

## 11.2.4  WTO agreements with relevance to investment

One useful way to summarize most of the fifty-plus Uruguay Round agreements being implemented at the WTO—and to illustrate their implications for MNEs and other firms—is to classify them as covering transactions concerning *goods, services,* or *intellectual property.*[3]

*Goods.* The modification of the existing GATT through an agreement called GATT1994, plus other agreements concerning goods, further lowered tariffs on trade in agricultural and manufactured goods, expanded restrictions on a

---

[3] In technical legal terms, the agreements that are focused on these three types of transactions appear as three 'annexes' to the Marrakesh Agreement Establishing the World Trade Organization, i.e. annexes 1A, 1B, and 1C. There are also some plurilateral agreements administered by the WTO, even though their signatories include relatively small subsets of the WTO membership; there are four such agreements: government procurement, civil aircraft, dairy, and bovine meat.

The basic texts of all of the agreements together total about 550 pages. However, there are 33 volumes totaling over 10,000 pages, including the individual countries' (and the EU's) tariff schedules on goods and their specific commitments on services. The basic texts and all of the supplementary materials are available in GATT (1994*b*) and on the WTO website at <*http://www.wto.org*>. Also see *International Legal Materials* and the website of the American Society of International Law at <*http://www.asil.org*>.

Responsibilities for monitoring and implementing the agreements lie with the General Council and its three specialized functional appendages, the Councils on Goods, Services, and Intellectual Property. They all meet continually in Geneva and provide a mechanism for the national governments to represent their interests directly. These councils are in addition to the bi-annual Ministerial Conferences, which meet in different parts of the world (the first three were in Singapore, Geneva, and Seattle). Analyses of WTO institutional features are available in Krueger 1998.

Table 11.3  Summary characteristics of major multilateral and regional

| Characteristics | Multilateral | | | | |
|---|---|---|---|---|---|
| | WTO[b] | | | OECD[c] | |
| | GATS | TRIMs | TRIPs | Cap | Cur |
| Binding | yes | yes | yes | yes | yes |
| Year | 1994 | 1994 | 1994 | 1963 | 1963 |
| Country coverage (number) | 135[g] | 135[g] | 135[g] | 26 | 26 |
| Objectives | Establish services trade & investment framework | Limit performance requirements in manufacturing | Protect intellectual property rights | Liberalize restrictions on capital transactions | Liberalize restrictions on capital transactions |
| Features | Complex architecture | Narrowly focused | Includes technology protection & technology transfer | Covers many types of capital transfers | Focused on balance of payments current account transactions |

*Notes* [a]Strictly agreements which include investment provisions, since they may also relate to trade, technology etc. The European Union has been excluded from this table, because it does not formally include an investment agreement; but the EU is far ahead of other organizations in terms of its degree of integration, and the inclusion of elements such as competition policy which would be included in a comprehensive investment agreement.
[b]WTO agreements are: GATS—General Agreement on Trade in Services; TRIMs—Trade Related Investment Measures; TRIPs—Trade Related Intellectual Property Rights. TRIPs is not an investment agreement *per se* but has major, direct implications for MNEs and FDI.

variety of non-tariff barriers, and addressed a series of traditional GATT issues (safeguards, balance of payments emergencies, anti-dumping, subsidies, countervailing measures, and rules of origin). A subsequent Information Technology Agreement (ITA) eliminates tariffs on a broad range of products, including for instance many IT products that are widely used in telecommunications. The agreement on Trade-Related Investment Measures (TRIMs) covers such measures as domestic content and trade-balancing requirements that are sometimes imposed on foreign direct investment projects by host

investment agreements in effect in 2000[a]

| OECD[c] | | Regional/Sectoral ECT[d] | Regional NAFTA[e] | APEC[f] |
|---------|---|---|---|---|
| NTI | MNE | | | |
| no | no | yes | yes | no |
| 1976 | 1976 | 1994 | 1993 | 1994 |
| 26 | 26 | 51 | 3 | 18 |
| Establish national treatment principles | Establish guidelines for firms' behavior | Liberalize energy, trade & investment in Central and Eastern Europe | Liberalize regional trade and investment | Liberalize regional trade and investment |
| Many sectoral exceptions | Brief statements on selected issues | Detailed sector-specific and region-specific coverage | Detailed coverage of numerous issues | General principles to follow in establishing national rules |

[c]OECD Agreements are: Cap—Code of Liberalization of Capital Movements; Cur—Code of Liberalization of Current Invisible Operations; NTI—National Treatment Instrument; MNE—Guidelines for Multinational Enterprises.
[d]Energy Charter Treaty.
[e]North American Free Trade Agreement.
[f]Asia Pacific Economic Cooperation (APEC) Non-Binding Investment Principles.
[g]At 20 March 2000.

*Source* Adapted from Brewer and Young 2000c, Table 11.1

governments. On issues concerning trade in goods, see especially Hoekman and Kostecki (1995).

*Services.* The General Agreement on Trade in Services (GATS) establishes a variety of 'general obligations' such as transparency and MFN nondiscrimination in a framework of rules for trade *and investment* in all service sectors. In addition, however, there are complex multi-tiered 'schedules of specific commitments', which since the entry into force of the WTO on 1 January 1995 have been amended by agreements on telecommunications services and financial services. Both of these sector-specific agreements represent significant expansions of WTO rules into obviously major service sectors in the global economy and in the national economy of every member of the WTO. There has also been renewed interest in some quarters in further liberalization of restrictions on environmental services, but as of mid-2000 it was not clear how much interest there would be in moving purposefully in that sector. In any case, the GATS commitments are subject to 'progressive liberalization' according to the agreement, and in fact a new round of negotiations towards further reductions in barriers to trade and investment in services commenced in March 2000. On FDI issues in GATS, see especially Sauvé (1995).

Thus, the GATS as a multilateral agreement, clearly and directly affects MNEs' location decisions in the services sector. The GATS is also particularly significant because of the size and growth rates of services sectors domestically and internationally. Furthermore, many services industries are still undergoing deregulation and privatization and may thus be open to the possibility of increased foreign investment.

*Intellectual property.* The agreement on Trade-Related Aspects of Intellectual Property Rights (TRIPs) includes new rules that standardize protection standards across countries and obligate their governments to provide transparent and non-discriminatory processes to enforce them. These standards pertain to copyrights, trademarks, and other forms of intellectual property protection. Such protection is especially important to firms in a variety of consumer goods and entertainment industries, as well as chemicals, pharmaceuticals, telecommunications, and information systems. Enhanced intellectual property protection increases the attractiveness of foreign production locations for firms through international licensing arrangements and international joint ventures.

## 11.2.5 WTO disputes

Although WTO disputes are between governments as a matter of legal technicality, the governments that initiate them are in fact typically responding to political pressures from firms. The firms, of course, typically want more access to foreign markets (including factor markets) and/or protection from foreign competition in domestic markets. The firms sometimes are acting individually, sometimes through industry associations, and sometimes in *ad hoc* coalitions. In some high-profile dispute cases, the political involvement of particular firms has become common knowledge—for instance, Kodak obtaining US government help in the 'Japanese film' case, and Chiquita obtaining US government help in the 'EU bananas' case.

These cases are suggestive of a much more extensive involvement by corporations in diverse industries in the complainant countries, and the cases are indicative of the wide-ranging consequences for corporations in the respondent countries. Like the governments that represent their interests, some corporations are winners and some are losers as a result of the outcomes of the dispute cases. Further, the structure of industries at the global level is sometimes at stake in the cases. Yet, as we will see in more detail in Section 3 of this chapter, the strategy literature has not yet reflected this important development. For further information on disputes and the dispute settlement process, see especially Shoyer (1998); Jackson (1998); Petersmann (1997); *The International Lawyer* (1998); Brewer and Young (1999*a*).

The implications of WTO dispute cases for corporations can be illustrated by a variety of dispute settlement cases. The cases selected for illustrative purposes here concern diverse industries, diverse types of international economic transactions, and all three of the principal categories of agreements noted above (goods, services, intellectual property).

*Manufactured goods: automobile TRIMs in Brazil and Indonesia.* In the Brazilian and Indonesian cases concerning trade-related investment measures (TRIMs) affecting the automobile industry, there were separate but similar complaints by Japan, the EU, and US. From 1993 Indonesia granted tax and tariff benefits to producers of autos based on the local content of the finished vehicle. In 1996 the Indonesian government established the 'National Car Program' which granted 'pioneer' companies similar benefits. The effect was that PT Timor Putra Nasional, a pioneer company, was given the right to import 45,000 finished cars from its Korean partner, Kia Motor Corporation. A WTO dispute panel found these Indonesian policies to be in violation of the GATT1994, the TRIMs agreement, and the Subsidies and Countervailing Duties agreements. A similar set of cases involving Brazilian TRIMs in the form of domestic content requirements in the auto industry was settled among the disputants without a formal dispute panel ruling. Together, these cases established that TRIMs, which have been prevalent in the motor vehicle industry around the world and which have affected many corporations' international production and sourcing strategies, would have to be reduced or even eliminated. In that respect, the cases facilitate the adoption of more nearly global strategies and the concomitant discontinuance of multidomestic strategies. There were significantly different implications for individual corporations, however. General Motors and Ford, on the one hand, and Chrysler, on the other, had adopted different strategies for serving the Brazilian market. Whereas the former already had engaged in direct investment in Brazil, the latter was serving the market by exporting from the US. The former had already met the Brazilian TRIMs requirements and thus were granted relatively low tariff levels for the parts and additional vehicles that they imported, whereas the latter faced much higher tariffs because it did not have facilities in Brazil at that time.

*Agricultural goods, services, and FDI: EU bananas.* In the European Union case concerning the regime for the importation, sale, and distribution of bananas, the complaints by Ecuador, Guatemala, Honduras, Mexico, and the US highlight different international business strategy issues. The EU's banana regime, which provided preferential access to bananas from ACP (Africa, Caribbean, and Pacific) countries over those from Central and South America, was deemed to be illegal. The US government was a complainant even though there are of course no bananas exported from the US to the EU. Rather, the US government's interest in the issue stems from the combination of the fact that a US-based firm, Chiquita, would like to export more to the EU from its plantations in Central American countries and the fact that the owners of the firm have been major contributors to candidates of both major parties for the congress and the presidency for the past several elections. Thus, foreign direct investment in the agricultural sector by a US-based firm has transformed a Central American–European trade dispute into a trans-Atlantic investment-related dispute as well.

*Intellectual property rights and import quotas in India.* In the Indian cases concerning patent protection for pharmaceutical and agricultural chemical products, complaints by the United States and by the EU alleged that the Indian government had not met its obligations under the TRIPs. The WTO ruled that India must establish a 'mailbox' system for filing patent applications and provide exclusive marketing rights for pharmaceuticals and agricultural chemicals—as had been required by the TRIPs agreement by 1 January 1995. This was required even though the developing countries such as India would have ten years to phase in their new patent protection regimes in full.

In the Indian cases concerning quantitative restrictions on imports of agricultural, textile, and industrial products, a complaint by the United States and separate complaints by Australia, Canada, and New Zealand focused on India's import quotas on over 2,700 agricultural and industrial products. These quotas had been maintained for a lengthy period of time under the balance of payments exceptions of GATT (Article XVIII and other articles and agreements). From the US perspective, the aim was to show that these restrictions were unnecessary, and also to preempt widespread use of a balance of payments exception in the wake of the Asian financial crisis. The WTO panel decisions in both sets of cases against the Indian government demonstrate the extent to which developing countries, which had often been exempted from the application of liberalization rules in the GATT system, are now expected to comply with WTO rules more fully. In that respect, this represents a significant geographic expansion of the effective scope of the multilateral trade-investment regime and its implications for international business strategy.

## 11.3 CONTRIBUTIONS AND LIMITATIONS OF THE LITERATURE

Since much of the most relevant research has been interdisciplinary, it is difficult and even arbitrary to classify many studies by discipline. Yet many of them do have clear disciplinary tendencies or emphases so that they can be considered within some standard categories. Here we find it useful to group them into: political science and legal studies that examine the institutional context; then studies that focus specifically on FDI-related issues; and finally on studies with business strategy aspects. Each group, of course, has its distinctive contributions and limitations.

### 11.3.1 Institutional context: law and political science

There is a vast literature on international trade law, including GATT/WTO and other institutional arrangements. Legal scholarship on the WTO quite naturally focuses on the details of provisions in the agreements, including their structure and their application in cases, as well as other institutional procedures. The book-length analysis by Jackson (1997) is especially noteworthy. In addition, there is a rapidly increasing literature on dispute cases; see especially Petersmann (1997); *International Lawyer* (1998); Jackson (1998). Among the law-oriented international trade journals are the *Journal of World Trade* (formerly *Journal of World Trade Law*), and the *Journal of International Economic Law* (which began publication in 1998). *Law and Policy in International Business* has included articles on both trade and investment. See also *The CEPMLP Internet Journal*, which focuses on energy issues at *www.dundee.ac.uk/cepmlp/journal*.

Foreign direct investment protection and promotion are the focus of *ICSID Review* (published by the World Bank), and there have been many articles on that topic in *Transnational Corporations*. Fatouros (1993) contains a large collection of legal studies on FDI and MNEs. Muchlinski (1995) and Sornarajah (1994) provide extensive analyses of the legal doctrines and traditions concerning investment protection and promotion. An extensive statement and explication of principles of investment protection and promotion—with associated studies—is available in World Bank (1992); this publication reflects the results of an ambitious exercise to codify and legitimize *Guidelines on the Treatment of Foreign Investment*, principally at the national and bilateral levels, but also including the multilateral level. Brewer (1995, 1996) focuses on investment dispute settlement procedures in a variety of international institutional arrangements.

In sum, this legal literature is useful for its descriptive details about institutional arrangements, the specific contents of the provisions of agreements, and the legal issues involved in dispute cases and dispute settlement procedures. However, the trade law literature does not generally concern itself with investment issues; indeed, FDI is often considered just another mode of 'trade', as in the services agreement. On the other hand, the legal literature concerning investment protection and promotion focuses on unilateral and bilateral policies, without much attention to the WTO. Its multilateral interests lie rather in the World Bank's International Centre for the Settlement of Investment Disputes (ICSID) and the network of other public and private institutional arrangements for dispute resolution procedures (see Brewer 1995). There is an important recent exception in the legal literature—a wide-ranging analysis by Waelde (1999) discusses FDI regulatory issues at all levels: multilateral, regional, sectoral, and bilateral.

In the political science literature, two strands of research are especially relevant—the 'international regimes' literature, including studies of the GATT/WTO in particular, and the domestic politics of trade literature. The literature on international regimes has appeared mostly in the journal *International Organization*; see, for instance, Haggard and Simmonds (1987). That literature is reviewed and applied in a preliminary way to issues of business strategy in Brewer (1997). For the literature on domestic politics, especially in the United States, see Chapter 8 by Spar in this volume; also see more generally articles in the journals, *International Studies Quarterly*, and *Foreign Policy*. Like the international regimes literature, the literature on the domestic politics of GATT/WTO policy is principally concerned with trade, not FDI, issues. Although there many studies of the domestic politics of the FDI and MNE policies of host governments and home governments, these studies do not include a consideration of policies toward the WTO. A collection of diverse studies of investment policies and trade policies is available in Brewer (1999).

The MAI negotiations spawned a wide range of critical contributions, with calls for the regulation of international business and control of MNEs. Much of this information can be found on the websites of organizations such as: Public Citizen, Preamble, Consumer International, Friends of the Earth-International, World Development Movement, Oxfam, as well as international trade unions and many others.

## 11.3.2  FDI: economics and institutions

Economists with an interest in FDI have generally ignored the GATT/WTO, while those with an interest in GATT/WTO have generally ignored FDI. As a result, the most relevant literature focuses on trade and financial capital flows. These are the focal topics of Chapter 9 by Ostry, and Chapter 10 by Guisinger and Berg in this volume. Hoekman and Kostecki (1995) provide an extensive treatment of the political economy of the substantive policy issues in the WTO regime, but with little attention to FDI in particular. An extensive assessment of the entire range of agreements, without specific reference to FDI issues or from the perspective of any particular group of countries, is available in Schott (1994).

Some studies by economists have addressed very broad business strategy issues from a normative standpoint and in terms of criteria for evaluating public policies. This literature includes analyses of: 'market contestability' (Graham and Lawrence 1997; Sauvé 1997); 'modal neutrality' (Julius 1994); and 'policy coherence' (UNCTAD 1996a). Broad-based economic studies (Hoekman and Kostecki 1995; Krueger 1998) of the political and economic context and implications of the WTO system, however, do not address issues of business strategy.

For book-length studies of FDI issues at the WTO, there are analyses by Brewer and Young (2000c), Graham (1996), and Sauvé and Schwanen (1996). An excellent discussion of many FDI-related issues is contained in an annual report by the WTO (1996). See Sauvé (1994) for an article-length review of the results of the Uruguay Round negotiations and agreements that is focused on FDI issues; Sauvé (1995) focuses specifically on the GATS, with particular reference to FDI. Further, for an analysis of FDI issues from the perspective of developing countries, see Mashayekhi and Gibbs (1999). The agreement on subsidies, with some reference to FDI-related issues, is discussed in Zampetti (1995).

*Transnational Corporations*, published by UNCTAD in Geneva, has had numerous articles on institutional aspects of the subject: see, for instance, Karl (1996), Brewer and Young (1996), Shahin (1997), Tuselmann (1997); and also Ganesan (1997) and Robinson (1998) on 'development friendliness' criteria in multilateral investment agreements, and Smythe (1998) on the venue (OECD or WTO) for investment negotiations. There is also an UNCTAD *Series on Issues in International Investment Agreements*, which consists of monograph-length expositions of key issues; see UNCTAD (1999a, 1999b, 1999c) and subsequent studies in the series. Also, an annual *World Investment Report* by UNCTAD (1996a) covers several key issues, and a useful collection of the texts of agreements is contained in UNCTAD (1996b). The OECD also has published several items of relevance; see, for instance, OECD (1996).

Collectively, the publications in this sub-section (3.2) represent the core literature for understanding the basics of the multilateral regime and key substantive public policy issues concerning it, particularly in regard to FDI. Many of these items are also useful, even essential, to an understanding of the implications for MNEs' international business strategies and operations. However, they are not by themselves sufficient for that purpose, for they do not address explicitly the types of strategic implications mentioned above in this chapter.

### 11.3.3 Business strategy

Kobrin (1997: 243) presents a 'threefold categorization of the role that politics and [nation-] states have played in the IB literature'. The categories are:

1. Firm–state interaction—including political risk, MNE-government bargaining, and the role of FDI in development.
2. Strategic management—including especially studies that consider firm–state interactions in the context of firm strategy and industry structure.
3. International political economy—including the impact of MNEs on the nation-state system (see his contribution to this volume).

The topic of this chapter, if its scope were conceived broadly, could incorporate elements of all three of these categories. However, since its focus is the implications of the WTO regime for business strategy and operations, the discussion of the chapter falls principally within the second category.

Studies that include an explicit strategic business perspective on the WTO are rare. Two introductory surveys prepared soon after the completion of the Uruguay Round (EIU 1994; International Trade Centre 1996) provide useful overviews of the importance to business of the agreements. However, neither study contains detailed or conceptual analyses of issues of business strategy or business–government relations; this is despite the claim in the title of the latter that it is a *Business Guide.*

There have been some sectoral studies, including in particular telecommunications services. See, for instance, Lee (1996) and Fredebeul-Krein and Freytag (1999) and the journal *Telecommunications Policy.*

There is a business school teaching case about the implications of the Uruguay Round agreement on agriculture for the sugar industry (Weston and Koehn 1996). Although it is specifically concerned with the implications of the agriculture agreement for the UK-based firm of Tate & Lyle, it contains much information about the consequences for worldwide patterns and trends in sugar production and consumption—and thus for international investment and trade. Because it was written just as the agreement was being finalized and before its implementation, however, the specifics of the process of 'tariffication' and the implementation of other elements of the agreement were of course unknown. Further, because it is a case that has been developed for pedagogical purposes, its value as a contribution to the literature on the business strategy implications of the WTO is naturally limited.

Another business school teaching case is available on environmental issues at the GATT (Prewitt, Markovich, and Reinhardt 1994). However, it does not include an explicit consideration of business strategy issues, though it is informative about multilateral environmental agreements and the diverse attitudes towards trade-environment issues among business groups and others.

A conference paper by Brewer and Young (1999b) presents a simple matrix (Figure 11.1) for structuring strategic analyses. However, this is only an introductory, first attempt to link the substance of WTO agreements and disputes, on the one hand, and business strategy issues, on the other.

As for empirical research, there is little evidence as to whether investment agreements matter to firms or how they are working (Wells 1998). UNCTAD (1998: 117–30) provides a thorough consideration of the impact of international policy frameworks on FDI flows and highlights the paucity of evidence. It concludes that a possible multilateral framework on investment would 'improve the enabling environment for FDI, to the extent that it would contribute to greater security for investors and greater stability, predictability and transparency in investment policies and rules. This, in turn, could encourage higher FDI flows and potentially some redistribution of those flows' (UNCTAD 1998: 129–30).

In any case, the existence of the WTO means less freedom for national governments for recourse to unilateral approaches to disputes and trade policy issues more generally. Yet, despite these trends, in a number of corporations interviewed in Washington DC, in 1998 (Brewer and Young 2000a), there was still a focus on issues that could be dealt with through the US political process; there was a built-in bias towards American policy questions. Several companies spoke of the danger of US-centrism in their trade and investment policies, and indeed, of Washington-centrism. One firm, which was about to implement a matrix management system involving global business units and market development organizations, remarked on a need for government affairs to become less focused on US domestic policy matters. Yet, there appeared to be a continuing US-centrism in the perspectives in the sense that there was still a focus on US government actions, even within the context of the broader WTO system. There was little recognition of the global importance of the newly expanded and strengthened WTO-centered regime. This study follows a lengthy tradition of work on public affairs and business–government relations, beginning with Boddewyn (1972), through to Shaffer

| Issues for Business Strategy | | | | |
|---|---|---|---|---|
| | Location of production | Access to markets | Structure of industry | Management of functions |
| General rules in agreements | GATS: national treatment | GATT: tariff bindings | Anti-dumping, e.g. in steel | TRIPs: technology transfer (R&D) |
| Industry-specific rules in agreements | Integration of textile regime (MFA) into WTO | Zero tariffs in pharmaceuticals | Tariffication of sugar quotas | Visa liberalization in tele-communications (HRM) |
| Dispute cases | TRIMs prohibited | EU bananas regime | Aircraft manufacture subsidies | Packaging/ labelling (Mktg.) |
| Other institutional features: committees, TPRM, others | Committee on Trade and Investment | Pressures to liberalize in policy reviews (TPRM) | Committee on Trade and Competition | Committee on Trade and Labor |

(row label, left axis: Elements of WTO Regime)

**Fig. 11.1 Illustrative implications for business strategy of the WTO regime**

and Hillman (2000); however, very little of this literature concerns relations with and responses to multilateral institutions.

As for WTO dispute cases, the Kodak–Fuji case is the subject of an analysis by Baron (1997) in the context of a discussion of a conceptual framework for analyzing firms' 'non-market' strategies. However, that analysis treats the case as a unilateral US 301 case, which it originally was, and does not include information about subsequent developments as a WTO dispute case. Tsurumi and Tsurumi (1999) have conducted a study of the same case from the perspective of firm behavior in an oligopolistic industry, but that analysis does not include a consideration of WTO dispute settlement procedures or the implications for firms.

An analysis by Brewer (1997) suggests that the literature of business strategy could be enriched by incorporating the literature of political science on international regime change and that the combination could be used to facilitate understanding of the implications for international business strategy of the WTO regime.

The themes, contributions, and limitations of this body of literature can be summarized as follows: *in toto*, the studies demonstrate the relevance and importance of the WTO system for MNEs' decisions about FDI and other strategic issues, including for instance mode of market entry, location of production, and the formation of strategic alliances. The studies provide information about a small number of industry and firm cases. They also provide the beginnings of conceptual analyses that may be useful in subsequent studies. They do not, however, represent a substantially developed body of literature, as required by the increasing importance and timeliness of the topic. Yet, in combination with the other bodies of literature discussed above, these studies may offer an incipient corpus that can be drawn upon in future research.

# 11.4 RESEARCH FRONTIERS

The implications for international business research of these observations about the multilateral investment system and the literature concerning it can be conveniently classified into several topics: industry structure, production location, market access, strategic mode, functional management, government relations, and issues of complexity and uncertainty.

## 11.4.1 Industry structure

Many key industries have clearly been experiencing major episodes of restructuring during the last decade of the twentieth century and the first decade of the twenty-first century; this includes in particular financial services and telecommunications services, as well as motor vehicle manufacturing. These industry restructurings, in part, have been facilitated by the liberalization of national policies within the context of the WTO and other international fora, and they have been conducted within the constraints of multilateral rules embodied in WTO agreements and other international agreements. Thus, the effects on the structure of industries of the evolving multilateral regime for FDI are an important but largely ignored topic.

This relative neglect may be substantially due to the absence of a competition (anti-trust) component in the regime. Thus, the large number of international acquisitions, mergers, and strategic alliances of recent years have been undertaken without being subject to any multilateral rules concerning their implications for industry structure or competition. There has been periodic unilateral or bilateral involvement by the EU and US in some cases, and there are continuous processes of monitoring in place in the EU and the US. But the international regulatory and institutional issues concerning international acquisitions, mergers, and alliances remain under-researched. They are under-researched relative to their importance at the micro-level of firms' strategic and competitive issues and the meso-level of particular industries, as well as the macro-level of national and global economic and policy issues.

## 11.4.2 Production location

As industry structure changes, the international location of production changes. Thus, one theoretical implication of the increasing importance of the multilateral regime for FDI is that hypotheses about the L in the 'OLI paradigm' (Dunning 1988, 1998) of FDI and MNEs need to take into account the effects of the WTO agreements and dispute cases on firms' strategic decisions about the location of their facilities. This is true not only of macro-level country variables, but also industry-level, firm-level, product-level, and project-level features—all of which can be related to the WTO agreements and disputes and their consequences for location decisions.

## 11.4.3 Market access

Issues concerning international market access have always been at the centre of the process of liberalization. Whether the details of multilateral negotiations and agreements concern tariffs on manufactured goods, subsidies in the agricultural sector, domestic regulations in services, or any of the other types of barriers to international business transactions, an underlying issue is always access to foreign markets for some firms (or protection of domestic markets for their competitors). Studies of when, how, and why firms respond to new market-opening rules are thus needed.

## 11.4.4  Strategic mode

Other issues of business strategy also emerge from the analysis of the chapter. For instance, given the lowering of tariffs and non-tariff barriers to imports in most countries in a specific industry, should a firm change a strategy of using foreign licensing partners or FDI projects rather than exporting? The effects of the agreements and the dispute cases on firms' strategic decisions, including their location decisions, can be assessed in part with the concept of 'modal neutrality' (Julius 1994). A condition of modal neutrality would exist if decisions among firms' exporting, FDI, and other strategic modes of serving a market would not be skewed toward or away from any one mode. An immediate, comprehensive liberalization of trade and investment policies in all industries in a given country would tend to create a regulatory framework of 'modal neutrality' for firms.

In reality, of course, the liberalization process is incremental and piecemeal, and it is inconsistent across industries, types of barriers to trade and investment, and types of international business transactions. Thus, the WTO-centered liberalization process leads to a continually changing mixture of deviations from 'modal neutrality'. These observations suggest several questions for research: To what extent and in what ways do changes in multilateral rules alter the relative advantages and disadvantages of modes of entry? Are the changes tending toward greater or lesser modal neutrality? What are the variations across industries in these effects? What types of firms are the winners and losers in their competitive positions within their industries?

## 11.4.5  Management functions

The managerial function issues created by changing multilateral rules are as diverse as the functions themselves. In finance and marketing, the issues include the implications of tariff reductions for transfer pricing practices. Assume, for example, that a firm is importing components into an affiliate's manufacturing facility in a host country that lowers the tariff on the imported good but maintains a relatively high corporate income tax. Should the firm raise the transfer price on the imported component in order to reduce the taxable income of the affiliate? In marketing, the issues also include more generally a variety of questions about product, price, promotion, and distribution decisions. Similarly in finance, there are diverse issues about when, where, and how to move funds internationally, as well as issues about how to raise funds and how to allocate them among potential investments and operational needs.

Human resources issues include, for instance, changes in the location and duration of personnel assignments in various countries. Labor relations issues associated with production process decisions are also raised. For example, will a decision in a particular country to switch from an international licensing arrangement with a local manufacturer to a wholly owned foreign subsidiary create new problems of labor–management relations?

## 11.4.6 Government relations

There are wide-ranging issues of business–government relations, including relations with firms' home governments as well as other governments, issues that arise across the entire spectrum of government relations' issues. MNEs' monitoring of the political environment has become more difficult because of the increasing importance of international agreements and institutions, including the WTO. There may be important differences between US-based and European-based corporations in their responses to these new circumstances. In particular, European-based firms seem to have a greater awareness of the changes in the multilateral regime for investment and trade. Further research in the strategic planning and government affairs staffs may confirm this difference. In any case, at least until the Seattle ministerial in December 1999, US firms seemed less able and less willing to analyze the implications of the global WTO system than is warranted by the increasing importance of the system to firms' interests.

A variety of questions arise: What kinds of political strategies for protection and/or market opening do firms have within the context of the new multilateral system? What kinds of firms tend to seek help from their governments to challenge their rivals by filing WTO dispute complaints? What are the patterns of outcomes? What are the tendencies—and deficiencies—in current MNE approaches to the government-relations issues associated with the evolution of the WTO system? How do firms and industry associations and other nongovernmental organizations (NGOs) approach the 'new' issues on the multilateral agenda—issues such as environmental issues?

## 11.4.7 Complexity and uncertainty

Thus, as noted in the introduction to this chapter, the multilateral regime for FDI entails additional sources of complexity and uncertainty for firms in their international institutional and regulatory environment. There is an irony in this, of course, since one of the central rationales for the development of the system is precisely that it should reduce complexity and uncertainty for firms and thereby facilitate international investment, trade, and technology transfer. A multilateral regime should reduce complexity and uncertainty by harmonizing and standardizing national policies and by imposing institutionalized multilateral legal restraints on national policy change. In fact, the WTO system does tend to accomplish these objectives—at least in the aggregate and in the long term. In specific instances, however, and in the short term the effects are often to increase complexity and uncertainty in the regulatory environment of firms. For a new layer of rules that is superimposed on and co-exists with national, bilateral, and regional policies increases complexity, and changes—or potential changes—in the rules add uncertainty. Thus, an interesting set of issues for research concerns the elements of complexity and uncertainty associated with the regime, whether and in what ways they become more and/or less problematic for firms, and how firms do or should respond.

## 11.4.8 Analytic approaches for the research agenda

Such a research agenda will require studies that are *multi-level, multi-functional,* and *multi-disciplinary.* One of the analytic challenges for future research is to incorporate more than one level of analysis. Indeed, any one or more of the following might be an appropriate level of analysis for a particular topic: global, regional, national, industry, firm, product, function. For instance, a study of the implications for the market entry strategies of firms in telecommunications services might require not only an analysis of the worldwide structure of the industry and the strategic alternatives of individual firms within it, but also the sub-sector level and product level specific commitments of individual countries in their schedules of commitments in the GATS. And this analysis might have to be conducted on each of four different modes of supply, including, but not only, FDI. Further, it might require an analysis of tariff levels on electronic goods, such as computers and switches, that are widely used in providing telecommunications services; this would necessarily mean an examination of GATT1994 and the ITA. Such a study might also require an analysis of topics in marketing and finance as well as business–government relations, in addition to strategy.

Multi-disciplinary studies will also be needed. They will need to draw upon central concepts of international law, such as right of entry and national treatment. They will need to draw upon political science studies of international regime change. They will need to draw upon economic studies of the macro-level and micro-level impacts of barriers to investment and trade in general and in particular industries. And of course such studies will need to incorporate concepts and information from industry studies and company studies in the business strategy literature.

In short, there is plenty of research to be done, and there are several bodies of literature to build upon. It thus seems likely that the multilateral regime for FDI and its implications for business strategy will become an increasingly salient topical focus in international business studies.

# APPENDIX 11.1

## WTO Principles

There are several core principles that pervade the WTO agreements. These include, in particular, two principles of nondiscrimination—national treatment (UNCTAD 1999a) and most favored nation treatment (UNCTAD 1999c). In the US, MFN is now sometimes technically referred to as 'normal trade relations', especially in regard to China's membership in the WTO.

*National treatment*, in relation to trade, refers to nondiscrimination against foreign-produced products, as for example through taxes or other regulations that put foreign-produced goods at a competitive disadvantage against similar domestically produced goods. In relation to FDI, national treatment refers to nondiscrimination against foreign-owned firms. For example, restrictions on the percentage of allowable foreign ownership of firms in a particular industry deny pre-establishment national treatment, and they thus limit foreign firms' right of establishment. According to some conventions of usage, it is important to note, the term national treatment is used specifically only in reference to post-establishment issues—that is, whether there is discrimination against a foreign-owned firm, for instance, through special regulations requiring a minimum number of local nationals on the board of directors. National treatment, as applied to investment issues, is thus an expansive and intrusive concept with sensitive implications within the domestic political system and economy of the host country.

The principle of national treatment only disallows discrimination against foreign products or firms. It does not require equal treatment, nor does it prohibit discrimination against domestic products or firms. In fact, subsidies granted by governments to foreign firms to encourage inward FDI are inherently discriminatory in favor of those firms and against domestic firms. Although there has been interest in restricting inward FDI subsidies, proposals for developing an international agreement to limit FDI subsidy competition in the OECD and/or the WTO have not gained much support (Brewer and Young 1997; UNCTAD 1996d).

*Most favored nation treatment* (MFN) refers to nondiscrimination among the foreign products or firms of members of the WTO on the basis of their nationality. National treatment and MFN are thus complementary: the former prohibits discrimination against foreign products and firms relative to domestic ones, while MFN prohibits discrimination against the products or firms of one foreign country (member of the WTO) relative to those of another foreign country (member of the WTO). In international investment protection law, there is a third principle of nondiscrimination, namely fair and equitable treatment; however, it is not so fully developed as the principles of national treatment or MFN.

Another principle that is embodied in WTO agreements is *transparency*. Though it is a difficult concept to define in operational terms and though it is a difficult principle to enforce because of the complexity and ambiguities of many government regulations, the basic notion is clear: The provisions of governments' policies should be stated clearly and made readily available to interested parties such as foreign firms; they should be implemented in ways that are open to public scrutiny; the relevant administrative and judicial procedures should be fair; and changes in policies should be notified to the WTO.

# REFERENCES

BARON, DAVID P. (1997). 'Integrated Strategy, Trade Policy, and Global Competition', *California Management Review*, 39: 145–69.

BODDEWYN, J. J. (1972). 'The External Relations of American Multinational Enterprises', *International Studies Quarterly*, Dec.: 433–53.

BREWER, THOMAS L. (1995). 'International Investment Dispute Settlement Procedures: The Evolving Regime for Foreign Direct Investment', *Law and Policy in International Business*, 26(3): 633–73.

—— (1997). 'International Political Economy and MNEs' Strategies: New Directions for Interdisciplinary Research', in Iyanatul Islam and William Shepherd (eds.), *Current Issues in International Business*. Cheltenham: Edward Elgar: 69–83.

—— (ed.) (1999). *Trade and Investment Policy*, 2 vols. Cheltenham: Edward Elgar.

—— and YOUNG, STEPHEN (1995). 'European Union Policies and the Problems of Multinational Enterprises', *Journal of World Trade Law*, 29(1): 33–52.

—— —— (1997). 'Investment Incentives and the International Agenda', *World Economy*, 20(2): 175–98.

—— —— (1999a). 'Developing Countries and Disputes at the WTO', *Journal of World Trade*, 33(5): 169–82.

—— —— (1999b). 'Location Determinants of Multinational Firms', paper prepared for the Seventh Sorbonne International Conference on Multinational Firms' Strategies. (Paris).

Brewer, Thomas L., and Young, Stephen (*cont.*) (2000*a*). 'The World Trade Organization: Global Rule Maker?', in Stephen Young and Neil Hood (eds.), *The Globalization of Multinational Enterprise Activity and Economic Development*. London: Macmillan, and New York: St Martin's, 251–77.

—— —— (2000*b*). 'American Corporate Planning and International Economic Disputes', in Thomas L. Brewer and Gavin Boyd (eds.), *Globalizing America*. Cheltenham: Edward Elgar, 173–89.

—— —— (2000*c*). *The Multilateral Investment System and Multinational Enterprises*. Oxford: Oxford University Press.

Caves, R. E. (1996). *Multinational Enterprise and Economic Analysis*, 2nd edn. Cambridge: Cambridge University Press.

Christy, P. B. (1991). 'Negotiating Investment in the GATT: A Call for Functionalism', *Michigan Journal of International Law*, 12(4), Summer: 743–98.

Croom, John (1995). *Reshaping the World Trading System*. Geneva: World Trade Organization.

Dunning, John H. (1988). 'The Eclectic Paradigm of International Production', *Journal of International Business Studies*, 19(1): 1–31.

—— (1998). 'Reappraising the Eclectic Paradigm in an Age of Alliance Capitalism', *Journal of International Business Studies*, 26(3): 461–91.

Economist Intelligence Unit (EIU) (1994). *The EIU Guide to the New GATT*. London: EIU.

Eden, Lorraine (1996). 'The Emerging North American Investment Regime', *Transnational Corporations*, 5(3): 61–98.

European Union (EU) (1999). *Report on United States Barriers to Trade and Investment*. Brussels: EU.

Fatouros, A. A. (ed.) (1993). *Transnational Corporations: The International Legal Framework*. United Nations Library on Transnational Corporations, Vol. 20. London: Routledge, on behalf of the United Nations.

Fredebeul-Krein, M., and Freytag, A. (1999). 'The Case for a More Binding WTO Agreement on Regulatory Principles in Telecommunications Markets', *Telecommunications Policy*, 23(9).

Ganesan, A. V. (1997). 'Development-Friendliness Criteria for a Multilateral Investment Agreement', *Transnational Corporations*, 6(3): 135–42.

General Agreement on Tariffs and Trade (GATT) (1994*a*). *Guide to GATT Law and Practice*, 6th edn. Geneva: GATT.

—— (1994*b*). *The Results of the Uruguay Round of Multilateral Trade Negotiations: The Legal Texts*. Geneva: GATT.

Gestrin, Michael, and Rugman, Alan M. (1996). 'The NAFTA Investment Provisions: Prototype for Multilateral Investment Rules', in OECD, *Market Access after the Uruguay Round*. Paris: OECD, 63–78.

Graham, Edward M. (1996). *Global Corporations and National Governments*. Washington, DC: Institute for International Economics.

—— and Lawrence, Robert Z. (1997). 'Measuring the International Contestability of Markets: A Conceptual Approach', *Journal of World Trade*, 30(5): 5–20.

Griffith-Jones, S., with Kimmis, J. (1999). 'Stabilizing Capital Flows to Developing Countries: the Role of Regulation', in S. Picciotto and R. Mayne (eds.) (1999),

*Regulating International Business.* London: Macmillan, and New York: St Martin's Press, 161–82.

HAGGARD, S., and SIMMONS, B. (1987). 'Theories of International Regimes', *International Organization*, 41: 491–517.

HOEKMAN, BERNARD M., and KOSTECKI, MICHAEL M. (1995). *The Political Economy of the World Trading System.* Oxford: Oxford University Press.

*International Herald Tribune* (2000). 'For Zhu, Trade Accord Is Boost for His Program', 17 Nov.: 7.

*International Lawyer, The* (1998). Special Issue, 'First Three Years of the WTO Dispute Settlement System,' Fall.

INTERNATIONAL TRADE CENTRE, UNCTAD/WTO and Commonwealth Secretariat (1996). *Business Guide to the Uruguay Round.* Geneva: International Trade Centre and Commonwealth Secretariat.

JACKSON, JOHN H. (1997). *The World Trade System.* Cambridge, Mass.: MIT Press.

—— (1998). 'Designing and Implementing Effective Dispute Settlement Procedures: WTO Dispute Settlement, Appraisal and Prospects', in Anne O. Krueger (ed.), *The WTO as an International Organization.* Chicago: University of Chicago Press, 161–80.

JULIUS, DEANNE (1994). 'International Direct Investment: Strengthening the Policy Regime', in Peter B. Kenen (ed.), *Managing the World Economy.* Washington, DC: Institute for International Economics, 269–86.

KARL, J. (1996). 'Multilateral Investment Agreements and Regional Economic Integration', *Transnational Corporations*, 5(2): 19–50.

KHALIL, M. I. (1992). 'Treatment of Foreign Investment in Bilateral Investment Treaties', *ICSID Review: Foreign Investment Law Journal*, 7: 339–83.

KOBRIN, STEPHEN J. (1995). 'Regional Integration in a Globally Networked Economy', *Transnational Corporations*, 4(2): 15–33.

—— (1997). 'Transnational Integration, National Markets, and Nation-States', in Brian Toyne and Douglas Nigh (eds.), *International Business: An Emerging Vision.* Columbia, South Carolina: University of South Carolina Press, 242–56.

—— (1998). 'MAI and the Clash of Globalizations', *Foreign Policy*, 112.

KRUEGER, ANNE O. (ed.) (1998). *The WTO as an International Organization.* Chicago: University of Chicago Press.

LEE, K. (1996). *Global Telecommunications Regulation: A Political Economy Perspective.* London: Pinter.

LEY, ROBERT (1989).'Liberating Capital Movements', *OECD Observer*, 159 (Aug.–Sept.): 22–6.

—— (1996). 'Multilateral Rules to Promote the Liberalisation of Investment Regimes', in OECD, *Towards Multilateral Investment Rules.* Paris: 69–73.

MASHAYEKHI, MINA, and GIBBS, MURRAY (1999). 'Lessons from the Uruguay Round Negotiations on Investment', *Journal of World Trade*, 33(6): 1–26.

MUCHLINSKI, PETER T. (1995). *Multinational Enterprises and the Law.* Oxford: Blackwell.

ORGANIZATION FOR ECONOMIC COOPERATION AND DEVELOPMENT (OECD) (1976a). *International Investment and Multinational Enterprises.* Paris: OECD.

ORGANIZATION FOR ECONOMIC COOPERATION AND DEVELOPMENT (OECD) (*cont.*)
(1976*b*). *Guidelines for Multination Enterprises.* Paris: OECD.
—— (1993*a*). *Code of Liberalisation of Capital Movements.* Paris: OECD.
—— (1993*b*). *Code of Liberalisation of Current Invisible Operations.* Paris: OECD.
—— (1994). *National Treatment for Foreign-Controlled Enterprises,* OECD working
papers, No. 34, ii. Paris: OECD.
—— (1996). *Towards Multilateral Investment Rules.* Paris: OECD.
PETERSMANN, E-U. (1997). *The GATT/WTO Dispute Settlement System.* London:
Kluwer Law International.
PICCIOTTO, S. (1999). 'Introduction: What Rules for the World Economy?' in
S. Picciotto and R. Mayne (eds.), (1999). *Regulating International Business.* London:
Macmillan, and New York: St Martin's Press.
—— and MAYNE, R. (eds.) (1999). *Regulating International Business.* London: Mac-
millan, and New York: St Martin's Press.
PREWITT, EDWARD, MARKOVICH, PATRICIA, and RIENHART, FOREST L. (1994). 'Envir-
onment and International Trade', Harvard Business School Case, 9-794-018.
ROBINSON, P. L. (1998). 'Criteria to Test the Development Friendliness of International
Investment Agreements', *Transnational Corporations,* 7(1): 83–9.
RUGMAN, ALAN M. (ed.) (1994). *Foreign Investment and NAFTA.* Columbia: University of South Carolina Press.
—— (2000). *The End of Globalisation.* Oxford: Oxford University Press.
—— and VERBEKE, ALAIN (1990). *Global Corporate Strategy and Trade Policy.* London: Routledge.
SAUVÉ, PIERRE (1994). 'A First Look at Investment in the Final Act of the Uruguay
Round', *Journal of World Trade,* 28(5): 5–16.
—— (1995). 'Assessing the General Agreement on Trade in Services', *Journal of World
Trade,* 28(5): 125–45.
—— (1997). 'Q's and A's on Trade, Investment, and the WTO', *Journal of World Trade,*
28: 5–16.
—— and SCHWANEN, D. (eds.) (1996). *Investment Rules for the Global Economy.*
Toronto: C. D. Howe Institute.
SCHOTT, JEFFREY J. (1994). *The Uruguay Round: An Assessment.* Washington, DC:
Institute for International Economics.
SHAFFER, B. S., and HILLMAN, A. J. (2000). 'The Development of Business–Govern-
ment Strategies by Diversified Firms', *Strategic Management Journal,* 21(2): 175–90.
SHAHIN, MAGDA (1997). 'Multilateral Investment and Competition Rules in the World
Trade Organization: An Assessment', *Transnational Corporations,* 6(2): 171–212.
SHOYER, ANDREW W. (1998). 'The First Three Years of WTO Dispute Settlement:
Observations and Suggestions,' *Journal of International Economic Law,* 1: 277–302.
SMITH, A. (1996). 'The Development of a Multilateral Agreement on Investment at the
OECD', in OECD, *Towards Multilateral Investment Rules.* Paris: OECD, 31–8.
SMYTHE, E. (1998). 'Your Place or Mine? States, International Organization and the
Negotiation of Investment Rules', *Transnational Corporations,* 7(3): 85–120.
SORNARAJAH, M. (1994). *The International Law on Foreign Investment.* Cambridge:
Cambridge University Press.

TSURUMI, Y., and TSURUMI, H. (1999). 'Fujifilm-Kodak Duopolistic Competition in Japan and the United States', *Journal of International Business Studies*, 30(4): 813–30.

TUSELMANN, H.-J. (1997). 'The Multilateral Agreement on Investment: The Case for a Multispeed Convergence Approach to Liberalization', *Transnational Corporations*, 6(3): 87–111.

UNITED NATIONS CONFERENCE ON TRADE AND DEVELOPMENT (UNCTAD) (1996*a*). *World Investment Report 1996: Investment, Trade and International Policy Arrangements*. New York: UN.

—— DTCI (1996*b*). *International Investment Instruments: A Compendium, I: Multilateral Instruments*. Geneva: UN.

—— (1996*c*). 'Draft United Nations Code of Conduct: Transnational Corporations (1983 Version)', in *International Investment Instruments: A Compendium*. Geneva: UN, 161–80.

—— (1996*d*). *Incentives and Foreign Direct Investment*. New York: UN.

—— (1998). *World Investment Report: Trends and Determinants*. New York: UN.

—— (1999*a*). *Admission and Establishment*, UNCTAD Series on Issues in International Investment Agreements. New York: UN.

—— (1999*b*). *Investment-Related Trade Measures*, UNCTAD Series on Issues in International Investment Agreements. New York: UN.

—— (1999*c*). *Most-Favoured-Nation Treatment*, UNCTAD Series on Issues in International Investment Agreements. New York: UN.

—— (1999*d*). *World Investment Report 1999: Foreign Direct Investment and The Challenge of Development*. New York: UN.

UNITED STATES, DEPARTMENT OF STATE (1948). *Havana Charter for an International Trade Organization, Including a Guide to the Study of the Charter*. Washington, DC: US Government.

UNITED STATES TRADE REPRESENTATIVE (USTR) (1999). *National Trade Estimate*. Washington, DC: US Government.

WAELDE, THOMAS (1999). 'International Law of Foreign Investment: Towards Regulation by Multilateral Treaties', *Business Law International*, 1: 50–79.

WELLS, L. T., JR. (1998). 'Multinationals and the Developing Countries', *Journal of International Business Studies*, 29(1): 101–14.

WESTON, MAX, and KOEHN, NANCY F. (1996). 'The World Sugar Industry and Tate & Lyle', Harvard Business School, Case 9-794-119.

WITHERELL, W. (1996). 'Towards an International Set of Rules for Investment', in OECD, *Towards Multilateral Investment Rules*. Paris: OECD, 17–29.

WORLD BANK (1992). *Guidelines on the Treatment of Foreign Investment*. Washington: The World Bank.

WORLD TRADE ORGANIZATION (1996). *Annual Report 1996*. Geneva: WTO.

YOUNG, STEPHEN, and BREWER, THOMAS L. (1999). 'Multilateral Investment Rules, Multinationals and the Global Economy', in Nicholas A. Phelps and Jeremy Alden (eds.), *Foreign Direct Investment and the Global Economy*. London: The Stationery Office, 13–29.

YOUNG, STEPHEN, and BREWER, THOMAS L. (in progress). 'Nonmarket Strategies and the Globalization of Business'.

ZAMPETTI, A. B. (1995). 'The Uruguay Round Agreement on Subsidies: A Forward-Looking Assessment', *Journal of World Trade*, 29(6): 5–29.

# PART III

# STRATEGY FOR MNES

# CHAPTER 12

# STRATEGY AND THE MULTINATIONAL ENTERPRISE

## STEPHEN B. TALLMAN

## GEORGE S. YIP

## 12.1 INTRODUCTION

THIS chapter uses a strategy analysis framework to examine the key strategic issues facing multinational enterprises (MNEs). While much of the discussion of international business has to do with the external conditions of international markets and industries, and much of the discussion of MNEs addresses their organizational analysis and structuring, we believe that a distinct role exists for multinational strategy. Using an explicitly strategic perspective is meant to emphasize this position. Within this overall framework, we will discuss strategic considerations of the multinational enterprise specifically and will show how different aspects of strategic analysis are emphasized in different contexts.

As teachers and researchers in international business, we are often asked, 'what is different about international strategy from domestic strategy?' Our answer is that international strategy has its own special issues and institutional contexts that require the application of classic strategic analysis techniques. Hence, our approach in this chapter is to view the strategic analysis process and international strategy issues as orthogonal to each other. We first review the strategic analysis process, then identify issues of international strategy, and lastly, examine these issues using the strategic analysis process. We do not aim to be comprehensive but to identify the most salient issues of international strategy and to set an agenda for debate and further research.

## 12.2 ANALYTICAL FRAMEWORK

Business strategy involves identifying and exploiting the resources and capabilities of the firm in the marketplace for the purpose of gaining competitive advantage and superior financial performance. Inherent in this definition is the need to continuously renew these resources and capabilities, to determine a set of goals and objectives for the enterprise when it does gain competitive advantage, to understand the structure of the marketplace and of the competitive situation faced by the firm, and to devise, assess, and choose among a set of strategic options for the firm. A fully developed strategy must also be suitable to the macro-environment of the enterprise and must develop organizational solutions to execute otherwise abstract plans. In the setting of this handbook, though, these macro and organizational issues are largely covered in other chapters, and we will focus on the core issue of strategy making in multinational enterprises (MNEs).

The major aspects of strategy analysis include: setting goals and objectives, performing competitive and industry analysis, analyzing resources and capabilities, developing strategic options, choosing a strategy, and implementing that strategy, with feedback loops among all the processes. Figure 12.1 shows this in a simplified model. There is, of course, a large strategy literature dealing with both the content of strategy and its implementation (e.g. Ansoff, 1965; Andrews, 1971; Steiner, 1979; Lorange, 1982; Porter, 1980 and 1985; Hax and Majluf, 1991; Grant 1998; Barney, 1996). In this chapter we focus on the international strategy process as far as 'strategic options'. Other chapters in this book deal with issues of implementation (while recognizing the inherent inseparability of strategy formulation and implementation, perhaps best summed up in the idea of 'implementable strategies' often espoused by management consulting firms).

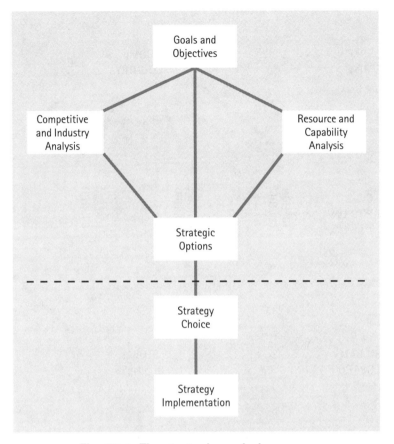

**Fig. 12.1 The strategic analysis process**

International business involves a specific set of issues whose strategic resolution ties into the generic strategic analysis framework in Figure 12.1. These
international strategy issues are presented in Figure 12.2 and involve (1) increasing geographic spread (often referred to as 'internationalization'), (2) achieving local adaptation (often referred to as 'responsiveness'), (3) building global
integration (sometimes referred to as 'globalization' or 'global strategy'), and
(4) multi-business, multi-country, and often multi-firm issues such as international strategic alliances and global mergers and acquisitions. The general
structure of the chapter will follow that of Figure 12.2, moving through the
international strategy issues, except for the fourth issue—multi-business,
multi-firm, multinational moves—which will be mostly covered in the next
chapter on strategic alliances. At each stage of the process, though, we will refer
to the strategic analysis processes in Figure 12.1 as they become relevant.

In general, the more basic issues in international strategy require more
use of the more basic issues in strategy analysis, as illustrated in Figure 12.3,

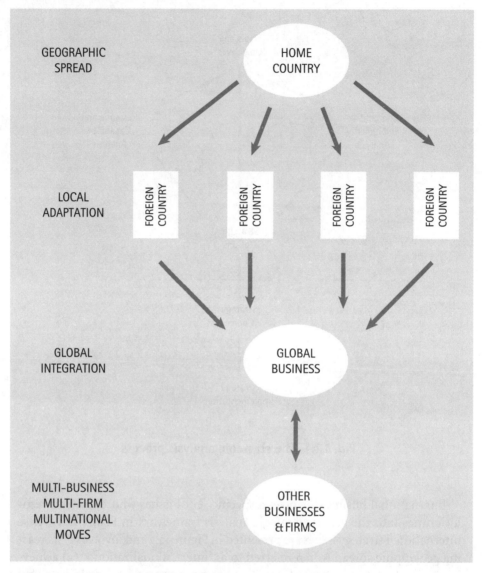

**Fig. 12.2 International strategy issues**

although the last international issue of multi-business/multi-firm/multinational moves tends to require heavy emphasis on all five strategic analysis processes. We see heavy reliance on goal setting, industry analysis, and resource assessment as firms expand internationally. Adaptation and integration are driven largely by issues developed through competitive analysis and resource assessment, while integration must also consider issues revealed by different means of assessing strategic conditions and opportunities.

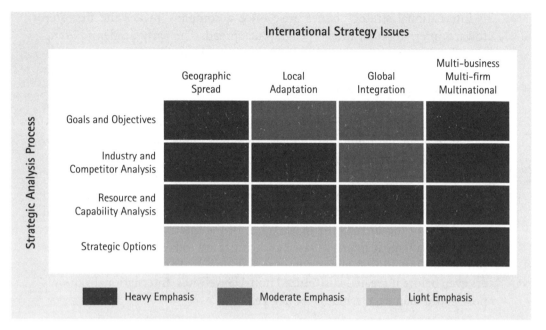

**Fig. 12.3  Mapping of international strategy issues and the strategic analysis process**

# 12.3 GEOGRAPHIC SPREAD

The defining aspect of multinational strategy is that it involves expansion of the operating horizon of the enterprise beyond the borders of the home nation. Through a combination of trade, licensing, alliance, and foreign direct investment, the MNE accesses customers and factors of production that are not available to the domestic firm. It also encounters competitive conditions and rival firms that would not affect the domestic company in a domestic business. From these unique encounters with the international environment, the multinational may finally develop a set of capabilities and competencies that it would otherwise never see.

International strategy issues arise once a company makes the first step toward internationalization—geographic spread. The early academic literature focused on exports as the minimum requirement to become an international company and foreign direct investment as a stricter requirement (e.g. Dunning 1988). Today, with internationalization of not just sales or production, but of other parts of the business system such as procurement or research, and with the advent of the Internet, *we consider internationalization to occur with any cross-border geographic spread of activities, whether physically or electronically.*

Internationalization has become more a matter of perceptual horizons and the scope of strategic intent than of specific means for foreign market entry. In the future, even the breadth of strategic vision will be subordinated to global access, not of the firm to the market, but of the international market to the firm. After all, most Internet-based companies are today born global whether or not they intend it. Amazon.com was making sales to international customers even before it created customized non-US websites. Internationalization is now, more than ever, a matter of degree.

## 12.3.1 Goals and objectives of geographic spread

Most academic literature, fuelled by the perspective of economics, has focused on the question of why companies should go international. In the perfect markets of neoclassical economics, companies can always sell the international rights to internationally exploitable assets and capabilities. Hence, most of the literature has focused on market imperfections, such as indivisibilities, that prompt a company to undertake foreign activities. But if you speak to multinational managers today, their question is seldom that of, 'should we go international?', but rather is, 'why should we not?' and 'what is the best way to do so?' Perhaps the most poignant example of failure to internationalize at the right time is provided by RCA, the original commercializer of television sets. Rather than go international, it sold the international rights to production, only to find decades later that its domestic business was almost entirely captured by foreign producers (a sort of international 'boomerang' effect). Given the long time span involved, a financial analysis might conclude that RCA did the right thing. Today's far faster moving markets imply that not going international incurs very severe competitive risks. Would anyone suggest that Microsoft should have licensed its international rights? In addition, various studies, particularly Gestrin, Knight, and Rugman (1998), show a very strong correlation between the financial performance of firms and the degree of internationalization of their revenues.

But, as usual, we face a problem of cause and effect. A strategy perspective would particularly argue that competitive advantage drives both financial performance and the ability to internationalize. Returning to the admittedly extreme case of Microsoft, one could hardly argue that internationalization is the cause of their financial performance (although failure to internationalize would have eventually threatened their dominance).

But let us return first to the traditional perspectives on why companies might go international. Many authors have listed many reasons, a particularly comprehensive list being provided by Root (1987). A common top consideration for most businesses as they expand geographically, whether locally, nationally, or internationally, is the desire to access larger markets. Even large domestic markets will be saturated by the successful firm as it expands distribution, increases its product range, develops new manufacturing sites, and so forth. Such a company, however, is likely to possess at least some resources that are not completely engaged, particularly managerial resources that increase with application and learning so that they can organize ever larger operations efficiently. Penrose (1959) tells us that the response of the business firm to excess resources that are 'lumpy' or indivisible, so that they cannot be evenly trimmed to fit its current position, is continual expansion. Once the national market is filled, the business firm will turn to international markets. Of course, this is an extreme and theoretical sequence. The reality of many companies is that they turn rapidly to international markets, even as they expand domestically. The outcome and objectives are the same, though, whether a company waits to fill every accessible corner of its national market or is looking to international possibilities early in its history. Larger operations open the way for economies of scale and scope, faster access to learning curve effects, market power as buyer and supplier, and other benefits of size. As technology has improved, the efficient scale of more and more industries has become larger than any one market, even those of the largest industrial nations, can absorb. Therefore, increasing geographical spread allows firms to become more efficient and thus more competitive, while at the same time providing them with the market power to dominate smaller, weaker, less widespread competitors.

The benefits of size are commonly cited as important to multinational firms, but access to wide ranging markets also improves the efficiency of smaller, smarter firms. The 'new economy' gives many examples of information age firms that seek regional and global audiences for their highly volatile products. Even in the old economy, we see examples of such strategies. Mascarenhas (1986) showed in a study of second tier firms that such enterprises moved into international markets when they perceived that they could not overcome more powerful rivals in the home market. Well-known companies such as Honda and Sony, for instance, became fixtures in the American market while they were still struggling with Toyota and Matsushita, respectively, in Japan. Morck and Yeung (1991) show that firms with extensive international operations often achieve superior performance. Myles and Shaver (1993) found that firms facing foreign challenges in their home markets needed to expand internationally in order to survive.

## 12.3.2 Resources and capabilities for geographic spread

The concept of resources and capabilities developed in the strategy literature (e.g. Wernerfelt, 1984; Grant, 1991) applies very well to the international strategy issue of geographic spread. Companies that own or access unique resources and capabilities—demonstrating unique core competencies in Hamel and Prahalad's terms—find that international expansion gives them vast new opportunities to leverage these expensive and valuable skills. A variety of studies have shown that for American (Hitt, Hoskisson, and Kim 1997) and British (Grant 1987) MNEs, international expansion leads to greater profitability, presumably because they can leverage such resources. Competencies typically involve large investments in capital and managerial energy, incurring high fixed costs. Firms that can expand their operations widely can earn greater returns to these investments, while potentially improving the competencies through previously unconsidered applications. International markets offer many of the advantages of product proliferation while allowing the firm to remain in its primary line of business.

MNEs can also access resources and build capabilities through international expansion. While many firms go abroad seeking new, more accessible markets, others (and even the same firms examined from a different perspective) go abroad to access resources that are in short supply in the home market. This was true historically of natural resource firms—if RTZ mines copper, they must locate mines where there is copper in deposits rich enough for economical extraction. Agricultural product firms such as Dole make millions growing bananas and other tropical fruits, but must locate (or access) production facilities in the tropics to do so. Other firms move abroad in search of less expensive labor in overpopulated developing countries, as has been seen historically for American firms locating plants in Mexico or South East Asia. Essentially, access to traditional sources of comparative advantage—cheap land, labor, or resources—is a key objective of many internationalization moves. Many such companies still see themselves as essentially domestic, but they are actually totally reliant on international sources of supply for their domestic markets. When the resources cannot move (or cannot move in sufficient quantity) to the producer, the producer must move to the resources. We will see that this move may be through market arrangements, alliance, or foreign ownership, much like market access, but the means and the objectives are not identical.

In today's knowledge-intensive business world, asset-seeking investment is moving away from traditional natural resource endowments. More firms go abroad to access constructed, or man-made assets. Porter (1990) focuses on the role of social institutions in developing home country advantages that can be exploited in foreign markets, but it is equally the case that international expansion can access location-bound competencies that have developed in other countries. So, asset-seeking expansion may be looking for skilled labor educated and conditioned in foreign systems (often a driver of investment from less developed countries (LDCs) into the United States or Europe), technologies that have arisen in foreign industrial clusters, or business processes that are embedded in a foreign location. Companies may also seek institutional conditions more friendly to their activities, moving their financing arms to financial centers, production to areas with less restrictive labor laws, or research to countries with strong intellectual property rights enforcement. The definition of location-based assets has changed, but the objectives of asset-seeking international expansion have not, at least, not in any real sense.

## 12.3.3 Risk and return in international strategy

Another consideration in international expansion is risk reduction, whether financial, business, or environmental. International expansion offers the opportunity to move into markets that are not perfectly in phase with the home market. We see in 2000, for instance, that the US economy is booming, but perhaps nearing the end of an up-cycle; that Western Europe is edging out of a period of stagnation or recession; and that East Asia is recovering, rapidly at times, from the 1997 crash. In the same way that product portfolio strategies are used to reduce cash flow variances, international market portfolio strategies can be used to manage diversifiable risks. Access to a broader base of financial markets may also reduce the basic market risk, particularly for firms from developing economies that can access developed markets. Recent studies have shown that international spread reduces financial betas for multinational firms, but also have shown that volatile currency markets have vastly increased the impact of exchange risk, so that the net variance in cash flows is higher today for multinational firms (Reeb, Kwok, and Baek 1998). This empirical evidence suggests that it is premature to say that multinationals have found a way to eliminate the risk-return relationship. However, it does seem to be the case that firms can simultaneously increase returns to fixed assets and take a portfolio approach to financial risk management by increased internationalization.

While financial risk reduction seems to be less clear-cut today, business risk reduction strategies through international expansion seem to continue to be attractive. If we look at business risk as exposure to unexpected events, international markets offer several advantages. First, extended product life-cycles, while perhaps less apparent than in the past (Vernon 1979), still seem possible in many industries. Firms that can shift sales of outdated product in industrialized countries to developing countries can gain ongoing returns on their initial investment and may also be able to avoid sudden replacement by new technologies or innovative products. Much evidence also exists to show that strategic maneuvering in concentrated industries is most successful when used by international firms against domestic firms. Hamel and Prahalad (1985) point to the impact of price competition by internationalized Japanese firms in the consumer electronics industry on American companies that could only respond in their domestic market, and that eventually exited the industry. Finally, political and other environmental risks can be difficult to manage for companies committed to one or a few national markets, while more internationalized firms can shift production, promotion, distribution, even development among a number of markets to take advantage of (or avoid) local conditions or to increase bargaining power.

## 12.3.4 Industry and competitor analysis for geographic spread

Classic industry and competitor analysis (Porter 1980 and 1985) can be applied to geographic spread. Firms usually need an initial competitive advantage that they can leverage into international markets. Recent research by Yip, Gomez, and Monti (2000) shows that for newly internationalizing firms, the initial competitive advantage is the single greatest determinant of international success, outweighing the process used in internationalization. In the case of geographic expansion, this advantage need only be relative to each specific country entered. Hence, a firm with weak competitive advantages at home may still have a competitive advantage in foreign markets. This would be particularly the case for firms moving from more developed economies to less developed ones. This effect is illustrated by the 'pyramid of international competitive advantage' in Figure 12.4. In this pyramid, firms selling 'down' to less developed economies (which usually but not always have less demanding markets) find it relatively easy to have a competitive advantage in the entered market. Firms selling 'sideways' to economies of similar development need to

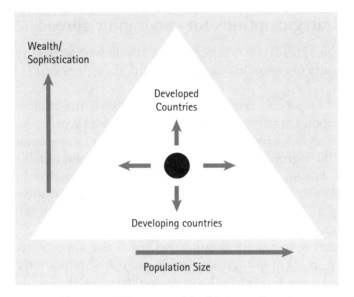

**Fig. 12.4 The pyramid of international competitive advantage**

*Source* George S. Yip (1999)

work a bit to create an advantage perhaps through local adaptation. Lastly, firms selling 'up' to more developed economies have to work really hard to establish a competitive advantage, perhaps through lower prices or by focusing on a market niche.

Then, in addition to the initial competitive advantage, companies need to conduct classic industry analysis in each market, as by using Porter's (1980) five forces framework to establish for each potential foreign market what the likely prospects are for above average returns. But the Porter (1980) framework does not directly address international issues. Instead, other industry level frameworks, such as that of Porter (1986), which examines the potential of industries for international dispersion and coordination of operations, or of Yip (1992), which describes the various industry drivers of global versus local strategies, may be applied. More comprehensive market-specific frameworks, especially that of Root (1987), also may be applied. This latter framework examines the classic issues of country attractiveness as well as whether the individual foreign entrant can build a viable and profitable business and is followed below.

## 12.3.5 Strategic options for geographic spread

In geographic spread, two types of strategic options arise: first, the choice of foreign country or region to enter, and second, the type of entry or participation mode.

*Choice of country to enter*: as mentioned above, the choice of country depends first on attractiveness analysis. But after several individual countries have been analyzed, a method needs to be applied to choose among them, or at least for the sequence of entry. Here, strategy portfolio techniques such as that of the Boston Consulting Group's growth-share matrix become very relevant (Henderson 1979). This matrix has been adapted in various ways for arraying countries rather than businesses or products (see Larréché, 1980; and Yip 1992, ch. 3).

Recent developments in globalization make the issue of sequence less germane. In an era of low transportation, poor communications, high trade barriers, and large differences between countries, MNEs had to take each country more or less one at a time. In the modern era of rapid transportation, instant electronic communications, low trade barriers, and converging country conditions, MNEs increasingly seek simultaneous rather than sequential international expansion. The ultimate case was provided by Microsoft's launch of Windows 95, which became the first major product in any category to be launched in virtually every country of the world on the same day. That has become the new standard. Again, Internet-based products achieve global reach even more quickly, with zero time lags.

The era of global strategies also requires MNEs to look beyond country-by-country choices on the basis of standalone attractiveness. Instead they also need to consider the global strategic importance of countries. According to Yip (1992, ch. 3), there are several ways in which a country can be globally strategic as a market:

- large source of revenues or profits
- home market of global customers
- home market of global competitors
- significant market of global competitors
- major source of industry innovation.

Activities of subsidiaries of MNEs in such markets cannot profitably be isolated from other operations in other parts of the world—they must be integrated into a global system.

*Choice of entry mode*: an extensive literature exists on the choice of entry mode (summarized in Root 1987 and 1994). These choices include: export entry modes (indirect, direct agent/distributor, direct branch/subsidiary), contractual entry modes (licensing, franchising, technical agreements, service contracts, management contracts, construction/turnkey contracts, co-production agreements), and investment entry modes (direct entry, acquisition, joint venture). Many of these considerations are addressed in other chapters in this book. Suffice it for us to say that the structure of entry mode is absolutely essential to successful implementation of international strategy.

Johanson and Vahlne (1977) showed that in the postwar era firms tended to internationalize in a typical sequence of exporting, allying, and investing. However, as more firms have more international experience, this pattern is less commonly seen. Hill, Hwang, and Kim (1990) provide a useful unifying framework in arguing that a firm's choice of entry mode depends on the strategic relationship the firm envisages between operations in different countries. Birkinshaw and Morrison (1995) show that the role and status of the individual subsidiary are dependent on the industry and strategy of the parent company. Tallman (1992) suggests that the application of capabilities beyond national boundaries is dependent on the interaction of firm strategy and national market characteristics. Capabilities do not always translate. Entry mode must be considered in the context of the industry, the overall international strategy, the management capabilities of the parent firm, and the expected role of the individual subsidiary.

Porter's (1990) Diamond Model, and other models such as Rugman and Verbeke's (1993) Double Diamond of national competitive advantage, go beyond simple economic development in determining preferred locations for activities. MNEs can base key product lines in order to access local competencies or regional clusters and then can apply these skills to the benefit of the entire MNE. Even within general categories of national development, regional specialization is common to many industries. Firms that plan to excel in a particular industry must be present in such clusters or industrial districts, but without the ability to move the products of such location-based advantage efficiently and to combine them with other capabilities, advantage is localized and benefits are severely limited. This is a key point that distinguishes local adaptation strategies from globally integrated strategies. Those are the topics of the following two sections.

International spread is generally associated with superior performance (Grant 1987; Hitt, Hoskisson, and Kim 1997), as might be expected for firms applying their particular capabilities in a wider market. However, other studies have shown less apparent benefit, even for American firms (Tallman and Li 1996). Longitudinal studies of Japanese multinational firms suggest that increased international sales actually predict lower levels of accounting performance, although they are more likely to reflect faster sales growth (Geringer, Tallman, and Olsen 2000). The marginal costs of entering international market may well surpass the marginal benefits at some point, resulting in an eventual competitive disadvantage to ever-greater geographical spread.

# 12.4 LOCAL ADAPTATION

As firms move into international markets, they soon discover that all potential customers do not have identical needs and desires. International expansion is often based, at least initially, on exports or licenses that provide goods identical to those sold at home to customers abroad. In many cases, though, firms find that foreign customers actually prefer somewhat different products, and that adapting their outputs to local tastes and preferences provides considerable competitive advantage in local markets. This is particularly appropriate for products with high cultural content, such as foods or personal-care products; for products or product mixes that are sensitive to levels of economic development, such as automobiles or farm equipment; or for services that involve high levels of personal interaction or are regulated, such as accounting or other professional services. Ohmae (1989) says that consumers do not like averages. That is, even in products with technology content such as automobiles, customers around the world may not want a 'world car', they may want a vehicle that corresponds to the needs and fashions of their nation. This is not to say that at least some models will not sell in some numbers in multiple markets, but the mix of models and demand for any one will vary from market to market.

So the longstanding conventional wisdom has been that the wise MNE will adapt to demand, not continue to sell standard offerings. (In the next section on Global Integration we will present the arguments questioning this conventional wisdom.) Political pressures may be high for products that, while lacking any need for different characteristics, might be seen as strategic goods. This category often includes defense equipment, but may also be extended to various technology intensive categories—computers, software, telecommunications, transportation, and many others—that are seen as critical to the nation's functioning. These categories also offer opportunities to improve the technology base of the host nation if production takes place locally, involving local scientists, engineers, technicians, and managers. Therefore, host governments often prefer local operations in what they consider sensitive industries.

Whatever the reason, and those given above are only a small sample, preference is often given to local firms, or firms that operate locally. The influence of the GATT and the WTO has steadily improved the situation for market access via imports, but many countries still have in place a variety of trade barriers and local subsidies. These may be formal barriers, such as tariffs and quotas, production subsidies, price supports, or investment incentives, or they may be informal 'buy local' campaigns, nationalistic biases, bureaucratic delays, and the like. Countries or regions also may have laws or regulations concerning environmental protection, labor practices, consumer protection, and so forth that are not intended as trade barriers, but which significantly affect the business environment in local or regional markets. Beyond barriers, though, MNEs need to be close to customer preferences, particularly in industries subject to rapid change, in order to shorten logistical lines, to understand how to advertise in a different culture, and to provide attentive sales and service require local responsiveness in many parts of the value-added chain for most products. Even among firms that keep their research, product development, and manufacturing centralized at global or regional levels, downstream operations are very likely to be decentralized and specialized to the demands of particular locations.

Many popular models of multinational strategy from the last few decades have treated responsiveness and global integration as competing demands. The more sophisticated approaches, though, have come to see that both pressures exist simultaneously, and that successful MNEs have learned to provide both. Prahalad (1975) and Prahalad and Doz (1987) developed the widely used and adapted Integration–Responsiveness Grid which shows these two pressures as orthogonal, and that companies need to judge the degree of strategic emphasis on both dimensions simultaneously rather than treating them as alternatives. Ghoshal (1987) proposed further that different businesses within a corporation, and different activities within a business area, would require different balances of integration and responsiveness, while Bartlett and Ghoshal's (1989) work on 'transnational strategies' set an agenda for the last decade that calls for both objectives to be satisfied in most industries.

## 12.4.1 Goals and objectives of local adaptation

The goals and objectives of local adaptation are fairly straightforward—to achieve the maximum fit with local constituencies whether customers, suppliers, partners, or regulators. Country managers have typically taken such objectives to heart and tried to run their local business as if it were their own. But it is not quite that simple. The essence of an MNE is sharing and leverage across countries. Total local adaptation would reduce the MNE to a loose collection of autonomous businesses that enjoys little synergy while incurring the overheads of a large MNE, as happened with Philips (the Dutch multinational) and others in the 1980s and 1990s. So MNEs have to constantly balance the needs of local adaptation and global integration.

## 12.4.2 Industry and competitor analysis for local adaptation

A strategy of local adaptation allows the MNE subsidiary manager to straight-forwardly apply industry and competitor analysis techniques to the local country. But the manager should be aware of extra-country opportunities and threats. Indeed, a primary criticism of the Porter Five Forces framework is that it does not directly address cross-border issues. In most cases, but not always, the addition of cross-border possibilities increases the strength of competitive forces. For individual countries, managers need to consider the openness of the market, not just in terms of government barriers (trade, investment, and regulatory) but also in terms of logistical access and customer openness to foreign products. For example, India prior to the reforms of the early 1990s was primarily closed in terms of governmental barriers and logistical access but somewhat open in terms of customer acceptance. New Zealand after its reforms became very open in terms of governmental barriers and customer acceptance but still suffers from logistical barriers given its geographic location at the end of the world. France today has few logistical barriers but some governmental barriers and significant barriers of customer resistance to foreign products.

The effect of country openness varies for each of Porter's five forces. Particularly for the threat of new entrants and rivalry among existing firms, increased country openness heightens competition by increasing its geo-graphic scope. Increased country openness also increases the pressure from substitutes by increasing the geographic scope of where these substitutes might come from. Country openness reduces the power of suppliers by allowing local subsidiaries to bring in supplies from outside. Conversely, country openness increases the power of buyers by allowing them to seek off-shore providers.

Globalization, in general, can also change the fundamental strategy required for managing competitive forces. In *Competitive Strategy*, published in 1980, Porter, effectively recommended that companies seek to compete in markets with weak competitors and weak customers. In *The Competitive Advantage of Nations*, published in 1990, Porter argues instead for participat-ing in national markets with the strongest rivals and most demanding custom-ers, in order to build international competitiveness. One difference between his two positions is explainable by the difference between a closed, domestic industry and an open, globalized industry. In a closed, domestic industry, a company accustomed to weak competitors and undemanding customers has little to fear—there is no source of new competitors who might grow strong in more demanding competitive arenas. In an open, globalized industry, such newly strong competitors abound. Porter, together with other international strategists, has also come to recognize the importance of learning in international environments in addition to simply exploiting old capabilities in new locations.

## 12.4.3 Resource and capability analysis for local adaptation

MNE subsidiaries clearly need resources and capabilities in order to be able to adapt and operate successfully. Conn and Yip (1997) found that the transfer of critical capabilities was the single most important determinant of subsidiary success. In addition, country openness and the fact of being a subsidiary of an MNE, typically competing with both other MNE subsidiaries and local firms, combine to raise a game theoretic issue for resources and capabilities. The local subsidiary can choose to play a 'local' game which may mean a submaximal deployment of parent company resources or can choose a 'global' game in which the full resources of the parent are brought to bear. Specifically, the MNE needs to decide how much to subsidize its activities in particular countries and how much strategic freedom to give to its subsidiary managers (Birkinshaw, Chapter 14 in this volume). Playing a global game in a specific country raises the stakes, rivalry, and risks. By definition, an MNE cannot subsidize every country operation unless it brings in resources from other lines of business, so the MNE has to husband its resources for subsidizing strategic markets, as defined earlier. In terms of local adaptation, that would typically mean more effort expended. For example, many Western MNCs recognized in the 1980s and 1990s that Japan was a strategic market and made extra efforts at local adaptation, while others, notably US automakers, were criticized for insufficient adaptation.

## 12.4.4 Strategic options for local adaptation

The key strategic choice in local adaptation lies in the combination of actual and presented degree of adaptation. The MNE subsidiary has to decide not just how much to adapt but how to present its degree of adaptation. In the latter choice, at one extreme the MNE can present itself and its products as totally local and at the other extreme as totally foreign or global. The extensive literature on 'country of origin effects' deals with this issue (e.g. Johansson 1989). The pyramid of international competitive advantage (Figure 12.4) provides guidance. In general, MNEs selling up the pyramid (from a less advanced home country to more advanced market countries) will want to hide their country of origin, either by claiming local identity or a third country identity. MNEs selling down the pyramid (from a more advanced home country to less advanced market countries will want to emphasize their country of origin. In addition, as is well known and discussed (e.g. Porter 1990) economic development does not correlate perfectly with sophistication in a given category (e.g. Germany for cars but Italy for clothing). Adaptation can match the needs of a given set of customers closely, but typically requires certain compromises with the equally important benefits of targeting a global market, as we see next.

# 12.5 GLOBAL INTEGRATION

Globalization is generally defined as integrating the activities of the MNE across international markets. Traditionally, globalization has been seen as a strategy concerned primarily with efficiency goals, as integrating worldwide operations permitted larger plants with greater economies of scale, bigger distribution systems with greater economies of scope, wider brand exploitation, and the like. This 'simple global' strategy (Porter 1986) was characterized by Bartlett and Ghoshal (1989) as a 'Japanese' strategy of efficient production and central control. More recently, though, global integration is recognized as important to differentiation strategies, providing more unique, more usable, more effective goods and services through the impact of multiple markets, superior intellectual inputs, and new organizational competencies. Without integration, MNEs act as national firms in multiple markets. While this strategy may exploit certain firm-specific resources more widely, it limits the ultimate ability of the MNE to take advantage of its geographic spread. Differentiating activities from location to location while tying these various operations together through corporate level processes can provide considerable cost benefits and can also generate new capabilities that are based on combinations of skills and resources from many places. Both efficiency and superior product offerings often are enhanced by integrating operations around the world.

## 12.5.1 Goals and objectives of global integration

Ohmae (1985) and other authors promote the need to compete in all parts of the Industrial Triad (the United States, Europe, and Japan) in order to exploit fully the benefits of integrated international operations. But with the advance of developing economies in Asia and Latin America, Ohmae's Triad should be expanded to the 'Quartet' of North America, Latin America, Europe, and Asia—or perhaps simply the entire world. Others, such as Rugman (2000), see integration taking place primarily within the regional groupings of nations. In either case, looking at markets that are larger than any single country satisfies a variety of objectives for the MNE. By looking to regional or global markets, firms can offer wider product ranges to the much larger customer base, and are also likely to find more product concepts by accessing a larger range of demand in an organized manner. While we no longer see efficiency as the only benefit of integrating across markets, economies of scale in all value-adding activities are certainly enhanced by global strategies. Product development, manufacturing, distribution systems, marketing, brands, and so forth are all subject to certain levels of fixed costs that can be dramatically reduced on an item by item basis through market integration. Many firms are beginning to centralize administrative services on a regional basis and policies worldwide, reducing the bureaucratic costs of running the organization—human resource policies, accounting, information systems, reward systems, and the many other maintenance items of a large company—to a much smaller proportion of the cost of doing business. Finally, a company's ability to pay for expensive technology and new product development is greatly enhanced if these innovative activities can be targeted at a larger-than-national customer base.

Global integration offers a variety of advantages, often acting to emphasize or greatly increase some of the benefits of international spread. Comparative (location or country-specific) and competitive (firm-specific) advantages are enhanced if the MNE is able to leverage these benefits across its entire range of markets, not just to focus on the single host market. For instance, the global firm can locate value-adding activities where local conditions are most appropriate and coordinate its value-added chain globally. Kogut (1985a) shows that even in the simplest economic terms, different levels of development across nations suggest specialization in different value-adding activities. The locally responsive MNE can use this idea to determine appropriate products and production processes for each country. The global firm can move the entire worldwide operation for a value-adding stage to the appropriate country—labor-intensive steps to NICs, technology-intensive stages to the United States or Japan—and then integrate transshipment of components and intermediate goods throughout its system to optimize its global efficiencies.

Global integration also provides benefits to internal organizational cap-abilities beyond simply exploiting the advantages of multiple locations world-wide. Again, Kogut (1985*b*) addresses benefits in market operations. A key advantage is to be able to arbitrage labor markets, tax benefits, exchange rates, and other location characteristics. The global firm, by shifting different activities among national markets while continuing to coordinate them on a worldwide basis, can greatly expand the scope of its 'buy low, sell high' efforts, giving it considerable advantage over the local or regional firm. This ability to shift operations also gives considerable leverage to the global MNE in its relationships with suppliers, buyers, and other stakeholders. Access to alternative production facilities has allowed MNEs to stave off nationalization threats, tap large tax concessions, and gain favorable labor settlements. Glob-alization also permits firms to shift funds internally, using profit sanctuaries in one region to subsidize expansion efforts in another. Indeed, Hamel and Prahalad (1985) consider financial cross-subsidy as one of the defining char-acteristics of the globally integrated strategy. While more efficient inter-national capital markets may reduce the advantage of simple access to funds, large, integrated MNEs still can get preferred rates, but even more can use internal funds to support strategic moves that financial markets might not support.

## 12.5.2 Industry and competitor analysis for global integration

The key industry issue in global integration is to figure out which industries lend themselves to more or less global integration. Clearly, there are differ-ences—at one extreme, the computer industry provides a primarily global industry. At the other extreme, the food industry is still in many ways a multilocal industry. Global industries have been defined in various ways: Hout, Porter, and Rudden (1982) defined a global industry, in contrast to a multidomestic industry, as one in which a firm's competitive position in one country market is significantly affected by its competitive position in other country markets; Bartlett and Ghoshal (1989) defined a 'transnational indus-try' as being driven by simultaneous demands for global efficiency, national responsiveness, and worldwide learning; Morrison (1990) characterized a global industry as having intense levels of international competition, competi-tors marketing a standardized product worldwide, industry competitors that have a presence in all key international markets and high levels of interna-tional trade. These definitions have the common thread of the need and opportunity to integrate strategy across countries.

Yip (1989 and 1992), building on Porter (1986), provides a comprehensive framework for diagnosing industry globalization potential. This framework uses industry globalization drivers: market, cost, government, and competitive. Each set of drivers has its proponents, with market drivers (e.g. globally common customer tastes) being particularly associated with Levitt (1983), cost drivers (e.g. global scale economies) with Porter (1986), government drivers (e.g. absence of trade restrictions) with Doz (1979), and competitive drivers (e.g. cross-country subsidization) with Hamel and Prahalad (1985). The industry diagnosis then requires certain strategic choices (discussed below). In terms of cross-industry empirical studies, Kobrin (1991) examined fifty-six manufacturing industries containing US-based firms and found technological intensity and advertising intensity to be key industry drivers of global integration by firms, while manufacturing scale economies was not a significant driver. Johansson and Yip (1994) examined industries involving thirty-six American and Japanese MNCs and found market and cost drivers to be the most significant for globalization while government and competitive drivers were not significant. Birkinshaw and Morrison (1995), in a study of 128 foreign subsidiaries in six countries, found that competitive and market drivers, rather than cost drivers, differentiated industries on their need for local responsiveness.

In terms of single industry empirical studies, Yip and Coundouriotis (1991) found in the chocolate confectionery business that market and competitive drivers provide the strongest spurs to globalization, while government drivers do not pose significant barriers, nor are cost drivers crucial. Baden Fuller and Stopford (1991) challenge the common view that mature industries are always ripe for global strategies. Based on 1975–87 data from the European domestic appliance industry, they found that changing economic conditions can diminish the value of global strategies. Critical in these shifts were simultaneous rises in demand for variety (that eroded the benefits of scale and continental market share) and decreases in manufacturing scale (that permitted new supply options), which reduced the extent of the strategic market to national dimensions. In contrast, Whirlpool, a leading participant in this worldwide industry is now aggressively pursuing global strategy both worldwide and in Europe (Maruca 1994).

There is also a strong school of thought that most industries are not global but regional. Rugman (2000) argues that far from taking place in a single global market, most business activity by large firms takes place in regional blocks. If this is indeed case, there is no uniform spread of American market capitalism nor are global markets becoming homogenized. Government regulations and cultural differences divide the world into the triad blocks of North America, the European Union, and Japan; and rival multinational enterprises from the triad compete for regional market shares and so enhance economic efficiency. However, other perspectives suggest that regional consolidation is a stage in the movement of industries toward global integration. In any case, many of the benefits of cross-border integrated strategies are as applicable, if on a smaller scale, to regional as to global contexts.

The regionalization and globalization of industry are tied to the evolution of competition and of capabilities of individual firms, and are dependent on the development of technology. Cross-border integration has become ever more feasible as transportation, communication, and data-processing technologies have progressed—could global 'just-in-time' inventory systems have existed in the days of telegraph communications, much less sailing ship transport? At the same time, demands for improved technology and better pricing together with relaxed regulation have allowed multinationals in various industries to consolidate their operations. The auto industry, for instance, was seen not long ago as differentiated by unique customer demand. Customer benefits and economic pressures, however, moved it toward regional competition over the last decades of the twentieth century. Now, as the new millennium dawns, consolidation across regions—for instance the Daimler-Benz acquisition of Chrysler in the United States in 1998 and its purchase in 2000 of a controlling share in Mitsubishi's automotive operations (strategic actions matched by several of their competitors)—presages truly global competition in this traditional industry.

## 12.5.3  Resource and capability analysis for global integration

Global integration both requires and develops resources and capabilities. Established MNEs that are run in multilocal fashion typically need some slack resources before they can become more globally integrated. For example, Ford incurred heavy organizational costs in its attempts to develop its first world cars (the Escort, Mondeo, and Focus). In contrast, younger MNEs can save resources by operating on a globally integrated fashion from the start, skipping the very expensive stage of multilocal value chains. The capabilities developed for operating a loose network of largely independent subsidiaries are not the same as those needed to integrate worldwide operations, but the organizational heritage of the MNE, as argued by Bartlett and Ghoshal (1989), is remarkably difficult to change.

Global MNEs also develop new capabilities and competencies as they engage in global activities. Most analysis focuses on access to location-based advantage, whether from traditional resources or from constructed advantage based on specialized competitive diamonds. Globally integrated firms, however, also develop and hone capabilities for transmitting such knowledge rapidly throughout their network of subsidiaries and affiliates. In complementary fashion to the advantage of efficient distribution networks for real goods, described by Hamel and Prahalad (1985), the efficient distribution of knowledge has become an essential part of competitive advantage in today's information centered world of commerce. Global integration of organizational learning is a critical advantage, particularly in technology-intensive firms. Companies that can develop or source knowledge from cutting edge locations; internalize, understand, and incorporate new knowledge into existing operations and products; and transmit knowledge throughout the firm have considerable benefits over fragmented, locally focused firms with shorter learning horizons and limited learning capacities. Such sophistication in knowledge management is the particular focus of multi-product, multi-firm multinationals.

Cantwell and Piscitello (1999) and Hitt, Hoskisson, and Kim (1997) provide evidence to suggest that firms competing in multiple product markets domestically develop management capabilities for integrating multiple activities that are convertible into managing multiple national units. At the same time, global firms often begin to find new products and businesses in foreign markets that they can profitably add to their product portfolio. The skills at operating a complex international network then get applied to managing the new business as an integral part of the global firm. The intensity of competition in recent years has driven MNEs in many industries, but especially in technology fields, to find new products and capabilities not internally, but in other companies. We see increasing rates of merger and acquisition activity, but in a development tied to the increased capability of communication media, we also see rapidly expanding use of what Nohria and Ghoshal (1997) call 'differentiated networks' of formal and informal alliances. The 'Flagship Firm' of the global network (Rugman and D'Cruz 1997) is no longer the clear-cut hierarchy of the past with internal subsidiaries and external market relationships. Rather, it has become an integrated network of extended, but not ownership based, connections. Efficiency calls for long-term supplier relationships, but flexibility demands that these suppliers can be changed on short notice if they fail to maintain standards for technology, quality, or service. The capability to manage multiple product lines across multiple countries via a network of multiple differentiated relationships is an increasing source of advantage to the MNEs that can find it. The competing objectives of cutting edge product technology, price competitiveness, and local adaptability called for by Bartlett and Ghoshal in their model of the transnational firm are indeed coming together, but only in this most complex organization. The cost of managing such complexity is high, and is not yet advantageous in all industries. These issues of global organization are further discussed in other chapters of this book.

## 12.5.4 Strategic options for global integration

Firms already find it hard to choose among strategic options for single country operations. MNEs find it even more difficult when facing choices of global or regional integration strategy. Prior literature and empirical studies have clearly established that forms of global strategy are multidimensional. These dimensions include:

1. *Global market participation* such as building major share in strategic as opposed to profitable countries (Ohmae 1985; Porter 1990; Rugman and D'Cruz 1993).
2. *Global product standardization* rather than local product adaptation (Levitt 1983; Kogut 1985*a*; Walters 1986; Samiee and Roth 1992).
3. *Global activity location* such as building a global value chain rather than self-sufficient local value chains (Hout, Porter, and Rudden 1982; Kogut 1985*b*; Bartlett and Ghoshal 1989), exemplified by the Japanese approach in many industries (Yip 1995) and increasingly by the MNCs of other countries. A global location strategy also includes global sourcing (Murray, Masaki, and Wildt 1995).
4. *Globally uniform marketing* such as global brand names or advertising rather than more locally responsive approaches (Quelch and Hoff 1986; Takeuchi and Porter 1986; Douglas and Craig 1989; Jain 1989). The use of global marketing is often criticized. But Syzmanski, Bharadwaj, and Varadarajan (1993), using the PIMS data base, found that performance relationships to marketing resource allocations were similar for businesses operating in the United States, Canada, or Western Europe, suggesting that it is possible to use a standardized approach in serving multiple national markets. Yip (1997) found extensive use of global marketing for certain elements of the marketing mix, particularly branding. Schuh (1999) found that most MNEs apply global marketing even in markets significantly different from the home bases of the MNEs, in his study, the markets of Central and Eastern Europe.
5. *Globally integrated competitive moves* such as cross-subsidized competitive moves or sequenced moves rather than only local moves (Hamel and Prahalad 1985; Porter 1986; Kotler, Fahey, and Jatusripitak 1985).

Yip (1989 and 1992) tied these different dimensions into a common framework, and Johansson and Yip (1994) provided validation on a sample of thirty-six American and Japanese worldwide businesses. Other studies have tried to identify clusters of strategies, at least one being a global strategy of some sort. Morrison and Roth (1992) identified, in a study of 115 business units, a 'quasi-global, combination strategy' as distinct from a domestic, product specialization strategy, an exporting, high quality offerings strategy, and an international, product innovation strategy. Roth (1992) found that selective globalization (in which the firm defines its global strategy around a narrow subset of the value chain) may lead to the most effective outcomes.

A number of case-study type articles have described the global strategies of individual companies with conflicting emphases. Some stress how these companies succeed via localization in global strategy: Honda (Sugiura 1990), BHP Broken Hill Proprietary (Lewis 1988), and Vicks/Procter and Gamble (Das 1993). Some stress a balanced global and local approach: GFT, an Italian company that is the world's largest manufacturer of designer apparel (Howard 1991), and Asea Brown Boveri (Taylor 1991). Lastly, some studies stress how some companies primarily use globally integrated strategy: Caterpillar, Ericsson, and Honda Motor (Hout, Porter, and Rudden 1982), Volkswagen (Avishai 1991), Thomson SA (McCormick and Stone 1990), and Whirlpool (Maruca 1994). The differences reported among companies, and between different articles on the same company (e.g. Honda Motors), suggest inevitably that successful global strategies have both local and global elements.

The advocates for regional strategy promote regional solutions as *balanced* compromises to meet both the challenges of globally efficient integration and local organizational responsiveness (e.g. Morrison, Ricks, and Roth 1991; Morrison and Roth 1992). These authors suggest that benefits from globalization and localization challenges could indeed be exploited *simultaneously* and therefore express skepticism whether global strategies always represent the right choice for multinationals. Accordingly, Morrison and Roth (1992: 45) define 'regional strategy' as the: 'cross-subsidization of market-share battles in pursuit of regional production, branding and distribution advantages. A transnational corporation with a regional strategy locates strategic decision-making within the region; market share battles are designed, waged and monitored within the region, and company operations are geared to regional-scale requirements.' Clearly, regions can share commonalities and be distinct from other regions in many ways, sufficient to justify regional strategies as well as national and global strategies. Yip (1998 and 2000) has developed a regional strategy framework and applied it to the major economies of Asia-Pacific, and Kozminski and Yip (2000) have done so for the economies of Central and Eastern Europe.

The ultimate determinant of which type or types of global integration strategies a firm should use depends on performance. The evidence tends to favor globally integrated strategies. Studies have provided limited evidence, all in favor of, or at least neutral toward, global strategy. Roth and Morrison (1990) found no significant difference in profit performance among businesses facing (1) global integration pressures, (2) local responsiveness pressures, and (3) both pressures. A narrower study, by Kotabe and Omura (1989) found that the market share and profit performance of 71 European and Japanese firms serving the US market was negatively related to the extent to which products were adapted for the US market, i.e. businesses with globally standardized products performed better. More broadly, Johansson and Yip (1994) found a strong positive relationship between the use of global strategy and superior performance in terms of relative market share and relative profitability. Morrison (1990) found that in his sample of global industries, companies with a 'global, combination' strategy had the best performance on measures of return on assets and those with an 'international, product innovation' strategy had the best performance on return on investment, while the companies with the worst fit—'domestic, product specialization' strategy—had the poorest performance. Birkinshaw and Morrison (1995) found that subsidiaries that were 'Specialized Contributors' performed significantly worse than either 'Local Implementors' or 'World Mandate' subsidiaries, perhaps because contributors were so integrated into the worldwide system that they could not differentiate their real profits from the multinational system. It is not the case that integration into a global system is always best for a subsidiary, or that an overall integrated strategy is the preferred international solution to world markets for all firms in all industries.

The limited evidence on performance also argues against regional strategies. Conn and Yip (1997) found in a study of 35 MNEs and their 120 subsidiaries that the use of regional strategies was associated with poorer performance, but the use of global strategies with better performance. Schlie and Yip (2000) found in a study of the automotive industry that car producers should first strive to become a global company, in order to efficiently and selectively regionalize only in a second step. So they recommend the counterintuitive strategy of *regional follows global*. Thus, regional strategies could be associated with a more rather than less advanced stage in the evolution of a company's global strategy.

# 12.6 CONCLUSIONS AND ISSUES FOR FURTHER RESEARCH

International strategy issues can be usefully analyzed with the tools of classic strategy frameworks, but also constitute a domain in their own right. To a certain extent, international strategies reflect extreme versions of the market segmentation, size-related efficiencies, market imperfections, and powerful competition that are concerns in all strategies. However, differences in political, legal, currency, macroeconomic, competitive, and technological regimes are so much greater in international markets than domestic markets that they really represent a new environment. The growth of regional multi-lateral economic unions has created a world of multi-tiered regulatory regimes that vary dramatically from region to region, exacerbating any differences and increasing the complexity of the international business environment significantly. Likewise, capabilities at handling highly diverse customers in many places, coordinating production across a widespread and highly diverse set of subsidiaries, financing operations in many currencies, and managing widespread and highly independent subsidiaries go beyond a simple scaling up of ordinary corporate practices. The idea behind the 'transnational' of Bartlett and Ghoshal, that MNEs must become adept at satisfying demands for efficiency, adaptation, and technological competency *simultaneously* but to a degree that varies across industry, location, and firm, suggests the complexity of global strategy. Domestic firms just do not need to manage the same degree of complexity.

The pressures of the 'new economy' for the information age business, can only make this analysis more difficult and more important. As we have said, Internet firms are 'born global', and must deal with the strategic conditions, issues, and choices presented here for the large and experienced firm, while still new and inexperienced. At the same time, their information basis suggests a strong cultural and language component to their content, and the resulting need to adapt from market to market. Finally, their essential attachment to technology suggests that rapid worldwide organizational learning, both from competitors in many markets and from successful subordinate units, is the essential component, the key source of competitive advantage for such companies. Isolation in a single market is a recipe for failure, but so too is a message that cannot be adapted to sophisticated audiences in many markets.

Several issues require further research. First, the issue of performance remains central, as it does in the broader field of strategy. Second, the performance issue is tied up with the continuing debate of national versus regional versus global strategies. It is also related to both home country and choice of foreign markets, as strategies interact with institutional factors and macro conditions to generate different levels of performance for the same or similar strategy and governance structure. Third, how can MNEs effectively make transitions from one type of international strategy to another, without incurring huge costs and delays? Fourth, is size an essential attribute of the successful MNE, or can global strategies be effectively pursued by lesser competitors? Finally, issues of strategy implementation lie behind most of our questions and concerns. Many more strategies are destroyed by poor implementation than are disrupted by poor analysis and planning. This issue will be addressed in subsequent chapters, but must be considered in its strategic context at all times. As we have said, the key question for firms is no longer 'Should we be international?' but has become 'Why should we not be ... and when, how, and with what resources do we go about it?'

## REFERENCES

ANDREWS, KENNETH R. (1971). *The Concept of Corporate Strategy*. New York: Dow-Jones Irwin.

ANSOFF, H. IGOR (1965). *Corporate Strategy: An Analytical Approach to Business Policy for Growth and Expansion*. New York: McGraw-Hill.

AVISHAI, BERNARD (1991). 'A European Platform for Global Competition: An Interview with VW's Carl Hahn', *Harvard Business Review*, 69/4 (July/Aug.).

BADEN-FULLER, C. W. F., and STOPFORD, J. M. (1991). 'Globalization Frustrated: The Case of White Goods', *Strategic Management Journal*, 12/7: 493–507.

BARNEY, JAY B. (1996). *Gaining and Sustaining Competitive Advantage*. Reading, Mass.: Addison-Wesley.

BARTLETT, CHRISTOPHER A., and GHOSHAL, SUMANTRA (1989). *Managing Across Borders: The Transnational Solution*. Boston: Harvard Business School Press.

BIRKINSHAW, JULIAN, and MORRISON, ALLEN (1995). 'Configurations of Strategy and Structure in the Multinational Subsidiary', *Journal of International Business Studies*, 26/4: 729–54.

CANTWELL, JOHN A., and PISCITELLO, L. (1999). 'The Emergence of Corporate International Networks for the Accumulation of Dispersed Technological Competencies', *Management International Review*, 39/1 (special issue): 123–47.

CONN, H. P., and YIP, G. S. (1997). 'Global Transfer of Critical Capabilities', *Business Horizons*, 40/1 (Jan.–Feb.): 22–31.

DAS, GUCHARAN (1993). 'Local Memoirs of a Global Manager', *Harvard Business Review*, 71/2 (Mar./April).

DOUGLAS, SUSAN P., and CRAIG, C. SAMUEL (1989). 'Evolution of Global Marketing Strategy: Scale, Scope and Synergy', *Columbia Journal of World Business*, 24/3 (Fall).

DUNNING, JOHN H. (1988). 'The Eclectic Paradigm of International Production: A Restatement and Some Possible Extensions', *Journal of International Business Studies*, (Spring).

GERINGER, J. M., TALLMAN, S., and OLSEN, D. M. (2000). 'Product and International Diversification Among Japanese Multinational Firms', *Strategic Management Journal*, 21/1: 51–80.

GESTRIN, MICHAEL, KNIGHT, RORY, and RUGMAN, ALAN M. (1998). *The Templeton Global Performance Index*. Oxford: Templeton College Executive Briefing.

GHOSHAL, SUMANTRA (1987). 'Global Strategy: An Organizing Framework', *Strategic Management Journal*, 8: 425–40.

GRANT, ROBERT M. (1987). 'Multinationality and Performance Among British Manufacturing Companies', *Journal of International Business Studies*, (Fall): 79–89.

—— (1998). *Contemporary Strategy Analysis*, (3rd edn.). Oxford: Blackwell.

—— (1991). 'The Resource-Based Theory of Competitive Advantage', *California Management Review*, 33/3: 114–35.

HAMEL, GARY, and PRAHALAD, C. K. (1985). 'Do You Really Have a Global Strategy?', *Harvard Business Review*, (July-Aug.): 139–48.

HAX, ARNOLDO C., and MAJLUF, NICOLAS S. (1991). *The Strategy Concept and Process: A Pragmatic Approach*. Englewood Cliffs, NJ: Prentice Hall.

HENDERSON, BRUCE D. (1979). *Henderson on Corporate Strategy*. New York: New American Library.

HILL, CHARLES, W. L., HWANG, PETER, and KIM, W. CHAN (1990). 'An Eclectic Theory of the Choice of International Entry Mode', *Strategic Management Journal*, 11: 117–28.

HITT, MICHAEL A., HOSKISSON, ROBERT E., and KIM, HICHEON (1997). 'International Diversification: Effects on Innovation and Firm Performance in Product-Diversified Firms', *Academy of Management Journal*, 40: 767–98.

HOUT, THOMAS, PORTER, MICHAEL E., and RUDDEN, EILEEN (1982). 'How Global Companies Win Out', *Harvard Business Review*, (Sep.–Oct.): 98–108.

HOWARD, ROBERT (1991). 'The Designer Organization: Italy's GFT Goes Global', *Harvard Business Review*, 69/5 (Sep./Oct.).

JAIN, SUBHASH C. (1989). 'Standardization of International Marketing Strategy: Some Research Hypotheses', *Journal of Marketing*, 53(Jan.): 70–9.

JOHANSON, JAN, and VAHLNE, J. E. (1977). 'The Internationalization Process of the Firm', *Journal of International Business Studies*, 8 (Spring/Summer): 23–32.

JOHANSSON, JOHNY K. (1989). 'Determinants and Effects of "Made in" Labels', *International Marketing Review*, 6/1 (Spring): 47–58.

—— and YIP, GEORGE S. (1994). 'Exploiting Globalization Potential: US and Japanese Strategies', *Strategic Management Journal*, 15 (Oct.): 579–601.

KOBRIN, STEPHEN J. (1991). 'An Empirical Analysis of the Determinants of Global Integration', *Strategic Management Journal*, 12 (Summer edn.).

KOGUT, BRUCE (1985a). 'Designing Global Strategies: Comparative and Competitive Value-Added Chains', *Sloan Management Review*, (Summer): 27–38.

—— (1985b). 'Designing Global Strategies: Profiting from Operational Flexibility', *Sloan Management Review*, (Fall): 27–38.

KOTABE, MASAAKI, and OMURA, GLENN S. (1989). 'Sourcing Strategies of European and Japanese Multinationals: A Comparison', *Journal of International Business Studies*, 20/1 (Spring): 113–30.

KOTLER, PHILIP, FAHEY, LIAM, and JATUSRIPITAK, S. (1985). *The New Competition*. Englewood Cliffs, NJ: Prentice-Hall.

KOZMINSKI, ANDRZEJ K., and YIP, GEORGE S. (eds.) (2000). *Strategies for Central and Eastern Europe*. London: Macmillan Business.

LARRÉCHÉ, JEAN-CLAUDE (1980). 'The International Product-Market Portfolio', in Jean-Claude Larréché and Edward E. Strong (eds.), *Readings in Marketing Strategy*. Palo Alto, Calif.: The Scientific Press.

LEVITT, THEODORE (1983). 'The Globalization of Markets', *Harvard Business Review*, (May–June): 92–102.

LEWIS, GEOFFREY, CLARK, JOHN, and MOSS, BILL (1988). 'BHP Reorganizes for Global Competition', *Long Range Planning*, 21/3 (June edn.).

LORANGE, PETER (1982). *Implementation of Strategic Planning*. Englewood Cliffs, NJ: Prentice-Hall.

MARUCA, REGINA FAZIO (1994). 'The Right Way to Go Global: An Interview with Whirlpool CEO David Whitwam', *Harvard Business Review*, (Mar.–April): 134–49.

MASCARENHAS, BRIANCE (1986). 'International Strategies of Non-Dominant Firms', *Journal of International Business Studies*, 17/1: 1–25.

McCORMICK, JANICE, and STONE, NAN (1990). 'From National Champion to Global Competitor: An Interview with Thomson's Alain Gomez', *Harvard Business Review*, 68/3 (May/June).

MITCHELL, WILL, SHAVER, J. MYLES, and YEUNG, BERNARD (1993) 'Performance Following Changes of International Presence in Domestic and Transition Industries', *Journal of International Business Studies*, 24/4: 647–70.

MORCK, RANDALL, and YEUNG, BERNARD (1991). 'Why Investors Value Multinationality', *Journal of Business*, 64/2: 165–87.

MORRISON, ALLEN J. (1990). *Strategies in Global Industries: How US Businesses Compete*. Westport, Conn.: Quorum Books.

—— and ROTH, K. (1992). 'The Regional Solution: An Alternative to Globalization', *Transnational Corporations*, 1/2: 37–55.

—— RICKS, D. A., and ROTH, K. (1991). 'Globalization Versus Regionalization: Which Way for the Multinational?', *Organizational Dynamics*, 19/3: 17–29.

MURRAY, JANET Y., KOTABE, MASAAKI, and WILDT, ALBERT R. (1995). 'Strategic and Financial Performance Implications of Global Sourcing Strategy: A Contingency Analysis', *Journal of International Business Studies*, 26/1 (first quarter).

NOHRIA, NITIN, and GHOSHAL, SUMANTRA (contrib.) (1997). *The Differentiated Network: Organizing the Multinational Corporation for Value Creation*. San Francisco: Jossey-Bass.

OHMAE, KENICHI (1985). *Triad Power: The Coming Shape of Global Competition*. New York: Free Press.

—— (1989). 'Managing in a Borderless World', *Harvard Business Review*, (May/June).

PENROSE, EDITH (1959). *The Theory of the Growth of the Firm*. New York: Wiley.

PORTER, MICHAEL E. (1980). *Competitive Strategy: Techniques for Analyzing Industries and Competitors*. New York: Free Press.

—— (1985). *Competitive Advantage*. New York: Free Press.

—— (1986). 'Changing Patterns of International Competition', *California Management Review*, 28/2 (Winter): 9–40.

—— (1990). *The Competitive Advantage of Nations*. New York: Free Press.

PRAHALAD, C. K. (1975). 'The Strategic Process in a Multinational Corporation', unpublished doctoral dissertation, Harvard Business School.

—— and DOZ, YVES L. (1987). *The Multinational Mission: Balancing Local Demands and Global Vision*. New York: Free Press.

QUELCH, JOHN A., and HOFF, EDWARD J. (1986). 'Customizing Global Marketing', *Harvard Business Review*, (May–June): 59–68.

REEB, DAVID M., KWOK, CHUCK C. Y., and BAEK, H. YOUNG (1998). 'Systematic Risk of the Multinational Corporation', *Journal of International Business Studies*, 29: 263–80.

ROOT, FRANKLIN R. (1987). *Entry Strategies for International Markets.* Lexington, Mass.: D. C. Heath, and San Francisco: Jossey-Bass, (rev. 1994).

ROTH, KENDALL (1992). 'International Configuration and Coordination Archetypes for Medium-Sized Firms in Global Industries', *Journal of International Business Studies*, 23/3 (third quarter).

—— and MORRISON, ALLEN J. (1990). 'An Empirical Analysis of the Integration-Responsiveness Framework in Global Industries', *Journal of International Business Studies*, 21/4 (fourth quarter): 541–64.

RUGMAN, ALAN M. (2000). *The End of Globalization.* London: Random House Business Books.

—— and D'CRUZ, JOSEPH (1997). 'The Theory of the Flagship Firm', *European Management Journal*, 15/4: 403–12.

—— and VERBEKE, ALAIN (1993). 'How to Operationalize Porter's Diamond of International Competitiveness', *The International Executive*, 35/4 (July/Aug.): 283–99.

SAMIEE, SAEED, and ROTH, KENDALL (1992). 'The Influence of Global Marketing Standardization on Performance', *Journal of Marketing*, 56/2 (April): 1–17.

SCHLIE, ERIK, and YIP, GEORGE S. (2000). 'Regional after Global: Strategy Mixes in the World Automotive Industry', *European Journal of Management*, 18/4: 343–54.

SCHUH, ARNOLD A. (1999). 'Global Standardization as a Success Formula for Marketing in Central Eastern Europe?' WU-Wien (Vienna): working paper presented at the Academy of International Business Conference.

STEINER, GEORGE A. (1979). *Strategic Planning: What Every Manager Must Know.* New York: Free Press.

SUGIURA, HIDEO (1990). 'How Honda Localizes Its Global Strategy', *Sloan Management Review*, 32/1 (Fall).

SYZMANSKI, DAVID M., BHARADWAJ, SUNDAR G., and VARADARAJAN, P. RAJAN (1993). 'Standardization versus Adaptation of International Marketing Strategy: An Empirical Investigation', *Journal of Marketing*, 57 (Oct.): 1–17.

TAKEUCHI, HIROTAKA, and PORTER, MICHAEL E. (1986). 'Three Roles of International Marketing in Global Strategy', in *Competition in Global Industries*, (ed. Porter). Boston, Mass.: Harvard Business School Press, 111–46.

TALLMAN, S. B. (1992). 'A Strategic Management Perspective on Host Country Structure of Multinational Enterprises', *Journal of Management*, 18/3: 455–71.

—— and LI, J. T. (1996). 'The Effects of International Diversity and Product Diversity on the Performance of Multinational Firms', *Academy of Management Journal*, 39/1: 179–96.

TAYLOR, WILLIAM (1991). 'The Logic of Global Business: An Interview with ABB's Percy Barnevik', *Harvard Business Review*, 69/2 (March/April).

VERNON, RAYMOND, (1979). 'The Product Cycle Hypothesis in a New International Environment', *Oxford Bulletin of Economics and Statistics*, 41: 255–67.

WALTERS, PETER G. P. (1986). 'International Marketing Policy: A Discussion of the Standardization Construct and its Relevance for Corporate Policy', *Journal of International Business Studies*, (Summer): 55–69.

WERNERFELT, BIRGER, (1984). 'A Resource-Based View of the Firm', *Strategic Management Journal*, 5 (April–June): 171–80.

YIP, GEORGE S. (1989). 'Global Strategy...In a World of Nations?', *Sloan Management Review*, 31/1 (Fall): 29–41.

—— (1992). *Total Global Strategy: Managing for Worldwide Competitive Advantage*. Englewood Cliffs, NJ: Prentice Hall.

—— (1997). 'Patterns and Determinants of Global Marketing', *Journal of Marketing Management*, 13: 153–64.

—— (1998). *Asian Advantage: Key Strategies for Winning in the Asia-Pacific Region*. Reading, Mass.: Addison Wesley/Perseus Books; and *Updated Edition: After the Crisis*. Cambridge, Mass.: Perseus Books, 2000.

—— and COUNDOURIOTIS, GEORGE A. (1991). 'Diagnosing Industry Globalization Potential: The World Chocolate Confectionery Industry', *Planning Review*, (Jan./Feb.): 4–14.

—— GOMEZ, J. B., and MONTI, J. (2000). 'Role of the Internationalization Process in the Performance of Newly Internationalizing Firms', forthcoming, *Journal of International Marketing*.

# CHAPTER 13

# THE MULTINATIONAL ENTERPRISE AS AN ORGANIZATION

## D. ELEANOR WESTNEY
## SRILATA ZAHEER

## 13.1 INTRODUCTION: WHAT IS SPECIAL ABOUT THE MULTINATIONAL ENTERPRISE AS AN ORGANIZATION?

THE study of organizations in international business has focused almost exclusively on the multinational enterprise (MNE). Its fundamental feature as an organization is that it maintains multiple units operating in multiple environments, although even within the IB field there is no consistency on the number of countries in which a company must operate to qualify as a multinational. It is this multi-country organizational presence that defines the MNE. A leading contemporary organizational theorist, Richard Scott has described the distinctive features of the MNE as follows:

One of the most influential modern organizational forms—the multinational corporation (MNC)—must simultaneously adapt to and operate within multiple societies and, hence, multiple environments... Their central management is confronted with the challenge of designing systems than retain sufficient unity and coherence to operate as a common enterprise and, at the same time, to allow sufficient latitude and flexibility to adapt to greatly varying circumstances. (Scott 1992: 138)

His description captures two important elements of writing on the multinational: the normative challenges of managing this complex multi-environment system, and the analytic challenges of understanding the MNE as an organizational form. This chapter focuses on the latter.

An essential feature of this form is that internationalization of activities is a process that unfolds across time and space. The basic assumption that the activities and features of its organization change predictably with internationalization gives models of the MNE a strongly evolutionary character. The organizational changes include the structure and design of the organization, the distribution of power and the nature of internal conflicts, and the cognitive and normative patterns within the organization.

Both the theories on which studies of MNE organization have been grounded and the phenomenon of the MNE itself have changed over the past three decades in significant ways, and show signs of even more radical transformation in the near future. In this chapter, we survey the changing models of MNE organization over the last three decades, examine their theoretical underpinnings, and assess their potential for understanding the future evolution of organizations in international business.

# 13.2 EVOLUTIONARY THEORIES OF MULTINATIONAL ORGANIZATION

Change over time has been a central feature of models of the MNE because internationalization is an incremental process. A company typically starts as a domestic enterprise and becomes more and more international over time, as the number of countries in which it operates, the number of sub-units which it must manage, and the range of activities in which it is engaged, expand. Although evolutionary theory has often been associated with highly deterministic theories of environmental selection, there are many variants that allow for strategic choices and for multiple evolutionary paths (March 1994; Aldrich 1999). Evolutionary theories of organization are in the broadest sense theories about patterned change over time, where changes are driven by selection pressures that move organizations in a direction common to other organizations that share the same trajectory (as in life cycle theories) or environment. Those pressures can be either internal (i.e. attributable to the dynamics within the organization) or external, or both.

Internationalization provides the basis for the selection forces that characterize the evolutionary models of the MNE. Internal selection pressures arise from the increasing scale, growing complexity and internal diversity, and intensifying coordination requirements that accompany international expansion. These strain the existing organization to the point that key features of the organization must change if it is to continue to grow or perhaps even survive. External selection pressures, those rooted in the environment, can be attributed to two different levels of analysis. The first and often the most salient, are the multiple country environments, including both home and host nations. There is also a global meta-environment, whose selection mechanisms can operate at the industry or supranational institutional levels.

# 13.3 THE EARLY WORK: INTERNAL SELECTION MECHANISMS

The early work on MNE organization included three distinct approaches. One focused on the paths by which MNE organizational structure evolved. A second school, originating in Sweden, dealt with the path by which MNE activities evolved in terms of mode and location, and a third approach centered on the evolution of managerial mind-sets.

The structural evolution approach had its conceptual roots in one of the most influential evolutionary models of enterprise, Alfred Chandler's *Strategy and Structure* (1962) and its empirical roots in the Harvard Multinational Enterprise Project, which began in 1966 as the first large-scale empirical study of multinational organization. The first stage of the project included 187 American MNEs, all Fortune 500 firms with manufacturing subsidiaries in five or more countries. The studies grounded in this database identified a number of MNE organizational structures, and proposed a model of the stages through which a company changed its structures as it internationalized. Like Chandler's work, these studies identified internal selection forces, such as the management stresses caused by diversification, as the primary drivers of structural change. Where Chandler focused on product diversification, the IB scholars combined this with geographic diversification.

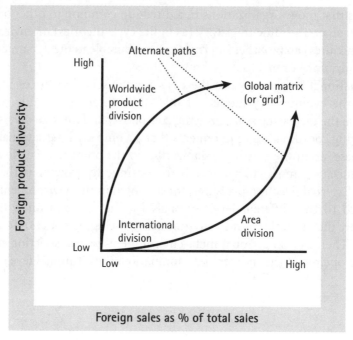

**Fig. 13.1 Evolutionary model of MNE organization (a)**

*Source* J.M. Stopford and L.T. Wells (1972)

The most notable work in this area was done by Fouraker and Stopford (1968) and Stopford and Wells (1972). They define the different stages through which MNE organization evolved, starting from Chandler's three-stage model of evolution of domestic firms from the enterprise run by the individual entrepreneur to a functional organization to a divisional structure (driven first by increasing scale and then by growing product diversity). Stopford and Wells portray firms as beginning their international expansion by putting foreign activities into a separate international division, followed by a move to either an area organization or a worldwide product organization or some hybrid of the two. They portrayed the most advanced structure as a matrix, which they called a grid (Figure 13.1).

Other scholars added alternative forms to the Stopford and Wells model. Larry Franko (1976) found that the first stage of internationalization for many European companies was not the international division but what he called the 'mother–daughter' structure, in which the heads of foreign subsidiaries reported directly to the head of the parent company. Other characteristics of the mother–daughter structure were relatively autonomous subsidiaries, informal, personalized relationships, organic rather than mechanistic controls, and the rotation of home-country personnel internationally (Hedlund 1984). Another structure identified in the 1970s was the worldwide functional

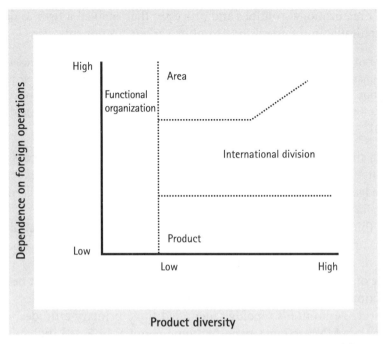

**Fig. 13.2 Evolutionary model of MNE organization (b)**

*Source* J. Daniels, R. Pitts, and M. Tretter (1984)

organization (Dymsza 1972). Both these were variants of the first stage of the evolution of an MNE.

This model did not go unchallenged. Chris Bartlett's dissertation (1979) found the international division structure to be viable at very high levels of product diversity and international sales. Davidson and Haspeslagh (1982) found that firms that moved from an international division to a global product organization actually experienced a drop in sales abroad. Such research implicitly argued against a unilinear model of MNE evolution. Other researchers proposed alternative models of structural evolution. For example Daniels, Pitts, and Tretter (1984) collected data from ninety-three US MNEs, and derived an alternative model that positioned the various forms very differently on the product diversity/dependence on foreign sales grid (Figure 13.2).

The second approach paid little attention to formal organization structure and focused instead on the evolution of MNE activities in terms of value-adding activities (from export to sales offices to production facilities to full value-chain subsidiary), mode of operations (from arm's length transaction through partnerships with locals to wholly-owned operations), and location (from more familiar to less familiar country locations). The force moving a firm across these stages was what we would now call the enhancement of capabilities: the incremental development of managerial skills and knowledge and of organizational routines and processes that enabled a firm to diversify geographically. In the words of two of its earliest proponents, it is

a model of the internationalization process of the firm. The model focuses on the development of the individual firm, and particularly on its gradual acquisition, integration and use of knowledge about foreign markets and operations and on its successively increasing commitment to foreign markets. (Johanson and Vahlne 1977: 23)

As with the structure approach, the primary drivers of change across stages were internal to the organization, in this case being the growth in experiential knowledge that changed the calculation of the risks and rewards of internationalization.

The third approach, which focused on the evolution of managerial mindsets, was proposed by Perlmutter (1969). Perlmutter argued that 'the living reality of an international firm' (p. 11) could not be captured by data on volume of foreign sales or by the number of foreign employees but needed to 'give serious weight to the way executives think about doing business around the world'. Perlmutter's typology identified three primary attitudes towards building an MNE: ethnocentric or home-country oriented, polycentric or host-country oriented, and geocentric or world-oriented. These attitudes shape three distinctive constellations of organizational patterns which involve the locus of decision-making, standards for evaluation and control, incentive systems, the directional flows of information and staffing patterns. He saw firms evolving across these three over time, in life-cycle fashion, as they expanded internationally:

There appears to be evidence of a need for evolutionary movement from ethnocentrism to polycentrism to geocentrism. The polycentric stage is likened to an adolescent protest period during which subsidiary managers gain their confidence as equals by fighting headquarters and proving 'their manhood' after a long period of being under headquarters' ethnocentric thumb. (Perlmutter 1969: 17)

All three approaches built evolutionary models that were essentially unilinear, in which the features of the MNE itself (its expanding international activities, its product diversification, its changing level of collective experience and knowledge) created the impetus to move from stage to stage. The first two focused on different aspects of organization design: one on formal structure, the other (the learning model) on the distribution and ownership of value-adding activities across locations. Both approaches were extended in the succeeding decade. William Egelhoff (1982, 1988a, 1988b) in particular drew on Galbraith's information-processing paradigm of organization design to provide a more theoretically grounded approach to the evolution of MNE formal structure, in terms of the kind of information flows facilitated by each type of formal structure. Applying information-processing theory to the

MNE was easier conceptually than empirically, as Egelhoff (1993) has pointed out: the complexity of information processing and the number of units in the MNE made the actual measurement of flows extremely difficult. The second approach, the analysis of incremental internationalization, was expanded in the 1980s by Bruce Kogut (1983), who pointed out that MNEs not only add activities in an existing location; they also often deepen them by, for example, increasing the sophistication and complexity of products manufactured in an established foreign plant. The third approach—Perlmutter's focus on mind-sets and managerial culture—was frequently invoked through subsequent years, as the focus on MNE organization in terms of its culture or social construction became an increasingly important aspect of the work on the MNE (see for example Hedlund 1986; Kobrin 1994). Influential as the ethno-centric–polycentric–geocentric model proved to be, by its very nature it did not lend itself to significant extension and further development.

Both the design and the cultural aspects of MNE organization received considerable attention from the IB field in these early years. However, there was relatively little focused and systematic exploration of the political aspects of MNE organization. But in the late 1970s and early 1980s, the potential for conflict and contention for influence over decision-making from different sets of actors within the MNE provided the touchstone for some major developments in the analysis of the MNE as an organization.

# 13.4 THE 1980S: EXTERNAL SELECTION MECHANISMS

The early 1980s saw the development of a highly influential framework that brought the environment to the fore as a selection mechanism for MNE evolution (the Integration-Responsiveness framework), and shifted the analysis of organization design from formal structure to managerial processes. The 1980s was a particularly fertile period for organizational studies of the MNE, and the concepts and frameworks developed then have provided much of the grounding for research and teaching about MNE organization to the present day.

The integration-responsiveness framework was developed by C. K. Praha-lad, Yves Doz, and Chris Bartlett, who all came to the doctoral program at the Harvard Business School in the 1970s with backgrounds as managers in international companies, and who shared both an experience-based under-standing of the complex internal workings of MNEs and a strong commit-ment to managerial relevance (for a brief overview of their dissertations and early work, see Doz and Prahalad 1993). Individually and jointly they pro-duced a series of papers in which the reader can see the gradual emergence of a new framework of the environment confronting MNEs, which provided an analytical grounding for the tension noted by Brooke and Remmers as early as 1970: 'A characteristic of the multinational company is the conflict between the geographical and the product-group projections of the organization,' (Brooke and Remmers 1970: 14).

In his earliest work, C. K. Prahalad (1976) portrayed this conflict in terms of internal forces—conflicting demands for managerial diversity and managerial interdependence. Yves Doz (1980: 27) put the locus of the conflict in the environment, attributing it to the tension between the political imperative (defined as 'adjustments made necessary by the demands of host govern-ments') and the economic imperative ('requirements for economic survival and success'). By 1981, an article jointly authored by Doz, Bartlett, and Prahalad described the parameters of the conflict as 'the often contradictory demands for global competitiveness and national responsiveness' (Doz, Bart-lett, and Prahalad 1983: 63). The terminology changed somewhat in later work, but this identification of two dimensions of environmental forces paralleled the contingency theory of Lawrence and Lorsch. By the mid-1980s, Bartlett's labeling of the two dimensions of the framework made the kinship with organizational contingency theory explicit, with 'forces for global integration' and 'forces for national differentiation' (Bartlett 1986: 377), while Doz and Prahalad favored 'pressures for global integration' and 'pressures for local responsiveness' (Prahalad and Doz 1987). Prahalad and Doz provide a succinct summary of the various factors included in each of the two dimensions in their 1987 book (Table 13.1).

By identifying two orthogonal sets of environmental forces, the Integra-tion-Responsiveness framework made it possible to map industries into a more complex conceptual space and allowed greater scope for managerial choice than did a single continuum from domestic (or multi-domestic) to global (as proposed by Levitt 1983 and Porter 1986). In part the opportunity for strategic choice stemmed from the fact that 'both forces are present to some degree in all businesses'(Bartlett 1983: 140), and since each 'force' was composed of multiple factors, managers could choose to focus on meeting certain pressures at the cost of ignoring or compensating for others. But equally important, these two factors clustered complex multi-variable envir-onmental forces in terms of their effects on organization (pressures to inte-grate, pressures to differentiate locally), and the strength of those pressures on any particular organization would obviously be affected by the firm's existing configuration. Therefore, although the primary use of the 'I-R grid' was to

MULTINATIONAL ENTERPRISE ORGANIZATIONS 357

## Table 13.1 Environmental pressures for global integration and for local responsiveness

| Pressures for global integration | | Pressures for local responsiveness |
|---|---|---|
| for strategic coordination | for operating integration | |
| Importance of multinational customers | Scale economies | Differences in customer needs/tastes |
| Importance of multinational competitors | Pressures for cost reduction | Need for substitutes |
| Investment intensity | Homogenous needs/tastes | Market/distribution structures |
| | Technology intensity | Host government demands |

*Source* Adapted from Prahalad and Doz (1987)

map industries, and therefore to indicate what strategy a firm should pursue (a global strategy in a business high on forces for integration and low on forces for national responsiveness, for example), it could also be used for mapping the strategies of different companies within an industry, whose managers might choose somewhat different positions in the competitive space based on what Bartlett called 'their administrative heritage'. Just as the environmental forces were seen to constrain but not determine organizational strategy, so the firm's organization influenced but did not dictate the strategy chosen.

The grid could be used to map to some extent the organization designs so central to the research of the 1970s: a global product structure for high I/low R industries, and an area-based structure for low I/high R industries. But the strategically most interesting kind of industry, high on both kinds of pressures, defied an easy organization design solution. Formal matrix structures had proven to be difficult to implement, and no formal structural alternative was emerging. Instead, Bartlett, Doz, and Prahalad all focused on other elements of organization design—processes and systems—with an especially strong focus on those that could help manage the inherent conflict built into the MNE. They pointed out (Doz, Bartlett, and Prahalad 1981) that the conflicting pressures for integration and local responsiveness were not only external; the very nature of the MNE ensured that they were internalized:

Some managers, attuned to local needs and sensitive to the power of host governments and national interest groups, favor, on almost any issue, more subsidiary
autonomy and greater freedom in responding to national demands. Other managers,
more concerned with world-wide competitive strategies, strive to increase coordination and integration across geographic boundaries. In trying to gain power and in
defining their own areas of responsibility, these managers unearth different facts,
analyze them differently, and propose different strategic decisions. (Doz *et al.* 1981: 65)

MNEs trying to balance high demands for both integration and responsiveness therefore had to shape decision-making processes, the perceived interests
of individual managers, and the composition of political coalitions by carefully designing an array of linking mechanisms such as task forces, committees, teams, integrator roles, and IT systems, and by aligning resources and
incentives with the task requirements of these linking mechanisms and with
the broad strategic needs of the organization. Human resource development
systems were critical in this process, especially the design of training programs
and careers that gave managers broad experiences across functions and units
and increased informal networks across units.

In short, organization design was crucially important for MNEs operating
in the 'H/H' environment, not so much in terms of formal structure ('grouping' in the current language of organization design—see Nadler and Tushman
1998) as in the expansion of cross-unit linking mechanisms and alignment
systems. These produced a shared mind-set that was an essential condition of
success in this type of MNE—'to develop a group of managers with a willingness and the ability to represent a particular perspective, an understanding
of other needs, and an appreciation that overall corporate objectives may
require different perspectives to prevail' (Doz *et al.* 1981: 71). Over the course
of the 1980s, the power and politics elements of the organizational analysis of
the MNE diminished somewhat, as the proponents of the new model of the
MNE looked to organization design and cultural aspects of the organization
for the tools to manage the political problems that it entailed.

It was not until the latter half of the 1980s that this emerging organizational
model had a name. For Bartlett it became the 'transnational' (Bartlett 1986);
for Prahalad and Doz (1987) the multi-focus firm. The distinctive labels
signaled a shift towards a more unilinear evolutionary model than can be
discerned in the writings of the early 1980s, where different environments
would tend to select for different kinds of model and where the organization
trying to cope with an 'H/H' environment was the focus of study not because
it was seen as the highest form of the MNE but because it was the most
difficult to manage. By the mid-1980s, however, it became the focus of
attention because it was seen as the model to which most MNEs would
evolve, as more and more environments seemed to experience an intensifica-
tion of both types of forces. As a growing number of MNEs moved into the
terrain of 'H/H' on the I-R grid, this led to a unilinear evolutionary model

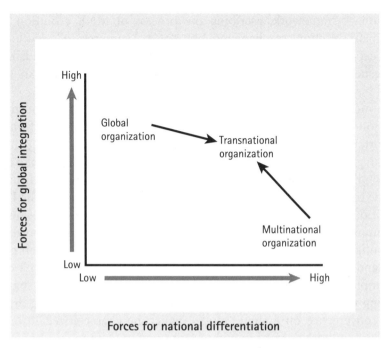

**Fig. 13.3 Evolutionary model of the 1980s: the transnational**

*Source* From Bartlett (1986), 377

similar in structure, though not content, to the convergence model of Stop-ford and Wells (see Figure 13.3).

An alternative term for the multinational of the future was proposed at much the same time by Gunnar Hedlund (1986), of the Stockholm School of Economics: the 'heterarchy'. Hedlund's approach had greater continuities with earlier work in the IB field, in that the drivers of change were portrayed as internal rather than environmental (the drive to exploit firm-specific advantages, especially the emergent advantages of being multinational, which connected both to the early work of Hymer and the more recent work of Kogut 1983). In some ways, however, his was a more radical recon-ceptualization of the emerging organizational form of the MNE, centered not on decision-making processes but on innovation and learning. Hedlund's model of the heterarchy shared with the 'transnational' and 'multi-focal' models the importance of multiple centers integrated by cross-unit ties unmediated by headquarters, the importance of integration through norma-tive controls and shared experience, and internal variety. But he went further in suggesting that the MNE was a 'meta-institution' that had both the resources and the strategic incentives to encourage experimentation and learning in its dispersed units, within units and cooperatively across units, and was constantly creating new 'institutional arrangements', and therefore acting to 'speed up evolution' (1986: 23). Hedlund explicitly invoked the evolutionary framework, ascribing the process of MNE evolution not to Darwinian selection mechanisms but to 'a "Lamarckian" development, where experience is accumulated, experiments fully exploited and memory over "generations" kept intact' (1986: 24). Evolutionary processes are thereby moved inside the MNE.

One more framework of the mid-1980s deserves brief mention: the 'configuration/coordination' framework of Michael Porter (1986a and b). Given that Porter established his reputation by providing frameworks for mapping the strategic environment of businesses (the Five Forces model in 1980 and the 'Diamond' of national competitiveness in 1990), it is somewhat ironic that when he turned his attention to global competition, he eschewed the I-R grid in favor of his own model that mapped strategies on a two-dimensional grid made up not of environmental but of organizational variables (coordination and configuration, the latter being defined as a continuum between concentrated and dispersed). Despite his insistence that the I/R grid didn't capture the complexity of a firm's international strategic choices, Porter shared the emerging unilinear view of international competition as entailing organizational convergence on a single model, which he characterized in terms of rising levels of both dispersion and of coordination. Although many in the IB field found configuration and coordination useful concepts, the main contribution of Porter's brief foray into the analysis of MNE organization was to reinforce the increasingly widespread perception of convergence on a single dominant model of the MNE.

The I/R grid became a basic teaching tool in IB even before it became a research framework, thanks in large part to a portfolio of Harvard Business School cases (with very helpful teaching notes) that provided the anchor for the organization and management component of IB classes throughout the United States and Europe. The concept of the transnational, however, quickly entered the mainstream of IB research and drew the attention of strategists and organization theorists, largely because of the joint work of Chris Bartlett and Sumantra Ghoshal in the mid-1980s, which expanded significantly the model of the transnational and provided unparalleled comparative information about organization and management in MNEs from the three major regions of the 1980s Triad world system. Their carefully designed project focused on managerial and innovation processes in three industries (consumer electronics, telecommunications switches, and branded package goods), involving three MNEs in each of the industries—one based in the United States, one in Europe, and one in Japan. The data generated in the project continued to provide the base for an influential stream of publications into the following decade (Bartlett and Ghoshal 1986, 1987a, 1987b, 1989, 1990; Ghoshal and Bartlett 1988, 1990; Ghoshal and Nohria 1990, 1998).

Bartlett and Ghoshal identified four models of the MNE, depicted in Figure 13.4: two variants of the multi-domestic firm, the multinational and the

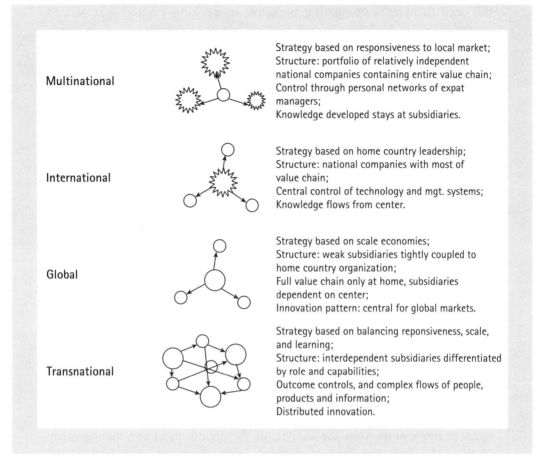

Multinational — Strategy based on responsiveness to local market; Structure: portfolio of relatively independent national companies containing entire value chain; Control through personal networks of expat managers; Knowledge developed stays at subsidiaries.

International — Strategy based on home country leadership; Structure: national companies with most of value chain; Central control of technology and mgt. systems; Knowledge flows from center.

Global — Strategy based on scale economies; Structure: weak subsidiaries tightly coupled to home country organization; Full value chain only at home, subsidiaries dependent on center; Innovation pattern: central for global markets.

Transnational — Strategy based on balancing reponsiveness, scale, and learning; Structure: interdependent subsidiaries differentiated by role and capabilities; Outcome controls, and complex flows of people, products and information; Distributed innovation.

**Fig. 13.4 Bartlett and Ghoshal's models of MNE organization**

international, which had subsidiaries that were locally oriented and contained most or all of the value chain; the global firm, where value-adding activities were concentrated in the home country; and the transnational, where capabilities were distributed across subsidiaries. The first three were 'hub-and-spoke' models with the MNE home country as the hub; the transnational was an integrated network of interdependent subsidiaries.

Bartlett and Ghoshal used the I-R framework not only to map these models and the industries they studied, but also to map companies within an industry, functions within a company, and activities within a function (Bartlett and Ghoshal 1989: 96–8). But in their discussion of the environmental forces pushing MNEs to the transnational model they added a third factor: 'forces for world-wide innovation': the competitive pressures to leverage the MNE's dispersed capabilities for innovation. In the Bartlett and Ghoshal work, it is this need for cross-border learning and innovation, more than the need to balance competing pressures in decision-making that was so central in the work of the early 1980s, that drives the development of processes and systems in the 'integrated network' model of the MNE, the alternative label for the transnational which became increasingly widely used in the 1990s. Organizationally, the transnational is defined by its networks: in contrast to the hub-and-spoke models of the multidomestic or global firm, the transnational's subunits are linked to each other directly, in a variety of ways. The nature and density of the cross-unit networks are shaped by each subunit's role, which is in turn shaped by a combination of the resources of the environment, the capabilities of the subunit itself, and the political and decision-making processes of the MNE (this is discussed in more detail in Chapter 14 by Julian Birkinshaw).

The Bartlett and Ghoshal work on the transnational had a strong influence on the IB field, in part because of the richness of the information it provided on the MNEs in the study, and in part because its normative prescriptions for managing the MNE of the future resonated strongly with managers and MBA students, providing IB faculty with powerful teaching tools. It also gave researchers and graduate students a demonstration of the power of a careful research design and a rich data base comprising both quantitative data (see Ghoshal and Bartlett 1990; Ghoshal and Nohria 1989) and detailed case studies. But it also had an impact well beyond the IB field: it resonated with the burgeoning organization theory literature on the new 'network organization' (see Powell and Smith-Doerr 1994: 370).

While Bartlett, Ghoshal, Doz, and Prahalad themselves tended over the 1990s to move away from the analysis of the organization and management of the MNE into the field of strategy, others built research agendas on the concept of the transnational or integrated network. We turn now to those agendas and to the other streams of research that characterized the 1990s.

# 13.5 THE 1990s: DIFFERENTIATED THEORIES AND RICHNESS TO RIGOR

Evolutionary approaches to MNE organization were still in evidence in the 1990s, but they differed considerably from those of earlier decades, in part because of the continuing dominance of the 1980s models, which portrayed the transnational as the endpoint of MNE evolution, and in part because the primary focus of analysis was the large, established MNE rather than the internationalizing enterprise. However, established MNEs were becoming so large and so diversified that their complexity defied comprehensive unitary empirical analysis. Even the studies of the 1980s, including Bartlett and Ghoshal's, had focused on a very few business units within each MNE, rather than on the company as a whole. Research in the 1990s tended to focus on ever more narrowly-defined and specialized activities within the multinational such as R&D, innovation, or human resource management (HRM); on a specific line of business, such as the studies of currency trading (Zaheer, 1995a and b; 2000); or, as discussed in Chapter 14, headquarters–subsidiary relationships.

The 1990s were dominated by three streams of research, all of which built on the frameworks and models of the 1980s. One extended and deepened the analysis of the transnational model, taking the managerial challenges of the MNE as the starting point and drawing on management and organization theories as they seemed to fit the context. The other two approaches began with theory, and focused on bringing together the analysis of the MNE and recent developments in theory. One centered on organization theory (primarily institutional theory and network theory), the other on emerging theories in the field of strategy (the resource-based view of the firm and the dynamic capabilities model). In this respect the study of the MNE was part of a much larger trend: organization theory and strategy increasingly engaged in dialogue over the 1990s, as strategy framed more of its analyses of competitive advantage in terms of organizational capabilities, and as even macro-organization theory attempted to integrate strategic choice and agency into its paradigms. Along with the movement to connect with theory, the nineties also saw the work on MNE organization move increasingly to large sample studies and accepted canons of empirical rigor, with researchers often adopting methods currently favored by social science disciplines, such as formal network analysis and survival analyses. A factor in these changes may well have been that IB researchers faced growing institutional pressures to publish their work in mainstream journals that were *not* primarily oriented toward international issues, largely because they increasingly found themselves located in strategy or organization theory oriented groups within their academic institutions.

Most of the work in all three streams continued to look at change over time in the organization of MNEs, and in doing so many researchers attempted to integrate the internal and the external drivers of change, and to move away from simple unilinear models of evolution. Issues of innovation and knowledge transfers became increasingly central to all three streams of work, and by the end of the decade, international management researchers were quite far into integrating the three perspectives.

The first stream of research, which explicitly addressed the managerial challenges of the integrated network MNE, had several distinct currents. One, itself part of the growing subfield of the internationalization of R&D (covered elsewhere in this volume by John Cantwell), centered on the link between the network model of the MNE and the organization of R&D and innovation (Nonaka 1990; Granstrand, Hakanson, and Sjolander 1992; Hedlund and Ridderstrahle 1995). Another topic of concern was the change process undergone by MNEs trying to move to the new model. Thomas Malnight (1996, 2000) employed detailed case studies in financial services and in pharmaceuticals to analyze the incremental processes by which MNEs actually shifted to a more transnational model. Murtha, Lenway, and Bagozzi (1998) collected data on changes over time in the 'mind-sets' of managers at the corporate and operating unit levels in terms of integration, local responsiveness, and changing role of country subsidiaries in a company trying to leverage its international presence more effectively, finding that over the thirty months of the study the attitudes and expectations of the corporate and operating managers tended to converge. Sölvell and Zander (1995) expanded on two different models of the MNE of the future: the home-based model advocated by Porter (1990) and the heterarchy or transnational model of the 1980s IM literature. But perhaps the greatest attention was paid to one of the key elements of the transnational: the evolution of subsidiary strategy and organizational roles, a literature discussed in detail in Chapter 14 by Julian Birkinshaw.

In the 1990s, however, much of the literature on MNE used the MNE as a venue for testing and expanding paradigms in organization theory and in strategy rather than addressing primarily the challenges of management (although of course these two approaches are far from mutually exclusive, and indeed increasingly drew on each other in the 1990s). Recognition of the importance of the MNE has been greater in the last decade in the field of strategy, where 'global strategy' became increasingly central in the field (see for example the special issue of *Strategic Management Journal* vol. 12 on global strategy) than in organization theory (OT). While organization theorists have shown occasional interest in what the multinational environment can teach them (for example, Hannon, Carroll, Dundon, and Torres 1996), there has as yet been no sustained interest in MNE organization, despite intermittent pleas from both sides for organization theorists to pay more attention to the MNE (e.g. Evans 1981; Ghoshal and Westney 1993). A conference held at INSEAD in 1989 brought together researchers in International Business who focused on MNE organization and a number of organization theorists whose focus was the interaction of organizations and environments. The papers presented there (published in revised form in Ghoshal and Westney 1993) looked at the MNE through a number of organizational theory lenses, but most of the authors were from IB rather than from OT. The conference revealed some of the sources of resistance in the OT community to the MNE as a venue for organizational research: the difficulty of assembling in the international domain the kinds of data to which OT researchers are accustomed domestically, the sheer complexity of MNE organization, and a visceral resistance to the strong pressures for normative or 'useful' theory that could guide the actions of managers.[1]

However, from the IB side there has been considerable interest in linking organization theory and the study of the MNE, and one of the principal avenues has been institutional theory. The 'new institutionalism' in OT can be traced to highly influential articles by Meyer and Rowan (1977) and, even more important, DiMaggio and Powell (1983). These writers argued that established models of environmental pressures on organizations in social and economic theory (contingency theory and population ecology, for example) over-emphasized evolutionary pressures for competitive efficiency and 'fit' with the resource environment and under-estimated the importance of a very different kind of evolutionary process: isomorphic pressures on organizations to adapt to other organizations around them—the 'organization field' in which they are embedded. Institutional theory was developed largely against the backdrop of the relatively unitary environment faced by a purely domestic firm, but it clearly had considerable potential for theoretically grounding the organizational effects of the 'pressures for integration' and the 'pressures for local responsiveness' of the I-R framework. An important element of the former is isomorphic pressure from the other units and headquarters of the MNE and from other MNEs that are defined as significant competitors or reference points, whereas the organizational field in each host country generates pressures for locally isomorphic organizational patterns (Westney 1988, 1989, 1993; Rosenzweig and Singh 1991).

During the 1990s a number of studies used empirical data to test and further develop institutional analysis of the MNE, not in terms of the formal structures of the 1970s models or even the managerial processes emphasized in the work in the 1980s, but in terms of specific routines and practices (reflecting the shifting level of analysis in organizational research in general). Rosenzweig and Nohria (1994) empirically explored the extent of isomorphism in organizational patterns and practices, and suggested a set of factors that would moderate the extent of local isomorphism, which they found in some HRM practices but not in others. Robinson (1994) looked at US owned subsidiaries in Japan in terms of the similarity of their HRM practices to local versus parent patterns. Zaheer (1995) linked isomorphism with strategic outcomes, showing that subsidiaries that imported successful home-country practices showed better performance than those that copied successful local practices.

---

[1] Organizational sociology has traditionally focused on understanding organizations, rather than providing tools for managers to control them more effectively.

Kostova (1997, 1999) developed a multi-level model of individual, organizational, and locational factors that influence the successful transfer of organizational practices within the MNE. Kostova measured successful transfer along several dimensions including the extent to which the practice was institutionalized in the receiving subsidiary, by assessing to what extent individuals in the receiving unit attached value and meaning to the practice. This work also explicitly examined the extent to which the level of acceptance of a practice by a unit is influenced by the acceptance of the practice in the country of location. An off-shoot of the work on institutional approaches is the work on organizational legitimacy of the MNE (Kostova and Zaheer 1999; Miller 1999; Dhanaraj 2000) that takes the MNE as an example of an organization with multiple subunits in multiple locations and attempts to disaggregate the concept of legitimacy at the parent and subunit levels of analysis, assessing how positive and negative legitimacy spillovers across MNE subsidiaries and across firms might occur. In a fashion not always matched by single-country research in the institutional paradigm but increasingly advocated by leading institutional theorists (e.g. DiMaggio 1988), empirical research on the MNE in the 1990s tended not only to cover several levels of analysis, but also to incorporate elements of strategy and choice and agency. Zaheer and Mosakowski (1997) in their study of the factors influencing the liability of foreignness, for example, examined both local and global competitive pressures as well as factors clearly driven by managerial choice, such as control systems. And the same authors, in a later paper (Mosakowski and Zaheer 1999), drew on economic theories of information as well as organization theory to establish that MNEs can gain certain informational advantages just from their organizational form.

Most of the work using institutional theory has focused on firms that are multinational, as opposed to firms that are becoming multinational. A notable exception is the work of Mauro Guillen, who combines institutional theory, development theory, and theories of the MNE to analyze how the institutional environment in middle-income countries (Argentina, Spain, Korea, and Taiwan) influences the way in which local firms participate in the global economy (Biggart and Guillen 1999; Campa and Guillen 1999; Guillen 2001).

The networks of the MNE constituted another major area of research and publication in the 1990s where developments in organization theory served to ground data analysis and advance the understanding of the MNE. Much of this literature is discussed in Birkinshaw's chapter on MNE subsidiaries, and we shall touch on it only briefly here. The rich data collected in the course of the Bartlett–Ghoshal studies of the mid-1980s, augmented by questionnaire data collected from a larger number of MNEs, provided a resource for further developing and testing the network model of the MNE in terms of three types of linkages: within each national subsidiary, between headquarters and subsidiary, and across subsidiaries (Nohria and Ghoshal 1993, 1997). Nohria and Ghoshal used these linkages to identify four types of MNE organization—structural uniformity, differentiated fit, *ad hoc* variation, and the differentiated network. Only the first of these requires the same design structure across all subsidiaries. While they clearly portrayed the differentiated network model as superior for innovation, they stopped short of suggesting an evolution of all firms toward the differentiated network. Gupta and Govindarajan (2000) analyze a larger set of companies (75 MNCs headquartered in the US, Europe, and Japan) to assess the predictors of seven types of knowledge flows into and out of subsidiaries (both between headquarters and subsidiary and across subsidiaries). They found their organizational predictors most successful in explaining parent–subsidiary knowledge flows, and suggest that this is both because MNEs have more success with such vertical as opposed to horizontal flows, and because 'the parent corporation continues to serve as the most active creator and diffuser of knowledge within the corporation', (2000: 490).

Interest in knowledge generation and transfer was also becoming increasingly central to work on the MNE that drew on and extended theories in the strategy field. As other chapters in this volume make clear, theories of the internationalization of firms had long recognized the importance of the firm's knowledge base as a source of the competitive advantage that enabled it to internationalize despite the 'liability of foreignness'. But as the primary interest of the IB field shifted from the internationalizing firm to the international firm, the focus changed from the advantage that enabled a firm to internationalize to the strategic competitive advantages that a firm derived from being international. Over time, the focus also shifted from the financial advantages (Agmon and Lessard 1977) to the organizational: first, the operating advantages of being able to shift activities in the value chain to advantaged locations within the MNE (Kogut 1985*a* and *b*), then the advantages in generating innovations (Hedlund 1986; Bartlett and Ghoshal 1989) and, in the 1990s, in transferring knowledge (Kogut and Zander 1995). With these shifts in focus came a steady increase in interest in the organizational features of the MNE that facilitate the effective generation, transfer, and use of knowledge within the MNE and the link between the competitive and institutional contexts of MNEs and the organizational patterns that underlie capabilities in cross-border knowledge management. It is around these issues that we have seen growing interaction across the three streams of research on MNE organization in the last decade.[2]

---

[2] Zaheer (1995), for example, highlighted the greater difficulty firms face in transferring knowledge or copying practices from other firms relative to transferring practices within their own firm, resonating with the Kogut and Zander work.

## 13.6 CHALLENGES FOR THE FUTURE

Research on MNE organization is quite likely to have an evolutionary framing, either explicitly or implicitly, for the foreseeable future, as the development of border-crossing capabilities, learning across units in different contexts, and the adjustments of organizational patterns to changing intra-MNE networks and changing external contexts continue to be the focus of work on MNE strategy and organization. But evolutionary framing can draw on increasingly sophisticated theorizing in the social sciences, as the recognition of the importance of a variety of selection forces (both internal and external), multiple evolutionary paths, strategic choice, and the complexities of the co-evolution of organizations and environments have reshaped evolutionary thinking (March 1994). MNEs are complex organizations facing complex environments, and those environments are changing in many ways, opening up new arenas for research.

The emergence of the new information and communication technologies of the Internet era promises to increase the variety of options for MNE organization and for the form of the MNE itself. Among these changes are the growing possibilities for the disaggregation of value chains across locations, the emergence of virtual MNEs, and the potential for small and medium enterprises (SMEs) to extend their activities across borders. The field is somewhat handicapped in approaching these issues because of the long-standing bias of research on MNE organization toward the very largest MNEs. The few studies of third-world MNEs (Wells 1983; Dawar and Frost 1999) and of the internationalization of small and medium enterprises (Roth 1992) pay less attention to organizational patterns than to strategy and performance issues. A further handicap stems from the fact that while the MNE is fundamentally defined by geography, the social and political complexities of location factors and their interactions with the organization of the MNE have received less attention in the literature than they deserve. When Porter (1986) raised the issue of 'configuration', he did a disservice to the field by defining it simply as a continuum between dispersion and concentration, while the more interesting configurational issues have to do with the MNE's portfolio of locations worldwide and how it distributes its value adding activities across this portfolio of locations (Zaheer 2000). Another locational issue is imprinting by sequence—i.e. the way in which learning processes and organizational capabilities of the firm are shaped by the locations in which it first establishes international operations. Firms from the same home country and industry might well follow very different sequences in going abroad, and one would expect to find as a result that they exhibit systematic differences in such factors as how or even whether they transfer knowledge and capabilities and how they staff key positions in subsidiaries. These questions are going to become more important as we attempt to understand the effects of technologies that contribute to increasing digitization of content and delivery, and to the associated possibility of remotely accessing value-adding activities. The role of location and nation in international organization may well return to the center-stage, as MNEs strive to benefit from the new technologies.

Another challenge is that much of the research on the organization and management of cross-border alliances and external networks has been conducted largely independently of the research on internal MNE networks. The literature has tended to assume that cross-border activities are either organized through external networks or conducted internally, whereas MNEs more and more appear to use both, either in parallel or in an integrated fashion. One example is the use of external but dedicated offshore software development centers by firms such as GE, whose development teams could include internal and external members. Increasingly, understanding the organization and management of MNEs requires us to analyze simultaneously their internal and external networks. As Nohria and Ghoshal (1997) have pointed out, the MNE is not simply an internally integrated network, but an extended network as well with multiple external linkages. This is even more the case for small firms, particularly in new economy industries such as software and media, where activities are primarily organized by project and these projects often cross country as well as firm boundaries.

Finally, the evolutionary bias of the field in the 1970s and the 1980s rested on certain unspoken assumptions that implied a limited set of evolutionary paths ending in convergence and a certain inevitability in movement along that path. More sophisticated evolutionary theories allowing for equifinality will be needed to accommodate firms from an increasing variety of home countries, entering the international arena at different points in time. They face very different organizational choices from the international economic, institutional, and technological regimes in place when they internationalize, and from the nature of their domestic business systems at the time their advance abroad begins. These period effects can cast a long shadow on patterns of organizational evolution, as the field has long recognized (e.g. Bartlett and Ghoshal 1989). But even more important, the strong unilinear, monotonic bias toward international expansion found in much evolutionary theory in IB has caused the field to neglect several categories of organizational change, such as contraction of international operations, or experimentation in location and configuration choices that produces exits and re-entries and patterns of change not conceivable in terms of standard incremental models. The field has also paid little attention to the stable international firm, which maintains a limited set of operations in a small number of countries (usually but not always in the same region). Nor is there much research on the non-MNE that extends its reach across borders through its networks of suppliers, alliance partners, technology sources, and even customers. Most important are the challenges facing researchers in analyzing the internationalization patterns of the emerging firms of the Internet age, some of whom engage in border-crossing activities very early in their existence.

Studies of MNE organization will therefore have to deal with two very different categories of MNE in the future: the large, established multi-country and multi-business MNEs that have for so long been the primary focus of research, and the internationalizing firms in newly emerging industries and in emerging market economies. This second category of firms is much more difficult to map; there is no equivalent of the Fortune International 500 to provide a base mailing list for questionnaires or a population from which to select 'representative' case studies. But they will grow in importance, and their analysis should build on the insights generated by decades of research on internationalization processes. Researchers must also continue to reach beyond the IB field for conceptual and theoretical tools, however—to today's more complex models of organization design, which encompass linking mechanisms and alignment systems as well as formal structures, and rules and routines as well as large-scale systems and processes. They must also recognize, as the researchers of the early 1980s did so well, that the MNE is a political system as well as an organization design, with conflicts of interest built into its configuration, and that it is also, as both the institutional theorists and the cross-cultural comparativists remind us, a social construction with many different 'constructors'. Research on MNE organization is demanding and difficult, and calls for careful selection and use of conceptual tools, but as Dick Scott has pointed out, it is one of the most influential organizational forms in the world today, and few of the questions that dominate international business today can be answered without taking MNE organization into account.

# APPENDIX 13.1

## MNE ORGANIZATIONAL STRUCTURES

The basic models of formal MNE structure identified in the 1960s and 1970s are still relevant today. This continuity is hardly surprising: there are three basic parameters involved in 'drawing the boxes' of the organization—function, business or product, and geography. All multi-location companies must decide how to deal with all three (even domestic companies often have geographic sales territories, for example). The key structural question for the MNE is how to deal with geography, and the charts in Figures 13.5–10 provide a highly simplified view of the various architectures for doing this.

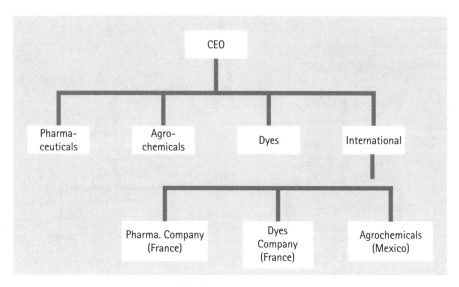

**Fig. 13.5 MNE organizational structures: international division organization**

For many US MNEs, the structure first used for international expansion involved separating international activities from the rest of the organization by creating an export division, which, as international activities expanded, evolved into an international division (Figure 13.5). Geography usually dominates in the next tier of the international division, which is commonly organized by country or region. Domestic activities can be organized by a completely different factor, such as function or product. IBM, for example, long maintained a variant of this structure by housing its international activities in the IBM World Trade Corporation. The advantage of this model is that it fosters a commitment to international expansion and an accumulation of country-specific and cross-border expertise within the international division. However, the separation of international activities from the domestic organization can result in a lack of strategic and operating coordination between international and home country organizations, especially on product development (which tends to be in the hands of the latter). This can result in tension and conflict between international and domestic managers. It also tends to foster the development of two distinct cultures: the 'parochial' home country and the 'cosmopolitan' international division. Chris Bartlett (1983) has discussed some management processes that firms can use to reduce the potential disadvantages of this structure and leverage its strengths.

The area or geographic structure makes geography the primary vector for the entire company's organization, usually with regional units supervising the next layer of the organization, which is commonly the country subsidiary (Figure 13.6). The advantage of this structure is that it gives priority to the requirements of local markets and to the strategies of local responsiveness, making it well suited to the expansion of international activities. The potential disadvantages are excessive differentiation, inefficient duplication of activities, and lack of cross-regional and cross-country learning and

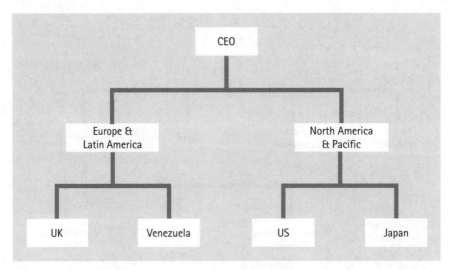

**Fig. 13.6 MNE organizational structures: area (or geographic) organization**

strategic coordination. The political tensions in this organization tend to involve country rivalries, which can become particularly acute in periods of contraction, competitive pressures, and rationalization. Culturally, this structure epitomizes Perlmutter's 'polycentric' environment of multiple different but coexisting mind-sets. A variant of the area structure is the 'mother-daughter' structure described by Franko (1976) and Hedlund (1984), in which the regional level is missing and country subsidiaries report directly to the CEO.

The global product structure (Figure 13.7) makes each separate business unit responsible for the international dimensions of its business. In some cases, the country organization ceases to exist, and each business unit sets up a separately incorporated local subsidiary. More often, the country organization provides an umbrella for support activities (such as accounting and human resource management) while the main reporting structure follows the lines of the business unit. This allows for a globally coordinated strategy at the business level, which is especially valuable in businesses where the firm faces the same competitors in most major markets. Its potential weakness is a lack of responsiveness to local needs and to local customers whose demands do not fit the profile expected by the business unit, and an inability to leverage potential synergies across product lines within a country or region. Where the country organization continues to exist, country managers can feel marginalized by local product managers, and local product managers can feel over-ridden by the global product managers. Ideally, the culture fits Perlmutter's 'geocentric' model, except where home country product managers take over global responsibilities without shedding their ethnocentric orientations.

Another approach is this worldwide functional organization (Figure 13.8), in which each local function reports to the central functional head. Usually R&D is centralized in this structure, and only manufacturing and marketing are distributed across

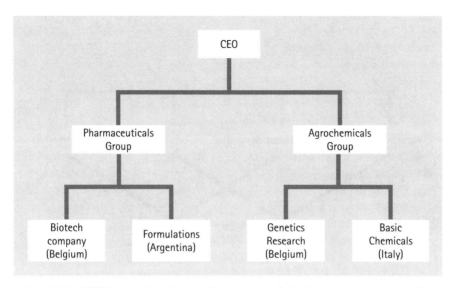

**Fig. 13.7  MNE organizational structures: global product organization**

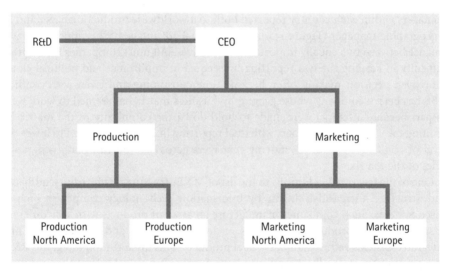

**Fig. 13.8  MNE organizational structures: global functional organization**

locations. This structure is appropriate for industries with very long product life cycles and complex systems of production that are concentrated in a few locations. The main advantage is the ability to leverage strong functional capabilities worldwide. The principal disadvantage of functional organization in general is slow cross-functional coordination, and this is magnified when the organization stretches across borders.

To address the longstanding tensions between geography and product, MNEs in the 1970s and early 1980s often turned to a matrix of geography and business, in which

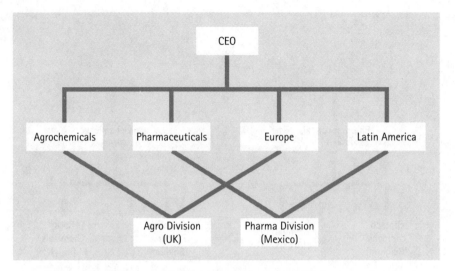

**Fig. 13.9  MNE organizational structures: matrix organization (business and geography)**

managers within each country reported both to a worldwide product manager and to a geographic manager (Figure 13.9). The potential advantage of this approach was a balance between two equally important perspectives, but most companies found great difficulty in keeping the two reporting lines equal in importance and political clout. Moreover, decision making often became time consuming and riven with conflict. ABB has been a company whose geography-business matrix has seemed to work well, in part because attempts were made to hold down the complexity of the matrix by limiting the number of managers with dual reporting lines. ABB also tried to lower the level of conflict by routinely moving managers across the business and geography sides of the matrix.

One of the few recent additions to the list of MNE structures is the 'front-end/back-end' structure, increasingly in use by Information Techonology companies such as Cisco Systems. Such companies manufacture an array of products with very different technologies and production processes, including software, and yet customers buy integrated systems rather than individual products. This organization integrates R&D and production in the 'back-end' product organization, but because the customer wants to see a 'single face' it puts sales and service into integrated marketing organizations that are organized geographically (Figure 13.10). The advantage of this structure is that it provides efficient integration of technology development and production in the 'back end', and customer focus and expertise on the 'front end', without the complexities of the matrix. However, it requires excellent linking mechanisms across the front and back ends to ensure that customer requirements are adequately integrated into technology development. Some of the same political struggles between a standardization-oriented technology organization and a locally-oriented customer organization that characterize both the international division and the global product organization can also be found here.

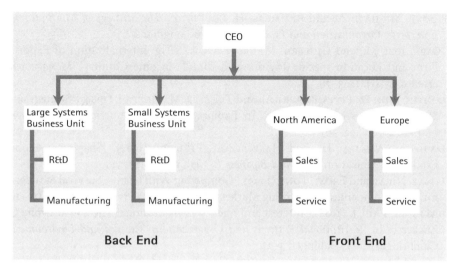

**Fig. 13.10 MNE organizational structures: front-end/back-end organization**

# REFERENCES

AGMON, T., and LESSARD, DONALD (1977). 'Investor Recognition of Corporate International Diversification', *Journal of Finance*, 32: 1049–55.

ALDRICH, HOWARD (1999). *Organizations Evolving*. London: Sage Publications.

BARTLETT, CHRISTOPHER A. (1983). 'MNCs: Get off the Reorganization Merry-go-round', *Harvard Business Review*, 61(2): 138–46.

——(1986). 'Building and Managing the Transnational: The New Organizational Challenge', in Michael E. Porter (ed.), *Competition in Global Industries*. Boston, Mass.: Harvard Business School Press, 367–404.

——and GHOSHAL, SUMANTRA (1986). 'Tap Your Subsidiaries for Global Reach', *Harvard Business Review*, 64(4): 87–94.

————(1987a). 'Managing Across Borders: New Strategic Requirements', *Sloan Management Review*, 28(4): 7–17.

————(1987b). 'Managing Across Borders: New Strategic Requirements', *Sloan Management Review*, 29(1): 43–53.

————(1989). *Managing Across Borders: The Transnational Solution*. Boston, Mass.: Harvard Business School Press.

————(1990). 'Matrix Management: Not a Structure, a Frame of Mind', *Harvard Business Review*, 68(4): 138–45.

BIGGART, NICOLE WOOLSEY, and GUILLEN, MAURO F. (1999). 'Developing Difference: Social Organization and the Rise of the Auto Industries of South Korea, Taiwan, Spain, and Argentina', *American Sociological Review*, 64(5): 722–47.

BROOKE, MICHAEL Z., and REMMERS, H. LEE (1970). *The Strategy of Multinational Enterprise: Organization and Finance*. London: Longmans.

CAMPA, JOSE M., and GUILLEN, MAURO F. (1999). 'The Internalization of Exports: Firm and Location-specific Factors in a Middle-income Country', *Management Science*, 45(11): 1463–78.

DANIELS, JOHN D., PITTS, ROBERT A., and TRETTER, MARIETTA J. (1984). 'Strategy and Structure of US Multinationals: An Exploratory Study', *American Management Journal*, 27(2): 292–307.

DAVIDSON, WILLIAM H., and HASPESLAGH, PHILIPPE (1982). 'Shaping a Global Product Organization', *Harvard Business Review*, 60(4): 125–32.

DAWAR, NIRAJ, and FROST, TONY (1999). 'Competing With Giants: Survival Strategies for Local Companies in Emerging Markets', *Harvard Business Review*, 77(2): 119–29.

DIMAGGIO, PAUL J. (1988). 'Interest and Agency in Institutional Theory', in Lynne G. Zucker (ed.), *Institutional Patterns and Organizations: Culture and Environment*. Cambridge, Mass.: Ballinger, 3–22.

—— and POWELL, W. W. (1983). 'The Iron Cage Revisited: Institutional Isomorphism and Collective Rationality in Organizational Fields', *American Sociological Review*, 48(2): 147–60.

DOZ, YVES L. (1979). *Government Control and Multinational Strategic Management: Power Systems and Telecommunication Equipment*. New York: Praeger.

—— (1980). 'Strategic Management in Multinational Companies', *Sloan Management Review*, 21(1): 27–46.

—— BARTLETT, CHRISTOPHER A., and PRAHALAD, C. K. (1981). 'Global Competitive Pressures vs. Host Country Demands: Managing Tensions in Multinational Corporations', *California Management Review*, 23(3): 63–74.

—— and PRAHALAD C. K. (1993). 'Managing DMNCs: A Search for a New Paradigm', in Sumantra Ghoshal and D. Eleanor Westney (eds.), *Organization Theory and the Multinational Corporation*. London: Macmillan, 24–50.

DYMSZA, WILLIAM A. (1972). *Multinational Business Strategy*. New York: McGraw-Hill.

EGELHOFF, WILLIAM G. (1982). 'Strategy and Structure in Multinational Corporations: A Revision of the Stopford and Wells Model', *Administrative Science Quarterly*, 27(3): 435–58.

—— (1988). *Organizing the Multinational Enterprise: An Information Processing Approach*. Cambridge, Mass.: Ballinger.

—— (1993). 'Information Processing Theory and the Multinational Corporation', in Sumantra Ghoshal and D. Eleanor Westney (eds.), *Organization Theory and the Multinational Corporation*. London: Macmillan, 24–50, 184–210.

EVANS, PETER B. (1981). 'Recent Research on Multinational Corporations', *Annual Review of Sociology*, 7: 199–223.

FOURAKER, LAWRENCE E., and STOPFORD, JOHN M. (1968). 'Organizational Structure and the Multinational Strategy', *Administrative Science Quarterly*, June, 13(1): 47–64.

FRANKO, LAWRENCE (1976). *The European Multinationals*. Greenwich, Conn.: Greylock.

GHOSHAL, SUMANTRA, and BARTLETT, CHRISTOPHER A. (1988). 'Creation, Adoption, and Diffusion of Innovations by Subsidiaries of Multinational Corporations', *Journal of International Business Studies*, 19(3): 365–87.

——— ——— (1990). 'The Multinational Corporation as a Differentiated Organizational Network', *Academy of Management Review*, 15(4): 603–25.

——— KORINE, HARRY, and SZULANSKI, GABRIEL (1994). 'Interunit Communication in Multinational Corporations', *Management Science*, 40(1): 96–110.

——— and NOHRIA, NITIN (1989). 'Internal Differentiation in Multinational Corporations', *Strategic Management Journal*, 10: 323–37.

——— ——— (1993). 'Horses for Courses: Organizational Forms for Multinational Corporations', *Sloan Management Review*, 33(2): 23–35.

——— and WESTNEY, D. ELEANOR (eds.) (1993). *Organization Theory and the Multinational Corporation*. London: Macmillan.

GRANSTRAND, OVE, HAKANSON, LARS, and SJOLANDER, SOREN (1992). 'Introduction and Overview', in Ove Granstrand, Lars Hakanson, and Soren Sjolander (eds.), *Technology Management and International Business: Internationalization of R&D and Technology*. Chichester: John Wiley, 1–18.

GUILLEN, MAURO F. (2001). *The Limits of Convergence: Organizational Change in Argentina, South Korea, and Spain*. Princeton: Princeton University Press.

GUPTA, ANIL K., and GOVINDARAJAN, VIJAY (2000). 'Knowledge Flows Within Multinational Corporations', *Strategic Management Journal*, 21(4): 473–96.

HANNON, M. T., CARROLL, G. R., DUNDON, E. A., and TORRES, J. C. (1995). 'Organizational Evolution in a Multinational Context: Entries of Automobile Manufacturers in Belgium, Britain, France, Germany, and Italy', *American Sociological Review*, 60: 509–28.

HEDLUND, GUNNAR (1984). 'Organization In-between: The Evolution of the Mother–Daughter Structure of Managing Foreign Subsidiaries in Swedish MNCs', *Journal of International Business Studies*, xv(2): 109–24.

——— (1986). 'The Hypermodern MNC: A Heterarchy?', *Human Resource Management*, 25: 9–35.

——— (1993). 'Assumptions of Hierarchy and Heterarchy, with Application to the Management of the Multinational Corporation', in S. Ghoshal and D. E. Westney (eds.), *Organization Theory and the Multinational Corporation*. London: Macmillan, 211–36.

——— and RIDDERSTRAHLE, JONAS (1995). 'International Development Projects: Key to Competitiveness, Impossible, or Mismanaged?', *International Studies of Management and Organization*, 25(1/2): 158–84.

JOHANSON, J., and VAHLNE, J.-E. (1977). 'The Internationalization Process of the Firm: A Model of Knowledge Development and Increasing Foreign Market Commitments', *Journal of International Business Studies*, 8(1): 23–32.

KOBRIN, STEPHEN J. (1994). 'Is There a Relationship Between a Geocentric Mind-set and Multinational Strategy?', *Journal of International Business Studies*, 25(3): 493–511.

KOGUT, BRUCE (1983) 'Foreign Direct Investment as a Sequential Process', in Charles Kindleberger and David Audretsch (eds.), *The Multinational Corporation in the 1980s*. Cambridge, Mass.: MIT Press, 38–56.

——— (1985a). 'Designing Global Strategies: Comparative and Competitive Value Added Chains', *Sloan Management Review*, Summer: 15–28.

——— (1985b). 'Designing Global Strategies: Profiting from Operational Flexibility', *Sloan Management Review*, Fall: 27–38.

Kogut, B. (*cont.*) and Zander, U. (1993). 'Knowledge of the Firm and the Evolutionary Theory of the Multinational Corporation', *Journal of International Business Studies*, 24(4): 625–45.

Kostova, T. (1997). 'Country Institutional Profile: Concept and Measurement', *Academy of Management Best Paper Proceedings*, Lloyd Dosier and J. Bernard Keys (eds.), Georgia Southern Univ., (8–13/97): 180–4.

—— (1999). Transnational Transfer of Strategic Organizational Practices: A Contextual Perspective', *Academy of Management Review*, 24(2): 308–24.

—— and Zaheer, S. (1999). 'Organizational Legitimacy under Conditions of Complexity: The Case of the Multinational Enterprise', *Academy of Management Review*, 24(1): 64–81.

Levitt, Theodore (1983). 'The Globalization of Markets', *Harvard Business Review*, 61(3): 92–102.

Madsen, T., Mosakowski, E., and Zaheer, S. (1999), 'Static and Dynamic Variation and Firm Outcomes', in J. Baum and W. Mckelvey (eds.), *Variations in Organization Science: In Honor of Donald T. Campbell*. Thousand Oaks, Calif.: Sage, 213–36.

Malnight, Thomas W. (1996). 'The Transition from Decentralized to Network-based MNC Structures: An Evolutionary Perspective', *Journal of International Business Studies*, 27(1): 43–66.

—— (2000). 'Toward a Model of Accelerating Organizational Change', in P. Christopher Early and Harbir Singh (eds.), *Innovations in International and Cross-Cultural Management*. Thousand Oaks, Calif.: Sage, 267–310.

Meyer, John W., and Rowan, Brian (1977). 'Institutionalized Organizations: Formal Structures as Myth and Ceremony', *American Journal of Sociology*, 83(3): 340–63.

Mosakowski, E., and Zaheer, S. (1999), 'The Global Configuration of a Speculative Trading Operation: An Empirical Study of Foreign Exchange Trading', *Organization Science*, 10(4): 401–23.

Murtha, Thomas P., Lenway, Stefanie Ann, and Bagozzi, Richard P. (1998). 'Global Mind-sets and Cognitive Shift in a Complex Multinational Corporation', *Strategic Management Journal*, 19(2): 97–114.

Nadler, David A., and Tushman, Michael L. (1997). *Competing by Design: The Power of Organizational Architecture*. New York: Oxford University Press.

Nohria, Nitin, and Ghoshal, Sumantra (1997). *The Differentiated Network: Organizing Multinational Corporations for Value Creation*. San Francisco: Jossey-Bass.

Nonaka, Ikujiro (1990). 'Managing Globalization as a Self-renewing Process: The Experience of Japanese MNCs', in Christopher Bartlett, Yves Doz, and Gunnar Hedlund (eds.), *Managing the Global Firm*. London: Routledge & Kegan Paul, 69–94.

Perlmutter, H. (1969). 'The Tortuous Evolution of the Multinational Corporation', *Columbia Journal of World Business*, 5(1): 9–18.

Porter, M. E. (1986a). 'Changing Patterns of International Competition', *California Management Review*, 28(2): 9–40.

—— (1986b). 'Competition in Global Industries: A Conceptual Framework', *Competition in Global Industries*. Boston, Mass.: Harvard Business School Press, 15–60.

PRAHALAD, C. K. (1976). 'Strategic Choices in Diversified MNCs', *Harvard Business Review*, 54(4): 67–78.

—— and DOZ, Y. (1987). *The Multinational Mission: Balancing Local Demands and Global Vision*. New York: The Free Press.

ROBINSON, PATRICIA (1994). 'Applying Institutional Theory to the Study of the Multinational Enterprise: Parental Control and Isomorphism among Personnel Practices in American Manufacturers in Japan', MIT Sloan School of Management.

ROSENZWEIG, P., and SINGH, J. (1991). 'Organizational Environments and the Multinational Enterprise', *Academy of Management Review*, 16(2): 340–61.

ROTH, KENDALL (1992). 'International Configuration and Coordination Archetypes for Medium-sized Firms in Global Industries', *Journal of International Business Studies*, 23(3): 533–49.

SCOTT, W. RICHARD (1992). *Organizations: Rational, Natural and Open Systems*, 3rd edn. Englewood Cliffs, NJ: Prentice-Hall.

SÖLVELL, ÖRJAN, and ZANDER, IVO (1995). 'Organization of the Dynamic Multinational Enterprise: The Home-based and the Heterarchical MNE', *International Studies of Management and Organization*, 25(1/2): 17–38.

STOPFORD, J. M., and WELLS, L. T., JR. (1972). *Managing the Multinational Enterprise: Organization of the Firm and Ownership of the Subsidiaries*. New York: Basic Books.

WESTNEY, D. ELEANOR (1988). 'Isomorphism, Institutionalization, and the Multinational Enterprise', paper presented at the Academy of International Business annual meetings, San Diego.

—— (1993). 'Institutionalization Theory and the Multinational Corporation', in S. Ghoshal and D. E. Westney (eds.), *Organization Theory and the Multinational Corporation*. London: Macmillan.

ZAHEER, A., and ZAHEER, S. (1997). 'Catching the Wave: Alertness, Responsiveness and Market Influence in Global Electronic Networks', *Management Science*, 43(11): 1493–509.

ZAHEER, S. (2000), 'Time-Zone Economies and Managerial Work in a Global World', in P. C. Earley and H. Singh (eds.), *Innovations in International and Cross-Cultural Management*. Thousand Oaks, Calif.: Sage.

—— (1995a). 'Overcoming the Liability of Foreignness', *Academy of Management Journal*, 38(2): 341–63.

—— (1995b). 'Circadian Rhythms: The Effects of Global Market Integration in the Currency Trading Industry', *Journal of International Business Studies*, 26(4): 699–728.

—— and MOSAKOWSKI, E. (1997). 'The Dynamics of the Liability of Foreignness', *Strategic Management Journal*, 18(6): 439–64.

CHAPTER 14

# STRATEGY AND MANAGEMENT IN MNE SUBSIDIARIES

## JULIAN BIRKINSHAW

## 14.1 INTRODUCTION

THE purpose of this chapter is to review the large and growing literature on MNE subsidiaries, and to offer some perspectives on how it may evolve in the future. There is clearly some overlap between the content of this chapter, and a number of other chapters—notably those concerned with the strategy and structure of the MNE as a whole, and the chapter about alliances and joint ventures in MNEs. What makes this chapter distinctive is its focus on the *wholly-owned subsidiary company as the primary unit of analysis* (where the subsidiary is defined as a value-adding activity outside the MNE's home country). The research reviewed here typically is concerned with the activities and/or responsibilities of the subsidiary company, and how the subsidiary company relates to other entities inside and outside the MNE. And from an applied perspective, it is typically directed towards the agenda of the subsidiary president.

While this sounds clear, it is important to recognize that the reality is much more complex. Researchers of MNE subsidiaries, in fact, find themselves in a rather strange position. On the one hand, the subsidiary is at the heart of the action in the MNE, especially with regard to such issues as integration and responsiveness, inter-unit coordination, knowledge transfer, and strategic control. On the other hand, the subsidiary company *per se* is something of an endangered species. Most MNEs have now moved towards some variant of the global business unit structure in their international operations, and a corresponding dilution in the power and responsibilities of the country manager. The result is that the *national* subsidiary no longer exists in most developed countries.[1] Instead, there is a series of discrete value-adding activities (a sales operation, a manufacturing plant, an R&D centre) each of which reports through its own business unit or functional line.

So while the issues around managing MNE subsidiaries are as important as ever, the problem of defining the subsidiary is becoming more acute. The approach taken here is to define the subsidiary as a discrete value-adding activity outside the home country, in other words at a level *below* the national subsidiary. This is appropriate because such entities can readily be identified, and can therefore be compared across countries and across MNEs. It does not solve all the problems, because there are still important interlinkages between subsidiaries in a single country, but it at least avoids the potential criticism that the study of MNE subsidiaries is an anachronism.

This chapter is in two parts. The first part is a selective review of the last thirty years of literature on MNE subsidiaries. The objective of this review is not to cover all studies of MNE subsidiaries, but to provide a roadmap of the field by highlighting the various empirical and theoretical issues that have been studied over the years. In the course of doing this, some attempt will also be made to evaluate the prospects for further research in different areas.

The second part of the chapter provides a more detailed examination of the issue of subsidiary strategy. For some people the term subsidiary strategy is an oxymoron, because they believe the subsidiary should be acting as an instrument of the MNE. For others (including the author) the idea that the MNE subsidiary has its own strategy is *necessary* if the MNE is to make effective use of its far-flung network. This section provides a discussion of what exactly strategy means at the subsidiary level, and some insights into how it is being affected by changes in the business environment and in the strategic direction of MNEs as a whole.

---

[1] Developing countries are often an exception to this rule. In countries such as China, India, and Indonesia the norm is still to have a distinct national subsidiary with a strong country manager. This is for several reasons—the need to have good political connections and a strong presence, the importance of national responsiveness in marketing strategy, and the need for a strong leader to build the business.

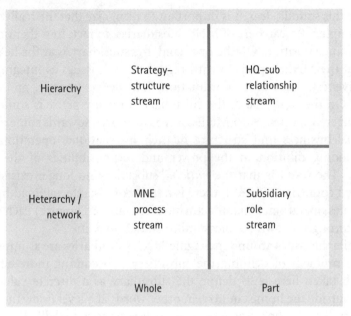

Fig. 14.1  Streams of MNE research

# 14.2 The MNE Subsidiary Literature

The MNE subsidiary literature can be traced back to the 1960s, though most of the early writing focused on the MNE, or the MNE-subsidiary relationship, as the primary unit of analysis. Thus, if we are to be strict about only considering literature on the MNE subsidiary *per se*, the field took shape in the early 1980s (Bartlett and Ghoshal 1986; Otterbeck 1981; Poynter and Rugman 1982; White and Poynter 1984), with a few isolated studies in the 1970s (e.g. Brandt and Hulbert 1977; Sim 1977).

## 14.2.1  The earlier literature

A previous review by the author sought to capture the shift in perspective from MNE to subsidiary using the framework in Figure 14.1 (Birkinshaw 1994). Four streams were identified in this review, as follows:

1. *The strategy–structure stream*: this literature focused on the strategies and structures of MNEs from a classic hierarchical perspective (e.g. Daniels *et al.* 1984; Egelhoff 1982; Stopford and Wells 1972). These studies were concerned with understanding why MNEs adopted certain structures (global product division, area division, matrix), though with a lack of convergence in their findings. Subsidiaries were given very little explicit attention in this stream of literature.

2. *The HQ–subsidiary relationship stream*: while this literature was the first to give explicit attention to MNE subsidiaries, it was essentially concerned with how the centre could control its subsidiaries. Thus, common themes in this literature were the centralization and formalization of decision-making, and approaches to coordination and integration across the portfolio of subsidiaries (Brandt and Hulbert 1977; Cray 1984; Gates and Egelhoff 1986; Hedlund 1980; Otterbeck 1981; Picard 1980).

3. *The MNE process stream*: this stream grew out of the strategy process literature, and it focused on such issues as strategic decision-making and organizational change in MNEs. Whereas the previous two streams of literature had assumed a traditional hierarchical relationship between the parent company and its subsidiaries, this body of research showed that reality was far more complex. Subsidiaries often had unique access to key resources; they often operated with far more degrees of freedom than was officially condoned; and formal structure was often less important than management systems or culture as a way of controlling subsidiary managers (Bartlett 1979; Doz 1976; Hedlund 1986; Prahalad 1976; Prahalad and Doz 1981). However, just as with the strategy–structure stream, the primary unit of analysis was the MNE as a whole, not the subsidiary.

4. *The subsidiary role stream*: this stream built explicitly on the MNC process stream by moving the level of analysis down to the subsidiary. Following Ghoshal's (1986) study of innovation processes, a long line of studies sought to understand the different roles that subsidiaries play within the MNE. There was also a long tradition of research in Canada looking at the roles of foreign-owned subsidiaries from both corporate and public policy perspectives (Crookell 1986; Etemad and Dulude 1986; Rugman and Poynter 1983; White and Poynter 1984). Underlying all this work was the idea that the subsidiary is not just an instrument of the parent, but has certain degrees of freedom in shaping its own destiny.

This categorization provides a useful perspective on how the field has evolved, but it also has several limitations. First, it gives little regard to theoretical issues—it distinguishes between the hierarchical and heterarchical perspectives using transaction cost economics, but it neglects the other theories that have been developed in the literature. Second, it stops in the early 1990s (the article was published in 1994), so it gives no sense of how the field has evolved subsequently. Which is a major problem given the large and varied body of literature that has emerged in the 1990s.

So it is important to consider what the new trends and issues are in the MNE subsidiary literature. Most of the recent literature, in fact, falls into the subsidiary role stream so it is necessary to make a more fine-grained analysis. The approach taken here is to make a split between the empirical and theoretical literatures, and to pick out the major streams of work in each.

## 14.2.2  Recent empirical literature

Considering the empirical research first, four distinct streams of research can be discerned. The first focuses on the increasingly *specialized roles taken by subsidiaries within the MNE*. The idea that subsidiaries have differentiated roles is now well established in the literature (Bartlett and Ghoshal 1986; Birkinshaw and Morrison 1996; Jarillo and Martinez 1990; Taggart 1997; White and Poynter 1984), but over the last decade this idea has been extended in a number of directions. Research has begun to look at the emergence of so-called centres of excellence, which are typically viewed as specific functional activities that the subsidiary is recognized for (Fratochii and Holm 1998; Frost, Birkinshaw, and Ensign 2000; Holm and Pedersen 1999; Surlemont 1998). A related line of research has explored the different roles of R&D units in subsidiaries (Kuemmerle 1998; Nobel and Birkinshaw 1998). There are also several studies looking at the emergence in subsidiaries of regional headquarters (Lehrer and Asakawa 1999; Schutte 1998), and divisional headquarters (Forsgren *et al.* 1995; Invest in Sweden Agency 1999).

The second stream of literature is concerned with the *evolution of subsidiary roles over time*. It has long been recognized in the international business field that foreign direct investment is a sequential process, whereby the initial investment leads to waves of additional, typically higher-quality investment (Kogut 1983, Chang 1995; 1996). However it is only recently that researchers have begun to address how this process of sequential investment affects the subsidiary. Malnight (1994, 1996) for example, has shown how the roles of subsidiaries evolve with the level of maturity of the MNE. Chang and Rosenzweig (1998), Delany (1998), Birkinshaw and Hood (1997), and Peters (1999) have documented case studies of subsidiary evolution, and the factors driving it.

Of central importance to this stream of literature is the idea that subsidiary evolution can be driven from within (i.e. through the initiative of subsidiary managers) or from without (i.e. investment from the parent company or external forces). Not surprisingly, those studies that are written from the corporate perspective tend to assume that parent company managers drive the subsidiary evolution process (Chang 1995; Malnight 1996), whereas those that are written from the subsidiary perspective put more emphasis on subsidiary initiative (Birkinshaw 1997). The reality is some combination of the two (Birkinshaw and Hood 1998a).

The third stream of literature looks at the *flows of information between the subsidiary and its network*, where the network can be either inside or outside the MNE. Considering the internal network first, research by Gupta and Govindarajan (1991, 1997, 2000) has looked at the patterns of information flow between subsidiaries and HQ, and the factors explaining that pattern. Arvidsson (1999) has studied the capabilities of foreign subsidiaries, and the flows of information between them in the search for 'best practices'. And there is an emerging body of research looking at the transfer of best practices between units, though not all of it is concerned explicitly with MNEs (Szulanski 1996).

In terms of the subsidiary's external network, research has focused on the nature and strength of the linkages between the subsidiary and its local business environment. One line of research uses patent citation analysis to show that subsidiaries draw from and contribute to the knowledge pool in their local environment (Almeida 1996; Almeida and Kogut 1999; Frost 1998, 2000; also Kuemmerle 1996). A second looks at the extent to which subsidiaries are 'embedded' in their local environment and how that affects their internal network relationships (Andersson 1997; Blankenburg-Holm 1996; Grabher 1993). And a third models the subsidiary as the interface between a leading-edge industry cluster and a leading-edge MNE (Sölvell and Zander 1998; Sölvell and Birkinshaw 2000; Enright 2000).

The fourth stream of literature is concerned with various aspects of the *headquarters–subsidiary relationship*. This is certainly not a new issue, but nonetheless, some interesting new approaches have been put forward in recent years. Most notable is the line of research by Kim and Mauborgne (1991, 1995a, 1995b; see also Taggart 1997) in which the concept of procedural justice is applied to the HQ–subsidiary strategic planning process. Gupta and Govindarajan (1999) examined the related concept of feedback-seeking behaviour in subsidiary managers. And a number of studies (Arvidsson 1999; Birkinshaw *et al.* 2000; Holm *et al.* 1995) focused on the notion of perception gaps between HQ and subsidiary managers, and the consequences of such gaps.

This review is certainly not comprehensive, but it provides an overview of the major empirical issues that have occupied the academic journals over the last decade. Of equal importance, however, is the theoretical perspectives that have been used to study MNE subsidiaries. Here the story is rather more complex.

## 14.2.3  Recent theoretical literature

Applying theory to MNE subsidiary research is troublesome for a couple of reasons. First, the relevant level of analysis for most theory is the MNE as a whole, not the subsidiary. As a result, there is often a problem in translating or applying the firm-level theory to the subsidiary unit. Second, the theories used in MNE research are eclectic and often incommensurable,[2] with the result that they cannot easily be brought together or compared. But having said that, it is still valuable to consider how various theories have been applied, and their prospects for further development.

The most widely used theory in MNE research is of course the *transaction cost-based theory of international production*. This theory seeks to explain the existence of MNEs in terms of ownership-specific advantages *vis-à-vis* incumbent domestic competitors, location-specific advantages that favour investment in the local country, and intermediate market failure that favours 'internalization' over other forms of contractual arrangements (Buckley and Casson 1976; Dunning 1980; Rugman 1981). Applying this theory to the MNE subsidiary is however troublesome because implicitly it assumes that ownership advantages originate in the MNE's home country, whereas the reality is that they often arise in subsidiaries as well.

Rugman and Verbeke (1992, 2000) have done the best job of applying the transaction cost-based theory of international production to the subsidiary context. In their 1992 paper they argued that ownership-specific advantages could arise anywhere in the MNE, and could be location-bound or non location-bound. They also suggested that location-specific advantages could either be leveraged internationally or used *in situ*. In their 2000 paper, they took this analysis a stage further by developing the concept of a subsidiary-specific advantage that emerges through the interaction of ownership- and location-specific advantages (see also Moore 1996).

This is a useful advance, but with the caveat that we are trying to make sense of a phenomenon through a theoretical lens that was not really designed for the task. The result is a theory that is—with some tweaking—consistent

---

[2] For example, the transaction-cost based theory of the MNE seeks to explain why firms exist across borders. The resource-based view is concerned with how the MNE's resources can lead to competitive advantage. And the network perspective seeks to describe the interrelationships between units of the MNE and the system in which it is embedded.

with the empirical evidence. Whether this theory then offers any additional insights into the phenomenon under investigation is more debatable.

As suggested in Figure 14.1, most subsidiary-level research has gravitated towards a *network conceptualization of the MNE*. Network thinking has been explicitly applied to the MNE for the last ten years (Ghoshal and Bartlett 1990: Forsgren and Johanson 1992), though its roots in social exchange theory go much further back (e.g. Emerson 1962). Increasingly, it is also being applied to subsidiary-level research (e.g. Birkinshaw and Hood 1998*b*; Gupta and Govindarajan 2000).

The advantage of the network perspective is that the subsidiary moves from being a subordinate entity (within the MNE hierarchy) to a node in a network—with links to external and internal actors, greater degrees of freedom, and so on. For those researchers concerned with how subsidiaries evolve and how they exchange information with other actors, the network perspective is obviously very attractive. Its weakness, however, is that it is frequently used in a purely descriptive way, which makes it unfalsifiable, and therefore detracts from its power as a theory. For the network perspective to fulfil its potential in MNE subsidiary research, then, it needs to be used in a more precise way, perhaps by drawing on recent advances in social exchange theory and social capital (cf. recent work by Hansen 1999, and Tsai and Ghoshal 1998).

The *resource based view of the firm* is currently the dominant conceptual paradigm in strategic management, and as such would appear to offer great potential to the study of the MNE. It argues that under certain conditions a firm's unique bundle of resources and capabilities can generate competitive advantage (Barney 1991). There are also related schools of thought that focus on the development of dynamic capabilities and knowledge as drivers of competitive advantage (Teece *et al.* 1997; Grant 1996).

Curiously, there has been little explicit attention given to the resource based view of the firm in the MNE literature, though Rugman and Verbeke (2000) and Birkinshaw and Hood (1998*a*) are recent exceptions. Part of the reason for this is again the level of analysis. The resource based view implicitly assumes that resources and capabilities are developed and held in a monolithic firm, whereas the reality in the MNE is that some are likely to be held at a firm level while others are held at a subsidiary level. Thus, rather than simply analysing subsidiary-level resources in terms of their potential for competitive advantage, the issue is more one of combining or leveraging them on a global basis. This approach would appear to have great potential, and some provisional thoughts are offered in the final part of this chapter.

*Institutional theory* became popular as a lens for studying the MNE during the 1990s, through the pioneering work of Westney (1990, 1994) and Rosenzweig and Singh (1991). Institutional theory provides a way of understanding why competing firms are often so similar. It argues that through a variety of pressures firms will deliberately adopt practices and behaviours that are similar ('isomorphic') to those in their task environment or 'organizational field' (Meyer and Rowan 1977; DiMaggio and Powell 1983). Westney's approach was to argue that MNE subsidiaries face competing isomorphic pulls—from the host country environment and from the rest of the MNE. Thus, by comparing the practices of the MNE subsidiary to those in the host country and the MNE, implications could be drawn about the MNE's strategy.

This line of thinking was applied in a number of empirical studies of MNE subsidiaries, including Rosenzweig and Nohria (1995), Robinson (1995), and Westney (1990). However, enthusiasm for institutional theory in MNE research appears to have dwindled in recent years, and it remains to be seen if it will be rekindled.

A number of other theoretical perspectives have also been used in MNE subsidiary research. The author (Birkinshaw 1999) has attempted to frame *the MNE as an internal market system* in which subsidiary companies compete with one another for charters, but it is not yet clear if this approach will yield any valuable insights. Several concepts have also been lifted from the *social psychology* literature, including procedural justice (Kim and Mauborgne 1995*a*) and feedback-seeking behaviour (Gupta *et al.* 1999), to model the HQ–subsidiary relationship. Agency theory has also been used in this way (Chang and Taylor 1999).

In sum, there would seem to be considerable scope for more careful application of theory to the study of MNE subsidiaries. Much of the research discussed earlier is well done but lacking in strong theoretical underpinnings, and for the field to move forward it is important for this deficiency to be remedied. The resource based view and social exchange theory, in particular, are rich theories that appear to have the potential for generating new insights about MNE subsidiaries.

# 14.3 RECONCEPTUALIZING SUBSIDIARY STRATEGY

The second part of this chapter builds on some of the issues raised in the first part, notably the need for more explicit grounding in existing theory. Its purpose is to reconsider the concept of subsidiary strategy, with a view to providing some insights into the appropriate role of the subsidiary general manager, and the ways that the subsidiary can add value to the MNE as a whole.

## 14.3.1  Subsidiary strategy vs. subsidiary role

A distinction is often made in the literature between the concepts of subsidiary strategy and subsidiary role. A subsidiary's *role* is assigned to it by the parent company—to sell the MNE's products in Australia, or to manufacture a line of products for the European market—the implication being that the subsidiary is simply following orders. Subsidiary *strategy*, by contrast, suggests some level of choice or self-determination on the part of the subsidiary. Obviously there are constraints on the subsidiary's strategy imposed from above and by the marketplace, but the underlying premise is that decisions are made by subsidiary managers, not HQ managers on their behalf.

We can, in other words, picture a spectrum of MNE subsidiaries with increasing degrees of freedom. To the left the subsidiary manager is simply an instrument of the headquarters, working to rather precise instructions about what to make or who to sell to. This subsidiary has a role that is shaped and managed from headquarters. To the right, the subsidiary manager is a free agent, operating within certain HQ-defined parameters but basically free to develop the business as s/he sees fit. Here, we can more usefully use the term 'strategy' to describe what the subsidiary is doing and what it is planning to do in the future. Of course, most cases lie somewhere between these extremes, in that there is a requirement to operate within certain product/market/resource constraints, but management are still able to take developmental initiatives within those constraints (Birkinshaw 1997; Birkinshaw and Hood 1998*a*).

## 14.3.2  Subsidiary strategy

Let us now consider the concept of subsidiary strategy in greater detail, on the assumption that most subsidiaries lie towards the middle or right of the spectrum depicted above.

Subsidiary strategy is defined as the positioning of the subsidiary *vis-à-vis* its competitors and its customers, and with regard to its underlying resources and capabilities (Andrews 1971; Porter 1980; Wernerfelt 1984).[3] In other words, there is a market-positioning component to strategy, and there is a

---

[3] Note that it is not appropriate to talk in terms of the link between strategy and competitive advantage for the subsidiary, because it is only one part of the whole corporation. Indeed, competitive advantage is commonly argued to arise as a result of the unique configuration and coordination of a corporation's activities (Porter 1996).

resource development component. Strategy is about how those two components are brought together. As noted earlier, a subsidiary is any value-adding unit outside the home country—a sales unit, an R&D centre, or a manufacturing plant. Thus, it is important to realize that many of the subsidiary's customers and even competitors will be other units within the corporation.

In the light of the earlier discussion, two questions need to be addressed. First, to what extent can these two components of strategy be understood at the level of the subsidiary, rather than the level of the MNE as a whole? Second, how many of the elements of subsidiary strategy are typically under the control of the subsidiary manager?

## 14.3.3 Market positioning

According to the traditional model of the MNE, subsidiaries had the conceptually straightforward task of selling the MNE's products in the local market. The centre would develop new products, and manufacture them as well in the early stages of the lifecycle (Vernon 1966), but the subsidiary had considerable discretion in figuring out the best way of selling them in their market.

Today, the situation is much more complex. Staying with the definition introduced earlier, there are sales and marketing subsidiaries that are responsible for selling locally, sales and marketing subsidiaries with global mandates, manufacturing subsidiaries with external customers, manufacturing subsidiaries with internal customers, R&D subsidiaries with internal customers, and so on. The point is that by working with the individual value-adding activity as the unit of analysis, there end up being many different types of market, only one of which is the 'traditional' local market.

This approach has some important implications, because it suggests that most subsidiaries actually have far less control over their market positioning than the traditional approach would suggest. Most manufacturing subsidiaries serving internal customers are part of an integrated supply chain. For example, back in the early 1990s Volkswagen's plant in Barrie, Ontario made wheels and other parts under precise specifications from assembly plants in Germany and Mexico. Its customers were those plants, and continued to be so for as long as the plant was part of the VW group. Equally, many sales subsidiaries are now part of global sales organizations, and have fairly few degrees of freedom in choosing how they will serve their local customers. Moreover, there are a number of trends underway that all serve to limit further the subsidiary's degrees of freedom in shaping its market positioning.

1. In many industries global customers are emerging who are demanding consistent products and services on a worldwide basis. MNEs are responding to global customers by setting up 'global accounts' that allow the customer to negotiate products, prices, and service agreements centrally. The net result for foreign sales subsidiaries is that many of their largest customers have been taken out of their hands. They still have to service such customers on a local basis, but a lot of what they traditionally did locally is now done centrally.

2. Mirroring the emergence of global customers is the global integration of the supply chain. Most large MNEs have recognized the need to make their purchasing and manufacturing activities more efficient. Some have opted to outsource major parts of their manufacturing to independent contractors, others have rationalized their manufacturing processes and streamlined their purchasing on a global basis. For foreign subsidiaries involved in such activities, though, the net effect is typically a reduction in their degrees of freedom as their activities are integrated with those in other parts of the world.

3. The R&D organizations of large MNEs are also coming under pressure to deliver more efficient outputs, typically through greater use of contract relationships with their business units. Again, the net result for the individual R&D unit tends to be less degrees of freedom in choosing how they will spend their time.

4. E-commerce is creating an unprecedented level of transparency in the global marketplace, as customers are able to compare products from multiple suppliers without leaving their office. The implication of this, in the context of the current chapter, is simply that it increases the pressure on MNEs to integrate and streamline their global activities in the ways described above.

5. Even in cases where activities are still configured on a local-for-local basis, competition is increasingly global. In these situations, MNEs have to be able to manage their portfolio of subsidiaries in a coordinated way (Prahalad and Hamel 1985) rather than as stand-alone entities. All of which again decreases the degrees of freedom of the individual subsidiary manager.

All these trends have the effect of reducing the MNE subsidiary's degrees of freedom *vis-à-vis* its customer base. In other words, the market-oriented aspects of subsidiary strategy are becoming more constrained, and to some degree being taken out of the hands of subsidiary managers. At very least, we are seeing that choice about what product-markets to serve and what competitive positions to adopt is increasingly made on a coordinated basis. Thus, there are increasing interdependencies between subsidiaries that are managed through regional and global business teams, board meetings, global account managers, and such like.

What is interesting, however, is that at the same time there is a broad 'empowerment' trend in management practice, through which subsidiary managers are encouraged to act more entrepreneurially (e.g. Ghoshal and Bartlett 1997). So on the one hand subsidiary managers find their choice of customers and markets constrained by the high-level changes sweeping through their organizations, while on the other hand they are being exhorted to take initiative and seek out new ways of adding value. We will return to this dilemma shortly.

## 14.3.4  Resource development

The resource side of strategy refers in this case to the internal resources and capabilities held by the subsidiary that are deployed in the marketplace. Resources are defined here as the stock of available factors owned or controlled by the firm, and capabilities are a firm's capacity to deploy resources, usually in combination, using organizational processes to effect a desired end (Amit and Schoemaker 1993). But if—as argued here—the subsidiary is a valid unit of analysis in its own right, it should be possible to split resources and capabilities up between the subsidiary and the MNE, as shown in Table 14.1. Considering resources first, most tangible resources (plant, equipment, people) are held primarily at the subsidiary level, while most intangible resources (financial, organizational, reputational) are held at the firm level. Of course, there are plenty of exceptions to this rule, such as employees or equipment that are moved between locations, or a reputation that is specific to the local subsidiary, but the key point is that it is possible to make such a split in the first place.

Capabilities are much harder to split between firm and subsidiary levels of analysis. Some are clearly held at a firm level and shared across subsidiaries, such as a particular organizational culture. Others are more likely to be specific to a particular subsidiary, such as handling local labour relations or working with government contracts. Most capabilities, however, sit somewhere between the two levels. Consider a hypothetical example like total quality manufacturing in Ford Motor Company. Ford has around fifty-five assembly plants around the world. Quality levels are measured in each plant, and it is found that year after year the highest quality ratings are achieved by the same plant in Belgium. The Belgian plant is therefore used as the benchmark that other plants should strive for, and it gets a stream of visitors from these other plants, all of whom are seeking to learn from and apply its 'best

Table 14.1 Examples of resources and capabilities at two levels of analysis

|  | Subsidiary level | Firm level |
|---|---|---|
| Resources | Physical resources such as plant, equipment, and locally sourced raw materials; Human resources employed in the subsidiary; Reputation with local customers and suppliers. | Financial resources such as firm's borrowing capacity; Access to suppliers that is controlled centrally; Organizational resources such as the formal reporting system; Technological resources such as patents or trademarks. |
| Capabilities | Rapid product innovation; Lean production system; Effective distribution; Customer focused marketing; Data processing skills; Etc.... | Firm-specific capabilities such as an organizational culture supporting innovation, quality, etc.; Ability to leverage capabilities from the left-hand column on a firm-wide basis. |

*Source* Adapted from Grant (1997)

practice'. Every year their quality levels creep up, but so does the quality of the Belgian plant.

So is the 'total quality management' capability held at the level of the Belgian plant, or at the firm level? The answer is a bit of both. The capability somehow originated in the Belgian plant, but it has also been successfully leveraged on a firm-wide basis. The suggestion, in other words, is that many capabilities have their origin in a single location. The extent to which such capabilities are dispersed throughout the firm depends on the ability of the firm to identify and leverage them—the so called 'transfer of best practices'. It also depends on the extent to which they are effective in different contexts—the adoption of Japanese approaches to lean production in America, for example.

In sum, then, the argument is that many firm resources and capabilities are actually developed at the subsidiary level. And a key feature of these capabilities is that they are system-dependent or 'embedded' to such an extent that they cannot be easily disentangled from their local context. Furthermore, the ability to nurture and develop such capabilities is clearly the responsibility of subsidiary managers, because it is they who have the local contacts and the intimate knowledge of local activities, not the people at HQ.

This discussion helps to clarify an important point, namely that the criteria used to evaluate resources in the resource based view (valuable, rare, non-imitable, non-substitutable) are not really relevant at the subsidiary level. Because the subsidiary is just one part of the whole, its resources and capabilities need to be complementary to other resources and capabilities elsewhere in the corporation, not necessarily unique. Each building block has a value in itself, but it is the ability to put those building blocks together in a unique, non-imitable way that is the source of advantage, not the independent value of the various blocks. As seen in cases of acquisitions, the price the buyer is prepared to pay is not a function of the stand-alone value of the acquired firm's resources, but a function of how much those resources are worth when combined with the buying firm's resources.

## 14.3.5  Bringing the two sides together

So what are the implications of this discussion for the concept of subsidiary strategy? It has been argued that choices about product-market positioning are increasingly being taken out of the hands of subsidiary managers and taken up to a corporate level. But those aspects of subsidiary strategy that are concerned with resource and capability development are still—and indeed should be—under the control of subsidiary managers. This potentially creates great problems, because strategy-making is all about ensuring that the market and resource sides of the equation fit together. Corporate-level managers are ill-equipped to do this because they do not understand the unique resources and capabilities in the subsidiary, whereas subsidiary managers have the knowledge, but not necessarily the power to fulfil this role.

How should this dilemma be solved? The easiest way to answer this question is to start by looking at how MNEs resolve it in practice. Without claiming that this is a comprehensive list, the following are some common approaches that can be observed.

1. Systems for ensuring that subsidiary managers are involved in market-facing decisions. For example many MNEs have regional or global business teams with representatives from all the countries involved. These teams have collective responsibility (at a corporate level) for marketing decisions, but subsidiary managers are able to provide input about their subsidiary's particular needs or expectations, and they can also feed information back to their colleagues. Likewise, most global account management programs have supervisory boards and global account 'executive' roles for national subsidiary managers to ensure their buy-in and involvement.

2. A shift in emphasis in subsidiary roles towards greater depth and less breadth. Thus, rather than having several factories working on duplicate product lines, each would be given a world mandate for a single product. This is a way of achieving global economies of scale while still ensuring that

each individual factory has its own customer. The term 'focused factory' is often used to describe this approach.

3. Internal-market structures. The paradoxical idea here is that efficient global integration can sometimes be achieved better by disaggregating activities than by leaving them together. ABB, for example, forces its R&D centres to compete for work, by linking the vast majority of R&D funding to contracts with business units. As a result, R&D subsidiaries are more closely integrated with the business units than they used to be, while at the same time they are very customer-oriented because funding is provided on a contract basis. Another example of this is Ericsson which created profit centres out of its R&D units. Whereas before these R&D centres were 'stuck in the bowels of the ship' they are now managed with a commercial mindset.

4. Systems for sharing knowledge. This involves a host of things from IT-based knowledge exchanges to informal networks to international teams. The idea in all cases is that subsidiary managers need to be tied into the corporate network more effectively in order that they can make the link between the market and resource sides of the strategy equation.

The common theme across these four points is that systems and structures have to be put in place within the MNE to ensure that the subsidiary manager is her own boss *and* an integral part of the corporate network. At first glance this is just a re-expression of the need to be globally integrated *and* nationally responsive, but it is actually subtly different because the axes are now reversed. In the traditional model, responsiveness was about tailoring the MNE's offerings to different national markets, while integration was concerned with managing the MNE's resources efficiently. The approach proposed here is that the market-facing side of strategy is becoming increasingly integrated, while the resource side is heterogeneous and needs to be managed with considerable degrees of freedom if it is to be truly effective.

## 14.4 CONCLUSIONS

This chapter provides a broad overview of the state-of-play in MNE subsidiary research. In the first part the objective was to cover the breadth of the field by picking up on the evolution of the literature and then considering the various strands of research that are currently ongoing. The second part provided a more in depth look at one central issue, namely the concept of subsidiary strategy. The argument, in a nutshell, was that subsidiary strategy is increasingly concerned with resource development rather than market positioning, which is the exact opposite of what we would traditionally argue. Of course, this is a deliberately provocative position to take, and the reality is rather more complex and nuanced than this bald statement would indicate. But it represents an interesting point for debate as this field of research moves forward in the years ahead.

# REFERENCES

AMIT, R., and SCHOEMAKER, P. (1993). 'Strategic Assets and Organizational Rent', *Strategic Management Journal*, 14: 33–46.

ANDERSSON, U. (1997). 'Subsidiary Network Embeddedness: Integration, Control and Influence in the Multinational Corporation', doctoral thesis, Department of Business Studies, Uppsala University.

ANDREWS, K. (1971). *The Concept of Corporate Strategy*. New York: Dow Jones-Irwin.

ARVIDSSON, N. (1999). The Ignorant MNE: The Role of Perception Gaps in Knowledge Management, doctoral dissertation, Stockholm School of Economics.

BARNEY, J. (1991). 'Firm Resources and Sustained Competitive Advantage', *Journal of Management*, 17(1): 99–120.

BARTLETT, C. A. (1979). Multinational Structural Evolution: The Changing Decision Environment in International Divisions, unpub. doctoral dissertation, Harvard University.

BARTLETT, C. A., and GHOSHAL, S. (1986). 'Tap Your Subsidiaries for Global Reach', *Harvard Business Review*, 64(6): 87–94.

BIRKINSHAW, J. M. (1994). 'Approaching Heterarchy: A Review of the Literature on Multinational Strategy and Structure', *Advances in Comparative Management, Research Annual*, 9: 111–44.

——(1995). Entrepreneurship in Multinational Corporations: The Initiative Process in Canadian Subsidiaries, unpub. doctoral dissertation, Western Business School, Univ. of Western Ontario.

——(1997). 'Entrepreneurship in Multinational Corporations: The Characteristics of Subsidiary Initiatives', *Strategic Management Journal*, 18(3): 207–29.

——(1999). 'Globalization and Multinational Corporate Strategy: An Internal Market Perspective', in N. Hood and S. Young (eds.), *The Globalization of Multinational Enterprise Activity and Economic Development*. London: Macmillan.

——HOLM, U., THILENNIUS, P., and ARVIDSSON, N. (2000). 'Impact of Perception Gaps on Control and Cooperation in HQ-subsidiary Relationships', *International Business Review* (forthcoming).

——and HOOD, N. (1997). 'An Empirical Study of Development Processes in Foreign-owned Subsidiaries in Canada and Scotland', *Management International Review*, 37(4): 339–64.

—— —— (1998a). 'Multinational Subsidiary Development: Capability Evolution and Charter Change in Foreign-owned Subsidiary Companies', *Academy of Management Review*, 23(4): 773–95.

—— —— (1998b). *Multinational Corporate Evolution and Subsidiary Development*. London: Macmillan.

—— and MORRISON, A. (1995). 'Configurations of Strategy and Structure in Subsidiaries of Multinational Corporations', *Journal of International Business Studies*, 26(4): 729–54.

BLANKENBURG-HOLM, D. (1996). Business Network Connections and International Business Relationships, doctoral thesis, Department of Business Studies, Uppsala University.

BRANDT, W. K., and HULBERT, J. M. (1977). 'Headquarters Guidance in Marketing Strategy in the Multinational Subsidiary', *Columbia Journal of World Business*, 12 (Winter): 7–14.

BUCKLEY, P. J., and CASSON, M. C. (1976). *The Future of the Multinational Enterprise*. London: Macmillan.

CHANG, E., and TAYLOR, S. (1999). 'Control in Multinational Corporations (MNCs): The Case of Korean Manufacturing Subsidiaries', *Journal of Management*, 25(4): 541–65.

CHANG, S-J. (1995). 'International Expansion Strategy of Japanese Firms: Capability Building Through Sequential Entry', *Academy of Management Journal*, 38(2): 383–407.

—— (1996). 'An Evolutionary Perspective on Diversification and Corporate Restructuring: Entry, Exit and Economic Performance During 1981–1989', *Strategic Management Journal*, 17(8): 587–612.

—— and ROSENZWEIG, P. (1998). 'Functional and Line of Business Evolution Processes in MNC Subsidiaries: Sony in the USA, 1972–1995', in J. M. Birkinshaw and N. Hood (eds.), *Multinational Corporate Evolution and Subsidiary Development*. London: Macmillan, 299–332.

CRAY, DAVID (1984). 'Control and Coordination in Multinational Corporations', *Journal of International Business Studies*, 15(3): 85–98.

CROOKELL, HAROLD H. (1986). 'Specialization and International Competitiveness', in Hamid Etemad and Louis Seguin Dulude (eds.), *Managing the Multinational Subsidiary*, London: Croom Helm, 102–11.

DANIELS, JOHN D., PITTS, ROBERT A., and TRETTER, MARYANN J. (1984). 'Strategy and Structure of US Multinationals: An Exploratory Study', *Academy of Management Journal*, 27(2): 292–307.

DELANY, E. (1998). 'Strategic Development of Multinational Subsidiaries in Ireland', in J. M. Birkinshaw and N. Hood (eds.), *Multinational Corporate Evolution and Subsidiary Development*. London: Macmillan.

DIMAGGIO, P. J., and POWELL, W. W. (1983). 'The Iron Cage Revisited: Institutional Isomorphism and Collective Rationality in Organizational Fields', *American Sociological Review*, 48: 147–60.

DOZ, YVES L. (1976). *National Policies and Multinational Management*, unpublished doctoral dissertation, Boston: Harvard Business School.

DUNNING, JOHN H. (1980). 'Towards an Eclectic Theory of International Production; Some Empirical Tests', *Journal of International Business Studies*, 11: 9–31.

EGELHOFF, WILLIAM G. (1982). 'Strategy and Structure in Multinational Corporations: An Information-processing View', *Administrative Science Quarterly*, 27: 435–58.

EMERSON, R. M. (1962). 'Power-dependence Relations', *American Sociological Review*, 27: 31–41.

ENRIGHT, M. (2000). 'Regional Clusters and Multinational Enterprises: Independence, Dependence or Interdependence?', *International Studies of Management and Organization*, 30(2): 114–38.

ETEMAD, HAMID, and DULUDE, LOUIS SEGUIN (1986). *Managing the Multinational Subsidiary*. London: Croom Helm.

FORSGREN, MATS, and JOHANSON, JAN (1992). *Managing Networks in International Business*. Philadelphia: Gordon & Breach.

——HOLM, U., and JOHANSON, J. (1995). 'Division Headquarters go Abroad: A Step in the Internationalization of the Multinational Corporation', *Journal of Management Studies*, 32(4): 475–91.

FRATOCCHI, L., and HOLM, U. (1998). 'Centres of Excellence in the International Firm', in J. M. Birkinshaw and N. Hood (eds.), *Multinational Corporate Evolution and Subsidiary Development*. London: Macmillan, 189–212.

FROST, T. S., (1998). 'The Geographic Sources of Foreign Subsidiaries' Innovations', working paper, Richard Ivey School of Business, Ontario.

——BIRKINSHAW, J. M., and ENSIGN, S. (2000). 'Centres of Excellence in Multinational Corporations', working paper, Richard Ivey School of Business.

GATES, STEPHEN R., and EGELHOFF, WILLIAM G. (1986). 'Centralization in Headquarters-subsidiary Relationships', *Journal of International Business Studies*, 17(2): 71–92.

GHOSHAL, SUMANTRA (1986). 'The Innovative Multinational: A Differentiated Network of Organizational Roles and Management Processes', unpublished doctoral dissertation, Boston: Harvard Business School.

——and BARTLETT, CHRISTOPHER A. (1990). 'The Multinational Corporation as an Interorganizational Network', *Academy of Management Review*, 15(4): 603–25.

————(1997). *The Individualized Corporation*. London: Harper Business.

GRABHER, G. (1993). 'Rediscovering the Social in the Economics of Inter-firm Relations', in G. Grabher (ed.), *The Embedded Firm*. London: Routledge.

GRANT, R. (1998). *Contemporary Strategy Analysis*. Oxford: Blackwell.

GUPTA, ANIL K., and GOVINDARAJAN, VIJAY (1991). 'Knowledge Flows and the Structure of Control within Multinational Corporations', *Academy of Management Review*, 16(4): 768–92.

————(1994). 'Organizing for Knowledge within MNCs', *International Business Review*, 3(4): 443–57.

————(1999). 'Feedback-seeking Behaviour within Multinational Corporations', *Strategic Management Journal*, 20(3): 205–25.

————(2000). 'Knowledge Flows within Multinational Corporations', *Strategic Management Journal*, 21(4): 473–96.

HALAL, W. (1994). 'From Hierarchy to Enterprise: Internal Markets are the New Foundation of Management', *Academy of Management Executive*, 8(4): 69–83.

HANNAN, M., and FREEMAN, J. (1977). 'The Population Ecology of Organizations', *American Journal of Sociology*, 82: 929–64.

HANSEN, M. (1996). 'Knowledge Integration in Organizations', unpub. Ph.D. dissertation, Stanford University.

HEDLUND, G. (1981). 'Autonomy of Subsidiaries and Formalization of Headquarters-subsidiary Relationships in Swedish MNCs', in L. Otterbeck (ed.), *The Management of Headquarters-subsidiairy Relations in Multinational Corporations*. Hampshire: Gower Publishing.

—— (1986). 'The Hypermodern MNC: A Heterarchy?', *Human Resource Management*, 25: 9–36.

HOLM, U., JOHANSON, J., and THILENIUS, P. (1995). 'Headquarters' Knowledge of Subsidiary Network Contexts in the Multinational Corporation', *International Studies of Management and Organization*, 25(1–2): 97–120.

—— and PEDERSEN, T. (1999). *The Emergence and Impact of Centres of Excellence*. London: Macmillan.

HYMER, STEPHEN (1960/1976). *The International Operations of National Firms: A Study of Foreign Direct Investment*, Ph.D. dissertation, Massachusetts Institute of Technology: MIT Press.

INVEST IN SWEDEN AGENCY (1999). 'I huvudet på ett företag' (in the mind/head of the company). Stockholm: Invest in Sweden Agency.

JARILLO, J-C., and MARTINEZ, J. I. (1990). 'Different Roles for Subsidiaries: The Case of Multinational Corporations', *Strategic Management Journal*, 11: 501–12.

KIM, C., and MAUBORGNE, R. (1991). 'Implementing Global Strategies: The Role of Procedural Justice', *Strategic Management Journal*, 12 (summer special issue): 125–44.

—— (1993a). 'Effectively Conceiving and Executing Multinationals Worldwide', *Journal of International Business Studies*, 24(3): 419–49.

—— (1993b). 'Procedural Justice, Attitudes, and Subsidiary Top Management', *Academy Of Management Journal*, 36(3): 502–27.

KOGUT, B. (1983). 'Foreign Direct Investments as a Sequential Process', in C. P. Kindleberger and D. Audretsch (eds.), *The Multinational Corporation in the 1980s*. Cambridge, Mass.: MIT Press.

KUEMMERLE, W. (1996). 'Home Base and Foreign Direct Investment in Research and Development: An Investigation into the International Allocation of Research Activity by Multinational Enterprises', unpub. doctoral dissertation, Harvard Graduate School of Business.

LEHRER, M., and ASAKAWA, K. (1999). 'Unbundling European Operations: Regional Management and Corporate Flexibility in American and Japanese MNCs', *Journal of World Business*, 34(3): 267–86.

MALNIGHT, T. (1994). 'Globalization of an Ethnocentric Firm: An Evolutionary Perspective', *Strategic Management Journal*, 16: 119–41.

—— (1996). 'The Transition from Decentralized to Network-based MNC Structures: An Evolutionary Perspective', *Journal of International Business Studies*, 27(1): 43–66.

MEYER, J. W., and ROWAN, B. (1977). 'Institutionalized Organizations: Formal Structure as Myth and Ceremony', *American Journal of Sociology*, 83(2): 340–63.

MOORE, KARL (1996). 'Capturing International Responsibilities in the Canadian Pharmaceutical Industry', *Industry Canada Working Paper*.

NOBEL, R., and BIRKINSHAW, J. M. (1998). 'Patterns of Control and Communication in International Research and Development Units', *Strategic Management Journal*, 19(5): 479–98.

OTTERBECK, LARS (ed.) (1981). *The Management of Headquarters-subsidiary Relations in Multinational Corporations*. Hampshire: Gower Publishing.

PENROSE, E. T. (1959). *The Theory of the Growth of the Firm*. Oxford: Basil Blackwell.

PETERS, E. (1999). 'Plant Subsidiary Upgrading: Some Evidence from the Electronics Industry', in N. Hood and S. Young (eds.), *The Globalization of Multinational Enterprise Activity and Economic Development*. London: Macmillan.

PICARD, J. (1980). 'Organizational Structures and Integrative Devices in European Multinational Corporations', *Columbia Journal of World Business*, 15: 30–5.

PORTER, M. E. (1996). 'What is Strategy?', *Harvard Business Review*, 74(6): 61–80.

POYNTER, THOMAS A., and RUGMAN, ALAN M. (1982). 'World Product Mandates: How Will Multinationals Respond?', *Business Quarterly*, Autumn: 54–61.

PRAHALAD, C. K. (1976). 'The Strategic Process in a Multinational Corporation', unpub. doctoral dissertation, School of Business Administration, Harvard University.

——and DOZ, YVES L. (1981). 'An Approach to Strategic Control in MNCs', *Sloan Management Review*, Summer: 5–13.

——and HAMEL, G. (1985). 'Do You Really Have a Global Strategy?', *Harvard Business Review*, 63(4): 139–45.

ROBINSON, PATRICIA A. (1996). 'Applying Institutional Theory to the Study of the Multinational Enterprise: Parental Control and Isomorphism Among Personnel Practices in American Manufacturers in Japan', unpub. doctoral dissertation, MIT.

ROSENZWEIG, P., and NOHRIA, N. (1995). 'Influences on Human Resource Management Practices in Multinational Corporations', *Journal of International Business Studies*, 25(2): 229–52.

——and SINGH, J. (1991). 'Organizational Environments and the Multinational Enterprise', *Academy of Management Review*, 16(2): 340–61.

RUGMAN, ALAN M. (1981). *Inside the Multinationals: The Economics of Internal Markets*. London: Croom Helm.

——(1983). *Multinationals and Technology Transfer*. New York: Praeger.

——and BENNETT, J. (1982). 'Technology Transfer and World Product Mandating in Canada', *Columbia Journal of World Business*, 17(4): 58–62.

——and DOUGLAS, S. (1986). 'The Strategic Management of Multinationals and World Product Mandating', *Canadian Public Policy*, 12(2): 320–28.

——and VERBEKE, ALAIN (1992). 'A Note on the Transnational Solution and the Transaction Cost Theory of Multinational Strategic Management', *Journal of International Business Studies*, 23(4): 761–72.

————(2000). 'Subsidiary-specific Advantages in Multinational Enterprises', *Strategic Management Journal* (forthcoming).

SCHUTTE, H. (1998). 'Between Headquarters and Subsidiaries: The RHQ Solution', in J. M. Birkinshaw and N. Hood (eds.), *Multinational Corporate Evolution and Subsidiary Development*. London: Macmillan.

SIM, A. B. (1977). 'Decentralized Management of Subsidiaries and Their Performance', *Management International Review*, 2: 45–52.

SÖLVELL, Ö, and BIRKINSHAW, J. M. (2000). 'Leading Edge Multinationals and Leading Edge Clusters', *International Studies of Management and Organization*, 30(2): 3–10.

——and ZANDER, I. (1998). 'International Diffusion of Knowledge: Isolating Mechanisms and the Role of the MNE', in A. Chandler, P. Hagstrom, and Ö. Sölvell (eds.), *The Dynamic Firm*. Oxford: Oxford University Press.

STOPFORD, JOHN M., and WELLS, LOUIS T. (1972). *Managing the Multinational Enterprise: Organisation of the Firm and Ownership of the Subsidiaries*. New York: Basic Books.

SURLEMONT, B. (1998). 'A Typology of Centers Within Multinational Corporations: An Emprical Investigation', in J. M. Birkinshaw and N. Hood (eds.), *Multinational Corporate Evolution and Subsidiary Development*. London: Macmillan.

SZULANSKI, G. (1996). 'Exploring Internal Stickiness: Impediments to the Transfer of Best Practices Within the Firm', *Strategic Management Journal*, 17 (special issue): 27–44.

TAGGART, J. H. (1997). 'Autonomy and Procedural Justice: A Framework for Evaluating Subsidiary Strategy', *Journal of International Business Studies*, 28(1): 51–76.

TEECE, D. J., PISANO, G., and SHUEN, A. (1997). 'Dynamic Capabilities and Strategic Management', *Strategic Management Journal*, 18: 509–34.

TSAI, W., and GHOSHAL, S. (1998). 'Social Capital and Value Creation: The Role of Intrafirm Networks', *Academy of Management Journal*, 41(4): 464–77.

VERNON, RAYMOND (1966). 'International Investment and International Trade in the Product Cycle', *Quarterly Journal of Economics*, May: 191–207.

WERNERFELT, B. (1984). 'A Resource Based View of the Firm', *Strategic Management Journal*, 5: 171–80.

WESTNEY, D. ELEANOR (1990). 'Internal and External Linkages in the MNC: The Case of R&D Subsidiaries in Japan', in C. A. Bartlett, Y. Doz, and G. Hedlund (eds.), *Managing the Global Firm*. London: Routledge, 279–302.

——(1994). 'Institutionalization Theory and the Multinational Corporation', in S. Ghoshal and D. E. Westney (eds.), *Organization Theory and the Multinational Corporation*. New York: St Martin's Press, 53–76.

WHITE, RODERICK E., and POYNTER, THOMAS A. (1984). 'Strategies for Foreign-owned Subsidiaries in Canada', *Business Quarterly*, Summer: 59–69.

# CHAPTER 15

..................................................

# STRATEGIC
# ALLIANCES

..................................................

## ANDREW C. INKPEN

OVER the past few decades there has been an enormous increase in the
formation of international strategic alliances and in the research efforts
devoted to understanding alliances. This chapter provides an analysis of the
major issues and research questions that have been studied in the international alliance area. Although the objective is to be as comprehensive as
possible, the enormous output in alliance studies, especially in the 1990s,
necessitates that various areas can be discussed only peripherally. The chapter
begins with a brief overview of alliance forms and then moves on to consider
alliance formation and governance structures, alliance performance, control
issues, bargaining power, the role of trust, evolutionary processes, and alliance
networks. Within each section, key research areas and questions are identified
and the major supporting research and associated findings are discussed.

## 15.1 STRATEGIC ALLIANCE FORMS
..................................................

Strategic alliances are collaborative organizational arrangements that use
resources and/or governance structures from more than one existing organ-

ization. Strategic alliances have three important characteristics. First, the two (or more) firms partnering remain independent subsequent to the formation of the alliance. Second, alliances possess the feature of ongoing mutual interdependence, in which one party is vulnerable to the other (Parkhe 1993). Mutual interdependence leads to shared control and management, which contributes to the complexity of alliance management and often creates significant administrative and coordination costs. Third, because the partners remain independent, there is uncertainty as to what one party is counting on the other party to do (Powell 1996).

The previous alliance definition includes a broad range of organizational forms, including equity joint ventures, licensing arrangements, and shared product development projects. To this definition we add the notion of cross-border flows and linkages. Thus, international strategic alliances are the relatively enduring interfirm cooperative arrangements that utilize resources from autonomous organizations based in two or more countries (Parkhe 1991). Figure 15.1 lists examples of alliance types. The two types of interfirm relationships excluded from the strategic alliance definition are market-based transactions undertaken by two firms and the merger of firms. Although some authors have treated mergers and acquisitions as a form of alliance, this is inconsistent with the concept of an alliance. The new organization that results from a merger or acquisition does not depend on two or more existing organizations for its survival, as does an alliance.

Figure 15.1 indicates an ascending order of involvement and interaction by the organizations creating the alliance (Contractor and Lorange 1988). The first alliance on the list, technical training, has an almost negligible amount of interorganizational interaction. The last form, equity joint ventures, has an extremely high degree of interorganizational interaction. In that sense, an equity joint venture is the most 'intimate' form of alliance. Until the late 1980s, the equity joint venture was viewed virtually synonymously with the term alliance. More recently, and concurrent with the vast number of new alliance formations, researchers have been investigating a much broader set of international collaborative arrangements (e.g. Hagedoorn 1993).

# 15.2 WHY ALLIANCES ARE FORMED

A variety of theoretical reasons have been suggested to explain firms' motives for forming international alliances. These reasons are examined in this section

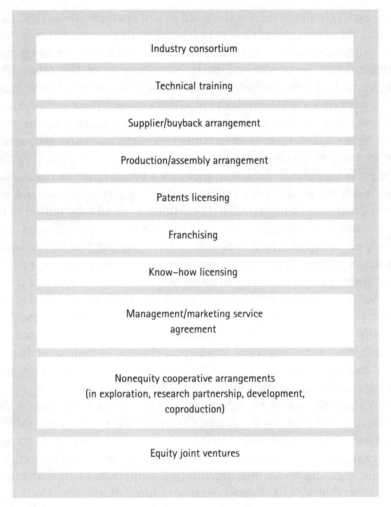

**Fig. 15.1 Types of strategic alliances**

by addressing two key questions: what are the strategic objectives in forming an alliance and why is an alliance the preferred organizational arrangement? Although the questions are addressed separately, in practice they are intertwined in a firm's decision to collaborate.

## 15.2.1 Strategic objectives

The overall strategic objective of alliance partners is the pooling of resources to create value in a way that each of the parents could not achieve by acting alone. Value creation refers to the process of combining the capabilities and resources of the partners to perform a joint task that has the potential to create monetary or other benefits for the partners. Although the perceived value to each of the parents need not be the same, each alliance partner must gain some benefits for an alliance to be the preferred option (Porter and Fuller 1986). For example, GM's strategic objectives for its NUMMI joint venture with Toyota may have included access to North American production of high quality small cars for the United States market and access to the Toyota manufacturing technology. Toyota's objectives were very different. As Toyota's first attempt at building cars in North America, the joint venture provided the company with an opportunity to develop an understanding of the North American manufacturing environment. Thus, the parties in an alliance will not necessarily value a relationship in the same way but will see it as a means to their individual ends.

The strategic objectives of alliances are discussed extensively in the alliance literature (e.g. Contractor and Lorange 1988; Gulati 1998; Harrigan 1986; Hennart 1991, 1988; Kogut 1988; Osborn and Hagedoorn 1997; Porter and Fuller 1986). The feature that links the objectives is that they are aimed at improving the firm's strategic positioning *vis-à-vis* rivals (Kogut 1988). The objectives, or benefits of alliances, can be broadly classified in several categories. Although discussed individually, firms will often have concurrent strategic objectives in forming alliances.

The first objective is to gain economies of scale by pooling economic activities such as raw materials supply, manufacturing, and marketing and distribution. A second objective is to reduce risk and promote stability. Alliances may be an attractive option for large, risky projects because neither partner bears the full cost of the venture activity. A third objective is legitimacy (Oliver 1990). Firms may seek established partners to capitalize on the partner's reputation. This objective may be prevalent in cases where small firms seek cooperative relationships with larger firms. Legitimacy concerns also may exist when firms try to enter international markets. A local partner may provide the necessary legitimacy for firms that are unfamiliar and uncertain about local conditions.

A fourth objective is to gain access to another firm's knowledge or ability to perform an activity where there are asymmetries between firms. Porter and Fuller (1986) referred to this benefit as one of access: firms seek access to such things as distribution channels and specialized know-how. Using alliances to enter foreign markets or to bring foreign products to local markets can give the firm access to resources that would not be available if the firm attempted the strategy alone. Firms may pool complementary resources in order to diversify into new product or geographic markets. Firms also may seek new technology in their core business area and therefore use an alliance to gain access to that knowledge.

The potential costs of alliance strategies must also be considered. First, there are the costs of coordinating the often divergent interests of the partners (Killing 1983). Second, when proprietary expertise and market access are transferred to partner firms, alliances have the potential to create competitors. For example, Reich and Mankin (1986) discussed the competitive implications of sharing technology across borders with potential competitors. Third, alliances can create an adverse bargaining position when one partner captures a disproportionate share of the value created by an alliance (Hamel 1991; Inkpen and Beamish 1997).

## 15.2.2 The preferred organizational arrangement

The four benefits discussed above provide a strategic rationale as to why firms form alliances. However, strategic explanations alone are not sufficient to explain the formation of an alliance because for each of the objectives, alternative organizational arrangements or modes could be chosen to achieve the same objective (Buckley and Casson 1996; Hennart 1988). Therefore, the question of why an alliance is preferred to another structure, such as a wholly-owned subsidiary or a market-based contract, must be addressed. In this section, the question of choice of organizational arrangement is considered while keeping in mind that theories of strategic and structural choice are complementary rather than opposing theories.

The transaction cost explanation for the formation of alliances is based on the approach proposed by Williamson (1981, 1975). Williamson's main argument was that hierarchically organized firms will replace the market for transactions in situations where the market for intermediate goods is inefficient. This inefficiency arises when there is uncertainty about the outcome or value of the transactions (i.e. a high degree of asset specificity) and when there is difficulty in creating the proper performance incentives for each party in the transaction. Williamson proposed that firms choose how to transact with the objective of minimizing transaction and production costs. These arguments are similar to those proposed by Thompson (1967) in explaining organization design. Using the concepts of uncertainty and domain, Thompson argued that organizations attempt to put boundaries around their activities to eliminate uncertainty.

Transaction cost theories of alliances must explain why a firm prefers an alliance over both arm's-length transactions and over the options of internal development or mergers and acquisition. Based on the transaction cost perspective, internalization theory proposes that the rational, profit-maximizing multinational corporation (MNC) would tend to use wholly-owned subsidiaries to achieve its international strategic objectives. According to Calvet (1981), organizing within the MNC provides channels for the transfer of knowledge and slows the dissipation of information to competitors. However, using transaction costs theory, persuasive arguments for the formation of alliances as an alternative to the MNC can be made (e.g. Beamish and Banks 1987; Contractor 1990; Dunning 1995; Hennart 1991, 1988; Madhok 1997). Madhok (1997) argued that markets may be unable to adequately bundle together the relevant tacit resources and capabilities. Beamish and Banks (1987) and Contractor (1990) proposed that alliances are preferable to MNCs when the transactional difficulties of opportunism, bounded rationality, uncertainty, and small numbers condition can efficiently be dealt with in an alliance. As well, alliances reduce the transaction and coordinating costs of arm's-length market transactions (Dunning 1995). Specifically, an alliance can be a more rapid means of establishing a competitive position than through replication or internal development. This implies that alliances may be more likely to occur in industries undergoing rapid structural change. The telecommunications industry in the late 1990s is a good example of an industry with rapidly evolving technology and a multitude of international alliances.

Another situation where alliances may be preferable to acquisition occurs when acquiring the desired firm-specific assets also means acquiring other businesses that are foreign to the buyer (Chi 1994; Hennart 1988). Thus, an alliance can be more economically feasible and involve a less irreversible commitment than acquisition. Because there is no transfer of ownership rights, the relationship may be rescinded at a relatively low cost. Hennart (1988) outlined specific circumstances of narrow imperfect markets that are likely to lead to internalization between parents and alliances. These include the markets for some raw materials and components, types of knowledge, loan capital, and distribution. Given the inefficient market for these goods, firms may attempt to bypass the market by forming a cooperative link with another firm.

Transaction cost explanations provide a compelling economic rationale for the formation of alliances and in particular for the superiority of the alliance mode of organization under specific circumstances. However, the transaction cost perspective is somewhat restrictive because it neglects more behavioral issues and implies too strongly a tractable economic analysis in understanding cooperative relationships. As Robins (1987: 83) argued, the effort to explain structural change solely on the basis of microeconomic processes obscures the role of historical and social forces that influence the competitive environment. In addition, the emphasis on structural arrangements and tangible assets (Lorenzoni and Lipparini 1999) makes some implicit assumptions that organization design can be equated with structure when in fact, organization design includes variables besides the physical structure. These include the people, task, reward systems, and decision and information processes and in particular the intangible assets associated with learning and knowledge.

### 15.2.3 Organizational learning as an alliance motive

Value creation in an alliance occurs after the venture is formed. Much of the alliance research is concerned with how to manage the collaborative process to maximize value creation. In recent years, there has been much greater attention focused on individual firm value appropriation through monetary and long-term competitive gains. An organizational learning motive provides a viable theoretical rationale for alliance formation. Coupled with the strategic objective of access to a partner's knowledge and skills, a learning motive represents a logical objective for firms involved in alliances. Therefore, although there are strong economic arguments as to why a firm chooses the alliance mode, organizational reasons cannot be ignored and may help to explain the prevalence of alliances in the international environment.

Alliances provide a platform for organizational learning, giving firms access to the knowledge of their partners. Through the shared execution of the alliance task, mutual interdependence and problem solving, and observation of alliance activities and outcomes, firms can learn from their partners. Unlike other learning contexts, the formation of an alliance reduces the risk that the knowledge will dissipate quickly (Powell 1987). Thus, alliances provide an ideal platform for learning. Two or more organizations are brought together because of their different skills, knowledge, and strategic complementarity. The differences in partner skills and knowledge provide the catalyst for learning by the alliance parents.

There is a significant body of theoretical research (Inkpen, 2000; Kogut 1988; Kumar and Nti 1998; Larsson, Bengtsson, Henriksson, and Sparks 1998; Makhija and Ganesh 1997; Mody 1993; Parkhe 1991; Pucik 1991) and empirical studies (Dodgson 1993; Hamel 1991; Inkpen and Crossan 1995; Inkpen and Dinur 1998; Lane and Lubatkin 1998; Mowery, Oxley, and Silverman 1996; Powell, Koput, and Smith-Doerr 1996; Simonin 1997, 1999) addressing the issue of alliances and learning. This stream of research addresses some of the important questions associated with the conditions under which organizations exploit alliance learning opportunities.

Various different learning perspectives have been examined in the alliance literature. Learning processes, as Doz (1996) argued, are central to the evolution of an alliance. From the alliance partner's point of view, learning can be examined from two perspectives: (1) learning about the alliance partner, which can be an antecedent to the development of interfirm trust and (2) learning from the alliance partner. Doz and Hamel (1998) emphasized that the motivations and effects of the two types of partner learning are very different. They referred to learning *about* the alliance partner as skill familiarity that supported the alliance partner's ability to jointly create value. Learning *from* an alliance partner is a very different type of alliance learning and is a key determinant of alliance bargaining power (Hamel 1991; Inkpen and Beamish 1997; Yan 1998). In turn, partner learning influences the extent of control one firm can exert over its alliance. Firms that can learn quickly are able to acquire partner skills, reducing dependence and increasing bargaining power. Inkpen and Beamish (1997) used these arguments to develop a framework of instability and international joint ventures.

Taking a different tack, Kogut (1991) suggested that alliances may be investments that provide firms with expansion opportunities. Faced with uncertainty and a desire to learn, firms may prefer an alliance to acquisition. If one partner has the option to purchase the other's equity in the venture, that partner can utilize the alliance as a means of acquiring complex knowledge about the business. Once the party with the option to buy has acquired (i.e. learned) the skills of the partner firm, further investment in the venture might not be warranted. At this point the buy option may be exercised and the alliance terminated.

Various other alliance studies have incorporated learning perspectives. For example, Makhija and Ganesh (1997) linked learning and control in a conceptual framework. Khanna, Gulati, and Nohria (1998) examined how the tension between cooperation and competition affects the dynamics of learning alliances. The authors developed the concept of private and common benefits to the alliance partners and suggested that firms often fail to understand the magnitude of partner asymmetric differences. Lyles and Salk (1996) examined the factors that influenced knowledge acquisition by the joint venture organization from the foreign parent. Given the interest in learning theories in other business disciplines it is likely that learning will continue to be a focus for alliance researchers in years to come.

# 15.3 ALLIANCE PERFORMANCE

International alliances are often described, particularly in the business press, as inherently unstable organizational forms that are prone to failure. Gulati

(1998) listed various factors that practitioners have identified to explain alliance performance: flexibility in management of the alliance, trust, information exchange, management of conflict, continuity of boundary spanning personnel, and managing partner expectations. Various researchers have observed that alliances involve significant costs in terms of coordination, reconciling goals with an independent entity, and creating competitors. Porter (1990) suggested that these costs make many alliances transitional rather than stable arrangements and therefore, alliances are rarely a sustainable means for creating competitive advantage. Supporting this argument, several empirical studies of alliances have found instability rates of close to 50 per cent (e.g. Kogut 1988). Based on the finding that twenty-four of the forty-nine international alliances they studied were considered failures by one or both partners, Bleeke and Ernst (1991) suggested that most alliances will terminate, even successful ones.

Despite conventional wisdom about the difficulty of alliance management, the measurement of alliance performance has bedeviled alliance researchers for decades. The difficulties of measuring alliance performance is rooted in both theoretical and methodological challenges. Because alliances are formed for a variety of purposes (Contractor and Lorange 1988; Hennart 1988) and often in highly uncertain settings, performance evaluation becomes a very difficult task (Anderson 1990). One perspective argues that alliance performance should be evaluated as a mutual outcome and take into account the perspectives of the multiple partners (Beamish 1988). A different perspective suggests that performance should be viewed in terms of value creation. Because each partner will have different cooperative objectives and abilities to appropriate alliance benefits, the focus should be on the individual monetary and competitive gains of each partner (Hamel 1991). A further perspective is that alliances should be evaluated as stand-alone entities seeking to maximize their own performance, not the partners' (Anderson 1990). Finally, alliance stability or survival has been extensively used as an indicator of performance (Gomes-Casseres 1989; Kogut 1989; Park and Russo 1996).

Empirical studies of alliance performance have mainly dealt with equity joint ventures. Geringer and Hebert (1991) identified the various performance measures used in international joint venture studies: profitability, growth, and cost position; venture survival; duration; instability of ownership; renegotiation of the alliance contract. Geringer and Hebert's empirical work found that an objective measure of joint venture performance was correlated with a measure based on venture performance relative to initial objectives. More recently, authors have developed extensive surveys (e.g. Parkhe 1993) with the objective of capturing partner asymmetries in perceptions of performance. This area should prove to be a fruitful avenue for future research.

## 15.3.1  Instability

With a focus primarily on equity joint ventures, several definitions of instability have been used in the alliance literature. Franko (1971) defined a joint venture as unstable when parent holdings changed and crossed 50 per cent or 95 per cent ownership, a parent sold its joint venture interest, or the venture was liquidated. Killing (1983) considered both a shift in alliance control and venture termination as evidence of instability. Other researchers have adopted a narrower view. For example, Kogut (1989) used venture termination as the sole indicator of instability. However, as Kogut indicated, an alliance cannot be considered unstable simply because its lifespan is short. All relationships between firms face challenges that threaten to change or terminate the basis for cooperation. Sometimes terminations are planned and anticipated by the parties involved. Ventures may also be terminated as a matter of policy when there is a change in parent ownership or management. In other cases, difficulties associated with ending a relationship may create a rationale for maintaining an existing alliance that would otherwise be terminated.

Inkpen and Beamish (1997) argued that instability in equity joint ventures should be linked with *unplanned* equity changes or major reorganizations. They defined instability as a major change in relationship status that was *unplanned* and *premature* from one or both partners' perspectives. Usually, instability will result in premature alliance termination, either when one partner acquires the alliance business or the venture is dissolved. A complicating factor is that alliance termination will not always be a mutual decision (Parkhe 1991). Premature termination may be precipitated by the actions of one partner. For example, when one firm is trying to learn from its partner in order to reduce its dependency, the partner doing the learning may have very different longevity objectives than the partner that is the knowledge source. Yan (1998) extended these arguments by drawing on structural instability and structural inertia perspectives to trace the destabilizing forces in international joint ventures. Yan suggested that alliance researchers should move away from the assumption that stability produces success whereas instability produces failure.

## 15.3.2  Culture and partner compatibility

Compatibility between the partners and congruency in partner cultural factors are often cited as critical to alliance success (e.g. Barkema and Vermeulen 1997; Shenkar and Zeira 1992). Compatibility can be viewed from multiple perspectives, including organizational fit, strategic symmetry, resource complementarities, and alliance task-based factors. Research linking partner compatibility with performance, including partner selection studies (e.g. Beamish 1987), has not yielded consistency in results. One stream of research posits that the more culturally distant two firms are, the greater the differences in their organizational and administrative practices, employee expectations, and accordingly, the less likely it is that the alliance will be successful. For example, Lane and Beamish (1990) argued that cultural compatibility between the partners is the most important factor in the endurance of an international alliance. Empirical research, however, does not bear this out. In a study of Japanese–US joint ventures, Park and Ungson (1997) found that organizational measures of compatibility were not important in dissolution rates. Luo (1997) found that the link between partners' sociocultural distance and joint venture performance was not significant. One of the problems, as Osborn and Hagedoorn (1997) pointed out, is that measurement of compatibility is more illusive than its definition.

# 15.4 CONTROL OF STRATEGIC ALLIANCES

Management control is the organizational process which aligns subunits and individuals with the interests and objectives of the organization (Tannenbaum 1968; Yan and Gray 1994). Control in the alliance context refers to the process by which partner firms influence an alliance entity to behave in a manner that achieves partner objectives and satisfactory performance. The process includes the use of power, authority, and a range of bureaucratic, cultural, and informal mechanisms (Geringer and Hebert 1989).

In alliances, control issues are often at the heart of management conflict between the partners. Alliances are formed when two or more partners, often with disparate skills and objectives, pool a portion of their resources to form a new entity. As Killing (1982) pointed out, the primary problems in managing alliances stem from one cause: there is more than one parent. Thus, the ability of an owner to exercise control over its alliance is a function not only of its influence over its alliance managers but also of the influence over the other partner (Child, Yan, and Lu 1997). The owners of alliances are often visible and powerful; they can and will disagree on just about anything. Given the potential for partner conflict, control issues are usually an important consideration for alliance partners (Geringer and Hebert 1989; Killing 1983; Yan and Gray 1994). However, in comparison with wholly-owned subsidiaries, exercising effective control over alliances is often difficult for the parent firms, especially if they are unable to rely solely on their ownership position (Geringer and Hebert 1989).

Various approaches have been employed to develop an understanding of alliance control and in particular its relationship with alliance performance. Geringer and Hebert (1989) made a significant contribution in analyzing the approaches and identifying three dimensions of control: (1) the mechanisms used by the parents to exercise control; (2) the extent of control achieved by the parents; and (3) the scope of activities over which parents exercise control. While Geringer and Hebert argued that the dimensions are complementary and interdependent, there is a paucity of empirical work to support their arguments. Child, Yan, and Lu (1997) made a distinction between contractual and noncontractual resource inputs as sources of bargaining power and, hence, control over alliance activities. Empirical research has tended to focus either on control over a range of decision or activities (e.g. Killing 1983) or mechanisms of control, such as contribution of key managers, board membership, or alliance structure and policies (e.g. Yan and Gray 1994). Work in the area of performance and control has been particularly ambiguous and suggests that deeper study into the roles of trust and learning should contribute valuable insights.

## 15.4.1 The control–performance relationship

A prominent theme in the literature on international alliances, and especially involving equity joint ventures, is the relationship between control and performance. A variety of mechanisms are available to parents for exercising effective control. Various terms have been used to describe different types of control mechanisms (see Martinez and Jarillo 1989 for a review of research on control and coordination mechanisms in multinational firms). To describe alliance controls, the terms formal and informal have gained acceptance (Makhija and Ganesh 1997). Formal controls tend to be predictable, regular, and involve explicit information transfers. Informal controls are more uncertain, ambiguous, and organizationally embedded (Deakin and Wilkinson 1998). Informal and non-contractual safeguards are more likely when there is a high level of trust between the partners. For example, in cases of high trust, the alliance agreement may be less detailed because of perceptions of a low probability of opportunism. Governance costs under conditions of distrust will be greater and procedures will be more formal, such as more detailed contract documentation, more frequent board meetings, closer scrutiny by lawyers, and more communication between partner headquarters and the alliance. These procedures will result in additional transaction costs to the alliance partners (Dyer 1997). Parkhe (1993) found support for the hypothesis that elaborateness of safeguards and the perception of opportunistic behavior are strongly related.

In the equity joint venture area, ownership has most widely been investigated as the basis for establishing parent control. While ownership and control do not correspond perfectly (Hennart 1991), majority ownership provides the basis for a high degree of management control. Blodgett (1992), using ownership to measure control and stability to measure performance, found that 50–50 shared management arrangements had a greater chance for long life than majority owned ventures. Blodgett argued that when partners have equal ownership, there will be pressure on both sides to make accommodations to the alliance to protect their investments and, therefore, both partners will be committed to making the venture successful. In a majority-owned venture, one partner may have the ability to configure the venture in a manner that is undesirable to the other partner(s).

Conceptualizing control in terms of the locus of decision-making and the *extent* of control exercised by partner firms provides the basis for an alternative view of performance and control. Killing's (1982) early work identified three categories of alliances based on the extent of shared decision-making: dominant parent, shared management, and independent ventures. The primary determinant of the alliance type was the degree of parent involvement in the decision-making of the alliances and the extent to which both parents had active roles. In making the link between control and performance, Killing (1982) found that dominant partner alliances were more likely to be successful than shared partner ventures. Killing argued that when a single parent controlled the venture's activities, the risks associated with coordination and potential conflicts were reduced. While there is conflicting evidence about this relationship (see Beamish and Banks' (1987) study of developing country alliances), Killing's argument is persuasive, especially when interpreted within a transaction cost framework. Coordination between partners entails significant costs that make many alliances transitional rather than stable arrangements. Reducing the risks associated with coordination can minimize transaction costs and stabilize the alliance. Following this logic, alliances in which a dominant partner has decision-making control should perform better than ventures where control is shared.

In an empirical setting, Mjoen and Tallman (1997) combined an ownership-focused control model with a resource input-based bargaining power model. Their results rejected an approach to joint venture governance based solely on ownership as the basis for control, arguing instead for a bargaining power-based model of control. Taking a different perspective, several studies have suggested that firms with different national backgrounds have different preferences in ownership (Erramilli 1996, Pan 1997). For example, Pan (1997) suggested that North American MNCs were more likely than Japanese firms to form wholly-owned subsidiaries. Interpreting these results are problematic because of the many strategic variables that must be controlled for.

Clearly, as Geringer and Hebert (1989) concluded: the relationship between dominant control and alliance performance is far more complex and less direct than scholars originally perceived. In recent years, the search for direct links between control and performance have faded as a major issue for alliance researchers, perhaps because of a renewed emphasis on bargaining power and the dynamics of alliance relationships.

# 15.5 ALLIANCES AND BARGAINING POWER

Viewing alliances from a bargaining power and dependence perspective is an area that has its roots in work by Emerson (1962) and generalized to the organizational level in Pfeffer and Salancik's (1978) resource-dependence model. The essence of the model is that the possession or control of key resources by one entity may make other organizations dependent on that entity. This notion of resource fit assumes that relationships are terminated for the inverse of the reasons for which they were formed (Seabright, Levinthal, and Fichman 1992).

In a cooperative relationship, dependence can be a source of power for the firm controlling key resources because to some degree, each firm can increase, or withhold, resources which are attractive to its partner (Bacharach and Lawler 1980). When one firm controls an 'irreplaceable' alliance resource or input, a dependency situation is created (Hamel 1991). While the dependency is voluntary in that firms choose to form alliances, once the alliance is operational, firms depend on their partners for specific resources and inputs. A firm that has the option to contribute or withhold an important resource or input can use that option as leverage in bargaining with its partner (Pfeffer 1981).

The notion of 'cooperative' may seem at odds with dependence and power. However, the key point is that at the time an alliance is formed, each partner is dependent on the other(s) for critical alliance inputs. Thus, the firms must cooperate to ensure that these critical inputs are transformed into a productive entity, i.e. the alliance. Over time, the dependence may change and as a result, bargaining power may tilt in favor of one partner. When that happens, the alliance partner holding the increased bargaining power has access to more available partners and other options, including venture termination, than does the partner with limited bargaining power (Yan and Gray 1994).

The bargaining power perspective is particularly appropriate for the examination of alliance stability because all alliances involve a negotiated bargain between the partners. At a general level, bargaining power in alliances arises out of the relative urgency of cooperation, available resources, commitments, other alternatives, and the strengths and weaknesses of each partner (Schelling 1956). Yan and Gray's (1994) inductive study, the most systematic exploration of the concept of bargaining power in international joint ventures to date, identified both resource-based and context-based components of bargaining power. The resources and capabilities committed by the partners to the alliance were a major source of bargaining power. Local knowledge in areas such as local sourcing, domestic distribution, and personnel management was the main resource contributed by the local partners (Yan and Gray 1994). For the foreign partners, resource contributions included expertise and technology for production management and global support.

To link the partner resource contributions directly to bargaining power and to understand the process of bargaining power shifts, concepts of organizational knowledge management must be incorporated in the framework. The pace of knowledge acquisition by one alliance partner is an important process dimension because, as Hamel (1991) argued, this dimension is very much within the firm's control. Because of this controllability, Hamel identified learning as the most important element in determining relative bargaining power. Substantial knowledge acquisition by one partner over time can erode the value of the knowledge contributed by the other partner, breaking down the bargaining relationship between the partners and enabling one firm to eliminate its dependency on its partner.

# 15.6 THE ROLE OF TRUST

International alliance research over the past decades (e.g. Beamish and Banks 1987; Buckley and Casson 1988; Inkpen and Beamish 1997; Inkpen and Currall 1998; Madhok 1995; Yan and Gray 1994) has repeatedly argued that mutual trust is essential for successful alliances. Ariño and de la Torre (1998), in their study of a failed joint venture, concluded that in the absence of a reserve of trust, alliances that encounter threats to stability will not be sustainable. Yan (1998: 786) wrote that 'lack of trust between the partners at the international joint venture formation can be a major source of structural instability'. As noted by Child and Faulkner (1998), trust is particularly fragile in international alliances because risk and uncertainty involved in a domestic alliance are heightened in the alliance context by cross-national differences between partner firms with respect to culture, law, politics, and trade policy.

Inkpen and Currall (1998) discussed alliance trust antecedents and consequences and argued that trust plays a crucial role in the overall nature of alliance processes. As well, alliance trust should be viewed as an evolving rather than static concept. Over time, as the partners and partner managers learn about each other and the alliance becomes an operating entity, the level of interpartner trust will change. Trust requires familiarity and mutual understanding and, hence, depends on time and context (Nooteboom, Berger, and Noorderhaven 1997). As the relationship ages, previous successes, failures, and partner interactions will influence the level of trust in the alliance. Furthermore, unlike most economic commodities, trust may grow rather than wear out through use (Hirschman 1984). Trust may also decrease over the life of the relationship. For example, when an alliance is formed, there is a subjective probability that a partner will cooperate. Experience will lead to adjustment of the probability, which in turn may lead to a shift in the level of trust.

Risk is a precondition for the existence of trust, and the trustor must be cognizant of risk (Mayer, Davis, and Schoorman 1995; Sitkin and Pablo 1992). The risk of negative outcomes must be present for trust to operate and the trustor must be willing to be vulnerable. In the absence of risk, trust is irrelevant because there is no vulnerability. The greater the risk, the higher the confidence threshold required to engage in trusting action. The nature of risk and its relationship with trust has received limited research attention in the international alliance literature.

## 15.6.1 Trust and performance

Although it has generally been argued that trust enhances alliance performance (e.g. Harrigan 1986; Saxton 1997), the argument that performance leads to trust has merit as well. Yan and Gray (1994) suggested that performance may have a feedback effect on trust. Poor performance may cause distrust between the partners, which in turn leads to poor long-term alliance performance (Killing 1983). A firm's review of past alliance results, in comparison with expectations, can lead to a firm's prediction of the extent to which the partner firm will follow through on its current promises (i.e. is trust in the partner warranted?). If alliance performance is worse than expected, alliance partners are likely to question the competence and capabilities of their partners. The level of trust in the relationship will therefore suffer accordingly. In turn, performance may suffer because the alliance managers become embroiled in conflict, resulting in a deviation-amplifying loop where a decrease in alliance performance leads to a decrease in trust, which continues to amplify the problem with performance.

The strongest empirical support for the trust-to-performance relationship in an interfirm context can be found in the marketing literature on channel relationships (e.g. Aulakh, Kotabe, and Sahay 1996; Mohr and Spekman 1994; Robichaux and Coleman 1994; Smith and Barclay 1997). In the equity joint venture literature, despite numerous conceptual arguments, there is limited empirical support. Using perception of opportunistic behavior as a proxy for trust, Parkhe (1993) found a strong relationship between perception of opportunistic behavior and alliance performance. Inkpen and Currall (1997) found support for the argument that trust has an indirect effect on performance mediated by forbearance. In their qualitative study of United States–China joint ventures, Yan and Gray (1994) identified trust as a mechanism that moderated the relationship between formal management control and venture performance. Park and Ungson (1997) and Saxton (1997) found a positive relationship between antecedents of trust and alliance outcomes.

# 15.7 EVOLUTIONARY PROCESSES IN ALLIANCES

Over the course of their life, successful alliances will go through a series of transitions. Alliances must evolve if they are to survive and, according to Lorange (1997), can be seen as always in a temporal stage and always on the way to something else. The study of alliance evolution is an area with great promise and, currently, limited output. As Yan (1998) stated, although the formation and termination events have been studied extensively, there has been limited attention given to the mid-life of alliances and the developmental dynamics of alliances.

Some recent work provides important understanding in the area of strategic alliance evolution. Doz (1996) proposed that successful alliances go through an evolutionary process involving sequential interactive cycles of learning, reevaluation, and readjustment. In contrast, failing projects were highly inertial and characterized by little learning or divergent learning. Child and Faulkner (1998) considered the evolution of trust-based relationships and suggested that trust tends to develop gradually over time as the partners move from one stage to the next. Ariño and de la Torre (1998) examined the interaction between two partners in a failed international joint venture. They found that positive feedback loops were critical in the evolutionary process and that procedural issues were critical in fostering a climate for positive reinforcement and mutual trust and confidence in the relationship.

## 15.7.1 Attachment

In addition to learning processes and structural developments, alliance dynamics are shaped by attachment. Attachment is the binding of one party to another (Salancik 1977). Attachment between partners develops through experience in the collaborative relationship and through investments the partners make in the relationship over time (Seabright, Levinthal, and Fichman 1992). When the partners have developed a strong attachment, there may be inertial forces that block the pressures for change in relationship status (Blau 1964; Salancik 1977). If firms have worked together in the past, they will have basic understandings about each other's skills and capabilities (Heide and Miner 1992). According to Parkhe (1993: 803), 'the older a relationship, the greater the likelihood it has passed through a critical shakeout period of conflict and influence attempts by both sides'. Because of prior relationships, firms often form alliances with firms with whom they have transacted in the past. For example, in a study of forty joint ventures, Inkpen (1995) found that in twenty-four cases, the partners had previously worked together. An MNC's knowledge about its local partner, generated through previous interactions, can also play an important role in determining its equity position in the host country (Sohn 1994).

Attachments in collaborative relationships may be the result of individual or structural ties that reflect the prior history of the relationship (Seabright, Levinthal, and Fichman 1992). Individual attachment reflects the socialization by individuals during their involvement in exchange activities. In alliances, individual attachment may be represented by personal relationships between partner managers. Continuing business relationships often become overlaid with social content that generates strong expectations of trust and forbearance (Granovetter 1985). Thus, attachment can lead to alliances that begin their existence with an existing stock of 'relationship assets' (Fichman and Levinthal 1991) and a high degree of inter-partner trust (Gulati 1995). Parkhe (1991) suggested that unplanned alliance termination is more likely when firms are working together for the first time. Kogut (1989) found that structural ties between alliance partners were negatively related to alliance dissolution. Kogut's variable for structured ties was a composite of three types of relationships: supply, other alliances, and licensing agreements.

# 15.8 ALLIANCES AND NETWORKS

The study of interorganizational networks has become a field unto itself, with specialized methodologies and well-developed theoretical frameworks. As well, the field has introduced some confusing terminology, such as alliance networks, industry networks, and constellations (Gomes-Casseres 1996). Although the ultimate definition of networks depends on arbitrary identification of boundaries, from an alliance and collaborative perspective, networks can be defined as a set of organizations linked by a set of social and business relationships that create strategic interfirm opportunities for the organizations. Although strategy research in the domestic arena has begun examining the social context (e.g. Lorenzoni and Lipparani 1999) of networks within which firms are embedded, the international alliance literature has not yet examined this in any detail. As Gulati (1998) pointed out, a social network perspective on alliances can have both descriptive and normative outcomes that provide valuable insights for various organizational theories.

The international business research has made some inroads into the examination of networks. Some network research as been comparative in nature. For example, using Japanese and American automotive suppliers as the basis for empirical examination, Dyer (1997) examined how firms in a production network could maximize production value. Other studies have tried to explain international expansion and the role of network affiliation. Along this vein, Sarkar, Cavusgil, and Aulakh (1999) examined the international expansion of telecommunication carriers and the influence of network characteristics. Finally, the study by Holm, Eriksson, and Johanson (1996) examined business network connections for European and US suppliers and customers and concluded that the alliance development process has to be coordinated with ongoing processes with other partner relationships. The authors hypothesized that network connections may play a significant role for market entry decisions.

# 15.9 FUTURE ALLIANCES RESEARCH ISSUES

Although the international alliance literature is rich and multi-disciplinary in nature, many exciting research opportunities remain. Two can be specifically singled out as warranting attention. The first major research opportunity is in the area of alliance evolutionary processes. There is a real need for greater understanding of what happens once an alliance is formed. For example, how does trust at one organizational level shape and influence trust at another level? How do contractual changes in the alliance influence interactions between managers? What are the evolutionary phases that characterize successful alliances? If, as Madhok and Tallman (1998) suggested, refraining from opportunistic behavior may have little to do with the development of trust and more to do with good business, how do managers analyze the cost-benefits associated with the likelihood of opportunism and non-opportunism over the life of the alliance? These research questions and many others associated with evolutionary processes have the potential to generate a new chapter in international alliance research.

The second major research opportunity is expanded understanding of new alliance forms and in particular, E-commerce-based alliances. These new alliance forms promise to challenge accepted wisdom and theories about how international alliances are formed and managed. In the Internet economy, alliances will become easier to create, and terminate, and location and firm size will become less critical variables. New forms of open-ended collaboration will be quickly formed and dissolved. The classic market entry bricks and mortar equity joint venture will decline in relevance as firms discover that relationships can be easily and efficiently established electronically. In the international arena, alliances will provide firms with enormous reach and opportunities to partner anywhere in the world. Studying these new alliance forms will introduce an exciting theoretical and empirical thrust to the field of strategic alliances.

## REFERENCES

ANDERSON, E. (1990). 'Two Firms, One Frontier: On Assessing Joint Venture Perform-
ance', *Sloan Management Review*, 18 (Winter): 19–30.
ARIÑO, A., and DE LA TORRE, J. (1998). 'Learning From Failure: Towards an Evolu-
tionary Model of Collaborative Ventures', *Organization Science*, 9: 306–25.
AULAKH, P. S., KOTABE, M., and SAHAY, A. (1996). 'Trust and Performance in Cross-
Border Marketing Partnerships: A Behavioral Approach', *Journal of International
Business Studies*, 27: 1005–32.
BACHARACH, S., and LAWLER, E. J. (1980). *Power and Politics in Organizations*. San
Francisco, Calif.: Jossey-Bass.
BARKEMA, H. G., and VERMEULEN, F. (1997). 'What Differences in the Cultural Back-
grounds of Partners are Detrimental for International Joint Ventures?', *Journal of
International Business Studies*, 28: 845–64.
BEAMISH, P. W. (1987). 'Joint Ventures in LDCs: Partner Selection and Performance',
*Management International Review*, 27: 23–37.
——(1988). *Multinational Joint Ventures in Developing Countries*. London: Rout-
ledge.
——and BANKS, J. C. (1987). 'Equity Joint Ventures and the Theory of the Multi-
national Enterprise', *Journal of International Business Studies*, (Summer): 1–16.
BLAU, P. M. (1964). *Exchange and Power in Social Life*. New York: Wiley.
BLEEKE, J., and ERNST, D. (1991). 'The Way to Win in Cross-Border Alliances', *Harvard
Business Review*, 69(6): 127–35.
BLODGETT, L. L. (1992). 'Factors in the Instability of International Joint Ventures: An
Event History Analysis', *Strategic Management Journal*, 13: 475–81.
BUCKLEY, P. J., and CASSON, M. (1988). 'A Theory of Cooperation in International
Business', in F. Contractor and P. Lorange (eds.), *Cooperative Strategies in Inter-
national Business*. Lexington, Mass.: Lexington Books, 31–53
——(1996). 'An Economic Model of International Joint Venture Strategy', *Journal of
International Business Studies*, 27: 849–76.
CALVET, A. L. (1981). 'A Synthesis of Foreign Direct Investment Theories of the
Multinational Firm', *Journal of International Business Studies*, (Spring/Summer):
43–59.
CHI, T. (1994). 'Trading in Strategic Resources: Necessary Conditions, Transaction
Cost Problems, and Choice of Exchange Structure', *Strategic Management Journal*,
15: 271–90.
CHILD, J., and FAULKNER, D. (1998). *Strategies Of Cooperation: Managing Alliances,
Networks, and Joint Ventures*. New York: Oxford University Press.
——YAN, Y., and LU, Y. (1997). 'Ownership and Control in Sino-Foreign Joint
Ventures', in P. Beamish and J. Killing (eds.), *Cooperative Strategies: Asian Pacific
Perspectives*. San Francisco, Calif.: New Lexington, 181–225.
CONTRACTOR, F. J. (1990). 'Contractual and Cooperative Forms of International
Business: Towards A Unified Theory of Modal Choice', *Management International
Review*, 30(1): 31–54.
——and LORANGE, P. (1988). 'Why Should Firms Cooperate: The Strategy and
Economics Basis for Cooperative Ventures', in F. Contractor and P. Lorange

(eds.), *Cooperative Strategies In International Business*. Lexington, Mass.: Lexington Books, 3–30.

DEAKIN, S., and WILKINSON, F. (1998). 'Contract Law and the Economics of Inter-organizational Trust', in C. Lane and R. Bachmann (eds.), *Trust Within and Between Organizations*. Oxford: Oxford University Press, 146–72.

DODGSON, M. (1993). 'Learning, Trust, and Technological Collaboration', *Human Relations*, 46: 77–95.

DOZ, Y. (1996). 'The Evolution of Cooperation in Strategic Alliances: Initial Conditions or Learning Processes?', *Strategic Management Journal*, 17 (Summer special issue): 55–84.

——and HAMEL, G. (1998). *Alliance Advantage: The Art of Creating Value Through Partnering*. Boston, Mass.: Harvard Business School Press.

DUNNING, J. H. (1995). 'Reappraising the Eclectic Paradigm in an Age of Alliance Capitalism', *Journal of International Business Studies*, 26: 461–92.

DYER, J. H. (1997). 'Effective Interfirm Collaboration: How Firms Minimize Transaction Costs and Maximize Transaction Value', *Strategic Management Journal*, 18: 535–56.

EMERSON, R. M. (1962). 'Power Dependence Relationships', *American Sociological Review*, 27 (Feb.): 31–41.

ERRAMILLI, M. K. (1996). 'Nationality and Subsidiary Ownership Patterns in Multinational Corporations', *Journal of International Business Studies*, 27: 225–48.

FICHMAN, M., and LEVINTHAL, D. A. (1991). 'Honeymoons and the Liability of Adolescence: A New Perspective on Duration Dependence in Social and Organizational Relationships', *Academy of Management Review*, 16: 442–68.

FRANKO, L. (1971). *Joint Venture Survival In Multinational Companies*. New York: Praeger.

GERINGER, J. M., and HEBERT, L. (1989). 'Control and Performance of International Joint Ventures', *Journal of International Business Studies*, 20: 235–54.

——(1991). 'Measuring Performance of International Joint Ventures', *Journal of International Business Studies*, 22(2): 253–67.

GOMES-CASSERES, B. (1996). *The Alliance Revolution: The New Shape of Business Rivalry*. Cambridge, Mass.: Harvard University Press.

——(1989). 'Joint Ventures in the Face of Global Competition', *Sloan Management Review*, 17 (Spring): 17–26.

GRANOVETTER, M. (1985). 'Economic Action and Social Structure: The Problem of Embeddedness', *American Journal of Sociology*, 78: 481–510.

GULATI, R. (1995). 'Does Familiarity Breed Trust? The Implications of Repeated Ties for Contractual Choice in Alliances', *Academy of Management Journal*, 38: 85–112.

——(1998). 'Alliances and Networks', *Strategic Management Journal*, 19: 293–318.

HAGEDOORN, J. (1993). 'Understanding the Rationale of Strategic Technology Partnering: International Modes of Cooperation and Sectoral Differences', *Strategic Management Journal*, 14: 371–85.

HAMEL, G. (1991) 'Competition for Competence and Inter-Partner Learning Within International Strategic Alliances', *Strategic Management Journal*, 12 (special issue): 83–104.

HARRIGAN, K. R. (1986). *Managing for Joint Venture Success*. Lexington, Mass.: Lexington Books.

HEIDE, J. B., and MINER, A. S. (1992). 'The Shadow of the Future: Effects of Anticipated Interaction and the Frequency of Contact on Buyer-Seller Cooperation', *Academy of Management Journal*, 35: 265–91.

HENNART, J. F. (1988). 'A Transactions Costs Theory of Equity JVs', *Strategic Management Journal*, 9: 361–74.

—— (1991). 'The Transactions Cost Theory of Joint Ventures: An Empirical Study of Japanese Subsidiaries in the United States', *Management Science*, 37: 483–97.

HIRSCHMAN, A. O. (1984). 'Against Parsimony: Three Easy Ways of Complicating Some Categories of Economic Discourse', *American Economic Review*, 74: 88–96.

HOLM, D. B., ERIKSSON, K., and JOHANSON, J. (1996). 'Business Networks and Cooperation in International Business Relationships', *Journal of International Business Studies*, 27: 1033–53.

INKPEN, A. C. (1995). 'Organizational Learning and International Joint Ventures', *Journal of International Management*, 1: 165–98.

—— (2000). 'Learning Through Joint Ventures: A Framework of Knowledge Acquisition', *Journal of Management Studies*, 37: 1019–43.

—— and BEAMISH, P. W. (1997). 'Knowledge, Bargaining Power and International Joint Venture Stability', *Academy of Management Review*, 22: 177–202.

—— and CROSSAN, M. M. (1995). 'Believing is Seeing: Joint Ventures and Organization Learning', *Journal of Management Studies*, 32: 595–618.

—— and CURRALL, S. C. (1997). 'International Joint Venture Trust: An Empirical Examination', in P. W. Beamish and J. P. Killing (eds.), *Cooperative Strategies: North American Perspectives*. San Francisco, Calif.: New Lexington Press, 308–34.

—— —— (1998). 'The Nature, Antecedents and Consequences of Joint Venture Trust', *Journal of International Management*, 4: 1–20.

—— and DINUR, A. (1998). 'Knowledge Management Processes and International Joint Ventures', *Organization Science*, 9: 454–68.

KHANNA, T., GULATI, R., and NOHRIA, N. (1998). 'The Dynamics of Learning Alliances: Competition, Cooperation, and Relative Scope', *Strategic Management Journal*, 19: 193–210.

KILLING, J. P. (1982). 'How To Make a Global Joint Venture Work', *Harvard Business Review*, 60(3): 120–27.

—— (1983). *Strategies For Joint Venture Success*. New York: Praeger.

KOGUT, B. (1988). 'Joint Ventures: Theoretical and Empirical Perspectives', *Strategic Management Journal*, 9: 319–22.

—— (1989). 'The Stability of Joint Ventures: Reciprocity and Competitive Rivalry', *The Journal of Industrial Economics*, 38: 183–98.

—— (1991). 'Joint Ventures and the Option to Expand and Acquire', *Management Science*, 37(1): 19–33.

KUMAR, R., and NTI, K. O. (1998). 'Differential Learning and Interaction in Alliance Dynamics', *Organization Science*, 9: 356–67

LANE, H. W., and BEAMISH, P. W. (1990). 'Cross-Cultural Cooperative Behavior in Joint Ventures in LDCs', *Management International Review* (special issue), 30: 87–102.

LANE, P. J., and LUBATKIN, M. (1998). 'Relative Absorptive Capacity and Interorganizational Learning', *Strategic Management Journal*, 19: 461–77.

LARSON, A. (1992). 'Network Dyads in Entrepreneurial Settings: A Study of the Governance of Exchange Relationships', *Administrative Science Quarterly*, 37: 76–104.

LARSSON, R., BENGTSSON, L., HENRIKSSON, K., and SPARKS, J. (1998). 'The Interorganizational Learning Dilemma: Collective Knowledge Development in Strategic Alliances', *Organization Science*, 9: 285–305.

LORANGE, P. (1997). 'Black-Box Protection of Your Core Competencies in Strategic Alliances', in P. W. Beamish and J. P. Killing (eds.), *Cooperative Strategies: European Perspectives*. San Francisco: New Lexington Press, 59–73.

LORENZONI, G., and LIPPARINI, A. (1999). 'The Leveraging of Interfirm Relationships as a Distinctive Organizational Capability: A Longitudinal Study', *Strategic Management Journal*, 20: 317–38.

LUO, Y. (1997). 'Partner Selection and Venturing Success: The Case of Joint Ventures with Firms in the People's Republic of China', *Organization Science*, 8: 648–62.

LYLES, M. A., and SALK, J. E. (1996). 'Knowledge Acquisition from Foreign Parents in International Joint Ventures: An Empirical Examination in the Hungarian Context', *Journal of International Business Studies*, 27: 877–903.

MADHOK, A. (1995). 'Revisiting Multinational Firms' Tolerance for Joint Ventures: A Trust-Based Approach', *Journal of International Business Studies*, 26: 117–38.

—— (1997). 'Cost, Value, and Foreign Market Entry Mode: The Transaction and the Firm', *Strategic Management Journal*, 18: 39–61.

—— and TALLMAN, STEPHEN B. (1998). 'Resources, Transactions, and Rents: Managing Value Through Interfirm Collaborative Relationships', *Organization Science*, 9: 326–39.

MAKHIJA, M. V., and GANESH, U. (1997). 'The Relationship Between Control and Partner Learning in Learning-Related Joint Ventures', *Organization Science*, 5: 508–20.

MARTINEZ, J. I., and JARILLO, J. C. (1989). 'The Evolution of Research on Coordination Mechanisms', *Journal of International Business Studies*, 20: 489–514.

MAYER, R. C., DAVIS, J. H., and SCHOORMAN, F. D. (1995). 'An Integrative Model of Organizational Trust', *Academy of Management Review*, 20: 709–34.

MJOEN, H., and TALLMAN, S. (1997). 'Control and Performance in International Joint Ventures', *Organization Science*, 8: 257–74.

MODY, A. (1993). 'Learning Through Alliances', *Journal of Economic Behavior and Organizations*, 20: 151–70.

MOHR, J., and SPEKMAN, R. (1994). 'Characteristics of Partnership Success, Partnership Attributes, Communication Behavior, and Conflict Resolution Techniques', *Strategic Management Journal*, 15: 135–52.

MOWERY, D. C., OXLEY, J. E., and SILVERMAN, B. S. (1996). 'Strategic Alliances and Interfirm Knowledge Transfer', *Strategic Management Journal*, 17 (special issue, Winter): 77–92.

NOOTEBOOM, B., BERGER, H., and NOORDERHAVEN, N. G. (1997). 'Effects of Trust and Governance on Relational Risk', *Academy of Management Journal*, 40: 308–38.

OLIVER, C. (1990). 'Determinants of Interorganizational Relationships: Integration and Future Directions', *Academy of Management Review*, 15(2): 241–65.

OSBORN, R., and HAGEDOORN, J. (1997). 'The Institutionalization and Evolutionary Dynamics of Interorganizational Alliances and Network', *Academy of Management Journal*, 40: 261–78.

PAN, Y. (1996). 'Influences on Foreign Equity Ownership Level in Joint Ventures in China', *Journal of International Business Studies*, 27: 1–26.

PARK, S. H., and RUSSO, M. V. (1996). 'When Competition Eclipses Cooperation: An Event History of Joint Venture Failure', *Management Science*, 42: 875–90.

—— and UNGSON, G. R. (1997). 'The Effect of National Culture, Organizational Complementarity, and Economic Motivation on Joint Venture Dissolution', *Academy of Management Journal*, 40: 279–307.

PARKHE, A. (1991). 'Interfirm Diversity, Organizational Learning, and Longevity in Global Strategic Alliances', *Journal of International Business Studies*, 22: 579–602.

—— (1993). 'Strategic Alliance Structuring: A Game Theoretic and Transaction Cost Examination of Interfirm Cooperation', *Academy of Management Journal*, 36: 794–829.

PFEFFER, J. (1981). *Power In Organizations*. New York: Pitman.

—— and SALANCIK, G. R. (1978). *The External Control Of Organizations: A Resource Dependence Perspective*. New York: Harper & Row.

PORTER, M. E. (1990). *The Competitive Advantage of Nations*. New York: Free Press.

—— and FULLER, M. B. (1986). *Coalitions and Global Strategy*. In M. E. Porter (ed.), *Competition In Global Industries*. Boston, Mass.: Harvard Business School Press, 315–43.

POWELL, W. W. (1987). 'Hybrid Organizational Forms', *California Management Review*, 30, 1: 67–87

—— (1996). 'Trust-Based Forms of Governance', in R. M. Kramer and T. R. Tyler (eds.), *Trust In Organizations: Frontiers Of Theory And Research*. Thousand Oaks, Calif.: Sage, 51–67.

—— KOPUT, K. W., and SMITH-DOERR, L. (1996). 'Interorganizational Collaboration and the Locus of Innovation: Networks of Learning in Biotechnology', *Administrative Science Quarterly*, 41: 116–45.

PUCIK, V. (1991). 'Technology Transfer in Strategic Alliances: Competitive Collaboration and Organizational Learning', in T. Agmon and M. A. Von Glinow (eds.), *Technology Transfer in International Business*. New York: Oxford University Press, 121–38.

REICH, R. B., and MANKIN, E. D. (1986). 'Joint Ventures with Japan give away Our Future', *Harvard Business Review*, 64(2): 78–86.

ROBICHAUX, R. A., and COLEMAN, J. A. (1994). 'The Structure of Marketing Channel Relationships', *Journal of the Academy of Marketing Science*, 22(1): 38–51.

ROBINS, J. A. (1987). 'Organizational Economics: Notes on the Use of Transaction-Cost Theory in the Study of Organizations', *Administrative Science Quarterly*, 32: 68–86.

SALANCIK, G. R. (1977). 'Commitment and the Control of Organizational Behavior and Belief', in B. Staw and G. Salancik (eds.), *New Directions in Organizational Behavior*. Chicago: St Clair Press, 1–54.

SARKAR, M. B., CAVUSGIL, S. T., and AULAKH, P. S. (1999). 'International Expansion of Telecommunication Carriers: The Influence of Market Structure, Network Characteristics, and Entry Imperfections', *Journal of International Business Studies*, 30: 361–82.

SAXTON, T. (1997). 'The Effects of Partner and Relationship Characteristics on Alliance Outcomes', *Academy of Management Journal*, 40: 443–61.

SCHELLING, T. C. (1956). 'An Essay on Bargaining', *American Economic Review*, 46: 281–306.

SEABRIGHT, M. A., LEVINTHAL, D. A., and FICHMAN, M. (1992). 'Role of Individual Attachments in the Dissolution of Interorganizational Relationships', *Academy of Management Journal*, 35: 122–60.

SHENKAR, O., and ZEIRA, Y. (1992). 'Role Conflict and Role Ambiguity of Chief Executive Officers in International Joint Ventures', *Journal of International Business Studies*, 23: 55–75.

SIMONIN, B. L. (1997). 'The Importance of Collaborative Know-How: An Empirical Test of the Learning Organization', *Academy of Management Journal*, 40: 1150–74.

—— (1999). 'Ambiguity and the Process of Knowledge Transfer in Strategic Alliances', *Strategic Management Journal*, 20: 595–624.

SITKIN, S. B., and PABLO, A. L. (1992). 'Reconceptualizing the Determinants of Risk Behavior', *Academy of Management Review*, 17: 9–38.

SMITH, J. B., and BARCLAY, D. (1997). 'The Effects of Organizational Differences and Trust on the Effectiveness of Selling Partner Relationships', *Journal of Marketing*, 61 (January): 3–21.

SOHN, J. H. D. (1994). 'Social Knowledge as a Control System: A Proposition and Evidence from the Japanese FDI Behavior', *Journal of International Business Studies*, 25: 295–324.

TANNENBAUM, A. S. (1968). *Control In Organization*. New York: McGraw-Hill.

THOMPSON, J. D. (1967). *Organizations In Action*. New York: McGraw-Hill.

WILLIAMSON, O. E. (1975). *Markets and Hierarchies: Analysis and Antitrust Implications*. New York: Free Press.

—— (1981). 'The Economics of Organization: The Transaction Cost Approach', *American Journal of Sociology*, 87(3): 548–77.

YAN, A., and GRAY, B. (1994). 'Bargaining Power, Management Control, and Performance in United States–China Joint Ventures: A Comparative Case Study', *Academy of Management Journal*, 37: 1478–517.

—— (1998). 'Structural Stability and Reconfiguration of International Joint Ventures', *Journal of International Business Studies*, 29: 773–96.

# PART IV

## MANAGING THE MNE

CHAPTER 16

# INNOVATION AND INFORMATION TECHNOLOGY IN MNE

## JOHN CANTWELL

## 16.1 FROM THE TRANSFER OF 'HIGH TECHNOLOGY' PRODUCTS TO INNOVATION IN THE MNE

IN recent years there has been a steady expansion in the literature that relates the internationalization of production to the development and transfer of technology by multinational enterprises (MNEs). It is a literature that can be dated back at least to John Dunning's (1958) seminal study of the impact of US MNEs upon UK technology and productivity, and Ray Vernon's (1966) development of the product cycle model (PCM) as an explanation of the technological dynamism associated with the growth of US foreign direct investment (FDI) in Europe in the 1950s and 1960s. Most of the issues that have attracted increasingly detailed research attention since that time had been anticipated in at least outline form in these early studies (see Cantwell 1992, for a discussion of how Dunning's initial framework was elaborated upon in later research, and Cantwell 1999a, for an elaboration of how Dunning and Vernon each anticipated key aspects of the current perspective on innovation and the MNE). However, what is new in subsequent research is the greater focus upon the firm as a unit of analysis, and upon the theory of the firm or a theory of business, in place of the earlier focus upon the level of the country or the product.

Four lines of investigation suggested by Dunning and Vernon became the subject of extensive later research. First, the PCM offers one account of how paths of internationalization may be opened up through the technological creativity of firms in a centre of innovation (an account extended by Magee 1977, in terms of the technological development of an industry). Some later explanations of the co-evolution of FDI and technological development from the viewpoint of a wider range of countries, and from the perspective of inward as well as outward FDI, drew a link between the degree of technological sophistication of the FDI it attracts and to which it gives rise (Lall 1987; Ozawa 1992; Dunning and Narula 1996). Other work has paid attention to the paths followed by the internationalization of the process of technology creation itself, which is achieved in large firms through the internationalization of the research and development (R&D) function (see for example, Mansfield, Teece, and Romeo 1979; Lall 1979; Håkanson and Zander 1988; Kuemmerle 1999a; Pearce 1999). In one such study, Cantwell (1995) discusses the extent to which some of the original propositions of the PCM still hold good in the light of a wider set of historical and cross-country evidence on the internationalization of R&D.

Second, Dunning's (1958) book examined the technological impact on indigenous firms of the local presence of foreign-owned companies that enjoy technological superiority and possess higher levels of productivity, an approach he later extended from the UK to Europe as a whole (Dunning 1970). Many subsequent country studies have also looked at the technological effects on national economies of inward and outward FDI (see e.g. Dunning 1985). However, the greatest interest in the latest research has been over the local technological spillovers generated by foreign-owned firms (Kokko 1994; Perez 1997), and the localization of the knowledge sources of the foreign-owned affiliates themselves (Almeida 1996; Cantwell and Iammarino 2000). Allied to these efforts has been an increasing awareness of the importance of absorptive capacity on the part of recipient firms (Cohen and Levinthal 1989) as a necessary condition for beneficial spillovers to occur. The role of absorptive capacity has become clearer from empirical evidence on some of the difficulties of technology transfer between countries (Teece 1977; Zander 1999), and in technology-based alliances between firms (Mowery and Rosenberg 1989; Sachwald 1998).

Third, a crucial related theme in both Dunning's and Vernon's work was the association of FDI with technology gaps between countries, and how FDI may sometimes act (and sometimes not act) to narrow these gaps and permit 'catching up'. Dosi (1984) extended the framework for analysing technology gaps, while Cantwell (1989) showed how in the case of US FDI in Europe the local technological impact depended upon the extent of absorptive capacity in indigenous firms. It was when the local industry in a host European country had inherited a strong technological tradition from the past (such as in the case of the German chemical industry) that inward FDI precipitated an indigenous revival and a closing of the postwar technology gap with the US. Thus, technological change is a localized and context-specific process as argued by Nelson and Winter (1982), and some models of international technology transfer (such as that of Perez 1998, with some antecedents in Lapan and Bardhan 1973) have attempted to accommodate the implications of this insight. It is not only the possibility of favourable spillovers from MNE affiliates to indigenous firms that depends upon the existent level of local capabilities, but also the feasibility of licensing the technological knowledge of MNEs to local partners as opposed to developing and exploiting technology entirely internally within the MNE. Indeed, locally technologically creative FDI and inter-firm licensing are generally complements rather than substitutes, as emphasized in the latest literature (such as Kogut and Chang 1991; Sachwald 1998; or Cantwell, Iammarino, and Noonan 2000) on how MNE affiliates depend upon localized knowledge sources in their own local knowledge generation.

Indeed, the realization that FDI is both easiest to attract and has the most favourable effects the greater is the innovativeness of indigenous companies, has led to an increasing interest in corporate capabilities and in the firm as a level of analysis alongside the country or the product levels. Linked as well to the current understanding that innovation and imitation or adaptation are complementary parts of a common process rather than alternatives, attention has shifted from the MNE simply as an agent of technology transfer and towards the MNE as a technology creator across national boundaries. This fourth stream of ideas was also anticipated in the earliest research to some extent, which had supposed that FDI was based upon the technological leadership and creativity of MNEs, or what Dunning (1995) later termed their 'ownership advantages'. However, while the early question was 'why do technologically advantaged firms go abroad to exploit their advantage (and transfer their technology internally to be able to do so)?', with the rapid expansion of FDI in now-established MNEs and of FDI from a wider range of home countries the question became 'why do existing MNEs source technology creation internationally through an internal network of geographically dispersed affiliates?' (see also John Dunning's Chapter 2 in this volume on the shift in the theoretical focus of attention in the international business literature, and Julian Birkinshaw in Chapter 14 on the competence-creating role of affiliates). This has led to a greater interest in the competence-based theory of the firm in the analysis of the MNE (Cantwell 1991; Cantwell and Piscitello 2000), and in the role of inter-company alliances in the capability generation of partner MNEs (Chesnais 1988a; Hagedoorn and Narula 1996).

Behind the shift of attention away from technology transfer *per se* lies another shift in terms of how technology itself is defined and conceptualized. In the earliest research in accord with the conventional approach in economics, technology was defined narrowly as scientific and engineering knowledge and blueprints, which in large firms are principally the outcome of R&D. The transfer of this codified knowledge and blueprints across national boundaries (whether within the MNE or by licensing to other local companies) then constituted technology transfer. Instead, the tendency is now to think of technology in broader terms, as encompassing the corporate capability to operationalize and effectively use in production this knowledge. While innovation can be defined as the introduction of new products and processes, technology is the capability to efficiently sustain these processes that generate quality products. Indeed, the creation of technology in this broader sense relies upon the corporate capacity to absorb new knowledge as an input into further learning in production, and hence in the generation of new capabilities. From this perspective technology transfer is a misnomer. While codified knowledge and blueprints can be transferred, corporate technological capabilities cannot be transferred through market-like exchange. These capabilities must be internally learned, whether the process of learning is externally assisted or not. In the next section we examine the issue of how to define technology further, before returning in the third section to the relationship between FDI and the construction of corporate technological capabilities in the MNE, and in the fourth section to a further examination of intra- and inter-firm international networks for technological development. The fifth section extends the discussion to the role of information and communications technology (ICT) within such international MNE networks.

# 16.2 THE CONCEPTUALIZATION OF TECHNOLOGY

One reason why the narrow definition of technology as an engineering concept was so readily accepted in the literature on MNEs and innovation was that MNEs were regarded as being distinctive from other firms only for their role in international technology transfer or diffusion. Therefore, even writers whose interests extended beyond technology transfer to issues of innovation, generally began by considering innovation as it applied to all firms, before considering the particular contribution of MNEs as agents of technology diffusion (see, for example, Parker 1974). What is internationally diffused both between firms and within MNEs is principally scientific and engineering knowledge, and so it was natural to focus upon this. It is only quite recently that attention has shifted away from the MNE for its contribution to technology transfer, and towards the MNE as an institution for international technology creation and innovation (Chesnais 1988a). With an increasing intra-firm integration of affiliates since the late 1960s (Dunning 1992), MNEs have established international networks for combined cross-border technological development (Cantwell 1989). This involves a coordinated change in production structures, or in other words technological change in its broadest sense conducted at an international level.

By comparison with the traditional literature on MNEs and technology transfer, some new discussions of MNEs and innovatory activities have started to find it convenient to take a wider view of technology, even though the measurement of technology continues to rely on more restrictively defined proxies such as R&D expenditure or patent counts. The new approach to MNEs and innovation has drawn heavily on an evolutionary view of the firm and the industry (Nelson and Winter 1982), examining the accumulation of technology within the international networks of MNEs as a path-dependent corporate learning process (Cantwell 1989, 1991). Other representatives of this new evolutionary approach have focused on organizational change within the MNE as a learning process (Kogut 1990; Teece 1991). Successful learning establishes technological competence (Cantwell 1991) or organizational capabilities (Teece 1991). What is specific about MNEs in this respect is their use of international networks for innovation, which is one aspect of the recent growth of network organization in the MNE (Hedlund 1986; Bartlett and Ghoshal 1989). The new approach to MNEs and innovation also implies a different perspective on technology transfer, being concerned with its interaction with learning processes and not just with the immediate exchange of knowledge.

Under the new broader definition of technology as a system for production, two components of technology can be distinguished (Cantwell 1991, 1994). First is the potentially public knowledge element of technology, which encompasses codifiable items as represented in the engineering blueprints and designs and the scientific knowledge that constitute the narrower definition of technology, and to which can be added management manuals, handbooks describing organizational methods and the like in the new broader definition. However, even this first element of technology ranges somewhat beyond the underlying scientific and engineering (or management) principles that can be easily written down and (when they are novel) patented. The potentially public element of technology includes individual practitioners' knowledge of the way such scientific and engineering principles are applied, or in other words the way things work in practice (Nelson 1992). While this type of knowledge may be difficult or cumbersome to write down in full and needs to be individually learned through practice to be completely understood, it is possible to communicate such practical information between those that are already skilled in the art in question. Taken as a whole, this potentially public aspect of technology is therefore analogous to information, in that in principle it can be exchanged between knowledgeable scientists, engineers, and practitioners or managers. The term public knowledge is qualified here as being at least potentially public, since devices such as patents or secrecy may delay its actual entry into the public domain.

Unlike the first, the second element of technology is not akin to information but is tacit, and is specific to particular firms or MNEs. This tacit element of technology is embodied in the organizational routines and collective expertise or skills of specific production teams (Nelson and Winter 1982). This is the part of technology which differentiates firms or MNEs, and which cannot be exchanged between them as it is derived from and tied to the localized and collective learning experience of the teams of a given company through their own development of production. Hence, the new more comprehensive definition of technology incorporates that element which describes firm-specific competence in production. While the first element of technology may be traded between firms, the second element is the essence of firm-specific competitive advantage, which is non-tradable and relies instead on internal group learning processes (Cantwell 1991; Kogut and Zander 1993, 1995).

The two elements of technology are strictly complementary, and cannot be used to create a functioning production system without one another. Thus, even though potentially public knowledge can be exchanged, to make it operational it is necessary to develop some supporting expertise of a tacit kind. In doing so it is possible for one firm to imitate the tacit capability of another, but it can never copy it exactly since the learning experience of each firm and the route actually followed by a production team is unique. The precise course taken by any firm depends partly on chance but also upon its own past technological experience as encapsulated in its existing routines and team skills. Where inter-firm agreements for technological cooperation extend to technical assistance the costs of imitation may be reduced, but it is still necessary for each firm to go through its own particular learning process, with or without assistance.

The firm-specific character of the tacit element of technology is also likely to lead to a differentiation of the codifiable knowledge and designs that are actually used, and to lead to some potentially public knowledge remaining firm-specific for a time. This is obvious where there are major differences in the technological competence of firms. The nature and the range of scientific principles and engineering designs employed by General Electric and by a Latin American based MNE producing electrical goods are quite different, even where they are serving the same market. Yet there is also a differentiation of the blueprints and knowledge used by say, General Electric, Westinghouse, and Philips when serving the same market. The specific organizational routines of each company run in parallel to specialized knowledge in certain branches of science and engineering and to a particular set of codes devised to represent the designs in use in a style that is familiar to the members of its own production team. Thus, even the codifiable element of technology requires adaptation if it is exchanged between firms. Specific blueprints and the practical skills that accompany them sometimes appear to be technological advantages, partly because the blueprints can be patented, but more importantly because these designs and skills provide a reflection of a firm's tacit capacity, which is the true source of such competitive advantage.

Nelson (1982, 1992) has described the two complementary components of technology as its public and private elements. The public element of technology is an expression of generic knowledge, or of knowledge which is potentially generic in the sense that it is capable of being understood by suitably trained scientists, engineers, and practitioners or managers in other firms or other countries. All that is needed is some translation of the specific codes typically used to articulate the knowledge for the purposes of the company that originally developed and applied it. Summarizing information in a form in which it can be disseminated externally is sometimes undertaken by the firm itself, where it is involved in the exchange of knowledge or in a patent application. The first element of technology is a combination of actual and potential generic knowledge. It is a latent public good, in that once it has been created (and after allowing for the costs of adaptation to a general form) it can be made freely available to others.

# 16.3 INTERNATIONAL EXPANSION AND CORPORATE TECHNOLOGICAL ACCUMULATION IN MNES

The term 'technological accumulation' encapsulates the view that the development of technology within a firm is a cumulative process. That is, the creation of new technology is to be understood as a gradual and painstaking process of continual adjustment and refinement, as new productive methods are tested and adapted in the light of experience. In any firm, there is a continual interaction between the creation of technology and its use in production. For this reason, although a group of firms in a given industry are likely to have similar lines of technological development (similarities which may be increased through collaborative R&D projects, through drawing on the results of publicly funded research, and through imitation), the actual technological path of each is to some degree unique and differentiated. The acquisition of new skills, and the generation of new technological capacity, partially embodied in new plant and equipment, must be a goal of every firm in an oligopolistic industry, if it is to maintain and increase its profits. Even where new technology is acquired from outside the firm, it must be gradually adapted and integrated with its existing production methods.

The notion of technological accumulation is consistent with the ideas of Rosenberg (1976 and 1982), Usher (1929), and the earlier work of Marx on technological change through systematic adaptation. More recently, Atkinson and Stiglitz (1969), Nelson and Winter (1977), and Stiglitz (1987) have spoken of 'localized' technological change in the context of the previous technological evolution and learning experience of the firm.

While the product cycle theory supposed that an individual act of technology creation was then diffused abroad, in the technological accumulation approach the use of technology in new environments feeds back into fresh adaptation and (depending upon the state of local scientific and technical capability) new innovation. When production is located in an area that is itself a centre for innovation in the industry concerned, the firm may gain access to research facilities which allow it to extend technology creation in what are for it previously untried directions. In recent years technological accumulation has frequently been organized in international networks, or in other words integrated MNEs. At one time MNEs may have been simply the providers of technology and finance for scattered international production; today they have become global organizers of economic systems, including systems for allied technological development in different parts of the world.

The technological accumulation approach therefore addresses the question of why it is that technology is developed in international networks, rather than in a series of separately owned plants. Part of the answer is provided by internalization theory, which focuses on why MNEs as opposed to purely national firms have come into existence (Buckley and Casson 1976). That is, if the initiating firm is to appropriate a full return on its technological advantage, and if it is to coordinate the successful introduction of its new technology elsewhere, then it must exercise direct control over the network as a whole. However, this may be not so much a feature of the market for technological knowledge which is the focus of internalization theory, as a feature of the very nature of technological development itself (Kogut and Zander 1993, 1995). In the alternative evolutionary view, technological knowledge is not an immediately usable intermediate product in its own right, but is rather an input into the collective corporate learning process by which tacit capability and hence technology as a whole is generated. As such, it is an input that normally has its greatest relevance to the learning process of the firm that created it and set the problem-solving agenda to which it represents a response, and thus it is likely to be of the greatest value to the originating company (Cantwell 1991, 1994).

The different focus of attention in these two accounts may be understood in terms of two approaches to profits (Cantwell 1999*b*). The standard internalization approach addresses concerns over individual opportunism and rent-seeking behaviour in the context of conventional profit maximization, the objective being to find the organizational mode that minimizes the transaction costs associated with problems of this kind. In the evolutionary technological accumulation approach instead firms search for higher profits through innovation (Nelson and Winter 1982), and by generating new value-creating technological capabilities. From this perspective the firm's incentive to invest is a (usually positive) function of the intensity of technological competition, which implies that the industry-level interaction between firms regulates the investment behaviour of each company, rather than simply a set of internal transaction cost calculations under 'make or buy' alternatives. The key indicator of inter-company differences of potential for firm growth is the ability of each firm to generate tacit capability or corporate technological competence (Cantwell 1991). While this approach to comparative firm growth became established in the MNE field by around 1990 (Cantwell 1989 and 1991), it has since become very fashionable in the form of the competence-based theory of the firm in economics and the resource-based view of the firm in management strategy (e.g. Nelson 1991; Foss 1993; Teece, Pisano, and Shuen 1997; Hodgson 1998; Loasby 1998; Chandler, Hagström, and Sölvell 1998); just as Buckley and Casson's (1976) work on the MNE preceeded a wave of fascination with transaction cost economics from the 1980s onwards.

Suppose for a moment that the act of exchanging technological knowledge between firms does not present a problem, in that a reasonable price for such an exchange can always be readily agreed, such as in a framework of cross-licensing agreements. Now consider an international industry in which constituent firms produce more or less identical products for the same international markets. However, each firm has its own quite specific process technology, derived from a distinct technological tradition (say, different chemical processes with a similar end result). In this situation, if technological accumulation is continuous in each firm, raising its productivity or lowering its costs along a given line of technological development, then no existing firm would abandon its existing pattern of innovation and buy in all its technological knowledge from a competitor. It would be far more costly, and perhaps even infeasible, for an existing firm to switch into a completely new line of technological development, by comparison with the costs of the potential seller of technology simply extending its own network. It is because technology is differentiated across countries even within the same firm, but especially between different firms, that technology transfer is a costly process (as demonstrated by Teece 1977). Some exchanges of technological knowledge between existing firms will take place, since alternative lines of technological accumulation in the same industry are often complementary to one another, and so spillovers occur and may be facilitated through inter-company alliances in which knowledge is exchanged and occasionally jointly developed. However, where technological knowledge is bought in it must be adapted to the specific context of the firm's own tacit capability (the other necessary component of any operational technology) and then incorporated into an existing stream of innovation, and this adaptation becomes part and parcel of the on-going process within an established firm of generating its own technology.

In the case outlined, the retention of technology within each firm has little to do with any failure or malfunctioning of the market for technological knowledge, but everything to do with the close association between the generation and the utilization of a distinctive type of technology within each firm. By extending its own network, each firm extends the use of its own unique line of technological development, and by extending it into new environments it increases the complexity of this development. The expansion of international production thereby brings gains to the firms as a whole, as the experience gained from adapting its technology under new conditions feeds back new ideas for development to the rest of its system. For this reason, once they have achieved a sufficient level of technological strength in their own right, firms are particularly keen to produce in the locations from which their major international rivals have emanated, which offer them access to alternative sources of complementary innovation. This offers one explanation of the increase in intra-industry FDI in the industrialized countries (Cantwell 1989).

The notion that the geographical dispersion of technological development enhances innovation in the network of the MNE as a whole is founded on the belief that innovation is location-specific as well as firm-specific (Cantwell 1989). The scientific and technological traditions of each country, the shared experience of its researchers and production engineers and the communication between them across companies, the nature of its educational system, and its common business practices all contribute to the distinctiveness of the path of technology development undertaken in each location (Nelson 1993, 1995). By drawing on innovations of various kinds depending upon the conditions prevailing in the relevant local research centre MNEs develop a more complex technological system. The attractiveness of locations for other research-related investments may well be strengthened in the process. The involvement of foreign MNEs in research in centres of innovation has a direct effect on broadening the scope of local technological capability, and an indirect effect through its competitive stimulus encouraging other firms to extend their local research programmes. The process helps to establish locational poles of attraction for research-related activity. The increased role of locationally dispersed sourcing of technology from the major centres of excellence through the international networks of more globally integrated MNEs (Cantwell 1995) has led to a growing interest in the asset-acquiring motive for FDI (Cantwell 1989; Kogut and Chang 1991; Dunning 1992, 1995, 1996; Pugel, Kragas, and Kimura 1996; Cantwell and Janne 1999; Cantwell and Piscitello 2000), and in the greater decentralization in the management of international R&D to capture 'home-base augmenting' benefits (Pearce and Singh 1992; Papanastassiou and Pearce 1997; Pearce 1997, 1999; Kuemmerle 1999*a*, 1999*b*).

The technological accumulation approach suggests two major reasons why the growth in international production has been associated with sustained technological competition between MNEs in manufacturing industries. Firstly, internationalization has supported technological diversification since the form of technological development varies between locations as well as between firms (Zander 1997; Cantwell and Janne 1999; Cantwell and Piscitello 2000). By locating production in an alternative centre of innovation in its industry the MNE gains access to a new but complementary avenue of technological development, which it integrates with its existing lines. By increasing the overlap between the technological profile of firms competition between MNEs is raised in each international industry, but so also are cooperative agreements as the numbers of knowledge spillovers between firms increase as well. Spillovers occur where technological knowledge is created by a firm which lies outside its own major lines of development, but which may be of greater use within the main traditions of another firm.

Secondly, and partly because of the first factor, today there are a growing number of connections between technologies which were formerly quite separate. This greater technological interrelatedness has brought more firms, and especially MNEs, into competition with one another. These two elements have been associated with the growth of what are sometimes called 'technological systems' in MNEs. Where MNEs in a competitive international industry are all attracted to certain centres of innovation to maintain their overall strength, then research and research-related production may tend to agglomerate in these locations (Cantwell 1987). Closely allied to these arguments, a recent literature has examined the emergence of the multi-technology corporation to take advantage of increased technological

interrelatedness (Pavitt, Robson, and Townsend 1989; Granstrand and Sjölander 1990; Kodama 1992; Granstrand, Patel, and Pavitt 1997; Granstrand
1998; Piscitello 1998; Gambardella and Torrisi 1998; Cantwell and Fai 1999;
Cantwell and Santangelo 2000); and a rise in the number of technologically
motivated inter-firm alliances reflecting the need of companies to draw on a
more diversified knowledge base (Teece 1996; Loasby 1998; Mowery, Oxley,
and Silverman 1998; Sachwald 1998).

Inward FDI may have competitive or anti-competitive effects on host
country industries (Cantwell 1989). It has been argued that in modern international industries a competitive impact from MNE growth in one location
and an anti-competitive effect in another are two sides of the same coin
(Cantwell 1987). Where indigenous firms enjoy a strong technological tradition in the sector in question the growth of international production provides
a competitive stimulus which encourages an increase in local research-related
activity; while where such a tradition is weaker the research of local firms
may be displaced by simpler assembly types of production organized by
foreign MNEs. The faster growth and upgrading of activity in one location
is then achieved at the direct expense of the downgrading of another, as
different stages of production become geographically separated. The positive
case in which a field characterized by a stronger indigenous technological
tradition is more likely to be associated with beneficial knowledge and hence
productivity spillovers between foreign-owned and local companies has
recently attracted much attention (Blomström 1989; Kokko 1994; Kokko,
Tansini, and Zejan 1996; Perez 1997, 1998; Cantwell and Iammarino 1998,
2000).

# 16.4 INTRA- AND INTER-FIRM INTERNATIONAL NETWORKS FOR INNOVATION AND LEARNING

The increasing appreciation of the role of technological accumulation and
learning within the MNE has been facilitated by the recent trend for MNEs to
establish international networks to support this process. These networks are
of two kinds. First are the networks of international production and international R&D facilities organized within MNEs. Such networks are the logical
outcome of the shift by MNEs away from local market-oriented investments

towards internationally integrated strategies that began in the late 1960s (Hedlund 1986; Bartlett and Ghoshal 1989; Dunning 1992). An interactive international network of MNE affiliates replaces a system of satellites or miniature replicas. Second are the inter-firm networks in which MNEs increasingly participate. These include the growing number of strategic alliances between MNE competitors, and a greater variety of local networks that link MNE affiliates with their suppliers and customers. Although each of these networks has various purposes, perhaps the most prominent motive prompting MNEs to enter into them has been that joint learning processes are believed to be a means of raising the rate of innovation of the MNE, and hence its technological competitiveness.

The establishment of integrated internal networks of R&D and production within MNEs has helped to foster a growing interest in the internationalization of R&D, and a gradual change in the way in which the literature has viewed this phenomenon. The early literature on the internationalization of R&D (reviewed by Pearce 1989) tended to depict R&D as a centrally provided service within the firm, the location of which may be partially dispersed according to the strength of centripetal forces relative to the significance of centrifugal forces. In other words, the R&D requirements of individual affiliates by and large could be treated separately. The central R&D facilities of the firm would provide knowledge to all the affiliates, and whether particular affiliates had locally supporting R&D of their own depended (for example) on the size of their local market and on the extent of its differentiation from the home market. The extent of the need for local testing, the adaptation of products to local requirements, the use of locally available materials, and meeting local government regulations could then be assessed against the gains from economies of scale in the locational concentration of R&D.

Many of the early writings on international R&D were also aware that it may have a monitoring function, tapping into local skills and acquiring foreign knowledge, as is clear in the paper by Mansfield, Teece, and Romeo (1979), and was originally outlined by Dunning (1958). However, some early articles spoke of this as 'reverse technology transfer', the implication being that knowledge was essentially disseminated outwards from the centre of the MNE, with allowance for feedbacks from the recipient affiliates. The notion of an active interchange between parts of a MNE network has only been picked up more recently, as MNEs have adopted internationally integrated strategies in a number of industries (Granstrand 1979; Granstrand, Håkanson, and Sjölander 1992). One reason why this possibility was not noted previously is that much of the earlier work understated the significance of the internationalization of R&D, asserting that as a rule the bulk of R&D is centralized in the parent company. It now seems clear that the empirical basis for this contention was the relatively low share of R&D located abroad by US

MNEs. While US and Japanese MNEs incur less than 10 per cent of their total world R&D expenditure in foreign facilities, for the MNEs that emanate from all the more industrialized European countries the equivalent proportion is at least 10 per cent (Cantwell and Harding 1998).

For many European MNEs, R&D has been quite strongly internationally dispersed since at least the 1960s. For these firms it is an easier process to switch towards the establishment of international networks for knowledge generation. They have often, although not always, geared affiliate R&D towards the fields of local technological specialization as a means of accessing the most relevant new knowledge being created in other major centres (Cantwell and Hodson 1991).

With the shift towards international networks for technology creation, US and Japanese MNEs have begun to follow suit. For this purpose, American MNEs have been steadily increasing the internationalization of their R&D facilities. This has not been true of Japanese MNEs, in which the very rapid growth of R&D in Japan has outstripped the extension of their operations abroad. However, the R&D of Japanese MNEs located in the US and Europe has also been growing quite fast, and it seems that such Japanese-owned R&D has been especially aimed at tapping into the strongest areas of local expertise and skills (Kogut and Chang 1991; Mowery and Teece 1992; Graham 1992; Ozawa 1991, 1992). In other words, in the international R&D that Japanese MNEs have undertaken, technology acquisition has been a prominent and perhaps the most important motive.

In the formation of a network for technological learning and research the location of R&D may again be subject to forces that point to either centralization or decentralization. On the one hand, R&D is increasingly drawn to the major centres of excellence in which the best researchers and most skilled production teams are clustered. This tends to increase the locational concentration of R&D and its centralization in the home country centre *vis-à-vis* countries in which local technological capability is weak. On the other hand, as part of the same process some R&D projects may be moved out of the home country to important foreign centres better able to undertake them, which contributes to decentralization. To examine conflicting trends of this kind further it is necessary to move beyond the rather simple single dimensional measure that has dominated the literature in this area to date, namely the share of R&D located abroad. A more complex indicator of geographical dispersal is required, and the data that are now available (Casson 1991) make this feasible, although progress in this direction is only just beginning.

Among the issues to be addressed concerning the international location of R&D by MNEs, two strands of analysis can be discerned. First, there are scholars that are interested in the R&D function as such, and with the changing requirements for the management of international R&D in the

MNE (Håkanson 1990; De Meyer 1992; Pearce 1989; Casson, Pearce, and Singh 1991; Pearce, and Singh 1992). This has become an important area of investigation as MNEs increasingly integrate their international R&D networks, and as there is a continuing rise in the reliance of innovation on new scientific and engineering know-how, the potentially public knowledge component of technology. However, this line of enquiry examines only one aspect of the international creation of technology by MNEs, since as argued above technology is not reducible to the output of R&D facilities. Instead, the R&D function is one (particularly important) contributor to the learning process that characterizes innovation, and leads to the creation of new technology in the sense of new production systems.

The second type of analysis directs attention to the international networks of MNEs that support technological innovation as a whole, through the development of new production systems (Cantwell 1989, 1995; Teece 1986; Patel and Pavitt 1991). In this kind of study, evidence on the internationalization of R&D and knowledge creation or invention is typically used as a proxy measure rather than as a means of focusing on the R&D function as such. The R&D-intensity of production is a measure of the technological sophistication of activity in each location, while the specific types of knowledge being created reflect the fields in which tacit capability or competence has been especially accumulated (that is, they provide a measure of technological specialization).

Of course, basic R&D may be located away from tacit capability, feeding knowledge to more development-based R&D facilities in other production centres. This is one important reason for preferring patent statistics in place of data on R&D facilities when measuring the international location of inventions by MNEs from the perspective of the broader process of technological innovation. Patent statistics generally provide a better indication of the location of the development component of R&D which tends to be linked to local production, rather than the location of pure research. Hence, patent grants better measure the location of underlying technological capability or competence. Equally, they may be misleading with respect to the location of basic R&D facilities.

Even where MNEs establish networks in which technological activity is locationally specialized across the major centres this does not usually destroy the distinctiveness of their national origins. As stressed above, firms follow differentiated paths to learning even when their fields of research are similar. Hence the nature of their tacit capability is path-dependent, and reflects their starting point in nationally differentiated types of expertise (see, for example, Kogut 1987, 1990). Moreover, the home centre of the MNE normally continues to be the most important individual source of knowledge and capability, a theme that is emphasized by Patel and Pavitt (1991). While the international R&D of MNEs is certainly significant it is quite possible that by reinforcing locational specialization among the major centres it may sustain rather than erode national systems of innovation (Archibugi and Michie 1995).

Nonetheless, as MNEs have moved towards the construction of international networks so the number of overlaps in their areas of knowledge creation in a given industry have increased. Nationally specific but overlapping patterns of technological development have helped to promote international joint ventures (Mowery and Rosenberg 1989). In addition, technological relatedness has been rising such that formerly separate branches of technology have been increasingly brought together in recent innovations. An important element in this process has been described as a trend towards technology fusion (Kodama 1991, 1992). While it is true that, as argued previously, the knowledge created by a firm is usually of greatest value to itself given its own particular experience in production, it may still be of some value to other companies after allowing for the costs of converting it for use in a somewhat different setting. R&D projects also tend to create potential spinoffs that the firm itself decides not to pursue, but which are increasingly likely to be of interest to some other firms as the extent of technological overlaps rises.

The increasing scope for technological interchanges between MNEs has provided a greater incentive for companies not to restrict themselves to creating their own intra-firm international networks but also to join with other MNEs in inter-firm networks in selected areas of parallel lines of activity. There are now a growing number of such technology-based strategic alliances (Chesnais 1988a, 1988b; Hagedoorn and Schakenraad 1992; Gugler and Dunning 1992; Hagedoorn and Narula 1996). Their purpose is not only to extend the existing arrangements for information sharing between firms, by regulating for and promoting the mutual exchange of knowledge. The objective is also to organize collaborative efforts in joint ventures where the paths of learning being followed by the firms are complementary to one another (Mowery, Oxley, and Silverman 1998; Sachwald 1998; Cantwell and Colombo 2000). Joint ventures may be superior to cross-licensing agreements as a means of mutual assistance towards technology improvements where tacit capability is more complex and most important relative to the sharing of knowledge (Mowery and Rosenberg 1989). The production and research set up in these joint ventures thereby establish a common learning experience on which all partners to a venture can draw, in return for their own specific contribution. The need for such ventures is further evidence of the difficulty of technology transfer between firms, requiring close cooperation if the tacit capabilities of different MNEs are to be combined in some way. Of course, from the viewpoint of the R&D function as such a further reason for entering into alliances is to share the very high costs of some R&D projects.

## 16.5 THE ROLE OF INFORMATION TECHNOLOGY IN THE MODERN MNE

The increasing significance of technological interrelatedness and fusion is one aspect of what has been described as a new techno-economic paradigm (Freeman and Perez 1988). In this context a techno-economic paradigm is a system of scientific and productive activity based on a widespread cluster of innovations that represent a response to a related set of technological problems, relying on a common set of scientific principles and on similar organizational methods. The old paradigm was based on energy and oil-related technologies, and on mass production with its economies of scale and specialized corporate R&D. In recent years this has gradually been displaced by a new paradigm grounded on the economies of scope derived from the interaction between flexible but linked production facilities, and a greater diversity of search in R&D. Individual plant flexibility and network linkages both depend upon the new information and communication technologies.

Part of the reason for the increased extent of technological interactions within and between firms lies in the more sophisticated modern system of production as well in the more intensive linkages between science and technology in the current techno-economic paradigm, which relies on flexibility through computerization and diversity through new combinations drawing upon a wider range of disciplines. Firms increase the returns on their own R&D through suitably adapting their underlying tacit capability so that they can absorb and apply the complementary knowledge acquired from other locations or from other firms more intensively in their own internal learning process. This is especially pertinent for MNEs developing technology in more than one location, as potential opportunities for cross-border learning have been enhanced by an increased take-up of ICT technologies (Santangelo 1999). ICT specialization seems to amplify the firm's technological flexibility by enabling it to fuse together a wider range of formerly separate technologies. In this sense, in the current ICT-based paradigm government intervention is better geared towards the promotion of cross-firm and cross-border knowledge flows (presuming that firms follow the model of a continually interactive search for better methods and improved products, and hence a search for higher profits through experimental innovation); rather than to provisions to protect the monopolistic and separate exploitation of knowledge by those that have independently invested in its creation (which could be more easily represented through an underlying model of static profit maximization by firms through the exercise of market power) (Cantwell 1999b).

However, the creation of technology may be locationally concentrated or dispersed according to the degree of complexity embedded in it. Some kinds of technologies are geographically easily dispersed, whilst the uncodified character of others makes cross-border learning within and across organizations much more difficult. Thus, although multinationals have shown a greater internationalization of their R&D facilities recently, it depends upon the type of technological activity involved. The development of science-based fields of activity (e.g. ICT, biotechnology and new materials) and an industry's core technologies appear to require a greater intensity of face-to-face interaction (Cantwell and Santangelo 2000). Nonetheless, it may sometimes still be the case that science-based and firm- and industry-specific core technologies are dispersed internationally. The main factors driving the occasional geographical dispersion of the creation of these kinds of otherwise highly localized technologies are either locally embedded specialization which cannot be accessed elsewhere, or company-specific global strategies that utilize the development of an organizationally complex international network for technological learning (Cantwell and Santangelo 1999).

The more typical pattern of international specialization in innovative activity within the MNE is for the development of technologies that are core to the firm's industry to be concentrated at home, while other fields of technological activity may be located abroad, and in this sense the internationalization of research tends to be complementary to the home base. Thus, when science-based technology creation is internationally dispersed it is most often attributable to foreign technology acquisition by the firms of 'other' industries—for example, chemical industry MNEs developing electrical technologies abroad, or electrical equipment MNEs developing specialized chemical processes outside their home countries (Cantwell and Santangelo 1999, 2000).

Evidence has now emerged that the choice of foreign location for technological development in support of what is done in the home base of the MNE depends upon whether host regions within countries are either major centres for innovation or not (termed 'higher order' or 'lower order' regions by Cantwell and Iammarino 1998, 2000). Whereas most regions are not major centres and tend to be highly specialized in their profile of technological development, and hence attract foreign-owned activity in the same narrow range of fields; in the major centres much of the locally sited innovation of foreign-owned MNEs does not match very well the specific fields of local specialization, but is rather geared towards the development of technologies that are core to the current techno-economic paradigm (notably ICT) or earlier paradigms (notably mechanical technologies) (Cantwell, Iammarino, and Noonan 2000). The need to develop these latter technologies is shared by the firms of all industries, and the knowledge spillovers between MNEs and local firms in this case may be inter-industry in character. Thus, ICT development in centres of excellence is not the prerequisite of firms of the ICT industries, but instead involves the efforts of the MNEs of other industries in these common locations.

It may also be the case that the development of the capability to manage a geographically complex international network lies in a firm's specialization in ICT. The opportunities created for the fusion of formerly unrelated types of technology through ICT has made feasible new combinations of activities, the best centres of expertise for which may be geographically distant from one another. The enhanced expertise in ICT seems to provide a company with greater flexibility in the management of its geographically dispersed network, and an enhanced ability to combine distant learning processes in formerly separate activities. If this is the case for manufacturing companies in general, it is all the more true for electrical equipment and ICT specialist companies. Affiliate networks are increasingly used to source new technology. Accordingly, global learning has become an important mechanism for corporate technological renewal within MNEs.

The key importance of ICT to the now more complex management of innovation in MNEs is that it enables firms to better exploit their corporate technological diversification across national boundaries (Cantwell and Piscitello 2000), owing to the role of ICT as a means of combining fields of knowledge creation that were previously kept largely apart (or what Kodama 1992, terms technology fusion). However, while this use of ICT has led many smaller firms to extend the breadth of their technological diversification to create new combinations, in some of the very largest MNEs the extent of technological diversification has been reduced, so as to better focus on the most promising possible combinations from amongst the broader initial dispersion of innovative activity that such companies have inherited from the past (Cantwell and Santangelo 2000). Thus, we find some convergence in the average degree of technological diversification across large firms, including amongst others in the pharmaceutical industry (Cantwell and Bachmann 1998).

Freeman and Perez (1998) had argued that in the latest techno-economic paradigm ICT has become a 'carrier branch' or a 'transmission belt' for the transferral of innovation across sectors, analogous to the role played by the capital goods sector in the mechanization paradigm in the nineteenth century (Rosenberg 1976). Company evidence now suggests more than this that ICT has become also a core connector of potential fields of technological development within firms (or between firms in technology-based alliances) that facilitates the technological fusion of a formerly disparate spread of innovative activity. Thus, while in the past the machine-building industry simply passed knowledge of methods from one field of mechanical application to another, ICT potentially combines the variety of technological fields themselves and so increases the scope for wider innovation. Hence, innovation has become a still more central part of MNE development in the ICT age. To return to where we began, this role of ICT as a promoter of innovation within the MNE is a further key factor in the shift from the MNE as an institution for technology transfer between established activities frequently organized along miniature replica lines in different locations, and towards the MNE as a developer of international networks for technology creation, which combine formerly unconnected streams of innovation. Internationalization through the MNE and the corporate development and application of ICT have become intertwined in a new era of innovative capitalism.

## References

ALMEIDA, P. (1996). 'Knowledge Sourcing by Foreign Multinationals: Patent Citation Analysis in the US Semiconductor Industry', *Strategic Management Journal*, 17/ Winter: 155–65.

ARCHIBUGI, D., and MICHIE, J. (1995). 'The Globalisation of Technology: A New Taxonomy', *Cambridge Journal of Economics*, 19/1: 121–40.

ATKINSON, A. B., and STIGLITZ, J. E. (1969). 'A New View of Technological Change', *The Economic Journal*, 79/3: 573–78.

BARTLETT, C. A., and GHOSHAL, S. (1989). *Managing Across Borders: The Transnational Solution*. Boston, Mass.: Harvard Business School Press.

BLOMSTRÖM, M. (1989). *Foreign Investment and Spillovers: A Study of Technology Transfer to Mexico*. London: Routledge.

BUCKLEY, P. J., and CASSON, M. C. (1976). *The Future of the Multinational Enterprise*. London: Macmillan.

CANTWELL, J. A. (1987). 'The Reorganisation of European Industries after Integration: Selected Evidence on the Role of Multinational Enterprise Activities', *Journal of Common Market Studies*, 26/2: 127–51.

—— (1989). *Technological Innovation and Multinational Corporations*. Oxford: Basil Blackwell.

—— (1991). 'The Theory of Technological Competence and its Application to International Production', in D. G. McFetridge (ed.), *Foreign Investment, Technology and Economic Growth*. Calgary: University of Calgary Press.

—— (1992). 'Innovation and Technological Competitiveness', in P. J. Buckley and M. C. Casson (eds.), *Multinational Enterprises in the World Economy: Essays in Honour of John Dunning*. Aldershot: Edward Elgar.

—— (1994). 'Introduction', in J. A. Cantwell (ed.), *Transnational Corporations and Innovatory Activities*. London: Routledge.

—— (1995). 'The Globalisation of Technology: What Remains of the Product Cycle Model?', *Cambridge Journal of Economics*, 19/1: 155–74.

—— (1999a). 'From the Early Internationalization of Corporate Technology to Global Technology Sourcing', *Transnational Corporations*, 8/2: 71–92.

—— (1999b). 'Innovation as the Principal Source of Growth in the Global Economy', in D. Archibugi, J. Howells, and J. Michie (eds.), *Innovation Policy in a Global Economy*. Cambridge: Cambridge University Press.

——and Bachmann, A. (1998). 'Changing Patterns in Technological Leadership: Evidence from the Pharmaceutical Industry', *International Journal of Technology Management*, 21/1: 45–77.

——and Colombo, M. G. (2000). 'Technological and Output Complementarities, and Inter-firm Cooperation in Information Technology Ventures', *Journal of Management and Governance*, 4 (1–2).

——and Fai, F. M. (1999). 'The Changing Nature of Corporate Technological Diversification and the Importance of Organisational Capability', in S. Dow and P. Earl, (eds.), *Contingency, Complexity and the Theory of the Firm: Essays in Honour of Brian J. Loasby*. Cheltenham: Edward Elgar.

——and Harding, R. (1998). 'The Internationalisation of German Companies' R&D', *National Institute Economic Review*, 163/Jan.: 99–115.

——and Hodson, C. (1991). 'Global R&D and UK Competitiveness', in M. C. Casson, (ed.), *Global Research Strategy and International Competitiveness*. Oxford: Basil Blackwell.

——and Iammarino, S. (1998). 'MNCs, Technological Innovation and Regional Systems in the EU: Some Evidence in the Italian Case', *International Journal of the Economics of Business*, 5/3: 383–408.

————(2000). 'Multinational Corporations and the Location of Technological Innovation in the UK Regions', *Regional Studies*, 34/3: 317–32.

————and Noonan, C. (2000). 'Sticky Places in Slippery Space: The Location of Innovation by MNCs in the European Regions', in N. Pain (ed.), *Inward Investment, Technological Change and Growth*. London: Macmillan.

——and Janne, O. E. M. (1999). 'Technological Globalisation and Innovative Centres: The Role of Corporate Technological Leadership and Locational Hierarchy', *Research Policy*, 28/2–3: 119–44.

——and Piscitello, L. (2000). 'Accumulating Technological Competence: Its Changing Impact on Corporate Diversification and Internationalisation', *Industrial and Corporate Change*, 9/1: 21–51.

——and Santangelo, G. D. (1999). 'The Frontier of International Technology Networks: Sourcing Abroad the Most Highly Tacit Capabilities', *Information Economics and Policy*, 11/1: 101–23.

————(2000). 'Capitalism, Innovation and Profits in the New Techno-economic Paradigm', *Journal of Evolutionary Economics*, 10/1–2: 131–57.

Casson, M. C. (ed.) (1991). *Global Research Strategy and International Competitiveness*. Oxford: Basil Blackwell.

——Pearce, R. D., and Singh, S. A. (1991). 'A Review of Recent Trends', in M. C. Casson (ed.), *Global Research Strategy and International Competitiveness*. Oxford: Basil Blackwell.

Chandler, A. D., Hagström, P., and Sölvell, Ö (eds.) (1998). *The Dynamic Firm: The Role of Technology, Strategy, Organization, and Regions*. Oxford: Oxford University Press.

Chesnais, F. (1988a). 'Multinational Enterprises and the International Diffusion of Technology', in G. Dosi, C. Freeman, R. R. Nelson, G. Silverberg, and L. L. G. Soete (eds.), *Technical Change and Economic Theory*. London: Frances Pinter.

CHESNAIS, F. (*cont.*) (1988*b*). 'Technical Cooperation Agreements Between Firms', *STI Review*, 4: 51–119.

COHEN, W. M., and LEVINTHAL, D. A. (1989). 'Innovation and Learning: The Two Faces of R&D', *Economic Journal*, 99/Sep.: 569–96.

DE MEYER, A. (1992). 'Management of International R&D Operations', in O. Granstrand, L. Håkanson, and S. Sjölander (eds.), *Technology Management and International Business: Internationalisation of R&D and Technology*. Chichester: John Wiley.

DOSI, G. (1984). *Technical Change and Industrial Transformation: The Theory and an Application to the Semiconductor Industry*. London: Macmillan.

DUNNING, J. H. (1958). *American Investment in British Manufacturing Industry*. London: Allen & Unwin.

—— (1970). *Studies in International Investment*. London: Allen & Unwin.

—— (ed.) (1985). *Multinational Enterprises, Economic Structure and International Competitiveness*. Chichester: John Wiley.

—— (1992). *Multinational Enterprises and the Global Economy*. Wokingham: Addison-Wesley.

—— (1995). 'Reappraising the Eclectic Paradigm in an Age of Alliance Capitalism', *Journal of International Business Studies*, 26/3: 461–91.

—— (1996). 'The Geographical Sources of the Competitiveness of Firms: Some Results of a New Survey', *Transnational Corporations*, 5/3: 1–29.

—— and NARULA, R. (1996). 'The Investment Development Path Revisited: Some Emerging Issues', in J. H. Dunning and R. Narula (eds.), *Foreign Direct Investment and Governments: Catalysts for Economic Restructuring*. London: Routledge.

FOSS, N. J. (1993). 'The Theory of the Firm: Contractual and Competence Perspectives', *Journal of Evolutionary Economics*, 3/2: 127–44.

FREEMAN, C., and PEREZ, C. (1988). 'Structural Crises of Adjustment, Business Cycles and Investment Behaviour', in G. Dosi, C. Freeman, R. R. Nelson, G. Silverberg, and L. L. G. Soete (eds.), *Technical Change and Economic Theory*. London: Frances Pinter.

GAMBARDELLA, A., and TORRISI, S. (1998). 'Does Technological Convergence Imply Convergence in Markets?: Evidence from the Electronic Industry', *Research Policy*, 27/5: 445–64.

GRAHAM, E. M. (1992). 'Japanese Control of R&D Activities in the United States: Is This a Cause for Concern?', in T. S. Arrison, C. F. Bergsten, E. M. Graham, and M. C. Harris (eds.), *Japan's Growing Technological Capability: Implications for the US Economy*. Washington, DC: National Academy Press.

GRANSTRAND, O. (1979). *Technology Management and Markets: An Investigation of R&D and Innovation in Industrial Organisation*. Göteborg: Svenska Kulturkompaniet.

—— (1998). 'Towards a Theory of the Technology-based Firm', *Research Policy*, 27/5: 465–90.

—— HÅKANSON, L., and SJÖLANDER, S. (eds.) (1992). *Technology Management and International Business: Internationalisation of R&D and Technology*. Chichester: John Wiley.

——Patel, P., and Pavitt, K. L. R. (1997). 'Multi-technology Corporations: Why They Have "Distributed" Rather Than "Distinctive Core" Competencies', *California Management Review*, 39/4: 8–25.

——and Sjölander, S. (1990). 'Managing Innovation in Multi-technology Corporations', *Research Policy*, 19/1: 35–60.

Gugler, P., and Dunning, J. H. (1992). 'Technology Based Cross-border Alliances', mimeo, Rutgers University.

Hagedoorn, J., and Narula, R. (1996). 'Choosing Organizational Modes of Strategic Technology Partnering: International and Sectoral Differences', *Journal of International Business Studies*, 27/2: 265–84.

——and Schakenraad, J. (1992). 'Leading Companies and Networks of Strategic Alliances in Information Technologies', *Research Policy*, 21: 163–90.

Håkanson, L. (1990). 'International Decentralisation of R&D: The Organisational Challenges', in C. A. Bartlett, Y. Doz, and G. Hedlund (eds.), *Managing the Global Firm*. London: Routledge.

Håkanson, L., and Zander, U. (1988). 'International Management of R&D: The Swedish Experience', *R&D Management*, 18/3: 217–26.

Hedlund, G. (1986). 'The Hypermodern MNC: A Heterarchy?', *Human Resource Management*, 25/Spring: 9–25.

Hodgson, G. M. (1998). 'Competence and Contract in the Theory of the Firm', *Journal of Economic Behavior and Organization*, 35/2: 179–202.

Kodama, F. (1991). *Analysing Japanese High Technologies: The Techno-Paradigm Shift*. London: Frances Pinter.

——(1992). 'Technology Fusion and the New R&D', *Harvard Business Review*, July–Aug.: 70–8.

Kogut, B. (1987). 'Country Patterns in International Competition: Appropriability and Oligopolistic Agreement', in N. Hood and J.-E. Vahlne (eds.), *Strategies in Global Competition*. London: Croom Helm.

——(1990). 'The Permeability of Borders and the Speed of Learning Among Countries', in J. H. Dunning, B. Kogut, and M. Blomström, *Globalization of Firms and the Competitiveness of Nations*. Lund: Lund University Press.

——and Chang, S. J. (1991). 'Technological Capabilities and Japanese Foreign Direct Investment in the United States', *Review of Economics and Statistics*, 73: 401–13.

——and Zander, U. (1993). 'Knowledge of the Firm and the Evolutionary Theory of the Multinational Corporation', *Journal of International Business Studies*, 24/4: 625–45.

————(1995). 'Knowledge, Market Failure and the Multinational Enterprise: A Reply', *Journal of International Business Studies*, 26/2: 417–26.

Kokko, A. (1994). 'Technology, Market Characteristics and Spillovers', *Journal of Development Economics*, 43: 279–293.

——Tansini, R., and Zejan, M. C. (1996). 'Local Technological Capability and Productivity Spillovers from FDI in the Uruguayan Manufacturing Sector', *Journal of Development Studies*, 32/4: 602–11.

Kuemmerle, W. (1999a). 'The Drivers of Foreign Direct Investment into Research and Development: An Empirical Investigation', *Journal of International Business Studies*, 30/1: 1–24.

KUEMMERLE, W. (*cont.*) (1999*b*). 'Foreign Direct Investment in Industrial Research in the Pharmaceutical and Electronic Industries: Results from a Survey of Multinational Firms', *Research Policy*, 28/2–3: 179–93.

LALL, S. (1979). 'The International Allocation of Research Activity by US Multinationals', *Oxford Bulletin of Economics and Statistics*, 41/4: 313–31.

—— (1987). 'Multinationals and Technology Development in Host LDCs', in J. H. Dunning and M. Usui (eds.), *Structural Change, Economic Interdependence and World Development: Proceedings of the Seventh World Congress of the International Economic Association, Vol. 4: Economic Interdependence*. London: Macmillan.

LAPAN, H., and BARDHAN, P. (1973). 'Localized Technical Progress and Transfer of Technology and Economic Development', *Journal of Economic Theory*, 6: 585–95.

LOASBY, B. J. (1998). 'The Organisation of Capabilities', *Journal of Economic Behavior and Organization*, 35/2: 139–60.

MAGEE, S. P. (1977). 'Multinational Corporations, the Industry Technology Cycle and Development', *Journal of World Trade Law*, 11: 297–321.

MANSFIELD, E., TEECE, D. J., and ROMEO, A. (1979). 'Overseas Research and Development by US Based Firms', *Economica*, 46: 187–96.

MOWERY, D. C., OXLEY, J. E., and SILVERMAN, B. S. (1998). 'Technological Overlap and Interfirm Cooperation: Implications for the Resource-based View of the Firm', *Research Policy*, 27/5: 507–24.

—— and ROSENBERG, N. (1989). *Technology and the Pursuit of Economic Growth*. Cambridge: Cambridge University Press.

—— and TEECE, D. J. (1992). 'The Changing Place of Japan in the Global Scientific and Technological Enterprise', in T. S. Arrison, C. F. Bergsten, E. M. Graham, and M. C. Harris (eds.), *Japan's Growing Technological Capability: Implications for the US Economy*. Washington, DC: National Academy Press.

NELSON, R. R. (1982). 'The Role of Knowledge in R&D Efficiency', *Quarterly Journal of Economics*, 96: 453–70.

—— (1991). 'Why Do Firms Differ, and How Does it Matter?', *Strategic Management Journal*, 12/1: 61–74.

—— (1992). 'What is "Commercial" and What is "Public" About Technology, and What Should Be?', in N. Rosenberg, R. Landau, and D. C. Mowery (eds.), *Technology and the Wealth of Nations*. Stanford: Stanford University Press.

—— (ed.) (1993). *National Innovation Systems: A Comparative Analysis*. Oxford: Oxford University Press.

—— (1995). 'Co-evolution of Industry Structure, Technology and Supporting Institutions, and the Making of Comparative Advantage', *International Journal of the Economics of Business*, 2/2: 171–84.

—— and WINTER, S. G. (1977). 'In Search of a Useful Theory of Innovation', *Research Policy*, 5/1: 36–76.

—— and WINTER, S. G. (1982). *An Evolutionary Theory of Economic Change*. Cambridge, Mass.: Harvard University Press.

OZAWA, T. (1991). 'Japan in a New Phase of Multinationalism and Industrial Upgrading: Functional Integration of Trade, Growth and FDI', *Journal of World Trade*, 25/1: 43–60.

—— (1992). 'Foreign Direct Investment and Economic Development', *Transnational Corporations*, 1/1: 27–54.

PAPANASTASSIOU, M., and PEARCE, R. D. (1997). 'Technology Sourcing and the Strategic Roles of Manufacturing Subsidiaries in the UK: Local Competences and Global Competitiveness', *Management International Review*, 37/1: 5–25.

PARKER, J. E. S. (1974). *The Economics of Innovation: The National and International Enterprise in Technological Change*. London: Longman.

PATEL, P., and PAVITT, K. L. R. (1991). 'Large Firms in the Production of the World's Technology: An Important Case of "non-globalisation"', *Journal of International Business Studies*, 22: 1–21.

PAVITT, K. L. R., ROBSON, M., and TOWNSEND, J. (1989). 'Technological Accumulation, Diversification and Organisation in UK Companies, 1945–1983', *Management Science*, 35/1: 81–99.

PEARCE, R. D. (1989). *The Internationalisation of Research and Development by Multinational Enterprises*. London: Macmillan.

—— (1997). *Global Competition and Technology: Essays in the Creation and Application of Knowledge by Multinationals*. London: Macmillan.

—— (1999). 'Decentralised R&D and Strategic Competitiveness: Globalised Approaches to Generation and Use of Technology in Multinational Enterprises (MNEs)', *Research Policy*, 28/2–3: 157–78.

—— and SINGH, S. (1992). *Globalising Research and Development*. London: Macmillan.

PEREZ, T. (1997). 'Multinational Enterprises and Technological Spillovers: An Evolutionary Model', *Journal of Evolutionary Economics*, 7/2: 169–92.

—— (1998). *Multinational Enterprises and Technological Spillovers*. Chur: Harwood.

PISCITELLO, L. (1998). 'Corporate Diversification, Coherence, and the Dialectic Relationship between Technological and Product Competencies', Ph.D. thesis, Politecnico di Milano.

PUGEL, T. A., KRAGAS, E. S., and KIMURA, Y. (1996). 'Further Evidence on Japanese Direct Investment in US Manufacturing', *Review of Economics and Statistics*, 78: 208–13.

ROSENBERG, N. (1976). *Perspectives on Technology*. Cambridge: Cambridge University Press.

—— (1982). *Inside the Black Box : Technology and Economics*. Cambridge: Cambridge University Press.

SACHWALD, F. (1998). 'Cooperative Agreements and the Theory of the Firm: Focusing on Barriers to Change', *Journal of Economic Behavior and Organization*, 35/2: 203–28.

SANTANGELO, G. D. (1999). 'Multi-Technology, Multinational Corporations in a New Socio-Economic Paradigm based on Information and Communications Technology (ICT): The European ICT Industry', Ph.D. thesis, University of Reading.

STIGLITZ, J. E. (1987). 'Learning to Learn, Localised Learning and Technological Progress', in P. Dasgupta and P. Stoneman (eds.), *Economic Policy and Technological Performance*. Cambridge: Cambridge University Press.

TEECE, D. J. (1977). 'Technology Transfer by Multinational Firms: The Resource Costs of Transferring Technological Know-how', *Economic Journal*, 87/2: 242–61.

TEECE, D. J. (*cont.*) (1986). 'Profiting from Technological Innovation: Implications for Integration, Collaboration, Licensing and Public Policy', *Research Policy*, 15: 285–305.

—— (1991). 'Reconceptualising the Corporation and Competition', in G. R. Faulhaber and G. Tamburini (eds.), *European Economic Integration: The Role of Technology*. Boston, Mass.: Kluwer.

—— (1996). 'Firm Organisation, Industrial Structure and Technological Innovation', *Journal of Economic Behavior and Organization*, 31/2: 193–224.

—— PISANO, G., and SHUEN, A. (1997). 'Dynamic Capabilities and Strategic Management', *Strategic Management Journal*, 18/7: 537–56.

USHER, A. P. (1929). *A History of Mechanical Inventions*. Cambridge, Mass.: Harvard University Press.

VERNON, R. (1966). 'International Investment and International Trade in the Product Cycle', *Quarterly Journal of Economics*, 80/2: 190–207.

ZANDER, I. (1997). 'Technological Diversification in the Multinational Corporation: Historical Evolution and Future Prospects', *Research Policy*, 26/2: 209–28.

—— (1999). 'How Do You Mean "Global"? An Empirical Investigation of Innovation Networks in the Multinational Corporation', *Research Policy*, 28/2–3: 195–213.

CHAPTER 17

···········································································

# CONTEMPORARY RESEARCH TRENDS IN INTERNATIONAL MARKETING: THE 1990s

···········································································

## MASAAKI KOTABE

INTERNATIONAL marketing underwent fundamental changes over the last two decades. Global, political, and economic liberalization trends created tremendous business opportunities and challenges for international marketers. The opening up of new markets in Eastern Europe and a tendency toward economic liberalization in the developing world have spawned new business opportunities. Similarly, the emergence of regional trading blocs in the form of the EU (European Union), the NAFTA (North American Free Trade Agreement), and MERCOSUR (Mercado Común del Sur) have necessitated reorganization in the production and marketing strategies of

The author acknowledges Shruti Gupta for providing research assistance during this project.

firms. The changes in strategy include serving different markets from one production source or the shifting of production facilities for greater efficiency.

At the same time, the Asian financial crisis in the latter half of the 1990s provided a significant reality check on the wisdom of globally integrated strategy development. Wildly fluctuating exchange rates make it difficult for multinational companies to manage globally integrated but geographically scattered activities. Indeed, many companies are scurrying to speed steps toward making their procurement, manufacturing, and marketing operations in Asian countries more local. Japanese companies seem to be one step ahead of US and European competitors in this localization strategy. Since the yen's sharp appreciation in the mid-1980s, Japanese manufacturers have moved to build an international production system less vulnerable to currency fluctuations by investing in local procurement and local marketing (*Nikkei Weekly* 1998).

Two fundamental counteracting forces have always shaped the nature of marketing in the international arena over the years. The same counteracting forces have been revisited by many authors in such terms as 'standardization vs. adaptation' (1970s), 'globalization vs. localization' (1980s), and 'global integration vs. local responsiveness' (1990s). Terms have changed, but the quintessence of the strategic dilemma that multinational firms face today has not changed and will probably remain unchanged for years to come. However, they are no longer an either/or dichotomous issue. Forward-looking, proactive firms have the ability and willingness as well as the necessity to strive to accomplish both tasks simultaneously.

The importance of these changes is reflected in the development of new research streams in international marketing (Li and Cavusgil 1991; Douglas and Craig 1992; Aulakh and Kotabe 1993; Pieters *et al.* 1999), those of market globalization (Levitt 1983; Douglas and Wind 1987; Jain 1989; Firat 1997), and collaborative business arrangements (including strategic alliances) (Thorelli 1986; Harrigan 1988; Contractor 1990; Beamish and Killing 1997).

These trends have imparted added importance to research in international marketing, but it is not clear how research in the field has coped with this broadened responsibility in a fast-changing environment. Past reviews of international marketing research (Boddewyn 1981; Bilkey and Nes 1982; Albaum and Peterson 1984; Bradley 1987; Aulakh and Kotabe 1993) highlighted deficiencies of the discipline in two aspects: that international marketing research was fragmentary and exploratory without a strong theoretical framework, and that it lacked the methodological rigor compared to the generic (or domestic) research in marketing. While the first deficiency in international marketing research was attributed to the opportunistic nature (Albaum and Peterson 1984) and lack of synthesis (Bradley 1987) of international marketing research, the latter was attributed to the inherent difficulties encountered in research involving more than one country (Aulakh and Kotabe 1993). Difficulties stemmed from financial constraints in data collection, problems of data comparability in cross-cultural research and the implementation of methodological techniques in foreign markets. There have been various attempts to address the problems encountered in international marketing research (e.g. Craig and Douglas 2000).

We examine the state of the art in research in international marketing in the 1990–9 period, with particular emphasis on the conceptual framework and theory development in the field. This decade is deliberate as it provides a fairly broad time frame to probe any significant changes in the field, both in terms of the substance of research and methodologies used, and to see to what extent these two fundamental concerns raised in the 1980s have been addressed. Thus the study takes stock of research in international marketing to see if the discipline has overcome the deficiencies outlined in the previous review articles.

Earlier review articles (e.g. Li and Cavusgil 1991; Cavusgil and Li 1992; Douglas and Craig 1992; Aulakh and Kotabe 1993) classified the research streams fairly broadly, encompassing macro-environment issues to marketing management to consumer behavior. To make this decade-long review of the international marketing literature comparable to those of the 1980s, the literature classification employed in Douglas and Craig (1992) is also employed here.

# 17.1 ADVANCES IN INTERNATIONAL MARKETING (1990–9)

This chapter reviews both macro- and micro-environmental topics in international marketing. Research for this review spanned more than 200 articles in the journals from marketing and other related business areas that are listed on the ProQuest database. A list of journals represented in this survey is provided in the Appendix at the end of this chapter. Although the list is not comprehensive, it covers sufficiently the domain of research international marketing. A large majority of articles published in the 1990s deal specifically with issues related to marketing management rather than macro-environments that affect marketing management practices.

## 17.1.1 The macro-context

The macro-environmental context in which the issues of area studies, consumerism in society, and institutional infrastructure are addressed is not examined in detail here. It is due primarily to the lack of substantial and specific research addressing those macro-environmental issues in the 1990s. As can be seen from the rest of this chapter, research focus in the 1990s was predominantly on international marketing strategy issues. However, the discussion on the micro-environmental issues familiarizes the reader with the countries or regions that have captured the attention of the researchers in the area of international marketing. No articles were identified on the issue of consumerism in society. As for the issue of institutional infrastructure, the discussion centered around international retailing, with just two articles cited in the review spanning ten years. Those two articles are summarized here as follows:

The standardization/differentiation debate is discussed in the context of the international retail sector and the contribution that such factors as consumer homogeneity and the creation of trading blocs make to this debate is explored (Segal-Horn and Davison 1992). It is suggested that retail companies can derive economies from sourcing, distribution, and many aspects of marketing, both within and across trading blocs. The need for definitional clarity of retail internationalization is advanced which provides the basis for internationalization in order to understand fully the extent and degree of standardization that can take place within the international retail context (Brown and Burt 1992).

## 17.1.2 The micro-context

The micro-context of research in international marketing constitutes the bulk of research conducted in the field. Although there is no single best way to arrange various topics, they are arranged as follows. First, we examine research in both organizational and personal consumer behavior as it represents the initial interfaces between firms and customers. In particular, the effect of country of origin in consumer behavior received a significant amount of research attention. Second, research in various modes of entry and their performance implications is examined. Third, the literature on the marketing mix strategy is highlighted as it constitutes the crux of marketing. Fourth, research in global strategy and strategic alliances is covered. Both marketing and strategy researchers generally share common research interest in these strategy-related issues. Researchers in marketing tend to be more interested in

## Table 17.1 A mapping of the topics covered under the micro-context

| | |
|---|---|
| 1. Organizational and consumer behavior | 1.1 Organizational buying behavior |
| | 1.2 International negotiations |
| | 1.3 Consumer behavior |
| | 1.4 Country of origin (COO) |
| 2. Market entry decisions | 2.1 Initial mode of entry |
| | 2.2 Specific modes of entry |
| |     2.2.1 Exporting |
| |     2.2.2 Joint ventures |
| 3. Local market expansion: marketing mix decisions | 3.1 Global standardization vs. local responsiveness |
| | 3.2 Marketing mix |
| |     3.2.1 Product policy |
| |     3.2.2 Advertising |
| |     3.2.3 Pricing |
| |     3.2.4 Distribution |
| 4. Global strategy | 4.1 Competitive strategy |
| |     4.1.1 Conceptual development |
| |     4.1.2 Competitive advantage versus competitive positioning |
| |     4.1.3 Sources of competitive advantage and performance implications |
| | 4.2 Strategic alliances |
| |     4.2.1 Learning and trust |
| |     4.2.2 Recipes for alliance success |
| |     4.2.3 Performance for different types of alliances |
| | 4.3 Global sourcing |
| |     4.3.1 Global sourcing in a service context |
| |     4.3.2 Benefits of global sourcing |
| |     4.3.3 Country of origin issues in global sourcing |
| | 4.4 Multinational performance |
| |     4.4.1 Determinants of performance |
| |     4.4.2 A different interpretation of performance |

| Table 17.1 *Continued* | |
| --- | --- |
| 5.  Analytical techniques in cross-national research | 5.1 Measurement issues<br>5.2 Reliability and validity issues |

market performance implications of global strategy and strategic alliances, while strategy researchers seem to place more emphasis on theoretical reasoning for those strategies. Fifth, we review research methodologies examined in the literature. A mapping of the topics covered under the micro-context is summarized in Table 17. 1.

# 17.2 ORGANIZATIONAL AND CONSUMER BEHAVIOR

## 17.2.1 Organizational buying behavior

Only one article was cited in this area. A study of organizational buyer behavior of the Gulf states was examined by Baker and Abu-Ismail (1993). In examining the organizational environment and its impact on buying decisions, five specific issues were considered—buying tasks, the composition of the buying group and its behavior, the impact of bureaucracy on buying decisions, the concept of time, and the influence of country of origin effects.

### 17.2.1.1 *International negotiations*

The review in this area revealed a paucity of research. The articles identified mostly focused on building a conceptual framework to understand the dynamics of cross-cultural/national negotiation process. In addition, two articles also offered some dos and don'ts for managers engaged in international negotiations.

*Conceptual Framework*: International negotiations project a complexity that makes them a challenge to describe, explain, and improve (Weiss 1993). To meet the challenge, the same author proposes a new analytic perspective that focuses on three key facets of negotiation (also labeled the RBC perspective)—parties' relationships, parties' behavior and influencing conditions, and their basic interaction. The RBC framework has the following distinct characteristics: first, a relationship orientation that emphasizes the interactive nature of negotiation process. Second, multiple levels and units for behavioral analysis and third, an internationally applicable representation of influencing conditions.

The process and outcomes of international negotiations are an outcome of the two contextual variables—environmental and immediate (Phatak and Habib 1996). The environmental context refers to the forces in the environment that are beyond the control of either party involved in the negotiations. The immediate context includes such aspects as the relative power of the negotiators and the nature of their interdependence. Additionally, Trumbore (1998) examined the conditions under which public opinion can act as a domestic constraint on the ability of international negotiators to reach agreement.

*Dos and Don'ts of Successful Negotiations*: With globalization of American business, a study examines how international negotiations are different from domestic negotiations on the cross-cultural platform and provides some guidelines for increasing one's likelihood for success when conducting international cross-cultural negotiations (Mayfield *et al.* 1998). Factors that lead to successful cross-cultural negotiations are discussed by Herbig and Kramer (1992). The key success factors are: to understand the national negotiating style, to understand what each party wants from the negotiations, to accept and respect their cultural beliefs, and to be conscious of personal mannerisms.

### 17.2.1.2  *Consumer behavior*

International consumer behavior studies provide an alternative to international marketing research by focusing on consumers, instead of relying on countries as a basis for analysis (Wang 1999). However, it is noted by the same author that the area of international consumer behavior suffers from three key problems—a lack of theories, a lack of measurement reliability, and an ignorance of moderating variables. Research in this area has been extensive and mostly can be grouped under the following subtitles:

(1)  impact of culture on consumer behavior;
(2)  universality of American consumer behavior models to the international context;
(3)  debate over global consumer homogeneity versus heterogeneity;
(4)  descriptions of international consumer behavior.

*Culture and Consumer Behavior*: The impact of culture on salient consumer behavior constructs of perception, information processing, value systems, and self concept is reviewed (McCort and Malhotra 1993). The impact of religion (a key determinant of culture) on consumer behavior is studied with a sample of Japanese and American Protestant consumers (Sood and Nasu 1995). The impact of culture in moderating consumer's opinion exchange behavior is explored by Dawar, Parker, and Price (1996). Results indicate that the cultural characteristics of power distance and uncertainty avoidance influence the focus of consumers' product information search activities, but not their tendencies to share product-related opinions with others.

*Universality of American Consumer Behavior Models*: Samli, Wills, and Jacobs (1993) alert the reader to the assumption that existing American consumer behavior knowledge is applicable to all cultures is a deterrent to international consumer behavior theory development. The effectiveness of international marketing strategies depends largely on the understanding of international markets at the macro level, and of consumer behaviors. It is in this context that Wills, Samli, and Jacobs (1991) suggest that separately developed consumer behavior models versus a global one would prove to be more effective in international marketing strategy. Such a consumer behavior model would incorporate the following dimensions—learning, involvement, diffusion-adoption, and culture context. Samli (1994) offers an international consumer behavior model that focuses on environmental and cultural factors and dwells on the theory that culture forms personality, which in turn modifies consumer behavior. Another consumer behavior framework called the A-B-C-D paradigm is proposed by Raju (1995). The framework suggests that the marketer should examine four stages—access, buying behavior, consumption characteristics, and disposal covering the entire spectrum of consumer behaviors with respect to product/service. Chao (1993) questions how international consumers evaluate products that are produced by strategic alliances involving multiple firms and multiple countries. In this research, a more complex form of the country of origin effect of product evaluation is examined.

Despite the above, Lee and Green (1991) found support for the applicability of the Fishbein's Behavioral Intentions Model in a South Korean consumer sample.

*Descriptive Consumer Behavior*: Research was conducted on the attitudes of Japanese consumers towards foreign countries and products (Nishina 1990). The results showed that in comparison to domestic products, foreign products were thought to be appealing in terms of design and individuality, but, not necessarily in terms of function and quality. From the impact that global philanthropy has on consumer behavior, Collins (1993) makes the observation that in the 1990s, on a global scale, a more 'caring' global consumer seems to be evolving. Difference between the consumer behavior of oil producing and non-oil producing nations in their decisions to purchase imported goods is observed by Metwally (1993). In a sample drawn from Japanese consumers, the study revealed differences on issues of ethics among the consumers that provide theoretical support for expanded research in the domain of cross-national consumer ethics and highlights the needs for managers to consider possible differences in the ethical behavior of consumers when entering a new international market (Erffmeyer, Keillor, and LeClair 1999).

*Consumer heterogeneity versus homogeneity*: In a consumer behavior survey of comparable samples from the United States, Mexico, Netherlands, Turkey, Thailand, and Saudi Arabia, the results suggest the existence of both a global consumer segment that transcends national boundaries and a local consumer segment (Yavas, Verhage, and Green 1992). In a sample representing thirty-eight nationalities, it is found that there are few differences in the use of quality signals across cultures for a high priority segment of consumers globally (Dawar and Parker 1994).

### 17.2.1.3 *Country of origin (COO)*

Although the COO research falls under the domain of consumer behavior research, it will be treated separately as it has carved out its own niche in international marketing research. This line of research has continued to be a breeding ground for extensive academic research. The pattern of research in this domain can be traced to the following themes:

(1) conceptual refinement;
(2) COO and information processing;
(3) establishing further proof for robustness of COO measure;
(4) proof against robustness of COO measure;
(5) measurement issues.

*Conceptual Refinement*: The COO construct is decomposed into the following components—country of product design, country of parts manufacture, and country of product assembly—by Insch and McBride (1998). Their results indicate that these three country-of-origin components do affect consumer perceptions of design quality, manufacturing quality, and overall quality for each product in distinctly different ways. In a cross-national survey of Chinese and Canadian respondents, it was indicated that both sets of consumers put more emphasis on country of design and country of assembly than on brand names in their product evaluations (Ahmed and d'Astous 1999). A study reveals that COO effects can only be understood with respect to consumer ethnocentrism, where low ethnocentric consumers are more likely to use country cues as objective information about product quality (Brodowsky 1998). Further, Klein, Ettenson, and Morris (1998) add that consumer animosity toward a country has a significant negative impact on buying decisions above and beyond the effect of consumer ethnocentrism.

*COO and Consumer Information Processing*: A schema based knowledge representation framework is developed to examine the effects of COO on product evaluations (Kochunny *et al.* 1993). Results indicate that consumers possess a COO schema and that COO schema affect consumers' retention of information about products as well as their judgments. The cognitive structures that influence a person's use of the COO factor in product evaluation are discussed (Janda and Rao 1997). Its is suggested that the COO may be an outcome of a combination of two processes—cultural stereotypes and personal beliefs

*Establishing Further Proof for Robustness of COO Measure*: Research was conducted to identify consumer expertise and the type of attribute information as moderating the effects of COO on product evaluations (Maheswaran 1994). A study found that in buying foreign products, US consumers base their decision not simply on COO cue, but on tradeoffs with price, warranty, and other product attributes (Lee and Kim 1992). Research shows that perception of quality was most strongly affected by COO followed by product evaluations other than quality. COO had its smallest effect on purchase intention (Lim, Darley, and Summer 1994). The extent to which the risk attitudes, political convictions, and COO associations of individuals affect the buying decision of a product from a controversial source country is explored with special reference to Eastern Europe (Johansson, Ronkainen, and Czinkota 1994). Chao and Gupta (1996) found that while COO did not affect the amount of pre-purchase search, it had a significant impact on the efficiency of consumer choices. In a meta analysis, it is indicated that COO has a larger effect on perceived quality than on attitude towards the product or purchase intention (Verlegh and Steenkamp 1999). COO with brand name is found to be a robust determinant in consumer decision making in a cross-cultural context (Hulland 1999). An initial test of the animosity model of foreign product purchase in PRC revealed that animosity towards a foreign nation will negatively affect the purchase of products produced by that country independent of judgment of product quality (Klein, Ettenson, and Morris 1998). In an experimental setting, the salience of COO was tested along with global brand name on product evaluation (Tse and Gorn 1993). In contrast to the general notion that a well-known global brand will override the COO effect, it was found that the COO was an equally salient and more enduring factor in consumer product evaluation. Research by Thakor and Katsanis (1997) indicates that while foreign branding affects product evaluations more than COO, the uni-cultural or multi-cultural nature of the research context is influential in determining which brands are seen as 'foreign'.

*Proof Against Robustness of COO Measure*: In a large scale, cross-national consumer survey conducted in US, Canada, UK, Netherlands, France, West Germany, Greece, and Hungary, the study provided some tentative evidence that product images may influence, or may be influenced by country images (Papadopoulos and Heslop 1990). Using conjoint analysis, the study found that the influence of COO on product evaluation is relatively weak when examined in the context of multi-attribute modeling (Akaah and Yaprak 1993). In two separate studies, Ahmed and d'Astous (1996) found that favorableness of a brand or country of origin cue is considerably modified when a consumer is provided with additional product-related information. In a study of Dutch consumers, they were found to place little importance on country of origin as a choice cue and trusted more on their ability to evaluate the product themselves (Liefeld *et al.* 1996).

*Measurement Issues*: Tests of internal reliability and validity were conducted across different countries and samples to assess the strength of a final fourteen-item semantic differential scale with success (Martin and Eroglu 1993).

# 17.3 MARKET ENTRY DECISIONS

## 17.3.1 Initial mode of entry

Research in this area has focused its attention in four areas:

(1) to lay a conceptual foundation for understanding the choice of entry mode;
(2) entry mode choice in service firms and how they differ from manufacturing firms;
(3) managerial how-tos—in other words, how managers make their decisions on the choice of entry mode;
(4) tools for market entry.

*Conceptual Foundation*: The literature continues to draw from the transaction cost/internalization and organizational capability perspectives, and even draws on concepts from the economics of industrial organization (Otto 1997).

Bjorkman and Eklund (1996) address the question why some companies follow the sequence of operational modes used by foreign investors as explained by the Uppsala internationalization model, while others deviate from the 'traditional' establishment chain as proposed in the above model.

Buckley and Casson (1998) present a fully integrated analysis of foreign market entry decisions encompassing a choice between exporting, licensing, joint venturing, and wholly owned foreign investment. A special feature of the model is the distinction between investment in production facilities and investment in distribution facilities—a distinction that according to the authors has been overlooked in international business literature.

An evolutionary perspective in analyzing MNEs' entry and expansion in the global market proposes four stages of development—preparation, entry, expansion, and experienced (Geng 1998). The model explores the evolving objectives of the MNE at each stage and discusses the strategic transitions with respect to mode and scale, operations management, marketing strategies, and human resources. However, the above study was based on the experiences of MNEs in China.

Camino and Cazorla (1998) examine the foreign market entry decisions by small and medium sized enterprises and indicate that meaningful differences in the internationalization of firms do exist, although most SMEs follow the sequential or evolutionary process predicted by internationalization theory. Using the case of Upjohn company, the test for reliability and validity of the internalization and internationalization theories in the context of market entry is performed by Fina and Rugman (1996).

A multi-dimensional measure of managers' perception of international market entry risk is developed by Tan (1996). Lampert and Jaffe (1996) examine the country of origin effects on international market entry that determines the consumer protection of imported products and their value. A study examines the contraction of foreign market operations and exit from foreign markets when MNEs face market turbulence and decline (Hadjikhani and Johanson 1996).

A comparison and contrast of the mode of foreign market entry decision is presented with the recommendation that the organizational capacity framework is better adapted to today's business context (Madhok 1997). Using the theories of transaction cost, internalization, and resource based view of the firm, a new framework of entry mode choice is developed where six different types of entry modes are distinguished based on location factors and complementarity (Moon 1997). A conceptual framework examines how host country, home country, and industry specific factors, along with operation related factors such as location and the level of local government, affect the mode of entry decision and formation of alliances (Tse and Yigang 1997).

*Entry mode choice in service firms*: A mail survey of 175 US service firms exhibited a wide diversity in the choice of entry mode patterns (Erramilli 1990). Foreign market entry behavior in industries dominated by hard services, such as software and engineering, appears to be similar to that observed in the manufacturing sector. However, wide differences were observed in the behavior of soft-service industries and manufacturing firms. Further findings from the survey reveal that customized services are more likely to be marketed via highly integrated entry modes that give the firm a great degree of control over its international marketing operations.

Following debate over how service firms choose their modes of entry, this study advances a classification scheme that allows some services to be grouped with manufactured goods in terms of entry mode choice (Ikechi and Sivakumar 1998). A conceptual model of factors affecting the entry mode choice of service firms is also proposed.

*Managerial how-tos*: Based on a series of interviews with managers at two international companies, the results of this study reveal that managers' mental models or representations developed for domestic markets guide the choice of entry mode for international markets (Maignan and Lukas 1997). Another study attempts to devise a strategy for entry into the Chinese market by British companies (Zhang and Kelvin 1999). This can be achieved by forming appropriate relationships with organizations to promote sales of products and technology into Chinese enterprises. In a study examining the experience of entering the Chinese market by six UK companies, it is suggested that equity joint ventures are a major route into the Chinese market (Wilson 1997). A list of strategies for US firms entering the restructured markets of Poland, Hungary, and Czechoslovakia are offered by DeDee and Pearce (1995). Further, in another study, baseline information about how US companies entered the opening markets of the former Soviet bloc countries that are fraught with risk of different types and of different levels is provided by Sharma (1995).

*Tools for market entry*: The approach of brand alliances is suggested as a more effective market entry tool given the large expenditures that firms face in order to build brand awareness and brand image in a foreign market (Voss and Tansuhaj 1999). A systematic understanding of the new product learning that takes place between consumers in two countries—a pair of lead and lag countries—can provide insights for a firm's international market entry decisions (Ganesh, Kumar, and Subramaniam 1997). Market entry strategy is also identified by Li (1995) as one of the determinants of survival of foreign subsidiaries in international markets. Another study by Mitchell, Shaver, and Yeoung (1994) reveals that successful foreign market entry is related to the extent of foreign presence in an industry at the time of entry.

## 17.3.2 Specific modes of entry

### 17.3.2.1 *Exporting*

Exporting has been one of the most frequently studied areas in the literature. Most of the academic work revolved around the following issues:

- conceptual understanding
- exporting and the marketing mix
- determinants of exporting
- export performance
- exporting and small business
- factors of export success
- barriers to exporting
- exporting and strategic alliances.

*Conceptual foundation*: Leonidou and Katsikeas (1996) provide a comprehensive review of the main models on the export development process, identify their structural characteristics, evaluate the methodologies used for their validation, and analyze the key conceptual issues emerging from their assessment. An integrative approach that combines the behavioral and attitudinal dimensions is offered to define export commitment (Stump, Athaide, and Axinn 1998). The concept of relational exchange between exporters and importers is explored through a model that hypothesizes that cultural distance influences relational exchange which is in turn mediated by exporting performance and opportunism (Lee 1998*a*).

*Exporting and the marketing mix*: A study defines export pricing strategies and processes currently being used by exporting firms, what influences the adoption of these strategies, and how these strategies differ across cultures (Myers 1997). The transformation of the export product portfolios is examined from a sample in Greece (Chryssochoidis 1996). According to the main findings, the foreign versus domestic market dependence of the focus exporters had a major effect in the transformation of the export product portfolios from initiation to development of exports. Export market characteristics such as local government regulation, infrastructure differences, export market lag, cultural differences, end-user differences in tastes and preferences, and competitive intensity affecting ideal and actual product adaptation are investigated by Johnson and Arunthanes (1995).

*Determinants of exporting*: The impact of organizational culture in a firm's export intention is explored by Dosoglu-Guner (1999). The four dimensions of organizational culture are market, adhocracy, hierarchy, and clan cultures. The results indicate that clan culture decreases and adhocracy culture increases the firm's probability of exporting.

*Export performance*: A longitudinal study of exporting firms examines the relationships among the managers' beliefs about exporting, their export intentions, subsequent exporting behavior, and future exporting intentions (Axinn *et al.* 1995). A structural model for the prediction of export performance conceived in Austria is outlined by Holzmuller and Stottinger (1996). Using a sample of New Zealand exporting firms, the study indicated that segmenting the managers based on their awareness levels of export schemes can lead to better export performance (Brendan 1997). Patterson, Cicic, and Shoham (1997) suggest that the satisfaction with the export relationship contributes to export performance and future export intentions. Morgan and Katsikeas (1998) discovered that the strength of perceived exporting problem is inversely related to the export intensity of the firm. The role of managerial characteristics as influences on the export behavior of the firm are reviewed (Leonidou, Katsikeas, and Piercy 1998). A generalized export performance measure, the EXPERF scale that can be applied to multiple countries is developed by Zou, Taylor, and Osland (1998).

*Exporting and small business*: In the context of small and medium size firms, the factors that make a small firm a successful exporter are discussed (Gray 1997; Nakos, Brouthers, and Brouthers 1998; Zafarullah, Ali, and Young 1998). Earlier, Calof (1994) examined the direct and indirect effects of firm size by studying three dimensions of export behavior—propensity to export, countries exporting to, and export attitudes for manufacturers. A survey of characteristics of the internationalization processes pursued by small Italian exporting companies confirms the validity of some premises of the stages theory, but it noted that companies are free to follow other routes and/or pursue individualized processes of development abroad (Dalli 1994).

*Factors for export success*: The adequacy of government export incentive programs as well as managers' awareness of these incentives are identified as the two key determinants of the success of export development strategies (Kotabe and Czinkota 1992; Kumcu, Harcar, and Kumcu 1995). The findings show that level of export interest, export exploration and company size have a higher explanatory power on awareness than other company characteristics. When exporting to developing countries, the findings of the study by Sriram and Manu (1995) highlight the importance of taking the country of destination into account when planning export marketing strategies. Two marketing factors identified to be most important to successful exporting were gathering marketing information and communicating with markets (Howard 1995). Finally, a study investigates managerial characteristics as influences on the export behavior of firms (Leonidou, Katsikeas, and Piercy 1998).

*Barriers to exporting*: An attempt is made to review, assess, and synthesize existing empirical research on factors impeding the initiation, development, or sustainment of export activities (Leonidou 1995). The role of cultural distance and managerial decision-making style are explored, as are explanatory variables as to why some firms perceive barriers to export as being more important than other firms, or why some firms perceive a given barrier as more important than it is for another company (Shoham and Albaum 1995).

*Exporting and strategic alliances*: A model is advanced that suggests the determinants of exporters' intentions to form strategic alliances with their foreign exchange partners (Lee 1998*b*). Relational exchange, exporting performance, and the duration of the business relationship are identified as factors affecting exporters' intentions to form strategic alliances.

### 17.3.2.2 *Joint ventures*

Research in this area examined the following issues:

- joint venture performance
- selection of international joint ventures
- the element of learning in joint ventures.

*JV performance*: One study examined the performance of international joint ventures in the context of a global aerospace industry (Dussauge and Garrette 1995). Strategic value analysis as an indicator of performance is applied in the evaluation of a Chinese joint venture (Mills and Chen 1996). In the context of international strategic technology partnerships, joint ventures are disproportionately represented in relatively mature industries (Hagedoorn and Narula 1996). Factors that explain joint ventures performance in China are identified as level of partner commitment, the number of joint venture partners, sociocultural distance among partners, product/industry characteristics, foreign control, and joint venture location in China (Hu and Chen 1996). International joint ventures in the context of developing countries are studied to reveal four types of IJVs, and four patterns of IJV development (Kim 1996).

*Selection of international joint ventures*: In a study that examines whether wholly owned subsidiaries are better than joint ventures, Chao and Yu (1996) indicate that for a small open economy under tariff protection, the desirable policy is 100 per cent foreign ownership of subsidiaries, coupled with export-share requirement. A model offers a range of predictions about the formation of joint ventures within industries, across industries, across locations, and over time (Buckley and Casson 1996).

*Learning in joint ventures*: Organizational characteristics, structural mechanisms, and contextual factors that influence knowledge acquisition from the foreign parent in international joint ventures are examined (Lyles and Salk 1996).

### 17.3.2.3 *Country-choice strategies*

In order for product introduction to be successful, corporations must identify countries and test market cities that offer a good fit with the firm's overall marketing strategy (Hoffman 1997). A two-stage model is presented by the author that combines the concepts of marketing strategy, the management science technique of goal programming, and micro computer technology for an efficient and effective evaluation of international markets.

International market choice of small entrepreneurial high-tech firms is largely shaped by the interests of various network players (Coviello and Munro 1995). These influential networks can be both formal and informal. Early relationships with large firms are recognized as being particularly influential in the entrepreneurial high-tech firm's internationalization process.

# 17.4 LOCAL MARKET EXPANSION: MARKETING MIX DECISIONS

This section examines the studies relating to the global standardization debate, followed by a discussion on the international marketing mix variables of product policy, advertising, pricing, and distribution.

## 17.4.1 Global standardization vs. local responsiveness

Four isolated studies were identified in the international marketing literature reviewed for this chapter. The findings of each study are summarized below:

1. Kotabe and Duhan (1991, 1993) examine Japanese executives' perceptions of the veracity of various PIMS (profit impact of market strategy) strategy principles developed from analysis of the pooled experience of businesses in the United States. While some differences exist, their findings generally suggest that most of the PIMS principles and strategic orientations found to exist in the United States are perceived by Japanese executives to apply in Japan.
2. A new perspective on the marketing mix standardization debate suggests that clusters should be a function of the marketing mix elements instead of the more popular country clustering approach (Ayal and Nachum 1994).
3. Sullivan (1992) points to the conflict or tension between global standardization and local responsiveness in multinationals.
4. An empirical investigation of MNEs that implement a global standardization program versus those that do not revealed that there were no

identifiable performance differences between the two samples (Samiee and Roth 1992).

The common theme in the above studies is that focus amongst the academicians seems to be on evaluating the effectiveness of a global standardization program in the context of multinationals.

## 17.4.2 Marketing mix

### 17.4.2.1 *Product policy*

The bulk of the studies in this domain examined the following two key concepts: (1) determinants of new product development and management in international markets, and (2) the success of new products.

*Determinants of new product development*: As new technologies are becoming more complicated, R&D consortia are becoming a popular tool for new product development (Hongcharu 1999). The marketing-R&D interface exerts a positive impact on new product performance in foreign markets (Li 1999). In a study of thirteen Japanese, American, and European multinational companies, observations reveal that global new product development processes vary in terms of the involvement of overseas subsidiaries in project teams and the generation of new product concepts (Mohan, Rosenthal, and Hatten 1998). It was found that when the knowledge about different product design requirements among overseas markets or plants is tacit, firms employ cross-national product development teams and use overseas subsidiaries as sources of new product concepts. The literature suggests that product innovation introduced later in a country results in faster diffusion as the consumers in the lag market have an opportunity to learn about the new product from the consumers in the lead market. This finding is used to provide some preliminary guidelines for manufacturers regarding the selection of foreign markets and the timing and order of entry decisions for new products (Ganesh, Kumar, and Subramaniam 1997). Investigating the relationship between marketing and new product development, a study based on East Asia revealed that marketing skills derived from marketing resources and the proficiency in conducted marketing activities are important in new product development (Song, Montoya-Weiss, and Schmidt 1997). The role of the Internet overseas in new product development is also examined (Quelch and Klein 1996).

*Success of new products*: Speed in new product introduction in the market is a critical dimension of competition faced by many firms in the global marketplace. A model explains that new product success is largely determined by the speed to market, which in turn is an outcome of technological familiarity, product differentiation, competitive intensity, and internal R&D skills (Yeoh 1994). A study conducted in PRC indicated that relative product advantage and the acquisition of marketing information were highly correlated with new product success (Parry and Song 1994). Unlike the findings from Canadian firms, the level of competitive activity, the timing of the product launch, and the level of proficiency in executing activities in the early stages of the product development process were identified as other indicators of new product success in China. A country's innovativeness contributes to the successful introduction of new products in the global markets (Lee 1990).

On a more applied setting, with the emergence of the European Union, diffusion rates of new products were found to be different between those introduced during the first and second half of the unification process (Ganesh 1998).

In addition to the above two discussed core areas, isolated studies examined the ability of a firm to develop new products as being crucial for an industrial firm to start exporting (Rynning and Anderson 1994); and how in a multicountry environment, variations in media availability has predictable effects on the speed and pattern of new product sales (Tellefsen and Takada 1999).

## 17.4.2.2 *Advertising*

The bulk of the literature in this domain has struggled with the issues surrounding the standardization versus adaptation debate, as can be seen in the volume of studies cited below. Some work has also been conducted in the area of international advertising strategy and its impact on other marketing related decisions. Therefore, the two key areas that have received most of the research attention are:

(1) advertising standardization versus customization;
(2) international advertising strategy.

Other studies have also examined advertising effectiveness in an international context. Here, the use of culturally relevant stimuli in international advertising is investigated to determine how these culturally relevant aspects are interpreted by the intended audience (Leach and Liu 1998). Visual advertisements have been found to be more effective than verbal ones in a global campaign (Kernan and Domzal 1993). Attitude toward the ad and advertised product in a collectivist cultural setting is found to be more positive when the advertisements depict consistencies in cultural norms and roles than when inconsistencies exist (Gregory and Munch 1997).

*Advertising standardization*: In a review of a forty-year debate over standardization versus adaptation advertising issues, Agarwal (1995) indicates that academicians have mostly advocated the adaptation approach, while the practitioners have alternated between the two approaches with a trend towards standardization. The degree of advertising standardization adopted by firms, and what is standardized varies across a standardization spectrum (Harris 1994). However, the opportunities for advertising standardization are most likely to occur in less affluent, developing markets (James and Hill 1991). Additionally, advertising standardization is more likely to be effective in country clusters which are segregated based on their economic and cultural similarity and their media availability and usage (Sriram and Gopalakrishna 1991). In spite of this finding, another study found US firms to generally prefer localized advertising over standardized versions (Kanso 1991).

In the context of Asian markets such as Hong Kong, Taiwan, Singapore, and PRC, a regionalization approach is found to be more effective than a global standardization perspective for advertising (Tai 1997). Contrasting this finding, Zandpour and Harich (1997) provide evidence that countries that are not necessarily a part of a geographic region may exhibit similar advertising preferences in spite of cultural differences and lack of regional proximity. Counteracting the benefits of a regionalization approach, Nevett (1992) indicated that British and American consumers had very different preferences in terms of their advertising needs. However, in terms of standardization, Alexander and King (1995) highlight the universality of leisure themes in international advertising across a sample of 500 billboard and print advertisements from thirty-three nationalities.

The scope of multi-country campaigns has deserved much attention and has often been overshadowed by the standardization-adaptation debate (Hill and Shao 1994). Additionally, the role of the advertising agency has been found to be negligible in the decision to standardize. One study has found evidence that suggests that standardization of advertising is on the decline (Kanso 1992).

*International advertising strategy*: One study showed unique characteristics at each stage of internationalization for a firm from a newly industrialized country (Cho, Choi, and Yi 1994). International advertising in addition to several other factors was identified as one of the major factors affecting the decisions of Middle Eastern consumers to purchase imported goods (Metwally 1993). The impact of international advertising of processed foods and beverages, pharmaceuticals, tobacco, and alcoholic beverages has also been examined (Baudot 1991).

## 17.4.2.3 *Pricing*

Many authors note that research in international pricing issues is a neglected area in international marketing management when compared to the other marketing mix variables (Aulakh and Kotabe 1993; Samli and Jacobs 1994; Myers and Cavusgil 1996). Therefore our literature search revealed that research in this domain tends to be scattered with no observable pattern or trend.

In a conceptual framework, Myers and Cavusgil (1996) identify the factors that influence the export pricing process and the reasons why firms adopt the export pricing strategies that they do. The relationship between a firm's strategies in international pricing and performance is explored. Research has tried to build a set of rules and processes for international price setting (Cavusgil 1996). An empirical study investigated the relationship between international pricing and Western European economic integration (Gaul and Lutz 1994). The results suggested that price differences that can be observed in the Western European market decrease when the influence on final prices exerted by exporting firms increases. A survey of US multinationals revealed that most firms tend to standardize their prices in the world markets and that this type of procedure is more successful in the short run (Samli and Jacobs 1994). Research on how to set international pricing suggests a technique called strategic choice that can help a manager understand tradeoffs made by different customer segments to set price discrimination and product differentiation policies (Sinclair 1993). More recently, Clark, Kotabe, and Rajaratnam (1999) have developed a conceptual framework to link international marketers' pricing strategy to the impact of exchange rate pass-through on international pricing and offered testable propositions.

### 17.4.2.4 *Distribution*

The only article that reflected on the conceptual underpinnings of international channels of distribution was the research by Kale and McIntyre (1991). The study suggested that international channel relationships should reflect the underlying cultural tenets of the society. Research in this area focused on the following broad issues:

- channel cooperation and conflict
- channel performance
- channels and MNE performance
- standardization versus adaptation debate
- applied issues.

*Channel cooperation and conflict*: This is a popular area of research in this field. Shoham, Rose, and Kropp (1997) examine this issue within the context of international channels. Two determinants of international channel conflict are identified—distribution system quality and cultural distance between exporters' home and international target countries. In a study of 135 British International Trade intermediaries, discussion centered around the factors that enhance cooperation and reduce conflict between an intermediary and its suppliers, and the impact of conflict and cooperation on the maintenance of long-term relationships (Balabanis 1998).

*Channel performance*: Channel performance can be enhanced by relying on certain nonmarket forms of governance—control and flexibility (Gilliland and Bello 1997). Of the two forms of control, output control along with flexibility is identified as enhancing export channel performance, with process control having no performance effect. Gillespie and McBride (1996) indicate that with smuggling as a popular form of illegal channel in emerging markets competing with more legitimate channels of distribution, US multinationals will face new challenges relating to strategic planning, etc. With respect to Canadian operations, a mail survey revealed that the lower the financial performance in the foreign market relative to Canadian operations, the lower the satisfaction with the international marketing channel (Klein and Roth 1993). Within the context of the Saudi car market, it is indicated that the level of economic development and culture affect the channel structure, operations, and its performance (Ahmed and Al-Motawa 1997).

*Channels and MNE performance*: Appropriate distribution channels along with high commitment of top management are identified as important determinants of international marketing success in large multinational corporations (Cavusgil and Kirpalani 1993). Access to the distribution channel is identified as a market entry barrier (among several others) in international consumer markets (Karakaya 1993).

*Standardization vs. adaptation debate*: It is noted that in the existing literature on this issue, both academicians and practitioners concur that market channels cannot be standardized. However, given this challenge, a conceptual framework for the possible standardization of global marketing channels is presented (Rosenbloom, Larsen, and Mehta 1997).

*Applied issues*: Fahy and Taguchi (1995) point to the changing landscape of the Japanese distribution system that is less intimidating and relatively more easily accessible by US multinationals. However, three years later, research continues to point to the complexity of the Japanese distribution system as a signal to foreign firms to use non-store retailing (Grossman 1998). On a last note, how to pick the right foreign distributors by small and medium sized firms (who lack sophisticated market research/decision analysis tools to assist them) is answered by the Analytical Hierarchy Process, which serves as a highly flexible and versatile substitute (Yeoh and Calantone 1995).

# 17.5 GLOBAL STRATEGY

The literature review was performed to advance the knowledge in the four sub-areas as identified by Douglas and Craig (1992). They are: competitive strategy, strategic alliances, sourcing, and multinational company performance. Search for articles in these four areas was conducted within an international or global context.

## 17.5.1 Competitive strategy

Three broad issues seem to be dominant in the mainstream research:

(1) theoretical and conceptual development to help in understanding the role of competitive strategy;
(2) difference between competitive advantage and competitive positioning; and
(3) sources of competitive advantage in international marketing strategy and performance implications.

### 17.5.1.2 *Conceptual development*

A resource-based strategic management model of MNE market entry demonstrates the value of this new conceptual framework to the understanding of competitive strategy of MNEs (Tallman 1991). The integration-responsiveness framework in the choice of the models of international strategy is less helpful for devising competitive strategy (Taggart 1998). A contingency framework illustrates how national and political institutions of a country impact the effectiveness of an MNE's international strategies (Murtha and Lenway 1994). Application of the Porter-Dunning Diamond model of international competitiveness is used to explain the current situation and the further development of the international competitive strategy of mainland China's manufacturing sector (Liu and Song 1997).

### 17.5.1.3 *Competitive advantage versus competitive positioning*

Strategy literature in the 1990s has tried to differentiate between two sources of competitive strategy—competitive advantage and competitive positioning. A firm experiences competitive advantage in terms of its core competencies. A firm's competitive positioning, on the other hand, raises the need for important strategy choices beyond the core competencies of a single corporation.

Such an overall strategy then combines the internal competencies of each company as core competencies of the entire competitive system. Competitive positioning strategy interacts with internationalization strategy in the formulation of an overall strategy (Morrison and Roth 1992).

### 17.5.1.4 *Sources of competitive advantage and performance implications*

Firms' competitive strategy along with other key variables such as market orientation, experience, and product characteristics, plays an important role in the development of International Manufacturing Configuration (IMC) strategies (DuBois, Toyne, and Oliff 1993). Competitive advantage is a key determinant of international marketing strategy (Lim, Sharkey, and Kim 1993). In a study of fifty-six large US-based multinational firms in Latin America, competitive advantages were found to be significant in firm performance. The only advantages that were consistently significant were, proprietary technology, firm's goodwill based on brand or company name, and economies of scale in production (Grosse 1992). This study identifies the sources of competitive advantage that significantly impact firm performance. Manufacturing policies are identified as a primary source of sustainable competitive advantage (Carr 1993). The three additional Ps of service firms (physical evidence, participants, and process) are also identified as sources of competitive advantage (Collier 1991).

Samli and Jacobs (1995) suggest that in order to achieve the strongest international competitive advantage, there must be cooperation between the public and business sectors. In other words, a nation will maximize its competitive advantage when both government and firms pool their competitive advantages together. Competitive advantage along with location-specific advantages should be integrated in the design of a firm's overall international strategy. In other words, the basic task of strategy is to identify the geographical location of firm's functional activities and to integrate these activities across the various locations. The study suggests that selective globalization (when a firm defines its global strategy around a narrow subset of the value chain) may lead to the most effective outcomes (Roth 1992).

## 17.5.2  Strategic alliances

The value of cooperation realized in the 1980s in the strategy literature is still recognized as an important contributor to firm success in a global economy (Amin, Hagen, and Sterrett 1995). The only article identified on the conceptual foundation of strategic alliances defines it as a manifestation of inter-organizational cooperative strategies, entailing the pooling of specific resources and skills by the cooperating organizations in order to achieve common goals (Varadarajan and Cunningham 1995). The motives for firms to enter into strategic alliances as identified by the above authors are: gaining access to new markets, accelerating the pace of entry into new markets, sharing of research and development, manufacturing, and/or marketing costs, broadening the product line/filling product, and learning new skills.

With the exception of the above research piece, literature in this area has focused its interest in three broad areas:

(1) issues of learning and trust in alliances
(2) recipes for alliance success
(3) performance issues for different types of alliances.

### 17.5.2.1 *Learning and trust*

Work by Varadarajan and Cunningham (1995) provides a conceptual foundation for understanding strategic alliances and the role of marketing in the nature of such alliances. Inkpen (1998) investigates into the potential of international strategic alliances for learning and knowledge acquisition. A study by Hamel (1991) suggests that not all alliance partners are equally adept at learning and that asymmetries in learning might alter the relative bargaining power of partners. A difference between convenience- and strategic-alliances affects the nature of learning. It is maintained that although all international corporate alliances provide for learning, this learning does not necessarily always lead to strategic learning (Samli, Kaynak, and Sharif 1996). The notion of trust in a special form of strategic alliance—non-equity based international cooperative alliance—was examined. Results showed that partner cultural sensitivity was an important contributor to trust building in such alliances (Johnson, Cullen, and Sakano 1996).

### 17.5.2.2 *Recipes for alliance success*

Interfirm relationship networks are strategic resources that can be shaped by managerial action and industry events (Ravindranath, Balaji, and Prescott 1998). Managing relationships with strategic alliance partners in addition with their customers, employees, channel partners, etc. is key to a firm's long-term success in a global economy (Beckett-Camarata, Camarata, and Barker 1998). There are different types of alliances each with its own type of performance implication (Dussauge and Garrette 1995). A framework is developed to analyze the likely success factors of international strategic alliances and to assist companies in their efforts to avoid picking the wrong alliance partners

(Brouthers, Brouthers, and Wilkinson 1995). Strategic alliances defined as interfirm partnering analyze the stability of alliance networks in a global context and whether market leaders tend to dominate the alliance partnership. To achieve a mature and coherent global order in a rapidly changing world, it is suggested that governments and businesses must reconcile economic interests by fostering collaborative international alliances (Halal 1993).

### 17.5.2.3 *Performance for different types of alliances*

Patterns of similarities and differences in the forms of strategic alliances among the triad powers are examined. The US and Europe are similar to each other in that they each have a balanced distribution of joint ventures, contractual agreements, and equity participation forms. Equity participation plays a somewhat larger role in the USA. Japan on the other hand, was characterized by a dominance of contractual agreements over joint ventures and equity participation forms (Terpstra and Simonin 1993). An analysis of 473 strategic alliances revealed that equity joint ventures are preferred to contracts when cultural differences between partner firms are greater and when alliances involve upstream rather than downstream value chain activities (Sengupta and Perry 1997). Real application of the performance of international strategic alliances (ISA) is examined in the case of China, where results show that ISAs outperform joint ventures and wholly owned subsidiaries. However, ISAs also bear more financial risks in terms of liquidity and solvency (Luo 1996).

# 17.6 GLOBAL SOURCING

Isolated studies examined the role of global sourcing as a critical factor in a variety of competitive strategies, differentiated between opportunistic and strategic sourcing (Samli, Browning, and Busbia 1998) and offered suggestion on how to reduce uncertainty associated with supplier selection in global markets (Min, LaTour, and Williams 1994). However, the three broad areas most popularly studied in this domain are the following:

(1) global sourcing in a service context
(2) benefits of global sourcing
(3) country of origin effects.

## 17.6.1 Global sourcing in a service context

A growing area of interest has been to investigate into the comparability of product versus services sourcing strategy. The market performance of global sourcing strategy of service firms is investigated by Kotabe, Murray, and Javalgi (1998). Using the TCA paradigm, Murray and Kotabe (1999) investigate the locational (domestic vs. global sourcing) and the ownership (internal vs. external sourcing) aspects of service sourcing strategy. Performance implications are also discussed.

## 17.6.2 Benefits of global sourcing

Despite eroding market share, US firms have consolidated their global profitability levels by skillfully exploiting their technological prowess through technology transfer and offshore sourcing (Kotabe and Swan 1994). The sourcing strategies used by European and Japanese firms hold implications for the transferability of the firm's product and manufacturing process technology (Kotabe 1993). Lower costs are not the only benefit of global sourcing. Some of the other more strategic benefits include potential for a lasting advantage in technical supremacy, penetration of growth markets, and high speed (Fagan 1991). Global sourcing is identified as one of the reasons that allows for relationship building between firms and their suppliers (Sharma and Sheth 1997). A contingency framework studies the moderating influence of product innovation, process innovation, and asset specificity on the relationship between the sourcing strategy and the product's strategic and financial performance (Murray and Kotabe 1995). The results show that the moderators are significant for only financial performance, and not strategic. In a study of US-based subsidiaries of foreign MNEs, the study shows that internal component sourcing and internal sourcing of non-standardized components from abroad is related to the highest sales growth (Murray, Kotabe, and Wildt 1995a; Murray, Wildt, and Kotabe 1995b).

## 17.6.3 Country of origin issues in global sourcing

Global sourcing is addressed as a type of commodity bundling of components with implications for the country of origin effect (Choi 1993). In this case, the 'made in a developing country' might pose as a problem for the company (Choi 1993; Witt and Rao 1992).

# 17.7 MULTINATIONAL PERFORMANCE

The literature here has focused on two sets of issues:

(1) determinants of performance—what leads to high MNE performance
(2) an environmental interpretation of performance.

## 17.7.1 Determinants of performance

The chosen mode of ownership (joint ventures or wholly-owned subsidiaries) is associated with the behavior and performance of overseas subsidiaries (Chowdhury 1992). Financial performance was found to be higher when management practices in the multinational work unit were congruent with the national culture (Newman and Nollen 1996). Performance was found to be enhanced by budget communication between subunits of multinationals when reliance on budget control and environmental dynamism are high (Hassel and Cunningham 1996). Sources of competitive advantage such as proprietary technology, goodwill based on the firm's brand and company name, and economies of scale in production are significant predictors of multinational performance (Grosse 1992). The need to develop better international products and to improve the multinational performance in international marketing efforts is mentioned by Wills, Samli, and Jacobs (1991), which, simply stated, means that managers should know when to globalize or localize marketing practices. Kotabe (1990) notes that the interaction between product and process innovation is a crucial determinant of market performance of European and Japanese multinationals.

## 17.7.2 A different interpretation of performance

Corporate environmental performance is different from the traditional interpretation of performance in financial terms (Epstein and Roy 1998). In this perspective, a multinational's performance depends on whether it adopts global or local standards to meet the environmental requirements. Yet another determinant of performance is stakeholder satisfaction (Greeno and Robinson 1992). The study revealed that companies that aggressively consider the environmental implications of all parts of their organization, processes, and products, as they set strategies for the future to satisfy stakeholder needs, will be high performers in the future.

# 17.8 ANALYTICAL TECHNIQUES IN NATIONAL AND CROSS-NATIONAL RESEARCH

The two broad concerns with cross-national research still pertain to measurement and reliability and validity issues of scales and measures used. These two concerns are reflected in the research review as follows:

## 17.8.1 Measurement issues

A measurement instrument developed by Keillor *et al.* (1996) provides a means by which the results of cross-culture and cross-national research can be empirically tested and on which more rigorous theory building can be based.

Four measurement issues involved in cross-national research that lead to risk of inferential errors are discussed in a paper by Singh (1995). They are: standardized versus unstandardized coefficients, the impact of measurement error and unequal reliability, the overall error rate, and simultaneous analysis and construct equivalence. Additionally, the nature of each of these problems, the likely impact they can have on substantive conclusions, and the approaches for tackling these problems are explained.

Three aspects of cross-national comparative research—measurement equivalence, translation equivalence, and calibration equivalence are identified as being critical to establish cross-national reliability and the validity of items used to measure theoretical constructs (Mullen 1995). Two techniques of multiple group LISREL and optimal scaling are suggested for use in diagnosing cross-national measurement equivalence. Optimal scaling is suggested by Mullen, Milne, and Didow (1996) as a technique for examining metric equivalence for the practice of comparing means cross-nationally in survey research.

## 17.8.2 Reliability and validity issues

A study tests the factor structure and reliability along with the nomological validity of the CETSCALE (consumer ethnocentrism) using samples from the US, Japan, France, and West Germany (Netemeyer, Durvasula, and Lichtenstein 1991). Variances in how cross-cultural or national respondents understand and evaluate the value measurement task are studied in a sample from Canada and Denmark (Grunert and Muller 1996). The findings revealed significant differences between the two samples on the understanding of real and ideal life values. This highlights the need for greater attention to be paid to the measurement methodology for obtaining value data. The validity of the CYMYC cosmopolitanism scale for Korean consumers is reported which provides some support for the scale (Yoon, Cannon, and Yaprak 1996).

# 17.9 Critique and Directions for Future Research

Having surveyed the international marketing literature published in the 1990s, we have to ask if the research deficiencies addressed in the last two decades have been addressed. In the early 1990s, Douglas and Craig (1992) lamented that strategy issues were a sadly neglected area in international marketing and that marketing's role in global strategy was largely ignored. Based on the 1990–9 international marketing literature, we have to repeat the same concern. Researchers in international marketing continue to borrow concepts and theories from the management and strategy literature, and tend to relate them to market performance. Management and strategy researchers tend to focus on the supply side of the dyadic relationships between firms and customers, while marketing researchers tend to focus on the demand side of the relationships. In a positive light, international marketing researchers complement management and strategy researchers in subjecting supply-side theories to demand-side considerations. However, studies in international marketing do not appear to have affected the direction of management and strategy research in any significant way.

Market segmentation and target marketing are two major concepts uniquely developed in the marketing literature with focus on the demand (customer) side. Yet, studies in these areas are scarce in both domestic and international marketing literature. This area of research would have some profound impact on supply-side strategy research if sufficiently developed. In particular, benefit and intermarket segmentation concepts appear promising for further development in the international marketing literature.

In the generic (domestic) context, marketing as a discipline has gradually migrated away from economic issues to behavioral issues. For example, marketing was developed as a study of distribution channels and logistics at the dawn of the twentieth century. Today, logistics is not generally considered as part of the marketing discipline. Even the economics of new product development is increasingly considered as being outside the mainstream marketing field. On the other hand, behavioral research, as well as quantitative applications, in consumer behavior, promotion, and channel management has become mainstream. In the international area, the same forces have been at work. Consequently, there have been an unproportionately large number of studies in consumer behavior (particularly country-of-origin effects), modes of entry (particularly exporting), and channel performance.

The focal area of marketing is the marketing mix strategy, encompassing product, price, promotion, and distribution management. Studies that address various aspects of the marketing mix were limited to the standardization vs. adaptation issue. Part of the limited attention to each aspect of the marketing mix is due to the difficulty of conducting empirical research. Product development has become so technically and technologically complex that this area is increasingly better examined by researchers in the engineering fields, or jointly by those in engineering and marketing fields. Pricing has always been one of the most difficult areas of research in marketing as firms are not willing to share pricing and cost information. Promotion—in particular, advertising-related research, such as advertising effectiveness and global advertising—as well as consumer behavior has attracted many marketing researchers. It is due mainly to the relative ease of collecting data and theory development from psychology literature. Research in distribution management is more or less limited to such behavioral issues as dyadic trust and power (control) relationships. Although global sourcing issues (including procurement and supply chain management) are considered part of the broadly defined domain of marketing (Douglas and Craig 1992), studies in these areas appear to be gradually migrating into the strategy literature away from the contemporary domain of marketing.

One area where marketing has genuine strengths is in research methodology. As the marketing discipline has evolved into a strongly psychology-based behavioral discipline, researchers have paid serious attention to the reliability and validity of measurement issues. In the last decade, we have seen a trickle-down effect of an increased call for more methodological scrutiny in international marketing research. However, it should be noted that international marketing research is faced with many more operational difficulties and pitfalls in conducting empirical research than is generic, domestic-bound research (Craig and Douglas 2000). Consequently, international marketing researchers may not be able to address those measurement and other methodological issues as effectively as would be possible in domestic research.

Another issue that shaped the nature of international business in the 1990s is that of regionalization as evidenced by the formation of various trading blocs including the European Union, the NAFTA, and the MERCOSUR, among others and by regional crises in South East Asia and Latin America. As a result, the fundamental strategic dilemma between integration (supply-side consideration) and local responsiveness (demand-side consideration) has intensified rather than attenuated. Until the mid-1990s the frame of mind of most business researchers and practitioners was that management of the configuration and coordination of globally scattered value-chain activities was possible. But since the second half of the 1990s we have begun to doubt the wisdom of such simplicity. We posit that a more self-contained localized 'delivery' systems perspective will gain prominence as the unexpected and wild fluctuations of the exchange rates will prevent multinational firms from effectively managing the set of globally scattered value-chain activities. Regional trade blocs will form currency areas in which exchange rates are stable relative to each other, which will reinforce localization of production and marketing. Regionalization of global strategy may be an apt characterization. If so, then how to manage global marketing in fragmented production and delivery systems can become an important managerial issue that begs for further investigation.

The emergence of E-commerce in recent years will also have a pervasive impact on the way marketing is practised around the world. Due to some time lag in conducting research, and the publication process, we expect a flurry of research publications on E-commerce to start appearing in the first decade of the twenty-first century. Thanks to the Internet revolution, information lag as well as geographical distance between countries has shrunk enormously. One fundamental assumption about the physical and mental distance behind the international product cycle thesis has become irrelevant for strategy development. It does not necessarily mean, however, that market needs are converging. Indeed, people around the world are expressing their ethnic and cultural differences more openly than ever before. Therefore, despite some regional integrations on the rise, other regions are Balkanizing across cultural and religious lines even within the same country (e.g. the Basque region in Spain, and Scotland in the UK). Thus, the fundamental strategic dilemma between integration and local responsiveness remains. With the advancement of the Internet and E-commerce in international business, the first decade of the twenty-first century may well be characterized by an *online scale* vs. *offline market sensitivity* dilemma.

In general, international marketing researchers have always been interested in the ever-changing market environments and/or methodological rigor as cherished by their domestic counterparts for research publication purposes. As a result, international marketing researchers have tended to focus their research attention either on topics *de jour* or on research areas in which a large database can be developed. The first group of international marketing researchers tends to focus on interesting but unstructured topics that are difficult to theorize on or apply existing theory to, and thus engage in exploratory research. Although exploratory research is interesting, it tends to lack transferability of its research framework and findings in explaining other related topics. The second group of international marketing researchers tends to focus on such behavioral research areas as country-of-origin, modes of entry, and trust/power relationships in the marketing channel, in which rigorous research methodology is applied for scholarly publication. Both groups of international marketing researchers face different criticisms. The first group is criticized as conducting atheoretical research, while the second group is criticized as overdoing research in mature areas in which additional contribution to the literature is increasingly very limited.

In conclusion, there remain many important research areas that have eluded serious academic inquiry. The increased technical complexity of marketing issues, particularly the marketing mix strategy, calls for more interdisciplinary work across traditional functional confines than in the past. Collaborative work by a group of researchers across national boundaries also facilitates data collection and promotes cultural sensitivity in conducting marketing research.

# APPENDIX 17.1
## LIST OF JOURNALS REVIEWED

### Marketing Journals

*European Journal of Marketing*
*Industrial Marketing Management*
*International Journal of Advertising*
*International Journal of Research in Marketing*
*International Marketing Review*
*Journal of Consumer Marketing*
*Journal of Advertising Research*
*Journal of Consumer Research*

### General Business Journals

*Academy of Management Journal*
*Business Horizons*
*International Journal of Management*
*Journal of Business Research*
*Journal of Business Strategy*
*Journal of Economic Psychology*
*Journal of International Business Studies*
*Journal of Management Studies*

Journal of Euro-Marketing
Journal of Global Marketing
Journal of International Consumer
  Marketing
Journal of International Marketing
Journal of International Marketing and
  Marketing Research
Journal of Macromarketing
Journal of Marketing
Journal of Marketing Research
Journal of Marketing Theory and Practice
Journal of the Academy of Marketing
  Science
Psychology and Marketing

Journal of Product Innovation
  Management
Journal of World Business
Long Range Planning
Management International Review
Organization Science
Review of Business
Sloan Management Review
Strategic Management Journal

## REFERENCES

AGARWAL, M. (1995). 'Review of a 40–year Debate in International Advertising', *International Marketing Review*, 12 (1), 26–49.

AHMED A., and AL-MOTAWA A. (1997). 'Communication and Related Channel Phenomena in International Markets: The Saudi Car Market', *Journal of Global Marketing*, 10 (3), 67–82.

AHMED S., and D'ASTOUS, A. (1996). 'Country of Origin and Brand Effects', *Journal of International Consumer Marketing*, 9 (2), 93–115.

—— (1999). 'Product-country Images in Canada and in the People's Republic of China', *Journal of International Consumer Marketing*, 11 (1), 5–22.

AKAAH, I., and YAPRAK, A. (1993). 'Assessing the Influence of Country of Origin on Product Evaluations', *Journal of International Consumer Marketing*, 5 (2), 39–53.

ALBAUM, G., and PETERSON, R. A. (1984). 'Empirical Research in International Marketing', *Journal of International Business Studies*, 15 (Spring/Summer), 161–73.

ALEXANDER, J., and KING, N. D. (1995). 'Leisure Themes in International Advertising: A Content Analysis', *Journal of International Consumer Marketing*, 8 (1), 113–14.

AMIN S. G., HAGEN A., and STERRETT, C. R. (1995). 'Cooperating to Achieve Competitive Advantages in a Global Economy: Review and Trends', *S.A.M. Advanced Management Journal*, 60 (4), 37–41.

AULAKH, PREET S., and KOTABE, MASAAKI (1993). 'An Assessment of Theoretical and Methodological Development in International Marketing: 1980–1990', *Journal of International Marketing*, 1 (2), 5–28.

AXINN, C. N., SAVITT R., SINKULA J. M., and THACH, S. V. (1995). 'Export Intentions, Beliefs and Behaviors in Smaller Industrial Firms', *Journal of Business Research*, 32 (1), 49–56.

AYAL, I., and NACHUM, L. (1994). 'A Fresh Look at the Standardization Problem: Classifying LDCs in the Marketing Mix Content', *Journal of International Marketing and Marketing Research*, 19 (1), 17–36.

BAKER, M., and ABU-ISMAIL, F. (1993). 'Organizational Buying Behavior in the Gulf', *International Marketing Review*, 10 (6), 42–61.

BALABANIS, G. (1998). 'Antecedents of Cooperation, Conflict and Relationship Longevity in an International Trade Intermediary's Supply Chain', *Journal of Global Marketing*, 12 (2), 25–46.

BAUDOT, B. (1991). 'International Issues in the Advertising of Health-related Products', *European Journal of Marketing*, 25 (6), 24–37.

BEAMISH, P. W., and KILLING, J. P. (1997). *Cooperative Strategies*. San Francisco: New Lexington Press.

BECKETT-CAMARATA, J. E., CAMARATA, M., and BARKER, R. T. (1998). 'Integrating Internal and External Customer Relationships Through Relationship Management: A Strategic Response to a Changing Global Environment', *Journal of Business Research*, 41 (1), 71–81.

BILKEY, W. J., and NES, E. (1982). 'Country-of-origin Effects on Product Evaluations', *Journal of International Business Studies*, 13 (Spring/Summer), 89–100.

BJORKMAN, I., and EKLUND, M. (1996). 'The Sequence of Operational Modes Used by Finnish Investors in Germany', *Journal of International Marketing*, 4 (1), 33–55.

BODDEWYN, J. J. (1981). 'Comparative Marketing: The First Twenty-five Years', *Journal of International Business Studies*, 12 (Spring/Summer), 61–79.

BRADLEY, M. F. (1987). 'Nature and Significance of International Marketing: A Review', *Journal of Business Research*, 15, 205–19.

BRENDAN, J. G. (1997). 'Profiling Managers to Improve Export Promotion Targeting', *Journal of International Business Studies*, 28 (2), 387–420.

BRODOWSKY, G. H. (1998). 'The Effects of Country of Design and Country of Assembly on Evaluative Beliefs About Automobiles and Attitudes Toward Buying Them: A Comparison Between Low and High Ethnocentric Consumers', *Journal of International Consumer Marketing*, 10 (3), 85–113.

BROUTHERS, K., BROUTHERS, L., and WILKINSON, T. (1995). 'Strategic Alliances: Choose Your Partners', *Long Range Planning*, 28 (3), 18–36.

BROWN, S., and BURT, S. (1992). 'Conclusions: Retail Internationalization', *European Journal of Marketing*, 26 (8), 80–5.

BUCKLEY, P. J., and CASSON, M. (1996). 'An Economic Model of International Joint Venture Strategy', *Journal of International Business Studies*, 27 (5), 849–76.

—— (1998). 'Analyzing Foreign Market Entry Strategies: Extending the Internalization Approach', *Journal of International Business Studies*, 29 (3), 539–61.

CALOF, J. (1994) 'The Relationship Between Firm Size and Export Behavior Revisited', *Journal of International Business Studies*, 25 (2), 367–87.

CAMINO D., and CAZORLA, L. (1998). 'Foreign Market Entry Decisions by Small and Medium-sized Enterprises: An Evolutionary Approach', *International Journal of Management*, 15 (1), 123–29.

CARR, C. (1993). 'Global, National and Resource Based Strategies: An Examination', *Strategic Management Journal*, 14 (7), 551–68.

CAVUSGIL, S. T. (1996). 'Pricing for Global Markets', *Journal of World Business*, 31 (4), 66–78.

—— and KIRPALANI, V. H. (1993). 'Introducing Products into Export Markets: Success Factors', *Journal of Business Research*, 27 (1), 1–15.

CAVUSGIL, S. T., (cont.) and LI, T. (1992). *International Marketing: An Annotated Bibliography.* Chicago: American Marketing Association.

CHAO C., and YU, E. (1996). 'Are Wholly Foreign Owned Enterprises Better than Joint Ventures?', *Journal of International Economics*, 40 (1), 225–47.

CHAO, P. (1993). 'Partitioning Country of Origin Effects: Consumer Evaluations', *Journal of International Business Studies*, 24 (2), 291–306.

—— and GUPTA, P. B. (1995). 'Information Search and Efficiency of Consumer Choices of New Cars: Country of Origin Effects', *International Marketing Review*, 12 (6), 47–59.

CHO D. S., CHOI, J., and YI, Y. (1994). 'International Advertising Strategies by NIC Multinationals: The Case of a Korean Firm', *International Journal of Advertising*, 13 (1), 77–93.

CHOI, C. J. (1993). 'A Note on Commodity Bundling and Global Sourcing', *Journal of Global Marketing*, 7 (2), 117–23.

CHOWDHURY, J. (1992). 'Performance of International Joint Ventures and Wholly Owned Subsidiaries', *Management International Review*, 32 (2), 115–34.

CHRYSSOCHOIDIS, G. M. (1996). 'Successful Exporting: Exploring the Transformation of the Export Product Portfolios', *Journal of Global Marketing*, 10 (1), 7–31.

CLARK, T., KOTABE, M., and RAJARATNAM, D. (1999). 'Exchange Rate Pass-through and International Pricing Strategy: A Conceptual Framework and Research Propositions', *Journal of International Business Studies*, 30 (2), 249–69.

COLLIER, D. A. (1991). 'New Marketing Mix Stresses Service', *Journal of Business Strategy*, 12 (2), 42–6.

COLLINS, M. (1993). 'Global Corporate Philanthropy', *European Journal of Marketing*, 27 (2), 46–59.

CONTRACTOR, F. J. (1990). 'Contractual and Cooperative Forms of International Business: Towards a United Theory of Model Choice', *Management International Review*, 30, 31–54.

COVIELLO, N., and MUNRO, H. J. (1995). 'Growing the Entrepreneurial Firm: Networking For International Market Development', *European Journal of Marketing*, 29 (7), 49–62.

CRAIG, C. S., and DOUGLAS, S. P. (2000). *International Marketing Research*, 2nd edn. New York: Wiley.

DALLI, D. (1994). 'The Exporting Process: The Evolution of Small and Medium Sized Firms Towards Internationalization', *Advances in International Marketing*, 6, 85–110.

DAWAR, N., and PARKER, P. (1994). 'Marketing Universals: Consumers' Use of Brand Name, Price', *Journal of Marketing*, 58 (2), 81–96.

—— PARKER, P., and PRICE, L. (1996). 'A Cross-cultural Study of Interpersonal Information Exchange', *Journal of International Business Studies*, 27 (3), 497–516.

DEDEE, J. K., and PEARCE, J. A. (1995). 'Eastern Euro-markets: Strategies for United States firms', *International Journal of Management*, 12 (3), 315–25.

DOSOGLU-GUNER, B. (1999) 'An Exploratory Study of the Export Intention of Firms: The Relevance of Organizational Culture', *Journal of Global Marketing*, 12, 45–63.

DOUGLAS, S. P., and CRAIG, C. S. (1992). 'Advances in International Marketing', *International Journal of Research in Marketing*, 9 (4), 291–318.

—— and WIND, Y. (1987). 'The Myth of Globalization', *Columbia Journal of World Business*, 22 (Winter), 19–30.

DuBois, F. L., TOYNE, B., and OLIFF, M. D. (1993). 'International Manufacturing Strategies of US Multinationals', *Journal of International Business Studies*, 24 (2), 307–33.

DUSSAUGE P., and GARRETTE, B. (1995). 'Determinants of Success in International Alliances', *Journal of International Business Studies*, 26 (3), 505–31.

EPSTEIN M., and ROY, M. J. (1998). 'Managing Corporate Environmental Performance: A Multinational Perspective', *Academy of Management Journal*, 16 (3), 284–96.

ERFFMEYER, R. C., KEILLOR, B. D., and LeCLAIR, D. T. (1999). 'An Empirical Investigation of Japanese Consumer Ethics', *Journal of Business Ethics*, 18 (1), 35–50.

ERRAMILLI, M. K. (1990). 'Entry Mode Choice In Service Industries', *International Marketing Review*, 7, 50–63.

FAGAN, M. (1991). 'A Guide to Global Sourcing', *Journal of Business Strategy*, 12 (2), 21–6.

FAHY, J., and TAGUCHI, F. (1995). 'Reassessing the Japanese Distribution System', *Sloan Management Review*, 36 (2), 49–62.

FINA, E., and RUGMAN, A. (1996). 'A Test of Internalization Theory and Internationalization Theory: The Upjohn Company', *Management International Review*, 36 (3), 199–213.

FIRAT, A. F. (1997). 'Educator Insights: Globalization of Fragmentation: A Framework for Understanding Contemporary Global Markets', *Journal of International Marketing*, 5 (2), 77–86.

GANESH, J. (1998). 'Converging Trends Within the European Union: Insights From an Analysis of Diffusion Patterns', *Journal of International Marketing*, 6 (4), 32–48.

—— KUMAR, V., and SUBRAMANIAM, V. (1997). 'Learning Effects in Multinational Diffusion of Consumer Durables: An Exploratory Investigation', *Journal of the Academy of Marketing Science*, 25 (3), 214–28.

GAUL W., and LUTZ, U. (1994). 'Pricing in International Marketing and Western European Economies', *Management International Review*, 34 (2), 101–25.

GENG, C. (1998). 'The Evolutionary Process of Global Market Expansion: Experiences of MNCs in China', *Journal of World Business*, 33 (1), 87–110.

GILLESPIE, K., and McBRIDE, B. (1996). 'Smuggling in Emerging Markets: Global Implications', *Journal of World Business*, 31 (4), 40–54.

GILLILAND, D., and BELLO, D. C. (1997). 'The Effect of Output Controls, Process Controls and Flexibility on Export Channel Performance', *Journal of Marketing*, 61 (1), 22–38.

GRAY, B. J. (1997). 'Profiling Managers to Improve Export Promotion Targeting', *Journal of International Business Studies*, 28 (2), 387–420.

GREENO, L., and ROBINSON, S. (1992). 'Rethinking Corporate Environmental Management', *Columbia Journal of World Business*, 27 (3), 222–32.

GREGORY, G. D., and MUNCH, J. M. (1997). 'Cultural Values in International Advertising: An Examination of Familial Norms and Roles in Mexico', *Psychology and Marketing*, 14 (2), 99–119.

GROSSE, R. (1992). 'Competitive Advantages and Multinational Enterprises in Latin America', *Journal of Business Research*, 25 (1), 27–43.

GROSSMAN, R. P. (1998). 'Japanese Culture and the Acceptance of Non-store Selling Methods by Japanese Housewives', *Journal of International Consumer Marketing*, 10 (3), 43–61.

GRUNERT, S. C., and MULLER, T. E. (1996). 'Measuring Values in International Settings: Are Respondents Thinking "Real" Life or "Ideal" Life?', *Journal of International Consumer Marketing*, 8, 169–215.

HADJIKHANI, A., and JOHANSSON, J. (1996). 'Facing Foreign Market Turbulence: Three Swedish Multinationals in Iran', *Journal of International Marketing*, 4 (4), 53–74.

HAGEDOORN, J., and NARULA, R. (1996). 'Choosing Organizational Modes of Strategic Technology Partnering: International and Sectoral Differences', *Journal of International Business Studies*, 27 (2), 265–85.

HALAL, W. E. (1993). 'Global Strategic Management in a New World Order', *Business Horizons*, 36 (3), 5–11.

HAMEL, G. (1991). 'Competition for Competence and Inter-Partner Learning Within International Strategic Alliances', *Strategic Management Journal*, 12, 83–104.

HARRIGAN, K. R. (1987). 'Strategic Alliances: Their New Role in Global Competition', *Columbia Journal of World Business*, 22 (Summer), 67–9.

HARRIS, G. (1994). 'International Advertising Standardization: What do the Multinationals Actually Standardize?', *Journal of International Marketing*, 2 (4), 13–31.

HASSEL, L. G., and CUNNINGHAM, G. M. (1996). 'Budget Effectiveness in Multinational Corporations: An Empirical Test of the Use of Budget Controls Moderated by Two Dimensions of Budgetary Participation Under High and Low Environmental Dynamism', *Management International Review*, 36 (3), 245–66.

HERBIG, P. A., and KRAMER, H. E. (1992). 'Do's and Don'ts of Cross-cultural Negotiations', *Industrial Marketing Management*, 21 (4), 287–99.

HILL, J. S., and SHAO, A. T. (1994). 'Agency Participants in Multicountry Advertising: A Preliminary Examination of Affiliate Characteristics and Environments', *Journal of International Marketing*, 2 (2), 29–49.

HOFFMAN, J. (1997). 'A Two-stage Model for the Introduction of Product into International Markets', *Journal of Global Marketing*, 11 (1), 65–86.

HOLZMULLER, H., and STOTTINGER, B. (1996). 'Structural Modeling of Success Factors in Exporting: Cross Validation and Further Development of Export Performance Models', *Journal of International Marketing*, 4 (2), 29–55.

HONGCHARU, B. (1999). 'An Analysis of Different Opinions on Consortia for Research and Development and Consortia for Manufacturing in New Product Development', *Journal of International Marketing and Marketing Research*, 24 (1), 35–44.

HOWARD, D. (1995). 'The Role of Export Management Companies in Global Marketing', *Journal of Global Marketing*, 8 (1), 95–110.

HU, M., and CHEN, H. (1996). 'An Empirical Analysis of Factors Explaining Foreign Joint Ventures Performance in China', *Journal of Business Research*, 35 (2), 165–73.

HULLAND, J. S. (1999). 'The Effects of Country-of-brand and Brand Name on Product Evaluation and Consideration: A Cross-country Comparison', *Journal of International Consumer Marketing*, 11 (1), 23–40.

IKECHI, E., and SIVAKUMAR, K. (1998). 'Foreign Market Entry Mode Choice of Service Firms', *Journal of the Academy of Marketing Science*, 26 (4), 274–92.

INKPEN, A. C. (1998). 'Learning and Knowledge Acquisition Through International Strategic Alliance', *Academy of Management Executive*, 12, 69–80.

INSCH, G., and McBRIDE, B. (1998). 'Decomposing the Country of Origin Construct: An Empirical Test of Country of Design, Country of Parts and Country of Assembly', *Journal of International Consumer Marketing*, 10 (4), 69–91.

JAMES, W. L., and HILL, J. S. (1991). 'International Advertising Messages: To Adapt or Not to Adapt', *Journal of Advertising Research*, 31 (3), 65–72.

JANDA, S., and RAO, C. P. (1997). 'The Effect of Country of Origin Related Stereotypes and Personal Beliefs on Product Evaluations', *Psychology and Marketing*, 14 (7), 689–702.

JOHANSSON, J., RONKAINEN, I., and CZINKOTA, M. (1994). 'Negative Country of Origin Effects: The Case of New Russia', *Journal of International Business Studies*, 25 (1), 157–76.

JOHNSON, J. L., and ARUNTHANES, W. (1995). 'Ideal and Actual Product Adaptation in US Exporting Firms: Market Related Determinants and Impact on Performance', *International Marketing Review*, 12 (3), 31–47.

—— CULLEN, J. B., and SAKANO, T. (1996). 'Setting the Stage for Thrust and Strategic Integration in Japanese–US Cooperative Alliances', *Journal of International Business Studies*, 27 (5), 981–1004.

KALE, S., and McINTYRE, R. P. (1991). 'Distributional Channel Relationships in Diverse Culture', *International Marketing Review*, 8 (3), 31–46.

KANSO, A. (1992). 'International Advertising Strategies: Global Commitment to Local Visions', *Journal of Advertising Research*, 32 (1), 10–15.

KARAKAYA, F. (1993). 'Barriers to Entry in International Markets', *Journal of Global Marketing*, 7 (1), 7–25.

KEILLOR, B. D., HULT, G. T. M., ERFFMEYER, R. C., and BABAKUS, E. (1996). 'NATID: The Development and Application of a National Identity Measure for Use in International Marketing', *Journal of International Marketing*, 4, 57–73.

KERNAN, J. B., and DOMZAL, T. J. (1993). 'International Advertising: To Globalize, Visualize', *Journal of International Consumer Marketing*, 5 (4), 51–72.

KIM, S. C. (1996). 'Analysis of Strategic Issues for International Joint Ventures: Case Studies of Hong Kong–China Joint Venture Manufacturing Firms', *Journal of Euro Marketing*, 4 (3), 55–70.

KLEIN, J. G., ETTENSON, R., and MORRIS, M. D. (1998). 'The Animosity Model of Foreign Product Purchase: An Empirical Test in the People's Republic of China', *Journal of Marketing*, 62 (Jan.), 89–100.

KLEIN, S., and ROTH, V. J. (1993). 'Satisfaction with International Marketing Channels', *Journal of the Academy of Marketing Science*, 21 (1), 39–45.

KOCHUNNY, C., BABAKUS, E., BERL, R., and MARKS, W. (1993). 'Schematic Representation of Country Image: Its Effects on Product Evaluations', *Journal of International Consumer Marketing*, 5 (1), 5–26.

KOTABE, M. (1990). 'Corporate Product Policy and Innovative Behavior of European and Japanese Multinationals', *Journal of Marketing*, 54 (2), 19–34.

KOTABE, M. (*cont.*) (1993). 'Patterns and Technological Implications of Global Sourcing Strategies: A Study of European and Japanese Multinational Firms', *Journal of International Marketing*, 1 (1), 26–43.

—— and CZINKOTA, M. R. (1992). 'State Government Promotion of Manufacturing Exports: A Gap Analysis', *Journal of International Business Studies*, 23 (4), 637–58.

—— and DUHAN, D. F. (1991). 'The Perceived Veracity of PIMS Strategy Principles in Japan: An Empirical Inquiry', *Journal of Marketing*, 55 (Jan.), 26–41.

—— —— (1993). 'Strategy Clusters in Japanese Markets: Firm Performance Implications', *Journal of the Academy of Marketing Science*, 21 (Winter), 21–31.

—— MURRAY, J. Y., and JAVALGI, R. G. (1998). 'Global Sourcing of Services and Market Performance: An Empirical Investigation', *Journal of International Marketing*, 6 (4), 10–31.

—— and SWAN, S. K. (1994). 'Offshore Sourcing: Reaction, Maturation and Consolidation', *Journal of International Business Studies*, 25 (1), 115–40.

KUMCU, E., HARCAR, T., and KUMCU, M. E. (1995). 'Managerial Perceptions of the Adequacy of Export Incentive Programs: Implications for Export Lead Economic Development Policy', *Journal of Business Research*, 32 (2), 163–75.

LAMPERT, S., and JAFFE, E. D. (1996). 'Country of Origin Effects on International Market Entry', *Journal of Global Marketing*, 10 (2), 27–52.

LEACH, M. P., and LIU, A. H. (1998). 'The Use of Culturally Relevant Stimuli in International Advertising', *Psychology and Marketing*, 15 (6), 523–46.

LEE, C. (1990). 'Determinants of National Innovativeness and International Market Segmentation', *International Marketing Review*, 7 (5), 39–60.

—— and GREEN, R. (1991). 'Cross-cultural Examination of the Fishbein Behavioral Intent', *Journal of International Business Studies*, 22 (2), 289–96.

LEE, D. (1998*a*). 'The Effect of Cultural Distance on the Relational Exchange Between Exporters and Importers: The Case of Australian Exporters', *Journal of Global Marketing*, 11, 7–22

—— (1998*b*). 'Developing International Strategic Alliances Between Exporters and Importers: The Case of Australian Exporters', *International Journal of Research in Marketing*, 15, 335–48.

LEE, H., and KIM, C. (1992). 'The Relative Effects of Price, Warranty and Country of Origin on Consumer Products Evaluations', *Journal of Global Marketing*, 6 (2), 55–80.

LEONIDOU, L. (1995). 'Empirical Research on Export Barriers: Review, Assessment and Synthesis', *Journal of International Marketing*, 3 (1), 29–43.

—— and KATSIKEAS, C. S. (1996). 'The Export Development Process: An Integrative Review of Empirical Models', *Journal of International Business Studies*, 27 (3), 517–51.

—— —— and PIERCY, N. F. (1998). 'Identifying Managerial Influences on Exporting: Past Research and Future Directions', *Journal of International Marketing*, 6, 74–102.

LEVITT, T. (1983). 'The Globalization of Markets', *Harvard Business Review*, 61 (May–June), 92–102.

LI, J. (1995). 'Foreign Entry and Survival: Effects of Strategic Choices on Performances in International Markets', *Strategic Management Journal*, 16 (5), 333–51.

LI, T. (1999). 'The Impact of the Marketing-R&D Interface on New Product Export Performance: A Contingency Analysis', *Journal of International Marketing*, 7 (1), 10–33.

—— and CAVUSGIL, S. T. (1991). 'International Marketing: A Classification of Research Streams and Assessment of Their Development from 1982 to 1990', paper presented at the 1991 American Marketing Association Summer Educators' Conference.

LIEFELD, J. P., HESLOP, L. A., PAPADOPOULOS, N., and WALL, M. (1996). 'Dutch Consumer Use of Intrinsic, Country-of-origin, and Price Cues in Product Evaluation and Choice', *Journal of International Consumer Marketing*, 9 (1), 57–81.

LIM, J., DARLEY, W., and SUMMER, J. (1994). 'An Assessment of Country of Origin Effects Under Alternative Presentation Formats', *Journal of the Academy of Marketing Science*, 22 (3), 274–82.

LIM J., SHARKEY, T., and KIM, K. I. (1993). 'Determinants of International Marketing Strategy', *Management International Review*, 33 (2), 103–31.

LIU, X., and SONG, H. (1997). 'China and the Multinationals: A Winning Combination', *Long Range Planning*, 30 (1), 74–83.

LUO, Y. (1996). 'Evaluating the Performance of Strategic Alliances in China', *Long Range Planning*, 29 (4), 534–42.

LYLES, M., and SALK, J. (1996). 'Knowledge Acquisition From Foreign Partners in International Joint Ventures', *Journal of International Business Studies*, 27 (5), 877–903.

MADHOK, A. (1997). 'Cost, Value and Foreign Market Entry Mode: The Transaction and the Firm', *Strategic Management Journal*, 18 (1), 39–61.

MAHESWARAN, D. (1994). 'Country of Origin as Stereotype: Effects of Consumer Expertise and Attribute Strength on Product Evaluations', *Journal of Consumer Research*, 21 (2), 354–66.

MAIGNAN, I., and LUKAS, B. A. (1997). 'Entry Mode Decisions: The Role of Managers' Mental Models', *Journal of Global Marketing*, 10 (4), 7–22.

MARTIN, I., and EROGLU, S. (1993). 'Measuring a Multi-dimensional Construct: Country Image', *Journal of Business Research*, 28 (3), 191–210.

MAYFIELD, J., MAYFIELD, M., MARTIN, D., and HERBIG, P. (1998). 'How Location Impacts International Business Negotiations', *Review of Business*, 19 (Winter), 21–4.

McCORT, D. J., and MALHOTRA, N. (1993). 'Culture and Consumer Behavior: Toward an Understanding of Cross-cultural Consumer Behavior in International Marketing', *Journal of International Consumer Marketing*, 6 (2), 91–128.

METWALLY, M. M. (1993). 'Attitudes of Middle Eastern Consumers Towards Imported Products', *Journal of International Marketing and Marketing Research*, 18 (2), 81–93.

MILLS, R. W., and CHEN, G. (1996). 'Evaluating International Joint Ventures Using Strategic Value Analysis', *Long Range Planning*, 29 (4), 552–62.

MIN, H., LaTOUR, M., and WILLIAMS, A. (1994). 'Positioning Against Foreign Supply Sources in an International Purchasing Environment', *Industrial Marketing Management*, 23 (5), 371–82.

MITCHELL, W., SHAVER, J. M., and YEUNG, B. (1994). 'Foreign Entrant Survival and Foreign Market Share: Canadian Companies Experience in United States Medical Sector Markets', *Strategic Management Journal*, 15 (7), 555–67.

MOHAN, S., ROSENTHAL, S. R., and Hatten, K. J. (1998). 'Global New Product Development Processes: Preliminary Findings and Research Propositions', *Journal of Management Studies*, 35 (6), 773–96.

Moon, H. C. (1997). 'The Choice of Entry Modes and Theories of Foreign Direct Investment', *Journal of Global Marketing*, 11 (2), 43–64.

Morgan, R., and Katsikeas, C. (1998). 'Exporting Problems of Industrial Manufacturers', *Industrial Marketing Management*, 27, 161–76.

Morrison, A., and Roth, K. (1992). 'A Taxonomy of Business-level Strategies in Global Industries', *Strategic Management Journal*, 13 (6), 399–418.

Mullen, M. R. (1995). 'Diagnosing Measurement Equivalence in Cross-national Research', *Journal of International Business Studies*, 26 (3), 573–97.

——Milne, G. R., and Didow, N. M. (1996). 'Determining Cross-cultural Metric Equivalence in Survey Research: A New Statistical Test', *Advances in International Marketing*, 8, 145–57.

Murray, J. Y., and Kotabe, M. (1999). 'Sourcing Strategies of US Service Companies: A Modified Transaction Cost Analysis', *Strategic Management Journal*, 20 (9), 791–809.

—— —— and Wildt, A. R. (1995a). 'Global Sourcing Strategies of US Subsidiaries of Foreign Multinationals', *Management International Review*, 35 (4), 307–24.

—— —— —— (1995b). 'Strategic and Financial Performance Implications of Global Sourcing', *Journal of International Business Studies*, 26 (1), 181–205.

Murtha, T. P., and Lenway, S. A. (1994). 'Country Capabilities and the Strategic State: How National Political Institutions Affect Multinational Corporations Strategies', *Strategic Management Journal*, 15, special issue, 113–30.

Myers, M. B. (1997). 'The Pricing Processes of Exporters: A Comparative Study of the Challenges Facing US and Mexican Firms', *Journal of Global Marketing*, 10 (4), 95–115.

—— and Cavusgil, S. T. (1996). 'Export Pricing Strategy-performance Relationships: A Conceptual Framework', *Advances in International Marketing*, 8, 159–78.

Nakos, G., Brouthers, K., and Brouthers, L. E. (1998). 'The Impact of Firm and Managerial Characteristics on Small and Medium-sized Greek Firms' Export Performance', *Journal of Global Marketing*, 11 (4), 23–47.

Netemeyer, R. G., Durvasula, S., and Lichtenstein, D. R. (1991). 'A Cross-national Assessment of the Reliability and Validity', *Journal of Marketing Research*, 28 (3), 320–27.

Nevett, T. (1992). 'Differences Between American and British Television Advertising: Explanations and Implications', *Journal of Advertising*, 21 (4), 61–72.

Newman, K. L., and Nollen, S. D. (1996). 'Culture and Congruence: The Fit Between Management Practices and National Culture', *Journal of International Business Studies*, 27 (4), 753–79.

*Nikkei Weekly* (1998). 'Manufacturers Reshape Asian Strategies', 12 Jan., 1, 5.

Nishina, S. (1990). 'Japanese Consumers: Introducing Foreign Products/Brands into the Japanese Markets', *Journal of Advertising Research*, 30 (2), 35–46.

Otto, A. (1997). 'Internationalization and Market Entry Mode: A Review of Theories and Conceptual Frameworks', *Management International Review*, 37 (2), 27–42.

Papadopoulos, N., and Heslop, L. (1990). 'National Stereotypes and Product Evaluations in a Socialist Country', *International Marketing Review*, 7 (1), 32–48.

Parry M. E., and Song, X. M. (1994). 'Identifying New Product Successes in China', *Journal of Product Innovation Management*, 11 (1), 15–41.

PATTERSON, P., CICIC, M., and SHOHAM, A. (1997). 'A Temporal Sequence Model of Satisfaction and Export Intentions of Service Firms', *Journal of Global Marketing*, 10 (4), 23–43.

PHATAK, A. V., and HABIB, MOHAMMED M. (1996). 'The Dynamics of International Business Negotiations', *Business Horizons*, 39 (3), 30–9.

PIETERS, R., BAUMGARTNER, H., VERMUNT, J., and BIJMOLT, T. (1999). 'Importance and Similarity in the Evolving Citation Network of the *International Journal of Research in Marketing*', *International Journal of Research in Marketing*, 16 (June), 113–27.

QUELCH, J., and KLEIN, L. (1996). 'The Internet and International Marketing', *Sloan Management Review*, 37 (3), 60–76.

RAJU, P. S. (1995). 'Consumer Behavior in Global Markets: The A-B-C-D Paradigm and its Application to Eastern Europe and the Third World', *Journal of Consumer Marketing*, 12 (5), 37–57.

RAVINDRANATH M., BALAJI, R. K., and PRESCOTT, J. (1998). 'Networks in Transition: How Industry Events Reshape Interfirm Relationships', *Strategic Management Journal*, 19 (5), 439–59.

ROSENBLOOM, B., LARSEN, T., and MEHTA, R. (1997). 'Global Marketing Channels and the Standardization Controversy', *Journal of Global Marketing*, 11 (1), 49–64.

ROTH, K. (1992). 'International Configuration and Coordination Archetypes', *Journal of International Business Studies*, 23 (3), 533–50.

RYNNING, M. R., and ANDERSON, O. (1994). 'Structural and Behavioral Predictors of Export Adoptions', *Journal of International Marketing*, 2 (1), 73–90.

SAMIEE, S., and ROTH, K. (1992). 'The Influence of Global Marketing Standardization on Performance', *Journal of Marketing*, 56 (2), 1–18.

SAMLI, A. C. (1994). 'Towards a Model of International Consumer Behavior: Key Considerations and Research Avenues', *Journal of International Consumer Marketing*, 7 (1), 63–85.

—— BROWNING, J. M., and BUSBIA, C. (1998). 'The Status of Global Sourcing as a Critical Tool of Strategic Planning: Opportunistic Versus Strategic Dichotomy', *Journal of Business Research*, 43 (3), 177–87.

—— and JACOBS, L. (1994). 'Pricing Practices of American Multinational Firms: Standardization vs. Localization Dichotomy', *Journal of Global Marketing*, 8 (2), 51–73.

—— —— (1995). 'Achieving Congruence Between Macro and Micro Generic Strategies: A Framework to Create International Competitive Advantage', *Journal of Macromarketing*, 15 (2), 23–33.

—— KAYNAK, E., and SHARIF, H. (1996). 'Developing Strong International Corporate Alliances: Strategic Implications', *Journal of Euro-Marketing*, 4 (3), 23–36.

SAMLI, C., WILLS, J. R., and JACOBS, L. (1993). 'Developing Global Products and Marketing Strategies: A Rejoinder', *Journal of the Academy of Marketing Science*, 21 (1), 79–84.

SEGAL-HORN, S., and DAVISON H. (1992). 'Global Markets, the Global Consumer and International Retailing', *Journal of Global Marketing*, 5 (3), 31–62.

SENGUPTA, S., and PERRY, M. (1997). 'Some Antecedents of Global Strategic Alliances Formation', *Journal of International Marketing*, 5 (1), 31–50.

SHARMA, A. (1995). 'From Exploiting to Investing: An Empirical Study of Entry Strategies of US Firms to the Former Soviet Bloc', *Academy of Management Journal*, Best Paper Proceedings, 197–200.

—— and SHETH, J. N. (1997). 'Supplier Relationships: Emerging Issues and Challenges', *Industrial Marketing Management*, 26 (2), 91–100.

SHOHAM, A., and ALBAUM, G. (1995). 'Reducing the Impact of Barriers to Exporting: A Managerial Perspective', *Journal of International Marketing*, 3 (4), 85–106.

—— ROSE, G. M., and KROPP, F. (1997). 'Conflict in International Channels of Distribution', *Journal of Global Marketing*, 11 (2), 5–22.

SINCLAIR, S. (1993). 'A Guide to Global Pricing', *Journal of Business Strategy*, 14 (3), 16–20.

SINGH, J. (1995). 'Measurement Issues in Cross-national Research', *Journal of International Business Studies*, 26 (3), 597–620.

SONG, M., MONTOYA-WEISS, M. M., and SCHMIDT, J. B. (1997). 'The Role of Marketing in Developing Successful New Products in South Korea and Taiwan', *Journal of International Marketing*, 5 (3), 47–69.

SOOD, J., and NASU, Y. (1995). 'Religiosity and Nationality: An Explanatory Study of their Effect on Consumer Behavior in Japan and the United States', *Journal of Business Research*, 34 (1), 1–10.

SRIRAM, V., and MANU, F. A. (1995). 'Country of Destinations and Export Marketing Strategy: A Study of US Exporters', *Journal of Global Marketing*, 8 (3), 171–91.

—— and GOPALAKRISHNA, P. (1991). 'Can Advertising be Standardized Among Similar Countries?: A Cluster Based Analysis', *International Journal of Advertising*, 10 (2), 137–50.

STUMP, R., ATHAIDE, G. A., and AXINN, C. N. (1998). 'The Contingent Effect of the Dimensions of Export Commitment on Exporting Financial Performance: An Empirical Examination', *Journal of Global Marketing*, 12 (1), 7–25.

SULLIVAN, D. (1992). 'Organization in American MNCS: The perspective in Europe', *Management International Review*, 32 (3), 237–51.

TAGGART, J. H. (1998). 'Strategy and Control in the Multinational Corporation: Too Many Recipes', *Long Range Planning*, 31 (4), 571–85.

TAI, S. H. C. (1997). 'Advertising in Asia: Localize or Regionalize?', *International Journal of Advertising*, 16 (1), 48–61.

TALLMAN, S. B. (1991). 'Strategic Management Models and Resource-based Strategies Among MNEs in a Host Market', *Strategic Management Journal*, 12 (Summer), 69–82.

TAN, S. J. (1996). 'Risks Assessment in International Market Entry: A Multi Dimensional Approach', *International Journal of Management*, 13 (3), 370–80.

TELLEFSEN, T., and TAKADA, H. (1999). 'The Relationship Between Mass Media Availability and the Multicountry Diffusion of Consumer Products', *Journal of International Marketing*, 7 (1), 77–96.

TERPSTRA, V., and SIMONIN, B. L. (1993). 'Strategic Alliances in the Triad: An Exploratory Study', *Journal of International Marketing*, 1 (1), 4–26.

THAKOR, M. V., and KATSANIS, L. P. (1997). 'A Model of Brand and Country Effects on Quality Dimensions: Issues and Implications', *Journal of International Consumer Marketing*, 9 (3), 79–100.

THORELLI, H. B. (1986). 'Networks: Between Markets and Hierarchies', *Strategic Management Journal*, 7 (1), 37–51.

TRUMBORE, P. (1998). 'Public Opinion as a Domestic Constraint in International Negotiations: Two Level Games in the Anglo-Irish Peace Process', *International Studies Quarterly*, 42 (3), 545–65.

TSE, D., and GORN, G. (1993). 'An Experiment on the Salience of Country of Origin in the Era of Global Brands', *Journal of International Marketing*, 1 (1), 57–77.

—— and YIGANG, P. (1997). 'How MNCs Choose Entry Modes and Form Alliances: The China Experience', *Journal of International Business Studies*, 28 (4), 779–805.

VARADARAJAN, P. R., and CUNNINGHAM, M. H. (1995). 'Strategic Alliances: A Synthesis of Conceptual Foundations', *Journal of the Academy of Marketing Science*, 23 (4), 282–96.

VERLEGH, P., and STEENKAMP, J.-B. E. M. (1999). 'A Review and Meta Analysis of Country of Origin Research', *Journal of Economic Psychology*, 20 (Oct.), 521–46.

VOSS, K. E., and TANSUHAJ, P. (1999). 'A Consumer Perspective on Foreign Market Entry: Building Brands Through Brand Alliances', *Journal of International Consumer Marketing*, 11 (2), 39–58.

WANG, C. C. L. (1999). 'Issues and Advances in International Consumer Research: A Review and Assessment', *Journal of International Marketing and Marketing Research*, 24 (1), 3–21.

WEISS, S. E. (1993). 'Analysis of Complex Negotiations in International Business: The RBC Perspective', *Organization Science*, 4 (2), 269–302.

WILLS, J., SAMLI, A. C., and JACOBS, L. (1991). 'Developing Global Products and Marketing Strategies: A Construct and a Research Agenda', *Journal of the Academy of Marketing Science*, 19 (1), 1–11.

WILSON, I. (1997). 'Entering the Chinese Market', *Journal of International Marketing and Marketing Research*, 22 (3), 139–46.

WITT, J., and RAO, C. P. (1992). 'The Impact of Global Sourcing on Consumers: Country of Origin Effects on Perceived Risk', *Journal of Global Marketing*, 6 (3), 105–29.

YAVAS, U., VERHAGE, B. J., and GREEN, R. T. (1992). 'Global Consumer Segmentation Versus Local Market Orientation', *Management International Review*, 32 (3), 265–72.

YEOH, P. L. (1994). 'Speed to Global Markets: An Empirical Prediction of New Products', *European Journal of Marketing*, 28 (11), 29–53.

—— and CALANTONE, R. J. (1995). 'An Application of the Analytical Hierarchy Process to International Marketing: Selection of a Foreign Distributor', *Journal of Global Marketing*, 8 (3), 39–65.

YOON, S., CANNON, H. M., and YAPRAK, A. (1996). 'Evaluating the CYMYC Cosmopolitanism Scale on Korean Consumers', *Advances in International Marketing*, 7, 211–32.

ZAFARULLAH, M., ALI, M., and YOUNG, S. (1998). 'The Internationalization of the Small Firm in Developing Countries: Exploratory Research from Pakistan', *Journal of Global Marketing*, 11 (3), 21–40.

ZANDPOUR, F., and HARICH, K. R. (1996). 'Think and Feel Country Clusters: A New Approach to International Advertising Standardization', *International Journal of Advertising*, 15 (4), 325–44.

ZHANG, J., and KELVIN A. (1999). 'Strategic Entry for Products and Technology into China', *Journal of International Marketing and Marketing Research*, 24 (2), 85–98.

ZOU, S., TAYLOR, C. R., and OSLAND, G. E. (1998). 'The EXPERF Scale: A Cross-national Generalized Export Performance Measure', *Journal of International Marketing*, 6 (3), 37–58.

# CHAPTER 18

# CULTURE AND HUMAN RESOURCES MANAGEMENT

## JOHN L. GRAHAM

... different people have to be managed differently.

Peter Drucker

## 18.1 INTRODUCTION

THE efficient transaction of international business is made more challenging because of several kinds of obstacles—geographical, financial, legal/political, and cultural. Cultural barriers include several factors that make human interactions more difficult—differences in language, values, and behaviors.

In many ways this last category is the most daunting because cultural differences are often hidden and are certainly the most difficult to quantify. Miles, time zones, exchange rates and such are easily measured. Laws and policies are stated in black and white, although enforcement is obviously a key issue. Alternatively, cultural differences are often not obvious and associated problems are neither easily diagnosed nor corrected. The focus here is on these 'mushy' cultural issues that often have a huge impact on the efficiency of international enterprise, and particularly on the management of people.

Every year for the last seven years senior executives of 250 southern California firms have been surveyed regarding their firms' international business activities (Aigner and Kraemer 1994–2000). Through these years executives have identified 'cultural differences' as the most serious and persistent problem affecting their international sales and operations. 'Financial considerations' were particularly important during the Mexican and Asian financial crises during 1994–5 and 1998–9, respectively. 'Foreign government regulations' were also consistently mentioned as problem areas. But, the problems associated with cultural differences have been most salient for these American executives managing mostly high technology companies. This was found to be so even though, as mentioned above, the cultural barriers are often hidden. The good news in the data is that during these years the 'heights' of all these barriers have been apparently shrinking. International business is becoming easier to conduct. The interviewees suggest that the Internet is helping overcome time and distance barriers and is making communications, even the cross-cultural ones, more efficient. European unification has also played a role. These trends are very encouraging. Although, it may be that the unusually large cash flows typical at southern California companies in the late 1990s has made all problems seem less severe.

Culture has a pervasive impact on the management of human resources (Adler 1997). Culture influences how blue- and white-collar workers respond to pay and non-pay incentives, how international firms are organized, and even how executives compose and implement business strategies. Thus, the remainder of this chapter is organized as follows: First, the central notion of culture will be defined including discussion of its dimensions and measurement. Next, culture's influences on interpersonal behaviors and negotiation styles are presented. Third, human resources policies are outlined that take into account cultural differences in employee groups. The final section focuses on culture's impact on managers' strategic thinking.

# 18.2 CULTURE: ITS DEFINITIONS AND DIMENSIONS

Perhaps the most instructional definitions of culture are the metaphorical ones. Geert Hofstede (1991) refers to culture as the 'software of the mind'. James Day Hodgson, former US Ambassador to Japan describes culture as a 'thicket', that is, difficult to traverse, but with effort and insight it is something you can get through (Hodgson, Sano, and Graham 2000). Then there is anthropologist Edward T. Hall, the seminal writer in this area—he reports:

The people we were advising [State Department] kept bumping their heads against an invisible barrier... We knew that what they were up against was a completely different way of organizing life, of thinking, and of conceiving the underlying assumptions about the family and the state, the economic system, and even Man himself. (Hall 1959: 23)

Hall's first point is an important one. If managers and policy makers do not take culture into account they will experience pain. Think of the last time you bumped your head really hard—it hurt. Executives, companies, and even countries get hurt if cultural differences are ignored.

Most scientific definitions of culture revolve around the notion that it is represented by the values, expectations, and behaviors that are *learned*, *shared* by a group of people (i.e. a 'cultural group'), and *transmitted* from generation to generation (cf. Erez and Earley 1993). Most often country or nation is used to define cultural groups even though most researchers working in the area fully recognize the associated limitations. That is, all countries are culturally diverse—India, for example, includes the eleven principle languages spoken on the subcontinent on each ten-rupee note. Or, consider Belgium and Canada where substantial portions of the population speak different first languages. However, most international data available have been collected at the national level, so using national culture as a point of departure in the area is convenient. Moreover, despite the obvious limitations, using nation as a proxy unit for culture has proven quite useful.

A second key limitation associated with the notion of culture has to do with the extent to which its study promotes stereotypes. That is, not everyone in a culture behaves the same way. Yes, culture does influence values, expectations, and behaviors. But, so do personality, economic status, social context, and a wide variety of other factors. Therefore, implied in most writing and research on the topic are the descriptors of cultural norms, behavioral averages, or typical behaviors. For example, the typical American will use threats during business negotiations (e.g. 'If you can't give me a lower price, I'll buy from someone else.'). However, not every American will use threats. Au (1999) provides a very important discussion of the potential problems of such *intra-cultural* variation.

Finally, despite both limitations, culture has proven a most useful concept. Knowing employees' or business partners' cultural backgrounds helps managers predict and understand their values, expectations, and behaviors. Taking into account cultural background helps managers do a better job. Next we describe the most important dimensions of culture as reported in the management literature.

## 18.2.1 Silent languages (Edward T. Hall)

The leading thinker in the area of culture and international business is anthropologist Edward Hall. His own background is pertinent. When he began writing about culture and business contexts in the 1960s his colleagues in anthropology eschewed the topic (Graham and Gronhaug 1988). In the field there was a general disdain for multinational companies—they were seen to 'disrupt' cultures. Hall did not share this phobia of international business—his father was an advertising executive for a multinational company (MNC). Growing up in an ad man's house (Hall 1992) taught him to appreciate the connections between commerce and culture that his associates seemed to have forgotten about until the 1990s.

His article, 'The Silent Language in Overseas Business', which appeared in the *Harvard Business Review* in 1960 remains a most worthwhile read. Based on his book published a year earlier (Hall 1959) it makes the fundamental point that we are not aware of the power of culture, because it tends to communicate below our level of consciousness in 'silent languages'. Hall specifies five such silent languages, those of time, space, things, friendship, and agreements. Thus, he defined five useful dimensions of culture using his years of fieldwork (among Native Americans, African-Americans, Japanese, Latin Americans, and other peoples) as evidence for their veracity.

Hall describes in much detail how *time* communicates differently across cultures. Schedules are important in Germany and not so important in Mexico. Such cross-cultural differences in the salience of time seem to be born out in recent empirical work—see Table 18.1 wherein thirty-one countries are compared. More recently, Hall and Hall (1990) have more deeply delineated cultural differences in perceptions of time. *Space* also communicates. The size of one's office is important in the United States, but says little about executives' status in Arab countries. Hall contrasts the materialism (a love of *things*) of Americans with the spirituality of India. He compares the quick *friendships* common in the US to the slow developing, but hugely

## Table 18.1  A measure of the relative importance of time

Rank of 31 countries for overall pace of life (combination of three measures: minutes downtown pedestrians take to walk 60 feet; minutes it takes a postal clerk to complete a stamp-purchase transaction; and accuracy in minutes of public clocks)

|  | Overall ranking | Walking 60 feet | Postal service | Public clocks |
| --- | --- | --- | --- | --- |
| Switzerland | 1 | 3 | 2 | 1 |
| Ireland | 2 | 1 | 3 | 11 |
| Germany | 3 | 5 | 1 | 8 |
| Japan | 4 | 7 | 4 | 6 |
| Italy | 5 | 10 | 12 | 2 |
| England | 6 | 4 | 9 | 13 |
| Sweden | 7 | 13 | 5 | 7 |
| Austria | 8 | 23 | 8 | 3 |
| Netherlands | 9 | 2 | 14 | 25 |
| Hong Kong | 10 | 14 | 6 | 14 |
| France | 11 | 8 | 18 | 10 |
| Poland | 12 | 12 | 15 | 8 |
| Costa Rica | 13 | 16 | 10 | 15 |
| Taiwan | 14 | 18 | 7 | 21 |
| Singapore | 15 | 25 | 11 | 4 |
| United States | 16 | 6 | 23 | 20 |
| Canada | 17 | 11 | 21 | 22 |
| South Korea | 18 | 20 | 20 | 16 |
| Hungary | 19 | 19 | 19 | 18 |
| Czech Republic | 20 | 21 | 17 | 23 |
| Greece | 21 | 14 | 13 | 29 |
| Kenya | 22 | 9 | 30 | 24 |
| China | 23 | 24 | 25 | 12 |
| Bulgaria | 24 | 27 | 22 | 17 |
| Romania | 25 | 30 | 29 | 5 |
| Jordan | 26 | 28 | 27 | 19 |
| Syria | 27 | 29 | 28 | 27 |
| El Salvador | 28 | 22 | 16 | 31 |
| Brazil | 29 | 31 | 24 | 28 |
| Indonesia | 30 | 26 | 26 | 30 |
| Mexico | 31 | 17 | 31 | 26 |

*Source* Levine 1997
Reprinted with permission from *American Demographies.* Copyright 1997.

important strong social ties and reciprocity in Latin America. Finally, he discusses the differences in *agreements*—in America the details of a written contract are crucial, in other places the qualities of the interpersonal relationship between business people are much more salient than any piece of paper.

In a subsequent book Hall (1976) details another important dimension of cultural difference. He distinguishes between low-context cultures and high-context cultures. In low-context cultures the social context of communication (e.g. who says it, when it is said, how it is said, where it is said, etc.) has little to do with the interpretation of what is said. Alternatively, in high-context cultures what is said can be understood only with a deep knowledge of the important social contextual factors surrounding the communication. In high-context cultures social hierarchy and relationships are important—'it's not *what* you know, it's *who* you know that's important'. Hall identifies the United States and Germany as low-context countries (information is salient) and Japan and Mexico as high-context countries (personal relationships are salient).

## 18.2.2 Cultural values (Geert Hofstede)

Hofstede is the most frequently cited author in international management, and with good reason. Hofstede's background is also pertinent—he grew up in the Netherlands, a country, as he puts it, on the 'cultural' border between northern (Protestant) and southern (Catholic) Europe. Hofstede's work (1980, 1991) draws heavily on Hall's ideas and the empirical work of Haire, Ghiselli, and Porter (1966) and Triandis (1972, 1995) for the theoretical justification of his empirical explorations.

Between 1968 and 1972 Hofstede had more than 100,000 employees of IBM in more than fifty countries complete a questionnaire regarding work values. Based on analyses of those data he defined four dimensions of culture—individualism/collectivism index (IND), power distance index (PDI), uncertainty avoidance index (UAI), and masculinity/femininity index (MAS). Moreover, he assigned numerical scores to each of fifty-one countries and two regions for each of the dimensions. In subsequent work with Michael Bond (Hofstede and Bond 1988), a Canadian teaching in Hong Kong, he identified a fifth dimension, long-term orientation (LTO).

Hofstede's work is important theoretically. But, its primary utility is based upon the scores he reports for the fifty-one countries and regions. These scores have been incorporated into hundreds of international management studies. His work has been heavily criticized (see West and Graham 1998, or Erez and Earley 1993 for summaries). However, three of the dimensions he

## Table 18.2  Several dimensions of culture

| Country | IND | PDI | UAI | TICPI 1999 | Df Eng | Primary language |
|---|---|---|---|---|---|---|
| Australia | 90 | 36 | 51 | 8.7 | 0 | English |
| Great Britain | 89 | 35 | 35 | 8.6 | 0 | English |
| Ireland | 70 | 28 | 35 | 7.7 | 0 | English |
| New Zealand | 79 | 22 | 49 | 9.4 | 0 | English |
| US | 91 | 40 | 46 | 7.5 | 0 | English |
| South Africa* | 65 | 49 | 49 | 5 | 0.6 | Afrikaans |
| Canada* | 80 | 39 | 48 | 9.2 | 0.9 | English |
| Austria | 55 | 11 | 70 | 7.6 | 1 | German |
| Germany | 67 | 35 | 65 | 8.0 | 1 | German |
| Jamaica* | 39 | 45 | 13 | 3.8 | 1 | Creole |
| Netherlands | 80 | 38 | 53 | 9.0 | 1 | Dutch |
| Switzerland* | 68 | 34 | 58 | 8.9 | 1.6 | German |
| Belgium* | 75 | 65 | 94 | 5.3 | 1.7 | Flemish |
| Denmark | 74 | 18 | 23 | 10.0 | 2 | Danish |
| Norway | 69 | 31 | 50 | 8.9 | 2 | Norwegian |
| Sweden | 71 | 31 | 29 | 9.4 | 2 | Swedish |
| Argentina | 46 | 49 | 86 | 3.0 | 3 | Spanish |
| Brazil | 38 | 69 | 76 | 4.1 | 3 | Portuguese |
| Chile | 23 | 63 | 86 | 6.9 | 3 | Spanish |
| Columbia | 13 | 67 | 80 | 2.9 | 3 | Spanish |
| Costa Rica | 15 | 35 | 86 | 5.1 | 3 | Spanish |
| El Salvador | 19 | 66 | 94 | 3.9 | 3 | Spanish |
| Ecuador | 8 | 78 | 67 | 2.4 | 3 | Spanish |
| France | 71 | 68 | 86 | 6.6 | 3 | French |
| Greece | 35 | 60 | 112 | 4.9 | 3 | Greek |
| Guatemala | 6 | 95 | 101 | 3.2 | 3 | Spanish |
| Iran | 41 | 58 | 59 | – | 3 | Farsi |
| Italy | 76 | 50 | 75 | 4.7 | 3 | Italian |
| Mexico | 30 | 81 | 82 | 3.4 | 3 | Spanish |
| Pakistan | 14 | 55 | 70 | 2.2 | 3 | Panjabi |
| Panama | 11 | 95 | 86 | – | 3 | Spanish |
| Peru | 16 | 64 | 87 | 4.5 | 3 | Spanish |
| Portugal | 27 | 63 | 104 | 6.7 | 3 | Portuguese |
| Spain | 51 | 57 | 86 | 6.6 | 3 | Spanish |

**Table 18.2** *Continued*

| Country | IND | PDI | UAI | TICPI 1999 | Df Eng | Primary language |
|---|---|---|---|---|---|---|
| Uruguay | 36 | 61 | 100 | 4.4 | 3 | Spanish |
| Venezuela | 12 | 81 | 76 | 2.6 | 3 | Spanish |
| Yugoslavia | 27 | 76 | 88 | 2 | 3 | Serbo-Croatian |
| India* | 48 | 77 | 40 | 2.9 | 3.7 | Indo-Aryan |
| Finland | 63 | 33 | 59 | 9.8 | 4 | Finnish |
| Japan | 46 | 54 | 92 | 6.0 | 4 | Japanese |
| Korea | 18 | 60 | 85 | 3.8 | 4 | Korean |
| Turkey | 37 | 66 | 85 | 3.6 | 4 | Turkish |
| Israel | 54 | 13 | 81 | 6.8 | 5 | Hebrew |
| Arabic countries | 38 | 80 | 68 | – | 5 | Arabic |
| Hong Kong | 25 | 68 | 29 | 7.7 | 6 | Cantonese |
| Singapore* | 20 | 74 | 8 | 9.1 | 6 | Taiwanese |
| Taiwan | 17 | 58 | 69 | 5.6 | 6 | Taiwanese |
| Indonesia | 14 | 78 | 48 | 1.7 | 7 | Bahasa |
| Malaysia* | 26 | 104 | 36 | 5.1 | 7 | Malay |
| Philippines* | 32 | 94 | 44 | 3.6 | 7 | Tagalog |
| Thailand | 20 | 64 | 64 | 3.2 | 7 | Thai |

*A substantial portion of the population is bilingual.

Columns = 1. (IND) Individualism Index (Hofstede 1991); 2. (PDI) Power Distance Index (Hofstede 1991); 3. (UAI) Uncertainty Avoidance Index (Hofstede 1991); 4. (TICPI) Transparency International Corruption Perception Index (*www.transparency.de*), 10 = least corrupt, 0 = most corrupt; 5. (Df Eng) Distance from English (West and Graham 2000); in some countries a secondary language is prevalent. For example, in South Africa 60% of the people speak Afrikaans as their first language and 40% speak English as their first language. The Distance from English of Afrikaans is 1, so the weighted average for the country is 0.6. The scores for the other mixed-language countries such as Canada and Belgium are calculated in the same way; 6. Primary language spoken.

identifies have been shown to be useful in many studies—IND, PDI, and UAI—so those three are discussed in some detail here. Readers interested in more detail regarding MAS and LTO are referred to the articles cited above and Hostede's new book on MAS (1998).

Hofstede's scores for each of the fifty-one countries he studied are listed in Table 18.2. In the more individualistic countries (e.g. the United States is rated highest on the IND scale with a score of 91) group membership is not so important and social ties are relatively loose. In highly collectivistic countries such as Japan group cohesion is a central value. In high power distance countries like Mexico social hierarchies are salient and behaviors, even language use, differ according to social status. In low PDI countries like Australia egalitarian values strongly influence behavior and social status distinctions are often ignored and even denigrated. Differences in uncertainty avoidance are perhaps demonstrated by a comparison of Japan (quite high on UAI) and Hong Kong (quite low). Hofstede would explain that while Japanese avoid risks the Chinese in Hong Kong are attracted to risky situations and uncertainties. Perhaps UAI helps explain the great affinity for horse racing in Hong Kong!

Hofstede (1980) notes a high correlation between IND and PDI (r = .67, p < 0.05) suggesting that the two values frequently coincide. He also bases his theoretical discussions of both concepts on Hall's (1976) high/low context concept. That is, cultures such as the Japanese Hall labels high-context, and they tend to be collectivistic and hierarchical. This has led Houston and Graham (2001) to propose a single dimension of culture subsuming IND, PDI, and high/low context labeled 'Social Context Salient Cultures' (SCSC). Japan and Mexico would be examples of countries where social context is salient, or high SCSC.

Most recently the Project GLOBE group consisting of some 160 scholars around the world has collected data in 64 countries and identified eight dimensions of leadership-related values (House *et al.* 2000). Similar to Hofstede they include uncertainty avoidance, power distance, and collectivism; they distinguish between gender egalitarianism and assertiveness; and they add future orientation, performance orientation, and humane orientation. These new data and dimensions will allow for even better understandings of how cultures differ with regard to managerially relevant values.

## 18.2.3  A measure of corruption (transparency international)

Ethics and notions of corrupt behavior are known to vary across cultures. During the last few years a non-governmental organization headquartered in Germany has endeavored to develop an accurate measure of the corruptness of countries. The Corruption Perception Index produced by Transparency International (TICPI) is now widely recognized as the best such measure. The TI website (*www.transparency.de*) provides a wealth of information regarding methodological details which are only summarized here. The TICPI integrates scores from six survey sources such as Gallup International and the DRI/

McGraw-Hill Global Risk Service. The reported correlations among the diverse sources range between 0.64 and 0.97. 'The index is a poll of polls, putting together the subjective evaluations of business people, political analysts, and the general public.' TI defines corruption in a very *western* way as, 'the misuse of public power for private benefits, e.g. the bribing of public officials, taking kickbacks in public procurement, or embezzling public funds'. A sampling of the 98 countries they rate is included in Table 18.3, and the complete listing can be downloaded from their website. They explain the meaning of their scores, 'A ten stands for a highly clean country while a zero equals a country where business transactions are entirely dominated by kickbacks, extortion, bribery, etc.'

Houston and Graham (2001) report the TICPI to have good validity characteristics (i.e. both convergent and nomological). They also describe in some detail the Western European bias inherent in the definition of corruption specified in the TI survey materials. Even so, they conclude the TICPI provides international managers an answer to the question about which countries have a 'widespread history of corruption'. Further, the TICPI definition of corruption as bribery is quite close to those serving as the bases for the American Foreign Corrupt Practices Act and the other similar policies being adopted in the European Union, the OECD, and the Organization of American States. The information provided in the TICPI, in conjunction with other sources, can be useful in making both strategic and operational decisions about foreign sales and operations.

## 18.2.4 Linguistic distance

Language is a crucial aspect of culture. The important role of language spoken on management styles is most clearly articulated by Jean-Claude Usunier (1998). Relatedly, recent empirical studies (West and Graham 1998) indicate that a new concept, linguistic distance, may prove to be another useful metric for cultural differences. Over the years linguistics researchers have determined that languages around the world conform to 'family trees' based on the similarity of their forms and development (Chen, Sokal, and Huhlen 1995). For example, Spanish, Catalan, Italian, French, and Portuguese are all classified as Romance languages because of their common roots in Latin. Distances can be measured on these linguistic trees. If we assume English to be the starting point, German is one branch away, Danish two, Spanish three, Japanese four, Arabic five, Chinese six, and Thai seven. These 'Distance from English' scores are listed for the fifty-one cultures in Table 18.2.

We are now learning that this measure of distance from English predicts other important aspects of culture—some of Hofstede's (and the Project GLOBE) cultural values and the Transparency International Corruption Perception Index (Houston and Graham 2001). That is, as linguistic distance from English increases Hofstede's individualism decreases (correlation coefficient r = .71, p < 0.05), power distance increases (r = .56, p < 0.05), and corruption increases (r = .58, p < 0.05). These studies are the first in this genre and much more work needs to be done. However, the notion of linguistic distance appears to hold promise for better understanding and predicting cultural differences in management behaviors and values.

## 18.2.5 Summary

So far we have presented the most salient dimensions of cultural differences as yet developed. They are related to one another conceptually and empirically. Hofstede's data include fifty-one countries, the Project GLOBE data at least sixty, the Transparency International ninety-eight countries, and the Linguistic Distance data provide a metric for culture for all countries. Indeed, the Linguistic Distance may prove the most useful of all because it can be applied for ethnic/cultural groups, indeed even individuals within countries as well. The fundamental point is that knowing what language someone speaks appears to provide some information for predictions about values and behaviors.

Moreover, the relationship between language spoken and cultural values holds even deeper implications. That is, as English spreads around the world circa 2000 via school systems and the Internet (*American Prospect* 2000), cultural values of individualism and egalitarianism will spread with it. For example, both Chinese Mandarin speakers and Spanish speakers must learn two words for 'you' (*ni* and *nin*, and *tu* and *usted*, respectively). The proper usage of the two depends completely on knowledge of the social context of the conversation. Respect for status is communicated by use of *nin* and *usted*. In English there is only one form of 'you'. Speakers can ignore social context and status and still speak correctly. It is easier and social status becomes less important.

Now we turn to the implications of culture for managers of international human resources.

# 18.3 INTERPERSONAL BEHAVIORS AND INTERNATIONAL NEGOTIATION STYLES

International managers negotiate in a wide variety of circumstances—with customers, distributors, licensees, suppliers, labor unions, governmental officials, headquarters or subsidiary personnel, joint venture partners, and supervisors. We know from a variety of studies that culture influences how people behave in interpersonal job situations such as teamwork (e.g. Song, Xie, and Dyer 2000), job interviews, and supervisor/subordinate interactions. However, because face-to-face negotiations are ubiquitous in international business our discussion focuses on that fundamental management activity. And, certainly much of the information provided regarding negotiations applies to these other kinds of work-related interactions.

The material in this section is based on a systematic study (Graham, Mintu, and Rodgers 1994; Hodgson, Sano, and Graham 2000) over the last two decades in which the negotiation styles of more than 1,000 businesspeople in eighteen countries (twenty cultures) were considered. The countries studied were: Japan, Korea, Taiwan, China (northern and southern), Hong Kong, Vietnam, the Philippines, Russia, the Czech Republic, Norway, Germany, France, the UK, Spain, Brazil, Mexico, Canada (English speakers and French speakers), and the United States.

Looking broadly across the several cultures two important lessons stand out. The first is that regional generalizations usually are not correct. For example, Japanese and Korean negotiation styles are quite similar in some ways, but in other ways they could not be more different. The second lesson learned from these studies is that Japan is an exceptional place: On almost every dimension of negotiation style considered, the Japanese are on or near the end of the scale. Sometimes, Americans are on the other end. But actually, most of the time Americans are somewhere in the middle. The reader will see this evinced in the data presented below. The Japanese approach, however, is most distinct, even *sui generis*.

Cultural differences cause four kinds of problems in international business negotiations—at the levels of:

(1) language
(2) nonverbal behaviors
(3) values
(4) thinking and decision-making processes.

The order is important; the problems lower on the list are more serious because they are more subtle. For example, two negotiators would notice immediately if one is speaking Japanese and the other German. The solution to the problem may be as simple as hiring an interpreter or talking in a common third language, or it may be as difficult as learning a language. Regardless of the solution, the problem is obvious. Cultural differences in nonverbal behaviors, on the other hand, are almost always hidden below our awareness. That is to say, in face-to-face negotiations participants nonverbally—and more subtly—give off and take in a great deal of information. Some experts argue that this information is more important than the verbal information. Almost all this signaling goes on below our levels of consciousness. When the nonverbal signals from foreign partners are different, negotiators are most apt to misinterpret them without even being conscious of the mistake. For example, when a French client consistently interrupts, Americans tend to feel uncomfortable without noticing exactly why. In this manner, interpersonal friction often colors business relationships, goes on undetected, and, consequently, uncorrected. Differences in values and thinking and decision-making processes are hidden even deeper and therefore are even harder to cure. We discuss these differences below, starting with language and nonverbal behaviors.

## 18.3.1 Differences in language and nonverbal behaviors

The verbal behaviors of negotiators in fourteen of the cultures (six negotiators in each of the fourteen groups) were videotaped. The numbers in the body of Table 18.3 represent the percentages of statements that were classified into each category listed. That is, 7 per cent of the statements made by Japanese negotiators were classified as promises, 4 per cent were threats, 7 per cent were recommendations, and so on. The verbal bargaining behaviors used by the negotiators during the simulations proved to be surprisingly similar across cultures. Negotiations in all fourteen cultures studied were comprised primarily of information-exchange tactics—questions and self-disclosures. Note that the Japanese appear on the low end of the continuum of self-disclosures. Their 34 per cent (along with the Spaniards and the English-speaking Canadians) was the lowest across all fourteen groups, suggesting that they are the most reticent about giving information. Overall, however, the verbal tactics used were surprisingly similar across the diverse cultures.

Table 18.4 provides the analyses of some linguistic aspects and nonverbal behaviors for the fourteen videotaped groups. While these efforts merely scratch the surface of these kinds of behavioral analyses, they still provide indications of substantial cultural differences. Note that, once again, the Japanese are at or next to the end of the continuum on almost every

Table 18.3 Verbal negotiation tactics (the 'what' of communications)

| Bargaining behaviors | Cultures (for each group, n = 6) | | | | | | | | | | | | | |
|---|---|---|---|---|---|---|---|---|---|---|---|---|---|---|
| | JPN | KOR | TWN | CHN* | RUSS | GRM | UK | FRN | SPN | BRZ | MEX | FCAN | ECAN | USA |
| Promise. A statement in which the source indicated its intentions to provide the target with a reinforcing consequence, which source anticipates target will evaluate as pleasant, positive, or rewarding. | 7† | 4 | 9 | 6 | 5 | 7 | 11 | 5 | 11 | 3 | 7 | 8 | 6 | 8 |
| Threat. Same as promise, except that the reinforcing consequences are thought to be noxious, unpleasant, or punishing. | 4 | 2 | 2 | 1 | 3 | 3 | 3 | 5 | 2 | 2 | 1 | 3 | 0 | 4 |
| Recommendation. A statement in which the source predicts that a pleasant environmental consequence will occur to the target. Its occurrence is not under source's control. | 7 | 1 | 5 | 2 | 4 | 5 | 6 | 3 | 4 | 5 | 8 | 5 | 4 | 4 |
| Warning. Same as recommendation, except that the consequences are thought to be unpleasant. | 2 | 0 | 3 | 1 | 0 | 1 | 1 | 3 | 1 | 1 | 2 | 5 | 0 | 1 |
| Reward. A statement by the source that is thought to create pleasant consequences for the target. | 1 | 3 | 2 | 1 | 3 | 4 | 5 | 3 | 3 | 2 | 1 | 1 | 3 | 2 |
| Punishment. Same as reward, except that the consequences are thought to be unpleasant. | 1 | 5 | 1 | 0 | 1 | 2 | 0 | 3 | 2 | 3 | 0 | 2 | 1 | 3 |

| Behavior | | | | | | | | | | | | | |
|---|---|---|---|---|---|---|---|---|---|---|---|---|---|
| **Positive normative appeal.** A statement in which the source indicates that the target's past, present, or future behavior was or will be in conformity with social norms. | 1 | 1 | 0 | 1 | 0 | 0 | 0 | 0 | 0 | 0 | 1 | 0 | 1 |
| **Negative normative appeal.** Same as positive normative appeal except that the target's behavior is in violation of social norms. | 3 | 2 | 1 | 0 | 0 | 1 | 1 | 0 | 1 | 1 | 2 | 1 | 1 |
| **Commitment.** A statement by the source to the effect that its future bids will not go below or above a certain level. | 15 | 13 | 9 | 10 | 11 | 9 | 13 | 10 | 9 | 8 | 9 | 8 | 14 | 13 |
| **Self-disclosure.** A statement in which the source reveals information about itself. | 34 | 36 | 42 | 36 | 40 | 47 | 39 | 42 | 34 | 39 | 38 | 42 | 34 | 36 |
| **Question.** A statement in which the source asks the target to reveal information about itself. | 20 | 21 | 14 | 34 | 27 | 11 | 15 | 18 | 17 | 22 | 27 | 19 | 26 | 20 |
| **Command.** A statement in which the source suggests that the target perform a certain behavior. | 8 | 13 | 11 | 7 | 7 | 12 | 9 | 9 | 17 | 14 | 7 | 5 | 10 | 6 |

* Northern China (Tianjin and environs).

† Read '7 percent of the statements made by Japanese negotiators were promises'.

*Source* Cateora and Graham, forthcoming 2002

# Table 18.4 Structural aspects of language and nonverbal behaviors ('how' things are said)

| Bargaining behaviors (per 30 minutes) | Cultures (for each group, n = 6) | | | | | | | | | | | | | |
|---|---|---|---|---|---|---|---|---|---|---|---|---|---|---|
| | JPN | KOR | TWN | CHN* | RUSS | GRM | UK | FRN | SPN | BRZ | MEX | FCAN | ECAN | USA |
| *Structural aspects* | | | | | | | | | | | | | | |
| 'No's.' The number of times the word 'no' was used by each negotiator. | 1.9 | 7.4 | 5.9 | 1.5 | 2.3 | 6.7 | 5.4 | 11.3 | 23.2 | 41.9 | 4.5 | 7.0 | 10.1 | 4.5 |
| 'You's.' The number of times the word 'you' was used by each negotiator. | 31.5 | 34.2 | 36.6 | 26.8 | 23.6 | 39.7 | 54.8 | 70.2 | 73.3 | 90.4 | 56.3 | 72.4 | 64.4 | 54.1 |
| *Nonverbal behaviors* | | | | | | | | | | | | | | |
| Silent periods. The number of conversational gaps of 10 seconds or longer. | 2.5 | 0 | 0 | 2.3 | 3.7 | 0 | 2.5 | 1.0 | 0 | 0 | 1.1 | 0.2 | 2.9 | 1.7 |
| Conversational overlaps. Number of interruptions. | 6.2 | 22.0 | 12.3 | 17.1 | 13.3 | 20.8 | 5.3 | 20.7 | 28.0 | 14.3 | 10.6 | 24.0 | 17.0 | 5.1 |
| Facial gazing. Number of minutes negotiators spent looking at opponent's face. | 3.9 | 9.9 | 19.7 | 11.1 | 8.7 | 10.2 | 9.0 | 16.0 | 13.7 | 15.6 | 14.7 | 18.8 | 10.4 | 10.0 |
| Touching. Incidents of bargainers touching one another (not including handshaking). | 0 | 0 | 0 | 0 | 0 | 0 | 0 | 0.1 | 0 | 4.7 | 0 | 0 | 0 | 0 |

* Northern China (Tianjin and environs).
*Source* Cateora and Graham, forthcoming 2002

dimension of the behaviors listed. Their facial gazing and touching are the least among the fourteen groups. Only the northern Chinese used the words 'no' less frequently and only the Russians used more silent periods than did the Japanese.

A broader examination of the data in Tables 18.3 and 18.4 reveals a more meaningful conclusion: The variation across cultures is greater when comparing linguistic aspects of language and nonverbal behaviors than when the verbal content of negotiations is considered. For example, notice the great differences between Japanese and Brazilians in Table 18.3 *vis-à-vis* Table 18.4.

Following are further descriptions of the distinctive aspects of each of the fourteen cultural groups videotaped. Certainly, conclusions about the individual cultures cannot be drawn from an analysis of only six business people in each culture, but the suggested cultural differences are worthwhile to consider briefly:

*Japan*: Consistent with most descriptions of Japanese negotiation behavior, the results of this analysis suggest their style of interaction is among the least aggressive (or most polite). Threats, commands, and warnings appear to be deemphasized in favor of the more positive promises, recommendations, and commitments. Particularly indicative of their polite conversational style was their infrequent use of 'no' and 'you' and facial gazing, as well as more frequent silent periods.

*Korea*: Perhaps one of the more interesting aspects of the analysis is the contrast of the Asian styles of negotiations. Non-Asians often generalize about the Orient; the findings demonstrate, however, that this is a mistake. Korean negotiators used considerably more punishments and commands than did the Japanese. Koreans used the word 'no' and interrupted more than three times as frequently as the Japanese. Moreover, no silent periods occurred between Korean negotiators.

*China (northern)*: The behaviors of the negotiators from northern China (i.e. in and around Tianjin) are most remarkable in the emphasis on asking questions at 34 per cent. Indeed, 70 per cent of the statements made by the Chinese negotiators were classified as information-exchange tactics. Other aspects of their behavior were quite similar to the Japanese, particularly the use of 'no' and 'you' and silent periods.

*Taiwan*: The behavior of the businesspeople in Taiwan was quite different from that in China and Japan but similar to that in Korea. The Chinese on Taiwan were exceptional in the time of facial gazing—on the average almost 20 out of 30 minutes. They asked fewer questions and provided more information (self-disclosures) than did any of the other Asian groups.

*Russia*: The Russians' style was quite different from that of any other European group, and, indeed, was quite similar in many respects to the style of the Japanese. They used 'no' and 'you' infrequently and used the most silent periods of any group. Only the Japanese did less facial gazing, and only the Chinese asked a greater percentage of questions.

*Germany*: The behaviors of the Western Germans are difficult to characterize because they fell toward the center of almost all the continua. However, the Germans were exceptional in the high percentage of self-disclosures at 47 per cent, and the low percentage of questions at 11 per cent.

*United Kingdom*: The behaviors of the British negotiators are remarkably similar to those of the Americans in all respects.

*Spain*: *Diga* is perhaps a good metaphor for the Spanish approach to negotiations evinced in our data. When you make a phone call in Madrid, the usual greeting on the other end is not *hola* (hello) but is, instead, *diga* (speak). It is not surprising, then, that the Spaniards in the videotaped negotiations likewise used the highest percentage of commands (17 per cent) of any of the groups and gave comparatively little information (self-disclosures, 34 per cent). Moreover, they interrupted one another more frequently than any other group, and they used the terms 'no' and 'you' very frequently.

*France*: The style of the French negotiators is perhaps the most aggressive of all the groups. In particular, they used the highest percentage of threats and warnings (together, 8 per cent). They also used interruptions, facial gazing, and 'no' and 'you' very frequently compared to the other groups, and one of the French negotiators touched his partner on the arm during the simulation.

*Brazil*: The Brazilian businesspeople, like the French and Spanish, were quite aggressive. They used the second highest percentage of commands of all the groups. On average, the Brazilians said the word 'no' 42 times, 'you' 90 times, and touched one another on the arm about 5 times during 30 minutes of negotiation. Facial gazing was also high.

*Mexico*: The patterns of Mexican behavior in our negotiations are good reminders of the dangers of regional or language-group generalizations. Both verbal and nonverbal behaviors are quite different than those of their Latin American (Brazilian) or continental (Spanish) cousins. Indeed, Mexicans answer the telephone with the much less demanding *bueno* (short for good day). In many respects, the Mexican behavior is very similar to that of the negotiators from the United States.

*French-speaking Canada*: The French-speaking Canadians behaved quite similarly to their continental cousins. Like the negotiators from France, they too used high percentages of threats and warnings, and even more interruptions and eye contact. Such an aggressive interaction style would not mix well with some of the more low-key styles of some of the Asian groups or with English speakers, including English-speaking Canadians.

*English-speaking Canada*: The Canadians who speak English as their first language used the lowest percentage of aggressive persuasive tactics (threats, warnings, and punishments totaled only 1 per cent) of all fourteen groups.

Perhaps, as communications researchers suggest, such stylistic differences are the seeds of interethnic discord as witnessed in Canada over the years. With respect to international negotiations, the English-speaking Canadians used noticeably more interruptions and 'no's' than negotiators from either of Canada's major trading partners, the United States and Japan.

*United States*: Like the Germans and the British, the Americans fell in the middle of most continua. They did interrupt one another less frequently than all the others, but that was their sole distinction.

## 18.3.2 Differences in values

Three values—objectivity, competitiveness, and punctuality—which are held strongly and deeply by most Americans seem to frequently cause misunderstandings and bad feelings in international business negotiations.

*Objectivity*: 'Americans make decisions based upon the bottom line and on cold, hard facts.' 'Americans don't play favorites.' 'Economics and performance count, not people.' 'Business is business.' Such statements well reflect American notions of the importance of objectivity.

The single most important book on the topic of negotiation, *Getting to YES* (Fisher, Ury, and Patton 1991), is highly recommended for both American and foreign readers. The latter will learn not only about negotiations but, perhaps more important, about how Americans think about negotiations. The authors are quite emphatic about 'separating the people from the problem', and they state, 'Every negotiator has two kinds of interests: in the substance and in the relationship.' This advice may be worthwhile in the United States or perhaps in low SCSC Germany, but in most places in the world such advice is nonsense. In most places in the world, personalities and substance are not separate issues and cannot be made so.

For example, consider how important nepotism is in Chinese or Hispanic cultures. Experts tell us that businesses don't grow beyond the bounds and bonds of tight family control in the burgeoning 'Chinese Commonwealth' (Redding 1993). Things work the same way in Spain, Mexico, and the Philippines by nature. And, just as naturally, negotiators from such countries not only will take things personally but will be personally affected by negotiation outcomes. What happens to them at the negotiation table will affect the business relationship regardless of the economics involved.

*Competitiveness*: One of the most important sentences written in English appears in Adam Smith's *The Wealth of Nations* (1776): 'By pursuing his own interests he frequently promotes that of society more effectually than when he really intends to promote it.' This 'invisible hand' justification is the philosophical underpinning of Western capitalism as it spreads across the globe circa 2000. This philosophy also underpins the approach to negotiations commonly accepted among American businesspeople. Thus, Americans take what Rubin and Brown (1975) called an *individualistic* approach to negotiations. They tend to see it as a competitive 'game' wherein each side takes care of itself. This is very different from the approach taken in more collectivistic cultures where long-term, mutually beneficial relationships are the goal. Perhaps managers in places like Japan and Mexico focus on the word 'frequently' in their interpretations of Smith's central sentence. From their perspective a business negotiation is one of those circumstances where competitiveness is dysfunctional and cooperation should be emphasized. Indeed, a recent study by Esteban, Ockova, Tang, and Graham (2000) provides empirical evidence that businesspeople in more individualistic cultures behave more competitively.

*Time*: 'Just make them wait.' This is one of the most powerful negotiation tactics when the opponents are from cultures that place high value on time (Hall 1960; Hodgson *et al.* 2000). See the top of the list in Table 18.1 for countries where time is more highly valued, and time-related negotiation strategies and tactics can be expected to be more effective.

## 18.3.3 Differences in thinking and decision-making processes

When faced with a complex negotiation task, most Westerners (notice the generalization here with which some will disagree, e.g. Allinson and Hayes, 2000) divide the large task up into a series of smaller tasks. Issues such as prices, delivery, warranty, and service contracts may be settled one issue at a time, with the final agreement being the sum of the sequence of smaller agreements. In Asia, however, a different approach is more often taken wherein all the issues are discussed at once, in no apparent order, and concessions are made on all issues at the end of the discussion. The Western sequential approach and the Eastern holistic approach do not mix well.

For example, American managers report great difficulties in measuring progress in Japan. After all, in America, you are half done when half the issues are settled. But in Japan, nothing seems to get settled. Then, surprise, you are done. Often, Americans make unnecessary concessions right before agreements are announced by the Japanese (Hodgson *et al.* 2000). In negotiations with Chinese managers Americans were found to complain often about the Chinese bringing up issues they thought were already settled (Lee and Graham 2001).

Western bargainers should anticipate such a holistic approach and be prepared to discuss all issues simultaneously and in an apparently haphazard order. Progress in the talks should not be measured by how many issues have been settled. Rather, Western negotiators must try to gauge the quality of the business relationship.

All these differences across the cultures are quite complex, and this material by itself should not be used to predict the behaviors of foreign counterparts. Instead, great care should be taken with respect to the aforementioned dangers of stereotypes. The key here is to be aware of these kinds of differences so that the Japanese silence, the French threat, or the 'Chinese lack of organization' are not over- or misinterpreted.

# 18.4 HRM in the International Context

The design and management of an international workforce must of course take into account all the cultural differences in values, expectations, behaviors, and negotiation and communication styles described above. The implications of culture for organizational design and employee recruiting, selection, training, motivation, compensation, evaluation, and control are now considered.

## 18.4.1 Designing the organization

The first step in managing an organization is its design. Based on analyses of current and potential market conditions, the local work environment, competition, and the firm's resources and capabilities, decisions must be made regarding the numbers, characteristics, and assignments of personnel. All these design decisions are made more challenging by the wide variety of circumstances in the global work- and marketplaces.

Mode of entry is the initial design decision to be made. In sourcing products and services the decision ranges from arm's-length purchasing agreements with foreign suppliers, to contract manufacturing agreements, to establishing green-field manufacturing facilities. Foreign market entry decisions range from simply selling to home country exporters, to working

524 JOHN L. GRAHAM

with a variety of foreign intermediaries, to establishing a local sales force. The discussion to follow assumes the last two options—choosing to establish either a green-field manufacturing operation or a local sales force in a foreign country.

In either case the second decision to be made is the make up of the management team—particularly how many expatriates (see Black, Gregersen, Mendenhall, and Stroh 1999 for the most complete discussion of expatriate issues), local nationals, and/or third-country nationals. The input of local nationals will be crucial in all the next steps. Factory and labor force design will consider available skill levels and culturally appropriate work flow patterns. For example, the prevalence of labor unions will affect all such decisions (Warner 2000). Sales force design must comprehend aspects such as territory allocation and customer call plans. Many of the most advanced operations research tools can be applied in foreign markets, of course, with appropriate adaptation of inputs.

For example, one company has provided such tools to help international firms create balanced territories and find optimal locations for sales offices in Canada, Mexico, and Australia (*www.terralign.com*). However, the use of such high-tech resource allocation tools requires the most intricate knowledge of not only geographical details, but also appropriate call routines. Many things can differ across cultures—length of sales cycles, the kinds of customer relationships, and the kinds of interactions with customers. Indeed, more than one study has identified substantial differences in the importance of referrals in the sales of industrial services in Japan *vis-à-vis* the United States (Money, Gilly, and Graham 1999; Pornpitakpan 2000). The implications are that in Japan sales calls must be made not only on customers, but also on the other key people, such as bankers, in the all-important referral networks.

## 18.4.2 Recruiting labor, service, sales, and management personnel

The job of recruiting a labor force has received little attention in the literature. However, with unemployment levels at record lows in the United States, companies are paying more attention to the problem. 'Signing bonuses' are now being given at some McDonald's restaurants! Of course, the labor market works very differently across countries. In China contractors are hired to recruit factory workers from rural provinces in the center of the country to work in the coastal manufacturing areas. In Tijuana, Mexico where unemployment is now virtually zero, large vans prowl city streets with loudspeakers blaring to attract workers that have flocked from southern states and other

Central American countries. Indeed, workers there are encouraged to bring in family members to apply for factory jobs. American phobias about nepotism make no sense at all in such a high SCSC culture and such a 'hot' job market.

The number of management personnel from the home country assigned to foreign countries varies according to the size of the operation and the availability of qualified locals. Increasingly, the number of home-country nationals (expatriates) assigned to foreign posts is smaller (Forster 2000) as the pool of trained, experienced locals grows. Several American MNCs, including PepsiCo, Black & Decker, and Hewlett-Packard, have established policies to minimize the number of expatriate personnel.

The largest white-collar personnel requirement abroad for most companies is the sales force, recruited from three sources: expatriates, local nationals, and third-country nationals. A company's staffing pattern may include all three types in any single foreign operation, depending on qualifications, availability, and a company's needs. Sales and other executives can be recruited via the traditional media of advertising (including newspapers, magazines, job fairs, and the Internet), employment agencies/executive search firms, and the all-important personal referrals. The last source will be even more crucial in many foreign countries, particularly the high SCSC ones.

Finally, while it is common practice in some countries (e.g. the US) to hire away experienced managers from competitors, suppliers, and/or even customers, the same approach in other countries will not work well, if at all. In places like Japan employees are more loyal to their companies and therefore are difficult to lure away even for big money. College recruits can also be hard to hire in Japan because the smartest students are heavily recruited by the largest Japanese firms. Smaller firms and foreign firms are seen in Japan as much more risky employment opportunities. In this way problems relating to recruiting can prove to be a substantial entry barrier to Japan.

## 18.4.3  Selecting personnel

The selection of employees in most circumstances will depend on the advice and perhaps the consent of local managers. In international settings MNC policies can conflict with local laws and customs. For example, many American firms refuse to do business with other firms that 'discriminate either in hiring or in employment practices' or that use 'child labor' (Mattel 2000).

To select personnel for international management positions effectively, management must define precisely what is expected of its people. A formal job description can aid management in expressing those desires for long-range needs as well as for current needs. In addition to descriptions for each management or marketing position, the criteria should include special requirements indigenous to various countries. Most selection criteria lists include several characteristics essential for overseas success (Rykken 2000; Cateora and Graham, forthcoming 2002): maturity, emotional stability, breadth of knowledge, a positive outlook, flexibility, cultural empathy, and an affinity for travel.

Most of these traits can be assessed during interviews and perhaps during role-playing exercises (Kirazov, Sullivan, and Tu 2000). Paper and pencil ability tests, biographical information, and reference checks will be of secondary importance. Indeed, as previously mentioned, in many countries referrals will be the best way to recruit managers and sales representatives, making reference checks during evaluation and selection processes irrelevant.

There is also some evidence that some traits that make for successful new hires in one country may not be important in other countries. In one study, sales representatives in the electronics industries in Japan and the United States were compared. For the American representatives, valence for pay and education were both found to be positively related to performance and job satisfaction. In Japan they were not. That is, the Americans who cared more about money and were more educated tended to perform better in and to be more satisfied with their sales jobs. Alternatively, the Japanese sales representatives tended to be more satisfied with their jobs when their values were consistent with those of their company (Money and Graham 1999). The few systematic studies in this genre suggest that selection criteria must be localized, and management practices must be adapted in foreign markets.

## 18.4.4 Training

Training for expatriates focuses on the customs and the special foreign management and marketing problems that will be encountered, whereas local personnel require greater emphasis on the company, its products, technical information, and selling methods. In training either type of personnel, the training activity is burdened with problems stemming from long-established behaviors and attitudes. Local personnel, for instance, cling to habits continually reinforced by local culture. Nowhere is the problem greater than in China or Russia (Clarke and Metalina 2000), where the legacy of the communist tradition lingers. The attitude that whether you work hard or not, you get the same rewards, has to be changed if training is going to hold. Expatriates, as well, are captives of their own habits and patterns. Before any training can be effective, open-minded attitudes must be established.

Continual training may be more important in foreign markets than in domestic ones because of the lack of routine contact with the parent company and its marketing personnel. In addition, training of foreign employees must be tailored to the recipients' ways of learning and communicating. For example, the Dilbert cartoon characters theme that worked so well in ethics training courses with a company's American employees did not translate well in many of its foreign offices.

Finally, one aspect of training is frequently overlooked: Home-office personnel dealing with international operations need training designed to make them responsive to the needs of the foreign operations. In most companies, the requisite sensitivities are expected to be developed by osmosis in the process of dealing with foreign affairs. However, the best companies provide home-office personnel with cross-cultural training and send them abroad periodically to increase their awareness of the problems of the foreign operations (Forster 2000).

The Internet now makes some kinds of training much more efficient. Users can study text on screen and participate in interactive assessment tests. Sun Microsystems estimates that its use of the Internet can shorten training cycles by as much as 75 per cent. And in some parts of the world where telecommunications facilities are more limited, CD-ROM approaches have proven quite successful. Lockheed-Martin uses an interactive CD-ROM based system to train its employees worldwide on the nuances of the Foreign Corrupt Practices Act and associated corporate policies and ethics.

## 18.4.5 Motivation

Motivation is especially complicated because the firm is dealing with different cultures, different sources, and different philosophies (Neelankavil, Mathur, and Zhang 2000). In one study (Money and Graham 1999) sales representatives in comparable Japanese and American sales organizations were asked to allocate 100 points across an array of potential rewards from work. The results were surprisingly similar. Both groups allocated the most points to an 'increase in pay'. The only real difference between the two groups was in 'social recognition', which predictably, the Japanese rated as more important. However, the authors of the study concluded that although individual values for rewards may be similar, the social and competitive contexts still require different motivational systems.

Individual incentives that work effectively in individualistic cultures like the US can fail completely in other cultures. For example, with Japan's emphasis on paternalism and collectivism and its system of lifetime employment and seniority, motivation through individual incentive does not work well because Japanese employees seem to derive the greatest satisfaction from being comfortable members of a group. Thus, an offer of an individual financial reward for outstanding individual effort could be turned down because an employee would prefer not to appear different from peers and possibly attract their resentment. As such, Japanese bonus systems are usually based on group effort, and individual commission systems are quite rare. Japanese employees are more motivated by the social pressure of their peers than the prospect of making more money based on individual effort. Likewise, compensation packages in Eastern European countries typically involve a substantially greater emphasis on base pay than in the US (Kiriazov *et al.* 2000) and performance-based incentives have been found to be less effective (Fey, Bjorkman, and Pavlovskaya 2000). While some point out that motivational practices are changing even in Japan (Shibata 2000), such patterns do not change very quickly or without substantial efforts (Gupta and Govindarajan 2000).

Working conditions are a crucial aspect of motivation. With increasing frequency the working conditions that may be acceptable in less developed countries are being scrutinized by labor and humanitarian groups in the more affluent countries. This scrutiny is producing positive changes in many countries. For example, Mattel's (2000) manufacturing principles now include positive statements about factory and living quarters conditions and prohibitions against corporal punishment.

Communications are also important in maintaining high levels of motivation; foreign managers need to know the home office is interested in their operations, and, in turn, they want to know what is happening in the parent country. Everyone performs better when well informed. However, differences in languages, culture (Harvey and Novincevic 2000), and communication styles can make mutual understanding between managers and sales representatives more difficult. Cultural differences can even be expected to influence the adoption of new communication media, that is the Internet (Cateora and Graham, forthcoming 2002).

## 18.4.6 Designing compensation systems

Developing an equitable and functional compensation plan that combines balance, consistent motivation, and flexibility is extremely challenging in international operations. This is especially true when a company operates in a number of countries, when it has individuals who work in a number of countries, and/or when the management and/or sales force is composed of expatriate and local personnel. Fringe benefits play a major role in many

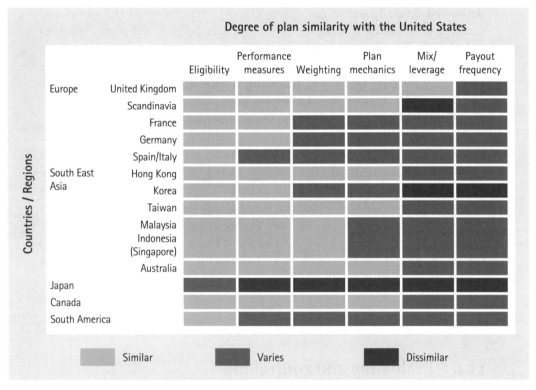

**Fig. 18.1 Global similarity to US compensation plans
(from Schick and Cichelli 1996)**

countries (Peterson, Napier, and Shul-Shim 2000). Those working in high-tax countries prefer liberal expense accounts and fringe benefits that are nontaxable instead of direct income subject to high taxes.

The issue of compensation plans becomes particularly difficult for global companies. Compensation plans of any one firm often vary substantially around the globe, reflecting the economic and cultural differences in the diverse markets served. As reflected in Figure 18.1, some experts feel compensation plans are most different from the standard US approach in Japan and Southern Europe.

One company has gone possibly the farthest to homogenize its worldwide compensation scheme. Beginning in 1996 IBM rolled out what is perhaps the most global approach to compensating a worldwide sales force (Marchetti 1998). The plan was developed in response to 'global' complaints from sales representatives that the old plan was confusing, that it did not provide for work done outside one's territory (e.g. when global customers are involved), and therefore did not promote cross-border team work. At first glance it may appear that IBM is making the cardinal error of trying to force a plan developed centrally onto sales offices literally spread around the world and across diverse cultures; however, the compensation plan still allows substantial latitude for local managers. Compensation managers in each country determine the frequency of incentive payouts and the split between base and incentive pay, while still following a global scheme of performance measures. Thus, the system allows for a high incentive component in countries like the US and high base-salary components in countries like Japan.

Of course, the trend for manufacturing firms is to follow the low wages wherever they might lead. Most MNCs have found that once the right motivational mix has been discovered workers in most countries are capable of efficiently producing to global standards. Circa 2000 wages vary within China as follows (Mattel 2000): in Hong Kong the typical plastics molder makes $1735/month and an engineer $4400/month; in Shenzhen the labor prices are $190/month for a molder and $1100 for an engineer; and in Nanjing the prices drop to $140/month and $800/month respectively. So, Mattel is now developing sourcing from two new factories in Nanjing.

## 18.4.7  Evaluating and controlling

Evaluation and control of employees in the US is a relatively simple task. Emphasis is placed on individual performance measures. However, in many countries the evaluation problem is more complex, particularly in the more collectivistic cultures, where teamwork is favored over individual effort. Performance measures require closer observation and may include the opinions of customers, peers, and supervisors. Of course, on the other hand, managers operating in more collectivistic cultures may see measures of individual performance as relatively unimportant. Shibata (2000) and others report that things are changing even on the factory floor in Japan where some companies are trying individual performance measures and incentives. However, the obstacles to change remain great.

One study comparing American and Japanese sales representatives' performance illustrates such differences (Money and Graham 1999). Supervisors' ratings of the representatives on identical performance scales were used in both countries. The distribution of performance of the Japanese was statistically normal—a few high performers, a few low, but most in the middle. The American distribution was different—a few high, most in the middle, but almost no low performers. In the US poor performers either quit (because they are not making any money) or they are fired. In Japan the poor performers stay with the company and are seldom fired. Thus, sales managers in Japan have a problem their American counterparts do not: how to motivate poor performers. Indeed, sales management textbooks in the United States usually include material on how to deal with 'plateaued' sales-people, but say little about poor performers because the latter are not a problem.

The primary control tool used by American sales managers is the incentive system. With the Internet and fax machines, more and more American sales representatives operate out of offices in their homes and see supervisors infrequently. Organizations have become quite flat and spans of control increasingly broad in recent years. However, in many other countries spans of control can be quite narrow by American standards—even in Australia and particularly in Japan. In the latter country, supervisors spend much more time with fewer subordinates. Corporate culture and frequent interactions with peers and supervisors are the means of motivation and control of sales representatives in more collectivistic and hierarchical cultures like Japan.

# 18.5 CULTURE'S INFLUENCE ON STRATEGIC THINKING

Perhaps Lester Thurow in his book *Head to Head* (1992) provides the most articulate description of how culture influences managers' thinking about business strategy. He distinguished between the British–American 'individua-listic' kind of capitalism and the 'communtarian' form of capitalism in Japan and Germany. The business systems in the latter two countries are typified by cooperation among government, management, and labor, particularly in Japan. Contrarily, adversarial relationships among labor, management, and government are more the norm in the UK, and particularly in the United States. We see these cultural differences reflected in Hofstede's (1991) results—on the IND scale the US is 91, the UK is 89, Germany is 67, and Japan is 46.

We also find evidence of these differences in a comparison of the performance of American, German, and Japanese firms (Anterasian, Graham, and Money 1996). In the less individualistic cultures labor and management cooperate—in Germany labor is represented on corporate boards, and in Japan management takes responsibility for the welfare of the labor force. Because the welfare of the workforce matters to Japanese and German firms their sales revenues are more stable over time. American style layoffs are eschewed. The individualistic American approach to labor–management relations is adversarial—each side takes care of itself. So we see damaging strikes and huge layoffs that result in a more volatile performance for American firms.

Circa 2000 the American emphasis on competition looks like the best approach. But, it is important to recall that key word in Adam Smith's justification for competition—'frequently'. It's worth repeating here, 'By pursuing his own interest he frequently promotes that of society...' Smith wrote *frequently*, not *always*, *most of the time*, or even *often*. A competitive, individualistic approach works well in a context of economic boom. During the late 1990s American firms have dominated Japanese and European ones. The latter seem stodgy, conservative, and slow in the current hot global information economy. However, downturns in a competitive culture can be ugly things. A review of the performance and layoffs at Boeing during the commercial aircraft bust of the late 1990s is instructive.

It should also be mentioned that Thurow and the others writing in the area omitted a fourth kind of capitalism—that common in Chinese cultures. Its distinguishing characteristics are a more entrepreneurial approach and an emphasis on *guanxi* (see Standifird and Marshall 2000) as the coordination principle among firms. Gordon Redding's excellent book, *The Spirit of Chinese Capitalism* (1993), provides the best description of this fourth form of capitalism. And this fourth form is predicted by culture as well. Chinese cultures tend to be high on the salience of social context (SCSC) and the strong reciprocity implied by the notion of *guanxi* fits well. Additionally, the Chinese firms tend to be smaller, limited by the size of extended family relations. Indeed, Leslie Young (1998) at Chinese University in Hong Kong points out an additional distinction in the evolving Chinese business system. He suggests that in southern China the emphasis will be on small, entrepreneurial firms while in northern China the big, state-owned heavy industries will evolve into a structure similar to that of the Japanese *keiretsu* forms of families of large companies.

## 18.6 CLOSING THOUGHTS

In the first half of this chapter my purpose was to quantify culture. Most anthropologists will have disdain for this approach—they would argue that culture can only be truly understood in the richness of the field. Culture must be experienced, not added up! While I appreciate this view, I do not share it.

I would certainly agree that not much credence should be put in any one number supplied, particularly when careers and/or cash are being decided upon. Rather the numbers provide the reader with a notion of how different cultures can be. Swiss and Mexicans do indeed think very differently about time, and both Swiss managers and Mexican managers benefit from this knowledge when they are involved commercially. This knowledge allows both to be more patient.

In the second half of the chapter the evidence is quite clear that culture affects thinking and behavior of both factory floor workers and CEOs (Harrison, McKinnon, Wu, and Chow 2000; Shane 1994; Wiersema and Bird 1993). Thus, two conclusions are paramount here: (1) Human Resources Management practices must be applied globally with consideration of cultural differences and consultation with locals. The latter is crucial, but a point often lost on ethnocentric home-office folks. (2) Corporate executive boards dominated by one cultural group, as they are in the United States, are bound to make huge mistakes of omission. Breadth of thinking is crucial in the culturally diverse global marketplace. I agree with Nick Forster (2000) that there are no global *managers*. Global *management teams* are the real key to future success in international enterprise.

In closing I am quite encouraged by the publication of the new book, *Culture Matters* (Harrison and Huntington 2000). It is an edited book including some twenty-two articles on topics related to culture and its influence on economic progress. My favorite title among them is Lucian Pye's 'Asian Values: from Dynamos to Dominos'. Hopefully the book will help rekindle the interest in culture's pervasive influences that Max Weber (1930) and others initiated so long ago.

# REFERENCES

ADLER, NANCY J. (1997). *International Dimensions of Organizational Behavior* (3rd edn.). Cincinnati, Oh.: Southwestern.

AIGNER, DENNIS J., and KRAEMER, KENNETH L. (1994–2000). *Orange County Executive Survey*. Irvine, Calif.: Graduate School of Management, University of California.

ALLINSON, CHRISTOPHER W., and HAYES, JOHN (2000). 'Cross-National Differences in Cognitive Style: Implications for Management', *International Journal of Human Resource Management*, 11/1: 161–70.

*American Prospect* (2000). 'The Internet and Linguistic Diversity', Mar. 27–April 10.

ANTERASIAN, CATHY, GRAHAM, JOHN L., and MONEY, R. BRUCE (1996). 'Are US Managers Superstitious about Market Share?', *Sloan Management Review*, 37/4: 67–77.

Au, Kevin Y. (1999). 'Intra-Cultural Variation: Evidence and Implications for International Business', *Journal of International Business Studies*, 30/4: 799–812.

Black, J. Stewart, Gregersen, Hal B., Mendenhall, Mark E., and Stroh, Linda K. (1999). *Globalizing People through International Assignments*. Reading, Mass.: Addison-Wesley.

Cateora, Philip R., and Graham, John L. (forthcoming, 2002). *International Marketing*. Burr Ridge, Ill.: Irwin/McGraw-Hill.

Chen, Jiangtian, Sokal, Robert R., and Ruhlen, Merritt (1995). 'Worldwide Analysis of Genetic and Linguistic Relationships of Human Populations', *Human Biology*, 67/4: 595–612.

Clarke, Simon, and Metalina, Tanya (2000). 'Training in the New Private Sector in Russia', *International Journal of Human Resource Management*, 11/1: 19–36.

Drucker, Peter F. (1999). *Management Challenges for the 21st Century*. New York: HarperBusiness.

Erez, Miriam, and Earley, P. Christopher (1993). *Culture, Self-Identity, and Work*. New York: Oxford University Press.

Esteban, A. Gabriel M., Ockova, Alena, Tang, Sara, and Graham, John L. (2000). 'Cultures' Influence on Marketing Negotiations: An Application of Hofstede's and Rokeach's Ideas', working paper, Graduate School of Management, University of California.

Fey, Carl F., Bjorkman, Ingmar, and Pavlovskaya, Antonina (2000). 'The Effect of Human Resource Management Practices on Firm Performance in Russia', *International Journal of Human Resource Management*, 11/1: 1–18.

Fisher, Roger, Ury, William, and Patton, Bruce (1991). *Getting to Yes*, 2nd edn. Boston: Houghton Mifflin.

Forster, Nick (2000). 'The Myth of the "International Manager"', *International Journal of Human Resource Management*, 11/1: 126–42.

Graham, John L., and Gronhaug, Kjell (1989). 'Ned Hall Didn't Have to Get a Haircut, or Why We Haven't Learned Much about International Marketing in the Last 25 Years', *Journal of Higher Education*, 69/2: 152–97.

——Mintu, Alma, and Rodgers, Waymond (1994). 'Explorations of Negotiation Behaviors in Ten Cultures Using a Model Developed in the United States', *Management Science*, 40/1: 72–95.

Gupta, Anil K., and Govindarajan, Vijay (2000). 'Managing Global Expansion: A Conceptual Framework', *Business Horizons*, Mar.–April: 45–54.

Haire, Mason, Ghisell, Edward E., and Porter, Lyman W. (1966). *Managerial Thinking, an International Study*. New York: Wiley.

Hall, Edward T. (1959). *The Silent Language*. New York: Anchor Books.

——(1960). 'The Silent Language in Overseas Business', *Harvard Business Review*, May–June: 87–96.

——(1976). *Beyond Culture*. New York: Anchor Books.

——(1992). *An Anthropology of Everyday Life*. New York: Anchor Books.

——and Hall, Mildred R. (1990). *Understanding Cultural Differences*. Yarmouth, Me.: Intercultural Press.

HARRISON, GRAEME L., McKINNON, JILL L., WU, ANNE, and CHOW, CHEE W. (2000). 'Cultural Influences on Adaptation to Fluid Workgroups in Taiwan and Australia', *Journal of International Business Studies*, 31/3: 489–506.

HARRISON, LAWRENCE E., and HUNTINGTON, SAMUEL P. (eds.) (2000). *Culture Matters*. New York: Basic Books.

HARVEY, MICHAEL, and NOVICEVIC, MILORAD M. (2000). 'Staffing Global Marketing Positions: What We Don't Know Can Make a Difference', *Journal of World Business*, 35/1: 80–94.

HODGSON, JAMES DAY, SANO, YOSHIHIRO, and GRAHAM, JOHN L. (2000). *Doing Business with the New Japan*. Boulder, Colo.: Rowman & Littlefield.

HOFSTEDE, GEERT (1980). *Culture's Consequences*. Beverly Hills, Calif.: Sage.

—— (1991). *Culture and Organizations*. London: McGraw-Hill.

—— and BOND, MICHAEL H. (1988). 'The Confucius Connections: From Cultural Roots to Economic Growth', *Organizational Dynamics*, 16/4: 4–21.

—— and associates (1998). *Masculinity and Femininity, the Taboo Dimension of National Cultures*. Thousand Oaks, Calif.: Sage.

HOUSE, ROBERT J., HANGES, PAUL J., RUIZ-QUINTANILLA, S. ANTONIO, DORFMAN, PETER W., JAVIDAN, MANSOUR, DICKSON, MARCUS, and about 170 GLOBE Country Co-Investigators (2000). 'Cultural Influences on Leadership and Organizations: Project GLOBE', in W. Mobley (ed.) *Advances in Global Leadership*, 1. Greenwich, Conn.: JAI Press.

HOUSTON, H. RIKA, and GRAHAM, JOHN L. (2000). 'Culture and Corruption in International Markets: Implications for Policy Makers and Managers', *Consumption, Markets, and Culture*, 4/3.

KIRIZOV, DIMITER, SULLIVAN, SHERRY E., and TU, HOWARD S. (2000). 'Business Success in Eastern Europe: Understanding and Customizing HRM', *Business Horizons*, Jan.–Feb.: 39–43.

LEE, KAM-HON, and GRAHAM, JOHN L. (2001), 'Analyzing Videotapes of Chinese and Americans in International Business Negotiations', working paper, Graduate School of Management, University of California.

LEVIN, ROBERT (1997). 'The Pace of Life in 31 Countries', *American Demographics*, 19/11: 20–9.

MARCHETTI, MICHELE (1996). 'Gamble, IBM Replaces Its Outdated Compensation Plan with a World Wide Framework, Will It Pay Off?', *Sales & Marketing Management*, July: 65–9.

MATTEL (2000). *Global Manufacturing Principles*. Hawthorne, Calif.: Mattel, Inc.

MONEY, R. BRUCE, GILLY, MARY C., and GRAHAM, JOHN L. (1998). 'National Culture and Referral Behavior in the Purchase of Industrial Services in the United States and Japan', *Journal of Marketing*, 62/4: 76–87.

—— and GRAHAM, JOHN L. (1999). 'Sales Performance, Pay, and Job Satisfaction: Tests of a Model Using Data Collected in the US and Japan', *Journal of International Business Studies*, 30/1: 149–72.

NEELANKAVIL, JAMES P., MATHUR, ANIL, and ZHANG, YONG (2000). 'Determinants of Managerial Performance: A Cross-Cultural Comparison of Perceptions of Middle-Level Managers in Four Countries', *Journal of International Business Studies*, 31/1: 121–40.

PETERSON, RICHARD B., NAPIER, NANCY K., and SHUL-SHIM, WON (2000). 'Expatriate Management: A Comparison of MNCs Across Four Parent Countries', *Thunderbird International Business Review*, 42/2: 145–66.

PORNPITAKPAN, CHANTHIKA (2000). 'Trade in Thailand: a Three-Way Cultural Comparison', *Business Horizons*, Mar.–April: 61–70.

REDDING, S. GORDON (1993). *The Spirit of Chinese Capitalism*. Berlin: de Gruyter.

RUBIN, JEFFREY Z., and BROWN, B. R. (1975). *The Social Psychology of Bargaining and Negotiation*. New York: Academic Press.

RYKKEN, ROLF (2000). 'Square Pegs, Hiring the Wrong Person for an Overseas Assignment Can Lead to Disaster', *Global Business*, Feb.: 58–61.

SCHICK, DAVID G., and CICHELLI, DAVID J. (1996). 'Developing Incentive Compensation Strategies in a Global Sales Environment', *ACA Journal*, Autumn: 34–50.

SHANE, SCOTT (1994). 'The Effect of National Culture on the Choice Between Licensing and Direct Foreign Investment', *Strategic Management Journal*, 15: 627–42.

SHIBATA, HIROMICHI (2000). 'The Transformation of the Wage and Performance Appraisal System in a Japanese Firm', *International Journal of Human Resource Management*, 11/2: 294–313.

SMITH, ADAM (1776). *The Wealth of Nations*. New York: Modern Library (1994).

SONG, X. MICHAEL, XIE, JINHONG, and DYER, BARBARA (2000). 'Antecedants and Consequences of Marketing Managers' Conflict-Handling Behaviors', *Journal of Marketing*, 64/Jan.: 50–66.

STANDIFIRD, STEPHEN S., and MARSHALL, R. SCOTT (2000). 'The Transaction Cost Advantage of *Guanxi*-Based Business Practices', *Journal of World Business*, 35/1: 21–42.

TERRALIGN (2000). www.terralign.com.

THUROW, LESTER (1992). *Head to Head*. New York: William Morrow.

TRANSPARENCY INTERNATIONAL (2000). www.transparency.de.

TRIANDIS, HARRY C. (1972). *The Analysis of Subjective Culture*. New York: Wiley.

—— (1995). *Individualism and Collectivism*. Boulder, Colo.: Westview Press.

USUNIER, JEAN-CLAUDE (1998). *International and Cross-Cultural Management Research*. London: Sage.

WARNER, MALCOLM (2000). 'Introduction: The Asia-Pacific HRM Model Revisited', *International Journal of Human Resource Management*, 11/2: 171–82.

WEBER, MAX (1930). *The Protestant Ethic and Spirit of Capitalism*. London: George Allen & Unwin (1976).

WEST, JOEL, and GRAHAM, JOHN L. (1998). 'Language's Consequences: A Test of Linguistic Based Measures of Culture', *Academy of Management Proceedings*, August, San Diego.

—— (2001). 'A Linguistic-Based Measure of Cultural Distance and Its Relationship to Managerial Values', working paper, Graduate School of Management, University of California.

WIERSEMA, MARGARETHE F., and BIRD, ALLAN (1993). 'Organizational Demography in Japanese Firms: Group Heterogeneity, Individual Dissimilarity, and Top Management Team Turnover', *Academy of Management Journal*, 36/5: 996–1025.

YOUNG, LESLIE (1998). A lecture delivered at the Chinese University of Hong Kong.

CHAPTER 19

# ENVIRONMENTAL POLICY AND INTERNATIONAL BUSINESS

ALAN M. RUGMAN

ALAIN VERBEKE

## 19.1 INTRODUCTION

THIS chapter analyses the interactions between environmental policy and international business. More specifically, a conceptual framework is developed which allows us to classify the various types of environmental regulations facing firms engaged in international business. In addition, an analysis is performed of the different environmental strategies that can be pursued by multinational enterprises (MNEs).

During the past few decades, environmental issues have increasingly come to the forefront, both on public policy agendas and in corporate boardrooms. Specialized academic journals have been introduced that focus exclusively on environmental issues; these include the *Journal of Environmental Economics and Management, Ecological Economics, Journal of Environmental Management, Business Strategy and the Environment,* and *Journal of Environmental Planning and Management.*

Moreover, many of the mainstream economics and management journals now regularly publish articles dealing with the environmental policy–corporate strategy interface. However, only a few publications have, so far, included conceptual insights specifically useful to international business. In contrast, this chapter focuses specifically on international business research issues.

In the area of environmental policy, two issues are of particular importance to international business thinking. First, the implications for business of the rapid increase in international environmental regulations. Second, the specific challenges and strategic opportunities faced by MNEs as compared to domestic firms.

## 19.2 The Increase in International Environmental Regulations

Table 19.1 clarifies from an institutional perspective what can and should be included in research on the linkages between environmental policy and international business. The horizontal axis suggests that environmental regulations can be imposed at five levels of government:

(1) multilateral rules, such as those established under the General Agreement on Tariffs and Trade (GATT) and World Trade Organization (WTO);
(2) regional level rules, such as in the European Union (EU) and in the North American Free Trade Agreement (NAFTA);
(3) national State level rules;
(4) sub-national rules, such as state and provincial laws;
(5) municipal or local regulations, in cases where these are not under provincial or state jurisdiction.

The vertical axis distinguishes among four types of firms potentially affected by environmental regulations, namely (a) domestic firms; (b) home based exporters; (c) home based (centrally run) MNEs; and (d) transnational (decentralized) MNEs. Each type of firm may be affected in a very different

## Table 19.1 Environmental regulation–business linkages

| Type of corporation | Level of environmental regulations | | | | |
|---|---|---|---|---|---|
| | Multilateral (GATT/WTO) | Regional (EU/NAFTA) | National | Sub-national (State/Province) | Municipal |
| Domestic firms | 1 | 2 | 3 | 4 | 5 |
| Home-based exporter | 6 | 7 | 8 | 9 | 10 |
| Home-based MNE | 11 | 12 | 13 | 14 | 15 |
| Transnational (decentralized) MNE | 16 | 17 | 18 | 19 | 20 |

way and may also react differently to environmental regulation at each institutional level. Rugman, Kirton, and Soloway (1997) (1999) and Rugman and Verbeke (2000a) provide an analysis.

The critical point to be made is that while all twenty cells are potentially relevant to firm and government policy interactions, in this chapter we shall focus on the international business scholarship in cells 11, 12, 13, 16, 17, and 18 of Table 19.1. These six cells capture the key linkages between international and national environmental regulations and the behaviour of multinational enterprises. These linkages are explored in the remainder of this chapter.

International environmental regulation is growing rapidly for five reasons. First, many environmental challenges have an international or even a global scale and can therefore be 'managed' most effectively at this level of policy making, especially to avoid 'free rider' problems (Esty 1994; Vogel 1995; Haas 1999).

Second, when a change in environmental policy entails 'winners' and 'losers' international cooperation is required, *inter alia*, to negotiate adequate compensations for the 'losers' (e.g. the nations trailing in environmental regulation and performance) (Kolk 1998).

Third, even if environmental problems can, in principle, be dealt with adequately at the national or subnational levels, a divergence in policies across jurisdictions may have economic effects in terms of influencing the relative competitive position of domestic versus foreign firms (Nehrt 1998).

Fourth, the increase in regional integration, e.g. through institutions such as the European Union (EU) and the North American Free Trade Agreement (NAFTA) has led to the inclusion of environmental issues as one component of a much broader array of issues in regional policy integration (Rugman, Kirton, and Soloway 1999; and Buysse, Coeck, and Verbeke 1999).

Fifth, many of the most important environmental problems at the global level, such as the pollution of the oceans, the ozone layer depletion, and the disposal of nuclear waste will have mainly long-term rather than short-term effects, perhaps exerting their full blown influence only on future generations. There is usually substantial uncertainty as regards optimal public policy as well as high 'costs' associated with effectively managing such problems. These costs may be highly visible and strongly felt today by firms and other pollution generating actors, whereas the benefits may only materialize in the distant future. Thus, a (perverse) incentive arises for governments at the national and subnational level to bring these issues to an international policy forum. In this way, domestic pressure groups pushing for environmental policy reform can be appeased and the difficult dossiers which can bring little rewards in terms of voting gains are removed from the domestic policy agenda.

## 19.3 THE IMPACT OF INTERNATIONAL ENVIRONMENTAL AGREEMENTS

A substantial body of literature now exists on international environmental agreements. First, it exists within the context of regional/multilateral environmental policy initiatives signed by governments (see for example Abbott 1996; Audley 1997; Esty 1994; Levy 1997; Haas *et al.* 1993; Keohane and Levy 1996; Mitchell 1994; Rugman and Kirton 1999; Young 1994). Second, it exists in the form of voluntary agreements among firms and sometimes other stakeholders such as international institutions, environmental non-government organizations (ENGOs), trade unions, and professional associations (Kolk *et al.* 1999; Prakash 1999; Rondinelli and Vastag 1996; UNCTAD 1996).

Both types of international agreements lead to specific compliance problems. In the case of regional/multilateral agreements, the question arises whether the governments involved are both willing and capable to introduce an effective administrative enforcement apparatus. This is not always easy as each country may be characterized by a very different national environmental policy regime and its economic system may be affected in a special manner by a new international policy regime (Andrew 1994; OECD 1993; Scholl 1996; Wallace 1995).

The voluntary initiatives include behavioural guidelines, i.e. general codes of conduct such as the International Chamber of Commerce Business Charter for Sustainable Development, and sectoral codes such as Responsible Care in the chemical industry. They also include environmental management standards such as ISO 14001 (adopted by the International Organization for Standardization) and EMAS (the Eco-Management and Audit Scheme). Kolk (2000) provides a comparative analysis. Self-regulation has the advantage that it is voluntary and allows flexibility in its implementation. Its main weakness is the free-rider problem, whereby non-subscribing or non-complying firms may benefit from the self-regulation of other firms.

At the level of the firm targeted by international environmental initiatives, the corporate response in terms of compliance depends upon its expected economic benefits (Rugman and Verbeke 1998*b*). These economic benefits can be high or low, as shown on the vertical axis of Figure 19.1. A second issue (on the horizontal axis) is whether these benefits are driven primarily by expected improvements in industrial performance (for example market share, profitability, growth, etc.) as is usually the case with voluntary initiatives, or by sanctions associated with non-compliance. In the latter case, it is mainly the strength of the administrative enforcement apparatus which determines compliance. For a discussion on the benefits of compliance see Barrett 1991; Henriques and Sadorsky 1996; Nehrt 1998; Walley and Whitehead 1994; Prakash 2000.

The four possible managerial responses are the following. In quadrant 1, performance driven compliance prevails. International environmental regulation is welcomed, for example, because it facilitates global benchmarking efforts irrespective of enforcement, which is viewed from a strategy perspective as a non-issue. This is the opposite situation to quadrant 3, where economic benefits consist primarily of avoiding costly sanctions, that is, compliance is enforcement driven.

Quadrants 2 and 4 reflect cases for which compliance leads to low net economic benefits. In quadrant 2, administrative enforcement is not an issue as compared to the absence of any contribution to improving the firm's industrial performance, which leads to unconditional non-compliance. This occurs, for example, when international environmental regulation is viewed by firms as political lip service to environmental pressure groups, without any serious government commitment to implementation. In contrast, quadrant 4 reflects conditional non-compliance. This is the case of environmental regulations for which government shows a genuine interest in implementation, but the design or operationalization of an administrative enforcement

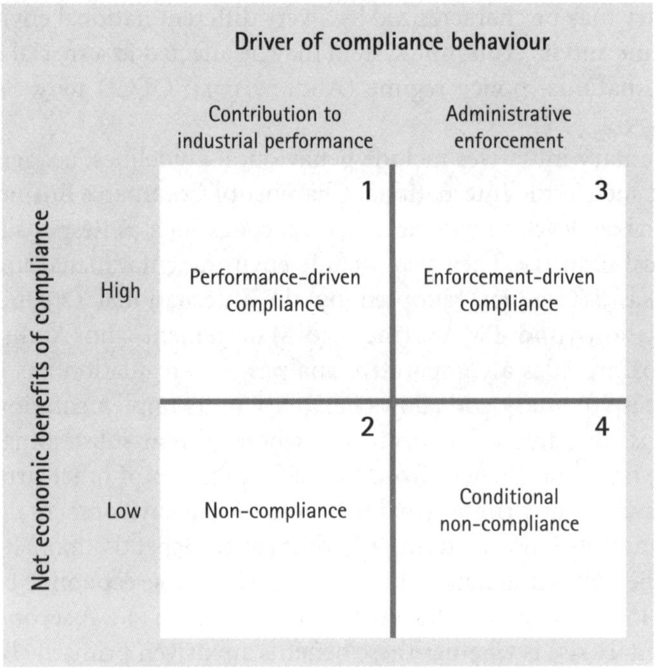

**Driver of compliance behaviour**

|  | Contribution to industrial performance | Administrative enforcement |
|---|---|---|
| **High** | **1** Performance-driven compliance | **3** Enforcement-driven compliance |
| **Low** | **2** Non-compliance | **4** Conditional non-compliance |

*Net economic benefits of compliance*

**Fig. 19.1 A managerial perspective on compliance with international environmental policies**

apparatus is lagging because of a lack of resources or other implementation barriers. Once the administrative enforcement apparatus functions properly, a shift to enforcement driven compliance (quadrant 3) may occur.

The four types of compliance behaviour that emerge from Figure 19.1 are induced by the characteristics of the environmental regimes faced by firms. Thus, we have placed, for illustrative purposes, in each of the four quadrants of Figure 19.1, a number of major international environmentally related policies, regulations, and environmental agreements on the basis of the firm responses that they have induced. In this way the agreements can be classified as follows:

Quadrant 1:  OECD non-binding environmental regulations, policies, and principles.

Quadrant 2:  International agreements with weak enforcement provisions, e.g. the United Nations Conference on Environmental Development's (UNCED) Rio Declaration of 1992 and the Kyoto Conference of 1997.

Quadrant 3:  The environmental standards of the EU, and its 'eco-labels'. Multilateral Environmental Agreements (MEAs) with strong enforcement provisions, such as the Montreal Protocol.

Quadrant 4:    NAFTA and the Commission for Environmental Cooperation
(CEC). GATT/WTO trade disciplines on environmental regulations.

The positioning of these international agreements requires further explanation. In the remainder of this section we shall highlight the key provisions in
each agreement which determine placement in the framework. It should be
emphasized that the positioning of each agreement on the horizontal axis of
Figure 19.1 was determined on the basis of the main driver of firm behaviour
(issue of contribution to industrial performance versus issue of administrative
enforcement). A position on the left hand side of Figure 19.1 implies that firms
fundamentally do not take into account enforcement issues.

The environmental measures of the OECD are in quadrant 1 of Figure 19.1.
The OECD does not enact binding environmental regulations on its members, yet its recommendations about environmental policy are extremely
influential with firms who see the OECD as setting useful benchmarks for
international business. Especially, multinational enterprises (MNEs) have
been highly responsive to the OECD's investment codes (Safarian 1993; Rugman and Gestrin 1997).

However, in quadrant 2 of Figure 19.1, firms do not adjust their behaviour
to respond to environmental regulations. This is because such regulations are
not perceived as contributing positively to industrial performance. For example, although the UNCED has promoted international environmental
concerns, as evidenced by the attendance of over 100 heads of state at the
Rio Summit in 1992, it has not been taken seriously by most firms. Many firms
viewed the Summit as a mere public relations exercise dominated by ENGOs
with poor political commitment to actual realization. Similarly, while the
Kyoto conference declaration of December 1997 requires states to adopt
carbon emissions standards, most potentially affected firms fail to see any
micro-level benefit potentially contributing to their industrial performance.
More importantly, they also assume that many states worrying about its costs
will refuse to ratify the declaration and offset the ENGOs, except in the
stronger advocacy areas such as the EU.

NAFTA is largely in quadrant 4 of Figure 19.1, since its relatively strong
environmental provisions have certainly captured the attention of most firms
doing business in North America. However, only when the CEC becomes a
credible bureaucracy to administer trade and environmental interaction,
consistent with the intent of the three NAFTA signatories, with active dispute
settlement procedures and active investigations to prevent trade-related environmental disputes (as its mandate permits), will NAFTA likely move from
quadrant 4 to quadrant 3. To date, there is no evidence to support the
placement of NAFTA in quadrant 3, since the CEC has not yet become active
in seeking to investigate and mediate any of the trade-related environmental

disputes identified in Vogel and Rugman (1997), of which there have been over twenty between the United States and Canada in the first five years of NAFTA, 1994–8.

In contrast to NAFTA, the EU has, through the actual enforcement by the European Commission, been able to make its environmental regulations widely applied by most EU companies, placing environmental regulations, such as the EU 'eco-labels' in quadrant 3. The eco-labels (on fine paper, for example), can even be used as a barrier to entry against foreign firms unable to comply with them (Rugman 1995; Vogel 1995). Similarly, MEAs such as the Montreal Protocol on Ozone Depletion are also in quadrant 3, as the signing governments have taken measures to guarantee enforcement in the form of specific domestic legislation. Other MEAs with trade-related environmental measures (TREMs) which may be in quadrant 3 include the Basle Convention of Hazardous Wastes (1989), and the convention on the International Trade in Endangered Species (CITES) (1973). In all these cases the main driver of compliance is not related to any potential improvement of industrial performance, but rather the negative sanctions associated with non-compliance.


# 19.4 The Complexity of Environmental Policy for MNEs

The interactions between environmental policy and the strategies of multinational enterprises are much more complex than the equivalent business–government interactions at the national level. This complexity results from six elements:

First, environmental policies often diverge across countries. In such cases, a choice needs to be made by MNEs to either tailor their environmental strategies to individual country regulations (including subnational regulations) or to set global standards, which must meet the most stringent regulatory requirements. In addition, environmental policy differences among countries may change the MNE's configuration of country specific advantages benefiting its value added activities in various locations; they could therefore, in principle, affect location choices. A further complexity is that a number of developing countries such as China may actually impose more stringent environmental regulations on foreign MNEs than on domestic firms (Tsai and Child 1997).

Second, given the option to implement global standards, and to diffuse 'best practices' across borders to the entire MNE network, substantial potential may exist to gain scope economies in the environmental strategy area. International knowledge transfer is, however, usually associated with a number of managerial and organizational challenges.

Third, given the potential to gain scope economies, MNEs face stronger incentives than domestic firms to interact with public policy makers so as to develop international environmental standards, for example through supranational regulations (Cairncross 1992; Schmidheiny 1992).

Fourth, when engaging in pro-active environmental strategies, MNEs may choose to develop green firm specific advantages (FSAs), i.e. proprietary assets and skills in the environmental area that may contribute to competitive advantage. A key challenge is then to develop an 'optimal mix' between 'location bound' and 'non-location bound' FSAs (these concepts are explained in the next section).

Fifth, the MNE's environmental reputation at the international level may be strongly affected by environmental problems occurring in one specific country. The danger of a negative externality affecting the entire MNE network requires a set of effective environmental strategy monitoring mechanisms.

Sixth, environmental policy may be used as a tool to create shelter, i.e. entry barriers against foreign rivals. The impact of such shelter-driven behaviour (by the firm itself or by competitors) should be taken into account by the MNE.

The practical relevance of the above elements has been demonstrated by Rugman and Verbeke (2000b), who have developed a new framework to analyse the greening strategies of multinational enterprises in response to environmental regulations. In this framework government regulations are added as an explicit 'sixth force' to Porter's basic 'five forces' model to guide strategy development. The new framework consists of three parts. First, shifts in corporate strategy are shown to occur as a response to either market forces or regulators, recognizing that it is possible for simultaneous shifts in strategy to occur. Second, the advantage of being a first mover is examined, again in response to either market forces or regulators. This recognizes that first mover behaviour is a multidimensional strategic issue. Third, a resource-based perspective on 'green' strategies is developed in an explicit international context. It is shown that firms can develop either 'location bound' or 'non-location bound' (internationally transferable) 'green' capabilities. When applying this three-part framework to the strategies of six MNEs, it is found that four of these MNEs have developed internationally transferable green capabilities (DuPont, Honeywell, McDonald's, and Xerox). One (Laidlaw) has a location bound capability and one has none (Allied Signal).

# 19.5 ENVIRONMENTAL PRACTICES
## OF MNEs

The environmental practices of MNEs have been analysed in a number of recent studies. Levy's (1995) study on the environmental practices in US plants of eighty large MNEs from the triad (North America, Europe, Japan) led to three important conclusions.

First, a high degree of multinationality (in terms of proportion of sales outside the home country) is associated with a better environmental performance. The reasons why this is the case are not entirely straightforward: (a) a higher degree of multinationality may lead to more potential for scope economies, when diffusing 'best practices' abroad; (b) the United States represent a high cost location for pollution intensive production, given the relatively stringent environmental regulations in most sectors, so that firms with a higher degree of multinationality may choose to locate their worst environmental performance activities in, for example, developing countries. The present empirical validity of such a 'pollution haven' hypothesis remains doubtful however (OECD 1997; Rugman and Verbeke 1998a; Rugman, Kirton, and Soloway 1999; Walter 1982; Leonard 1988; and Low 1992); (c) a higher degree of multinationality leads to a higher public visibility, for example as a result of global brand names, and to higher pressure by external stakeholders to improve environmental performance. The danger of negative externalities affecting the entire MNE network when faced with environmental performance problems in one location may also be much stronger.

Second, larger MNEs appeared to have more advanced environmental policies and procedures but a poorer environmental performance. This implies that, for example, their better dissemination of environmental information and more comprehensive environmental policies did not translate into lower emissions. Therefore, good environmental policy formulation is not necessarily associated with effective environmental policy implementation. The latter may be severely hampered by a greater inertia and bureaucratic complexity in larger firms.

Third, a major difference appeared to exist between Japanese and European owned plants in the United States. The Japanese owned plants showed a consistently worse environmental performance than the other plants, perhaps because the Japanese companies built their production facilities very fast in the rapidly expanding US markets. In the European plants, a positive relationship was found between environmental policies and environmental performance, in contrast to the sample as a whole.

The above findings suggest that there is a country (or regional) effect in both environmental practices and performance. This should not be surprising as the Levy (1995) study was based on the UNCTAD (1993) report on corporate environmental management of large MNEs. The UNCTAD report concluded that home country legislation was the single most important factor leading to changes in environmental management. This factor was cited as a catalyst for change by 60 per cent of respondents. Host country legislation was mentioned by only one fifth of firms. However, Asian firms attached more importance to domestic legislation than North American and especially European firms. In contrast, North American firms experienced much more change, driven by host country legislation, than did European and Asian firms.

Andrews (1994) has described government policies to encourage the adoption of clean technologies and found substantial differences in regulatory tradition among countries, especially in terms of the openness of the decision-making process and the flexibility of regulatory enforcement. The United States has both a very open decision-making process with wide public participation and information diffusion in the policy formulation stage, but a very rigid and legalistic approach to enforcement, with a high probability of litigation in cases of conflict. The EU is characterized by a kaleidoscopic situation in terms of policy instruments used (Scholl 1996), but in general the policy formulation process is much less transparent than in the United States, whereas the enforcement process is much more flexible, leaving ample room for *ex post* negotiation. The Japanese situation is positioned closer to the EU than the US situation (see also Kolk 2000). Here, it should be recognized that environmental regulation is changing rapidly, whereby, for example, the conventional US liability and litigation approach is now being complemented by regulation that allows more flexibility, including voluntary agreements.

Domestic environmental policy does not appear to have, by itself, negative effects on international competitiveness at the macro level, according to a survey of more than 100 empirical studies in the US manufacturing industry (Jaffe *et al.* 1995). The difficulties faced by MNEs result, however, precisely from being faced simultaneously with environmental regulation at the global level, the level of regional trade and investment blocks (e.g. EU and NAFTA), the level of various individual countries, the subnational level, and the local level (see Rugman and Verbeke 2000*a*).

In this context, a recent empirical study conducted by Buysse, Verbeke, and Coeck (2001) on the differences in environmental strategies between domestic firms in a small open economy and foreign MNEs led to five important conclusions.

First, foreign MNEs appeared to have much more pro-active environmental strategies than domestic firms.

Second, the regulatory pressures exerted by the government of the small open country had an impact on the environmental strategies of domestic firms, in terms of shifting from a reactive to a proactive mode whereas this was not the case for the foreign MNE subsidiary strategies.

Third, and this is in contrast with the impact of conventional views on the impact of home country regulation on MNE subsidiaries, MNEs do not appear to design environmental strategies based primarily on their home country regulations. Therefore, the Porter and van der Linde (1995) perspective, which argues that stringent environmental regulation at home can offer home producers a competitive edge as first-movers in international markets, was not supported.

Fourth, both shareholder pressures and perceived economic opportunities are important drivers of proactive environmental management, whereas other individual stakeholder pressures exert less influence.

Fifth, the choice of a proactive environmental strategy in MNEs also appears to be affected by the pressure exerted by rivals and the importance attached to good relationships with local communities (i.e. a nationally responsive approach).

Rondinelli and Berry (2000) provide an overview of the wide diversity of elements present in a modern, proactive environmental strategy in large MNEs, building upon a content analysis of the environmental performance reports of thirty-eight MNEs. Their conclusions are largely consistent with the above analysis: the potential to improve industrial performance as well as environmental performance is a key driver of proactive environmental strategies, whereas government regulation clearly is somewhat less important. In this context, it also appears that the projects geared directly towards environmental improvement, building upon interactions with external stakeholders, are far less important in terms of environmental expenditures than internal environmental practices intended to generate both financial returns and beneficial environmental results. They also point out that international environmental regulation (including self regulation) is viewed as increasingly important by MNEs.

# 19.6 THE DEVELOPMENT OF GREEN FSAS IN MNES

A large literature has emerged on the interactions between environmental policy and corporate strategy. Rugman and Verbeke (1998a) and Nehrt (1998)

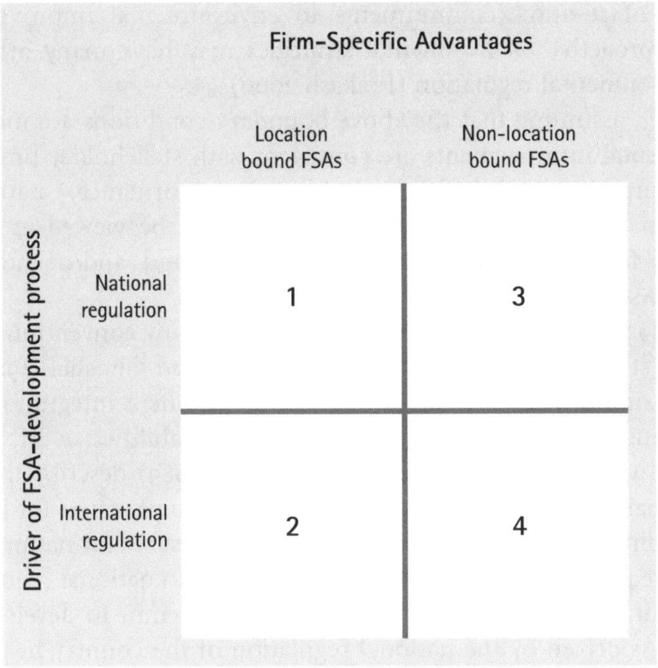

**Firm–Specific Advantages**

Fig. 19.2 The development of 'green'
firm-specific advantages

provide recent syntheses of this work. Two key questions face managers in MNEs. First, whether or not to develop an FSA in greening, i.e. a capability in the environmental area that would allow the firm to outperform its rivals and would ultimately contribute to the firm's industrial performance. Second, whether to develop such a capability in a location bound or non-location bound fashion.

A location bound FSA reflects a strength in environmental management that is unique, difficult to imitate, and perceived as valuable by relevant stakeholders (consumers, shareholders, etc.) However, this strength is not transferable internationally, but can only be exploited in one or a limited number of locations, for example when it was developed in response to the specific stakeholders' pressures prevailing in one nation. In contrast, a non-location bound FSA represents a 'best practice' which, in so far as it consists of knowledge, is easily transferable internationally.

The choice that often needs to be made in MNEs between developing location bound and non-location bound FSAs, is represented on the horizontal axis of Figure 19.2. The drivers of green FSA development include both national and international environmental regulation. Rugman and Verbeke (1998*a*) have argued that green FSA development will usually only take place in the presence of leveraging effects benefiting industrial performance and flexibility of resource commitments to environmental improvements. In addition, proactive environmental strategies may have many other drivers than environmental regulation (Prakash 2000).

However, assuming that the above boundary conditions are met, i.e. that environmental improvements are consistent with stakeholder pressures and complementary to the firm's industrial performance, national and international environmental regulations can then be viewed as the actual co-drivers for the development of location bound and/or non-location bound FSAs.

Figure 19.2 represents a reinterpretation of the now conventional work on corporate strategy and globalization by Bartlett and Ghoshal (1989). It is a relatively simple resource based application of their integration-national responsiveness matrix, in which the strategic capabilities of MNEs can be analysed. In their matrix, Bartlett and Ghoshal (1989) describe the tensions faced by managers of MNEs, between responding to pressures for integration (often leading to global scope economies) and pressures for national responsiveness (requiring global standards to be adapted to national requirements).

In Quadrant 1 of Figure 19.2, MNE affiliates attempt to develop location bound FSAs driven by the national regulation of the country in which they operate. In Quadrant 2, it is international regulation that invites firms to develop such location bound FSAs. In both cases, this implies that the MNE's affiliates in each country are given substantial autonomy to engage in proactive environmental behaviour most appropriate to their specific local circumstances. Quadrant 3 reflects the situation whereby the firm's response to national environmental regulation is used to develop non-location bound FSAs in the environmental area. The potential occurrence of this situation constitutes a powerful incentive for governments to introduce stringent environmental regulation, so as to trigger innovation and thereby provide a first mover advantage to domestic firms operating in international markets (Porter and van der Linde 1995). However, the validity of the claim that such 'environmental innovation policy' can be effective is doubtful (Rugman and Verbeke 1998a). In any case, it is possible that stringent environmental regulations in one country may push MNEs to develop more advanced global benchmarks and company wide best practices, for example in the area of production technology (Lundan 1996).

Finally, in Quadrant 4 it is international regulations that push firms to develop non-location bound FSAs (Rugman, Kirton, and Soloway 1999). In practice, it appears that various types of regulations facing MNEs may lead to a differentiated response, covering the four cells of Figure 19.2 depending upon, for example, the type of foreign direct investment (FDI) undertaken (resource seeking, market seeking, efficiency seeking, strategic asset seeking), the specific value activity involved, the requirements imposed by customers, the age of the production equipment in a specific country, the environmental strategies of local business system partners (suppliers, joint-venture partners, etc.) (Kolk 2000).

# 19.7 THE PORTER HYPOTHESIS ON HOME-BASED ENVIRONMENTAL REGULATIONS

The previous section contrasted domestic (home country) and international environmental regulations. In this section, we focus on the specific case of two countries with strong trading relationships, in which one country has a much larger market size than the second one. It should be noted that there is no discussion here of the use of green strategies in relation to other market-based firm strategies, such as the three generic strategies of Porter (1980). Such work is attempted by Rugman and Verbeke (1998a) and Shrivastava (1995).

Porter and van der Linde (1995) argue that it is good policy for a government to pass strict environmental regulations. Then firms based in that country (e.g. the United States) will have to develop new core competencies in environmentally sensitive manufacturing. Eventually, these firms can go abroad and use their strong home base as a staging ground to outperform other less environmentally sensitive firms in global markets. This point has been endorsed by US Vice-President Al Gore (1992). The Porter hypothesis presumes that other countries will not 'compete' by inconveniently raising their own domestic environmental regulations too soon (before the US-based firms have developed innovations at home), and that the regional and multi-lateral organizations also follow along, rather than initiate new and diverging environmental regulations. Thus it is a matter of timing. If the US government is a first mover, it can spur US-based firms to be the first green MNEs, and their environmental credentials should help them outperform competitor firms on the world stage, once the world stage also becomes green.

In Figure 19.3 on the impact of environmental regulations on firms, the Porter and van der Linde (1995) propositions can be illustrated. Actually, the same point can be traced back to Porter (1990), where he first argued that stringent environmental standards and regulations could put pressure on firms to upgrade the foundations of their competitive advantage. If the home government imposes strong environmental regulations and enforces these tightly, then domestic firms are forced to comply. In time, the

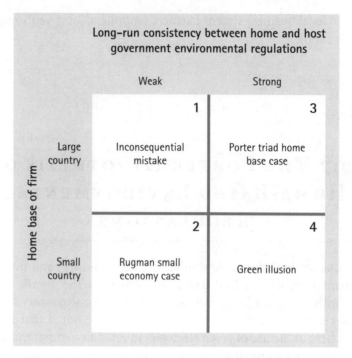

**Fig. 19.3 Impact of home versus host government environmental regulations**

investments made by such home firms will improve their environmentally related competitive advantages. Porter also states that home-based firms could then expect to go abroad and be able to outperform foreign firms which have not yet been exposed to such tight environmental regulations. Two caveats are important. First, this only happens when the home government has sufficient foresight to anticipate the environmental regulations of all other countries, which will be modelled after those of the home country. Second, it only works for a very large, triad-based economy (like the United States or Germany) whose economic influence on the world economy is immense; it will not work for smaller countries, as discussed below.

The horizontal axis of Figure 19.3 measures the long run consistency between home and host country environmental regulations. The vertical axis identifies whether a particular firm has a small or large country as its home base. The Porter and van der Linde hypothesis is placed in quadrant 3 of Figure 19.3. Domestic firms from a large country are highly responsive to home government regulations, and a long run consistency of domestic environmental policy with that prevailing in a small host country provides competitive advantages to domestic firms.

In contrast, the case described by Rugman (1995) is positioned in quadrant 2 of Figure 19.3. Even large MNEs in smaller countries will not benefit from tight domestic environmental regulations, according to Rugman, since the relevant environmental regulations are those of their foreign customers. These firms, from smaller countries, need to monitor the environmental regulations of host countries, rather than those of the home country. Only rarely will a small country's home government (like Canada) be able to anticipate international environmental trends for the benefit of home-based MNEs, which thus reflects a 'green illusion' in quadrant 4.

The problem with the Porter hypothesis, from a Canadian perspective, is that it is difficult to think of any sector where it could be applied. Virtually all of Canada's larger MNEs sell far more abroad than at home. The average ratio of foreign to total sales for Canada's largest twenty MNEs is over 70 per cent (Rugman 1990). Thus, if the Canadian government were to impose tight new environmental regulations, Canadian-based MNEs would have to invest and restructure for a market which takes a minority of their sales. These firms would prefer to adapt their manufacturing, and possibly increase outward FDI to suit the environmental regulations of their major customers abroad (especially when the big market for Canadian firms is the United States). In short, as far as Canadian competitiveness is concerned, the Porter hypothesis could be misleading. By forcing Canadian-based firms to take on board stronger, new environmental regulations, the Canadian government would likely reduce the international competitiveness of such firms, or force them to engage in outward FDI. In contrast, if the US government incorrectly antici- pates consistency between its own standards and Canadian standards, this would be an 'inconsequential mistake' for most US firms (quadrant 1 of Figure 19.3), given the relatively small size of the Canadian market compared to the US one.

# CONCLUSION

This chapter has focused on the managerial choice of specific environmental strategies in MNEs. It has been argued that these choices are strongly influenced by external elements such as compliance incentives provided by public agencies, the divergence/consistency among national environmental policy regimes, regional integration trends, etc.

In addition, the chapter has highlighted the particular opportunities and threats faced by MNEs when designing environmental strategies. We found that important choices need to be made regarding the development of location bound (poorly internationally transferable) or non-location bound (internationally transferable) green capabilities. The presence or absence of leveraging effects benefiting industrial performance, as well as the flexibility of resource commitments to environmental improvements, are critical in the choice to develop green capabilities. However, little research so far has been conducted on the internal, firm-specific variables that determine the development of green capabilities in MNEs.

A resource-based perspective, with an emphasis on the requirement of complementary assets in the MNE, may be a fruitful avenue for further research. Christmann (2000) has adopted such an approach, albeit in the context of domestic firms. Her approach does suggest, however, that the successful development and international transfer of global best practices in the environment area is unlikely to be suitable to all MNEs. For example, the impact on performance of early timing of environmental innovations and their international transfer is very likely to depend on the MNE's general capability to obtain first-mover advantages through process innovations and their rapid international transfer, within the MNE network.

## References

ABBOTT, F. (1996). 'From Theory to Practice: The Second Phase of the NAFTA Environmental Regime', in R. Wolfrum (ed.), *Enforcing Environmental Standards.* Berlin: Springer, 451–78.

ANDREWS, C. (1994). 'Policies to Encourage Clean Technology', in R. Socolow, C. Andrews, F. Berkhout, and V. Thomas (eds.), *Industrial Economy and Global Change.* Cambridge: Cambridge University Press, 405–22.

AUDLEY, J. (1997). *Green Politics and Global Trade: NAFTA and the Future of Environmental Politics.* Washington, DC: Georgetown University Press.

BARRETT, S. (1991). 'Environmental Regulations for Competitive Advantage', *Business Strategy Review* 2(1): 1–15.

BARTLETT, C., and GHOSHAL S. (1989). *Managing Across Borders: The Transnational Solution.* Boston: Harvard Business School Press.

BUYSSE, K., COECK C., and VERBEKE A. (1998), 'The International Co-ordination of Environmental Policy from an EU Perspective', in W. Meeusen (ed.), *Economic Policy in the European Union: Current Perspectives.* Cheltenham: Edward Elgar.

——VERBEKE A., and COECK C. (2001). 'The Greening of Corporate Strategies', in D. Van Den Bulcke and A. Verbeke (eds.), *Globalisation and the Small Open Economy.* Cheltenham: Edward Elgar.

CAIRNCROSS, F. (1992). 'UNCED, Environmentalism and Beyond', *Columbia Journal of World Business*, 27(3–4): 15–16.

CHRISTMANN, P. (2000). 'Effects of "Best Practices" of Environmental Management on Cost Advantage: the Role of Complementary Assets', *Academy of Management Journal*, 43(4): 663–80.

ESTY, D. (1994). *Greening the GATT*. Washington, DC: Institute for International Economics.

GORE, A. (1992). *Earth in Balance: Ecology and the Human Spirit*. Boston: Houghton Mifflin.

HAAS, P. M. (1999). 'Social Constructivism and the Evolution of Multilateral Environmental Governance', in A. Prakash and J. A. Hart (eds.), *Globalization and Governance*. London: Routledge.

HAAS, P., KEOHANE, R., and LEVY, M. (eds.) (1993). *Institutions for the Earth: Sources of Effective International Environmental Protection*. Cambridge, Mass.: MIT Press.

HENRIQUES, I., and SADORSKY, P. (1996). 'The Determinants of an Environmentally Responsive Firm: An Empirical Approach', *Journal of Environmental Economics and Management* 30: 381–95.

JAFFE, A. B., PETERSON, S. R., PORTNEY, P. R., and STAVINS, R. N. (1995). 'Environmental Regulation and the Competitiveness of US Manufacturing: What Does the Evidence Tell Us?', *Journal of Economic Literature*, 33: 132–63.

KEOHANE, R., and LEVY, M. (eds.) (1996). *Institutions for Environmental Aid: Pitfalls and Promise*. Cambridge, Mass.: MIT Press.

KOLK, A. (1998). 'From Conflict to Cooperation: International Policies to Protect the Brazilian Amazon', *World Development*, 26(8): 1481–93.

——(2000). *Economics of Environmental Management*. Harlow: Pearson Education.

——VAN TULDER R., and WELTERS, C. (1999). 'International Codes of Conduct and Corporate Social Responsibility: Can Transnational Corporations Regulate Themselves?', *Transnational Corporations*, 8(1): 143–80.

LEONARD, H. J. (1988). *Pollution and the Struggle for the World Product*. Cambridge: Cambridge University Press.

LEVY, D. L. (1995). 'The Environmental Practices and Performances of Transnational Corporations', *Transnational Corporations*, 4(1): 44–67.

——(1997). 'Business and International Environmental Treaties: Ozone Depletion and Climate Change', *California Management Review*, 39(3): 54–71.

LOW, P. (ed.) (1992). *International Trade and the Environment*. Washington, DC: World Bank, discussion paper 159.

LUNDAN, S. (1996). *Internationalization and Environmental Strategy in the Pulp and Paper Industry*. Ph.D. dissertation, Newark: Rutgers University.

MITCHELL, R. (1994). *International Oil Pollution at Sea: Environmental Policy and Treaty Compliance*. Cambridge, Mass.: MIT Press.

NEHRT, C. (1998). 'Maintainability of First Mover Advantages When Environmental Regulations Differ Between Countries', *Academy of Management Review*, 23(1): 77–97.

OECD (1993). *Pollution Abatement and Control Expenditure in OECD Countries*. Paris: OECD.

OECD (*cont.*) (1997). *Foreign Direct Investment and the Environment: An Overview of the Literature.* Paris: OECD.

PORTER, M. E. (1980). *Competitive Strategy.* New York: Free Press.

—— (1990). *The Competitive Advantage of Nations.* New York: Free Press.

—— and VAN DER LINDE, C. (1995). 'Towards a New Conception of the Environment-competitiveness Relationship', *Journal of Economic Perspectives*, 9(4): 97–118.

PRAKASH, A. (1999). 'A New-institutionalist Perspective on ISO 14000 and Responsible Care', *Business Strategy and the Environment*, 8: 322–35.

—— (2000). *Greening the Firm: The Politics of Corporate Environmentalism.* Cambridge: Cambridge University Press.

RONDINELLI, D. A., and BERRY, M. A. (2000). 'Environmental Citizenship in Multinational Corporations: Social Responsibility and Sustainable Development', *European Management Journal*, 18(1): 70–84.

—— and VASTAG, G. (1996). 'International Environmental Standards: An Integrative Framework', *California Management Review*, 39(1): 106–22.

RUGMAN, A. M. (1990). *Multinationals and the Canada–United States Free Trade Agreement.* Columbia, SC: University of South Carolina Press.

—— (1995). 'Environmental Regulations and International Competitiveness: Strategies for Canada's West Coast Forest Products Industry', *The International Executive*, 37(5): 451–65.

—— and GESTRIN, M. (1997). 'New Rules for Multilateral Investment', *The International Executive*, 39(1): 21–34.

—— and KIRTON, J. (1999). 'Multinational Enterprise Strategy and the NAFTA Trade and Environment Regime', *Journal of World Business*, 33(4): 438–54.

—— —— and SOLOWAY, J. (1997). 'NAFTA, Environmental Regulations and Canadian Competitiveness', *Journal of World Trade*, 31(4): 129–44.

—— —— —— (1999). *Environmental Regulations and Corporate Strategy: A NAFTA Perspective.* Oxford: Oxford University Press.

—— and VERBEKE, A. (1998a). 'Corporate Strategies and Environmental Regulations: An Organizing Framework', *Strategic Management Journal*, 19(4): 363–75.

—— —— (1998b). 'Corporate Strategy and International Environmental Policy', *Journal of International Business Studies*, 29(4): 819–34.

—— —— (2000a). 'Environmental Regulations and the Global Strategies of Multinational Enterprises', in Aseem Prakash and Jeffrey Hart (eds.), *Coping With Globalization.* London: Routledge, 77–93.

—— —— (2000b). 'Six Cases of Corporate Strategic Responses to Environmental Regulations', *European Management Journal*, 18(4): 377–85.

SAFARIAN, A. E. (1993). *Multinational Enterprises and Public Policy.* Cheltenham: Edward Elgar.

SCHMIDHEINY, S. (1992). *Changing Course.* Cambridge, Mass.: MIT Press.

SCHOLL, G. (1996). 'Sustainable Product Policy in Europe', *European Environment*, 6(1): 183–93.

SHRIVASTAVA, P. (1995). 'The Role of Corporations in Achieving Ecological Sustainability', *Academy of Management Review*, 20(4): 936–60.

TSAI, S. H. T., and CHILD, JOHN (1997). 'Strategic Responses of Multinational Corporations to Environmental Demands', *Journal of General Management*, 23(1): 1–23.

UNCTAD (1993). *Environmental Management in Transnational Corporations. Report on the Benchmark Corporate Environmental Survey.* New York: United Nations.

—— (1996). *Self-regulation of Environmental Management. An Analysis of Guidelines Set by World Industry Associations for Their Member Firms.* New York: United Nations.

VOGEL, D. (1995). *Trading Up: Consumer and Environmental Regulations in a Global Economy.* Cambridge, Mass.: Harvard University Press.

—— and RUGMAN, A. M. (1997). 'Environmentally-related Trade Disputes Between the United States and Canada', *The American Review of Canadian Studies*, 27(2), Summer: 271–92.

WALLACE, D. (1995). *Environmental Policy and Industrial Innovation. Strategies in Europe, the US and Japan.* London: Earthscan/Royal Institute of International Affairs.

WALLEY, N., and WHITEHEAD, B. (1994). 'It's Not Easy Being Green', *Harvard Business Review*, 72(3): 46–52.

WALTER, I. (1982). 'Environmentally Induced Industrial Relocation to Developing Countries', in S. J. Rubin and T. R. Graham (eds.), *Environment and Trade.* Allanheld: Osmun Publishers.

YOUNG, O. (1994). *International Governance: Protecting the Environment in a Stateless Society.* Ithaca, NY: Cornell University Press.

..........................................................................

# CHAPTER 20

# INTERNATIONAL FINANCIAL MANAGEMENT AND MULTINATIONAL ENTERPRISES

..........................................................................

MICHAEL BOWE

JAMES W. DEAN

## 20.1 INTRODUCTION

..........................................................................

THIS chapter provides a selective, critical survey of the academic literature on the financial management policy of multinational enterprises (MNEs). The focus of much current research interest can be captured in two major themes which also dominate this analysis. The first is financial management policy in

The authors wish to thank Mo Yamin and Laura Stanciu for their comments on a previous draft. The support of ESRC grant R022250131 in facilitating part of this research is gratefully acknowledged.

relationship to the increasing volatility of real and financial asset prices in the international financial environment within which MNEs operate. This dictates one theme of this chapter: the impact of financial risk, in particular market risk,[1] on MNEs and an appraisal of evolving financial risk management practices.

The second theme is international market segmentation (Choi and Rajan 1997). The globalization of international business activity has evolved along with increasing financial market integration, particularly in capital markets. To a limited extent this has been accompanied by increased harmonization and standardization of both international regulatory and accounting practices (Roberts *et al.* 1998). Despite such trends, the asymmetric incidence of accounting standards, regulations, and taxation has had significant tactical and strategic financial management implications for MNEs (Choi and Levich 1990, 1997; Gray *et al.* 1995; Meek *et al.* 1995; Oxelheim *et al.* 1998). We evaluate the nature, incidence, and implications of such market segmentation for selected aspects of MNE financial management activity.

It is clear from the context of our analysis that we believe financial factors to have important implications for the comparative advantage of MNEs located in different jurisdictions, and also that financial management plays a critical role in deciding an MNE's competitive prosperity. This belief is supported by surveys of MNEs (Rawls and Smithson 1990; Marshall 2000). Marshall (2000) reports the results of a survey of the 200 largest MNEs which reveal that 87 per cent of Asian Pacific-based MNEs, 68 per cent of UK-based MNEs, and 55 per cent of the US-based MNEs state that foreign exchange risk management is at least as important as business risk management. Nonetheless, to date no generally accepted theoretical underpinning has yet been provided demonstrating that financial factors alone are both necessary and sufficient to rationalize the existence of MNEs.[2] We further discuss this issue in the context of modes of market entry and participation in a later section.

The remainder of the chapter is easily summarized. Section 2 discusses the enhanced importance of recent increases in asset price volatility, relating it to

---

[1] To define financial risk, we must first select the financial variable(s) of interest. The value of the MNE's portfolio of assets and liabilities, corporate earnings, equity capital, or a specific cash flow arising from an operating or contractual exposure, are all natural candidates. Focusing on the former variable for illustrative purposes, financial risk can be defined as *unexpected* changes in the valuation of a multinational corporation's portfolio of assets and/or liabilities arising either: (i) from changes in the value of financial instruments, or (ii) consequent upon the corporation's activities in financial markets. Unexpected movements in the prices of financial instruments, such as exchange rates, interest rates, commodity and equity prices, collectively termed market risk, are the major sources of financial risk for most MNEs.

[2] The irony of this fact has not escaped the attention of many commentators (see e.g. Lessard 1997), given that many of the building blocks for the modern theory of the MNE were established following Hymer's critique of the 'international capital flow' theory of FDI which stimulated much early theoretical work on MNEs.

country risk and international investment appraisal. The classification and measurement of risk exposure is considered in section 3. Particular attention is given to recently developed techniques such as value-at-risk and cash-flow-at-risk. Section 4 is concerned with the management of financial risk by MNEs. In particular, a distinction is made between management policies designed primarily to hedge risk, and those intending to exploit its potential to create competitive advantage. This section also evaluates empirical studies of MNE risk management. Section 5 addresses issues relating to the effective implementation of a risk management system within the governance structure of an MNE. Brief concluding remarks follow together with some suggestions for future research.

# 20.2 THE NATURE OF FINANCIAL RISK

Our emphasis on financial risk and the evolution of MNE risk management practices has been motivated by a number of factors, the most important being the trend toward increasing global financial market integration (Lessard 1997) and the enhanced volatility in the financial environment within which MNEs operate.[3] We later evaluate studies which argue that these factors can confer certain advantages to internationalization of a firm's activities. In preparation for this analysis we chronicle certain major recent developments in the global financial environment, which indicate the increasing importance of market risk in global financial markets.

## 20.2.1 Exchange rate variability

Following the collapse of the Bretton Woods system of fixed exchange rates in the early 1970s, exchange rate fluctuations have become increasingly volatile, punctuated by occasional episodes of exchange rate crises. Between 1970 and

[3] We note that this trend is not universal. While the global financial environment incorporates an increasingly integrated core, there remains a large periphery including many LDCs ostracized by debt overhang and incomplete contracting regimes which in Lessard's words is 'dependent upon but only loosely linked to the core international market'. For further discussion of the impact of debt on capital market access see Bowe and Dean 1997.

mid-2000, the Yen/US dollar exchange rate has moved from 361 to 107 and the Deutschmark/US dollar rate has fallen from 4.2 to 1.9. However, the dollar has appreciated by about two-thirds against sterling over the same period. The crisis in the European Monetary System (ERM) in September 1992 led to significant falls in the value of sterling and the Italian Lira, while the currencies of Thailand, Indonesia, Malaysia, the Philippines, and South Korea lost between one-third and three-quarters of their value in the second half of 1997. There have also been major movements in exchange rates following shifts in the monetary policy stance of certain governments, such as the tighter monetary policy followed in the early days of the Thatcher administration in the UK. Indeed, the average volatility of exchange rates, which is in the region of 10–15 per cent per year, is sufficient to eliminate the average profit margin for the typical multinational corporation.

## 20.2.2  Interest rate variability

Interest rate volatility has similarly affected corporate funding costs, cash flows, and net asset values since the early 1970s. Inflationary pressures caused interest rates to increase in the first half of the 1970s in the US, and although they subsequently declined, a change in policy by the Federal Reserve caused a sharp increase in both the level and volatility of rates in 1979. Interest rates peaked in 1981, and then fell slowly. Since 1983, there have been four more US interest rate cycles. According to Jorion (1996), the increase in 1994 eliminated over $1.5 trillion dollars from fixed income portfolios. Interest rates have also become more volatile since many central banks began to abandon targeting interest rates as a policy objective in favour of targeting money supply growth or inflation. In the UK, interest rates shot up in the late 1980s and early 1990s due to inflationary pressures caused by a relaxation in monetary policy, but then fell substantially with sterling's withdrawal from the ERM in September 1992.

## 20.2.3  Equity market variability

Equity markets have also become extremely volatile. During the inflationary periods of the early 1970s, prices increased significantly only to fall sharply during the bear market of 1974–5 following a 300 per cent hike in the price of oil. A global recovery then ensued, with minor price reversals in 1982–3, and the market peaked in 1987. On Black Monday, 19 October 1987, prices plunged. US equities lost 23 per cent of their value, equivalent to over US$1 trillion in equity capital. This was followed by another recovery over the next ten years, sustained worldwide with the exception of Japan, where the Nikkei index fell from 39,000 in 1989 to 17,000 in 1992, a capital loss of US $2.7 trillion. Finally from mid- to end 1997, the stock markets of Bangkok, Jakarta, Kuala Lumpur, and Manila lost US $370 billion, or 63 per cent of the four countries' combined GDP, while the Seoul stock market declined 60 per cent.

## 20.2.4 Commodity price variability and other sources of increased risk

Commodity prices, particularly those in primary product markets, have also been subject to large fluctuations since the 1970s, a trend established subsequent to the oil price rises of 1973–4. This variability also had spillover effects in other financial markets, particularly equity markets, thereby corroborating the view that it is fundamentally incorrect to treat financial markets in isolation from one another. Significant regulatory and legal changes, the globalization of the financial services industry, and the emergence of offshore financial activity have also increased financial risks. Finally, risk associated with the enhanced global nature of competition has become apparent. Systemic regional and global risk has resulted from increased levels of world trade, major changes in trade policy, the economic and political transition of the former Soviet bloc, the growth of the EU, and the emergence of the Asian 'tiger' economies as economic powers.[4]

## 20.2.5 Country risk[5]

This increasing financial market volatility has potentially important consequences for both the issue of international investment appraisal, and also the appropriate measure of country risk.[6] Before we consider methodological

---

[4] For a recent survey of MNE activity in relation to emerging markets see Errunza 1997.

[5] This section draws heavily on an excellent series of papers on equity risk premiums by Aswath Damodaran which can be found on *http://www.stern.nyu.edu/~adamodar.*

[6] This analysis makes no attempt to consider the important issues surrounding the appropriate theoretical framework for international capital budgeting decisions in terms of present value versus real option approaches. Appropriate discussion can be found in Dixit and Pindyck

issues relating to the measurement of country risk, there are some commentators who argue that country risk is diversifiable (unsystematic) and that there should be no correction for country risk premium in evaluating international investment decisions. Recent asset pricing behaviour in international financial markets provides substantial evidence of cross-market correlation (systematic risk) suggesting country risk is non-diversifiable even in a global portfolio, and hence should be incorporated.[7] On the measurement aspects, Damodoran (2000) has argued that the risk premium in any equity market can be conceptualized as:

Equity Market Risk Premium in Country A = Base Premium for Mature Equity Market (US) + Country Premium for Country A.

In calculating the base premium for the US market, an approach based upon historical premium remains standard. Here, actual equity returns are estimated over a sufficiently long time frame and compared to the actual returns earned on default-free (usually government) securities. The annualized difference is then calculated and represents the historical premium. This method yields substantial differences in the premiums we observe being used in practice: even for the case of the USA estimates range from 4 per cent to 12 per cent. This is all the more surprising given that most calculations use identical data, the Ibbotson Associates database of historical returns.

We conjecture several reasons exist for this divergence. First: differences in time periods used. Proponents of the use of shorter time periods argue that such estimates are more relevant, as the average risk aversion of investors changes over time. This consideration is likely overwhelmed by the fact that to obtain reasonable standard errors one requires very long time periods (at least twenty-five years).[8] Indeed, the standard errors from ten-year estimates often exceed the risk premium estimates, making the estimates redundant.[9] Second, the risk-free rate chosen in estimating the premium must be consistent with the risk-free rate used in calculating expected returns, in other words the method must match up the duration of the cash flows being discounted (Damodoran 2000). If the yield curve is upward sloping, the risk premium will be larger when estimated relative to short-term government securities.

1994, 1995; Sercu and Uppal 1994, 1995; Brennan and Trigeorgis 2000; and Buckley 2000. A thorough analysis of surveys (e.g. Oblak and Helm 1980; Wicks Kelly and Philippatos 1982; Shao and Shao 1993; Buckley *et al.* 1996), of the actual practice of MNE international investment appraisal, is contained in Buckley 2000.

[7] Classic studies in this area include Solnik 1974; Jacquillat and Solnik 1978; Severn 1974; and Roll 1993. The debate is treated in Buckley 2000.

[8] Even though such estimates are plagued by survivor bias.

[9] This precludes direct estimates of equity market premium for emerging markets, where reliable data rarely pre-dates the mid-1980s, and annual standard deviations in equity returns are substantial.

Consistency is required and given the previous comments, the use of equity premium calculated relative to long-dated government bonds seems appropriate for most cases. Third, a debate exists over how to compute the average returns on stocks and bonds, in particular whether to use arithmetic or geometric averages. While conventional wisdom argues for use of arithmetic averages, strong arguments can be made in favour of the geometric alternative. Specifically, empirical studies indicate equity returns are negatively correlated over time, implying the use of arithmetic averages (which assume zero correlation) will exaggerate the premium. Moreover, while assets pricing models are typically single period models, their use to generate expected returns over long periods (say ten years) suggests the 'single period' is much longer than the data period used in their estimation (typically one year). In such a case the argument for geometric premiums is enhanced.

A further issue questions whether one should incorporate a country premium, and if so how it is to be estimated. The first question has already been answered in the affirmative. The second issue requires an ability to: (i) measure country risk, (ii) convert the estimate into a risk premium, and then (iii) evaluate individual MNE's exposure. On measurement, country sovereign bond ratings provided by rating agencies incorporate current market risk perceptions, and have the advantage of being measured as spreads relative to US treasuries. However, they only measure default risk, not equity risk. A crude method of converting them to the latter involves adjusting the default spread of the country concerned for the volatility of its equity market in relation to its bond market ($\sigma$ (equity)/$\sigma$ (bond)). The country's equity premium is set equal to the country default spread multiplied by ($\sigma$ (equity)/$\sigma$ (bond)). This equity premium will increase if either the country's rating drops or its equity market volatility increases.[10] Finally, on evaluating MNEs' individual exposure, one has to identify the MNE's exposure to country risk in relation to all other market risks it faces. This requires detailed analysis of the process used to estimate beta. Not only is this beyond the scope of this paper, but it also represents an ongoing research activity over which a concensus has yet to emerge.[11]

Finally, we contend that further research attention should be given to alternative methods of estimating country risk premium that do not require corrections for country risk in the manner indicated above. Damodoran (2000) suggests use of implied equity premiums derived from the following equity market valuation model, which essentially measures the present value of dividends growing at a constant rate:

[10] It is also sensitive to the time horizon over which measurement is made. The equity premium converges to the bond premium as one looks at longer term spreads.

[11] Certain issues are fairly clear. In particular, it is generally incorrect to assume that all companies in a country are equally exposed to country risk, or that it is proportional to exposure to other market risks, measured by the standard beta.

Value of Corporation = Expected Dividends next period/(required rate of return of equity − expected growth rate in dividends).

The only unobservable input in this model is the required rate of return on equity. This relation can therefore be solved to generate an implied expected return on equity, which in turn will generate an equity risk premium once a correction is incorporated for the risk free rate. This approach has two main advantages. It does not require historical data and it reflects current market perceptions. The drawback is that it assumes the market overall is accurately priced, which is problematic in the case of emerging markets. More analysis in this important area would be most welcome.

# 20.3 THE CLASSIFICATION AND MEASUREMENT OF RISK EXPOSURE

With increased volatility in financial markets, MNEs have learned that their value has become more subject to the risks occasioned by changes in their financial environment. There are a number of approaches MNEs have adopted to deal with this risk. Some early commentators (Rodriguez 1981) report that the overall strategy of many MNEs in foreign exchange risk management is defensive in that they attempt to minimize the impact of market risk.[12] However, more recent analysis has identified that the key MNE objectives when managing market risk are cash flow management (Copeland and Joshi 1996; Cummins et al. 1998; Marshall 2000) and the smoothing of earnings fluctuations (Marshall 2000). While both are important for UK and US-based MNEs, smoothing earnings is of particular relevance for the larger MNEs and those based in the Asia Pacific region, while cash flow management is held to be more important for MNEs with a high degree of internationalization. These findings for MNEs are consistent with previous single country studies of domestically domiciled firms in the UK and US (see Bodnar et al. 1995, 1996, 1998; and Grant and Marshall 1995). One avenue for further exploration is to what extent the regional differences noted above can be explained by company characteristics.

---

[12] Other studies of the foreign exchange risk management behaviour of US and UK corporates include those by Collier and Davies 1985; Mathur 1985; Davies et al. 1991; Berg and Moore 1991; Joseph and Hewins 1991; and Belk and Glaum 1990.

## 20.3.1 Classifying a multinational firm's exposure to market risk

The central question confronted by an MNE's financial director or treasury department is to what extent the value of the firm's cash flows or earnings are exposed to changes in financial asset prices. In the context of foreign exchange risk, three classifications are commonly adopted in the literature, namely transaction or contractual exposure, translation exposure, and economic or operating exposure. These are not mutually exclusive, rather they are overlapping. They are also easily generalized to other sources of market risk. MNEs are normally exposed to more than one type, and there is still no general agreement as to which exposure needs to be emphasized from the financial management perspective, although several authors have taken a strong stance on this issue.

Contractual exposure arises from a MNE's fixed contractual obligations: accounts payable/receivable, long-term purchase/sale contracts, and financial positions expressed in foreign currency. If the source of information on contractual exposure is accounting data, then it becomes relatively transparent and easy to quantify for most types of market risk. Moreover, contractual cash flows are fixed either in domestic (reference) currency units or in units of the firm's output. Their nominal value in domestic currency then changes in the same proportion as the change in the exchange rate, foreign currency price, or amount sold, other things equal. Alternatively stated, contractual exposures have an elasticity of one.

Empirical studies of MNEs based in the UK, US, and Asia Pacific suggest that most tend to focus upon the management of contractual rather than translation or economic exposure. Berkman and Bradbury (1996), Berkman *et al.* (1997), Belk and Edelshain (1997), Duangploy *et al.* (1997), Khoury and Chan (1988), Joseph (2000), and Marshall (2000) all report that MNE foreign exchange risk management focuses on contractual exposure. This emphasis is understandable in view of the immediate impact of contractual risk on cash flows and earnings, and the relative ease with which it is measured.

There is a wide-ranging debate as to whether translation exposures, the effect of unexpected foreign exchange fluctuations upon a MNE subsidiary's financial statements, should be actively managed. Many authors (Shapiro 1999; and Sercu and Uppal 1995; among others), argue that as translation exposure is purely an accounting concept with no impact on future cash flows it need not be actively managed. However, surveys by Rodriguez (1977) for the USA, Collier *et al.* (1992), and Joseph (2000) for the UK, and Marshall (2000) for both the above regions plus the Asia Pacific, confirm that translation exposure *is* actively managed by most MNEs, particularly in the

Asia Pacific.[13] We conjecture that the decision to manage such exposure is influenced by market segmentation considerations, in particular differential financial reporting requirements in the reporting country, which will affect the MNE's financial statements (Hakkarainen *et al.* 1998).[14] The importance Asia Pacific MNEs attribute to translation exposure could also be explained by survey timing, especially in relation to the relative strength of the reporting currency in the context of this parameter's influence on the value of overseas assets and liabilities.

Buckley (2000), Sercu and Uppal (1995), Glaum (1990), and Kohn (1990) all maintain that a central, if not the most important, risk management activity for an MNE is the management of economic exposure. Moreover, the importance of this type of exposure is recognized by MNEs. In this context, it is perhaps surprising that it has not been more systematically managed. In an early survey, Blin *et al.* (1980) found that adjustment was made for economic exposure in less than one third of companies. One possible explanation is that economic exposure is very difficult to quantify, as it requires a detailed understanding of the firm's competitive position and the macroeconomic environment in which it operates (Oxelheim and Wihlborg 1987, 1989*a*,*b*).[15]

We consider some recent developments in the complex task of measuring economic exposure in the following section. However, despite these advances, Marshall's (2000) survey results indicate that it generally continues to receive less risk management emphasis than other forms of exposure. The exception is for the MNEs based in the Asia Pacific, where the 1997 financial crisis may have eroded competitive advantage beyond the realm of managing transaction and translation exposures.

## 20.3.2 Quantifying MNE exposure to market risk

There are several means available to MNE treasury departments for quantifying exposure to market risk. As many of these techniques are relatively recent,

[13] Collier *et al.* 1990 indicate that financial managers in certain UK and US-based MNEs are concerned about the adverse impact of translation risk on leverage, distributable reserves, and overall balance sheet value. See also Schooley and White 1995.

[14] For further discussion of the financial management implications for MNEs of the asymmetric incidence of accounting standards, regulations, and taxes see Gray *et al.* 1995; Meek *et al.* 1995; and Roberts *et al.* 1998.

[15] Moreover, as fluctuations in exchange rates impact on operating cash flows in both domestic and foreign currency the total resulting impact could imply an elasticity greater or less than one. Capturing operating exposures through accurate elasticity estimates is critical to cash flow sensitivity analysis. How corporations obtain elasticity estimates, for example using economic models or simulations, will vary. Indeed, this translation of financial price risk into

we will discuss them in some detail. Broadly speaking, they can be divided into two types: internal and market-based measures. We begin with the former.

### 20.3.2.1 *Internal measures of market risk: value at risk (VaR)*

Most of the recently developed internal techniques for measuring financial risk recognize that market risk should not be considered as exposure to individual financial asset price changes, but rather as exposure to an integrated set of interrelated asset price changes. Moreover, any proposed definition must be both easily understood, and easily communicated to the MNE's senior management. This has led to the development of probability-based summary measures of exposure, the most notable being value-at-risk (VaR).

VaR is a valuation technique based upon the current net asset value of the portfolio. It is specified in terms of a confidence level (Jorion 1996), and enables the risk manager to calculate the maximum that the corporation can lose over a specified time horizon at a specified probability level. This calculation is undertaken using historical simulation of past data, Monte Carlo simulation, or analytic variance-covariance methods. The method chosen should depend on the composition of the portfolio and the desired time horizon. The calculated VaR is then translated in to a probability statement about likely changes in portfolio valuation resulting from financial asset price changes over a given time period. For example, the risk manager should be able to define the maximum loss for a one-day, one-week, one-month period that the firm will incur with 95 per cent probability (implying that this loss should be exceeded on only five occasions in one hundred).

### 20.3.2.2 *The relevance of VaR*

The VaR concept, while not a panacea for risk measurement difficulties, has been embraced by many multinational corporations, particularly those where the MNE's value is linked closely to the current net asset value of its portfolio. These firms are market value driven, with business assets marked to market daily. Typically securities and derivatives trading is a primary business focus, and the company's investment horizon is measured over short time periods. They would, therefore, have a keen interest in managing the volatility of their current asset value. Hence, VaR is particularly suitable for financial

changes in the corporation's operating performance is perhaps the most challenging aspect of ascertaining cash flow exposure. It also compels multinational treasurers to be explicit about their operating parameters, and these parameters can then be re-evaluated in the context of the model(s) used.

institutions, institutional investors, and the treasury divisions located in manufacturing corporations where such trading divisions function as profit centres. An example of the later is British Petroleum, where BP Finance not only manages the company's natural financial risk exposures, but is also expected to trade foreign exchange and interest rate financial instruments with the intention of contributing to BP's profits.

### 20.3.2.3 *Alternatives to VaR: cash flow at risk*

For other multinational corporations, however, the VaR approach is potentially less relevant. These corporations can be characterized as cash flow driven, and their value is linked closely to the judicial exercise of the real growth options arising from their investment and research and development activities. In these corporations, business assets are marked to market infrequently, derivatives are used only as tools to manage financial risks, and investment horizons are measured in months or even years. Their primary focus therefore is to manage cash flow volatility so that they can judicially exercise their growth options at the appropriate time.

Corroboration of such an interpretation is provided by the surveys of MNEs mentioned earlier, which concluded that a majority of MNEs stated that their primary risk management objective was to reduce cash flow volatility. The issue then becomes how best to translate this information into a summary, operational measure of financial exposure which focuses on the impact of price changes on the firm's cash flows: in other words, a cash flow analogue to VaR. This would relate the magnitude and timing of cash inflows to a corporation's contractually committed liabilities and investment opportunities, as suggested by Froot *et al.* (1993). Smithson (1998) refers to this as *cash flow sensitivity analysis*, while Dowd (1998) terms it *cash flow at risk*. Smithson proposes the following cash flow based measure of exposure: *A corporation's consolidated exposure to financial risk is the probability that the company will fail to satisfy its performance targets over a given time period as the result of unexpected changes in financial asset prices.*

The practical relevance of these internal risk measurement procedures revolves around identifying the appropriate procedures for their implementation. Smithson (1998) argues that the desired model must be sufficiently rich to capture the interactions between commodity inputs, product prices, foreign and domestic operations, and contractual payment obligations. The corporation's planning model could provide a useful place to begin this exercise, but it would have to be supplemented to address two critical shortcomings. First, appropriate simulation exercises would have to be undertaken with variable prices in order to model realistically the various pricing scenarios that the firm is likely to face in the future. Second, an acceptable method would have to be found for modelling the relationship between the impact of market risk and MNE cash flows.[16] This is complex because the operating cash flows of the corporation depend on both the economic environment the firm faces, and how, given this competitive environment, the corporation's strategy is impacted by unexpected changes in financial asset prices, including the exchange rate.

### 20.3.2.4 *Market based measures of financial risk*

As their name suggests, market based measures of financial risk utilize market determined values of financial data to measure the market's perception of how changes in the corporation's value (or other preselected measure of financial performance) are related to changes in the prices of financial assets. Market based approaches to risk measurement vary in the details of their implementation, but can be broadly be said to use economic and/or statistical models to estimate the sensitivity of a corporation's earnings, cash flow or share price to movements in the value of selected financial prices. These include changes in selected exchange rates, interest rates, and commodity prices. The models can also be used to estimate the exposures of the MNE's main competitors, providing an input into the firm's strategic decision making, and contributing insights into the competitive environment. Whether the firm chooses to use internal or market based systems, the following section considers the appropriate organizing framework within which an MNE can coordinate its risk management policies.

# 20.4 THE MANAGEMENT OF FINANCIAL RISK EXPOSURE BY MNES

Froot (1994) highlights the lack of a comprehensive framework for the MNE's management of market risk exposures. Clearly, any risk management strategy should be undertaken if and only if it increases the expected discounted value of the MNE's cash flows or earnings. It is of critical importance, however, to distinguish between two classes of risk management policies. In the first class

---

[16] The nature of the company's operations is a critical determinant of its ability to model successfully the dependency of cash flows upon market risk. Multinational corporations with global production operations are obviously at the complex end of the modelling spectrum relative to single product or commodity driven firms.

are those policies commonly denoted hedging, which serve purely to reduce the long term volatility of the MNE's cash flows or earnings, thereby reducing the expected costs of financial distress. The second class consists of policies designed to respond to financial risk by tactically and/or strategically exploiting asset price volatility to create competitive advantage. The emphasis in the financial risk management literature is overwhelmingly placed on the hedging aspects. We believe this focus on hedging may have generated a misplaced emphasis in the empirical literature which attempts to identify MNE's risk management practices, a point to which we return below. At this point, it is sufficient to note that using exposure to financial price volatility to create competitive advantage requires adjustments in operational decisions which involve a complex set of tactical, strategic, and organizational issues additional to hedging. We note that neither the hedging nor the responsive motives for dealing with financial risk rely on the MNE's management exhibiting risk averse behaviour.

In view of these considerations, it is clear that in practice MNEs would adopt a variety of risk management techniques, usually identified in the literature under the categories of internal and external (Hakkarainen *et al.* 1998). Internal techniques are an integral component of the MNE's financial management, and do not give rise to special contractual arrangements outside the core-subsidiary network. External techniques use bilateral external contractual arrangements for risk management purposes. For short-run risk management considerations, the major internal techniques identified in the literature are balance sheet hedging, currency matching, leading and lagging, netting of cash flows, and pricing policy. To generate flexibility in the management of longer term cash flows or earnings volatility, the literature highlights international diversification in manufacturing and distribution, which confer the MNE with enhanced operational flexibility, thereby enhancing its competitive advantage (Allen and Pantzalis 1996; Kogut and Kulatilka 1994; Buckley and Casson 1998; Rangan 1998).[17]

External techniques focus on the management of financial risk using off-balance sheet financial instruments, generally known as derivatives: forwards, futures, swaps, and options. These instruments provide the building blocks that enable MNEs to use both standardized exchange-traded instruments and customized financial products obtained in over-the-counter markets, to manage the risks associated with currency, interest rate, and commodity price fluctuations far more flexibly, cheaply, and efficiently than is possible with on-balance sheet strategies. We begin with a discussion of the more conventional hedging motives.

---

[17] For a critique see Lewent and Kearney 1990; and Glaum 1990.

## 20.4.1 Risk management and motives for hedging financial risk

Theories of optimal hedging are designed to demonstrate how financial risk management can increase firm value in the presence of capital market imperfections by reducing the volatility of cash flows or earnings. The relation between the present value of a corporation's cash flow and its financial policies was demonstrated in a classic paper by Modigliani and Miller (1958), which developed the seminal 'M&M' propositions. These propositions imply that in the absence of capital market imperfections, investors can undertake their own hedging policies just as effectively as the firm's managers, by holding diversified investment portfolios. The relevance of the M&M proposition for strategic risk management becomes evident by considering its corollary: a necessary condition for strategic risk management to affect firm value is that it impacts upon the firm's taxes, transaction costs, or investment decision. While necessary, this is not sufficient. Given the incentives created by capital market imperfections, a corporation's choice to use derivative instruments depends also on its level of financial risk exposure, the availability of internal hedging mechanisms, and the costs of managing financial risk. In the following section we adopt a framework developed by Geczy *et al.* (1997) in order to organize the various theories explaining a firm's hedging strategy.

### 20.4.1.1 *Managers*

Managers of international firms invest much of their human capital or intangible wealth in the corporation. They may also hold significant amounts of common shares. If management are averse to bearing uncompensated risk, the value of these two components of their wealth will be significantly adversely affected by volatility in the corporation's earnings. As hedging reduces the volatility of the value of the firm, management will direct the firm to hedge if it can do so at a lower cost than compensating the managers for bearing the additional risk through, for example, a management compensation scheme containing share options (Smith 1983; Stultz 1984; Smith and Stultz 1985). DeMarzo and Duffie (1995) suggest an alternative but complementary argument focusing upon managerial reputation. A corporation's value is determined both by the quality of managerial decisions relating to its core business competencies, and also by financial risk, which impacts on the firm's earnings but which lies outside the domain of managerial control. Managers may choose to manage the effect of financial risk through hedging, as the information content of corporate earnings as a signal of managerial ability is thereby enhanced. Managerial labour markets and the market for corporate control are then more able to isolate the effects of good luck from good judgement when assessing managerial performance.

### 20.4.1.2 *Bondholders*

Bondholders of the corporation have an incentive to support strategic risk management activity in order to reduce the probability, and therefore the expected costs of financial distress (or bankruptcy). Financial distress arises when the firm's income stream is insufficient to cover its liabilities, or its probability of default rises to due increased volatility in its income stream. The associated costs include not only the direct costs associated with bankruptcy or liquidation, but also the indirect costs of a deterioration or loss of long-term relationships with suppliers and customers or a reduction in the firm's borrowing capacity through a downgrading of its credit rating. We note that a risk management strategy will only reduce expected financial distress costs if the firm can credibly commit to following a hedging strategy, through for example bond covenants or credit agreements.

As first demonstrated by Myers (1977), financial distress costs also induce suboptimal investment decisions (see also Bessimbinder 1991). As the perception that the firm may encounter financial distress increases, it becomes more difficult and costly to raise external finance. This leads to capital rationing constraints and the consequent rejection of profitable investment opportunities. Froot *et al.* (1993) develop this argument, noting that hedging mitigates this underinvestment problem by reducing not only the costs of raising finance externally, but also the firm's reliance on external funds.

### 20.4.1.3 *Equityholders*

Smith and Stultz (1985) were the first to demonstrate that risk management can increase shareholders' expected wealth when the firm operates in a fiscal environment where corporate tax rates increase more than in proportion to corporate income. This is known as a convex tax liability schedule. The existence of tax preference items, such as various forms of tax credits, which are subtracted from pre-tax income, indirectly create convexity in the tax liability schedule, since the present value of unused tax shields decreases as they are postponed to future periods. As Mian (1996) among others has pointed out, by reducing the variance of corporate earnings, risk management increases the expected value of tax shields because the probability of using preference items increases with the level of a firm's taxable income. DeMarzo and Duffie (1991) have also shown that equityholders in the corporation will support risk management when the firm's managers have better information about the risks which affect the corporation's earnings. As hedging reduces the volatility of the firm's earnings, it enables equityholders to better distinguish the effects of luck and managerial ability, and consequently make better informed portfolio optimization decisions.

We now consider those financial risk management policies which are motivated primarily by a desire to respond to real and financial asset price volatility in order to exploit an MNE's comparative and competitive advantage. This risk management response incorporates both a tactical and a strategic dimension, and we begin with the former.

## 20.4.2  Risk management to create competitive advantage

Many of the tactical responses to financial risk, especially over short time horizons, involve the exploitation of arbitrage opportunities which create a comparative advantage for certain MNEs in a particular segment of the international capital markets (see Oxelheim *et al.* 1998). These situations arise as a result of international financial market segmentation in one form or another, and can be utilized by MNEs to create a competitive advantage, for example by reducing corporate funding costs, or the costs of capital, in a manner not open to single country firms.

### 20.4.2.1  *Reducing funding costs by arbitraging markets*

The appropriate use of derivative instruments can exploit artificial market segmentation caused by an asymmetric incidence of governmental regulation or tax treatment. Barriers to entry are standard in many international capital markets. For example, prior to 1992, the Subcommittee for Foreign Issues of the Central Capital Markets Committee regulated the timing and amount of new issues in the German external bond markets by establishing monthly quotas for deutschmark-denominated bond issuance. Since the supply of securities was thereby artificially restricted, their price was higher than the market determined price, and accordingly the instruments carried below market interest rates. The corporations or other end users with privileged access to the market could exploit this anomaly through judicious borrowing combined with the appropriate derivative positions.

Differences in national taxation practices can also present arbitrage opportunities; these can again be exploited through derivative portfolios and other balance sheet strategies (Kramer *et al.* 1993).[18] Withholding taxes on offshore

---

[18] Giovannini 1989 discusses several mechanisms for tax shifting. A particularly interesting one, cited in Lessard 1997, is when an MNE structures foreign operations as a branch of a domestic subsidiary that can be consolidated or unconsolidated at the parent's discretion. This facilitates a continuous movement from deferred to non-deferred treatment, thereby creating an

borrowings in certain countries give rise to such opportunities. In the 1980s the Australian government levied a withholding tax on interest payments made by Australian companies on all offshore borrowings denominated in Australian dollars. This tax, combined with high interest rates in Australia and a relatively stable currency prompted a substantial volume of currency swap-driven Australian dollar eurobond issues in early 1986. A similar situation arose in New Zealand in 1990. Other examples arise when differences in taxation laws provide incentives to raise capital in one country to finance investment in another. Historically, generous capital consumption allowances in some European countries, such as France, implied that interest expenses provided only a minimal tax shield in those countries. MNEs then had an incentive to raise finance in countries where interest expenses provide a considerable tax shield, and to invest the funds in countries with high depreciation allowances.[19] This procedure, while reducing funding costs, provides a foreign exchange exposure in at least one currency, the risk of which can be managed with the appropriate derivatives portfolio.

In the same context of corporate funding requirements, there is some evidence that the choice of location for an MNE's equity market listing is infuenced by differential international accounting and regulatory disclosure requirements. Saudagaran and Biddle (1995) analysed over 450 internationally traded MNEs listed on nine stock exchanges in eight countries at the end of 1992. They found that choice of listing location is significantly determined by financial disclosure variables, in addition to an MNE's business profile, measured by the level of exports from the MNE to the listing locality.

Froot (1989, 1990) argues that MNEs based in countries with currencies that have undergone significant real appreciation can benefit from a reduced liquidity premium in that currency. This generates a window of opportunity enabling them to place a higher value on overseas investments, thereby acting as a stimulus for overseas asset acquisition or capital expenditure. Such opportunities may not be reciprocally shared by overseas competitors (Kester and Luehrman 1989). However, it still remains an open question why this should take the form of real, as opposed to portfolio investment.

### 20.4.2.2  *Reducing funding costs through embedded options*

MNEs may also be able to reduce their funding costs by issuing hybrid debt, essentially debt which contains an implicit or embedded option: for example a bond with an equity warrant attached, a convertible bond, or a callable bond. There is some evidence to suggest that historically this option feature of the

---

international mechanism for shifting tax losses, which cannot be obtained using portfolio management techniques.

[19]  For further discussion see Radebaugh and Gray 1997.

debt has been underpriced by investors in the terms of the debt contract. Astute financial management would lead the corporation to sell an asset (perhaps another option) with the same or similar features after issuing such a bond. Following amortization of the price received for this asset, the corporation has effectively issued debt at below market rates.

### 20.4.2.3 *Reducing funding costs by reducing transaction costs*

Transaction costs such as the bid-ask spread in a financial market, the costs of acquiring information, and those associated with liquidity, are the natural consequences of raising funds in any financial market. MNEs can to some extent mitigate these costs by the appropriate use of certain derivative instruments which allow them to separate the cash flow obligations on their original borrowing from the ultimate cash flow characteristics they face. For example, a MNE may be able to exploit a comparative advantage across different segments of the international capital market with a currency swap.[20] This is undertaken by raising funding in that currency segment of the international capital markets where it can be obtained relatively cheaply. This is then swapped to create synthetic funding in the most appropriate currency for business purposes.

## 20.4.3 Market segmentation, competitive advantage, and costs of capital

The evidence is now fairly convincing that models which are based upon complete international capital market integration have difficulty in explaining the extant pattern of the international distribution of portfolio holdings or the behaviour of financial asset returns. (See Cooper and Kalpanis 1986, 1994; Jorion and Schwartz 1986; Hietela 1989; French and Poterba 1991; Tessar and Werner 1995.) It follows that in order to generate a framework for international capital market decision making, it is necessary not only to introduce costs of international investment which induce market segmentation into international investment models (Black 1984, Stultz 1981), but also to modify the standard capital budgeting rules found in corporate finance (Adler and Dumas 1975a, b, 1983; and Stapleton and Subrahmanyan 1977).

---

[20] The market anomalies (or inefficiencies) which may give rise to such opportunities are extensively discussed in Bowe 1988, and most leading international finance texts, e.g. Buckley 2000.

The implication for MNE real investment decisions is that it is necessary to incorporate market segmentation considerations when calculating the costs of capital for international investment decisions. Most existing models either assume complete market integration or complete segmentation or introduce it in an *ad hoc* fashion (Errunza and Losq 1985; Abuaf and Chu 1994; Godfrey and Espinosa 1996; and Stultz 1995).[21] Cooper and Kaplanis (2000) by deriving optimal capital budgeting rules in an extension of the Stultz (1981) model, is the only example in the literature familiar to us which provides a robust framework for devising corporate finance decision rules for MNEs in segmented markets.

In this model, differential costs of access to capital arises not from money illusion, or segmentation between money and bond markets inducing different effective real interest rates to companies domiciled in different countries,[22] but from equity market segmentation. Required returns differ for MNEs undertaking the same investment differ as the investment has different marginal risks and returns for their investor clients. This in turn affects MNEs' international competitiveness and motives for FDI as shown by Lessard (1991).[23] An interesting avenue for future research is suggested in that in principle one could estimate the required rates of return for different projects, (which will depend on the MNE making the investment), and link this back to motives for FDI and its impact upon competition in product markets.

## 20.4.4 Market segmentation and strategy: the choice of participation mode

The consequences of international capital market segmentation are relevant not only in terms of investment evaluation as addressed in the previous section, but also in terms of its impact upon modes of market participation and entry. Consider the choice of alternatives to full equity ownership such as: joint ventures, strategic alliances, licensing agreements, project finance, or incentive management contracts. These financial arrangements are customarily viewed as motivated by the need to provide contractual structures which align incentives for those participants who are able to influence outcomes. Our view is that financial factors are possibly a major if largely neglected component in the determination of these contractual structures. Devoting

[21] An insightful discussion of the cost of capital as a competitive variable is presented in Lessard 1997. See also Oxelheim *et al.* 1998.

[22] These types of approaches are critiqued in Kester and Luehrman 1992; and Lessard 1997.

[23] The model thereby explains the 'home-bias' results of Cooper and Kaplanis 1986, 1994; and French and Poterba 1991.

further attention to this issue is perhaps more important in the context of recent evidence that certain mergers and acquisitions often reduce corporate value (for example, Berger and Ofek 1995).

To take a particular example, consider market entry or participation by an MNE through a joint venture. The motives and gains for joint ventures are usually rationalized in terms of synergy sharing (McConnell and Nantell 1985; Berkovitch and Narayanan 1993; Maquiera et al. 1998); the efficient governance of expropriation threats, hold-up problems, or other transactional barriers arising for example from asset specificity (Alchian and Woodward 1987; Klein et al. 1978; Williamson 1979, 1983); or efficient risk sharing between upstream and downstream firms (Weston et al. 1990).[24]

An additional, complementary rationale relates to their use as financing vehicles (Johnson and Houston 2000), in particular for vertical joint ventures. Under a market length contract the supplier typically owns and finances the productive capacity. Using standard asymmetric information arguments (Myers and Majluf 1984), one can demonstrate that firms may face constraints in raising external financing which leads them to refuse orders from buyers which require new production capacity if the seller has exhausted internal sources of funds. This is a standard underinvestment problem. Organizing a market participation or new entry as a vertical joint venture enables the supplier to provide non-financial resources while the buyer provides financing. This financing is provided at lower cost than another provider, as the buyer can more easily monitor the joint venture, and has more secure collateral. To test this motive one could refer to the literature on finance constraints and investment (Fazzari et al. 1988) to find proxy variables for firms facing financing constraints. For example it has been suggested that firms which pay little or no dividends in the period immediately prior to the joint venture may be 'internal funds constrained'. A similar logic could be applied to the analysis of strategic alliances, although the fact that they do not involve equity investments or the creation of a third organizational form suggests that they have less well-defined property rights (Chan et al. 1997). We believe these would be profitable areas for future research.

## 20.4.5 Empirical evidence on MNEs' financial management approaches

Evidence indicates that the vast majority of large MNEs use both internal and external risk management instruments (Stanley and Block 1980; Khoury and

---

[24] The references are selective as these motives are considered at length elsewhere in this volume.

Chan 1988; Tufano 1996; Hakkarainen *et al.* 1998). The choice of instrument reflects both the types of exposure they face, and certain characteristics of the firm, in particular its size and degree of internationalization.[25] Moreover, the use of external hedging instruments by MNEs is much more widespread than for domestic firms, as evidenced by comparing the survey results in Joseph (2000) with those of, for example, Bodnar *et al.* (1995).

In terms of internal techniques, Joseph (2000) suggests the following. For contractual exposure, inter-company netting and home currency invoicing are the most commonly used hedging techniques; for translation and economic exposure matching currency inflows and outflows and asset/liability management are the dominant hedging techniques. Phillips (1995), Joseph (2000), and Marshall (2000) all report that forward contracts are the main external method for managing contractual exposure, while Joseph (2000) indicates that foreign currency borrowing and lending is the primary method for hedging translation and economic exposure, especially the former. The use of foreign exchange options and futures are relatively low for all classes of exposure, although options are more widely used than futures (Glaum and Belk 1992; Phillips 1995; Joseph 2000). The low use of futures may be due to the daily settlement characteristic of these contracts which may impact adversely on liquidity and cash flow management.

We are now in a position to ask to what extent is the available empirical evidence on the use of risk management techniques consistent with the motives which have been identified? As the recent evidence indicates both that external techniques play a more important role in risk management than internal techniques, and that the explanatory power of empirical procedures is much stronger for external techniques, we focus on evidence relating thereto.[26] Concerning managerial motives for hedging, Geczy *et al.* (1997) argue that empirical proxies for managerial risk aversion are positively correlated with derivatives usage, while Francis and Stephan (1990) found strong evidence for the managerial signalling arguments using multivariate and time series empirical techniques. Both sets of results are in accordance with *a priori* theoretical expectations. The available evidence is also broadly consistent with the use of risk management tools to avoid the costs of financial distress as advocated by Froot *et al.* (1993) and Smith and Stultz (1985). A significant relationship has been found between a corporation's derivative usage and the following variables: its level of debt service coverage (negative), its leverage (positive), its level of foreign operations (positive), and changes in its credit

---

[25] See Riehl and Rodriguez 1977; McRae and Walker 1980; Joseph and Hewins 1991; Shirreff 1994; Ramaswamy *et al.* 1996; and Joseph 2000. Sullivan 1994 develops an index of internationalization of the firm.

[26] Moreover, some studies, such as Nance *et al.* 1993; and Dolde 1995, only study external methods for managing risk.

rating (negative). The signs in parentheses refer to the directions of the relationships, which are in accordance with the theory. Finally, the available evidence is also weakly consistent with the view that risk management is used to increase shareholder wealth by reducing taxes. Positive relationships have been uncovered between both tax loss carryforwards and tax credits and the use of derivatives. These results are encouraging in the sense that not only do theoretical arguments demonstrate how corporations should be managing risk in order to maximize their shareholders wealth, but empirical evidence demonstrates they appear to be behaving in accordance with the theory.

However, one interesting finding which we believe merits further research is contained in Joseph (2000), who argues that the use of certain risk management techniques is (surprisingly) associated with an increase in variability of certain financial measures. Apart from the implications for leverage in some hedging decisions, the maturity mis-match of exposures and certain derivatives,[27] and the concerns related to the non-linearity of options payoffs raised by Giddy and Dufey (1995),[28] the rationale for these findings is not addressed in the existing theoretical or empirical literature. In the light of previous discussion, we conjecture that one possible explanation may lie in the distinction introduced earlier between risk management techniques which respond to volatility to create competitive advantage, and those which are intended explicitly for hedging purposes. If the MNEs are using external techniques to secure funding or cost of capital advantages, then their use may clearly increase the volatility of cash flows or earnings in the short-term.

# 20.5 IMPLEMENTING AN EFFECTIVE RISK MANAGEMENT STRATEGY WITHIN AN MNE

Implementing an effective risk management strategy within an MNE basically involves establishing corporate governance processes which deliver the requisite knowledge and ensure appropriate accountability. Once the objective of financial management activity is clarified, and financial risks have been identified and measured, it is important they are not considered in isolation,

---

[27] See Mello and Parsons 1995.
[28] A closely related reference is Ware and Winter 1988.

but rather form part of some integrated corporate strategy for dealing with risk. Smithson (1998) suggests how this might be achieved. The framework he proposes is now presented in increasing order of strategic complexity in terms of management requirements.

1. *Integrate market risks*: Many non-financial firms such as Intel, Hewlett-Packard, and Hyundai attempt to implement a portfolio measure of risk by combining all the sources of risk arising from changes in financial prices, and considering their net impact. However, according to Bodnar *et al.* (1996), two out of three derivatives users still manage risk on a transaction by transaction basis. Corroboration of this finding is provided in another survey, which concluded that of over 500 multinational firms, only one quarter had centralized treasury operations.

2. *Integrate market risk and insurance*: Effectively this requires the combination of these two risk management functions, and involves a realization that the distinction between financial risk and insurance is becoming blurred. Indeed, certain insurance corporations such as Swiss Re and Cigna Property & Casualty now offer insurance policies resembling options on financial price variables. MNEs such as Honeywell and Union Carbide are proponents of such a risk management strategy, and have integrated financial price risk management with the corporation's insurance activities.

3. *Integrate financial with manufacturing and marketing risks*: This is the most complex approach to risk management, and involves integrating the treasury department's activities, decisions on how best to handle liquidity, operational and legal risk, and the firm's core businesses. Smithson (1998) notes that the most prominent example of this practice is Merck & Company, which requires that the treasury function become an integral part of managing the corporation rather than simply providing the financing once business decisions have been made. Such a system of 'enterprise-wide risk management' potentially involves major structural changes, and commitments of managerial time. Oldfield and Santomero (1995) suggest that this requires a comprehensive review of all the major business activities along the following lines. First, the specific risks of each business activity must be identified and measured, where possible. Second, risk management must 'begin at the point nearest to the assumption of risk' in order to ensure that management control is maintained, data is generated in a consistent fashion, and needless exposure to risk is eliminated. Finally, senior management (the Board of Directors) must have a clearly formulated and effective overall risk management strategy, closely integrated into the corporation's business planning and management control processes.[29]

[29] It is the responsibility of the MNE's Board of Directors to: (i) understand how risk management affects the corporation's overall business plan; (ii) ensure that the team of managers entrusted with implementing the corporation's risk management policies have the

## 20.5.1 Monitoring and evaluation of the corporate risk management strategy

The data derived from the selected risk management strategy must be used as an informational input into a centralized system of evaluation and performance monitoring. It is crucial that this system of monitoring and evaluation should be independent of the activity itself, and that whatever the strategy selected, corporate management be constantly appraised of the value of the portfolio of risk management instruments. The analytics of such a system have been concisely summarized by Dowd (1998), and include: (i) data verification procedures, (ii) systems to monitor compliance with constraints imposed on those taking decisions (for example position limits on traders), (iii) systems to acquire and analyse data for performance evaluation and adjustments in the riskiness of the MNE's position, and (iv) ensuring that risk management systems are valid and appropriate for the task at hand. Research in this area is still in its infancy. In particular, we await the results of comparative analysis of the success rates of different corporate governance structures established to implement an MNE's overall risk management strategy.

# 20.6 CONCLUSION

This chapter maintains that the advent of an increasingly integrated global capital market system, characterized by volatility in real and financial asset prices and macroeconomic risks, enhances not only the competitive impact of MNE financial risk management, but augments the potential gains from integrating financial management considerations into key strategic and operating decisions. With the possible exception of routine hedging, financial decisions are not a function which can be isolated from the underlying strategic and operating decisions which effectively determine an MNE's cash flows or earnings in a volatile macroeconomic environment.

Several areas have been identified where further work is needed. First, attention should be given to alternative methods of estimating country risk

required expertise; (iii) evaluate the performance of the risk management activity, and ensure it is reviewed periodically.

premium that do not rely on the analysis of historical data. The use of implied equity premiums derived from equity market valuation models is one possibility which is identified. Second, more investigation is required of the reasons for regional differences observed in MNEs' stated risk management objectives and revealed risk management practices. Third, attention must be given to the appropriate procedures MNEs should adopt when implementing internal risk management processes such as cash-flow-at-risk or variants of value-at-risk. Fourth, the implications of differences in capital costs arising from equity market segmentation (Oxelheim *et al.* 1998; Cooper and Kaplanis 2000) on the motives for FDI and its impact upon competition in international product markets needs investigating. Finally, a case has been made that financing considerations are a relevant, but largely neglected, determinant of the choice of mode of market entry. Further attention should be paid to this issue, particularly in the light of recent findings that certain mechanisms for market entry appear to reduce corporate value.

# REFERENCES

ABUAF, N., and CHU, Q. (1994). *The Executive's Guide to International Capital Budgeting.* 1994 update, Solomon Brothers: New York.

ADLER, M., and DUMAS, B. (1975*a*). 'Optimal International Acquisitions', *Journal of Finance*, 30(1), 1–19.

—— (1975*b*). 'The Long-Term Financial Decisions of the Multi-National Corporation', in: E. J. Elton and M. J. Gruber (eds.), *International Capital Markets*. Amsterdam: North Holland.

—— (1983). 'International Portfolio Choice and Corporation Finance: A Synthesis', *Journal of Finance*, 38, 925–84.

ALCHIAN, A., and WOODWARD, S. (1987). 'Reflections on the Theory of the Firm', *Journal of Institutional and Theoretical Economics*, 143, 110–36.

ALLEN, L., and PANTZALIS, C. (1996). 'Valuation of the Operating Flexibility of Multinational Enterprises', *Journal of International Business Studies*, 27, 633–53.

BELK, P. A., and EDELSHAIN, D. J. (1997). 'Foreign Exchange Risk Management: the Paradox', *Managerial Finance*, 23(7), 5–24.

—— and GLAUM, M. (1990). 'The Management of Foreign Exchange Risk in UK Multinationals: an Empirical Investigation', *Accounting and Business Research*, 21, 3–13.

BERG, M., and MOORE, G. (1991). 'Foreign Exchange Strategies: Spot, Forward and Options', *Journal of Business Finance and Accounting*, 18, 449–57.

BERGER, P., and OFEK, E. (1995). 'Diversification's Effect on Firm Value', *Journal of Financial Economics*, 37, 39–66.

BERKMAN, H., and BRADBURY, M. (1996). 'Empirical Evidence on the Corporate Use of Derivatives', *Financial Management* 25, 5–13.

BERKMAN, H., (*cont.*)BRADBURY, M. E., and MAGAN, S. (1997). 'An International Comparison of Derivative Use', *Financial Management*, 26(4), 69–73.

BERKOVITCH, E., and NARAYANAN, M. P. (1993). 'Motives for Takeover: An Empirical Investigation', *Journal of Financial and Quantitative Analysis*, 28, 347–62.

BESSEMBINDER, H. (1991). 'Forward Contracts and Firm Value: Investment Incentive and Contracting Effects', *Journal of Financial and Quantitative Analysis*, 26, 519–32.

BLACK, F. S. (1974). 'International Capital Market Equilibrium with Investment Barriers', *Journal of Financial Economics*, 1, 337–52.

BLIN, J. M., GREENBAUM, S. I., and JACOBS, D. P. (1980). *Flexible Exchange Rates and International Business*. Washington, DC: USA.

BODNAR, G. M., HAYT, G. S., and MARSTON, R. C. (1996). '1995 Wharton Survey of Derivative Usage by US Non-Financial Firms', *Financial Management*, 25(4), 113–33.

—— (1998). '1998 Wharton Survey of Derivative Usage by US Non-Financial Firms', *Financial Management*, 27(4), 70–92.

—— HAYT, G. S., MARSTON, R. C., and SMITHSON, C. W. (1995). '1994 Wharton Survey of Derivative Usage by US Non-Financial Firms', *Financial Management*, 24(2), 104–5.

BOWE, M. (1988). *Eurobonds*. Homewood, Illinois: Dow-Jones Irwin.

—— and DEAN, J. W. (1993). 'Debt-Equity Swaps: Investment Incentives and Secondary Market Prices', *Oxford Economic Papers*, 45, 130–45.

—— —— (1997). 'Has the Market solved the Sovereign Debt Crisis?', *Princeton Studies in International Finance*, 83, 1–64.

BRENNAN, M., and TRIGEORGIS, L. (2000). *Project Flexibility, Agency, and Competition: New Developments in the Theory of Real Options*. Oxford: Oxford University Press.

BUCKLEY, A. (2000). *Multinational Finance*, 4th edn. London: Prentice Hall.

—— BUCKLEY, P., LANGEVIN, P., and TSE, K. (1996). 'The Financial Analysis of Foreign Investment Decisions by Large UK-based Companies', *European Journal of Finance*, 2, 181–206.

BUCKLEY, P., and CASSON, M. (1998). 'Models of the Multinational Enterprise', *Journal of International Business Studies*, 29, 539–61.

CHAN, S., KENSINGER, J., KEOWN, A., and MARTIN, J. (1997). 'Do Strategic Alliances Create Value?', *Journal of Financial Economics*, 46, 199–222.

CHOI, F. D. S., and LEVICH, R. M. (1990). *The Capital Market Effects of International Accounting Diversity*. New York: Dow-Jones Irwin.

—— —— (1997). 'Accounting Diversity and Capital Market Decisions', in F. D. S. Choi (ed.), *International Accounting and Finance Handbook*, 2nd edn. New York: John Wiley.

CHOI, J. J., and RAJAN, M. (1997). 'A Joint Test of Market Segmentation and Exchange Risk Factor in International Capital Markets', *Journal of International Business Studies*, 28, 29–50.

COLLIER, P. A., and DAVIS, E. W. (1985). 'The Management of Currency Transaction Risk by UK Multi-National Companies', *Accounting and Business Research*, 16(3), 327–34.

—— DAVIS, E., COATES, J., and LONGDEN, S. (1990). 'The Management of Currency Risk: Case Studies of US and UK Multinationals', *Accounting and Business Research*, 20, 206–10.

———————(1992). 'Policies Employed in the Management of Currency Risk: Case Study Analysis of US and UK', *Managerial Finance*, 18 (13/4), 41–52.

COOPER, I. A., and KAPLANIS, E. (1986). 'Costs to Crossborder Investment and International Equity Market Equilibrium', in A. Edwards (ed.), *Recent Advances in Corporate Finance*. Cambridge, UK: Cambridge University Press.

———(1994). 'Home Bias in Equity Portfolios, Inflation Hedging and International Capital Market Equilibrium', *Review of Financial Studies*, 7(1), 45–60.

———(2000). 'Partially Segmented International Capital Markets and International Capital Budgeting', *Journal of International Money and Finance*, 19, 309–29.

COPELAND, T. E., and JOSHI, Y. (1996). 'Why Derivatives Don't Reduce FX Risk', *Risk Management*, 43(7), 76–9.

CUMMINS, J. D., PHILLIPS, R. D., and SMITH, S. D. (1998). 'The Risk of Risk Management', *Economic Review*, 83(1), 15–21.

DAMODARAN, A. (2000). 'Estimating Equity Risk Premiums', and 'Estimating Risk Parameters', http://www.stern,nyu.edu/~adamodar.

DAVIES, E., COATES, J., COLLIER, P., and LONGDEN, S. (1991). *Currency Risk Management in Multinational Companies*. Hertfordshire: Prentice Hall.

DEMARZO, P., and DUFFIE, D. (1995). 'Corporate Incentives for Hedging and Hedge Accounting', *The Review of Financial Studies*, 8, 743–71.

DOLDE, W. (1993). 'The Trajectory of Corporate Financial Risk Management', *Continental Bank Journal of Applied Corporate Finance*, 6, 33–41.

——(1995). 'Hedging, Leverage, and Primitive Risk', *The Journal of Financial Engineering*, 4, 187–216.

DOWD, K. (1998). *Beyond Value at Risk*. Chichester: John Wiley.

DUANGPLOY, O., BAKAY, V. H., and BELK, P. A. (1997). 'The Management of Foreign Exchange Risk in US Multinational Enterprises: An Empirical Investigation', *Managerial Finance*, 23(7), 85–100.

ERRUNZA, V. (1997). 'Emerging Markets in Global Finance', in B. Toyne and D. Nigh (eds.), *International Business: An Emerging Vision*. Columbia: University of South Carolina Press.

——and LOSQ, E. (1985). 'International Asset Pricing Under Mild Segmentation: Theory and Test', *Journal of Finance*, 40, 105–24.

FAZZARI, S., HUBBARD, R. G., and PETERSEN, B. (1988). 'Financing Constraints and Corporate Investment', in *Brookings Papers on Economic Activity*. Washington, DC: Brookings Institution.

FRANCIS, K., and STEPHAN, J. (1990). 'Characteristics of Hedging Firms', in R. Schwartz and C. Smith, Jnr., *Advanced Strategies in Financial Risk Management*. New York Institute of Finance, 615–35.

FRENCH, K., and POTERBA, J. (1991). 'Investor Diversification and International Equity Markets', *American Economic Review*, 81, 222–26.

FROOT, K. A. (1989). 'Buybacks, Exit Bonds, and the Optimality of Debt and Liquidity Relief', *International Economic Review*, 30, 49–70.

——(1990). 'Multinational Corporations, Exchange Rates and Direct Investment', in W. Branson, J. Frankel, and M. Goldstein (eds.), *International Policy Coordination and Exchange Rate Determination*. Chicago: Chicago University Press.

FROOT, K. A., (*cont.*) SCHARFSTEIN, D., and STEIN, J. (1993). 'Risk Management: Co-ordinating Corporate Investment and Financing Policies', *Journal of Finance*, 48, 1629–58.

—— —— —— (1994). 'A Framework for Risk Management', *Harvard Business Review*, 72(6), 91–103.

GECZY, C., MINTON, B., and SCHRAND, C. (1997). 'Why Firms Use Currency Derivatives', *Journal of Finance*, 52, 1323–54.

GIDDY, I., and DUFEY, G. (1995). 'Uses and Abuses of Currency Options', *Bank of America Journal of Applied Corporate Finance*, 8, 49–57.

GIOVANNINI, A. (1989). 'Capital taxation', *Journal of Economic Policy*, Oct: 345–86.

GLAUM, M. (1990). 'Strategic Management of Exchange Rate Risks', *Long Range Planning*, 23, 65–72.

—— and BELK, P. (1992). 'Financial Innovations: Some Empirical Evidence from the United Kingdom', *Managerial Finance*, 18, 71–86.

GODFREY, S., and ESPINOSA, R. (1996). 'A Practical Approach to Calculating Costs of Equity for Investments in Emerging Markets', *Journal of Applied Corporate Finance*, 9(3), 80–9.

GRANT, K., and MARSHALL, A. P. (1997). 'Large UK Companies and Derivatives', *European Financial Management*, 3(2), 191–208.

GRAY, S. J., MEEK, G. K., and ROBERTS, C. B. (1995). 'International Capital Market Pressures and Voluntary Annual Report Disclosures by US and UK Multinationals', *Journal of International Financial Management and Accounting*, 6, 43–68.

HAKKARAINEN, A., JOSEPH, N., KASANEN, E., and PUTTONEN, V. (1998). 'The Foreign Exchange Exposure Management Practices of Finnish Industrial Firms', *Journal of International Financial Management and Accounting*, 9, 34–57.

HIETALA, P. T. (1989). 'Asset Pricing in Partially Segmented Markets: Evidence from the Finnish Market', *Journal of Finance*, 44, 697–718.

JACQUILLAT, B., and SOLNIK, B. (1978). 'Multinationals are Poor Tools for Diversification', *Journal of Portfolio Management*, 4, 8–12.

JESSWEIN, K. R., KWOK, C. Y., and FOLKS, W. R. (1995). 'Corporate Use of Innovative Foreign Exchange Risk Management Products', *The Columbia Journal of World Business*, 30, 70–82.

JOHNSON, S. A., and HOUSTON, M. B. (2000). 'A Re-examination of the Motives and Gains in Joint Ventures', *Journal of Financial and Quantitative Analysis*, 35, 67–85.

JORION, P. (1996). *Value at Risk*. New York: McGraw-Hill.

—— and SCHWARTZ, E. (1986). 'Integration vs. Segmentation in the Canadian Stock Market', *Journal of Finance*, 41, 603–14.

JOSEPH, N. (2000). 'The Choice of Hedging Techniques and the Characteristics of UK Industrial Firms', *Journal of Multinational Financial Management*, 10, 161–84.

—— and HEWINS, R. (1991). 'Portfolio Models for Foreign Exchange Exposure', *International Journal of Management Science*, 19, 247–58.

—— —— (1997). 'The Motives for Corporate Hedging among UK Multinationals', *International Journal of Finance and Economics*, 2, 151–71.

KESTER, C., and LUEHRMAN, T. A. (1989). 'Are We Feeling Competitive Yet? The Exchange Rate Gambit', *Sloan Management Review*, 30, 19–28.

—————(1992). 'What Makes you Think US Capital is so Expensive?', *Journal of Applied Corporate Finance*, 5(2), 29–41.

KHOURY, S., and CHAN, K. (1988). 'Hedging Foreign Exchange Risks: Selecting an Optimal Tool', *Midland Corporate Finance Journal*, 5, 40–52.

KLEIN, B., CRAWFORD, R., and ALCHIAN, A. (1978). 'Vertical Integration Appropriable Rents, and the Competitive Contracting Process', *Journal of Law and Economics*, 21, 297–326.

KOGUT, B., and KULATILAKA, N. (1994). 'Operating Flexibility, Global Manufacturing and the Option Value of a Multinational Network', *Management Science*, 40, 123–39.

KOHN, K. (1990). 'Managing Foreign Exchange Risk Profitability', *Columbia Journal of World Business*, 25, 203–7.

KRAMER, A., McDERMOTT, W., and HESTON, J. (1993). 'An Overview of Current Tax Impediments to Risk Management', *Continental Bank Journal of Applied Corporate Finance*, 6, 73–80.

LESSARD, D. R. (1990). *The Tactician*, 3(3), Citibank.

—————(1991). 'Global Competition and Corporate Finance in the 1990s', *Continental Bank Journal of Applied Corporate Finance*, 3, 59–72.

—————(1997). 'Finance and International Business', in B. Toyne and D. Nigh (eds.), *International Business: An Emerging Vision*. Columbia: University of South Carolina Press.

LEVI, M., and SERCU, P. (1991). 'Erroneous and Valid Reasons for Hedging Foreign Exchange Rate Exposure', *Journal of Multinational Financial Management*, 1, 25–37.

LEWENT, J., and KEARNEY, A. (1990). 'Identifying, Measuring and Hedging Currency Risk at Merck', *Continental Bank Journal of Applied Corporate Finance*, 2, 19–28.

MAQUIERA, C., MEGGINSON, W., and NAIL, L. (1998). 'Wealth Creation Versus Wealth Redistributions in Pure Stock-for-Stock Mergers', *Journal of Financial Economics*, 48, 3–33.

MARSHALL, A. P. (2000). 'Foreign Exchange Risk Management in UK, USA and Asia Pacific Multinational Companies', *Journal of Multinational Financial Management*, 10, 185–211.

MATHUR, I. (1985). 'Managing Foreign Exchange Risks: Strategy Considerations', *Managerial Finance*, 11, 7–11.

McCONNELL, J., and MUSCARELLA, C. (1985). 'Corporate Capital Expenditure Decisions and the Market Value of the Firm', *Journal of Financial Economics*, 14, 399–422.

—————and NANTELL, T. J. (1985). 'Corporate Combinations and Common Stock Returns: The Case of Joint Ventures', *Journal of Finance*, 40, 519–36.

McRAE, T., and WALKER, D. (1980). *Foreign Exchange Management*. London: Prentice Hall.

MEEK, G. K., ROBERTS, C. B., and GRAY, S. J. (1995). 'Factors Influencing Voluntary Annual Report Disclosures by US, UK and Continental European Multinational Corporations', *Journal of International Business Studies*, 26, 555–72.

MELLO, A., and PARSONS, J. (1995). 'Maturity Structure of a Hedge Matters: Lessons from the Metallgesellschaft Debacle', *Bank of America Journal of Applied Corporate Finance*, 8, 106–20.

MIAN, S. (1996). 'Evidence on Corporate Hedging Policy', *Journal of Financial and Quantitative Analysis*, 31, 419–30.

MODIGLIANI, F., and MILLER, M. (1958). 'The Cost of Capital, Corporation Finance, and the Theory of Investment', *American Economic Review*, 48, 261–97.

MYERS, S. (1977). 'The Determinants of Corporate Borrowing', *Journal of Financial Economics*, 5, 147–75.

——— and MAJLUF, N. (1984). 'Corporate Financing Decisions when Firms have Information that Investors do not Have', *Journal of Financial Economics*, 13, 187–221.

NANCE, D., SMITH, C., and SMITHSON, C. (1993). 'On the Determinants of Corporate Hedging', *Journal of Finance*, 48, 267–84.

OBLAK, D. J., and HELM, R. J. (1980). 'Survey and Analysis of Capital Budgeting Methods used by Multinationals', *Financial Management*, Winter, 37–41.

OLDFIELD, G., and SANTOMERO, A. (1995). 'The Place of Risk Management in Financial Institutions', working paper, Wharton School, University of Pennsylvania.

OXELHEIM, L., and WIHLBORG, C. (1987). *Macroeconomic Uncertainty: International Risks and Opportunities for the Corporation*, 4th edn. Chichester: John Wiley.

——— (1989a). 'Competitive Exposure: Taking the Global View', *Euromoney Corporate Finance*, Feb., 24–9.

——— (1989b). 'Taking the Sting out of Economic Exposure', *Euromoney Corporate Finance*, March, 28–34.

——— STONEHILL, A., RANDAY, T., VIKKULA, K., DULLUM, K., MODÉN, K-M. (1998). *Corporate Strategies to Internationalise the Cost of Capital*. Copenhagen: Copenhagen Business School Press.

PHILLIPS, A. L. (1995). '1995 Derivatives Practices and Instruments Survey', *Financial Management*, 24(2) 115–25.

RADEBAUGH, L. H., and GRAY, S. J. (1997). *International Accounting and Multinational Enterprises*. 4th edn. New York: John Wiley.

RAMASWAMY, K., KROECK, K., and RENFORTH, W. (1996). 'Measuring the Degree of Internationalization of a Firm: A Comment', *Journal of International Business Studies*, 27, 167–77.

RANGAN, S. (1998). 'Do Multinationals Operate Flexibly? Theory and Evidence', *Journal of International Business Studies*, 29, 217–37.

RAWLS, S., and SMITHSON, C. (1990). 'Strategic Risk Management', *Continental Bank Journal of Applied Corporate Finance*, (Winter), 6–18.

RIEHL, H., and RODRIGUEZ, R. (1977). *Foreign Exchange and the Money Markets*. New York: McGraw-Hill.

ROBERTS, C., WEETMAN, P., and GORDON, P. (1998). *International Financial Accounting: A Comparative Approach*. London: FT Pitman Publishing.

RODRIGUEZ, R. M. (1981). 'Corporate Exchange Rate Risk Management: Theme and Aberrations', *Journal of Finance*, (May), 427–39.

——— (1977). *Foreign-Exchange Management in US Multinationals*. Toronto: Lexington Books.

ROLL, R. (1993). Untitled paper presented at the Whitmore Conference on the International Capital acquisition process, Michigan.

SAUDAGARAN, S. M., and BIDDLE, G. C. (1995). 'Foreign Listing Location: A Study of MNCs and Stock Exchanges in Eight Countries', *Journal of International Business Studies*, 26, 319–42.

SCHOOLEY, D., and WHITE, H. (1995). 'Strategies for Hedging Translation Exposure to Exchange Rate Changes: Theory and Empirical Evidence', *Journal of Multinational Financial Management*, 5, 57–72.

SERCU, P., and UPPAL, R. (1994). 'International Capital Budgeting Using Options Pricing Theory', *Managerial Finance*, 20, 3–21.

—— (1995). *International Financial Markets and the Firm*. London: Chapman-Hall.

SEVERN, A. K. (1974). 'Investor Evaluation of Foreign and Domestic Risk', *Journal of Finance*, 29, 545–50.

SHAO, A. P., and SHAO, L. T. (1993). 'Capital Budgeting Practices Employed by European Affiliates of US Transnational Companies', *Journal of Multinational Financial Management*, 3, 95–109.

SHAPIRO, A. C. (1999). *Multinational Financial Management*, 6th edn. New York: John Wiley.

SHIRREFF, D., (1994). 'Fill that Gap!', *Euromoney*, 304, 28–32.

SMITH, C. (1993). 'Risk Management in Banking', in R. Schwartz and C. Smith (eds.), *Advanced Strategies in Financial Risk Management*. New York: Englewood Cliffs, 147–62.

SMITH, C., JR., and STULTZ, R. (1985). 'The Determinants of Firm's Hedging Policies', *Journal of Financial and Quantitative Analysis*, 20, 391–405

SMITH, M. (1996). 'Shareholder Activism by Institutional Investors: Evidence from CallPERS', *Journal of Finance*, 51, 227–52.

SMITHSON, C. (1998). *Managing Financial Risk*. New York: McGraw-Hill.

SOLNIK, B. (1974). 'Why Not Diversify Internationally Rather Than Domestically?', *Financial Analysts Journal*, 30, 48–54.

STANLEY, M., and BLOCK, S. (1980). 'Portfolio Diversification of Foreign Exchange Risk: An Empirical Study', *Management International Review*, 20, 83–92.

STAPLETON, R. C., and SUBRAHMANYAN, M. G. (1977). 'Market Imperfections, Capital Market Equilibrium and Corporation Finance', *Journal of Finance*, 32(2), 307–19.

STULZ, R. M. (1981). 'On the Effects of Barriers to International Investment', *Journal of Finance*, 36, 923–34.

—— (1984). 'Optimal Hedging Policies', *Journal of Financial and Quantitative Analysis*, 19, 127–40.

—— (1995). 'The Cost of Capital in Internationally Integrated Markets: The Case of Nestle', *European Financial Management*, 1(1), 11–22.

—— (1996). 'Why Does the Cost of Capital Differ Across Countries? An Agency Perspective', *European Financial Management*, 2(1), 11–22.

SULLIVAN, D. (1994). 'Measuring the Degree of Internationalization of a Firm', *Journal of International Business Studies*, 25, 325–42.

TESSAR, L. L., and WERNER, I. M. (1995). 'Home Bias and High Turnover', *Journal of International Money and Finance*, 14(4) 467–92.

TUFANO, P. (1996). 'Who Manages Risk? An Empirical Examination of Risk Management Practices in the Gold Mining Industry', *Journal of Finance*, 51, 1097–137.

WARE, R., and WINTER, R. (1988). 'Forward Markets, Currency Options and the Hedging of Foreign Exchange Risk', *Journal of International Economics*, 25, 291–302.

WEETMAN, P., and GRAY, S. J. (1991). 'A Comparative International Analysis of the Impact of Accounting Principles on Profits: The USA Versus the UK, Sweden and the Netherlands', *Accounting and Business Research*, 21, 363–79.

WESTON, J. K., CHUNG, K., and HOAG, S. (1990). *Mergers, Restructuring and Corporate Control*. Hertfordshire: Prentice-Hall.

WICKS KELLY, M. E., and PHILIPPATOS, G. C. (1982). 'Comparative Analysis of the Foreign Investment Evaluation Practices by US-based Manufacturing Multinational Corporations', *Journal of International Business Studies*, 13, 19–42.

WILLIAMSON, O. (1979). 'Transaction Cost Economics: the Governance of Contractual Relations', *Journal of Law and Economics*, 22, 233–61.

—— (1983). 'Credible Commitments: Using Hostages to Support Exchange', *American Economic Review*, 73, 519–40.

...............................................................................................

# CHAPTER 21

# TAXES, TRANSFER PRICING, AND THE MULTINATIONAL ENTERPRISE

...............................................................................................

## LORRAINE EDEN

## 21.1 INTRODUCTION

...............................................................................................

I can find only one functional area in which governments have made a serious effort to reduce the conflicts or resolve the ambiguities that go with the operations of multinational enterprises. The industrial countries have managed to develop a rather extraordinary web of bilateral agreements among themselves that deal with conflicts in the application of national tax laws. Where such laws seemed to be biting twice into the same morsel of profit, governments have agreed on a division of the fare. Why governments have moved to solve the jurisdictional conflict in this field but not in others is an interesting question. Perhaps it was because, in the case of taxation, the multinational enterprises themselves had a major stake in seeing to the consummation of the necessary agreements. (Vernon 1985: 256)

Transfer pricing—the pricing of cross-border intrafirm transactions between related parties—used to be a term known only to a few international tax specialists. No longer. Transfer pricing is now the top international taxation issue faced by multinational enterprises (MNEs) according to surveys (Ernst and Young 1997, 1999). Books on transfer pricing, particularly professional books written by international tax lawyers and accountants, are multiplying rapidly.[1] In the past year, both the United Nations (UNCTAD 1999) and *The Economist* (2000) have published major pieces on transfer pricing. Thus, the transfer pricing domain has spread from an obscure area to a subject of informed public knowledge.

The reasons for this change are not hard to understand. Since every cross-border transaction means that two governments are involved in regulating the transfer price, there is always the possibility for conflict. First, as Rugman and Eden (1985) argued, the MNE sees differences in corporate income taxation systems as exogenous market imperfections that can be arbitraged through tax avoidance strategies, such as tax deferral, financial maneuvers (for example double dipping), and transfer price manipulation (over- or underinvoicing intrafirm transfers of goods, services, or intangibles).[2] Second, concern about inappropriate (too much or too little, but particularly too little) tax paid by the MNE has led national tax authorities to devise evermore sophisticated national tax systems to regulate transfer pricing. Third, disputes between home and host governments over MNE taxes has led national tax authorities to reach out to the international level to devise a series of bilateral and international institutional responses.

Over the 1986–94 period, the US Treasury revised its corporate income tax legislation and regulations in this area, responding to pressures of globalization, heavy inward foreign direct investment (FDI), and the growing international trade in services and intangibles. The 1994 US rules are much more complicated, detailed, and onerous than their predecessors (Eden 1998). In addition, in 1995, the OECD's Committee of Fiscal Affairs (CFA) issued the first major update of its 1979 transfer pricing guidelines for its member states (OECD 1995). These regulatory changes have generated a domino-like round of changes in other jurisdictions, including Canada, Mexico, Australia, New Zealand, and most recently the United Kingdom (Eden, Dacin, and Wan, forthcoming). At the dawn of the twenty-first century, an international

---

[1] Particularly useful books on the topic include Aitkinson and Tyrrall (1999), Cole (1999), Coopers and Lybrand (1993), Easson (1999), Eden (1998), Emmanuel and Mehafdi (1994), Feinschreiber (1998), King (1994), Lowell, Burge, and Briger (1998), Lowell and Governale (1997), Pagan and Wilkie (1995), Plasschaert (forthcoming), Rugman and Eden (1985), and Tang (1993, 1997).

[2] See Hines (1999) for a detailed and thorough review of the empirical work on MNE responses to international taxation in terms of foreign direct investment (size and location) and tax avoidance (tax havens, transfer price manipulation, and fiscal maneuvers). Hines concludes that MNEs do react to international tax differentials, both by shifting location decisions and by engaging in tax avoidance strategies.

transfer pricing regime, administered by national tax authorities, for regulating cross-border intrafirm transactions is now visible.

The purpose of this chapter is to outline, for the reader, the complex issue of transfer pricing, as seen by MNE managers and by governments faced with the daunting task of taxing business profits. The paper is organized as follows. First, we briefly discuss transfer pricing from the MNE's perspective and the problems that this raises for national governments. We then review the basic rules of international taxation as they apply to MNE profits. The specific rules and procedures that apply to transfer pricing, as practiced in the United States and recommended by the OECD, are then outlined. We conclude with a discussion of unresolved problems that are likely to plague transfer pricing from 2000 to 2005.

# 21.2 MOTIVATIONS FOR TRANSFER PRICING

A *transfer price* is the price charged in transactions between firms that are related, for example, trade between a parent company and its foreign subsidiary or between two foreign affiliates. MNEs normally set their transfer prices based on either production costs or market prices; surveys suggest that about two-thirds of transfer prices are cost based (Tang 1997, 1993).

There are both internal and external motivations for the MNE to establish transfer prices for intrafirm trade in goods, business services and/or intangibles, which have been well established in the literature. Many foreign affiliates are run as profit centers; as a result, the rewards of the top management team in these affiliates depend on their affiliate's profits. The setting of transfer pricing can therefore be internally driven, as a way to both motivate managers and monitor subsidiary performance. Externally, MNEs have to pay corporate income taxes on their domestic and foreign source income, necessitating that they set transfer prices for cross-border trade flows. Customs authorities also require transfer prices for intrafirm imports of parts, components, and finished goods, either for customs duties or rules of origin purposes.

*Transfer price manipulation*—as distinct from transfer pricing—is the over- or under-invoicing of related party transactions in order to avoid government regulations (e.g. underinvoicing to avoid paying *ad valorem* tariffs) or to exploit cross-border differences in these rates (for example, shifting deductible expenses to the high tax location and revenues to the low tax location in order to reduce overall corporate tax payments). It is not transfer pricing that is the problem; it is the potential for transfer price *manipulation* that governments fear and want to prevent through regulation. However, what one party sees as legitimate forms of price setting may be seen by the other as evasive and illegitimate manipulation.

Ernst and Young (1997, 1999) surveyed more than 500 tax and finance directors of major multinationals about their internal and external motivations for setting transfer pricing policies. Table 21.1 reports these results. In 1997, maximizing operating performance was the main priority for 45 per cent of respondents; another 29 per cent identified operating performance as important but not the top priority. Financial efficiencies, another internal motivation, was the main priority for 24 per cent of respondents, and a second-level priority for 48 per cent. Two external motivations were addressed in the survey: optimizing tax arrangements (25 per cent top priority, 51 per cent second tier priority) and preparing transfer pricing documentation in preparation for a tax audit (25 per cent top priority, 48 per cent second tier). Performance incentives, another internal motivation, was ranked as the lowest motivation by the participants.

In 1999, Ernst and Young repeated the survey but split the respondents into parents and foreign subsidiaries. The noticeable change in the table is the rise in documentation as the main priority, up from 25 per cent to 35 per cent for parents and an astonishing 52 per cent for subsidiary respondents. As we show below, this change reflects the new emphasis, particularly in the United States, on contemporaneous documentation of the MNE's transfer pricing policies for tax purposes. The 'bottom line', as evidenced in this recent survey, is that multinationals continue to see transfer pricing policies as primarily driven by internal resource allocation issues, and not by tax minimization reasons. To the extent that taxes are driving transfer pricing policies, the motivations used to be equally split between optimizing tax arrangements and documenting transfer pricing policies; now documentation requirements have surpassed minimizing taxes as the primary external motivation for establishing transfer pricing policies within the multinational enterprise.

# 21.3 THE PROBLEM: HOW TO TAX MULTINATIONALS?

Multinational enterprises create particular problems for tax authorities that do not occur when taxing domestic firms. The MNE is an integrated business

# Table 21.1 Factors shaping MNE transfer pricing policies

| Factors shaping MNE transfer pricing policies | Percent of respondents who identify factor as: | | | | | | | | | | | |
|---|---|---|---|---|---|---|---|---|---|---|---|---|
| | Main priority | | | Important but not main priority | | | Not very important | | | Not important at all | | |
| | 1999 | | 1997 | 1999 | | 1997 | 1999 | | 1997 | 1999 | | 1997 |
| | Parents | Subs | | Parents | Subs | | Parents | Subs | | Parents | Subs | |
| *Internal motivations* | | | | | | | | | | | | |
| Maximizing operating performance | 40 | 42 | 45 | 33 | 32 | 29 | 19 | 14 | 22 | 8 | 8 | 4 |
| Financial efficiencies | 25 | 25 | 24 | 45 | 42 | 48 | 22 | 24 | 48 | 8 | 6 | 6 |
| Performance incentives | 12 | 15 | 11 | 27 | 26 | 27 | 39 | 37 | 44 | 22 | 18 | 18 |
| *External (tax-related) motivations* | | | | | | | | | | | | |
| Optimizing tax arrangements | 23 | 23 | 25 | 45 | 51 | 51 | 25 | 16 | 20 | 7 | 7 | 4 |
| Documentation in preparation for transfer pricing audit | 35 | 52 | 25 | 38 | 29 | 48 | 20 | 14 | 21 | 7 | 1 | 6 |

*Source* Ernst and Young (1999: 14; 1997: 10)

group consisting of several related affiliates located in different countries, under common control, with common goals, and sharing a common pool of resources. Governments are defined, and limited, by their borders; MNEs have a global reach. *Ipso facto*, the MNE's activities cross national borders and create interjurisdictional issues for national tax authorities.

From the MNE's perspective, as the number of jurisdictions rises, the costs and risks of multiple levels of authority increase. The enterprise is faced with higher cross-border transactions costs, greater interaction costs with a wider variety and number of governments, and increased levels of political risks (Sundaram and Black 1992; Kostova and Zaheer 1999). As Vernon (1998: 38) notes:

> where taxes are involved, multinationals have always been obliged to navigate through a sea of conflicting national claims. With every national tax code differing from the code of its neighbor, the multinationals have constantly been exposed to the risk that the same dollar of their global profit might be taxed by more than one tax authority.

From the government's perspective, the global reach of the multinational raises three types of taxation problems: *jurisdiction, allocation,* and *valuation.* The first issue, jurisdiction, asks which government has the right to tax the multinational's income, and if two governments both claim the same right to tax, should one government's claim have priority over the other's? What if the tax base arises in more than one country? Which government should have the right to tax this income base? Should tax relief be given by one of the governments in order to prevent double taxation of the MNE's income?

The global reach of MNEs raises additional jurisdictional issues since it gives multinational enterprises the ability to avoid the national reach of government regulations, engaging in practices that reduce their overall tax payments. Low tax jurisdictions, such as tax havens, provide inviting locations for MNEs, but at the same time create tax competition between nation-states. How can governments prevent MNEs from using these multiple jurisdictions to hide profits and reduce taxes on a worldwide basis? How can governments curtail destructive international tax competition among national tax authorities, preventing a 'race to the bottom'?

A second issue is allocational. Affiliates of the MNE share common overheads and resources. From the MNE's perspective, these resources should be allocated where they provide the greatest overall advantage to the MNE group. National trade and tax barriers distort this allocation and raise transactions and governance costs for the MNE. From the government's perspective, how should the costs of, and income from, these resources be allocated among jurisdictions? Common resources are a source of competitive advantage for the members of the MNE family, but they are also a source of interdependencies that make it difficult to disentangle the MNE's global income for tax purposes. Setting transfer prices for intragroup transactions in services and intangibles is therefore an activity prone to international disputes.

A third issue is valuation. The MNE's income and expenses must not only be allocated to one or more members of the MNE group, but they must also be valued. This directly leads us to the issue of transfer pricing: the valuation of intrafirm transfers. Because the MNE is an integrated entity, with the ability to exploit international differentials and generate integration economies not available to domestic firms, transfer prices are unlikely to be the same prices arm's-length parties would negotiate. The prices of traded tangibles, intangibles, and services within the various units of the enterprise are basically accounting or bookkeeping prices set for internal reasons. However, since MNE activities cross national borders, transfer prices must be provided to tax authorities and used to calculate both border taxes (tariffs, export taxes) and corporate income taxes. Therefore internal and external factors will influence the MNE's choice of transfer prices. The fear of tax authorities is that external factors will dominate and the MNE will set its transfer prices so as to avoid or evade taxes.

Lastly and more generally, the common goals and common control of the MNE group are also potential sources of conflict. The MNE group has an overarching goal, the maximization of global after-tax profits, which brings the individual units into immediate conflict with the geographically limited but overall broader economic, social, and political goals of nation-states. 'There is one and only one social responsibility of business—to use its resources and engage in activities designed to increase its profits so long as it stays within the rules of the game.'[3] Overall control by the parent firm implies that key output, sales, trade, and pricing decisions are generally made outside national jurisdictions, creating potential conflicts between MNEs and host country governments concerned with eroding sovereignty (the MNE evading national regulations) and extraterritoriality (the MNE as Trojan horse for the home country government). At the same time, 'ownership' and 'control' are becoming increasingly fuzzy terms since non-equity alliances may involve *de facto* control (for example auto assemblers and their first tier suppliers) and the same opportunities to manipulate cross-border prices as traditional intrafirm transactions. Thus, the boundaries of the MNE for tax purposes are becoming increasingly fuzzy.

The basic problem for national tax authorities is that the MNE is an *integrated, complex network of related firms that spans across multiple tax jurisdictions but has externally fuzzy organizational boundaries,* much like a multi-headed ever-moving hydra. The integrated nature of the multinational enterprise makes it difficult to regulate MNEs at the domestic level alone. The characteristics of the MNE—common control, common goals, and common

---

[3] Milton Friedman, as quoted in Vernon (1998: 131).

resources—complicate international allocation and valuation of the MNE revenues and expenses, and thus the taxation of its worldwide profits, creating interjurisdictional conflicts not only between MNEs and nation-states but also between home and host governments.

In any international tax situation, there are, in effect, three parties: the MNE and the two tax authorities. When one government taxes an MNE unit (parent, subsidiary, branch), it has implications for the tax base of the other country since, in any intrafirm transaction, a higher tax base in country A implies a lower base in country B. Thus, Stopford's (1994) model of triangular bargaining best applies to the conflicts between home and host countries over which country has the right to tax (the jurisdiction issue), what the tax base and tax rates should be (the allocation issue), and how the MNE's revenues and expenses should be priced (the valuation issue).

# 21.4 THE SOLUTION: CREATING AN INTERNATIONAL TAX REGIME

## 21.4.1 International regimes

International regimes are sets of functional and behavioral relationships among national governments that have been established in response to problems at the international level in particular issue areas. For example, in situations where there is no clear legal framework establishing property rights and liability, markets for information are imperfect, or there are incentives for governments or MNEs to behave opportunistically, setting up an international regime can improve global welfare by providing rules of behavior, supplying information and formalizing dispute settlement mechanisms. Thus, international regimes can be useful for managing interdependencies among nations. Regimes embody principles, norms, rules, and procedures.

Regimes can be defined as sets of implicit or explicit principles, norms, rules, and decision-making procedures around which actors' expectations converge in a given area of international relations. *Principles* are beliefs of fact, causation, and rectitude. *Norms* are standards of behavior defined in terms of rights and obligations. *Rules* are specific prescriptions or proscriptions for action. *Decision*-making *procedures* are prevailing practices for making and implementing collective choice. (Krasner 1983: 2; italics added)

## 21.4.2 The international tax regime

In the international tax area there are a variety of national tax policies, bilateral tax treaties (BTTs), and model treaties and guidelines developed by institutions such as the Organization for Economic Cooperation and Development (OECD), and the United Nations. International bodies of experts such as the OECD's Committee on Fiscal Affairs (CFA) and the International Fiscal Association (IFA) have played important roles in developing international policies and norms.

At the bilateral level, most OECD countries have negotiated bilateral tax treaties (BTTs) to define the tax base, set up transfer pricing rules, and arrange for dispute settlement procedures under so-called *competent authority* provisions. At the multilateral level, the CFA, made up of senior tax officials from the OECD's member countries, has played the major role in developing tax codes and guidelines for its members. These are not binding commitments, but most member countries have used the OECD codes and guidelines to set up their own tax systems. Within the CFA, the key policy-maker country (not surprisingly since it is home to the largest number of MNEs) has been the United States as represented by the US Treasury and the Internal Revenue Service (IRS).

We argue that the combination of these government policies can be seen as constituting an *international tax regime*, albeit one that is at present primarily confined to OECD countries (Eden 1998, ch. 2). The regime reduces transactions costs associated with international capital and trade flows; resolves tax disputes between tax authorities and multinationals, and between home and host governments; and reduces the possibilities for opportunistic behavior by MNEs and nation-states by formalizing rules and dispute procedures. The Committee on Fiscal Affairs at the OECD has been the critical international organization developing international norms, rules, and procedures for taxing MNEs:

Since 1956 the OECD has sought to build up a set of internationally accepted 'rules of the game' which govern the ways in which Member countries tax profits arising from international transactions. The main instrument used to achieve an internationally consistent approach to the taxation relating to such international transactions has been the development of an OECD Model Tax Convention....[Its] purpose is the avoidance of international double taxation and to assist tax authorities in counteracting tax evasion and avoidance. (OECD 1993: 1)

The OECD has, since its 1963 model tax convention, endorsed the concept of the *separate entity* as the underlying basis for allocating taxing rights to business income between countries. The right to tax depends on the existence of a connection or *nexus* between the taxing jurisdiction and the business enterprise. The nexus differs under the source and residence principles.

Under the *source principle*, a government has the right to tax business profits if the firm has a permanent establishment (fixed place of business) in the country. Permanent establishments within a country are treated as separate legal entities from their parents. The tax authority has jurisdiction over the income and assets of this separate entity, earned or received within the country, up to its *water's edge*. Where MNEs are involved, affiliates are treated as separate legal entities and income is apportioned between them assuming intrafirm transactions take place at arm's length prices. The traditional tax on business profits is the corporate income tax (CIT). In addition, withholding taxes, at rates from 5–30 per cent, are levied on business income that leaves the country; for example, interest, dividends, rents, royalties, and management fees normally attract a withholding tax.

Under the *residence principle*, the definition of residency can vary between countries. In some countries (e.g. the United States), a business is resident in the jurisdiction where it is incorporated; in others (e.g. Canada, the United Kingdom, Australia), location of the 'seat of management' exercising *de facto* control over the entity determines residency. The residence country normally levies a corporate income tax on the enterprise's business profits, allowing the enterprise to deduct expenses incurred in the production of the income. Generally, the net income from all business units within a country are consolidated for tax purposes. The residence country has the right to choose to tax businesses on either their domestic income only (exempting foreign source income from tax), on their worldwide income (taxing all income wherever earned), or some combination of the two. The most common method is to defer taxation of foreign source income until it is remitted from the MNE's foreign affiliates.[4]

Since both home and host countries have the right to tax business profits, double taxation of MNE income is a clear possibility. As a result, under the jurisdictional norms promoted by the OECD's Model Income Tax Convention, the 'first crack' (primary) right to tax business profits is given to the source country, with the residence country having the primary right to tax most other categories of income. The residence country is then obligated to eliminate double taxation of business profits by modifying its own tax rules so as to take account of source country taxation. The most common method is to give a tax credit, against the home country corporate income tax, for foreign income taxes (including the withholding tax) paid on repatriated profits.

The tax boundaries established in OECD countries are therefore basically the same: each government taxes the worldwide income of its residents and the domestic source income of its nonresidents. Many governments, including the United States, tax the worldwide income of their residents

---

[4]  See Altshuler (2000) for a summary of the recent US debate over tax deferral.

but allow tax deferral on foreign source income until it is repatriated. Once the income is repatriated, a foreign tax credit is granted for the corporate income taxes and withholding taxes paid in the host country, up to the level of the home country tax. A few governments (e.g. France) exempt foreign source income from tax, while others exempt certain categories of foreign source income while taxing others as earned (e.g. Canada exempts active business income but taxes passive income in tax havens on an accrual basis).

Most bilateral tax treaties are based on the OECD Model Tax Convention. A BTT clarifies which income and transactions can be taxed, the share of the tax base assigned to each country, and a method for settling tax disputes. One key purpose of a BTT is to determine the types and levels of withholding taxes levied by the source country on income outflows. Where two countries do not have a BTT, withholding rates tend to be high and there is no easy method for resolving interjurisdictional taxation disputes.

# 21.5 THE TAX TRANSFER PRICING REGIME

Nested within the international tax regime is the *international tax transfer pricing regime*, centered around the international norm of the arm's length standard (Eden 1998, ch. 2). Government cooperation in the transfer pricing area is based on national corporate income tax regulations and bilateral tax treaties. The OECD's Committee on Fiscal Affairs and the US Treasury have played the two key roles in developing the arm's length standard as the centerpiece of this regime.

## 21.5.1 The arm's length standard

The solution that tax authorities in OECD countries have adopted to reduce the probability of transfer price manipulation is to develop specific transfer pricing regulations as part of the corporate income tax code. These regulations are based on the concept of the *arm's length standard* (ALS), which requires two related parties to set the same transfer price for an intrafirm

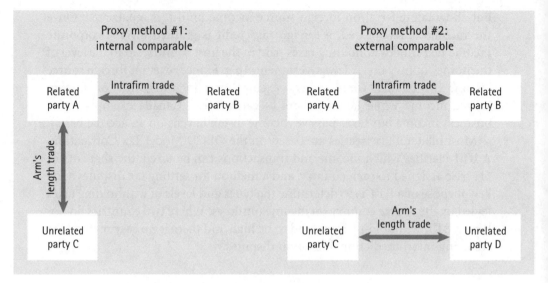

**Fig. 21.1 The arm's length standard**

transaction as two unrelated parties would have set if they had been engaged in the same or similar transaction under the same or similar circumstances. Under the arm's length standard, the associated enterprises are treated as separate entities for tax purposes, rather than as parts of an integrated multinational enterprise. Each entity must price its related party transactions as if (i.e. under the hypothetical assumption that) the entities are at arm's length. The *arm's length price* is therefore the price two unrelated parties would reach through bargaining in a competitive market. The OECD guidelines recognize that it may be impossible to determine a single one arm's length price so an *arm's length range* of 'equally reliable' prices may be acceptable because 'transfer pricing is not an exact science' (OECD 1995: 1.45).

The arm's length standard asks the question: What price would the parties have negotiated if the entities had been unrelated? Since the firms *are* related, the answer to this question has to be hypothetical. The OECD and US Treasury argue that the best answer is a proxy calculated in one of two ways.

In the first method, the price set by one of the related parties in a comparable transaction under comparable circumstances with an unrelated party could be used as an estimate. Where the MNE either buys outside or sells outside, under comparable circumstances, the price negotiated with unrelated parties can be used as the arm's length price. That is, in the left hand graph in Figure 21.1, suppose A buys an intermediate good from its sister affiliate B, and also buys the same good from unrelated party C. Then the price that A pays to C is used as a proxy for the transfer price that A should pay to B in order to satisfy the arm's length standard. This arm's length price is called an *internal comparable*. Similarly, if A sells the same product to B and to C, the price charged to C can be used to proxy for the transfer price for B.

In the second method, the price negotiated by two other unrelated parties which were engaged in a comparable transaction under comparable circumstances is a proxy for the arm's length price in the transaction in question. In this case, the regulator looks for two other firms, unrelated and engaged in similar activities as the related parties in question, and then uses the price negotiated by the unrelated firms, adjusted if necessary for differences in product and functional characteristics, as the arm's length price. As Figure 21.1 shows, the arm's length price negotiated between firms C and D is used to proxy for the transfer price between the related firms A and B. This arm's length price is called an *external comparable*.

In summary, the fundamental principle underlying the tax rules on transfer pricing is that transfer prices should approximate the arm's length price which two unrelated parties would have chosen if the transaction had taken place in the external market. For example, the preamble to the 1994 IRS Section 482 regulations states this quite clearly (IRS 1994):

The purpose of section 482 is to ensure that taxpayers clearly reflect income attributable to controlled transactions, and to prevent the avoidance of taxes with respect to such transactions. Section 482 places a controlled taxpayer on a tax parity with an uncontrolled taxpayer by determining the true taxable income of the controlled taxpayer... The district director may allocate income, deductions, credits, allowances, basis, or any other item or element affecting taxable income. In determining the true taxable income of a controlled taxpayer, the standard to be applied in every case is that of a taxpayer dealing at arm's length with an uncontrolled taxpayer. A controlled transaction meets the arm's length standard if the results of the transaction are consistent with the results that would have been realized if uncontrolled taxpayers had engaged in the same transaction under the same circumstances (arm's length result).

The key to determining an arm's length price is *comparability* of the related party and independent transactions. Comparability means there should be no differences in the 'economically relevant characteristics' of the two situations that could materially affect the pricing method or that such differences can be taken into account (OECD 1995: 1.15). The economically relevant characteristics include:

characteristics of the property or services transferred, the functions performed by the parties (taking into account assets used and risks assumed), the contractual terms, the economic circumstances of the parties, and the business strategies pursued by the parties. (OECD 1995: 1.17)

The OECD's 1995 transfer pricing guidelines are in the process of being adopted by all OECD members and some non-OECD countries (e.g. Brazil, Argentina, Chile, China). Thus, the arm's length standard has been widely adopted as the international norm for pricing cross-border intrafirm transactions. The currently acceptable transfer pricing methods within the OECD are outlined below.

## 21.5.2 Transfer pricing rules

Since the mid-1990s, there has been a growing uniformity in acceptable transfer pricing methods (the *rules* of the transfer pricing regime) across OECD countries. Led by the Internal Revenue Service, which published new section 482 regulations in 1994, and the OECD, which issued new transfer pricing guidelines for its member states a year later, these methods diffused first to Mexico and Canada, and more recently to countries as geographically dispersed as New Zealand, the United Kingdom, and Venezuela. From 2000–2005 these methods are likely to be adopted and used by most tax authorities in the developed and emerging market economies. As the tax rules for pricing intrafirm transactions spread and become more similar across the globe, tax disputes might in theory be expected to decline. However, transfer pricing is a question of fact and circumstances. Which method to use and how to employ it will remain contentious issues, even as the understanding of the methods improves for all parties.

Figure 21.2 outlines the currently acceptable methods for pricing intrafirm transactions in goods, services, and intangibles.[5] There are two main categories of methods: transactional and profit based. The old or 'traditional' methods are transactional, so-called because they focus on finding a price for a transaction. Within the transactional methods, are two groups: product comparables and functional comparables, so distinguished by the way each calculates the transfer price.

### 21.5.2.1 *Transaction-based methods*

In 1968, the US Internal Revenue Service issued its first set of transfer pricing regulations. The regulations specified five types of intrafirm transactions: loans, rentals, or sales of tangible property, transfer or use of intangible property, and performance of various business services. General rules were established for all five types to satisfy the arm's length standard. In addition,

---

[5] There are some differences not discussed here, particularly in the US regulations. For example, for goods, a product comparable is called CUP (comparable uncontrolled price), for intangibles, a CUT (comparable uncontrolled transaction); CPM should only be used for pricing intangibles where all other methods fail, etc. The interested reader is referred to the actual regulations and guidelines for specific details.

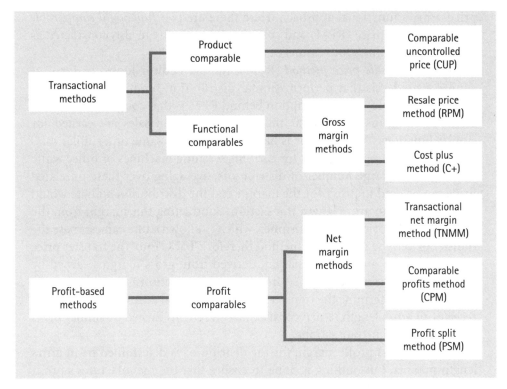

**Fig. 21.2 Acceptable transfer pricing methods**

for sales of tangible property (goods), three specific transfer pricing methods were developed: the comparable uncontrolled price method (CUP), the resale price method (RPM), and the cost plus method (C+).

The *comparable uncontrolled price* (CUP) is a product comparable method. Under CUP, the price of a transaction between two unrelated parties for the same product traded under the same circumstances is used as the transfer price. CUP looks for a comparable product to the transaction in question, either in terms of the same product being bought or sold by the MNE in a comparable transaction with an unrelated party, or the same or similar product being traded between two unrelated parties under the same or similar circumstances. The product so identified is called a *product comparable*. All the facts and circumstances that could materially affect the price must be considered, for example the characteristics of the product, the market location, the trade level of the firms, and the risks involved. Adjustments are made to the external price to more closely estimate the arm's length price.

Where a product comparable is not available, so that the CUP method cannot be used, an alternative method is to focus on one side of the transaction, either the manufacturer or the distributor, and to estimate the transfer price using a functional approach. Here there are two *functional comparable* methods: resale price (RPM) and cost plus (C+); both are also considered as *gross margin methods* for reasons outlined below.

Under the *resale price method* (RPM), the tax auditor looks for firms at similar trade levels that perform similar distribution functions (i.e. a functional comparable). The assumption behind RPM is that competition among distributors means that similar margins (returns) on sales are earned for similar functions. A distributor is likely to charge the same or a similar sales margin for carrying TV sets as for carrying washing machines or other white goods. Given a large number of distributors, averaging over these unrelated firms can be used to proxy for the margin that the distribution affiliate would have earned in an arm's length transaction. Subtracting this margin from the retail price (the price to the consumer, which is known), one can estimate the transfer price. The resale price method therefore 'backs into' the transfer price by subtracting a gross profit margin, derived from gross margins earned by comparable distributors engaged in comparable functions, from the known retail price to determine the transfer price. The method ensures that the buyer receives an arm's length return consistent with returns earned by similar firms engaged in similar transactions.

Since the gross profit margin for the distributor is determined in an arm's length manner, but nothing is done to ensure that the manufacturer's profit margin is consistent with margins earned by other manufacturers, the adjustment is only one-sided. Under RPM, having determined the buyer's arm's length margin, all excess profit on the transaction is assigned to the seller. Because RPM is a one-sided method, it tends to overestimate the transfer price, giving all unallocated profits on the transaction to the upstream manufacturer. RPM is best used when the distributor adds relatively little value to the product so that the value of its functions is easier to estimate and intangibles are less likely to be missed or under-valued. In effect, this method assumes the affiliate is a contract distributor, contracting out the distribution stage to the lowest bidder.

The other functional comparable method is the *cost plus method* (C+), where the gross markup that would be charged by unrelated firms performing the same function(s) as the related-party seller under the same circumstances is added to the standard cost of the related party to determine the transfer price. In C+, the tax auditor looks at the other side of the transaction: the manufacturer or supplier. The method starts with the costs of production, measured using recognized accounting principles,[6] and then adds an appro-

---

[6] In order to use C+, the cost basis of the related and unrelated parties must be the same. For example, do both parties use *actual cost* or *standard cost* (costs which have been standardized for cyclical fluctuations in production)? Are only *manufacturing costs* included or does the cost base include some portion of *operating costs* (i.e. selling, general and administrative expenses, and R&D costs)? The larger the cost base (i.e. the more items put below the line and thus into the

priate markup over costs. The appropriate markup is estimated from those earned by similar manufacturers. The assumption is that in a competitive market the percentage markups over cost that could be earned by other arm's length manufacturers would be roughly the same. Thus, this method is also a functional comparable like RPM.

As a one-sided method, the cost plus method focuses only on the profit markup of the seller and insists that the seller should earn only what arm's length sellers engaging in similar transactions would earn in a competitive market. Therefore C+ tends to underestimate the transfer price because it gives all unallocated profits from the transaction to the buyer, implicitly assuming the supplier is a contract manufacturer. Therefore, C+ works best when the producer is a simple manufacturer without complicated activities so that its costs and returns can be more easily estimated.

### 21.5.2.2 *Profit-based methods*

Until 1995, these three were the only acceptable transfer pricing methods within the OECD countries, with the exception of 'other methods'. Unfortunately, actual experience in the United States showed that both IRS auditors and the US tax courts relied more and more heavily in the 1980s on 'other methods' such as profit splits and profit ratio comparisons. The most serious problem was (and remains) the lack of arm's length comparables, making CUP, RPM, and C+ difficult to use in practice and necessitating the use of fourth methods. This was particularly true in the case of intangibles where external market prices were often nonexistent. In addition, existing US tax law allowed American multinationals to transfer the ownership of intangibles generated from (tax deductible) R&D expenditures to offshore affiliates where the income from these intangibles could remain untaxed by the US government. These problems were aggravated when foreign MNEs were involved since foreign information was often not available. As a result, in the 1980s, transfer pricing regulation was an acrimonious area of US tax law with dozens of tax court cases, many dragging on for up to a decade and more through the court process.

In order to deal with these problems, the US Congress in 1986 added a sentence to section 482 requiring that transfers of intangibles be priced *commensurate with the income* (CWI) from the intangibles. For eight years, the Internal Revenue Service drafted a variety of regulations designed to integrate the CWI standard into the 482 regulations. The outcome, the 1994 section 482 regulations, applies the CWI standard to all intrafirm transactions. The new regulations require that MNEs select and apply the 'best method', taking into account the facts and circumstances of the case, and

---

cost base), the smaller should be the profit markup, or gross margin, over costs. Functional comparability is key so the cost definitions must be the same.

the quality and quantity of available data. Taxpayers must prepare a functional analysis (an economic evaluation of the activities, responsibilities, resources, and risks of each of the related parties) and provide contemporaneous documentation of their transfer pricing policies. Periodic adjustments (re-evaluations) of intangible prices can be made be the IRS if transfer prices diverge from the CWI standard. In addition, two new profit-based methods were added to supplement the transactions methods: the comparable profits method (CPM) and the profit split method.

The *comparable profits method* (CPM) is a *profit-based method*, whereby the industry average net profit margin earned by comparable firms is used to 'back into' the transfer price. One of the two related firms is chosen as the tested party, usually the one with the simplest functions and for which the best data are available. Unrelated firms engaged in the same product(s) or business segment are selected as comparable firms, with adjustments to their balance sheets being made for differences in responsibilities, risks assumed, resource capabilities, and any other material differences relative to the tested party. A profit level indicator (e.g. return on assets, return on sales) is used to calculate a net profit margin for each of the uncontrolled firms. The net profit margin for the tested party is then compared to the interquartile range of the unrelated firms, and if the margin falls within the interquartile range, the transfer price is deemed to be inside the arm's length range. If the firm's net profit margin lies outside the interquartile range, the tax authority sets the margin at the median of the range, and then 'solves backwards' for the arm's length transfer price. All remaining profit on the transactions or line of business in question is assigned to the other related party. CPM is therefore a one-sided method since it focuses only on the net margins of the tested party. In addition, the method ensures that the tested party is as profitable as the median of the comparable unrelated firms.

A very different approach is taken by the *profit split method* (PSM). PSM assumes that the profit on an intrafirm transaction should be split between the two related parties based on their relative contributions to the transaction. Various ratios can be used to split the profits; the most commonly recommended ones are return on operating assets or return on sales. A second version of this method is the residual profit split, which first allocates an arm's length return to basic functions performed by each party, and then splits any residual profit between the two parties based on their shares of output, sales, or capital employed.

Both CPM and PSM were very controversial when first proposed by the Internal Revenue Service because the methods were based on profit comparables rather than product or functional comparability. The profit split was criticized for ignoring both external and internal comparables (the foundation of the arm's length standard) and for simply relying on a ratio (pulling a rabbit out of a hat) to allocate profits between the two affiliates.

The key criticism of CPM was that, in practice, the method would degenerate into simply finding the transfer price that ensured the tested party earned the average rate of return of other firms in the same industry. Given the widespread use of COMPUSTAT data, and its equivalents, it would be very easy to calculate average rates of returns and back into meaningless transfer prices. For example, one transfer pricing expert commented that 'CPM is destined to be widely used because it is so simple to apply... As with alcohol, tobacco, and firearms, "widely used" ultimately may mean "widely abused", rather than "wisely used"' (Horst 1993: 1444).

In the early 1990s, the OECD's Committee on Fiscal Affairs (CFA), made up of senior tax officials from the OECD's member countries, first strongly criticized the proposed and temporary IRS transfer pricing regulations (OECD 1993), but then finally adopted similar versions of the same five methods in its 1995 guidelines. As a fig leaf to the arm's length standard, CPM was given the awkward name of *transactional net margin method* (TNMM) and governments were told to apply the method from the bottom up (focusing on comparable transactions) rather than from the top down (focusing on comparable firms). That is, TNMM calculates the industry average net profit margin earned by arm's length parties on comparable transactions and uses that net margin to 'back into' the transfer price.

In practice, there is little difference between CPM and TNMM. Culbertson (1995), who developed CPM while in the US Treasury, argues that they get to the same destination (the arm's length range) by different routes (comparability of firms for CPM, comparability of transactions for TNMM):

The OECD guidelines use a transactional emphasis as a shortcut to get to the same place that the US regulations reach via their lengthy comparability analysis. Accordingly, the final guidelines' emphasis on the transactional character of its TNM[M] method is fully consistent with the comparability-based CPM set forth in the US regulations. (Culbertson 1995: 1344)

In effect, CPM starts by searching for comparable parties, and then works down to the most narrowly identifiable business activity that incorporates the intrafirm transaction. TNMM starts by searching for comparable transactions and scales up to a set of transactions for which data can be found. Culbertson also argues that CPM can trump the gross margin methods (resale price and cost plus) in cases where publicly available data are insufficiently detailed to allow the application of a gross margin method. He suggests three possible cases: where data are reported on a business segment basis, cost accounting adjustments are needed but the particular costs cannot be identified, or the firms perform different functions (Culbertson 1995: 1343).

Table 21.2 lists a variety of intrafirm transactions, ranging from sales of goods to technology sharing arrangements, the percentage of firms which see these transactions as vulnerable to government tax audits, and the percentage of firms applying different transfer pricing methods for each transaction category. The top four vulnerable transactions are: administrative/managerial charges (39 per cent); sales of finished goods (36 per cent); royalties (26 per cent); and technical services (25 per cent). The most cited transfer pricing methods are cost plus (cited by more than 60 per cent of all respondents for all nine transactions categories) and CUP (cited by more than 50 per cent for all categories). Resale price is cited by approximately 30 per cent of the respondents. The profit-based methods (CPM, TNMM, profit splits) are cited significantly less often (15 per cent for CPM and PSM, about 7 per cent for TNMM). Overall, the Ernst and Young survey suggests that the transactional methods are used significantly more often than the profit-based methods in practice.

Partly, the lower reliance on profit-based methods stems from their lower acceptability by OECD governments. Table 21.3 summarizes the currently acceptable transfer pricing methods in selected countries. It is clear, for example, that the US Internal Revenue Service is an outlier in its support for the comparable profits method. What is also clear from the table is how the transactional and profit based methods are being widely adopted, not just by OECD countries, but more generally.

## 21.5.3 Dispute settlement procedures

Under the corporate income tax, governments normally tax the net income of firms located in their jurisdictions, minus any tax deductions or credits. Net income is defined as gross revenues (product sales to households and other firms, royalty income, license fees, etc.) minus cost of goods sold (factor costs, purchased materials), general expenses, and other allowable expenses. Where buyers and sellers are unrelated, governments take intermediate and final product prices as market based (at arm's length) and accept the transactions as being determined in the market place. However, where the firms are related, governments insist that the MNE prove that its transfer prices are equivalent to those that would have been negotiated by unrelated parties engaged in comparable transactions, or the national tax authority will substitute its calculation of arm's length prices for the MNE's transfer prices.

At the national level, most bargaining games occur behind closed doors between 'large case' tax auditors and MNE tax departments. The negotiations take place over several years, from the date of the first tax audit through to the completion (win, lose) of enormously complicated tax court cases that can cost millions of dollars. Only at the last stage, if the negotiations end up in tax court, is the bargaining made public. As a result of the growing number and

**Table 21.2 Transfer pricing methods used by multinationals by type of transaction**

| Type of intrafirm transaction | Number of responses | Percent of respondents that see transaction as vulnerable | Percent of respondents using transfer pricing method | | | | | | | | | |
|---|---|---|---|---|---|---|---|---|---|---|---|---|
| | | | Transaction-based methods | | | | Profit-based methods | | | | Other methods | |
| | | | CUP | CUT | Resale price | Cost plus | Cost | CPM | TNMM | Profit split | Historic practice | Other |
| Sales of finished goods | 363 | 36 | 52 | 11 | 31 | 60 | 12 | 17 | 7 | 11 | 20 | 12 |
| Sales of raw materials | 254 | 18 | 57 | 13 | 33 | 61 | 13 | 18 | 6 | 13 | 19 | 13 |
| Administrative or managerial services | 418 | 39 | 53 | 11 | 21 | 66 | 14 | 14 | 7 | 9 | 18 | 16 |
| Technical services | 352 | 25 | 55 | 12 | 25 | 64 | 15 | 15 | 8 | 9 | 17 | 16 |
| Commissions for sales of goods | 232 | 19 | 56 | 12 | 27 | 61 | 12 | 16 | 6 | 14 | 20 | 13 |
| Technology cost sharing agreements | 191 | 15 | 54 | 11 | 26 | 71 | 20 | 16 | 6 | 12 | 16 | 19 |
| Royalties for intangibles | 247 | 26 | 55 | 15 | 30 | 68 | 13 | 18 | 8 | 12 | 20 | 15 |
| Inter-company financing | 456 | 23 | 51 | 11 | 23 | 61 | 13 | 14 | 7 | 10 | 19 | 15 |
| Others | 52 | – | 61 | 13 | 15 | 65 | 15 | 15 | – | 10 | 17 | 19 |

Note Multiple selections allowed.
Source Ernst and Young (1999: 21, 28)

## Table 21.3 Transfer pricing methods accepted in selected countries

| | Transaction-based methods | | | Profit-based methods | | |
|---|---|---|---|---|---|---|
| | CUP CUT | Resale price | Cost plus | CPM | TNMM | Profit split |
| Australia | yes | yes | yes | no | yes | yes |
| Belgium | yes | yes | yes | no | yes | yes |
| Brazil | yes | yes | yes | no | no | no |
| Canada | yes | yes | yes | no unless as TNMM | last resort | yes |
| China | yes | yes | yes | no | yes | deemed profit |
| Denmark | yes | yes | yes | no | yes | yes |
| France | yes | yes | yes | no | yes | yes |
| Germany | yes | yes | yes | no | last resort | last resort |
| Japan | yes | yes | yes | no | no | yes |
| Italy | yes | yes | yes | yes ? (profit comparisons) | yes | yes |
| Korea | yes | yes | yes | no | last resort | last resort |
| Mexico | yes | yes | yes | no | yes | yes |
| Netherlands | yes | yes | yes | no | yes | yes |
| New Zealand | yes | yes | yes | yes | yes | yes |
| South Africa | yes | yes | yes | no | yes | yes |
| Spain | yes | yes | yes | no | no | yes |
| United Kingdom | yes | yes | yes | last resort | last resort | last resort |
| United States | yes | yes | yes | yes | seen as same as CPM | yes |
| OECD guidelines | yes | yes | yes | no | last resort | last resort |

*Source* Based on UNCTAD (1999: 33); and Aitkinson and Tyrrall (1999: 232)

length of these cases, and the IRS's propensity to lose the cases in tax court, the procedures used by the IRS to handle transfer pricing disputes are also changing. A new *Advance Pricing Agreement* procedure was introduced in 1991 whereby a taxpayer and the IRS negotiate an agreed transfer pricing methodology that is binding on both parties for a specified time period, generally three years. In 1994, the Service and Apple Computer first used *binding arbitration* to settle their transfer pricing dispute rather than going to the tax courts; however, even though both parties were happy with the outcome, the method has not been used since. New *penalty regulations* for transfer pricing misvaluations were also added to the Internal Revenue Code in order to ensure MNE compliance with the new section 482 rules.

The traditional bilateral approach has been through *competent authority* provisions of bilateral tax treaties that bring the two tax authorities together to settle transfer pricing disputes. Given that most intrafirm trade takes place within the Triad, where tax rates are roughly similar, real disputes can arise over apportionment of the MNE's tax base between the two tax jurisdictions, not just between the MNE and the nation-state. Where tax rates are the same, the location of the tax base determines which country has the right to tax under the first crack principle and therefore which government will receive most or all of the tax revenues. Since the jurisdiction rules (i.e. which country has the right to tax which income) are seldom changed, transfer pricing policies are a second method by which national governments can reallocate taxable income in their favor. Double taxation is more likely when governments engage in confiscatory transfer pricing policies.

With the development of the global economy, it is estimated that over 90 per cent of current transfer pricing disputes concern two or more developed (and high-tax) countries in which an MNE conducts operations, each taking a different view of what the MNE's pricing policy on a particular transaction should be. Each country is concerned with protecting its own share of tax take; tax avoidance, as such, is not the real issue. (Pagan 1994: 163)

# 21.6 AN ALTERNATIVE APPROACH TO TAXING MNES: FORMULARY APPORTIONMENT

The arm's length standard is based on the *separate accounting* or *separate entity approach*. The borders of a firm are defined according to national boundaries; this is known as the 'water's edge'. Domestic affiliates and foreign branches are consolidated with the parent firm for tax purposes, but foreign subsidiaries and other affiliates of the MNE are treated as separate firms. Income of the multinational is measured using separate accounting for the domestic and international units of the MNE. Since the parent's tax return is consolidated with its domestic affiliates and foreign branches, transfer prices for intrafirm transactions among these affiliated parts of the MNE are not required for tax purposes. However, intrafirm transactions between the parent and its foreign affiliates must be measured and accounted for.

The arm's length standard is not the only norm that could be used to guide the international tax transfer pricing regime, nor is the standard without its critics. A basic criticism is that a separate accounting approach to taxing MNEs is inappropriate because it is difficult to separate out the contribution each affiliate makes within an integrated MNE group. More specifically, the transactional methods are difficult to apply in practice and the profit-based methods are easily abused. As Vernon notes:

The underlying problem of course, is that the national tax authorities are trying to place an exact figure on a concept that does not exist, namely, the 'true' profit that arises in each national taxing jurisdiction. In the real world, the profit allocated to each country by a multinational enterprise commonly is an artifact whose size is determined largely by precedent and by the debating skills of lawyers and accountants.... When round pegs are being shoved into square holes, both the pegs and the holes are bound to get heated in the process. (Vernon 1998: 40–41)

The alternative would be to tax multinationals on a worldwide consolidated basis using a *global formulary method (a.k.a. unitary taxation)* for taxing MNE profits. Under a global formulary approach, each affiliate's share of certain factors (e.g. sales, employment, assets), as a percentage of the worldwide MNE amount of these factors (however weighted), would be multiplied by the MNE's total worldwide income to compute the tax to be paid in that jurisdiction. A global formulary approach requires three steps: (1) determining the boundaries of the MNE for tax purposes, (2) accurately estimating the MNE's global profits, and (3) establishing the formula for allocating the global profits among the various national tax jurisdictions (OECD 1995: para 3.59).

Unitary taxation has been little used in practice. As Table 21.3 shows, most of the countries listed do not allow formulary approaches to transfer pricing. The US states and Canadian provinces use formulary methods to allocate subfederal corporate tax revenues among themselves. A few US states, notably California, have attempted, mostly unsuccessfully, to tax MNEs in their jurisdiction on a *pro rata* share of the MNE's worldwide income. Most recently, the IRS has signed several advance pricing agreements with international banks, using a formulary approach to allocate their income from global (24–hour) trading.

Respected academics such as Ray Vernon (1985, 1998), Richard Bird (1986, 1988), Charles McLure (1984), and Stanley Langbein (1986) have been strongly supportive of formulary approaches. However, the OECD dislikes and has actively discouraged the use of global formulary methods on the grounds that they are arbitrary and do not satisfy the norm of the arm's length standard (OECD 1995: paras 3.58–3.74).

# 21.7 WHERE DO WE GO FROM HERE?

At the end of the twentieth century, there are three trends that will have major impacts on international taxation and the regulation of MNE transfer prices. The first driver is globalization. Globalization increases the spread and mobility of multinational enterprises. Transnational strategies encourage the fragmentation of MNE value adding activities, with each plant distributed according to its highest value adding location. This means that national tax authorities are faced with a disarticulated MNE (a part of the whole) for tax purposes, where the local unit is heavily engaged in network-like complex forms with sister affiliates, subcontractors, and strategic alliance partners of intrafirm two-way flows of goods, services, and intangibles. This suggests that MNE-state disputes should increase in number and intensity, with more governments involved and more difficulty in assigning tax bases and determining transfer prices.

The second driver is regionalization. The growing number of preferential trading arrangements, and the deepening and broadening of existing arrangements such as the European Union and NAFTA, suggests that MNEs will be developing and strengthening their regional core networks. Thus, the need for regionally based tax systems becomes more acute, in order to avoid a growing number of bilateral disputes. One might expect increasing use of formulary apportionment models as a way to allocate tax bases at the regional level. Withholding tax rates are likely to be reduced to zero within regional trading areas. Financial and real intrafirm trade flows are likely to increase in number and complexity as a result.

The third driver is the Internet. The Internet creates the possibility to buy and sell globally without a nexus for tax purposes. It allows and encourages the development of supplier–buyer intranets that engage in intrafirm transactions in E-space. New industries, such as 24-hour global trading and outsourcing of business services such as airline reservations, are created by the ability to move funds and intangibles around the world instantaneously. The taxation implications have only just begun to be understood (e.g. the US Treasury, Revenue Canada, and the OECD all are studying the E-commerce issue), and are particularly acute in the financial sector.

These three drivers have, at the present time, unclear implications for *global governance* in terms of deepening and broadening the international tax and tax transfer pricing regimes. Why and how is the regime likely to spread and deepen? Many non-OECD countries are adopting the arm's length standard (e.g. Venezuela, Brazil, Chile), suggesting that the geographic scope of the regime is broadening; is this likely to continue? As MNEs adopt more transnational network structures, will harmonization of national dispute settlement mechanisms (APAs, penalties, documentation requirements) occur? Will regionalization facilitate deepening within the regime, for example, could North America shift from three bilateral tax treaties to one trilateral tax treaty?

New types of transfer pricing and taxation problems are also caused by globalization and the Internet. As the knowledge content of MNE activity continues to rise, intrafirm services and intangible transfers will displace physical transfers as the primary form of intrafirm trade. Historically, for intangible assets, royalty rates based on downstream sales were used to price these assets; now rapidly growing cost sharing arrangements among strategic alliances suggest that the traditional arm's length methods may become increasingly inappropriate.

Twenty-four hour global trading may be the bell-wether industry here, just as the automotive industry has traditionally been the bell-wether for other manufacturing industries. As MNEs adopt complex network structures based on mutual interdependence among their affiliates, will some form of formula apportionment be the only way to value intrafirm transactions and MNE group profits? The new IRS global dealing regulations suggest this may be the case.

# 21.8 CONCLUSIONS

Taxing multinational enterprises has always been a difficult and complex task. Globalization is likely to make it more so. Governments have responded by developing a network of bilateral tax treaties, based on the OECD model tax convention, designed around the source and residence principles and the arm's length standard. This separate accounting framework worked reasonably well in the 'horse and buggy' days when multinationals were stand-alone replicas of their parents and most intrafirm transactions were in finished goods. As E-business spreads and more MNEs adopt transnational strategies and complex matrix structures, it will become increasingly difficult to apply separate accounting rules. The IRS has led the way by applying a formulary apportionment method to the global trading industry; perhaps this will be a bell-wether for future approaches to taxing MNEs in the twenty-first century.

# REFERENCES

AITKINSON, MARK, and TYRRALL, DAVID (1999). *International Transfer Pricing: A Practical Guide for Finance Directors.* London: Financial Times Management.

ALTSHULER, ROSANNE (2000). 'Recent Developments in the Debate on Deferral', *Tax Notes International,* 3 April: 1579–95.

BIRD, RICHARD (1986). 'The Interjurisdictional Allocation of Income', *Australian Tax Forum,* 3/3: 333–53.

—— (1988). 'Shaping a New International Tax Order', *International Bureau of Fiscal Documentation Bulletin,* July: 292–9.

COLE, ROBERT T. (1999). *Practical Guide to US Transfer Pricing.* New York: Aspen Publishers.

COOPERS and LYBRAND (1998). *International Transfer Pricing.* Chicago, Ill.: CCH.

CULBERTSON, ROBERT (1995). 'A Rose by Any Other Name: Smelling the Flowers at the OECD's Last Resort', *Tax Notes International,* Aug. 7: 370–82.

EASSON, ALEX (1999). *Taxation of Foreign Direct Investment: An Introduction.* London: Kluwer Law International.

*Economist, The* (2000). 'The Mystery of the Vanishing Taxpayer. A Survey of Globalization and Tax', 29 Jan.

EDEN, LORRAINE (1998). *Taxing Multinationals: Transfer Pricing and Corporate Income Taxation in North America.* Toronto: University of Toronto Press.

—— DACIN, TINA, and WAN, WILLIAM (forthcoming). 'Standards Across Borders: The Arm's Length Standard in North America', *Accounting, Organizations and Society.*

EMMANUEL, CLIVE, and MEHAFDI, MESSAOUD (1994). *Transfer Pricing.* San Diego, Calif.: Academic Press.

ERNST and YOUNG (1997). *Global Transfer Pricing Survey.* Washington, DC: Ernst and Young International.

—— (1999). *Global Transfer Pricing Survey.* Washington, DC: Ernst and Young International.

FEINSCHREIBER, ROBERT (ed.) (1998). *Transfer Pricing Handbook,* 2nd edn. New York: Wiley.

HINES, JAMES (1999). 'Lessons from Behavioral Responses to International Taxation', *National Tax Journal,* 52/2: 305–22.

HORST, THOMAS (1993). 'The Comparable Profits Method', *Tax Notes International*, 14 June: 1443–58.

Internal Revenue Service (1994). *Intercompany Transfer Pricing Regulations under Section 482. T.D. 8552.* Washington, DC: US Government Printing Office.

KING, ELIZABETH (1994). *Transfer Pricing and Valuation in Corporate Taxation: Federal Legislation vs. Administrative Practice.* Boston: Kluwer Academic Publishers.

KOSTOVA, TATIANA, and ZAHEER, SRILATA (1999). 'Organizational Legitimacy Under Conditions of Complexity: The Case of the Multinational Enterprise', *Academy of Management Review*, 24: 64–81.

KRASNER, STEPHEN (1983). 'Structural Causes and Regime Consequences: Regimes as Intervening Variables', in Stephen Kraser (ed.), *International Regimes*. Ithaca: Cornell University Press.

LANGBEIN, STANLEY (1986). 'The Unitary Method and the Myth of Arm's Length', *Tax Notes: Tax Analysts Special Report*. 17 Feb.: 625–81.

LOWELL, CYM H., BURGE, MARIANNE, and BRIGER, PETER L. (1998). *US International Transfer Pricing*, 2nd edn. Boston: Warren, Gorham and Lamont.

——and GOVERNALE, DACK P. (1997). *US International Taxation: Practice and Procedure.* Boston: Warren, Gorham and Lamont.

McLURE, CHARLES E. (1984). 'Defining a Unitary Business', in Charles E. McLure (ed.), *The State Corporate Income Tax: Issues in Worldwide Unitary Combination.* Stanford: Hoover Institution Press.

OECD (1979). *Transfer Pricing and Multinational Enterprises.* Paris: OECD.

——(1993). *The United States Proposed Regulations Dealing with Tax Aspects of Transfer Pricing Within Multinational Enterprises.* Paris: OECD, Committee on Fiscal Affairs.

——(1995). *Transfer Pricing Guidelines for Multinational Enterprises and Tax Administrations.* Paris: OECD, looseleaf updates.

PAGAN, JILL (1994). 'An Open Letter to Jeffrey Owens, Fiscal Affairs Division, OECD, From Jill C. Pagan', *Tax Notes International*, 17 Jan.: 161–67.

——and WILKIE, J. SCOTT (1995). *Transfer Pricing Strategy in a Global Economy.* Amsterdam: IBFD.

PLASSCHAERT, SYLVAIN (ed.) (forthcoming). *Transfer Pricing and Taxation.* London: Routledge, United Nations Library on Transnational Corporations, Vol. 14.

RUGMAN, ALAN, and EDEN, LORRAINE (eds.) (1985). *Multinationals and Transfer Pricing.* London and New York: Croom Helm, and St Martin's Press.

STOPFORD, JOHN M. (1994). 'The Growing Interdependence Between Transnational Corporations and Governments', *Transnational Corporations*, 3: 53–76.

SUNDARAM, ANANT, and BLACK, J. STEWART (1992). 'The Environment and Internal Organization of Multinational Enterprises', *Academy of Management Review*, 17/4: 729–57.

TANG, ROGER Y. W. (1993). *Transfer Pricing in the 1990s: Tax and Management Perspectives.* Westport, Conn.: Quorum Books.

——(1997). *Intrafirm Trade and Global Transfer Pricing Regulations.* Westport, Conn.: Quorum Books.

United Nations Conference on Trade and Development (UNCTAD) (1999). *Transfer Pricing.* New York: UNCTAD.

VERNON, RAYMOND (1985). 'Sovereignty at Bay: Ten Years After', in Theodore Moran (ed.), *Multinational Corporations: The Political Economy of Foreign Direct Investment*. Lexington, Mass.: Lexington Books.

—— (1998). *In the Hurricane's Eye: The Troubled Prospects of Multinational Enterprises*. Cambridge, Mass.: Harvard University Press.

# PART V

## REGIONAL STUDIES

CHAPTER 22

..................................................................

# JAPAN

..................................................................

## D. ELEANOR WESTNEY

THE rapid expansion of Japanese multinational enterprises in the 1980s changed the nature of competition in several major industries and attracted wide popular and scholarly attention. Japanese MNEs are arguably the most studied population of MNEs next to those from the United States, and in some aspects—particularly the extent to which home country practices and systems are carried across borders—they have been more exhaustively analyzed than those from any other country. In part, the volume of research can be attributed to the rapidity of the emergence of Japanese firms as international competitors, and in part to the fact that they constitute the first population of non-Western MNEs. But perhaps the most significant factor is that they are seen to differ significantly from both US and European MNEs, and this has attracted attention from a broad spectrum of researchers: International Business scholars for whom the Japanese MNE is a special case of the MNE; scholars of Japanese business for whom it is a special case of Japanese management and organization; and researchers in comparative organizations and the sociology of work, for whom the efforts of Japanese MNEs to instill their systems in their subsidiaries provide a rich case of change in established patterns of work practices and management systems.

Summarizing this extensive literature poses a formidable challenge. This chapter tries to accomplish three things. First, it provides an overview of the scope, timing, and destination of Japanese foreign direct investment (FDI)—three of the fundamental topics of interest in international business—in order to supply a basic map of when and where Japanese companies extended their operations abroad. Second, it takes the research on Japanese MNEs conducted in the 1970s as a benchmark to examine their evolution over time. Finally, it briefly looks at Japan as a host country for foreign multinationals.

# 22.1 THE PATTERNS OF INTERNATIONALIZATION: SCALE, DESTINATION, AND TIMING

## 22.1.1 The first century: 1884–1971

The prevailing image of Japanese MNCs today is shaped by the auto transplants and electronics factories in North America and England that have been the focus of so much academic research and media attention in the last two decades. But the first century of Japanese FDI was dominated not by manufacturing firms but by trading companies, banks, and companies in other service sectors, and the main destination was not the West but Japan's Asian neighbors (Taiwan, Korea, and China).

The trading companies were the first Japanese companies to set up international subsidiaries. Mitsui and Company, one of Japan's first *sogo shosha* (general trading companies) set up its first overseas office in Shanghai in 1874; by 1910 it had forty-six branches in Asia, five in Europe, two in the United States, and one in Australia (Mason 1999: 18–19). Other trading companies and other Japanese service firms (primarily banks and transport services) followed, providing the infrastructure for Japanese trade. Mira Wilkins's observation about Japanese trade with the United States before World War II applies to Japan's activities throughout the world:

Japanese banks in the United States financed Japanese trade; Japanese insurance companies insured the cargoes; the Japanese trading companies with offices in the United States handled the bulk of Japanese commerce (including the movement of intangibles, technology transfer, and assisting the arrangements for American companies' joint ventures in Japan), and last but not least, Japanese ships transported the goods in both directions. (Wilkins 1994: 264)

In Asia, one would have to add the key role of Japanese-financed and owned railways, which transported the goods on land.

Japanese manufacturing companies were somewhat slower to set up operations abroad, but Japan's growing colonial possessions (Taiwan was annexed in 1895, Korea in 1910) and spheres of influence in China drew increasing numbers of Japanese manufacturers into ventures abroad. For example, in a pattern that prefigures the market-defending nature of much of Japan's postwar FDI, Japanese textile firms set up factories in China in the 1920s to defend local markets won by their exports, and by 1936 Japanese-owned cotton mills accounted for 40 per cent of China's total production of machine-spun yarn and 57 per cent of its machine-woven cloth (Duus 1989: 79). Japan's military expansion into China in the 1930s drew further infrastructure and manufacturing investment from Japan, often into army-affiliated ventures: by the early 1940s, 159 of 522 Japanese-owned operations in China were either owned or controlled by the Japanese military (Mason 1999: 22).

Defeat in the Pacific War marked a major disruption in some aspects of Japanese FDI. Japanese overseas assets were confiscated, and many of Japan's most international companies were the targets of anti-*zaibatsu* 'trust-busting': the largest prewar multinational firm, the Mitsui trading company, for example, was split into over 100 separate entities, which gradually coalesced over the ensuing decade. Japanese companies in general faced severe restrictions on any movement of capital out of Japan. Moreover, they had more urgent concerns than resuming overseas operations; they were preoccupied with surviving the hardships of the postwar economy, the transformation of industrial relations, and Occupation policies that targeted firms associated with the wartime regime (Dower 1999: 532). Even when the Occupation ended and postwar recovery was well underway, Japanese companies continued to face severe government regulations on capital outflows. Moreover, the markets that Japanese firms had dominated before 1945 were now closed to them: China and North Korea by Communist revolution, and South Korea by nationalist revulsion at Japanese colonialism (South Korea prohibited Japanese investments completely until 1965). When in the late 1950s Japanese companies once again began to extend their activities abroad, Taiwan, Hong Kong, and Singapore were the major destinations.

Although the geographic pattern of Japanese FDI within Asia changed considerably after World War II, however, Asia remained the primary target of Japanese companies' FDI. Indeed, the overall continuities with prewar patterns were considerable, and remained so until the early 1970s. Non-manufacturing companies predominated, led again by the trading companies, which were granted government permission to set up offices overseas as early as 1950. The banks, insurance companies, and shipping companies that had provided the infrastructure of Japanese trade in the prewar period also resumed their activities in the 1950s. The anxiety about Japan's low domestic supplies of key natural resources meant that much of this infrastructure in the

1950s and 1960s was directed to natural resource projects and to facilitating trade in commodities (Tsuru 1993: 193). Trading companies were the leaders in such activities, and were also active in helping Japanese manufacturing companies set up operations abroad, especially medium and smaller-scale enterprises. Yoshi Tsurumi found that 'approximately one-half of the Japanese manufacturing subsidiaries abroad that had been established by 1972 included at least one Japanese trading firm as one of its initial participants' (Tsurumi 1976: 138). The facilitating role played by the trading company is widely seen as one of the reasons for the unusually large part of pre-1970s Japanese FDI attributable to small and medium-sized firms (Yoshino 1976).

When Japan's manufacturing firms did begin to extend their operations internationally in the late 1950s and the 1960s, they continued to face obstacles put up by a government determined to foster a favorable balance of trade and to restrict capital outflows. In general, offshore subsidiaries were not allowed to produce for the home market: the Japanese government made a prohibition of reverse imports a condition of allowing such investments to be made (Mason 1999: 29–30). Most of the ventures abroad by Japanese firms, therefore, were driven by a desire to keep or expand local markets that had initially been won by exports. One of the industries that was most aggressive in developing production abroad was the textile industry, which accounted for 25 per cent of the stock of Japanese manufacturing FDI as late as the early 1970s, making it the most international of Japan's industries. Firms in consumer products, whose goods were often well-suited to Asian markets, began to expand in the late 1950s and the 1960s. Consumer electronics and appliance firms were especially active, setting up locally focused assembly plants first in Taiwan and then in Southeast Asia to reach expanding but protected local markets. Some firms ventured beyond Asia: NEC set up its first foreign venture in Taiwan in 1958, and then expanded to Pakistan in 1965, Mexico and Brazil in 1968—focusing its FDI in this period, like nearly all Japanese manufacturing firms, on developing countries (Kobayashi 1989: 101–2). By 1971, approximately 66 per cent of Japanese manufacturing subsidiaries abroad were located in Asia, and another 20 per cent in Latin America (Tsurumi 1976: 71).

In markets which could be served by exports from Japan—primarily the developed country markets such as the United States—Japan's manufacturing firms set up sales offices to expand the penetration of Japan-produced goods. In a pattern subsequently followed by other Asian firms, Japanese consumer electronics firms were particularly successful in exporting to the world's largest single market through America's mass market retailers (Gereffi 1997). One account estimates that between 1963 and 1975, Sears alone sold over 60 per cent of all Japanese color television sets made for export (Wolf 1983: 20). In Asia, in contrast, the leading Japanese firms followed their home country pattern of building a retail and service network of brand-exclusive shops to reach consumers with their entire product range of household appliances and electronics. These extensive distribution and service activities were usually housed in a sales and distribution subsidiary; manufacturing operations were incorporated separately. Instead of a single country subsidiary, therefore, as was the pattern in most Western MNEs, Japanese parent firms set up functionally separate subsidiaries.

By the early 1970s, therefore, Japanese firms were expanding abroad, in two distinct patterns. They were setting up marketing and manufacturing operations on a locally oriented basis in developing countries, primarily but not exclusively in Asia, and they were building relationships with retailers and setting up marketing organizations in the developed countries, serving them from their Japanese factories.

Most accounts of Japanese FDI identify 1971 (in retrospect) as one of two major turning points in the postwar internationalization of Japanese companies (the second being 1985), due to three major factors. The government's gradual relaxation of controls on outward foreign direct investment was of fundamental importance, but two other factors both strengthened the motivation for Japanese manufacturing firms to go abroad and played a role in the government's willingness to allow—even encourage—them to do so. One was the 1971 ending of the postwar regime of fixed exchange rates, which led to a rapid strengthening of the yen *vis-à-vis* the dollar and most other Asian currencies. The other was the growing threat of retaliation against Japanese exports into major western markets, especially in the sector of Japan's greatest success—consumer electronics in the United States, where in 1971 the US Tariff Commission ended a four-year investigation of dumping complaints by finding against the Japanese manufacturers. These two factors—a strengthening yen and threats of retaliation against Japanese exports—continued to be important factors shaping the level and direction of the internationalization of Japanese manufacturing firms for the rest of the century (Itagaki 1997: 1–2).

## 22.1.2  From crisis to crisis: Japanese FDI 1971–2000

In the remaining three decades of the twentieth century, Japanese firms expanded their international operations to an extent that virtually no one could have anticipated from the vantage point of the early 1970s. Even as acute an observer as Michael Yoshino, in his otherwise insightful analysis of Japanese MNEs written in the mid-1970s, stated that:

Japan's inability to generate major innovative technologies will almost certainly limit the multinational spread of her industries and will particularly inhibit large-scale entry of Japanese manufacturing activities into the US market. For the foreseeable future, then, Japanese enterprise will scarcely challenge the dominance of US-based multinational enterprises. (Yoshino 1976: 90)

Given that MNE theory in the 1960s and 1970s strongly emphasized product innovation as the key firm-specific advantage with which a company could expand abroad, Yoshino's assessment should not be surprising. It does remind us how much the Japanese firms' ability to ground a competitive advantage on process innovations and the organization of work changed our models of multinational enterprise—and indeed our models of strategy—in the 1980s and 1990s.

These three decades were marked by dramatic shifts in the scale and direction of Japanese FDI. In 1977, Japan provided about 6 per cent of the total world FDI flows. At its peak in 1989, Japanese FDI accounted for 30 per cent of world flows, and Japan was the world's single largest foreign investor (Froot 1989). By 1997, Japan ranked fifth among the sources of FDI (after the US, the UK, France, and Germany) and once again accounted for about 6 per cent of the vastly expanded world total FDI flow of $423.7 billion. The internationalization of Japanese firms was punctuated by dramatic turning points: *endaka* (the sudden strengthening of the yen in the aftermath of the Plaza Accords in 1985), the bursting of the Bubble economy in 1990–1, and the Asia financial crisis of 1997 (see Table 22.1).

In the early 1980s, the low value of the yen relative to the dollar had greatly helped Japanese firms to penetrate US markets from their production base in Japan (and also made Japanese goods less expensive in the dollar-linked markets of the rest of Asia). The US–Japan trade tensions produced by Japanese import penetration had already led the firms in the motor vehicle industry to set up production plants in the United States in order to get around the so-called Voluntary Export Restraints negotiated by the US and Japanese governments. Honda led the way with its plant in Ohio in 1982; Nissan followed with a truck plant in 1983 and Toyota with a joint venture, NUMMI, with GM in California in 1984. But in the aftermath of the Plaza Accord of 1985 the value of the yen strengthened dramatically, from 252 yen to the dollar in 1984 to 160 in 1986, and Japan suddenly became a high-cost location relative to both Western and other Asian countries. The existing Japanese auto transplants quickly expanded capacity, and others followed suit. They drew with them many of their Japanese suppliers: by 1990 nearly 300 Japanese auto parts companies had set up production in North America (Gelsanliter 1990: 7–8). The large-scale move of the Japanese auto firms into North America challenged the industry that had, more than any other, exemplified America's industrial might for decades, and did so less with alternative products than with an alternative way of organizing. It is probably the most intensively studied single case of FDI in history.

## Table 22.1  Japan's foreign direct investment by year 1980–98

| Year | Total outward FDI | 1980 total =100 (US$ base) | 1980 total =100 (yen base) | Manufacturing FDI | 1980 total =100 (yen base) | Manufacturing as % of total FDI |
|---|---|---|---|---|---|---|
| 1980 | 4,693 | 100 | 100 | 1,706 | 100 | 36.3 |
| 1981 | 8,932 | 190 | 185 | 2,305 | 131 | 25.8 |
| 1982 | 7,703 | 164 | 180 | 2,076 | 134 | 26.9 |
| 1983 | 8,145 | 173 | 182 | 2,588 | 160 | 31.8 |
| 1984 | 10,155 | 216 | 227 | 2,505 | 154 | 24.7 |
| 1985 | 12,217 | 260 | 274 | 2,352 | 145 | 19.2 |
| 1986 | 22,320 | 476 | 352 | 3,806 | 166 | 17.0 |
| 1987 | 33,364 | 710 | 453 | 7,832 | 293 | 23.5 |
| 1988 | 47,022 | 1002 | 567 | 13,805 | 316 | 29.3 |
| 1989 | 67,540 | 1439 | 876 | 16,284 | 581 | 24.1 |
| 1990 | 56,911 | 1213 | 775 | 15,486 | 593 | 27.2 |
| 1991 | 41,584 | 886 | 526 | 12,311 | 429 | 29.6 |
| 1992 | 34,138 | 727 | 406 | 10,057 | 329 | 29.4 |
| 1993 | 36,025 | 768 | 377 | 11,131 | 320 | 30.9 |
| 1994 | 41,051 | 875 | 394 | 13,783 | 364 | 33.6 |
| 1995 | 50,694 | 1080 | 443 | 18623 | 452 | 36.7 |
| 1996 | 48,019 | 1023 | 492 | 20258 | 570 | 42.2 |
| 1997 | 53,972 | 1150 | 613 | 19,325 | 604 | 35.8 |
| 1998 | 40,747 | 868 | 502 | 12,252 | 415 | 30.1 |

Unit = $US million

The late 1980s witnessed the peak of Japanese FDI. The combination of the strengthening yen and the 'Bubble Economy', which gave firms ready access to low-cost capital to finance expansion abroad, stimulated manufacturing firms to expand rapidly their production operations outside high-cost Japan. The 'push' factors to expand abroad included labor shortages, which were becoming a problem for technology-intensive firms. Both availability of capital and the perceived need for technical talent encouraged a sudden expansion in the number and scale of Japanese-owned R&D centers in the United States and Western Europe (Westney 1993; Pearce 1997). Some of these centers were set up to increase a firm's ability to develop products that suited local customer needs more effectively; others were intended primarily to tap into local centres of science and technology to expand the firm's knowledge base. Often these R&D centers followed the pattern set up in earlier expansions of the value chain internationally, and were separately incorporated. Japanese firms tended therefore to have an array of subsidiaries within a country, instead of a single country subsidiary (Nissan, for example, in the early 1990s had four subsidiaries in the United States: a sales company, a manufacturing company, a design center in California, and an R&D center in Ohio; Matsushita had nineteen subsidiaries, five of them focused on R&D).

Difficult as it is to recall clearly today, after a decade of recession in the Japanese domestic economy, the lengthy crisis in the Japanese banking system, and widespread recognition of the low level of competitiveness in many of Japan's industries,[1] the international expansion of Japanese firms was widely viewed as a serious threat in both the United States and Western Europe in the late 1980s. Some of the FDI flowing into the United States involved real estate transactions, some of them highly symbolic, such as Mitsubishi Real Estate Company's 1989 purchase of Rockefeller Center in New York City, and others with significant impacts on local communities (such as Japanese purchases of hotels, golf courses, and residential real estate in Hawaii). The highly publicized ventures of Sony and Matsushita into Hollywood, with Sony's purchase of Columbia Pictures in 1989 and Matsushita's acquisition of MCA/Universal in 1990, also seemed to symbolize a transfer of influence as well as of capital. Japanese banks expanded their offices abroad, and began competing aggressively with their US and European counterparts. When the bubble burst in 1990–1, however, Japan's economy fell into recession and Japanese FDI fell off rapidly from its 1989 peak; moreover, Americans began to realize that most Japanese companies had significantly over-paid for their acquired US assets (Matsushita, for example, sold off MCA/Universal at a significant loss). US anxieties about Japanese expansion receded accordingly.

Japan's manufacturing firms continued to invest at fairly steady levels through the early 1990s, largely in response to the continued volatility of the yen (see column 5 in Table 22.1). Although data on Japanese FDI are invariably presented in US dollars, even in Japanese government statistics, it is useful to look at the trends in terms of yen as well. Japanese managers operate in a yen world, as Itami (1997: 339) has pointed out, even though their actions are

---

[1] For an excellent overview of the problems of the 1990s in Japan, see T. J. Pempel (1998).

Table 22.2  Geographic distribution of Japanese outward FDI flows
1980–98

| Region | 1980 | 1985 | 1989 | 1995 | 1998 |
|---|---|---|---|---|---|
| North America | 34.0% | 45.0% | 50.2% | 44.9% | 26.9% |
| Europe | 12.3 | 15.8 | 21.9 | 16.7 | 34.4 |
| Asia | 25.3 | 11.7 | 12.2 | 24.2 | 16.0 |
| Latin America | 12.5 | 21.4 | 7.8 | 7.6 | 15.9 |
| Oceania | 9.5 | 4.3 | 6.8 | 5.5 | 5.4 |
| Other | 6.4 | 1.8 | 1.1 | 1.0 | 1.4 |
| TOTAL (US$ million) | $4,693 (100%) | $12,217 | $67,540 | $50,594 | $40,747 |

interpreted through the lenses of the dollar world. The dollar-based data exaggerate somewhat the ups and downs of investment flows. For example, the combination of the strong yen and the increase in FDI meant that the dollar value of Japanese FDI flows jumped by 83 per cent in 1986 over the previous year. The yen value increase is much less dramatic, although still substantial at 46 per cent. In dollar terms, Japanese FDI in manufacturing during the Bubble peaked in 1989, and in the 1990s in 1996; in yen terms, the peaks were delayed: the Bubble high point was 1990, and it exceeded that peak in 1997.

The geographic targets of Japanese FDI shifted over time. Although investment in Asia increased steadily, by 1980, North America accounted for 34 per cent of total Japanese outward FDI and Asia for 25 per cent, and North America remained the primary destination for Japanese FDI throughout the 1980s and 1990s. By the end of the 1980s, Europe had replaced Asia as the second most important target of Japanese FDI. The relative positions of Europe and Asia as targets of Japanese FDI shifted again in the mid-1990s, until the 1997 Asian crisis caused Japanese firms to reduce the flow of investment into the region (Table 22.2). Asia remained the second most important target of manufacturing FDI, however, well ahead of Europe, and indeed for a brief period (1994–6) Asia became the top destination of manufacturing FDI flows, exceeding even North America.

As a result of the continuing investment in foreign plants, the overseas production rations of Japan's manufacturing industry rose rapidly. As Table 22.3 shows, while the level of overseas production remained considerably

Table 22.3 Overseas production ratios of Japanese, US, and German manufacturing industries

|  | 1985 | 1990 | 1995 |
|---|---|---|---|
| Japan | 3.0% | 6.4% | 10.0% |
| United States | 16.6 | 24.1 | 25.2 |
| Germany | 16.6 | 17.9 | NA |

*Note* Calculated as sales of overseas manufacturing subsidiaries as a percentage of sales of domestic manufacturing industry.

*Source Jetro White Paper on Foreign Direct Investment, 1996,* Available *www.jetro.gv.jp/it/e/pub/whitepaper/invest1996/index.html/* Table 16; and *OECD Economic Surveys Japan, 1996* p. 30.

Table 22.4 Export ratios of some of Japan's leading manufacturing firms 1981–99
% of production from Japan factories that is exported

| Company | 1981 | 1991 | 1999 |
|---|---|---|---|
| Hitachi | 30 | 24 | 25 |
| Toshiba | 24 | 26 | 39 |
| NEC | 33 | 18 | 20 |
| Canon | 74 | 70 | 82 |
| Fujitsu | 15 | 14 | 22 |
| Fanuc | 46 | 31 | 52 |
| Nikon | 51 | 49 | 66 |
| Toyota | 43 | 35 | 56 |
| Nissan | 53 | 41 | 49 |

*Source Japan Company Handbook* (various years)

below that of the United States or Germany, the rate of increase was dramatic. However, despite the continuing emphasis on trade tensions and exchange rates as reducing the comparative advantage of Japan as a location for international production, in many of the companies most active in extending their production networks abroad, the export ratio of the Japanese factories fell very little, and in some cases even rose considerably (see Table 22.4).

The fact that even firms with extensive international production networks have such high proportions of their high-priced Japanese production go to foreign markets has, like the large Japanese trade surpluses that persisted through the 1990s, challenged analysts to understand and explain the organizational patterns of internationalization of Japanese business.

## 22.2 DIVERGENCE AND CONVERGENCE: ARE JAPANESE MNCs DIFFERENT?

Research on Japanese MNEs began in the 1970s, at a fairly early point in their internationalization. Over the following decades some of the patterns in strategy and organization observed in these early studies changed considerably; others persisted to a remarkable degree. How much Japanese MNEs differed from the US and European companies to whom they were constantly compared, how to explain these differences, and the likelihood of convergence in the future have been the questions that have dominated the research agenda for nearly three decades, and they show no signs yet of being definitively answered.

Explanations for the differences have centered on three sets of factors, whose weight and nature has shifted somewhat over time: period effects (system-level factors related to the timing of internationalization, including technology, international trade and investment regimes, relative position in the world order, and dominant management models and ideologies), home country effects (the influence of the company's country of origin, in terms both of the political economy and the patterns of strategy and organization institutionalized in the domestic business system), and life cycle effects (firm-level factors related to the length and range of a company's international experience). Period and home country effects are sources of imprinting, differentiating one country's MNEs from another's. They posit a long-term impact that changes only very slowly over time. Life cycle effects, in contrast, build on general models of MNE evolution and have tended to imply convergence across MNEs from different countries over time (see Chapter 13). How any analysis assesses the prospects for Japanese MNEs converging with Western patterns depends heavily on the combination of factors invoked to explain differences.

Serious academic studies of Japan's MNEs were stimulated by that landmark in MNE research, the Harvard Multinational Enterprise Project, which provided both a set of categories for analyzing MNE activities and a touchstone for comparison.[2] The 1970s studies identified a number of differences between the internationalization patterns of Japan's firms and those of the American firms that dominated contemporary models of the MNE. Some of these were discussed in the preceding section: the differences in industry, in destination (the strong orientation to developing countries, compared to the strong developed-country focus of US and European MNEs), and in the high salience of small and medium-sized firms and of the trading companies. In addition, all the studies of the 1970s noted the much higher use of joint ventures (JVs), particularly minority-owned JVs, compared to the strong tendency for US MNEs to set up wholly-owned subsidiaries, a marked preference for greenfield plants rather than acquisitions, and a strong tendency for a number of Japanese firms in an industry to enter a new location at much the same time—a clustering that often drew local resentment. The studies that looked more closely at the organizational features of Japanese operations abroad also identified the following traits:

(1) relatively loose control structures and a strong local market orientation, compared to the US MNEs' strong central control and globally integrated strategies (Tsurumi 1976: 4, 75–9);

(2) predominance of international divisional structure, versus the trend to global product divisions or matrix organizations in US MNEs (Yoshino 1976: 136; Yoshihara 1979);

(3) high proportions of expatriate managers, much higher than US or European firms (Yoshino 1976: 167–73; Tsurumi 1976: 250–7; Yoshihara 1979: 194–205; 258–9);

(4) strong proclivity for transferring Japanese management and production systems to foreign subsidiaries, which Tsurumi calls 'the creation of Little Japans' (1976: 194).

Explanations for the distinctive features of Japanese MNCs in the 1970s drew on a range of factors. One category of period effects, *late development factors*, was widely invoked to explain built on the fact that, despite the remarkable economic growth of the 1950s and 1960s, Japan in the 1970s was

---

[2] Of five major studies in the 1970s, only one (Yoshihara 1979) undertook to replicate the HMEP methodology, but both Yoshino (1976) and Tsurumi (1976) were at Harvard and were stimulated to look at Japanese MNEs by Ray Vernon's work. Kobayashi (1980), which although published in 1980 was based on fieldwork conducted throughout the 1970s, drew on many of the same measures and concepts. Ozawa (1979) provided an analysis based in political economy rather than management, and was the first in a line of research challenging the firm-level analysis of Japanese MNEs, arguing that what required observation was the internationalization of the Japanese system (defined by Ozawa as the double structure of advanced and labor-intensive industries). A more recent example in a similar vein is Hatch and Yamamura (1996).

still at a different level of development from that of the highly industrialized societies of North America and Western Europe. Therefore Japanese companies focused on markets that were at a still earlier stage of development, where they had a competitive advantage, and where industries squeezed for labor by the rapid changes in Japan's industrial structure could find affordable workers. Late development was therefore invoked to explain both the industry patterns and the destination of Japanese FDI, and also to explain patterns in mode (i.e. the willingness to use JVs). Japanese firms had fewer advanced technologies to protect than their Western counterparts, and were therefore more willing to share control—and also more willing, as late developers, to make concessions to local interests in exchange for market entry. Entering less-developed markets, they were also less likely to find local firms that provided good acquisition opportunities.

Kojima (1978) and Ozawa (1979), on the other hand, each working from a base in political economy rather than management, stressed system-level home country factors rather than period effects. They highlighted the role of the Japanese government (provider of tied aid to Japan's Asian neighbors, information on foreign markets, and export financing) and its close cooperation with business. They saw the trading companies less as facilitating the entry of small and medium-sized firms into foreign location (as did Tsurumi and Yoshino) than as playing a key role linking government, business, and foreign markets. This systemic cooperation encouraged Japanese firms to enter certain foreign locations, especially favoring Asia, and helped provide an infrastructure that allowed them to maintain their 'Japanese-ness'. For Ozawa, the internationalization of Japanese firms in the 1960s and 1970s represented an export of Japan's 'double structure' of labor-intensive traditional industries (which went abroad) and capital-intensive modern heavy industry (which stayed primarily at home). Framing the internationalization of Japanese firms as a system-level rather than a firm-level phenomenon—the export of the Japanese development model—continued to be a feature of political economy approaches to Japanese MNEs throughout the following decades (for more recent formulations, see Dicken 1992; Hatch and Yamamura 1996; Doremus et al. 1998).[3]

Home country effects at the firm level contended with life cycle effects in explanations of the organizational departures from US models. Yoshino (1976) and Tsurumi (1976) both attributed the high proportion of expatriate Japanese in key management positions and the tendency to transfer Japanese

---

[3] See e.g. Peter Dicken (1992: 77): 'Some of the distinctive features of Japanese transnational activity are explicable in terms of two factors which are virtually unique to the Japanese situation. The first is the close involvement of the national government, the second is the key role played by the giant Japanese trading companies.' And again (p. 176): 'Overseas investment by Japanese firms came to be seen as an integral part of Japanese industrial policy. It is not something that has "just happened"; it has been positively encouraged.'

organizational patterns into overseas subsidiaries to the management systems of Japanese companies at home, especially the decision-making systems (which emphasized intense face-to-face information-sharing and negoti-ation), the human resource management systems (lifetime employment and the cultivation of company loyalty), and the coordination and control systems (based on dense human networks), all of which meant that, in the prescient words of Mike Yoshino (1976: 173), 'The most serious problem of the Japanese management system in the multinational setting is that it cannot effectively integrate local nationals into the mainstream of management in the foreign subsidiaries.' Japan-based scholars, on the other hand, while recogniz-ing that home country factors played a part, tended to put more emphasis on life cycle factors—that is, on the relatively short experience of Japan's com-panies abroad (Yoshihara 1979; Kobayashi 1980; Enatsu 1984).

If life cycle factors were the primary cause of the distinctive patterns, then the differences between Japanese and Western MNE organizations would fade naturally over time, as Japan's companies expanded their international activ-ities. If home country factors were the primary cause, then convergence with Western models, if it occurred at all, would be slow and painful. In the 1970s, the American-based scholars had no doubt that such convergence was neces-sary: to quote Yoshino again, who eloquently sounded a theme that would echo repeatedly in the coming decades,

In order to undertake international expansion internationally, the Japanese must bring about basic changes in their management system—changes that will not be easy to achieve. And in the process, they may well sacrifice those elements that have made their system so effective. (Yoshino 1976: 178)

A survey by Kobayashi in the late 1970s, however, found that many Japanese managers envisioned another possibility: the development of an alternative model of a Japanese-style MNE: 52 per cent of the managers in 82 companies surveyed expected that Japan's international companies would in future develop a distinctive Japanese model, 35 per cent expected the development of a hybrid of Japanese and Western models, and only 6 per cent said Japanese MNEs would become like European and American MNEs (Kobaya-shi 1980).[4]

The view that Japanese MNEs were different because they were being observed at an earlier stage of their evolution than had been possible with US and European firms (an evolution that would naturally move them towards established MNE models over time) and the contrary view that they would evolve in distinctive ways could each find validation in Yoshihara's replication of the Harvard Multinational Enterprise Project methodology in the 1970s. Using the HMEP criteria, Yoshihara (1979) could find only

---

[4] 6 per cent gave no response to the question.

thirty-seven companies that fit the definition in 1975 (i.e. listed among Japan's 500 largest manufacturing firms, and with manufacturing subsidiaries in five or more countries with an ownership ratio of at least 25 per cent—or 15 per cent when two or more Japanese partners were involved). The largest industry represented was the textile industry (eight firms), followed by electrical equipment (covering consumer electronics and appliances) with seven firms, chemicals with six, and food products with five. These 'true MNEs' were outnumbered by another category of international firm not covered by the HMEP, which Yoshihara called 'export-oriented firms': forty-eight companies that had sales companies in five or more countries and an export ratio of over 20 per cent for the previous three years. The representation of industries in this category has a far more familiar ring today than the ordering of the 'true' Japanese MNEs of the day: electrical equipment (11), transport equipment (10), steel (9), and precision machinery (8).

In the early 1980s, it was these 'export-oriented firms' that took center-stage and provided an alternative to the dominant model of multinational enterprise. Their dramatic success in penetrating US and European markets from their production base in Japan led strategy experts such as Michael Porter to identify them as the epitome of global firms:

The purest global strategy is to concentrate as many activities as possible in one country, serve the world from this home base, and tightly coordinate those activities that must inherently be performed near the buyer. This is the pattern adopted by many Japanese firms in the 1960s and 1970s, such as Toyota. (Porter 1986a: 18)

This model of course was based not on Japanese subsidiaries in Asia, which followed a more conventional pattern, but on the US and European operations of these 'export-oriented companies'. Porter, like others who identified the Japanese as exemplars of global strategy (Hout et al. 1982; Gluck 1983; Hamel and Prahalad 1985; Bartlett 1986; Bartlett and Ghoshal 1989), saw period effects as the key to explaining this Japanese strategy and organization: changes in transportation and communications technologies and the postwar trade regime allowed Japanese companies to do what most US and European managers would have preferred to do but couldn't in earlier eras, and could do only with great difficult in the present, given their extensive investments in dispersed subsidiaries.[5] Japanese MNEs in the 1980s were also seen to excel in the use of international strategic alliances, which allowed them to build on a capability honed by their extensive networks of alliances in their domestic setting (Westney 1988).

[5] 'Japanese multinationals had the advantage of embarking on international strategies in the 1950s and 1960s when the imperatives for a global approach to strategy were beginning to accelerate, but without the legacy of past international investments and modes of behavior.' (Porter 1986b: 45)

The 1985 strengthening of the yen revealed the risks of such global strategies, however, and as Japan's 'global' companies scrambled to expand production abroad, they ceased to be lauded as exemplars of a bold new model of the MNE (although the late-1980s wave of investment abroad intensified general views of Japanese companies as major competitive threats to US and European firms and as exemplars of management best practice in a number of domains). As the transnational model of a dispersed network of capable, interdependent subsidiaries (Bartlett 1986; Hedlund 1986; Bartlett and Ghoshal 1989) became increasingly popular among both international business researchers and MNE managers in the late 1980s and the 1990s, Japanese managers adopted much of its rhetoric, and tried to increase the amount of local value added in their American and European subsidiaries, often adding R&D centers and even setting up regional headquarters to provide an umbrella organization for their numerous local sales and manufacturing subsidiaries (Okumura 1989a, 1989b; Iwai 1991; Ishii 1992).

The companies that faced these challenges differed in significant ways from the Japanese MNEs of the 1970s. For one thing, there were far more of them: Yoshihara found in a replication of his earlier study that the number of 'true' Japanese MNEs had grown from thirty-seven in 1974 to 149 by 1994 (Yoshihara 1996). For another, they had far more extensive international operations (from an average in 1974 of eleven overseas affiliates to twenty-six), and those affiliates were far less likely to be joint ventures, especially in North America, where 64 per cent of affiliates were wholly-owned, and Europe, with 57 per cent (Yoshihara 1996: 5–6). This suggested strongly that the earlier patterns of ownership were shaped by a combination of host country effects and life cycle effects, and that in terms of ownership structure, Japanese MNEs were indeed becoming more similar to MNEs from other advanced countries.

But some of the patterns of the 1970s persisted, particularly the high proportion of expatriate managers (Bartlett and Yoshihara 1988; Okumura 1989b; Lifson 1992) and the propensity to try to transfer home country patterns of organization abroad. Other patterns reinforced the model of the Japanese MNE as distinctively home-country-driven. Even at the end of the 1990s, after a decade of expanding their R&D networks abroad, Japanese MNEs did far less innovation abroad than US and European MNEs.[6] In Asia, the locally focused, loosely controlled subsidiaries were a thing of the past, replaced by production networks that were integrated across the region and carefully coordinated from Japan (Hatch and Yamamura 1996). Japan continued to be the locus of much of the high value-added manufacturing in

---

[6] Discussing Cantwell and Harding's 1997 study of the research locations revealed in US-filed patents, Dunning summarizes their findings as follows: 'Between 1991 and 1995, 11 per cent of the US registered patents of the world's largest firms were attributable to research locations outside the home country of the parent company. Only in the case of Japan was there not a rise in the proportion of patents registered by foreign affiliates since the early 1970s.' (Dunning 1998: 51).

its MNEs, as well as of the R&D for its worldwide businesses. The strong cross-border functional networks (linking a 'sister' plant in Japan to siblings in other countries, and R&D centers abroad to the main R&D organizations in Japan) made for home-country centered communication and coordination linkages. The regional headquarters tended to be staffed by and controlled from the parent in Japan. In short, Japanese MNEs continued to exemplify a more home-country-centric model of the MNE than their US or European counterparts.

The explanations for the persistence of this model involved elaborations of the sets of factors invoked in the 1970s. Advocates of the life cycle approach could point to the fact that the major expansion of Japan's MNEs took place after 1985, relatively recently compared to US and European internationalization (see for example Campbell 1994). Moreover, Japanese MNEs continued to expand abroad by building up the capabilities of established subsidiaries (Song 1998), an approach that favored a very gradual diminution of central control, rather than by acquiring well-established firms, the mode favored by many European and US MNEs and one that lent itself to more transnational strategies. In this view, the home-country-centered model would inevitably give way to more 'integrated network' systems over time.

On the other hand, advocates of the importance of period effects as conducive to the development of distinctive organizational models could point to the fact that the world economic regime and the technological changes of the late 1980s and the 1990s, when Japanese internationalization accelerated, actually made possible much more rapid and efficient 'hub-and-spoke' models of the sort epitomized by the Japanese. Indeed, in the 1990s many US firms strengthened global product structures and 'centers of excellence' in R&D, suggesting that the communication and information technological revolution whose initial stages in the early 1980s had been seen as opening the way for more heterarchical and horizontal organizational structures had in fact, as they unfolded in the 1990s, increased the potential for effective and efficient central coordination.

Home country effects loomed much larger than period effects, however, in explanations of the persistence of the home-country-centered MNE model. To the factors cited in the 1970s—the decision-making and human resource management systems, the language problems, ethnocentrism—the extensive research on Japanese companies in the 1980s and 1990s added another: the vertical, centralized nature of organizational networks even within Japan itself. One factory was often designated as the lead factory even for the domestic production network, and organizational networks both within the company and across its boundaries tended to be strongly hierarchical (e.g. Fruin 1997).

However, in the past few years the case of Japan has reminded us that home country factors, although slow to change, are far from static. The Japanese business system is changing at home, as the human resource management systems and vertical networks of Japan's leading companies are undergoing experimentation and modification. Even the accounting systems are changing, from the unconsolidated basis (which tended to encourage under-reporting of profits abroad in order to bolster the performance of the home company) to a consolidated basis. Whether the dynamics of change in Japan will move MNEs towards their US and European counterparts or produce the next generation of the home-country-centered model will be a topic to challenge researchers for at least the next decade.

One aspect of Japan's home-country-centered MNE model—the propensity to transfer home country organizational patterns to foreign subsidiaries—was arguably the most widely studied aspect of the organization of multinational enterprise in the 1980s and the 1990s, and although international business scholars certainly played a significant role, research on the topic involved scholars from a wide range of social science disciplines and management fields, many of whom had never before manifested an interest in the MNE. The efforts of Japanese manufacturing companies to transfer their production systems first to the US and then to Europe (predominantly the UK)—countries where labor markets, employment systems, and the social context more generally differed so greatly from those of Japan—was intensively studied by both Japanese and Western scholars. The 'auto transplants'—the very term used suggests the perceived uniqueness of the endeavor—draw most of the attention, especially in the United States, but the electronics plants also attracted considerable research. Initial questions about whether it was possible to transfer Japanese patterns at all soon gave way to increasingly detailed analyses of how the patterns replicated or departed from the Japanese systems on which they were based (for a good recent compendium of empirical research, see Liker *et al.* 1999). Some studies focused primarily on the outcomes, such as those of Abo's research group, which conducted careful and detailed analyses of 'application vs. adaptation' in Japanese-owned auto, semiconductor, and electronics plants in the United States (Abo 1994) and Taiwan and Korea (Itagaki 1997). Others focused more on the processes by which adaptation occurred (e.g. Sumi 1998; Brannen *et al.* 1999).

The studies agreed in finding systematic variations in the degree of transfer across industries (greater in autos, much less in electronics), although not in explaining the differences. One of the key factors explaining variation across industries was strategic intent: efforts at transfer were much greater in industries where the organizational patterns of the production system were viewed by Japanese managers as key to competitive advantage, and the human resource systems were seen as important to the production system. Another factor put forward was location: the electronics plants tended to be located in California, whereas most of the auto firms carefully chose mid-Western, non-industrial locations where there were few immediately accessible competing models of factory organization (Sumi 1998). But another factor was surely the legitimacy of the Japanese patterns in local eyes, which was in turn linked both to critical mass and to competitive dominance: Japan's auto firms were seen in the 1980s as competitively superior to America's 'Big Three', embodying the 'next generation' of post-Fordist production, whereas in the much more variegated, multi-player fields of electronics, Japanese were far less dominant and were in less innovative sectors of the industry.

One of the puzzles of this body of work for IB is why so much research has been devoted to the transfer of home country organizational patterns to subsidiaries in the case of the Japanese transplants and so little to this issue in non-Japanese MNEs. A host of plausible explanations comes to mind—the competitive advantage of MNEs was historically assumed to be product technology rather than organizational systems; the factory-centered patterns of the Japanese production system were more readily accessible to researchers than the management-based distinctive features of Western MNEs; the differences in organizational systems and social context between Japan and the United States and the UK drew attention because they seemed to dwarf any previous differences between developed nations that were the locus of most MNE activity. Nevertheless, it is somewhat embarrassing that there was so little research in IB on the cross-border transfer of organizational systems that could serve as a touchstone for the research on the Japanese transplants, and we can surely expect that the topic will have a higher salience in IB research in the future.

There are at least two other issues raised by the internationalization of Japanese firms that ought to become more central to the IB field in the decades to come. One is posed by the continued insistence by both Western and Japanese IB scholars that Japanese MNEs would have to change at home if they were to internationalize successfully, a theme sounded from the 1970s to the present day. Why should this be uniquely true of Japanese companies? Has the IB field not focused somewhat too heavily on what firms have done abroad, and too little on what changes they were making as a result at home? Since the classic works of the 1970s on the change of formal organizational structure (see Chapter 13), the management of subsidiaries has attracted far more attention than the changes in the home country organization that have undoubtedly accompanied the expansion of international activity and changes in its nature. How does the home country R&D organization change as R&D expands abroad, for example, or the information networks in a global business unit as it extends its international reach? There has been some interesting normative work in this area (e.g. Bartlett and Ghoshal 1989, 1996) but relatively little empirical research.

Finally, the Japanese case has raised and continues to raise questions about the strong proclivity of the IB field for convergence theories of the MNE (an issue discussed in more detail in Chapter 13). Japanese MNEs constitute the first significant population of non-Western MNEs to participate in the global economy, but they are unlikely to be the last. The relative salience of period effects and home country effects versus the life cycle effects emphasized by established models of the MNE is likely to be an important area for theory and research in the field in the future.

# 22.3 JAPAN AS A HOST COUNTRY FOR MNEs

Research on FDI into Japan and the operations of foreign-affiliated companies there has had much less impact on the international business field than research on Japanese MNCs, largely because the small amount of inward FDI and the nature of foreign operations there have posed relatively few problems for the established paradigms in the field (see for example Dunning 1996). But the mismatch between the scale of Japanese FDI abroad and FDI into Japan has been a serious public policy issue for the United States for two decades, and the challenges of doing business in Japan have provided material for IB courses for nearly as long. No discussion of Japan and the IB field would be complete without some attention to Japan as a host country for FDI.

Foreign business operations in Japan date back to the sixteenth century, when traders from Portugal, Holland, and England established outposts there as part of their worldwide trading networks (Boxer 1986; Goodman 1986; Van de Velde and Bachofer 1992; Weinstein 1996). These were eliminated when the Tokugawa Shogunate closed the country in the 1630s, restricting Western contacts to a small settlement of Dutch traders in Nagasaki, isolated on a small artificial island and allowed only one shipment into and out of Japan each year. The arrival of Commodore Perry in 1853 and the subsequent negotiations with Western governments resulted in Japan's opening once again to foreign trade and investment, with the designation of six 'treaty ports' where Westerners could establish operations subject only to the laws of their own countries (Hoare 1994). The 'unequal treaties' imposed in the 1850s took control of tariffs out of Japanese hands, setting standard low tariff rates for imported goods and making it virtually impossible for the Japanese authorities to protect their own industries. Japan gradually regained some of its power to regulate foreign interactions, but it was not until the end of the nineteenth century that the last elements of the unequal treaties were formally eliminated and Japan regained full control of the terms of its involvement in the world economy. Japanese discussions of foreign trade and investment have drawn metaphors and terminology from this history ever since, including *sakoku* (the policy of closing the country) and *kuro-fune* (the 'Black Ships' of Commodore Perry that forced Japan at gunpoint to allow foreigners into its markets, a metaphor for a foreign market invasion).

In the prewar era, despite the forbidding challenges of distance and language and the legacy of the nineteenth century restrictions on foreign investment, Western firms entered Japan in significant numbers. By 1931, according to a Japanese government count, there were fifty-nine foreign-affiliated firms in Japan: thirteen wholly owned and managed by foreigners; ten majority-owned and managed by foreigners; and thirty-six joint ventures managed by Japanese (Yamamura 1986). Kozo Yamamura (1986) has argued that the technical capabilities transferred to Japan by firms like Ford, GM, RCA, and Western Electric ironically helped to make feasible the growing autarky of Japan's military government in the 1930s, which forced foreign-affiliated companies to divest their ownership stakes. World War II of course completed Japan's isolation from Western trade and investment.

The postwar Occupation authorities, sharing the Japanese government's concern with the revival of Japanese industry, did little to open Japan's economy to foreign firms. Through the Occupation and well into the 1960s, the stringent controls on outward FDI (discussed in section 1 above) were more than matched by controls on inward investment. Foreign firms wanting to set up operations in Japan had to find a Japanese joint venture partner or set up a 'yen' company that was not allowed to repatriate profits. The few exceptions (such as IBM and Texas Instruments) were painstakingly negotiated, and usually were granted in exchange for licensing technology to their Japanese competitors to 'level the playing field' (for more detailed analysis that focuses on the US–Japan relationship, see Mason 1992).

However, the same GATT requirements that led the government to remove restrictions on outward FDI in the late 1960s operated with equal force on the restrictions on inward investment. Anxiety about the possibility of Western 'black ships' invading the Japanese market by acquisition led the government to encourage firms to strengthen their cross-shareholding networks in the late 1960s and early 1970s in advance of the removal of investment restrictions, as a protection against takeovers. However, perhaps because of the macro-economic uncertainties stemming from the Oil Shocks of the 1970s, the liberalization of inward FDI was not followed by a rush of Western companies into Japan. By 1980, Japan had a relatively open investment regime, with no formal restrictions on ownership, and the effects can be seen in the age structure of foreign-affiliated companies at the close of the 1990s (shown in Table 22.5): two-thirds of the subsidiaries operating in 1998 had been founded after 1980.

**Table 22.5  Age structure of foreign companies' affliates in Japan 1999 (Total number of foreign-affiliated companies listed = 3,320)**

| Year of establishment | % of total |
| --- | --- |
| Before 1970 | 14.7% |
| 1971–5 | 9.7 |
| 1976–80 | 8.5 |
| 1981–5 | 13.8 |
| 1986–90 | 19.9 |
| 1991–5 | 14.9 |
| 1996–9 | 18.5 |

*Source* Toyo Keizai and Dun and Bradstreet (eds.), 2000

Inward FDI was dominated by American companies (Table 22.6). No other single country came close to matching the volume of US investment, although European investment overall was almost as high as that of the US.

The efforts of foreign companies to establish themselves in Japan provided fodder for the International Business courses of the 1980s and early 1990s, as quintessential examples of the necessity of local adaptation. Kentucky Fried Chicken and McDonald's provided examples of the value of working with strong local partners, IBM Japan and Coca-Cola of the contributions made by building a strong local management team and innovating in response to local market needs; Fuji-Xerox and Yokogawa Hewlett-Packard of the advantages of having a strong organizational presence in an innovation center (both subsidiaries played a role in their quality control programmes of their parent companies in the 1980s and early 1990s). There were a number of success stories: foreign-affiliated enterprises were the most profitable companies in Japan, and especially after the yen appreciation of the mid-1980s they made significant contributions to the worldwide profits of their parent organizations (Christopher 1986; Huddleston 1990).

But inward FDI, although it continued to grow, was a steadily diminishing fraction of Japan's outward FDI, as the latter grew at a much greater pace. This made Japan increasingly an outlier among the nations who accounted for much of the world's outward FDI (see Table 22.7).

This was especially resented by the United States, Japan's major trading partner and the target of much of Japanese companies' expansion abroad.

## Table 22.6  Country of origin of foreign direct investment into Japan 1999

| | Percentage of total investment |
|---|---|
| North America | 49.8% |
| (United States) | (47.5%) |
| Europe | 40.2% |
| (Germany) | (10.2%) |
| (UK) | (8.2%) |
| (France) | (6.5%) |
| Asia | 8.6% |
| Other | 1.5% |
| TOTAL | 100.1% |

*Source* Toyo Keizai and Dun and Bradstreet (eds.), 2000

## Table 22.7  Inward FDI stock as a percentage of outward FDI stock, selected countries

| | 1973 | 1980 | 1990 |
|---|---|---|---|
| Japan | 15.5% | 8.1% | 5.9% |
| United States | 20.3 | 37.1 | 95.4 |
| UK | 87.7 | 78.1 | 84.0 |
| Germany | 149.2 | 84.9 | 60.2 |

*Source* Calculated from data in John H. Dunning (1996), 62

The US ratio of inward to outward investment was moving in a very different direction, as it changed from being the world's major provider of FDI to the largest target of inward investment, and this difference in trends fueled American resentment of Japanese patterns. The resentment was increased by growing recognition of the fact that trade and investment were not substitutes for each other but were in fact complementary: in the early 1990s, foreign-affiliated companies in Japan accounted for less than 3 per cent of Japan's GDP but 17 per cent of its imports (Jordan 1996: 196).

From the 1980s on, the Japanese were able to argue convincingly that there were few formal barriers to inward FDI, but Japan's dismantling of formal restrictions on imports and inward investment had made little apparent difference to the overall imbalance. Why then did inward FDI continue to be so low? The principal cause was that Japan was widely perceived to be a difficult business environment for foreign firms, for a number of reasons. As Mark Mason (1992) points out, the Japanese government had historically cooperated with industry to restrain foreign competition until Japan's companies were technologically competitive, and by the 1980s any potential foreign entrant faced the prospect of strong competitive reaction from well-established local incumbents. Building a customer base took time and resources: in consumer markets, because of the need to establish relationships in the complex, multi-layered distribution network, and in industrial markets, because of the prevalence of long-established supplier relationships, especially in the vertical *keiretsu* system, and high requirements for reliability of delivery and (often) customization. Hiring qualified staff was an especially difficult challenge in Japan, where the prestige and stability of employment in the large Japanese corporations meant that few Japanese were willing to take the risk of joining a foreign subsidiary, in which organization and strategy might change at the whim of a distant head office. And from the mid-1980s on, the strong yen that made established foreign affiliates in Japan so profitable also made new entry and expansion seem very expensive to a foreign parent. In many countries, the difficulties of building a local presence could be short-circuited by the acquisition of a capable local company. But in Japan, complex cross-shareholding patterns and shareholding by banks and other financial institutions meant that it was almost impossible for a foreign company to acquire a significant stake in any but seriously troubled companies—and often even they resisted any attempts at a takeover.

As Japanese often pointed out, all these problems except the strong yen also faced new Japanese entrants to the market, and therefore Japan was not discriminating against foreign firms. However, as Japanese investment in the United States ballooned in the late 1980s, US industry put pressure on the American government to find some way to 'level the playing field', leading the Bush administration to launch in 1989 an unprecedented policy effort—the Structural Impediments Initiative, which identified features of Japan's business system that made it difficult for foreign companies to penetrate the Japanese market and demanded that the Japanese government take steps to change these. The SSI identified six categories of impediments: Japanese patterns of savings and investment (high personal savings rates that reduced consumption, and low public investment); land use patterns that, among other problems, kept real estate prices unnecessarily high;

complex distribution systems; exclusionary business practices; the *keiretsu* system; and price mechanisms, including government regulation of the domestic market and weak enforcement of the anti-monopoly laws (Hsu 1994: 341–5). The irony of the Americans simultaneously demanding that Japan's government de-regulate and reduce its role in the economy and that it force massive changes in the way business was organized in Japan (including the enforcement of quotas to raise imports) was not lost on either Japanese or Western critics of the initiative. The Japanese responded with an extensive list of American structural impediments to trade and investment (such as the American legal system), and extended negotiations produced little result.

The pressures were eased by the Japanese recession of the 1990s. This made Japan a less attractive market, and American companies that had been demanding that the US government improve access to Japan turned their attention elsewhere. In addition, Japan's rapid transformation from economic juggernaut to seriously troubled economy meant that US policy-makers changed their view of the threat that Japan posed to the world trading system from one of dominance to one of collapse. American policy-makers continued to urge de-regulation on the Japanese, but more as a vehicle for economic recovery than as a window for US companies to move into Japanese markets.

What US pressure could not do, however, the lengthy recession and the massive problems of the financial sector have begun to do. The scale of acquisitions in Japan has increased enormously, as Japan's leading companies are shedding businesses in their efforts to reduce debt, and as capable but debt-saddled companies seek desperately for a means of survival. Carrier International has been able to acquire Toshiba's air conditioning business, for example; Ford has expanded its stake in Mazda to give it effective control of the company; Renault has bought into Nissan. Even more important in the long run, perhaps, has been the large-scale entry of US firms into financial services: Merrill-Lynch has acquired many of the offices and personnel of the bankrupt Yamaichi Securities, GE Capital has bought into a range of leasing businesses and established new businesses, and the Travelers Insurance acquisition of one of Japan's major insurance companies was on a scale that pushed the 1997 value of foreign acquisitions to an unprecedented level.

As the number of US financial service firms operating on a significant scale in Japan increases, it is quite possible that they will have a catalytic effect on Japanese companies comparable to that of the Japanese transplants on American manufacturing in the 1990s. As in that case, the result will not be the widespread 'cloning' of the foreign-based models by local firms, but rather a complex learning process born of intensified competition and the presence of alternative modes of organization and management that have demonstrably succeeded in the local environment. And some of the research issues raised by the Japanese transplants around the transfer and adaptation of organizational patterns in the cross-border transfer of organizational capabilities may well make the next generation of foreign firms in Japan a much more central locus of research in international business.

## References

ABO, TETSUO (1989). 'The Emergence of Japanese Multinational Enterprises and the Theory of Foreign Direct Investment', in K. Shibagaki, M. Trevor, and T. Abo (eds.), *Japanese and European Management: Their International Adaptability.* Tokyo: University of Tokyo Press.

—— (ed.) (1994). *Hybrid Factory: The Japanese Production System in the United States.* New York: Oxford University Press.

ADLER, PAUL S. (1999). 'Hybridization: Human Resource Management at Two Toyota Transplants', in Jeffrey K. Liker, W. Mark Fruin, and Paul S. Adler (eds.), *Remade in America: Transplanting and Transforming Japanese Management Systems.* New York: Oxford University Press, 75–116.

BARTLETT, C. A. (1986). 'Building and Managing the Transnational: The New Organizational Challenge', in M. E. Porter (ed.), *Competition in Global Industries.* Boston, Mass.: Harvard Business School Press, 367–404.

—— and GHOSHAL, S. (1989). *Managing Across Borders: The Transnational Solution.* Boston, Mass.: Harvard Business School Press.

—— —— (1990). 'Managing Innovation in the Transnational Corporation', in C. A. Bartlett, Y. Doz, and G. Hedlund (eds.), *Managing the Global Firm.* London: Routledge.

—— and YOSHIHARA, H. (1988). 'New Challenges for Japanese Multinationals: Is Organization Adaptation their Achilles Heel?', *Human Resource Management,* 27(1), 19–43.

BEAMISH, PAUL W., DELIOS, ANDREW, and LeCRAW, DONALD J. (1997). *Japanese Multinationals in the Global Economy.* Cheltenham: Edward Elgar.

BEECHLER, SCHON, and BIRD, ALLAN (eds.) (1999). *Japanese Multinationals Abroad: Individual and Organizational Learning.* New York: Oxford University Press.

BRADLEY, G. E., and BURSK, E. C. (1972). 'Multinationalism and the 29th Day', *Harvard Business Review,* 50(1), 37–47.

BRANNEN, MARY YOKO, LIKER, JEFFREY K., and FRUIN, W. MARK, 'Recontextualization and Factory-to-Factory Knowledge Transfer from Japan to the United States: The Case of NSK', in Jeffrey K. Liker, W. Mark Fruin, and Paul S. Adler (eds.), *Remade in America: Transplanting and Transforming Japanese Management Systems.* New York: Oxford University Press, 117–53.

CAMPBELL, N. (1994). 'Introduction', in N. Campbell and F. Burton (eds.), *Japanese Multinationals: Strategies and Management in the Global Kaisha.* London: Routledge, 1–8.

CHRISTOPHER, ROBERT (1986). *Second to None.* Tokyo: Charles Tuttle.

DeNero, H. (1990). 'Creating the "Hyphenated" Corporation', *McKinsey Quarterly* (4), 153–73.

Dore, R. P. (1987). *Taking Japan Seriously*. London: Athlone Press.

Doremus, Paul N., Keller, William W., Pauly, Louis W., and Reich, Simon (1998). *The Myth of the Global Corporation*. Princeton: Princeton University Press.

Dower, John W. (1999). *Embracing Defeat: Japan in the Wake of World War II*. New York: W. W. Norton/The New Press.

Dunning, John H. (1996). 'Explaining Foreign Direct Investment in Japan: Some Theoretical Insights', in Masaru Yoshitomi and Edward M. Graham (eds.), *Foreign Direct Investment in Japan*. Cheltenham: Edward Elgar, 8–63.

—— (1998). 'Location and the Multinational Enterprise: A Neglected Factor?', *Journal of International Business Studies*, 21(1), 45–66.

Duus, Peter (1989). 'Zaikabo: Japanese Cotton Mills in China 1895–1937', in Peter Duus, Ramon H. Myers, and Mark R. Peattie (eds.), *The Japanese Informal Empire in China 1895–1935*. Princeton: Princeton University Press, 65–100.

Enatsu, Kenichi (1984). *Takokuseki Kigyo Yoron*. Tokyo: Bunshindo.

Froot, Kenneth A. (1989) 'Japanese Foreign Direct Investment', NBER working paper no. 3737.

Gelsanliter, David (1990). *Jump Start: Japan Comes to the Heartland*. New York: Farrar, Straus, Giroux.

Gluck, F. (1983). 'Global Competition in the 1980s', *Journal of Business Strategy*, 3(4), 22–7.

Hamel, G., and Prahalad, C. K. (1985). 'Do You Really Have a Global Strategy?', *Harvard Business Review* (5), 139–48.

Hatch, Walter, and Yamamura, Kozo (1996). *Asia in Japan's Embrace*. Cambridge: Cambridge University Press.

Hoare, J. E. (1994). *Japan's Treaty Ports and Foreign Settlements: The Uninvited Guests 1858–1899*. Folkestone: Japan Library.

Hout, T., Porter, M. E., and Rudden, E. (1982). 'How Global Companies Win Out', *Harvard Business Review*, 60(5), 98–108.

Hsu, Robert C. (1994). *The MIT Encyclopedia of the Japanese Economy*. Cambridge, Mass.: MIT Press.

Huddlestone, Jackson N., Jr. (1990). *Gaijin Kaisha: Running a Foreign Business in Japan*. Tokyo: Charles Tuttle.

Ishii, Masashi (1992). *Nihon Kigyo no Kaigai Jigyo Tenkai*. Tokyo: Chuo Koronsha.

Itagaki, Hiroshi (1997). 'Higashi Ajia Nikkei Kojo no Bunseki Shikaku', in Itagaki Hiroshi (ed.), *Nihonteki Keiei. Seisan Shisutemu to Higashi Ajia*. Tokyo: Mineruba Shobo, 1–24.

Itami, Hiroyuki (1997). 'International Development of Manufacturing', in Japan Commission on Industrial Performance (ed.), *Made in Japan: Revitalizing Japanese Manufacturing for Economic Growth*. Cambridge, Mass: MIT Press, 335–58.

Iwai, Masakazu (1991). *Toshiba no 'Guro-baruka' Senryaku*. Tokyo: Diamond-sha.

Kobayashi, Koji (1989). *Koso to Ketsudaku: My Years with NEC Corporation*. Tokyo: Diamond-sha.

Kobayashi, Noritake (1980). *Nihon no Takokuseki Kigyo*. Tokyo: Chuo Koronsha.

Kojima, K. (1978). *Japanese Foreign Direct Investment*. Tokyo: Charles E. Tuttle.

KUDO, AKIRA (1989). 'Kao Corporation's Direct Investment and Adaptation in Europe', in Kazuo Shibayaki, Malcolm Trevor, and Tetsuo Abo (eds.), *Japanese and European Management: Their International Adaptability*. Tokyo: University of Tokyo Press, 107–17.

LIFSON, T. B. (1992). 'The Managerial Integration of Japanese Business in America', in S. Kumon and H. Rosovsky (eds.), *The Political Economy of Japan Vol. 3: Cultural and Social Dynamics*. Stanford: Stanford University Press, 231–66.

LIKER, JEFFREY K., FRUIN, W. MARK, and ADLER, PAUL S. (eds.) (1999). *Remade in America: Transplanting and Transforming Japanese Management Systems*. New York: Oxford University Press.

MASON, MARK (1992). *American Multinationals and Japan: The Political Economy of Japanese Capital Controls 1899–1980*. Cambridge, Mass.: Harvard University Press.

—— (1999). 'The Origins and Evolution of Japanese Direct Investment in East Asia', in Dennis J. Encarnation (ed.), *Japanese Multinationals in Asia*. New York: Oxford University Press, 17–45.

OKUMURA, A. (1989a). 'The Globalization of Japanese Companies', in K. Shibayaki, M. Trevor, and T. Abo (eds.), *Japanese and European Management: Their International Adaptability*. Tokyo: University of Tokyo Press, 31–40.

—— (1989b). 'Guro-barize-shon to Nihonteki Keiei no Shinka', in A. Okumura and M. Kato (eds.), *Guro-baru Kiko to Kaigai Shinshutsu Butai: Takokuseki Kigyo to Kokusai Soshiki*. Vol. 15. Tokyo: Tokyo Daiichi Hoki Shuppan KK, 318–31.

OZAWA, T. (1979). *Multinationalism, Japanese Style*. Princeton: Princeton University Press.

PEARCE, ROBERT (1997). *Global Competition and Technology: Essays in the Creation and Application of Knowledge by Multinationals*. Houndmills: Macmillan Press.

PEMPEL, T. J. (1998). *Regime Shift: Comparative Dynamics of the Japanese Political Economy*. Ithaca: Cornell University Press.

PORTER, M. E. (1986a). 'Changing Patterns of International Competition', *California Management Review*, 28(2), 9–40.

—— (1986b). 'Competition in Global Industries: A Conceptual Framework', in Michael E. Porter (ed.), *Competition in Global Industries*. Boston, Mass: Harvard Business School Press, 15–60.

SONG, JAEYONG (1998). *Firm Capabilities, Technology Ladders, and Evolution of Japanese Production Networks in East Asia*. Ph. D. dissertation, Department of Management, The Wharton School of the University of Pennsylvania.

SUMI, ATSUSHI (1998). *Japanese Industrial Transplants in the United States: Organizational Practices and Relations of Power*. New York: Garland Publishing Company.

TREVOR, M. (1983). *Japan's Reluctant Multinationals*. London: Pinter.

TSURU, SHIGETO (1993). *Japan's Capitalism: Creative Defeat and Beyond*. Cambridge: Cambridge University Press.

TSURUMI, Y. (1976). *The Japanese are Coming: A Multinational Interaction of Firms and Politics*. Cambridge, Mass.: Ballinger Publishing.

VAN DER VELDE, PAUL, and BACHOFER, RUDOLF (1992). *The Deshima Diaries: Marginalia 1700–1740*. Tokyo: The Japan–Netherlands Institute.

WEINSTEIN, DAVID (1996). 'Structural Impediments to Investment in Japan: What Have we Learned Over the Last 450 Years?', in Masaru Yoshitomi and Edward M.

Graham (eds.), *Foreign Direct Investment in Japan*. Cheltenham: Edward Elgar, 136–72.

WESTNEY, D. E. (1988). 'Domestic and International Learning Curves in Managing International Competitive Strategies', in Farok Contractor and Peter Lorange (eds.), *Cooperative Strategies in International Business*. Lexington, Mass.: Lexington Books.

WILKINS, M. (1970). *The Emergence of Multinational Enterprise: American Business Abroad from the Colonial Era to 1914*. Cambridge, Mass.: Harvard University Press.

—— (1994). 'Epilogue: More than One Hundred Years: A Historical Overview of Japanese Direct Investment in the United States', in Tetsuo Abo (ed.), *Hybrid Factory: The Japanese Production System in the United States*. New York: Oxford University Press, 257–96.

WOLF, MARVIN J. (1983). *The Japanese Conspiracy: Their Plot to Dominate Industry World-wide, and How to Deal With it*. New York: Empire Books.

YAMAMURA, KOZO (1986). 'Japan's Deus ex Machina: Western Technology in the 1920s', *Journal of Japanese Studies*, 12(1), 65–94.

YOSHIHARA, H. (1979). *Takokuseki Kigyo Ron*. Tokyo: Hakuto Shobo.

—— (1996) 'Japanese Multinationals (Manufacturing)', Discussion Paper series no. 68, Research Institute for Economics and Business Administration, Kobe University, Japan.

YOSHINO, M. Y. (1968). *Japan's Managerial System: Tradition and Innovation*. Cambridge, Mass.: MIT Press.

—— (1976). *Japan's Multinational Enterprises*. Cambridge, Mass.: Harvard University Press.

CHAPTER 23

# INTERNATIONAL BUSINESS IN LATIN AMERICA

ROBERT GROSSE

## 23.1 INTRODUCTION AND HISTORICAL CONTEXT

THIS chapter examines international business activity in Latin America, from Mexico in the north to Argentina and Chile in the south. The structure of this chapter follows a fairly standard format of examining first the historical context in which international business takes place in Latin America, followed by subcategories of analysis by issue, and to a limited extent by industry sector and by country. The overarching goal is to identify and clarify four issues that are central to international business in Latin America at the start of the twenty-first century. They are:

1. The *government/business relationship* and its great significance in Latin America relative to that in the US. The reform of the government sector and the institutionalization of democracy have greatly affected the IB environment in Latin America. Likewise, the relationship of these countries to the US is key to international business in the region.

I would like to thank To Nhu Dao for her excellent research assistance on this project.

2. The impact of *subregional integration schemes* on competition in the region, including that between local and multinational firms. The question is: what kind of regional economic integration can best support economic development?

3. *Financial flows* into the region and policies to avoid *financial crises*. Financial flows have been dominated by foreign direct investment in the 1990s, but this has not precluded recurring episodes of financial crisis in the region.

4. The *entry and operation of foreign MNEs*, and the *reaction of local firms to the onslaught of MNEs* from the US, Europe, and elsewhere. At the same time, local firms are expanding internationally, demonstrating new capabilities that enable these firms to compete.

An added theme is considered briefly as well, though it falls out of the mainstream of the international business literature:

5. The relation of the *informal economy* to international business in the region. This part of the economy, constituting easily more than 1/3 of the total economy in many countries, undoubtedly has an impact on the international business conducted there.

Let us begin with a look at some history of international business in the region. Until the end of the eighteenth century, all of the countries in the region were colonies of European powers, mostly Spain, and in Brazil's case, Portugal. The United States gained independence first in the hemisphere, separating from England in 1783. The Latin American colonies followed into nationhood in the early 1800s. International business in the colonial period was tightly tied to the home country, and in that sense was not even 'international' if we consider colonies part of the home country. So, to avoid debate over that issue, and since little data is available to discuss in the period before 1800, the discussion is limited to the post-independence period.

In Latin American economies international business has played a major role since the creation of independent nations, when most of the region broke away from Spain between 1810 and 1825 (Brazil gained independence from Portugal in 1822). Indeed, probably the first major type of international business in the region was financing of Latin American governments for the wars of independence during 1810–25. Most of this debt was in the form of bonds issued in the London market—and most of it defaulted during the crash of 1825–6 in Europe[1] (not wholly unlike the situation in the 1980s, except for the form of the debt) (Marichal 1989).

Even before the move to independence, the Latin American colonies of Spain and Portugal were heavily involved in international business in the form of exchange of raw materials, such as gold and silver exported from

---

[1] This situation is described in Marichal (1989: 12–67).

## Table 23.1  Long-term capital flows into Latin America in the 1800s

| Source and date | Long-term bond issues | Foreign direct investment |
| --- | --- | --- |
| 1822–5<br>United Kingdom | £21 million by London banks for various Latin American governments | More than 40 joint-stock companies formed to extract raw materials in the region |
| 1825<br>France | FF30 million issued by the government of Haiti on the Paris Stock Exchange (Bourse) | |
| 1826–50<br>United Kingdom | £18 million by London banks for various Latin American governments | No new joint-stock Wrms founded to operate in Latin America |
| 1851–80<br>United Kingdom | £130 million by London banks for various Latin American governments | Railways built in several countries, including Peru and Brazil |
| 1870–9<br>France (ann. avg.) | FF1.5 billion issued by various Latin American governments on Paris Bourse | FF32 million of private-sector shares and bonds issued on Paris Bourse |
| 1881–1900<br>United Kingdom | £105 million net increase in Latin American bond issues on London Stock Exchange | £147 million FDI in railways during1880–90; other private stock and bond investment rose by £256 million during 1880–1900 |
| 1880–1900<br>France | FF2.1 billion issued by various Latin American governments on Paris Bourse | FF2.3 billion of private-sector shares and bonds issued on Paris Bourse |

*Source* United Nations (1965), 5–12

Latin America, for products from Europe, such as clothing, iron, and manu-factured goods. The raw materials and commodities bias still characterizes trade today between these countries and the US and European Union. For most of the last two centuries Latin American primary products, especially metals and agricultural products, have been extensively traded in exchange for European and later US manufactures (Bulmer-Thomas 1994).

This process of highly 'dependent development' with respect to trade flows was paralleled by one of more independent interaction between borrowers in the region and lenders in Europe for much of the nineteenth century. Table 23.1 shows a sketch of major long-term capital investments in Latin America during that century.

Foreign direct investment began as early as the mid-nineteenth century, with projects in mining and also development of infrastructure such as railways and then telegraph/telephone systems (Wilkins 1970; Miller 1993).

In the twentieth century Latin America became a major trading partner for the United States, providing natural resources and low-cost assembly of manufactures such as clothing and electronic products (Wilkins 1974). Often, the production of the natural resources, such as oil, copper, bauxite, and bananas, attracted foreign direct investment to build and operate the large-scale mines or plantations that produced competitive outputs for international sales (principally in the US). Other natural resource exports, such as sugar, coffee, and cocoa, were largely produced by local companies and exported to international markets.

The markets of Latin American countries attracted some limited foreign direct investment to serve local demand, but this was largely attracted to the big three—Argentina, Brazil, and Mexico—until the past two decades. This market-seeking FDI was typically in manufactures that required relatively small capital commitments, such as production of processed foods and some low-tech machinery and electrical goods (Grosse 1989).

Today Latin America is the fourth largest region in the world in measures of international business, trailing the US and Canada, the European Union, and East Asia. International trade of Latin American countries amounted to over $US 300 billion in 1998 (see Appendix Table 23.A1), and incoming foreign direct investment was over $US 70 billion in 1998. Several measures of the size of international business activity in Latin America appear in Table 23.2.

# 23.2 THE GOVERNMENT–BUSINESS RELATIONSHIP

## 23.2.1 History of the policy environment toward international business

The government policy frameworks throughout Latin America followed pendulum swings during the twentieth century. For almost the full first-half of the century, the competitive and bargaining advantages of foreign multinationals gave the companies an insurmountable edge in dealing with Latin

Table 23.2  Trends in international business in Latin America and the
Caribbean (US$ millions)

| Activity | 1950 | 1960 | 1970 | 1980 | 1990 | 1998 |
|---|---|---|---|---|---|---|
| Exports | 6,611 | 9,264 | 15,923 | 103,719 | 139,611 | 275,055 |
| Imports | 5,855 | 9,622 | 17,241 | 113,795 | 124,715 | 356,644 |
| Current account balance of payments | −140 | −1168 | −3,573 | −27,436 | −2,436 | −93,214 |
| Foreign direct investment inflow | 372* | −521 | 1,077 | 5,709 | 8,339 | 70,388 |
| US FDI *stock* by industry | | | | | | |
| • Total | 4,735 | 8,366 | 12,961 | 38,275 | 71,539 | 196,655 |
| • Manufacturing | 780 | 1,521 | 4,541 | 14,489 | 23,733 | 48,008 |
| • Petroleum | 1,408 | 3,122 | 2,703 | 4,336 | 4,140 | 9,711 |
| • Mining and smelting | 628 | n.a. | 1,712 | 1,408 | n.a. | 2,403 |
| • Other | 1,919 | 3,723 | 4,005 | 18,042 | 43,720 | 138,936 |

*Data for 1951

*Sources* International Monetary Fund, *Direction of Trade Yearbook* (1999); *Balance of Payments Statistics* (1999); US Department of Commerce, *Survey of Current Business* (various issues); CEPAL archives

American governments and local competitors. That is, their financial resources, managerial and technological capabilities, and access to industrial-country markets gave multinationals an advantage that permitted them to overcome competitors throughout the region and to gain concessions from governments in negotiating tax and other regulatory treatment.

This situation resulted in a fairly permissive environment for MNE entry and operation in Latin America. However, trade barriers did exist, and exporting within the region was quite limited by tariff barriers. (This was not a particularly burdensome problem for MNEs, since their business was often extractive, with sales in industrial countries or market-serving in local markets, because transportation costs were quite high between countries of the region.) Thus, the regulatory environment was fairly open with respect to rules on establishment, but fairly restrictive with respect to trade barriers.

After World War II the situation changed to some extent, as Latin American companies grew in size and experience, enabling some of them to compete with foreign multinationals. Also, governments became better able to negotiate with the multinationals, based on the MNEs' growing interest in local markets, and improvements in transportation and communications that enabled even government-owned natural resource companies to reach world markets more directly (i.e. without MNE intervention to provide that access).

Latin American governments imposed increasingly restrictive policies on foreign MNEs, toward the end of import-substituting industrialization and promoting domestically owned business. This policy perspective was strongly supported by the United Nations Economic Center for Latin America (CEPAL), and is often called the Cepalista view (Prebisch 1950).

The period of increasing restrictions lasted until the debt crisis of the 1980s, when economic conditions forced Latin American governments to look for foreign financial, technical, and managerial resources more openly. At the very end of this inward-looking period, controls on foreign business included the barriers listed in Table 23.3. Notice that across a wide range of activities, foreign firms were limited in their ownership and control of business in Latin America. This inward-looking policy bias started with rules that (in the Andean Pact countries and Mexico) called for local ownership of at least 51 per cent of most companies, and included rules on profit remittances and royalty payments, that were limited through exchange controls, taxes, and quantitative restrictions.

The impact of the external debt crisis, which arrived with Mexico's declaration in August 1982 of the government's inability to service its foreign bank debt, led to almost a decade of financial contraction and economic recession, or even depression. This situation, along with the demise of the communist model at the end of the 1980s, led to a new wave of economic opening (*apertura económica*) beginning in Mexico in 1986, when that country joined GATT and began dismantling tariff and other business barriers. By 1991 Argentina, Bolivia, Chile,[2] Colombia, and Peru had joined the groundswell to make the region generally highly open to private sector business and to foreign business in particular.

Looking at the same policy issues as above, the conditions in 1997, ten years later, are depicted in Table 23.4.

---

[2] Chile, of course, is viewed as the leader in economic opening in Latin America. When General Pinochet's government installed a University of Chicago-recommended free market regulatory system in 1976, this shift from protectionism stood in stark contrast to the rest of the region for more than a decade. Chile remains the most open economic system in Latin America at the turn of the century, though Argentina and Mexico have become similarly quite open by this time.

Table 23.3 Selected rules affecting affiliates of foreign MNEs in 1987

| Country | Ownership | Profit remittance | Technology transfer | Exchange controls | Local content | Price controls | Tariffs | Non-tariff barriers |
|---|---|---|---|---|---|---|---|---|
| Argentina | Unrestricted | Supplementary tax on remittances above 12% of registered capital. | Unrestricted; pharmaceuticals not patentable. | Extensive controls | 80% required on autos | Repeated price freezes since 1985; most products controlled. | Range of 0–60% *ad valorem* | Imports must have certificate of necessity from DJNI; government imports must be on Argentine flat vessels. |
| Brazil | De facto government pressure for majority Brazilian ownership. | Supplementary tax on remittances above 12% of registered capital. | Licenses must be registered; royalties allowed of 1–5% of sales. | 2-tiered exchange rate; access to official rates is heavily controlled. | Required on many products; over 90% on autos. | Repeated price freezes since 1986; most products affected. | Range of 0–400% *ad valorem* | Anti-dumping duties; government purchases should be from suppliers or imported on Brazilian vessels. |
| Mexico | 49% foreign is maximum | Unrestricted except by general exchange controls. | Licenses must be registered; royalties allowed up to 7% of sales. | 2-tiered exchange rate. | Required on many products; 60% on autos. | 3-tiered system of limits, on most products. | Range of 0–45% *ad valorem* | Imports of luxury cars and vans prohibited. Advance deposit of full duties on imported motor vehicles. |
| Chile | Unrestricted | Unrestricted | | Open market | No restrictions | On few products | 10% uniform tariff *ad valorem* | Import payment must be made 120 days after shipment; license required on all imports. |

Andean Pact:

| | | | | | | | |
|---|---|---|---|---|---|---|---|
| Bolivia | Decision 24 | Decision 24 | 2-tiered exchange rate | n.a. | On some products categories of products. | 80% *ad valorem* | 33% of products imported; quotas on raw materials. |
| Ecuador | Decision 24 | Decision 24 | Fairly strict | Required in autos | On drugs and some foods. | Range of 0–200% *ad valorem* | License required for most imports; 180-day prior deposit required. |
| Peru | Desision 24 | Decision 24 | 2-tiered exchange rate | 25–50% in many sectors | On all products | Average 57% on mfg; 25% on raw materials *ad valorem*. | 300 products prohibited; license required on all imports; no prior deposit. |
| Venezuela | Decision 24 | Decision 24 | 3-tiered exchange rate | Required in many sectors | On 150 categories or products. | Range of 0–500% *ad valorem* | License required for many products; coffee, salt; some clothing articles prohibited. |

*Note* Decision 24 of the Andean Pact required fade-out of foreign ownership in foreign direct investment projects to a maximum of 49% over a 15-year period. Also, profit remittances were limited to 20% of registered capital per year, and payments for technology transfer from parent to subsidiary firm are not allowed. These rules are not strictly enforced in any of the countries, and many exceptions are allowed. Decision 24 was formally dropped by the group in 1987.

*Sources* Business International Corporation (1987), *Investing, Licensing, and Trading Conditions*, (New York); Price Waterhouse (1985), *Guide to Doing Business in Bolivia* (New York: Price Waterhouse); Price Waterhouse, *Guide to Doing Business in Chile* (New York) current editions.

Table 23.4 Selected rules affecting affiliates of foreign MNEs, 1997

| Country | Ownership | Profit remittance | Technology transfer | Exchange controls | Local content | Price controls |
|---|---|---|---|---|---|---|
| Argentina | No limit | No restriction | No restriction | Fixed (to $US) exchange rate; open foreign exchange market. | Maximum 40% foreign parts in autos. | On utilities, telecom tariff, and credit card interest. |
| Brazil | Relatively few limits | 15% tax | Required approval removed | Float freely although still have 2-tier exchange rate. | No explicit requirement | On public goods and services |
| Chile | Unrestricted | Unrestricted | No restrictions | None | No limits | Very few |
| Colombia | Certain restrictions for financial and public sector. | Ceiling removed | | Floating exchange rate | Applied for car assembly. | Applied for 11 product categories |
| Ecuador | | No restriction | | Floating after Feb. 1999; fixed to US dollar in 2000. | 50–60% for export products to other LA countries. | On fuels, drugs, and some foods |
| Mexico | Largely unrestricted | Unrestricted | No restriction | Floating rate | 34% for cars | No price controls |
| Peru | Largely unrestricted | | | 'Dirty' float | | On many products |
| Venezuela | Some restrictions, esp. on natural resources. | Restrictions removed | Most restrictions removed | Floating rate | 33% in automobile industry, but limit was dropped in 1999. | On agricultural and some pharmaceutical products. |

Source Economist Intelligence Unit, Investing, Licensing, and Trading Conditions (various issues)

Notice the dramatic shift in policy characteristics, with all countries demonstrating a large degree of openness and lack of quantitative barriers. The most restrictive countries in the region today are Brazil and Venezuela, each of which nonetheless permits relatively free entry and operation of foreign firms in most sectors.

An important research question that arises today concerns the policy environment that will prevail in the next decade. There appear to be strong underpinnings for a continued reliance on market-based capitalist development at present. However, issues such as the chronic currency and banking crises that have hit most countries of the region once or even twice during the 1990s lead many observers to anticipate a new interventionism, at least in financial markets. Perhaps the free trade policy framework that currently exists piecemeal through the region will lead to the proposed Free Trade Area of the Americas—but there is certainly no guarantee of that outcome.

### 23.2.1.1. *Privatizations*

Privatization of state-owned enterprises has been one central step of the economic opening process, and one vitally linked to FDI (Birch and Haar 2000). In the process of selling off state-owned infrastructure companies and others, Latin American governments have attracted the world leaders in these sectors as direct investors and members of consortia that include technical experts, financial groups, and local powerful companies.

The process of privatization in Latin America has encompassed most of the airlines, telephone companies, electric power companies, and banks that were either begun as state monopolies or nationalized during the previous half-century. For example, the telephone companies throughout the region were founded and developed mostly by the US-based ITT (International Telephone & Telegraph) early in the twentieth century. These telephone monopolies were nationalized in most countries during the 1970s, and then re-privatized during the 1990s (Ramamurti 1996; Wellenius 2000).

Electric power companies, as well, were mostly set up by a few foreign firms. Local power companies were acquired and developed throughout Latin America by American & Foreign Power Company (a subsidiary of GE) in the 1920s (Wilkins 1974). They were later nationalized and operated as government-operated monopolies, with the re-privatizations only occurring in the 1990s. This sector has been slower to be moved to private-sector management, and even in Mexico today the electric power sector is operated as a state monopoly in both generation and distribution (Grosse 2000).

Airlines were a very sensitive sector, since the national flag-carrier airline not only represented the country in international flights, but under international airline transport agreements, the national airline was often the only one permitted landing rights in other countries. With the enormous financial losses in commercial airline business during the late 1980s and early 1990s, most governments in the region chose to sell off the airline, rather than incur continuing losses and lack of competitiveness (Ramamurti 1996).

As a final example, commercial banks were largely privatized throughout Latin America during the late 1980s and the 1990s, as governments chose to let this sector operate more competitively and to retain a national development bank along with the central bank as public-sector entities. The banking systems of the region now operate largely as competitive sectors, with significant state supervision and regulation (Grosse 2000).

Interestingly, in each of these sectors the tendency has been for multinational firms in conjunction with local investors to dominate the business. In telecommunications, Telefónica from Spain along with GTE and Bell South have become the dominant carriers in Latin America. In electric power, Endesa from Spain and Houston Energy, AES, and Duke Power are leading distributors and generators in much of the region today. In banking, Banco Santander-Central Hispano and Banco BilbaoVizcaya Argentaria from Spain, along with Citibank and HongKong Bank have built regionwide networks of affiliates, and currently lead this sector. In airlines, the picture is less concentrated for domestic flights, but international flights are dominated by American Airlines, United Airlines, and Continental Airlines.

New research is needed into issues such as the evolving government/business relationship in the 2000s, and bargaining strategies for international firms in dealing with Latin American governments. Some of the changing conditions include the competition among countries to attract foreign direct investment, and the regulation of companies by state governments that also may compete to attract them. The issue of a 'new form of dependencia' is also worth careful exploration, as the new economy continues to develop, and as technology returns as a key advantage of foreign firms.


# 23.3 REGIONAL ECONOMIC INTEGRATION

Regional integration in Latin America has a history as long as that of the countries in the region, with the original goal of the Liberator, Simon Bolivar, to unite South America as one country in the 1820s. Since World War II, there have been several major integration efforts, beginning with the Latin

American Free Trade Area (LAFTA or ALALC) in 1960. This arrangement never achieved its free-trade goals, and it spawned several subregional efforts to group fewer countries with greater integration. The first was the Andean Pact, among Bolivia, Chile, Colombia, Ecuador, Peru, and Venezuela (Mytelka 1979). This group, initiated in 1967, developed a highly restrictive, anti-multinational policy framework including a foreign investment code (Grosse 1983), which at first caused some decline in investment in the sub-region, but later was found to permit enough exceptions such that FDI and multinational activities were not further reduced. In 1987 the Andean Pact dropped the restrictive policy regime and began to promote FDI into the region, as well as moving toward full tariff elimination among the member countries.

Another subregional integration effort is Mercosur, grouping Argentina, Brazil, Uruguay, and Paraguay (Roett 1999). This group has added Chile and Bolivia as associate members, and generally has served to open up trade between Argentina and Brazil. Mercosur has been hampered greatly by the Brazilian crisis of 1998–9, from which the devaluation of the real caused tremendous antagonism with Argentina, whose currency remains tied to the US dollar. While some analysts see Mercosur as a major potential contributor toward building a southern cone single market, the wide disparities in economic conditions and especially in economic policies between Brazil and Argentina do not augur well for continued trade barrier reductions and harmonized policies.

The most successful economic integration agreement in Latin America thus far has been the North American Free Trade Area, grouping Mexico with the United States and Canada since 1994. This agreement has produced a region-leading rate of economic growth in Mexico, despite the financial crisis of 1994–5, and a dramatic jump in foreign direct investment into Mexico (McClenahen 2000; McKinney 1999). To be sure, NAFTA's explicit focus is on trade barrier reductions—and trade between the US and Mexico grew by 113 per cent during 1994–9, faster than US trade with any other major trading partner. However, the really powerful impacts of NAFTA have been on decisions to locate production. Many multinational firms from the US, Europe, and Asia have chosen to use Mexico as a staging location for production to be sold in all of North America, especially the United States. The growth of direct investment into Mexico has also been among the world's fastest. And the integration of both Mexican and Canadian production into global strategies of multinational firms has advanced dramatically during NAFTA's short existence (Blank and Haar 1998).

The logic for these growth rates and company strategy shifts has a lot to do with the explicit reduction of policy barriers to trade and investment. Still, the average US tariffs on Mexican exports were less than 4 per cent *ad valorem* in the early 1990s, so the restrictions were not severe even before NAFTA. This logic also has to do with the increased confidence that investors feel now that Mexico is tightly tied to the US market and the US policy framework. Investors are anticipating a much more stable and transparent policy framework for MNEs to deal with, thus encouraging them to include Mexico as a 'safe' location for globally integrated production and distribution. Without a similar link to the US, Mercosur will never achieve a similar level of investor confidence, nor the integration of MNE activities that Mexico has experienced.

### 23.3.1  Barriers to trade and investment in Latin America in the twenty-first century

The restrictions on international trade and mobility of people in Latin America today are largely due to geographic and cultural barriers rather than legal ones. With economic policies promoting international trade in most countries, the problems of transportation costs and quality are what defeat firms' efforts to integrate the region more extensively. While transportation costs have fallen over time, there still remains the reality that high mountains and wide jungle separate population centers in Latin America. Most development remains on the coasts, and so transportation tends to be by air or by boat, with land transport between countries still lagging in quality and availability. These problems cannot be eliminated by tariff reductions or other government policies.

The case should not be overstated, either, that policy barriers to trade and investment in Latin America have been reduced but not eliminated. There still remain numerous policies that restrict foreign company activities in some industry sectors, some state-owned firms that are protected against competition, and some degree of inconsistency in both policy implementation and policy continuation as regards MNE activities.

### 23.3.2  The always-contentious relationship with the United States

The relationship between Latin American countries and the United States has been problematic since the United States became the leading industrial power at the beginning of the twentieth century. As Latin American countries became more and more dependent on the US for capital, technology, management skills, and also as a huge target market for their exports, the 'devil to the north' became more threatening. This reality has not changed very much at the beginning of the twenty-first century, except that some of the countries of the region have diversified their international business to some degree, including Europe as another major target market and buying more from European and Asian suppliers. The love/hate relationship with the United States remains.

This relationship has produced eras of political intervention, as the US defined its geopolitical interest to include the Americas (following the Monroe Doctrine of 1823), marked by direct military intervention in Nicaragua, the Dominican Republic, Panama, and even Cuba. It has also produced eras of relative calm such as immediately after World War II and again in the 1990s, as the Latin American countries unilaterally chose to follow policies more in line with US perceived interests.

The ultimate relationship between each Latin American country and the United States will evolve as interests shift and develop over time. Economic interests are driving such relationships at this point in the twenty-first century. The decision by Mexico's government to join the US and Canada in NAFTA is perhaps the strongest demonstration of the willingness to open the national economy to competition from the US companies in exchange for open access to that market, including the attraction of US companies to produce in Mexico for sales in the US market. This strategy has placed Mexico's economy on a fast-track growth path with an expectation of fewer major economic shocks in the future. (The Mexican elections of 2000 demonstrated to some extent the security of the growth path; every previous election for four presidencies had produced a major devaluation and economic crisis; the 2000 election was a striking exception to this recent history.)

The lesson from this experience may be that it is better to join the US rather than fight it. Certainly, opening up the economies to increased trade flows has proven highly successful in the period of *apertura económica* since 1990. The results of opening up financial flows to the market are less convincing, in the aftermath of Mexico's Tequila Crisis of 1994–5 that spread throughout the region, and the Asian crisis of 1997–8, which also dragged down Latin American financial markets in its wake.

It is expected that more and more Latin American and Caribbean countries will pursue greater economic integration with the United States in the next decade. To fight its economic crisis, Ecuador has recently adopted the US dollar as its official currency, thus linking itself to US monetary policy and currency valuation. To build its globally oriented economy, Chile has been seeking for almost a decade to join the US in a free trade agreement, since 1994 looking to become a fourth member of NAFTA. The Caribbean Common Market countries as well as the members of the Central American Common Market have likewise been pursuing efforts to link themselves in free trade with the

US. Because the expected benefits (and costs) are small for the US, the US government has not actively responded to these initiatives thus far.

Further research in this area is needed on subjects such as the impacts of NAFTA and Mercosur, and the question of whether or not a tie to the US is needed for regional integration efforts to make significant economic progress. Latin America is fertile ground for empirical exploration of the costs and benefits of economic integration schemes.

# 23.4 FINANCIAL MARKETS, FLOWS, AND CRISES

## 23.4.1 Foreign financing in Latin America

Foreign financing of Latin American countries for the past two centuries was initially in the form of bond issue and some bank loans in the London market, and subsequently was led by bank loans and some portfolio investment based primarily in the New York market, as described at the beginning of this chapter. For the past decade, foreign direct investment has boomed, due principally to the elimination of barriers to FDI in the region, especially in the context of major privatizations, and also to the rapid growth rate of Latin American economies in the 1990s. Table 23.5 shows the distribution of financial flows to the region in 1998.

Clearly, foreign direct investment in 1998 dwarfed both bank lending and official development finance, as it has for the whole decade of the 1990s. Despite the decline in bank lending and portfolio investment into Latin America in 1998 in the wake of the Asian financial crisis, FDI continued to grow in the region and continued to dominate the other financial flows.

### 23.4.1.1 *Financial crises and policies to deal with them*

A key concern of Latin American countries today is the problem of financial crisis that has become more pronounced as a result of the financial opening of the region to international capital flows. Beginning with the Mexican crisis of 1994–5, the Latin American countries have seen vivid evidence that balance-of-payments problems can lead to major capital flight episodes, resulting in maxi-devaluations, banking crises, and severe recessions.

Table 23.5  Net aggregate resource flows to Latin America, 1998
(US$ millions)

| Country | Total flow | Official flows | Private debt flows | Foreign direct investment |
|---|---|---|---|---|
| Argentina | 21,537 | −2 | 15,889 | 5,650 |
| Brazil | 14,956 | 3,836 | −13,283 | 24,403 |
| Chile | 9,508 | 547 | 3,874 | 5,087 |
| Colombia | 4,506 | 204 | 1,376 | 2,926 |
| Mexico | 13,661 | −1,104 | 4,035 | 10,730 |
| Peru | 3,898 | 717 | 789 | 2,392 |
| Venezuela | 8,412 | 90 | 4,547 | 3,775 |
| TOTAL Latin America | 83,201 | 6,126 | 17,624 | 59,451 |

Source World Bank, *Global Development Finance* (1999), 171

This lesson was brought into sharper focus when the Asian LDCs faced a major crisis in 1997–8, which spilled over into emerging markets everywhere, but particularly in Latin America. Argentina's fixed exchange rate policy (dollarization) was heavily tested both in the Tequila crisis and after the Asian crisis by these spillover or contamination effects. Other Latin American countries also experienced capital outflows and pressures on their currencies.

The country whose economy suffered most after the Asian crisis was Brazil, whose currency faced severe speculative pressures in the fall of 1998 and eventually devalued sharply in January 1999. This resulted in a recession that lasted for the entire year and a lack of investor confidence that was only reversed in the new century.

The solution to these problems is certainly to look for ways to protect the Latin American economies against the severe capital flow shifts allowed by completely open financial markets. The best way to protect against the massive short-term capital movements is not clear, but an enormous effort is under way to explore alternatives, from dollarization of the whole region, to Chilean-style capital controls, to bail-out funds for short-term help, to identifying monetary policies that might reduce the likelihood of such crises.

New research is needed into topics such as the appropriateness of dollarization of Latin American economies as a response to financial crises. And the broader question of how to mitigate the frequency and impact of financial crises, for example through capital controls, remains a very crucial subject after two major rounds of financial turmoil in 1994–5 and 1998–9. In addition, the key characteristics of a viable financial market, whether it includes a local stock and bond market or not, is a major concern for Latin America today.

# 23.5 MULTINATIONAL ENTERPRISES IN LATIN AMERICA

## 23.5.1 Foreign multinationals in Latin America today

Latin America attracted an enormous inflow of foreign direct investment in the 1990s, rebounding from the decade-long economic downturn of the 1980s. In terms of value, much of the new inflow of investment has involved privatizations of state-owned enterprises in industries such as telecommunications, electric power, petroleum, banking, and airlines. For example, the privatization of YPF (oil company) in Argentina brought in $US 4 billion in 1993, and the ultimate sale of the company to Repsol of Spain in 1998 brought in another $US 7 billion to Argentina. (Portfolio capital inflows also rose dramatically during this period through privatizations. For example, the sale of Telmex brought in over $US 3 billion in 1991, and the sale of Telebras as twelve separate companies brought in both direct and portfolio investment of about $US 19 billion in 1998.)

Foreign firms count for a significant part of output in all Latin American countries, and they tend to dominate the high-tech and capital-intensive sectors. Notice that after the big three state-owned oil companies, the list of the largest firms in Latin America is dominated by foreign oil and auto companies, followed by telecom and electric power companies, which are now also dominated by foreign owners. Interestingly, there are only nine consumer goods firms in the top fifty, the rest coming from natural resources, public services, and industrial goods (See Table 23.6).

There are three types of important FDI in Latin America: extractive, maquila, and market-serving. The extractive and market-serving public utility investments came first, beginning in the nineteenth century with ventures in gold, silver, and copper mining, along with railroads and telegraph service (Stone 1968). In the early twenty-first century, the extractive ventures remain

## Table 23.6  The largest fifty firms in Latin America (ranked by sales)

| Rank 1998 | Rank 1997 | Company | Country | Sector | 1998 sales (in $US m) | Market value 1998 |
|---|---|---|---|---|---|---|
| 1 | 2 | Pemex | Mexico | oil/gas | 27,267 | 15,572 |
| 2 | 1 | PDVSA | Venezuela | oil/gas | 25,256 | 31,763 |
| 3 | 3 | Petrobras | Brazil | oil/gas | 14,903 | 17,982 |
| 4 | 6 | Telmex | Mexico | telecom | 7,872 | 10,635 |
| 5 | 8 | CFE | Mexico | electricity | 7,562 | n.d. |
| 6 | 7 | General Motors | Mexico | autos | 7,452 | n.d. |
| 7 | 13 | Electrobras | Brazil | electricity | 7,163 | 49,636 |
| 8 | 9 | Volkswagen | Brazil | autos | 6,653 | 457 |
| 9 | 15 | General Motors | Brazil | autos | 6,445 | n.d. |
| 10 | 10 | Chrysler | Mexico | autos | 6,199 | n.d. |
| 11 | 5 | Petrobras Dist. | Brazil | oil/gas | 6,196 | 1,203 |
| 12 | 16 | Carrefour | Brazil | retail stores | 5,836 | n.d. |
| 13 | 11 | YPF | Argentina | oil/gas | 5,496 | 7,204 |
| 14 | 23 | Cifra | Mexico | retail stores | 5,179 | 2,662 |
| 15 | 29 | Volkswagen | Mexico | autos | 4,920 | 863 |
| 16 | 22 | Ipiranga | Brazil | oil/gas | 4,724 | 752 |
| 17 | 64 | Exxel Group | Argentina | holding co. | 4,700 | n.d. |
| 18 | 20 | Odebrecht | Brazil | holding co. | 4,503 | 1,310 |
| 19 | 14 | Shell | Brazil | oil/gas | 4,502 | 883 |
| 20 | — | Tele Norte Leste | Brazil | telecom | 4,432 | 7,663 |
| 21 | 12 | Fiat | Brazil | autos | 4,309 | 1,218 |
| 22 | 26 | Cemex | Mexico | cement | 4,298 | 3,872 |
| 23 | 18 | Vale Rio Doce | Brazil | mining | 4,253 | 8,035 |
| 24 | 19 | Ford | Mexico | autos | 4,205 | 806 |
| 25 | — | Light | Brazil | electricity | 3,949 | 1,912 |
| 26 | 17 | Ecopetrol | Colombia | oil/gas | 3,944 | 1,575 |
| 27 | 47 | CBD | Brazil | retail stores | 3,627 | 804 |

Table **23.6**  *continued*

| Rank 1998 | Rank 1997 | Company | Country | Sector | 1998 sales (in $US m) | Market value 1998 |
|---|---|---|---|---|---|---|
| 28 | 25 | Alfa | Mexico | holding | 3,626 | 2,024 |
| 29 | 32 | Furnas | Brazil | electricity | 3,608 | 8,475 |
| 30 | 28 | GrupoCarso | Mexico | holding co. | 3,597 | 1,970 |
| 31 | 43 | Telefónica | Argentina | telecom | 3,435 | 3,184 |
| 32 | 24 | Telesp | Brazil | telecom | 3,388 | 9,297 |
| 33 | 38 | Femsa | Mexico | beverages | 3,373 | 1,482 |
| 34 | – | Embratel | Brazil | telecom | 3,309 | 4,559 |
| 35 | 39 | Enersis | Chile | electricity | 3,270 | 1,656 |
| 36 | 30 | Cesp | Brazil | electricity | 3,239 | 13,123 |
| 37 | 50 | Telecom | Argentina | telecom | 3,173 | 2,693 |
| 38 | 67 | Nortel | Argentina | telecom | 3,173 | 1,372 |
| 39 | 35 | Texaco | Brazil | oil/gas | 3,130 | 410 |
| 40 | 27 | Ford | Brazil | autos | 3,036 | −124 |
| 41 | 41 | Varig | Brazil | airline | 2,997 | 78 |
| 42 | 34 | Copec | Chile | oil/gas | 2,890 | 4,280 |
| 43 | 21 | Eletropaulo | Brazil | electricity | 2,878 | 1,922 |
| 44 | 56 | Panamco | Mexico | beverages | 2,773 | 1,978 |
| 45 | 53 | Ceval | Brazil | foods | 2,747 | 469 |
| 46 | 31 | Codelco | Chile | copper | 2,730 | n.d. |
| 47 | 48 | Sabritas | Mexico | foods | 2,638 | n.d. |
| 48 | 40 | Usiminas | Brazil | steel | 2,616 | 2,615 |
| 49 | 57 | Brahma | Brazil | beverages | 2,611 | 1,182 |
| 50 | 37 | Nestlé | Brazil | foods | 2,580 | 542 |

*Source* 'Las 500 de Latinoamerica', *America Economia* (1999–2000 issue)

very important, ranging from coal mines and oil wells to the traditional copper mines.

EXXON is among the largest companies in the region, owning coal, oil, and natural gas resources and production facilities throughout South America. Likewise, Shell has long been a major investor in the region, and is very active today in exploration and production of oil and natural gas. The key change from the twentieth century in this area is that foreign multinationals are being allowed to invest once again in major natural resource projects, from oil wells to coal mines to natural gas exploration, after a strong resistance to their presence during the past thirty years.

Maquila, or offshore-assembly investment, has become very significant in Latin America since the 1970s. As low-cost imports of cars, steel, electronics, and clothing from Asia and elsewhere entered the US market in recent decades, many US firms and also European and Asian ones have invested heavily in Latin American and Caribbean assembly plants for producing clothes, consumer electronics including computers, cars, and auto parts, and various other products. The maquila business in Mexico alone accounted for more than one million jobs and over $US 50 billion of export sales (mainly to the US) by 1999 (*www.mexicomaquila.com*).

Market-serving direct investment has evolved into many consumer and industrial sectors since the early beginnings in transportation and public utilities. All of the major global competitors in consumer products are actively involved in Latin America; Nestlé and Unilever rank among the largest firms in the region, along with several automakers. Much of the market-serving investment is used to carry out final assembly of products (for example, local assembly of auto kits, formulation of pharmaceuticals and chemicals), rather than basic production. When economies of scale are less important, full local production is often undertaken (for example, by the food processing companies, and by clothing companies that import designs but use local fabrics). General Motors has more than a dozen auto assembly plants through the region, using many imported parts but local labor to assemble the vehicles. By contrast, Nestlé has more than one hundred plants in Latin America, typically producing entire ranges of products locally and importing others for local sales.

## 23.5.2 Local economic groups going international

Increasingly in the 1990s, with the process of economic opening largely completed in many countries of the region, the large family-based corporate groups from Latin America have been investing overseas as US and European industrial leaders have done through the twentieth century. These direct investments are not yet numerous, but they are increasing and placing several Latin American firms in the ranks of global leaders. Beyond the natural-resource-based groups, which are generally not family-based organizations, there are dozens of powerful groups from Latin American countries. They include the Grupo Diego Cisneros from Venezuela; Grupo Alfa from Mexico; Grupo Luksic from Chile; and Perez Companq from Argentina (Peres 1998).

The Cisneros group has expanded overseas with several of its major companies, including the Venevision television network, which is the largest in Latin America (and its US affiliate, Univision), and several telecom ventures based on its Telcel domestic cellular phone company. In 1999 the group jointly invested with America Online to own half of the AOL-Latin America business. The group was originally based in retailing, holding the main Pepsi franchising operation for Venezuela, and banking. After the Venezuelan economic crisis of the early 1990s the Cisneros group has moved heavily into media and telecommunications and away from its traditional food and beverages activities.

Grupo Alfa is just one of the major holdings of the Garza Sada family in Mexico. This group holds major investments in steel (Hylsamex), petro-chemicals (Alpek), telecommunications (Onexa, a joint venture with AT&T), and food (Sigma). Each of these firms has overseas FDI; for example, Hylsamex owns the SIDOR steel company in Venezuela. As with many of the other leading groups in the region, Alfa is moving into less cyclical, less resource-based businesses to stabilize its financial position and to promote growth.

Grupo Luksic from Chile has realigned its businesses extensively during the 1990s, such that today the group is heavily involved in copper (Madeco), beer (CCU), telecommunications (VTR), and banking (Banco Edwards). Luksic investment in banking formerly included two of the largest banks in Chile, but under government pressure after the merger of two Spanish banks that were also involved, the Luksic's sold their interest and subsequently bought the smaller Banco Edwards. This group has placed a significant part of its resources into telecommunications in recent years.

Perez Companq in Argentina has pursued a restructuring very similar to those of the comparable leading groups in other countries of Latin America. Once largely a shipping company that diversified into other assorted businesses, in the 1990s Perez Companq focused increasingly on the oil and gas, telecommunications, and electric power sectors. After YPF (now Repsol), Perez Companq has been and remains the second-largest energy company in Argentina, with investments abroad in several mostly southern-cone countries. Moving downstream, Perez Companq owns key electric power generation and distribution companies, including Central Costanera and Edesur.

When the Argentine telecom sector was opened to competition in 1990, Perez Companq bought a major interest in one of the two main operating companies, Telecom.

The strategies of these firms tend to be based on the following key competitive advantages: knowledge of and access to local markets; ability to deal successfully with governments, including in the context of privatizations; and production of relatively low-cost products. It is clear that they are never leaders in creating new technology in the global context, but still these firms tend to be able to jump in and manage the lower-tech aspects of high-tech sectors—such as sales, distribution, negotiating with governments, and financial management (Peres 1998; Dawar and Frost 1999).

In addition to the private-sector groups, state-owned companies that remain in natural resource ventures are becoming more active in foreign direct investment. These include such firms as the three oil giants: Pemex, PDVSA (from Venezuela), and Petrobras. All three have important businesses in the United States, ranging from PDVSA's ownership of Citgo Oil to Pemex's petrochemical plants in several states.

An important research question in the early twenty-first century concerns the industrial structure that will prevail once the privatizations are completed and the markets opened to foreign investors that choose to take ownership positions in firms in the region. Will the local firms become largely irrelevant or, at most, partners with foreign investors in some sectors? Will the economies of the region become dominated by a handful of firms in each industrial sector, as is the trend in many sectors in the US, Japan, and Europe? It does appear that the tendency is in that direction, though there are some anomalies such as the active participation of Spanish firms in several sectors such as banking, electric power, telecommunications, and insurance.[3]

New research is clearly needed to better understand the successful strategies of those Latin American firms that have weathered the storm of foreign MNE entry and competition, as well as those of Latin American firms that are going international in their activities. What are their key competitive advantages, and how likely is it that other firms can develop similar capabilities? Also, the use of alliances, which has long been a key part of Latin firms' strategies, is expanding rapidly, and should be studied in much more detail.

[3] The Spanish 're-conquest' may be a temporary phenomenon, as the European market opens more widely, and other large firms look to acquire the Spanish leaders.

# 23.6 THE INFORMAL ECONOMY'S IMPACT ON BUSINESS IN LATIN AMERICA

The informal (underground) economy in Latin America during the late 1900s was estimated to be as large as one-half of the total economy in many countries (De Soto 1985; Portes *et al.* 1989). This economy is defined simply as the unrecorded part of the total economy, and it includes both 'legitimate' business such as personal services and transactions that are pursued to evade taxes and 'illegitimate' business such as narcotics trafficking and smuggling. As noted in great detail by De Soto, the legal environments in Latin American countries for many years made it extremely difficult for businesspeople to follow all of the sometimes obscure and contradictory rules. Thus, there was a large stimulus to move business into the informal economy when possible, to avoid dealing with these inefficient barriers. Unfortunately, this pressure produced a large unreported economy in Latin American countries, which facilitated the activities of criminals involved in activities ranging from drug trafficking to illegal arms sales to smuggling of electronics and clothing, etc.

Today, with the economic opening that has occurred in the region, the need for operating in the underground economy has lessened, though inefficient government policies have not disappeared entirely. Still, because of the inertia developed in doing business underground, it is a slow process to bring all or most of the economy into the reported, formal sector. Even today, much of the non-urban economy of Latin American countries remains in the informal sector.

Multinational firms tend to ignore or minimize this activity, though in the case of consumer products, smuggling often acts to hurt the interests of the producers of stereos, clothing, refrigerators, and even toothpaste and hairbrushes that are sold in the black (underground) market. Certainly, multinationals try to avoid dealing in the underground economy, for fear of being caught and penalized (and gaining very bad press) for such activity.

# 23.7 CONCLUSIONS

International business in Latin America has boomed in the 1990s, and now looks much more like that among European countries than ever before. There has been a dramatic change in the policy environment toward permitting foreign company and private sector participation in all Latin American economies. The role of Latin American companies in the new context remains to be developed. Certainly, with their smaller average size than leading multinationals from the US, Europe, and Japan, there is a risk of losing ownership of many industries to foreign investors and importers.

The arrival of the new economy has hit Latin America almost as hard as the industrial countries, but it is less noticeable in Latin America—not the least because of all the other changes that are taking place in the sweep to more open business systems. The growth of Internet business is global, and so not limited to Latin America, but the growth of Latin America-based Internet business is definitely rapid and threatening to traditional business. Thus far, E-businesses tend to be related to existing bricks and mortar firms, so the impact is more in developing new distribution channels rather than replacing existing businesses. As Latin America's economies continue to globalize, the roles of both foreign and local multinationals will continue to grow relative to smaller local firms, and the role of electronic commerce will continue to threaten the existing order.

Table 23.A1 Value of international trade in Latin America, 1997 (US$ millions)

| Exporter | Importer | | | | | | | | | | | | |
|---|---|---|---|---|---|---|---|---|---|---|---|---|---|
| | Arg. | Brazil | Chile | Col. | CR | Ecu. | Gua. | Mex. | Peru | Uru. | Ven. | US | World |
| Argentina | — | 8,120 | 1,837 | 208 | 0 | 0 | 14 | 236 | 248 | 791 | 315 | 1,986 | 28,172 |
| Brazil | 6,824 | — | 1,243 | 514 | 77 | 189 | 63 | 869 | 333 | 802 | 768 | 9,408 | 61,253 |
| Chile | 681 | 995 | — | 253 | 37 | 172 | 25 | 372 | 452 | 63 | 158 | 2,711 | 17,811 |
| Colombia | 89 | 126 | 201 | — | 125 | 527 | 34 | 124 | 348 | 6 | 887 | 4,576 | 13,951 |
| Costa Rica | 0 | 2 | 24 | 14 | — | 6 | 89 | 77 | 15 | 2 | 8 | 2,263 | 3,795 |
| Ecuador | 112 | 28 | 259 | 385 | 4 | — | 22 | 61 | 90 | 14 | 32 | 2,073 | 4,542 |
| Guatemala | 0 | 5 | 35 | 10 | 117 | 2 | — | 80 | 6 | 0 | 13 | 1,403 | 4,048 |
| Mexico | 600 | 1,186 | 1,076 | 594 | 244 | 157 | 478 | — | 256 | 52 | 675 | 94,531 | 92,599 |
| Peru | 50 | 284 | 119 | 159 | 14 | 122 | 11 | 142 | — | 5 | 139 | 1,571 | 6,754 |
| Uruguay | 364 | 980 | 58 | 18 | 0 | 6 | 1 | 35 | 80 | — | 15 | 163 | 4,068 |
| Venezuela | 63 | 1,048 | 273 | 1,599 | 132 | 289 | 184 | 421 | 365 | 88 | — | 13,081 | 14,574 |
| United States | 6,068 | 14,344 | 4,333 | 5,430 | 2,226 | 1,675 | 1,714 | 82,182 | 2,602 | 433 | 6,608 | — | 867,038 |
| World | 26,487 | 56,069 | 17,789 | 12,551 | 4,641 | 5,792 | 3,978 | 108,700 | 6,787 | 3,099 | 25,912 | 762,834 | 5,469,600 |

Source International Monetary Fund, Direction of Trade Statistics Yearbook (1999)

## REFERENCES

AGOSIN, M. (ed.) (1995). *Foreign Direct Investment in Latin America.* Washington, DC: Inter-American Development Bank.

AHARONI, Y. (1966). *The Foreign Investment Decision Process.* Boston: Harvard Business School Press.

ALIBER, R. (1970). 'A Theory of Direct Foreign Investment', in C. Kindleberger (ed.), *The International Corporation.* Cambridge, Mass.: MIT Press.

AUSTIN, J. (1990). *Managing in Developing Countries.* New York: Free Press.

BENNETT, DOUGLAS, and SHARPE, KENNETH (1985). *Transnational Corporations Versus the State.* Princeton, NJ: Princeton University Press.

BIRCH, MELISSA, and HAAR, JERRY (eds.) (2000). *The Impact of Privatization in the Americas.* Coral Gables, Fla.: North-South Center Press.

BLANK, STEPHEN, and HAAR, JERRY (1985). *Making NAFTA Work: U.S. Firms and the New North American Business Environment.* Coral Gables, Fla.: North-South Center Press.

BUCKLEY, P. J., and GHAURI, P. N. (1991). *The Internationalisation of the Firm.* Oxford: Oxford University Press.

BULMER-THOMAS, VICTOR (1994). 'The Economic History of Latin America Since Independence', *Cambridge Latin American Studies*, 77 (Dec.).

CEPAL (1998). *Foreign Investment in Latin America and the Caribbean.* Santiago, Chile: United Nations, (E.98.11.G.14).

DARWENT, C. (1996). 'Investors Cut a Dash Away from the US Border', *Corporate Location*, May/June: 56–61.

DAWAR, NIRAJ, and FROST, TONY (1999). 'Competing with Giants: Survival Strategies for Local Companies in Emerging Markets', *Harvard Business Review*, Mar.–April: 119–29.

DE SOTO, HERNANDO (1985). *El otro sendero.* Lima: Instituto de Libertad y Democracia.

DUNNING, J. H. (1980). 'Toward an Eclectic Theory of International Production: Some Empirical Tests', *Journal of International Business Studies*, 11/1: 9–31.

ECONOMIST INTELLIGENCE UNIT (various issues). *Business Latin America.* www.eiu.com.

ERB, C. B., HARVEY, C. R., and VISKANTA, T. E. (1996). 'Political Risk, Economic Risk, and Financial Risk', *Financial Analysts Journal*, 52/6: 29–46.

FAGRE, N., and WELLS, JR., L. T. (1982). 'Bargaining Power of Multinationals and Host Governments', *Journal of International Business Studies*, 13/2: 9–23.

FEENSTRA, R. C., and HANSON, G. H. (1997). 'Foreign Direct Investment and Relative Wages: Evidence from Mexico's Maquiladoras', *Journal of International Economics*, 42/3–4: 371–93.

FRANK, A. G. (1969). *Capitalism and Underdevelopment in Latin America.* New York: Monthly Review Press.

FROOT, KENNETH (ed.) (1993). *Foreign Direct Investment.* Chicago: University of Chicago Press.

GARTEN, J. (1997). *The Big Ten: The Big Emerging Markets and How They Will Change Our Lives.* New York: Basic Books.

GOMEZ-MEJIA, L. R., and PALICH, L. E. (1997). 'Cultural Diversity and the Performance of Multinational Firms', *Journal of International Business Studies*, 28/2: 309–35.

GREEN, R., and CUNNINGHAM, W. (1975). 'The Determinants of US Foreign Investment: An Empirical Examination', *Management International Review*, 15: 113–20.

GROSSE, R. (1983). 'The Andean Foreign Investment Code's Effect on Foreign Direct Investment', *Journal of International Business Studies*, Winter: 121–33.

—— (1989). *Multinationals in Latin America*. London: Routledge.

—— (1997). 'Foreign Direct Investment in Latin America', in Robert Grosse (ed.), *Generating Savings for Development in Latin America*, Nov. 135–53. Coral Gables: North-South Center Press.

—— (2000). 'Moving Beyond Privatization: The Government–Business Relationship in Latin America', *North/South Agenda*, April. Coral Gables: North-South Center Press.

—— (Forthcoming). 'Investment Promotion Policies in Latin America', in E. Huber (ed.), *Models of Capitalism and Latin American Development in the 21st Century*. Pennsylvania: Pennsylvania State University Press.

—— and KUJAWA, D. (1995). *International Business: Theory and Managerial Applications*. 3rd edn. Homewood, Ill.: Irwin.

GRUBAUGH, S. (1987). 'Determinants of Direct Foreign Investment', *Review of Economics and Statistics*, 69/1: 149–52.

HOFSTEDE, G. (1980). *Culture's Consequences: International Differences in Work-Related Values*. Beverly Hills: Sage Publications.

HOUDE, M. F. (1994). 'Mexico and Foreign Investment', *OECD Observer*, 190: 10–13.

HUFBAUER, GARY, and SCHOTT, JEFFREY (1994). *Western Hemisphere Economic Integration*. Washington, DC: Institute for International Economics.

INTERNATIONAL MONETARY FUND (1998). *International Financial Statistics*, CD-ROM.

JUN, K. W., and SINGH, H. (1996). 'The Determinants of Foreign Direct Investment in Developing Countries', *Transnational Corporations*, 5/2: 67–105.

KINDLEBERGER, CHARLES (1969). *Foreign Direct Investment Abroad*. New Haven: Yale University Press.

KOBRIN, S. J. (1976). 'The Environmental Determinants of Foreign Direct Manufacturing Investment: An Ex-Post Empirical Analysis', *Journal of International Business Studies*, 7: 29–42.

KOGUT, B. (1983). 'Foreign Direct Investment as a Sequential Process', in C. Kindleberger and D. Audretsch (eds.), *The Multinational Corporation in the 1980s*. Cambridge, Mass.: MIT Press.

LALL, SANJAYA, and STREETEN, PAUL (1977). *Foreign Investment, Transnationals, and Developing Countries*. London: Macmillan.

LATIN AMERICAN INFORMATION SERVICES (various dates). *Lagniappe Letter*. New York: Latin American Information Services, *www.lais.com*.

LEWIS, CLEONA (1938). *America's Stake in International Investment*. Washington, DC: Brookings.

LOREE, D. W., and GUISINGER, S. (1995). 'Policy and Non-Policy Determinants of U.S. Equity Foreign Direct Investment', *Journal of International Business Studies*, 26/2: 281–99.

MANZETTI, LUIGI (ed.) (2000). *Regulatory Policy in Latin America: Post-Privatization Realities*. Coral Gables: North-South Center Press.

MARICHAL, CARLOS (1989). *A Century of Debt Crises in Latin America*. Princeton: Princeton University Press.

McCLENAHEN, J. (2000). 'NAFTA Works', *Industry Week*, 10 Jan.: 5–6.

McKINNEY, J. (1999). 'NAFTA: Four Years Down the Road', *Baylor Business Review*, Spring: 22–3.

MILLER, R. (1993). *Britain and Latin America in the 19th and 20th Centuries*. New York: Longman.

MORAN, T. (1974). *Multinational Corporations and the Politics of Dependence: Copper in Chile*. Princeton: Princeton University Press.

MUDAMBI, R., and RICKETTS, M. (1998). 'Economic Organisation and the Multinational Firm', in R. Mudambi and M. Ricketts (eds.), *The Organisation of the Firm: International Business Perspectives*. London: Routledge.

MYTELKA, LYNN (1979). *Regional Development in a Global Economy: The Multinational Corporation, Technology, and Andean Integration*. New Haven: Yale University Press.

NIGH, D. (1985). 'The Effect of Political Events on United States Direct Foreign Investment: A Pooled Time-Series Cross-Sectional Analysis', *Journal of International Business Studies*, 16/1: 1–17.

OECD (1996). *OECD Benchmark Definition of Foreign Direct Investment*. Paris: OECD.

PERES, WILSON (ed.) (1998). *Grandes Empresas y Grupos Industriales Latinoamericanos*. Santiago, Chile: CEPAL.

POLITICAL RISK SERVICES (1980–97). *International Country Risk Guide*. Syracuse, NY: PRS Group (formerly Frost and Sullivan), published monthly.

PORTES, ALEJANDRO, CASTELLS, MANUEL, and BENTON, LAUREN (eds.) (1989). *The Informal Economy*. Baltimore: Johns Hopkins University Press.

PREBISCH, RAUL (1950). *The Economic Development of Latin America and Its Principal Problems*. New York: United Nations. (Reproduced as 'The Economic Development of Latin America and Its Principal Problems', *Economic Bulletin for Latin America*. Santiago, Chile: CEPAL (1962), 7/1: 1–51.)

RAMAMURTI, RAVI (ed.) (1996). *Privatizing Monopolies: Lessons from the Telecommunications and Transport Sectors in Latin America*. Baltimore: Johns Hopkins University Press.

RAMSARAN, RAMESH (1985). *US Investment in Latin America and the Caribbean*. New York: St Martin's Press.

RIPPY, J. FRED (1959). *British Investment in Latin America, 1822–1949*. Minneapolis: University of Minnesota Press.

ROBINSON, RICHARD (1976). *National Control of Foreign Business Entry*. New York: Praeger.

ROETT, RIORDAN (ed.) (1999). *Mercosur: Regional Integration, World Markets*. Boulder, Colo.: Lynne Reiner Publishers.

ROOT, F., and AHMED, A. (1979). 'Empirical Determinants of Manufacturing Direct Foreign Investment in Developing Countries', *Economic Development and Cultural Change*, 27/4: 751–67.

SCHNEIDER, F., and FREY, B. (1985). 'Economic and Political Determinants of Foreign Direct Investment', *World Development*, 13/2: 161–75.

STONE, IRVING (1968). 'British Long-Term Investment in Latin America', *Business History Review*, Autumn: 311–39.

UNITED NATIONS (1965). *External Financing in Latin America*. New York: United Nations.

—— (1978). *Transnational Corporations in World Development*. New York: United Nations.

UNITED NATIONS CENTRE ON TRANSNATIONAL CORPORATIONS (1992). *The Determinants of Foreign Direct Investment*. New York: United Nations, (ST/CTC/121).

UNITED NATIONS CONFERENCE ON TRADE AND DEVELOPMENT (1999). *World Investment Report*. New York: United Nations.

VAITSOS, CONSTANTIN (1973). 'Foreign Investment Policies and Economic Development in Latin America', *Journal of World Trade Law*, Nov.–Dec.: 619–65.

WELLENIUS, BJORN (2000). 'Regulating the Telecommunications Sector: The Experience of Latin America', in Luigi Manzetti (ed.), *Regulatory Policy in Latin America: Post-Privatization Realities*. Coral Gables: North-South Center, 189–241.

WILKINS, MIRA (1970). *The Emergence of Multinational Enterprise*. Cambridge, Mass.: Harvard University Press.

—— (1974). *The Maturing of Multinational Enterprise*. Cambridge, Mass.: Harvard University Press.

WOODWARD, D., and ROLFE, R. (1993). 'The Location of Export-Oriented Foreign Direct Investment in the Caribbean Basin', *Journal of International Business Studies*, 24/1: 121–44.

CHAPTER 24

# CHINA AND INTERNATIONAL BUSINESS

## JOHN CHILD

CHINA requires special consideration for a number of reasons. With 1.2 billion people, it has the world's greatest population, is the second largest economy adjusting for purchasing power, and is projected to become the largest by around the year 2020 (World Economic Forum 1999). The country's sheer scale and diversity make it an economic region in its own right. China's political economy is also quite distinctive. It is pursuing its own mode of transition from socialism through policies and institutional arrangements that are to a large extent *sui generis*.[1] This transition includes a progressive engagement with international business.

China's scale and growing involvement with international business mean that it cannot be ignored, even though the ideological and institutional differences between China and other major economic powers create numerous difficulties. The protracted negotiations over China's entry to the WTO bear witness to the problem. As an environment for foreign-investing firms, China presents an unusual degree of complexity and uncertainty that does

---

[1] In this chapter China denotes 'Mainland China'. In other words it excludes the Hong Kong and Macau Special Administrative Regions of the PRC.

not necessarily favor the strategies MNCs pursue elsewhere. Many firms are disappointed with the returns they have secured from this investment and some have withdrawn. At the same time, Chinese firms investing abroad have often run into difficulties. China's role in international business therefore presents a challenge both for practice and theory.

# 24.1 CHINA'S GROWING ROLE IN INTERNATIONAL BUSINESS

## 24.1.1 Trade and inward FDI

China's program of economic reform, launched in December 1978, has centered on the twin tracks of putting government at arm's-length from business and opening up the economy to the outside world. The country continues to move along these tracks with further business reforms such as the official legitimation of private business in 1999, and entry to the WTO (on China's economic reform see Naughton 1995; Rawski 1999; *China Quarterly* 1999).

Under the economic reform program, China has grown rapidly and progressively entered the world economy. Although since the mid-1990s its rate of GDP growth has fallen below the heady double-digit figures previously recorded, at around 8 per cent it remains one of the highest rates in the world.[2] China has increased its level of external trade from almost zero in 1978 to the point where it is now the eleventh largest trading nation in the world. China weathered the Asian economic crisis of 1997–8 relatively well, maintaining an upward trend in its value of foreign trade and a large trade surplus (*China Economic News*, 2000a; *Asian Wall Street Journal*, 2000). WTO membership will draw China further into the world economy, though whether it can at the same time sustain such strong current account performance is more doubtful.

The passing of legislation over the years since 1979, permitting various forms of foreign business ownership such as equity joint ventures and wholly foreign-owned enterprises (WFOEs), has provided foreign companies with

---

[2] Some doubt has to be attached to China's official economic growth figures, which in recent years have become a political virility symbol for the regime. Reported energy output growth figures, for instance, are considerably lower. International economists agree that GDP growth is probably 0.5–2.0 per cent lower than recorded (EIU 1999: ch. 1: 39).

structures for investing in China. Since 1992, China has attracted more FDI than any other emerging economy, ranking second only to the United States as a global destination for such investment. Approximately half of the Fortune 500 companies have now invested in China. According to estimates published by UNCTAD (1999: Annex B), China had an internal stock of actual FDI amounting by the end of 1998 to just over US $261 billion or about one-quarter of its GDP. The countries or territories by rank order with the largest total stock of FDI in China were Hong Kong, Japan, the USA, Taiwan, Singapore, and South Korea. The UK ranked eighth and Germany ninth. The unknown amount of domestic capital 'round-tripping' through Hong Kong to obtain preferential tax treatment exaggerates FDI figures for China as well as Hong Kong's leading position as a source of funds. Nevertheless, the rankings reflect the presence of a significant Asia-Pacific regional economic cluster in which China plays a major part (Lee 1996).

This inward investment is making a major contribution to the development of China's economy, in terms of technology, expertise, and external trade. In 1998, firms with foreign investment (including joint ventures) accounted for 13 per cent of China's total investment in fixed assets, and for 22 per cent of the nation's total industrial output value. Such firms employed around 18 million people, or about 10 per cent of the urban workforce. They were responsible for 44.1 per cent of China's exports and 48.7 per cent of its total foreign trade (National Bureau of Statistics 1999). They also contributed over 14 per cent of national tax revenues. The fact that the national added value contributed by foreign-invested firms is over 10 per cent greater than their proportion of national output reflects their generally superior technology and know-how (*The Economist*, 1999; *China Economic News*, 2000*b*).

The form of investment carried out by multinational corporations (MNCs) in China has evolved since the start of the process in the early 1980s. To begin with, in an unfamiliar environment, most investors were cautious and limited their commitment. Some exported goods to China, often as knockdown kits, and backed this with limited technology transfer. Others began with relatively small investments in joint ventures, expanding these later on and often acquiring larger shares of joint venture equity. Much of the surge in inward FDI between 1992 and 1997 was attributable to MNCs deciding to invest in larger projects and increasingly taking 100 per cent ownership. In 1997 the number of newly contracted WFOEs in China exceeded that of new joint ventures for the first time.

From the mid-1990s, many MNCs faced increasing competition in China both from other MNCs entering the market and from improving domestic enterprises. While a few have withdrawn, others have responded by expanding their operations, purchasing shares of domestic companies, or establishing greenfield facilities that incorporate relatively advanced technologies. As they diversify their activities, such companies have tended to establish a China corporate office or to move their regional headquarters to China. Such a move not only recognizes the growing importance of their China business but also helps to provide co-ordination, realize scale economies, and utilize funds more effectively as between different China units (Meier *et al.* 1995; EIU 1999: ch. 9). Motorola is a leading example. It has become the largest US investor in China, with a total of US $1.2 billion in 1999. It has its North Asia headquarters in Tianjin, operates several production plants, repair and maintenance centers, a 'Motorola University', and technological cooperation projects. A second prominent example is Daimler Chrysler which, following its merger, established its Northeast Asia headquarters in Beijing.

## 24.1.2 Motives and entry mode

The predominant motive for companies investing in China has been to gain access to the domestic market (Daniels *et al.* 1985; Child 1994). Although based on a low average per capita income, this market had the alluring combination of a large population and rapid economic growth. Many of the companies entering China early, such as Hewlett-Packard and Volkswagen, gave priority to gaining a strategic position and strong business presence ahead of their competitors and were prepared to wait for profits in the longer term. This policy has generally paid off in superior profitability and market share (Pan, Li, and Tse 1999). Some investment from nearby high-cost locations, notably Hong Kong, Japan, and Taiwan, has also been attracted by the lower costs of labor and sourcing in China (Thorburn *et al.* 1990; Child and Yan 2001). This is understandable in view of these territories' factor-cost profiles combined with their geographical proximity to China. Looking to the future, it is likely that an increasing number of MNCs will also use China for asset-seeking purposes, such as a location for R&D given the high quality of much Chinese technical education.

The most singular case in terms of motives for investment in China, however, is that of Hong Kong companies. For many of them, escaping the pressures of rising land prices and employment costs have tended even to outweigh the attraction of the China market. Indeed, some use facilities established in the Mainland to produce primarily for export outside China rather than for the domestic market (Child *et al.* 2000). Hong Kong firms also tend to be interested in opportunities for transfer pricing benefits and tax breaks (Child and Yan 2001; Lin 1996).

Pan and Chi (1999) investigated the impact of entry timing, mode of entry, market focus, and location advantages on the financial performance and survival of MNCs in China. They assessed profitability in terms of percentage of profit on sales revenue and survival in terms of whether or not MNCs had closed their operations between the two years surveyed: 1992 and 1993. The more profitable MNCs tended to be those which had entered China in an earlier year, operated through equity joint ventures rather than cooperative (normally contractual) operations or WFOEs, and were located in major cities rather than elsewhere. Another study (Pan, Li, and Tse 1999) examined interactions between timing and mode (EJV or WFOE) of entry to China. Its findings suggest that earlier entry increases market share, but that when taken together neither variable has a significant effect on profitability.

Since entering China, many foreign companies have endeavored to convert their joint ventures into wholly owned subsidiaries, or at least secure a substantial majority of equity ownership. Disappointing levels of profitability and difficulties with local partners have given rise to a conventional wisdom that, in China at least, it is best to have sole ownership and control (Vanhonacker 1997). In the words of the Economist Intelligence Unit (1999: ch. 9: 10–11):

Foreign investors now opt for the WFOE option whenever possible, loth to entangle themselves in what will almost certainly be an unhappy union... The balance is also changing among existing ventures as foreign multinationals aggressively buy out useless joint-venture partners to bring their investments toward profitability.

Although this statement reflects a widely held belief among both commentators and executives, evidence on the relation between investment form and performance in China does not admit of any straightforward conclusion. Hu and Chen (1994) found from a survey of 382 Hong Kong subsidiaries and ventures operating in China, that wholly-owned subsidiaries were more likely to be successful than equity joint ventures or those based on contractual agreements.[3] A study of seventy MNCs by AT Kearney in 1998 found that a higher proportion of investment projects using the WFOE mode were profitable, and had shorter break-even times, compared to those formed as joint ventures (EIU 1999: ch. 9: 11). Wang, Zhi, and Tan (2000) found that foreign partner rights to key managerial appointments in joint ventures, underwritten by majority ownership, were associated with greater satisfaction with JV performance among both foreign and Chinese managers.

On the other hand, a large-scale survey using data from China's 1995 industrial census concluded that while WFOEs on average achieved a higher market share than did equity joint ventures, they had an inferior level of profitability (Pan, Li, and Tse 1999). This finding for profitability is supported by more detailed data from Jiangsu Province (Luo 1996). Among Sino-foreign

---

[3] The results must, however, be treated with caution since there were only 27 wholly-owned subsidiaries in the sample, and very indirect measures of performance were employed: duration of the alliance and total partner investment in it.

joint ventures, an EIU/Andersen Consulting study found that the most profitable ones had a lower average foreign equity share (54 per cent) than did the unprofitable ones (68 per cent) (EIU/Andersen Consulting 1995: 24). Beamish's (1993) review of studies also suggested that in China shared joint venture ownership and control is conducive to better performance.

A resolution of this issue would clearly be of considerable interest to companies investing in China, while accounting for FDI performance also poses a theoretical challenge. There are several possibilities that deserve further investigation. The studies reporting a performance advantage for WFOEs or majority-owned joint ventures tend to have been conducted more recently than those presenting the contrary finding. It is possible that changing circumstances are favoring sole or majority ownership. These include the easing of regulatory restrictions on WFOEs, an advance of foreign companies up the China learning curve which reduces their reliance on partners, and the multiple locations through which many MNCs now operate in China across which economies can be gained if their management and resource allocation is coordinated through unified ownership. The context of foreign operations in China also needs to be taken into account more carefully in future research. Thus sole foreign ownership is not an option in certain strategic industries. In other cases, local monopolies mean that only a Chinese partner can deliver entry into a market. Smaller foreign companies may not have the resources or experience to operate on their own in China.

## 24.1.3 Outward FDI

The other side to China's growing participation in the regional and world economy lies in its growth of outward FDI. Before the late 1970s, outward FDI was minimal and was mainly to service trade (Cai 1999). By 1998, however, China's outward stock of FDI had risen to a total of US $22.1 billion (UNCTAD 1999: Annex B). According to Chinese official figures, outward FDI had been invested in some 6,000 enterprises in 140 countries, but these data are significant underestimates because many Chinese firms invest overseas without seeking official approval. Even allowing for underreporting, the stock of outward FDI is still small compared to the inward stock. It accounted for just 2.2 per cent of GDP in 1997, as against the 23.5 per cent accounted for by the stock of inward FDI. Nevertheless, the value of outward stock compared to GDP grew rapidly during the 1990s, having risen from only 0.7 per cent in 1990 (UNCTAD 1999: Annex B). China is expected to maintain its rapid growth of outward direct investment as the internationalization of domestic enterprises proceeds.

There are several motives for outward FDI from China. Some is related to the expansion and support of foreign trade, frequently to developing countries, where it often takes the form of joint ventures to circumvent trade barriers. Other outward FDI is market-seeking, with the Haier company providing a prominent example. Outward FDI has also been prompted by the desire to acquire a stable supply of raw materials, and a search for foreign technology and management skills.

Outward FDI has progressed through three main stages (Cai 1999; Tseng 2000). In the first stage lasting until the mid-1980s, only state owned import-export corporations and enterprises seeking foreign economic and technological cooperation under the auspices of the Foreign Trade Commission had permission to invest abroad. During this period, some 185 non-trading enterprises contracted outgoing FDI mainly in developing countries and in catering, engineering, finance, and insurance. The second stage lasted from 1985 to 1990, during which companies with a separate legal entity, sufficient capital, technical and operational know-how, and a suitable overseas partner could invest abroad with the permission of the foreign trade ministry (MOFERT). In this period, 577 overseas enterprises were established in over 90 countries. Many of these hosts were developed countries and the spread of business widened considerably. It was during this stage that the first transnational corporations emerged from China. These were import and export companies, such as the China National Metals and Minerals Import and Export Corporation which by 1989 already had 49 companies, joint ventures, and representative offices in 23 countries and regions.

The third stage characterized the 1990s, during which both inward and outward FDI increased dramatically. For a while, in the first half of the 1990s, China provided the second largest FDI outflow among developing countries after Taiwan, though this was later exceeded by countries such as South Korea and Malaysia (UNCTAD 1999: Annex B). The range of Chinese enterprises investing abroad widened beyond foreign trade corporations to include foreign business-oriented conglomerates such as CITIC and Guangdong Enterprises, large industrial companies such as Shougang Steel, entrepreneurially led state-owned enterprises (SOEs) like Haier, and SMEs such as Kelon, Galanz, and Huawei. Shougang, for example, has fifteen overseas enterprises and offices with an accumulated FDI of US $13.2 million. Haier has plants in the Philippines, Indonesia, and Malaysia and has invested US $30 million in a new South Carolina factory to produce refrigerators. Kelon, which started as a township enterprise, is listed on the Hong Kong Stock Exchange, has moved its headquarters to Hong Kong, and in 1996 invested 1.1 billion Japanese Yen to establish a subsidiary in Japan to undertake R&D for electronic appliances (Bruton, Lan, and Lu 2000).

There are certain characteristics of Chinese firms' foreign market entry strategy (Zhang and Van den Bulcke 1996). Their capital outlay tends to be small and there is a preference to form joint ventures in order to reduce investment risk. Most China investors are unlikely to consider alternative countries in deciding on FDI, but rely instead quite heavily on ethnic and cultural links. These measures to reduce risk and psychic distance are an attempt to compensate for an unfamiliarity with local business conditions and a shortage of qualified staff who possess appropriate language skills and international business experience. Nevertheless, we shall see that problems continue to arise.

## 24.2 PROBLEMS ATTENDING CHINA'S ROLE IN INTERNATIONAL BUSINESS

### 24.2.1 Inward investment

'The golden days of foreign investment in China are over', according to the EIU (1999: ch. 9: 1), which describes the problems that many foreign companies have experienced there. Annual sums of newly contracted FDI to China fell from 1996 onward, and there was a particularly dramatic fall in 1999.[4] China only received an additional US $41 billion of new foreign investment during 1999, a decline of 21 per cent from 1998, while foreign investment actually used fell by over 11 per cent (*China Economic News* 2000c). If allowance is made for the fact that China commitments sold by one foreign company to another are counted as 'fresh' foreign capital, the true figure is certainly lower (*The Economist* 1999).

The decline in FDI inflow reflects the increasing difficulty that many foreign-investing firms have experienced in making an acceptable return on their investment. From its 1998 study, AT Kearney estimated that some 60 per cent of Sino-foreign joint ventures were not making money and that about one-quarter of all multinationals had pulled out of at least one China operation. When asked the reason for withdrawing, some 44 per cent said a lack of profitability (Wonacott 1999). China is regarded as a land of promise, but for many investors that promise has yet to be fulfilled. An analysis of industrial

[4] However, the hazard of focusing on just one year is demonstrated by a subsequent rise in newly contracted FDI of 27 per cent during the first quarter of 2000 (*Asian Wall Street Journal*, 2000). Moreover, inward FDI is expected to rise substantially following China's accession to the WTO.

census data concludes that the median return on equity of foreign companies in China was only 3.1 per cent in 1996 (Li and Tse 1999*a*). Some companies have pulled out of China altogether, including the Royal Bank of Canada, South-western Bell, Fosters, and Marks & Spencer (from Shanghai). In the case of Southwestern Bell the problem lay in regulatory obstacles. Fosters failed to make any profit in China's oversupplied beer market.

A more common reaction has been retrenchment. Unilever, for example, has cut costs by replacing expensive expatriate employees with local staff and moving to a leaner structure through consolidating fourteen joint ventures into just three operating companies (Jacob 2000). Also many new projects have been put on hold (Harding 1999). On the other hand, there are also many companies that are still making money, and surveys of Hong Kong and European firms with operations in China indicate that many remain satisfied with their performance (Fiducia 1999; Child *et al.* 2000). It is therefore extremely difficult to generalize about experience in such a huge and diversified country.

It is, nevertheless, possible to identify factors in China as an investment environment that have obliged many foreign firms to reconsider their position there. These stem essentially from the combination of a less benign economic environment, in which growth is slowing and competition intensifying, with the continuing presence of governmental inhibitors on the ability of foreign companies to compete with a free hand and to invest where returns are most favorable. The quality of China's business support infrastructure, in terms of intermediate institutions and managerial competence, also compares unfavorably with many other countries, although this aspect of the environment is improving rapidly.

## 24.2.2 China as an environment for inward FDI

The growth of domestic competition has resulted both from market entry by foreign companies and from the rise of local market leaders. The latter has been quite striking in some sectors. In white goods, local companies such as Haier and Kelon have beaten back foreign brands, which is one of the reasons why Whirlpool from the USA withdrew from the refrigerator and air conditioner markets. In the PC market, Compaq Computer was the leader in 1994 with a 21 per cent share of China's personal computer business. By 1999, it only had 9 per cent, while Legend Computer based in Beijing had become the country's most successful PC maker with a 17 per cent market share (Sesser 1999). Some of the growing competition has come from domestic private and collective firms which, according to the 1996 data already mentioned, achieved median returns on equity of 19.5 and 9.4 per cent respectively (Li and Tse 1999*a*). In addition, certain key SOEs have benefited from government subsidies and cheap loans, and domestic producers as a whole tend to gain from informal regulatory assistance in ways that are illustrated below.

The huge inventories accumulating in some industries have also discouraged foreign investors. These have resulted from a combination of slowdown in the economy, market saturation in many traditional industries, and over-investment. China experienced over two years of continuous deflation, up to the middle of 2000. From a portfolio investor's perspective, it is undesirable to invest in a company holding inventories during a period of deflation, since they will eventually cause large losses. Direct investors such as multinationals are reluctant to commit to building new plants for fear of exacerbating excess capacity. Consumer durable industries, such as producers of refrigerators, televisions, and washing machines, are particularly badly affected by excess capacity. For example, Changhong is China's largest and most respected manufacturer of television sets. In 1999 it had 30 per cent of its annual production stuck in inventory, and other TV makers were in a similar position. The industry was beset with massive over-capacity, indicated by the gap between its production capacity of 35 million units per year and a demand running at only 25 million units. Changhong responded in April 1999 by slashing its prices by 20 per cent and initiating a price war (Chang 1999; Tsiang 1999).

A competitive market, the growth policies pursued by new entrants, and more sophisticated buyers, are creating pressures to offer open credit terms. Dun and Bradstreet's 1998 survey of 104 foreign companies in China, revealed that the percentage under pressure to ease credit terms had more than doubled to 40 per cent from the previous year. Days sales outstanding (DSO), which indicates the average time it takes a company to receive payment, of between forty and ninety days were the most common among the respondents, peaking in the sixty to ninety day period. Bad debt was also a problem, though less so among more recently established companies (Dun & Bradstreet 1998).

It has become clear that, as competitive pressures mount, regulators in China are prepared to defend domestic firms and to preserve national control over key sectors, if necessary by taking measures hostile to foreign-investing firms. Thus the government's concern to support domestic producers has led it to issue what are, in effect, 'buy local' orders for industries such as mobile telecommunications equipment, certain pharmaceutical products, and some kinds of power generation equipment. This places foreign producers at a significant disadvantage. Examples continue to be reported of non-tariff barriers that are erected by Chinese bureaucrats to protect local companies against foreign competition (e.g. Johnson 2000). Moreover, the periodic tightening of foreign exchange controls creates further difficulties for foreign firms seeking to repatriate earnings or to purchase from abroad. A European Union survey in 1999 found 40 per cent of companies claiming that they were slowing or canceling investments involving foreign-currency related financing (Seidlitz and Murphy 1999). The US–China Business Council reported that nearly 50 per cent of its members had decided 'to reconsider, delay or even cancel intended' investment because of difficulties in importing goods and services and in repatriating profits (Harding 1999).

The Chinese government is also determined to retain control in what it considers to be key sectors. This is illustrated by the order of the Ministry of Information Industry that contracts made under the so-called China-China-Foreign formula are illegal. Under this formula, foreign investors such as Sprint, Welcom, NTT, France Telcom, and Siemens had participated indirectly in China's second largest telecoms group (China Unicom) through second joint ventures that they controlled (Parkes 1999). At the time of writing, the issue of foreign ownership in sectors such as financial services and telecoms was not finally resolved despite protracted negotiations. The liberalization that foreign investors had expected to occur in the later 1990s, especially in services, did not take place.

Consistent with their emphasis on preserving control, Chinese regulators continue to place restrictions on the use of one of the main contemporary vehicles for attracting investment by MNCs, namely acquisition. The announcement of a new enterprise reform campaign in September 1997 appeared to open up opportunities for foreign investors to buy up struggling state-owned enterprises. What has actually transpired is a continuation of a practice already in place by which companies could buy into SOEs, usually through joint venture or joint stock arrangements, rather than buy them outright. One notable exception, clearly regarded as experimental by Chinese regulators, may however open the door to acquisition as a normal process in the future. This was Kodak's purchase in March 1998 of the assets of three ailing SOE film manufacturers through the establishment of a 'joint-share' company (EIU 1999: ch. 9: 37).

A further widespread cause of complaint from foreign companies operating in China concerns the weak enforcement of intellectual property right protection (EIU 1999: ch. 10). China ranked forty-eighth out of the fifty-nine countries surveyed by the World Economic Forum for strength of IPR protection and fifty-fourth for compliance with court rulings (World Economic Forum 1999). There is a major risk of technological leakage and reverse engineering, while there have also been many cases of brand piracy. The source of this problem lies not so much in a lack of statutory provision for legal protection as in the central government's inability to ensure the enforcement of such provision. Indeed, the paradox of widespread government involvement in business affairs, coupled with weak enforcement at the local level, gives rise to local anomalies which the central authorities may not be able to resolve.

The quality of factor inputs and business support services available in China is improving, aided by the institutional reforms and policies of technology transfer which are discussed later in this chapter. Nevertheless, they generally fall below world standards. As an indication, the World Economic Forum survey ranked China fiftieth out of fifty-nine countries for both loan availability and sophistication of financial markets, and fifty-sixth for overall quality of management (World Economic Forum 1999).

The nature of China as an environment for foreign investment can be clarified by reference to Porter's (1990) 'diamond' of determinants of national competitive advantage. Porter argues that different locations vary in their competitive advantages and, by extension, in the advantages or otherwise that they offer to firms operating in a given location. Locational factors include both demand and supply conditions, many of which can be affected by government policies. On the demand side, the size, growth, and sophistication of the market are considered important factors, as is the strength of local competitive pressures to improve quality and performance. On the supply side, the availability of production factors and supporting industries and business service providers are regarded as significant (see also Porter 1994). In China's case, government intervention and the legal system are important additional institutional determinants of the conditions facing foreign investing companies.

In the main, China's attraction as an environment for foreign investment lies in its market rather than on the supply side (World Economic Forum 1999). This explains why the great majority of companies providing inward FDI have done so for market-seeking reasons and why increasing competition in the domestic market has led to disappointment. Nevertheless, the combination of a large domestic market with the growing range of services and other inputs available in rapidly developing centers such as Shanghai, is encouraging companies to locate their regional offices in China. These offices are also well placed to facilitate exports from China plants to other parts of the Asia-Pacific region.

The factors in Porter's 'diamond' are also likely to have a bearing upon the preferences of foreign investors concerning the governance of their operations in China. The combination of market-seeking opportunities with poorly developed supply conditions, including the supply of high quality local managers and partners, will encourage the push towards a controlling level of ownership already noted. The argument is broadly as follows. The more favorable the demand conditions prevailing in a host country, the greater the attraction for inward market-seeking investment and the more prepared international companies will be to commit high levels of investment giving them sole or dominant ownership in local operations. Similarly, if a host country is deficient in the quality of its factors of production or in the development of supporting industries, the foreign investor will need to make good these deficiencies either through a direct injection of capital and non-capital resources and/or by contracting for necessary supporting inputs. For the same reason, it will need to inject more direct managerial support. These moves signify greater involvement in ownership and control. On the other hand, rivalry from sophisticated domestic producers may increase the willingness of foreign investors to take such producers on as joint venture partners, thus diluting their ownership stake. This is because the domestic producers represent a threat as independent competitors, and they can also offer value by way of distinctive competencies.

China is thus suggestive of the ways in which host location conditions act as contingencies for the corporate governance of FDI. This is an issue that merits further research.

## 24.2.3 Outward investment[5]

Although it is on a much smaller scale than inward FDI, China's outward foreign investment has been accompanied by a number of problems, some of them also related to government involvement. Government is heavily involved in controlling and steering the outward FDI process. Depending on the type, scale, and location of direct, non-trade, investments being proposed, approvals are required from different levels of government. Projects valued at US $1 million or above require central government approval, whereas smaller investments are approved either by local provincial and municipal governments or by ministries responsible for the prospective investment. Using this administrative framework, the Chinese government has been active in encouraging specific types of outward FDI that it considers will generate benefits for the domestic economy and link in with its development assistance programs. It employs tax incentives, subsidies, national bank loans with preferential terms, and better access to the domestic market for goods produced by Chinese overseas affiliates. As Cai (1999: 870) notes, 'in any analysis of Chinese outward FDI, it is . . . important to point out that political considerations always play an important role'.

This highly administered system of outward FDI is, however, deficient in a number of respects. The government does not have a specific policy for such FDI and as a result its guidance and incentive policies also lack clarity. Relevant laws with respect to Chinese foreign affiliates are lacking, and

---

[5] This section draws heavily on Cai (1999).

a mechanism to conduct post-approval supervision and evaluation is not in place.

Since Chinese foreign affiliates are still mainly SOEs, they tend to be managed like their parent companies in a centralized and inflexible manner. Lacking the necessary autonomy regarding personnel, finance, and compensation levels, they are run inefficiently and without scope for local initiative. Many Chinese parent companies still suffer from the absence of any strategic orientation within the previous command economy. They do not have a clear strategy for their overseas business or an effective evaluation and supervision system. Another inherited problem lies in the tendency of government enterprises to appoint to overseas managerial positions on the basis of administrative connection rather than managerial ability, a practice that encouraged notoriously ill-judged behavior in the mid-1990s among the so-called 'Red Chip' companies registered and listed in Hong Kong.

While some of these problems stem from what Cai (1999: 876) calls 'the lingering legacy of the previous command economy', they are exacerbated by the fact that China is still a long way down the learning curve in respect of its engagement in the international economy. Many of its firms investing abroad lack a good understanding of host country environments or a basis on which to assess the credibility of local partners. Moreover, their affiliates usually lack qualified personnel with international management skills, sufficient host country knowledge, and a sound understanding of international standards.

This combination of governmental influence and inexperience has in many cases resulted in the under-achievement of outward Chinese FDI. It is unlikely, however, to preclude a continuing growth in such FDI, effected increasingly through the internationalization of entrepreneurial firms like Haier that have succeeded in breaking away from old ways and restrictions.

# 24.3 CHINA'S INSTITUTIONAL CONTEXT

It is apparent from the previous discussion that a fundamental characteristic of Chinese society is the deep involvement of officialdom with business life. This characteristic is associated with many of the difficulties experienced by both inward and outward investors. The interventionist role of government has deep roots in Chinese history and is not simply a product of the socialist legacy, even though this has been a reinforcing factor (Gernet 1982). The role of the state in Chinese society is based on an assumption that its officials have the legitimacy to represent the collective interest over that of individual or sectional interest. Hence government intervenes frequently in both inward and outward FDI projects. Walder (2000: 64) has noted that 'the continuing role played by government at all levels in the management of enterprises and the guidance of local economies' confounds the expectations of many experts on economic transition. Thus the government's role in China is not confined to regulation and taxation. Chinese officials actively manage enterprises in villages, towns, and smaller cities, play an active role in assisting the development of local firms, and invest in the private economy. They regard it as their function to work for the interests of the enterprises under their purview in any deals with foreign investors and in respect of any competitive threats from foreign-invested companies.[6]

The power of officialdom to intervene, and the temptation to abuse such power, is a particular source of complexity and uncertainty for foreign firms investing in China. Even though China is now engaged in major institutional change under its continuing program of economic reform, it would be very sanguine to expect deeply entrenched official values and behavior patterns simply to melt away with the signing of formal commitments such as membership of the WTO. The practical and theoretical issues raised by China's growing engagement in international business have to be considered in the light of this institutional context. It is appropriate to do so through the lens offered by institutional theory.

I have argued elsewhere (Child 2000a) that the impact of global forces upon firms is mediated by institutions at the supra-national level (such as the WTO), the regional level (such as the EU and NAFTA), and at the national level. Global forces are both material and ideational. The former consist primarily of the economic and technological developments associated with trade liberalization and IT. The latter consist of the ideas, tastes, and values that are now circulating more widely and freely around the world than ever before. How these global forces impact upon the operations of business within a given context depends importantly on the institutions active in that context, as well as local culturally informed norms. It is particularly important to take account of this institutional mediation in China because it is more entrenched and pervasive than in most other countries.

A growing body of research has identified the key national institutions that impact upon the policies and operations of firms, and which hence constitute distinctive contexts for business (Orru, Biggart, and Hamilton 1997; Biggart

---

[6] The maintenance of substantial state paternalism is, however, also characteristic of some other transition economies such as Russia and the Ukraine. See Ch. 25 by Meyer in this volume.

and Guillén 1999; Whitley 1992*a*, 1992*b*, 1999). Such research suggests an analytical framework that focuses on three main categories of institution: government, business system, and intermediate institutions. The characteristics related to government include the extent to which markets are administratively regulated, the degree of centralization in government economic policy, and the extent of government ownership in business. The nature of ownership and corporate governance, and openness to foreign capital and international trade are highly significant features of business systems. Intermediate institutions include the legal, financial, production, distribution, and management development systems of the country concerned. Some institutions, such as the educational system, help to form organizational competencies. Others, such as the banking and insurance system, provide intermediate services, and other support services such as health care. Yet others impose legal and regulatory constraints. In China's case, governmental bodies are involved in each of these roles through public ownership and/or active policy determination.[7]

### 24.3.1 Government

China's government operates through a complex system of state legislative and executive bodies, central ministries such as MOFTEC (Ministry of Foreign Trade and Economic Cooperation), a wide range of local authorities, intermediate institutions such as banks and the judiciary, and SOEs. It has been the primary source of changes introduced to the country since China embarked on its transition and opening to international business in 1979. In introducing these changes, the central government has followed two complementary principles: pragmatism and the preservation of social stability. These principles are likely to be maintained into the future.

Pragmatism is evident in the experimental approach adopted towards reforms. Most have followed a set pattern: a change is introduced experimentally within a geographically defined area, the reform is then modified in the light of experience and subsequently legitimized by the central government for economy-wide adoption (Child 1994; Naughton 1995). Deng Xiaoping's famous aphorism was that reform should advance by 'taking two steps forward, one step back'. While this approach has provided an uncontroversial means for China to reform almost continuously, its inherent non-linear flexibility can create uncertainties for international firms as to the exact

---

[7] Child and Tse (2001) provide a fuller analysis of China's business related institutions.

speed and direction of evolving reforms. The fact that the 'steps back' are normally taken by governmental fiat in response to major obstacles adds to the uncertainty. While China's economic reform is incremental in its stepwise nature, and is path-dependent insofar as it is conditioned by existing institutional structures, it is also recursive.

The second principle is the preservation of social stability. At a number of critical times, most notably in 1981 and 1989, there were marked shifts in policy that balanced the pace of reform with the need for stability. Attempts to maintain this balance continue to give rise to instability in government policy, such as an oscillation between encouragement and discouragement of bank lending to ailing enterprises (Rawski 1998). The authorities face the dilemma that growth is a requirement for social stability because it provides new employment, yet the enterprise restructuring needed to create the conditions for performance-led growth threatens social disruption in the shorter term.

The constant interplay between reform and the need for stability has also led China to evolve into a highly differentiated economy (Nee 1992). It contains centrally planned sectors, such as oil refining, still dominated by enterprises with hybrid governmental and commercial features, as well as entirely market driven sectors such as food processing with a full range of enterprise forms (Luo 2000). To circumvent open conflict between reform and conservative factions, the Chinese leadership has creatively called this a 'market system with socialist characteristics'.

China's central government has decentralized authority from central to lower level governmental units at provincial, city, and village levels. These 'local' governments are now able to formulate their own policies for attracting investment and for business operations under their jurisdictions, within a general framework set by the central government. Decentralization is also underway in China's ministries, where provincial sub-units are encouraged to fund their own budgets independently. These moves towards decentralization have been motivated by the inability to manage activities at the micro level in an increasingly complex and sophisticated economy. The financial drain on the central budget of maintaining a centrally planned system has reinforced the move to decentralization (Li and Tse 1999).

The process of decentralization has, however, not proceeded smoothly (Feinerman 1998) and there have been sharp oscillations within the central–local power balance. Often, the central government has not been able to find effective institutional mechanisms to ensure that local initiatives are prudent and consistent with overall national interests. It has resorted instead to periodic administrative interventions. The fundamental problem is that China has not yet been able to work out its own system of federalism (Pei 1999), and this will continue to generate considerable uncertainty in the Chinese business environment.

## 24.3.2 The business system in China

The heart of China's industrial structure lies in the relationship between firms and government. Through ownership ties and mutual dependence, many firms are integrated with government at various levels. Scholars have described this relationship as 'network capitalism' (Biggart and Hamilton 1992; Boisot and Child 1996), and it has been associated with *guanxi* as a special Chinese cultural characteristic. It has survived in China despite the considerable changes since the economic reform began in 1979. The multi-level *guanxi* system sustains a fragmented economy in which few firms dominate (Li and Tse 1999*b*).

From an economy that in 1980 was dominated by SOEs commanding 76 per cent of industrial output, China today has a wide range of firms that are differently constituted in terms of their ownership. According to Nee (1992), and Boisot and Child (1996), there are four main categories of firm in China. These are non-marketized and marketized state-owned enterprises (contributing 28.2 per cent of industrial output in 1998), collective enterprises (38.4 per cent of industrial output), private enterprises (17.1 per cent of industrial output), and other types of firm, primarily foreign-invested ones (22.9 per cent) (National Bureau of Statistics 1999: Table 13.3). Except for some in the first category, these firms secure resources and dispose of outputs through markets. From the early 1990s, a significant development has been the conversion of SOEs to joint-stock companies (JSCs). The number of such companies rose from 2,751 in 1991 to 12,500 in 1997. By 1996, 530 JSCs were listed on the Shanghai and Shenzhen stock exchanges, over fifty were listed in Hong Kong, and about twenty in New York (Lau and Tse 1999*b*). The conversion of SOEs into JSCs offers new opportunities for international firms seeking to buy into local companies.

Since their inception under China's economic reform, private enterprises have had to survive the harshest environment (IFC 2000). They mostly comprise entrepreneurial and small businesses, without the superior technology and management skills of foreign firms, or the institutional sponsorship afforded to other types of Chinese firm. The private sector is, however, the fastest-growing in China, and massive lay-offs from restructured SOEs have produced many more entrepreneurs. Private enterprises now employ over 13 million people. Realizing their substantial economic contribution, the government in February 1999 amended the country's constitution to provide private firms with the same legal rights as the publicly owned part of the economy, and so remove their previous handicaps. The establishment of new venture capital funds should provide needed financial capital to the promising few, and is a sign of developments to come. While few private firms have so far become joint venture partners or acquisition targets for foreign firms, some of them will become more attractive in the future especially in areas such as software and Internet development (Becker 1999; *China Economic News* 1999; *The Economist* 1999).

The changes in progress, such as the further reform of SOEs and the legitimation of private business, will permanently alter China's business system. So far, Chinese leaders have advanced the reform of SOEs through greater marketization, as a way of reducing economic distortions, and through increasing privatization. Rather than building South Korean type Chaebols, the government has encouraged the break-up of large SOEs with some exceptions, into small units for sale to other firms. Accordingly, mergers and acquisitions are likely to dominate the business scene in China (*South China Morning Post* 1999). MNCs have eagerly participated in these mergers in Internet firms and airlines.

It is expected that some successful JSCs and SOEs will capitalize on the opportunity to expand their operations through the input of additional funds, technology, and even export opportunities. Government sources envisage that some large SOEs will develop into international firms featuring among the Fortune 500. A survey revealed that 70 per cent of the top three brands in fifty consumer product markets derive from local firms (Hong Kong Trade Development Council 1998). Given the size of the China market, these firms can leverage their domestic market power to expand internationally, a strategy that has proved to be effective among newly emerged Asian companies such as Acer and Lucky Gold Star. As noted earlier, an increasing number of Chinese firms are expanding into overseas markets. Whether many of them can catch up the enormously powerful giant global corporations, however, remains an open question (Nolan 1999).

## 24.3.3 Intermediate institutions

The government is also leading the development of the systems that support the operation of business. These primarily comprise the legal, production, finance, distribution, and management education systems. Each has gone through many changes since 1979 and their future development will have a significant bearing on the capacity of China's firms to compete internationally as well as on the environment that China offers to foreign firms.

Historically, China did not have a legal system independent of the state. Since 1979, there has been continuous legal reform in the field of business. This includes regulations governing the status of foreign firms and investment, and a body of new commercial laws. Yet, the implementation of China's laws remains a major source of uncertainty for MNCs. One problem lies in the use of ad hoc administrative amendments to regulations. Another stems from the central–local tension within government. The interpretation of laws is often left to local officials. Local interpretations frequently deviate from the original legislative intention and can change as one official replaces another. Therefore, despite continued legal reform evidence suggests that the law in China remains 'a tool of state administration' (Lubman 1995: 2).

China's technological system was the first to undergo dramatic changes. Licensing agreements and equity joint ventures were important vehicles for introducing modern production technologies into Chinese firms on an unprecedented scale. Recently, many foreign high-tech firms have set up R&D centers in China and some have acquired local Internet service providers. In reverse, some Chinese firms are establishing offices in major high-tech regions such as Silicon Valley to acquire technology first hand. Chinese firms are now exposed to global advances in technology through the Internet.

The most obvious milestones in the development of China's financial system are the establishment of its stock markets in Shanghai and Shenzhen in the 1990s. Yet the gradual reform of its banking system is equally significant, though the banking and financial sector has not yet been totally opened to international firms. In its negotiation to join WTO, the Chinese government has committed to a series of further reforms including the participation of foreign financial institutions. The availability of services from international financial institutions would considerably help in the provision to foreign-invested firms of working capital, trade finance, and insurance. Internal resistance to these proposals has, however, been strong.

Since 1992, however, the entry of foreign ventures in the retail sector has created some fundamental and far-reaching changes. Most retail development has been initiated by private enterprises and foreign ventures (Hong Kong Trade Development Council 1999). The reform of SOEs is likely to promote further changes in China's distribution system because many wholesalers are owned by the government. In addition, the development of China's railway and other transportation systems is facilitating the expansion of its distribution network. The current explosive growth of computers among the general population suggests that there will also be a rapid spread of electronic shopping and other forms of electronic commerce.[8]

Another significant factor in China's business environment is the supply of its human resources, especially those available to business (Warner 1995). So far, the development of its education system, particularly higher education, has been slow (UNDP 1999). The strength of China's major universities has been in technical subjects rather than commercial and management studies. The demand for management education far exceeds supply, with most graduates

---

[8] It is reported that in June 2000 there were approximately 10 million Internet subscribers in China with the figure expected to double every six months (Sheridan 2000).

receiving multiple job offers. To meet their immediate needs, many foreign-investing firms in China organize in-house executive programs or send their staff to management programs offered by different business schools outside of China and some domestic universities, such as Tsinghua and Fudan. However, new developments are apace including the formation of consortia with foreign schools to promote the development of business and management education.

China's intermediate institutions are developing quite rapidly, but this process still has a long way to go. While the country is by and large no longer a resource shortage economy in terms of basic physical services (power, water, and waste) or most raw materials, it remains short of the support services that intermediate institutions are expected to provide. A survey recently conducted by the author and colleagues of over 600 Hong Kong firms with operations in China is revealing on this point (Child *et al.* 2000). The availability of adequate support resources emerged as a significant predictor of how well their China business performs, especially the availability of marketing and technical know-how, and of trained staff. Many of these firms still experience the need to source such support from outside mainland China.

# 24.4 IMPLICATIONS FOR THEORY AND POLICY

The impact of globalization on China continues to be importantly mediated by that country's institutions. Although much of China's previous command economy has now been dismantled, governmental agencies continue to have an important impact on its relations with the international business community. It may well be that the country's rapid economic development and integration into the world community will result in the continued further disengagement of government from the highly interventionist position it still occupies. The trend towards privatization, and entry into the WTO, are clearly steps in that direction. However, an analysis of the present situation and the foreseeable future must take government intervention and its consequences into account.

The nature of government economic intervention can be conceptualized as pragmatic, experimental, and particularistic. As already noted, pragmatism has led to variability in the maintenance and application of policies and regulations. Experimentation has given rise to diversity, especially in the forms of business now extant in China, including those engaging in outward FDI. The strong element of particularism in Chinese culture (Trompenaars 1993) has a practical significance for business transactions there in terms of who you know and the basis on which the relationship is understood to rest. This accounts for the considerable attention given to the notion of *guanxi* that captures this characteristic. It contrasts with universalism, which denotes that it is culturally appropriate to apply the same rules and standards whoever the person may be. Given the latitude that local officials generally enjoy in dealing with the foreign firms located within their purview, particularism adds considerably to the uncertainty that China presents as an environment for international business.

The application of these concepts, combined with a recognition of the mediating role played by China's institutions, can generate a better understanding of that country's relevance to the theory and practice of international business. The final section of this chapter will illustrate this assertion in two ways. First by examining the nature of complexity in China's business environment and strategies available to foreign investing firms for coping with this. Second by exploring the relevance of China's differentiated business system for modes of engagement between Chinese and international firms.

## 24.4.1 The nature of China's complex environment

People with experience of China as an environment for doing business are very likely to emphasize its complexity and variability. Boisot and Child (1999) applied Kaufmann's (1993) analysis to depict the contours of this complexity. Briefly, Kauffman makes the following distinctions in a system consisting of nodes interlinked with varying degrees of density:

1. N refers to the number of parts in the system under consideration. Each part makes a fitness contribution which depends upon that part and on K other parts among the N.
2. K in effect reflects how richly cross-coupled the system is. With K=0 for example, there are no interactions. With K=N(N−1), on the other hand each node in the network is affected by every other node and we obtain the largest value for K.
3. P is a control parameter, ranging between 1.0 and 0.5, that tunes the behavior of the links between nodes. In this way they can be made to exhibit order, chaos, or a phase transition between those two states that is labeled 'the edge of chaos'. A high value for P reflects a high degree of

stability and structure, whereas low P, close to 0.5, is low in stability and structure

China as a socio-economic system displays a high level of Kaufmann's N. It consists of many and differentiated elements. We have highlighted the existence of different levels of government and multiple forms of enterprise. There are the additional complexities of many regions that contrast in wealth, education, and sub-cultures (Child and Stewart 1997). This differentiation lends China the character of a complex cellular society.

The cellular nature of China's society means that it is characterized by a high N but low levels of K between its constituent units. At the same time, levels of K are high *within* the system's constituent units, especially within local communities which have close-knit networks embracing administrative, political, and business groups. This combination creates tensions between the central and local levels in the governance system, and consequent ambiguities about their respective jurisdictions. While laws and regulations are formulated centrally, coordination between national government bodies is often ineffective and, in addition, laws and regulations are administered locally. This can give rise to considerable ambiguity as to who is 'the government' and inconsistencies between different agencies and localities.

Ambiguity about governmental jurisdictions and powers contributes to a low level of stability within the Chinese system and hence a low level of P. The form of complexity in China (low overall K combined with high local K and low P) poses far greater difficulties for those engaged in economic relationships, than does a high N *per se*. For it describes a situation in which economic governance tends to be organized through intensive relations coordinated according to implicit rules which can vary both between locations and over time.

The cognitive complexity (low P) which is caused by ambiguities as to the locus of power and initiative in the Chinese system, is added to by the lack of transparency of many Chinese laws and/or their uncertain enforcement, as is the case with intellectual property rights. Local governmental agencies have powers to interpret regulations, issue licenses, and impose taxes, which furnish ample scope for negotiation and corruption. The system is characterized by what Gell-Mann (1995) termed 'effective complexity', deriving from its irregularity, inherent tensions, and hence unpredictability.

This high level of complexity and uncertainty poses problems for local Chinese business people as well as foreign investors. Historically, the Chinese have sought to adapt to these contingencies by forming relational networks with lower numbers but denser inter-personal links than those typical of Western countries. These specific relationships, based on trust and implicit (non-codified) norms, fall into two broad categories. These are the family and the network based on reciprocated assistance and favor (*guanxi*). Therefore, to an important extent, transactions within the Chinese business system have been governed by relatively tacit norms and expectations, rather than by the more codified rules characteristic of transactions regulated either by hierarchical rules or by laws of contract applied to market dealings (Boisot and Child 1996). This is the backdrop against which a rapid implementation within China of formal WTO provisions may well prove to be a long and difficult process.

## 24.4.2 Strategies for handling environmental complexity

Despite the increasing codification and transparency of information in the Internet world, it is arguable that the breakdown of old structures in areas such as new flexible value chain arrangements and employment patterns are moving the system of international transactions closer to the effective complexity model. If this is the case, the transactional options available for handling China's complexity should enrich our appreciation of international business policy alternatives more generally.

Two broad approaches—complexity reduction and complexity absorption—have developed as cultural responses to the specific conditions of Western and oriental societies respectively over long periods of time. Complexity *reduction* entails the attempt to control complexity by reducing it to known proportions and routines, including attempts at reducing it via environmentalenactment such as lobbying. Complexity *absorption*, by contrast refers to the attempt to ride with complexity. Baumard (1999: 229) comments that organizations 'escape ambiguity when they cease concentrating on the reduction of complexity, but, on the contrary, direct their efforts towards its penetration'. Complexity absorption involves the creation of options and risk-hedging strategies often through networking with individuals or organizations having their own special knowledge of, and connections to, events. This response is broadly consistent with the management of uncertain opportunities by pursuing a number of high-variance outcomes as 'real options' (McGrath 1999).

MNCs entering China have a strategic choice in how to cope with the complexity they experience. The first option is to apply their standard policies and practices, which are well understood and compatible with their worldwide activities. They endeavor to do this by securing sufficient control over their affiliates and external influence so as to enact critical aspects of the Chinese environment. This is the strategy of reducing complexity by bringing it under apparent control. Reducing reliance on partners and external relationships will lower the transaction costs of social exchange, but most likely raise the transaction costs of exercising direct managerial control using expensive expatriates. Moreover, this policy could be of limited effectiveness in reducing risk because it places low value on the support of local partners and may also alienate powerful officials in the institutional environment. These factors point to a distinct limitation in the ownership advantages enjoyed by foreign firms operating in China, which may contribute significantly to their often disappointing performance in that country.

The second option is to try to absorb the complexity of the Chinese situation and this is the approach for which historically the Chinese have shown a cultural preference. Given the difficulties of gaining access to local networks and their implicit modes of operation, this approach requires the support of local partners. Absorption entails a greater degree of participation in local relational systems and hence raises the transaction costs of social exchange. It also engages the foreign firm in a greater level of variance than it is familiar with which may limit its ability to relate its policies and practices in China to its worldwide system. On the other hand, this policy can increase the firm's ability to learn and open up a greater range of options for it. This approach essentially attempts to reduce risk by co-opting those who can help to anticipate and interpret change and who can suggest a range of alternative actions. Such co-optation should also reduce the transaction costs of exercising direct managerial control.

Policy choices of this kind are clearly relevant to the basis on which international firms engage with Chinese counterparts. They illustrate how the particular case of China offers an opportunity to examine the trade-off between different kinds of transaction costs in the process of risk reduction. This is a theoretical avenue worth pursuing further, particularly if it is combined with an examination of relevant contingencies. Thus certain conditions may bear upon the ability of firms to enact their environments and adopt a complexity reducing approach successfully, or alternatively to handle complexity via the absorption approach. For firms operating in China, their ability to enact local environmental conditions will clearly be a function of factors such as their global reputation, and their skill at generating political goodwill. Smaller firms may not have either the resources, standing, or experience to adopt this policy, and will hence tend to rely more heavily on coping with China's complex environment through the assistance of partners.

The merit of developing a contingency analysis lies in the way it avoids the temptation to apply over-simple 'one-best-way' solutions to what is a quite varied set of circumstances. In recent years, something of a mythology has arisen extolling the virtues for foreign-investing firms of running their China affiliates as wholly-owned subsidiaries (e.g. Vanhonacker 1997). This is consistent with the implications, noted earlier, of applying Porter's locational advantages analysis to the prediction of FDI governance preferences. Yet, as we have also seen, the available evidence on the performance of foreign affiliates in China does not support such a simple universalistic nostrum and suggests instead that further more specific firm-level contingencies are in play.

We suggest that the contingency approach can be further informed by a close examination of specific cases. For instance, a detailed study of British firms with operations in China has given rise to two main conclusions that contribute in this way. First, the specific location of foreign operations within China's highly differentiated business system does not always make sole or controlling ownership a viable option. Government regulations do not permit it in some sectors, while in others partnership may be the price to pay for delivery of market access. Second, different ownership regimes can be successful, but a condition for such success is that the approach of the foreign partner to the ongoing processes of management and relationship building should suit the configuration of ownership and control that applies (Child 2000b).

## 24.4.3 Modes of engagement between Chinese and international firms

With the growth of both inward and outward FDI, it is becoming increasingly relevant to ask how Chinese firms are coming to engage with other firms within the international division of labor. Most of the integration that has been achieved thus far has been within China's domestic economy through the medium of alliances and subsidiaries. The contingency approach, just discussed, draws attention to several factors that have a bearing on the chosen mode of integration. One is governmental regulation, which restricts the form of Sino-foreign business cooperation in certain sectors. Another is the status of foreign-investing firms, with large MNCs generally having a preference for sole ownership and the financial strength to bear the additional risk this may entail. SME foreign investors are, by contrast, more likely to seek the help of local partners. A third factor is the order of entry into China, with early entrants tending towards the partnership mode and later entrants tending towards either a dominant equity share in joint ventures or sole ownership (Pan, Li, and Tse, 1999). A fourth factor is nationality of the foreign-investing firm. When they form joint ventures, partners from Western countries and Japan are more likely to choose SOEs and larger collective enterprises, whereas investors from overseas Chinese territories have often chosen small collectives or private firms as partners (Tse, Pan, and Au 1997).

A characteristic of China's business system noted earlier is the differentiation of Chinese firms into several categories, promoted in large measure by government classifications and policies. The various types of Chinese firm may well come to play a different role in overseas expansion. In strategic sectors, the Foreign Trade Corporations and large SOEs that remain under the guidance and patronage of the central government are likely to retain the edge in internationalization opportunities. With expertise in international operations and better business information, such firms prefer to invest in advanced technological firms in developed economies and in large raw material extraction projects through acquisitions and mergers (Cai 1999). Their relationship with MNCs is likely to be a primarily competitive one, since the Chinese government has hitherto balked at the prospect of foreign involvement in its strategic industries and also harbors ambitions for selected larger SOEs to join the ranks of the Fortune 500. As noted earlier, whether such ambitions can actually be realized through catching up with the leading MNCs remains an open question.

In other sectors, efficient joint stock and private firms, which have secured a strong position in the domestic market, may be the leaders in international expansion. Although firms like Haier have so far preferred to establish greenfield investment projects, some of these firms may consider joining alliances with foreign companies in order to profit from learning opportunities, much as many Japanese firms did previously (Hamel 1991). Some could also become potential targets for acquisition by MNCs, especially if they become financially over-stretched. Given the range of Chinese and international firms, there is a variety of ways in which both may be expected to engage with each other in international business. Table 24.1 sets these out.

The possibility of a matrix of modes of international business engagement arises from the *differentiation* among categories of firm on both the Chinese and international sides of the relationship. Firms by virtue of their size, focus, and level of experience tend to find different locations within the international division of labor, and this has implications for the kind of linkages they will form. Whereas large strategic SOEs will strive to compete on a par with MNCs and to remain independent of them, other Chinese firms without a political imperative behind them and/or not enjoying the same financial and technological strength are more likely to seek to form partnerships with international firms. The same logic applies to foreign internationalizing SMEs as well. Small effective Chinese firms may more rationally transact with MNCs and international SMEs as contractors of specialized local production and service provision, including high-tech development services. Overseas Chinese firms are already extending their regional networks to include mainland Chinese joint stock and private sector firms; such networks represent yet another means whereby Chinese firms are entering international business.

The implication of this analysis is that different types of Chinese firm will internationalize to varying extents and by contrasting routes. Large SOEs are expected to favor technology transfer agreements and overseas acquisition

Table 24.1 Emerging modes of business engagement between Chinese firms and international firms

| | Large strategic SOEs | Other SOEs (and large collectives) | Joint stock companies | Private sector firms (collectives, private cos.) |
|---|---|---|---|---|
| MNCs | Mainly competitors, some global alliances but mergers unlikely. Major SOE moves are government directed. | Mainly a JV relationship. | JVs and acquisitions by MNCs. | JVs, acquisitions by MNCs, and contracting to MNCs of specialized local production and services. |
| International SMEs | International SMEs supply specialized technologies to SOEs, as contractors, licensors, or JV partners; acquisitions of foreign SMEs by large internationalizing SOEs. | Mainly JVs, but some international SMEs may become contractors or licensors. | JVs and some acquisitions of foreign SMEs to facilitate market entry or consolidate market position. | JVs and private sector Chinese firms act as contractors of specialized local production and services to international SMEs. |
| Overseas Chinese firms | Few transactions or other business relationships. Operate in different sectors. | Mainly JVs. | JVs and regional network partners. | JVs and mutual network partners; some acquisitions by firms in both categories. |
| Most likely route to internationalization by Chinese firms | 1. Technology transfer agreements.<br>2. Acquisition of overseas firms and greenfield investment. Possible JVs in marketing and distribution. | Little or no internationalization. | 1. Overseas marketing.<br>2. Acquisitions primarily to strengthen market position. | 1. Contracts with overseas firms, esp. overseas Chinese.<br>2. Some mutual ownership (e.g. JVs).<br>3. Members of extensive regional networks. |

or greenfield investment. Few smaller SOEs and larger collectives have the resources to seek international expansion. Reformed JSCs are expected to market overseas from their domestic base. They seek acquisitions outside China in order to strengthen their position in foreign markets. Now that they have received official recognition, private sector firms are expected to enter into various contractual and joint venture arrangements, initially within overseas Chinese communities to which they have cultural and social links. They are therefore likely to expand their international presence through networks.

While this discussion remains somewhat speculative, recognition of the differentiation between the categories of Chinese and international firm alerts us to a range of likely ownership and transactional linkages between them, and hence to different bases on which Chinese firms will engage in international business. MNCs themselves are expected to form different kinds of relationship to the various categories of Chinese firm. This qualifies our earlier application of Porter's 'diamond' to the prediction of foreign investor ownership and control preferences in China as an investment location. A simple prediction is hazardous because the range of domestic firms both as competitors and potential partners is so extensive. The analysis also elaborates on the conventional assumption that MNCs investing in transition economies will follow a linear progression from dependence to independence, with sole ownership as the end point (cf. Prahalad 1997).

Moreover, the identification of a *range* of ways in which Chinese and foreign firms can engage together in international business suggests that the current debate on whether or not firms from developing and transition economies can compete in the global marketplace is being conducted in oversimplified terms. The example of China suggests that there are various possibilities involving a range of strategies on the part of both categories of firm which themselves cannot be treated as one of a kind.

# 24.5 Avenues for Further Inquiry

A comparison of this chapter and that by Meyer in the same volume indicates some of the unique features of China's transition from socialism. Taken as a whole, China is unquestionably a success story (Nolan 1995; Rawski 1999). This is one of the reasons why China has become such an important environment for MNCs and other international businesses, and why some of its own enterprises are themselves beginning to play an active role in global business.

China's policy makers have, however, insisted that certain fundamental features shall be retained in the course of the country's reform, above all the pervasive role of the state as the guardian of national and party interests. The distinctive structure of business and the interventionist industrial policies which arise from this insistence raise the fundamental question of how well strategies pursued in other parts of the global economy will succeed in China (Peng 2000). There is a general need for further research on institutions and their influence on corporate strategies and behaviors, and some of this could profitably proceed in China. It would also seem useful to apply Porter's framework to this research, but from the perspective of national or regional environments as conditions for FDI strategies rather than just from the original perspective of national competitiveness.

Two salient characteristics of China as a business environment underlie its complexity. These are the internal differentiation of its governmental and business systems, and its non-linear path of reform. China presents an opportunity for international business research to advance its understanding of contextual complexity and the alternative strategies available to firms for coping with it. We are at the beginning of this avenue of inquiry, which promises to have wider relevance in a world that is evidencing increasing 'effective complexity'. The challenge is to see whether conclusions derived from the specific case of China can be theorized and then tested for their general applicability.

Privatization has become a significant aspect of China's reform, first almost by default and now encouraged by the authorities. The private sector provides much of the country's growth and the evolution of this sector deserves close study. Such research should throw light on the ways that entrepreneurship can flourish within a highly controlled environment and in relation to the non-private sector which the Chinese authorities are committed to preserve in strategic industries. China is likely to remain a mixed-mode business system, in contrast to the Anglo-Saxon model and continuing comparisons between the two will highlight both the contingencies that sustain them and their relative strengths and weaknesses.

Examination of the variety of ways in which Chinese and foreign firms engage together in international business draws attention to the fact that firms are situated differentially with regard to the international economy. This is a function of the resource and other endowments that characterize their specific locations and sectors; it is also a consequence of firm-level characteristics such as size, ownership, and experience. How Chinese firms will form part of international business networks, and the basis on which they will relate with MNCs, SMEs, and overseas Chinese firms are issues that will be of increasing consequence for the future shape of international business.

Last, but by no means least, this chapter has taken China as a pre-eminent example of the contribution that an institutional and context-sensitive analysis can make to the study of international business. Business contexts that are unconventional to the main contemporary perspectives in this field of study can only serve to generate the discomfort that stimulates learning. China provides this kind of challenge to academics and practitioners alike.

# REFERENCES

*Asian Wall Street Journal* (2000). 'Chinese Growth Accelerates', 17 April: 3.

BAUMARD, PHILIPPE (1999). *Tacit Knowledge in Organizations.* Thousand Oaks, Calif.: Sage.

BEAMISH, PAUL W., (1993). 'The Characteristics of Joint Ventures in the People's Republic of China', *Journal of International Marketing*, 1: 29–48.

BECKER, JASPER (1999). 'Fortune at China's fingertips', *South China Morning Post Saturday Review*, 28 Aug.: 1.

BIGGART, NICOLE W., and HAMILTON, GARY G. (1992). 'On the Limits of a Firm-based Theory to Explain Business Networks: The Western Bias of Neoclassical Economics', in Nitin Nohria and Robert G. Eccles (eds.), *Networks and Organizations.* Boston, Mass.: Harvard Business School Press: 471–90.

—— and GUILLÉN, MARIO F. (1999). 'Developing Difference: Social Organization and the Rise of the Auto Industries of South Korea, Taiwan, Spain and Argentina', *American Sociological Review*, 64: 722–47.

BOISOT, MAX, and CHILD, JOHN (1996). 'From Fiefs to Clans and Network Capitalism: Explaining China's Emerging Economic Order', *Administrative Science Quarterly*, 41 (4): 600–28.

—— (1999). 'Organizations as Adaptive Systems in Complex Environments: The Case of China', *Organization Science*, 10: 237–52.

BRUTON, GARRY D., LAN, HAILIN, and LU, YUAN (2000). 'China's Township and Village Enterprises: Kelon's Competitive Edge', *Academy of Management Executive*, 14: 19–27.

CAI, KEVIN G. (1999). 'Outward Foreign Direct Investment: A Novel Dimension of China's Integration into the Regional and Global Economy', *China Quarterly*, 160, Dec.: 856–80.

CHANG, LESLIE (1999). 'China's TV Price War Puts Economic Division in Focus', *Asian Wall Street Journal*, 7–8 May: 1, 12.

CHILD, JOHN (1994). *Management in China During the Age of Reform.* Cambridge: Cambridge University Press.

—— (2000*a*). 'Theorizing About Organization Cross-nationally', *Advances in Comparative International Management*, 13: 27–75.

—— (2000*b*). 'A Configurational Analysis of International Joint Ventures Drawing Upon Experience in China', working paper no. 2000-004-01, Chinese Management Centre, University of Hong Kong.

CHILD, JOHN, (*cont.*) CHUNG, LEANNE, DAVIES, HOWARD, and NG, SEK HONG (2000). *Managing Business in China.* Hong Kong: Hong Kong General Chamber of Commerce.

——and STEWART, SALLY (1997). 'Regional Differences in China and Their Implications for Sino-Foreign Joint Ventures', *Journal of General Management*, 23/3: 65–86.

——and TSE, DAVID K. (forthcoming 2001). 'China's Transition and its Implications for International Business', *Journal of International Business Studies*, 32.

——and YAN, YANNI (forthcoming 2001). 'National and Transnational Effects in International Business: Indications from Sino-Foreign Joint Ventures', *Management International Review.*

*China Economic News* (1999). 'Constitution Amendment Gives Solid Legal Support to Private Businesses', 15 March: 1–2.

——(2000*a*). 'How Does China's Foreign Trade do in 1999?', 14 Feb.: 7–8.

——(2000*b*). 'Foreign Investment in China', 3 Jan.: 6–7.

——(2000*c*). 'An Account of Foreign Investment Used in China From Jan–Dec 1999', 6 March: 13.

*China Quarterly* (1999). Special issue on 'The People's Republic of China after 50 years', no. 159.

DANIELS, J. D., KRUG, J., and NIGH, D. (1985). 'US Joint Ventures in China: Motivation and Management of Political Risk', *California Management Review*, 27: 46–58.

DUN & BRADSTREET (1998). *The 1998 Dun and Bradstreet Survey of Accounts Receivables and Credit Systems.* Shanghai: Dun & Bradstreet, China.

*Economist The*, (1999). 'China's Private Surprise', 19 June: 103–4.

EIU (Economist Intelligence Unit) (1999). *China Hand.* Hong Kong: EIU.

——and Andersen Consulting (1995). *Moving China Ventures Out of the Red into the Black.* Hong Kong: EIU.

FEINERMAN, JAMES V. (1998). 'The Give and Take of Central–Local Relations', *China Business Review*, Jan–Feb: 16–23.

FIDUCIA LTD. (1999). *European Investment in China.* Hong Kong: Fiducia Ltd.

GELL-MANN, MURRAY (1995). *The Quark and the Jaguar: Adventures in the Simple and the Complex.* London: Abacus.

GERNET, JACQUES (1982). *A History of Chinese Civilization.* Cambridge: Cambridge University Press.

HAMEL, GARY (1991). 'Competition for Competence and Inter-partner Learning Within International Strategic Alliances', *Strategic Management Journal*, 12: 83–103.

HARDING, JAMES (1999). 'End of the China Goldrush', *Financial Times*, 25 March: 19.

HONG KONG TRADE DEVELOPMENT COUNCIL (1998). *China's Consumer Market.* Hong Kong: Hong Kong Trade Development Council.

——(1999). *Expanding China's Distribution Channels: A Practical Guide.* Hong Kong: Hong Kong Trade Development Council.

HU, MICHAEL Y., and CHEN, HAIYANG (1994). 'The Performance of Hong Kong Foreign Subsidiaries in China', *Advances in Chinese Industrial Studies*, 4: 185–98.

IFC (International Finance Corporation) (2000). *Private Enterprise in China.* Washington, DC: IFC.

JACOB, RAHUL (2000). 'Chinese Clean-up Operation', *Financial Times*, 18 May: 12.

JOHNSON, IAN (2000). 'China Continues to Hobble Foreign Firms', *Asian Wall Street Journal*, 23 March: 1, 5.

KAUFFMAN, STUART (1993). *The Origins of Order*. Oxford: Oxford University Press.

LAU, CHUNG MING, and TSE, DAVID K. (1999). 'New Ownership Forms in Transitional Economies: Emergence, Characteristics and Performance of China's Joint Stock Companies', working paper no. 1999-003-01, March, Chinese Management Centre, University of Hong Kong.

LEE, JOSEPH S. (ed.) (1996). *The Emergence of the South China Growth Triangle*. Taipei: The Chung-Hua Institution for Economic Research.

LI, SHAOMIN, and TSE, DAVID K. (1999*a*). *China Industrial Markets Yearbook 1999*. Hong Kong: City University of Hong Kong Press.

——— (1999*b*). 'The "Visible" and "Invisible" Hands On Firm Performance in China: An Institutional Approach', working paper, Marketing Department, City University of Hong Kong.

LIN, DANMING (1995). 'Sino–Hong Kong Joint Ventures: Strategies, Structures and Performance', unpublished Ph.D. thesis, University of Hong Kong.

LUBMAN, STANLEY (1995). 'Introduction: The Future of Chinese Law', *China Quarterly*, special issue on 'China's Legal Reform', 141: 1–21.

LUO, YADONG (1996). 'Evaluating the Performance of Strategic Alliances in China', *Long Range Planning*, 29: 534–42.

——— (2000). *Multinational Corporations in China*. Copenhagen: Copenhagen Business School Press.

McGRATH, RITA G. (1999). 'Falling Forward: Real Options Reasoning and Entrepreneurial Failure', *Academy of Management Review*, 24: 13–30.

MEIER, JOHANNES, PEREZ, JAVIER, and WOETZEL, JONATHAN R. (1995). 'Solving the Puzzle: MNCs in China', *The McKinsey Quarterly*, 1995/2: 20–33.

NATIONAL BUREAU OF STATISTICS (1999). *China Statistical Yearbook 1999*. Beijing: China Statistics Press.

NAUGHTON, BARRY (1995). *Growing Out of the Plan: Chinese Economic Reform 1978–1993*. New York: Oxford University Press.

NEE, VICTOR (1992). 'Organizational Dynamics of Market Transition: Hybrid Forms, Property Rights and Mixed Economy in China', *Administrative Science Quarterly*, 37 (1): 1–27.

NOLAN, PETER (1995). *China's Rise, Russia's Fall: Politics, Economics and Planning in the Transition from Stalinism*. Basingstoke: Macmillan.

——— (1999). 'Restructuring China's Large Enterprises in the Epoch of Explosive Globalisation: Challenge and Response', Judge Institute of Management Studies, University of Cambridge.

ORRU, MARIO, BIGGART, NICOLE W., and HAMILTON, GARY G. (eds.) (1997). *The Economic Organization of East Asian Capitalism*. Thousand Oaks Calif.: Sage.

PAN, YIGANG, and CHI, PETER S. K. (1999). 'Financial Performance and Survival of Multinational Corporations in China', *Strategic Management Journal*, 20: 359–74.

——— LI, SHAOMIN, and TSE, DAVID K. (1999). 'The Impact of Order and Mode of Market Entry on Profitability and Market Share', *Journal of International Business Studies*, 30: 81–103.

PARKES, CHRISTOPHER (1999). 'Investors Prepare to Fight for Contracts "revised" by Beijing', *Asian Wall Street Journal*, 17 Nov.: 6.

PENG, MIKE W. (2000). *Business Strategies in Transition Economies*. Thousand Oaks, Calif.: Sage.

PEI, MINXIN (1999). 'Is China stable?', *Asian Wall Street Journal*, 28 July: 10.

PORTER, MICHAEL E. (1990). *The Competitive Advantage of Nations*. New York: Free Press.

——(1994). 'Competitive Strategy Revisited: A View From the 1990s', in Paula B. Duffy (ed.), *The Relevance of a Decade*. Boston, Mass.: Harvard Business School Press: 245–85.

PRAHALAD, C-K. (1997). 'The Role of Joint Ventures in India', Proceedings of the Conference on Strategic Alliances in Transitional Economies, University of Michigan William Davidson Institute working paper, no. 99, May.

RAWSKI, THOMAS G. (1998). '8 per cent Growth: Mission Impossible?', *China Perspectives*, 20, Nov.–Dec.: 8–15.

——(1999). 'Reforming China's Economy: What Have we Learned?', *The China Journal*, 41: 139–56.

SEIDLITZ, PETER, and MURPHY, DAVID (1999). 'Prolonged Crackdown on Forex Cheats Strangles Foreign Ventures', *South China Morning Post* (Money Section), 25 April: 3.

SESSER, STAN (1999). 'Local Legend takes Lead over PC rivals in China', *Asian Wall Street Journal*, 31 May: 13.

SHERIDAN, MICHAEL (2000). 'Internet Breaks Down China's Walls of Secrecy', *Sunday Times*, 4 June: 28.

*South China Morning Post* (1999). 'China's SOE Reform', 26 Aug.

THORBURN, J. T., LEUNG, H. M., CHAU, E., and TANG, S. H. (1990). *Foreign Investment in China Under the Open Policy: The Experience of Hong Kong Companies*. Aldershot: Avebury.

TROMPENAARS, FONS (1993). *Riding the Waves of Culture*. London: Economist Books.

TSE, DAVID K., PAN, YIGANG, and AU, KEVIN Y. (1997). 'How MNCs Choose Entry Modes and Form Alliances: The China Experience', *Journal of International Business Studies*, 28(4): 779–805.

TSENG, CHOO-SIN (2000). 'The Development of Chinese Multinationals', paper given to the Workshop on the Evolution of the Chinese Firm, Chinese Management Centre, University of Hong Kong, February.

TSIANG, RICHARD (1999). 'China Bursts at the Seams With Unsold Goods', *Asian Wall Street Journal*, 15 March: 12.

UNCTAD (United Nations Conference on Trade and Development) (1999). *World Investment Report 1999*. New York: United Nations.

UNDP (United Nations Development Programme) (1999). *The China Human Development Report*. New York: United Nations.

VANHONACKER, WILFRIED (1997). 'Entering China: An Unconventional Approach', *Harvard Business Review*, 75/2: 130–40.

WALDER, ANDREW G. (2000). 'China's Transitional Economy', in J. T. Li, Anne S. Tsui, and Elizabeth Weldon (eds.), *Management and Organizations in the Chinese Context*. Basingstoke: Macmillan, 63–83.

WANG, PIEN, ZHI, YUNDE, and TAN, KONG YAM (2000). 'Control and Performance in Sino–Foreign Equity Joint Ventures', in J. T. Li, Anne S. Tsui, and Elizabeth Weldon (eds.), *Management and Organizations in the Chinese Context*. Basingstoke: Macmillan, 131–56.

WARNER, MALCOLM (1995). *The Management of Human Resources in Chinese Industry*. London: Macmillan.

WHITLEY, RICHARD D. (1992*a*). *Business Systems in East Asia*. London: Sage.

——(ed.) (1992*b*). *European Business Systems*. London: Sage.

——(1999). *Divergent Capitalisms: The Social Structuring and Change of Business Systems*. Oxford: Oxford University Press.

WONACOTT, PETER (1999). 'China Worries are Deterring Foreign Firms', *Asian Wall Street Journal*, 28 April: 4.

WORLD ECONOMIC FORUM (1999). *The Global Competitiveness Report 1999*. Geneva: World Economic Forum.

ZHANG, HAI-YAN, and VAN DEN BULCKE, DANIEL (1996). 'International Management Strategies of Chinese Multinational Firms', in John Child and Yuan Lu (eds.), *Management Issues in China: Volume II, International Enterprises*. London: Routledge, 141–64.

CHAPTER 25

...................................................

# INTERNATIONAL BUSINESS RESEARCH ON TRANSITION ECONOMIES

...................................................

## KLAUS E. MEYER

## 25.1 INTRODUCTION

...................................................

UNTIL 1989, the countries of the Soviet bloc traded primarily in autarky from the world economy. The small volumes of East–West business were conducted on the basis of counter-trade negotiated with state-trade monopolies (e.g. Neale and Shipley 1990). Only few Western businesses operated within the

This work benefited from discussions with colleagues in direct and indirect ways. I thank Alan Rugman for initiating this work, and Tom Brewer, Klaus Uhlenbruck, and Snejina Michailova, as well as other contributors to the handbook for their helpful comments. Special thanks go to Arnold Schuh (Vienna) for his help with the marketing literature.

region, including Occidental Petroleum and Great Northern Telecom (Jacobsen 1997) who offered services considered vital by the socialist leadership.

The revolutions of 1989 brought dramatic changes for existing business relationships (e.g. Salmi and Møller 1994) and opened major business opportunities for the first time since respectively 1917 in Russia and 1945 in Central Europe. The region from Prague to Vladivostok embarked on reform from similar starting positions and with comparable objectives, yet with increasingly divers development since.[1] The transition economies in Central and Eastern Europe (CEE) become similar to other medium-income market economies, while most successor states of the Soviet Union are lagging especially in building market-oriented institutions.

The international policy framework evolved very favourably for international business, with rapid reduction of trade barriers and liberalization of foreign investment regulation. Membership in international organizations, such as WTO, facilitated this process. The westernmost countries signed 'Europe Agreements' with the European Union that further reduced trade barriers *vis-à-vis* the union, and became stepping stones towards eventual membership in the union (e.g. Lavigne 1998).

Western businesses were quick to position themselves in the new markets, as is illustrated by the acceleration of foreign direct investment (FDI) in the region,[2] see Figure 25.1, and the dramatic reorientation in the pattern of international trade (EBRD 1999). However, businesses operating in the region face a distinct institutional environment, which pre-determines the strategic opportunities for businesses (Peng 2000; Hoskisson *et al.* 2000). This creates challenges for managers of both local firms and Western business partners that differ not only from Western experience, but also among transition economies. On the other hand, outward international business from the region has been slow to evolve, and rarely been studied (but see Svetličič *et al.* 1999). However, the comparison with China or Latin America (Child 2001; Grosse 2001) suggests that it will be of increasing importance in the near future.

International business research has so far focused on Western multinational firms operating in the region. Research has approached the transition economies in different ways:

---

[1] Readers interested in comprehensive reviews of economic transition are recommended to consult Lavigne (1999) as well as reviews commissioned by multilateral institutions (e.g. World Bank 1996, Havrylyshyn and McGettigan 1999, Fisher and Sahay 2000, EBRD annually). Independent studies are published e.g. in the *Journal of Comparative Economics, Economics of Transition,* and *Comparative Economic Studies.* This author maintains a website with information on recent research and links: *http://www.econ.cbs.dk/institutes/cees/*

[2] Concise surveys of recent trends of FDI are provided by EBRD (annually), and UN (annually). For a critical evaluation of the data see Brewer (1994), Meyer (1995), and Meyer and Pind (1999).

(1) by testing the validity of general theories in the specific context of transition; and

(2) by exploring and explaining the specific features of the business context and their implications for business operating in the region.

The former is prominent in leading management journals, and offers insights for those pursuing development and refinement of theory in their respective fields. The latter research is generally more exploratory and generates novel insights on the functioning of business in transition economies, and theoretical frameworks to analyse it. It contributes to our understanding of the interaction between firms and their environment, which in turn can stimulate research on the relationships between firm behaviour and institutions in mature market economies. This review focuses on challenges faced by businesses in the transition context drawing upon research beyond mainstream business journals.

This review is structured as follows: section two summarizes the microeconomic aspects of economic transition, taking the development of new institutions as starting points as they set the stage for developments in the enterprise sphere. The third section discusses multinational firms entering the region, considering their motives, and their strategies to deal with the specific context. Section four addresses some managerial challenges that arise for multinational firms operating in the region. Section five concludes with perspectives for future research.

## 25.2 TRANSITION

### 25.2.1 New institutions: what kind of capitalism?

The essence of economic transition 'from plan to market' (World Bank 1996) is the replacement of one set of institutions governing economic activity by a different one. Institutions, albeit frequently neglected in economic theorizing, have an essential role in setting the 'rules of the game' by which individuals interact in a market economy (North 1990). They ensure the competitiveness of markets, for instance by preventing or regulating monopolies, insider trading, and negative externalities. Only with a solid framework set by institutions does the free interaction of agents lead to efficient allocation of goods and services.

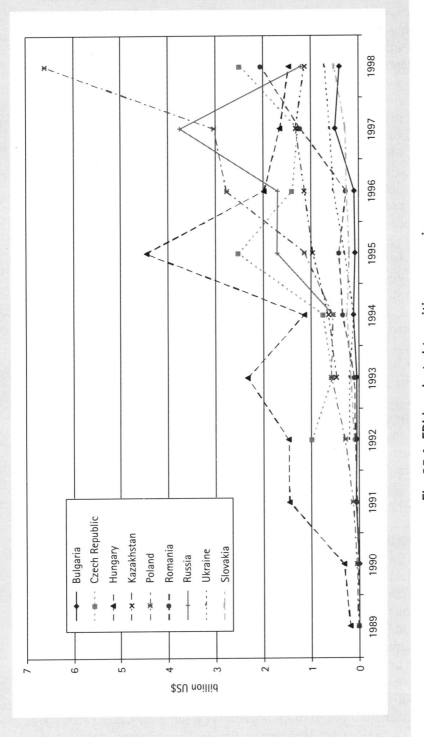

**Fig. 25.1  FDI in selected transition economies**

*Note* Net inflows recorded in the balance of payments

*Source* EBRD 1999, Table 3.1.6.

The Western market economies have built their institutions over decades, if not centuries, and they vary as a result of both different historical evolution and underlying cultures (North 1981). The institutions are supported by strong and impartial states, for example as guarantors of law enforcement and an independent judiciary. The path dependency of institutional frameworks let to a variety of 'business systems' that differ not only between the US, Asia, and Europe but even within Western Europe (Whitley (ed.) 1992).

Eastern Europe is building its institutions under strong outside influence, especially from the Anglo-Saxon sphere. Yet, new institutions cannot be superimposed from above as they must meet not only an efficiency test, but also be socially acceptable (Offe 1995). The distinct cultural and systemic inheritance influences especially informal institutions such as norm and values. In addition, the political development during the early years of transition influenced the way new institutions have been set up, notably the methods of privatization (Stark 1992; Hare *et al.* 1999). Policy choices made during the period of radical change around 1990 created institutions and established distribution of power. In many countries, the weak legal framework permitted a large extent of opportunistic behaviour, rent shifting, bribery, and corruption (e.g. Nelson *et al.* 1998). In some countries, vested interests have been created that would not benefit from further reform (Stiglitz 1999; EBRD 1999). Due to path dependency of institutions, policies during that 'window of opportunity' and the inheritance from the previous regime shape the future institutional frameworks (North 1990; Stark 1992). Consequently, Eastern Europe may develop a distinctive form of capitalism.

In the 1990s, the institutional frameworks were unstable and rapidly changing. The fundamental change in the environment may prompt an expectation of equally radical change of behaviour, but this did not happen in many CEE organizations (Whitley and Csaban 1998a). Even where formal institutions were established quickly, for example by copying laws from elsewhere, informal institutions are slow to evolve. Consequently, the process of building institutions in transition economies takes more time than most reform scenarios envisaged in 1990 (Murrell 1992; Kogut 1996). During this process, agents face the additional challenge that they cannot base their decisions on present institutions, which are unstable, and possibly inconsistent. Flexibility and short-term objectives should thus be the norm.

The distinctiveness of the CEE business systems, be it temporary or permanent, limits the transferability of Western business strategies and organizational concepts. Hence, strategies observed in transition economies differ from those in developed economies (Peng and Heath 1996), and strategies applied successfully in one country may fail in another. Corporate strategies in the transition economies can thus be explained only by incorporating the specific institutional context in the analysis. This holds for China (Peng 2000; Child 2001) as well as for Hungary or Russia. Some generalizations across these countries may be helpful, yet one has to be cautious as the variation among transition economies may be just as large as that between transition and mature market economies. The following sections review the evolution of the enterprise sector in this context, starting with the central institution of the market economy—the market.

## 25.2.2 From plan to market: change of coordination mechanisms

During socialism, the central plan was the core institution coordinating economic activity. The societies thus had strong vertical coordination, but failed, among other reasons, because horizontal linkages between firms were weak (Vlachoutsicos 1998) leading to high transaction costs between enterprises within supply chains. In addition, the plan focused on quantitative output targets with few incentives for quality and customer service.

The main purpose of transition was to introduce markets as more efficient coordination mechanisms. Yet, the old economic system disintegrated before the institutions supporting a market economy were in place. The absence of, among other, systems providing information, accounting, and auditing as well legal enforcement of contracts allowed extensive information asymmetries and opportunities for opportunistic behaviour, thus increasing transaction costs (Swaan 1997). The politically motivated push towards creating markets before creating institutions (Hare *et al.* 1999) has been especially drastic in the areas of capital markets. Mass privatization quickly brought firms on the stock exchanges, notably in the Czech Republic. Yet as institutions were not in place, this led to multiple opportunities for abuse by insiders, and in fact very slow restructuring of enterprises (Spicer *et al.* 2000).

In particular, the lack of informal institutions such as routines, knowledge, and procedures at the individual and organizational level provoked market failure. Essentially, administrators had to act as independent economic agents from the day the central plan was dissolved. They had to act on markets that did not yet exist; they lacked the (often tacit) knowledge on how to use the market mechanism, and who potential partners and competitors are. Without experience, they had to identify potential types of business and preferences of customers; and they had to assess the composition of demand and supply, and estimate demand elasticity. Thus, agents engaged in considerable search processes to set up transactions and to find the right prices (Swaan 1997).

The lack of institutions increases transaction costs, especially for new business relationships, and thus inhibits many potential transactions, in particular those of complex or long-term nature. The resulting coordination failure has been a major cause of the deep recession of the early 1990s (Blanchard and Kremer 1996; Swaan 1997). The most visible consequence of failing markets is the widespread use of barter in several successor states of the former Soviet Union (Gaddy and Ickes 1998; Commander and Momsen 1999; Seabright 2000). Yet it also affects international businesses with the transition economies. Western MNEs lack information on their partners; have to negotiate with persons inexperienced in business negotiations (Antal-Mokos 1998); and confront unclear regulatory frameworks, inexperienced bureaucracy (Thornton and Mikheeva 1996), and the weak enforcement of property rights.

The weaknesses of market institutions, and constraints on internalizing transactions, led to the widespread use of alternative, intermediate mechanisms of exchange through informal networks in CEE (Stark 1996; Clark and Soulsby 1995; Todeva 2000), and even more in Russia (Puffer *et al.* 1996; Holden *et al.* 1998; Salmi 1996, 1999). The post-socialist economies inherited systems of personal networks that served to overcome shortage under the central plan. These networks connected firms to authorities, especially the communist party and the plan ministries, and focused on influencing plan targets and delivery of crucial inputs.

The central plan regime created large interdependent production units. They were split into separate enterprises, but retained a high degree of asset specificity and resource dependencies. Many firms reacted by recreating inter-firm relationship by informal means to establish industrial groups (Stark 1996; Hayri and McDermott 1998). In Hungary, Stark (1996) observed 'recombinant networks' of firms with interlocking ownership and other formal and informal arrangements between related companies. In Russia financial-industrial groups developed close ties with banks and political institutions and became significant power bases. Where conventional strategies of internal or external growth are inhibited because the markets for relevant resources are defunct, 'network-based growth strategies' offer an alternative (Peng and Heath 1996). Businesses react to imperfect markets by network-based coordination.

Informal networks have retained their importance as a coordination mechanism, due to structural and cultural characteristics. However, they do not necessarily reflect the needs of a market economy. Many focus on extraction of rents from the state through collusion between businesses, and between business and units (or individuals) of the government, in particular municipal authorities. In a market economy, networks also serve an important role in relating interdependent business and overcoming various market imperfections. Yet clear legal and ethical codes prevent transactions that cause harm to third parties. Restructuring the networks to serve the needs of a market economy is thus an essential component of transformation.

## 25.2.3 Privatization and corporate governance

Enterprises in socialist countries had been set up to achieve the objectives
defined by socialist ideology and the central plan, notably the fulfilment of
quantitative plan targets. The transition places enterprises at a different place
in society, redefining the purpose of their existence. This change involves a
formal, legal change and an informal, internal transformation. This section
reviews the changes in formal structures through privatization and systems of
corporate governance, and the next section discusses the organizational
transformation.

Privatization in transition differs from Western experiences by the scope of
the task, the absence of efficient capital markets, and the lack of private
domestic savings that could be invested. These obstacles were overcome by
novel routes of privatization, most notably mass privatization based on
voucher schemes. More conventional modes included direct sales to outside
investors, management–employee buy-outs, and restitution to former owners
(Brada 1996; World Bank 1996; Bornstein 1997).

Privatization is, however, not a sufficient condition to trigger enterprise
restructuring. Many privatizations other than by sales to outside investors
failed to create powerful incentives that would guide managers in transforming firms. Therefore corporate governance has become the most debated issue
in the transition economics literature (e.g. Frydman *et al.* 1997; La Porta,
Lopez-de-Silanes, and Shleifer 1999; Estrin and Wright 1999). The collapse of
communism left state-owned firms without mechanisms for the state to
enforce control, and weak internal structures to handle the new demands of
the marketplace.

Frequently, managers and/or worker councils attained considerable influence, *de facto* or *de jure*, especially in Poland and many CIS countries. In many
cases, insiders managed to convert their *de facto* control into formal ownership by opting for privatization modes that gave them preferential access to
shares. As a result, many firms, particularly in Poland and the former Soviet
Union, have managers and employees as minority or even majority shareholders (e.g. Åslund 1995; Blasi *et al.* 1995). Therefore, theories considering
stakeholders, rather than solely shareholders, have been revived to analyse
corporate governance in transition economies (Buck *et al.* 1998; Berglöf and
von Thadden 1999; Mygind 1999).

Corporate governance problems also arose as a result of voucher privatization. Most transition countries (with the notable exception of Hungary) have
implemented a voucher scheme as a main pillar of their mass privatization
(e.g. World Bank 1996; Estrin and Stone 1996). It permitted the creation of
widespread popular ownership of industrial equity and the redistribution of
the wealth to citizens in a 'fair' way, thus generating popular support for
reform. The Czech scheme—the first and most publicized—privatized a

major share of the country's assets in several waves of multiple-auction bidding processes. Investment funds attained considerable power through the accumulation of vouchers and bidding on behalf of individuals (Coffee 1996). They now control major Czech businesses, but themselves are often owned by (largely state owned) banks. This creates interdependent institutions without clear monitoring and control structures, but with multiple agents that have hold-up power (Hayri and McDermott 1998). The resultant lack of effective corporate governance has frequently been blamed for the slow progress of enterprise restructuring (e.g. Nellis 1999).

In Poland, the large privatization was delayed due to political conflicts over its conditions. In 1996, shares of some 500 enterprises were allocated to government-sponsored investment funds, which in turn were privatized through vouchers that are now traded on the Warsaw stock exchange. Each enterprise was initially owned by a fund holding 33 per cent of equity, plus minority shareholdings by the other funds, workers, and the government. While overcoming defaults of corporate governance in the Czech voucher privatization, the Polish scheme still suffers from conflicts between different control institutions. In Russia, mass privatization has been rapid and created a substantial private sector—but dominated by insider ownership (e.g. Boyko et al. 1995; Blasi et al. 1997; Earle and Estrin 1997; Wright et al. 1998). The resulting management and employee ownership may have positive effects on motivation and labour productivity (Ben-Ner and Jones 1995), but can be a major obstacle for restructuring in large firms, if lay-offs or access to outside finance are required.[3]

Following privatization, the emergence of local equity markets is crucial. The need to raise fresh capital should induce insider-controlled firms to accept new outsider equity stakes and provide acquisition opportunities. However, progress has been slow (Earle and Estrin 1996; Filatochev et al. 1996) and ownership patterns are relatively stable (Jones and Mygind 1999a; Anderson et al. 1999). Especially in the former Soviet Union, it is difficult to obtain ownership and effective control of privatized firms, among other reasons because legal stock market institutions such as protection of minority shareholders are not in place.

However, competition is at least as important as privatization for enterprises to improve their efficiency—a result consistent with empirical research on privatization in the West (e.g. Vickers and Yarrow 1988). Yet while many

---

[3] The empirical evidence on performance implications is hotly debated as many Western advisors see it as a key obstacle to restructuring (e.g. Havrylyshyn and McGettigan 1999). Several studies suggest that manager-ownership outperforms employee ownership (e.g. Frydman et al. 1997). Yet other studies find positive effects of employee ownership compared to dispersed shareholding or state-ownership on production efficiency (Smith et al. 1997, Jones and Mygind 1999b), on labour productivity (Earle and Estrin 1997, Djankov 1999b), and on product, input, and asset restructuring (Estrin and Rosevear 1999).

major Western privatizations are in industries with natural monopolies that require complex regulation to create competition, most firms privatized in Eastern Europe enjoy monopoly powers courtesy of past or present government policy. After privatization, the key difference is 'not how competition affects firm performance, but in the degree to which market forces in transition are either softened or distorted' (Bevan *et al.* 1999: 14). Firms in transition frequently face soft budget constraints and obtain protected market positions of various sorts. In Russia, a particular problem appears to be the lack of domestic entry, and thus contestable markets, in part due to protective intervention by regional authorities (Broadman 1999). In other countries, new entrants are a major source of competition (see section 25.2.5).

Thus the transition economies are poised to retain corporate governance systems that differ from those in mature market economies, even taking into account the variation found for instance between the US and Continental Europe. Some of the largest firms in the region are subject to weak governance while enjoying close contacts to government and, in some ex-Soviet Union states, considerable barriers to entry. Yet other firms have gone very far in shedding these legacies of the twentieth century. This diversity of governance mechanisms and of competition patterns is likely to be a continuing feature of the region for years to come.

## 25.2.4 Organizational transformation

In the socialist regime, firms' overriding objective was plan-fulfilment.[4] The incentives created by central planning led however to severe distortions, such as the production of large volumes of standardized low quality products, lack of concern for consumer demand, disregard for externalities of any kind, notably for the environment. By establishing positions rather than creating jobs, firms employed far more people than necessary to achieve their output target as labour costs were not a constraining variable. Employment relationships were effectively based on life-time employment and enterprises provided many of the social needs of both current and retired employees. The enterprise sector was reasonably efficient in allocative efficiency, but failed dramatically in innovation (Berliner 1976; Murrel 1990; Kogut and Zander 2000). In this system, management had few incentives, or in fact opportunities, to act as business leader or entrepreneur in a Western sense.

---

[4] On the nature of firms in the real existing socialism see e.g. Berliner (1952), Kornai (1980, 1992), and Lawrence and Vlachoutsicos (1990).

As this brief characterization makes clear, firms have a very different role in socialist and in capitalist societies (Heidenreich 1993). Consequently they have different resource configurations, skill and capability reservoirs, and ways of organizing themselves. As transformation involves all these areas—and I do not contend this would be a complete list—it is a complex task.

It typically started with defensive adjustments aimed at survival under hard budget constraints, for example laying off workers or shifting the product mix (see reviews by Brada 1996; Carlin 2000; Bevan *et al.* 1999; EBRD 1999). Productivity improved, even before privatization, as management reacted to external pressures. However, further strategic and organizational restructuring is necessary to attain sustainable competitiveness (Meyer 1998*b*). Few domestic-owned firms have been able to pursue corporate strategies that would lead to a viable position in the international competition (Brada 1996; Wright *et al.* 1998; Stiglitz 1999). Foreign-owned firms engaged in more strategic change such as development of new products, investment in new production facilities, entry into new markets and establishing marketing, new brand names, and distribution channels (e.g. Carlin *et al.* 1995; Estrin *et al.* 1997; Newman and Nollen 1998; Djankov 1999*a*; Hooley *et al.* 1996).

At the onset of transition, many advisors focused on productivity improvements, promoting redundant assets, and downsizing to reduce over-employment. However, excessive reliance on cost cutting has been criticized for undermining firms' ability to develop new strategies. A certain degree of slack can be an important resource for innovation (Nohria and Gulati 1996), for managerial learning (Geppert 1996), and thus for transformation. Many firms undoubtedly had excess slack. However, some firms, notably in East Germany, seem to have cut the workforce to such extent that the morale was undermined, and no slack left that could become a source for new growth (Thomson and Millar 1999).

Beyond downsizing, the reconfiguration of resources needs a pro-active approach to acquiring complementary resources, through both investment in complementary assets and organizational learning (Uhlenbruck *et al.* 2000). Especially in the area of marketing, firms have to improve their basic competences in terms of structure, systems and processes, organizational culture, and human resources (Batra 1997). The learning begins with top managers, who are often not well prepared to lead the transformation process. Many essential management capabilities were not developed under socialism because other skills were asked for. Managerial learning (see section 25.4.2) and employee training thus are crucial elements of the resource upgrading.

These organizational changes also include the methods of organizing production. The labour process in the socialist period was designed on

Taylorist principles, with high degrees of division of labour and technical job specialization, and close supervision. Yet, the frequency of distortions in supplies, inadequate machinery, and to some extent shortage of skilled labour made the full realization of the cost advantages impossible. As Taylorism has been the norm of industrial production in the 1950s, but passed into history in most sectors in industrial countries, it was expected that transition would instigate the shift to post-Taylorist production (Sorge 1993; Meyer and Møller 1998). Yet evidence from Hungary shows that in some firms, notably locally owned ones, the opposite occurred. Firms refined their 'scientific management' and reduced costs by more precise division between skilled and unskilled workers and more rigorous supervisory control. In the short-term, these firms showed above average productivity and profitability (Whitley and Csaban 1998b; Taplin and Frege 1999). Yet it is doubtful if such a strategy will enhance competitiveness in the longer term.

Also other empirical evidence points to continuity rather than radical change. Observing twenty-seven Hungarian case firms, Whitley and Csaban (1998a) conclude that by most criteria, they showed a remarkable degree of continuity, for instance in terms of product mix, production technology, and markets. Although top management had often been replaced, the new leaders were typically promoted internally. Interdependence led firms to continue existing relationships rather than to seek business opportunities with different partners (Stark 1996; Todeva 2000). The continuity of personnel, the persisting importance of the political environment, and limited role of product market competition contributed to continuity in management strategies and behaviour (Martin 1999; Newman and Nollen 1998).

This continuity is natural, according to the evolutionary view of transformation. Resource reconfiguration requires the acquisition of new capabilities, which have to be developed from existing ones, in combination with imported know-how. Organizations thus evolve, rather than reincarnate themselves overnight, when facing change—even radical change—in their environment. Consequently, Spicer, McDermott, and Kogut (2000) are concerned that privatization was too radical and broke up existing industry networks and thus inhibited the effective use of co-specialized resources. Kogut (1996) thus sees a priority for learning through experimentation and internal development of new routines and capabilities adapted to the specific context, rather than the wholesale imposition of imported routines. Lieb-Dóczy and Meyer (2000) suggest that foreign acquirers especially risk losing valuable local capabilities if they concentrate on transfer of their established best practice and neglect development of variety by fostering indigenous capabilities.

In conclusion, Enterprise Transformation and the ensuing managerial challenges are complex phenomena that cannot be analysed satisfactorily with established theoretical frameworks only. Having reached the limits of conventional economic analysis, further analysis may extend the resource-based view of the firm to explore specific challenges of emerging and transition economies (Hoskisson *et al.* 2000). I see potential in complementing this perspective with organizational learning theory (Uhlenbruck *et al.* 2000), evolutionary theory (Lieb-Dóczy and Meyer 2000), or theory of coordination games (Meyer 2000*c*) to analyse the changing resource base during ET.

## 25.2.5 The growth of entrepreneurial start-ups

Despite the major efforts in privatization, much of the recent economic growth in the transition economies comes from newly established firms. Especially in Poland, the new private sector is flourishing while much of the former state sector is stagnating (e.g. Johnson and Loveman 1995; EBRD 1999). These new firms are often the most dynamic units in the region. Peng (2000) points to four groups of individuals that become entrepreneurs by setting up their own businesses in transition economies:

1. Scientists and other professionals pursue entrepreneurial activity in reaction to the rapid decline in real income at their job in the public sector or a privatizing firm. Often this starts as a part-time job, notably for academics seeking to better their income through consultancy (Webster and Charap 1993; Kirby *et al.* 1996).
2. Former cadres frequently become entrepreneurs especially in Russia, capitalizing on their control over key resources, including physical and financial assets, and most importantly network connections to the bureaucracy (Rona-Tas 1994; Parish and Michelson 1996).
3. Individuals who were left at the bottom of society after losing their previous position may survive as street traders, and gradually upgrade to bazaar traders, and to shop owner-managers. They thus mature from the grey economy to the official economy.
4. Farmers may have enjoyed private ownership of their plots, as in Poland, which provided them with initial resources for entrepreneurial activity in related sectors.

The pressure of enterprise transformation created strong push factors for specialists to leave the uncertainty of a privatizing firm, and seek their own fortune. Many, however, retain close business relationships with their former employer, more than spin-offs in the West typically do (Kirby *et al.* 1996). Entrepreneurial firms thus grow as part of the new corporate networks in the region (Stark 1996). They are joined by managers who attained control, with or without formal ownership, over privatized enterprises.

The newly established businesses benefit, compared to privatized ones, from simple governance structures, low fixed costs, and flexibility to switch from unpromising markets to more attractive ones (Johnson and Loveman 1995; Puffer *et al.* 2000). Moreover, without the burden of inheritance from a predecessor organization, entrepreneurs have the freedom to hire selectively the most suitable employees. In the early years of liberalization, many newly established firms were extremely profitable, in part because they offered products not previously available, or served niche markets, and second-movers were slow.

However, the opportunities for entrepreneurs are often constrained by their lack of resources and by the institutional context. Financial resources have been a major constraint for many given the underdeveloped capital markets (Holmström 1996; Johnson and Loveman 1995). Venture capital funds have only recently been established in the region and are gradually developing expertise in assessment and monitoring of entrepreneurial firms in the transition context (Karsai *et al.* 1997). Yet equally important are human capital as well as political and social capital, i.e. access to key decision-makers in politics and business (Batjargal 2000).

Institutional change permitting the establishment of new businesses and simplifying licensing procedures was the starting call for entrepreneurship. Yet obstacles in the institutional framework are still the main hindrance for further development of entrepreneurial firms, especially in the less advanced transition economies. This includes high informal barriers to entry, weak protection of property rights, excessive bureaucracy, and corruption. For instance, newly established firms pay on average over 5 per cent in 'bribe tax' compared to around 4 per cent for privatized and state-owned firms (EBRD 1999). Johnson, McMillan, and Woodruff (1999) found that reinvestment of profits has been especially constrained by the weak protection of property rights. Moreover, entrepreneurs continue to be obstructed by a weak investment climate and indirect barriers to entry (EBRD 1999; Broadman 1999).

Entrepreneurship research on transition economies stands—unless major contributions have escaped my attention—very much at the beginning.[5] However, it ought to be as important as the transformation of existing SOE for the future of these economies, as well as for Western businesses looking for suitable partners in the region.

---

[5] A starting point may be the series of short research notes on transition economies in the *Journal of Small Business Management* in 1995 to 1997.

# 25.3 STRATEGIES OF MULTINATIONAL BUSINESSES

## 25.3.1 Motivations

Theoretical research has pointed to the importance of factor cost advantages (e.g. Ozawa 1992), as has a comparison of CEE with East Asia (Urban 1992; UN 1995; Meyer 2000b). FDI was expected to utilize factor differences and to build export oriented production. CEE still has low labour costs compared with Western Europe although higher than some locations in South East Asia. Factor cost advantages may also arise from the low cost of locally extracted raw materials.

However, there is almost undisputed evidence that markets are the main attraction of the region, as reported in the large number of surveys conducted among Western firms with investments in CEE and among joint-ventures within the region (e.g. Meyer 1998a; Pye 1998; OECD 1995; Lankes and Venebles 1996). Many MNEs considering entry expect considerable long-term growth of demand, especially as the income of the middle class, their prime customers, grows faster than the average measured by GDP (Batra 1997). Several features make the markets in CEE particularly attractive (Estrin and Meyer 1998).

First, consumers in CEE had previously had little or no access to consumer goods and brands available in other countries at similar levels of per capita income. Trade liberalization unleashed a catch-up demand, especially for consumer durables for which West European markets are saturated. The high status of Western goods was in part a result of Western media penetration, even before 1989. It was sustained through effective advertising and brand-building in the newly liberalized local media.

Second, entry in CEE may be a strategic move by MNEs to sustain or enhance their global strategic position. Global leaders may invest to prevent challenges from their rivals or the emergence of new competitors from within the region. Firms dominated by a larger competitor may see early entry in new markets as an opportunity to gain competitive advantages. MNEs established in both Western and Eastern Europe may have superior opportunities to exploit price discrimination, product differentiation, or vertical integration. In industries with major network externalities, such as consultancy and financial services, presence in the region may be necessary to offer global coverage for their globally operating customers.

Third, several underdeveloped sectors of industry are being reestablished to accelerate productivity growth across the economy. Governments in CEE are therefore inviting foreign investors to upgrade telecommunications, power generation and distribution, and transportation infrastructure. They encourage selective private entry, for example licensing of new service providers or concessions to operate existing public infrastructure (EBRD 1996). In addition, the privatization of utilities, especially in the telecommunications sector, attracts substantial FDI capital inflows. The infrastructure development furthermore creates opportunities for those providing inputs, such as construction firms, turnkey-plant engineers, and manufacturers of telecommunications equipment.

Factor cost oriented FDI has picked up since the early 1990s. While fewer in number, this includes some high profile FDI projects and substantial capital inflows. Many projects may initially have focused on local markets, but as these were saturated and productivity in the new affiliate increased, they started exporting to other nodes in the investors' multinational network.

CEE has comparative advantages in intermediate technical skills as the level of technical education in the region was relatively high, although it has considerably deteriorated since 1990, at least in Russia (Clarke and Metalina 2000). At the same time, unit labour costs have risen substantially but are still significantly below West European, especially German, levels. Economic policy has strengthened this advantage in some countries through an effective undervaluation of exchange rates or incomes policy, such as constraints on wage increases.

Low factor costs attract especially SME and firms from the neighbouring countries who exploit the cost differential through outward-processing with or without equity investment. The relocation of production has been important in a small number of industries including textiles, clothing, furniture, or musical instruments. It gained in relative importance in the mid 1990s as cost-seeking investors were under less time-pressure than market-seekers.

However, many cost-oriented investors were deterred by low productivity, lack of telecommunication and transportation infrastructure, and bureaucracy (OECD 1995; Meyer 1998a; Pye 1998). In addition, investors face obstacles in identifying suitable local partners and suppliers able to provide inputs and services at the required level of quality.

## 25.3.2 Entry strategies

Since most Western businesses entered the region only in the 1990s, CEE provides an excellent laboratory to study international business entry. Entry strategies encompass a number of interrelated strategic variables, however, researchers have preferred to analyse the different components separately, and so will this review. First, there are locational choices, which have been discussed in the previous section. Second, entrants select an entry mode, such as export, contractual cooperation, or FDI. Direct investors furthermore have to decide the share of their equity ownership, and whether to invest in a greenfield project or by acquiring an existing firm. Third, the timing and speed of entry is crucial for instance for those pursuing first-mover advantages. Moreover, a successful entry requires an appropriate strategy for marketing, e.g. branding of products, and for human resource management.

### 25.3.2.1 *Entry mode strategies*

The choice of entry mode soon became a foremost research topic of IB scholars interested in Eastern Europe (e.g. Brouthers *et al.* 1998; Meyer 1997, 1998a; Pye 1998). Initially, entrants preferred modes with low exposure to country risk, especially exports and contracting. Ten years into the transition, this still applied in some countries of the former Soviet Union, but less in Central Europe. Most businesses started with exporting, but accelerated soon with contractual and investment modes. Many firms moved quickly along the internationalization process, some even establishing FDI in their first activity (Engelhard and Eckert 1993; Ali and Mirza 1996; Czinkota *et al.* 1997).

Contractual modes were particularly important before legal constraints had been fully removed, and when investment risks were perceived to be high. Beyond the standard forms, this included for instance management- technology- and turnkey-contracts. Franchising became popular as eager local entrepreneurs looked to franchisers to provide them with both resources and managerial training. At the same time, those managing global brands found franchising a fast way of expansion while limiting their investment risk. Subcontracting has been particularly popular with German and Italian SMEs relocating selected stages of their production process (e.g. Pellegrin 1998). New contractual arrangements have been developed to facilitate the region's infrastructure investments. For instance, build-operate-transfer contracts permit private investment and ownership, yet with ultimate transfer to the public sector.

### 25.3.2.2 *Ownership of FDI*

In the early 1990s, a JV was the only legally permissible mode to establish a direct investment (OECD 1995; Hood and Young 1994; Hunya 1996). Yet, the ownership patterns have rapidly changed since then. Regulations have been relaxed in many small steps, and by 1992 FDI was fairly unregulated in most countries (EBRD 1994), though it took far longer in Russia.

This explains the initially high share of joint-ventures, and the massive shift towards fully-owned affiliates in the mid 1990s by both new investors and by old investors increasing their equity share (Sharma 1995). Many acquisitions in the privatization process occurred in a staggered pattern, and were thus registered as JV although from the beginning the investor attained management control and envisaged the acquisition of full ownership (Perotti and Gulati 1993; Lieb-Dóczy and Meyer 2000). These 'transitory alliances' (Hagedoorn and Sadowski 1999) are means of implementing acquisitions in a particular institutional context, and share little of the characteristics typically observed in joint-ventures (cf. Beamish and Killing 1997). As temporary arrangement they offer advantages to both partners. Governments obtain some control over the firm's restructuring, and thus externalities for the local economy, while capitalizing on the probable appreciation of the share value as the transition economy becomes less uncertain (and avoid embarrassment over initial underpricing). Governments may also be reluctant to transfer control over firms deemed strategic, or trading with governmental institutions (Wright et al. 1993) for both political and economic reasons. The investor obtains access to local institutions and networks while sharing investment risk.

Investors normally aim for full control of acquired businesses, not only to reduce transaction costs but to be able to enforce faster turnaround of former state-owned enterprises (Aulakh and Kotabe 1997). However, many entrants, at least initially, accept lower degrees of involvement. A local partner may be useful in many ways, notably in accessing local business and government networks. Especially in Russia, such informal networks are vital for business, substituting many functions of the institutional framework in mature market economies (Thornton and Mikheeva 1996; Puffer et al. 1996; Holden et al. 1998). Consequently, entry modes with higher capital commitment are preferred in the advanced transition economies, while low risk modes are employed where institutional frameworks are still unstable or of low repute.

Formal tests of the determinants of entry modes mostly find support for the same factors as studies elsewhere, especially with respect to firm and industry specific variables, thus confirming the validity of the respective theoretical framework. For instance, Brouthers et al. (1998) showed the influence of cultural attributes of both home and host country, in addition to cultural distance. CEE-specific aspects emerge with the factor endowment of the local economy and the institutional framework, which influence the transaction costs in pertinent markets and thus investors' internalization preferences (Meyer 1998a).

The performance of FDI has been analysed on the basis of survey data, for example in Hungary (Lyles and Baird 1994; Meschi 1997), Russia (Fey 1995; Thornton and Mikheeva 1996), and Kazakhstan (Charman 1998). The success of a JV depends mainly on issues such as the compatibility of the objectives of the parents, and establishment of mutual trust while avoiding dominant control by either partner. International business experience of the local partner is important, as is the Western partner's management training. However, wholly owned operations are judged to perform better in investors' own assessment (e.g. Lyles and Baird 1994).

### 25.3.2.3 *Acquisition or greenfield*

Foreign investors wishing to establish a wholly-owned operation could often do so only through an acquisition in the privatization process. This, however, requires complex negotiations with multiple governmental authorities (Brouthers and Bamossy 1997; Antal-Mokos 1998; Marinova 2000) as well as with management and work councils (Bak and Kulawczuk 1997). Moreover, the investor has to take responsibility for enterprise transformation (cf. section 25.3), and may face considerable post-acquisition investment in resource upgrading and organizational change while being constrained by stipulations of the privatization contract (see section 25.4.1).

As this post-acquisition investment often exceeds the initial investment, the project takes on features normally associated with greenfield investment, and different from conventional acquisitions. Such 'brownfield' investment (Meyer and Estrin 1999) can substitute both greenfield strategies where crucial local assets are not available in unbundled form, and acquisition strategies where the resources of local firms are too weak to face international competition.

Investors prepared to commit to enterprise restructuring and technological upgrading, find acquisitions attractive to access valuable human capital in local firms, especially their technological skills, and to (informal) local networks, and to government agencies. Local brand names and distribution networks are also valuable assets in some consumer goods industries. Acquirers furthermore report fewer bureaucratic obstacles to acquiring land and obtaining the permits required to start or expand production (Estrin *et al.* 1997).

Despite these advantages, investors increasingly bypass the restructuring of local firms and set up greenfield operations. This allows them to implement their corporate strategy without having to incorporate the heritage of an acquired firm. Small firms that lack the managerial and financial resources to lead enterprise restructuring, are even more avoiding acquisitions in the privatization process (Estrin and Meyer 1998). Consequently, the share of greenfield investment is increasing in CEE, in contrast to worldwide trends.

### 25.3.2.4 *Strategies for timing and acceleration of entry*

Many MNEs in industries with worldwide oligopolistic structures were among the first entrants (Marton 1993; Kogut 1996). They pursued first-mover advantages that are perceived to be very important in consumer goods industries where brand names are crucial competitive assets (e.g. Arnold and Quelch 1998). Expected long-term benefits include brand recognition, control of distribution channels, and preferential access to local suppliers and governments. One way to attain such advantages is to acquire the dominant local firm in the industry. Moreover, early entrants may even be able to influence the local regulatory environment in their favour. The perceived importance of first-mover advantages is highlighted by Lankes and Venebles (1996) who report a bimodal distribution on the first-mover motive: very important for 39 per cent of investors, especially for those targeting the local market, but unimportant for most others.

Is this euphoria about first-mover advantages justified? Liebermann and Montgomery (1998) cast doubt on the first-mover argument by showing that product innovators rarely became market leaders. An optimal product specification and a marketing strategy to penetrate a mass market are more important for lasting success. The entry in Eastern Europe poses different challenges as the products in question are mature, and their marketing methods have been tested elsewhere. Even so, first entrants have to overcome obstacles in the local environment, and strategic decisions on, for example, location and partner choice incur considerable sunk costs. Moreover, brand names may be worth less where brand loyalty is low as consumers still experiment with new products. Case evidence suggests that some first-movers failed to realize their expected benefits, and second-movers could build a larger market-share or a more profitable operation (Meyer and Estrin 1998; Bridgewater *et al.* 1995).

Later entrants benefit from local bureaucrats' improved understanding of the needs of business, and from first-movers' investment in training and introduction of new types of products to 'build the market'. 'Fast-seconds' can learn from successes and failures of the first-mover and adapt their strategies for marketing and government relations accordingly.

Aiming for the best of both strategies, many investors followed a foothold strategy that provides an entry to the market, but delays commitment of substantive capital investment. Such 'platform investment' (Kogut 1983), for example a representative office, permits the investor to learn about the local environment while investigating business opportunities. The local base permits a rapid response to emerging business opportunities. Foothold strategies were important for the first investors in Hungary (Marton 1993) and in the volatile environment of Russia (Fey 1995).

Some authors have developed more detailed typologies of strategies that they observed in Eastern Europe (Hooley *et al.* 1993; McCarthy and Puffer 1997; Bridgewater *et al.* 1995). By distinguishing entrants by their strategic investment motives and the speed of resource commitment, they observe some noteworthy strategies.

Many investors are client-followers in that they enter Eastern Europe to serve customers they have served before (Bridgewater *et al.* 1995). Their investment decisions are thus linked to the strategies of major customers. This applies in particular in the automotive industry (van Tulder and Ruigrok 1998; Meyer 2000*b*) and in the financial sector, but also ordinary products such as soft drinks can draw bottling companies and manufacturers of modern packaging to the East. The client provides a sufficiently large and secure demand to merit the commitment, and from that base the follower may expand on the local market. Last, but not least, many Western accountants and consultants supply projects funded by Western agencies such as the EU (Gilbert 1998).

Investors in the oil and gas industry face heavy up-front investment, especially for extraction and refining (McCarthy and Puffer 1997). The sector attracts a major share of FDI in Russia and her neighbours to the south, but investors have to be cautious not only because of high sunk costs, but because they need to cooperate closely with key local players in governments and among state-owned or privatized monopolies. Investment consortia between major multinationals are thus common, both to share the risk, and to negotiate with the authorities.

### 25.3.2.5 *Marketing strategies*

Beyond entry mode choice, marketing scholars have addressed issues of market penetration, consumer behaviour, and marketing management (reviewed by Schuh and Springer 1997). A major concern is the trade-off between standardization and differentiation. Batra (1997), and Arnold and Quelch (1998) recommend a multi-tier product strategy to serve not only the high-end segments but also the middle and lower price segments of the markets. They suggest that foreign companies should adjust their product mix to the purchasing power given the low average household income in these countries. Adaptation of consumer electronics, for example, may strip-out of existing sophisticated products those features—with the corresponding costs—that are not highly valued yet, and provide products that are more reliable and need less servicing (Batra 1997).

However, empirical research suggests that foreign investors typically position their products at the upper end of the market, leaving the lower end to local brands, in anticipation of market growth with the emergence of the middle class (Schuh 2000). Many of the first entrants were global-oriented companies that create products pro-actively and adapt them passively, pursuing highly standardized marketing strategies in CEE with limited adaptation, for example of labelling, package design, and brands (e.g. Church 1992; Hooley *et al.* 1993). Classic country-related differentiation can only be found in the consumer goods industry and is often connected to the acquisition of local companies (Dahm, 1995). In fact, several incidences have reported that investors discontinued an acquired local brand, but later reintroduced it after realizing the loss of the mass market (Meyer and Estrin 1998; Lieb-Dóczy 2000).

Research into marketing mix and distribution channels points to major challenges for multinational entrants. Distribution channels are often fragmented, with small retailers accounting for a large share of consumer markets. Reliable marketing information is scarce. Channels of mass communication are less developed and less effective where consumers prefer to rely on personal experiences. This suggests a need for high distribution intensity and multiple marketing partners rather than exclusive distributors. Extensions of successful brands ('Umbrella branding') and multi-tier product strategies to cover high- and middle-price segments of the market have proven to be successful. However, consumers are very price sensitive such that markets tend to be price competitive. TV and event sponsorship are reported to be most effective to establish brand names if used considerate to local cultural, political, and religious sensitivities (Sharma 1992; Batra 1997; Arnold and Quelch 1998).

Consumer behaviour has been volatile and varying across the region, making it hard to give definitive answers on issues such as buying behaviour, attitudes to country of origin, and impact of advertising. Most marketing researchers essentially benchmark CEE against the West thus failing to address issues of specific relevance to countries in transition (Schuh and Springer 1997). Future research may thus pay more attention to issues such as national marketing systems, specifics of marketing in CEE by country and industry, marketing at different stages of enterprise transformation, and establishment of effective marketing institutions and networks in CEE.

Reviewing the marketing literature, one notices a variety of innovative strategies proposed. Yet few authors provide convincing evidence of superior performance of these strategies. Counter-intuitive evidence, such as first-mover failures, suggest caution. Future research may focus more on the long-term performance implications.

# 25.4 MANAGEMENT CHALLENGES

Western businesses operating within transition economies face a number of specific challenges that arise from the transition context. This section focuses on the implications of running a formerly state-owned firm, knowledge transfer, managerial training, and cultural diversity within the organization.

## 25.4.1 Privatization acquisition

Owning and managing a privatized business unit confronts businesses with national politics. From the investor's perspective, it is a case of 'mergers and acquisitions'; yet buying a firm from the government results in a number of peculiarities. Privatization aims to break the link between governments and firms. Yet, the political social and economic context of privatization constrains post-privatization strategies (Uhlenbruck and DeCastro 2000):

1. Government sell firms not only to maximize their financial revenues, but to pursue broader social objectives (e.g. Estrin 1994). The corporate strategy pursued by the (formerly) state-owned firm is interdependent with other aspects of public policy. For instance, the divestment of social assets (kindergartens, health care facilities, etc.) is interdependent with the ability of other providers, municipal or otherwise, to provide these services. Layoffs are constrained by the social consequences of unemployment.

2. The negotiation process is complicated not only by the broader set of objectives of the seller but by the multiplicity of interest groups involved in the process and by the relative inexperience by the local negotiators (Antal-Mokos 1998). Brouthers and Bamossy (1997) and Arens and Brouthers (1999) analyse the role of the government using the concept of the 'key stakeholder'.

3. After completing the sale, governments often continue to be indirectly involved with the privatized firm. They can create tools to control the actions of the acquirer as an agent by extending the contract beyond outright sales. This occurs in CEE through retained minority shareholding, conditions imposed on the acquirer (Stark 1992; Uhlenbruck and DeCastro 1998), and competition policy. At the same time, governments may support privatized firms by securing financing, guarantee procurement, tax breaks, restrictions on import competition, etc. (EBRD 1994, 1999).

'Staggered divestment' especially (Perotti and Guney 1993) allows privatization agencies a temporary influence on post-acquisition management. If the acquirer attains management control, the influence of the government on operational management is limited. The foreign investor may not like the possible government interference in strategic decisions, but would appreciate the risk sharing and the lower amount of capital to be raised at the outset. Furthermore, the interests of the government, especially regional or local authorities, are becoming more aligned with those of the business if they share the profits of the venture. This should reduce undue bureaucracy and regulatory interference, while providing access to important local networks.

One might expect weaker performance of firms in mixed ownership because the government may aim at obtaining social rather than financial returns. At the same time, the private partner faces weaker incentives arising from the lower share in profits, and may benefit from some form of transfer pricing. (The MNE has to share any profit of the JV, but keeps all if it is accounted for elsewhere.) Compared to local firms, JVs do not show better performance than local firms, as would be expected given their more proactive restructuring (section 25.2.3). Managers themselves assess performance of firms with residual government ownership more negatively (e.g. Lyles and Baird 1994). However, Uhlenbruck and DeCastro (2000) find that firms with residual state-ownership actually perform better in terms of sales growth.

With the acquisition, the investor takes responsibility for the enterprise transformation process. This requires substantial additional investment in upgrading of equipment, organizational restructuring, and training. Foreign acquirers thus face an uphill struggle, although compared to local firms, they have a number of advantages:

1. They have access to complementary resources, in particular finance and managerial knowledge.
2. They can establish clear control structures, and thus avoid most of the corporate governance problems associated with other forms of privatization in CEE.
3. They can better initiate organizational change through the experience in leading competitive businesses and thus provide vision and a strategy for the restructuring.
4. They can create market access by integrating the acquired business into their international production networks (Schwartz and Zysman 1998 Meyer 2000a).

The importance of investing in the acquired business is illuminated not only by the frequency of brownfield investment in the region (Meyer and Estrin 1999), but by the fact that investment is the only strategic variable that Uhlenbruck and DeCastro (2000) and others found clearly associated with better performance. Also research on joint-ventures suggests that support from the foreign partner is crucial (Lyles and Baird 1994; Lyles et al. 1996; Fey 1995). The investor has to create a comprehensive strategy for the post-acquisition restructuring and integration (Obloj and Thomas 1998; Meyer and Møller 1998; Thomson and McNamara 1998). A central part of this strategy is the learning process of the local organization.

## 25.4.2 Managing the learning and education process

Firms have to upgrade their managerial capabilities far more fundamentally than is catered for by conventional management training. Technological skills were on a high level due to good general education in natural sciences, especially mathematics and engineering. Yet managerial and social skills were deficient due to both the change of skills and capabilities required in the new institutional setting, and the separation from modern social sciences. Incumbent leaders were often insufficiently prepared as they had different tasks and developed other skills in the central plan system. In fact the required capabilities are often beyond the experience-horizon of individuals used to the central-plan system. What is worse, the new private sector in Russia makes very little provision for training of their employees, while locally available training is limited and relatively expensive (Clarke and Metalina 2000). The required new skills are often based on tacit know-how, which requires an interactive learning process (Swaan 1997). They can be described on three levels (Child 1993; Villinger 1996):

1. At the technical level, new and specific techniques have to be acquired such as methods for quality measurement, scientific and engineering techniques, or the construction of samples for market research.
2. At the systemic level, new systems and procedures have to be adopted, which requires integrative learning emphasizing coordination, relationships, and links. Examples include coordination of integrated production systems, or production control and budgeting systems. Already at this level, the learner not only has to unlearn acquired routines and replace them by new ones, but to reassess attitudes and value systems underlying behaviour within the organization under the old and the new regimes (Michailova 1997; Meyer and Møller 1998).
3. At the strategic level, senior managers have to change their cognitive framework for doing business and conducting the tasks of management. They need to reassess their criteria of business success and factors contributing to that success. This requires understanding of technological and managerial processes in such depth that they can engage in innovation, select and adapt technology, and take strategic decisions.

The acquisition and adaptation of this complex, and in many cases tacit, knowledge is inhibited by the cultural and institutional context of its transfer (Jankowicz 1994; Kostera and Wicha 1996; Geppert 1996). Managerial learning, and in particular the internalization of new knowledge, is modified by the connection made by recipients between new ideas, information and experiences, and their prior knowledge and experiences. The content of received knowledge is filtered through the mind set of the recipient in CEE and their experiences in the socialist society (Soulsby and Clark 1996).

Most academic observers therefore stress the need to contextualize the contents and methods of training in Eastern Europe (e.g. Jankowicz 1994, 1996; Child and Czegledy 1996). Yet, a fundamental discrepancy separates Western training methods, which are grounded in extensive research, and the expectations of Eastern course participants. The contextualization of training programmes thus faces the dilemma that formalization of delivery methods, as preferred by many participants, cannot achieve the objectives of the training, i.e. inducing managers to think for themselves on a strategic level (Hollinshead and Michailova 1999).

Those transferring management knowledge to the East often took, especially in the early 1990s, an ethnocentric perspective, believing in the superiority of the Western way of doing things and being disrespectful, or unaware, of local traditions, cultures, and accomplishments (Hollinshead and Michailova 1999). Western consultants in particular are resented, delivering reports of little practical use because they fail to understand the institutional context of the CEE firms (Soulsby and Clark 1996). This leads to considerable 'consultancy fatigue' (Gilbert 1998) especially if the consultants obtain only superficial information on the ground and, as they are paid for by international institutions, are more concerned about Brussels or Washington than with Novgorod or Vladivostok.

This literature advises to employ individuals that relate modern management and post-communist reality. For instance, Soulsby and Clark (1996) report that local consultants with Western training and émigrés returning to their roots have been highly appreciated by local managers. In Central Europe, the intellectual and cultural gap between Western and local managers is narrowing, yet finding persons capable of communicating effectively in the former Soviet Union is still a considerable challenge.

Vlachoutsicos and Lawrence (1996) argue that positive change in managerial practice will come about only if continuities with the values and decision-making processes of the Russian traditional collective are preserved, and the natural behaviour of Russian managers are integrated into newly introduced managerial systems and practices. From the perspective of evolutionary and institutional economics, new practices have to be built on existing attitudes and value systems, preserving selectively what is worthy, and using experimentation to discover new best practices suitable for transition economies (Kogut 1996; Spicer et al. 2000). JV research confirms the importance of incorporating local management as 'shared management' is generally associated with better performance (Lyles and Baird 1994; Fey 1995).

The gradual development of capabilities is however challenged by the radical nature of the organizational change faced by many firms. The turbulence, the dramatic shortfall of available resources, and the fundamental threats created for many people have inhibited, if not undermined, their willingness to learn (Hedberg 1991; Villinger 1996). In the face of high uncertainty, imitation of imposed practices may be preferred to an internalization of new knowledge (Child and Czegledy 1996). Newman and Nollen (1998) thus observe an inverse-U-shaped relationship between firms' ability to learn and to restructure, and the gap between existing and required capabilities. This suggests that training should be based on a step-wise learning process, with clearly delimitated intermediate targets.

## 25.4.3  Managing cultural diversity

Western investors managing acquired businesses or joint-ventures in transition economies experience considerable cultural diversity, and consequently conflicts between different groups within the organization (e.g. Child and Markoczy 1993; Puffer and McCarthy 1997). Managing such conflicts of organizational culture is a major challenge for joint-ventures, especially in Russia (Puffer *et al.* 1996; Michailova 2000; Fey and Beamish 1999). As Russian culture is often seen as not conducive to successful market-based management, managers, as well as researchers, face a major challenge in how to change organizational culture (Fey and Denison 1999). Yet what are the origins of such cross-cultural conflicts?

### 25.4.3.1  *The cultural legacy of socialism*

The business culture in transition economies is in flux, and therefore hard to define. Three distinct cultural forces are, metaphorically, battling for the hearts and minds of East European people. These are, first, the historical cultural roots that have been loosened, but not lost, with the arrival of socialism. Second, the socialist experience bears upon those who grew up under the system. Third, many people are willing to shed either legacy to adapt Western culture, or what is received of it through the media, business contacts, and tourists. Thus, culture is unusually unstable and shows considerable discrepancies between the cultural norms and behaviours communicated in public and those people actually internalized (Todeva 1999). Feichtinger and Fink (1998) describe the volatility of culture in the 1990s, and the corresponding confusion at the individual level, as 'collective culture shock'. This analogy suggests that after a period of disorientation, the societies will recover and prosper with the new cultural identity. In the Western parts of the region, culture is converging towards Western European patterns, with regional specialties such as egalitarian and religious values.

Socialism left behind a 'bloc culture' (Sztompka 1993). This is not the officially propagated philosophy of Marxism–Leninism, but the reality of values and attitudes of individuals within real existing socialism. Despite the communitarian ideology, socialist regimes were low-trust regimes. Distrust was institutionalized through networks of informers of KGB or its partner institutions, fostering suspicion even when it was without foundation. In consequence people drew a sharp separation between their private and public circles. As a double legacy of socialism, 'individuals are likely to have a high degree of trust in their immediate social network, and a high degree of distrust in the formal institutions of the state' (Rose *et al.* 1997: 10). Low levels of trust in institutions continue in the transition period, reinforced by insider privatization that benefited the old nomenklatura, the growth of the Mafia, and corrupt politicians. Transition thus has to build trust in institutions, beyond the personal level.

Russian business culture has however roots that go deeper than socialism. Several researchers aim at explaining this culture and the emerging cross-cultural discrepancies in Russian–Western organizations (Lawrence and Vlachoutsicos 1990; Puffer *et al.* 1996; Michailova 2000; Holden and Cooper 1994; Holden *et al.* 1998; Elenkov 1998). Vlachoutsicos (1998) presents a comprehensive analysis of 'the inner logic of Russian management' based on its roots in both Russian history and the influences of seventy years of socialism. He outlines the 'matrioshka' structure of Russian organizations with strong vertical ties, but weak horizontal coordination, and the traditional decision-making process. This is typically top-down on strategic matters, but contains a major consultative element on issues of implementation, if only in a ritualized fashion.

These traditions influence Russian managers' interactions with Western counterparts. For instance, Russians are reported to act short-term orientated, averse against planning, and they typically expect the leaders to take strategic decisions, but discuss methods of implementation (Michailova 2000). Yet there is considerable variation of behaviour and belief systems between, say, a Soviet-area senior executive and a young entrepreneur (e.g. Puffer *et al.* 1997, 2000).

### 25.4.3.2 *Networking*

Bonding and other forms of network activities have a central role in Russian business. They arise from both cultural traditions and as substitute to legal institutions such as contract enforcement. East European managers are well versed in developing personal business networks, and in making informal arrangements to compensate for the breakdowns in formal resource allocation and distribution systems (Child and Czegledy 1996; Martin 1999). At least the former is, while commonly overlooked in economic models, an important part of business in any economic system, and fostered in modern management under the title of the 'network organization'.

In Russia, networking occurs more at a personal level activity rather than between institutions. Several studies emphasize the importance of personal relationships, as Russians typically do not distinguish between personal friends and business relations (Salmi 1999; Meyer *et al.* 2000). Social activities thus are part of business dealings. This arises from cooperative value systems, distrust towards strangers, and traditions such as *blat* (Ledeneva 1999). To overcome initial mistrust, Russians are reported not to engage in business before they have shared social activities, and substantial amounts of vodka. Western partners are expected to participate in such bonding activity (Holden *et al.* 1998).

The reliance on informal relationships raises pertinent issues of business ethics for local and in particular foreign business persons operating in the region. The emphasis on connections may undermine the introduction of new and objective standards of performance by creating distrust and dissatisfaction (Cyr and Schneider 1996). Moreover, there is a thin line between networking and unethical or illegal activity. For example Russians consider violation of insensible laws as normal, yet can it be for a Western investor? It may be infeasible to do business if one was to obey all the rules at all times (Puffer and McCarthy 1995). Experienced investors claim that there are many ways to cope with the situation, e.g. building contacts at the highest level in the authorities, knowing the law precisely, and exchanging experiences with other Western expatriates. Yet, Russia is not for beginners.

### 25.4.3.3 *Human resource management*

Human resource management has to accommodate the cultural diversity. An area where this appears particularly difficult is the recruitment and remuneration of people for the local operation. Many investors assign expatriates to all top management positions, and aim at recruiting and training local personnel to take over these positions after a few years. This however proved difficult, especially for finance and marketing personnel. The small number of qualified people in these fields, often younger than their Western counterparts, found themselves head-hunted by Western investors. Yet, beyond this small élite, managerial labour markets hardly function at all because of the shortage of key personnel (Peiperl and Estrin 1997).

Local firms have a generally low turnaround of managers. Three years into transition, 78 per cent of top and second tier management positions in the Czech Republic were still held by former nomenklatura managers. Most changes occurred at the position of the CEO and the personnel managers, often the party representative, who were mostly replaced internally (Clark and Soulsby 1996; Newman and Nollen 1998). Management change is more frequent in firms facing competition and hard budget constraints (EBRD 1999: 139) and, where outsiders were recruited, associated with better performance (Claessens and Djankov 1998), suggesting that active recruitment will eventually take hold in the region.

Western HRM approaches have been adopted in the region, for instance by creating a wider spread of salaries (Basu *et al.* 1997; Clark and Soulsby 1996). Incentive-based pay has been introduced, especially by Western investors, but with mixed success, as it sometimes conflicts with the egalitarian local culture (Mueller and Clarke 1998; Cyr and Schneider 1996). As in other areas of management, HRM practice in Central Europe converges towards West European models, while Russians still have a high level of suspicion over the introduction of Western management ideas (Holden *et al.* 1998; Shekshina 1998). MNEs adapted their HRM policies to the local context to varying degrees. While performance appraisal and promotion were standardized, recruitment, training, and financial reward systems were locally adapted, especially in Russia (Björkman and Ehrnrooth 1999). Only some of the HRM policies adopted in Russian firms were found to actually improve performance (Fey *et al.* 2000).

An often underestimated HRM challenge is the communication across cultural and linguistic divides (Villinger 1996; Cyr and Schneider 1996; Jankowicz 1994). Effective communication is important to convey to the entire workforce the strategic direction of the business, to obtain direct feedback, and to build personal relationships and trust. It requires that both partners are sensitive to each other's cultural and historical context and share a common language (Villinger 1996; Michailova 2000). In particular, the communication has to overcome the culturally conditioned differences in key concepts such as 'time', 'plan', and 'control' (Michailova 2000), which is a particularly serious problem in Slavonic languages where expressions for certain Western business terminology have not been developed prior to 1990.

# 25.5 Perspectives for Future Research

The study of business in transition economies offers opportunities not only to understand 'transition' but to generate insights, concepts, and theoretical frameworks for international business in general. The transition economies provide a laboratory for business; and insights gained here will contribute to the discourse on global economy in the twenty-first century. Research challenges include questions on how businesses evolve during radical organizational change, and how institutions shape corporate behaviour. Scholars may venture more inductive research, and develop new concepts and frameworks relevant beyond the region.

In the 1990s, research focused on issues that were specific to the start of transition and the opening to international business. Research needs to move on, from privatization to new entrepreneurial businesses, from entry strategies to operations strategies, and from negotiating acquisitions to managing subsidiaries. Yet this research needs to consider the business context that, as proposed in section 25.2.1, has developed specific institutional characteristics that are likely to persist for the next decades.

The analysis of institutions and their influence on corporate strategies and enterprise behaviour can be taken beyond Peng (2000) to explain not only the differences of strategies between capitalist and transition economies, but to explain variations within regions. China followed a different path of transition, with gradual reform since the late 1970s, but observers detected interesting similarities with transition in Europe at the level of enterprises (Child and Markoczy 1993; Batra 1997; Peng 2000). Yet researchers need to be cautious about generalizing across emerging economies—as evident from comparing this paper with its companion on China (Child 2001). Challenges faced by enterprises vary considerably due to different macroeconomic and institutional contexts even within the region. Hungary and Poland, for example, converge with Western Europe, while Russia will retain distinct features for many years.

For example, the legal-institutional framework cannot yet guarantee property rights, which creates interesting challenges for contracting under uncertainty and without external enforcement mechanisms. Corporate ownership and governance exhibits specific features such as a high share of employee-ownership, staggered privatization, and close relations between businesses and governments. This implies that managers have to pursue profits as well as non-monetary objectives set by the firm's shareholders and stakeholders.

Firms design their corporate strategies and management procedures in response to these institutions, in particular by building business relationships that rely not only on markets as coordination mechanism. Consequently, we observe innovatory strategies such as conglomerate building in form of 'recombinant property' (Stark 1996) and 'network-base growth strategies' (Peng and Heath 1996). Further research may explore in more depth how different institutions influence the design of business organizations. This requires the development of more sophisticated analytical tools concerning the link between institutions and strategy.

Foreign investors too select and adjust their modes of business. They develop new forms of non-equity cooperation, engage in 'transitory alliances' (Hagedoorn and Sadowski 1999) and 'brownfield investment' (Meyer and

Estrin 1999). Businesses moreover face major challenges in understanding the local business cultures and in developing appropriate approaches to cross-cultural management and to change management—areas where applied research could be of great value. Last, but not least, technological advances may permit the region to leap-frog stages of technological development and innovate business, e.g. in E-commerce.

The analysis of business in an unusual context provides a laboratory to explore aspects that are less observable in mature market economies. Novel concepts and analytical frameworks may feed back into theories used in mainstream international business research. In addition to the institutional perspective, Hoskisson *et al.* (2000) point to the potential of adapting transaction cost theory and the resource-based view of the firm to the specific challenges of emerging markets. However to enrich these frameworks, researchers have to be venturous in their approaches, and apply exploratory research methods. Existing theories help analysts by concentrating attention on important variables and relationships—but they fail if important variables or relationships are missed. Few region specific insights are born out of hypothesis testing of standard theory. We need inductive research to understand new or unconventional business contexts. Longitudinal studies and linkages to related literature in, for example, transition economics and sociology may help to develop new, relevant, and dynamic theoretical frameworks.

# REFERENCES

ALI, SHAUKAT, and MIRZA, HAFIZ (1996). 'Entry Mode and Performance in Hungary and Poland: The Case of British Firms', AIB(UK) conference proceedings, Aston University, March: 1–23.

ANDERSON, JAMES H., KORSUN, GEORGES, and MURREL, PETER (1999). 'Ownership, Exit and Voice After Mass Privatization: Evidence From Mongolia', *Economics of Transition*, 7: 215–43.

ANTAL-MOKOS, ZOLTAN (1998). *Privatisation, Politics, and Economic Performance in Hungary.* Cambridge: Cambridge University Press.

ARENS, PATRICK, and BROUTHERS, KEITH D. (1999). 'Key Stakeholder Theory and State-owned versus Privatized Firms', London, mimeo.

ARNOLD, DAVID J., and QUELCH, JOHN A. (1998). 'New Strategies in Emerging Markets', *Sloan Management Review*, 39(3): 7–20.

ARROW, KENNETH (1985). 'The Economics of Agency', in J. Pratt and R. Zeckhauser (eds.), *Principals and Agents: the Structure of Business.* Boston, Mass.: HBS Press, 37–51.

ÅSLUND, ANDERS (1995). *How Russia Became a Market Economy.* Washington, DC: Brookings Institution.

AULAKH, P. S., and KOTABE, MIKE (1997). 'Antecedents and Performance of Channel Integration in Foreign Markets', *Journal of International Business Studies*, 28, 145–75.

BĄK, M., and KULAWCZUK, P. (1997). 'Foreign Investment Withdrawals from Poland: Case Studies and Recommendations', mimeo, The Institute for Private Enterprise and Democracy, Warsaw.

BARBERIS, NICHOLAS, BOYKO, MAXIM, SHLEIFER, ANDREI, and TSUKONOVA, NATALIA (1996). 'How Does Privatization Work? Evidence from Russian Shops', *Journal of Political Economy*, 104: 764–90.

BASU, SWAIT, ESTRIN, SAUL, and SVEJNAR, JAN (1997). 'Employment and Wage Behaviour of Industrial Enterprises in Transition Economies: The Cases of Poland and Czechoslovakia', *Economics of Transition*, 5: 271–89.

BATJARGAL, BAT (2000). 'The Impact of Resources and Resource Combination on Firm Performance in Russia', mimeo, London Business School, January.

BATRA, RAJEEV (1997). 'Marketing Issues and Challenges in Transitional Economies', *Journal of International Marketing*, 5(4): 95–114.

BEAMISH, PAUL W., and KILLING, J. P. (eds.) (1997) *Cooperative Strategies: North American Perspectives*. San Francisco: Lexington.

BEN-NER, AVNER, and JONES, DEREK C. (1995). 'Employee Participation, Ownership and Productivity: A Theoretical Framework', *Industrial Relations*, 34: 532–54.

BERGLÖF, ERIK, and VON THADDEN, ERNST-LUDWIG (1999). 'The Changing Corporate Governance Paradigm: Implications for Transition and Developing Countries', mimeo, Stockholm and Lausanne.

BERLINER, JOSEPH S. (1952). 'The Informal Organization of the Soviet Firm', *Quarterly Journal of Economics*, 64: 34265.

—— (1976). *The Innovation Decision in Soviet Industry*. Cambridge: MIT Press.

BEVAN, ALAN A., ESTRIN, SAUL, and SCHAFFER, MARK (1999). 'Determinants of Enterprise Performance during Transition', CERT working paper no. 99/03, Heriot-Watt University, Edinburgh.

BLANCHARD, OLIVER, and KREMER, MICHAEL (1996). 'Disorganization', *Quarterly Journal of Economics*, 62: 1091126.

BLASI, JOSEPH, KROUMOVA, MAVA, and KRUSE, DOUGLAS (1997). *Kremlin Capitalism: Privatizing the Russian Economy*. Ithaca: Cornell University Press.

BJÖRKMAN, INGMAR, and EHRNROOTH, MATS (1999). 'HRM in Western Subsidiaries in Russia and Poland', *Journal of East–West Business*, 5(3): 63–79.

BORNSTEIN, MORRIS (1997). 'Non-standard Methods in the Privatization Strategies of the Czech Republic, Hungary and Poland', *Economics of Transition*, 5(2): 323–38.

BOYKO, MAXIM, SHLEIFER, ANDREI, and VISHNY, ROBERT W. (1996). 'A Theory of Privatization', *Economic Journal*, 106: 309–19.

BRADA, JOSEF C. (1996). 'Privatization is Transition: Or is it?', *Journal of Economic Perspectives*, 10: 67–86.

BREWER, THOMAS L. (1994). 'Indicators of Foreign Direct Investment in the Countries of Central and Eastern Europe: A Comparison of Data Sources', *Transnational Corporations*, 3(2): 115–26.

BRIDGEWATER, SUSAN (1999). 'Networks and Internationalisation: The Case of Multinational Corporations Entering Ukraine', *International Business Review*, 8: 99–118.

—— KIERAN, R., and WENSLEY, R. (1995). 'Strategic Investment Decisions by Western Firms in Ukraine: The Role of Relationships in Home and Host Market Networks', *Journal of East West Business*, 1(3): 17–35.

BROADMAN, HARRY G. (ed.) (1999). *Russian Enterprise Reform: Policies to Further the Transition*. Washington, DC: World Bank.

BROUTHERS, KEITH D., and BAMOSSY, GARY (1997). 'The Role of Key Stakeholders in International Joint-Venture Negotiations: Cases from Eastern Europe', *Journal of International Business Studies*, 28: 285–308.

—— BROUTHERS, LANCE E., and NAKOS, GEORGE (1998). 'Central and Eastern European Investment: A Comparison of US, Dutch and German Firm Activities', in G. Hooley, R. Loveridge, and D. Wilson (eds.), *Internationalization: Process, Context and Markets*. London: Macmillan Press.

BUCK, TREVOR, FILATOCHEV, IGOR, and WRIGHT, MIKE (1998). 'Agents, Stakeholders and Corporate Governance in Russian Firms', *Journal of Management Studies*, 35: 81–104.

CARLIN, WENDY (2000). 'Empirical Analysis of Corporate Governance in Transition', in E. Rosenbaum, F. Bönker, and H.-J. Wagener (eds.), *Privatization, Corporate Governance and the Emergence of Markets*. London: Macmillan, forthcoming.

—— VAN REENEN, JAN, and WOLFE, TOBY (1995). 'Enterprise Restructuring and Dynamism in Transition Economies', *Economics of Transition*, 3: 427–58.

CHARMAN, KEN (1998). 'The Structure and Charactistics of International Joint-Ventures in Kazakhstan', unpubl. Ph.D. thesis, London Business School.

CHILD, JOHN (1993). 'Society and Enterprise between Hierarchy and Market', in J. Child *et al.* (eds.), *Societal Change between Market and Organization*. Aldershot: Avebury.

—— (2001). 'China and International Business', in *Oxford Handbook of International Business*. Oxford: Oxford University Press, forthcoming.

—— and CZEGLEDY, ANDRE P. (1996). 'Managerial Learning in the Transformation of Eastern Europe: Some Key Issues', *Organization Studies*, 17: 167–80.

—— and MARKOCZY, LIVIA (1993). 'Host-country Managerial Behaviour and Learning in Chinese and Hungarian Joint-ventures', *Journal of Management Studies*, 30: 611–31.

CHURCH, N. (1992). 'Advertising in the Eastern Bloc: Current Practices and Anticipated Avenues of Development', *Journal of Global Marketing*, 5(3): 109–29.

CLAESSENS, STIJN, and DJANKOV, SIMEON (1998). 'Managers, Incentives and Corporate Performance: Evidence from the Czech Republic', mimeo, World Bank, April.

CLARK, E., and SOULSBY, A. (1995). 'Transforming Former State Enterprises in the Czech Republic', *Organization Studies*, 16: 215–42.

CLARKE, SIMON, and METALINA, TANYA (2000). 'Training in the New Private Sector in Russia', *International Journal of Human Resource Management*, 11: 19–36.

COFFEE, J. C., JNR (1996). 'Institutional Investors in Transitional Economies: Lessons from the Czech Experience', in R. Frydman, C. W. Gray, and A. Rapazynski (eds.), *Corporate Governance in Central Europe and Russia*, vol. 1. London and Budapest: Central European University Press.

COMMANDER, SIMON, and MOMSEN, CHRISTIAN (1999). 'Understanding Barter in Russia', EBRD working paper no. 37, December.

CYR, DIANE J., and SCHNEIDER, SUSAN C. (1996). 'Implications for Learning: Human Resource Management in East-West Joint Ventures', *Organization Studies*, 17: 207–26.

CZINKOTA, M. R., GAISBAUER, H., and SPRINGER, R. (1997). 'A Perspective on Marketing in Central and Eastern Europe', *The International Executive*, 39: 831–48.

DAHM, M. (1995). 'Strategische Marktbearbeitungsentscheidungen internationaler Markenartikel-unternehmen am Beispiel Ungarns', *Der Markt*, 34: 122–32.

DJANKOV, SIMEON (1999a). 'Ownership Structure and Enterprise Restructuring in Six Newly Independent States', *Comparative Economic Studies*, 41: 75–95.

—— (1999b). 'The restructuring of Insider-dominated Firms: A Comparative Analysis', *Economics of Transition*, 7: 467–80.

EARLE, JOHN S., and ESTRIN, SAUL (1996). 'Employee-Ownership in Transition', in R. Frydman, C. Gray, and A. Rapaczynski (eds.), *Corporate Governance in Central Europe and Russia*. Budapest: CEU Press.

—— (1997). 'After Voucher Privatization: The Structure of Corporate Ownership in Russian Manufacturing Industry', CEPR working paper no. 1736, London: CEPR, December.

EBRD (European Bank for Reconstruction and Development) (annually since 1992), Transition Report, London: EBRD.

ELENKOV, DETELIN S. (1998). 'Can American Management Concepts work in Russia: A Cross-Cultural Comparative Study', *California Management Review*, 40(4): 133–56.

ENGELHARD, JOHAN, and ECKERT, STEFAN (1993). 'Markteintrittsverhalten deutscher Unternehmen in Osteuropa', *Der Markt: Zeitschrift für Absatzwirtschaft und Marketing*, 32(4): 172–88.

ERNST, M., ALEXEEV, M., and MARER, P. (1996). *Transforming the Core: Restructuring Industrial Enterprises in Russia and Central Europe*. Boulder, Colo.: Westview Press.

ESTRIN, SAUL (ed.) (1994). *Privatization in Eastern Europe*. London: Longman.

—— HUGHES, KIRSTY, and TODD, SARAH (1997). *Foreign Direct Investment in Central and Eastern Europe*. London: Cassell.

—— and MEYER, KLAUS (1998). 'Privatization-Acquisition: Who Buys State-owned Enterprises?', *MOST: Economic Policy in Transitional Economies*, 7: 159–72.

—— and ROSEVEAR, ADAM (1999). 'Enterprise Performance and Corporate Governance in Ukraine', *Journal of Comparative Economics*, 27: 442–58.

—— and STONE, ROBERT (1996). *Taxonomy of Mass Privatization, Transition*. World Bank: Nov: 8–9.

—— and WRIGHT, MIKE (1999). 'Corporate Governance in the Former Soviet Union: An Overview', *Journal of Comparative Economics*, 27: 398–421.

FEICHTINGER, CLAUDIA, and FINK, GERHARD (1998). 'The Collective Culture Shock in Transition Economies: Theoretical and Empirical Implications', *Leadership and Organizational Development Journal*, 19(6): 302–24.

FEY, CARL (1995). 'Important Design Characteristics for Russian–Foreign Joint-Ventures', *European Management Journal*, 13: 405–15.

—— and BEAMISH, PAUL (1999). 'Strategies for Managing Russian International Joint Venture Conflict', *European Management Journal*, 17: 99–106.

—— BJÖRKMAN, INGMAR, and PAVLOVSKAYA, ANTONIA (2000). 'The Effect of Human Resource Management Practices on Firm Performance in Russia', *International Journal of Human Resource Management*, 11: 1–18.

—— and DENISON, D. R. (1998). 'Organizational Culture and Effectiveness: The Case of Foreign Firms in Russia', Institute of International Business, Stockholm School of Economics, research paper no. 10/98.

FILATOTCHEV, I., HOSKISSON, R. E., BUCK, T., and WRIGHT, M. (1996). 'Corporate Restructuring in Russian Privatizations: Implications for US Investors', *California Management Review*, 38(2): 87–105.

FISHER, STANLEY, and SAHAY, RATNA (2000). 'The Transition Economies after Ten Years', NBER working paper no. 7664, Cambridge, Mass.

FRYDMAN, ROMAN, GRAY, CHERYL, and RAPACZYNSKI, ANDRZEJ (eds.) (1996). *Corporate Governance in Central Europe and Russia, vol. 1*. London and Budapest: CEU Press.

—— —— HASEL, MAREK, and RAPACZYNSKI, ANDRZEJ (1997). 'Private Ownership and Corporate Performance: Evidence from Transition Economies', EBRD working paper no. 26, London, December.

GADDY, C. G., and ICKES, B. W. (1998). 'Russia's Virtual Economy', *Foreign Affairs*, 77: 53–67.

GEPPERT, MIKE (1996). 'Paths of Managerial Learning in the East European Context', *Organization Studies*, 17: 249–68.

GILBERT, KATE (1998). 'Consultancy Fatigue: Epistomology, Symptoms and Prevention', *Leadership and Organizational Development Journal*, 19(6): 340–46.

GROSSE, ROBERT (2001). 'International Business in Latin America', in *Oxford Handbook of International Business*. Oxford: Oxford University Press, forthcoming.

HAGEDOORN, J., and SADOWSKI, B. (1999). 'Exploring the Potential Transition from Strategic Partnering to Mergers and Acquisitions', *Journal of Management Studies*, Jan.

HARE, PAUL, BATT, JUDY, CAVE, MARTIN, and ESTRIN, SAUL (1999). 'Introduction', in P. Hare, J. Batt, and S. Estrin (eds.), *Reconstituting the Market, The Political Economy of Microeconomic Transformation*. Amsterdam: Harwood Academic, 1–30.

HAVRYLYSHYN, OLEH, and McGETTIGAN, DONAL (1999). 'Privatization in Transition Countries: A Sampling of the Literature', working paper of the International Monetary Fund, no. 99/6.

HAYRI, AYDIN, and McDERMOTT, GERALD (1998). 'The Network Properties of Corporate Governance and Industrial Restructuring: A Post-Socialist Lesson', *Industrial and Corporate Change*, 7: 153–94.

HEDBERG, BO (1991). 'How Organizations Learn and Unlearn', in P. C. Nystrom and W. H. Starbuck (eds.), *Handbook of Organizational Design*. Oxford: Oxford University Press.

HEIDENREICH, MARTIN (1993). 'Vom volkseigenen Betrieb zum Unternehmen: Transformationsprobleme betrieblicher Produkt-, Organizations- und Personalkonzepte in Ostdeutschland', *Koelner Zeitschrift für Soziologie und Sozialpsychologie*, 45: 46–96.

HOLDEN, NIGEL, and COOPER, CARY (1994). 'Russian Managers as Learners: Implications for Theories of Management Learning', *Management Learning*, 25: 503–22.

HOLDEN, NIGEL, and COOPER, CARY (*cont.*) and CARR, JENNIFER (1998). *Dealing with the New Russia: Management Cultures in Collision*. Chichester: John Wiley.

HOLLINSHEAD, GRAHAM, and MICHAILOVA, SNEJINA (1999). 'Blockbusters or Bridge-builders? The Role of Western Trainers in Delivering New Entrepreneurialism in Eastern Europe', mimeo, Bristol and Copenhagen, June.

HOLMSTROEM, BENGT (1996). 'Financing of Investment in Eastern Europe: A Theoretical Perspective', *Industrial and Corporate Change*, 5: 205–37.

HOOD, NEIL, and YOUNG, STEPHEN (1994). 'The Internationalization of Business and the Challenge of East European Development', in P. Ghauri and P. Buckley (eds.), *The Economics of Change in East and Central Europe*. London: Academic Press.

HOOLEY, GRAHAM J., BERACS, JOSEF, and KOLOS, K. (1993). 'Marketing Strategy Typologies in Hungary', *European Journal of Marketing*, 27(11/12): 80–101.

——Cox, TONY, SHIPLEY, DAVID, FAHY, JOHN, BERACS, JOZEF, and KOLOS, KRISTINA (1996). 'Foreign Direct Investment in Hungary: Resource Acquisition and Domestic Competitive Advantage', *Journal of International Business Studies*, 27(4): 683–709.

HOSKISSON, ROBERT E., EDEN, LORRAINE, LAU, CHUNG MING, and WRIGHT, MIKE (2000). 'Strategy in Emerging Markets', *Academy of Management Journal*, 25(3).

HUNYA, GABOR (1996). 'Foreign Direct Investment in Hungary: A Key Element of Economic Modernization', research report no. 226, Vienna Institute for Comparative Economic Studies (WIIW), February.

JACOBSEN, KURT (1997). 'The Great Northern Telegraph Company: A Danish Company in the Service of Globalisation since 1969', in S. Tønnesson, J. Koponen, N. Steensgaards, and T. Svensson (eds.), *Between National Histories and Global History*. Helsinki: FHS.

JANKOWICZ, D. (1994). 'The New Journey to Jerusalem: Mission and Meaning in the Man', *Organization Studies*, 15: 479.

——(1996). 'On Resistance to Change in the Post Command Economies and Elsewhere', in M. Lee, H. Letiche, R. Crashaw, and M. Thomas (eds.), *Management Education in the New Europe*. London: Jutil Thompson Business Press, 139–62.

JOHNSON, SIMON, and LOVEMAN, GARY W. (1995). *Starting Over in Eastern Europe: Entrepreneurship and Economic Revival*. Cambridge, Mass.: HBS Press.

——McMILLAN, JOHN, and WOODRUFF, CHRISTOPHER (1999). 'Property Rights, Finance, and Entrepreneurship', mimeo, MIT and UCSD.

JONES, DEREK C., KLINEDIENST, MARK, and ROCK, CHARLES (1998). 'Productive Efficiency during Transition: Evidence from Bulgarian Panel Data', *Journal of Comparative Economics* 26: 446–64.

——and MYGIND, NIELS (1999a). 'The Nature and Determinants of Ownership Changes after Privatization: Evidence from Estonia', *Journal of Comparative Economics*, 27: 422–41.

——— (1999b). 'Ownership and Productive Efficiency: Evidence from Estonia', working paper no. 24, Center for East European Studies, Copenhagen Business School.

KARSAI, J., WRIGHT, M., and FILATOTCHEV, I. (1997). 'Venture Capital in Transition Economies: The Case of Hungary', *Entrepreneurship Theory and Practice*, 21(4): 93–110.

KIRBY, D. A., JONES-EVANS, D., FUTO, P., KWIATKOWSKI, S., and SCHWALBACH, J. (1996). 'Technical Consultancy in Hungary, Poland, and the UK', *Entrepreneurship Theory and Practice*, 20(4): 9–23.

KOGUT, BRUCE (1983). 'Foreign Direct Investment as a Sequential Process', in C. P. Kindleberger and D. Audretsch (eds), *The Multinational Corporation in the 1980s*, Cambridge, Mass.: MIT Press.

—— (1996). 'Direct Investment, Experimentation, and Corporate Governance in Transition Economies', in R. Frydman, C. W. Gray, and A. Rapaczynski (eds.), *Corporate Governance in Central Europe and Russia, vol. 1*. London and Budapest, Central European University Press, 293–332.

—— and ZANDER, UDO (forthcoming 2000). 'Did Socialism Fail to Innovate? A Natural Experiment of the Two Zeiss Companies', *American Journal of Sociology*.

KORNAI, JANOS (1980). *Economics of Shortage*. Amsterdam: North-Holland.

—— (1992). *The Socialist System: The Political Economy of Communism*. Princeton, NJ: Princeton University Press.

KOSTERA, MONIKA, and WICHA, MACIEJ (1996). 'The "Divided Self" of Polish State-owned Enterprises: The Culture of Organization', *Organization Studies*, 17: 83.

LANKES, HANS PETER, and VENEBLES, ANTHONY (1996). 'Foreign Direct Investment in Economic Transition: The Changing Pattern of Investments', *Economics of Transition*, 4: 331–47.

LAPORTA, RAFAEL, LOPEZ-DE-SILANES, FLORENCIO, and SHLEIFER, ANDREI (1999). 'Corporate Ownership around the World', *Journal of Finance*, 54: 471–517.

LAVIGNE, MARIE (1998). 'Conditions for Accession to the EU', *Comparative Economic Studies*, 40: 38–57.

—— (1999). *Economics of Transition*, 2nd edn. London: Macmillan.

LAWRENCE, PAUL R., and VLACHOUTSICOS, CHARALAMBOS A. (eds.) (1990). *Behind the Factory Walls: Decision-making in Soviet and US Enterprises*. Boston, Mass.: HBS Press.

LEDENEVA, ALENA V. (1998). *Russia's Economy of Favours: Blat, Networking and Informal Exchange*. Cambridge: Cambridge University Press.

LIEB-DÓCZY, ENESE E. (2000). *Transition to Survival: Enterprise Restructuring in Twenty East German and Hungarian Companies*. Aldershot: Ashgate.

—— and MEYER, KLAUS E. (2000). 'Context Sensitivity of Post Acquisition Restructuring: An Evolutionary Perspective', CEES working paper no. 36, Copenhagen Business School, June.

LIEBERMANN, MARVIN B., and MONTGOMERY, DAVID B. (1998). 'First-mover (Dis)-advantages: Retrospective and Link with the Resource-based View', *Strategic Management Journal*, 19: 1111–25.

LYLES, MARJORIE A., and BAIRD, INGA S. (1994). 'Performance of International Joint-Ventures in Two Eastern European Countries: The Case of Hungary and Poland', *Management International Review*, 34: 313–29.

—— CARTER, NANCY M., and BAIRD, INGA S. (1996). 'New Ventures in Hungary: The Impact of US Partners', *Management International Review*, 36: 355–70.

—— and SALK, JANE E. (1996). 'Knowledge Acquisition from Foreign Parents in International Joint Ventures: An Empirical Examination in the Hungarian Context', *Journal of International Business Studies*, 27: 877–903.

MAIER, CHARLES S. (1997). *Dissolution: The Crisis of Communism and the End of East Germany*. Princeton: Princeton University Press.

MARINOVA, SVETLA (2000). 'The Process of FDI Privatization in Bulgaria: Relationships between the Parties Involved', Ph.D. thesis, Faculty of Business and Economics, Copenhagen Business School.

MARTIN, RODERICK (1999). *Transforming Management in Central and Eastern Europe*. Oxford: Oxford University Press.

MARTON, KATHERIN (1993). 'Foreign Direct Investment in Hungary', *Transnational Corporations*, 2: 111–34.

McCARTHY, DANIEL, and PUFFER, SHEILA M. (1997). 'Strategic Investment Flexibility for MNE Success in Russia: Evolving Beyond Entry Modes', *Journal of World Business*, 32: 293–319.

McMILLAN, CARL H. (1993). 'The Role of Foreign Direct Investment in the Transition from Planned to Market Economies', *Transnational Corporations*, 2: 97–119.

MESCHI, PIERRE-XAVIER (1997). 'Longevity and Cultural Differences of International Joint Ventures: Toward Time-based Cultural Management', *Human Relations*, 50: 211–28.

MEYER, KLAUS E. (1995). 'Foreign Direct Investment in the Early Years of Transition: A Survey', *Economics of Transition*, 3: 301–20.

—— (1997). 'International Market Entry: Beyond Markets and Hierarchies', AIB conference, Banff.

—— (1998a). *Direct Investment in Economies in Transition*. Cheltenham: Edward Elgar.

—— (1998b). 'Enterprise Transformation and Foreign Investment in Eastern Europe', *Journal of East–West Business*, 4: 7–28.

—— (2000a). 'Direct Investment in East Asia and in Eastern Europe: A Comparative Analysis', in P. Artisien-Maksimienko and M. Rojec (eds.), *Direct Investment in Eastern Europe*. London: Macmillan.

—— (2000b). 'International Production Networks in Central Europe', *Comparative Economic Studies*, 62(1): 135–50.

—— (2000c). 'Enterprise Transformation as Coordination Game: The Leadership Challenge', *Journal of East European Management Studies*, forthcoming.

—— and ESTRIN, SAUL (1998). 'Opportunities and Tripwires for Foreign Investors in Eastern Europe', *Thunderbird International Business Review*, 40: 209–34.

—— —— (1999). 'Entry Mode Choice in Emerging Markets: Greenfield, Acquisition and Brownfield', CISME working paper no. 51, London Business School, January.

—— and MØLLER, INGER BJERG (1998). 'Managing Deep Restructuring: Danish Experiences in Eastern Germany', *European Management Journal*, 16: 411–21.

—— and PIND, CHRISTINA (1999). 'The Slow Growth of Foreign Direct Investment in the Successor States of the Former Soviet Union', *Economics of Transition*, 7: 201–14.

—— TIND, ANE, and JACOBSEN, MAAR KLINGE (2000). 'National Internationalization Processes: SME on the Way to Eastern Europe', CEES working paper no. 37, Copenhagen Business School, June.

MICHAILOVA, SNEJINA (1997). 'Inertia: Organizational Culture of Bulgarian Industrial Companies between Stability and Change', Ph.D. thesis, Faculty of Economics and Business, Copenhagen Business School.

——(2000). 'John, we are Not in the West Any Longer: Expatriates and Planning Change in a Russian Context', *Academy of Management Executive*, forthcoming, Nov.

MUELLER, STEPHEN L., and CLARKE, L. D. (1998). 'Political Economic Context and Sensitivity to Equity: Differences between the United States and the Transition Economies of Central and Eastern Europe', *Academy of Management Journal*, 41: 319–29.

MURRELL, PETER (1990). *The Nature of Socialism: Lessons from East European Foreign Trade*. Princeton: Princeton University Press.

——(1992). 'The Evolution in Economic and the Economic Reform of the Centrally Planned Economies', in C. C. Clague and G. Rausser (eds.), *The Emergence of Market Economies in Eastern Europe*. Cambridge, Mass.: Blackwell, 35–53.

MYGIND, NIELS (1999). 'Enterprise Governance in Transition: A Stakeholder Perspective', mimeo, CEES working paper no. 30, Copenhagen Business School, December.

NEALE, C. W., and SHIPLEY, D. (1990). 'Empirical Insights into British Countertrade with Eastern Bloc Countries', *International Marketing Review*, 7(1): 15–31.

NELLIS, JOHN (1999). *Time to Rethink Privatization in Transition Economies?* Washington, DC: World Bank/IFC working paper no. 38.

NELSON, JOAN, TILLY, CHARLES, and WALKER, L. (eds.) (1998). *Transforming Post Communist Political Economies, Task Force on Economies in Transition*. National Research Council, Washington, DC: National Academy Press.

NEWMAN, KAREN (2001). 'Radical Versus Incremental Change: The Role of Capabilities, Competition and Leaders', in D. Denison (ed.), *Managing Organizational Change in Transition Economies*, Mahwah, NJ: Lawrence Erbaum Associates.

——and NOLLEN, STANLEY D. (1998). *Managing Radical Organizational Change: Company Transformation in Emerging Market Economies*. Thousand Oaks, Calif.: Sage.

NOHRIA, NITIN, and GULATI, R. (1996). 'Is Slack Good or Bad for Innovation?', *Academy of Management Journal*, 39: 1245–64.

NORTH, DOUGLAS (1981). *Structure and Change in Economic History*. New York: Norton.

——(1990). *Institutions, Institutional Change and Economic Performance*. Cambridge: Cambridge University Press.

OBLOJ, KRYSTOF, and THOMAS, HOWARD (1996). 'Transforming State-owned Companies into Market Competitors in Poland', *European Management Journal*, 16(4): 390–9.

OECD (Organisation for Economic Cooperation and Development) (1995). *Assessing Investment Opportunities in Economies in Transition*. Paris: OECD.

OFFE, CLAUS (1995). 'Designing Institutions for East European Transitions', in J. Hausner, B. Jessop, and K. Nielsen (eds.), *Strategic Choice and Path Dependency in Post-Socialism: Institutional Dynamics in the Transformation Process*. Cheltenham: Edward Elgar, 47–66.

OZAWA, TERUTOMO (1992). 'Foreign Direct Investment and Economic Development', *Transnational Corporations*, 1: 27–54.

PARISH, W., and MICHELSON, E. (1996). 'Politics and Markets: Dual Transformations', *American Journal of Sociology*, 101: 1042–59.

PEIPERL, MAURY, and ESTRIN, SAUL (1997). 'Managerial Markets in Transition in Central and Eastern Europe: A Field Study and Implications', *International Journal of Human Resource Management*, 8.

PELLEGRIN, JULIE (1998). 'Market Linkages and the Dynamics of Regional Integration in Europe: Theoretical Considerations and Empirical Evidence at the Macroeconomic Level', in B. Bastida (ed.), *Integrating the Enterprise Sphere of Central European Countries in Transition into European Corporate Structures*. ACE project no. 95P-2003-R, printed by GATE, Universidad de Barcelona, 61–76.

PENG, MIKE W. (1997). 'Firm Growth in Transitional Economies: Three Longitudinal Cases From China: 1989–96', *Organization Studies*, 18: 385–413.

—— (2000). *Business Strategies in Transition Economies*. Thousand Oaks, Calif.: Sage.

—— and HEATH, P. S. (1996). 'The Growth of the firm in Planned Economies in Transition: Institutions, Organizations, and Strategic Choice', *Academy of Management Review*, 21: 492–528.

PEROTTI, ENRICO C., and GUNEY, SERHAT E. (1993). 'The Structure of Privatization Plans', *Financial Management*, 22: 84–98.

PUFFER, SHEILA M. (1996). *Business and Management in Russia*. Cheltenham: Edward Elgar.

—— and MCCARTHY, DANIEL (1995). 'Finding the Common Ground in Russian and American Business Ethics', *California Management Review*, 37: 29–46.

—— MCCARTHY, DANIEL J., and NAUMOV, ALEXANDER I. (1997). 'Russian Managers Beliefs about Work: Beyond Stereotypes', *Journal of World Business*, 32: 258–76.

—— —— —— (2000). *The Russian Capitalist Experiment*. Cheltenham: Edward Elgar.

PYE, ROBERT (1998). 'Foreign Direct Investment in Central Europe, Experiences of Major Western Investors', *European Management Journal*, 16: 378–89.

RONA-TAS, A. (1994). 'The First Shall be Last? Entrepreneurship in Communist Cadres in the Transition from Socialism', *American Journal of Sociology*, 100: 40–69.

ROSE, RICHARD, MICHLER, W., and HAERPFER, C. (1997). *Getting Real: Social Capital in Post-Socialist Societies*. Glasgow: Strathclyde University, CSPP.

SALMI, ASTA (1996). 'Russian Networks in Transition: Implications for Managers', *Industrial Marketing Management*, 25: 37–45.

—— (1999). 'Entry into Turbulent Business Networks: The Case of a Western Company on the Estonian Market', *European Journal of Marketing*, 34.

—— and MØLLER, KRISTIAN (1994). 'Business Strategy During Dramatic Environmental Change: A Network Approach for Analysing Firm-level Adaptation to the Soviet Economic Reform', in P. Buckley and P. Ghauri (eds.), *The Economics of Change in East and Central Europe*. London: Academic Press.

SCHUH, ARNOLD (2000). 'Global Standardization as a Success Formula for Marketing in Central Eastern Europe?', *Journal of World Business*, 35, May/June: 133–48.

——and SPRINGER, REINER (1997). 'Marketing in Central and Eastern Europe: An Assessment of Past and Future Research', in P. Chadraba and R. Springer (eds.), *Proceedings of the 5th Annual Conference on Marketing Strategies for Central and Eastern Europe*. Vienna: Wirtschaftsuniversität Wien.

SCHWARTZ, ANDREW, and ZYSMAN, JOHN (eds.) (1998). *Enlarging Europe: The Industrial Foundations of a New Political Reality*. Berkeley: BRIE; and Vienna: Kreisky Forum.

SEABRIGHT, PAUL (ed.) (2000). *The Vanishing Rouble: Barter and Currency Substitution in Post-Socialist Societies*. Cambridge: Cambridge University Press, forthcoming.

SHARMA, AVRAHAM (1992). 'Transforming the Consumer in Russia and Eastern Europe', *International Marketing Review*, 9(5): 43–59.

——(1995). 'Entry Strategies of US Firms to the Newly Independent States, Baltic States and East European Countries', *California Management Review*, 37(3): 90–109.

SHEKSHNIA, STANISLAV (1998). 'Managing People in Russia: Challenges for Foreign Investors', *European Management Journal*, 12: 298–305.

SMITH, STEPHEN C., CIN, BEOM-CHEOL, and VODOPIVEC, MILAN (1997). 'Privatization Incidence, Ownership Forms and Firm Performance: Evidence from Slovenia', *Journal of Comparative Economics*, 25: 158–79.

SORGE, ARNDT (1993). 'Arbeit, Organisation und Arbeitsbeziehungen in Ostdeutschland', *Berliner Journal für Soziologie*, 4: 549–67.

SOULSBY, ANNA, and CLARK, ED (1996). 'The Emergence of Post-Communist Management in the Czech Republic', *Organisation Studies*, 17: 227–48.

SPICER, ANDREW, McDERMOTT, GERRY, and KOGUT, BRUCE (2000). 'Entrepreneurship and Privatization in Central Europe: The Tenuous Balance between Destruction and Creation', *Academy of Management Review*, 25: 630–49.

STARK, DAVID (1992). 'Path Dependence and Privatization Strategies in East Central Europe', *East European Politics and Society*, 6: 17–54.

——(1996). 'Recombinant Property in East European Capitalism', *American Journal of Sociology*, 101: 993–1027.

STIGLITZ, JOSEPH (1999). 'Whither Reform? Ten Years of the Transition', Washington: World Bank Annual Conference on Development Economics.

SVETLIČIČ, MARJAN, ROJEC, MATJA, and TRTNIK, ANDREJA (1999). 'Outward Foreign Investment by Central European Firms and Restructuring: The Case of Slovenia', AIB Conference, Charleston, South Carolina, Nov.

SWAAN, WIM (1997). 'Knowledge, Transaction Costs and the Creation of Markets in Post-Socialist Economies', in P. G. Hare and J. Davis (eds.), *Transition to the Market Economy*, vol. II. London: Routledge, 53–76.

SZTOMPKA, PJOTR (1993). 'Civilizational Incompetence: The Trap of Post-Communist Societies', *Zeitschrift für Soziologie*, 22(2): 85–95.

TAPLIN, IAN M., and FREGE, CAROLA M. (1999). 'Managing Transitions: The Reorganization of Two Clothing Manufacturing Firms', *Organization Studies*, 20: 721–40.

THOMSON, J. NEIL, and MILLAR, CARLA (1999). 'The Role of Slack in Transforming Organisations', mimeo, FH, Nuremberg; and City University, London.

THOMSON, J. NEIL, (cont.) and MCNAMARA, PETER (1998). 'Two-way Learning in West/East Mergers and Acquisitions: Short-Term and Long-Term Viewpoints', *Journal of East European Management Studies*, 3: 164–88.

THORNTON, J., and MIKHEEVA, N. N. (1996). 'The Strategies of Foreign and Foreign-Assisted Firms in the Russian Far East: Alternatives to Missing Infrastructure', *Comparative Economic Studies*, 38(4): 85–120.

TODEVA, EMANUELA (1999). 'Models for Comparative Analysis of Culture: The Case of Poland', *International Journal of Human Resource Management*, 10: 606–23.

—— (2000). 'Comparative Business Network in Eastern Europe', *Journal of East–West Business*, 6(2).

VAN TULDER, ROB, and RUIGROK, WINFRIED (1998). 'International Production Networks in the Auto Industry', in A. Schwartz and J. Zysman (eds.), *Enlarging Europe: The Industrial Foundations of a New Political Reality*. Berkeley: BRIE; and Vienna: Kreisky Forum.

UHLENBRUCK, KLAUS, and DE CASTRO, JULIO (1998). 'Privatization from the Acquirer's Perspective: A Mergers and Acquisitions Model', *Journal of Management Studies*, 35: 619–40.

—— —— (2000). 'Foreign Acquisitions in Central and Eastern Europe: Outcomes of Privatization in Transitional Economies', *Academy of Management Journal*, 25 (3).

—— HITT, MICHAEL, and MEYER, KLAUS (2000). 'Organizational Transformation in Transition Economies: Resource-based and Organizational Learning Perspectives', CEES working paper no. 35, Copenhagen Business School, June.

UN (United Nations) (annually). World Investment Report, Geneva: UN.

URBAN, WALTRAUT (1992). 'Economic Lessons for the East European Countries from Two Newly Industrializing Countries in the Far East?', Wiener Institut für International Wirtschaftsvergleiche, Forschungsbericht 182.

VICKERS, J., and YARROW, G. (1988). *Privatization: An Economic Analysis*. Boston, Mass.: MIT Press.

VILLINGER, ROLAND (1996). 'Post-acquisition Managerial Learning in Central East Europe', *Organization Studies*, 17: 181–206.

VLACHOUTSICOS, CHARALAMBOS (1998). 'Russian Communitarianism: An Invisible Fist in the Transformation Process in Russia', working paper no. 120, William Davidson Institute, University of Michigan Business School, January.

—— and LAWRENCE, PAUL R. (1996). 'How Managerial Learning can Assist Economic Transformation in Russia', *Organization Studies*, 17: 311–26.

WEBSTER, L., and CHARAP, J. (1993). 'The Emergence of Private Sector Firms in St Petersburg: A Survey of Firms', World Bank technical paper, no. 228, Washington, DC: World Bank.

WHITLEY, RICHARD (ed.) (1992). *European Business Systems*. London: Sage.

—— and CZABAN, LASLO (1998a). 'Institutional Transformation and Enterprise Change in an Emerging Capitalist Economy: The Case of Hungary', *Organisation Studies*, 19: 259–80.

—— —— (1998b). 'Ownership, Control and Authority in Emergent Capitalism', *International Journal of Human Resource Management*, 9: 99–115.

WORLD BANK (1996). *World Development Report: From Plan to Market*. Washington, DC: Oxford University Press.

WRIGHT, MIKE, HOSKISSON, ROBERT E., FILATOCHEV, IGOR, and BUCK, TREVOR (1998). 'Revitalizing Privatized Russian Enterprises', *Academy of Management Executive*, 12(2): 74–85.

——THOMPSON, STEVEN, and ROBBIE, KEN (1993). 'Finance and Control in Privatisation by Management Buy-out', *Financial Accountability and Management*, 9(2): 75–99.

CHAPTER 26

················································································

# THE SMALLER ECONOMIES OF PACIFIC ASIA AND THEIR BUSINESS SYSTEMS

················································································

## GORDON REDDING

WHAT came to be known as the Asian miracle took place in a number of quite varied contexts in countries outside the major states Japan and China, and the way in which these smaller economies have built their development trajectories in the forty years after 1960 has been a matter of serious attention among policy makers worldwide. Japan and China are given specific attention elsewhere in this volume and so this section considers the rest of Pacific Asia. It cannot pay attention to every country as the number is large and many are still of small relevance in international business, but its aim is to outline the systems of business which have come to characterize the following clusters of countries: first South Korea which stands on its own as a distinct case; second Hong Kong, Taiwan, and Singapore which are essentially Chinese in their ethnic make-up, their current political structures, and their business behaviour, but which nevertheless display great differences among themselves; third the ASEAN group outside Singapore, that is Malaysia, Indonesia, Philippines, and Thailand, again containing variety but with certain key common denominators. Brief note will also be taken of Vietnam.

The Asian crisis of 1997/98 has tended to dull the business reputation built up in the area over the previous decades but, except for a late return to health of Indonesia, recovery is now in progress, and there are grounds for believing that the lessons learned have been salutary in most contexts. In this process of adjustment one over-riding issue of interest and speculation has been whether the region would become more recognizably Western in its methods of operating, or whether the new forms evolving would retain their distinctive nature, reflecting Asian ideals, or the somewhat controversial 'Asian values'. To understand the context of this question, and the implications for doing business in the region, it is necessary to come to terms with the forces of history and culture as well as the rationalities of economic and technical forces, all of which are in play here.

Real GDP growth-rates for East Asia averaged 7.3 per cent for 1965–80, 8 per cent for 1980–90, and 8.1 per cent for 1990–8. Poverty and illiteracy declined dramatically, and very clear advances were made in calorie intake, life expectancy, status equalization, democratic norms, and civil liberties. The outcome of the widely adopted policy of export-oriented labour intensive manufacturing is visible in the ratings for 1997 for percentage of GDP accounted for by exports. Worldwide, Singapore was first, Malaysia second, Hong Kong third, Indonesia fourth, Thailand fifth, Taiwan seventh, and Korea tenth. This widely used policy has resulted in work for the labour force and especially its female component, and in consequence high savings rates, lower levels of dependency, increases in productivity, and the attraction of foreign investment. It has also fostered continual reskilling and the ability to switch into new industries as time goes on, an example here being the industries connected with information technology either in its manufacturing or service aspects.

The crisis caused less social suffering than might have been expected. Despite currency devaluations of up to 40 per cent and recession during 1998 and 1999, the long accumulated savings came into play along with the traditions of family and village network support. Company misery was shared by managers. The global connections were maintained and as the global economy continued to surge in traditional markets for Asian products, the recovery was fast and the recovering economies now have leaner and more efficient companies. They have however not noticeably become copies of Western companies in this process of re-emergence.

As a framework for understanding, the notion will be adopted of the business system existing in a society, with most, but not all, societies defined within a political boundary. The business system is an evolving and constantly changing pattern of features and it owes its shape to its heritage in the way a society chooses to deal with modernization. The features of the system are aspects of the way economic behaviour is held together in stable patterns. An example is the norm of going to the stock-market for capital, or having trade unions, or operating mainly with family business. These stable patterns affect three features of the total structure: the way in which ownership holds organizations together, with different forms of ownership producing different forms of company, such that variations are seen in the use of professional management, nepotism, firm size, decision-making, etc.; second, the way in which an economy may be tied together horizontally and vertically in ways which affect the workings of competition, such alliances and understandings being often invisible; and third, the way organizations in a particular society typically go about the job of holding people together in conditions of cooperation within the organization.

These elements of the business system are embedded in the way a society chooses to modernize, specifically how it works out the creation and availability of financial capital, human capital (skill and talent and their availability), and social capital or trust. These in turn are embedded in the culture of the society, and especially the rules for vertical and horizontal order which influence relationships. All of these interactions are constantly affected by the rational logics of price and efficiency, and the changes wrought by technology.

# 26.1 HISTORICAL BACKGROUND

It is difficult to understand the region as a whole without coming to terms with the historical influences which have seeped into it from the great civilizations surrounding it. Prime among these has been the influence of China, and especially the ideals of social comportment and order stemming from Confucianism. This has been of most obvious relevance to the ethnic Chinese who moved south into the region, mainly in the late nineteenth century, and who now have such significant influence in regional business. It has also had a marked effect on the social and political structuring of South Korea and Vietnam, both tributary states of the Chinese empire for very long periods. It is clearly manifest in Hong Kong, Taiwan, and in Singapore.

The influence of Islam also has a long history, especially in the south of the region, and it is highly significant in the social fabric of Indonesia and Malaysia. This is based on centuries of trading and cultural absorption. Thailand has remained predominantly Buddhist and also independent of foreign control for many centuries, with a clear sense of national identity focused on the royal family. The Philippines is predominantly Catholic after four hundred years of Spanish rule, although the base layer of animism is never far from the surface. This latter feature applies also in much of the region more generally.

The colonial period saw the addition of Western influences to this mixture. These came via the colonization of Hong Kong, Singapore, and what is now Malaysia, by the British, of Indonesia by the Dutch, Vietnam by the French, and the Philippines by the USA. There was also a significant Japanese colonial period in the first half of the twentieth century in the histories of Taiwan and Korea.

These colonial powers left different legacies, but they all established patterns of relationships between government and business, structures of law, and an institutional fabric in the society, which are still visible in present-day systems. For example, business philosophy and practice in Hong Kong has been consistently *laissez–faire*, with excellent infrastructure but no government involvement in business itself. This reflects long-standing British attitudes, especially in the colonial context. In both Taiwan and Korea the Japanese ideal of state involvement in the design and managing of the economy is clearly reflected. Company law in Indonesia reflects much Dutch thinking and practice. The legal and educational structures of the Philippines display American norms. Vietnam still has many basic regulatory structures which go back to the French regime.

The end of the colonial period was spread over the third quarter of the twentieth century, a time of great regional instability, typified in the Korean War, the French and American Wars in Vietnam, the 'confrontasi' between Malaysia and Indonesia, and almost permanent high tension between China and Taiwan. There was also a spilling out of tension from a highly unstable and seemingly aggressive China between 1967 and 1977 as it went through the chaos of the Cultural Revolution. But in the late 1970s a change came over the region as stability returned and there began a period of more or less unbroken peace lasting into the new millennium and gradually strengthening in its likelihood of continuation. This provided the context for rising confidence in business investments, and those investments were themselves boosted by the opening of world markets, and especially the Western markets for consumer goods in the US and Europe. The establishing of such trading relationships then led to the growth of external investment into the region, a phenomenon which grew steadily through the 1980s and then exploded in the 1990s, culminating in the serious overdosing on low cost Western capital in search of 'emerging markets' which contributed significantly to the crisis of 1997/98. During these times also there grew a flourishing intra-regional trade and pattern of investment led by the regional ethnic Chinese, an example of one of its outcomes being the dominance of Taiwan as an investor in Vietnam.

# 26.2 General Characteristics of the Region

The most significant feature of the region is the variety within it. This begins with differences in religion and social philosophy, in language, and in historical legacies. A country such as Thailand which has never been colonized, and is Buddhist and royalist, is unlikely to display much similarity to one such as Indonesia which is Islamic, patrimonial, and heavily influenced by the legacies of a Dutch colonial structure. There are also radical differences in size, ranging from the 200 million population of Indonesia to the 2.6 million of Singapore. Levels of income per capita range from the Hong Kong and Singapore levels which exceed that of the UK, to the extreme poverty found in parts of Indo-China, not least in Vietnam. There are nevertheless, despite the variety, certain common denominators.

Two features of the business environments of the region are found widely, and tend to be seen as challenging by many companies going in from the outside. The first is the level of government involvement in the economy, and the second is the level of uncertainty and volatility which the business environment of these countries can display.

# 26.3 Involved Government

The kinds of development processes which many Western countries have gone through have included the historically slow taking over of the role of the state by the capitalist sector. Thus, put simply, in most Western capitalist systems the accessing of capital is now a largely private sector activity organized by institutions such as banks and stock-markets which are essentially self governing. This is seen as legitimate as long as the interests of society are served. So too the shaping of education and the skilling of people, and the building of large-scale enterprise, have been strongly marked by the wishes of the business world. An infrastructure of institutions then grew, including the significant components of professionalism in accounting and commercial law, which serves to guarantee order, but government has not directly put it there. It grew largely because it was needed by the people doing business, and they instigated it. There is of course in this process a constant flow of interaction between the parties concerned, and a long series of adjustments and negotiations. One of the outcomes is an ability to devolve decision making to managers in the organizations in the base of the economy without destabilizing the order of society. Creativity and entrepreneurship are then fostered.

When countries develop later, they cannot afford to wait for this infrastructure to grow naturally, as that could take centuries, and government is induced to play a strong role in the shaping of the business system, in effect filling the vacuum. They do this in different ways and with differing degrees of success, and the end results include different kinds of organization and of business system.

The smaller countries of Pacific Asia may be seen in three categories in this regard: first the cases of Korea, Taiwan, and Singapore, where the state has filled the vacuum very forcefully and taken on the role of prime mover in designing and managing the shape of the economy; second, the ASEAN states outside Singapore where the governments have monopolized much economic power but have so far failed to produce what some observers regard as authentic capitalism. This latter problem emerges from a combination of starting late, implementing weakly, and the obstacles such as cronyism and corruption which derive from a patrimonial heritage. A third case is that of Vietnam where political will for radical change is weak and where reform struggles against much residual dogma. Hong Kong is a special case of a policy of 'positive non-intervention' by government, and perhaps only possible at that level of success within the confines of a city state.

In the cases of South Korea and Taiwan, their governments took the view that catching up with the advanced countries was a matter of using their indigenous talent and resources to pursue growth by export oriented manufacturing industry. What was lacking was risk capital, a tradition of applied science in industry, and experience of large-scale organization at competitive world standards. These governments then set out to define the ideal shapes of their economies and to deal with what was lacking. In the case of Korea, beginning with the regime of Park Chung Hee in the 1960s, a series of five-year plans was launched, and key entrepreneurs found to implement them. Their organizations grew into the *chaebol*. The reward and the incentive for the huge tasks involved was the retention of ownership by the founder families. The choice of industry was guided by government planners, and government shared risk by making public funds available to support the growth. Government also shaped the economy in favour of the national aim by controlling union power, by the support of education and research, especially in engineering, and by spearheading and coordinating the drive for export markets. The consequence was that, with government support, it was possible to grow major global corporations, plus large numbers of effective smaller companies in their supply chains. Korea grew from a situation of total devastation at the end of the Korean War to the world's thirteenth largest economy by the late 1990s.

This fast evolution brought change with it, and especially in the degree to which government could continue so much to dictate strategy and control, including union power. Recent years have seen the state loosening its grip. Unions have grown along with democratization and the role of the *chaebol* has come under attack as their use of their advantaged position meets public opposition. A great deal of adjustment is now taking place in Korea as the roles of government, big business, small business, and the public at large, form a new pattern. The extreme dependence of some *chaebol* on government funding was revealed dramatically in the US $73 billion debt of the Daewoo group.

In Korea, the government was for most of the period since the 1960s in effect a military dictatorship, and largely unaffected by the kind of stakeholder arguments which go with democracy. It also tended to behave with impressive professionalism in matters of development policy, relying on an élite group of civil servants attached to the office of successive prime ministers. These policy-makers appear to have been driven by an ideal of national development, and to have been uncorrupted by their access to such power (as opposed to some of their more political colleagues). In Taiwan also this high level of professionalism in the bureaucratic élite, and its dedication to state development, marked the rise of Taiwan as an economic powerhouse, eventually accumulating more foreign reserves than any other country.

In other respects the Taiwan formula was different. There the continuation of the Japanese ideal of the strong state was interpreted in such a way that certain key sectors of the economy such as the banking sector, major utilities, and industries such as steel, fell under government control. The aim was the same as that of Korea but the mechanism was not to sponsor major private corporations to do the work. Instead it was to leave the big players in the economy under the control of the state élite and then to let the rest of the economy survive by its wits in the international market. The rest of the economy would come to consist of very large numbers of small firms, following Chinese intuitions about the legitimacy of family business and the retention of personal control. The entrepreneurship of which they then became capable served to give them important power in several world markets. Such markets are those servable by networks of small firms, working in commodity chains connecting them into the markets of the developed world, thus computer components, toys, electrical goods, specialized engineering products, etc. But in Taiwan, the market was still being managed by the government. It did so by the feeding of credit, technical assistance, and skilled labour, via the large scale sector into the small, and by setting the strategic direction for the large scale sector, influencing the shape of the profit opportunities available further down in the economy.

The case of Singapore is different again, although the principle of the strong state guiding the economy remains consistent with Korea and Taiwan. At the early stages of its development Singapore had few resources, little capital, and a small population. It took the view that its development would be dependent on making itself attractive to large foreign corporations as investors and it set out to do that. At the same time, as in Taiwan, the government of Singapore developed a highly professional civil service élite to manage industrial policy, and that élite became strongly involved in the command of significant parts of the infrastructure, and later in investment risk-taking in industry on behalf of government. Apart from the support of indigenous banks, the rest of the local economy was effectively marginalized, in favour of the multinationals. The latter responded with heavy investments, and now make up the major part of the economy. The Singapore government has remained dedicated to the idea of control, and unlike the governments of Korea and Taiwan, has used the legitimacy it has gained from increasing national wealth to perpetuate a single party state. There are some indicators that the stifling of pluralist debate and of democratic opposition may have had side effects on the society's capacity for spontaneous business creativity, and this policy of control may not survive the passing of the present élite.

In the ASEAN states other than Singapore, the government records have been less impressive as far as economic growth is concerned. An early tendency was to discourage foreign investment, and to attempt to develop local industry behind tariff walls, and other restrictions such as keeping out foreign executives. This changed slowly during the 1980s as the worldwide dominance of market capitalism began to assert itself. The crisis of 1997 gave further impetus to this trend.

In Korea, Taiwan, and Singapore, élite civil service groups dedicated to growth and modernization achieved great respect internationally for their clarity of vision, and their capacity to achieve its implementation by business people on the ground. In these ASEAN states, the record is one of less clarity, and also of greater difficulty in achieving implementation. These economies started later than their Confucian neighbours, and have grown respectably but not so spectacularly, as the late flying geese in the formation.

The largest of these states, Indonesia, was for most of its recent history controlled by powerful leaders with military backing, initially Sukarno, and then Soeharto, up to the point of the crisis. The long Marcos regime in the Philippines was similar in nature. Thailand's much more varied recent political history included long periods of military-backed government. Malaysia has been under the strong control of Mahathir Mohamed as prime minister since 1981. Each government chose its own format for dealing with economic growth. In Indonesia the main growth has been achieved by ethnic Chinese Indonesians in collaboration with the governing élite, a collaboration which has included some sharing of the economic gains in exchange for the granting of licences and privileged access to markets. In the Philippines the rampant corruption of the Marcos era weakened the country and left his democratically elected successors severely handicapped. In this case a traditional land-owning élite was joined by ethnically Chinese Filipinos in the process of taking the development opportunities. Here again, government connections were often crucial to the securing of access to opportunity. In Thailand, where business is dominated by Chinese Thai families, mainly of Chiu Chow origin, the connections between the business élite and the government have always been strong, but in this case one of the mechanisms is the involvement of the business sector in government itself via membership of the Senate. In Malaysia, the long serving prime minister has vigorously pursued a policy of industrialization which has aimed to protect the indigenous Malay people who account for just over half of the ethnic make-up. This has required some control of ethnic Chinese business expansion, and the encouragement of outside investments which would foster technology transfer.

In all of these countries, the government is heavily involved in economic processes. For outsiders this is most immediately visible in the negotiation of access to the economy. After that the level of government control of business behaviour in such fields as employment, technology, finance, and governance, is higher than most Westerners are accustomed to. In some countries corruption is part of the challenge and companies may be faced with explaining to head office extra costs due to this. These are still patrimonial states in which the duty of the élite is to maintain order, but that carries with it a right to extract benefits.

# 26.4 Uncertainty and Opaqueness

The second main characteristic of most Asian business environments is their opaqueness. These are business systems in which reliable public information on business matters is rare. Part of this stems from the late catch-up effect and the 'vacuum' referred to earlier, and caused by the absence of a deep layer of advanced institutions designed to foster order and independent of government. The second influence is the tendency of many indigenous business people, especially but not exclusively the ethnic Chinese, to keep tight control of their companies. This means that disclosure about corporate performance and assets is inhibited. To the outsider it becomes clear that key knowledge is seen as an important and rare possession, and is available on restricted networks, access to which becomes an important pre-condition of survival. The general high level of uncertainty is exacerbated by the volatility which goes with such fast growth, and the highly competitive search for the opportunities thrown up by the expansion.

The Asian formula for the securing of enough information to make decisions about business is to use interpersonal trust and a set of connections as key assets developed by individuals. The more of these you have the more you can achieve, but there are limits to how many such bonds a person can construct and maintain, as they are expensive in terms of both social time and attendant obligations. This puts a limit on the range of a person's field of effectiveness, and most Asian business people appear to act with this in mind, staying in fields they have come to understand well, and allying with partners they trust personally.

Having outlined the nature of these Asian business environments as being in general terms characterized by involved government and by high levels of uncertainty, we now turn to a consideration of the business systems which result within the more specific national cultures.

# 26.5 SOUTH KOREA

At both the societal and firm level, the theme which sheds light on South Korea is the transition from centralized authoritarianism to decentralized participation. Both politically and organizationally this process of transition is ongoing. It is not complete by any means but the direction of movement is clear and seemingly likely to persist.

The rescue of the country from its condition of destitution was achieved, as noted earlier, by a strong government co-opting the help of entrepreneurs to put into practice the national five-year plans for export-oriented industrial growth. Thus emerged the *chaebol*, large family dominated conglomerates in which those families are now under pressure to release their grip on ownership. Family ownership ranges from 39 per cent to 61 per cent, with an 'official' acceptable maximum of 40 per cent and a government aim of 25 per cent. Change is occurring fast as the government intention to favour in future those who go along with its wishes is being taken more seriously. There is in consequence a rise in the influence of professional managers and a decline in the salience of the personal vision of the owner.

At the same time, these organizations have had several decades in which to set a particular style of operating and this is likely to change less quickly. The characteristics of the large Korean organization which stem from this familistic history are:

1. A high level of authoritarianism in the exercise of authority, such that the metaphor most commonly used to describe them is 'militaristic'. An aspect of this is a formal approval process involving senior authority in many minor decisions proposed from below.
2. The use of a central control office, the 'Chairman's office', to gather performance data in detail about the company's activities.
3. Tall hierarchies, with few staff and many line functions, and controlled by strong functional departments in planning, finance, and personnel.
4. Loosely defined roles lower down in the hierarchy, and thus high dependence on the boss, a feature which also brings with it high flexibility.
5. Executive networks within the firm, which are often regionally based or stem from education connections. This makes for a significant level of informal organization.
6. A concern with harmony through the vertical levels, a feature which reduces the negative effects of the authoritarianism, and which fosters a search for consensus.
7. A strong work ethic, at least in part stimulated by pride in Korean achievement, especially *vis-à-vis* Japan.
8. Relatively weak horizontal communications within the organization, with coordination remaining a central preserve.
9. Unions with only recent acceptance and structured around an industry rather than an enterprise.

The style overall is paternalistic, a feature which is reflected in the rest of the economy made up of small and medium enterprises. But the concern with ownership, and the centralization of power have other effects in addition. There is a strong tendency for the *chaebol* to behave competitively towards each other, and to resist building alliances. This is in strong contrast to the position in Japan where alliances run horizontally throughout the economy. An outcome of this has been a tendency for the large Korean groups to incorporate too many fields within themselves in the general interest of firm growth, but to cause duplication in the economy at large. This is currently a field of battle with government.

It could be argued that the great strength of the *chaebol* has derived from the ambition and the visions of the owners who ran them, and the availability of government investment to back them, and that as these elements are diluted they will be hard to replace. Such centralization of power does bring great capacity to inspire creativity and to respond to change. The new form of *chaebol* will be predictably similar in many ways, and it may simply turn out that the newly rising professionals will be able to perpetuate much of the successful social psychology of the past, while eliminating its negative effects. It is as yet too early to find evidence of the new patterns.

The Korean business system is then dominated by changing family conglomerates with a traditional high dependence on government, an unwillingness to cooperate among themselves, and powerfully personal and authoritarian corporate cultures. What is the societal bedrock in which this formula evolved? Why is Korean business so distinct?

Financial capital in Korea has tended to derive from government, either directly, or via a tightly controlled banking system. Access to wider public and international sources of capital has been constrained by the concern with retention of control, the closing to outside influence of the Korean finance system, and the sheer size of the capital requirements to achieve the growth actually delivered. This could not have been done without special allowances being made for low financial efficiency. The entire scheme was a calculated alliance between government and business for a set purpose, and in the longer perspective it has worked. It has however left public shareholders as only marginally relevant until now, and other stakeholders dealt with when the pressure rose but not until.

Human capital in Korea has grown also as a result of the government–business alliance. Skills needed for the growth of specifically identified industries were produced by the education system as part of the national plans. Heavy investments in education and training by firms were also encouraged fiscally, and the end product is a society very rich in industry-related skill, especially in engineering.

Social capital in Korea, or the nature of trust and its workings, derives largely from the Confucian ideals which still penetrate the upbringing of Korean children. You look upwards for people to trust to look after you, and if the father figure ideal can be replicated in the organization then that has high psychological appeal. Vertical order is instinctive. Horizontal order is much more conditioned, and trust only works naturally in that dimension if prior socialization has created the network of references on which to base it, thus school and university groups, and region of origin connections. The rest are to be dealt with guardedly, and an instinctive competitiveness towards others outside the network is natural.

The end result is that the *chaebol* come from the tradition of Confucian order which is so much a part of Korean history, but because of government support they have grown well beyond the normal limits of family business. They appear to stand halfway between the Japanese form which is large but professional, and the Chinese form which is small and familistic. This form is large and familistic. Its impact on world markets has been impressive and it will probably retain its strength. We cannot yet say what the new form will be but it is reasonable to argue that it will continue to reflect Korean norms and traditions.

# 26.6 HONG KONG, TAIWAN, AND SINGAPORE

These three economies have been notable for their success as (along with Korea) the 'four little dragons' which followed rapidly in the wake of Japanese economic success. They have a common denominator in their ethnic dominance by people of Chinese stock, and this has brought with it strong doses of Confucian ideals about the ordering of social, political, and business life. It has also brought with it, perhaps as part of a refugee experience for so many of them or their near forebears, a pragmatic insistence on taking responsibility for their own fate and setting about its becoming more secure. The Confucian work ethic is founded in insecurity and helps also in the acceptance of authority. These common denominators have however been exercised in quite different settings with quite different routes to their eventual common success. They are now all rich in foreign reserves and Hong Kong and Singapore are rich in per capita terms also. Between 1981 and 1996 per capita income in Taiwan went from 26 per cent to 46 per cent of the US level. In Singapore and Hong Kong it went from 40 per cent to close on parity.

## 26.6.1 Taiwan

In Taiwan, the arrival of the Kuomintang refugees from China led to a social divide in the country between the mainlanders and the Taiwanese. This still affects much networking although it is fading slowly with time. As noted earlier, the policy for development was to structure an economy based on two sectors: the major industries and infrastructure elements under the control of the government related élite; and the small and medium enterprise sector which was left to grow under conditions of openness to world competition. Government would guide the economy by its control of the banking sector and the major industries, and would also assist in the development of human capital.

The end result is a business system with a vibrant and healthy small and medium sector, strongly connected into world markets, and highly flexible in responding to changes in demand. Its main role is the supply either of components into vertically integrated chains, or finished products which themselves go further into a chain of marketing with someone else's brand name. Examples of the former are bicycle gears or computer switchgear, of the latter Nike shoes or Canon cameras. As Taiwan has found itself competing with other low-cost labour countries it has moved much investment offshore into countries such as China or Vietnam, where it can continue to control costs and not lose its international connections into markets. The Taiwanese economy, like that of the Japanese, extends widely into the region as a result. A further consequence of this loss of comparative advantage in the home base has been the upgrading of much Taiwanese industry in terms of its technical sophistication. The computer industry is a case in point and this adaptation illustrates the key nature of connections into the US for the acquisition of knowledge, and technology.

## 26.6.2 Singapore

Singapore is very different. It has an economy based heavily on foreign investment by transnationals, and its environment is conducive to that. The local small business sector was marginalized earlier and despite regular government attempts to re-inject entrepreneurialism it has not thrived with anything like the efflorescence so visible in Taiwan or Hong Kong. Other than the transnationals, what remains in Singapore is largely government dominated, although playing by market rules and managed with professionalism.

## 26.6.3 Hong Kong

Hong Kong, now a Special Administrative Region of China, was formed in large measure under conditions of open free market competition as the ultimate *laissez-faire* economy, although a closer reading of the situation would lead one to qualify that simple view. The government's long standing and continuing policy of non-involvement in business meant that it did not get involved in taking financial risk or in setting industrial policy. It did however provide subsidized housing for half the population, and it controlled the prices of transport, of utilities, key foods, and crucially of land and thus property. A property cartel of major developers has taken a heavy proportion of the ownership of the capital value in the stock market and done so by its skill in maintaining good relations with the administrative élite, always a relatively small and closed group.

Industry in Hong Kong is similar in many ways to the small and medium sector in Taiwan, but it does not have the same government supported large scale industrial superstructure, and its banking system is entirely independent. Significantly, though, the major part of Hong Kong manufacturing industry has migrated to China, principally to the neighbouring province of Guangdong. Ownership has remained in Hong Kong, and the net effect has been a massive increase *de facto* in the industrial base, even though it is no longer inside the same political boundary. This is similar to what happened in Taiwan with the regional dispersal of its industry, also in that case predominantly into China.

## 26.6.4  The Chinese family business

The principal economic instrument found in Taiwan and Hong Kong is the family business. We shall also note later that it has high significance for the economies of Malaysia, Indonesia, Philippines, and Thailand. It is also worthy of note that its re-emergence in China in recent years adds greatly to its reach. It is now becoming significant again in Vietnam, after some decades of withdrawal. One of the characteristics of this type of organization is that the majority of them are small or medium in size. Because of this they are able to fit into a wide range of business environments and adapt themselves to local circumstances This business system is not bounded within a political border. Instead it penetrates the region widely. It also operates with a network of regional connections as if its natural arena were all the countries bordering the South China Sea.

Although Chinese family business is most commonly found at small and medium scale, there are many examples of conglomerate structures run under Chinese family control and employing tens of thousands of people. Such organizations have grown successfully in recent decades but almost always retain their original ownership structure and a management style of central-

THE SMALLER ECONOMIES OF PACIFIC ASIA

ized control. Strategy making is a family monopoly. Questions are constantly posed about whether they will 'learn' to make the transition to being standard multinationals with public ownership and professional management throughout. A parallel question is whether the second generation will 'reform' them. Another related question is about their instability at the time of transition from the founding generation to the next.

To be able to answer such questions requires an understanding of their context. As long as the business environments of the region remain (a) politicized, and (b) opaque, then the appropriate organization to thrive in such circumstances will be one in which:

(1) negotiating power for the organization is concentrated in one set of hands with full authority;
(2) the chief executive sees it as a key role to cultivate political allies;
(3) the chief executive sees it as a key role to build a network of trusted contacts with whom to exchange information, share risk, and share opportunity in the interest of long-term mutual benefit, thus counteracting the opaqueness.

The Chinese family business at large scale exhibits these characteristics. It will change its nature when it has to, that is, when the environments change. That shows little signs of happening in any significant measure yet. So what happens to these large conglomerates when the original founding owner passes on? The most common response is that they are divided between family members and the units start again the process of growth, some succeeding and some failing. Because the units are virtually always independent businesses then the chances of success are not handicapped by the breaking up of a delicately coordinated structure. This is a version of creative destruction which, seen from the standpoint of the business system as a whole, is healthy.

Creative destruction also accounts for much of the vibrancy and ability to adapt in the small and medium sector of the economy. Here, firms of a hundred or so employees, predominantly in medium technology manufacturing, but also in services, are run by their owners. What might appear to be diseconomies of scale are counteracted by flexible networking, and this makes it possible for firms to specialize in very particular aspects of a total process, knowing that the system as a whole can put together products such as fashion garments, toys, electronic and electrical goods, and so on, at world standards of cost efficiency and flexibility of response. Coordination is often managed by buying agencies, or trading houses. Transaction costs within the system are kept low by the use of interpersonal trust networks, by the reduction of bureaucratic process and legal contracting, and by a widespread dedication to cost control. This efficiency is helped by the concentration of decision making power in the hands of owners, each usually having a very hands-on knowledge of the business and the industry. Such individuals can transact with each other at high speed, can build up and pay off mutual obligations over long time periods, and can keep key information flowing around the system. Bonds of trust are specific, not general, but they are powerful means of coordinating economic behaviour.

Speaking generally, the fundamental *raison d'être* of the Chinese family business in the capitalist contexts of the region is to build up the wealth, and thus the security, of a family. This requires the searching for and taking of opportunities, but also the hedging of risk, and the preservation of some liquidity. The common pattern is to enter an industry and strive within it, often for decades, using family members nepotistically, but also key trusted employees who may be treated almost as family, to occupy key positions. Surplus is normally invested in property, seen as historically safe and potentially liquid. Risk is often spread geographically.

At larger scale, the roles tend to be rentier in nature and owners live off the benefits of cash flowing from assets. The bigger the entry barrier to the acquisition of such assets, and the closer such assets are to basic societal requirements like power, infrastructure, transport, hotels, communications, housing, then the safer the strategy. The risks of acquiring such seemingly unassailable positions are high and the time required is long, but the right political skills, and the right alliances will normally help.

Family business had been traditional in China for centuries, and in conditions where the growth of organizations to efficient large scale was inhibited by state interference and conservatism, by endemic mistrust in the absence of reliable trust-fostering institutions such as property rights and good public accounting, and by the Confucian placing of the family at the centre of the legitimate social system. Many Chinese left China in the later decades of the nineteenth century and settled in the countries to the south. Waves of this same exodus have continued in the twentieth century, with the result that there are now approximately 50 million people of Chinese ethnic origin in the region outside China.

The business system of the regional ethnic Chinese has family ownership of enterprise at its centre. Virtually all firms are under tight control and those which appear to have gone public tend to have large assets separated out into private domains and not accounted for publicly. Notions of stakeholder and shareholder involvement in policy making are irrelevant in this context. The key to the power structure in each firm is the owner-manager, and he or she normally dominates the making of strategy, this latter being rarely defined specifically. This person is also key to the building on behalf of the firm of strategic alliances to secure political 'coverage', well-judged information, and the sharing of risk and opportunity.

These personalized firms are operating in a general context of mistrust, and they make alliances to counter this, but only with very specific sets of chosen partners. Thus the 'network capitalism' most natural to the Chinese allows

tries considered here. The country is very large, both in extent and population, having 81 million people. Centuries of earlier autonomy left it with a very strong sense of national identity, but the decades of war against the Japanese, then the French, then the US, left the country weak and still psychologically divided. As with most totalitarian states the instruments of control are many, sophisticated, and deep in their penetration, and while Vietnam continues to talk about opening up and encouraging capitalist activity it continues to frustrate the business person with rules, regulations, and unpredictably changing controls.

The end result is that small business, operating close to the ground, and left to its own devices, can survive and even prosper. Businesses at larger scale have to navigate the world of political approval. Investors going in from advanced countries have had mixed experiences in recent years, and progress in opening the country to world trade and competition is slow. Income per capita is the lowest among the major countries of the region at US $400.

There is a strong sense among many observers of Vietnam that the country is at the same position China was at in the 1970s prior to the Deng Xiao Ping reforms of 1979. Freedom of economic behaviour in China was achieved by a process of decentralization and loosening of control. It was done slowly and is still far from complete, but there was at least an official endorsing of 'the glory of being rich', and private ownership expanded in line with the decline of the state sector. This same direction is being followed much more hesitantly in Vietnam and with much less clarity of endorsement from the very top. Instead policy is fought over between the liberals and the hard liners, and the truce line between them shifts constantly. The retention of power by party members drives much behaviour and the likelihood of fast progress is low.

# REFERENCES

BACKMAN, M. (1999). *Asian Eclipse*. Singapore: Wiley.

CHAN, S., CLARK, C., and LAM, D. (eds.) (1998). *Beyond the Developmental State*. London: Macmillan.

ENRIGHT, M. J., SCOTT, E. E., and DODWELL, D. (1997). *The Hong Kong Advantage*. Hong Kong: Oxford University Press.

HOSONO, A., and SAAVEDRA-RIVENO, N. (eds.) (1998). *Development Strategies in East Asia and Latin America*. London: Macmillan.

JOMO, K. S. (ed.) (1998). *Tigers in Trouble*. Hong Kong: Hong Kong University Press.

McVEY, R. (ed.) (1992). *Southeast Asian Capitalists*. Ithaca NY: Cornell University Press.

ORRU, M., BIGGART, N. W., and HAMILTON, G. G. (1997). *The Economic Organization of East Asian Capitalism*. London: Macmillan.

them to transcend their scale limitations and take part in the international economy via informal collaboration with fellow firms, such networks being flexible in the short term and basically stable in the long term.

The holding together of employees in cooperative relation with the firm is done largely by the application of principles of paternalism, another feature which inhibits the growth of individual firms. This exchange of obligation to employees downwards and loyalty, deference, and acceptance of authority upwards, is a social system rooted in Confucian ethics which give it moral force and sustainability.

The institutional fabric of the societies in which the Chinese family business system thrives tends to be one in which they keep separate as much as possible from government, and rely on their own sources of capital. The larger companies will build political friendships into government to secure access to opportunities. Some large ones will also tap into international finance markets while working hard to retain control. The system of human capital is influenced heavily by a very high sensitivity to the value of education, and a high level of individual responsibility in achieving it. This stems from the ethics of responsibility to family and the insecurity so commonly part of family folklore. In some states, the government has invested heavily in educational infrastructure, notably Hong Kong and Taiwan. In other cases such as Malaysia and Indonesia, ethnic discrimination has held them back from their full potential.

Skills are normally acquired by individuals in their pursuit of a career and are not provided by the firm. The use of skill is usually at the discretion of management and in most countries in the region is unaffected by labour union pressure. Social capital, or the availability of trust, is problematic in this business culture, but is solved by the networking. Limited but reliable networks provide the means of getting around the endemic mistrust.

The tendency for these responses to be visible across many countries is suggestive of certain common inclinations in Chinese culture. In particular, the salience of Confucian familism at the centre of the social order is clearly important. This provides high legitimacy for the holding of authority by the father figure and those who behave as such. So too are the ethics surrounding the obligations to friends. These provide the social glue which ties together the myriad business transactions at such high levels of efficiency. These ancient bases for vertical and horizontal order show no sign of declining in the socialization of the next generation, and it might therefore be supposed that this business system will continue to prosper in the conditions to which it is adapted.

A summary of the main characteristics of Chinese capitalist enterprises is as follows:

(1) owned and managed by the same person or family group;

(2) networked with other companies of the same type for the raising of capital, the hedging of risk, and the exchange of strategic information. Bonds of steady business relationships are also fostered like this;

(3) sensitive to the need for co-opting political support when operating at large scale;

(4) paternalistic in style of management;

(5) capable of operating at large scale especially via the use of alliances for the incorporating of technology, and brand names;

(6) extensively networked in small scale manufacturing of components which are assembled in vertical commodity chains with reach into advanced country markets;

(7) capable of high speed of response and flexibility;

(8) tend to grow in one field of specialism prior to later diversification for hedging, or opportunity taking;

(9) inhibited by limitations on trust from building large professionally managed and decentralized organizations. All growth tends to be in conditions of tight central control of strategy and of finance;

(10) internally very conscious of costs and externally able to limit transaction costs by the use of personalistic trust.

# 26.7 Indonesia, Malaysia, Philippines, and Thailand

It was noted earlier that these countries came relatively late to the Asian 'miracle'. They also suffered heavily from the crisis, especially Thailand and Indonesia. Three of them have huge populations (Philippines 65m, Indonesia 200m, Thailand 60m) and have found in them the basis of comparative advantage. Much investment has been attracted in on the basis of the volumes of skilled labour available at low cost.

Although the systems of capitalism vary in these countries there are certain common features. The kind of indigenous organizations found fall into two types. On the one hand are the ethnic Chinese organizations which tend to dominate and which appear in all sizes. On the other hand are the ethnically more local organizations, many of which have been favoured with government support. Some of these can be very large and examples of them are the companies associated with the military in Indonesia, the Bumiputra com-

panies in Malaysia, some of which took over previously colonial assets, the companies in the Philippines associated with the earlier land-owning élite. These large companies tend to exist as a result of government support or preference, and sometimes also as instruments of élite exploitation as occurred with the Suharto holdings in Indonesia or the Marcos holdings in the Philippines. At large scale, the ethnic Chinese companies have also been involved in this aspect of patrimonial extraction of benefits.

Networking across these economies takes place in conditions of what one observer has termed 'ersatz' capitalism. In other words these are states in which the level of order is low, institutions are unreliable or weak, and the government record in coordinating the various components of orchestrated economic development is weak. Thus capital market regulation is not sophisticated, reliable data are rare, law is negotiable in many instances, and government management of the economy is hesitant and reactive, lacking a clear, and fully worked out long-term vision. This criticism is less applicable to Malaysia where long standing policies are traceable and where government strength has been demonstrated. But an overall general conclusion is that the institutional fabric of these societies is not yet of the quality needed for the full development of market capitalism. Financial capital is still heavily influenced by personal or government connections. Human capital remains a field rich in potential but limited in development so far. Social capital is still a matter of personal connections.

The direction of movement in these countries is clear. They are dealing with their weaknesses with the intention of making themselves again significant competitors for the investments and the markets of the developed world. This will mean a rise in the quality of their business infrastructures, especially in banking and commercial law. One can also expect a continuation in education, especially technical, to produce the new skills needed. But the problems of order, and of coordination of policy, are immense in countries of such large size with traditions of weak government. The earlier resort to authoritarianism in the face of such challenges is less and less legitimate as democracy raises expectations.

# 26.8 Vietnam

Vietnam is a special case, being still heavily influenced in practice dogma, and being much further away from prosperity than the

REDDING, S. G. (1993). *The Spirit of Chinese Capitalism*. New York: de Gruyter.

TU WEI MING (ed.) (1996). *Confucian Traditions in East Asian Modernity*. Cambridge, Mass.: Harvard University Press.

VAN KEMENADE, W. (1997). *China, Hong Kong, Taiwan Inc.* New York: Alfred A. Knopf.

WADE, R. (1990). *Governing the Market*. Princeton NJ: Princeton University Press.

WEIDENBAUM, M., and HUGHES, S. (1996). *The Bamboo Network*. New York: Free Press.

WHITLEY, R. (1992). *Business Systems in East Asia*. London: Sage.

YEUNG, H. W. C., and OLDS, K. (eds.) (2000). *Globalization of Chinese Business Firms*. London: Macmillan.

# PART VI

## CONCLUSIONS

# CHAPTER 27

# METHODOLOGICAL CONTRIBUTIONS IN INTERNATIONAL BUSINESS AND THE DIRECTION OF ACADEMIC RESEARCH ACTIVITY

## BRUCE KOGUT

IT is one of the best-kept secrets of research that a methodological contribution is the most powerful engine for the replication and diffusion of an idea. Radical organizational innovations are far more influential than technological ones for the same reasons. Because they serve as complements to a wide array of industrial techniques, they can diffuse rapidly across the boundaries of a sector. Similarly, a major innovation in research design is far more powerful than a single technique or isolated idea.

The development of the field of international business has been strongly driven by innovations in research design and methodologies. I would like to emphasize this role in this concluding chapter in order to suggest to researchers, and to our doctoral students, that progress is engaged when a community collectively is able to ride upon common methods, schemas, and templates. The tendency in some fields, such as strategy, has been to suffer from the incentives for a proliferation of terms that represent the same idea. We thus have terms, such as 'multidomestic', 'multinational', and 'polycentric', that mean roughly the same thing. This proliferation is exacerbated by the applied mission of the strategy field and its proximity to the textbook and consulting industries. Yet in all fields, there is value for career advancement in generating and proliferating terms, a problem hardly unique to the managerial sciences.

Given these incentives, what then constitutes a good innovation in academic research? There are many answers to this question, but I prefer, as someone who likes historical sociology, a simple one. Good innovative research is what a community decides is interesting. However, this relativistic orientation is disciplined by an important caveat in the following form. The best measurement of this interest is its sustained allocation of subsequent scientific effort to produce, confirm, and extend the cumulative results associated with the innovation.

If we accept the definition of a 'good' research innovation as a contribution that can be verified by a community (much in the spirit of Robert Merton's emphasis on the importance of the cumulation of knowledge), then it follows that tools of research design can have powerful effects on the direction of academic activity. We often study the direction of research activity among industrial firms and ask why certain technologies have evolved, and others not. By now, we know the answer is not simply market demand. Some technologies provide richer avenues for development; they are 'generatively' more fecund and act as broad technological platforms into new uses.[1]

Not all research methods and designs are equal in this regard. Take for example the research on transaction costs. Ronald Coase established in 1937 the observation that the boundaries of the firm are determined by a comparison of the costs of using the external market relative to the costs of internal

My thanks to Janine Napahiet in suggesting the topic of methodology as a comment in passing, to the doctoral students at Wharton, Stockholm School of Economics, and INSEAD for their indulgence over the years, to Mark Casson for his comments, and to Jose Campa and his Spanish colleagues in testing these ideas with them.

[1] See the seminal NBER volume on the direction of inventive activity (Universities-National Bureau Committee for Economic Research 1962), from which the title of this chapter derives.

organization. This work laid dormant until the 1970s when Oliver Williamson (1975) forced a reconsideration of these ideas. Surely, there was a market for this reconsideration, for Williamson wanted to explain initially why anti-trust authorities should not break up large firms. His earlier efforts in this regard relied upon a brilliant, yet conventional, welfare analysis that compared the monopoly loss of a process innovation relative to the gains in efficiency. He subsequently developed a more radical approach, first expounded at length in his 1975 book *Markets and Hierarchies*.

Yet, this book was not clearly different than other approaches developed at the same time that stressed the importance of market imperfections, especially for knowledge and information. In the international field, Peter Buckley and Mark Casson (1976), two young scholars, offered a broader explanation for the existence of the firm (in the form of the multinational corporation) by analyzing the different sources of market imperfections and the incentives for 'internalization' of market activities (see also Dunning 1977). Their approach was also more general, for unlike Williamson, they did not have the goal of showing that the multinational corporation was 'globally' the most efficient way to organize production. They sought to provide a positive theory for why it exists. In addition to Buckley and Casson, there were other efforts, including that of McManus (1972) who contributed the important notion of a continuum of governance solutions and 'relational' contracting. Not long after, Jean-François Hennart (1982) offered a theory of the multinational corporation that relied heavily upon market imperfections for the sale of information *and* incentive conflicts among principal and agents. Rugman (1981) similarly suggested the efficiency explanations for the multinational corporation.

All of these contributions invoked subsequent lines of research. (In fact, I fall prey to a 'selection' bias in failing to investigate those many ideas of the mid-1970s that essentially died without further development—or, remembering the dormancy of Coase's early work, at least have yet to be developed.) Why has the term of 'transaction costs' come, however, to be the dominant construct in the discussions on the boundary of the firm? Why do we not have studies clearly focused on 'internalization' as opposed to transaction costs, especially outside the field of international business?

Of the many answers to this question, I would like to highlight one: Williamson (1979) provided a schema by which empirical research could proceed to test his ideas. This article proposed that transaction costs have three dimensions: asset specificity, frequency, and uncertainty. Up until then, transaction costs appeared as an unobservable construct that required data on production and market costs under two different governance regimes (i.e. within the firm and from the market). How could this be done? These dimensions, especially the first of asset specificity, provided the manifest constructs for subsequent researchers to investigate the relationship between an observable decision, e.g. to make rather than source a component, and the latent factor, called transactions costs. With this methodological and research design contribution, research in transaction costs established its industry. However, it is important to underline that the collection of such data, when using Williamson's prescription for 'microanalytic' detail, can be very difficult and demanding.

Research in international business has contributed its own methodological designs that serve as templates for subsequent efforts. I would like to document briefly three contributions: Raymond Vernon's multinational data base, foreign direct investment studies, and the choice of foreign entry mode. I turn then to two current areas of research (i.e. organizational ecology and comparative national systems) that might benefit from agreement on design and method. In focusing on these contributions, I neglect other major contributions to international business research, especially that of business history (as seen in Chandler 1990; Wilkins 1970, 1974, 1988) that has indisputably created successful research programs with defined methodologies; this topic is well treated in Wilkins' chapter in this volume.

# 27.1 The Harvard Multinational Enterprise Database

Raymond Vernon, following a successful career in government service and a series of influential studies on the economic geography of American cities and their loss of industry, became intrigued by the question: why does the United States dominate foreign direct investment flows. It is often forgotten that Vernon posed essentially a historical question regarding *country* patterns in direct investment. Of course, he knew that other firms from other countries invested overseas. But what explained the dominance of the United States in the current flows? By posing the product life cycle theory of international investment that emphasized the *home bias of innovation,* he could subsequently provide a research template that sought to correlate the life cycle of innovations to the pattern of investment in that industry (Vernon 1966).[2]

---

[2] This theme was picked up and amplified by Porter (1990).

He also recognized that, (1) innovations spawn oligopolies and that, (2) consequently the geographic direction of direct investment should be influenced by the gaming among these large American firms.[3]

It was essentially this second point that preoccupied Vernon in his research following his initial article on the innovative basis and home bias in direct investment. To investigate the international expanse of multinational corporations and the challenges they posed to foreign governments, he organized a massive research effort to collect data on the 180 largest American multinational corporations. The Ford Foundation, in those days, provided grants for business research, especially on a topic important for economic development. Vernon successfully bidded for Ford support, allowing him a degree of independence from the Harvard Business School tradition of case studies. In designing this effort, he made several important decisions. He defined a multinational corporation as consisting of six or more subsidiaries outside the United States. He thus began with an idea of what should constitute the population and sample. For his research purposes, this definition generated a population of the largest multinational corporations. He then traced their expansion overseas from the 1900s onward, and collected public and confidential data on their product diversity, spread, and overseas entries and exits (Vernon 1971).

In other words, Vernon created the first demographic database for the creation and expansion of firms, whether they be multinational or domestic. (See also Curhan and Vaupel 1973; Curhan *et al.* 1977.) Of course, this choice enters a certain bias for some kinds of studies. A study, for example, on survival requires that the population be created at the time of birth, not for a given cross-section; otherwise, we are sampling on survivors. But this was not Vernon's concern; he wanted to show the gradual and then explosive growth of American multinationals over the course of the 'American' century. As the American century came to crisis in the period of the Vietnam war, the database moved on to collect newer data on the American companies, but also on multinationals from other countries.

These data served Vernon's own research purposes, especially as seen in his magisterial study *Sovereignty at Bay*, which is an incisive analysis of the opposition of governments and multinational corporations (1971). Vernon's student Frederick Knickerbocker (1973) wrote and published his thesis on

---

[3] At the Harvard of the 1960s, one could not avoid ideas of games among oligopolists, given the presence of the influential managerial economics group under the leadership of Howard Raiffa. Lawrence Fouraker wrote an important book on bargaining in oligopolistic industries (Fouraker and Siegel 1963) and went on to co-author with John Stopford (1968), who later worked with Lou Wells in their influential study (Stopford and Wells 1972) on the strategy and structure of the multinational corporation; this study used the Harvard multinational database.

oligopolistic gaming and defensive investments on the basis of this research data. Stopford and Wells (1972) published the most important book on strategy and structure in the multinational business field using these data. Subsequent students, particularly William Davidson (1976, 1980), further developed the database and analyzed the entry patterns of multinational corporations. Karen Hladik (1985) and Ben Gomes-Casseres (1985) wrote their theses on alliances using these data. Gatignon and Anderson (1988), discussed below, also used these data. In 1993, Delacroix published a brilliant chapter on the demography of entry by American firms into Europe.

The above list is hardly exhaustive, but serves the purpose to show how a research design and project can diffuse far from its original intention. Did the design itself diffuse? Did other authors not use the data for testing other theories? Of course, but they did so within the constraints of the sampling design established by Raymond Vernon in collecting the data. He established therefore not only the raw data, but also a research program encoded in the decisions how and what to sample. The impressive and stunning contribution of Alfred Chandler to international business research, especially his 1990 book that compared the large firms of the US, the UK, and Germany, (*Scale and Scope: The Dynamics of Industrial Capitalism*), essentially established the same research framework of deriving statements about efficiency and advantage from comparisons among the largest firms.

In fact, when we sample on the side of host countries, we find that foreign direct investment has historically consisted of investments by many small and medium size firms. It is easy to forget this, and to conclude that size itself drove the success of multinational firms. The contrary hypothesis is that, in many cases, firms grew big because they had the knowledge of doing things better. As they grew, they invested overseas. In looking at foreign direct investment by American firms historically, I argued, with suggestive statistical analysis, that the growth and expansion of the US multinational rode upon the diffusion of better practices by US companies (Kogut 1992). The relationship of size and competitive advantage is partly a spurious result due to the omission of the underlying factors that drove the growth of the firm in the first place. More recent work in organizational demography has redressed this omission of analyzing growth, as we will see below.

One of the lessons of the Harvard Multinational Database project is that successful research templates bias subsequent studies away from other avenues of inquiry.

# 27.2 FOREIGN DIRECT
# INVESTMENT STUDIES

As discussed in many chapters in this volume, Hymer transformed the theory of direct investment by logically showing that competitive advantage at the firm level, not macroeconomic rates of return, explains the motives for outward investment by firms. Since then, direct investment and the multinational corporation have been indelibly linked. He proposed that since foreign firms were always at a disadvantage, they had to bring competitive advantages, e.g. scale economies, to overseas markets (Hymer 1960). However, he only tested this idea by correlating outward investment flows and concentration levels at the industry level (with the common belief of the time that industry concentration proxies for firm advantages). His thesis adviser Charles Kindleberger (1969) fought for the recognition of Hymer's contribution, which was not published until after the latter's death in a motor vehicle accident, by using Hymer's insight as the basis of a series of influential lectures on the current history of the multinational corporation.

In 1971, Richard Caves advanced this line of work by emphasizing the importance of the multinational firm for the transfer of 'intangible assets' across borders. This issue of 'transferability' of advantages, to use the current even if clumsy parlance, lies at the heart of the multinational corporation, for the costs of the transfer of the advantage must be less than the revenues derived from the investment. These ideas were far ahead of the debate at that time and were largely neglected. Instead, the ideas of entry barriers as derived from intangible assets appeared to be a succinct formulation of the Hymer line of analysis.

This article itself may have been remembered and footnoted as an early and intelligent treatment of the industrial economics of direct investment. Caves (1974), however, solidified his contribution by subsequently proposing a way to test the economic motivations of direct investment. His design consisted simply of regressing industry data on direct investment on measures of firm advantage, such as scale economies, R&D, advertising. These measures of firm advantage relied, in other words, on industry-level proxies that could be attained, with some difficulty, from government and public sources for some countries, in particular for Canada and the United States.

Having provided a statistical specification and a sampling methodology that relied on public data, Caves contributed a template that has been a standard design in direct investment research up to now. Of course, there have been some important modifications to this approach as well. One modification concerns the measurement of the dependent variable. Many studies, especially those that look at macroeconomic flows, rely on balance of payment data as published by the International Monetary Fund and by the Centre on Transnational Corporations. The balance of payments method does not include investments, for example, that are made by borrowing from the foreign country to be invested there. Some studies have used, as a result measures of plant and equipment when available (the US government provides such data for a fee); others have used sales data, sometimes net of imports. Other studies have used entry counts, which have been shown to be highly correlated with plant and equipment purchase data.

Another series of modifications regards the right hand variables. Because not all countries provide R&D or advertising data, some studies have used US data even when looking at investments by non-American firms. For example, the Netherlands publishes very skimpy R&D data, as collected by the OECD, because it cannot give figures for electronics without revealing private information of N. V. Philips, a Dutch electronics firm. Since R&D data, as well as other sectoral data such as scale economies and advertising, are correlated across countries, the use of American data as a proxy appears as reasonable.

But is it? Obviously, the use of American data is not reasonable when we are trying to explain differences in patterns across countries. Perhaps oligopolistic conditions are not the same across all countries. Can Japanese technological rivalry successfully lead to investments in American oligopolies? A possibility is that the American industry is not an oligopolistic in the same sector and the resident firms lack competitive advantage. (Of course, we also might be comparing an American sector of technological rivalry with the large firm dominance characteristic of Japan.) If we use only American data for describing American and Japan, we obviously cannot evaluate this possibility.[4]

But there is a more subtle point. The Hymer and Caves studies also shared the Vernon home bias assumption, namely, that firms go overseas on the basis of their home advantage. The home advantage pushes out investment. Yet, what happens if foreign countries pull investment because of location advantages? Traditionally, we thought of location advantages as differences in factor costs. Since direct investment is primarily among rich countries, we know that wages cannot be the explanatory cause for location decisions. Clearly then, home market access and technological sourcing (inclusive of productivity differentials) are factors that can pull investment.

John Cantwell (1989) was one of the first to explore the influence of technological pull on investment. In doing so, he relied upon a new source of data in the form of patent registrations. Unlike direct investment data, patent registrations exist over a long period of time. Increasingly, they are

---

[4] This small point was not, however, resolved in the empirical literature until Hideki Yamawaki published his study on Japanese exporting behavior using different observations on Japan and the United States (1988). Sea-Jin Chang and I (Kogut and Chang 1991) followed this approach to analyze Japanese direct investment in the United States.

accessible remotely through electronic databases, a process that can be easily automated. The ease of these data have already spawned an industry of studies. He also endorsed a particular measure of revealed technological advantage that indicates a country's relative propensity to innovate in a particular sector normalized for its overall innovative propensity in all sectors.

However, there is, as always, a serious bias in using data for proxy purposes. For example, investment into a country is pulled not only by technology in the strict definition, but by superior productivity in carrying out particular activities. The sources of this superior productivity might be organizational or institutional. An organizational source is the local diffusion of a particular practice within the borders of a nation, such as the diffusion of mass production in automobile manufacturing in the early part of the last century.[5] An institutional source is, for example, the corporate governance practices supported by the legal and financial institutions of a country. In either case, organizational and institutional sources do not easily diffuse across borders of countries. Consequently, a country might have a sustained location advantage in attracting investment and such advantages need not be reflected in patent data.

Again, we have the case that the success of a research strategy can steer a field in particular paths. One possible response from researchers in the area of patents is that technological output is complementary to innovative organizational practices. Thus, patents are a proxy of publicly registered technological outputs plus the tacit knowledge of how to innovate and, less obviously, of how to organize in general. We don't know how good, in general, an assumption this is, but it is possible to think of cases where it is a very bad one. Perhaps the clearest example is an industry where patents play a minor role, and yet direct investment flows show a country pattern. Advertising is a good case, where the US and the United Kingdom have long dominated and have attracted a great deal of foreign investment. There are other prominent industries as well, from cinema to industrial design to consulting. Patents are a bad measure of some important kinds of knowledge. However, given the template and the importance of studies on technology, location, and diffusion, studies using patents are riding currently a powerful trajectory that will, and should, expand further.

Are there proxies for knowledge in general? Lieberman and Demeester (1999) suggest that inventory levels proxy for the Japanese practice of just-in-time inventories and on this basis, they trace the diffusion of these

---

[5] For a full explanation, we have to explain why such organizational practices stay within the borders of a country despite the ability of firms within a country to imitate each other. An early attempt to address this question, and to propose a country explanation for firm advantage, is given in Kogut (1991).

practices within Japan. This study has the benefit of looking at an economic outcome, inventories, to measure presumed adoption. In this sense, it is a more direct measure of an economic effect that patents that are presumed, with several studies that validate this claim, to measure technological inputs. Some studies look at adoption of practices, such as divisional structures or quality control, without knowing the 'fidelity' of adoption or the economic consequence.

The alternative is the expensive but rewarding research design to collect data at the level of the practice itself. The MIT motor vehicle program, especially the research of John Paul MacDuffie (see MacDuffie 1993 for example), has collected data at the plant level across countries for organizational practices. However, because these data are limited to a single industry and are at the plant level, they cannot serve as a template for quantitative studies on relating the effect of organizational innovations on pulling or pushing direct investment. Such studies do serve as useful templates for research in national comparisons, a point to which we return later.

# 27.3 FOREIGN ENTRY MODE

The choice of the mode of entry by a multinational corporation has interested researchers in international business from the start of the field. Most of the early studies were based on case studies that provided rich insights into the choice. However, with the creation of the Harvard Multinational Enterprise Database, it became possible to explore more systematically the factors that influenced the choice of entry. Stopford and Wells (1972) looked at correlations to make predictions about the positive relationship between strategies and the degree of equity ownership, arguing that technology encouraged higher control relative to advertising. Fagre and Wells (1982) later asked: how did bargaining power between host government and foreign firm influence the degree of equity held in a local subsidiary? Wilson (1980) used the Harvard Multinational Database to look at the choice to acquire, using correlational analysis.

This concern with equity control gradually became relatively less interesting than the question of entry mode choice, that is, by wholly-owned, acquisition, joint venture, licensing, or exporting. It has been a common confusion in this literature to confuse mode with the choice between a greenfield versus brownfield investment, that is a new investment versus buying into an existing facility. Clearly, wholly-owned entry can also be conducted by an acquisition. However, the above framing has become the currency of research in this area.

An important breakthrough in the studies on entry mode choice occurred when Richard Caves and his student Mehra (1986) published their chapter in a book on international competition that included, among other things, a logit analysis of the entry choice. This contribution was inevitable given that the entry choice was discrete, but it was nevertheless Caves who gave the methodological template once again. This template consisted of collecting data on entry mode as the dependent variable and then regressing it on reasonable predictors. Again, an industry was launched, with no clear signs that its energies have yet been sapped.

Given the methodology, the scramble was now to refine the method and to name its theoretical implications. Gatignon and Anderson (1988), in this regard, made both of these fundamental contributions. Unlike an ordinary least squares regression, a qualitative-choice model does not provide a measure of explained variance. It does provide a goodness of fit test in the form of a Chi-square estimated from the likelihood function. This test has low power, which has usually not troubled researchers in management (or economics) who rarely conduct power tests. Gatignon and Anderson were troubled, however, that their data—to which we come in a second—consisted primarily of wholly-owned entries. They thus partitioned the data into several sets, ran their estimates, and then tested for the robustness of the results. This paper has become a standard fare in doctoral courses as a result of this rigor alone. In addition, the paper introduced multinomial choice models to the literature at a time when the software was not available in a package.[6]

The other contribution of the paper was to establish a template for future research emphasizing transaction cost explanations for entry choice. Stopford and Wells had argued that strategic motivations explained entry choice, such as the desire to control technology. They supported their point by correlating R&D expenditures with entry choice. Anderson and Gatignon (1986) argued that these motives are best seen as relating to transaction costs concerns. They reinterpreted, for example, the measures of R&D expenditures as a proxy for the hazard of transacting information in the market place. (Buckley and Casson 1976 made the same argument and empirical claims for the internalization of investment flows in their seminal study.) Effectively, they

---

[6]  Singh and I (Kogut and Singh 1988a), in fact, used their program for our paper published in the same year. Our paper introduced a measure of 'cultural distance' that by itself served as a vehicle for replication in other studies, another example of a methodological innovation allowing a field to develop, with some negative consequences in biasing attention away from other kinds of cultural studies. The success of this measure is due to riding the coat-tails of a more sweeping research program of Geert Hofstede (1990) on culture, which I do not review in this chapter though deserving of attention.

highjacked the direct investment and Harvard Multinational Enterprise templates for the purposes of ushering in the plethora of transaction costs studies that were to follow.

Given that we knew that the correlations between their proxy variables and control were already explored by Stopford and Wells for the same data, the results of their qualitative-choice models were not surprising, but surely were reassuring of the robustness of the earlier analysis. They noted, however, that it was difficult to predict the degree of equity control as opposed to the choice of entry. This finding suggested that firm considers the equity control decision subsequent to entry choice, with equity control influenced by bargaining and by other means to exercise control. Over all, the assumption of a monotonic relationship between control and equity share has been a difficult one to maintain in the empirical work on entry mode choice.

This finding of a two stage process was basically ignored until a paper by Myles Shaver (1998) exploited this insight to suggest a radical rethinking of the entry and strategy relationship. Shaver was perturbed by the finding of Hennart and Park (1993) that entry by acquisition lead to more stable entries by foreign firms. This claim troubled him, as it should. For if doing X is better, then we should see all firms doing X in the absence of barriers to imitation. Whereas we can construct scenarios whereby a firm is unable to imitate an acquisition, this construction is a far more sophisticated interpretation than justified by the original estimation.

Shaver proposes to separate out the entry decision of foreign firms into the United States along the lines of Gatignon and Anderson. First, we should understand the strategy choice to enter a country and second, we should test for the performance impact of this choice. After all, it is possible that acquisitions are encouraged in more profitable and fast growing industries, and it is this unobservable, called industry conditions, that also then influences the survival and performance of the entry.[7] There is, in other words, a potential Hausmann selection bias (Hausmann 1978). How do we then separate out the unobservable influence of industry conditions?

Shaver notes that we can, in fact, say something about this unobservable because we know already that firms have chosen to enter the United States by a particular entry choice. So step one is to estimate the coefficients to the predictors for choosing an entry mode, acquisitions or wholly-owned. These coefficients can then be used, in combination with the data for each firm, to generate the estimate for the likelihood that a firm will choose acquisition over wholly-owned entry.

Step two consists of taking this value and treating it as an independent variable in the equation that specifies the survival chances of a given entry. He shows acquisition, without this selection correction, is positively related to

---

[7]   Kogut and Singh (1988b), in fact, find this relationship to hold for their sample.

enhancing survival, but that this effect goes away when the selection bias is controlled. To drive home his point even further, he then conducts a counterfactual exercise, showing how mortality should rise if the entering firms chose the 'wrong' entry mode.

There are other examples in management studies where it is claimed that doing X has a monotonic effect on performance. Such claims, based on single equation and linear estimates, are vulnerable usually to the line of inquiry posed by Shaver; hence his contribution has opened a wide terrain of research in the strategy and management literatures in general. It is not surprising that other researchers are already jumping onto this moving train.

It should be noted that the Hausman selection bias is equivalent to the bias of incomplete sampling discussed above in the context of the Harvard Multinational Enterprise Database. Without correcting for selection, the bias is incurred by specifying the model as 'unconditioned'. In fact, the estimates are conditioned on the underlying sampling methodology. In the case of the Harvard data, small firms were left out and the multinationals that died by the time of the 1966 cross-section were left out. In the case of the Shaver study, the performance model was conditioned already on the choice of firms to choose an entry mode. In both cases, the error was failing to see that the estimations were conditioned on the sampling methodology.

# 27.4 ORGANIZATIONAL DEMOGRAPHY AND OPTION VALUATION

The article by Shaver belongs also to another research tradition called organizational demography. Vernon had, as we noted, started this line of work in international studies, but his choice of sampling on survivors entered a bias into the data. This bias is called a left-hand censoring bias and it arises whenever we reconstruct histories based on survivors. We have obviously lost data on multinational corporations that are no long surviving or no longer qualify as multinationals under Vernon's definition.

The adjacent field of organizational ecology and demography, particularly associated with the early studies of Hannon and Freeman (1977) and Carroll and Delacroix (1982), has heavily emphasized the importance of this kind of bias. They have made an important and remarkable contribution in establishing a clear template for demographic research regarding the importance of sampling on founders rather than survivors and of the effects of age on mortality. For example, many of the early studies on joint venture survival ignored that ventures may die faster when young, or that older ventures are already proven 'survivors'. It is simply unacceptable to compare organizations of different ages and make inferences on survival without correcting for these effects.

Of course, organizational ecology is more than the methods of demography. Ecology has also proposed a number of theoretical ideas, some no longer in repute, some that are still in development in the international area. One idea, though of less concern today, was the liability of newness, derived from Stinchcombe (1965), that suggested that young firms' die more rapidly than older ones because they have yet to establish legitimacy and to learn the ropes. Another theoretical claim is that firms' entry into markets rises and then declines with the density in that industry, and similarly mortality has also a quadratic relationship with density. Density is the number of firms in the industry.

The diffusion of these methods into the direct investment performance literature happened with a decade or more delay. In many ways, these methods and ideas resonated well with international business that had been preoccupied with entry and death from the time of Vernon and Burenstam Linder. The latter, in his remarkable study that launched the field of inter-industry trade (Burenstam Linder 1961), noted that international export is the extension of the home network overseas. In other words, international expansion is part of the theory of the growth of the firm.

These ideas were not actively explored, outside of the fascinating studies in business and economic history, by international business researchers until the 1990s. Many of these studies adopted population ecology theories along with the method, thus leading to a rich, sometimes overly complex theoretical discussion for the reasons for the growth and death of subsidiaries. The early studies were by Jiao-ti Li (1995) who looked, using the new methods, at the survival of foreign subsidiaries. They thus sampled on firms that already entered. This approach, with increasing sophistication, informed also the studies of Shaver and his two thesis advisers, Will Mitchell and Bernie Yeung, in their work (Mitchell *et al.* 1993; Shaver *et al.* 1997). The article by Shaver (1998) on selection bias, discussed above, was the outcome of this line of research.

Srilata Zaheer's studies on trading rooms represent a sophisticated treatment of this line of work. In her article on currency trading rooms, she looks at whether multinational financial companies that have foreign subsidiaries working as currency traders suffer from the Hymer disadvantage, which she labels the 'liability of foreignness' (Zaheer 1995). She finds evidence for the effect of a liability of foreignness, even for an industry where information diffuses rapidly and all traders have, in theory, equal access. Of course, we once again have Shaver's possibility, namely, firms that have decided to operate overseas already are a selected bunch.

The Zaheer study poses, however, the larger question if the importation of ecological ideas, as apart from the method, have been corroborated. In part, the problem is that ecology has itself not fully addressed issues in its own literature regarding the liability of newness and the reliance on reduced-equation models of entry and death. Both of these issues raise larger questions regarding whether demographic forces are lawful, independent of context, a larger issue we pick up in the next section.

The liability of newness hypothesis has not been satisfactorily tested in the literature. The early efforts imposed a parametric specification of the hazard model and then asked seemingly simple questions, such as is the slope negative. A parametric specification gives the hazard rate as a specific functional form; early choices were the Gomperz or Weibull. If the slope was negative, then this implies that young firms die at a higher rate than older firms. Of course, there are many problems with this estimate of the slope. First of all, most of the specifications were log-linear, whereas the data almost showed a rather non-linear trend, even when logged. Even when the slopes were estimated to be negative, the plots of the data suggested a far more complicated relationship. In particular, deaths usually picked up after an initial period. Efforts to fix this problem resulted in partitioning the sample into early and later periods or discussing complicated relationships between intercept and slope estimates.

But there is a more devastating objection to this hypothesis other than the resistance of the data to conform. All demographic samples of organizations consist of heterogeneous firms. This heterogeneity consists of observables such as size or product diversity. It also consists of unobservables, such as the inherent quality of the firm. Now here is the problem, and the beauty of a liability of newness prediction. It is mathematically true that any heterogeneous population will evidence a liability of newness. (See Heckman and Singer 1985 for a proof.)

It is simple to show why this would be true. Consider two populations, one consisting of dogs, the other of humans. Both have exponential hazard rates, that is, their hazard rates are constant regardless of age. (Now this is extreme, but it serves our purpose.) In Figure 27.1, we graph their constant hazard rates and assume that the hazard rate for dogs is higher. Now what would happen if we mix these two populations? It takes a moment of reflection to realize that we would begin at a point in between the two populations and then that the decline would asymptotically decline to the constant rate for the humans. Since the dogs are dying more rapidly, their contribution to the mixed population declines relatively faster; at some points, there are only

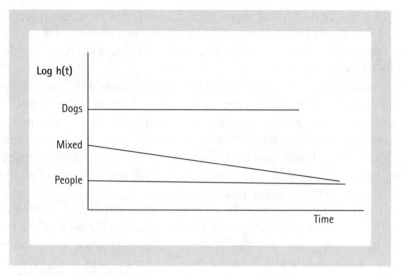

Fig. 27.1 Constant hazard rates and yet a liability of newness

people left. Heterogeneity always generates a liability of newness, even when the true populations have constant hazard rates.

Of course, there are some reasonable sources of heterogeneity. Size is an obvious one; we don't expect large firms to die as fast as small ones. We can try to control for these influences in a parametric model, but it is unlikely that heterogeneity can be controlled. (Efforts to specify mixed distributions, such as considering the happy conjugate of the gamma as a description of the unobserved error, have not lead to satisfactory resolutions.) The alternative is to avoid the claim of a liability of newness, specify exactly what are the causal sources that should cause young firms to fail, and to rely upon semi-parametric or non-parametric specifications to test their relationships. Implicitly, the literature has taken this direction without formally disclaiming the earlier claims to have found a liability of newness.

The weakness in trying to infer a law from a reduced equation raises the more important issue of whether it might be more interesting to think about the underlying mechanisms instead. The international literature began, as we noted, with an emphasis that international expansion is a consequence of the growth of a successful firm. This emphasis leads to a research design that samples the firms in a country and then analyzes their expansion overseas and the consequences of this expansion on firm mortality. Mitchell *et al.* (forthcoming) follow this strategy, arguing that international expansion actually increases the mortality (hazard) rate. This surprising result is consistent with earlier findings that suggest firms who are not succeeding at home often expand overseas first; successful ones would rather expand at home. (See Mascarenhas 1992; Yu and Ito 1988 for some evidence.) In other words, it raises Shaver's selection bias issue in trying to sort out the direct effect of expansion from the unobserved factors that might promote overseas expansion in the first place.[8]

These are complex issues, which are not helped by the plethora of organizational and economic theories for why firms grow in general and why they grow across national boundaries in particular. As in all cases, it is sometimes useful to remember a baseline case. This case consists of a firm that grows randomly but proportionately. In other words, growth is log-normal and is governed by the following process:

$$dS/S = a(t) + \sigma dZ$$

where the proportionate growth of the firm is equal to an expected mean growth (or drift) plus random variation drawn from a standard normal distribution and scaled by the variance of the firm.[9] Let's assume that a firm expands overseas once it has reached a certain size. (This size could be the volume of exports.) The hazard of expansion overseas is the probability that the size of the firm will hit a lower boundary given its size at a certain point in time. A hazard rate is, in other words, derived from a more fundamental structural model that expresses a theory of the growth of the firm.

This observation implies that every growth process can be understood as facing certain hazards. Sometimes, this hazard is a negative outcome, such as death; other times, it is positive, as when large size gives the possibility to expand overseas. We might then ask the question if changes in size allows a firm to go overseas, what is the value of this probability at a certain point of time? In other words, what is the value to the option that a firm expand in the future?

There is, in other words, a mathematic relationship between hazard rates and option values that also suggests a theoretical point. Firms have the potential to enter a country, or to withdraw from a country. We can under-

[8] For those interested in understanding the technical details in many of these models, it is useful to see the repetition in mathematic specification. The primary observation is thank the heavens for the exponential function. The second is that the treatment of selection, censoring, and truncation bias leads to the same methodology of calculating the probability density functions conditional on the remainder of the cumulative distribution function. A lot of the magic goes away when we see how the same tricks solve so many different problems.

[9] The specification of the hazard rate implies, in consequence, particular forms for the underlying structural process. I have never found a text or discussion that describes, for example, the implied process for a Weibull or Gomperz model. However, for the random walk, the conditional probability of hitting a boundary is the inverse Gaussian, a solution given first by Edwin Schroeder for the so-called first passage problem. However, it is important to note that the random walk is a reasonable model for firm growth only if the process is scaled, that is if the process is log-normal. Otherwise, we are assuming that a firm has the same dollar variance when it is worth a billion dollars as when it is worth 10 dollars. This would greatly overstate the chances that large firms will survive and greatly exaggerates the (correct) point that size matters to understanding hazard rates.

stand this potential as a probability, or hazard rate. We can also, if we are taking a more economic approach, evaluate the value of this potential. In other words, organizational demography leads directly to a consideration of option values, once we move from reduced forms (hazard rates) to considering the underlying stochastic process governing the value of the firm.[10]

Understanding the sources of the stochastic growth of the firm has proven to be a difficult and complex undertaking. Economics suggests that it might be more appealing to work with profit or cost functions, and let stochastic elements enter via exchange rates or other price movements. It is this approach explored by Dixit (1987) in his model on exports and hysteresis (see also Campa 1993) and by Kogut and Kulatilaka (1994) in their treatment of the multinational network as consisting of the options to respond flexibly.

While these models seem far removed from the concerns of organizational demographers, they are in fact mathematically related and substantively related in trying to understand the stochastic value of the firm to grow and coordinate its activities across borders. Thus, in empirical work on the relationship between exchange rates and foreign investment, Kogut and Chang (1996) relied principally upon the methods of organizational demography. They constructed a population of Japanese firms in the electronics industry listed on the Japanese stock market. They then looked at the influences of exchange rates, previous entries, and firm characteristics on the hazard of 'exercising the option' to enter the United States.[11] Thus, the template of organizational demography was brought to bear upon a problem of the economic analysis of foreign entry.

## 27.5 COMPARATIVE MANAGEMENT AND NATIONAL SYSTEMS

One of the most promising directions of organizational demography in recent years is its work on tracing the entry and exit of firms in a given industry

---

[10] Tuma and Hannon (1984) analyze models derived from stochastic growth as Ito processes; Ito processes are a standard in the options literature. Yet, the technical similarity between the approaches has been ignored, because the two literatures do not know each other, but also because organizational demography has not theoretically been disposed to the idea of 'exercising options', that is, to the idea of choice.

[11] Rangan 1998 offers a more direct test of the multinational switching hypothesis.

across borders.[12] As noted earlier, the chapter by Delacroix (1993) is a fascinating application of organizational ecology to foreign entry, using the Vernon database, which also is sensitive to country context. A good deal of this work is focused on the question if founding and death rates are density dependent. For the reasons given above on the liability of newness, this question is likely to be very sensitive to controlling for other factors, such as the size of firms and their concentration of sales in the local markets. But these efforts represent the most extensive efforts to collect comparable data since the Harvard Multinational Enterprise Database.

One of the principal questions that derived by looking at the rates of entry and exit across countries is the effect of institutions on economic behavior. Work in this area varies widely in approach and in conceptual rigor. Some approaches consist of the claim that countries are different in their business systems and offer a list of factors by which to make comparisons. Or sometimes an approach simply claims that institutions matter and countries differ in their political ideologies and economy in how they achieve social consensus. More ambitious approaches ride upon notions of institutional equilibria. In these approaches, a country is characterized by a number of actors who are institutionally represented. They achieve a political balance that also permits effective coordination in the workplace.

A good example of this latter approach is the work of David Soskice on Germany. Soskice (1990) proposes that Germany, as an ideal type of 'corporatist' solutions to social cooperation, is characterized by the institutions of labor, enterprise hierarchies, banking, and business associations. Each of these institutions are represented by formal institutions or dominant actors. (In other articles, the Central Bank and governments also play a role.) These institutional actors bargain to create a 'high equilibrium' that supports the coordination of work to produce quality export-oriented products.

This is a vast field that is rapidly expanding. Are there templates of methodology and research in this area?

There are certainly a number of possible avenues for researching institutions. The crude yet effective way is to collect data across countries, and then use country dummies to check for differences. There are variations on this method, ranging from random effects to log-linear models. However, these approaches do not provide deep insights into how institutions matter; the power of these tests, one suspects, is not in any event strong.

Comparative studies often, as a consequence, consist of rich country studies that try to isolate an effect by quasi-experimental design. For example, Bendix (1956), in his study on the relationship of authority systems to national development, chose Russia, the UK, Germany, and the United States as four countries, each which occupied a single cell in his two-dimensional

---

[12] See e.g. Delacroix and Carroll (1983) and Hannon *et al.* (1995).

framework. Since he had two causes and four countries, he effectively created a 2 by 2 factorial design.

The construction of experimental design using a small number of cases is a common template used in comparative research. Charles Ragin (1987) offers the most rigorous treatment of this approach that can serve as a canonical model in comparative international business research. Ragin formalizes and extends the comparative method of John Stewart Mills by using a few simple rules of Boolean algebra.[13]

Consider the argument of Masahiko Aoki (1990) that the strength of the Japanese firm relies upon three duality principles that can be summarized as the joint presence of the main banking system, vertical ranks for promotion, and horizontal control among workers and suppliers.[14] He argues that when these three elements are present, they produce a truth condition of a high performing economy. We can represent this by the following claim:

Main Bank   Vertical Rank   Horizontal Control   Truth Condition: Performance

1                    1                          1                                                1

The ones indicate that these conditions are present. Aoki proposes in other words a 3 factorial design. To consider all the possible cases (that is, combinations), we would need to look at $2^3$ or 8 combinations. Aoki does not engage in this comparison and is content to propose his theory as 'fitting' the Japanese case. Most of the studies conducted in relation to his theory have looked at variations within Japan, especially between firms that belong and do not belong to business groups. Of course, these studies run into a selection bias (they are already chosen to be members or not prior to looking at performance). They also do not test at all adequately the claim that all three principles must be present in order to achieve high performance. Yet, these studies are reasonable first approaches to look at how institutions influence performance *within* a country.

However, this approach is not adequate for deriving any solutions regarding whether these three duality principles have an effect on performance in other countries. This point is not minor, as there has been a significant amount of policy advice given to countries to adopt foreign institutions *as a whole* because of their jointness and their proven value in producing high performance outcomes.

The extrapolation of these findings to other countries is stymied by four problems. The first one is easily treated and is an example of spurious

---

[13] For a comparative institutional analysis that used experimental designs in a 2 country case, see Gittelman 2000. Note that Ragin is not simply Aristotle in new bottles, nor even Mills. Borrowing from cost minimization algorithms for the design of electrical circuits, Ragin proposes a way to reduce the cases to logical constellations, or complements.

[14] We do not have the space here to develop this notion of 'jointness' in relation to the recent work in complementarities. For such an analysis, see Kogut *et al.* 1999.

causality as delineated by Simon (1957). This problem is easily treated by Ragin's comparative Boolean methodology. In particular, we will utilize the following Boolean rule. A cause A can be present (denoted as A) or absent (denoted as 'a'). In one case AB are two factors that are both present and are associated with a truth condition of high performance. In a second case, factor A is still present but factor B is not, and yet the outcome is still high performance. By Boolean algebra, given that the truth condition is the same, AB + Ab = A. In other words, only cause A is causally related to the outcome of high performance. Indeed, for this comparison, A is *sufficient* to cause high performance. In the absence of other causes, A also appears as a *necessary* factor.

Lets reconsider the Aoki formulation more carefully. Using now our binary symbols of 1 and 0 rather than upper and lower case letters, we can represent Aoki's claim, as we saw, as mapping the combination of {1 1 1} to the condition of high performance. What if we found a second country, say Korea, that had only two of these conditions but still had high performance. Comparing the two cases, we have:

Japan: 1 1 1
Korea: 1 0 1

We can now conclude that only the first and third causes are causal; condition two is eliminated by Boolean algebra.

The second problem falls under the label of functional equivalence, as first analyzed and studied by Merton (1949). To illustrate this problem, consider the case that we compare Korea to a third country, say France, and both are high performing. (If it seems unfair to compare rich France to moderately rich Korea, keep in mind that there are much poorer countries than Korea. Sample selection issues remain critical to this methodology too!) By assumption, these two countries have the following configurations:

Korea: 1 0 1
France: 0 1 0

We cannot reduce these expressions further. They represent functionally equivalent institutional configurations to achieve high performance.

Now this conclusion might be troubling to our penchant to want matters to be more precise, such as there is one configuration that dominates all others. But as we have learned from the literature on the varieties of capitalism (e.g. Berger and Dore 1996), there are many ways by which countries can achieve similar performance outcomes despite different institutional configurations.

The problems of spuriousness and functional equivalence are easily dispatched by the application of a Boolean methodology. However, our third and fourth problems are not fully resolvable. The third is the problem of insufficient variety in the empirical data. As noted earlier, Aoki's three factorial design implies 8 distinct configurations. These are {0 0 0} {1 0 0} {1 1 0} {0 1 0} {0 0 1} {1 0 1} {0 1 1} {1 1 1}. What if history does not provide all these experiments? Or what if the research design did not generate a fully saturated model by the force of its sampling methodology?

It is easy to see that we can make an error. Consider the case in which we have sampled Japan and Korea as before in the first two rows and then subsequently consider the case of a third rich country called the US:

Japan: 1 1 1
Korea: 1 0 1
US: 0 1 0

Clearly, we can no longer decide to eliminate the second cause. In fact, this second cause appears as sufficient, but not necessary in order to have a rich outcome. We have now two configurations that are suggested by Boolean reduction. This analysis reduced the complexity of the three cases to two configurations.

Of course, we can in some cases generate 'what if' cases based on the empirical data. We know by de Morgan's law that these two statements are equivalent: both it rains and Johnny comes, and either it does not rain or Johnny does not come. We can use this rule on the empirically observed configurations to generate the counter factual cases.

The last problem is the perennial obstacle of omitted variables. It is always the case in empirical research (and in theorizing) that we have neglected variables that do not only matter but they also interact with the variables we have chosen. In econometrics, there are statistical treatments to eliminate unobserved heterogeneity (as discussed earlier), but these treatments are themselves guesses about the distribution of the unobserved error; they do not handle issues of complex interactions.

The effect of the problem of complexity is easily represented by Ragin's Boolean approach. Consider a comparison of Japan and Chad; Chad looks the same as Korea but is poor. We could conclude that the absence of the second factor is causally responsible for poverty by analyzing the following configuration.

Japan: 1 1 1
Chad: 1 0 1

But we already know that Korea has the same configuration as Chad and it is relatively rich. The contradiction indicates that there is a problem due to an omitted variable and an incomplete theory. If we add in a fourth condition, we might have:

Japan: 1 1 1 1
Korea: 1 0 1 1
Chad: 1 0 1 0

Now we see that the fourth variable is causally responsible. But we discovered this only because there was a logical contradiction, and because we expanded our theory to look at a variable in which Japan and Korea agree, but Chad differs. It almost looks as if we cooked the books. Theorizing country differences that do not permit testing is indeed an exercise in exotic and imaginary cuisines. Yet, theorizing is indisputably required in order to guide the choice of variables and to prevent the list-like presentation of country differences that is often to be found in the literature.

The national system literature presents countries as independent experiments, sometimes precariously balanced in an equilibrium in which all actors must continue to agree to perform. However, it is also clear that practices and institutions diffuse across borders. How can we understand the study of Eleanor Westney (1987) on the importation of organizational forms into Japan if we contend that organizational effectiveness is contingent upon rigid institutional configurations? Similarly, the work of John Paul MacDuffie (1993), discussed above, indicates that American factories can adopt Japanese practices (in configurations) and achieve high performance productivity in the US despite different institutions?

Diffusion presents thorny issues to national systems. The problem is that there has been a failure in theory at two levels. The first is to separate the effects of genesis from diffusion. It is perhaps true that certain institutional configurations gave rise to particular practices; this is historical causality. But once such practices are known, they may diffuse to other institutional conditions.

The second level is a failure to understand that actors are far more adaptive than implied by these comparisons and that these practices themselves undergo radical re-interpretations. Within the corporatist balance of Germany, practices at the firm or factory level may change, sometimes by diffusion, but in the context of a discursive search among actors to adapt these practices. It is surely more complex to adapt when practices challenge existing categorizations of work encoded in an existing division of labor, such as skill categories that are tied to prestige and to wages. Yet, even here, the political balance among corporatist actors at the macroeconomic level need not be tightly coupled with the changes in work practice adaptations at the microlevel of work and industrial organization.[15]

Work on diffusion is still pretty much trapped in fairly crude analyses that once characterized national comparisons. That is, studies look at how a practice diffuses and by what channels. There is a growing literature on the difficulty of adopting certain kinds of knowledge (e.g. Zander 1991) and a fledgling body on institutional and political resistance to the adoption of

---

[15] See Kogut and Parkinson (1998) for this argument, and also Kogut (1999) for an analysis of the adaptation of US work practices in Weimar Germany.

these practices. These studies need to be joined, but they are theoretically quite distant. And closer to our thesis, there is no clear research template by which to drive this research farther along. It is in need of a methodological innovation.

As a first pass, let's consider the case of the adoption of a practice by a European firm that is institutionally neutral. In this case, the problem is largely cognitive, for the adopting firm needs now only to understand the right causal combination and to adopt the various elements. Easier said than done! The European firm is organized as a hierarchy, with banking investors, and internal recruitment of top managers. We can characterize this system then:

| Hierarchy | Internal Recruiting | *Truth Values: Performance and Quality* | |
|---|---|---|---|
| 1 | 0 | 1 | 0 |

Consider now an American firm that has a different organizational structure of

| | | | |
|---|---|---|---|
| 0 | 0 | 1 | 1 |

In other words, the American firm produces at the same level of efficiency as the French firm but at better quality. What can the French firm do? It has control, subject to its negotiations with its managers, over the degree of hierarchy and its internal recruitment. (Indeed, the 1980s revolution in American corporate life saw flatter hierarchies and more external recruiting (Useem 1996)). Given this, the French firm can make three changes.[16]

| Hierarchy | Internal Recruiting | *Truth Values: Performance and Quality* | |
|---|---|---|---|
| 1 | 0 | ? | ? |
| 0 | 1 | ? | ? |
| **0** | **0** | **?** | **?** |

It becomes transparent right away that there are twelve experiments to run, as each configuration can take on four different combinations of truth values. This is complicated, so we can make our lives easy by assuming that productivity does not decline. The first two cases represent hybridization by recombining American and French practices. They represent two feasible paths from the French system. It is possible, of course, that these hybrids are superior to the American configuration, in which case there might be reverse diffusion. The third case (in bold) is Americanization, with the wholesale adoption of the American configuration. If the two first cases both lead to high quality and high productivity, then they are functionally equivalent. If neither work, then the firm is constrained to choose the American configuration.

---

[16] With two elements to perturb, there are 4 possible configurations; the firm's current configuration occupies one possibility.

It should be clear that even in this easy case, the finding of the right solution is not easy. We have restricted the choice to two factors. Of course, there might be more elements. In addition, a firm might be unable to run all these experiments. As a consequence, it might observe other firms that have experimented, or it might hire consultants. Even then, borrowing might be too inclusive and practices might be borrowed that have little to do with performance. They are like the hitching-hiking genes in genetics, bits of practices that have no clear causal outcome.

It is possible that even in the third case, the new configuration will not do well because of interactions with French institutions. In this case, the initial configuration might have to include the influence of the type of external financial market. In this extending consideration, the initial configuration is the following:

| Hierarchy | Internal Recruiting | Bank Finance | *Truth Values: Performance and Quality* | |
|---|---|---|---|---|
| 1 | 1 | 1 | 1 | 0 |

Here, a value of 0 for bank finance means that the firm relies upon equity markets. If the external financial institution is a fixed constraint, there are three possibilities:

(1)  how a firm finances does not matter to performance;
(2)  finance matters in conjunction with some configurations but not all;
(3)  how a firm finances is a *necessary* condition (with equity finance required in order to achieve quality).

The second possibility is the most interesting, for it suggests that French firms can adopt hybrid forms that suit the national conditions. For different countries, there will be different configurations of practices that generate both high productivity and high quality. An obvious point is that there is not a single best set of practices. But the more important point is what gets diffused, or should be diffused, from a source country (e.g. the US) varies from country to country. In Italy, given its small firm structure, the adoption of American corporate organization might well decrease productivity. At the same time, external recruiting of managers might help performance. The idea of *core practices* is, then, possibly wrong, for it presumes that there are *necessary* practices. As we have seen, diffusion of practices from one country to the next can be compatible with multiple configurations.

The last possibility poses the problem of institutional change. For if French firms wish to achieve both quality and productivity, then there will have to be changes in financial markets. Institutional change is different than adopting practices, for it concerns the social and political agreements among diverse actors. In this wider consideration, not only is cognition a point, or the internal politics of the firm, but also the credible commitments made by various parties to institutions.

Institutional change poses, then, particular problems for diffusion of practices. Of course, the example of superior American quality might seem anachronistic—if it was ever valid. But if we switch the truth value to radical innovation and the financial system under consideration to be venture capital (or its absence), we have indeed posed precisely the contentions in the popular press that financial markets are critical for the new economy success of the United States. And in fact, France, Germany, and other countries have introduced new stock markets to provide incentives (through initial public offerings) for venture capitalists.

Yet, even the simple idea of introducing a stock market for small firms can pose complex institutional interactions. We have not, therefore, entirely treated the problem of institutional change. For the problem is rarely simply altering a single institution, but rather the consideration of a change on the ensembly of interacting institutions.

Again, an illustration might help. If we return to Soskice's description of Germany, the corporatist economy is a fragile balance between competing interests. German financial institutions interact with central bank powers and with national and sectoral unions who bargain for wages. The logic of adopting new practices might require changes in an institution. However, changing a given institution might itself cause national agreements to decay.

Thus, it is not simply an issue of whether a firm should equity finance, but how this affects the strategic behaviors of other economic actors. The Eichel Plan to forgive taxing German companies for restructuring their holding companies has the appearance of creating more American capital market pressure on firms. However, the external shareholder representatives of American financial institutions still must sit on supervisory boards consisting of 50 per cent worker and managerial delegates. Whether such piecewise institutional changes are possible have yet to be fully observed. Clearly, such proposals are rejoined with an active debate among the institutional actors.

Boolean algebra does not eliminate all inherent complexity in causal relationships. It does provide, however, a methodology by which to sample countries (i.e. saturate the design) and to characterize the factorial combinations as necessary, sufficient, or causally unrelated. This approach has always been implicit in country comparisons, but yet rarely explicit as a template for conducting comparative research.

# 27.6 CONCLUSIONS

The field of international business has engaged the efforts of hundreds, if not thousands, of researchers over the decades. Despite these extensive efforts, doctoral students are not given clear definitions of methodological templates that can permit them to address important theoretical and empirical issues in a timely fashion. *Market demand* alone is not sufficient to create timely and high quality research.

International business has sometimes failed to lead in research on important international questions, such as transition in formerly communist countries or globalization. Other disciplines have made important contributions in these areas, even disciplines lacking the relatively homogeneous agreement in paradigm that characterizes economics. For example, in the area of transition economics, David Stark (1992) and Victor Nee (1989) made early contributions to understanding the importance of institutions and labor markets; Stark relied upon ethnographic and network analysis and Nee upon demographic techniques. Annalee Saxenian (1996) and Saskia Sassen (1998) used ethnographic methods to analyze differences in the performance of regions or the impact of globalization on different social strata. More recent studies, such as those by Ghemawat and Khanna (1998) and Hansen (1999), are attentive to context—be it country or company—and yet are branching into exciting new areas of research that are part of the legacy of the international business discipline.

It is important to consider, then, the value of emphasizing the role of coherent research methodologies that can speed research yet assure a high quality. International business, like many of its allied fields in management, has often resolved this issue by turning toward other disciplines, e.g. economics. We have failed to realize that international business' own history reveals that it has been most successful when research efforts have been able to rely upon broad methodological templates.

There is, in fact, a very simple implication in this discussion. The training of Ph.D. students should not be organized around timely topics but around research programs with defined methodological definitions. These definitions should engage students in understanding and utilizing frontier methods in statistical, comparative, historical, and ethnographic research. As illustrations of important methodological techniques that yet define broad theoretical research programs, I have cited above the examples of selection bias and Boolean comparative analysis, among others.

There is, of course, a broader implication regarding the desirability of international business to foster greater efforts to provide the equivalent of Vernon's multinational enterprise database. To a large extent, organizational demography has seized this opportunity for the comparative study across countries. These efforts should be embraced and endorsed in international business. After all, an origin of this approach is the Vernon research program that is surely the historical domain of the field of international business. We should look with caution at contributions that fail to utilize existing or create well-defined research methodologies that permit researchers, especially doctoral students, to acquire the broad skills to influence the future direction of academic research activity in international business.

## REFERENCES

ANDERSON, E., and GATIGNON, H. (1986). 'Modes of Foreign Entry: A Transaction Cost Analysis and Propositions', *Journal of International Business Studies*, 17, 1–26.

AOKI, M. (1990). 'Toward an Economic Model of the Japanese Firm', *Journal of Economic Literature*, 28, 1–27.

BAIN, J. S. (1956). *Barriers to New Competition: Their Character and Consequences in Manufacturing Industries*. Cambridge Mass.: Harvard University Press.

BENDIX, R. (1956). *Work and Authority in Industry; Ideologies of Management in the Course of Industrialization*. New York: Wiley.

BERGER, S., and DORE, R. (eds.) (1996). *National Diversity and Global Capitalism*. Ithaca: Cornell University Press.

BUCKLEY, P., and CASSON, M. (1976). *The Future of the Multinational Enterprise*. London: Macmillan.

BURENSTAM LINDER, S. (1961). *An Essay on Trade and Transformation*. Uppsala: Almquist & Wiksells.

CAMPA, J. M. (1993). 'Entry by Foreign Firms in the United States Under Exchange Rate Uncertainty', *Review of Economics and Statistics*, 75, 614–22.

CANTWELL, J. (1989). *Technological Innovation and Multinational Corporations*. Oxford: Blackwell.

CARROLL, G. R. (1997). 'Long-Term Evolutionary Change in Organizational Populations: Theory, Models and Empirical Findings in Industrial Demography', *Industrial and Corporate Change*, 6, 119–43.

—— and DELACROIX, J. (1982). 'Organizational Mortality in the Newspaper Industries of Argentina and Ireland: An Ecological Approach', *Administrative Science Quarterly*, 27, 169–98.

CAVES, R. E. (1971). 'International Corporations: The Industrial Economics of Foreign Investment', *Economica*, 38, 1–27.

—— (1974). 'Causes of Direct Investment: Foreign Firms' Shares in Canadian and United Kingdom Manufacturing Industries', *Review of Economic Statistics*, 56, 79–93.

—— and MEHRA, S. (1986). 'Entry of Foreign Multinationals into US Manufacturing Industries', in M. Porter (ed.), *Competition in Global Industries*. Boston: Harvard Business School Press.

CHANDLER, A. D. (1990). *Scale and Scope: The Dynamics of Industrial Capitalism.* Cambridge Mass.: Belknap Press of Harvard University.

COASE, R. (1937). 'The Nature of the Firm', *Economica,* 4, 386–405.

CURHAN, J. P., DAVIDSON W. H., and SURI, R. (1977). *Tracing the Multinationals: A Sourcebook on US-Based Enterprises.* Cambridge: Ballinger.

—— and VAUPEL, J. P. (1973). *The World's Multinational Enterprises; A Sourcebook of Tables Based on a Study of the Largest US and Non-US Manufacturing Corporations.* Boston: Division of Research, Graduate School of Business Administration, Harvard University.

DAVIDSON, W. H. (1976). 'Patterns of Factor-Saving Innovation in the Industrialized World', *Journal of Industrial Economics,* 32, 253–64.

—— (1980). 'The Location of Foreign Direct Investment Activity: Country Characteristics and Experience Effects', *Journal of International Business Studies,* 11, 1–22.

DELACROIX, J. (1993). 'The European Subsidiaries of American Multinationals: An Exercise in Ecological Analysis', in S. Ghoshal and E. Westney (eds.), *Organizational Theory and the Multinational Enterprise.* New York: Macmillan, 105–31.

—— and CARROL, G. R. (1983). 'Organizational Foundings: An Ecological Study of the Newspaper Industries of Argentina and Ireland', *Administrative Science Quarterly,* 28, 274–91.

DIXIT, A. K. (1987). 'Strategic Aspects of Trade Policy', in T. F. Bewley (ed.), *Advances in Economic Theory: Fifth World Congress.* New York: Cambridge University Press, 329–62.

DUNNING, J. (1977). 'Trade, Location of Economic Activity and the MNE: A Search for an Eclectic Approach', in B. Ohlin, P. O. Hesselborn, and P. M. Wijkman (eds.), *The International Allocation of Economic Activity: Proceedings of a Nobel Symposium Held at Stockholm.* London: Macmillan, 395–418.

FAGRE, N., and WELLS, L. T. (1982). 'Bargaining Power of Multinationals and Host Governments', *Journal of International Business Studies,* 13, 9–23.

FOURAKER, L. E., and SIEGEL, S. (1963). *Bargaining Behavior.* New York: McGraw-Hill.

—— and STOPFORD, J. M. (1968) 'Organization Structure and the Multinational Strategy', *Administrative Science Quarterly,* 13, 47–64.

GATIGNON, H., and ANDERSON, E. (1988). 'The Multinational Corporation's Degree of Control Over Foreign Subsidiaries: An Empirical Test of a Transaction Cost Explanation', *Journal of Law, Economics and Organizations,* 4, 305–36.

GHEMAWAT, P., and KHANNA, T. (1998). 'The Nature of Diversified Business Groups: A Research Design and Two Case Studies', *Journal of Industrial Economics,* 46, 35–61.

GITTELMAN, M. (1999). 'Scientists and Networks: A Comparative Study of Cooperation in the French and American Biotechnology Industry', Ph.D. thesis, Wharton School, University of Pennsylvania.

GOMES-CASSERES, B. (1985). 'Multinational Ownership Strategies', Ph.D. thesis, Harvard Business School.

HANNON, M. T., DUNDON, E. A., CARROLL, G. R., and TORRES, J. C. (1995). 'Organizational Evolution in a Multinational Context: Entries of Automobile Manufacturers in Belgium, Britain, France, Germany, and Italy', *American Sociological Review*, 60, 509–28.

HANNON, M. T., (*cont.*) and FREEMAN, J. (1977). 'The Population Ecology of Organizations', *American Journal of Sociology*, 82, 929–64.

HANSEN, M. T. (1999). 'The Search-Transfer Problem: The Role of Weak Ties in Sharing Knowledge Across Organization Subunits', *Administrative Science Quarterly*, 44, 82–111.

HAUSMANN, J. (1978). 'Specification Tests in Econometrics', *Econometrica*, 46, 1251–71.

HECKMAN, J. J., and SINGER, B. (1985). 'Social Science Duration Analysis', in J. J. Heckman and B. Singer (eds.), *Longitudinal Analysis of Labor Market Data*. New York: Cambridge University Press, 39–110.

HENNART, J.-F. (1982). *A Theory of Multinational Enterprise*. Ann Arbor: University of Michigan Press.

——and PARK, Y. R. (1993). 'Greenfield vs. Acquisition: The Strategy of Japanese Investors in the United States', *Management Science*, 39, 1054–68.

HLADIK, K. J. (1985). *International Joint Ventures: An Economic Analysis of US Foreign Business Partnerships*. Lexington, Mass.: Lexington Books.

HOFSTEDE, G. (1980). *Culture's Consequences: International Differences in Work Related Values*. Beverly Hills: Sage.

HYMER, S. (1960). 'The International Operations of National Firms: A Study of Direct Foreign Investment', Ph.D. dissertation, Cambridge: MIT Press.

KINDLEBERGER, C. (1969). *American Business Abroad: Six Lectures on Direct Investment*. New Haven: Yale University Press.

KNICKERBOCKER, F. (1973). *Oligopolistic Reaction and Multinational Enterprise*. Boston: Div. of Research, Graduate School of Business Administration, Harvard University.

KOGUT, B. (1991). 'Country Capabilities and the Permeability of Borders', *Strategic Management Journal*, 12, 33–47.

——(1992). 'National Organizing Principles of Work and the Erstwhile Dominance of the American Multinational Corporation', *Industrial and Corporate Change*, 1(2): 285–326.

——(1999). 'The Recoupling of a Somewhat Coupled System: Weimar Germany and American Work Practices', The Wharton School, University of Pennsylvania, in progress.

——and CHANG, S.J. (1991). 'Technological Capabilities and Japanese Foreign Direct Investment in the United States', *Review of Economics and Statistics*, 73, 401–13.

————(1996). 'Platform Investments and Volatile Exchange Rates: Direct Investment in the US By Japanese Electronic Companies', *Review of Economics and Statistics*, 78, 221–31.

——and KULATILAKA, N. (1994). 'Operating Flexibility, Global Manufacturing, and the Option Value of a Multinational Network', *Management Science*, 40, 123–39.

——MACDUFFIE, J. P., and RAGIN, C. (1999). 'Prototypes and Fuzzy Work Practices', Reginald H. Jones Center Working Paper Series, WP99-08, The Wharton School, University of Pennsylvania.

—— and PARKINSON, D. (1998). 'Adoption of the Multidivisional Structure: Analyzing History from the Start', *Industrial and Corporate Change*, 7, 249–73.

—— and SINGH, H. (1988a). 'The Effect of National Culture on the Choice of Entry Mode', *Journal of International Business Studies*, 19, 411–32.

—— —— (1988b). 'Entering the United States by Joint Ventures: Competitive Rivalry and Industry Structure', in F. Contractor and P. Lorange (eds.), *Cooperative Strategies in International Business*. Lexington, Mass.: Lexington Press.

—— and ZANDER, U. (1993). 'Knowledge of the Firm and the Evolutionary Theory of the Multinational Enterprise', *Journal of International Business Studies*, 24, 625–45.

LI, J. T. (1995). 'Foreign Entry and Survival: Effects of Strategic Choices on Performance in International Markets', *Strategic Management Journal*, 16, 333–51.

LIEBERMAN, M., and DEMEESTER, L. (1999). 'Inventory Reduction and Productivity Growth: Linkages in the Japanese Automotive Industry', *Management Science*, 45, 466–85.

MACDUFFIE, J. P. (1993). 'Human Resource Bundles and Manufacturing Performance: Organizational Logic and Flexible Production Systems in the World Auto Industry', *Industrial and Labor Relations Review*, 48, 197–221.

MASCARENHAS, B. (1992). 'Order of Entry and Performance in International Markets', *Strategic Management Journal*, 13, 499–510.

MCMANUS, J. C. (1972). 'The Theory of the International Firm', in: G. Paquet (ed.), *The Multinational Firm and the Nation State*. Don Mills, Ore.: Collier-MacMillan, 66–93.

MERTON, R. (1949). *Social Theory and Social Structure: Toward the Codification of Theory and Research*. Glencoe, Ill.: Free Press.

MITCHELL, W., SHAVER, J. M., and YEUNG, B. (1993). 'Performance Following Changes of International Presence in Domestic and Transition Industries', *Journal of International Business Studies*, 24, 647–69.

—— MORCK, R., SHAVER, J. M., and YEUNG, B. (forthcoming). 'Causality Between International Expansion and Investment in Intangibles, with Implications for Financial Performance and Firm Survival', in J.-F. Hennart (ed.), *Global Competition and Market Entry Strategies*. Amsterdam: North Holland.

NEE, V. (1989). 'A Theory of Market Transition: From Redistribution to Markets in State Socialism', *American Sociological Review*, 54, 663–81.

PORTER M. E. (1990). *The Competitive Advantage of Nations*. New York: Free Press.

RAGIN, C. (1987). *The Comparative Method*. Berkeley Calif.: University of California Press.

RANGAN, S. (1998). 'Do Multinationals Operate Flexibly? Theory and Evidence', *Journal of International Business Studies*, 29, 217–37.

RUGMAN, A. M. (1981). *Inside the Multinationals: The Economics of Internal Markets*. London: Croom Helm.

SASSEN, S. (1998). *Globalization and its Discontents. Essays on the New Mobility of People and Money*. New York: The New Press.

SAXENIAN, A. L. (1996). *Regional Advantage: Culture and Competition in Silicon Valley and Route 128*. Cambridge, Mass.: Harvard University Press.

SHAVER, J. M. (1998). 'Accounting for Endogeneity when Assessing Strategy Performance: Does Entry Mode Choice Affect FDI Survival?', *Management Science*, 44, 571–85.

——MITCHELL, W., and YEUNG, B. (1997). 'The Effect of Own-firm and Other-firm Experience on Foreign Direct Investment Survival in the United States', *Strategic Management Journal*, 18, 811–24.

SIMON, H. A. (1957). *Models of Man: Social and Rational; Mathematical Essays on Rational Human Behavior in a Social Setting.* New York: Wiley.

SOSKICE, D. (1990). 'Wage Determination: The Changing Role of Institutions in Advanced Industrialized Countries', *Oxford Review of Economic Policy*, 6, 36–61.

STARK, D. (1992). 'Path Dependence and Privatization Strategies in East Central Europe', *East European Politics and Societies*, 6, 17–51.

STINCHCOMBE, A. L. (1965). 'Social Structure and Organizations', in J. G. March (ed.), *Handbook of Organizations.* Chicago: Rand McNally, 142–93.

STOPFORD, J. M. and WELLS, JR., L. T. (1972). *Managing the Multinational Enterprise: Organization of the Firm and Ownership of Subsidiaries.* New York: Basic Books.

TUMA, N. B., and HANNON, M. T. (1984). *Social Dynamics: Models and Methods.* New York: Academic Press.

UNIVERSITIES-NATIONAL BUREAU COMMITTEE FOR ECONOMIC RESEARCH (1962). 'The Rate and Direction of Inventive Activity: Economic and Social Factors', NBER Special Conference Series no. 13, Princeton: Princeton University Press.

VERNON, R. (1966). 'International Investment and International Trade in the Product Cycle', *Quarterly Journal of Economics*, 80, 190–207.

—— (1971). *Sovereignty at Bay: The Multinational Spread of US Enterprises.* London: Basic Books.

WESTNEY, D. E. (1987). *Imitation and Innovation : The Transfer of Western Organizational Patterns to Meiji Japan.* Cambridge: Harvard University Press.

WILKINS, M. (1970). *The Emergence of Multinational Enterprise: American Business Abroad from the Colonial Era to 1914.* Cambridge, Mass.: Harvard University Press.

—— (1974). *The Maturing of Multinational Enterprise: American Business Abroad from 1914 to 1970.* Boston: Harvard University Press.

—— (1988). 'The Free-standing Company, 1870–1914: An Important Type of British Foreign Direct Investment', *Economic History Review*, 2nd series, 41, 259–82.

WILLIAMSON, O. (1975). *Markets and Hierarchies, Analysis and Antitrust Implications: A Study in the Economics of Internal Organization.* New York: Free Press.

—— (1979). 'Transaction-Cost Economics: The Governance of Contractural Relations', *Journal of Law and Economics*, 22, 233–61.

WILSON, B. D. (1980). 'The Propensity of Multinational Companies to Expand Through Acquisitions', *Journal of International Business Studies*, 11, 59–65.

YAMAWAKI, H. (1988). 'Import Share Under International Oligopoly with Differentiated Products: Japanese Imports in US Manufacturing', *Review of Economics and Statistics*, 70, 569–79.

YU, C-M. J., and ITO, K. (1988). 'Oligopolistic Reaction and Foreign Direct Investment: The Case of the US Tire and Textile Industries', *Journal of International Business Studies*, 19, 449–60.

ZAHEER, S. (1995). 'Overcoming the Liability of Foreignness', *Academy of Management Journal*, 38, 341–63.

ZANDER, U. (1991). 'Exploiting a Technological Edge: Voluntary and Involuntary Dissemination of Technology', doctoral dissertation, Stockholm School of Economics.

# CHAPTER 28

# MULTINATIONAL ENTERPRISES AND PUBLIC POLICY

## ALAN M. RUGMAN
## ALAIN VERBEKE

## 28.1 INTRODUCTION

IN this chapter we review and integrate representative literature on the exceptionally broad topic of multinational enterprises (MNEs) and public policy towards them. We will consider the literature on MNEs and public policy as it has emerged since 1970 and make projections ahead to the relevance of this literature for the year 2020, which is the target date for the members of the Asian-Pacific Economic Community (APEC) to realize full

Helpful comments have been received from Mark Casson, John Dunning, Michael Gestrin, and Stephen Guisinger. An earlier version of this chapter appeared in the *Journal of International Business Studies* 29(1), 1998: 115–36.

trade and foreign direct investment (FDI) liberalization. Such liberalization has already been implemented in the European Union, and has been started in NAFTA and Mercosur (Rugman 2000).

Three approaches to analysis of MNEs and public policy can be adopted. First is a 'normative' approach, using neoclassical welfare economics to review the benefits and costs of national government policies. Second is a 'behavioural' approach to public policy, based on the assumption that there are self-interested actors in the political domain who can influence public policy formation. Third, using the resource-based theory of the firm, is an explicit 'strategic' perspective for MNEs interacting with governments. This approach, adopted in this chapter, provides insight into the managerial aspects of the firm-level strategy process, dealing with core competencies and dynamic capabilities, that need to be integrated into the MNE-government literature. Furthermore, we carefully differentiate the policies of home and host governments and show how the institutional structuring of public policy and the corporate strategies of MNEs are relevant in the current international business literature.

The organization of this chapter is as follows. First, we shall review the efficiency aspects of MNEs and public policy. Next we develop an original analytical framework of our own to synthesize the literature on MNEs and public policy. Finally, we shall relate some of the key references in the literature on MNEs and public policy by others to our new analytical framework.

# 28.2 Efficiency Aspects of MNEs and Public Policy

The basic analytical approach adopted by economists such as Caves (1982, 1996) is to concentrate on the efficiency aspects of MNE activities in a world where, in reality, government regulations on MNEs are imposed for equity/distributional reasons. This distinction between efficiency and equity is extremely useful from the viewpoint of economists and it has been used by many writers on MNEs, e.g. Safarian (1966, 1993), Rugman (1980), Casson (1987), Dunning (1993a).

Analysis of the efficiency aspects of MNEs builds upon the normative foundation of neoclassical welfare economics (in which distributional issues are assumed away). The assumptions required for neoclassical welfare economics to work are that:

(1) each state attempts to maximize real national income;
(2) distributional issues are entirely separate from efficiency ones;
(3) each enterprise has a single 'home base' country to act as a numeraire;
(4) each MNE and nation-state operate in a competitive environment, with a downward sloping demand curve for the proprietary assets of MNEs and an upward sloping supply curve of MNE resource commitments for each nation;
(5) policy making by governments can discriminate between foreign and home based MNEs.

This provides us with a robust framework to analyse public policy towards MNEs. For example, in his classic text, using this welfare economics framework, Caves (1982) is able to analyse key issues such as:

(1) taxation;
(2) natural resource rents;
(3) competition policy;
(4) technology creation and transfer.

A flavour of the implications stemming from the welfare economics approach is given by the last issue of technology transfer. Many writers sympathetic to developing countries bemoan the perceived lack of technology transfer from the branch plant subsidiaries of foreign MNEs and allege lower ratios of R & D to sales by subsidiaries as evidence of this. Caves (1982), however, makes the brilliant point that technology transfer takes place when the consumers in developing countries have access to the goods and services that embody the technology. Thus, the focus is not upon the domestic production of technology-intensive goods and services in developing countries, but upon the end result of FDI, namely the consumption of technologically intensive goods and services. Whether they are provided by foreign-owned or domestic firms is relatively unimportant.

In the behavioural approach we allow for the self-interest of agents in government policy making. This is relevant for analysis of government policies which have aimed to regulate inward FDI as well as home government policies directed towards the promotion of FDI for market access reasons. The behavioural approach explains the actual focus of many governments on distributional issues and away from income maximization. Utility-maximizing electoral behaviour leads to redistribution at the expense of foreign MNEs because foreign equity holders cannot vote, and discrimination against foreigners may provide perceived utility to domestic citizens. In a second version of this approach, government policy is assumed to be the work of a coalition of government officials, who resent foreign MNEs mainly because of their ability to circumvent or avoid various types of regulation.

In both versions of the behavioural approach, discriminatory measures are imposed on foreign MNEs. These behavioural models, however, do not appear very useful in explaining government support for domestic MNEs engaged in outward FDI. This approach may have some validity when used to discuss the role of multilateral agencies which attempt to regulate or facilitate FDI and MNE activity.

A focus on the efficiency aspects of MNEs is fully consistent with the use of internalization theory (examined earlier by Hennart in Chapter 5 of this book) as the key theoretical explanation for the existence of MNEs. The early work using such a transaction cost approach to the MNE was pioneered by Buckley and Casson (1976), Rugman (1981), Hennart (1982), and others. All of these writers considered the public policy implications of the MNE in a similar manner to Caves (1982). This body of work is, of course, a significant departure from the seminal work of Hymer (1976), but based on his 1960 doctoral dissertation. Hymer and many political science-based writers on the MNE, such as Gilpin (1975, 1987) and Grieco (1982), are not really interested in the efficiency aspects of MNEs; rather they wish to discuss such issues as the relative power of MNEs versus the nation-state. This is also a theme of the recent explosion of books on the topic of globalization, some of which are reviewed in Rugman (2000).

There is a rich tradition of work looking into the relative power of the MNE versus the nation-state, with some of the more sensible observations being in Vernon (1971), Bergsten, Horst, and Moran (1978), Behrman and Grosse (1990), etc. Earlier chapters have reviewed these arguments in some detail, and considered the relationship of this work on MNEs to the relevant literature in international political economy (IPE) generated by Susan Strange (1988, 1997) and Eden (1991). In IPE, the focus is upon the interaction between MNEs and nation-states, with emphasis upon the ability of MNEs to transcend the traditional authority of the nation-state. Strange alleges that the MNE has increased its power relative to the state in the areas of natural resources, finance, and technology. In particular, US-based MNEs have developed control in these three 'market' areas, leading to an overall decline in the power of the 'state', but paradoxically to the reinforcement of US economic hegemony for most of the postwar period. Another relevant consideration is that non-governmental organizations (NGOs) and other sub-national groups are exercising an increasing amount of power in the Western democracies, Ostry (1997). The role of NGOs is especially important in analysis of trade and environment issues, (Vogel 1995; Vogel and Rugman 1997; Rugman and Verbeke 1998; Rugman, Kirton, and Soloway 1999).

In another advance on the efficiency-only perspective of MNEs, Stopford and Strange (1991) have addressed the relationships between MNEs and states in an IPE triangular diplomacy framework where there is a triad of bargaining relationships: state/state; state/firm; firm/firm. As another example of IPE work, Milner (1988) and Goldstein (1993) build on Krasner (1978), Keohane (1984), and Keohane and Nye (1977) to describe the role of institutional factors in the administration of US trade policy. Goldstein found that the US Congress protects the US domestic market by a variety of protectionist trade laws, such as anti-dumping (AD) and countervailing duty (CVD) measures (Rugman and Anderson 1987, 1997; Bhagwati 1988; Rugman 1996).

We do not devote any more attention to IPE, hegemonic stability theory, and related theories of MNE–government conflict, because today governments need to deal simultaneously with both inward and outward FDI. We shall develop a framework which considers the symmetry between these two types of FDI. Our approach is consistent with that of Dunning (1993a, 1997) who traces the changing nature of interaction between MNEs and governments over the last thirty years. In particular, governments have switched attention from questions of the distribution of rents and structural issues of technology transfer and regulation towards policies aimed at attracting the knowledge-based mobile FDI taking place in a global system of alliance capitalism.

# 28.3 THE SIMPLE ANALYTICS OF MNEs AND PUBLIC POLICY

In this section we shall develop an analytical framework consisting of three sequential components, which we now describe. The first component of the framework reflects the issue of consistency between MNE goals and government goals, in both home and host countries. Most of the international economics models on MNE–government relations build upon specific assumptions regarding this goal consistency, or lack thereof. Such assumptions determine both the substantive focus and the normative implications of these models. The four main possibilities in this area are shown in Figure 28.1.

In quadrant 1 of Figure 28.1, interactions between MNEs and both home and host governments are assumed to be driven by goal conflict. This reflects the tensions between the micro-efficiency-driven behaviour of MNEs and the macro-efficiency or distributional objectives of governments. The opposite situation arises in quadrant 4 of Figure 28.1; here the goals of MNEs and both home and host governments are complementary. In quadrant 2 there is consistency between MNE and home country goals, but conflicts with host

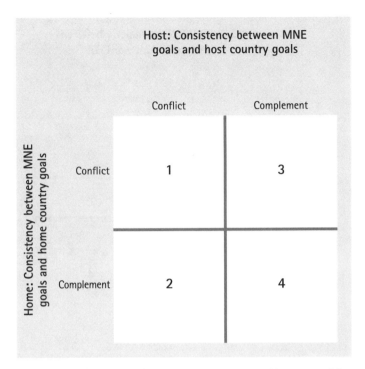

Fig. 28.1 The consistency between MNE and home and host
government goals

country goals. The reverse applies in quadrant 3. In the next section, we shall use this matrix to position a large part of the existing literature in international business and public policy.

The economist's perspective on the literature (as in Caves 1982) requires that each MNE has a clearly defined nationality, usually with a strong home base in which its Firm Specific Advantages (FSAs) are developed. The MNE has a centralized, hierarchical organizational structure to control the global production of each line of business. In terms of government regulation Caves (1982) makes a clear distinction between home and host country interests. Given that the Caves perspective is primarily one of synthesis, it is hardly surprising that literature covering the various quadrants of Figure 28.1 is discussed in his book, albeit with a focus largely situated in quadrant 1. Caves concentrates his focus on research dealing with conflict issues between MNEs and governments, for example, taxation and competition policy, bargaining over natural-resource rents, and technology transfer issues.

The second component of the framework builds upon more recent insights in the international business field. There, it is recognized that the institutional characteristics of specific MNEs and specific countries largely determine MNE–government interactions. In contrast to the macro-analysis provided

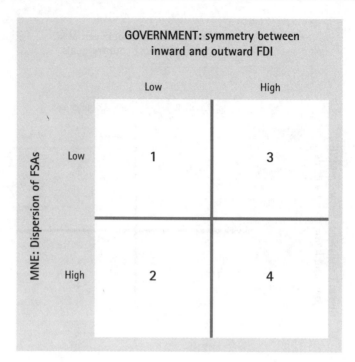

**Fig. 28.2 Institutional determinants of MNE–government interactions**

by the first component of our conceptual framework, which assumed a particular level of inherent goal congruence between firms and public agencies (largely based on ideological elements) this second component attempts to highlight the most important institutional elements determining MNE and government behaviour. These institutional elements are shown in Figure 28.2.

On the MNE axis, the key institutional issue is the dispersion of its FSAs across geographic borders. The FSAs of an MNE reflect its core competencies and dynamic capabilities (in terms of the resource-base theory of the firm). Incidentally, the FSA terminology precedes that of core competencies and dynamic capabilities (Rugman 1980, 1981). A conventional ethnocentric MNE will be characterized by a concentration of FSAs in the home country with a replication of home country production and managerial approaches in host nations. The product line manager in the home base controls the FSAs of the MNE. In contrast, a polycentric MNE is one with its FSAs dispersed into its various host nation subsidiaries. The country managers of the polycentric MNE develop and control the FSAs across whatever product markets they choose. Finally, a geocentric MNE attempts to develop a balance between the interests of product line and country managers. Here, some FSAs remain

concentrated in the home base, whereas other FSAs are developed autono-
mously in the various host country subsidiaries. An economist's perspective
on the literature, with a focus on adversarial interactions, especially between
the MNE and host nations, is justified only in the first case, of an ethnocentric
MNE. In both the latter two cases (of polycentric and geocentric MNEs) we
need to build upon a richer framework that would allow us to explain the
interaction between MNEs and governments when FSAs are developed and
controlled in several nations simultaneously.

On the government axis, the key parameter determining MNE–government relations is the symmetry between inward and outward FDI. This
parameter is viewed as an institutional element in this paper because a high
symmetry represents an *ex post* reflection of the willingness of government to
allow inward and outward FDI. A nation's policies towards MNEs will depend
on whether it is (i) a net exporter of FDI (with MNEs using a strong home
base), (ii) a net recipient of FDI (a typical host nation), or (iii) a 'dual' player
with both outward and inward FDI. In each of these cases, the incentive
structure facing governments in terms of regulating MNE behaviour is fundamentally different (Dunning 1993*b*). In Figure 28.2, we relate these two
determinants of MNE–government interactions. On the vertical axis for the
MNE we represent the dispersion of the MNE's FSAs, either low or high. On
the horizontal axis for government we place the symmetry between inward
and outward FDI, either low or high. As regards this latter parameter, we
assume a high absolute volume of FDI. If the FDI volume were low, the
symmetry issue would obviously not be critical.

The Caves (1982) perspective mainly describes one of the four cases in
Figure 28.2; it is in quadrant 1. Here, there is no recognition of the dispersion
of FSAs by the firm and a low degree of symmetry between inward and
outward FDI prevails. The view of MNEs as only demonstrating centralized
structures (i.e. they only develop FSAs in their single home-country base) and
the view of governments as acting narrowly in accordance with either home or
host nation perspectives allows for elegant, albeit often over-simplified, modelling by economists. In reality, three more complex cases may occur that do
not lend themselves to simple modelling. In quadrant 2 of Figure 28.2, firm-
driven national responsiveness may induce governments to provide national
treatment. This requires that governments understand the economic and
strategic significance of MNEs operating a network with dispersed FSAs.
Governments also need to be interested in the creation of sustainable value-
added domestically, whether by domestic or foreign MNEs. In contrast, in
quadrant 3, the symmetry between a country's inward FDI and outward FDI
positions provides incentives for the non-discriminatory regulation of foreign
MNEs, irrespective of their ethnocentric, polycentric, or geocentric strategies.
National treatment of foreign MNEs may then induce foreign MNEs to
become more nationally responsive themselves. Finally, in quadrant 4, there is

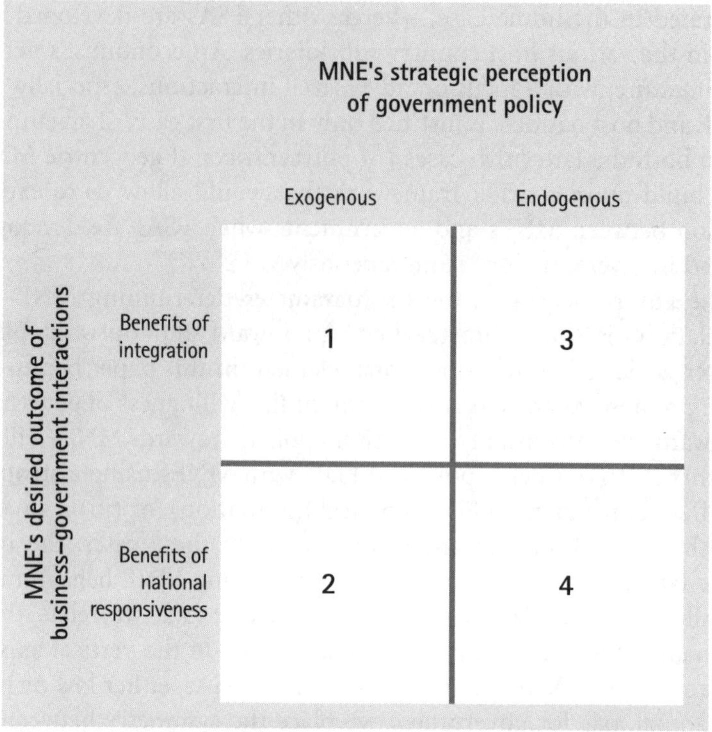

MNE's strategic perception
of government policy

Exogenous                    Endogenous

| | Benefits of integration | 1 | 3 |
| | Benefits of national responsiveness | 2 | 4 |

MNE's desired outcome of business–government interactions

Fig. 28.3 MNE's strategic approach to government policy

a government preference for global regulation and a firm preference for a 'supranational' approach to government policy. The reason for such preferences is that a symmetrical position of inward and outward FDI at the public policy level and a dispersed FDI configuration at the firm level leads to complexities in terms of optimal business–government interactions that cannot be solved at the national level.

To summarize, in the basic analysis by economists, such as Caves (1982), the MNE is a centralized, hierarchical organization that closely monitors and meters the use of its home-based FSAs. Government policy is systematically analysed from the viewpoint of either a host country (recipient of FDI) or a home country (exporter of FDI). Thus, the Caves perspective has a single MNE–government context in quadrant 1 of Figure 28.2. However, the institutional determinants of MNE–government interaction are now recognized to be more complex than this and so the other three quadrants of Figure 28.2 are necessary to properly explore the process of interactions between MNEs and home and host governments.

The third component of our new framework analyses the MNE's strategic approach to government policy in terms of strategic perspectives and desired outcomes. This is shown in Figure 28.3.

The strategic perspective on government policy reflects the extent to which it is viewed as either exogenous or endogenous by the managers of the MNE. If it is endogenous, this means that the MNE will attempt to alter the content and/or process of government policy in its favour. If exogenous, the MNE will work within the rules set by public agencies. Given this choice of interaction with governments, the MNE must design an appropriate strategy and structure to obtain either the benefits of integration or of national responsiveness, when interacting with home and host governments. This leads to several complex situations in Figure 28.3, only one of which is discussed in depth by Caves (1982). This is quadrant 1 where the MNE views government policy as exogenous and its objective is to achieve the benefits of integration, i.e. conventional efficiency benefits in the area of scale economies, economies of scope, and economies of exploiting national differences.

The other quadrants of Figure 28.3 represent the newer stream of international business literature. The four quadrants as a whole represent a 'transnational' approach to government policy. There the MNE has to make a strategic choice for each type of government regulation (or intervention) relevant to the firm. It does this within each region, for each SBU, and for each function and task. Each MNE has to decide two things. First, whether government policy will be viewed as an endogenous or exogenous variable; second, whether benefits of national responsiveness versus integration will be pursued in its business–government interaction. The latter decision depends on the relative importance of the MNE's location bound versus non-location bound FSAs. The location bound FSAs reflect proprietary competencies and capabilities which can be exploited in only a limited geographic region, e.g. an excellent local reputation, a well positioned retail network, privileged relationships with domestic economic actors, etc. If location bound FSAs represent the key to competitive success, the MNE will focus on those areas of government regulation that constitute an opportunity or threat to developing and exploiting such FSAs. In contrast, if the MNE builds primarily on non-location bound FSAs, such as global brand names and technologies that can easily be transferred internationally, either as an intermediate good or embodied in a final product, then its focus in government relations will be on protecting and exploiting such FSAs.

There are four cases in Figure 28.3. In quadrant 1 government policy is used as a lever for global competitiveness. In quadrant 2 there is the good corporate citizen approach building upon a strategy of national responsiveness. In quadrant 4 the strategy of national responsiveness is extended to one of nation bound bargaining, whereas in quadrant 3, the firm's interest may be in developing global bargaining strategies to be used when dealing with subnational, national, and supranational public agencies. In fact, it could be argued that in quadrant 4, the MNE will develop location bound FSAs in government relations in each country in which it operates, whereas in quadrant 3, the focus will be on non-location bound FSAs. This is a strategy of developing systemic advantages in dealing with public agencies across borders.

# 28.4 A NEW SYNTHESIS OF THE LITERATURE

In Figure 28.1A, where most of the conventional economics literature can be positioned, quadrants 1 and 4 are the polar extremes of the MNE–state debate. In quadrant 1 we have the Hymer (1976) quasi-Marxist view of the conflicts between MNEs and home and host governments. The focus is upon distributional issues and the power of the MNE versus the host nation-state (Dunning and Rugman 1985). We can also position *the Sovereignty at Bay* of Raymond Vernon (1971) in this quadrant. As Vernon (1991) himself states, the title of his book has been misinterpreted—he did not argue that the MNE would dominate the host nation-state, but rather that there would be antagonistic relations between them, as we show in quadrant 1. Also in this quadrant can be placed the Kojima hypothesis to the effect that trade and FDI are substitutes in the US experience but complements in the Japanese case, (Kojima 1973, 1975, 1978, 1985), i.e. that there can be both MNE–host and home government conflicts.

In contrast, in quadrant 4 of Figure 28.1A we suggest the complementary nature of MNE–home and host state relations. This is more consistent with Vernon (1966) and Knickerbocker (1973) where the MNE grows through a product life cycle of technology-intensive products developed initially in a strong home base, then manufactured by wholly-owned subsidiaries in host economies and finally (when the product is mature) anywhere in the world with the lowest factor input costs. This is an efficiency-based view of the MNE–state relationship (Rugman 1999). This quadrant is also consistent with early views of internalization theory in Buckley and Casson (1976), Rugman (1980, 1981), Dunning (1981), and Hennart (1982). The internalization of technological and managerial know-how within the internal market of the MNE leads to a positive externality which overcomes the Coase (1937) problem of knowledge as a public good. Johnson (1970) and Magee (1977) explored how the MNE could 'appropriate,' or own, firm-specific assets in know-how and in technology and thereby overcome the transaction cost of

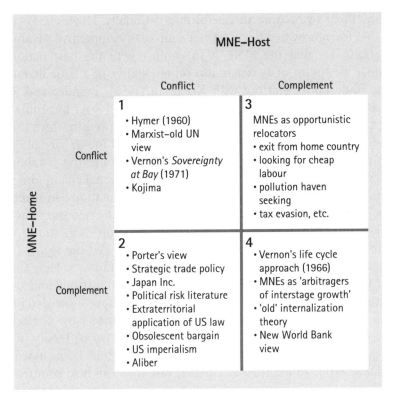

**MNE–Host**

|  | Conflict | Complement |
|---|---|---|
| **Conflict** | **1**<br>• Hymer (1960)<br>• Marxist–old UN view<br>• Vernon's *Sovereignty at Bay* (1971)<br>• Kojima | **3**<br>MNEs as opportunistic relocators<br>• exit from home country<br>• looking for cheap labour<br>• pollution haven seeking<br>• tax evasion, etc. |
| **Complement** | **2**<br>• Porter's view<br>• Strategic trade policy<br>• Japan Inc.<br>• Political risk literature<br>• Extraterritorial application of US law<br>• Obsolescent bargain<br>• US imperialism<br>• Aliber | **4**<br>• Vernon's life cycle approach (1966)<br>• MNEs as 'arbitragers of interstage growth'<br>• 'old' internalization theory<br>• New World Bank view |

(left axis label: **MNE–Home**)

**Fig. 28.1A  Examples of Figure 28.1**

knowledge as a public good. The process of internalization is efficiency based since the MNEs help both home and host nations to develop; indeed the MNE is the engine of economic development in quadrant 4 of Figure 28.1A. To the extent that national governments understand the value to their country of access to the MNE's FSAs, goal conflict can be largely avoided. Dunning (1994) has described why most governments are now 'acclaiming FDI as good news' after a period of hostility in the 1970s and early 1980s. In fact, this change in attitude reflects the understanding that the FSAs of MNEs cannot be simply unbundled or purchased as intermediate goods. This view has also been echoed in recent World Bank reports and it represents a welcome shift in the public policy perspective (Rugman 1999).

There are then two more complex cases in Figure 28.1A. In quadrant 2 we place the Porter (1990) view of MNEs with a strong home base. There is a complementary relationship between the home government and its MNEs. In fact, appropriate government policy for each of the determinants of Porter's national diamond of competitiveness (i.e. factor conditions, demand conditions, related and supporting industries, the firms' strategy, structure, and rivalry in a specific industry) will strengthen the domestic firms' home base and allow them to become successful internationally. However, Porter also argues that foreign-owned firms are not sources of competitive advantage for host nations, i.e. that the MNE is in conflict with the host nation. This quadrant 2 viewpoint of Porter is also representative of a large literature on strategic trade policy starting with Krugman (1986), Brander and Spencer (1985), and then misapplied to public policy by Tyson (1993) and Yoffie (1993), amongst others. Basically all of these writers develop cases in which the home government can subsidize its MNEs to develop first mover advantages in a zero-sum game. Strategic trade policy has home states giving discriminatory subsidies to home based MNEs, who then act as national champions to take global market shares away from MNEs based in host nations. In reality, such policies have mostly failed as few governments have the necessary knowledge and the required implementing apparatus to catapult domestic firms into becoming globally competitive MNEs (Rugman and Verbeke 1990). The earlier literature on Japan Inc. is also positioned in quadrant 2. Here the argument is that the Japanese keiretsus have developed in a strong and rivalrous home base and, helped by the Japanese government, have succeeded in global markets at the expense of host country firms (Ohmae 1985; Gerlach 1992; Nonaka and Takeuchi 1995; Fruin 1997). The Aliber (1970) theory of FDI is also in quadrant 2. He argues that a strong currency allows home based MNEs to capitalize expected earnings at a higher rate than can host country firms.

Finally the more conventional literature on political risk management, Kobrin (1982), Brewer (1983, 1985), Ghadar (1982), Nigh (1985), and others, is also in quadrant 2. The literature assumes that host governments should be able to regulate foreign MNEs, or otherwise change the political environmental parameters facing MNEs in the host nations. In this work, MNEs are often seen as modern instruments of colonization, bringing with them unwanted approaches (including managerial and labour practices) prevailing in their home nations. An extreme version of political risk is the obsolescing bargain hypothesis, Encarnation and Wells (1985), Kobrin (1984, 1987). This argues that the manufacturing or resource based MNEs in host economies have sunk costs in the form of factories, mines, and plantations, all of which could be nationalized by the host government and result in losses for the MNE. Here, the main point is that host government goals can only prevail at the expense of foreign MNE goals once the MNE has engaged in irreversible resource commitments and its bargaining position has weakened substantially. To help overcome this, there is still a US legal viewpoint that argues for extraterritorial application of its laws. The Helms-Burton Act on Cuba is the latest manifestation of this old-fashioned view that US MNEs can be used as instruments of US foreign policy (complementary) against the interests of the host governments.

In quadrant 3 we have the opposite situation. Here, there is a conflict between MNEs and their home governments, but a complementary relationship with host governments. An example is the pollution haven argument, whereby MNEs are alleged to flee tight home market regulations to go to lax host nation regimes. The cheap labour offshore assembly platform argument also fits here, as does the naïve viewpoint that MNEs engage in transfer pricing and seek out tax havens at the expense of their governments. There has been less research output in this quadrant than the larger literature in quadrant 2. What literature there is tends to refute the political science-led rationale for quadrant 3. For example, Eden (1985, 1997), building on earlier work, e.g. Copithorne (1971), Lall (1973), Nieckels (1976), Lessard (1979), Rugman and Eden (1985), finds no evidence for systematic transfer pricing by MNEs other than as a response to effective tax rate differentials and other exogenous market imperfections. The rationale for offshore assembly has been falling as most manufactured sectors reduce the labour content of their processes; there are some exceptions such as the offshore assembly of disc drives and other high technology commodity products. In NAFTA the role of Mexico as a cheap labour and pollution haven for Asian and European MNEs was offset by rules of origin for autos and textiles which protect 'insider' North American MNEs (Rugman 1994; Gestrin and Rugman 1994; Eden and Molot 1993; Hufbauer and Schott 1992, 1993; Lustig, Bosworth, and Lawrence 1992). In more general terms, it would be incorrect to assume that MNEs, faced with excessive goal conflicts in their home countries, seek cooperation with mostly poorer host nations, where goal complementarity is prevailing. However, institutional competition among potential host countries to attract FDI can lead to generous investment promotion programmes, even in the most developed economies, sometimes creating a situation of reverse discrimination.

Turning to Figure 28.2A we can see that the older literature in international business fits into quadrant 1, as this failed to address the ability of the MNE to disperse its FSAs globally, using its organizational structure and systems as a managerially based core competence. Indeed the literature up to Caves (1982), including early internalization theory, plus the Vernon (1966, 1971) and Porter (1990) work, all assume the creation of non-location bound FSAs in the home country of the MNE that would lead to profits abroad through exports, licensing, or FDI. Strategies for MNEs in quadrant 1 consist of replicating home country practices and are entirely dependent on decisions made in the home country concerning value chain configuration and coordination (Porter 1986). There is no recognition of the need to develop location bound FSAs in host countries that would lead to benefits of national responsiveness.

The turning point in recognizing the ability of the MNE to be nationally responsive can be traced to the neglected work of Doz (1986) and to the more influential book by Bartlett and Ghoshal (1989). These authors have added rigorous strategic modelling methods to the original insight by Perlmutter (1969) into the decentralized role of polycentric managers. In Bartlett and

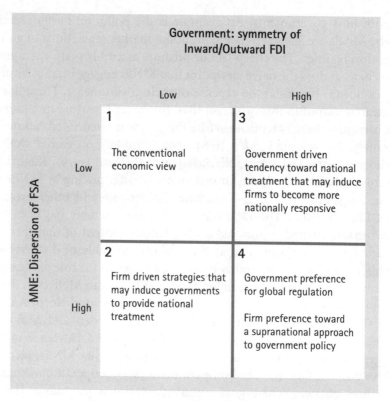

**Fig. 28.2A  Examples of Figure 28.2**

Ghoshal's work, it is also demonstrated that when MNEs feel sufficiently confident about the economic and strategic potential of a specific foreign subsidiary or business unit abroad, then non-location bound FSAs may actually be developed there. This gives the host nation a characteristic conventionally reserved to home nations, namely to become a source country for new innovations. This leads to a quadrant 2 situation in Figure 28.2A with firm driven strategies that may induce governments to provide national treatment.

The conventional literature, as in Caves (1982), also assumes a low symmetry between inward and outward FDI, which is a key parameter determining government regulation of MNEs. The 'old' politics of international institutions such as the GATT concerned themselves with tariff cuts and the negotiation of the removal of trade barriers. This was a focus on 'shallow integration' (Ostry 1997; Brewer and Young 1998). This shallow integration of successive GATT rounds assumed that little could be achieved on trade in services and in the FDI area because governments would be either a net exporter or a net recipient of FDI. The new agenda of the WTO and of a potential Multilateral Agreement on Investment (MAI) is to negotiate 'deep integration' and the removal of barriers to FDI. The objective of an MAI is to make domestic markets internationally contestable through the principle of national treatment, i.e. all MNEs are to be treated in the same manner as domestic firms by host governments (Rugman 2000). Thus in quadrant 3 of Figure 28.2A there is a new agenda for international relations which recognizes the reality of a high symmetry at the country level between inward and outward FDI characterizing many countries, including the United States, Canada, the EU, and Japan. This symmetry has led to the widespread adoption of the national treatment principle, i.e. it ends the discriminatory treatment of home and foreign firms by governments. This is consistent with Dunning (1994) who has suggested that inbound FDI may inject more market-oriented beliefs and practices in a domestic economic system and may alter the international competitiveness agenda of government.

The view that diverges the most sharply from the conventional economist's view is found in quadrant 4 of Figure 28.2A. Here, there is a mutual preference by both MNEs and governments for a 'supranational' approach to public policy. This will take into account the dispersion of MNE FSAs and the high degree of symmetry of inward and outward FDI at the national level. Given the general institutional trend towards quadrant 4 in Figure 28.2A some possible MNE strategies towards MNE–government relations are analysed in Figure 28.3A.

In Figure 28.3A we can incorporate the resource-based view of literature on MNE strategy and public policy developed in Rugman and Verbeke (1991). In this work a vital distinction is drawn between location bound FSAs and non-location bound FSAs. Location bound FSAs include those that lead to benefits of national responsiveness, whereas non-location bound FSAs are those that lead to integration benefits of scale, scope, and exploiting national differences. Application of this model to issues of strategic trade policy and shelter theory, competitiveness, and NAFTA, can be found in Rugman and Verbeke (1990) and Rugman (1996).

The prevailing view on the impact of MNE–public policy linkages on international competitiveness is that of Porter (1990), which can be positioned in quadrant 1 of Figure 28.3A. His use of the home base/cluster concept requires that the MNE adopts an integration strategy and regards the government policy as exogenous. The MNEs in the triad respond to, for example, home government subsidies and other policies strengthening the domestic 'diamond' (Porter 1990) and use their large home base to become globally competitive. This is partly consistent with the resource-based view, but it limits the public policy induced development of managerially based FSAs to those generated by home government stimulus. There is no room in this work for subsidiary managers or foreign governments to contribute to the FSAs, except in the implementation stage of integration-based strategies. Applications of this thinking have been made to trade and environment issues by Porter and van der Linde (1995).

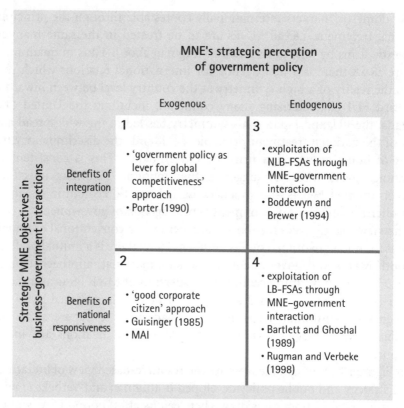

**Fig. 28.3A  Examples of Figure 28.3**

In quadrant 2 of Figure 28.3A, government policy is still viewed as exogenous, but here MNEs develop strategies (building upon such policies) whose aim is to achieve benefits of national responsiveness in the various countries where the firm operates. Government policy is not viewed as a major determinant of international competitiveness. This view is consistent with the proposition that public policy should focus on providing a level playing field rather than creating an international competitive advantage. Issues of public policy which are relevant in quadrant 2 of Figure 28.3A include work on negotiation of a subsidies code at the GATT and WTO. Here the research of Guisinger and Associates (1985), Hufbauer and Erb (1984), Gladwin and Walter (1980) is relevant. The work on an MAI would occur in this quadrant.

In contrast, quadrant 4 reflects a proactive strategy of national responsiveness. The MNEs here have a decentralized or matrix organizational structure and they outperform the average competitor through national responsiveness, as argued by Doz (1986), Prahalad and Doz (1987), and by Bartlett and Ghoshal (1989). An application of this has been made to corporate strategies and environmental regulations by Rugman and Verbeke (1998). In this work government policy is viewed as a parameter that can be influenced (endo-genized) through lobbying and negotiation. This is consistent with the con-clusions of a body of political risk literature which argues that such risk is largely determined by micro-environmental factors.

In quadrant 3 of Figure 28.3A it is also argued that government policy is endogenous, but this time the MNE aims to achieve the benefits of integra-tion-based FSAs. These are non-location bound. The danger associated with active MNE strategies in this area is that they sometimes represent a 'Trojan horse' approach. Firms themselves use strategic trade policy arguments to obtain government favours. First mover advantages at the international level, strategic entry deterrence, technological spill-overs, learning curve effects, credible retaliation to foreign support programmes, etc. may be among the effects lobbied for by firms. The end result should be domestic MNEs with stronger non-location bound FSAs. Unfortunately, such lobbying often dis-guises shelter-seeking strategies. These firms are unable to compete without artificial government support. Such behaviour has been variously defined as a political strategy by Boddewyn (1988) and by Boddewyn and Brewer (1994) or as a fourth generic strategy by Rugman and Verbeke (1990). Perhaps the most interesting feature of the above analysis is that some firms are now actually adopting a 'transnational' strategy, in the Bartlett and Ghoshal (1989) spirit, that may cover each of Figure 28.3A's four quadrants, depending upon the area of regulation, the relevant country, or the affected business unit.

# 28.5 CONCLUSIONS AND FUTURE RESEARCH

The conceptual framework described in this paper suggests that there is more to the analysis of MNE–government relations than is described in a basic economics-driven synthesis of the conventional literature, as in Caves (1982). The institutional reality driving much of today's business–government inter-actions is one whereby governments increasingly do not unambiguously represent either a home or a host country. The symmetrical status of countries both as source nations and as recipients of FDI makes it more difficult for governments to design specific incentive programmes and regulatory policies. At the country level, national treatment of foreign direct investment is often the appropriate policy. In addition, many large MNEs now have a dispersed structure of FSAs, which reduces their legal and strategic commitment to a single home base. Thus, national responsiveness has developed as the key strategy for many firms.

When the symmetry in FDI positions at the government level and the dispersion of FSAs at the firm level are taken into account simultaneously, both sets of actors will have a keen interest in international and multilateral trade and investment liberalization. Generally accepted rules need to guide MNE–government interactions. Finally, it is important to realize that the MNE's strategic approach to government policy is increasingly one in which choices tend to be made regarding the nature of the benefits sought (benefits of integration versus benefits of national responsiveness) and the extent to which actions will be undertaken to change or set the rules. This is the old issue of the extent to which government policy should be viewed as endogenous rather than exogenous to the firm. What is certain is that some MNEs have taken on board a broader spectrum of strategic alternatives in developing and exploiting their FSAs than was considered by the earlier work of economists interested in MNEs and public policy.

The next twenty years will see an international business literature develop which is based much more on this new thinking than on the earlier economic-driven literature. The next round of the WTO will probably focus on further liberalization of trade in services, issues of trade and the environment, and issues of investment and competition policy. New work on an MAI appears in Gestrin and Rugman (1995), Brewer and Young (1998) and this is consistent with earlier analysis of codes of conduct at the OECD by Safarian (1993) and Grosse (1980). The nature of networks and of R&D policy is also an area where our new framework provides guidance for future research. While the Japanese access Silicon Valley in the United States, US firms also draw R&D from Japan (Westney 1993). Work on alliance capitalism, as discussed in papers in Dunning (1997) and on strategic alliances and cooperative strategies, as discussed in Contractor and Lorange (1988), D'Cruz and Rugman (1997), Rugman and D'Cruz (2000), and in Beamish and Killing (1997) will grow in relevance. Networks and alliance capitalism may well supplement the development and exploitation of FSAs by home country-based MNEs as the focus of public policy.

The field of international business is expanding rapidly across these, and related, dimensions. Yet in terms of analysis of the MNE and public policy the earlier analytical insights of economists such as Caves (1982) provides a solid foundation for present and future research. The 'multiple perspectives' approach now being used to bring disciplinary insights into the activities, operations, and structures of MNEs is congruent with both the conventional static economic efficiency analysis and also the current dynamic resource-based theory of the firm viewpoint incorporated into the new framework developed here. The interaction between MNEs and governments has been, and will remain in the future, a lively area of research activity for scholarship in the field of international business.

# REFERENCES

ALIBER, ROBERT Z. (1970) 'A Theory of Direct Foreign Investment', in Charles P. Kindleberger (ed.), *The International Corporation*. Cambridge, Mass.: MIT Press, 17–34.

BARTLETT, CHRISTOPHER A., and GHOSHAL, SUMANTRA (1989). *Managing Across Borders: The Transnational Solution*. Boston: Harvard Business School Press.

BEAMISH, PAUL, and KILLING, PETER (1997). *Cooperative Strategies* (3 vols.). San Francisco: The New Lexington Press.

BEHRMAN, JACK N., and GROSSE, ROBERT E. (1990). *International Business and Governments: Issues and Institutions*. Columbia, SC: University of South Carolina Press.

BERGSTEN, C. FRED, HORST, THOMAS, and MORAN, THEODORE H. (1978). *American Multinationals and American Interests*. Washington, DC: Brookings Institution.

BHAGWATI, JAGDISH (1988). *Protectionism*. Cambridge, Mass.: MIT Press.

BODDEWYN, JEAN J. (1988) 'Political Aspects of MNE Theory', *Journal of International Business Studies*, 19: 341–63.

——and BREWER, THOMAS (1994). 'International Business Political Behaviour: New Theoretical Directions', *Academy of Management Review*, 19(1): 119–43.

BRANDER, JAMES, and SPENCER, BARBARA (1985). 'Export Subsidies and International Market Share Rivalry', *Journal of International Economics*, 18 (Feb.): 85–100.

BREWER, THOMAS L. (1983). 'The Instability of Controls on MNE's Funds Transfers and the Instability of Governments', *Journal of International Business Studies*, 14 (3): 147–57.

——(ed.) (1985). *Political Risks in International Business: New Directions for Research, Management and Public Policy*. New York: Praeger.

——and YOUNG, STEPHEN (1998). *Multinational Investment Rules and Multinational Enterprises*. Oxford: Oxford University Press.

BUCKLEY, PETER J., and CASSON, MARK (1976). *The Future of the Multinational Enterprise*. London: Macmillan.

CASSON, MARK. (1987). *The Firm and the Market*. Cambridge, Mass.: MIT Press.

CAVES, RICHARD E. (1982). *Multinational Enterprise and Economic Analysis*. Cambridge: Cambridge University Press, (2nd edn. 1996).

COASE, R. H. (1937). 'The Nature of the Firm', *Economica*, 4: 386–405.

CONTRACTOR, FAROK, and LORANGE, PETER (eds.) (1988). *Cooperative Strategies in International Business*. San Francisco: New Lexington Press.

COPITHORNE, L. W. (1971). 'International Corporate Transfer Prices and Government Policy', *Canadian Journal of Economics*, 4: 324–41.

D'Cruz, Joseph, and Rugman, Alan M. (1997). 'The Theory of the Flagship Firm', *European Management Journal*, 15(1): 403–11.

Doz, Yves (1986). *Strategic Management in Multinational Companies*. Oxford: Pergamon Press.

Dunning, John H. (1981). *International Production and the Multinational Enterprise*. London: Allen & Unwin.

—— (1993a). *Multinational Enterprises and the Global Economy*. New York: Addison-Wesley.

—— (1993b). *The Globalization of Business*. London: Routledge.

—— (1994). 'Re-evaluating the Benefits of Foreign Direct Investment', *Transnational Corporation*, 3(1): 23–51.

—— (ed.) (1997). *Governments, Globalization and International Business*. Oxford: Oxford University Press.

—— and Rugman, Alan M. (1985). 'The Influence of Hymer's Dissertation on the Theory of Foreign Direct Investment', *American Economic Review*, papers and proceedings, 75: 228–32.

Eden, Lorraine (1985). 'The Micro-economics of Transfer Pricing', in Alan M. Rugman and Lorraine Eden (eds.), *Multinationals and Transfer Pricing*. London: Croom Helm, 13–46.

—— (1991). 'Bringing the Firm Back in: Multinationals in IPE', *Millennium Journal of International Studies*, 20(2): 197–224.

—— (1997). *Taxing Multinationals: Transfer Pricing and Corporate Income Taxation in North America*. Toronto: University of Toronto Press.

—— and Molot, Maureen Appel (1993). 'Insiders and Outsiders: Defining 'Who is Us' in the North American Automobile Industry', *Transnational Corporations*, 3(2) (Dec.): 31–64.

Encarnation, Dennis J., and Wells, Louis T. Jr. (1985). 'Sovereignty en garde: Negotiating with Foreign Investors', *International Organization*, (Winter): 147–71.

Fruin, Mark (1997). *Knowledge Works*. Oxford: Oxford University Press.

Gerlach, Michael (1992). *Alliance Capitalism: The Social Organization of Japanese Business*. Berkeley: University of California Press.

Gestrin, Michael, and Rugman, Alan M. (1994). 'The North American Free Trade Agreement and Foreign Direct Investment', *Transnational Corporations*, 3(1): 77–95.

———— (1995). 'The NAFTA Investment Provisions: Prototype for Multilateral Investment Rules', Organization for Economic Co-operation and Development, *Market Access After the Uruguay Round: Investment, Competition and Technology Perspectives*. Paris: OECD.

Ghadar, Fariborz (1982). 'Political Risk and the Erosion of Control: The Case of the Oil Industry', *Columbia Journal of World Business*, 13 (2): 47–51.

Gilpin, Robert (1975). *US Power and the Multinational Corporation*. New York: Basic Books.

—— (1987). *The Political Economy of International Relations*. Princeton: Princeton University Press.

Gladwin, Thomas N., and Walter, Ingo (1980). *Multinationals Under Fire: Lessons in the Management of Conflict*. New York: John Wiley.

GOLDSTEIN, JUDITH (1993). *Ideas, Interests and American Trade Policy.* Ithaca: Cornell University Press.

GRANOVETTER, M. (1992). 'Problem of Explanation in Economic Sociology', in N. Nohria and R. Eccles (eds.), *Networks and Organizations.* Boston: Harvard Business School Press, 22–56.

GRIECO, JOSEPH M. (1982). 'Between Dependency and Autonomy: India's Experience with the International Computer Industry', *International Organization,* 36(3): 609–32.

GROSSE, ROBERT (1980). *Foreign Investment Codes and the Location of Direct Investment.* New York: Praeger.

GUISINGER, STEPHEN E., and Associates (1985). *Investment Incentives and Performance Requirements.* New York: Praeger.

HEDLUND, GUNNER (1994). 'A Model of Knowledge Management and the N-form Corporations', *Strategic Management Journal,* 15: 73–90.

HENNART, JEAN-FRANÇOIS (1982). *A Theory of Multinational Enterprise.* Ann Arbor, Mich.: University of Michigan Press.

HUFBAUER, GARY C., and ERB, JOANNA (1984). *Subsidies in International Trade.* Washington, DC: Institute for International Economics.

——and SCHOTT, JEFFREY J. (1992). *North American Free Trade Issues and Recommendations.* Washington, DC: Institute for International Economics.

————(1993). *NAFTA: An Assessment.* Washington, DC: Institute for International Economics.

HYMER, STEPHEN H. (1976). *The International Operations of National Firms: A Study of Direct Foreign Investment.* Cambridge, Mass.: MIT Press (originally, Ph.D. dissertation, MIT, 1960).

JOHNSON, HARRY G. (1970). 'The Efficiency and Welfare Implications of the Multinational Corporation', in Charles P. Kindleberger (ed.), *The International Corporation: A Symposium.* Cambridge, Mass.: MIT Press, 33–56.

KEOHANE, ROBERT O. (1984). *After Hegemony.* Princeton: Princeton University Press.

——and NYE, JOSEPH (1977). *Power and Interdependence.* Boston: Little Brown.

KNICKERBOCKER, FREDERICK T. (1973). *Oligopolistic Reaction and Multinational Enterprise.* Boston: Harvard University Graduate School of Business Administration, Division of Research.

KOBRIN, STEPHEN J. (1982). *Managing Political Risk Assessment.* Berkeley, Calif.: University of California Press.

——(1984). 'Expropriation as an Attempt to Control Foreign Firms in LDCs: Trends from 1960–79', *International Studies Quarterly,* 28(3): 329–48.

——(1987). 'Testing the Bargaining Hypothesis in the Manufacturing Sector in Developing Countries', *International Organization,* 41(4): 609–38.

KOGUT, BRUCE, and ZANDER, U. (1993). 'Knowledge of the Firm and the Evolutionary Theory of the Multinational Enterprises', *Journal of International Business Studies,* 24(4): 625–45.

KOJIMA, KIYOSHI (1973). 'Macroeconomic Approach to Foreign Direct Investment', *Hitotsubashi Journal of Economics,* 14: 1–21.

——(1975). 'International Trade and Foreign Investment: Substitutes or Complements?', *Hitotsubashi Journal of Economics,* 16: 1–12.

Kojima, Kiyoshi (*cont.*) (1978). *Direct Foreign Investment: A Japanese Model of Multinational Business Operations.* London: Croom Helm.

—— (1985). 'Japanese and American Direct Investment in Asia: A Comparative Analysis', *Hitotsubashi Journal of Economics*, 26: 1–35.

Krasner, Stephen (1978). *Defending the National Interest.* Princeton: Princeton University Press.

Krugman, Paul R. (ed.) (1986). *Strategic Trade Policy and the New International Economics.* Cambridge, Mass.: MIT Press.

Lall, Sanjaya (1973). 'Transfer Pricing by Multinational Manufacturing Firms', *Oxford Bulletin of Economics and Statistics*, 35: 173–95.

Lessard, Donald R. (1979). 'Transfer Prices, Taxes, and Financial Markets: Implications of Internal Financial Transfers Within the Multinational Corporation', in Robert G. Hawkins (ed.), *The Economic Effect of Multinational Corporations.* Greenwich, Conn.: JAI Press, 101–20.

Lustig, Nora, Bosworth, Barry P., and Lawrence, Robert Z. (1992). *Assessing the Impact of North American Free Trade.* Washington, DC: Brookings.

Magee, Stephen P. (1977). 'Information and Multinational Corporation: An Appropriability Theory of Direct Foreign Investment', in J. N. Bhagwati (ed.), *The New International Economic Order.* Cambridge, Mass.: MIT Press, 317–40.

Milner, Helen V. (1988). *Resisting Protectionism: Global Industries and the Politics of International Trade.* Princeton, NJ: Princeton University Press.

Nieckels, Lars (1976). *Transfer Pricing in Multinational Firms.* Stockholm: Almqvist and Wiksell.

Nigh, Douglas (1985). 'The Effect of Political Events on United States Direct Foreign Investment', *Journal of International Business Studies*, 16: 1–17.

Nonaka, Ikujiro, and Takeuchi, Hirotaka (1995). *The Knowledge-creating Company.* New York: Oxford University Press.

Ohmae, Ken-ichi (1985). *Triad power: The Coming Shape of Global Competition.* New York: The Free Press.

Ostry, Sylvia (1997). *The Post Cold War Trading System: Who's On First?* Chicago: University of Chicago Press.

Perlmutter, Howard (1969). 'The Tortuous Evolution of the Multilateral Corporation', *Columbia Journal of World Business*, 4(1): 9–18.

Porter, Michael G. (1990). *The Competitive Advantage of Nations.* New York: The Free Press.

—— and van der Linde, C. (1995). 'Green and Competitive', *Harvard Business Review*, 73(5): 120–34.

Prahalad, C. K., and Doz, Yves L. (1987). *The Multinational Mission.* New York: The Free Press.

Rugman, Alan M. (1980). *Multinationals in Canada: Theory, Performance and Economic Impact.* Boston: Martinus Nijhoff.

—— (1981). *Inside the Multinationals: The Economics of Internal Markets.* New York: Columbia University Press.

—— (ed.) (1994). *Foreign Investment and NAFTA.* Columbia: University of South Carolina Press.

—— (1996). *Multinational Enterprises and Trade Policy: Volume 2 of the Selected Scientific Papers of Alan M. Rugman*. Cheltenham: Edward Elgar.

—— (1999). 'Forty Years of the Theory of the Transnational Corporation', *Transnational Corporations*, 8(2): 51–70.

—— (2000). *The End of Globalization*. London: Random House. Also published by AMACOM/McGraw Hill (2001).

—— and ANDERSON, ANDREW (1987). *Administered Protection in America*. London: Routledge.

—— —— (1997). 'NAFTA and the Dispute Settlement Mechanisms: A Transaction Costs Approach', *The World Economy*, 20(7): 935–50.

—— and EDEN, LORRAINE (eds.) (1985). *Multinationals and Transfer Pricing*. London: Croom Helm.

—— and D'CRUZ, JOSEPH (2000). *Multinationals as Flagship Firms: Regional Business Networks*. Oxford: Oxford University Press.

—— and VERBEKE, ALAIN (1990). *Global Corporate Strategy and Trade Policy*. London: Routledge.

—— —— (1991). 'Environmental Change and Global Competitive Strategy in Europe', in Alan M. Rugman and Alain Verbeke (eds.), *Research in Global Strategic Management*, (Vol. 2), *Global Competition and the European Community*. Greenwood, Conn.: JAI Press, 3–28.

—— —— (1998). 'Corporate Strategies and Environmental Regulations: An Organizing Framework', *Strategic Management Journal*, 19(3) (March): 363–75.

—— —— KIRTON, JOHN, and SOLOWAY, JULIE (1999). *Environmental Regulations and Corporate Strategy: A NAFTA Perspective*. Oxford: Oxford University Press.

SAFARIAN, A. E. (1966). *Foreign Ownership of Canadian Industry*. Toronto: McGraw-Hill.

—— (1993). *Multinational Enterprises and Public Policy*. Aldershot: Edward Elgar.

STOPFORD, JOHN, and STRANGE, SUSAN (1991). *Rival States, Rival Firms: Competition for World Market Shares*. Cambridge: Cambridge University Press.

STRANGE, SUSAN (1988). *States and Markets: An Introduction to International Political Economy*. London: Pinter.

—— (1997). *The Retreat of the State: The Diffusion of Power in the World Economy*. Cambridge: Cambridge University Press.

TYSON, LAURA D'ANDREA (1993). *Who's Bashing Whom? Trade Conflict in High-technology Industries*. Washington, DC: Institute for International Economics.

VERNON, RAYMOND (1966). 'International Investment and International Trade in the Product Cycle', *Quarterly Journal of Economics*, 80: 190–207.

—— (1971). *Sovereignty at Bay: The Multinational Spread of US Enterprises*. New York: Basic Books.

—— (1991). 'Sovereignty at Bay: Twenty years after', *Millennium Journal of International Studies*, 20(2): 191–5.

VOGEL, DAVID (1995). *Trading Up: Consumer and Environmental Regulations in a Global Economy*. Cambridge, Mass.: Harvard University Press.

—— and RUGMAN, ALAN M. (1997). 'Environmentally Related Trade Disputes Between the United States and Canada', *American Review of Canadian Studies*, 27(4): 271–92.

WESTNEY, D. ELEANOR (1993). 'Institutionalization Theory and the Multinational Enterprise', in Sumantra Ghoshal and Eleanor Westney (eds.), *Organization Theory and the Multinational Enterprise*, London: Macmillian, 53–76.

YOFFIE, DAVID (ed.) (1993). *Beyond Free Trade: Firms, Governments and Global Competition*. Boston: Harvard Business School Press.

# SUBJECT INDEX

and sovereignty 183, 190, 192, 193–9
  *see also* anti-globalization movement
globaphobia 240
goals 320, 822
goods 209, 291, 295
governance 616, 696, 723–5
  and sovereignty 186, 187, 192, 201
government 186, 201, 271
    China 695, 696–7
    Pacific Asia 764–8
government relations 306
government–business relationship 652,
    655–62
Great Northern Telecom 717
green firm-specific advantages (FSAs) 548–51
green strategies 545
greenfield investment 634, 709, 734
Greenpeace 225
greens 245
gross margin pricing 606, 609 n.
growth 237, 241, 242
  China 682, 689
growth rates 260, 666, 761
Grupo Alfa 672
Grupo Luksic 672
Guangdong Enterprises 687
*guanxi* 218, 532, 698, 702, 703

Haier 687, 689, 694, 707
Hall, Edward T. 506–8
*Harvard Business Review* 506
Harvard Business School 360
Harvard Multinational Enterprise
    Database 788–90
Harvard Multinational Enterprise Project 351,
    634, 636
Havana Charter 287
hazard rates 801
Heckscher-Ohlin-Stopler-Samuelson theory,
    *see* factor intensities theory
hedging 571, 572, 579, 580
hedonism 238, 239
Helms-Burton legislation 189
heterarchy 359, 639
Hewlett Packard 170, 525, 581, 644, 684
hierarchical structures 183, 189, 195, 196, 639
  *see also* transaction cost theories
high-context cultures 508
Hofstede, Geert 508–11
holdup 139, 140
home bases 169–71
home country effects 633–42 *passim*

home-country-centric model 639, 640
Honda 170, 323, 628
Honeywell 581
Hong Kong 681 n., 683, 684, 694, 765, 773–4
horizontal activities 72, 82, 83, 85, 130 n.
host countries:
    and international trade theory 81, 84, 85
    Japan 642–8
hub-and-spoke models 361, 362, 639
human resources management (HRM) 358,
    503–33, 700, 744–5
human rights groups 221, 225
Hungary 746
hybrids 136
Hymer's theory, *see* industrial organization
    theories
Hyundai 581

Ibbotson Associates database 563
IBM 214, 371, 529, 643, 644
ICI-Dupont case 188
ICT, *see* information technology
IFA, *see* International Fiscal Association
ILO, *see* International Labor Organization;
    International Labour Organization
IMF (International Monetary Fund) 216, 247,
    287
imperialism 182
imports 210
incentives 284
    cultural factors 527–8
    and location advantages 155, 162
    and national policies 213, 214
    and theories of the MNE 134, 136 n.
income 240, 241
incorporation 192
incremental internationalization 355
India 198, 220, 233, 296
individualism/collectivism index 508
Indonesia 263, 295
    and national policies 211, 216, 221
    and SE Asian economies 767, 768, 778, 779
industrial organization theories 69, 71–2,
    130–1
industry analysis 320
    geographic spread 326–7
    global integration 336–8
    local integration 332
industry structure 303–4
inequality 240
infant industry protection 266
inflationary finance 265

# AUTHOR INDEX

*Note*: Multi-author works of three or more contributors are referred to by the name of the main author plus *et al.*

panies in Malaysia, some of which took over previously colonial assets, the companies in the Philippines associated with the earlier land-owning élite. These large companies tend to exist as a result of government support or preference, and sometimes also as instruments of élite exploitation as occurred with the Suharto holdings in Indonesia or the Marcos holdings in the Philippines. At large scale, the ethnic Chinese companies have also been involved in this aspect of patrimonial extraction of benefits.

Networking across these economies takes place in conditions of what one observer has termed 'ersatz' capitalism. In other words these are states in which the level of order is low, institutions are unreliable or weak, and the government record in coordinating the various components of orchestrated economic development is weak. Thus capital market regulation is not sophisticated, reliable data are rare, law is negotiable in many instances, and government management of the economy is hesitant and reactive, lacking a clear, and fully worked out long-term vision. This criticism is less applicable to Malaysia where long standing policies are traceable and where government strength has been demonstrated. But an overall general conclusion is that the institutional fabric of these societies is not yet of the quality needed for the full development of market capitalism. Financial capital is still heavily influenced by personal or government connections. Human capital remains a field rich in potential but limited in development so far. Social capital is still a matter of personal connections.

The direction of movement in these countries is clear. They are dealing with their weaknesses with the intention of making themselves again significant competitors for the investments and the markets of the developed world. This will mean a rise in the quality of their business infrastructures, especially in banking and commercial law. One can also expect a continuation in education, especially technical, to produce the new skills needed. But the problems of order, and of coordination of policy, are immense in countries of such large size with traditions of weak government. The earlier resort to authoritarianism in the face of such challenges is less and less legitimate as democracy raises expectations.

# 26.8 VIETNAM

Vietnam is a special case, being still heavily influenced in practice by socialist dogma, and being much further away from prosperity than the other countries considered here. The country is very large, both in extent and population, having 81 million people. Centuries of earlier autonomy left it with a very strong sense of national identity, but the decades of war against the Japanese, then the French, then the US, left the country weak and still psychologically divided. As with most totalitarian states the instruments of control are many, sophisticated, and deep in their penetration, and while Vietnam continues to talk about opening up and encouraging capitalist activity it continues to frustrate the business person with rules, regulations, and unpredictably changing controls.

The end result is that small business, operating close to the ground, and left to its own devices, can survive and even prosper. Businesses at larger scale have to navigate the world of political approval. Investors going in from advanced countries have had mixed experiences in recent years, and progress in opening the country to world trade and competition is slow. Income per capita is the lowest among the major countries of the region at US $400.

There is a strong sense among many observers of Vietnam that the country is at the same position China was at in the 1970s prior to the Deng Xiao Ping reforms of 1979. Freedom of economic behaviour in China was achieved by a process of decentralization and loosening of control. It was done slowly and is still far from complete, but there was at least an official endorsing of 'the glory of being rich', and private ownership expanded in line with the decline of the state sector. This same direction is being followed much more hesitantly in Vietnam and with much less clarity of endorsement from the very top. Instead policy is fought over between the liberals and the hard liners, and the truce line between them shifts constantly. The retention of power by party members drives much behaviour and the likelihood of fast progress is low.

# REFERENCES

BACKMAN, M. (1999). *Asian Eclipse*. Singapore: Wiley.

CHAN, S., CLARK, C., and LAM, D. (eds.) (1998). *Beyond the Developmental State*. London: Macmillan.

ENRIGHT, M. J., SCOTT, E. E., and DODWELL, D. (1997). *The Hong Kong Advantage*. Hong Kong: Oxford University Press.

HOSONO, A., and SAAVEDRA-RIVENO, N. (eds.) (1998). *Development Strategies in East Asia and Latin America*. London: Macmillan.

JOMO, K. S. (ed.) (1998). *Tigers in Trouble*. Hong Kong: Hong Kong University Press.

McVEY, R. (ed.) (1992). *Southeast Asian Capitalists*. Ithaca NY: Cornell University Press.

ORRU, M., BIGGART, N. W., and HAMILTON, G. G. (1997). *The Economic Organization of East Asian Capitalism*. London: Macmillan.

THE SMALLER ECONOMIES OF PACIFIC ASIA

them to transcend their scale limitations and take part in the international economy via informal collaboration with fellow firms, such networks being flexible in the short term and basically stable in the long term.

The holding together of employees in cooperative relation with the firm is done largely by the application of principles of paternalism, another feature which inhibits the growth of individual firms. This exchange of obligation to employees downwards and loyalty, deference, and acceptance of authority upwards, is a social system rooted in Confucian ethics which give it moral force and sustainability.

The institutional fabric of the societies in which the Chinese family business system thrives tends to be one in which they keep separate as much as possible from government, and rely on their own sources of capital. The larger companies will build political friendships into government to secure access to opportunities. Some large ones will also tap into international finance markets while working hard to retain control. The system of human capital is influenced heavily by a very high sensitivity to the value of education, and a high level of individual responsibility in achieving it. This stems from the ethics of responsibility to family and the insecurity so commonly part of family folklore. In some states, the government has invested heavily in educational infrastructure, notably Hong Kong and Taiwan. In other cases such as Malaysia and Indonesia, ethnic discrimination has held them back from their full potential.

Skills are normally acquired by individuals in their pursuit of a career and are not provided by the firm. The use of skill is usually at the discretion of management and in most countries in the region is unaffected by labour union pressure. Social capital, or the availability of trust, is problematic in this business culture, but is solved by the networking. Limited but reliable networks provide the means of getting around the endemic mistrust.

The tendency for these responses to be visible across many countries is suggestive of certain common inclinations in Chinese culture. In particular, the salience of Confucian familism at the centre of the social order is clearly important. This provides high legitimacy for the holding of authority by the father figure and those who behave as such. So too are the ethics surrounding the obligations to friends. These provide the social glue which ties together the myriad business transactions at such high levels of efficiency. These ancient bases for vertical and horizontal order show no sign of declining in the socialization of the next generation, and it might therefore be supposed that this business system will continue to prosper in the conditions to which it is adapted.

A summary of the main characteristics of Chinese capitalist enterprises is as follows:

(1) owned and managed by the same person or family group;

(2) networked with other companies of the same type for the raising of capital, the hedging of risk, and the exchange of strategic information. Bonds of steady business relationships are also fostered like this;

(3) sensitive to the need for co-opting political support when operating at large scale;

(4) paternalistic in style of management;

(5) capable of operating at large scale especially via the use of alliances for the incorporating of technology, and brand names;

(6) extensively networked in small scale manufacturing of components which are assembled in vertical commodity chains with reach into advanced country markets;

(7) capable of high speed of response and flexibility;

(8) tend to grow in one field of specialism prior to later diversification for hedging, or opportunity taking;

(9) inhibited by limitations on trust from building large professionally managed and decentralized organizations. All growth tends to be in conditions of tight central control of strategy and of finance;

(10) internally very conscious of costs and externally able to limit transaction costs by the use of personalistic trust.

# 26.7 INDONESIA, MALAYSIA, PHILIPPINES, AND THAILAND

It was noted earlier that these countries came relatively late to the Asian 'miracle'. They also suffered heavily from the crisis, especially Thailand and Indonesia. Three of them have huge populations (Philippines 65m, Indonesia 200m, Thailand 60m) and have found in them the basis of comparative advantage. Much investment has been attracted in on the basis of the volumes of skilled labour available at low cost.

Although the systems of capitalism vary in these countries there are certain common features. The kind of indigenous organizations found fall into two types. On the one hand are the ethnic Chinese organizations which tend to dominate and which appear in all sizes. On the other hand are the ethnically more local organizations, many of which have been favoured with government support. Some of these can be very large and examples of them are the companies associated with the military in Indonesia, the Bumiputra com-